# POLITICAL PARTIES & ELECTIONS in the UNITED STATES

## AN ENCYCLOPEDIA

### N–INDEX

GENERAL EDITOR

## L. Sandy Maisel

*Department of Government*
*Colby College*

ASSOCIATE EDITOR

## Charles Bassett

*Department of English and American Studies Program*
*Colby College*

GARLAND PUBLISHING, INC.
New York & London
1991

Library of Congress Cataloging-in-Publication Data

Political parties and elections in the United States : an encyclopedia /
    edited by L. Sandy Maisel.
      p.  cm. — (Garland reference library of social science:
vol. 498
    Includes index.
    ISBN 0-8240-7975-2
    1. Political parties—United States—Encyclopedias. 2. Elections—
United States—Encyclopedias. I. Maisel, Louis Sandy, 1945– .
II. Series.
JK2261.P633  1991
91-6940
324.273'03—dc20
CIP

Printed on acid-free, 250-year life paper
MANUFACTURED IN THE UNITED STATES OF AMERICA

# N

## Ralph Nader (1934– )

Consumer advocate. Ralph Nader has been the most influential consumer advocate in the United States since the 1960s. Born in Winsted, Connecticut, Nader received his B.A. from Princeton University in 1955 and his LL.B. degree from Harvard in 1958. Nader was an unknown lawyer when he published his first book, *Unsafe at Any Speed*, a scathing indictment of automobile safety in general and of the Chevrolet Corvair in particular. Nader's efforts thrust him in the public spotlight and sped passage of the Traffic and Motor Vehicle Safety Act of 1966.

He quickly became known as someone who defended the common person against the large corporations and other powerful interests. Nader's popularity soared too when it became known that he lived in a single room, did not own a car, and needed only about $5,000 a year to get by.

In the 1970s Nader then began to fight for consumers' rights on a wide variety of fronts. Over the years, he established a number of organizations, including the Center for Study of Responsible Law, the Corporate Accountability Research Group, the Public Interest Research Group, Congress Watch, and Public Citizen, Inc., among others. Those organizations are staffed with highly trained investigators, most of whom are attorneys; they have come to be known as "Nader's Raiders" for the quality and intensity of their work. Nader-inspired organizations have had a substantial impact on public policy, including the establishment of the Occupational Safety and Health Administration (OSHA). These groups also provide invaluable resources, such as the annual *Who Runs Congress,* for others who are interested in influencing the decision-making process. Nader's most notable defeat has been the failure of Congress to establish a consumers' protection agency.

*Charles S. Hauss*

## Joseph Napolitan (1929– )

Pioneer political media consultant. Joseph Napolitan began his career as a newspaper reporter in Springfield, Massachusetts, where he still maintains his permanent residence. His first experience in campaign management came in Springfield in 1957 when he organized the successful mayoral campaign of Thomas J. O'Connor, pioneering in the use of television advertising. Napolitan went on to work on Democrat John Kennedy's presidential campaign in 1960; he worked briefly in the Democrat Hubert Humphrey presidential campaign in 1968.

Napolitan founded and served as the first president of the American Association of Political Consultants; he co-founded and was president of the International Association of Political Consultants. Napolitan compares his work to that of an architect or an engineer who prepares blueprints for a successful building. Since his early days, Napolitan has masterminded an impressive number of successful campaign blueprints both in the United States and abroad, ranging from the Milton Shapp campaign for governor of Pennsylvania; to congressional and gubernatorial campaigns in Hawaii and other states; to those of Presidents Carlos Andreas Perez and Dr. Jaime Lusinchi of Venezuela,

Valéry Giscard d'Estaing of France, and Ferdinand Marcos of the Philippines.

President of Joseph Napolitan Associates with offices in Springfield, Massachusetts, London, and New York, Napolitan is also chairman of the board and chief executive officer of Public Affairs Analysis, a multinational public affairs consulting firm with headquarters in New York City. Napolitan conducts seminars on political techniques and also serves as consultant to private industry. He has lectured and conducted workshops at numerous colleges and universities including Harvard, Yale (where he served as Poynter fellow), MIT, Princeton, Occidental, Mount Holyoke, and the Eagleton Institute of Politics. He is the author of a pioneering book on campaign techniques, *The Election Game and How to Win It* (1972).

*See also:* Hubert Humphrey, John F. Kennedy

*Elinor C. Hartshorn*

## Thomas Nast (1840–1902)

One of the nation's most prominent political cartoonists. Thomas Nast joined the staff of *Harper's Weekly* in 1862, and before long his cartoons of major political figures dominated the popular imagination. He gained national prominence for his assaults upon the corruption of New York City's William Marcy Tweed and the "Tweed Ring." A staunch supporter of Ulysses S. Grant, Nast reached the zenith of his influence in the 1870s as he blasted the Liberal Republican movement and ridiculed its candidate, Horace Greeley.

Nast is credited with creating the Republican elephant and the Democratic donkey as symbols to counter the tiger of Tammany Hall. Among his targets were inflationary monetary policies, southern terrorism against Black citizens, communism, and the Catholic Church. Republican in his politics, in 1884 Nast broke with the Republican Party over the nomination of James G. Blaine in a biting series of cartoons that constituted his last great visual commentary on American politics.

*See also:* James G. Blaine, Ulysses S. Grant, Horace Greeley, Liberal Republicans, Tammany Hall, William Marcy Tweed

*Brooks Donohue Simpson*

REFERENCES

Keller, Morton. 1968. *The Art and Politics of Thomas Nast*. New York: Oxford U. Pr.

Leonard, Thomas C. 1986. *The Power of the Press: The Birth of American Political Reporting*. New York: Oxford U. Pr.

Paine, Albert Bigelow. 1904. *Thomas Nast: His Period and Pictures*. New York: Macmillan.

St. John, Thomas Nast. 1974. *Thomas Nast: Cartoons and Illustrations*. New York: Dover.

## National American Woman Suffrage Association

The National American Woman Suffrage Association (NAWSA) was formed in 1890, when two wings of the suffrage movement merged: the National Woman Suffrage Association, which had worked for a federal amendment while supporting other women's rights; and the American Woman Suffrage Association, which had concentrated solely on the right to vote, aiming to achieve passage state by state. Because of the inability to secure passage of a federal amendment, NAWSA chose state suffrage as its main goal. In its early years, the organization was led by Elizabeth Cady Stanton (1890–1892) and Susan B. Anthony (1892–1900).

By 1910 NAWSA had 75,000 members and branches throughout the nation. It was finally able to gain adherents in the South when the leader of one of the largest women's organizations—the Women's Christian Temperance Union—began to advocate suffrage. The existence of the progressive reform movement, together with growth of women's voluntary organizations, also helped the cause. Progressive demands for a more open government and the elimination of injustice encouraged mutual support. The National Consumers League, the Women's Trade Union League, and the settlement movement provided NAWSA with members and leaders. Additionally, the increasing numbers of women entering the public service brought legitimacy to the suffrage demand.

As NAWSA grew in size and respectability, its arguments for suffrage increasingly reflected the mainstream. Instead of promoting suffrage based on a natural rights doctrine as was done in the nineteenth century, NAWSA emphasized the traditional concept that women were morally superior and would bring decency to politics. This assertion of high-mindedness not only offered a response to political conservatives' arguments against suffrage, but it also attracted middle-class support.

Even so, the organization was at an impasse in 1913 when Alice Paul and a group advocating more militant tactics brought pressure on NAWSA to be more vigorous in the pursuit of a federal amendment. NAWSA rejected this strategy, and when Paul's group formed the National

Woman's Party, the suffrage movement was again divided.

Under Anna Howard Shaw's presidency (1904–1915), NAWSA clearly committed itself to state suffrage with its support of the ill-fated Shafroth-Palmer Amendment. This direction, plus NAWSA's failure to achieve victory in a four-state referendum effort in 1915, led to the overhaul of the organization with Carrie Chapman Catt returning to the presidency (1900–1904; 1915–1920). She was a clever strategist who devised a "Winning Plan" in which delegates from suffrage states obtained resolutions from their legislatures supporting a federal amendment, while others worked for state suffrage. This state emphasis was carefully coordinated with the national office's efforts to achieve a federal amendment. Under her presidency, NAWSA remained nonpartisan and as a result gained support from both Republicans and Democrats.

When the United States entered World War I, NAWSA argued for suffrage as a war measure. The organization maintained an overseas hospital in France and supported the war effort but continued to work primarily for suffrage. Once the Congress passed the Nineteenth Amendment in 1919, ratification was relatively smooth because of Catt's plan. After victory, the League of Women Voters, which had been created to educate women in their new responsibilities, became NAWSA's official successor.

*See also:* Susan B. Anthony, Carrie Chapman Catt, League of Women Voters, National Woman's Party, Nineteenth Amendment, Alice Paul, Elizabeth Cady Stanton, Women's Christian Temperance Union

*Joy A. Scimé*

REFERENCES

Flexner, Eleanor. 1959. *Century of Struggle: The Women's Rights Movement in the United States*. Cambridge: Belknap Press.

Scott, Anne F., and Andrew M. Scott. 1975. *One Half the People: The Fight for Woman Suffrage*. Philadelphia: Lippincott.

Woloch, Nancy. 1984. *Women and the American Experience*. New York: Knopf.

## National Association for the Advancement of Colored People

Founded in 1909 by W. E. B. Du Bois and other Black militants in coalition with white liberals galvanized by the Springfield, Illinois, race riot of 1908, the National Association for the Advancement of Colored People (NAACP) has long played an important leadership role in civil rights and African-American protest. In 1909 the organization's membership and leadership was predominantly white; Du Bois served as the only Black official of the organization, having been appointed editor of its official publication, *Crisis*.

From the beginning, the NAACP committed itself to what was then considered a militant program based on the Niagara Movement platform, which insisted upon equal educational opportunities, political privileges, and civil rights for African-Americans. The NAACP fought to achieve its goals primarily through legislation like antilynching laws and litigation aimed at ensuring the rigorous enforcement of the Fourteenth and Fifteenth amendments. Eventually its significant victories transformed American political and social life. For example, its successful challenge to the grandfather clause and the white primary expanded political opportunities to people of color. Other victories promoted more integrated housing patterns.

The strategy that brought the NAACP its most important triumph, however, was to attack the "separate but equal" doctrine established in *Plessy v. Ferguson* (1898), especially as it pertained to schools. In a series of cases beginning in 1938, NAACP attorneys convinced the Supreme Court that if separate facilities were not equal, they would have to be integrated. Gradually, lower courts agreed to consider intangible along with concrete components in the equality equation. Finally, in a landmark 1954 case, *Brown v. the Board of Education*, the Court ruled that, at least in the area of education, separate facilities were inherently unequal. From there, the NAACP easily litigated out the last vestiges of legalized segregation.

In addition to promoting new civil rights legislation and initiating suits in court, the NAACP serves as a watchdog to prevent the imposition of standards in areas that it considers as illegitimate discrimination on the basis of race. Therefore, along with other civil rights groups, the NAACP opposed the inauguration of a skills test by the state of Texas to be used as a criterion for admittance into teaching programs.

With 450,000 members, the NAACP remains a potent political force. At its 1988 national convention, the organization listed its recent key accomplishments. Despite the negative attitude of the Ronald Reagan administration, the NAACP pointed with pride to the fact that most civil rights legislation remained intact. They pointed to the effectiveness of their fight against the confirmation of the conservative Robert Bork to the Supreme Court and for a congressional override of Reagan's veto of the Civil Rights Restoration Act. The NAACP also actively promotes voter registration drives and campaigns to get out the vote. In fact, the theme of the convention was "Vote. Be Heard." It does not, however, directly endorse candidates, forbidden from doing so by its constitution.

Despite these achievements, since 1977, under the leadership of Benjamin Hooks, the NAACP has faced numerous difficulties. First, tensions between Blacks and their traditional white liberal allies, especially organized labor, over such issues as school busing and affirmative action in employment has caused membership to drop off. Moreover, while the organization still engages in such traditional civil rights battles as boycotting schools over allegedly racist policies or bringing suit to ensure that low- and middle-income housing will be built in predominantly white communities to foster integrated housing and education, many see the need for a new agenda to serve the needs of poor and uneducated African-Americans. The 1988 convention resolved to devote more of its resources to fighting drug and alcohol abuse, to countering rising crime and school drop-out rates, and to pregnancy counseling and other self-help programs.

*See also:* Civil Rights Legislation and Southern Politics, W. E. B. Du Bois, Fifteenth Amendment, Race and Politics, Ronald Reagan

*Roberta S. Alexander*

REFERENCES

Hughes, Langston. 1962. *Fight for Freedom: The Story of the NAACP.* New York: Norton.

Kellog, Charles Flint. 1967. *NAACP: A History of the National Association for the Advancement of Colored People. Vol. 1: 1909–1920.* Baltimore: Johns Hopkins U. Pr.

McPherson, James M. 1975. *The Abolitionist Legacy from Reconstruction to the NAACP.* Princeton: Princeton U. Pr.

Ovington, Mary White. 1947. *The Walls Came Tumbling Down.* New York: Harcourt, Brace and World.

Record, Wilson. 1964. *Race and Radicalism: The NAACP and the Communist Party in Conflict.* Ithaca: Cornell U. Pr.

Zangrando, Robert L. 1980. *The NAACP Crusade Against Lynching, 1909–1950.* Philadelphia: Temple U. Pr.

## National Association of Manufacturers

A business association of more than 13,000 corporate members (of which more than 300 operate political action committees [PACs] that contribute to congressional candidates). Established in 1895, the National Association of Manufacturers (NAM) is generally regarded as one of the four most powerful business lobbies in America. (It had the dubious distinction of being the focus of the first series of congressional investigations of lobbying activity in 1913.) The NAM represents the trade, business, and financial interests of manufacturers to government by monitoring and seeking to affect legislative, administrative, and judicial activities affecting industry. It is affiliated with the National Industrial Council, a federation of about 300 national, state, and local trade associations representing about 100,000 firms.

The NAM does not contribute directly to congressional candidates. It does operate as a bellwether organization for other business PACs by distributing information about congressional candidates. The NAM also publishes *The PAC Manager*, a newsletter identifying favorable candidates, and it has been active in assisting other businesses in forming PACs. In conjunction with the U.S. Chamber of Commerce, the NAM created the Business-Industry PAC (BIPAC) in 1963. Now distinct from NAM, BIPAC was the largest business PAC throughout the late 1960s and early 1970s. At present, BIPAC issues ratings of legislators and is extremely important as a "broker," giving direction to many pro-business PACs. Both NAM and BIPAC are actively courted by pro-business candidates seeking financial support because of the leadership role they play among contributors and supporters.

*See also:* Business-Industry Political Action Committee, Political Action Committees

*Clyde Brown*

REFERENCES

Drew, Elizabeth. 1982. "Politics and Money, Part I." December 6 *The New Yorker* 54.

Green, Mark, and Andrew Bushbaum. 1980. *The Corporate Lobby.* Washington: Public Citizen.

## National Committee for an Effective Congress

The oldest liberal nonconnected political action committee (PAC) in America. Founded in 1948 by advocates of Franklin Roosevelt's New Deal and Harry Truman's Fair Deal, the National Committee for an Effective Congress (NCEC) was one of the first interest groups to be almost exclusively interested in electoral activity as a means to promote political ideals; as such it was clearly a forerunner to modern ideological PACs.

The NCEC is a staff organization with a membership limited to 50 individuals. It raises funds from approximately 100,000 contributors, targets winnable congressional races for liberals, and provides liberal candidates with technical and financial support. Rather than providing direct contributions to candidates, most of its resources are funneled through the NCEC's Campaign Services Program, which provides less-expensive-to-the-campaign, in-kind technical services in the form of political consultants. These campaign professionals work on the basis of group rates to assist campaigns with precinct targeting, polling, media production, commercial-time buying, research, and fundraising (including appearances by celebrities). Initially involved only in Senate races, NCEC is now active in House races as well.

Historically among the largest ideological PACs in terms of money raised, expended, and contributed, the NCEC's influence grows out of the leadership and coordination it provides to liberal PAC contributors. Similar to the role AFL-CIO COPE plays for labor PACs and BIPAC for business PACs, NCEC is a major broker for liberal PACs in terms of identifying competitive races where contributions can make a difference. The NCEC's success in electing liberal congressional candidates in the early 1970s led conservatives to create similar political organizations. Despite its emphasis on electoral politics, the NCEC has been in the forefront of several legislative battles: the censure of Senator Joseph McCarthy in 1954, securing the passage of civil rights legislation in the House Rules Committee in 1965, opposition to the Vietnam War, reform of the seniority system in 1974, and efforts at campaign finance reform.

*See also:* AFL-CIO COPE, Civil Rights Legislation and Southern Politics, Political Action Committees, Vietnam War as a Political Issue

*Clyde Brown*

REFERENCES

Nugent, Margaret Latus. 1986. "When Is a $1,000 Contribution Not a $1,000 Contribution?" 3 *Election Politics* 13.

Peabody, Robert L., Jeffrey M. Berry, William G. Frasure, and Jerry Goldman. 1972. *To Enact a Law: Congress and Campaign Financing.* New York: Praeger.

Scoble, Harry M. 1967. *Ideology and Electoral Action.* San Francisco: Chandler.

## National Conservative Political Action Committee

Founded in 1975 by Charles Black, Jr., Roger Stone, and John T. (Terry) Dolan, the National Conservative Political Action Committee (NCPAC) first came into the spotlight in 1980. During that year, the Republican Party accepted conservatism as its central political dogma, offering Ronald Reagan as its ideological standard-bearer and providing him with a supporting cast of conservative Republican Senate and House candidates. Reagan won in a landslide, and the Republicans gained control of the U.S. Senate and 33 seats in the House.

Most political observers give NCPAC at least some of the credit for the Republicans' massive success in 1980. This committee spent large amounts of money in an effort to discredit the Jimmy Carter administration and specific Carter supporters in Congress. The result was a series of negative television and newspaper advertisements outlining what NCPAC deemed to be the "failings" of a liberal President and Congress. NCPAC targeted President Carter and six prominent, liberal Senate Democrats for defeat and spent anywhere from $3.3 million to $4.5 million in its attempts to achieve that goal. In addition to Carter's defeat, Senators Frank Church of Idaho, George McGovern of South Dakota, John Culver of Iowa, and Birch Bayh of Indiana also lost; Senators Alan Cranston of California and Thomas Eagleton of Missouri won.

In its most visible strategy, NCPAC has attempted to influence the campaigns of candidates who disagree with the policy positions of the committee. NCPAC differs from other political action committees, however, in several key ways: it tends indirectly to support challengers, whereas most other PACs opt for incumbents. In addition, NCPAC, as an ideological political action committee, exercises its influence through the use of independent expenditures on behalf of campaigns, rather than through direct contributions to candidates campaigns—the traditional means of influence peddling by PACs. By choosing this strategy, NCPAC has skirted several federal campaign regulations restricting PAC expenditures. Since NCPAC expresses opposition to candidates rather than endorsing their opponents, the organization can legally spend unlimited amounts of money on negative campaign ads. This news was received with dismay by Democrats, whose candidates received only 3 percent of the $14.2 million in independent expenditures spent by NCPAC and other ideological PACs.

Unlike many other political action committees, NCPAC was founded as an independent entity. Whereas labor unions and corporations often organize and fund their own PACs, NCPAC is accountable only to those few individuals directing it. In 1980 and 1982, NCPAC was criticized after the press quoted Terry Dolan, the organization's director, as having said, "a group like ours could lie through its teeth, and the candidate it helps stays clean." In fact, rival organizations charged that NCPAC deliberately distorted the records of Frank Church in 1980 and Maryland Senator Paul Sarbanes in 1981.

Loopholes in federal election laws and problems with enforcement still allow for strategies of influence by means of independent expenditure to succeed. Groups such as NCPAC and the Congressional Club, both of which support conservatives and Republicans, are limited in their effectiveness, however, because liberal and Democratic countergroups have formed to present opposing viewpoints. Indeed, since 1982, the impact of the National Conservative Political Action Committee has diminished appreciably.

*See also:* Birch Bayh, Jimmy Carter, Thomas Eagleton, George McGovern, Negative Advertising, Political Action Committees, Ronald Reagan

*Michael Heel*

REFERENCES

Sorauf, Frank J. 1984. *What Price Pacs?* New York: Twentieth Century Fund.

## National Democratic Party of Alabama

A political party formed in Alabama in 1968, the National Democratic Party of Alabama (NDPA) ran candidates for federal, state, and local office until 1976 as an alternative forum for liberal voters who could then participate in a party more closely aligned with the national Democratic Party than was the Alabama Democratic Party (ADP). The NDPA also sought to provide a way for Alabama voters to vote for the national Democratic presidential nominee rather than for Alabama governor George Wallace.

The NDPA's founders saw the effects of a split African-American vote in the 1966 gubernatorial primary, and they decided to found a party that would empower Blacks in state politics. The charter took effect on January 12, 1968.

The NDPA was unsuccessful in its bids to obtain recognition as the "loyalist" Democratic Party in Alabama by petitioning the Democratic National Convention in 1968 and 1972. In 1968, 1970, and 1972, the NDPA was successful in winning only countywide offices in rural coun-

ties in western Alabama's "Black Belt," where African-Americans constitute a majority of the electorate. NDPA was unable to succeed beyond the county level for several reasons: its platform was consistently more liberal than any favored by the Alabama electorate; it threatened the dominant ADP; and it was unsuccessful in obtaining the support of Black elites and white progressives. By 1978 NDPA had ceased to function as a political party, although many of its leaders and voters found a home in the post-Wallace ADP, which was much more receptive to African-Americans.

*See also:* George C. Wallace

*Samuel F. Mitchell*

REFERENCES

Frye, Hardy T. 1980. *Black Parties and Political Power: A Case Study.* Boston: G. K. Hall.

Hamilton, Charles V. 1960. *Minority Politics in Black Belt Alabama.* New York: McGraw-Hill.

Walton, Hanes, Jr. 1972. *Black Political Parties: An Historical and Political Analysis.* New York: Free Press.

## National Education Association

A self-described "professional association union," perhaps the first in American history, that endeavors to promote America's public schools in general and the education profession in particular. Lobbying and research help to support these goals. The National Education Association (NEA) also strives to enhance the welfare of its members by serving as a bargaining unit. In this activity, it is the rival to the smaller American Federation of Teachers, which is under the auspices of the AFL-CIO. The NEA's Government Relations office lobbies both the Congress and the executive branch to influence legislation of interest primarily to public-school teachers at the elementary and secondary levels. The NEA's political action committee (NEA-PAC) endorses and makes financial contributions to candidates for Congress and the presidency who are deemed to be friends of education. NEA has made clear its presidential selections only since 1976; all have been Democrats.

The largest professional education organization in the United States with more than 1.8 million members in 1987, the NEA is also presently the largest employee organization in the United States. Membership is open to all employees of educational institutions, including colleges and universities. The NEA evolved from the National Teachers Association (NTA), established in 1857. NTA's efforts in part prompted the federal government to set up a sub-Cabinet-level Department of Education in 1867. This post presaged another monument to NEA's prowess as a powerful lobby more than 100 years later. In 1979 President Jimmy Carter created a Cabinet-level Department of Education out of the former Department of Health, Education, and Welfare. A national Secretary of Education was a goal that NEA had sought since 1921. The newer AFT, which feels it has more influence in Congress and at the local level, opposed it.

NEA reorganized and adopted its current name in 1871. For the first four decades of the twentieth century, school administrators dominated NEA, emphasizing the development of more efficient methods of running schools rather than improving the salaries and working conditions of classroom teachers.

Among the public policy issues that NEA has taken a stance on over its history are lobbying for the passage of the Morrill Act that established land-grant universities in 1862; the endorsement of women's suffrage in 1911; lobbying to pass the G.I. Bill of Rights in 1944; public opposition to the confirmation of Clement Haynsworth and G. Harrold Carswell to the Supreme Court in 1969 because of their negative records on civil rights.

Although NEA members are delegates or alternates at both Republican and Democratic conventions, their influence has been much greater among the more politically liberal Democrats. At the 1984 Democratic convention, NEA representation was larger than that of any other organization or union.

*See also:* Jimmy Carter, Political Action Committees

*Frederick J. Augustyn, Jr.*

REFERENCES

Butler, Susan Lowell. 1987. *The National Education Association—A Special Mission.* Washington: National Education Association.

National Education Association. 1983. *NEA Handbook, 1983–84.* Washington: National Education Association.

West, Allan M. 1980. *The National Education Association: The Power Base for Education.* New York: Free Press.

## National Farmers' Alliance and Industrial Union

Often called the Southern Alliance, the National Farmers' Alliance and Industrial Union originated in Lampasas County, Texas, in September 1877 as a livestock protective association. Known as the Knights of Reliance, the organization soon changed its name to the Farmers' Alliance. In May 1878 the Farmers' Alliance organized on the state level in Texas, and by the autumn of 1887, state alliances had been established in Texas, Missouri, Louisiana, Mississippi, Alabama, and North Carolina. During that same year, the Alliance established a national organization known as the National Farmers' Alliance and Cooperative Union, with Charles McCune as president. Two years later the organization changed its name to the National Farmers' Alliance and Industrial Union in an unsuccessful attempt to unite with the National Farmers' Alliance, commonly known as the Northern Alliance or Northwestern Alliance. At that time, the Southern Alliance also intensified its recruiting in the Great Plains, particularly in Kansas and the Dakotas, where it competed with the less aggressive Northern Alliance.

By the mid-1880s, the Alliance primarily sought solutions to the economic problems in southern and western agriculture: the crop-lien system, low prices, and abusive railroad practices. It worked to establish cooperative stores to help farmers sell their commodities and to purchase needed items by eliminating the middleman. The Alliance also advocated nonpartisan support of politicians who supported its demands. Besides engaging in cooperative business practices and nonpartisan political lobbying, the Alliance served as a ritualistic secret order and as a social and educational organization similar to the Patrons of Husbandry or the Grange. The Alliance's constitution, however, limited its membership to rural whites, including teachers, doctors, and ministers. It did not distinguish between large planters, tenants, and farmworkers. Townsmen, merchants, bankers, lawyers, and Blacks could not join the organization.

In 1890 the National Farmers' Alliance and Industrial Union held its annual meeting in Ocala, Florida. There, the Southern Alliance began to expand its political influence by demanding a subtreasury, a circulating medium of at least $50 per capita, a graduated income tax, a tariff for revenue only, the abolition of national banks, the popular election of United States Senators, and the regulation of interstate commerce (particularly the railroads). The Alliance also sought legislation to compel railroads to lower rates, to break land monopolies, to destroy trusts, and to lower interest rates.

Although the Supreme Council of the Southern Alliance did not endorse the formation of a third party at the Ocala convention, by 1891 an increasing number of Alliance men realized that cooperative stores and nonpartisan politics would not solve the economic problems of southern and western farmers. Accordingly, they began to seek the formation of a third party. As a result, in 1892 the Alliance overwhelmingly supported the creation of the People's Party and its Omaha platform. Without a strong national organization or leadership, however, the loose confederation of state alliances lacked the discipline, authority, and financial base to remain a viable, nonpartisan political force and economic reform organization. After 1892 the People's Party overshadowed the National Farmers' Alliance and Industrial Union, and the Alliance essentially became a paper organization. During its short existence, however, the National Farmers' Alliance and Industrial Union gave enough farmers in the South and Great Plains sufficient experience in radical politics to make a third political party a reality.

The National Farmers' Alliance and Industrial Union met for a last time on a national basis in February 1897. During the late 1890s the Alliance also disappeared on the state and local levels, except in North Carolina, where it continued to meet until 1941. By the turn of the twentieth century, however, the Alliance no longer had political leverage or economic influence.

*See also:* Northern Farmers' Alliance, People's Party, Railroads

*R. Douglas Hurt*

REFERENCES

Barnes, Donna A. 1984. *Farmers in Rebellion: The Rise and Fall of the Southern Farmers' Alliance and People's Party.* Austin: U. of Texas Pr.

Goodwyn, Lawrence. 1976. *The Democratic Promise: The Populist Movement in America.* New York: Oxford U. Pr.

Hicks, John D. 1931. *The Populist Revolt.* Minneapolis: U. of Minnesota Pr.

McMath, Robert C., Jr. 1975. *Populist Vanguard: A History of the Southern Farmers' Alliance.* Chapel Hill: U. of North Carolina Pr.

## National Federation of Democratic Women

One of many women's organizations active in Democratic Party politics. Unlike their counterparts in the Republican Party, the Democratic women's clubs are chartered by the state committees rather than the national party. The National Federation of Democratic Women (NFDW) is headquartered in the home of the NFDW president—it has no office in Washington. State and local Democratic women's clubs have traditionally been supported by the Democratic National Committee (DNC) with its Office of Women's Activities (OWA). The OWA, abolished in 1985 by DNC chairman Paul Kirk, maintained a mailing list of Democratic women, sponsored a biennial campaign conference for Democratic women, and conducted regional workshops and conferences. The DNC currently has no formal organizational unit responsible for grass-roots organization of Democratic women. Responsibilities for women's activities are shared by one of the four vice chairs (elected by the whole DNC membership) and the chair of the DNC Women's Caucus (elected by the female members of the DNC). The NFDW president and two other members are designated by the Democratic Party Charter as members of the DNC. The DNC By-Laws stipulate that the vice chairs, the chair of the DNC Women's Caucus, and the NFDW president are all members of the DNC Executive Committee, which makes the majority of policy and administrative decisions in the period between formal meetings of the 350-member DNC.

The NFDW has proved to have little influence or presence on the DNC. The DNC Women's Caucus is a subset of national committee members, while the vice chair responsible for women holds a regular party office with other responsibilities. Neither has access to any formal party-controlled organization that links the national party to state and local Democratic women. At the 1988 Democratic National Convention, the Women's Caucus sponsored two-hour public meetings for delegates to discuss women's issues on four consecutive days of the convention. These meetings were subsidized by 15 nonparty women's political, professional, and feminist groups: National Women's Political Caucus–Democratic Task Force, Planned Parenthood, League of Women Voters, National Organization for Women, Emily's List, Fund for the Feminist Majority, American Association of University Women, American Nurses Association, National Association of Social Workers, National Abortion Rights Action League, National Women's Law Center, Voters for Choice, Women's Campaign Fund, Women's Legal Defense Fund, and Young Women's Christian Association. The NFDW, except for luncheons sponsored by individual state women's organizations, was largely invisible at the convention.

*See also:* Democratic National Committee, League of Women Voters, National Organization for Women

*Denise L. Baer*

REFERENCES

Cotter, Cornelius P., and Bernard C. Hennessy. 1964. *Politics Without Power: The National Party Committees.* New York: Atherton Press.

Freeman, Jo. 1988. "Women at the 1988 Convention." 61 *PS* 875.

## National Federation of Republican Women

One of the largest women's political organizations in the United States, the National Federation of Republican Women (NFRW) has approximately 160,000 members in over 2,600 clubs in the 50 states, the District of Columbia, Puerto Rico, Guam, and the Virgin Islands. In 1988, the Republican National Convention passed a resolution providing for a voting membership for the President of the NFRW on the Republican National Committee (RNC) Chairman's Executive Council, which controls the majority of the executive and administrative functions of the RNC between formal meetings of the RNC. The NFRW is also the only financially self-sufficient RNC affiliated organization with a yearly budget of over $1 million.

The NFRW was organized in 1938 by Marion Martin—then RNC assistant chairman and head of the Women's Division of the RNC—as a device to organize the proliferating numbers of local independent Republican women's clubs. The first recorded Republican women's club was organized in the early 1870s; by the late 1930s, Indiana alone supported 140 clubs. Eleven states joined as 1938 charter members of the NFRW: California, Colorado, Connecticut, District of Columbia, Indiana, Maryland, Michigan, Missouri, Montana, New Jersey, and Pennsylvania. The NFRW is directed by a national president who is elected at the biennial national convention; the Women's Division of the RNC has been traditionally headed by an assistant chairman (appointed by the RNC chairman). The Women's Division exercised effective control over the NFRW until 1948. Before then, the head of the Women's Division served as executive director of the NFRW, and since the NFRW president did not reside in the District of Columbia, she could not manage the NFRW on a day-to-day basis. This situation changed with the election of Elizabeth Farrington (1949–1953), whose husband was then a delegate to Congress from Hawaii. In 1952, the NFRW By-Laws were amended to abolish the office of executive director, and the president of the NFRW was designated as the official liaison between the NFRW and the RNC Executive Committee. Elizabeth Farrington was succeeded by Nora Kearns (1953–1957), whose husband was a Congressman from Pennsylvania. Nora Kearns established residence in Washington, D.C., at her own expense; by 1956 the NFRW provided a Washington residence for their president. Under the presidency of Ruth Parks (1961–1963), the NFRW greatly expanded its membership; by 1962 all 50 states and the District of Columbia had federated. This enlargement made the NFRW increasingly independent of the RNC since the RNC had subsidized approximately two-thirds of the NFRW budget. In 1977 the NFRW became completely self-sustaining financially.

In subsequent years, the NFRW achieved effective control over the Women's Division, establishing itself as the one organization representing elected Republican female public and party officials and volunteer activists. Recent NFRW presidents have held important RNC offices: Patricia Hutar, NFRW president from 1976 to 1978, served previously as assistant chairman of the RNC, and Betty Green Heitman served as co-chairman of the RNC from 1980 to 1985 following her NFRW presidency (1978–1980). At the 1988 Republican National Convention, the NFRW served as the communication center for Republican women delegates and public and party officials.

The NFRW has its independent headquarters in the Republican Complex on Capitol Hill and publishes *The Republican Woman* on a bimonthly basis. NFRW programs include both coordination of campaign volunteerism and professional training for women candidates and campaign managers. In 1989 the NFRW sponsored five regional weekend Campaign Management Schools for members, a program begun in 1979. The NFRW also sponsors a Women Candidates Seminar for Republican women running or considering a run for public office. The NFRW provides low-cost polling for Republican candidates by training its members as volunteer political pollsters in regional polling schools conducted by the Marketing Research Institute. In 1986 it is estimated that NFRW members contributed over 4 million hours to Republican candidates. The NFRW also encourages local community service through a "Caring for America" Program and provides college scholarships and Washington internships at the NFRW for young Republican women.

*See also:* Republican National Committee

*Denise L. Baer*

REFERENCES

Cotter, Cornelius P., and Bernard C. Hennessy. 1964. *Politics Without Power: The National Party Committees.* New York: Atherton Press.

"NFRW: Fifty Years of Leadership, 1938–1988." 1987. In *National Federation of Republican Women.* Washington: National Federation of Republican Women.

## National Nonpartisan League

A word that unlocks much of the National Nonpartisan League's history is diffusion. The NNPL was founded after commercial farmers in North Dakota mobilized behind a program of government intervention into the North Dakota economy. In 1916 the North Dakota Nonpartisan League successfully used the North Dakota Republican primary to capture control of most of North Dakota's executive offices. This success generated enormous optimism among the League's top leaders about the possibilities for repeating their "boring from within" tactics in other states. The North Dakota League's leaders decided to found a national organization for diffusing the North Dakota model to other states.

Headquarters of the NNPL were established in 1917 in St. Paul, Minnesota. From there the NNPL's top staff oversaw a sizable dissemination of propaganda for the organization of commercial (and in certain places tenant) farmers in north central, northwestern, southwestern, and western states. The premise of the National Nonpartisan League's staff was that state Leagues would quickly emerge if the NNPL provided an initial supply of organizers, money, and expertise. These areas were assumed to be full of discontented farmers waiting for political leaders capable of articulating their discontents. The NNPL also assumed that in those states a significant number of industry workers would also be attracted to the League's attacks on "Big Biz" and to its calls for public policies that would protect self-organization by workers.

The League's investment of political resources was a significant factor in the formation of the Minnesota Farmer-Labor Party (1918–1944), the Washington Farmer-Labor Party (1920–1924), the Idaho Progressive Party (1922–1926), and the Oklahoma Farmer-Labor Reconstruction League (1922). Upton Sinclair's EPIC (End Poverty In California) platform (1934) for his California gubernatorial campaign was patterned after the NNPL, since Sinclair strongly admired the League.

The League enjoyed friendly relations with President Woodrow Wilson (1912–1920). But the League had little direct impact on national public policy despite calls for institutionalizing those federal controls over the economy that Wilson had established. At the state level, however, the League had a far greater impact. It often shaped public policy even in the face of state and local accusation of radicalism, although in certain cases repression badly crippled it. The League had a lasting impact on credit markets— North Dakota established a state bank still in existence, and Minnesota and South Dakota both adopted rural credits in the post-WWI recession. Moreover, in Minnesota the League played a key role in the establishment of a modest level of iron ore taxation. League leaders envisioned a regional industrial policy—high, almost confiscatory iron ore taxes would force steel mills and automobile plants to locate in Minnesota or western Wisconsin. As a result, farmers would have larger and nearer urban markets, and trade unions would grow in strength.

*See also:* Woodrow Wilson

*Richard M. Valelly*

REFERENCES

Coleman, Patrick K., and Charles R. Lamb. 1985. *The Nonpartisan League, 1915–22: An Annotated Bibliography.* St. Paul: Minnesota Historical Society Press.

Morlan, Robert L. . 1985. *National Nonpartisan League Paper.* St. Paul, MN: Minnesota Historical Society.

———. 1985. *Political Prairie Fire: The Nonpartisan League, 1915–1922.* St. Paul: Minnesota Historical Society Press.

## National Organization for Women

Organized in 1966, the National Organization for Women (NOW) is the largest national feminist organization in the U.S. While the modern civil rights movement was well along in the 1940s, many of the women's organizations active during the suffrage movement had either ceased to exist or were in historian Jo Freeman's words, "a pale shadow of their former selves by the late 1950s." With no existing women's organization poised to take action, NOW was formed after the newly created Equal Employment Opportunity Commission refused to enforce the "sex" provision for equality of the 1964 Civil Rights Act. Betty Friedan, one of the founding members, became NOW's first president. Originally formed to lobby the executive branch, NOW grew rapidly as a grass-roots membership organization: between 1967 and 1974, NOW grew from 1,000 members in 14 chapters to 40,000 members in over 700 chapters. While organized on a federal basis, the national organization operates autonomously and has been strongly influenced by its former president, Eleanor Smeal. Under Smeal's leadership, ratification of the Equal Rights Amendment (ERA) to the Constitution became the primary focus; the national organization became heavily dependent on direct mail contributions and concentrated on mass rallies, colorful demonstrations, and nationally oriented television ads. Membership increased during Smeal's first tenure from 60,000 in 1977 to 220,000 by 1982. Nevertheless, the ERA failed, despite an extension that had been proposed by NOW, on June 30, 1982.

With the ERA receding as a national issue, other more traditional women's groups have become effective advocates for feminist issues. The smaller bipartisan National Women's Political Caucus (NWPC) has targeted its influence within the parties themselves. The membership of NOW has always been predominantly Democratic, but NOW first adopted a partisan role in the 1984 presidential election. In sharp contrast to its previously formal bipartisan stance, the national board of NOW under the presidency of Judy Goldsmith (1983–1985), Smeal's successor, interviewed Democratic candidates Walter Mondale, Gary Hart, and Jesse Jackson before endorsing Mondale in December 1983. The NOW endorsement was publicly perceived as crucial to Mondale's selection of U.S. Representative Geraldine Ferraro as his running mate. NOW was only one of many groups active in the Women's Presidential Project, which coordinated pressure for a woman vice presidential nominee. However, Mondale's selection was preceded by NOW's 1984 national conference during which NOW members warned Mondale publicly and in person that unless a woman was selected, there would be a "thunderstorm."

While women delegates to both Democratic and Republican conventions identify themselves more frequently as representatives of women's groups than of any other kind of interest group, NOW is probably more influential at the Democratic convention. In 1984 approximately 6 percent of Democratic delegates were members of NOW or the NWPC. However, the NOW national board endorsement of Mondale in 1984 did not exert much influence on Democratic delegates: female delegates identifying themselves as representatives of women's groups exhibited a slight preference for Gary Hart's candidacy.

Smeal defeated Goldsmith for reelection in 1985, attacking Goldsmith's coalition-building approach and claiming that NOW should renew the ERA campaign and attack the right on the abortion issue. Smeal, who stepped down in 1987, was succeeded by Molly Yard, then NOW's political director and Smeal's longtime ally and friend. Yard, an ERA activist and leader, defeated New York State NOW president Noreen Connell who was endorsed by Betty Friedan. Yard supports Smeal's confrontational tactics of big marches and demonstrations as well as support for women candidates.

*See also:* Direct Mail, Equal Rights Amendment, Geraldine Ferraro, Jesse Jackson, Walter Mondale, National Women's Political Caucus, Eleanor Smeal, Suffrage

*Denise L. Baer*

REFERENCES

Baer, Denise L., and David A. Bositis. 1988. *Elite Cadres and Party Coalitions: Representing the Public in Party Politics*. Westport, CT: Greenwood.

Fraser, Arvonne S. 1983. "Insiders and Outsiders: Women in the Political Arena." In Irene Tinker, ed. *Women in Washington: Advocates for Public Policy*. Beverly Hills, CA: Sage.

Freeman, Jo. 1983. "On the Origins of Social Movements." In Jo Freeman, ed. *Social Movements of the Sixties and Seventies*. New York: Longman.

Mansbridge, Jane J. 1986. *Why We Lost the ERA*. Chicago: U. of Chicago Pr.

## National Progressive Republican League

Officially formed in 1911, the National Progressive Republican League sought to wrest control of the Republican Party from its conservative leadership in Congress and to nominate a Progressive for President in 1912. The electoral shift of 1910 toward Progressive candidates and attrition through death or resignation of key congressional conservatives signaled an opportunity for insurgent Republicans to challenge the regular GOP leadership. Wisconsin Senator Robert La Follette, with the advice of Oregon reformer William S. U'Ren, outlined a program of political reforms at the state level, including the institution of initiative referendum recall, the corrupt practices act, and the direct election of Senators as well as delegates to presidential nominating conventions. Favorable responses from other prominent Progressives led La Follette to launch the National Progressive Republican League in January 1911. Oregon Senator Jonathan Bourne was president; Nebraska Congressman George Norris, first vice president; Michigan governor Chase Osborn, second vice president; Illinois businessman Charles Crane, treasurer. Nine Senators, sixteen Congressmen, four governors, and several prominent reformers endorsed the League. The League's two greatest weaknesses were its heavy midwestern composition and the absence of Theodore Roosevelt.

La Follette appeared to be the logical Progressive to challenge William Howard Taft's presidential renomination bid in 1912. His opportunity disappeared, however, when he gave a rambling, seemingly confused speech before the Periodical Publishers Association. La Follette alienated his audience and revealed his deteriorating powers of organization. Although the Wisconsin Senator refused to withdraw from the race, Theodore Roosevelt's subsequent declaration that he would challenge Taft effectively eliminated La Follette as a major contender. The League collapsed in disunity as several Progressives decided to support Roosevelt while the La Follette loyalists attacked Roosevelt.

*See also:* Robert La Follette, George Norris, Theodore Roosevelt, Robert Taft

*Nicholas C. Burckel*

REFERENCES

Margulies, Herbert F. 1976. "La Follette, Roosevelt and the Republican Presidential Nomination of 1912." 58 *Mid-America* 54.

Mowry, George E. 1972. "Election of 1912." In Arthur M. Schlesinger, Jr., et al., eds. *The Coming to Power: Critical Presidential Elections in American History.* New York: Chelsea House.

Thelen, David P. 1976. *Robert M. La Follette and the Insurgent Spirit.* Boston: Little, Brown.

## National Republicans

Politicians and voters who supported John Quincy Adams in 1828 and Henry Clay in 1832 against Andrew Jackson and the "Democratic Republicans" were the National Republicans. In Congress, where the National Republicans were led by Clay and Daniel Webster and through newspapers such as the *National Intelligencer*, they opposed Jackson's policies until 1834 when the National Republicans joined with disaffected Democrats and Antimasons to form the Whig coalition.

Although the New York politician and historian Jabez Hammond claimed to have founded the National Republican "party" in 1827, the term was applied indiscriminately during the campaign of 1828. That year the contesting forces were usually associated with the name of the candidate they championed or were designated "Administration" (Adams) and "Anti-Administration" (Jackson), labels that had appeared in the press earlier to describe interest blocs in Congress. As historians have used it, the term "National Republican" better reflects one position on the conflicts over policy that were splintering the Republican hegemony of the postwar decade; the group was not really an organized political party. Yet in the course of the next four years, people did refer to themselves as National Republicans, newspapers took up the cause, and, in certain areas, especially New England and the Middle States, an increasingly large organization was associated with the name. Thus, in December 1831, a "national republican" convention met in Baltimore to nominate Henry Clay for President and John Sergeant of Pennsylvania for Vice President. The convention was made up of 155 delegates from 18 states and the District of Columbia but was basically dominated by New England and the Middle States. (Tennessee for example was represented by only one delegate.) The convention did produce what has been considered the first nominating speech in American presidential history, an "Address to the People" lauding Clay and excoriating Jackson. A "Young Men's National Republican Convention" met a few months later, in May 1832, in Washington to ratify the choice of Clay as the party's candidate. This meeting was the first at which the candidate appeared to personally accept the nomination and the first to adopt a platform. In ten platform resolutions the National Republicans came out in favor of a protective tariff, internal improvements, the ultimate authority of the Supreme Court on constitutional questions, the prerogatives of the Senate; the platform inveighed against the spoils system and Jacksonian foreign policy on the northeast boundary and the Anglo-American settlement on West Indian trade. Only during the election did the national bank issue emerge.

The Jacksonians emphasized the conflict between the "Aristocracy and the People" and denied that Clay and the "new fangled" National Republicans were republicans at all. The election was something of a landslide for Jackson, who took 219 electoral votes to 49 for Clay and 7 for the Antimason candidate, William Wirt. Clay received only 37.5 percent of the popular vote although he did relatively well in southern New England, the Middle Atlantic States, and Ohio. Delaware, Maryland, and Clay's home state of Kentucky were the only slave states in which the National Republican ticket gained electoral votes.

*See also:* John Quincy Adams, Henry Clay, Election of 1828, Andrew Jackson, Daniel Webster

*William G. Shade*

REFERENCES

Remini, Robert. 1963. *The Election of 1828*. Philadelphia: Lippincott.

Schlesinger, Arthur M., Jr., and Fred L. Israel, eds. "The Election of 1828" and "The Election of 1832." *History of American Presidential Elections: 1789–1968.* New York: Chelsea House.

## National Rifle Association

Founded in 1871 in response to the poor marksmanship displayed by northern soldiers during the Civil War, the National Rifle Association (NRA) is probably the prototypic single-issue interest group in America. It promotes firearm possession and use for shooting, hunting, gun collecting and self-protection; it vigorously opposes gun control measures as an infringement of the Second Amendment to the Constitution. The Second Amendment reads, "A well regulated militia, being necessary to the security of a free state, the right of the people to keep and bear arms shall not be abridged." Interpretation of the amendment has been the subject of intense debate for more than a century, with the NRA vociferously advocating a pro-gun position.

The NRA is a multifaceted organization. First, it is a powerful, organized lobby at the local, state, and federal levels through its Institute for Legislative Action (ILA). In the late 1980s, the ILA had an $11 million budget (raised mostly from voluntary contributions) and 80 staffers, mostly professional lobbyists in Washington and in the field. But the NRA is more than a lobby group; it is also an immense service organization that trains law enforcement officers, conducts hunter safety programs, and supplies members with various fringe benefits, including insurance programs. For many years, it made available inexpensive government-surplus firearms and ammunition; the NRA also instructs Olympic shooters and sponsors shooting tournaments. The NRA has an affluent nonpartisan political action committee, NRA–Political Victory Fund (NRA-PVF), which regularly during the 1980s was among the top ten PACs in both funds contributed to candidates and independent expenditures. NRA-PVF endorsements and contributions are determined solely by a candidate's position on gun control. Finally, the NRA is an organization of 3.1 million members, often exerting significant political influence as single-issue voters. The NRA has a $60 million budget, 300 paid staff, 54 state groups, 10,000 local gun clubs, and two major publications (3 million subscribers). It is second only to the AFL-CIO in terms of spending on internal communications and is legendary for its ability to mobilize its members for letter-writing campaigns to legislators.

The NRA was successful in getting certain portions of the 1968 Gun Control Act relaxed in 1986, but it has found itself more and more at odds with many law enforcement organizations that favor gun control as a means to of combatting crime. The association has also had to fight numerous gun control initiatives at the state and local levels in recent years.

*See also:* Political Action Committees

*Clyde Brown*

REFERENCES

Corrigan, Richard. 1986. "NRA, Using Members, Ads and Money, Hits Police Line in Lobbying Drive." January 4 *National Journal* 8.

Spitzer, Robert J. 1988. "Gun Control." In Raymond Tatalovich and Byron W. Daynes, eds. *Social Regulatory Policy.* Boulder, CO: Westview Press.

## National Right to Life Committee

Formed in 1973 in reaction to the Supreme Court's ruling in *Roe v. Wade* that a woman had a right to obtain an abortion, the National Right to Life Committee (NRLC) has long been the largest and most influential interest group working to end legal abortions in the United States. The NRLC has chapters in all 50 states and also supports 2,500 local chapters. With national headquarters in Washington, D.C., NRLC lobbies members of Congress and federal agencies, offers congressional testimony, conducts research, maintains a speakers' bureau, issues a variety of publications, coordinates and promotes grass-roots activities, and grants awards. Its committees include the Federal Political Action Committee, and the National Right to Life Political Action Committee (LAPAC). NRLC's departments include Education, Legislative, News, and Public Relations. NRLC claims national membership of about 7 million and holds annual national conventions. It also opposes euthanasia.

NRLC has focused much of its effort on enacting statutory and constitutional restrictions to abortion practices. It has also pressured state legislatures to approve a call for a constitutional convention as an alternate means of amending the Constitution. Through its political action wing, it seeks to raise money in support of anti-abortion public officials and office seekers, and in opposition to pro-choice sympathizers. With the exception of the enactment of the Hyde Amendment—a federal restriction barring the use of federal Medicaid funds for abortion—right to life forces have failed to obtain their desired legislative restrictions on abortion, despite the election of right to life sympathizer Ronald Reagan to the presidency. NRLC has also filed friend of the court briefs to the Supreme Court in four abortion cases from 1973 to 1987.

NRLC has been considered more traditional in its political activities than other right to life groups, and it has engendered the ire of other more extreme elements of the right to life movement, such as the New York–based Right to Life Party. For example, the NRLC endorsed Ronald Reagan for President in 1980, while the RTLP endorsed the minor party's leader Ellen McCormack (the RTLP leaders considered Reagan's stand against abortion to be insufficiently enthusiastic).

While NRLC decries the use of violence and other illegal activities, including the firebombing of abortion clinics, it has disseminated information on tactical means for disrupting abortion activities. One of the NRLC's best-known activities has been coordination of an annual demonstration in Washington on the anniversary of the *Roe v. Wade* decision. The rise and persistence of the NRLC and other anti-abortion groups is symptomatic of the rise in single-issue politics in the 1970s and 1980s.

In its early days, NRLC was headed by Judie Brown. Her husband, Paul Brown, left a job as manager of a K-Mart store to head LAPAC. In the 1980s, NRLC has been headed by a medical doctor, Jack C. Willke.

*See also:* Ellen McCormack, Political Action Committees, Ronald Reagan

*Robert J. Spitzer*

REFERENCES

Tatalovich, Raymond, and Byron Daynes. 1981. *The Politics of Abortion.* New York: Praeger.

## National Silver Party

This party existed only briefly during the election of 1896. Its birth can be traced to the 1895 merger of three pro-silver organizations (the American Bimetallic League, the National Bimetallic League, and the National Executive Silver Committee) into the American Bimetallic Union and its political arm, the National Silver Party. The establishing conference called for a national convention in St. Louis in July 1896,

and the Populist Party then agreed to meet at the same time in the same city. The National Silver Party numbered no important politicians among its members except for Senator William M. Stewart and Senator John P. Jones of Nevada.

When the National Silver Party met in July, the Democrats had already nominated William Jennings Bryan and Arthur Sewall as their 1896 national ticket and had adopted a silver platform. Silver men had never supposed that the Democrats would take such a radical pro-silver action and thus found their own silver position seriously undercut. The National Silver Party had no choice but to endorse Bryan and Sewall unanimously, but when they met in conference with the Populists, agreement on Sewall proved impossible. The Populists stood by Tom Watson as their vice presidential candidate.

Nevertheless, Bryan went into the campaign with support from three political parties—the Democrats, the Populists, and the National Silverites. The latter maintained their organization but, in fact, were actually subordinate to the Democrats. The NSP's main role seemed to be to retain the large number of Republicans attracted to the pro-silver banner, voters who might otherwise have returned to the GOP. Mining money better financed the National Silver Party than the Populists or the Democrats, and it used its funds to campaign particularly strongly in Chicago, where some 600 silver clubs and a Women's Silver League flourished. When Bryan lost the election, however, the National Silver Party, like the Populists, faded from existence.

*See also:* William Jennings Bryan, Election of 1896, Populist (People's) Party

*John F. Marszalek*

REFERENCES

Coletta, Paolo E. 1964. *William Jennings Bryan: Political Evangelist 1860–1908.* Lincoln: U. of Nebraska Pr.

Glad, Paul W. 1964. *McKinley, Bryan, and the People.* Philadelphia: Lippincott.

Glass, Mary Ellen. 1969. *Silver and Politics in Nevada: 1892–1902.* Reno: U. of Nevada Pr.

Jones, Stanley L. 1964. *The Presidential Election of 1896.* Madison: U. of Wisconsin Pr.

## National Woman's Party

The National Woman's Party (NWP) emerged out of the twentieth-century women's suffrage campaign. In 1913, Alice Paul, an American participant in the British suffrage movement, was appointed chair of the Congressional Committee of the National American Woman

Suffrage Association (NAWSA). Within months, Paul and Lucy Burns formed the separate national Congressional Union that challenged NAWSA to devote all of its efforts to the passage of a federal suffrage amendment. When NAWSA's leadership rejected this strategy and removed Paul from her position, the other members of the committee resigned and coalesced around the Congressional Union. Using a technique borrowed from the British, they dedicated the new organization to achieving the suffrage amendment by holding the party in power—the Democrats—responsible for its passage.

In 1914 the Congressional Union campaigned against all Democratic candidates regardless of their individual stand on suffrage. Members concentrated their energies in the states where women were indeed able to vote and claimed credit for defeating 23 of 43 western Democrats. To transfer this effort successfully in the presidential campaign, they created the National Woman's Party in June 1916 and campaigned unsuccessfully to defeat Woodrow Wilson.

The NWP became a nationwide organization when it merged with the Congressional Union in 1917. The leadership turned to more militant tactics and began to picket the White House. NWP banners instigated altercations after the United States entered World War I because they featured slogans challenging the nation's devotion to democracy. Women were arrested and jailed, some for up to six months. When they went on hunger strikes, they were force fed and became martyrs to the cause. Their efforts attracted publicity, renewed vigor, and new members, all of which helped to bring about the successful passage of the Nineteenth Amendment giving women the vote.

Once the goal of suffrage was achieved, the party decided to remain in existence in order to eliminate all remaining forms of discrimination against women. To that end, the party leadership proposed that it would work to achieve an Equal Rights Amendment (ERA) with the same single-mindedness evident in the suffrage campaign. Some within the NWP wanted a more comprehensive program that would allow the party enough flexibility to express concern over issues involving discrimination against Blacks. The leadership prevailed and the ERA was introduced in Congress in 1923. The party also supported international versions: the Equal Rights Treaty and the Equal Nationality Treaty.

The party's unrelenting campaign for the amendment helped to create an irreparable division in the post-1920 women's movement. Other women's groups, including NAWSA's successor, the League of Women Voters, considered the ERA a threat to special labor laws created to protect women in the work force. This legislation had resulted from a long and hard fight by women reformers for limitations on the kind of work that women could do, for maximum hours, and for the elimination of night work for women.

The ERA split the women's movement so completely that the organizations were unable to cooperate on any issue again until the 1960s. The ERA represented not only a method for achieving equality but an ideological definition of it as well.

The NWP held that women were the equal of men on the basis of their shared humanity and that individual talent, not sexual differences, should determine a person's place in society. The party claimed that women would be made equal when they were allowed all the rights and responsibilities accorded men. It declared the ERA the most efficient means to eliminate discriminatory restrictions. While the party supported special labor laws for both sexes as protective, they condemned them as restrictive and inequitable when applied only to women.

The NWP worked for the ERA as it had suffrage, campaigning only for those office seekers who supported the amendment. The party also encouraged the election and appointment of women, claiming that success would not only bring the women's viewpoint into government but also would develop a women's bloc vote. The party successfully lobbied to get members like Jessie Dell appointed as Civil Service commissioner and Rebekah Greathouse as assistant U.S. district attorney in 1925. The NWP also supported those who were not members but were sympathetic to their principles, such as Democrat Ruth Bryan Owens in a 1928 Florida congressional contest. They were willing to oppose women who did not support the NWP, such as Republican Ruth Hanna McCormick who was critical of the party. In a 1930 New York congressional election, the NWP went so far as to endorse Socialist Heywood Broun and Democrat Louis Brodsky against incumbent Republican Ruth Baker Pratt who opposed the ERA. It was the only time, though, that the party opposed a woman and supported her male opponents.

Even so, the NWP was not a political party in the traditional sense, nor was it organized simply to take part in the political process. It also sponsored research on women's lives and investigated and acted on discrimination against women, reporting such efforts in the party journal, *Equal Rights*. The NWP was the only women's organization after 1920 that defined itself as feminist and was dedicated solely to pursuing rights for women.

For the most part, the organization was dominated by Alice Paul and controlled from the top by educated professional women from the upper-middle classes. Efforts were made to reach other classes through industrial and occupational councils in the 1920s and 1930s, but the majority of the party's funds came from wealthy members. Though the leadership's decisions were binding, disagreements in 1935 and 1947 resulted in short-lived schisms. Membership was estimated to be from 30,000 to 60,000 in the suffrage years, and afterward shrinking below 10,000.

In time, the ERA became more popular, especially when major political figures like Eleanor Roosevelt expressed support and the League of Women Voters finally joined the fight in 1959. A more unified women's movement took up the cause in the late 1960s, and the Equal Rights Amendment was passed by Congress in 1972. Despite their failure to achieve the ERA's ratification, the party continues to maintain headquarters in Washington, D.C.

*See also:* Equal Rights Amendment, National American Woman Suffrage Association, Nineteenth Amendment, Alice Paul, Eleanor Roosevelt, Woodrow Wilson

*Joy A. Scimé*

REFERENCES

Becker, Susan D. 1981. *The Origins of the Equal Rights Amendment: American Feminism Between the Wars.* Westport, CT: Greenwood.

Lunardini, Christine A. 1986. *From Equal Suffrage to Equal Rights: Alice Paul and the National Woman's Party, 1910–1928.* New York: New York U. Pr.

Nelson, Marjory. 1976. "Ladies in the Streets: A Sociological Analysis of the National Woman's Party, 1910–1930." Ph.D. dissertation, State U. of New York at Buffalo.

Scimé, Joy A. 1987. "Government Policy, Working Women and Feminism in the Great Depression: Section 213 of the 1932 Economy Act." Ph.D. dissertation, State U. of New York at Buffalo.

## National Women's Political Caucus

Established in July 1971, the National Women's Political Caucus (NWPC) was formed to increase the visibility of women in politics as well as to encourage women's election and appointment to public office. Among its founders were some of the most prominent leaders of the women's movement, including Shirley Chisholm, Bella Abzug, Gloria Steinem, Betty Friedan, and Patsy Mink. At NWPC's first national convention, Shirley Chisholm stated that "the function of the NWPC is not to be the cutting edge of the women's liberation movement, but the big umbrella organization which provides the weight and muscle for those issues which the majority of women in this country see as concerns." The NWPC was intended to be a vehicle through which women could better influence decision-makers; more importantly, it would eventually provide the requisite support to assist women themselves in becoming decision-makers.

The NWPC is one of a number of women's advocacy groups formed during the late 1960s and the early 1970s such as the National Organization for Women (NOW) and the Women's Equity Action League (WEAL). The NWPC came to symbolize a maturing women's movement as leaders of various entities realized that genuine change would occur only when women became active participants in the political process. The founding of the National Women's Political Caucus provided the women's movement with a political instrument to direct the efforts to place women in appointive and elective office, to lobby on behalf of women's issues, and to raise money for campaigns. The rapid growth of state and local caucuses is evidence of women's perceived need for just such an organization; one year after its founding, all fifty states, the District of Columbia, and Puerto Rico had active caucuses. Because of the very success of the network of state and local groups, the NWPC experienced some internal conflict when it decided to go national by opening a Washington lobbying office in 1973.

As stated in its literature, the NWPC is a multipartisan organization, aligned with neither of the two major parties. The majority of members are middle class and belong predominantly to the Democratic Party. Its members have been extremely active in local, state, and national politics: approximately 90 percent of the membership has worked in campaigns, and over a third of the members have held party leadership posts.

On the heels of its founding, the NWPC played an influential role in the 1972 Democratic

National Convention. Taking advantage of the McGovern-Fraser reforms in the delegate selection process, the NWPC's efforts allowed women to gain 40 percent of the delegate positions. The NWPC provided informational sessions for these female delegates in an attempt to make them more effective participants. Significantly, the NWPC authored a women's plank in the Democratic platform that included federal funding for child-care programs and support for the Equal Rights Amendment. The caucus also ran Frances "Sissy" Farenthold, a former gubernatorial candidate in Texas, for Vice President.

At the 1972 Republican National Convention, the NWPC realized less success. Only a relatively weak child-care plank was included in the GOP platform. Women did, however, comprise approximately 30 percent of the delegates, up from 17 percent in 1968.

While the 1972 presidential election was disappointing to a majority of NWPC members, the caucus achieved noteworthy results in its initial year. For example, more women than ever before sought elected office. The representation of women in state legislatures increased by 28 percent. Nationally, five new women were elected to the House of Representatives—four Democrats and one Republican.

The influence of the National Women's Political Caucus has widened over the years. The group was active in the passage of major legislation affecting women, such as the Equal Credit Opportunity Act of 1974 and the Women's Educational Equity Act of 1974. With the aid of the NWPC's Campaign Support Committee, female candidates have received money and other assistance requisite for electoral success.

*See also:* Bella Abzug, Shirley Chisholm, Equal Rights Amendment, Frances "Sissy" Farenthold, Betty Friedan, McGovern-Fraser Commission, National Organization for Women, Gloria Steinem, Women's Equity Action League

*Susan L. Roberts*

REFERENCES

Deckard, Barbara Sinclair. 1983. *The Women's Movement.* New York: Harper & Row.

Tinker, Irene, ed. 1983. *Women in Washington.* Sage Yearbooks in Women's Policy Studies. Vol. 7. Beverly Hills, CA: Sage.

## Negative Advertising

Primarily associated with television, negative advertising in campaigns became the focus of attention following the 1988 presidential election, an election noted for its negative campaigning and for its focus on personalities. The term "negative advertising" refers to advertising that portrays a candidate's opponent in an unfavorable light; it is also referred to as "comparison advertising." Although political caricatures such as those by Thomas Nast and the practice of adversary journalism such as that of the Muckrakers have been a familiar component of American politics, real concern over the use of negative advertising in campaigns is a relatively recent phenomenon.

Edwin Diamond and Stephen Bates, authors of *The Spot: The Rise of Political Advertising on Television*, credit the Democrats and Adlai Stevenson in 1956 with the first use of negative television advertising. Using footage of Dwight Eisenhower from one of his 1952 commercials addressing political corruption, the spot dramatized how well (or poorly) Eisenhower had kept his promises. Although subsequent television advertisements relied on comparisons between candidates, it was not until the 1964 "Daisy" commercial in the Lyndon Johnson–Barry Goldwater presidential campaign that negative television advertisements attracted considerable attention. The Johnson commercial merged the picture of a young girl plucking daisy petals with the countdown of a nuclear explosion, implying that Goldwater would involve the nation in a nuclear war. This commercial, now the quintessential symbol of negative political advertisements, was withdrawn after only one showing owing to its provocative nature.

The most celebrated negative advertisement of the 1988 presidential campaign was a George Bush television spot involving Willie Horton, a convicted murderer from Massachusetts who raped a woman while on furlough from prison. The commercial suggested that many other crimes were committed by prisoners on furlough in Massachusetts, painting a picture of Michael Dukakis as "soft" on crime. The use of negative advertising has been prevalent at the congressional level as well. The 1984 Senate race in North Carolina between Jesse Helms and Jim Hunt, for example, received national attention for both its record level of campaign expenditures as well as its abundance of negative advertising.

The heavy reliance on electronic media and image politics of the contemporary American political campaign raises a number of questions about the impact of negative advertising on the electorate. Does negative advertising contribute to cynicism on the part of voters and consequently lower the level of turnout? Does negative advertising devalue the issues and overemphasize personality politics? At what point is a negative strategy counterproductive? Central to a discussion of negative advertising among politicians is the question of whether or not it works. Although candidates realize the risks of appearing unfair or malicious in their advertising, the prevalence of negative advertising would seem to suggest that negativity is a risk that many candidates are willing to take.

*See also:* George Bush, Michael Dukakis, Dwight D. Eisenhower, Barry Goldwater, Jesse Helms, Lyndon B. Johnson, Adlai Stevenson II

*Susan L. Roberts*

REFERENCES

Broder, David S., and Paul Taylor. 1988. "How the Presidential Campaign Got Stuck on the Low Road." November 7 *The Washington Post National Weekly* 14.

Diamond, Edwin, and Stephen Bates. 1988. *The Spot: The Rise of Political Advertising on Television.* Cambridge: MIT Pr.

Jamieson, Kathleen Hall. 1984. *Packaging the President.* Oxford: Oxford U. Pr.

Kazee, Thomas A., and Patrick J. Sellers. 1987. "Poisoning the Atmosphere or Energizing the Electorate?: The Impact of Negative Advertising in Political Campaigns." Paper presented at the 1987 Annual Meeting of the American Political Science Association, Chicago.

## Harry S. New (1858–1937)

Republican National Chairman, United States Senator, and Postmaster General. Born into a political family, Harry Stewart New's father was Treasurer of the United States under Ulysses S. Grant and consul general at London under Benjamin Harrison. His father was also publisher of the Indianapolis *Journal*. New was educated at Butler University and began his career as a reporter on the *Journal*, rising to the position of editor. In 1896 he was elected both to the state senate and as a delegate to the Republican National Convention. After brief service in the Spanish-American War, he was chosen national committeeman from Indiana in 1900.

New was one of the new generation of Republican politicians recruited into the entourage of President Theodore Roosevelt in 1904 by George Cortelyou. New was in charge of the campaign literature in the Midwest regional office and was next elevated to the vice chairmanship of the national committee in 1906. He became acting chairman in January 1907, when Cortelyou resigned. The national committee confirmed New's status as national chairman in December 1907, and he served through the 1908

national convention. Between 1900 and 1912, New was generally considered "one of the most powerful political figures of the Middle West."

In 1912 New struggled to manage the divisive national convention on behalf of President William Howard Taft. He was elected United States Senator in 1917, appointed Postmaster General under Harding in 1923, and reappointed to that Cabinet post by Coolidge in 1925.

*See also:* Calvin Coolidge, George B. Cortelyou, Ulysses S. Grant, Warren G. Harding, Benjamin Harrison, Theodore Roosevelt, William Howard Taft

*Ralph M. Goldman*

## New Deal

Implemented during Franklin D. Roosevelt's presidency, the "New Deal" established the regulatory-welfare state of modern America, helped consummate the political realignment, producing the New Deal party system with its Democratic majority, and set the course of American politics and government for decades to come. When FDR became President in March 1933, the Great Depression had devastated the nation's economy. One-fourth of the work force was unemployed, millions more were impoverished, and both industrial production and farm income had fallen more than 50 percent below 1929 levels. The Roosevelt administration's efforts to achieve economic recovery, provide assistance to the jobless and destitute, and effect institutional and social reform through the New Deal had large and lasting consequences for electoral politics.

Politics and public policy were intertwined throughout the Roosevelt years. A repudiation of the incumbent Republican (Herbert Hoover) administration, the landslide 1932 election gave Roosevelt and the Democratic Party a mandate to try new approaches to deal with the cataclysmic Depression. The immediate result was the "First New Deal," implemented during FDR's fabled "Hundred Days" of 1933 and concerned especially with recovery by means of national planning and controls in industry and agriculture. Among its many initiatives, the early New Deal also assumed America's first federal responsibility for relief assistance to the poor, enacted important banking and stock-market reform, and helped financial institutions as well as middle-class Americans with measures to protect savings accounts and home and farm mortgages. Impressive Democratic gains in the 1934 election—counter to the long-established pattern of the President's party losing ground in off-year elections—provided early evidence of the political impact of the New Deal and facilitated the "Second New Deal" of 1935. More reformist than the First New Deal, the 1935 legislative agenda included such measures as the Works Progress Administration, with its innovative variety of work-relief programs; the Social Security Act for old-age pensions and unemployment insurance; the Wagner Act for organized labor; and progressive tax reform. The Second New Deal was partly the product of the shortcomings or termination of earlier New Deal programs, but it was the result of politics as well. Caught between increasingly intransigent opposition from the right and the "thunder on the left" from popular leaders like Huey Long and Francis Townsend, FDR, a practical politician, moved in 1935 toward the new reform programs—measures toward which his administration and the more liberal and Democratic Congress elected in 1934 were heading anyway.

The 1936 election resoundingly demonstrated the New Deal's impact on American politics. A massive affirmation of the New Deal and Franklin Roosevelt, the crushing Democratic landslide culminated the political realignment of the 1930s and established the Democrats as the nation's majority party. Turnout rose sharply, and millions of new voters, activated by allegiance to FDR and the New Deal, cast Democratic ballots. Including the traditional Democratic Solid South but distinguished especially by huge majorities among working-class, lower-middle-class, ethnic, and African-American voters in urban-industrial areas, the New Deal coalition enabled FDR to sweep three-fifths of the popular vote and 46 (all but Maine and Vermont) of the 48 states. The election was also a signal victory for the Democratic Party, which won overwhelming control of the Congress.

Despite the great victory of 1936, Roosevelt thereafter encountered a waxing conservative coalition of Republicans and anti-New Deal Democrats in the Congress and waning support in the electorate for extending the New Deal. Southern Democrats, typically senior Senators and Congressmen distressed about the new dominance of urban liberals in the Democratic Party and about a more assertive presidency under FDR, played a particularly important role in thwarting the New Deal. Reflecting also traditional American localism and antistatism, the conservative coalition was fueled by the 1937 "court-packing" episode, the sharp economic downturn of 1937 and 1938, FDR's attempt to "purge" anti-New Deal Democrats in the 1938 primaries, and Republican gains in the 1938 congressional elections. For all that, Roosevelt's second term was not without accomplishment, and some scholars have discerned in it the lineaments of an emerging "Third New Deal" of a reorganized and strengthened executive branch and of liberal Keynesian prescriptions to achieve both recovery and reform. Still, the New Deal had clearly lost momentum by the late 1930s. World War II then brought a changed political context of global priorities and defense prosperity that further militated against liberal reform. Despite Roosevelt's decisive and unprecedented third- and fourth-term victories in 1940 and 1944, liberal proposals for significantly expanding the New Deal at the end of the war did not eventuate. Nevertheless, Harry S Truman's 1948 victory reflected the degree to which the New Deal and the Roosevelt coalition had become established facts of the American polity.

What was the impact and legacy of the New Deal? The New Deal did not end the Depression (World War II did that); it did not provide adequate assistance for all those who needed it; and it did not radically restructure the nation's economy or society or effect a fundamental redistribution of power or wealth. Yet economic indexes generally improved after 1933; landmark federal programs for the first time provided relief assistance and a floor on living standards; and the New Deal reformed and strengthened the nation's economic institutions while implementing social reform and including such groups as organized labor, Catholics, Jews, Blacks, and women in national politics and government to an unprecedented degree. In pursuing that agenda, Roosevelt and the New Deal broker state paid attention to the "common man" as the federal government never had before and restored national confidence and optimism. For all those reasons and more, the New Deal helped make the Democrats—the minority party since the 1890s—the nation's new majority party, reduced the GOP to minority status, and accelerated the decline of the Socialist Party as a significant political force. It also established voting patterns and party differences that persisted far beyond the 1930s. Often described as but a "half-way revolution" in public policy, the New Deal was central to a dramatic and durable transformation of American politics.

*See also:* Elections of 1932, 1936, 1940, and 1944; Herbert Hoover; Huey Long; Franklin D. Roosevelt; Francis Townsend; Harry S Truman

*John W. Jeffries*

REFERENCES

Allswang, John M. 1978. *The New Deal and American Politics*. New York: Wiley.

Badger, Anthony J. 1989. *The New Deal: The Depression Years, 1933–1940*. New York: Noonday.

Blum, John M. 1976. *V Was for Victory: Politics and American Culture During World War II*. New York: Harcourt Brace Jovanovich.

Burns, James MacGregor. 1956. *Roosevelt: The Lion and the Fox*. New York: Harcourt, Brace & World.

————. 1970. *Roosevelt: The Soldier of Freedom*. New York: Harcourt Brace Jovanovich.

Jeffries, John W. 1979. *Testing the Roosevelt Coalition: Connecticut Society and Politics in the Era of World War II*. Knoxville: U. of Tennessee Pr.

Ladd, Everett C., Jr., and Charles D. Hadley. 1978. *Transformations of the American Party System: Political Coalitions from the New Deal to the 1970s*. 2d rev. ed. New York: Norton.

Leuchtenburg, William E. 1963. *Franklin D. Roosevelt and the New Deal, 1932–1940*. New York: Harper & Row.

Lubell, Samuel. 1965. *The Future of American Politics*. 3rd rev. ed. New York: Harper & Row.

Patterson, James T. 1967. *Congressional Conservatism and the New Deal: The Growth of the Conservative Coalition in Congress, 1933–1939*. Lexington: U. Pr. of Kentucky.

Sitkoff, Harvard, ed. 1985. *Fifty Years Later: The New Deal Evaluated*. New York: Knopf.

Stave, Bruce M. 1970. *The New Deal and the Last Hurrah: Pittsburgh Machine Politics*. Pittsburgh: U. of Pittsburgh Pr.

Weiss, Nancy J. 1983. *Farewell to the Party of Lincoln: Black Politics in the Age of FDR*. Princeton: Princeton U. Pr.

## New Deal Coalition

The New Deal was an exceptional period in American history, an era beginning with the inauguration of President Franklin D. Roosevelt in 1933 and ending during World War II. It was an era in American political life characterized by a new public philosophy, one in which the federal government assumed a major role in organizing and regulating the economy as well as providing for the material well-being of American citizens. This new role of the federal government as a "benevolent force" in the everyday life of individuals was wonderfully captured for a popular audience in John Ford's cinematic version of Steinbeck's *Grapes of Wrath* (1939), in which a federal housing camp is seen as an island of stability, prosperity, and community in an otherwise harsh and brutal world. Moreover, as political scientist Samuel Beer has argued, the New Deal stood for the nationalization of American politics and for the rapid democratization of political life. The balance of

political power during the New Deal shifted from the states to Washington, D.C. Under FDR's lead, Congress enacted legislation that substantially expanded the scope of national political authority, such as the Social Security Act of 1935, the National Labor Relations Act of 1935, and the Fair Labor Standards Act of 1938. In this way, a truncated version of the modern welfare state was introduced to America, and a national bureaucracy was made an integral part of the federal government.

But the New Deal did more than herald a new understanding of the role of the federal government in American politics. It also reinvigorated and transformed the American party system. For a generation, American parties had been in a state of decline, as seen by diminishing rates of voter turnout and the demise of local party organizations. But during the New Deal, national voting turnout increased with the rapid mobilization of nonactive voting groups into the electorate, and local party organizations were given new life because of a large infusion of federal funds to urban areas across America. The party benefiting most from this revival of the American party system, of course, was the Democrats. Whereas the Democratic Party had generally been the national minority party since the Civil War, its strength largely confined to the South, the Democrats were given new life in the 1930s as theirs became the national party of choice for a majority of Americans. Between 1933 and 1968, the Democrats held the presidency for 28 of the 36 years, were the majority in the Congress for 32 of the 36 years, and dominated many state and local governments. Rarely in American history had one political party so effectively controlled national and state electoral politics.

The electoral coalition that comprised the Democratic Party throughout the New Deal party system consisted of a wide array of different economic interests, regional alliances, and ethnic and racial voting groups. In terms of economic interests, the New Deal coalition joined together organized labor, poverty-stricken Americans, and capital-intensive manufacturing firms. In terms of regional alliances, the New Deal coalition was very inclusive, broadening the Democratic Party's base from its traditional stronghold in the South to new areas of voting strength, such as the urban centers of the North and Midwest, old mill and manufacturing towns in New England, and the agrarian West. In this way, two-party competition was returned to virtually every area of the United States (except the Senate). Finally, in terms of voter alignments, the New Deal coalition provided a broad base for political participation. The sociodemographic base of the New Deal coalition largely consisted of Catholics (especially of Irish and Polish origin); Jews; Blacks; working-, middle-, and upper-class southerners; union member families; and to a somewhat lesser degree, working-class Protestants.

The New Deal coalition brought together many diverse economic interests, regional alliances, and voting factions—all of which joined the ranks of the Democratic Party on economic policy grounds in support of an activist role for the federal government in directing the economy. But the New Deal coalition could not endure forever; too many cleavages split the New Deal coalition—such as the one between southerners and Blacks. Beginning in 1964, a majority of southern voters cast their ballots for non-Democratic presidential candidates. The only exception to this trend was in 1976, when the Democrats under Jimmy Carter temporarily revived a scaled-down version of the New Deal coalition. Catholic voters, now the beneficiaries of a growing economic prosperity and of relocation from large urban centers to the suburbs, began to vote increasingly on the basis of their economic status and not on their ethnic identification, with growing numbers defecting to the Republican Party. The only voting group that remained consistently loyal to the New Deal coalition throughout the 1932–1988 period were Black Americans, who voted overwhelmingly for Democratic candidates for office in national, state, and local elections. Although the New Deal coalition in the 1990s is no longer a consistent and effective voting bloc in presidential elections, it nevertheless remains a powerful symbolic and rallying force in American politics: Democratic presidential candidates continue to direct their appeals to this coalition that once so clearly dominated the American electoral landscape.

*See also:* Jimmy Carter, Franklin D. Roosevelt

*Richard A. Champagne, Jr.*

REFERENCES

Andersen, K. 1979. *The Creation of a Democratic Majority, 1928–1936*. Chicago: U. of Chicago Pr.

Axelrod, Robert. 1972. "Where the Votes Come From: An Analysis of Electoral Coalitions, 1952–1968." 66 *American Political Science Review* 11.

Beer, Samuel. 1978. "In Search of a New Public Philosophy." In Anthony King, ed. *The New American Political System*. Washington: American Enterprise Institute.

Burnham, Walter Dean. 1970. *Critical Elections and the Mainsprings of American Politics*. New York: Norton.

Clubb, Jerome, William Flanigan, and Nancy Zingale. 1980. *Partisan Realignment*. Beverly Hills, CA: Sage.

Garson, Robert. 1974. *The Democratic Party and the Politics of Sectionalism, 1941–1948*. Baton Rouge: Louisiana State U. Pr.

Kuttner, Robert. 1987. *The Life of the Party: Democratic Prospects in 1988 and Beyond*. New York: Viking.

Ladd, Everett Carll, with Charles Hadley. 1978. *Transformations of the American Party System*. New York: Norton.

Mollenkopf, J. 1983. *The Contested City*. Princeton: Princeton U. Pr.

Petrocik, John. 1981. *Party Coalitions: Realignments and the Decline of the New Deal Party System*. Chicago: U. of Chicago Pr.

Schattschneider, E. E. 1960. *The Semi-Sovereign People*. Hinsdale, IL: Dryden Press.

Sundquist, James. 1983. *Dynamics of the Party System*. Washington: Brookings.

## New Hampshire Primary

Every President elected from 1952 to 1988 has won the New Hampshire, "first-in-the-nation" primary election. This unbroken streak of ten straight elections has given this presidential primary a unique place in modern American electoral history. And it has also led to cries of foul by losing candidates and by politicians in other states.

New Hampshire now seems willing to do anything to retain its "first-in-the-nation" status, but that was not always the case. The Granite State first established a presidential primary in 1913 as part of the response to progressive calls for reforming the political parties. The original primary was to be held in late spring, but as typically frugal New Englanders, the New Hampshire legislators soon discovered that they could save money if they held the primary on the same day as their town meetings—the traditional form of local government in much of New Hampshire. Town meetings were held in early March, before spring mud season made rural roads impassable. Thus, the New Hampshire primary came first.

Still, the New Hampshire primary—and primaries in general—were largely ignored by American politicians during the first half of this century. In 1949, however, the New Hampshire state legislature added a presidential preference line to the primary ballot; voting on that line did not affect the selection of delegates, but it did give the winning candidate added publicity.

Primaries of this type became known as "beauty contest" primaries: they featured the presidential candidates' names, but a victory did not pay off in delegates to the national nominating convention. However, the publicity from winning the "beauty contest" was worth more than the relatively small number of party delegates apportioned to New Hampshire.

The New Hampshire primary first came to the nation's attention in 1952, when politicians interested in the candidacy of Dwight ("Ike") Eisenhower placed his name on the Republican ballot without seeking his permission. Massachusetts Senator Henry Cabot Lodge, who was leading the "Draft Eisenhower" effort, worked to assure that "Ike" won the "beauty contest" part of the election. When he did, soundly defeating the Republican establishment's candidate, Ohio Senator Robert Taft, the Eisenhower boomlet took off. On the same day, Tennessee Senator Estes Kefauver defeated President Harry Truman in the Democratic "beauty contest." Though Truman entered the contest late and claimed that he had decided much earlier not to seek reelection, the Kefauver victory certainly solidified the President's decision to retire. And these two results formed the basis for the reputation of the New Hampshire primary.

The New Hampshire primary has played critical roles in other nomination campaigns. In 1968, Senator Eugene McCarthy (D-Minn.), running on an antiwar platform, did much better in New Hampshire than analysts had projected (he still lost to Lyndon Johnson, even though the President's name did not appear on the ballot); McCarthy's showing was instrumental in Johnson's decision not to seek reelection. In 1972 Senator Edmund Muskie (D-Maine) did less well than pundits felt he should have, considering that he came from a neighboring state; his too-narrow victory in New Hampshire was the first blow to a campaign that never adjusted to a changing electoral climate. In 1976 a little-known former governor of Georgia won a surprise victory in New Hampshire; in spite of Jimmy Carter's failure to poll anywhere near a majority of the votes, his victory propelled him onto the national news shows, the covers of weekly magazines, and into the front-runner's position—a position he never relinquished. Ronald Reagan used the New Hampshire primary in 1980 to recover the momentum that he had lost to George Bush, who had won a surprising victory in the Iowa caucuses. Then the Vice President and presidential candidate George Bush, drawing on painful lessons from the past, spared no effort to be certain that he won a New Hampshire primary victory in 1988 in order to break any momentum that Senator Robert Dole (R-Kans.) had begun with his Iowa victory. New Hampshire led Bush to turn to negative advertising for the first time, demonstrating his willingness to use any technique to win this important contest.

Critics claim that the New Hampshire primary has become too important, citing the small size of the state and the relative unrepresentativeness of its population (e.g., few Blacks) as disqualifying factors. Until his death in 1981, critics also cited the undue influence of right-wing publisher William Loeb and his *Manchester Union-Leader*, a newspaper that dominated the state's political coverage until very recently. Each component can be explored independently. The *Union-Leader* is no longer as influential as it once was, largely because of population shifts to the southern part of the state, which relies more on the Boston media. The state is small, but its population is not wholly unrepresentative of the prominent ideological factions within the two parties. In fact, none of these ingredients alone seems to disqualify New Hampshire as a logical place to start the primary campaigns.

But what is clear is that this one state's primary, because it is first and does not face competition for media coverage from any other political event, commands a disproportionate amount of media attention. All of the candidates are in one place; the state is picturesque; the people are colorful Yankees and play their moment in the spotlight for all it is worth. Iowans have seen the advantages that accrue to New Hampshire, trying to copy this success with early caucuses. But New Hampshire still receives the most attention. Nearly a fifth of all of the national television coverage of the primaries and caucuses in recent years has been centered on this one small state.

Defenders of the "first-in-the-nation" status say that New Hampshire allows for "retail" politics—that candidates have the opportunity to meet the voters one-on-one and convince them that they merit support. To some extent this personalism is typical. Candidates do campaign door-to-door and in the country stores. In one traditional story, a reporter asks an old New Hampshire farmer which presidential candidate he is going to support. The farmer replies, "How do I know? I've only met them once or twice each." But New Hampshire politics has become media politics in recent campaigns. George Bush turned a losing effort into a winning one with last-minute television commercials, many on the Boston stations that blanket the more densely populated southern part of the state. He gave up on walking more country roads or ringing more doorbells.

Thus the fact remains that a small state, unrepresentative of the nation on a number of variables—including the number of union households and the percentage of minorities in the population—has a great deal of impact on electoral politics in the United States. The momentum that builds up from a New Hampshire victory, the media attention that comes from it, the boost that the winner receives in recognition among the electorate and in support in future primaries, all make this a prize sought after by every serious candidate. Because this primary comes first and because all of the serious candidates are contending for the prize guarantees that so long as the New Hampshire primary is held before any others—and so long as no other primaries are held on the same date—this northern New England ritual will continue to play a unique and important role in presidential nominating politics.

*See also:* George Bush, Jimmy Carter, Robert Dole, Dwight D. Eisenhower, Lyndon B. Johnson, Estes Kefauver, Henry Cabot Lodge, William Loeb, Eugene McCarthy, Media and Presidential Campaigns, Edmund Muskie, Ronald Reagan, Robert Taft, Harry S Truman

*L. Sandy Maisel*

REFERENCES

Brereton, Charles. 1979. *First Step to the White House: The New Hampshire Primary, 1952–1980*. Hampton, NH: Wheelabrator Foundation.

Orren, Garry R., and Nelson W. Polsby, eds. 1987. *Media and Momentum: The New Hampshire Primary and Nomination Politics*. Chatham, NJ: Chatham House.

Peirce, Neal R. 1976. *The New England States*. New York: Norton.

## New York City Reform Clubs

The first reform club in New York City—the Lexington Democratic Club—was established in 1949 by a group of young, well-educated political activists on the Upper East Side of Manhattan. Its members challenged the ruling hierarchy of the Democratic Party (the regulars) for political control of their assembly district.

The regulars had built political bases by providing patronage jobs and personal help to neighborhood voters. Typically, working-class Catholics of average educational and profes-

sional achievement controlled the regular clubs. The regulars' strength was greatest in poorer communities inhabited by immigrants and second generation Americans. The reformers were principally young Jewish professionals and, to a lesser degree, well-educated Protestants. They regarded as corrupt the kind of personal favoritism that the regulars used to win the allegiance of voters, and they accused the regulars of holding party control so tightly that interested citizens could not participate in the political process.

The philosophical debate inherent in these two different approaches to politics had often emerged during New York City election campaigns as a contest between the backers of the Democratic political machine and the supporters of reform-minded "Fusion" candidates for mayor. With development of the reform Democratic clubs, the contest became a struggle for control of the Democratic Party. To an extraordinary degree the battle was also a cultural collision between the working-class Catholic political professionals who controlled the regular wing, and the younger, better-educated, upper- and middle-income Jews who dominated the reform clubs.

Fueled by enthusiasm for Adlai Stevenson's presidential campaigns in 1952 and 1956, political activists in Jewish and Protestant neighborhoods in Manhattan founded a number of reform clubs. Others began to appear in Jewish neighborhoods elsewhere in the city by the end of the 1950s. In 1959 Herbert Lehman and Eleanor Roosevelt organized an umbrella group of reform clubs known as the Committee for Democratic Voters (CDV), the purpose of which was to unseat Carmine DeSapio, the Italian Catholic political boss of "regular" Tammany Hall. In the 1961 Democratic primary, in alliance with Mayor Robert Wagner who severed his ties with the regular wing that year and mounted an "anti-boss" campaign in his bid for reelection, the reformers won a resounding victory.

Since then, reform clubs have become permanent and influential institutions in the Democratic Party in New York City. The reformers have succeeded in electing candidates to Democratic Party positions, the New York City Council, the New York State Assembly and the New York State Senate, and the U.S. Congress. Edward I. Koch, first elected mayor of New York in 1977, began his career as a member of the Village Independent Democrats, one of New York City's best-known reform clubs. The

New Democratic Coalition (NDC), formed to coordinate reform club activity on a citywide basis in 1989, is weak and ineffective, even though reform clubs continue to have influence in many assembly districts.

While the philosophical differences between the regulars and the reform clubs have at times seemed great, in practice reformers have often used many of the same political techniques as regulars. More than anything else, the reform clubs emerged out of the desire of a generation of well-educated, middle-class Jews to have a voice in a Democratic Party controlled by working-class, Catholic politicians.

See also: Bosses, Carmine DeSapio, Election of 1952, Fusion Party of New York, Edward Koch, Eleanor Roosevelt, Adlai Stevenson II, Tammany Hall

*Christopher McNickle*

REFERENCES

Costikyan, Edward N. 1966. *Behind Closed Doors*. New York: Harcourt, Brace & World.

Heilbroner, Robert. 1954. "Carmine G. DeSapio: The Smile on the Face of the Tiger." July *Harper's Magazine* 26.

Lekachman, Robert. 1958. "How We Beat the Machine: Challenging Tammany at the District Level." April *Commentary* 290.

Wakefield, Dan. 1959. "Greenwich Village Challenges Tammany: Ethnic Politics and the New Reformers." October *Commentary* 307.

Wilson, James Q. 1962. *The Amateur Democrat*. Chicago: U. of Chicago Pr.

## Newberry v. United States
256 U.S. 232 (1921)

In a five-to-four decision in 1921, the Supreme Court in *Newberry* held that congressional authority to regulate elections as conferred by Article I, Section 4 of the Constitution does not extend to party primaries and nomination activities. Accordingly, the Court struck down the so-called Reed Amendment of the Publicity Act Amendments of 1911, which limited expenditures by U.S. Senate candidates to the lesser amount of a maximum of $10,000 or the ceiling established by state law.

Truman H. Newberry was a successful Republican candidate for U.S. Senate from Michigan in 1918. His campaign committee, according to its own report, spent nearly $180,000 pursuing the Republican nomination, almost 100 times the limit of $1,875 established by Michigan state law. He and 16 others (members of his campaign staff and supporters) were found guilty in 1920 of conspiring to violate the spending limits of the 1911 act. They appealed their conviction to the Supreme Court, arguing that Congress had no authority to regulate primaries and that Newberry and his codefendants had not violated the spending limit since it applied to a campaign committee, not the candidate or individual supporters. The Court based its decision of the former contention and, that being sufficient to reverse the lower court decision, did not consider the latter argument over interpretation of the statute.

In the opinion of the Court, Justice James McReynolds noted that "general provisions touching elections in Constitutions or statutes are not necessarily applicable to primaries—the two things are radically different." While nomination may be requisite to election, it is not part of the manner of holding elections. Nor is control over nominations necessary in order to effectuate the control over elections vested in Congress. To allow federal regulation of senatorial nominations would therefore "interfere with the purely domestic affairs of the state and infringe upon liberties reserved to the people." Justice Joseph McKenna concurred in this opinion "as applied to the statute under consideration which was enacted prior to the Seventeenth Amendment; but he reserve[d] the question of the power of Congress under that amendment." Four justices, including Chief Justice Edward White, dissented, arguing that the method of securing nominations is part of the manner of holding elections.

The Court's ruling generated some "doubt as to what Congress may . . . do" since McKenna's opinion left open the question whether, in light of the Seventeenth Amendment, "Congress may possibly have [the] power to pass a new statute limiting expenditures to secure nominations for senator." The legislature did not test the issue, adopting the Federal Corrupt Practices Act of 1925 without provisions for primary campaigns. But the Court returned to the question in 1941 and, in *United States v. Classic*, ruled that Congress had authority over primaries and nomination activities wherever state law made them part of the election process and wherever they effectively determine the outcome of the general election. The Congress, however, did not reassert its authority to promulgate regulations for primary campaigns until 1971, when it adopted the Federal Election Campaign Act.

See also: Federal Corrupt Practices Act of 1925, Federal Election Campaign Acts

*Anthony J. Corrado*

REFERENCES

Mutch, Robert E. 1988. *Campaigns, Congress, and Courts*. New York: Praeger.

Powell, Thomas Reed. 1921. "Major Constitutional Issues in 1920–21." 36 *Political Science Quarterly* 469.

## Reinhold Niebuhr (1892–1971)

Pastor, educator, theologian, and political philosopher. One political scientist, Hans Morgenthau, in 1962 called Reinhold Niebuhr "the greatest living political philosopher in America." Niebuhr was both thinker and activist. He served as pastor of the Bethel Evangelical Church in Detroit from 1915 to 1928 and then taught at Union Theological Seminary in New York from 1928 to 1960. Niebuhr wrote over 15 books and 1,000 articles; he was a principal founder of Americans for Democratic Action; he served as vice chairman of the Liberal Party in the state of New York; he edited *Christianity and Crisis* and other journals; and he participated in numerous governmental and quasi-governmental bodies. Martin Luther King, Jr., Adlai Stevenson, and Hubert Humphrey, among others, acknowledged Niebuhr's impact on their own thought and work.

Niebuhr was this country's conscience from the early 1940s through the 1960s. As the leading exponent of a prophetic and practical Christian realism, he helped shape the vital center in American foreign policy and domestic politics, seeking the middle ground between cynicism and sentimental idealism, between resignation and utopianism. He used the resources of the Bible and the Christian tradition—Paul, Augustine, Luther—to illuminate the events and ambiguities of our present experience. According to Niebuhr, human beings are sinners, persistently failing to accept the limitations of their own power, wisdom, and virtue, but they are nonetheless capable of, and should work toward, the achievement of greater justice in society. He believed that one ought to seek proximate solutions, not perfection. In 1940 Niebuhr finally broke with the Socialist Party over its idealistic pacifism and became an important spokesman in support of the war against Hitler. After World War II he endorsed resistance to Soviet political expansion in Europe. He was an early opponent of the Vietnam War.

*See also:* Americans for Democratic Action, Hubert Humphrey, Martin Luther King, Jr., Liberal Party, Socialist Party of America, Adlai Stevenson II

*David Hein*

REFERENCES

Bingham, June. 1961. *Courage to Change: An Introduction to the Life and Thought of Reinhold Niebuhr.* New York: Scribner's.

Brown, Robert McAfee, ed. 1986. *The Essential Reinhold Niebuhr: Selected Essays and Addresses.* New Haven: Yale U. Pr.

Fackre, Gabriel. 1970. *The Promise of Reinhold Niebuhr.* Philadelphia: J. B. Lippincott.

Fox, Richard Wightman. 1987. *Reinhold Niebuhr: A Biography.* San Francisco: Harper & Row.

Harland, Gordon. 1960. *The Thought of Reinhold Niebuhr.* New York: Oxford U. Pr.

Harries, Richard, ed. 1986. *Reinhold Niebuhr and the Issues of Our Time.* Grand Rapids, MI: Wm. B. Eerdmans.

Kegley, Charles W., and Robert W. Bretall, eds. 1956. *Reinhold Niebuhr: His Religious, Social, and Political Thought.* New York: Macmillan.

Landon, Harold R., ed. 1962. *Reinhold Niebuhr: A Prophetic Voice in Our Time.* Greenwich, CT: Seabury Pr.

Lovin, Robin. 1988. "Reinhold Niebuhr, Past and Future." 14 *Religious Studies Review* 97.

Merkley, Paul. 1975. *Reinhold Niebuhr: A Political Account.* Montreal: McGill–Queen's U. Pr.

Niebuhr, Reinhold. 1929. *Leaves from the Notebook of a Tamed Cynic.* Chicago: Meridian.

———. 1932. *Moral Man and Immoral Society.* New York: Scribner's.

———. 1941, 1943. *The Nature and Destiny of Man.* 2 vols. New York: Scribner's.

———. 1944. *The Children of Light and the Children of Darkness.* New York: Scribner's.

———. 1952. *The Irony of American History.* New York: Scribner's.

———. 1953. *Christian Realism and Political Problems.* New York: Scribner's.

———. 1959. *The Structure of Nations and Empires.* New York: Scribner's.

Scott, Nathan A., Jr., ed. 1975. *The Legacy of Reinhold Niebuhr.* Chicago: U. of Chicago Pr.

Stone, Ronald H. 1972. *Reinhold Niebuhr: Prophet to Politicians.* Nashville, TN: Abington Pr.

## Nineteenth Amendment

The impetus for a women's suffrage amendment began in the mid-nineteenth century. In the 1848 Seneca Falls Convention, Elizabeth Cady Stanton proposed that the right to vote be included in a Declaration of Sentiments outlining women's grievances. Convention delegates based their demand on a natural rights doctrine, claiming that the state could not legitimately govern women without their consent.

National events helped to turn suffrage into a major goal of the emerging women's rights movement. When the Fourteenth and Fifteenth amendments, guaranteeing rights to ex-slaves, were proposed, Stanton and Susan B. Anthony, perceiving the advantages of a federal amendment, insisted that women be included. This strategy was rejected by the ruling Republican Party, which feared it would jeopardize Black suffrage.

In an effort to achieve a federal suffrage amendment and support women's rights, Stanton and Anthony created the National Woman Suffrage Association in 1869. Through the years, they tried to align the NWSA with Republicans, Democrats, the National Labor Union, and even the Equal Rights Party for better political support. Lucy Stone and other New England reformers who were closely associated with the Republican Party formed the American Woman Suffrage Association in 1869 to work solely for suffrage on a state-by-state basis.

Neither group achieved success. Thus in the early 1870s, a colorful convert to the cause—Victoria Woodhull—made an effort to convince Congress that the Fourteenth and Fifteenth amendments had already enfranchised women. This was an argument first suggested by Virginia Minor, who claimed that the two amendments gave women the right of citizenship and thus the right to vote. Despite Woodhull's contention, Congress rejected attempts to pass enforcing legislation. This theoretical argument was finally put to rest in *Minor v. Happersett* (1875): the Supreme Court ruled that suffrage was not a right of citizenship but a privilege granted by each state.

In 1878 Senator Aaron A. Sargent of California introduced what was first known as the Sixteenth Amendment and later the Susan B. Anthony Amendment: "The right of citizens of the United States to vote shall not be denied or abridged by the United States or any state on account of sex." After hearings, the bill reached the Senate floor in 1886 and was defeated 34 to 6.

In 1890 opposing women's groups set aside disagreements to pursue both federal and state voting rights through a unified National American Woman Suffrage Association (NAWSA). Suffrage gained national support as the number of women's organizations increased and came to be considered a more legitimate demand as more women entered the public sphere. NAWSA became a respectable middle-class organization that based its appeal less on women's natural rights and more on the traditional concept that women's moral superiority would improve the political process. Suffrage gained additional conservative support when some supporters used racist arguments to claim that women would add to the educated white vote and negate the votes of Blacks, workers, and the foreign born. While NAWSA remained the largest organization, support for women's vote was also evident among Socialists, radicals, and the Progressive Party, which endorsed suffrage in its 1912 presidential platform.

Suffragists faced well-financed opposition from a liquor industry suspicious that a women's vote would bring prohibition. Other business opponents believed that women would support protective legislation for workers and end child labor. Male politicians, reluctant to share political power, worried that women voters would work to reform the political system. In particular, the South feared that an extension of suffrage would disrupt the disenfranchisement of Blacks below the Mason-Dixon line.

Opponents of suffrage often argued their position by an appeal to traditional sex-role division. They held that women's suffrage was unnecessary because men represented women in politics. They also claimed that women, by stepping out of their proper sphere, would disrupt the home and destroy themselves and the nation in the process. This opposition was so formidable that by 1910 only four states had enfranchised women.

The suffrage campaign was energized in 1913 when Alice Paul and others applied militant tactics learned in the British suffrage movement to a renewed drive for a federal amendment. Paul insisted on holding the party in power responsible for its passage and formed the National Woman's Party to campaign against Democrats regardless of the individual candidate's position. In 1914 Paul claimed partial credit for defeating 23 out of 43 Democrats in the nine western states where women could vote. Owing to her efforts and the dogged work of NAWSA, the suffrage amendment reached the Senate floor in 1914 and the House in 1915. Though it was defeated, the whole House was able to consider the amendment for the first time, and the Senate debated it for the first time since 1887.

NAWSA renewed its drive for the amendment while continuing to work for state suffrage under the presidency of Carrie Chapman Catt. In 1916 the organization attempted to woo politicians from both parties and achieved state suffrage planks in their platforms. Suffragists also were able to acquire Woodrow Wilson's support for a federal amendment. His stand partly contributed to his victory in ten of the twelve women-suffrage states.

When the United States entered World War I, both groups continued their campaign. Sophisticated lobbying, the contribution of women to the war effort, and even the passage of prohibition, helped to increase support for women's suffrage. Theodore Roosevelt encouraged Republicans to vote for the suffrage amendment, and Wilson advised Democrats to do the same. The increased number of women voting also put pressure on Congressmen, who finally approved the measure in 1918 (165 Republicans and 104 Democrats voted in favor; 33 Republicans and 102 Democrats opposed). When the Senate failed to pass the Nineteenth Amendment, women's organizations campaigned against selected opponents. They successfully defeated the antisuffrage candidates in Massachusetts and Delaware and effectively reduced their majorities in New Jersey and New Hampshire.

By the time the Senate reconsidered the amendment, it was faced with the political reality that women could vote in 20 states with 339 electoral votes. After further lobbying and a personal appeal by Wilson, a new Senate finally passed the amendment on June 4, 1919, with 36 Republicans and 20 Democrats voting in favor and 8 Republicans and 17 Democrats opposed.

Local suffrage organizations were instrumental in obtaining ratification in 35 states by August 1920. The final state—Tennessee—was the site of a pitched battle by suffragists and such opponents as the liquor, manufacturing, and railroad lobbies. After an intensive and flamboyant campaign with rumors of bribes, deals, and drunken legislators, Tennessee finally ratified the amendment by two votes. The Nineteenth Amendment became law on August 12, 1920, after 72 years of effort by women and their allies.

*See also:* Susan B. Anthony, Carrie Chapman Catt, Equal Rights Party, Fifteenth Amendment, Alice Paul, Progressive Party, Theodore Roosevelt, Elizabeth Cady Stanton, Lucy Stone, Suffrage, Woodrow Wilson, Victoria Woodhull

*Joy A. Scimé*

REFERENCES

Flexner, Eleanor. 1959. *Century of Struggle: The Women's Rights Movement in the United States.* Cambridge: Belknap Press.

Scott, Anne F., and Andrew M. Scott. 1975. *One Half the People: The Fight for Woman Suffrage.* Philadelphia: Lippincott.

Woloch, Nancy. 1984. *Women and the American Experience.* New York: Knopf.

## Richard M. Nixon (1913– )

Only President of the United States to resign from office. Richard Milhous Nixon entered politics in his native state of California as a young veteran of World War II. In his first race in 1946, Nixon ran successfully as a Republican candidate for the U.S. House of Representatives against the Democratic incumbent, Jerry Voorhis. That victory marked the start of a political career of remarkable proportions. Among other distinctions, Richard Nixon was the youngest person ever elected to the office of Vice President, only the second person (Franklin Roosevelt was the first) ever to be on the ticket of a major American political party five times, and the only American President ever to resign from office.

Nixon was reelected in 1948, a year in which the Republicans regained control of the House for the first time since 1930. As a member of the majority party, he was able to play an active role in the investigation of Communist influence in the federal government. He gained considerable notoriety for his efforts to reveal the alleged Communist ties of a career State Department official, Alger Hiss, in an investigation that relied heavily on the testimony of an admitted former Communist, Whittaker Chambers.

The Hiss-Chambers case provided unusual publicity for this second-term Congressman, providing the springboard for Nixon's successful run for the Senate in 1950. In that race, he undertook a slashing, wide-ranging campaign against fellow House member Helen Gahagan Douglas. Portraying her as a liberal who was soft on communism (the "Pink Lady") and brandishing his own credentials as an anti-Communist, Nixon won 59 percent of the vote and became California's junior Senator at the age of 36.

A year and half later, the Republican presidential nominee, Dwight Eisenhower, tapped Nixon to be his running mate. While Nixon hardly had the stature of most candidates for national office, he came to Eisenhower's attention for the political strengths that he was presumed to bring to the Republican ticket: his youth, his campaign acumen, his conservative reputation and support, and his residence in a large, western state.

Nixon's nomination soon stood on to the brink of disaster when press reports suggested that his congressional salary had been supplemented by private contributions from wealthy California businessmen. In a critical national television address, Nixon preserved his candidacy by explaining that the funds had been for campaign use only and by defending his actions in accepting them. A reference near the end of the speech to the family dog, Checkers, gave this speech its now historical sobriquet, the "Checkers speech."

Eisenhower and Nixon were elected with 55 percent of the popular vote in 1952 and again in 1956 with 57 percent of the vote. The relationship between the two men was never close, and many (unsubstantiated) reports have suggested that Eisenhower would have preferred to remove Nixon from the ticket in 1956.

In 1960 Nixon had very little opposition in his bid for the Republican nomination for President. At the convention in Chicago, he was nominated with overwhelming support on the first ballot. He selected Henry Cabot Lodge, a former Massachusetts Senator and then United States ambassador to the United Nations, as his running mate.

Nixon lost the 1960 election by the narrowest of margins to Senator John F. Kennedy of Massachusetts. He then returned to California to practice law. In 1962 he was the gubernatorial nominee of the California Republican Party, only to lose that contest to the incumbent governor, Edmund G. Brown, Jr. On the day following his defeat, Nixon held what he described as his "last press conference," in which he castigated the press for its treatment of him and said "you won't have Nixon to kick around any more."

For most of the next five years, Nixon practiced law with a large New York City law firm. During this time, he continued to travel the country, speaking at fundraisers and campaign events for Republican candidates. In 1968, at the age of 56, he began another race for the presidency. He was not regarded as a favorite at the outset, but his potential rivals—Governors George Romney of Michigan, Nelson Rockefeller of New York, and Ronald Reagan of California—faded quickly or never fully emerged. Nixon won important victories in the early primaries and got the Republican nomination on the first ballot in Miami Beach, Florida. He selected Governor Spiro Agnew of Maryland as his running mate.

In another close presidential race, Richard Nixon finally won the presidency in 1968, with 43.4 percent of the popular vote to 42.7 percent for the Democratic candidate, Senator Hubert Humphrey of Minnesota, and 13.5 percent for American Independent Party candidate Governor George Wallace of Alabama.

Nixon spent an eventful first term in office. The war in Vietnam continued while the Nixon administration sought to negotiate a peace and to withdraw American troops in a program known as "Vietnamization." In 1970 the war was expanded with an invasion of Cambodia by American and South Vietnamese forces and with the revelation that American troops had been active in Laos. Nixon and his national security adviser, Henry Kissinger, initiated secret discussions with the government of the People's Republic of China, eventuating in a visit by Nixon to China in February 1972, a first step in what later became a significant period of improved relations with China.

In other policy initiatives, Nixon's first term brought about a reorganization of the managerial and policy development apparatus in the executive office of the President, a sweeping but ultimately unsuccessful effort at welfare reform, approval of an antiballistic missile system, the institution of wage and price controls to dampen inflation, the enactment of general revenue sharing, and the rejection by the Senate of two of Nixon's Supreme Court nominees, Clement Haynsworth and G. Harrold Carswell.

In 1972 Richard Nixon was renominated by his party after facing only token opposition in the presidential primaries. In the general election he defeated his Democratic opponent, Senator George McGovern of South Dakota, by one of the largest popular vote margins in American history—60.7 percent to 37.5 percent.

In June 1972 a criminal break-in at the headquarters of the Democratic National Committee in the Watergate complex in Washington started Richard Nixon's downfall. While little noticed and of little effect during the election, that break-in stimulated an investigation that later revealed a massive program by Nixon partisans to upset the electoral process in 1972 so as to ensure Nixon's reelection. The "Watergate scandal" became the nation's most important news after Nixon's second inauguration. In the summer of 1973, a Senate committee headed by Senator Sam Ervin (D-N.C.) conducted nationally televised hearings on the Watergate scandal. Simultaneously, the national press began digging intensively into this story. The Nixon presidency was increasingly crippled by the nation's focus on Watergate and by the President's preoccupation with his own defense.

In 1974 several motions of impeachment were filed against Richard Nixon in the House of Representatives. The House Judiciary Committee began its own inquiry to determine whether or not to recommend impeachment. As this process moved forward, Nixon's popular support diminished almost to the vanishing point. Calls for his resignation began to emerge even from his former supporters. On August 9, 1974, before the House could vote to impeach him, Nixon resigned the presidency, the first incumbent ever to do so. He was succeeded by Vice President Gerald R. Ford.

Richard Nixon still looms over the post-Watergate political landscape as a man of enormous contrasts. No one doubts his staying power. For almost three decades, with but few lapses, he has been one of the nation's most prominent political figures. Many contemporary analysts regarded him as a clever political strategist and a perceptive and creative thinker in foreign policy. Though most of his political support was conservative, Nixon himself was rarely burdened by ideological constraints. In fact, his most enduring accomplishments—the reopening of relations with China, a cooling of tensions with the Soviet Union, the proposal for a Family Assistance Plan—seemed to run against the grain of much of his political support and a good deal of his own accumulated rhetoric.

But Nixon was also tragically flawed by a persistent, almost paranoid reaction to his political opponents. He took criticism and defeat personally and allowed these failures to corrode and ultimately undermine his substantial intellectual and political strengths. As a consequence, Nixon's contemporary reputation is dominated not by his innovative policy initiatives, though there were many of those; not by his lengthy stay at the pinnacle of national politics, though few others have ever matched it; but rather by the most all encompassing political scandal in American history.

See also: Spiro Agnew; American Independent Party; Edmund G. (Pat) Brown, Jr.; Whittaker Chambers; Elections of 1952, 1960, 1968, 1972; Gerald Ford; Hubert Humphrey; John F. Kennedy; Henry Cabot Lodge; George McGovern; Ronald Reagan; Theodore Roosevelt; United Nations; Vietnam War as a Political Issue; George Wallace; Watergate

*G. Calvin MacKenzie*

REFERENCES

Ambrose, Stephen. 1987. *Nixon: The Education of a Politician*. New York: Simon & Schuster.

Erlichman, John. 1982. *Witness to Power*. New York: Simon & Schuster.

Haldeman, H. R. 1978. *The Ends of Power*. New York: Times Books.

Nixon, Richard. 1978. *RN: The Memoirs of Richard Nixon*. 2 vols. New York: Grosset and Dunlap.

## Nixon v. Herndon
### 273 U.S. 536 (1927)

*Nixon v. Herndon* was the first of the "white primary cases" that represent the United States Supreme Court's effort in the early to mid-1900s to deal with racial discrimination in voting laws. In *Herndon*, the Supreme Court used the Fourteenth Amendment to fashion and protect the fundamental right to vote. *Herndon*, and its progeny, symbolize the Supreme Court's determination that the equal protection clause of the Fourteenth Amendment was drafted "with a special intent to protect the blacks from discrimination against them." Before *Herndon*, the equal protection clause of the Fourteenth Amendment was regarded primarily as a more limited prohibition against other, more blatant forms of discrimination, such as laws that denied Blacks citizenship and the accompanying constitutional rights.

In *Herndon*, an African-American citizen of Texas challenged the constitutionality of a 1923 Texas statute that prohibited Blacks from voting in state Democratic primary elections. The Supreme Court determined that private injury resulting from political activity was capable of redress in a court of law. The Court found the Texas statute unconstitutional because it withheld from African-Americans equal protection of the law that conferred upon selected citizens the right to vote. The Court recognized the state's right to require voters to meet certain reasonable qualifications but held unequivocally that race "cannot be the basis of a statutory classification affecting the right [to vote]." The Court held that the Texas law excluding Blacks from Democratic primary elections violated the equal protection guarantees of the Fourteenth Amendment. The Court in *Herndon*, therefore, did not feel compelled to consider possible Fifteenth Amendment violations, having determined that the provisions of the statute were a "direct and obvious infringement of the Fourteenth [Amendment]." The Supreme Court's reliance entirely upon the equal protection clause of the Fourteenth Amendment was a further indication of the Court's recognition that the clause clearly applied to voting rights and laws affecting them. The effect of *Herndon* was the abolition of the white primary; by 1950, with its progeny, *Herndon* had established protections for Blacks in the electoral process. *Herndon* turned out to be one legal impetus for the elimination of racial discrimination in the voting place—a struggle that continues to this day with varying degrees of success.

*See also:* Fifteenth Amendment, Voting Rights Act of 1965 and Extensions

*Morton A. Brody*

## George W. Norris (1861–1944)

Among the most significant progressive politicians of the twentieth century, George William Norris had a political career spanning five decades, and he had a lasting influence on national legislation and on policy in his home state of Nebraska. More so than most reformers, Norris was able to translate the causes for which he fought into legislation of lasting consequence.

George Norris was born in Ohio, the son of farmers. He excelled in school, later attending Baldwin University (now Baldwin-Wallace College) and Indiana Normal School (now Valparaiso University). After receiving his law degree, he was admitted to the Indiana bar in 1883. He finally moved to Beatrice, Nebraska, in 1885 where he established the first of several law offices in the state.

The Nebraska to which Norris moved was experiencing a vigorous economic boom. But in the depression-ridden 1890s, he found his own business ventures increasingly straitened. Norris was elected a prosecuting attorney in 1894; he defeated the Populist incumbent by two votes to become county judge in 1895. In 1902 Norris was the Republican candidate in the Fifth Nebraska Congressional District; he won the general election, defeating the Democratic incumbent by 181 votes of 30,000 cast.

Norris's early electoral experience set the stage for his subsequent political life: he was a deeply committed Republican who found himself running in areas that were dominated either by Populists, Democrats, or both. While Norris's Republicanism tied his early political career to the electoral fortunes of the national party, his constituency demanded that he be an unorthodox Republican, lest he fail in the next election.

Although Norris championed farming interests and the "little man" from the beginning of his political career, he was a loyal Republican in the House. During his 1904 reelection campaign Republican Speaker Joseph Cannon, the epitome of regular party leaders, came to his district to campaign vigorously on Norris's behalf. Of course, during his early years in the House, a progressive Republican could easily swim within the party's mainstream, the chief requirement being support of President Theodore Roosevelt's program. Yet as the Republicans became increasingly torn between progressive and reactionary elements, and as national Republicans such as William Howard Taft and Cannon rejected the tenants of Roosevelt Republicanism, progressive Republicans in Congress had trouble toeing the party line. When the conflict in the party reached its peak, Norris was right there in front.

The progressive-standpat split put Norris at the center of the most important parliamentary maneuver in the history of the U.S. House of Representatives. Norris was an early participant with a group of Republicans who were disturbed by the unilateral authority given Speaker Cannon under the House rules, especially since Cannon used that authority to thwart the plans of the progressives. These "insurgents" sponsored a resolution in 1908 to strip the Speaker of his control over the Rules Committee. The resolution failed, but they did manage to win passage in 1909 of a new rule providing for "Calendar Wednesday," a maneuver that promised to loosen the grip of the Speaker over the House's agenda.

Those insurgents who revolted against the Speaker and the rules paid dearly for their convictions: they were stripped of committee assignments and shunned by state and national GOP committees in their races to win reelection in 1908. Indeed, Norris won his 1908 reelection bid by only 22 votes of 41,000 cast, convincing him that he could no longer tie his political future too closely to the Republican Party.

On March 17, 1910, Norris rose on the House floor to "present a matter of privilege under the Constitution." Cannon, apparently unaware of what Norris had in mind, allowed him to make his motion. Norris then presented for immediate consideration a resolution that would require the House Rules Committee to be elected by the full chamber, rather than be appointed by the Speaker, and to prohibit the Speaker from serving on the committee. Cannon ruled the resolution out of order, but following a dramatic floor fight that lasted for a day and a half, Cannon's parliamentary ruling was overturned and Norris's resolution was adopted by a 191-

to-156 vote. This act marked the end of the period of a Speaker's "czar rule" in the House and laid the groundwork for a new era of weak Speakers, independent committees, and a nearly inviolable seniority system.

From this point on, Norris was a national leader of the progressive movement, although he remained a nominal Republican for decades to come. He was elected vice president of the National Progressive Republican League in 1911 and was an early supporter of the nomination of Robert M. La Follette for President on the Republican ticket. In addition, Norris took advantage of the rising tide of support for Republican progressivism in Nebraska to win the Republican nomination for Senate in 1912. He then went on to take the general election by a comfortable margin.

In the Senate Norris continued his advocacy of and leadership in progressive issues, including measures both of social reform and international isolation. Because Norris entered the Senate during a time of Democratic control, however, he also found himself contesting Senate rules and practices, especially caucus government, although he supported much of the substance of Woodrow Wilson's "New Freedom." On the foreign policy side Norris was one of the "little group of willful men" who opposed President Wilson's plans to arm merchant ships in war zones. Norris was one of the six Senators who voted against the entry of the United States into World War I, arguing that the war was precipitated by powerful financial and industrial interests. Similarly, he was opposed to the Treaty of Versailles that concluded the war.

During the period of Republican control of Congress in the 1920s, Norris won institutional leadership within the body. As chair of the Agriculture and Judiciary committees, Norris supported federal aid to agriculture, labor organizing, and a series of governmental reforms, among then the Twentieth Amendment to the U.S. Constitution, which ended the "lame duck" session of Congress by moving the presidential inaugural from March to January. At the same time Norris was instrumental in inducing the Nebraska legislature to amend the state constitution to create the only unicameral state legislature in the country, elected in nonpartisan elections.

It was during the 1930s that Norris broke formally with the Republican Party—a break generated by his experience during the 1930 primary. In 1930 conservative Republicans found another man named George W. Norris (branded "Grocer Norris" after his trade) to oppose the Senator in the Republican primary. The state was flooded with outlandish charges that Senator Norris was an immoral drunkard married to a Catholic; some evidence indicates that the source of these charges was the Republican National Committee. In the end, the "real" Norris was reelected, Grocer Norris was sentenced to jail on perjury charges, and Senator Norris dropped his party affiliation in 1936 to stand for reelection as an Independent.

Norris's formal break with the Republican Party also followed from his opposition to the renomination of Herbert Hoover in 1932 and his early support of Franklin Roosevelt. Following the 1932 election Norris was a regular supporter of the New Deal, elated that so many proposals he had long supported were now championed by the President and passed into law. Most significant was his sponsorship of the bill that created the river-taming, electricity-producing Tennessee Valley Authority. Norris was also instrumental in the enactment of the Rural Electrification Act and the Norris-Doxey Forestry Act.

Norris was defeated handily for reelection in 1942 by a more conservative and conventional Republican, Kenneth Wherry. Norris returned to Nebraska where he completed his autobiography six weeks before his death.

Norris left an indelible mark on American politics during the first half of the twentieth century. Unlike so many reformers before or since, he was a committed student of the institutions he inhabited, a keen practitioner of parliamentary practice and tactics, and a solid political success over a period of decades.

*See also:* Robert La Follette, National Progressive Republican League, New Deal, Franklin D. Roosevelt, Theodore Roosevelt

*Charles Stewart III*

REFERENCES

Richard, Lowitt. 1963. *George W. Norris: The Making of a Progressive, 1861–1913.* Urbana: U. of Illinois Pr.

———. 1971. *The Persistence of a Progressive, 1913–1933.* Urbana: U. of Illinois Pr.

———. 1978. *The Triumph of a Progressive, 1933–1944.* Urbana: U. of Illinois Pr.

## North Dakota Nonpartisan League

A student of the comparative politics of small, "open" economies might well be intrigued by the history of the North Dakota Nonpartisan

League. Its history can be briefly told in terms easily recognizable to such comparativists, terms that would emphasize both the political economy of economic protest movements in "open" economies and the larger political and economic constraints on the success of such protest movements.

The North Dakota Nonpartisan League was an agrarian protest movement born in 1915 in a jurisdiction whose small, homogeneous population was primarily engaged in producing an agrarian commodity (wheat) for export and sale outside the jurisdiction. The League sought to transcend commercial farmers' dependence on mainly external actors based in St. Paul and Minneapolis and, beyond the Mississippi, in Chicago and New York, who controlled such vital financial and marketing institutions as banks, railroads, grain terminal elevators, and commodity exchanges. Labeling the local politicians as tools of these outside interests, the League successfully focused farmers' attention on politics and public policy as a solution to their discontent with the political economy of wheat production. It organized an electoral coalition for gaining control of the North Dakota government, and the League developed the ingenious tactic of using a new institution—the primary election—for nominating a slate of candidates who, after securing nomination, would run under the aegis of the Republican Party, the dominant party in North Dakota.

Over the course of two primary elections and two general elections in 1916 and 1918 the League succeeded in gaining almost complete control of North Dakota's government. In very few other states has a political faction ever gained so much formal institutional control. The League legislated public housing and established financial and marketing institutions directly controlled by the state of North Dakota. It also established collective bargaining.

Yet by 1921 the League was in disarray, accused of scandal, corruption, and mismanagement; it was forced from office in a special recall election. Many of these charges were plausible. However, the League might have succeeded had it not faced a basic constraint: dependence on external finance. The fiscal basis of its reform program was bond finance. Yet North Dakota bonds sold poorly, and evidence indicates an organized boycott of these bonds in national capital markets. With the League's removal from office, a conservative faction of the North Dakota Republican Party resumed control of state government, backed by the Independent Voters Association, an organization that copied many of the League's tactics. In many ways then, the League had gone through a natural history that partly resembles, for instance, Chile's experience in the early 1970s with Unidad Popular, when a need for foreign exchange and foreign loans crippled Unidad Popular's program.

It should be noted that the North Dakota Nonpartisan League had a second, if different, incarnation after its defeat. It became a political club that functioned as the liberal wing of the North Dakota Republican Party. In the 1930s it supported a semi-Populist governor, William Langer. The League finally merged with the Democratic Party in 1956.

See also: Agrarianism, National Nonpartisan League

Richard M. Valelly

REFERENCES

Morlan, Robert L. 1985. *Political Prairie Fire: The Nonpartisan League, 1915–1922.* St. Paul: Minnesota Historical Society Press.

## Northern Farmers' Alliance

Milton George, editor of Chicago's *Western Rural*, founded the Northern Farmers' Alliance in 1880 to help farmers by supplementing the work of the Grange. Although George did not favor the formation of a new political party, he wanted farmers to work through existing parties to elect to public office men who would promote the interest of the agrarian classes. Convinced that railroads exerted too much influence in government, George called for federal regulation of interstate commerce and the abolition of "free" passes for travel on the railroad.

Heavily dependent on George for leadership and financial support, the Northern Alliance remained small in its early years. In 1886 its membership began to increase in Illinois, Nebraska, Iowa, Wisconsin, and Minnesota. The following year the Alliance revised its constitution to strengthen the power of state chapters and to make them better able to be self-supporting. George's power then waned, with the leadership shifting to men like Jay Burrows of Nebraska. Even then, the Northern Farmers' Alliance remained weakly organized and small compared to the more powerful Southern Farmers' Alliance.

The Northern Alliance's significance lies in the preparation that it gave members to become political Populists. When it met with the Southern Alliance at St. Louis in 1889, its platform called for the abolition of the national banking system, the issuance of money directly by the federal government, tariff reform, nationalization of railroads, the restriction of alien ownership of land, a graduated income tax, and the Australian ballot. In 1890 the Northern Alliance contributed to the formation of independent farmers' parties in Nebraska and Minnesota. In 1892 it joined other reform organizations in forming the People's Party.

*See also:* Australian Ballot, Populist (People's) Party, Railroads, Southern Farmers' Alliance

*William F. Holmes*

REFERENCES

Saloutos, Theodore. 1960. *Farmer Movements in the South, 1865–1933.* Berkeley: U. of California Pr.

Scott, Roy V. 1958. "Milton George and the Farmers' Alliance Movement." 45 *Mississippi Valley Historical Review* 90.

## Nuclear Freeze Movement

In February 1981, only a few weeks after Ronald Reagan took office as President of the United States, Soviet Premier Leonid Brezhnev announced a new policy officially stating the USSR's support for a "nuclear freeze." Taking their cue from that pronouncement, peace activists and organizations around the world coalesced about this "new" approach to peace in the nuclear age. In the United States, pressure on the new administration mounted slowly, as a carefully organized grass-roots campaign for the nuclear freeze sought to work both within the system and from the outside to gain political legitimacy and credibility for itself.

The nuclear freeze was really quite a simple concept and not a new idea as of 1981. Cessation of the production, development, and deployment of all nuclear weapons and delivery systems was the stated central goal of the nuclear freeze movement. In its infancy, the nuclear freeze captured the attention of an American public already concerned about the possibility of nuclear war. In June 1982, more than 750,000 people converged on Central Park in New York City to protest the U.S. Government's buildup of nuclear weapons, and in a mass show of support, the crowd's leaders insisted on the nuclear freeze as a policy alternative.

Led by Randall Forsberg, director of the Institute for Defense and Disarmament Studies, and Randall Kehler, national coordinator of the Nuclear Weapons Freeze Campaign, nuclear freeze managers spearheaded efforts to make the freeze a centerpiece of the government's debates on nuclear weapons. During the con-

gressional election year of 1982, in an unusual approach, nuclear freeze activists organized hundreds of smaller referendum campaigns in search of legitimized public support. The result was that over 500 towns, several dozen cities, and 9 states endorsed the principle of the nuclear freeze. The movement also drew the support of several organizations, including the Clergy and Laity Concerned, Common Cause, the National Education Association, and Friends of the Earth.

In the short term, the 1982 success energized the movement. As presidential contenders announced their candidacies throughout 1983, all of the Democrats came out in support of the nuclear freeze. Senator Alan Cranston from California even made the nuclear freeze the cornerstone of his campaign. In Congress, Democrats and liberal Republicans in the House passed several resolutions in the period 1982–1984 promoting the nuclear freeze as a policy of national security. In the Senate, however, Republicans and conservative Democrats continually rejected the nuclear freeze, opting for support of the President's policy. The official position of the Reagan administration called for a modernization and buildup of nuclear weaponry and delivery systems, followed by a negotiated reduction of these arms—the so-called "peace through strength" policy.

The nuclear freeze evolved into a partisan issue, endorsed by the Democratic Party, a development that initiated the movement's downfall. The landslide reelection of Ronald Reagan in the 1984 campaign, followed by his first of a series of summit meetings with Mikhail Gorbachev, served to deflate and then to dissolve the nuclear freeze movement. Likewise, the wide acceptance of the nuclear freeze by Democrats made that party appear weak on defense and may have inadvertently added to the magnitude of the defeat of the presidential ticket of Walter Mondale and Geraldine Ferraro in 1984.

*See also:* National Education Association, Ronald Reagan

*Michael Heel*

REFERENCES

Beres, Louis Rene. 1983. *Mimicking Sisyphus: America's Countervailing Nuclear Strategy.* Lexington, MA: Lexington Books.

## Nullification

The early-nineteenth-century constitutional doctrine asserting that each state could judge the constitutionality of any federal law and refuse to enforce it within its boundaries if it deemed the law unconstitutional. Nullification was built upon the distinction between the sovereignty exercised by the state conventions in ratifying the Constitution and the government it subsequently created. The Constitution was to act as a break on the dangerous tendencies of all governments to accumulate power, and the state's duly elected convention would be the final authority in interpreting the Constitution.

In the Virginia and Kentucky resolutions (written by James Madison and Thomas Jefferson in 1798), the legislatures of the two states asserted their right to interpose their sovereignty between their citizens and federal encroachment and declared the Alien and Sedition acts null and void, maintaining that "where powers are assumed which have not been delegated, a nullification of the act is the right remedy." Although Madison insisted that the resolutions were simply an "expression of opinion" seeking support from the other states, the Kentucky legislature defended its right to nullify unconstitutional legislation unilaterally.

The doctrine was revived in a more virulent form during South Carolina's economic troubles in the mid-1820s. Although the idea had been anticipated by other South Carolinians, such as Robert J. Turnbull, the theory of nullification was most clearly formulated by Vice President John C. Calhoun in "The South Carolina Exposition and Protest" written at the behest of the state legislature in 1828 following the passage of the so-called, "Tariff of Abominations." At first Calhoun's role was kept secret, but the "Fort Hill Address" publicly connected the Vice President with nullification.

The nullification crisis reached its peak in the winter of 1832–1833. It grew out of the economic problems of South Carolina following the panic of 1819 and was exacerbated by the personal animosities between Vice President Calhoun and President Andrew Jackson—a split that eventually led to the resignation of Calhoun. The tariff, which nearly doubled in the course of the decade, became a symbol of the economic and social ills of the Palmetto State, and in 1832 the nullifiers acquired a sufficient number of seats in the state legislature to call a convention to declare in the "Ordinance of Nullification" that the tariffs of 1828 and 1832 were unconstitutional and thus "null, void, and no law, nor binding upon this state." Drawing on the thought of those more radical than Calhoun, the Ordinance also threatened secession. In response, Jackson issued his "Proclamation to the People of South Carolina" and privately threatened to hang Calhoun. Because of its nationalistic tone (set by Secretary of State Edward Livingston who drafted it at Jackson's request), the Proclamation made southern states' rights supporters uneasy and drew acclaim from northern opponents like Daniel Webster. Jackson's focus, however, was on South Carolina's claim of the right of secession, and he maintained his general adherence to states' rights unionism. At the same time Calhoun worried about the maintenance of the Union and looked upon nullification (as opposed to secession) as a conservative means to redress his state's grievances. In the end both Jackson and Calhoun, along with Henry Clay, played crucial roles in the "Compromise of 1833" that provided for the gradual lowering of the tariff over the next decade and the abrogation of the Ordinance.

*See also:* Alien and Sedition Acts, John C. Calhoun, Henry Clay, Andrew Jackson, Thomas Jefferson, James Madison

*William G. Shade*

REFERENCES

Ellis, Richard E. 1987. *The Union at Risk: Jacksonian Democracy, States' Rights and the Nullification Crisis.* New York: Oxford U. Pr.

Freehling, William W. 1966. *Prelude to Civil War: The Nullification Controversy in South Carolina, 1816–1836.* New York: Harper & Row.

———, ed. 1967. *The Nullification Era.* New York: Harper & Row.

# O

## David R. Obey (1938– )

Democratic reform Congressman from Wisconsin. David R. Obey was among the earliest advocates of restricting the activities of political action committees (PACs). With former Congressman Tom Railsback (R-Ill.), Obey in 1979 won House passage of a bill that, as amended, would have limited members of the House to $70,000 in PAC contributions and would have reduced the amount that PACs could give to any House candidate from $10,000 to $6,000 per election. Obey's bill died in the Senate. In August 1990, Obey won House acceptance of a campaign finance bill amendment limiting individual contributions to $500, restricting aggregate PAC contributions to $220,000 per candidate, and providing public matching funds for contributions of $50 or less. The bill that passed in the Senate was different, and no compromise eventuated before the One Hundred First Congress adjourned in October.

An established and respected legislator after only a few terms, Obey exhibited reformist tendencies early as chairman of the House Commission on Administrative Review, which in 1977 pushed a massive ethics reform package through the House but failed to enact certain administrative and procedural changes. In 1979 Obey was elected chairman of the liberal Democratic Study Group; he also has chaired the Joint Economic Committee and served on the Budget Committee (almost winning the chair in 1980). In the mid-1980s, Obey frequently served as spokesman for liberals on a number of economic issues, while at the same time advocating reforms of the budget process and anathematizing excessive honoraria for members. At this writing, Obey serves as an activist chairman of the House Appropriations Committee's Subcommittee on Foreign Operations, where he frequently tangled with the Ronald Reagan and George Bush administrations on foreign aid questions such as support for Israel and aid to the Nicaraguan Contras. By 1988, at the age of 50, the 10-term veteran was judged "one of the most accomplished and effective of his generation of legislators in the House."

*See also:* Democratic Study Group, Political Action Committees

*John R. Johannes*

## Lawrence F. O'Brien (1917–1990)

During more than four decades as a Democratic Party activist, Lawrence Francis O'Brien became probably the foremost political campaign strategist and organizer of his time. O'Brien was also the Democratic Party chairman whose office was bugged and burglarized by members of President Richard Nixon's reelection team in June 1972.

As a Massachusetts teenager, O'Brien was introduced to politics by his father, a Democrat. In the Army during World War II, O'Brien entered politics on a full-time basis by managing the 1948 Massachusetts congressional campaign of Foster Furcolo, who asked O'Brien to accompany him to Washington as an administrative assistant. O'Brien found the work tedious. Approached in 1950 by Congressman John F. Kennedy (D-Mass.), O'Brien returned to campaign managing, serving as the chief organizer for Kennedy's successful races for the U.S. Senate in 1952 and 1958. O'Brien later recalled that he drew on these campaigns to develop his "O'Brien Manual," the organizational blueprint for Kennedy's successful 1960 presidential campaign as well as for presidential races in 1964 and 1968 and in political campaigns in a dozen foreign countries. O'Brien wrote in his autobiography that effective organization "can affect perhaps 3 to 5 percent of the total vote, enough to win or lose a close election."

After his election, Kennedy tapped O'Brien to serve as the White House congressional liaison, and during the next several years of the Kennedy administration, O'Brien worked to pass a number of liberal measures, including an increase in the minimum wage, an omnibus housing bill, and a constitutional amendment outlawing a state poll tax. But O'Brien achieved his greatest success by helping Lyndon Johnson, Kennedy's successor, push through the major "Great Society" legislation, including Medicare, aid to education, and the Voting Rights Act.

Johnson rewarded O'Brien by appointing him Postmaster General in November 1965, a traditional patronage position. O'Brien, however, worked seriously at improving what he saw as an antiquated postal service, and his proposal for postal reform was eventually enacted by President Richard Nixon.

O'Brien resigned his position in 1968 to direct the presidential bid of Robert Kennedy, successfully engineering victories in three of the four primaries that Kennedy entered. When Robert Kennedy was assassinated, O'Brien threw his support to Vice President Hubert Humphrey, working hard to achieve unity during the riot-torn 1968 Democratic National Convention in Chicago. After the convention, at Humphrey's urging, O'Brien accepted the position of chairman of the Democratic National Committee. His efforts to build an effective campaign organization despite funding difficulties helped narrow Nixon's lead over Humphrey during the final days of the 1968 presidential race.

After the election O'Brien resigned to work with a New York investment firm, but he returned to head the Democratic National Committee in 1970 at a time when the party was $9.3 million in debt and deeply divided over the Vietnam War and other domestic issues. O'Brien pushed the party to work on reforming the process of selecting presidential delegates; his labors ultimately led to more young people,

women, and minorities at the 1972 Democratic National Convention as delegates.

On June 17, 1972, burglars working for the Nixon presidential reelection committee broke into O'Brien's Watergate office, leading to the attempted cover-up and ultimately to Nixon's resignation.

*See also:* Democratic National Committee, Elections of 1960 and 1964, Hubert Humphrey, Lyndon B. Johnson, John F. Kennedy, Robert F. Kennedy, Richard M. Nixon, Vietnam War as a Political Issue, Voting Rights Act of 1965 and Extensions, Watergate

*Matthew J. Dickinson*

### REFERENCES

Anderson, Patrick. 1968. *The Presidents' Men (White House Assistants of Franklin D. Roosevelt, Harry S Truman, Dwight D. Eisenhower, John F. Kennedy and Lyndon B. Johnson).* Garden City, NY: Doubleday.

O'Brien, Lawrence. 1974. *No Final Victories: A Life in Politics from John Kennedy to Watergate.* New York: Ballantine Books.

## O'Brien v. Brown
### 409 U.S. 1 (1972)

This Supreme Court case involved challenges to the delegate selection rules for the 1972 national convention of the Democratic Party. The Credentials Committee recommended that the convention delegates refuse to seat 59 uncommitted Illinois delegates elected in a state primary on the basis of a party guideline requiring that slate making take place in a public process and recommended the unseating of 151 California George McGovern delegates on the ground that the winner-take-all primary violated the party's 1968 mandate to reform the selection process.

Brought to the Court on an expedited basis, the issue was delayed because the Court refused to settle the case on its merits, deciding instead that the complaints should be presented to the Democratic National Convention for initial resolution. Accordingly, the Court stayed the judgment of the U.S. Court of Appeals. But the Democrats were unable to resolve the difficulties, and the Court heard the case immediately thereafter.

Before *O'Brien*, several cases had apparently treated political party nominating processes as a public function, subject under the doctrine of state action to all of the constitutional limitations normally imposed on governmental bodies. *O'Brien* dismissed those cases with the words, "This is not a case in which claims are made that injury arises from invidious discrimination based on race in a primary contest within a single State."

The Court described the parties "as voluntary associations of individuals" and noted that credentials determinations and "the deliberative processes of a national political convention" have "heretofore [been] thought to lie in the control of political parties." It found no precedent for judicial intervention. Therefore, the Court refused to decide whether the actions of the parties should be considered state action subject to such constitutional provisions as the due process clause.

See also: Winner-Take-All Systems

*Stephen E. Gottlieb*

REFERENCES

Gottlieb, Stephen E. 1982. "Rebuilding the Right of Association: The Right to Hold a Convention as a Test Case." 11 *Hofstra Law Review* 191.

## Daniel P. O'Connell (1885–1977)

Boss of the Democratic Party machine in Albany, New York. Daniel Peter O'Connell, the son of a tavern owner, never completed high school. He served in the U.S. Navy during World War I, returning to his native Albany after the war to enter local politics. In 1919 O'Connell challenged the Republican organization by winning the post of city assessor. Two years later, with the help of his three brothers, he seized control of the relatively dormant Albany County Democratic Committee. That same year the O'Connells elected the first Democratic city administration in 22 years. In 1922 they duplicated their local success in races for positions in Albany County government, winning most of them for the Democrats.

All four O'Connell brothers were powerful figures, but Daniel, affectionately called "Uncle Dan" by his supporters, was their leader. Brother Edward was Albany Democratic county chairman until his death in 1939. Patrick became clerk of the state senate in 1933 but died the following year. John J., known to friends as "Solly," confined himself to overseeing the family's substantial brewery interests until his death in 1953.

The O'Connell machine patterned itself after Tammany Hall of New York City. Tales were told of stuffed ballot boxes, of slush funds drawn from gambling, and of public contracts awarded to a favored few. The most prominent of accusations hurled against the O'Connells was that they juggled local property tax assessments—raising them for opponents, lowering them for supporters.

The O'Connell machine survived several onslaughts. A two-year federal investigation of "baseball pool" gambling resulted in Daniel O'Connell's plea of guilty to a 1927 conspiracy charge. In 1929 O'Connell served a 90-day jail sentence for refusing to testify before a federal grand jury.

Dan O'Connell's most serious challenge came in 1945 from New York Republican governor Thomas E. Dewey. During the investigation, state accountants actually took possession of Albany City Hall, claiming that a shortage of funds existed. But the accusation was false, and no indictments resulted against O'Connell, a man who Dewey disparagingly labeled an "ex-convict."

In 1961 the New York State Commission of Investigation charged that there was "shocking inequities" in Albany property tax assessments, "laxity" in collections, and "possible conflicts of interest." Republican governor Nelson A. Rockefeller ordered the Democratic state comptroller to investigate. Once again, O'Connell emerged unscathed.

O'Connell held only one elected office—Albany city assessor from 1919 to 1921. After that, he confined himself to internal Democratic politics. He almost never made a public speech and was accessible only to a few reporters and close political associates. From 1922 to 1966, the Republicans never won office in Albany. The Roman Catholic O'Connells favored Democratic candidates from socially prominent, old-money, Protestant families, most notably Erastus Corning II, who served as mayor of Albany for 40 years.

The machine routinely delivered large Democratic majorities in local races as well as national ones. Once when former Democratic Congressman Leo W. O'Brien told O'Connell that he was tired of hearing critics of the machine refer to "Boss O'Connell," the Albany County leader replied, "But, Obie, I *am* the boss."

See also: Erastus Corning II, Thomas E. Dewey, Nelson Rockefeller, Tammany Hall

*John K. White*

REFERENCES

Moscow, Warren. 1948. *Politics in the Empire State.* New York: Knopf.

Weaver, Warren, Jr. 1977. "Daniel P. O'Connell Is Dead at 91; Old-Time Albany Democratic Boss." *New York Times*, March 1.

## James G. O'Hara (1925– )

Michigan Democratic Congressman and party reformer. In Congress, James Grant O'Hara was known as a hard worker and a good parliamentarian who actively supported education, civil rights, and labor causes throughout his legislative career. He was involved in the formation of the Democratic Study Group and served as its chairman from 1967 to 1969. He made a bid for Majority Leader in 1971, but his candidacy was unsuccessful.

O'Hara's first campaign in 1958 involved close races in both the primary and general elections. He captured the Democratic nomination by a scant 23 votes out of nearly 30,000 cast and then defeated the incumbent Republican by fewer than 3,000 votes. He was not seriously challenged again until 1972, when a combination of redistricting and an unpopular stand on school busing nearly cost him his seat. O'Hara restored his large electoral margin in the 1974 election by winning 72 percent of the vote.

Following the 1968 Democratic National Convention, O'Hara chaired a committee charged with writing the first formal rules for the Democratic Party in convention. The O'Hara Commission, officially known as the "Commission on Rules," established a credentials panel with strict procedures for seating delegates. This committee received little public attention in comparison to the more controversial McGovern-Fraser Commission. O'Hara served as parliamentarian for the 1972 Convention.

O'Hara gave up his House seat to run for the Senate when Philip Hart retired in 1976. He finished third in the Democratic primary to the eventual winner, Donald Riegle.

*See also:* Democratic Study Group, McGovern-Fraser Commission

*John A. Clark*

## Old Republicans

The Old Republicans were a faction of the Jeffersonian Republicans who believed that they alone carried the torch of true republicanism into the nineteenth century. Although John Taylor, John Randolph, and Nathaniel Macon have been described as the "Keepers of the Jeffersonian Conscience," they and their fellow Old Republicans were often at odds with the Sage of Monticello especially on questions concerning democracy. Randolph, Littleton Waller Tazewell, Benjamin Watkins Leigh, and younger men like Abel Parker Upshur and John Tyler fought both the extension of suffrage and the reapportionment of the legislature in the Virginia Constitutional Convention of 1829–1830. Their conservative interpretation of the republican tradition focused upon a nearly paranoid distrust of power emphasizing liberty from government and the right of individuals to "secure their own interests."

Like the "Country" party in eighteenth-century England, they represented the interest of the landowning gentry and took their oppositionist stance from Viscount Bolingbroke, the eighteenth-century British writer. The Old Republicans were men of little faith who looked upon change with a jaundiced eye and agreed with Randolph who assailed that "maggot, innovation." At every step they feared that the consolidation of power and the tyranny of numbers would undermine the "principles of '98" expressed in the Virginia and Kentucky resolutions.

The most important leaders of the Old Republicans were Virginians. Randolph spoke of himself in 1806 as one of "the old republicans," after he had broken with the Jefferson administration, and his contemporaries used the term distinguishing between the "old Party" and "the New one." The Old Republicans generally distrusted James Madison, and in 1808 they supported James Monroe's bid for the presidency.

During Madison's first term they often talked belligerently but rejected any increase in military appropriations emphasizing strict construction and economy. Although they accepted the declaration of war in 1812, the Old Republicans gave "Mr. Madison's War" only halfhearted support.

During the Era of Good Feelings, they led the states' rights revival that spread from Virginia across the lower South. Spencer Roane directly confronted the judicial nationalism of John Marshall and the Supreme Court, and Taylor served as the movement's major ideologue, attacking the tariff, the national bank, and federal aid for internal improvements as well as the pretensions of the federal judiciary. The Old Republicans of these years lay the groundwork for the emerging states' rights advocates of the lower South by explicitly connecting conservative republicanism to the defense of slavery. Any step in the direction of strengthening the federal government potentially threatened the "Peculiar Institution." In 1824 they promoted the candidacy of William H. Crawford, but in response to the nationalistic posture of the Adams administration, they moved into the

Jackson camp and staunchly supported his actions during his first administration. Many of the leading Old Republicans had died by the 1830s, and their younger colleagues, after turning against Jackson, joined forces briefly with the Whigs before gradually drifting into the extreme states' rights wing of the Democracy led by John C. Calhoun.

*See also:* John C. Calhoun, Election of 1808, Andrew Jackson, James Madison, Nathaniel Macon, James Monroe, John Randolph, John Taylor, John Tyler

*William G. Shade*

REFERENCES

Cunningham, Noble E., Jr. 1963. "Who Were the Quids?" 50 *Mississippi Valley Historical Review* 252.

Risjord, Norman K. 1965. *The Old Republicans: Southern Conservatives in the Age of Jefferson.* New York: Columbia U. Pr.

Shallhope, Robert E. 1980. *John Taylor of Caroline: Pastoral Republican.* Columbia: U. of South Carolina Pr.

## Floyd B. Olson (1891–1936)

Leader of the Minnesota Farmer-Labor Party in the 1930s. Floyd B. Olson governed Minnesota from 1931 to 1936, when he died in office of stomach cancer. At the time he was also ostensibly seeking a seat in the United States Senate but had in fact been too weak to campaign for several months. His death provoked an outburst of mass grief in Minnesota, similar to the national grief when Franklin Roosevelt and John Kennedy died. Olson is still revered today in Minnesota. His statue is located at one end of the Capitol mall in St. Paul.

As governor, Olson pushed the 1933 and 1935 legislatures for major reforms in the tax system, getting the lawmakers to design the tax system more progressively. He also pushed the 1933 legislature for a mortgage moratorium law to aid farmers. His state attorney general successfully defended the law before the U.S. Supreme Court, helping to lay the constitutional basis for the welfare state in America. Finally, Olson turned the Minnesota National Guard into a pro-labor policy instrument during the 1934 Minneapolis truckers' strikes. The two succeeding Farmer-Labor governors, Hjalmar Petersen and Elmer Benson, also used the Guard to aid labor.

Olson had good relations with Franklin D. Roosevelt, who did little to interfere with the Farmer-Labor Party's success in Minnesota and often aided it. Before 1935 Olson often spoke of organizing a national third party, but at his death he committed the FLP to aiding FDR's reelection.

*See also:* Minnesota Farmer-Labor Party, Franklin D. Roosevelt

*Richard M. Valelly*

REFERENCES

Mayer, George. 1951. *The Political Career of Floyd B. Olson.* Minneapolis: U. of Minnesota Pr.

## James Oneal (1875–1962)

A prolific author and active Socialist for over 60 years, James Oneal was one of the Socialist Party's most influential anti-Communist leaders. He played major roles both in the party's break with communism after World War I and in its schism in the mid-1930s.

The son of an Indianapolis iron puddler, Oneal left school in sixth grade to become an ironworker. He joined the Social Democracy in 1897 and subsequently enrolled in the Socialist Party. During the prewar period he was a talented "soap-boxer," won various state and national Socialist Party positions, wrote for the *New York Call,* and edited the *New York Worker.* His first book, *The Workers in American History,* was published in 1910.

Oneal went to Europe in 1919 as a party representative. He returned a fervent anti-Communist and was instrumental in pushing this view within the party. As an occasional candidate for office, a member of the party's national executive committee, and (from 1924) editor of the *New Leader,* Oneal fought any perceived communistic incursions. His career as an author served a similar purpose. His *American Communism* (1927), a very early work on the topic, was part scholarly study, part anti-Communist polemic. The same was true of his various later works. Oneal was a leader of the Old Guard faction in its battle with the "Militants" during the mid-1930s, denouncing his opponents as middle-class dilettantes with communistic tendencies. In 1936 he and other Old Guardsmen left the party and formed the Social Democratic Federation. He remained as editor of the increasingly moderate *New Leader* until 1940 and then moved to California. He continued to write, authoring a Socialist pamphlet for the Gene Debs People's Forum Foundation as late as 1958.

*See also:* Communism as a Political Issue, Socialist Party of America

*Gary L. Bailey*

REFERENCES

Johnpoll, Bernard K., and Harvey Klehr, eds. 1986. "James Oneal." *Biographical Dictionary of the American Left.* Westport, CT: Greenwood.

Oneal, James. 1910. *The Workers in American History.* Terre Haute: James Oneal.

——. 1927. *American Communism: A Critical Analysis of Its Origins, Development and Programs.* New York: Rand Book Store.

——. 1931. "Our Bourgeois Barbarians." In Samuel D. Schmalhausen, ed. *Behold America!* New York: Farrar and Rinehart.

——. 1934. *Some Pages of Party History.* New York: Privately printed.

Shannon, David A. 1955. *The Socialist Party of America: A History.* New York: Macmillan.

## Thomas P. (Tip) O'Neill (1912– )

Speaker of the U.S. House of Representatives for the longest continuous term in that chamber's history. Thomas Phillip (Tip) O'Neill's rise within Massachusetts politics paralleled the decline of Republican hegemony in that state; his rise within the hierarchy of the U.S. House of Representatives was prototypical of progress up through the ranks in the latter half of the twentieth century; and his service as Speaker was instrumental in guiding the development of the House of Representatives after the important committee and Democratic caucus reforms of the early 1970s.

Tip O'Neill's introduction to politics came through his father, an Irish immigrant and public employee in Cambridge, Massachusetts. The younger O'Neill began his political career in Cambridge in 1934, losing a bid for the Cambridge City Council by a narrow margin in a multicandidate field; two years later he was more successful, winning election to the Massachusetts state legislature. Befitting the man who popularized the expression "all politics is local," O'Neill spent these years paying particular attention to his district, dispensing patronage and tending the legislative fires for his working-class district. He was also an effective behind-the-scenes operator; when the Democrats gained control of the Massachusetts House in 1948 for the first time in a century, O'Neill was elected the first Democratic Speaker.

O'Neill was elected to the U.S. House of Representatives in 1952, replacing John F. Kennedy, who had given up this seat following his election to the U.S. Senate. O'Neill won the Democratic nomination in a close six-man race and then swept his Republican opponent in the general election with 70 percent of the vote. Tip

O'Neill held this seat until his retirement in 1987, never receiving less than 73 percent of the vote in any of his reelection campaigns.

Being a "New Deal Democrat" representing a working-class district made O'Neill a natural candidate for a leadership career track in the House. Personally sponsored by his Massachusetts colleague, John McCormack, then House Minority Whip, O'Neill was assigned to the House Rules Committee in his second term.

O'Neill's rise within the House leadership hierarchy began in the 1960s. As a member of the Rules Committee in the 1950s and early 1960s, he was loyal to the Democratic leadership, voting against the conservative coalition that had controlled the committee since the New Deal, but also staying aloof from its more liberal critics, such as the Democratic Study Group, who urged direct confrontation between party leaders and the Rules Committee's southern Democrats.

O'Neill's ultimate rise to the pinnacle of power in the House of Representatives was aided by both his astute understanding of institutional politics and luck. He first entered the leadership ladder when he was appointed Democratic Whip by Majority Leader Hale Boggs in 1971. O'Neill's rise to the top accelerated following Boggs's unexpected death in 1972. O'Neill was elected Majority Leader in the next Congress, winning after he forced his only opponent, Sam Gibbons (Florida), out of the race.

The retirement of Carl Albert following the 1976 election elevated O'Neill to the speakership in 1977 (95th Congress). O'Neill immediately took the opportunity to pursue a partisan Democratic program in the House, given a large House Democratic majority (292 Democrats to 143 Republicans) and a newly elected Democratic President, Jimmy Carter. But O'Neill often found himself frustrated in pushing the President's program, a problem he often attributed to President Carter's naiveté about the workings of Congress.

O'Neill's frustrations also eventuated from the tremendous institutional changes that engulfed the House in the 1970s—changes that were the product of both a series of formal institutional reforms initiated earlier in the decade, such as the "subcommittee bill of rights," and a rapid influx of new members. The formal institutional reforms had liberalized many House procedures, making the Rules Committee more accountable to the wishes of the Democratic Caucus, providing rank-and-file members with greater say in the conduct of committee business, making committee chairs subject to a vote of confidence from the caucus, and changing the process by which members were appointed to committees. Compared with Speakers earlier in the century, O'Neill had few of the resources with which to force his followers into compliance with the wishes of party leaders; the caucus itself had greater say in the performance of leaders and committees, and the rank and file could more easily evade leadership requests.

The influx of new members, best represented by the class of "Watergate babies" who entered the House in the 1974 election, also affected O'Neill's ability to lead House Democrats independently. Democrats who entered following the 1974 election were noted for being more independent of party leaders, in part because many represented former Republican districts and thus *had* to exhibit partisan independence in order to ensure their own reelection.

O'Neill responded to these changes in the texture of the House by promoting formal and informal institutional innovations. One such innovation begun under O'Neill was the "leadership task force," a maneuver that allowed the Speaker to create ad hoc committees to consider legislation that cut across committee jurisdictions. Another related formal innovation was "Speaker discharge" and multiple referral, stratagems that allowed the Speaker to refer complicated legislation to more than one committee and to require committee action by a certain date. These reforms were instituted not only to improve the quality of legislation in complex substantive areas but also to allow for innovative bargaining mechanisms in a context of few leadership sanctions.

Certainly the most difficult set of events that O'Neill had to face as Speaker was consideration of the legislative and budgetary program in the first Congress (the 97th) of Ronald Reagan's first presidential term. The actual diminution of federal domestic programs was personally painful to O'Neill, and President Reagan was able to see much of his own program passed because a core of southern Democrats was willing to desert O'Neill and support Reagan's policy proposals for most of 1981 and 1982. In a series of television advertisements sponsored by the Republican Party, O'Neill himself became a symbol of a bloated federal government. After the 1982 election, Democratic strength in the House was restored to its pre-1980 level, and until his retirement in 1987, O'Neill was able to lead a Democratic Party that was more unified than had been the case in the earliest years of the decade. Tip O'Neill retired to Massachusetts where he enriched his retirement with television commercial appearances and golf games.

*See also:* Carl Albert, Jimmy Carter, John F. Kennedy, John McCormack, Speaker of the House

*Charles Stewart III*

## Open Primary

A primary election in which voters may decide at the time of the election and in the privacy of the voting booth which party primary they wish to participate in is called an open primary. Voters need not express allegiance to any party before the primary election. Voters may not participate in the primary of more than one party in any election. As of 1986 open primary states included Hawaii, Idaho, Michigan, Minnesota, Montana, North Dakota, Utah, Vermont, and Wisconsin. The open primary differs from the blanket primary in that blanket primary states allow voters to vote in the primary of more than one party during one election. Voters in blanket states (Alaska, Louisiana, and Washington) may not vote in the same primary for the same office in more than one party.

Unlike the closed primary, independent voters may participate in any party's primary process. The system allows voters to engage in "raiding," where voters allied with one party can support the nomination of a weaker candidate in the opposition party in the hopes of facilitating the election of their own party's nominee. Although crossover voting frequently occurs in open primary states, little evidence suggests that it results in systematic raiding.

The open primary first appeared in Wisconsin and was a product of Progressive era reforms of the early twentieth century that were designed to open up the nomination process to all voters and encourage greater participation. Most traditionalist party leaders argue that the open primary undercuts the strength and control of party organizations.

*See also:* Blanket Primaries, Crossover Voting

*Robert J. Spitzer*

REFERENCES

Sorauf, Frank. 1984. *Party Politics in America.* Boston: Little, Brown.

## *Oregon v. Mitchell*
### 400 U.S. 112 (1970)

In this case the Supreme Court limited Congress' attempts to enact laws that define the scope of the equal protection clause of the Fourteenth Amendment. The *Mitchell* Court was faced with equal protection challenges to the constitutionality of certain provisions of the Voting Rights Act Amendments of 1970. The challenged provisions were those that lowered the minimum voting age from 21 to 18 in federal, state, and local elections; prohibited the use of state-imposed residency requirements for federal elections; and barred the use of literacy tests to determine voter qualifications. In a fragmented decision, the Supreme Court upheld all of the provisions except those that lowered the voting age in state and local elections. However, the Court appeared less concerned with equal protection and enforcement of civil rights than it was with determining the extent of Congress' power legislatively to define the reach of the equal protection clause.

Five years before *Mitchell*, in *Katzenbach v. Morgan*, the Supreme Court upheld federal legislation prohibiting literacy tests that Congress found to be discriminatory against certain classes of citizens. In *Katzenbach*, the Court held that Congress had the power, under Section 5 of the Fourteenth Amendment, to legislate as it deemed necessary and proper in order to remedy perceived violations of fundamental rights under the equal protection clause of the Fourteenth Amendment. The broader implications of *Katzenbach* were that Congress has the power to expand or restrict equal protection and that the federal judiciary and the state legislatures must accord deference to such congressional action.

Despite this apparent judicial acquiescence in congressional determination of the scope of the equal protection clause, the *Mitchell* Court backed away from *Katzenbach* and restricted the latitude within which Congress could act. The plurality in *Mitchell* held that Congress had usurped the power and responsibility of the federal judiciary and the state legislatures by restricting the states' autonomy over state and local elections (through the age requirements) without first finding that such restrictions were necessary to combat discrimination by the states. The Court concluded that Section 5 of the Fourteenth Amendment does not confer upon Congress unlimited power to determine the meaning of equal protection, particularly by preempting state legislation or federal court rulings.

In 1970 the *Mitchell* Court said that when Congress finds states discriminating against classes of citizens with respect to a fundamental

right, then it may legislate to broaden the scope of protection afforded by the Fourteenth Amendment. The Court determined, however, that there was no rational basis for finding discriminatory the restriction of the electoral franchise to persons age 21 or older. In this regard, the Court reaffirmed its previous holdings that states *may* impose reasonable restrictions on the right of suffrage. The Court made clear that in no instance can Congress restrict the scope or dilute the guarantees of the equal protection clause. The Court also said that any congressional action affecting the equal protection clause would be subject to review by the federal courts. The federal courts are not required to defer to congressional determinations on equal protection and fundamental rights. A federal Court can invalidate such action if it finds that the legislation either minimizes the protection afforded by the Fourteenth Amendment or unnecessarily restricts the autonomy of the states in establishing reasonable voter qualifications for state and local elections.

*Mitchell* helped to clarify the murky lines that existed between the powers of the states and the three branches of federal government in relation to the Fourteenth Amendment. While the boundaries that separate these powers will never be absolutely plain, *Mitchell* showed that as long as states do not discriminate against classes of citizens, they may retain authority and autonomy over the time, place, and manner of their own elections, subject only to review by the federal courts.

*See also:* Literacy Tests, Suffrage

*Morton A. Brody*

## James L. Orr (1822–1873)

South Carolina political leader before and after the Civil War. James Lawrence Orr was a southern politician who "thought nationally" and thus sought to build intersectional alliances. He was born in South Carolina, the son of a successful merchant. Admitted to the bar in 1843, he also edited the *Anderson Gazette* (1844–1846). Elected to the state legislature (1844–1848), he favored modernization: popular election of presidential electors, internal improvements, and educational reform. A generation younger than John Calhoun, Orr accepted intersectional party politics and opposed particularism as detrimental to national influence for South Carolina. Orr's service in the U.S. House of Representatives (1848–1859) was marked by support for sectional interests within the context of union. Initially opposed to compromise in 1850, he later organized a faction of National Democrats to promote its acceptance. At the 1856 Democratic convention, he supported Stephen A. Douglas and in 1857 was chosen House Speaker. Yet in 1858 he was denied a seat in the Senate, and in 1860 he was unable to prevent the break up of the Charleston Democratic convention. He signed South Carolina's secession ordinance and was involved in attempts to get President Abraham Lincoln to surrender Charleston's forts just before the outbreak of the Civil War. He served the Confederacy in its Provisional Congress and Senate. A Lincoln hater, Orr advocated negotiations with the North in the war's waning months. Following defeat, he was selected to help revise the South Carolina state constitution and then to serve as the state's first postwar governor. He cooperated fully with Andrew Johnson, following him into the National Union movement. Orr later advocated cooperation with the Republican Congress. A Republican by 1868, he served as circuit judge (1868–1870) and finally as Ulysses Grant's minister to Russia.

*See also:* John C. Calhoun, Stephen A. Douglas, Andrew Johnson, Abraham Lincoln, National Democrats, Secession, Speaker of the House

*Phyllis F. Field*

REFERENCES

Breese, Donald H. 1979. "James L. Orr, Calhoun, and the Cooperationist Tradition in South Carolina." 80 *South Carolina Historical Magazine* 273.

Leemhuis, Roger P. 1979. *James L. Orr and the Sectional Conflict.* Washington: U. Pr. of America.

## Moisei Y. Ostrogorski (1854–1919)

Russian intellectual and pioneer in empirical study of political parties. A fount of knowledge and ideas on Anglo-American political systems, Moisei Yakovlevich Ostrogorski's *Democracy and the Organization of Political Parties* served as the model for the later research of the two great German political sociologists, Max Weber and Robert Michels.

Ostrogorski acquired his legal education in St. Petersburg (now Leningrad) and then served in the Ministry of Justice. He later studied in France, where his writings on the rights of women in public law merited him the 1892 Paris Faculty of Law Prize. His magnum opus, *Democracy and the Organization of Political Parties*, published in 1902, resulted from extensive firsthand study of political parties in both England and the United States.

Ostrogorski was the first to argue for the need to go beyond the analysis of formal political institutions in order to study actual political behavior and institutions outside the governmental sphere. He was generally lauded for his conclusion that oligarchic controls, manipulation of the electorate, and a blurring of ideological differences are inherent in the organizational pressures on parties operating under conditions of universal suffrage. His proposed solution—discarding the use of permanent parties in favor of restoring and reserving a political party's essential character as a combination of citizens specially formed for a particular issue—met with much derision as being unrealistic and naive.

Ostrogorski published no other scholarly works. He returned to Russia after the revolution of 1905 and was elected to the first Duma (parliament) in 1906. Following its demise, Ostrogorski withdrew from active politics.

*Nancy C. Unger*

REFERENCES

Butler, David. 1958. *The Study of Political Behavior.* London: Hutchinson.

Ostrogorski, Moisei. 1964. *Democracy and the Organization of Political Parties.* Ed. Seymour Martin Lipset. Chicago: Quadrangle.

Ranney, Austin. 1962. *The Doctrine of Responsible Party Government: Its Origins and Present State.* Urbana: U. of Illinois Pr.

Weber, Max. 1946. "Politics as a Vocation." In H. H. Garth and C. W. Wills, eds. *From Max Weber: Essays in Sociology.* New York: Oxford U. Pr.

# P

## A. Mitchell Palmer (1872–1936)

Repressive Attorney General during the Red Scare. The word enigmatic aptly describes the career of A. Mitchell Palmer. Born a Quaker in Stroudsburg, Pennsylvania, he attended Swarthmore College, studied law, but devoted most of his life to politics.

The vicissitudes of Palmer's public life brought mixed results. Elected as a Democrat to Congress in 1908, he served until 1914, when he unsuccessfully challenged Pennsylvania's Republican Senator Boies Penrose. After allegedly declining the presidential nomination in 1912, Palmer sought a Cabinet appointment. He rejected Woodrow Wilson's offer of the War Department, citing his (Quaker-inspired) pacifistic beliefs, but Palmer made known his desire to be Attorney General. Initially thwarted, he became Alien Property Custodian in 1917, in spite of earlier doubts about his patriotism, and finally in 1919, he became Attorney General. He emerged as the favorite for the Democratic presidential nomination in 1920, but fears about his electability, the decline of the Red Scare, and organized labor's hostility worked against him. The Democrats did not nominate Palmer, and he retired from politics. He reemerged briefly in 1932, when he helped Franklin Roosevelt draft the Democratic platform.

Palmer's brief tenure as Attorney General is his most enduring legacy. Appointed at a time of heightened fear of domestic radicalism, Palmer, originally a friend of labor, acted in enmity, using the Lever Act of 1917, which gave the government the authority to act to ensure the adequate production and distribution of food, to break strikes. In June 1919 he planned a roundup and deportation of alleged alien radicals. With the able assistance of J. Edgar Hoover, the Justice Department raided the Union of Russian Workers and the Communist and Communist Labor parties in November 1919 and January 1920. Though no real threat of revolution in America existed, many superpatriots feared its imminence, and Palmer both shared their concern and hoped to parlay his response into political triumph. Though some might argue that Palmer simply reacted to public sentiment, his Justice Department's overtly repressive actions both subjugated basic American rights and ignored statutory procedures.

*See also:* Communism as a Political Issue, Election of 1920, Boies Penrose, Red Scare, Franklin D. Roosevelt, Woodrow Wilson

*Robert F. Zeidel*

REFERENCES

Coben, Stanley. 1963. *A. Mitchell Palmer: Politician.* New York: Columbia U. Pr.

Murray, Robert K. 1955. *Red Scare: A Study in National Hysteria, 1919–1920.* New York: McGraw-Hill.

Powers, Robert Gid. 1987. *Secrecy and Power: The Secret Life of J. Edgar Hoover.* New York: Free Press.

## Alton B. Parker (1852–1926)

Democratic presidential candidate in 1904. Chief Justice of the New York Court of Appeals, Alton Brooks Parker was a political novice. The conservative jurist suited gold-standard Grover Cleveland Democrats fed up at once with Roosevelt and with the Democratic radical, William Jennings Bryan. Parker personified an old-fashioned campaign strategy.

Parker, however, accepted the nomination reluctantly, hoping to maintain a judicious silence throughout the campaign. He wanted to conduct a front-porch campaign from Rosemount, his Hudson River estate in Esopus, New York, greeting visitors and speaking occasionally. By 1904, on the other hand, such campaigns were clearly anachronistic. Parker began paying what the New York *Evening Sun* called "the penalty of prominence." Rosemount was overrun with photographers who dogged the judge, even as he disrobed and plunged into the Hudson River for his morning swim. Similarly, he was hounded for policy statements on the major issues of the day. His telegram to the Democratic convention in support of the gold standard was not considered sufficiently enthusiastic.

By September, Democratic worries over a narcotized campaign forced Parker onto the stump. In late October, he began assailing President Roosevelt's "shameless" sellout to the corporations for campaign funds. But it was too late. Parker was trounced in a victory that testified to Roosevelt's popularity and to the revolution in candidate behavior that Bryan had unleashed during the 1896 and 1900 campaigns. Upon his defeat, Parker happily resumed his legal career.

*See also:* William Jennings Bryan, Grover Cleveland, Election of 1904, Theodore Roosevelt

*Gil Troy*

REFERENCES

Hollingworth, J. Rogers. 1963. *The Whirligig of Politics: The Democracy of Cleveland and Bryan.* Chicago: U. of Chicago Pr.

Pringle, Henry. 1956. *Theodore Roosevelt: A Biography.* Rev. ed. New York: Harcourt, Brace & World.

## Partisan Coalitions in the Electorate

The composition of the coalitions supporting each political party is a much-researched topic, and changes in these party coalitions are principal components of partisan realignments and party system shifts. V. O. Key's original articles on critical and secular realignment stress the importance of charting the changes in group ties to the parties. Although theoretically significant, such changes have been especially difficult to assess. Analyses of party coalitions have focused either on *overlapping* groups, such as Blacks and the working class, or on *exclusive* groups, such as white, middle-class Protestants. Yet neither approach is adequate: use of overlapping groups makes it impossible to tell which characteristics are the crucial determinants of party support; reliance on exclusive groups largely predetermines the research outcome because the critical groups have to be defined a priori.

The coalitional basis of the parties is the focus of this analysis. Evaluating the partisanship of individual group members from a multivariate perspective provides improved insights into the marginal difference made by membership in each group and into the makeup of a party's support coalition. An example of such an approach is this examination of the Democratic coalition over the past three decades. Results of this analysis strengthen conventional wisdom about individual partisan changes by African-Americans and southern whites but differ significantly with respect to the strength and timing of changes by these and other groups. In addition, the results underscore changes in the composition of the Democratic coalition. Although how one measures partisan changes, not what might motivate such changes, is our focus, the results delimit the possible reasons for those changes. Though the absence of one single, dramatic change leaves room for argument, but the best evidence supports Carmines and Stimson's conclusion that a partisan realignment centering on race occurred in the mid-1960s.

### Party Identification: Measurements of Changes in Group Support

Among studies of group partisanship, consensus on the manner of analysis is lacking. For example, two of the most prominent studies of group partisan change use superficially similar procedures that are in fact quite different. Axelrod (1972, 1986) analyzed the voting support of six groups for Democratic and Republican presidential candidates between 1952 and 1984, defining each group by a single characteristic (Table 1). Thus, individuals are partitioned into overlapping groups. Any given respondent could fall into two, three, four, five, or even all six groups that Axelrod defined. Contrarily, Petrocik analyzed the partisan identification shifts of 15 groups between the 1950s and the 1970s, defining each group by particular combinations of 7 characteristics (Table 2). Groups as defined in this way were exclusive; individuals could fall into only one of them.

# Table 1

## Party Coalitions and the Vote

### The Democratic Coalition, 1952–1984

| Year | Percentage Contribution= | | | | | | (Size | | | | | | x | Turnout | | | | | | x | Loyalty) | | | | | | + | (NT x NL) | |
|---|---|---|---|---|---|---|---|---|---|---|---|---|---|---|---|---|---|---|---|---|---|---|---|---|---|---|---|---|---|
| | P | B | U | C | S | CC | P | B | U | C | S | CC | | P | B | U | C | S | CC | | P | B | U | C | S | CC | | NT | NL |
| 1952 | 28 | 7 | 38 | 41 | 20 | 21 | 36 | 10 | 27 | 26 | 28 | 16 | | 46 | 23 | 66 | 76 | 35 | 68 | | 47 | 83 | 59 | 57 | 55 | 51 | | 65 | 44.4 |
| 1956 | 19 | 5 | 36 | 38 | 23 | 19 | 25 | 9 | 26 | 25 | 29 | 14 | | 40 | 23 | 64 | 72 | 39 | 63 | | 47 | 68 | 55 | 53 | 52 | 55 | | 60 | 42.0 |
| 1960 | 16 | 7 | 31 | 47 | 27 | 19 | 23 | 10 | 25 | 25 | 34 | 13 | | 46 | 31 | 60 | 74 | 50 | 74 | | 48 | 72 | 66 | 82 | 52 | 65 | | 64 | 49.7 |
| 1964 | 15 | 12 | 32 | 36 | 21 | 15 | 19 | 11 | 23 | 26 | 28 | 12 | | 45 | 42 | 69 | 72 | 49 | 65 | | 69 | 99 | 80 | 75 | 58 | 74 | | 63 | 61.1 |
| 1968 | 12 | 19 | 28 | 40 | 24 | 14 | 16 | 11 | 24 | 26 | 31 | 10 | | 44 | 51 | 61 | 68 | 53 | 63 | | 44 | 92 | 51 | 61 | 39 | 58 | | 62 | 42.7 |
| 1972 | 10 | 22 | 32 | 43 | 25 | 14 | 12 | 11 | 25 | 31 | 34 | 8 | | 37 | 47 | 58 | 65 | 44 | 60 | | 45 | 86 | 45 | 45 | 36 | 61 | | 56 | 37.5 |
| 1976 | 7 | 16 | 33 | 35 | 29 | 11 | 9 | 11 | 23 | 30 | 32 | 8 | | 32 | 44 | 62 | 55 | 45 | 58 | | 67 | 88 | 63 | 57 | 53 | 61 | | 54 | 50.1 |
| 1980 | 5 | 22 | 31 | 31 | 39 | 12 | 5 | 12 | 25 | 31 | 34 | 8 | | 34 | 45 | 57 | 54 | 50 | 51 | | 71 | 88 | 50 | 44 | 47 | 69 | | 54 | 41.0 |
| 1984 | 10 | 25 | 30 | 39 | 32 | 7 | 9 | 12 | 20 | 33 | 32 | 8 | | 28 | 41 | 59 | 59 | 45 | 58 | | 66 | 81 | 55 | 47 | 44 | 70 | | 53 | 40.5 |
| Column | 1 | 2 | 3 | 4 | 5 | 6 | 7 | 8 | 9 | 10 | 11 | 12 | | 13 | 14 | 15 | 16 | 17 | 18 | | 19 | 20 | 21 | 22 | 23 | 24 | | 25 | 26 |

| | |
|---|---|
| P | Poor (income under $3,000/yr. before 1980; $5,000/yr. since 1980) |
| B | Black (and other nonwhite) |
| U | Union member (or union member in family) |
| C | Catholic (and other non-Protestant) |
| S | South (including Border States) |
| CC | Central cities (of 12 largest metropolitan areas) |
| NT | National turnout |
| NL | National loyalty to Democrats |

### Percentage Deviation in Loyalty to Democrats

| Year | P | B | U | C | S | CC |
|---|---|---|---|---|---|---|
| 1952 | +2 | +38 | +14 | +12 | +10 | +6 |
| 1956 | +5 | +26 | +13 | +11 | +10 | +13 |
| 1960 | −2 | +22 | +16 | +32 | +2 | +15 |
| 1964 | +8 | +38 | +19 | +14 | −3 | +13 |
| 1968 | +1 | +49 | +8 | +18 | −4 | +15 |
| 1972 | +8 | +49 | +8 | +8 | −2 | +24 |
| 1976 | +17 | +38 | +13 | +7 | +3 | +10 |
| 1980 | +30 | +47 | +9 | +3 | +6 | +28 |
| 1984 | +25 | +40 | +14 | +6 | +3 | +29 |
| Column | 27 | 28 | 29 | 30 | 31 | 32 |

### The Republican Coalition, 1952–1984

| Year | Percentage Contribution= | | | | | | (Size | | | | | | x | Turnout | | | | | | x | Loyalty) | | | | | | + | (NT x NL) | |
|---|---|---|---|---|---|---|---|---|---|---|---|---|---|---|---|---|---|---|---|---|---|---|---|---|---|---|---|---|---|
| | NP | W | NU | P | N | NCC | NP | W | NU | P | N | NCC | | NP | W | NU | P | N | NCC | | NP | W | NU | P | N | NCC | | NT | NL |
| 1952 | 75 | 99 | 79 | 75 | 87 | 84 | 64 | 90 | 73 | 74 | 72 | 84 | | 72 | 67 | 61 | 58 | 73 | 61 | | 56 | 57 | 61 | 61 | 57 | 57 | | 63 | 55.1 |
| 1956 | 84 | 98 | 78 | 75 | 84 | 89 | 75 | 91 | 74 | 75 | 71 | 86 | | 67 | 64 | 58 | 56 | 69 | 60 | | 59 | 59 | 63 | 62 | 60 | 60 | | 60 | 57.4 |
| 1960 | 83 | 97 | 84 | 90 | 75 | 90 | 77 | 90 | 75 | 75 | 66 | 87 | | 70 | 68 | 65 | 61 | 71 | 63 | | 50 | 51 | 55 | 63 | 50 | 52 | | 64 | 49.5 |
| 1964 | 89 | 100 | 87 | 80 | 76 | 91 | 81 | 89 | 77 | 74 | 72 | 88 | | 67 | 66 | 61 | 60 | 68 | 63 | | 40 | 42 | 45 | 44 | 38 | 40 | | 63 | 38.5 |
| 1968 | 90 | 99 | 81 | 80 | 80 | 92 | 84 | 89 | 76 | 74 | 69 | 90 | | 65 | 63 | 62 | 60 | 66 | 62 | | 44 | 47 | 46 | 49 | 47 | 45 | | 62 | 43.4 |
| 1972 | 93 | 98 | 77 | 70 | 73 | 95 | 88 | 89 | 75 | 69 | 66 | 92 | | 58 | 57 | 55 | 53 | 62 | 55 | | 61 | 66 | 63 | 65 | 60 | 63 | | 56 | 60.7 |
| 1976 | 97 | 99 | 80 | 76 | 74 | 98 | 91 | 89 | 77 | 70 | 68 | 92 | | 56 | 56 | 52 | 54 | 59 | 54 | | 49 | 52 | 52 | 53 | 49 | 49 | | 54 | 48.0 |
| 1980 | 98 | 90 | 80 | 75 | 66 | 96 | 95 | 88 | 75 | 69 | 65 | 92 | | 55 | 55 | 53 | 54 | 56 | 54 | | 52 | 56 | 54 | 54 | 51 | 53 | | 54 | 50.7 |
| 1984 | 97 | 96 | 83 | 69 | 72 | 92 | 91 | 88 | 80 | 67 | 68 | 92 | | 56 | 55 | 52 | 51 | 57 | 53 | | 61 | 65 | 63 | 62 | 60 | 61 | | 53 | 58.8 |
| Column | 1 | 2 | 3 | 4 | 5 | 6 | 7 | 8 | 9 | 10 | 11 | 12 | | 13 | 14 | 15 | 16 | 17 | 18 | | 19 | 20 | 21 | 22 | 23 | 24 | | 25 | 26 |

| | |
|---|---|
| NP | Nonpoor (income over $3,000/yr. before 1980; $5,000/yr. since 1980) |
| W | White |
| NU | Nonunion |
| P | Protestant |
| N | Northern (excluding Border States) |
| NCC | Not in central cities of 12 largest metropolitan areas |
| NT | National turnout |
| NL | National loyalty to Republicans |

### Percentage Deviation in Loyalty to Republicans

| Year | NP | W | NU | P | N | NCC |
|---|---|---|---|---|---|---|
| 1952 | +1 | +2 | +6 | +6 | +6 | +2 |
| 1956 | +1 | +1 | +5 | +4 | +2 | +2 |
| 1960 | 0 | +1 | +5 | +13 | 0 | +2 |
| 1964 | +1 | +3 | +6 | +5 | −1 | +1 |
| 1968 | 0 | +3 | +2 | +5 | +3 | +1 |
| 1972 | +1 | +5 | +3 | +4 | −1 | +2 |
| 1976 | +1 | +5 | +4 | +5 | +1 | +1 |
| 1980 | +1 | +5 | +4 | +3 | +1 | +2 |
| 1984 | +2 | +7 | +4 | +3 | +1 | +2 |
| Column | 27 | 28 | 29 | 30 | 31 | 32 |

Source: Axelrod (1986), 282–283.

# Table 2

*The Sociodemographic Basis of Party Preference*

| Coalition Groups | Proportion of Population | Percent Democrat | Percent Independent | Percent Republican |
|---|---|---|---|---|
| Very high-status Protestants | 6% | 17 | 27 | 56 |
| Middle- and high-status Protestants | 10 | 13 | 27 | 51 |
| Lower-status Protestants | 12 | 34 | 29 | 37 |
| Border Southerners | | | | |
| middle and upper status | 2 | 48 | 25 | 27 |
| lower status | 4 | 58 | 19 | 23 |
| Deep South | | | | |
| immigrants | 3 | 35 | 31 | 35 |
| middle- and upper-status natives | 6 | 61 | 28 | 11 |
| lower-status natives | 9 | 67 | 20 | 13 |
| Catholics | | | | |
| Polish and Irish | 3 | 58 | 29 | 13 |
| other nationalities—higher status | 4 | 36 | 36 | 28 |
| other nationalities—middle and lower status | 7 | 53 | 230 | 18 |
| Jews | 3 | 58 | 34 | 8 |
| Blacks | 9 | 69 | 20 | 11 |
| Northern farmers | 4 | 37 | 20 | 44 |
| Union members | 19 | 51 | 29 | 20 |

Source: Petrocik (1981), 70.

The choice of whether to consider group membership in overlapping or exclusive terms seems both unnecessary and unfortunate. Choosing either rules out the opportunity to assess the marginal impact of *any* group membership on partisanship.

Axelrod's overlapping approach, for example, is highly appropriate if one wishes only to describe the partisanship of a group or to determine whether, say, African-Americans or union members account for a larger share of Democratic identifiers. Yet consider a result such as that the poor showed strong loyalty to the Democrats. Since the poor are often Black and often live in central cities and since both of these groups also showed strong Democratic tendencies, the observation about the poor might simply reflect the Democratic tendencies of either or both of the other two characteristics. With overlapping groups, one simply cannot tell.

An alternative is Petrocik's analysis. Reliance on exclusive groups merits consideration if few individuals have multiple group memberships or if it is known that the additional memberships only slightly alter the likely partisanship of individuals. However, group memberships are the rule, not the exception, and additional memberships do indeed affect an individual's likelihood of identifying with a particular party. That being the case, defining groups in exclusive terms typically leads the researcher to ignore some strong partisan ties. Moreover, reliance on exclusive groups can lead to inference problems similar to those noted for overlapping groups. For example, some have speculated that higher-status white native southerners are becoming less Democratic. This result could owe to the decreasing Democratic tendencies of being middle or upper status or of being a native white southerner. Of course, because exclusive groups are more narrowly defined than overlapping ones, the scope of the statements is more certain. There is yet a third problem: categorizing individuals into exclusive groups to a large degree assumes what should be tested. Categories of individuals like those above, for example, assume that status, race, and region dominate other characteristics such as religion and class.

Use of either overlapping or exclusive groups may also lead to erroneous cross-time inferences as a result of changes in group characteristics. For example, in recent years individuals in union-member households have become less likely to claim Democratic identification. But to conclude from this finding that belonging to this group is less likely to incline a member toward claiming Democratic identification is unwarranted. Such a group membership may give the same or an even greater nudge toward Democratic identification than in previous years, yet changes in other characteristics (for instance, union members may be less likely to identify with the working class) may have overridden the other factor.

Alternatively, misunderstandings about partisan trends might arise because of changes in the partisan disposing tendencies of multiple group memberships. Individuals in a given region of the country, for example, may have retained the same distributions of group memberships over the years, but the partisan tendencies of those other groups may have changed. Thus, the incremental partisan effect of living in that region may have remained the same, but the traditional group approach will falsely suggest a change.

To test competing hypotheses effectively—to determine whether changes should be ascribed to one group or to another and to establish whether shifting demographics or shifting partisan biases of multiple groups have produced observed changes—requires a multivariate approach. Here we will rely on multivariate logit. Like the more familiar ordinary least squares (OLS), logit is a multivariate technique that efficiently measures the impact of several independent variables. Logit is more suitable, however, because the potential dependent variables—claiming Democratic identification or voting Democratic—are dichotomies, not the continua OLS assumes. Moreover, logit better reflects our theoretical expectations. With OLS, a particular group membership would have the same partisan effect on all individuals, whatever the other memberships of an individual. With logit, the partisan impact of a group membership varies across individuals depending upon the other group memberships of those individuals: a group membership has little impact on those who are otherwise almost certainly Democratic or extremely unlikely to be Democrats; it has its greatest effect on those in the middle.

Taking this approach solves most but not all the problems of a group analysis of partisanship. While we do not have to assume a hierarchy of groups, for example, we still must explicitly include each relevant group. An analysis with "New Deal" groups will not by itself indicate the importance of new groups such as evangelicals, conservationists, or any groups that are not explicitly entered into the analysis. More fundamentally, neither a univariate or multivariate statistical analysis will prove causality. Nor, finally, will we be able to take full advantage of the theoretical specificity of effects identified by the logit technique. For some purposes an average effect seems sufficient even though we know that the effect varies across individuals depending upon their other group memberships. Nonetheless, a multivariate analysis of group support will avoid many of the problems of previous approaches and, in the present instance, will give us improved insight into group support for the Democrats over time.

### The Model

We focus on changing partisanship over the period 1952–1984, with special emphasis on the extent to which the New Deal coalition supporting the Democratic Party has deteriorated. We concentrate on party identification as the more durable indicator of partisanship. Thus we estimated a total of nine equations, one for each of the nine presidential elections from 1952 to 1984. Due to the greater independence from the parties since the mid-1960s and the poor showings of most Democratic presidential candidates since 1952, we also examined the same model using "pure" independents and "leaners" and Democratic presidential voting as the dependent variables. Except for Jews, each element of the New Deal coalition ended with appreciably higher likelihoods of claiming independence. The trends for voting Democratic [not shown here] show strong short-term fluctuations but essentially resemble those found for claiming Democratic partisanship. Also, the tendency of Democratic partisans to vote Democratic for President did not change during this period. Typically three-quarters of the Democratic partisans voted Democratic for President, showing greater loyalty in 1964 and less in 1972. No strong group differences prevailed in voter defection rates among partisans, except Blacks proved somewhat more loyal, southern whites less so.

In order to make the over-time comparisons meaningful, the same, exclusively group-based model is applied to each presidential election. (Although individuals identify with a party for many reasons other than their group memberships, the objective here is not to "explain" most of the variance in partisan identification but to trace the trends in group partisan ties since 1952.) The model includes the core elements of the New Deal coalition: white native southerners, Blacks, Jews, the working class, union members, and Catholics. A variable for gender is also included (Table 3).

# Table 3

*Variables in the Model*

**DEPENDENT VARIABLES:**

| | |
|---|---|
| Democratic | 1 if strong or weak Democratic identifier, 0 if apolitical, other, independent, or Republican |

**INDEPENDENT VARIABLES:***

| | |
|---|---|
| Black | 1 if Black, 0 otherwise** |
| Female | 1 if female, 0 otherwise** |
| Union HH | 1 if union member in household, 0 otherwise** |
| Working Class | 1 if self-reported working class, 0 otherwise** |
| Native Southern White | 1 if white native of South (grew up in Alabama, Arkansas, Florida, Georgia, Louisiana, Mississippi, North Carolina, South Carolina, Tennessee, Texas, or Virginia), 0 otherwise** |
| Catholic | 1 if Catholic, 0 otherwise** |
| Jewish | 1 if Jewish, 0 otherwise** |

*Whites migrating into the South, age, income, education, metropolitan residence, rural residence, blue-collar workers, white-collar workers, farmers, Protestant, Irish or Polish descent, and foreign-born parents were incorporated at earlier stages of the analysis but failed to exhibit a consistently significant relationship with Democratic partisanship or voting.

**"Otherwise" incorporates only other valid data codes. Missing data (primarily "not ascertained" cases) were excluded from the analysis.

## The Results

### Overall and Incremental Effects of Group Memberships

Beneath the stable relative strength of the Democratic and Republican identifiers and the shift of the whole population toward independence, Axelrod, Petrocik, and others have detected significant underlying partisan movements by groups. Measuring the percentage deviation of a group's Democratic vote relative to the national Democratic vote share, Axelrod found that three groups had decreasing loyalty to the Democrats: individuals in households with union members, Catholics, and southerners (although Jimmy Carter's candidacies recovered part of the earlier decreases among southerners). The poor, Blacks, and those residing in the central cities of the nation's 12 largest metropolitan areas showed increasing loyalty to the Democrats between 1952 and 1984 (Table 1). Analyzing shifts in party identification, Petrocik reported that only Blacks did not grow more independent, taking on instead a much stronger Democratic identification. Other groups all shared a marked tendency toward independence and a diminished partisan preference. Southern whites showed the sharpest decline in Democratic identification, although the drop was greatest for those with high social status. Jews became more independent and less pro-Democratic as did Catholics, although the Democratic dropoff was not as strong.

Our results confirm the sharpest of these movements—especially of Blacks and southern whites—but they differ in other respects.

First of all, once other variables are taken into account, being poor and residing in met-ropolitan areas did not incline individuals to-ward Democratic identification (i.e., they did not achieve statistical significance) in the 1952–1984 period. The tendency of the poor and of metropolitan residents to support the Democrats can be accounted for by their other characteristics. Two often-used indicators of status—education and income—were not related to Democratic identification, perhaps because subjective identification with the working class better revealed the connections of status to partisanship.

Given the nonlinearity of logit, the original coefficients (not shown) are less easily interpreted than in the case of linear regression. Yet each coefficient can be translated into a probability value indicating the marginal effect of that variable on the likelihood that the individual respondent will claim Democratic identification. As noted earlier, these probability values are dependent on all other characteristics of the individual and will vary from one individual to another as these other characteristics differ. While we make some use of these highly individualized probabilities, our initial presentation involves more aggregated summary values.

Two summary values are of special significance—the overall predicted mean probability of being a Democrat for each group and the incremental probability difference each group membership makes. For the first value, we began by calculating a predicted probability for each individual. This required applying the parameter estimates for each variable to data values for each individual, just as we might calculate a predicted score for each individual in an OLS analysis. The overall predicted probability for a group in a given year is then the average of the predicted probabilities for all group members in that year. Similarly, the incremental difference is the average of the difference for each group member between the individual's predicted probability and what the individual's probability would have been without the effect of the group membership.

Tables 4 and 5 show the overall and incremental impact of membership in each group. Table 4 presents the mean predicted probability that a group member would claim Democratic identification in each of the nine presidential election years. In other words, these probabilities show the frequency of Democratic identification in each group before imposing any controls for other group memberships. As such, they represent a useful baseline for comparisons below. Even these figures, however, show the plight of the Democrats. In 1964 and 1968, the average member of each group was more likely than not to identify with the Democrats. After 1976 this was true only of Blacks and Jews. But one need not contrast recent partisan ties with each group's most Democratic point to show Democratic decline. Comparisons of the chronological endpoints suffice. Table 4 shows that only Blacks significantly increases the probability of Democratic identification; white southerners registered the strongest decline. The

probability for white southerners declined 33 points in 32 years, but most of that decline came in the 20-point drop between 1964 and 1968 and the 10-point drop between 1976 and 1984. The probability of Democratic identification for Catholics, females, individuals in union member households, and self-identified members of the working class, although peaking in 1960 or 1964, later declined to levels below those of the 1950s. Jewish individuals registered lower probabilities in the middle years, rising in 1980 and 1984 to regain levels resembling those for 1952 and 1956, respectively.

But Table 4 presents an overall probability, not controlling for other group memberships. The incremental impact of a particular group membership is isolated in Table 5. Rather than asking whether Catholics, say, have remained loyal to the Democrats at the level that prevailed in the 1950s—or even asking whether they remained loyal compared to overall national (voting) figures, as Axelrod did—we ask whether being Catholic, taking into account the other group memberships of the individual, gives the same incremental push toward Democratic identification as it did previously. Such a marginal effect could remain constant even though the group exhibited a generally declining Democratic commitment.

## Table 4

*Overall Probability of Democratic Identification for Group Members, 1952–1984*

| Year | 1952 | 1956 | 1960 | 1964 | 1968 | 1972 | 1976 | 1980 | 1984 |
|---|---|---|---|---|---|---|---|---|---|
| Black | .53 | .50 | .45 | .79 | .85 | .68 | .70 | .70 | .65 |
| Catholic | .56 | .51 | .65 | .61 | .54 | .50 | .50 | .42 | .42 |
| Jewish | .70 | .60 | .50 | .52 | .54 | .52 | .57 | .69 | .59 |
| Female | .47 | .43 | .49 | .59 | .51 | .43 | .42 | .42 | .40 |
| Native Southern White | .75 | .70 | .72 | .71 | .52 | .50 | .52 | .46 | .42 |
| Union Household | .54 | .50 | .57 | .67 | .53 | .45 | .47 | .44 | .46 |
| Working Class | .54 | .48 | .51 | .64 | .55 | .45 | .46 | .44 | .42 |

Note: Cells are the mean of the predicted probabilities of Democratic identification for all group members in each year.

## Table 5

*Incremental Probability of Democratic Identification for a Particular Group Membership, 1952–1984*

| Year | 1952 | 1956 | 1960 | 1964 | 1968 | 1972 | 1976 | 1980 | 1984 |
|---|---|---|---|---|---|---|---|---|---|
| Black | .17 | .17 | .09 | .34 | .47 | .36 | .40 | .38 | .35 |
| Catholic | .20 | .18 | .29 | .17 | .17 | .19 | .20 | .09 | .12 |
| Jewish | .38 | .32 | .18 | .17 | .23 | .26 | .34 | .41 | .34 |
| Female | .00 | -.03 | .04 | .04 | .04 | .06 | .06 | .08 | .06 |
| Native Southern White | .43 | .41 | .41 | .33 | .17 | .20 | .24 | .17 | .13 |
| Union Household | .10 | .11 | .13 | .14 | .07 | .07 | .10 | .08 | .11 |
| Working Class | .12 | .09 | .09 | .12 | .09 | .07 | .08 | .07 | .06 |

Note: Cells are the average of the difference for each group member between the individual's predicted probability of Democratic identification and what the individual's probability would have been without the effect of the group membership.

The strongest movement over the years are as apparent in Table 5 as in Table 4. The Black increase, the southern white decrease, and the Jewish decline and recovery are all evident in Table 5 and are of about the same magnitude as in the overall results in Table 4. Yet the patterns are not identical to what has been observed using other approaches. Axelrod, for example, found that Blacks in 1952 were far more likely (by 38 percent) than the general population to support Democrats. That Democratic edge declined until 1964, when it rebounded to the same level as in 1952. Our results are not a direct contradiction because they involve slightly different questions (i.e., the marginal impact and partisan identification), but they suggest that being Black did not contribute strongly to being Democratic until 1964. Before that it had less marginal impact than, for example, being Catholic. In 1964 and later, however, the effect of being Black contributed much more significantly to a Democratic identification than it had at any time in the 1950s.

The marginal effect of being a native southern white declined precipitously, as did the overall probability of Democratic identification. That this coincides with Petrocik's results is due in part to the fact that in this instance Petrocik's narrowly defined group helps control for other factors (e.g., race and religion). Likewise, the large difference with Axelrod's results arises because he combined all southerners into one group. The impact of being Jewish declined between the 1950s and 1960s, but unlike Petrocik's trend, our results show a rebound even by 1972 when his series ended. This trend continued through 1980, leaving the marginal impact very nearly what it was at the start.

Though smaller and therefore less noticeable, the same contrast with earlier results is apparent among Catholics. Axelrod and Petrocik found the contribution of Catholics declining by 1972 and 1968, respectively. Our data suggest that except for the special circumstances of 1960, being Catholic stimulated a Democratic identification to about the same degree until 1980.

The sharpest contrast suggested by our approach occurs with members of union households. Here both Axelrod's earlier results and our own data on the overall probabilities suggest a decline in Democratic proclivities of about 5 percent to 8 percent. In contrast, the incremental push that comes from this characteristic appears to have changed very little over the last three decades. This difference may have come about in part because we were able to separate the effect of being working class from that of being in a union household. For self-identified members of the working class, there was a halving of the boost in the probability of Democratic identification between 1952 and 1984. Since many union members consider themselves working class, exclusion of the working class variable might erroneously indicate a decline in the effect of being in a union household.

Observe also the contrasting images created by the overall versus incremental probabilities for women. Females are less likely to identify themselves as Democrats in the 1980s than they were in the 1950s; at the same time, being female has given an increasingly larger boost to Democratic identification. Note, however, that this increment is not simply a Reagan phenomenon. Marginal feminine support for the Democrats goes all the way back to 1960, and it has been slowly but steadily increasing since then. Interestingly, the only reversal in the pattern is in Reagan's 1984 reelection. It remains to be seen whether or not this counterintuitive change continues.

A final way of using our multivariate approach is to ask whether changes in the mix of demographic characteristics have had a significant effect on the probability of claiming Democratic identification. It is possible, for example, that the decline in the number of females identifying with the working class and other such changes can largely account for the observed changes in tendencies toward Democratic partisanship. In 1952, 67 percent of the Catholics and 60 percent of the females claimed working-class status. In 1984 the percentages were 52 and 50, respectively. Another example: in 1952, 78 percent of the individuals in union households identified with the working class. In 1984 only 55 percent did so. Reliance on either overlapping or exclusive groups cannot easily address such possibilities. Here, however, there is a straightforward way to study this question. We can apply the coefficients from a later election year to an earlier distribution of individual group memberships (e.g., from the 1952 election survey) and contrast these hypothetical results with the actual ones for the later year. Such a comparison conveys the degree of partisan change arising from shifts in the coefficients (i.e., the partisan meaning of group memberships). By similarly varying the distribution of group memberships, one can gauge the degree of partisan change arising from shifting mixes of individual group memberships.

The two sets of coefficients for the endpoints 1952 and 1984 capture the partisan meanings of group memberships for those two years. What happens if the patterns of meanings for 1984 are applied to the 1952 data? The overall probability of Democratic identification for the group is not appreciably different whether one applies the 1952 coefficients to 1952 or 1984 data (first column, Table 6). Apparently the changing composition of groups made for very little partisan change. However, major differences in probabilities result from taking the data from 1952 and then applying the 1984 coefficients (second column, Table 6). Ignoring the signs, the mean change in probabilities for varying the data distribution is less than two points, for varying the coefficients 14 points. Such results suggest that the shifts in the meaning of group memberships far outweigh the partisan implications of demographic changes that decreased the multiplicity of Democratic inclined group memberships. Changes in the partisan meaning of group memberships, not declines in reinforcing group memberships, account for the decreasing probabilities of identifying with the Democrats. Although the demographic trends were not favorable to the Democrats, these trends were not so politically troubling as the changed partisan push of group ties.

## Group Support and Democratic Coalition

Our approach to the question of group support also gives us a new way of looking at the party coalitions. In addition to determining the marginal impact of a group characteristic (e.g., controlling for other group memberships, does claiming working-class status tend to make one more Democratic than not claiming such a status?), we can evaluate the contribution of a group characteristic to the party coalition (e.g., what impact does being a native southern white have on the size and shape of the Democratic coalition?). This resembles Axelrod's approach but provides a new perspective because it answers a qualitatively different question.

Axelrod's analysis reveals the extent to which the Democratic coalition is made up of Blacks, metropolitan residents, Catholics, southerners, the poor, and members of union households. If one wishes to know simply a group's share of the Democratic coalition, Axelrod's approach has much to recommend it. But studying groups within party coalitions—just as studying individual voting behavior—does not require us to treat the groups as if they were monolithic. The typical individual has several group ties that affect partisanship, and our multivariate approach explicitly acknowledges this. Since most individuals have multiple group characteristics, removing a single characteristic from the mix need not mean that all members of that group

## Table 6

*Contrasting the Effects of Changes in Group Characteristics and Group Democratic Tendencies, 1952 and 1984*

|  | **Vary Data Distribution** | **Vary Coefficients** |
|---|---|---|
| Hypothetical: | C:52 D:84 | C:84 D:52 |
| Actual: | C:52 D:52 | C:52 D:52 |
| **GROUP** | | |
| Black | -.02 | .12 |
| Catholic | .01 | -.14 |
| Jewish | -.05 | -.08 |
| Female | .00 | -.07 |
| Native Southern White | .02 | -.35 |
| Union Household | -.01 | -.09 |
| Working Class | .00 | -.13 |

Note: Cells represent the hypothetical minus the actual probabilities of Democratic partisanship. For example, -.02 in the center column for Blacks indicates that if Blacks had the pattern of group memberships that prevailed in 1984 among Blacks but the partisan meaning for those memberships that prevailed in 1952, Blacks as a group would have a mean probability for Democratic identification .02 lower than actually prevailed in 1952. More generally, notation such as "C:52 D:84" indicates coefficients from the 1952 model applied to the data distribution of 1984. Contrasting the resulting probabilities with those from "C:52 D:52" suggests the effects of changes in group characteristics, and the "C:84 D:52" with "C:52 D:52" contrast indicates the effects of changes in group Democratic tendencies. Comparable partisan changes are obtained if the actual results are for 1984, and varying the 1952 coefficients and data provide the hypothetical case.

desert the party. While Axelrod's findings reveal the coalition share that each group composes, his figures cannot reveal, for example, how many southern whites would remain Democrats if being a southern white gave no nudge toward Democratic identification. Nor can they show what the size of the Democratic coalition would be if that Democratic propensity was lost. In contrast, our approach yields both of these results.

Such results are hypothetical, of course, but they are what the party strategist would most like to know. If the party stopped appealing to southern whites as such, what would that do to the party coalition? How many southern whites would remain Democratic despite the changing appeals, and how much of a loss would the party sustain?

Answers to these questions, along with comparison figures of the type that Axelrod generated, are given in Table 7. The top of the table shows the proportion of Democratic identifiers in the United States and, below that, the percentage of the Democratic coalition with a given

## Table 7

*Size and Composition of the Democratic Coalition, 1952–1984*

**Proportion of Democratic Identifiers in the U.S.**

|  | 1952 | 1956 | 1960 | 1964 | 1968 | 1972 | 1976 | 1980 | 1984 |
|---|---|---|---|---|---|---|---|---|---|
| Nation | 47.3 | 43.7 | 47.3 | 52.9 | 45.5 | 40.3 | 39.5 | 39.3 | 38.0 |

**Percentage of Democratic Coalition with a Given Group Characteristic***

|  | 1952 | 1956 | 1960 | 1964 | 1968 | 1972 | 1976 | 1980 | 1984 |
|---|---|---|---|---|---|---|---|---|---|
| Black | 10.8 | 9.8 | 7.9 | 13.6 | 16.8 | 16.2 | 18.3 | 19.2 | 19.2 |
| Catholic | 26.1 | 24.8 | 27.3 | 25.2 | 26.3 | 29.7 | 31.5 | 25.0 | 31.0 |
| Female | 53.8 | 53.8 | 54.8 | 56.2 | 58.8 | 59.7 | 61.6 | 60.9 | 61.3 |
| Jewish | 4.8 | 4.3 | 3.4 | 2.8 | 3.3 | 2.9 | 3.5 | 5.8 | 4.1 |
| Native Southern White | 25.6 | 27.4 | 27.3 | 20.3 | 18.7 | 20.7 | 20.1 | 19.4 | 20.8 |
| Union Household | 31.5 | 31.7 | 33.1 | 29.6 | 28.6 | 28.9 | 27.6 | 29.3 | 25.7 |
| Working Class | 70.5 | 69.0 | 72.0 | 65.8 | 62.9 | 61.1 | 61.5 | 58.5 | 57.0 |

**Percentage of Group Claiming Democratic Identification After Democratic Tendency of Defining Group Characteristic Removed****

|  | 1952 | 1956 | 1960 | 1964 | 1968 | 1972 | 1976 | 1980 | 1984 |
|---|---|---|---|---|---|---|---|---|---|
| Black | 68 | 67 | 81 | 56 | 44 | 46 | 43 | 46 | 46 |
| Catholic | 64 | 65 | 55 | 71 | 69 | 63 | 59 | 79 | 73 |
| Female | 100 | 106 | 92 | 94 | 93 | 87 | 85 | 82 | 86 |
| Jewish | 46 | 48 | 63 | 68 | 58 | 50 | 40 | 41 | 42 |
| Native Southern White | 42 | 42 | 43 | 54 | 66 | 60 | 53 | 64 | 69 |
| Union Household | 81 | 79 | 78 | 80 | 87 | 85 | 79 | 82 | 77 |
| Working Class | 77 | 82 | 82 | 82 | 84 | 85 | 83 | 84 | 85 |

**Relative Size (%) of Democratic Coalition if Group Characteristic Removed*****

|  | 1952 | 1956 | 1960 | 1964 | 1968 | 1972 | 1976 | 1980 | 1984 |
|---|---|---|---|---|---|---|---|---|---|
| Black | 96.6 | 96.8 | 98.5 | 94.1 | 90.5 | 91.3 | 89.4 | 89.6 | 89.7 |
| Catholic | 90.7 | 91.3 | 87.9 | 92.6 | 91.4 | 89.1 | 87.1 | 94.7 | 91.6 |
| Female | 100.0 | 103.4 | 95.8 | 96.0 | 95.2 | 92.3 | 90.6 | 88.8 | 91.3 |
| Jewish | 97.5 | 97.7 | 98.7 | 99.0 | 98.7 | 98.5 | 98.0 | 96.4 | 97.6 |
| Native Southern White | 85.2 | 84.0 | 84.6 | 90.7 | 93.6 | 91.8 | 90.6 | 93.1 | 93.4 |
| Union Household | 93.9 | 93.1 | 92.6 | 93.2 | 96.0 | 95.8 | 94.2 | 94.7 | 93.9 |
| Working Class | 83.5 | 87.4 | 86.7 | 87.0 | 88.8 | 91.1 | 89.4 | 90.6 | 91.6 |

*The figures for relative group shares result from taking the mean predicted probability of Democratic identification for a group in a particular year multiplied by that group's number of respondents and dividing this product by the number of Democratic identifiers. (Cross tabulation could produce similar figures but not the subsequent findings about the effects of each group characteristic on the size and shape of the Democratic coalition.)

**Figures derived by recalculating the probabilities of Democratic identification without the effect of, say, working-class identification, then taking the mean of these probabilities for all respondents who claimed working-class status. The ratio of this revised mean probability to the mean probability with the effect of working class included gives the ratio of the hypothetical size to the actual one.

***The above calculations for the whole sample rather than just members of a particular group give indications of the reduced size of the Democratic coalition with particular characteristics removed.

group characteristic. The breakdown of the coalition is in terms of overlapping groups, making these percentages analogous to those presented for the Democratic vote by Axelrod. Not surprisingly (because of their size in the population), working-class identifiers and females consistently make up the largest shares of Democratic identifiers (54 to 72 percent). Blacks and Jews, despite their high Democratic loyalty, constituted the smallest shares of identifiers. Of course, the shares change over the years.

The results in the third panel of the table show what would have happened to each group if the Democratic increment due to the group characteristic were removed. Females, for example, would have been the least affected. Despite the gender gap, Democratic appeals to women as such have been sufficiently few, and women's other characteristics have been sufficiently pro-Democratic, that even in 1984, 86 percent of females would have continued to identify with the party even if there were no special push due to their gender. In contrast, less than half of the Blacks and Jews would have continued to identify with the party if it lost its special appeal to them as Blacks and Jews. As one would expect, the results do not coincide perfectly with the incremental probabilities, but Jews would have defected a bit more frequently. The main point of this comparison, however, is that the varied incremental probabilities translate into an even greater range in rates at which the party would have lost supporters in the various groups if the party had stopped its special appeals.

But what effect would such changes have had on the party coalitions? Surprisingly, the last panel in Table 7 shows that the loss of any of these group increments would never have reduced the coalition by more than 16 percent and that since 1980 the loss would have been between 6 percent and 10 percent for each group (except for Jews because of their small part in the overall population). In recent years the overlap among group memberships and the Democratic tendency of each membership has been such that the loss of appeal to one characteristic would entail no more than a 10 percent loss in identifiers (as significant as that would be), and the loss would be similar regardless of what the characteristic was. Of course, the overall size of the Democratic coalition has declined over these years, so the losses in the later years are taken from a reduced base.

As the top of Table 7 shows, the Democratic Party has consisted increasingly of Blacks and females and decreasingly of southern whites and the working class. These data also show clearly the widely varying proportions of each (overlapping) group within the Democratic coalition. But one can hardly conclude—either from the varying group sizes or from the changes over time—that the Democrats could ignore Catholics at much less peril than the working class, the south with much less risk than women, and so on. Despite the widely differing group sizes and incremental contributions of group characteristics, in terms of identifiers, the absence of each group characteristic from the coalition in recent years makes for losses of a rather similar magnitude. The Democratic Party is not as particularly dependent upon a couple of groups as it was in the 1950s, but almost equally dependent upon six.

*Conclusion*

Studies of the group basis of partisan coalitions defined groups in overlapping or exclusive terms, concealing rather than revealing the net partisan impacts of an individual's multiple group memberships. This review employed multivariate logit to assess partisan change, measuring the incremental impact of individual membership in selected groups on Democratic partisanship.

In large measure, the findings reported here strengthen current knowledge about shifting group loyalties. Being Jewish or being in a union household pushes an individual in the direction of being a Democrat as much as it did in the 1950s. Being Black or being female gives a greater push now than either did three decades ago. Catholics, native white southerners, and working-class members receive a lessened stimulus toward Democratic identification from such group memberships. In addition, our findings refine our understanding of the nature and timing of such changes as the increasing Democratic support among Blacks and women.

The possibility that demographic change reduced reinforcement of partisan tendencies from multiple, overlapping group memberships proved a far more potent link to the decline. We also noted that the contribution of the varying groups to the Democratic coalition was now so highly similar that a loss of appeal to any one group would be a strong blow to an already weakened party.

One type of partisan change was not found here. No group reversed its partisan meaning. Yet the strong changes by Blacks and native southern whites deserve special emphasis, because these two groups make up a sizable share of the voting-age population (almost 30 percent in 1984). The timing of the changes by these two groups (rapid shifts in the 1964–1968 period) suggest a racially inspired change in the group basis of the Democratic Party consistent with Carmines and Stimson's thesis of a racial realignment of the parties at that time. Of course, the fact that southern whites (and to a lesser degree Catholics, individuals in union households, and members of the working class) moved toward independence rather than the Republican Party means that one could call it a racially motivated dealignment. However, Beck's analysis of the partisan shifts among southern whites prior to the mid-1970s calls into question the links between such changes and racial motivations. But the point is that a large-scale change in the group foundation of the Democratic Party occurred during that decade.

But group affiliations are not the only ones that matters and these other things have not remained constant over the years. The incremental meanings of group membership for partisanship must be appreciated in the context of the declining tendency to identify with the Democrats and the recently dismal record of Democratic presidential campaigns. Partly because of these problems at the presidential level, some Democrats in the wake of the 1984 elections questioned the wisdom of a group-oriented political campaign such as Walter Mondale's, whether or not it was aimed at the traditional Democratic groups. In the light of the findings reported here, journalistic and party obituaries for the New Deal coalition appear harsher than the reality warrants. Native southern whites had a strong, prolonged decline in their incremental partisan impact, but the milder declines for most groups, coupled with the increases of females, Jews, and Blacks, suggest that the New Deal group basis of Democratic identification may not be dazzling but is far from dead.

One reason for the resilience of the New Deal coalition may turn on the observation that the arrival of a new partisan order does not require the obliteration of the old ties. Sundquist notes that even in a new realignment, the old realignment patterns endure—reduced, no doubt, but still detectable, the realignment process resembling a "collage of successive overlays." The New Deal group cleavage may be of this sort; it has not disappeared, but it may have been superseded by other cleavages. Traditional group partisan differences still endure, but new ones are now as prominent or more so. Groups such as feminists, evangelicals, environmentalists, residents of the Sunbelt and Frostbelt, young professionals, Hispanics, and workers in high-tech or smokestack industries suggest clusters of voters whose loyalties now might be eagerly sought. As for the New Deal coalition itself, it is clearly smaller than in the past. If the New Deal coalition is not alive and well, then at least its corpse has yet to disappear.

*See also:* Drop-off, Election of 1984, Gender Gap, V. O. Key, Jr., New Deal Coalition, Party Identification

*Harold W. Stanley*
*William T. Bianco*
*Richard G. Niemi*

REFERENCES

Axelrod, Robert. 1972. "Where the Votes Come From: An Analysis of Electoral Coalitions." 66 *American Political Science Review* 11.

———. 1986. "Presidential Election Coalitions in 1984." 80 *American Political Science Review* 281.

Beck, Paul Allen. 1977. "Partisan Dealignment in the Postwar South." 71 *American Political Science Review* 477.

Carmines, Edward G., and James A. Stimson. 1984. "The Dynamics of Issue Evolution." *Electoral Change in Industrial Democracies*. Princeton: Princeton U. Pr.

Key, V. O. 1955. "A Theory of Critical Elections." 17 *Journal of Politics* 3.

———. 1959. "Secular Realignment and the Party System." 21 *Journal of Politics* 198.

Petrocik, John R. 1981. *Party Coalitions: Realignment and the Decline of the New Deal Party System*. Chicago: U. of Chicago Pr.

Sundquist, James L. 1983. *Dynamics of the Party System: Alignment and Realignment of Political Parties in the United States*. Rev. ed. Washington: Brookings.

## Partisan Context of Congressional Recruitment

When Chicago's Mayor Richard Daley used to handpick his city's congressional delegation, he exercised a power that few party leaders have ever claimed. Typically, local party organizations rank elections to the U.S. House of Representatives relatively low on their list of priorities; congressional candidates are expected to run their own campaigns. This laissez faire attitude means that parties rarely control the nominations or outcomes of House races. Yet parties participate in candidate recruitment, even though they seldom send members to Congress who declare, as Daley's emissary did, that "I will go to Washington to help represent Mayor Daley." Local organizations, by shaping the political context in which an individual seeks a seat in Congress, exert a subtle yet significant influence over a prospective candidate's decision to run for the House of Representatives.

## The Rise of the Congressional Entrepreneur

Since the turn of the century, party organizations have steadily lost interest and authority in nominating congressional candidates. The patronage-poor post of U.S. Representative contributed less to party maintenance goals than did state and local offices, and the advent of the direct primary enabled individual lawmakers to challenge party nominating decisions. For these reasons, most party leaders did not consider it worthwhile to invest resources in dictating a party choice for the House. The placement of congressional candidates near the bottom of the ballot in many states perfectly symbolized the attitude of local parties toward the office of U.S. Representative.

At the same time, the decision of the House of Representatives in 1911 to fix its membership at 435 meant that congressional districts would steadily increase in population and encompass more and more county jurisdictions over time. As the number of party organizations in each constituency multiplied, so did the opportunities for playing off one against the other. Lawmakers became accountable to many party leaders and, hence, answerable to very few.

By the 1960s, the separation of House members from their local party organizations was firmly established. As one scholar observed, "Many Congressmen minimize their party affiliation in their bids for reelection. . . . They prefer to rely on personal supporters and staff after they have transformed the existing district organization into a personal campaign group." Although cities such as Chicago remained a notable exception to this general pattern, numerous studies of the period confirmed this view of House members as independent entrepreneurs. Indeed, the majority of congressional candidates described themselves as "self-starters" in their bid for office. Party intervention in the process of selecting candidates was most visible in unwinnable races when local organizations found it necessary to induce reluctant contestants to put their names on the ballot.

If lawmakers operated beyond the reach of party leaders, then in an era when partisan identification accounted for 90 percent of the vote in House elections, the gulf between them would inevitably widen further in the dealignment era of the 1980s. The rise of political action committees (PACs) also fueled independence as candidates raised a growing proportion of their campaign revenues from outside the district (about 36 percent from PACs on average by 1986). Voters, too, encouraged separation from the party by showing a growing proclivity for selecting candidates on the basis of personal performance rather than party label. Finally, three decades of reapportionment insured further divergence between district boundaries and county lines. In many urbanized states gerrymanderers cut across communities willy-nilly in their effort to protect sitting incumbents. In rural areas, on the other hand, the number of counties per district steadily increased. The cumulative effect of these changes was to reinforce the tendency among congressional candidates to view their decision to run as divorced from local party constraints. Case studies of candidate decision-making in the 1970s highlighted this pattern. Moreover, a survey of primary candidates in the 1978 election revealed that fewer than 20 percent of the respondents had the formal or informal backing of the party organization in their bid for a House seat. Only slightly more than a third of these politicians had even discussed their chances with local leaders before running. One scholar summarized the electoral efforts of House members and local parties as "separate organizations pursuing separate tasks."

Many observers of the contemporary Congress have seen the lack of party control over the selection of candidates as the primary source of weak party discipline on Capitol Hill. As one political analyst has noted, "In general, where strong local party organizations have controlled the nomination process, Congressmen have had a strong 'practical' streak, and have been followers rather than innovators in policy matters." Because members today seek election and reelection through their own efforts, the argument goes that they have few incentives to support their party or their President once they get to Washington. Some scholars carry this line of reasoning further by claiming that local partisan control over congressional nominations in the nineteenth century accounted for the high rates of party-line voting in the House so characteristic of the period.

Do congressional candidates truly operate outside the confines of local party organizations? Does party discipline begin—and end—at home? For several reasons dismissing the role of local parties in the recruitment of prospective House members seems premature. First, the criteria for assessing party influence over congressional nominations are overrestrictive, thus assuring that few local organizations will meet conventional standards of control. A looser definition of party participation in candidate recruitment yields a decidedly different picture. Second, the evidence supporting the view that congressional candidates are divorced from political parties is often sketchy and in some instances one-sided. A look at candidate decision-making within the broader context of American politics demonstrates how parties and party activists continue to play a part in the decisions of prospective House members.

### Defining Party Influence in Congressional Recruitment

Selecting candidates is the quintessential function of party organizations. As one of the classic works on political parties put it, "Whatever else they may or may not do, parties must make nominations." In the strictest sense, parties still do exercise this basic responsibility for House candidates; only a handful in any given election seek office without benefit of either the Republican or Democratic label. Fully 90 percent of all House candidates are nominated through party primaries, either contested or otherwise.

How much genuine influence is attached to these formalities is a subject for interpretation, however. Those who dismiss the role of parties in congressional recruitment emphasize two features of local organizations: first, that parties cannot assure their nominees a place on the ballot; and second, that they fail to groom candidates for the House of Representatives. On the other hand, some students of party politics stress the enormous variation in state and local parties, a situation that leaves a good deal of room for party influence over recruitment. Some even argue that the resurgence of national parties has been matched by a rejuvenation of lower-level organization. Therefore, a good deal of ambiguity surrounds the relationship between parties and congressional candidates.

These conflicting evaluations spring from different notions of what is implied by party influence over candidate recruitment. Traditionally, scholars who have written about party

organizations evaluate them according to bureaucratic standards. These include hierarchy, functional division of labor, and routinized procedures. American parties have never fared very well when judged by these standards, and when the standards are applied to candidate recruitment, party leaders clearly lack the authority to impose their choice, the resources to develop new talent, or the mechanisms for developing an orderly pattern of succession. As political scientist V. O. Key observed, "To assert that the party leadership of many states develops candidates is more an attribution of a duty stated in the textbooks than a description of real activity." The muddled jurisdictions of congressional districts merely compound an already disorganized situation, making inevitable the failure of local organizations to come close to the bureaucratic ideal.

Some students of political parties, however, have challenged the validity of the hierarchical model of party organization. They have also contended that scholarly preoccupation with the centralized decision-making of urban political machines has obscured a range of strategies that have enabled party organizations to adapt to their political environment. Although very little of this analysis addresses the recruitment of congressional candidates directly, it suggests certain connections between local party organizations and prospective House members that are worth exploring.

Putting aside the criteria of centralized control epitomized by the Daley organization in Chicago, what else might local parties do to shape the outcome of congressional nominations? Probably the most important party function is the coordination and dissemination of information about prospective candidates.

Given the pluralistic setting of American elections, aspiring candidates and their putative supporters have a pressing need for intelligence about rival factions. Especially in the inefficient media markets so typical of House districts, finding out which other candidates are considering the race and where they will find backers is difficult. These two pressing questions are ones that party leaders are well positioned to answer.

The great majority of local parties are now institutionalized to the point of having permanent headquarters and staff and relatively stable leadership. As such, they represent a solid feature in an otherwise fluid organizational system. Almost through default, party leaders become conduits for political discourse among activists by virtue of their very position.

In particular, local leaders are an important contact point for the national party organizations, including both the congressional campaign committees and the headquarters operations. The Republican Congressional Campaign Committee (RCCC) in Washington has become especially active in recruiting congressional candidates (as many as 100 men and women in the 1980 election). During their search for congressional competitors, the GOP scouts typically started with local leaders. In the 1980s, the Democratic Congressional Campaign Committee (DCCC) was also beginning to support candidates in targeted constituencies, albeit on a lesser scale. Although the DCCC had access to district information through its close ties to union locals, it relied on county chairpersons for political intelligence as well. By identifying promising challengers and evaluating the various contestants in open-seat races, party leaders thus influenced the flow of national party resources into House districts.

Party leaders are also the mainstays of the local media in their coverage of congressional candidates. Reporters require authoritative sources and therefore in their search for reliable facts and quotations gravitate toward those who hold formal positions on the local political scene. Comments from party officials are a regular part of the prenomination phase of a House campaign, and these statements can be critical in making a fledgling candidacy seem legitimate.

Finally, party leaders from one county are in a position to exchange information with their counterparts in other counties. Through participation in their state organizations, these men and women are among the few links binding otherwise autonomous local parties together. Such connections become especially important to aspiring House members in multicounty districts.

Two surveys of state party leaders in the early 1980s confirmed the prevalence of these informational and coordinative activities. One survey, carried out by the Advisory Commission on Intergovernmental Relations, reported that 85 percent of the Republican state party chairpersons and 53 percent of the Democratic state chairs have been involved with coordinating the recruitment of congressional candidates. The other survey, conducted by a group of scholars at the University of Wisconsin, Milwaukee, revealed that roughly two-thirds of the state party

officials surveyed claimed to have recruited candidates for the U.S. House. An additional study of county chairpersons undertaken by these same scholars produced similar findings: nearly two-thirds indicated that they were "very" or "somewhat" involved in recruiting congressional candidates.

These figures on leadership activity contrast vividly with the amount of contact that with party officials congressional candidates themselves report. As noted above, most House candidates describe themselves as self-starters. Relatively few primary contestants consulted party officials before making their decision to run, and only a small percentage reported that they received party support in their bid for a House seat. Despite an apparent inconsistency, such disparate views of the party's role in candidate recruitment are reconcilable.

First, the informational functions of party leaders described previously need not involve prospective candidates directly. Communication among various echelons of the party or with the press requires no action by the candidates themselves and may not even be visible to those who are thinking about running. Second, party leaders often use their informational resources to weed out wavering or weak candidates. Those who are warned off or discouraged by unsympathetic officials, of course, do not figure in most analyses of candidate decision-making. But the omission of these individuals from an assessment of party leadership activity leads inevitably to a biased view of the leaders' involvement. Third, most research on candidate recruitment takes place after a candidate has already decided to run and the campaign is well under way. Under these circumstances, faulty recall is certainly a possibility. But more likely is the disappointment most congressional candidates experience when their exaggerated expectations for organizational assistance are not met, which leads them to discount other aspects of the party as well.

In sum, if centralized control is the standard used to measure party influence in the recruitment of congressional candidates, then local organizations must be found lacking. If declared candidates and incumbent members of Congress serve as the sole source of information about what motivates individuals to run, then party leaders will surely be assigned a minor role. In fact, a recognition of the informational advantage of party leaders and their ability to shape the winnowing process among prospective candidates from behind the scenes will lead to a somewhat different conclusion. Party leaders may not dictate who runs for Congress, but they are not as impotent as many believe.

*Reexamining the Institutional Setting*

Individual motivation is the decisive factor in a person's decision to contest a House seat. Whatever the level of party engagement in recruitment, most congressional candidates enter a race in pursuit of their own personal ambitions rather than organizational goals. In seizing the initiative for higher office, House candidates evaluate the relative merits of a race (e.g., the costs and benefits of running, the probability of winning). How these calculations turn out, however, depends upon the favorability of the local context. The rules and norms of local party organizations can make a race look more or less promising, and hence they may well play a role in the candidate's decision to run.

Just how local parties enter into the deliberations of individual candidates is unclear. Relatively little is known about the differences among various party organizations, and even less is understood about the various ingredients that prospective House members consider in making up their minds whether or not to run. Still, one can piece together several features of the district context, features that define the level of party influence in recruitment. These include the level of primary competition, the structure of offices that prepare individuals for a House career, and the candidates' access to local contributors and volunteers.

In congressional elections, individual candidates bear most of the organizational costs, which are rapidly rising. Theirs is the responsibility to put together a personal campaign operation and raise the necessary funds to support it. Assistance may come from parties, PACs, or individuals, but the candidate has to mobilize these supporters and coordinate their electoral efforts. Increasingly, organizing is a full-time job requiring many months of intense activity, especially if the race is potentially competitive. The campaign is also an expensive endeavor: in 1986 the average candidate spent $210,000 to campaign and laid out more than twice that amount for an open seat.

Given the effort and expense attached to a successful bid for Congress, serious candidates cannot afford to make uninformed decisions. No matter what their personal desire for a career in the House, they must ground their ambitions in the realities of the local political scene. Party organizations are part of that environment.

One of the first concerns of would-be House candidates is their likelihood of winning the party primary. Conventional wisdom holds that primaries create political opportunities for a few prospective candidates who are able to run without the blessing of party leaders. But the evidence suggests that primaries vary significantly across states in their effect on congressional ambitions. Under some circumstances primaries seem to inhibit rather than encourage individuals from becoming candidates.

Statistical analysis of the number of candidates running in state legislative and congressional primaries, for example, reveals a strong relationship between the type of party organization within the state and the number of primary contestants: the more structured the party, the fewer the number of candidates. In addition, a recent study of legislative races in four states revealed that when primaries are closed—that is, when only registered partisans may vote— candidates are far more likely to consult with party leaders before running, to seek the party endorsement, and to avoid contested primaries. Not surprisingly, the winners in closed congressional primaries score higher in party support when they serve in Congress than do those Representatives who come from open primary states. Finally, a study of eight congressional districts in Minnesota indicated that relatively few of the candidates endorsed by the party organization were contested at the nominating convention, that the convention losers seldom challenged the endorsee, and that all eight endorsed candidates in 1986 won their primary bids.

This evidence is far from conclusive, but it does suggest that the participation and success of contestants in congressional primaries are connected in varying degrees to local party organizations. The same can be said of the public offices that candidates use in launching their congressional careers.

Although parties typically do not groom candidates for Congress, they take a much more active interest in recruiting men and women to fill state and local offices. As one scholar has noted, "Most state legislatures remain highly partisan . . . because party organizations have more control over who holds the position." Since most serious congressional candidates have had previous experience holding public office, their careers leading up to the House will likely bear the stamp of local party organizations. Indeed, fully half of the Representatives in Washington today have served in their state legislatures. Perhaps their decision to move up the ladder to Congress was a personal one, but their advantageous position cannot be separated from their earlier dealings with party leaders.

In deciding to run for the House of Representatives, prospective candidates have to consider where they will get money and volunteers to support their campaign. At first glance, the party seems an unlikely place to turn: party contributions and expenditures on behalf of the nominees represented just 4 percent of all funds contributed to House candidates in 1986. Individuals remain the greatest financial resource available to congressional contestants, providing roughly 60 percent of all monies raised.

Local party organizations, however, turn out to be the most effective channel for potential contributors. Individuals who contribute to campaigns tend to be registered partisans who strongly identify with their party. Moreover, the lone study conducted of donors to congressional campaigns revealed a high incidence of party-related activity among contributors, both as leaders and volunteers in local organizations. Considering how much money must be raised in a very short time, it is no surprise that candidates turn to the network of party activists for help in constructing their primary constituency.

In managing their grass-roots efforts, candidates also rely on local parties. Congressional candidates who responded to a survey conducted in 1984 gave local organizations relatively high marks for recruiting campaign volunteers; the candidates rated them even more favorably for their local efforts to get out the vote. Some evidence also suggests that the party activists of today are of greater use in a campaign than in the past because they are motivated by issue concerns and solidarity incentives rather than by economic self-interest. Thus, the highly personal, even episodic, organizations that spring up around congressional candidates have their roots in the local parties.

One scholar has called these loosely constructed groups "cadre parties," noting that such parties foster "opportunities for candidates to mobilize support within an organizational framework." He concluded that "primary nominations are not always as purely candidate-centered as they appear."

In general, candidates pursue their personal ambitions for a congressional career within a political context shaped to a significant degree by state and local party organizations. The likelihood of contesting a primary depends on such institutional rules as the closed primary and internal procedures regulating endorsements. The officeholding experience that makes a congressional bid feasible is often indicative of prior alliances with the party leadership. And the personal coalition that candidates tap for contributors and volunteers draws from a larger network of partisan activists.

*Future Prospects for Party Influence*

Predicting how the linkage between congressional candidates and party organizations will develop is difficult. The subtle connections and informal interactions described above could evolve into a more structured relationship.

Several commentators believe that renewed activity by the two national party organizations has already drawn local parties more directly into the recruitment of House candidates. By pouring resources into selected congressional races, the Republican and Democratic campaign committees have created incentives for local parties to pay more attention to their congressional contestants. Moreover, the national organizations have fostered connections between House nominees and other candidates through such tactical moves as establishing local telephone banks, stressing party themes in campaign advertising, and introducing professional managers and consultants into district contests. Finally, the special efforts of the GOP efforts to recruit state legislators may eventually produce a crop of potential congressional candidates with stronger ties to the party. In a recent book, Xandra Kayden and Eddie Mahe, Jr., concluded that such trends would produce a new kind of congressional candidate: "The independence exhibited by the old candidates is less likely to characterize the new . . . and as the party does more to recruit and train candidates, it will end up with a more homogeneous group who will be more inclined to be team players."

For all that, party leaders will probably be more interested in recruiting congressional candidates because the position of Representative has become more relevant to their own organization than in the past. As incumbent House members have expanded casework efforts and pursued federal grants for their constituents, they have become more vital to the organizational health of the local party. Few party leaders can afford to ignore the federal dollars and services that legislators channel into the community; therefore, they may try to forge stronger ties with the source of this largesse.

Whatever new patterns emerge, however, the relationship between congressional candidates and local leaders can never be one that the party controls. The responsibilities of federal lawmakers take them far beyond the reach of local organizations for long periods of time, and the formidable resources of incumbency insure them continued independence. But even for today's independent entrepreneurial legislators, local parties continue to make their presence felt.

*See also:* Closed Primary, Richard Daley, Party Identification, Political Action Committees

*Linda L. Fowler*

REFERENCES

Cotter, Cornelius P., et al. 1984. *Party Organizations in American Politics.* New York: Praeger.

Crotty, William. 1984. *American Parties in Decline.* 2nd ed. Boston: Little, Brown.

Epstein, Leon D. 1986. *Political Parties in the American Mold.* Madison: U. of Wisconsin.

Fishel, Jeff. 1973. *Party and Opposition.* New York: David McKay.

Fowler, Lina L., and Robert D. McClure. 1989. *Political Ambition: Who Decides to Run for Congress.* New Haven: Yale U. Pr.

Gibson, James L., et al. 1983. "Assessing Party Organizational Strength." 27 *American Journal of Political Science* 193.

———. 1985. "Whither the Local Parties?: A Cross-Sectional and Longitudinal Analysis of the Strength of Party Organizations." 29 *American Journal of Political Science* 139.

Haeberle, Steven H. 1985. "Closed Primaries and Party Support in Congress." 13 *American Politics Quarterly* 341.

Herrnson, Paul S. 1986. "Do Parties Make a Difference? The Role of Party Organizations in Congressional Elections." 48 *Journal of Politics* 589.

Huckshorn, Robert J., and Robert C. Spencer. 1971. *The Politics of Defeat: Campaigning for Congress.* Amherst: U. of Massachusetts Pr.

Jacobson, Gary C. 1987. *The Politics of Congressional Elections.* 2nd ed. Boston: Little, Brown.

Kayden, Xandra, and Eddie Mahe, Jr. 1985. *The Party Goes On: The Persistence of the Two-Party System in the United States.* New York: Basic Books.

Kazee, Thomas. 1980. "The Decision to Run for the U.S. Congress: Challenger Attitudes in the 1970s." 5 *Legislative Studies Quarterly* 489.

Key, V. O. 1956. *American State Political Parties.* New York: Knopf.

Kunkel, Joseph A., III. 1988. "Party Endorsement and Incumbency in Minnesota Legislative Nominations." 13 *Legislative Studies Quarterly* 211.

Leuthold, David. 1968. *Electioneering in a Democracy: Campaigning for Congress.* New York: Random House.

Maisel, Louis Sandy. 1982. *From Obscurity to Oblivion: Running in the Congressional Primary.* Knoxville: U. of Tennessee Pr.

Mayhew, David R. 1986. *Placing Parties in American Politics: Organization, Electoral Settings and Government Activity in the Twentieth Century.* Princeton: Princeton U. Pr.

Niemi, Richard G., Stephen Wright, and Lynda W. Powell. 1987. "Multiple Party Identifiers and the Measurement of Party Identification." 49 *Journal of Politics* 1093.

Polsby, Nelson W. 1981. "Coalition and Faction in American Politics: An Institutional View." In Seymour Martin Lipset, ed. *Party Coalitions in the 1980s.* San Francisco: Institute for Contemporary Studies.

Sabato, Larry J. 1988. *The Party's Just Begun: Shaping Political Parties for America's Future.* Boston: Little, Brown.

Seligman, Lester. 1961. "Political Recruitment and Party Structure: A Case Study." 55 *American Political Science Review* 77.

U.S. Advisory Commission on Intergovernmental Relations. 1986. *Transformation in American Politics.* Washington: ACIR.

## Partisan Dealignment

According to recent research on partisan realignment, each of the American political party systems has consisted of four phases: the realignment, a "stable" phase, a midsequence adjustment, and a "decay" phase. The concept of partisan dealignment is most closely linked with the last phase of a party system and is characterized by the gradual deterioration of the set of partisan coalitions that were initially created by the realignment. Although the study of partisan *realignments* remains more fully developed and extensive, some scholars have begun to explore the evolution of party systems, as opposed to merely their birth, and as a result have begun to recognize partisan *dealignment* as an important phenomenon in American political history.

With the passage of time, the onset of dealignment is stimulated by the declining importance of the issues and symbols that had earlier generated the preceding partisan realignment. Like realignment, dealignment is felt in both the electorate and, through elections, in government.

In the electorate, the issues and symbols of the last realignment increasingly fail to activate existing partisan loyalties. At the same time, more immediate issues appear and disrupt and crosscut them. Not only do the realignment's issues and symbols become less and less relevant to those voters who experienced them, they also become irrelevant to a larger and larger proportion of the electorate, which is increasingly filled with new voters who either did not experience the realignment or whose experience was indirect. Thus a generational effect combines with the weakening of established ties to effect the deterioration of the existing alignment. As a whole, the electorate is increasingly disengaged from the realignment and the crisis that precipitated it. It accordingly is particularly susceptible to third-party appeals, easily swayed by issues of the moment, and likely to generate inconsistent and unstable political support.

In the government, similar effects take place. Just as the last realignment grows more politically distant to the electorate, so does it to officeholders and office seekers. While the realignment issues and symbols cannot be wholly abandoned by political elites, they increasingly fail to provide a basis on which the parties can take clear and opposing positions to one another in electoral politics and in the government. Elite coalitions, like those in the electorate, are likely to splinter and fragment as leaders grapple with new issues that cross the party boundaries established by the previous realignment. The parties in government are likely to suffer internal divisions and thus to lose their ability to define coherent policy.

Owing to the deterioration of the established alignment at both the mass and the elite level, periods of partisan dealignment are likely to be characterized by divided partisan control of government and incremental, rather than comprehensive, policy change. Not surprisingly, the parties themselves become less meaningful symbols for both voters and political leaders. Most scholars agree, however, that dealignment does not lead directly or necessarily to realignment, which is still viewed as the consequence of severe domestic crisis.

Somewhat in contrast to the historical character of the realignment literature, much of the empirical analysis relevant to dealignment has focused on post-New Deal politics and, specifically, the erosion of the New Deal party system. "Party decline" over the last several decades has been examined in the electorate, in electoral campaigns, and in the Congress. For the contemporary period, party decline has been associated with a variety of factors such as decreasing levels of turnout and partisan identification, an increasing incidence of single-issue politics and third-party activity, the fragmentation of party blocs in Congress, and divided partisan control of government—exactly the factors that would characterize a party system undergoing dealignment.

While the manifestations of party decline in the post-New Deal era are consistent with the precepts of dealignment, they are also plausibly attributable to changes in electoral rules and institutional reform. It is therefore unclear whether the widely acknowledged disarray of the present party system is part of a historical process that has repeated itself several times or whether it is instead peculiar to the rules and structures that characterize the second half of the twentieth century.

Traditionally, scholars have characterized electoral behavior as the primary causal role behind dealignment. Despite this theoretical emphasis, other research suggests that institutional factors and, implicitly, governmental performance are the superior indicators of dealignment. A comparison of party systems has shown that no one set of electoral patterns alone distinguishes a period of dealignment from other phases of a party system—one exception being the consistent appearance of third parties. Rather, dealignment is apparently set in motion by the interaction between the deterioration of partisan alignments in the electorate and the effects of that deterioration in government—primarily the impetus that divided and unstable control of government gives to policy deadlock in the American federal system. At the institutional level, however, dealignment apparently takes different forms in different party systems. While dealignment in the present party system and its 1896 predecessor was characterized by declining levels of interparty conflict in the Congress, the present system is distinguished by a steady rather than erratic decrease in conflict and a steady increase in widespread consensus.

*See also:* New Deal, Partisan Identification, Third Parties in American Elections

*Melissa P. Collie*

REFERENCES

Beck, Paul Allen. 1974. "A Socialization Theory of Partisan Realignments." In *The Politics of Future Citizens*. San Francisco: Jossey-Bass.

Burnham, Walter Dean. 1973. *Critical Elections and the Mainsprings of American Politics*. New York: Norton.

———, and William Nisbet Chambers. 1975. "Party Systems and the Political Process." In Walter Dean Burnham and William Nisbet Chambers, eds. *The American Party Systems: Stages of Political Development*. New York: Oxford U. Pr.

Clubb, Jerome M., William M. Flanigan, and Nancy H. Zingale. 1980. *Partisan Realignment*. Beverly Hills, CA: Sage.

Collie, Melissa P. 1989. "Electoral Patterns and Voting Alignments in the U.S. House, 1886–1986." 14 *Legislative Studies Quarterly* 107.

Crotty, William. 1984. *American Parties in Decline*. 2nd ed. Boston: Little, Brown.

Sinclair, Barbara. 1982. *Congressional Realignment 1925–1978*. Austin: U. of Texas Pr.

Sundquist, James L. 1973. *Dynamics of the Party System*. Washington: Brookings.

## Partisan Voting in the Contemporary Congress

Congress is, above all, a partisan institution. In both the House of Representatives and the Senate political party organization and leadership—and partisan cleavage in policymaking—provide the dominant, longstanding, and prevailing features of the institution. Our national political parties first took shape as congressional caucuses. These congressional parties reflected sectional rivalries and emergent policy differences between adherents of Alexander Hamilton's program for national development and his opponents. That our national parties emerged first in the congressional vortex underscores the importance of the parties in Congress.

In the American constitutional system, congressional parties perform two vital functions. First, they enable governing coalitions to develop. In a decentralized political system such as ours, parties serve as essential mediating and integrating mechanisms. In a heterogeneous polity, partisan integration is always partial and constrained. The formation of coalitions is not an automatic process; party coalitions must be actively built by party leaders. Moreover, coalitions may be shifting, with varying quantities of overlap of the parties at the margins of issue or ideological support. Nevertheless, national political leadership could not be effective without party organization and behavior sufficient to permit the development of stable, collective decisions.

Second, congressional parties are significant channels of responsiveness and accountability. Broadly speaking, the parties in Congress partake in the transformation of voters' choices into responsible policy decisions. The American system of political accountability has many shortcomings to be sure, but congressional parties can be, and normally are, highly responsive to their national constituencies. The parties in Congress have become an important link between constituencies and governing decisions.

### The Congressional Parties

The congressional parties clearly illustrate the dominance of two political parties in American politics. Only the Republicans and the Democrats succeed in electing members. Once elected, Republicans and Democrats in Congress become part of a congressional party organization. The congressional parties are made up of caucuses, committees, and leaders. The majority party controls the key leadership positions—Speaker of the House, Majority Leader of the Senate, and all committee and subcommittee chairmanships.

In both houses, the parties choose a floor leader. For the House majority party, the floor leader works with the Speaker, who is the majority party leader. For the House minority party and the two parties in the Senate, the floor leader is the principal party leader. In the Senate, the Majority Leader manages and directs the work of the chamber. In both houses the two congressional parties maintain whip organizations made up of chief whips, deputy whips, and zone or regional whips. The whip organization is responsible for getting the party's members to the floor for key votes and for encouraging members to support their party's position on bills. All of the members of the Democratic and Republican parties in each house make up the party caucuses (called "conferences" by the Republicans), and each caucus has a chairman who is, accordingly, a member of his or her party's leadership group.

The congressional parties are organized into three types of party committees: policy committees, committees to choose members of standing committees of each house, and campaign committees. The policy committees gauge the stands of party members on major issues and then serve as forums for the discussion of policies before the House or Senate considers them. The House Democratic Steering and Policy Committee, chaired by the Speaker, also serves as the Democratic Party's committee on committees. In the Senate, the Democratic committee on committees is called the Steering Committee. Both House and Senate Republican committee assignments are made by distinct committees on committees. All four congressional parties maintain campaign committees whose purpose it is to assist in the reelection of incumbent members of the party.

The congressional parties are not monolithic, hierarchical organizations demanding the absolute or undying loyalty of their members. Some accounts of congressional political implicitly contrast the way the congressional parties work to a mythical parliament with extremely disciplined parties under absolute rule. This contrast makes the American congressional parties seem very weak. On the one hand, in no country with democratic parliamentary politics is party discipline absolute; on the other hand, congressional parties have a pervasive, even a major role in legislative decision-making. The degree of discipline of legislative or parliamentary parties in democratic countries is relative. In Congress, the parties are less highly disciplined than in many other national parliaments, reflecting the character of American politics; but the difference in degree is not so great as is often implied. The congressional parties matter.

*Party Voting in Congress*

The strength of political parties in a legislature or parliament may be gauged by the extent of interparty cleavage and the propensity of party members to vote together on major policy issues. The concept of party voting has come to have a particular empirical definition in analyses of congressional politics. Conventionally, a party vote is defined as a roll-call vote on which at least a majority of Republicans vote together in opposition to at least a majority of Democrats. We might say that this criterion for a party vote is moderately strong. In 1987, of the 488 roll-call votes taken in the House of Representatives, 64 percent were party votes in which the party majorities were divided; in the Senate, 41 percent of the 420 roll calls in 1987 were party votes.

Although the conventional definition of a party vote has been in terms of opposing party majorities, stronger criteria have been applied to congressional voting. If, in order to qualify as a party vote, 75 percent of the Democrats had to vote together against 75 percent of the Republicans, then in 1987 party voting would have amounted to 32 percent of all votes in the House and 20 percent in the Senate. Employing a very strict criterion, a 90 percent level for interparty opposition in voting, then only 10 percent of House votes and 9 percent of Senate votes were "party votes" in 1987. But these stricter gauges of party voting would understate the influence of party on legislation in the United States.

## Variations in Levels of Party Voting

In the contemporary era—that is, since World War II—levels of congressional party voting measured by the "party majorities in opposition" standard have waxed and waned. Figure 1 portrays oscillations in party voting in Congress from 1949 to 1987. Although the trajectories differ for the two houses over these years, party voting in both houses varies around nearly the same mean (for the House, 45.2; for the Senate, 45.1). Close inspection of Figure 1 confirms a marked regularity in the oscillations of party voting: generally, though not always, levels of party voting run higher in the first session of a Congress and lower in the second. Some scholars have called attention to this "session effect" in their analyses of party voting well before the period analyzed here, some stretching back into the 1830s. This interesting regularity may stem from the tendency of Congressmen to depart from partisanship in favor of nursing their constituencies in election years; or it may issue from a propensity to arrange the legislative agenda so that partisan issues come on to the schedule in the first part of a Congress.

Beyond the fluctuations from session to session, the House and Senate have in recent years produced intriguing patterns of party voting. In the House of Representatives, despite wide variation, the level of party polarization averaged about half of the roll calls (50.2 percent) from 1949 until the mid-1960s. During the ensuing decade, party voting in the House first declined quite significantly, bottomed out, and then began to rise (averaging 34.0 percent from 1966 to 1974). The level of party voting then unmistakably, if irregularly, increased, reaching a postwar high of 64 percent in 1987. For the Senate, the trajectory was different; there, levels of party voting dropped off in the early 1950s, oscillated sharply around a mean of about 44 percent until the mid-1960s, declined briefly in congruence with trends in the House, and then at last increased.

## Party Voting on Major Legislation

If congressional party cleavage falls, on average, somewhat below half of the total number of roll-call votes in the contemporary era, this modest average level of party voting occurs partly because Congress extracts a very large number of recorded votes from its members, many of these votes on minor, administrative, or noncontroversial issues. For instance, the staff of the Senate Democratic Policy Committee re-

# Figure 1

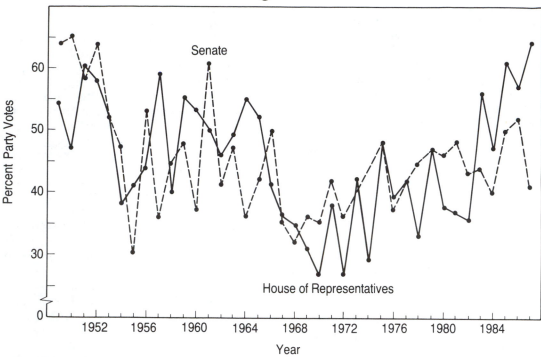

ported that fully 70 percent of the public laws passed by Congress in 1985 were "nonsubstantive" or dealt with minor administrative matters. These actions included naming a county courthouse in Kentucky for the late Congressman Carl D. Perkins (D-Ky.), designating "Benign Essential Blepharospasm Awareness Week," and deciding not to print certain public documents on parchment paper. If levels of congressional party voting were calculated on the basis of major policy issues considered by the House and Senate, rather than over the full repertoire of legislation, party influence and the targets of partisan cleavage would be brought into sharper focus.

Every year Congressional Quarterly, the major Washington, D.C., reporting service for congressional developments, selects the "key votes" cast by members of the House and Senate (i.e., congressional votes on major policy issues). Key votes are those cast on matters of major political controversy, concerning significant presidential or political power, and involving decisions "of potentially great impact on the nation and lives of Americans." These are issues about which the congressional party leadership groups are deeply concerned, and on these issues party leaders care seriously about voting outcomes.

# Table 1

| | House of Representatives | Senate |
|---|---|---|
| 1940s | 56.0 | 58.0 |
| 1950s | 72.1 | 67.3 |
| 1960s | 74.0 | 55.8 |
| 1970s | 73.7 | 61.1 |
| 1980s | 79.6 | 71.9 |

Large majorities of congressional votes on key issues are party votes, as Figure 2 shows. Oscillations in party voting on these major political issues shift substantially from year to year, and sometimes dramatic House-Senate differences do occur. The picture is clarified by comparing average party voting levels on key issues for the past five decades:

That the lion's share of key congressional votes divide the parties is exemplified in the fact that, in the 1980s, more than 80 percent of House votes and about 75 percent of Senate votes were party votes. On the average, congressional party voting on major political issues has been more pronounced in the 1980s than in previous post-WWII decades.

## Variations Across Issue Domains

Congressional party polarization is stronger in some domains than in others. Roll-call votes in Congress can be classified into five distinctive issue domains: government management of the economy, social welfare, civil liberties, international involvement, and agricultural assistance. In the 1950s and 1960s partisan cleavage was sharpest in the government management and social welfare domains and weakest in the international involvement domain. In the 1970s party voting on issues involving government economic management abated some as a regional split in the Democratic Party developed over energy and environmental policy issues; a steady partisanship prevailed on social welfare issues. Today, social welfare programs like social security enjoy some bipartisan support in Congress, but very dramatic party cleavage continues to characterize most social security votes.

Since the 1950s quite a marked shift has occurred in patterns of voting on civil liberties issues. Support for civil liberties legislation has grown among southern Democrats who in-

creasingly draw support from African-American voters. Conversely, Republican support for civil liberties has declined significantly. The political realignment of the South, with the advent of southern Republicanism, has largely removed race and urbanism as factors that could account for the voting of southern Congressmen. Party has become the most important variable in the voting of Congressmen from the South across a range of issues, including civil liberties.

Moreover, various changes have taken place in congressional voting on foreign policy questions. Until the 1960s considerable bipartisanship characterized voting on international issues, epitomized by the notion that party politics should "end at the water's edge." The bulk of "international involvement" votes through the 1960s dealt with foreign aid. Although a regional split persisted in both parties (northern v. southern Democrats; northeastern v. interior

## Figure 2

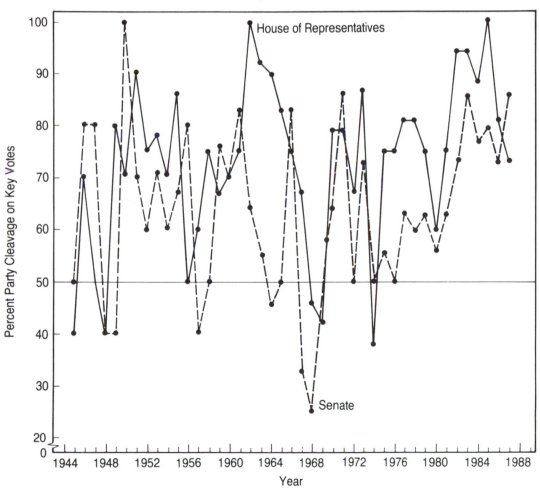

Republicans), the 1970s and 1980s saw foreign policy voting in Congress become more partisan. The greater partisan cleavage in foreign policy voting partly shows up as the response of congressional partisans to Presidents of their own party and partly as opposition to Presidents of the opposition party.

This pattern of contemporary congressional voting on international issues is neatly illustrated by the jockeying between the Democratic majorities of the House and Senate of the One Hundredth Congress and President Ronald Reagan over U.S. support for the Nicaraguan Contras (the guerillas battling against the leftist Sandinista regime). In 1987 a series of votes sharply split the parties over the use of defense appropriations to aid the Contras and over issues of humanitarian versus military aid. Republicans strongly supported the Reagan administration on Contra aid; Democrats were divided, with some southern Democrats voting to support Contra aid. Finally, when a cease fire agreement between the Contras and the Sandinistas was concluded, a Nicaraguan aid package was passed with bipartisan support.

Cutting across those major issue domains that give substance to congressional voting are budgetary decisions. Budgetary issues have come to be among the most partisan of congressional votes, particularly in the House of Representatives. In 1987 more than a third of the "strict" party votes in the House—on which 90 percent of the Democrats voted together against 90 percent of the Republicans—were votes on budget resolutions, reconciliation bills, and other fiscal policy issues. Of partisanship in budgeting, one House Budget Committee member said, "In the House we have always taken the view that the budget is the best way to demonstrate the difference between the parties." Senate budgetary decision-making is less partisan, but even there fully 30 percent of the "strict" party votes in 1987 were votes on budget issues.

## Leadership of the President

Party voting in Congress is, to a considerable extent, a reflection of support or opposition to the President's policy stands or initiatives. On the whole, Democrats in the House and Senate have overwhelmingly supported the position of Democratic Presidents on issues, and Republicans have likewise supported Republican Presidents. This reflection of party voting in presidential support is summarized in Table 1. In the more than three decades recorded in Table 1,

Presidents have been supported by their party's members in Congress at least two-thirds of the time, and sometimes much more.

At the same time, sometimes spectacular cross-party voting occurs. In 1981 President Reagan was able to win the support of a remarkable proportion of congressional Democrats on key budget votes. By the same token, by 1987 Reagan had lost a good deal of support even from Republicans in Congress; in nearly half the votes he lost in the Senate, Reagan could not win the support of even half the Republican Senators.

## The Ideological Basis of Party Voting

Congressional Democrats vote together against Republicans partly because Democrats tend to be ideologically liberal and Republicans tend to be conservative. The congressional party groups are more homogeneous ideologically today than has been true for most of the post-WWII era. House and Senate Republicans are more conservative, Democrats more liberal than in previous years.

Since the New Deal days of the 1930s, a so-called "conservative coalition" has sometimes developed in congressional voting—a combination of Republicans and southern Democrats. Conservative coalition votes appear when a majority of Republicans and southern Democrats vote together against a majority of northern Democrats. Although this voting combination appeared on nearly a third of House votes in 1971, the number of conservative coalition votes reached a post-WWII low in 1987. In author Alan Ehrnhalt's view, the evaporation of this conservative cross-party voting tendency reflects "the new arrangement in Congress: Democrats working together across regional and ideological lines, and Republicans united as a partisan bloc against them."

The liberalism or conservatism of members of Congress can be gauged by using the rating of the Americans for Democratic Action, a liberal organization that each year gives Representatives and Senators scores on the basis of roll calls showing a "clear-cut test of liberal-conservative differences." In 1987, for example, a congressional "liberal" opposed aid to the Nicaraguan Contras and favored aid to the homeless, favored arms reductions and opposed development of the strategic defense initiative (SDI), supported pro-labor legislation, advocated the "fairness doctrine" in broadcasting, and supported welfare programs. A "conservative" wanted to require

## Figure 3

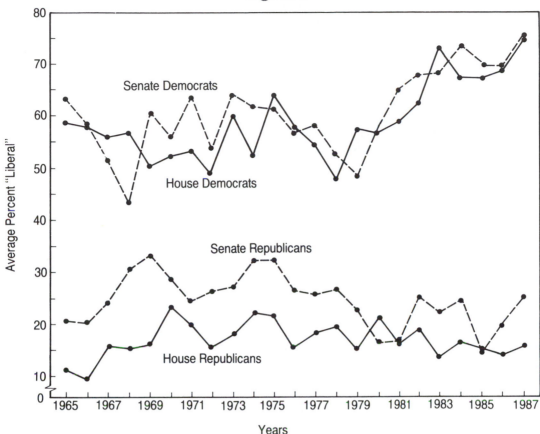

testing for the AIDS virus, supported nuclear testing and lie-detector tests, opposed abortions, and favored the confirmation of Robert H. Bork as an Associate Justice of the Supreme Court. A fully coherent political philosophy may or may not undergird these "clusters of ideas," but nevertheless Republicans and Democrats display distinctly different patterns of political behavior.

Figure 3 shows a sizable and widening ideological gap between congressional Republicans and Democrats, at least on the average. While Republicans have become somewhat more conservative since the mid-1970s, House and Senate Democrats have shown markedly greater liberalism. In the 1960s and 1970s the ideological gap between Democrats and Republicans first narrowed somewhat and then widened substantially. The magnitude of this gap was at some 40 percentage points in the early 1980s but grew to well over 50 percentage points by 1987.

The ideological character of congressional party polarization is further underscored by the roll-call analyses conducted by the *National Journal*. The 1987 study of 90 key votes—54 in the House and 36 in the Senate—showed dramatic party differences in ideological stance. In both congressional houses, Democrats were sharply more liberal than Republicans in three issue areas analyzed: economic issues, social issues, and foreign policy issues. Defining a "liberal" as a member who voted liberal in all three issue areas and a "conservative" as one who voted conservative on all three issues, the 1987 study showed the Democrats to be substantially liberal—70 percent in the House and 65 percent in the Senate—and the Republicans overwhelmingly conservative—93 percent in the House and 80 percent in the Senate.

Moreover, the ideological basis of much party voting in Congress and the ideological polarization of the 1970s and 1980s shows up in high correlations between the government management, social welfare, and civil liberties policy domains, on the one hand, and the ideological alignments, or "levels of ideological structure," of the congressional houses, on the other. Ideological cleavage appears, but less prominently, in the foreign policy domain; and agricultural issues show relatively little ideological structure.

## The Basis for Party Voting

Most of the research and analysis seeking to account for the occurrence of party voting in Congress has been concentrated on individuals. Focusing on the behavior of individual Congressmen, some scholars have sought to ferret out the effects of party and constituency on roll-call behavior. Others have accorded heavy explanatory weight to electoral effects in congressional districts or to constituency economic interests.

Still other students of congressional voting, more sensitive to the complexities of the internal politics of legislatures, have dealt in a much more elaborate fashion with the field of forces in which Congressmen decide how to vote and have constructed relatively well-specified models. Party voting is seen to emerge from the relationships of like-minded men and women, stimulated by patterns of party leadership in the legislative context.

A thinner vein of research has tried to account for fluctuations in party voting levels over time. Indeed, partisan cleavage occurs when partisan legislators have reason to vote on opposite sides of the fence. For all that, the impact of partisanship—who wins and who loses—takes place in the aggregate; party voting is a property of the legislative body as a whole. Investigations by a number of scholars establishes the historic impact of crucial electoral alignments on congressional party voting levels. Since the 1940s, party polarization in the House and Senate seems to have developed in response to distinctive forces. Party voting in the House is very heavily responsive to increased partisan conflict in the constituencies, to the partisanship of the President, to the homogeneity of the party memberships, and to the shape of the legislative workload. Senate party voting is largely dependent upon presidential partisanship; regardless of other influences, party voting in the Senate is greatest when the party of the President and the Senate majority is the same and follows the contours of voting to support the President's legislative program.

## Conclusion

Political parties, partisan strife, and party voting figure as central features of legislative life in the contemporary Congress. Indeed, most political issues of major national importance engender partisan division in the House and Senate. For a given meeting of the congressional houses, party cleavage emerges from commonalities of constituency interest, ideological or attitudinal agreement among partisans, and the exchange of behavioral cues in the Congress itself. Over time, levels of congressional party voting resonate to external partisan forces, legislative leadership, the work to be done, and the partisan behavior of the President. Partisanship in voting in Congress is not immutable and unswerving, but it is, by all odds, the most important thing.

See also: Majority Party Leadership in Congress, New Deal, Ronald Reagan, Speaker of the House

*Samuel C. Patterson*

### REFERENCES

Black, Merle. 1979. "Regional and Partisan Bases of Congressional Support for the Changing Agenda of Civil Rights Legislation." 41 *Journal of Politics* 665.

Brady, David W. 1988. *Critical Elections and Congressional Policy Making*. Stanford, CA: Stanford U. Pr.

Cherryholmes, Cleo H., and Michael J. Shapiro. 1969. *Representatives and Roll Calls: A Computer Simulation of Voting in the Eighty-eighth Congress*. Indianapolis: Bobbs-Merrill.

Clausen, Aage R. 1973. *How Congressmen Decide: A Policy Focus*. New York: St. Martin's.

Clubb, Jerome M., William H. Flanigan, and Nancy H. Zingale. 1980. *Partisan Realignment: Voters, Parties, and Government in American History*. Beverly Hills, CA: Sage.

Epstein, Leon D. 1986. *Political Parties in the American Mold*. Madison: U. of Wisconsin Pr.

Fowler, Linda L. 1982. "How Interest Groups Select Issues for Rating Voting Records of Members of the U.S. Congress." 7 *Legislative Studies Quarterly* 401.

Froman, Lewis A., Jr. 1963. *Congressmen and Their Constituencies*. Chicago: Rand McNally.

Garand, James C., and Kathleen M. Clayton. 1986. "Socialization to Partisanship in the U.S. House: The Speaker's Task Force." 11 *Legislative Studies Quarterly* 409.

Hoadley, John F. 1980. "The Emergence of Political Parties in Congress, 1789–1803." 74 *American Political Science Review* 757.

———. 1986. *Origins of American Political Parties, 1789–1803*. Lexington: U. Pr. of Kentucky.

Jackson, John E. 1974. *Constituencies and Leaders in Congress: Their Effects on Senate Voting Behavior*. Cambridge: Harvard U. Pr.

Kingdon, John W. 1981. *Congressmen's Voting Decisions*. 2nd ed. New York: Harper & Row.

MacRae, Duncan, Jr. 1958. *Dimensions of Congressional Voting*. Berkeley: U. of California Pr.

———. 1970. *Issues and Parties in Legislative Voting: Methods of Statistical Analysis*. New York: Harper & Row.

Matthews, Donald R., and James A. Stimson. 1975. *Yeas and Nays: Normal Decision-Making in the U.S. House of Representatives.* New York: Wiley.

Mayhew, David R. 1966. *Party Loyalty Among Congressmen: The Differences Between Democrats and Republicans 1947–1962.* Cambridge: Harvard U. Pr.

Norpoth, Helmut. 1976. "Explaining Party Cohesion in Congress: The Case of Shared Policy Attitudes." 70 *American Political Science Review* 1156.

Patterson, Samuel C. 1972. "Party Opposition in the Legislature: The Ecology of Legislative Institutionalization." 4 *Polity* 344.

———, and Gregory A. Caldeira. 1988. "Party Voting in the United States Congress." 18 *British Journal of Political Science* 111.

Peltzman, Sam. 1985. "An Economic Interpretation of the History of Congressional Voting in the Twentieth Century." 75 *American Economic Review* 656.

Poole, Keith T. 1988. "Recent Developments in Analytical Models of Voting in the U.S. Congress." 13 *Legislative Studies Quarterly* 117.

———, and R. Steven Daniels. 1985. "Ideology, Party, and Voting in the U.S. Congress, 1959–1980." 79 *American Political Science Review* 373.

Shaffer, William R. 1980. *Party and Ideology in the United States Congress.* Washington: U. Pr. of America.

———. 1982 "Party and Ideology in the U.S. House of Representatives." 35 *Western Political Quarterly* 92.

Shannon, W. Wayne. 1968. *Party, Constituency, and Congressional Voting.* Baton Rouge: Louisiana State U. Pr.

Shelley, Mack C., III. 1983. *The Permanent Majority: The Conservative Coalition in the United States Congress.* University: U. of Alabama Pr.

Shull, Steven A., and James M. Vanderleeuw. 1987. "What Do Key Votes Measure?" 12 *Legislative Studies Quarterly* 573.

Sinclair, Barbara. 1978. "The Policy Consequences of Party Realignment: Social Welfare Legislation in the House of Representatives, 1933–1954." *American Journal of Political Science* 22.

———. 1981. "Coping with Uncertainty: Building Coalitions in the House and the Senate." In Thomas E. Mann and Norman J. Ornstein, eds. *The New Congress.* Washington: American Enterprise Institute.

———. 1983. *Majority Leadership in the U.S. House.* Baltimore: Johns Hopkins U. Pr.

Smith, Steven S. 1981. "The Consistency and Ideological Structure of U.S. Senate Voting Alignments, 1957–1976." 25 *American Journal of Political Science* 780.

Truman, David B. 1959. *The Congressional Party: A Case Study.* New York: Wiley.

Turner, Julius. 1970. *Party and Constituency: Pressures on Congress.* Baltimore: Johns Hopkins U. Pr.

Wander, W. Thomas F., Ted Hebert, and Gary W. Copeland. 1984. *Congressional Budgeting: Politics, Process, and Power.* Baltimore: Johns Hopkins U. Pr.

Weisberg, Herbert G. 1978. "Evaluating Theories of Congressional Roll Call Voting." 22 *American Journal of Political Science* 554.

## Party Endorsing Procedures

Primary elections constitute a system of nomination that takes control of the party label out of the hands of political parties. Even in closed primaries, persons who have never been active in the party—and so have had nothing to do with giving value to the party label—are given the right to determine who shall be the party's standard-bearer in the general election.

One of the ways that political parties regain a measure of control over the assignment of their own label in states that have adopted the primary system is by making and publicizing their own endorsements before the primary election.

Special preprimary endorsing conventions are permitted in 17 states (and are in fact legally required in several of these). In Utah and Connecticut, only candidates who have won a certain number of votes at the preprimary convention are allowed on the primary ballot. In Utah, however, the party must endorse two candidates unless one receives 70 percent or more of the party's vote; in that case, the candidate is nominated without a primary. Six other states (Colorado, Delaware, New Mexico, New York, North Dakota, and Rhode Island) ensure a place on the ballot to any candidate winning the endorsement or with a specified percentage of convention votes, while requiring other candidates to qualify by petition. On the other hand, California, Florida, and New Jersey have all attempted to prevent political parties from making such endorsements, but the parties' right to do so has been affirmed by the courts.

Forty states have no laws regarding endorsements, and in several of these (Minnesota, Massachusetts, Wisconsin, Illinois, Pennsylvania, and Ohio) one or more of the parties do issue endorsements. Once California's laws prohibiting endorsements were ruled unconstitutional by the courts, the Democratic Party in that state began making endorsements. In both Wisconsin and California, party clubs (voluntary associations that are not officially part of the party) have sometimes been able to influence the outcome of primary contests with their endorsements. In general, however, endorsements with no legal significance—including those given by the party itself—are normally less well publicized and probably less effective in influencing the outcome.

Not all party activists believe the endorsement process is good for their party; some believe it weakens party unity and that endorsing conventions are unrepresentative of rank-and-file voters. However, most convention delegates support endorsements, arguing that they give political activists a more important role to play and that, in the words of Malcolm Jewell and David Olson, "the endorsement process strengthens the state and local party organizations and helps to unify the party, increasing its chances of winning the general election."

Wherever endorsements are issued, the fortunate endorsees are more likely to be unopposed: between 1960 and 1986, 57 percent of those endorsed in states with legal endorsement policies and 28 percent of those endorsed informally ran unopposed (however, also noteworthy is the fact that single candidates also ran uncontested in 20 percent of all primary elections without either kind of endorsement).

Winning the party's endorsement normally gives a candidate the support of party activists as well as other important resources (organizational assistance, financing) during the primary campaign. Although some have argued that preprimary endorsements indicated on the ballot serve as useful guides to the voters, enhancing the rationality of the voting decision, others believe that voters pay little attention either to the endorsement process or to its outcome. At best, the endorsement facilitates but by no means ensures victory: when endorsed candidates face opposition in the primary election, they win about 75 percent of the time. Timothy Conlan is probably correct in arguing that the usefulness of an endorsement varies according to "the formal or informal nature of the process, party organizational strength, and state political norms and culture."

*See also:* Blanket Primaries, Caucuses, Closed Primary, Louisiana's Nonpartisan Primary, Open Primary

*Kay Lawson*

REFERENCES

Conlan, Timothy. 1986. "State and Local Parties in Contemporary Politics: Decline, Adaptation, and Continuing Legal Constraints." In Advisory Commission on Intergovernmental Relations. *The Transformation in American Politics*. Washington: ACIR.

Costantini, Edmund, James Fay, Robert Girard, Kay Lawson, and Walter Layson. 1983. "The Deregulation of Political Parties." Position paper of California Committee for Party Renewal.

Jewell, Malcolm E., and David M. Olson. 1988. *Political Parties and Elections in American States*. 3rd edition. Chicago: Dorsey Press.

Lawson, Kay. 1987. "How State Laws Undermine Parties." In A. James Reichley, ed. *Elections American Style*. Washington: Brookings.

Morehouse, Sarah McCally. 1980. *State Politics, Parties and Policy*. New York: Holt, Rinehart, and Winston.

## Party Fundraising by Mail

Direct mail has emerged as the dominant means of political fundraising for political parties in the 1980s. The national committees of the Republican Party, the most successful of all direct mailers, generated over $200 million for the 1984 and 1986 campaigns, almost six times the amount collected by their Democratic counterparts. These huge sums of money, the ensuing Republican advantage, and generous contributions of PACs have changed dramatically the role of the national parties, their personnel, and the campaign funding for candidates.

Direct mail provides parties with a combination of advantages that no other political communication can match: repeat solicitations, personalization, concentration, and immediacy. The mailing process begins with a "prospect" list—names of persons who the mailer believes have political values similar to the ones being offered. Although "prospecting" often loses money (the typical response rate is only 1 percent or 2 percent), the sponsor is willing to incur these costs in order to obtain a "house list"—those persons who responded to the prospect mailing. This list is a precious asset in that mailings to persons on it have an average response rate to future mailings of over 10 percent; and, equally important, the sponsor can solicit the list again and again. This new technique constitutes a fundraising breakthrough. Volunteers find it embarrassing to go back two weeks after an individual has made a donation and ask for another, yet previous givers turn out to be the persons most likely to respond.

The ability to personalize and concentrate communications accounts for much of direct mail's success. The salutation is often directed to an individual by name, and the letter's form and substance always reflect the expected attributes and values of the recipient. Closely related to personalization is the ability to concentrate on particular audiences. By pulling the political and census geography together in a method called "digitizing," fundraisers can target their messages according to socioeconomic status. For example, the Republican Party in California can send out a mailing to all residents in precincts that voted over 60 percent for Ronald Reagan in 1984, with an average age of over 45, living in houses costing over $100,000.

Almost every political mailing follows the same order in its appeals, beginning with a short series of paragraphs that threaten the reader's values, asking for immediate help, and showing that the recipient's action can make a difference. After these initial paragraphs, the mailings provide an extended picture of the cause, the organization, and what actions the addressee can take to alleviate the threat. The last section of the text goes back to the opening themes. An example of a successful mailing by the National Republican Senatorial Committee and signed by President Reagan began

> I am writing you today to ask for your help.
>
> For you and I must take bold immediate action to ensure that everything this Administration stands for is not destroyed in the '84 elections.
>
> Specifically, we are in danger of losing Republican control of the U.S. Senate for the rest of this century.
>
> And I want to tell you, as plainly as I can, what this means—I cannot govern the country without a Senate Majority.
>
> If we lose the Senate, we will no doubt return to the policies of double digit inflation, massive tax increases, and a second rate military—the same policies that nearly ruined our nation.

The following nine paragraphs (plus a two-page insert) describe the task force and the benefits that an individual will receive should he join. The final paragraphs return to personal efficacy, threat, and immediacy:

> America's future for the next twenty years rests on who controls the U.S. Senate in 1984.
>
> I hope and pray that Senator Dick Lugar and I can count on your Task Force membership. Serious work needs to be done *now* to preserve our Senate majority.
>
> Please join today. Your membership will help make the difference!

Three important trends have emerged in the parties' use of direct mail marketing. First, the Republican Party has a distinct advantage over Democrats. Republicans raise more than four times as much money through direct mail as do Democrats, and these funds and corresponding independence from large contributors that direct mail makes possible have led to an increasingly powerful national Republican Party. Second, party mailings are seen by party elites as quite different from nonparty appeals. The parties stress traditional party issues, party loyalty, and citizen duty; they leave the more emotional single-issue appeals to PACs, citizen action groups, and individual candidates. Third, direct mail has created national parties whose staff are marketing specialists rather than traditional politicians. The use of volunteer workers at every level has declined as the parties increasingly rely on mass marketing techniques, a trend particularly evident in the Republican Party.

*See also:* Direct Mail, Political Action Committees

*R. Kenneth Godwin*

REFERENCES

Godwin, R. Kenneth. 1988. *One Billion Dollars of Influence: The Direct Marketing of Politics.* Chatham, NJ: Chatham House.

Kayden, Xandra, and Eddie Mahe, Jr. 1984. *The Party Goes On.* New York: Basic Books.

Nash, Edward L. 1982. *Direct Marketing: Strategy, Planning and Execution.* New York: McGraw-Hill.

Viguerie, Richard. 1981. *The New Right: We're Ready to Lead.* Falls Church, VA: The Viguerie Co.

## Party Identification

### The Concept of Party Identification

Party identification is a concept derived from reference group and small group theory asserting that one's sense of self may include a feeling of personal identity with a political party. In the United States, the feeling is usually expressed as "I am a Democrat" or "I am a Republican." Only in exceptional cases does this sense of individual attachment to party reflect a formal membership or active connection with a party organization. Moreover, one's sense of party identification does not necessarily connote a particular voting record, although the influence of party allegiance on electoral behavior is strong, and clear evidence has established a reciprocal relationship in which voting behavior helps constitute and then solidify or strengthen one's sense of party allegiance. The tie between individual and party is a psychological identification, an extension of one's ego to include feeling a part of a group. This tie can persist without legal recognition or formal evidence of its existence and even without either resting on or producing a totally consistent record of support for the party in attitude or act.

Those seeking a mode for describing the nature of party identification without direct reference to the world of politics sometimes turn to the example of religion for a comparison that is much more than an analogy. Partisan affiliation, like religious affiliation, often originates within the family, where it is established as a matter of early socialization in family values. In addition to the primary group (family) experience, however, a clear sense of belonging to a larger body of adherents or co-religionists is conveyed to the child. The sense of self in the religious context is clearly established by the sense of "We are Catholics" or "I am a Jew"; in politics "We are Democrats" or "I am a Republican." And an affirmative exclusivity attaches to the group identification. Neither religious identification nor party identification necessarily speaks to one's regard, positive or negative, for other persuasions.

*Functions of Party Identification*

To push the comparison another step or two, in matters of religion very few ordinary citizens are creative theologians, just as very few party identifiers are creative political ideologues. One of the roles of the church or the party is to provide structure to an ordinary person's understanding of the external world, specifying which of the phenomena of the secular world are relevant to one's religion, which to one's politics. Group leaders may specify the attitudes that are appropriate to one's affiliation and the values that are central to one's definition of that component of one's life. The function of theology, as with ideology, is often to provide structure, organization, and coherence to a person's thinking about matters that theology (or ideology) defines as relevant to religion (or politics). A central role is thus played by party ideology or sectarian theology in facilitating understanding of the nature of the world.

Beyond such contributions to cognitive structure, the role of faithful parishioner or party follower also provides many cues for affective assessments of the outside world. What is good, what is bad? What is acceptable, what is unacceptable? As a consequence of the many psychological functions generated by one's identification with the group, the citizen is given answers to a multitude of questions. What should I believe? What is the nature of reality? What should be done, what should not be done?

Beliefs relevant to the group, whether theological or ideological, are conveyed through group leaders. Thus political leaders, presidential candidates or presidents, and others perceived to be legitimate party spokespersons are those who articulate party ideology, or the party line, just as the minister or the rabbi, the bishop or the pope, are the authoritative articulators of church dogma. Leaders articulate the creed of the faithful, and they stand as symbols representing any and all of the variety of meanings to be attached to group affiliations. A strict definition of orthodox belief may follow from the homogeneity of leaders' views; a pluralism of heterogeneous beliefs and perspectives among followers may result from ideological factionalism among leaders. However, at the same time that the generic function of leadership is to articulate group values and beliefs, many individual leaders are perceived, at least in their early days of prominence, to possess the attributes associated with their party until, or unless, they establish a more or less unique personal identity. Party identifiers initially perceive in emerging leaders characteristics previously associated with the party. Although some leaders ultimately put their own stamp on the party and contribute to a reshaping of the party image, in the beginning they are often assumed to have the attributes of their predecessors.

Thus, party identification can be understood as serving, for the individual and his or her world of politics, a function similar to that which religious identification provides to the same individual in an organized religion. These identifications are ultimately voluntary choices of allegiance. At this level, they are both extensions of self. They provide partial answers of social reference to the questions of "Who am I, who are you? Who is she? What do they believe?" Such partisanship may be acquired in the first blush through family membership, but, like religious affiliation, political identity may subsequently be influenced by other social relationships and may be dramatically affected by life experiences well into later stages of a person's life. In both instances, the group leadership may be a highly personal leadership, as one can specify for many contemporary religions—Mary Baker Eddy, Joseph Smith, the Reverend Billy Graham—or in politics through a Franklin Roosevelt, or a Norman Thomas, or a Barry Goldwater, or, at the intersection of politics and religion, a Reverend Jerry Falwell, or a Reverend Pat Robertson, or a Reverend Jesse Jackson.

As new issues arise, and as new social problems develop, the leadership must decide and help define the appropriate beliefs and behaviors for the parishioner or the party identifier anent the new phenomena. However, we all know of creative thinking about the issues of the day within the party's rank and file. Although no mass electorate meets idealized standards for being so well informed as to encourage mass decision-making through direct democracy, large numbers of attentive citizens do formulate opinions and policy preferences on their own. But transforming the welter of individual opinion into a consensus for a party is the task of democratic politics and a challenge to party leaders.

*Operational Measures of Party Identification*

Most Americans have a sense of attachment to one party or the other, and for the individuals who do, the strength and direction of their party identifications are facts of central importance in determining attitudes and behavior. The importance of stable party loyalties has been universally recognized in electoral studies. However, the manner in which loyalty to party should be defined and measured has been a subject of much disagreement. In keeping with the conception of party identification as a psychological bond between the individual and the group, party identification has been measured in the research of the National Election Studies by asking individuals to describe their own sense of being a Democrat or Republican. Other studies, however, have chosen to measure stable partisan orientations using individuals' past voting records, or their attitudes on a set of enduring partisan issues. Thus, Republican and Democratic identifiers are sometimes defined as those who vote consistently for the same party and Independents as those who do not.

Such definitions should be characterized as definitions of partisanship, not of party identification, and as definitions of partisanship, they serve many practical and scholarly purposes. However, used as operational definitions of party identification, they serve many practical and scholarly purposes. However, used as operational definitions of party identification, they blur the distinction between the psychological state of one's identification with party and the consequences of that identification. Party identification cannot be measured by the vote or by the citizen's evaluation of partisan issues if, at the same time, the analyst is interested in exploring the influence of party identification on voting behavior or its policy-based determinants.

The extent to which behavioral measures confound the analysis of party identification becomes particularly apparent if the focus is on the study of change in party identification. The familiar phenomenon of ticket splitting, for example, is clearly related to party identification and is taken by some scholars to be measure of party identification. The stronger one's identification the less frequently one splits one's ticket;

the more clearly that one is an Independent, the more often one splits one's ticket. However, in the attempt to study change in party identification by looking at changes in ticket splitting, researchers have found that what has changed may just as well be the attractiveness of the opportunities to split one's ticket as it is the propensity to vote for all of the candidates of one's party.

More generally, given a multivariate view of the origin of personal opinions or individual behaviors, opinion or behaviors may well change as the result of change in any one of a number of origins or causes. Party identification is properly recognized, year in and year out, as the most important contributor to voting behavior, but it is nevertheless only one contributor. Changes in voting behavior may occur with no change whatsoever in a voter's sense of party identification; the changes may stem from other influences that contribute to the vote decision. When an independent measure of party identification is used, even strong party adherents at times may think and act in contradiction to their party allegiance. The observer can never establish the conditions under which this change will occur if the phenomenon of party identification is measured in terms of the consequences it is thought to produce.

The most appropriate and most widely accepted measures of party identification rest fundamentally on self-classification. Since 1952 the National Election Studies have repeatedly asked cross sections of the national electorate a sequence of questions inviting individuals to state the direction and strength of their partisan orientation. The dimension presupposed by these questions appears to have psychological reality for virtually the entire electorate.

The manifestation of party identification is provided by the question: "Generally speaking do you usually think of yourself as a Republican, a Democrat, an Independent or what?" Those who classify themselves as Republicans or Democrats are then asked, "Would you call yourself a strong Republican (or Democrat) or a not very strong Republican (or Democrat)?" This sequence permits the entire population to be arrayed on a continuum running from strong Republican to weak Republican to Independent to weak Democrat to strong Democrat. The effort to measure enduring group identification rather than transitory feelings of partisan preference is reflected in the phrase, *"Generally speaking, do you usually think of yourself . . . ?"*

The result of this choice of language is often visibly different from that produced by another widely used measure that begins "*In politics as of today*, do you consider yourself . . . ?"

### The Preferences of Non-Identifiers

For purposes other than measuring party identification, the National Election Studies' question sequence also continues for those individuals who do not think of themselves as Democrats or Republicans. Those who classify themselves as Independent or, more often, who volunteer the fact they have no party preference are asked the follow-up question: "Do you think of yourself as closer to the Republican or Democratic party?" This question permits a subdivision of the non-identifiers into three categories: one category professing a preference for the Republican Party, one professing a preference for the Democratic Party, and the third group consisting of those who twice resist any suggestion that they have a partisan predisposition or partisan inclination.

This subdivision of the non-identifiers proves useful for a number of purposes, including the use of the entire sequence as a powerful, seven-category predictor of the actual vote division. The same sequence, subdividing "Independents" into those with partisan preferences and those who are staunchly nonpartisan is, however, responsible for some confusion among analysts of electoral behavior. Americans who reject a sense of party identification but who do confess to a party preference are usually devoid of any psychological sense of loyalty or allegiance to a party; they may nevertheless behave very much like partisans. Their partisanship is sometimes more thoroughgoing than the partisanship of those who do identify with a party. Nevertheless, in such circumstances theirs is not a partisanship born of a sense of group identity or belonging but quite different consequence of the attractiveness of a particular leader or the coincidence of their preferences of one party's position on issues. Independent "leaners," or non-identifiers with party preferences, should not be confused with party identifiers despite such occasional treatment by scholars.

### The Stability of Party Identification

The fundamental distinction among citizens emerging from the party identification question is that produced by the initial root question separating the population into three categories: Republican identifiers, Democratic identifiers, and all others. In most studies of the stability of party identification, evidence that individuals "change" their party identification consists largely of evidence that, from election to election, variations within party designations of strong or weak partisanship take place, or shifts occur within the group of non-identifiers, to and from preferences with one or the other party. Those who thus "change" their party identifications, however, seldom cross the barrier between non-identification and identification with a party on either side of the central nonparty domain, and they almost always agree to retain their classifications as Democrats or Republicans.

The relative stability of party identification at both the level of national aggregate distributions and at the level of individual measurement through time is both impressive and necessary to the status of party identification as an analysis of mass electoral behavior. As should be true of one's sense of political self, measures of the stability and durability of various political attitudes consistently place party identification in the top rank, virtually unchallenged by feelings toward national political leaders or by commitments on matters of public policy as indicators of enduring political predispositions. Party identification is by no means an immutable commitment, but given accumulated evidence of its relatively strong stability, it is often used as the beginning point for studies of change in the more transitory perceptions, attitudes, and beliefs about candidates for election and policy alternatives involved in election-day decisions.

### The Origins of Party Identification

Despite the profound importance of party identification as a conditioner of individual behavior and as a shaper of the politics of the society, the origins of partisanship are not well established. The family was once thought to be all-important. The presumed centrality of the family in creating a sense of party was, in part, a direct consequence of early measurement practices among the professional students of electoral behavior. In many studies of political socialization, scholars put great reliance on individuals' *recall* of parental partisanship. These reports were used in lieu of data directly examining the shared sense of party within the context of the family (i.e., studies of both parent and child at the same time). In the virtual absence of appropriate evidence, heavy reliance was placed on after-the-fact reports of children, often "children" now in their adulthood, of their parent's partisanship, a partisanship that often existed decades in the past and was recalled with memories blurred by the passage of time. Not surprisingly, that partisanship was often remembered as being the same as the current partisanship of the "child." The early thesis that the family was the source of partisanship, and that the continuity of party identifications in the United States was a reflection of the conserving influence of family traditions of party loyalty, has been substantially modified by research that reveals evidence of great slippage between the partisanship of the hearth and the sense of party identification exhibited in later life.

Studies following a cohort of high school students and their parental families over the course of a number of years have suggested that the earliest sense of an almost content-free identification with party (evident in yet other studies of children at elementary school levels) may, over the decade leading up to later adolescence, be replaced by a growing sense of nonpartisan independence. That sense of independence from party ties or party loyalty may in part be engendered by the traditional civics-class-textbook emphasis on the value of political independence, on the value of voting for the person and not the party, on the importance of considering the issues rather than blindly accepting the party label. At the same time, however, some evidence points to the acquisition of party loyalties through one's association with one's secondary school peers, and, to a very limited extent, through association with one's teachers. The subsequent evolution of party identification in the electorate is a matter of social learning that apparently picks up in young adulthood and may extend throughout one's adult life.

As with initial childhood socialization, *the process* by which a high school senior's disdain for political party is replaced 20 years later by a strong sense of party loyalty has not been well documented. The beginning state and the end result have been well studied, but we do not know the mechanics of the process of transformation. Do people move from a sense of remoteness from both parties to a modest preference for one party, then to behavior reflecting that preference, and ultimately to a sense of self that is consonant with an established behavioral pattern? Or is the process much more a cognitive process of rationally deciding and choosing between the parties on the basis of one's maturing values, social perspectives, and preferences on matters of issues? Is the process much more a cognitive process of rationally deciding and choosing between the parties on the basis of one's maturing values, social perspectives, and preferences on matters of issues? Is the process one that is mobilized largely by the attractions of party leadership, or do questions of urgent public policy better facilitate the growth of party loyalties? It is clear that Americans, from early adulthood on, are faced with the repetitious recurrence of partisan elections. It is hard to be a good citizen in the United States without being a voluntary participant, and if one is going to participate, one's choices at the time of election are limited to a small number, and usually with the same party labels. The persistent obligation to vote, the accompanying exposure to political campaigns, and the repeated choice between only two party alternatives must somehow transform one's sense of a predominant partisanship into a sense of party loyalty.

Whatever the psychological mechanism that leads adult citizens to identify with a political party in such large proportions, recent decades have greatly increased our understanding of the external conditions that lead to new identifications or reinforce old ones. Some are conditions that are apolitical in origin, conditions of change in individual social locations. Going away to school, marrying, acquiring a job, and moving to a new home all intrude on original familial values and the political context of childhood. Thus sequentially experienced life cycle changes may produce changes in the social environment that, in turn, could produce changes in individual political identities. In some periods these kinds of changes may shift the geographic balance in partisan alignments, as with outward migrations from central city to suburbs—or as with the great mid-century migrations from the rural South to the West Coast or to the urban North. The political changes induced by such social change may have substantial political consequences, as in the erosion of the Democratic dominance of the one-party South. They are, however, often overshadowed by changes induced by more directly political causes.

Large, cataclysmic events of national scope and extended temporal duration may reshape the national limits of party identification. Two major epochs were formed by the Civil War of the 1860s and the Great Depression of the 1930s. The Civil War introduced 70 years of Republican domination of national politics, an epoch of one-party dominance that was overturned only after the Depression and Franklin Roosevelt's Democratic New Deal.

Although much of the evidence is indirect and the strongest arguments are inferential, both of these periods seem to have begun after pervasive changes occurred in citizens' party loyalties, changes that, once established, shaped the partisanship of families and communities for generations. But like the generic problem of understanding the establishment of an individual's party identification following an adolescence of political independence, the precise mechanisms driving these major historical transformations are not established. Particularly unclear for the post-Depression period in the twentieth century is how much credit should be given to the Democratic mobilization of previous nonvoters and how much should go to the conversion of Republican sympathies into Democratic loyalties. And whatever the balance between mobilization and conversion, what proportion of those who changed did so because of the appeal of the policies of the New Deal? How many simply expressed their bitter disappointment in the performance of Herbert Hoover and the Republican Party? And how many became Democrats because of the charismatic appeal of Franklin Roosevelt? Much is yet to be learned from the reconstruction of such periods of national upheaval.

*The Importance of Party Identification*

With the advent of new methods of social science research, and of survey research in particular, recent decades have produced major additions to our knowledge about the nature of party identification. Where the "importance" of party identification was once assessed largely in terms of its simple correlation with the voter's choice, credit is now given for its many "indirect" contributions as well. These occur as party identification shapes perceptions and transmits values to the attitudes and beliefs that, in turn, lead to the individual's choice at the ballot box. The contributions of both *direct* and *indirect* effects to the individual voting decision must be joined to an awareness of the importance of the national balance of partisan loyalties in any thoroughgoing appraisal of the role of party identification in national politics. When this conjunction is understood, for example, the recent history of Republican dominance of presidential politics in a nation that has, at the same time, voted Democratic for most other lesser offices becomes explicable. The analyst is now aware that party identifications, on which Democrats enjoy a plurality of support, are more important as a singular influence on the "other" vote decisions; these same party identifications are more often countered by candidate- and issue-oriented, short-term forces in the presidential contest.

Most significant recent theoretical advances have centered on decoding persistent sources of change in party identification. In one important development in the analysis on "issue voting," persuasive evidence indicates that citizens' retrospective evaluations of incumbent administrations make a separate contribution to their decisions on election day, above and beyond their issue preferences for future public policy decisions. Indeed, so persuasive is the evidence of retrospective evaluation of performance as an explanation of vote choice that a related thesis has developed to explain the impact of performance evaluations of party identifications. While firm party identifications may be strong influences on voters' evaluations of incumbents' performances, a "failed presidency" or visible evidence of an economy in trouble may be sufficient to override opinions that might otherwise flow from the voters' sense of party loyalty to an incumbent administration. The same negative evaluations of a President or his party that induce a temporary vote defection in favor of the challenger may also erode an earlier sense of party identification or justify a new self-identity.

The specific hypotheses on the impact of performance evaluations on voters' choices have been joined with other evidence that new issues and new candidates, even though short-term forces, can change the party identification of adult citizens. When combined with the demonstration that a vote defection, against the candidate of one's party, weakens party identification, a powerful new thesis emerges: party identification can be thought of as a "running tally" of one's political experience. This perspective does not necessarily question the nature or alter the conception of the roles subsequently played by party identification in shaping individuals' attitudes and behavior. It does, however, replace more primitive themes of habit and childhood experience with notions of rational adult decision-making as the source of developing or changing party loyalties.

A complementary but very different perspective has emerged from work that has captured some of the consequences of the social turmoil and political upheaval in the United States during the late 1960s and early 1970s. For example, an examination of the high school seniors in 1965 and their parents provides evidence of generational differences in the changes induced by the turbulent events surrounding the civil rights movement, the anti-Vietnam War protests, and the emergence of the counterculture. Disillusionment and dissatisfaction with virtually all of society's institutions did not spare political parties. During a period in their lives young adults normally would acquire or strengthen their sense of party identification, the cohort of the mid-1960s actually underwent a decline in party attachments. The antiparty sentiments of the period not only forestalled but also reversed the growth of their party identifications.

The subsequent return of national politics to something resembling normality permitted, or engendered, a stabilization of these young adults' party identifications but at a level markedly different from that of older Americans. The impact of the period on these older cohorts was also very visible in 1968 and 1972; but by 1984 they had returned to a level of party loyalty—and a balance of partisan forces—scarcely different from one that could have been predicted 20 years before. Not so for the younger generation; they continued to bear the scar of the period of national turmoil and thereby adopted a "generation gap" that may well persist through their days as members of the electorate.

Students of politics must understand the phenomenon of party identification because it has come to be seen as the foundation on which many attributes of America's political system rest. In addition to the restraints on third-party development imposed by our electoral system, the conserving influence of party identification inhibits the development of sustained third-party loyalties. As a conserving base for individual responses to politics, party identification sustains the political cleavages that separate social, cultural and economic groups in the society and thereby define party alignments. Geographic mobility and internal migration result in shifting national political contours because the individual migrants tend to take their party identifications with them, often into new settings where they give way only slowly under the influence of new contextual pressures. The maintenance of a high level of attachment to party means the maintenance of an important motive for political participation by large numbers of Americans. And the withering away of party loyalties exacerbates the problem of low turnout on election day. Although party identification exists within the individual as a very personal dimension of social life, its collective manifestations are a vital part of the institutions of politics and government in the United States.

*See also:* Barry Goldwater, Herbert Hoover, Ideology, Jesse Jackson, Marion G. Robertson, Franklin D. Roosevelt

*Warren E. Miller*

REFERENCES

Campbell, Angus, Philip E. Converse, Warren E. Miller, and Donald E. Stokes. 1960. *The American Voter*. Chicago: U. of Chicago Pr.

Clagget, William. 1981. "Partisan Acquisition Versus Partisan Intensity: Life Cycle, Generation and Period Effects, 1952–1976." 25 *American Journal of Political Science* 193.

Converse, Philip E. 1976. *The Dynamics of Party Support*. Beverly Hills, CA: Sage.

Green, Donald P., and Bradley Palmquist. 1990. "Of Artifacts and Partisan Instability." 34 *American Journal of Political Science* 872.

Jennings, M. Kent, and Richard G. Niemi. 1981. *Generations and Politics*. Princeton: Princeton U. Pr.

Miller, Warren E. 1990. "The Electorate's View of the Parties." In L. Sandy Maisel, ed. *The Parties Respond*. Boulder, CO: Westview Press.

## Party Leadership Selection in the Congress

It was Speaker Thomas B. Reed of Maine, the legendary "Czar" of the House of Representatives in the 1890s, who understood the ambiguity of legislative leadership in the Congress. As he stated in 1889

> Under our system of government . . ., the responsibilities and duties of this office [the speakership] are both political and parliamentary. So far as the duties are political, I sincerely hope that they may be performed with a proper sense of what is due to the people of this whole country. So far as they are parliamentary, I hope with equal sincerity that they may be performed with a proper sense of what is due to both sides of this chamber.

Legislative leaders operate differently from the leaders of other political structures. They neither hire nor can they fire their fellow members in the legislature. They must contend with anyone the electorates of hundreds of districts or dozens of states send to their assemblies. Leading those who may not wish to be led requires a special set of skills. Scholars have identified four different forms of legislative leadership: (1) issue leadership; (2) procedural leadership; (3) committee leadership; and (4) party leadership. Among these, party leadership is clearly the most demanding.

*Issue leadership* involves the presentation of particular legislative positions through the sponsorship of bills and motions designed to implement a particular public policy goal. Any member of a legislature can choose this role, making it the most democratic form of legislative leadership.

*Procedural leadership* exists in all legislatures. The need for a bill to receive a full and fair hearing through frank and informed discussions by the members requires an orderly arena for such discussion. It is the responsibility of the presiding officers to guarantee orderliness and to permit the members of all parties to conduct legislative business.

Within the committees, a more subtle form of leadership exists far from the notice of the assembly floors. It is the *committee leaders* who must sift through the vast array of legislative proposals, determine which can be acted upon, and navigate those bills through the committee so that they may be deliberated on the assembly floor.

*Party leadership* entails leading into the legislative fray a cohesive group of members whose commitment to winning on the chamber floor requires a willingness to subordinate any issues, alliances, and personal elements that divide them. Religion, region, social origin, and personal aspirations are only some of the many cross-cutting affiliations that have to be bypassed in the quest for party unity and ever-elusive legislative majorities.

Legislative leadership was prevalent among the 55 men who gathered in Philadelphia to draft the Constitution. Forty-two of the Founding Fathers had served in the Continental Congress, the first national assembly in this hemisphere. Of all these forms of leadership, none was more distrusted in 1787 than party leadership. Still, within two years of the new Republic's life, many of these same founders became party leaders in the Congress and were often at odds with one another.

*Speakership Elections*

It was in the House of Representatives that partisanship first emerged. The original hope had been that the Speaker, as was the custom in the House of Commons, would be chosen by the majority party when a vacancy in the chair occurred but would be continued in the chair indefinitely regardless of which party controlled the chamber.

Frederick A. C. Muhlenberg, the first Speaker, had presided over the Pennsylvania House and was presumed to be a moderate Jeffersonian. He was elected Speaker in a Federalist-dominated House—a time of limited partisanship. Muhlenberg stepped aside in the Second Congress (1791–1793) but was elected on the third ballot in the Third Congress, the first of 13 multiballot contests for the speakership in the first 36 Congresses.

Party lines become more evident after 1793, and the nonpartisan hopes of the Founding Fathers were dashed. This factionalism was further confirmed by Secretary of State Thomas Jefferson's departure from the Cabinet in 1793 and his subsequent challenge to John Adams in 1796. Adding to the bitterness was the lingering hostility from the battle over the ratification of the Jay Treaty in 1795.

The fragmentation of power within the Constitution was designed to create various issue factions too numerous for the concentration of power. The complexity of this structure with its elaborate set of checks and balances was such that the system would have dissolved into near-fatal governmental stalemate had it not been for the unifying role of political parties in transcending the institutional barriers. It was the parties and their leaders who gave the new Republic direction and focus.

Partisan elections for the speakership were soon followed by the use of committee assignments to insure party control of legislative business. Since the Speaker made these assignments, party leaders in the House had obviously taken over procedural and committee leadership roles.

In 1800 the victory of Jefferson's party, the Democratic-Republicans, began an unequaled era of party dominance over the elected branches of government, the presidency, the Senate, and the House. Democratic-Republican margins of victory grew to near unanimity in the presidential contest of 1820 while at the same time, their proportion of congressional seats in both chambers—90 percent in the Senate and 87 percent in the House—gave hope to those who believed that a one-party government might achieve what the Founding Fathers had originally sought—a cure for the "mischiefs of faction."

Factions can exist within parties as well as between them as became evident in the multiballot speakership contests that took place in the Sixth, Ninth, Eleventh, Sixteenth, Seventeenth, and Nineteenth Congresses. Most of these were Congresses controlled almost completely by the Democratic-Republicans and the contests featured members of the same party. Only Henry Clay of Kentucky, who served as Speaker for most of the years between 1811 and 1825, was able to gain election on the first ballot. Personal ambition and not partisan policy differences seemed to lie at the root of most of these contests.

Following the reorganization of the parties into Democrats and Whigs in the second American party system (1825–1861), the House parties appeared to have more internal coherence, but multiballot speakership battles continued.

The growing estrangement between northern and southern states over slavery was responsible for three extraordinarily contentious contests. In 1849, 63 ballots were needed to elect Georgia's Howell Cobb over the Whig incumbent, Robert C. Winthrop of Massachusetts. Six years later in 1855, Nathaniel Banks of Massachusetts, a candidate of the minor American Party, emerged as Speaker after 2 months and 133 ballots. In both cases, the House agreed to do away with the majority requirement for election. And the last of the pre-Civil War Congresses, the Thirty-sixth in 1859, cast 44 ballots before electing their Speaker, William Pennington, a freshman from New Jersey and the first Republican to hold the chair.

During the Civil War, party caucuses were first institutionalized. Moving the intraparty conflicts from the floor to the caucus room eliminated the multiballot speakership contest as members fought behind closed doors and voted with near unanimity on the floor for their party's speakership nominee. Only once in the past 130 years has there been a multiballot speakership contest: Progressive Republicans led a nine-ballot revolt in 1923 against incumbent Republican Speaker Frederick Gillet of Massachusetts.

The contests for the speakership have now been removed from public view; no longer is House business delayed by balloting for its highest office. And even within the party caucuses themselves, the speakership nominees for both parties are rarely challenged.

*House Floor Leadership Selections*

In the second session of the First Congress in 1790, the House decided to give the Speaker appointment power over all of the committees—standing committees as well as select and special ones. Thus the Speaker got the opportunity to select the chairs of the most powerful committees. From the ranks of these individuals emerged the majority leadership of the House.

Given the fact that the House's unique role in the Constitution was linked to its control over the revenue function, it was not surprising that the chairman of the House Ways and Means Committee emerged as the "first among equals" among the committee chairs and become the de facto majority party leader. Not until the twentieth century did the title gain official usage, but it was an identifiable leadership post as far back as 1795.

The post was appointive and one served at the pleasure of the Speaker. Pre-Civil War Speakers removed seven chairs of the Ways and Means Committee during their tenure in the chair. In 1805 Speaker Nathaniel Macon of North Carolina rebuffed President Jefferson's urging to rid the Ways and Means Committee of its erratic chairman, John Randolph of Roanoke, and found himself bypassed for Speaker by the Democratic-Republicans in 1807 in favor of Joseph B. Varnum of Massachusetts.

Throughout the pre-Civil War period, the Ways and Means chairs were the enforcers of the Speaker's message. To use the terminology of author Robert Bales's interaction process analysis, the floor leaders served as the "task leaders" of the House focussing the majority on the party's issue agenda, while the Speakers served as its "social leader" struggling to maintain decorum in a chamber increasingly beset with violent actions taken by members against one another.

During the Civil War, the money power was divided between the taxing committee, Ways and Means, and a new spending committee, Appropriations. Its first chairman, Thaddeus Stevens of Pennsylvania, left the chairmanship of Ways and Means to preside over the new committee, an indication that the two committees were to be perceived as equals. This parity was confirmed when post-Civil War Speakers put members of both committees beside them as fellow majority members of the five-man House Rules Committee. Thus, the majority leadership was shared between the chairmen of the Ways and Means and Appropriations committees.

In 1911 this selection system changed with the "overthrow" of Speaker Joseph G. Cannon of Illinois. The Republican Speaker, who had chaired the Rules Committee, was removed from that committee and his power to appoint members of committees, chairmen included, was lost.

Committee members were now chosen by each party's respective committee on committees, thus beginning the separation of party leadership from committee leadership. The Democrats chose their members of the Ways and Means Committee in caucus and gave them responsibility for other committee assignments. The Republicans created a separate committee on committees to handle their assignment selections.

Both parties used caucuses to select their floor leaders. For the majority party, this procedure represented a break from the committee-based power of the pre-1911 era. However, the minority party procedure continued a post-Civil War custom of asking the party's defeated speakership nominee to serve as the minority floor leader. It was in 1911 that James R. Mann of Illinois became the first to be designated "Chairman of the Minority Conference."

Since 1911 floor leaders in both House parties have been elected by their respective caucuses. The Republicans have had a livelier history than the Democrats with four of their leaders removed in the caucuses of 1919, 1931, 1959, and 1965; Democratic leaders have faced noisy but relatively nonfatal caucuses. Democratic contests almost invariably occur when a seat is open. The most closely contested election in recent years among the Democrats occurred in 1977 when three ballots were necessary to select Jim Wright of Texas over Philip Burton of California for Majority Leader. Only one vote divided them on the third ballot.

The most notable feature of the House Democratic selection process has been the prevalence of leaders from Massachusetts and Texas. From 1940 to 1989 four of the seven Democrats who served in the top two leadership posts came from these two states—Sam Rayburn of Texas (Majority Leader, 1937–1940; Speaker, 1940–1947, 1949–1953, and 1955–1961; Minority Leader, 1947–1949 and 1953–1955) and Jim Wright of Texas (Majority Leader, 1977–1987; Speaker 1987–1989) and John McCormack of Massachusetts (Majority Leader, 1941–1947, 1949–1953, and 1955–1961; Minority Whip, 1947–1949 and 1953–1955; Speaker, 1961–1971) and Thomas P. "Tip" O'Neill of Massachusetts

(Majority Whip, 1971–1973; Majority Leader, 1973–1977; Speaker, 1977–1987). In addition, two of the others—Carl Albert of Oklahoma (Majority Whip, 1955–1961; Majority Leader, 1962–1971; Speaker, 1971–1977) and T. Hale Boggs of Louisiana (Majority Whip, 1962–1971; Majority Leader, 1971–1972)—came from states adjacent to Texas. This linkage is sometimes known as the "Austin-Boston Connection."

Its ostensible purpose was to place in the House Democratic leadership members from the largest southern state with the smallest Black population (Texas) and from the largest northern metropolitan area with the smallest Black population (Boston). In this way, House Democrats selected as their leaders members whose careers were relatively independent of the divisive race questions that have plagued Democratic presidential candidacies in recent years.

In June 1989 Speaker Jim Wright was forced to resign from the House in the wake of an ethics investigation that contended that he had tried to circumvent House limitations on outside earned income by collecting unusually high royalties from the sale of a book containing his speeches and by the employment of his wife in a firm run by a business associate who had a direct interest in legislation. Wright was the first Speaker to resign from the House while under an ethics investigation.

Speaker Wright's departure and the retirement of Speaker O'Neill in 1987 brought an end to the "Austin-Boston" dynasty, which had ruled the House Democrats for almost 50 years.

O'Neill and Wright have been replaced by Speaker Thomas Foley of Washington and Majority Leader Richard Gephardt of Missouri. Race politics in the Democratic Party has evolved from containing the race question to accommodating it. This sensitivity to race on the part of national Democratic leaders led to the selection of a Black Majority Whip, William Gray of Pennsylvania, the House Democrats' third major leadership post.

Republican leaders cannot be characterized so easily. They have selected leaders from each of the nation's major regions. In terms of social status, leaders have often come from lower-income families. Joe Martin, who led the House Republicans from 1939 to 1959 and was its last Speaker (1953–1955) was the son of a Massachusetts blacksmith. Robert Michel, who has led the Republicans since 1981, is the son of a

Belgian-born maintenance man at an Illinois paint factory. Clearly, men of the people.

The quasi-permanent minority status of contemporary Republicans has shaped the party's leadership selection system. It has led to an alternation of the floor leadership between Republican leaders who can get along with the majority Democrats—Joe Martin (1939–1959), Gerald Ford of Michigan (Minority Leader, 1965–1973), and Robert Michel (Minority Whip, 1975–1981; Minority Leader, 1981–present) and those stronger partisans who wished to challenge the Democrats—Charles Halleck of Indiana (Minority Leader, 1959–1965) and John Rhodes of Arizona (Minority Leader, 1973–1980). The 1989 whip contest between Georgia's Newt Gingrich and Illinois' Edward Madigan turned directly on the issue of which candidate would most effectively confront the Democrats. Gingrich, who led the ethics battle against Speaker Wright, won by just two votes.

The most notable Republican floor leader in recent years was Gerald R. Ford, who won the post by overthrowing Charles Halleck in 1965. Congressman Ford served as Minority Leader for nine years until the resignation of President Richard Nixon's first Vice President, Spiro Agnew, in October 1973. Ford replaced Agnew and became the first person to become Vice President under the provisions of the Twenty-fifth Amendment, which enables the President and the Congress to fill vacancies in the vice presidency. Ten months later, in August 1974, Vice President Ford succeeded President Nixon who resigned over the Watergate scandal. He was the first House leader to become President since William McKinley (R-Ohio) in 1897.

### House Party Whip Selections

It was the late-nineteenth-century Republicans who first formalized the position of party whip. The whip's major responsibility is to make sure that the party's members are in the chamber at the time of a vote. Presumably, this assembly should enable the party to present a united front on the chamber floor.

The first Speaker to make use of the party whip was "Czar" Thomas B. Reed of Maine, who served as Speaker from 1889 to 1891 and from 1895 to 1899. Reed, whose Republican partisanship was legendary, used the whips to round up votes as one of his techniques to thwart the obstructionism of southern Democrats.

Democratic experience with whips has been uneven. Although they named a party whip before 1911, Speaker James B. "Champ" Clark of Missouri did not make consistent use of this position during his eight-year tenure in the chair (1911–1919). The post was not regularly filled by the Democratic leadership until 1921.

Selection methods have varied over time for this post. For Republicans, whips were appointed by the floor leadership from 1897 to 1919. In 1919 the Republican caucus elected the whip, but two years later, the selection was turned over to the party's Committee on Committees where it remained until 1965. In that year, the caucus made the post elective again. In each of the two transitions, the incumbent Republican whip selected by the earlier method was retained.

The longest-serving House leader in any position was Leslie Arends of Illinois, who served as Republican Party whip from 1943 to 1975. The whip post in the Republican Party has not been a steppingstone to the floor leadership position. Only Robert Michel, a protégé of Arends, has accomplished that feat in recent history. Also, the continuing minority party frustration of the House Republicans has led two of their most recent whips to seek career advancement beyond the House. Trent Lott of Mississippi, whip from 1981 to 1988, was elected to the Senate. And his immediate successor, Wyoming's Richard Cheney, left the whip's post to become Secretary of Defense less than three months after his election in 1989. Another intriguing development among recent Republican whips is their seemingly anomalous geographic location: Republican whips have come from such traditional Democratic strongholds as Mississippi (Lott) and Georgia (Gingrich).

The Democratic whip was appointed until 1987. Democratic Speakers and floor leaders had regularly contended that this post was theirs to fill. With the departure of Speaker O'Neill, the Democratic Caucus held its first election for whip. The initial winner was Tony Coelho of California, the party's most successful fundraiser. His term did not last long: Coelho left the House in 1989 during the investigation of Speaker Jim Wright. Coelho was fearful that his own questionable financial dealings with brokerage firms and savings and loan associations would further undermine the Democratic majority, and he chose to resign.

The House Democrats elected their next whip in June 1989. Coelho's successor was William Gray of Pennsylvania, the first Black member to hold a major leadership post in either branch of Congress.

Controlling the selection of the whip was another way in which the House Democratic leaders could determine the leadership succession system within their party. The regular procession of members from whip to floor leader to Speaker became known as the "leadership ladder." Given the fact that the Democrats have organized the House for all but two of the past thirty Congresses (1931–1991), this "ladder" gave the party leaders continuity and the membership predictability. The collapse of the Wright speakership in 1989 shook the "ladder" and the continuity and predictability that it provided.

For most of this century, the House Democratic leadership selection was hierarchically arranged in a tightly controlled system including its leadership ladder and appointed whips. The system was intended to minimize internal conflict. The end of the "Austin-Boston" dynasty, however, has led to a new selection system that places less importance upon seniority and the apprenticeship-protégé norms that had governed Democrats for so long. Being the protégé of a sitting leader will probably no longer guarantee any member a rung on future leadership ladders.

Other key changes involving the House Democrats have to do with the development of other party offices. Elections for chairman and vice chairman of the Democratic Caucus, posts that were not previously contested, have lately taken on more meaning. Further ramifications may follow from the 1989 leadership crisis, but their direction is unclear.

The House Republican leadership selection system remains stable. Throughout most of this century it has been relatively egalitarian with open competition and a dominant role for their membership. This competition has extended from the top party offices through the lesser ones. House Republicans have seen little need to control their leadership succession. However, they remain the minority party and until Republican control returns to the House, the party will continue to wrestle with what leadership stance they will take toward the Democrats.

*Senate Presiding Officer Selections*

The two positions of procedural leadership in the Senate emanate indirectly from the political parties. The President of the Senate is the Vice President of the United States, who occupies the post as a consequence of the presidential election and not because of selection by any party caucus. Interestingly enough, 11 of the last 12 Democratic conventions since 1944 have given vice presidential nominations to sitting or former United States Senators. The 1988 nomination of Lloyd Bentsen of Texas is the most recent example of this tendency among Democrats.

Republican conventions have been less inclined to select sitting or former Senators for the vice presidency. Only six of their thirteen selections since 1940 have come from the Senate. However, the most recent Republican Vice President, Indiana's J. Danforth Quayle, served in the Senate for eight years.

The sitting Senator whose duties include presiding over the chamber is the President *pro tempore*. This Senator is the senior member of the majority party in the Senate. Generally, this Senator's seniority not only qualifies him for the President *pro tempore* slot but also for the chairmanship of one of the Senate's major committees. Committee leadership duties outweigh procedural leadership ones, and the quotidian job of presiding over the Senate usually falls among the more junior members.

However, the Senate has seen contests for this post. Five times in this century, intraparty conflict has erupted over the post of President *pro tempore* of the Senate. Three times, Democrats were involved (1913, 1915, and 1949) and twice, Republican Senators challenged their party's senior claimant to the post (1916 and 1931). The 1931 contest saw 13 Republican insurgents denying their party's nominee for this post, Senator George Moses of New Hampshire, through 25 ballots. After more than two weeks of balloting, Vice President Charles Curtis used a parliamentary technicality to end the balloting and install Moses even though neither Moses nor Democratic Senator Key Pittman of Utah had secured a majority.

*Senate Floor Leadership Selection*

Floor leadership developed very slowly in the Senate. In 1885, 96 years after the convening of the First Congress, Woodrow Wilson contended that "No one is the Senator. No one may speak for his party as well as for himself; no one exercises the special trust of acknowledged leadership. The Senate is merely a body of individual critics."

Issue leadership had always been a feature of Senate life as Senators from throughout the nation would make use of the unlimited debate within that chamber to champion their various causes and attract a national audience for their views. Senators such as Daniel Webster of Massachusetts, Thomas Hart Benton of Missouri, John C. Calhoun of South Carolina, and Henry Clay of Kentucky were not men who were easily led by others.

Party leadership was another matter. Isolated from the American public by their lack of direct election and knowing that they had a six-year lease on their offices, nineteenth-century Senators could not be disciplined nor did they wish to be.

The 1890s left their mark on almost every part of the American political system. Among the effects were a much more active foreign policy as a consequence of the Spanish-American War, the closing of the American frontier, the growing power of the speakership under Thomas B. Reed, the assertive presidencies of Grover Cleveland and William McKinley, the judicial validation of racial segregation in *Plessy v. Ferguson* (1896), and the regional polarization of politics in the McKinley-Bryan elections of 1896 and 1900. The Senate could no longer remain isolated from these events.

Gathering regularly at the Washington home of Senator James McMillan of Michigan in the early years of this century were the Republican powers of the Senate—William Boyd Allison of Iowa and Nelson W. Aldrich of Rhode Island. Joined by Senators Orville Platt of Connecticut and John Coit Spooner of Wisconsin, these Republican Senators played poker and sought to routinize the business of the Senate by deciding among themselves the legislative agenda that they would pursue on the floor and in committee.

The chairman of the party conference assumed whatever party leadership role the Senate members were willing to grant. In his 1985 compilation of Senate floor leaders, Floyd Riddick, the Senate's parliamentarian emeritus, began his designation of Senate party leaders with chairmen of the party conferences from 1903 on, but he points out that the official minutes of the conferences only grant floor leadership to Democratic chairmen in 1921 and to Republican chairmen in 1925.

As a consequence of the relatively late developing of most of this post, there is no history in the Senate comparable to that in the House. Senator George Mitchell of Maine prevailed in a 1988 first-ballot victory over Senators J. Bennett Johnston of Louisiana and Daniel Inouye of Hawaii. It was only the third reported contest for floor leader among Senate Democrats in history. The others were the one-vote victory of

Alben Barkley of Kentucky over Pat Harrison of Mississippi in 1937 and the challenge of Florida's Lawton Chiles to West Virginia's incumbent leader Robert Byrd in 1984.

Senate Democrats have a relatively orderly leadership selection system. It does not have the dimensions of the "leadership ladder" of the House because the Senate Democratic floor leader also holds the titles of chairman of the Democratic Conference and chairman of the Policy Committee, and until 1989, chairman of the Steering Committee. This concentration of offices has the disadvantage of reducing the number of opportunities available to ambitious younger Democrats, but paradoxically, it may generate harmony by limiting the potential for conflict in the caucus.

Senate Republicans have had a curious pattern of leadership selection. For most of this century, from 1899 to 1949, the Republicans selected their Senate leaders without opposition from among the party's senior hierarchy. Since 1949 there have been seven contests for Republican floor leader. In all but the 1971 contest in which incumbent Hugh Scott of Pennsylvania defeated Howard Baker of Tennessee, the floor leader battles have occurred when that post was open. Unlike House Republicans, Senate Republicans seem not to challenge or overthrow their leaders.

The most hotly contested battle among Republicans took place in 1984 when a five-way race to replace retiring Floor Leader Howard Baker took five ballots to resolve. Kansas Senator Robert Dole eventually won over the Assistant Floor Leader Ted Stevens of Alaska.

### Selections for Other Senate Offices

Since 1913 Senate Democrats have continuously identified and filled the position of party whip. Senate Republicans filled the post from 1915 to 1935 and have continuously done so since 1944. The nine-year hiatus in the Roosevelt years occurred when Senate Republicans were too few in number to warrant a whip. The Senate Republicans changed the name of the office from "whip" to "assistant floor leader" in 1969.

Both parties have had vigorous contests for party whip, the second post in the Senate structure. Louisiana's Russell Long defeated John Pastore of Rhode Island in 1965 and was himself defeated by Edward M. Kennedy of Massachusetts in 1969. Kennedy, the youngest brother of the slain President, was elected a few months after his surviving brother, Senator Robert

Kennedy of New York, was assassinated in Los Angeles in 1968. In the aftermath of his own personal problems, Senator Kennedy was to lose this post in 1971 to Senator Robert Byrd of West Virginia.

For many years Republicans in the Senate used the position of whip to balance the floor leadership between the party's eastern moderates and the midwestern conservatives. As this conflict faded and the party became more uniformly conservative, contests depended less on philosophy and more on personal followings.

The Senate Republicans reorganized their leadership system in 1944 after the death of their longtime leader and 1940 vice presidential candidate, Charles McNary of Oregon, into a six-member hierarchy—floor leader, whip, chairman, and secretary of the Republican conference, and chairs of the policy and campaign committees. Not only did they reactivate the whip, but they limited leaders to only one position.

All of the Republican posts must be achieved through open competition. The Senate Republicans have had 27 open contests from 1949 to 1984, while Senate Democrats have had only 6 in the same period.

*Summary*

Each of the four "congressional parties" has evolved a different leadership selection system. The House Democrats, the most successful of the modern congressional parties, developed a selection system that permitted their large and highly variegated majorities to thrive as a semi-united legislative force without surrendering the extraordinary diversity that has had so much to do with Democrats winning most of the congressional elections in this country. It is a closed hierarchical system with limited competition, but it produces a short, highly selective list of leaders with widespread support in the House. By contrast, the House Republicans have a high degree of open competition for their posts, a feature that sometimes extends to overthrowing its leadership. It is the most competitive of the congressional parties. Senate Democrats have been the most quiescent. Centralizing as many as four different posts in the position of the Democratic floor leader has limited competition, and the lesser role of party loyalty in the Senate has minimized threats to existing leaders. Senate Republicans only challenged for the leadership in the years since 1949. Contests abound among the Senate's Republicans, but they appear to be more related to candidate popularity than to underlying conflicts within the party. As political circumstances change and shifts occur among the congressional parties, so too will their leadership selection systems.

*See also:* John Adams, Nelson Aldrich, Howard Baker, Robert Byrd, John C. Calhoun, Joseph Cannon, Henry Clay, Robert Dole, Tom Foley, Thomas Jefferson, George Mitchell, Speaker of the House, James Wright

*Garrison Nelson*

*REFERENCES*

Browne, Lynne P., and Robert L. Peabody. 1987. "Patterns of Succession in the House Democratic Leadership: The Choices of Wright, Foley, Coelho, 1986." Paper presented at the Annual Meeting of the American Political Science Association.

Canon, David T. 1989. "The Institutionalization of Leadership in the United States Congress." 14 *Legislative Studies Quarterly* 415.

Nelson, Garrison. 1976. "Leadership Position-Holding in the United States House of Representatives." *Capitol Studies.*

———. 1977. "Partisan Patterns of House Leadership Change, 1789–1977." 71 *American Political Science Review* 918.

———. 1985. "Leadership Selection in the U.S. Senate, 1899–1985: Changing Patterns of Recruitment and Institutional Interactions." Paper presented to the Annual Meeting of the American Political Science Association.

Oleszek, Walter J. 1985. *History and Development of the Party Whip System in the U.S. Senate.* Senate Doc. 98–45. Washington: U.S. Government Printing Office.

Peabody, Robert L. 1976. *Leadership in Congress: Stability, Succession and Change.* Boston: Little, Brown.

Riddick, Floyd M. 1985. *Majority and Minority Leaders of the Senate: History and Development of the Offices of the Floor Leaders.* Senate Doc. 99–3. Washington: U.S. Government Printing Office.

Ripley, Randall B. 1967. *Party Leaders in the House of Representatives.* Washington: Brookings.

Rothman, David B. 1966. *Politics and Power: The United States Senate, 1869–1901.* Cambridge: Harvard U. Pr.

Wilson, Woodrow. 1883. *Congressional Government: A Study in American Politics.* Boston: Houghton Mifflin.

## Party Lever in the Voting Booth

The problem of agreement on the best methods for voting are as old as the ancient Greek practice of casting little balls to express public choices. Before adoption of the Australian ballot (one ballot per person, printed at public expense, with choice among candidates and option for ticket splitting) by Massachusetts in 1888, voting was a partisan function involving limited voter choices, universal straight-ticket voting, intimidation, and sometimes even violence.

Voting machines were introduced in the twentieth century as a reform measure designed to ensure secrecy, to prevent ballot stuffing, to stop dishonest ballot counts, and to speed the process of voting and counting. Because voting is primarily a state responsibility, substantial variations exist in the ways that candidates are selected and presented to voters. In the Indiana system, under party names or symbols all candidates of various parties are listed in separate columns. Voters may mark a single spot at the top of a column to vote the whole party ticket or to make choices among candidates from various parties. The party lever on a voting machine mechanizes this process by means of a single party lever for individual candidates. The Massachusetts method lists all candidates irrespective of party labels in groups related to particular offices. Under this method voters have no option for straight-ticket or single-party voting, although they can seek out and vote for all candidates from the same party.

Little solid research or evidence shows how various state voting systems influence voting behavior, but a variety of assumptions and rights associated with each system has attracted strong advocates for both preservation and reform. Equally interesting appears to be the lack of logical pattern or explanation as to why particular states have one system rather than another. For example, straight-party ticket and nonpartisan systems are distributed randomly throughout the United States, except that straight-party ticket systems do not exist in the West.

Because the Indiana party-column method and the party lever facilitate straight-ticket voting, political scientists, party leaders, and candidates assume that this method compels blind, irrational voting behavior in which the best candidates suffer a disadvantage. This disadvantage is especially egregious if they are running for lower office, are at the end of the column, and are in the minority party. Defenders of straight-ticket voting argue that the two-party system is inherent in American democracy and the party lever facilitates this tradition. The party lever supposedly encourages collective party responsibility, discourages political fragmentation, disadvantages influential PAC candidates, provides appropriate guidance to voters confronted with a complicated mechanism, encourages high voter turnout, and speeds the voting process. Those against the party lever tend to be those unfriendly toward party gov-

ernment. They maintain that removal of the lever is consistent with the evolution of American democracy, that voters should be encouraged to seek out candidates based on their qualifications and records rather than on party labels, that removal of the lever would make elected officials more responsible, and that voters would be encouraged to be better informed before casting their ballots.

Connecticut is often cited for its reliance on the party lever. Before ratification of its 1965 constitution, Connecticut used a mandatory party lever in all elections, meaning that voters had to pull a party lever to initiate the voting process. For the next 20 years, Connecticut had an optional party lever. In 1985 Connecticut voters approved a constitutional amendment prohibiting the party lever in any state or local election. Studies of the consequences of this change are inconclusive. While some evidence points to a decline in voter turnout, to voter confusion in selecting candidates, and to delays in voting, little evidence either supports the advocates of the party lever, who tend to be Democratic, or the proponents of removal of the lever, who tend to be Republican. Nevertheless, voting specialists and professional politicians generally agree that the party lever on voting machines will soon be an election artifact more suitable for a museum than a polling center. In 1988 only 3 states among the 17 with optional straight-party voting systems used the party lever, and in none of these states was a party lever a mandatory function to initiate the voting process. Since no company manufactures the old Connecticut one-party lever machine, and since a variety of computerized machines with centralized tallying are available, few party-lever, straight-ticket voting machines will be in operation beyond the 1990s.

See also: Australian Ballot, Split-Ticket Voting

*Clyde D. McKee, Jr.*

REFERENCES

Calvert, Randall L., and John A. Ferejohn. 1983. "Coattail Voting in Recent Presidential Elections." 77 *American Political Science Review* 407.

Rusk, Jerrold G. 1970. "Effect of Australian Ballot Reform on Split-Ticket Voting 1876–1900." 64 *American Political Science Review* 1220.

## Party Organization in Historical Perspective

For much of American history, the subject of parties has meant, first of all, a distinctive American brand of patronage-based party organization. These structures have caught the eyes of observers and provoked hypotheses about relations among the public, parties, government, and policy. Thus, for example, the classic *American Commonwealth* by James Bryce (1888), *Democracy and the Organization of Political Parties* by Moisei Ostrogorski (1902), D. W. Brogan's *The American Political System* (1933), and E. E. Schattschneider's *Party Government* (1942).

Such structures have flourished at all three levels of government, though at different times. State-level organizations grew throughout the nineteenth century and peaked, in general, around 1900. At the federal level the leading decades were the 1830s through the 1880s. Local organizations, including city machines, grew in importance during the last half of the nineteenth century and stood up remarkably well during the first half of the twentieth. They were still thriving in the 1960s. Relations among the three levels have to be kept in mind. Patronage and influence have flowed among them as a matter of routine; furthermore, organizations at one level have sometimes been shaped or generated by entrepreneurs from another.

At the local level, political organizations like these lasted into a time when hundreds of scholars became available to take a close look at them. Numerous works from the 1950s and 1960s are especially useful. They permit a good fix on the geography of local patronage-based organizations as of the late 1960s, after which came a steep downhill slide in their fortunes. (See David Mayhew, *Placing Parties in American Politics* [1986] for a bibliographic essay on the subject; this work also tracks the geographic incidence-cum-prominence of such local organizations, as of the late 1960s, through application of a definition of "traditional party organization" [TPO].)

A "traditional party organization" has the following properties: (1) It has substantial autonomy. That is, its existence does not depend on the incentive structure of an organization operating mostly outside electoral politics (e.g., a union or a private corporation). The TPO might get resources from nonlocal levels of government, but it can operate as a substantially independent power base in dealing with such other levels. (2) The TPO lasts over decades or generations rather than over months or years. It can survive leadership changes. (3) Its internal structure has an important element of hierarchy. In fact, it is apt to be known by its leader's name, as in the case of Chicago's Daley organization or Albany's O'Connell organization. (4)

The TPO regularly tries to nominate candidates for a wide range of public offices, ordinarily including state assembly, state senate, and local or municipal offices, and sometimes judgeships and congressional and statewide offices. A TPO routinely tries to nominate convention or primary slates. (This definitional move excludes, from the TPO rubric, incumbent officials who use job patronage to their own end but do not impinge on nominating for other offices. They run their own shows, which come to an end when they leave office. Some mayors of Boston and Denver offer good instances, as do county commissioners' positions in Oklahoma.) (5) A TPO relies substantially on "material" incentives and not much on "purposive" incentives to get people to work for or to support the organization. Particularistic awards of jobs, contracts, tax abatements, statutory variances, among other things, amount to a distinctive political currency. Job patronage, in particular, in exchange for election work, makes possible the organizational hierarchy that in turn permits control of nominations.

Finally, for later purposes here, a "machine" can be said to be a "traditional party organization" that is able to exercise overall control over government at a city or county level. Not all TPOs have enjoyed that success. Some, for example, have been successful only in city wards or have channeled candidates into some public offices but not into mayoralties.

Given this five-pronged definition, thirteen states supported arrays of strong "traditional party organizations" as late as the 1960s: Rhode Island and Connecticut in southern New England; New York, New Jersey, Pennsylvania, Maryland, and Delaware (for which the evidence is notably scanty) in the Middle Atlantic area; Ohio, Indiana, and Illinois in the southern Midwest; and the noncoastal Border States of West Virginia, Kentucky, and Missouri. The pattern is substantially specific to each state. That is, all other sorts of variables held equal, knowing that a "traditional party organization" occurs somewhere locally in a state helps to predict whether it will turn up elsewhere in the same state—in urban, suburban, or rural areas. In Maryland, West Virginia, Kentucky, Missouri, and Indiana, TPOs have commonly taken a "factional" form. That is, local politics has featured competition for office and its effects between two or more TPOs operating in the same party in the same city or county. Places sustaining such factional-TPO politics have included

Jackson County (Kansas City), Missouri; Jefferson County (Louisville), Kentucky; Vanderburgh County (Evansville), Indiana; Kanawha County (Charleston), West Virginia; the city of Baltimore; and rural Queen Annes County in Maryland.

Outside these 13 states, "traditional party organizations" were, as of the 1960s, rare, weak, nonexistent, or at least quite recessive in the politics of their states. The other TPO outcroppings worth mentioning, mostly rural, appeared in Hispanic New Mexico, Mexican-American southern Texas, Francophone southern Louisiana (including the wards of New Orleans), and the southern Appalachian chain.

What accounts for this geographic pattern of the 1960s? Certainly not "regionalism" in any simple sense. The 13 prime TPO states do not constitute a "northeastern" or a "northeastern quadrant" bloc. Massachusetts, northern New England, Michigan, Wisconsin, and Minnesota showed no trace of such organizations in the 1960s. Relative size of immigrant populations offers little help. All of the states just named, and also New Hampshire, drew relatively more late-wave immigrants than any of the Border States or, for that matter, Ohio, Indiana, or Illinois. Relative size of urban population helps somewhat, not surprisingly, at least if all 50 states are taken as a comparison. But West Virginia, Kentucky, and Indiana are really not very urban.

History, going back at least two centuries, seems a better bet than cross-sectional analysis for explaining this late-1960s organizational map. Strikingly, on the one hand, all 13 "organization states" grew into polities early enough to win statehood by 1821 (West Virginia as part of its parent state). This date was well before statehood came for Michigan, Wisconsin, Florida, or California, to give some geographically scattered examples. Nearly a necessary condition, though hardly a sufficient one, it seems, for TPO politics to have existed in a state in the 1960s is some set of factors associated with the state before 1821 or their resonance since. "Nearly," because the Hispanic- or Mexican-background areas of Texas or New Mexico are not parts of pre-1822 states, though the U.S. electoral politics of both does date to the 1840s or 1850s. "Hardly a sufficient one" because even though seven of the original states appear on the list of 1960s organization states, six do not: New Hampshire and Massachusetts to the north of the contiguous bloc of such states, and Vir-

ginia, North Carolina (some mountain-area outcroppings notwithstanding), South Carolina, and Georgia to the south.

Tracing the historical background of modern party organization is not easy, since most of the considerable recent scholarship on party history has dealt with voter cleavages rather than party structure. The work that addresses structure, moreover, has only sometimes looked into institutional-maintenance features, patronage-based or otherwise. But enough pertinent work now exists to make possible a broad outline of the rise, incidence, and fortunes of patronage-based organization over the last two centuries or so. The story wends its way among local, state, and national levels of government, and it points to the antecedents, at least, of the 1960s geographic pattern of organization. The strict 1960s definition of "traditional party organization" need not be imposed beyond its time or (local) level, but the earlier lines of party structure to be discussed here follow more or less the same logic. Particularistic goods or favors produce organization hierarchy, which in turn allows influence over nominations and of public offices that generate goods and favors.

No one doubts that, on the East Coast, the modern New England (or Massachusetts, at least) versus Middle Atlantic versus southern Atlantic pattern of party organization has deep eighteenth-century roots. New York, New Jersey, and Pennsylvania, according to recent accounts, stood out as colonies and then as revolutionary-era states for their ethnic, religious, and economic heterogeneity. They generated exceptional conflict. These states had no dominant socioeconomic hierarchies, as was notably the case in Massachusetts, Virginia, and South Carolina, that could handle political matters relatively harmoniously and ward off a polarizing mobilization of the public. In the Middle Atlantic area, deference politics broke down. Professional political management, competing tickets of candidates, and statewide campaigns seem to have set in as standard features of politics by 1789. The three core Middle Atlantic States seem to have set the pace. But Rhode Island also was riven by a vigorous, mobilizing, two-sided factional politics throughout much of the middle and late eighteenth century. Delaware held excited and violent elections. And Maryland conducted statewide campaigns and pioneered in electioneering practices such as parades, speeches, and rallies.

The Middle Atlantic area developed in these early years some distinctive elite-level political practices. Was it generating a distinctive "political culture"? Not necessarily, if that term is taken to mean attitudes ingrained in the minds of the general population about how politics should be conducted. Only the elite-level practices can be documented. Still, these practices may be the whole story, or most of it, in the eighteenth century and later. Individual-level phenomena (e.g., the political outlook of the typical Pennsylvania German or Quaker) did not bring about political practices; the causative factors were evidently society-level phenomena (i.e., societal heterogeneity and the lack of a more or less unified ruling social hierarchy). And elite political practices once in place could be very tenacious.

Scholarship covering the period just after 1800 pins down another development in the Middle Atlantic area. State-centered spoils systems, tied to the organizational needs of electioneering, became prominent in the contemporary political universe. Evidence of spoils is especially good for New York and New Jersey, though Pennsylvania evidently had about the same. In these states at this time, electoral contesting took place between preparty "factions" rather than what are now called "parties." But to dwell on the distinction would probably be a mistake. Doing so can obscure the relatively seamless evolution of political practices from the eighteenth century into the nineteenth.

From here, the politics of the Middle Atlantic area progressed into the distinctively organization-centered mode, with a larger popular base than earlier, described by Richard P. McCormick in *The Second American Party System* (1973) for the Jacksonian period. (On New Jersey, see Levine 1974.) In New York, through something of a Darwinian process, Martin Van Buren's state-level Albany Regency moved to the fore first as a leading faction and then as a party in the 1820s and 1830s. It is the classic archetypal instance of a disciplined, job-awarding, electioneering enterprise. Thurlow Weed's Whig organization emerged in New York in the late 1830s as a carbon copy.

Organizations at lower levels show different patterns. When we think of twentieth-century parties in New York, New Jersey, Pennsylvania, and Maryland, we think at least of their distinctively powerful county organizations. Not much work has been done on the origins of these states' county systems, but what there is

suggests that their foundations were laid in the decades before the Civil War as state governments spun off powers and allocational authority to local governmental units, as happened in Maryland, for example, in the 1850s. New York City and Philadelphia, the two American municipalities with the longest continuous histories of city- or ward-level organizations based substantially on patronage, evidently had installed those institutions by Jacksonian times.

Parties, of course, along with some sorts of attendant mobilizing mechanisms, grew to prominence throughout most of the country during the Jacksonian period. But outside the Middle Atlantic area writ large, almost no state-, county-, city-, or ward-level party organization comes to light that had the hierarchy, discipline, material incentive structure, durability, and overall influence of the Albany Regency or early Tammany Hall. The chief exception seems to be New Hampshire's Hill Regency of the 1830s, which had much in common with the Albany organization, except its staying power; we do not know that the Hills outlived the friendly national administrations of the 1830s or had recognizable progeny. Massachusetts notably resisted a full-blown spoils system in pre-Jacksonian times, and in Ronald Formisano's recent treatment (1983) of that state's parties of the Jacksonian era, Albany Regency–like structures are notable for their absence.

Historians would pay less attention to Martin Van Buren's Albany Regency had it not played a leading role in two moves of national importance in the 1820s and 1830s. The first was to present a resonant ideological justification for building parties as disciplined, patronage-based organizations. In effect, new Jacksonian ideas were grafted onto old practices. An apparatus of such considerable substance, it was argued, could serve as a democratic battering ram against the socioeconomic privilege that controlled the political sector. And a spoils system, interpreted as the rotation-in-office principle, could embody the democratic statement that anybody is good enough to hold an appointive job.

The second move was the "Middle Atlanticization," more or less, of American national politics through the incorporation of the political practices of fast-growing New York and Pennsylvania into the federal parties and government. From the 1830s through the 1870s, after which came a tailing off, the Jacksonian Democrats, the Whigs, and then the Republicans built and tended nationally centered party organizations that drew considerable strength from the use of federal job patronage. Post offices and customhouses, in particular, served as nodes of party activity down in the cities and states.

Organization during this time commonly took the form of intraparty factions, rather than a leadership apparatus that enjoyed unified control of a party at some level of government. Such factions typically drew resources from, and operated at, federal levels but also at lower levels. By the 1870s, U.S. Senators had moved into the role of chief dispensers of federal patronage. Financial assessments of federal employees as well as kickbacks from private contractors (notably mail carriers) and duty payers (notably the liquor trade) brought the party in power considerable income for electioneering purposes. This particularistic fundraising, in contrast to the corporate financing that came later, may have allowed the parties to be relatively independent of broader societal interests. Federal patronage politics seems to have reached a high tide in the Stalwart Republican coalition of the 1870s that flourished under President Ulysses Grant. Its bases were the southern and Border State parties plus New York, Pennsylvania, and Illinois—"the home states of the three most prominent Republican machine politicians."

All three nineteenth-century American mass parties—the Jacksonian Democratic, Whig, and Republican—are instances of "internally mobilized" as opposed to "externally mobilized" parties. They took shape at times when their leaders held positions of governmental authority in a combination of federal (e.g., the Republicans after 1860) and state holdings (e.g., all three parties had strong bases in New York). A further condition, a lack of institutionalized bureaucracies, permitted the particularistic use of government resources to build patronage-based organizations. As a general proposition, these are evidently the circumstances in which such organizations are likely to arise.

J. G. A. Pocock has noted the irony that Americans waged a revolution against a patronage-based "connections" regime in the eighteenth century, the English system shaped by Walpole, only to build one themselves in the next century when the English were getting rid of theirs. The American system, however, in accord with federalism, remained relatively decentralized. And the strong civic base of the American regime probably put a limit on how much politics could hinge on material-incentive transactions. "Reform" grew as a tradition

too. At presidential nominating conventions, parties ordinarily found it wise, for electoral reasons, to nominate blue-ribbon candidates. Consequently no national "boss" arose. And the system's national-cum-state party factions bolstered by patronage ties commonly had identifying policy tendencies as well.

During and after Jackson's presidency the new patronage-oriented style of the national parties intruded downward into states where before it had been unimportant or absent. One of the interesting stories of the nineteenth century is the extent to which this intrusion, in some places at least, was resisted. In post-Civil War Massachusetts, Benjamin F. Butler drew on federal patronage to build a considerable organization in the Republican Party. But unlike comparable entrepreneurs in, say, Pennsylvania and Illinois, Butler failed to build a dominant, patronage-based state organization. No such organization was ever built. Massachusetts's influential Brahmin class of Republicans joined ranks to close Butler out. The elite remained committed to an idealistically individualistic style of politics that shied away from disciplined organization and featured, though the term sounds musty in 1870s Massachusetts, deference.

As in Massachusetts, so in the South. Democratic party elites in the South Atlantic and Gulf Coast states (but not in Maryland, Kentucky, and Tennessee) balked at the rotation-in-office principle of the Washington-centered spoils system. They largely stayed clear of the game from Jackson's presidency through Buchanan's. Particularly in the Carolinas and Virginia, elite gentries, expressing a republican ethic of individual public service, dominated politics until the Civil War. By New York standards, southern party organizations remained despised and underdeveloped.

Even if Whigs and Democrats competed closely at the state level, the picture below could be rather different. In North Carolina, relations of deference to notables built up large, safe majorities for one party or the other even at the county level. Alabama's Whigs, in their Black Belt strongholds of the 1840s, nominated candidates in direct primaries rather than in convention-generated slates. Alabama's hill-country Democrats ran against one another in considerable numbers in general elections in the 1840s just as they were running against one another in Democratic primaries a century later. All in all, the mechanism of spoils and slating seems to have failed to "take" at the local level in the coastal South even when Whigs rivaled Democrats at the state level. Political scientists err in so easily crediting the idiosyncratic structure of the South's parties to Democratic one-party dominance that grew in the late nineteenth century.

Especially in the southern Atlantic states, political elites kept up their resistance during and after Reconstruction, which was, among other things, an effort by Republicans to graft a national party style onto the South. In reaction, a *political* ethos as well as simply race or economics animated the defeated elites of Virginia and the Carolinas. Virtue—as measured by wealth, position, education, character, and manners—was supposed to prevail in politics, and in certain areas it did. The Democratic gentries of North Carolina and Virginia fought 30-year battles against the intrusion of ordinary, popular, mobilizing, patronage-based American parties, and around 1900 they won. In both cases, though more strikingly in Virginia, the result in the twentieth century was a distinctive kind of strong state Democratic Party organization that fended off the outside world and preserved local relations of deference through low suffrage. Progressivism, in these two states, is hard to disentangle from gentry restoration.

The trajectory differed in South Carolina, where deference politics attracted the opposition of turn-of-the-century "demagogues" like "Pitchfork Ben" Tillman (who assaulted the "aristocratic oligarchy") and Cole Blease. Much of the rest of the deep South generated similar figures sooner or later. But the particularly revealing analogy is Massachusetts, a New England state that produced instructive counterparts to Tillman and Blease in the versatile Benjamin F. Butler (who orated as well as organized) and later the "Brahmin Baiter" James Michael Curley. These were distinctive one-man oppositions that arose to oppose deference-politics regimes surviving well beyond the age of Jackson. But at this time in these environments, hierarchical, patronage-based parties could not easily be built. Massachusetts, like the Deep South, carried into the twentieth century an individualistic style of politics in which politicians seek and hold office on their own rather than as agents of disciplined party organizations. Boston had some influential ward organizations around the turn of the century, and Curley's later mayoralties were corrupt, but no Tammany-style organization has ever succeeded in dominating Boston or, so far as one can tell, any other sizable Massachusetts city.

As the federal government's material nourishment of the parties fell off after the 1870s, corporate money partly took up the slack, and organizational strength shifted downward to the states and cities. United States Senators, who until 1913 still needed the votes of state legislators to get elected, assembled and headed most of the exceptionally strong state party organizations that operated around 1900. New York, Pennsylvania, and Maryland—continuing the Middle Atlantic tradition—set the standard with their authoritative, material-incentive-based, statewide organizations that incorporated powerful city and county units and could ordinarily control state nominations and command state legislative majorities. Private corporations, in this region, normally played the roles of allies and something like equals. City or county machines figured importantly in the state party systems, united or faction based, of New Jersey, Ohio, Indiana, and Illinois. In general, outside the Middle Atlantic region and the Ohio Valley, strong turn-of-the-century state party organizations were extensions of private business—as in North Dakota, or in Michigan and Wisconsin that lacked dominant city machines in Detroit or Milwaukee to serve as organization bases. California and New Hampshire went further yet: railroad companies, not parties, quite directly organized the chief political hierarchies at the state level (e.g., in nominating conventions). Elsewhere, particularly in most of the South, no sort of party or party-like organization managed to dominate state electoral politics during the early years of the twentieth century.

At the local level, as these instances suggest, a geographic pattern of party organization had coalesced by 1900, one that resembled the later "traditional party organization" map of the 1960s. In general, significant material-incentive-driven organizations operated at ward, city, or county levels in the Middle Atlantic area and in the older states of the Ohio and Mississippi valleys—particularly in old sea and river ports. West of the Appalachians, Cincinnati, Indianapolis, Louisville, and New Orleans are examples, as are Chicago and Kansas City (Mo.). Not much is known about the pre-Civil War roots of such organizations west of Pennsylvania, but by about 1900 they emerge clearly in the records. Organizations arose, or would later arise, in many of the newer northern industrial cities of the older Ohio Valley states (e.g., in Cleveland, Toledo, South Bend, and Gary) but not, evidently, in similar new industrial cities a tier farther north (e.g., in Kenosha, Racine, or Grand Rapids) or at least such organizations would have less strength and durability farther north. It is true that TPOs flourished around 1900 in a few places where all traces of them would be gone by 1950 (e.g., in San Francisco and in some of the wards of Omaha and Boston). But in general the 1900 map looks like the 1960s map.

"Reform," of course, infused cities all over the country after 1900, but reform could occur and widely did without a city "machine" as an incumbent enemy. Often the target instead was, to use a distinction advanced by Raymond Wolfinger, "machine politics," or particularistic exchange relations without any party organization in the picture. In Milwaukee and Detroit, for example, private utilities and the liquor industry nickel-and-dimed individual city councilors whatever their party. Reform like this also occurred, to cite some well-documented instances, in Galveston, Beaumont, and Grand Rapids.

Most of the powerful state party organizations fell victim to Progressive reform, but city machines, surprisingly, had more of a future than a past in 1900. For one thing, *factional* party organizations, which had been the norm at the city level in the nineteenth century, gave way starting around 1900 to *unified* party organizations. Some of these were powerful enough to amount to machines, and they certainly became statistically more common. Tammany Hall, to give an example, was not able to consolidate its control over the Manhattan Democratic Party—putting down other nonreform factions—until 1890. Similar consolidations evidently occurred around 1900 in Philadelphia and New Orleans. And the geographic domain of material-incentive-based urban organization would shrink very little during the first half of the twentieth century, even as the factional variant gave way to the unified variant. Hence, most of the strong, memorable American city machines—Jersey City, Memphis, New Orleans, Kansas City, Albany, Gary, Providence, and Chicago—have been largely or entirely twentieth-century creations. The city machines of the Democratic Party were to lead an important late life as elements of ruling national coalitions under Franklin Roosevelt, Harry Truman, John F. Kennedy, and Lyndon Johnson. The most prominent of the last considerable array of ma-

terial-incentive-based organizations was, of course, Chicago's Daley machine of the 1950s and 1960s.

At local, state, or national levels, what are the overall effects of having parties based substantially on material incentives? In the American case, three arguments are often presented. First, leaders have thereby often built the significant support needed to govern fractious and heterogeneous populations. This is an argument about aggregation of coalitions. It has figured, for example, in interpretations of Lincoln's rule during the Civil War and the Democratic machine's control over Chicago. Second, since one, albeit not the only, alternative to "material" incentives in politics is "purposive" incentives some argue that issues, ideologies, and causes have played a less significant role in American material-incentive-driven environments than they perhaps otherwise would have. City machines, for example, have been relatively uninterested in issues. Third, other analysts maintain that patronage politics has delayed or diminished the growth of American governmental programs and, in general, the state. The long-term effect of patronage, stemming mostly from nineteenth-century political experience but echoing well beyond that, has been to undermine public belief in the administrative capacity of government, and to stave off or delay the growth of European-style bureaucracies that have their own expansionary dynamic.

*See also:* James Buchanan, Benjamin F. Butler, James Michael Curley, Richard Daley, Ulysses S. Grant, Jacksonian Democracy, Abraham Lincoln, Political Patronage, Reconstruction, Tammany Hall, Ben Tillman, Martin Van Buren, Thurlow Weed

*David R. Mayhew*

REFERENCES

Abrams, Richard M. 1964. *Conservatism in a Progressive Era: Massachusetts Politics, 1900–1912.* Cambridge: Harvard U. Pr.

Baker, Jean H. 1973. *The Politics of Continuity: Maryland Political Parties from 1858 to 1870.* Baltimore: Johns Hopkins U. Pr.

Banfield, Edward C. 1961. *Political Influence: A New Theory of Urban Politics.* New York: Free Press.

Barnes, Brooks M. 1981. "The Congressional Elections of 1882 on the Eastern Shore of Virginia." 89 *Virginia Magazine of History and Biography* 467.

Barnes, Samuel H., and Giacomo Sani. 1974. "Mediterranean Political Culture and Italian Politics: An Interpretation." 4 *British Journal of Political Science* 289.

Benedict, Michael Les. 1985. "Factionalism and Representation: Some Insight from the Nineteenth-Century United States." 9 *Social Science History* 361.

Bonomi, Patricia U. 1973. "The Middle Colonies: Embryo of the New Political Order." In Alden T.

Vaughan and George A. Billias, eds. *Perspectives on Early American History*. New York: Harper & Row.

Bourke, Paul F., and Donald A. DeBats. 1978. "Identifiable Voting in Nineteenth-Century America: Toward a Comparison of Britain and the United States Before the Secret Ballot." 11 *Perspectives in American History* 259.

Brogan, D. W. 1933. *The American Political System*. London: Hamish Hamilton.

Brown, M. Craig, and Charles N. Halaby. 1987. "Machine Politics in America." 17 *Journal of Interdisciplinary History* 587.

Bryce, James. 1959. *The American Commonwealth*. 2 vols. New York: Putnam's.

Carman, Harry J., and Reinhard H. Luthin. 1943. *Lincoln and the Patronage*. New York: Columbia U. Pr.

Christian, Ralph J. "The Folger-Chatham Congressional Primary of 1946." 53 *North Carolina Historical Review* 25.

Clark, E. Culpepper. 1980. *Francis Warrington Dawson and the Politics of Restoration: South Carolina, 1874–1889*. University: U. of Alabama Pr.

———. 1983. "Pitchfork Ben Tillman and the Emergence of Southern Demagoguery." 69 *Quarterly Journal of Speech* 423.

Cole, Donald B. 1970. *Jacksonian Democracy in New Hampshire, 1800–1851*. Cambridge: Harvard U. Pr.

———. 1984. *Martin Van Buren and the American Political System*. Princeton: Princeton U. Pr.

Cooper, William J., Jr. 1968. *The Conservative Regime: South Carolina, 1877–1890*. Baltimore: Johns Hopkins U. Pr.

Dinkin, Robert J. 1977. *Voting in Provincial America*. Westport, CT: Greenwood.

———. 1982. *Voting in Revolutionary America*. Westport, CT: Greenwood.

Dorsett, Lyle W. 1977. *Franklin D. Roosevelt and the City Bosses*. Port Washington, NY: Kennikat.

Escott, Paul D. 1985. *Many Excellent People: Power and Privilege in North Carolina, 1850–1900*. Chapel Hill: U. of North Carolina Pr.

Ettinger, B. G. 1985. "John Fitzpatrick and the Limits of Working-Class Politics in New Orleans." 26 *Louisiana History* 341.

Fish, Carl Russell. 1905. *The Civil Service and the Patronage*. New York: Longmans, Green.

Formisano, Ronald P. 1983. *The Transformation of Political Culture: Massachusetts Parties, 1790s–1840s*. New York: Oxford U. Pr.

Freehling, William W. 1966. "Spoilsmen and Interests in the Thought and Career of John C. Calhoun." 52 *Journal of American History* 25.

Greenberg, Douglas. 1979. "The Middle Colonies in Recent American Historiography." 36 *William and Mary Quarterly* 396.

Greenberg, Kenneth S. 1985. *Masters and Statesmen: The Political Culture of American Slavery*. Baltimore: Johns Hopkins U. Pr.

Harmond, Richard. 1968. "The 'Beast' in Boston: Benjamin F. Butler as Governor of Massachusetts." 55 *Journal of American History* 266.

Harrison, Robert. 1982. "Blaine and the Camerons: A Study in the Limits of Machine Power." 49 *Pennsylvania History* 157.

Heintzman, Ralph. 1983. "The Political Culture of Quebec, 1840–1960." 16 *Canadian Journal of Political Science* 3.

Isaac, Paul E. 1975. "Municipal Reform in Beaumont, Texas, 1902–1909." 78 *Southwestern Historical Quarterly* 409.

Jaenicke, Douglas W. 1986. "The Jacksonian Integration of Parties into the Constitutional System." 101 *Political Science Quarterly* 85.

Josephson, Matthew. 1938. *The Politicos: 1865–1896*. New York: Harcourt, Brace.

Kass, Alvin. 1965. *Politics in New York State, 1800–1830*. Syracuse: Syracuse U. Pr.

Key, V. O., Jr. 1948. *Politics, Parties, and Pressure Groups*. 2nd ed. New York: Crowell.

———. 1949. *Southern Politics in State and Nation*. New York: Knopf.

Kruman, Marc W. 1983. *Parties and Politics in North Carolina, 1836–1865*. Baton Rouge: Louisiana State U. Pr.

Levine, Peter. 1974. "The Rise of Mass Parties and the Problem of Organization: New Jersey, 1829–1844." 91–92 *New Jersey History* 91.

Luthin, Reinhard H. 1954. *American Demagogues: Twentieth Century*. Boston: Beacon.

Macy, Jesse. 1904. *Party Organization and Machinery*. New York: Century.

Mallam, William D. 1960. "Butlerism in Massachusetts." 33 *New England Quarterly* 186.

Mayhew, David R. 1986. *Placing Parties in American Politics: Organizations, Electoral Settings, and Government Activity in the Twentieth Century*. Princeton: Princeton U. Pr.

Mayo, Edward L. 1979. "Republicanism, Antipartyism, and Jacksonian Party Politics: A View from the Nation's Capital." 31 *American Quarterly* 3.

McCormick, Richard P. 1973. *The Second American Party System: Party Formation in the Jacksonian Era*. New York: Norton.

McKitrick, Eric L. 1967. "Party Politics and the Union and Confederate War Efforts." In William Nisbet Chambers and Walter Dean Burnham, eds. *The American Party Systems: Stages of Political Development*. New York: Oxford U. Pr.

Nelson, William E. 1976. "Officeholding and Powerwielding: An Analysis of the Relationship Between Structure and Style in American Administrative History." 10 *Law and Society Review* 187.

Ostrogorski, Moisei. 1902. *Democracy and the Organization of Political Parties*. Vol. 2. New York: Macmillan.

Perman, Michael. 1984. *The Road to Redemption: Southern Politics, 1869–1879*. Chapel Hill: U. of North Carolina Pr.

Peskin, Allan. 1985. "Who Were the Stalwarts? Who Were Their Rivals? Republican Factions in the Gilded Age." 99 *Political Science Quarterly* 703.

Pocock, J. G. A. 1980. "1776: The Revolution Against Parliament." In J. G. A. Pocock, ed. *Three British*

*Revolutions, 1641, 1688, 1776.* Princeton: Princeton U. Pr.

Prince, Carl E. 1964. "Patronage and a Party Machine: New Jersey Democratic-Republican Activists, 1801–1816." 21 *William and Mary Quarterly* 571.

Pulley, Raymond H. 1968. *Old Virginia Restored: An Interpretation of the Progressive Impulse, 1870–1930.* Charlottesville: U. Pr. of Virginia.

Rice, Bradley R. 1975. "The Galveston Plan of City Government by Commission: The Birth of a Progressive Idea." 78 *Southwestern Historical Quarterly* 365.

Schattschneider, E. E. 1942. *Party Government.* New York: Rinehart.

Shefter, Martin. 1977. "Party and Patronage: Germany, England, and Italy." 7 *Politics and Society* 403.

———. 1978. "The Electoral Foundations of the Political Machine: New York City, 1884–1897." In Joel H. Silbey, et al., eds. *The History of American Electoral Behavior.* Princeton: Princeton U. Pr.

Skowronek, Stephen. 1982. *Building a New American State: The Expansion of National Administrative Capacities, 1877–1920.* New York: Cambridge U. Pr.

Sorauf, Frank J. 1963. *Party and Representation: Legislative Politics in Pennsylvania.* New York: Atheneum.

Stone, Clarence N. 1963. "Bleaseism and the 1912 Election in South Carolina." 40 *North Carolina Historical Review* 54.

Strum, Harvey. 1981. "Property Qualifications and Voting Behavior in New York, 1807–1816." 1 *Journal of the Early Republic* 347.

Summers, Mark W. 1987. *The Plundering Generation: Corruption and the Crisis of the Union, 1849–1861.* New York: Oxford U. Pr.

Tanner, Mary Nelson. 1963. "The Middle Years of the Anthony-Brayton Alliance, or Politics in the Post Office, 1874–1880." 22 *Rhode Island History* 65.

Thompson, Margaret S. 1982. "Ben Butler versus the Brahmins: Patronage and Politics in Early Gilded Age Massachusetts." 55 *New England Quarterly* 163.

Thornton, J. Mills, III. 1978. *Politics and Power in a Slave Society.* Baton Rouge: Louisiana State U. Pr.

Travis, Anthony R. 1974. "Mayor George Ellis: Grand Rapids Political Boss and Progressive Reformer." 58 *Michigan History* 101.

Tregle, Joseph G., Jr. 1960. "The Political Apprenticeship of John Slidell." 26 *Journal of Southern History* 57.

Tunnell, Ted. 1984. *Crucible of Reconstruction: War, Radicalism and Race in Louisiana, 1862–1877.* Baton Rouge: Louisiana State U. Pr.

Van Noppen, Ina Woestemeyer, and John J. Van Noppen. 1973. *Western North Carolina Since the Civil War.* Boone, NC: Appalachian Consortium Press.

Wallace, Michael. 1968. "Changing Concepts of Party in the United States: New York, 1815–1828." 74 *American Historical Review* 453.

Watson, Harry L. 1981. *Jacksonian Politics and Community Conflict: The Emergence of the Second American Party System in Cumberland County, North Carolina.* Baton Rouge: Louisiana State U. Pr.

Wilson, James Q. 1973. *Political Organizations.* New York: Basic Books.

Wolfinger, Raymond E. 1974. *The Politics of Progress.* Englewood Cliffs, NJ: Prentice-Hall.

Wright, James. 1987. *The Progressive Yankees: Republican Reformers in New Hampshire, 1906–1916.* Hanover, NH: U. Pr. of New England.

## Party Organization in Nineteenth-Century America

Political organizations, most of them small scale and relatively undeveloped, appeared in colonial America long before national political parties existed. In many of the original colonies, contested popular elections were frequent enough to need some degree of organization. Candidates often nominated themselves or their friends did it for them, but collective activities to mobilize voters, convince them of what to do, and supervise election day activities, all occurred, in however rudimentary a form. In a strictly local society with relatively few voters, elaborate political organization was unnecessary. What structures there were, therefore, did not reach everywhere or last very long.

At the end of the eighteenth century and in the first third of the nineteenth century, particularly in the years after 1815, all of this informality changed, albeit slowly and at first, spottily. After 1789, a new national political arena established by the Constitution demanded more elaborate mechanisms for nominating major officeholders and to run the business of state and national legislatures fiercely debating alternative public policies. As political parties evolved in the 1790s to meet these responsibilities, organizational development followed. These early political organizations were often dominated by cadres of notables working together in the rarified atmosphere of nonpopular politics to secure a political advantage, a nomination or appointment, or a specific public policy. The characteristic organizational element at this time was the legislative caucus, a small self-created group that operated with minimal reference to the larger population of citizens outside of their numbers. Legislative caucuses set agendas, nominated candidates, and took the lead to shape and direct political activity.

While popular election campaign activities remained a minor key until the 1830s, they too had to be accepted more systematically than before when regular national elections became part of the American political scene after 1789. Nominating candidates became a more public act—the first national convention met in 1808 to nominate Federalist candidates for President and Vice President. A few more followed at the state and local level, but their form was far different from later mass politics conventions, attuned as they were to the elite-dominated past. And so were other election activities in what remained a nondemocratic political system.

After 1815, however, organizations filled out, growing rapidly in response to a new political environment. The number of voters increased as did their active participation in politics at all levels. In response to the growing number of voters and the wider geographic reach of political activity, party leaders constructed a framework to manage electoral politics—from nominations to campaigns to elections themselves. Voters had to be mobilized and managed in an increasingly contentious republic that featured a debate over a range of public policies, frequent elections, and a legislative system of constant activity. A new era of vigorous popular politics had dawned. Politics became more than the maneuvers of elite factions. Most important, despite the American political culture's lingering hostility to them, political parties took deep root on the American landscape and with them, followed many more organizational structures than had ever existed before. Parties articulated what was at stake in the political world, offered voters cues to behavior, staffed the government, and fought to achieve specific policy objectives. Parties espoused certain group values and then protected and promoted them against their enemies.

A quickened organizational imperative accompanied this vast party development. The organizational structures that the parties built were their mechanisms for accomplishing each party's many goals. The parties now grew from occasional and unusual factions into disciplined, wide ranging, complete forms—ones that reached throughout the nation and whose activities were increasingly routinized and repetitive in operation. Given their purpose and function in this environment, political organizations unsurprisingly became a major and characteristic aspect of the American political experience for the rest of the nineteenth century.

### The Chronological Frame

Like the party system itself, fully developed political party organizations did not appear all at once but grew up and spread unevenly over several decades. In the decade between the mid-1820s and mid-1830s, many of the elements that were to characterize effective political organization came into being and were unevenly

established for some immediate electoral purpose. This decade was the incubation period for most of the familiar institutions of political organization that have since come to distinguish the American scene.

Jacksonian Democrats took the lead. Introduced by the great political innovator, Martin Van Buren and his colleagues in New York State, new forms and directions took shape and came to dominate political life. In the 1820s, Van Buren's Albany Regency and New Hampshire Democracy's Concord Cabal were, in the words of Donald Cole, two prototypes "that served as fore-runners of modern political machines." Out of these two also appeared a new breed of professional politician (always male) who applied his managerial skills on an increasingly broad canvas. The emergence of these professional politicians led to the firm establishment of caucuses and conventions, first at the state level and then, in the early 1830s, nationally. Campaign organizations designed to mobilize voters through the activities of networks of party activists followed. American politics now existed as a pyramid with three levels. At the top was the leadership with its plans and ambitions. At the base of the pyramid were the increasing number of voters seeking direction and awaiting stimulation. Filling the space between was the organizational apparatus.

The presidential election of 1840 propelled these institutions most thoroughly onto the national landscape, where they sank deep and permanent roots. The impetus came from the leaders of the Whig Party; they organized a campaign to elect William Henry Harrison to the presidency by dramatizing the issues at stake in colorful and far-reaching ways. They set up caucuses and called conventions, created correspondence committees to coordinate nationwide activities, and built up a vigorous party press to spread the word. As a result, W. N. Chambers maintains that party organization "reached previously unprecedented levels. If the party was not yet a machine, it could muster a political drill that matched or over-matched the uniformed militia of the time. To rally the faithful, win recruits, and mobilize the voters—such was the militia style which the Harrison men brought to near perfection." The Whigs mobilized voters in numbers beyond anything previously known. Concomitantly, the Democrats were not far behind in this "hurrah campaign." Their leading political operative, Amos Kendall, in addition to running the party's electioneering activities, issued his "Address on Political Organization" in 1840; it was a handbook for party workers that was widely distributed, copied, and used.

This time, politics could not turn back. Organizational commitment became the intellectual and behavioral norm on the American political scene. The forms and structures built in the 1830s took root and matured. Close electoral competition in most areas of the country stimulated their growth and permanence. Political organizations, in a variety of sizes and styles, existed everywhere in the country. If organizational form differed from state to state (largely based on the degree of electoral competition between the parties), many common themes linked the organizations together into a whole. Both parties learned from each other, copied each other, and applied their joint lessons widely. Even among the Whigs, some of whom initially expressed hesitancy about and resistance to the new partisan imperatives, the commitment to organization became commonplace in the 1840s.

All of this activity added up to an incomplete but substantial edifice for carrying on the people's political business. The need to mobilize a mass electorate was clear enough. What was now crucial was the realization that in order to gain its specific policy objectives, each party had to pay attention to every part of the system, coordinating and managing contests at every level of politics, on behalf of one's party. Attention to one leader's fortunes at the top of the ticket every four years had to be replaced by constant, repeated concern all of the time for every office if the party wanted to accomplish policy objectives and protect gains already made.

After the 1840s, the existing organizational forms were further elaborated, although little new was added. Each party enjoyed a national reach and carried on its activities with an eye to all local, state, and national electoral prizes. Neither the style nor the structure of party organizations changed very much. The roots planted in the late 1830s and that built up over the next decade provided strong underpinnings for subsequent party campaign activities. The partisan age had established its characteristic way of doing business, a style that was maintained even when disruptive forces emerged to affect the political scene in the 1850s. The 1860s and 1870s continued this pattern. They were not innovative years; rather they were the decades of the political organization's most mature phase, when they ran at maximum effectiveness.

In this era right after the Civil War, the great state and national party bosses, leading massive political organizations, thoroughly dominated the playing fields of American politics.

*Shape, Structure, and Function*

The purposes of political organizations were clear enough to nineteenth-century Americans: to impose order on the political system; discipline its constituent elements; and prepare, direct, and promote all electoral, legislative, and administrative activities. The recruitment of candidates, the mobilization of voters, and the management of activities at every level had to be implemented. It was generally recognized that spontaneity in politics was no longer enough. As George Luetscher wrote, "when large bodies of men are drawn out to act [for some common purpose], their action cannot be effectual without organization and discipline. Ten men may perform a common work without formal regulations, but ten thousand cannot act without regular leaders and subordination." Therefore, another wrote, "party organization is as necessary to the success of principles as truth is to their usefulness and vitality."

Organizations of this kind were tripartite in location (local, state, and national), pyramidical in structure (consisting of hundreds of committees and conventions from the grass-roots through the state level to the national convention), and bivariate in approach (expressive and public on the one hand, introspective and hidden on the other). Participatory partisanship stimulated particular kinds of organizations. They were, first of all, deeply imbedded in local communities throughout the country. Political life originated in thousands of towns, rural crossroads, and big-city wards, where the polls were located, where the candidates appeared, and where the citizenry's original attitudes toward public life and policies formed and were expressed. There, as elsewhere, politics was carried on and managed by political organizations. Local structures of similar shape and purpose grew up to handle the party affairs of even a few hundred voters or less.

The centers of gravity of party organization were at the state level for most of our history, certainly until quite recent times. Although national in name and reach, both parties were decentralized, made up of blocs of state organizations, largely self-sufficient and administratively disunified no matter how hard they worked in a common cause. National campaign structures were established for each presidential and congressional election. A Democratic National Committee (first chaired by Benjamin Hallett of Massachusetts) appeared in 1848; the Whigs followed in 1852; the Republicans, under Edwin D. Morgan of New York, in 1856. These national committees were supported by small staffs and a number of campaign and finance committees. But, as Robert Marcus concludes in his study of the Republican organization after the Civil War, "decentralization was fundamental to American political life." State and local parties were "scarcely disturbed from outside" by the national party organizations, which were "the servant of the state parties."

Wherever they were, all political organizations looked the same; all adopted similar structures and behaved in similar ways. At every level of political activity, another pyramidical organizational structure developed. At the point of the apex was each organization's leadership. In the early days, newspaper editors—such as Isaac Hill, Amos Kendall, and Thurlow Weed—often were the main leaders of the organization, sharing power with an emerging class of professional politicians who had become "paid workers like everyone else" in nineteenth-century America. Later in the century, these professional politicians, often holding high government offices, ruled the party structures alone.

These full-time professionals became adept operators of the system through long experience. Their role late in the nineteenth century has been well described by Richard L. McCormick. New York's Boss Thomas Platt

> was a master at managing the hierarchy of party committees and at calling and running harmonious conventions. When the nominations were made, Platt knew how to mold the hundreds of party newspapers into an efficient propaganda machine to send the right Speakers to the right places, and to rouse voters' enthusiasm. On election day his organization spread the campaign fund judiciously, got the Republicans to the polls, and frustrated Democratic attempts at fraud. When Republicans won office, Platt made the most of the patronage their positions brought and strengthened the party for the next election.

State party leaders usually rose through the ranks of the multitiered political organizations they came to head. Platt of New York held in turn practically every position in the committee hierarchy of his own party: chairman of his county committee, national congressional campaign committeeman, chairman of the ex-ecutive committee of the state committee, chairman of the state committee, and national committeeman. During his years of training, he carefully refined the techniques of political management. Their effective application required years of actual experience, which Platt had. In Harold Gosnell's words, he and his colleagues in other states were "the general manager[s] of the organization."

Below Platt and his colleagues in the other states were the local "bosses"—county chairmen usually—who presided over affairs at the local level and who ran their venues with the same attention to detail as the state leaders did. The ballot boxes of American politics were placed in thousands of localities where county, town, ward, and precinct leaders kept close tabs on them. Precinct captains at the base of the pyramid established and maintained the regular face-to-face contacts with the voters who were considered vital to party success. New York State had 4,600 such local organizations, for one example, in the late nineteenth century.

What these men ran were networks of committees and conventions, both usually elected and guided by some form of the representative principle. American political parties tended to be "cadre" institutions, lacking masses of official members, and dependent on volunteers called together by the small group of local and state chairmen and secretaries. Yet, as suggested, the organizations were elaborate and encompassing. In 1840, Abraham Lincoln, one of the Whig Party's organizational mainstays in Illinois, laid out for his colleagues a meticulous plan of party activity from the county down into more local jurisdictions for that year's election. He wrote the following:

The Whig county committees should,

1st. Appoint one person in each county as county captain, and take his pledge to perform promptly all the duties assigned him.

Duties of the County Captain

1st. To procure from the poll-books a separate list for each Precinct of all the names of all those persons who voted the Whig ticket in August.

2nd. To appoint one person in each Precinct as Precinct Captain, and, by a personal interview with him, procure his pledge, to perform promptly all the duties assigned him.

3rd. To deliver to each Precinct Captain the list of names as above, belonging to his Precinct, and also a written list of his duties.

Duties of the Precinct Captain

1st. To divide the list of names delivered him by the county Captain, into Sections of ten who reside most convenient to each other.

2nd. To appoint one person of each Section as Section Captain, and by a personal interview with him, procure his pledge to perform promptly all the duties assigned him.

3rd. To deliver to each Section Captain the list of names belonging to his Section and also a written list of his duties.

Duties of the Section Captain

1st. To see each man of his Section face to face, and procure his pledge that he will for no consideration (impossibilities excepted) stray from the polls on the first Monday in November; and that he will record his vote as early on the day as possible.

2nd. To add to his Section the name of every person in his vicinity who did not vote with us in August, but who will vote with us in the fall, and take the same pledge of him, as from the others.

3rd. To *task* himself to procure at least such additional names to his Section.

The convention system was the centerpiece of political organization in nineteenth-century America. According to Richard P. McCormick, it defined and reflected the party system and its structural contrivances. The convention was "the key device of the new party organization," the organization's "crowning achievement." At first, conventions were little more than ad hoc mass meetings, called together in unsystematic and highly informal ways and attended by anyone inclined to come. Like everything else in the organizational sphere, only slowly did they become regular and powerful, reflect clearly defined rules of representation, and gain the ultimate power to direct and flesh out party organizations. Conventions became working meetings of party managers and political activists called together to nominate candidates and establish the organizational framework for each year's campaign. Here the party's business was carried on.

Conventions were called for every election and held at every level of electoral politics: district, county, state, and national. The local meetings at the town, ward, or precinct level, usually called the primary meetings, began the process that was elaborated at each subsequent level. Held at a convenient community center— a hotel, saloon, or church—they had three purposes. First, they nominated candidates, passed statements of policy, and drafted platforms. Second, they elected delegates to the higher level conventions still to meet. Third, they established the local committee apparatus that ran the campaigns and that also had the responsibility for running the parties' affairs between conventions. Conventions at each succeeding level—county, legislative district, congressional district, and state—repeated the same functions, each in turn. Every four years the whole was capped by the meeting of the national convention where all this political maneuvering came together. The national candidates, McCormick writes, were named and "a sense of unity" and "enthusiasm for a common cause" advanced strikingly.

Conventions came to be understood as having the party's sovereign powers. Their word was the party's law. No other institution of the organizational structure better reflected the theory of party operations or better illustrated the organizational imperatives underlying party activities. The convention system, like the partisan networks themselves, reflected nineteenth-century America's commitment to the norms of delegated democracy: the notion that in each increasingly wide arena of politics, delegates, "fresh from the people," in Andrew Jackson's words, represented the views and acted on behalf of the hundreds and then thousands of party members whom they had been selected to represent. Pyramidical structures—delegated in principle and resting on local primary meetings—expressed the American notion of party organization. Conventions more accurately characterized that notion than did anything else in nineteenth-century American political life.

Of course, the democratic features of a convention were never unalloyed. Party leaders and partisan officeholders, sharing similar values and loyalties to the party organization, dominated the meetings. Convention rules, such as the unit vote that bound everyone rather than allowing for individual expression, gave party leaders a great deal of clout while relegating dissenters to the status of outvoted minorities. Still, democratic regulators did exist. Party leaders in conventions, as elsewhere, were bound by some limits; they did have to consider what the rank and file wanted or would accept. They were never entirely free of some degree of supervision. As one experienced and prominent officeholder put it in 1852, party leaders paid constant "unacknowledged deference to public opinion." Public attitudes directly affected their behavior. They shaped platforms as they selected candidates: to represent the party's claims and reflect the desires of the party's constituent elements.

The point of the nominating and platform-writing phase of the campaign sequence was to provide for the general expression of preference by party members. Then, however, the convention moved into a second, reflective stage; party leaders shaped that expression according to the dictates of the need to solidify their coalition and maximize the party's electoral chances. Conventions first heard, the theory went, the expression of opinion based on interests, personal commitments, or prejudices; and then moved to another level, at which experience, shrewdness, and wisdom tamed the variety of expressions heard. (It is this later, reflective stage that has been extensively weakened in the late twentieth century.) The interaction between expression and reflection, in theory, and to a great extent in practice, gave conventions their central standing, role, and meaning within the parties' organizational structure and the partisan political culture.

Central to all of the convention's activity was the notion of collective discipline. Party leaders sought to impose order and obedience on the collective in pursuit of their common aim. One purpose of organization was to rationalize the procedures for selection of candidates and reduce the effect of internal party factionalism on the outcome of the election. Contentious individualism and group rivalries had to give way to the party's greater claims. As historian James Kehl sums it up, "state bosses were masters of enforcement. They recognized that disagreements must end when the nominee was chosen or [else] the party would face possible defeat at the polls." A common aphorism of mid-nineteenth-century politicians stated their aim well: "Union, harmony, self-sacrifice, everything for the cause, nothing for men."

The party committees appointed at these delegated meetings executed the will of the convention. The New York State Central Committee in the late nineteenth century, for example, was made up of one representative from each congressional district, elected by the state convention delegates from that district. The State Committee oversaw the day-to-day activities of the party in the campaign. Its purpose was voter mobilization. Each party's major goal was to construct those campaign structures that could manage the electoral process most efficiently. Exuberant ratification meetings, frequent rallies, parades, spectacular displays, and heavily attended public meetings were all norms of the campaign months. Behind all of this apparently spontaneous enthusiasm was a wide-ranging panoply of organization and management. Networks of speakers' bureaus and publicity and finance committees appeared. Often elaborate polling of individual voters went on as did constant supervision of all events. Nothing was left to chance.

All of these schemes required people, money, and instruments of expression and direction. State committees raised money in their own states. Often, they also asked the national committee to supplement local funds. They raised the money from both officeholders and well-endowed party supporters. As the century passed, the public arena and government patronage provided an increasing share of party resources through the assessments of each partisan officeholder. Finance committees organized part of this fundraising; local committeemen, as well as the very top leaders, also participated.

Partisan clubs, ethnic and otherwise, from the Tippecanoe Clubs of 1840 to the Republican Wide Awakes to Irish volunteer fire companies, engaged in electioneering activity at every level. Federal and state officeholders—postmasters, census takers, land agents, and others—served as particularly valuable foot soldiers for party organizations, largely because of their ability to distribute newspapers and pamphlets and to seek out and compile lists of voters. Their activities brought the mechanism of party organization directly onto the local scene everywhere in the country. Whereas conventions at every level set the policies and the boundaries of a party's activities, the local agents of the political organization provided the main instrument for directly carrying on party actions. Each campaign season always gave the locals a great deal to do.

Party organization also worked to insure victory. Election day organizational activity capped the whole sequence of events that had been initiated months before by the calls to local conventions. Parties, not the government, largely controlled the electoral apparatus. Each organization provided individual ballots or tickets to voters, got everyone out to the polls, and kept close watch on all matters dealing with the process. A story in the *New Hampshire*

*Statesman*, appearing just before the state elections in 1839, sums up this aspect of organizational activity very well. The election was the following week; the editor wrote,

"ARE YOU READY?"

Is every town properly, thoroughly organized?

How are the committees of vigilance? Are they on the alert?

Are the Whig lists completed, that every town knows its strength?

Are the names of the Whig voters on the check lists?

Are the names of those Tories [i.e., Democrats] who are not entitled to vote, stricken off?

Have arrangements been made to secure the attendance of every man at the polls? Carriages and attendants provided for the aged and infirm?

And, lastly, have the printed votes been received—the Whig votes—in every town?

At the polls, party workers supervised and guided (some said intimidated) eligible citizens to vote the right way. Finally, they saw to the counting of the votes after the polls had closed. Like everything else in the extraordinarily competitive partisan environment of American politics in the nineteenth century, all of these election day activities became even more elaborate and complex as the years passed. They capped each year's efforts and insured a hard won victory (at least for one party).

Linkage among all of these activities was always essential—and carefully seen to. Stump speakers and candidates, editors and legislators, all stayed in constant touch through an extraordinary communications network. Party platforms, drafted in conventions, provided the instructions and cues subsequently disseminated largely by newspapers, the main agency for transmitting party outlooks and strategies. The press transmitted information and exhortation in widening circles to the party committed through exchanges and correspondence between different areas. Before the Civil War, each party maintained a major national publication, situated in Washington, that published a partisan world view and issued directions to officials elsewhere. The Democrats' Washington *Globe* and then the *Union* exemplified these party organs of the 1830s, 1840s, and 1850s. Every state capital also saw the publication of a major newspaper for each party. Weed's Albany *Evening Journal* spread the Whig Party's word in New York State as did the Democratic Richmond *Enquirer* in Virginia. In both the state capitals

and in the national capital, party newspapers benefited from the governments' printing patronage, a boon that allowed them to concentrate on their main (partisan) purpose. Local newspapers in county seats repeating the word, exhorting the faithful, and detailing activities filled out the system. In every election special campaign newspapers appeared, filled with a single-minded devotion to the party's electoral fortunes.

Conditions in the newspaper world changed just before the Civil War, and the creation of the Government Printing Office in Washington in 1861 ended a very direct relationship between newspapers and government patronage. The press now had to depend less on government resources for survival but newspapers still served partisan purposes. Such newspapers as the *New York Tribune,* the *New York Times*, the *Chicago Tribune*, and other major regional dailies came to dominate the scene from the Civil War on; they were still party newspapers, however, espousing a partisan line and feeding it to the faithful in every place they reached. Most editors were not independent of party, nor did they want to be. Some, like Horace Greeley and Whitelaw Reid, ran for office. But their many energies were devoted primarily to communication. They served unstintingly as a major force in the political mobilization of the American voter.

Moreover, organizations issued pamphlets publicizing the party line and compiled campaign handbooks containing a representative sample of speeches, editorials, platforms, and statistics for the political guidance of the faithful. Campaign biographies of presidential candidates appeared early and became routine by mid-century. All of these publications were widely distributed and found their way into stump speeches at every level as well as into local newspapers. Their propaganda gave the faithful a fairly uniform and national picture of the party's outlook and activities. Styles of presentation were exhortative, simplified, vulgarized, and popular. Whatever the guise, the outpouring of printed material performed a major post-convention function in the politically charged atmosphere leading to election day.

All of this mobilization activity was rarely designed to persuade people to vote for a party that they usually did not support. In this extraordinarily partisan age of American politics, from the 1830s to the 1890s, individual and group party loyalty was deep, intense, powerful, and persistent. In this partisan era, strategic options were limited, obvious, and well understood. Party organizations worked primarily to arouse those already committed, unstintingly loyal, intensely partisan members of their own party, most of whom could be counted upon to vote if properly stimulated. Given the closeness of elections, no one could be forgotten. Parties were very unlikely to convert loyalists of the other side. The real problem was thus paramountly organizational—insuring unity and harmony, instilling discipline, and mobilizing the maximum turnout of the already committed. When turnout at the polls reached 90 percent of those eligible, as it did, the fruits of organizational activity were clearly seen.

The final purpose of party organization was to manage the government. Legislative caucuses, as noted, had long been a feature of state and national politics. In the 1820s and 1830s, the widespread introduction of patronage appointments to government offices became another firmly imbedded and characteristic element of the American political scene, bringing the disciplined party outlook directly into every area of government administration. Party leaders determined appointments. The state committeemen in the thirty-four congressional districts in late-nineteenth-century New York State, for example, were the clearinghouse for all federal and state government patronage. Party and government were more than symbolically entwined. The extent of the partisan organization's influence on government is suggested by the fact that several men who made their early reputations largely as soldiers or commanders in various party structures (Martin Van Buren, Abraham Lincoln, Franklin Pierce, Chester Alan Arthur) became Presidents. And no one succeeded in government without the organization's imprimatur.

### Scope and Assessment

Party organizations sometimes did add additional elements to their structures. Urban political machines took shape in large eastern cities from the 1850s onward. By the 1880s, they had developed their characteristic pattern to become the one new element added to political organization after the innovative period of the 1830s and 1840s. Machines functioned for similar purposes and had structures similar to the other parts of the organizational mechanism. Tammany Hall, after all, was the New York County Democratic Committee. Below it, and

other machines like it, was the usual array of precinct and ward committees, with their chairmen, secretaries, and other committeemen. Committee headquarters became less casual, however, as the lease on a few rooms above a tavern or in a storefront during the campaign season was replaced by more permanent arrangements, a base of operations (at every level) that stayed open throughout the year and were manned at least part of every day.

Of course, these urban political machines added new roles to the functions of political organizations. Their basic coin of exchange continued to be elections and patronage. In that, little had changed. Beyond campaign administration and electoral mobilization, however, urban machines played another role as well: they served as ombudsmen and social welfare agencies for their immigrant constituents. As a result, what now existed was a further stage of organizational development but one that was firmly rooted in existing structures and assumptions about parties and organization.

American political organization in its heyday never achieved the ideal model of systematic efficiency, scope, centralization, and permanence. Parties were nowhere near as thorough, systematic, and sustained as many thought necessary. Constant exhortations for some group to get going appeared in state party newspapers and attested to some lack of necessary activity. During campaigns, party organizations took frequent missteps, lacked coordination, and failed to raise enough money, while the various state campaigns did not always fully mesh. On the day after election, as one student has noted, "virtually the entire organizational edifice . . . entered into a mad race of dissolution." Party machinery largely disappeared or went into suspended animation.

On the other hand, importance of this dissolution can be exaggerated. Parties in America, Richard P. McCormick correctly remarks, have been "more heavily burdened with electoral tasks than those of any other democracy." Because elections in America were held so frequently, organizational machinery had almost always to be kept in place. State and local elections preceded the presidential election; not everyone voted on the same day. Few months of the year passed without their quota of elections. One set of party meetings and conventions ended, often to be succeeded quickly by another set for another office. This regularity and ubiquity had significant impact. One of the most repeated of historical cliches attests to the decentralized nature of American party organizations. Yet regular, repetitive, and similar decisions made and activities carried out suggest the existence of a powerful national organizational culture whatever the formal decentralization of activities and ultimate decision-making power.

Some of these organizational forms were expressive and popular: rallies and conventions, for example. Some were not, smoke-filled rooms being a major case in point. All served some purpose in electoral and policy mobilization. As has been noted, all were in theory, and to a degree in actuality, not dictatorially directed from the top but interactive. The notion of cynical bosses, corrupt activities, issueless and watered-down campaigns distinctive only for drama not for substance, permeates much of our understanding of nineteenth-century party organizations. No discussion of party organization can avoid the presence of charges of partisan and frequent political corruption, vote manipulation, bribery, and illicit financial activities for the benefit of individuals and parties. Corruption of this kind was always closely coupled, by unfriendly observers and the losing side, to the existence of party organizations and their activities. Parties were, after all, always looking for an advantage, always in need of money to lubricate their activities.

Some of these charges were true. But the democratic implications of the pyramidical shape of party organizations were not entirely fiction. Parties, led by elites but dependent upon the mass of voters, had to take into account the outlooks and perspectives of the commoners, a political fact that set boundaries on elite control. Organizational norms dictated a process of movement upward from local meetings to evermore central conclaves in a pattern of reciprocal understandings, exchanges, and ideas. Cadres of local leaders at the precinct, town, and county level contributed as much as the statewide boss to the organizational imperatives and the political wisdom shaping the decisions that dominated partisan politics. At the same time, political parties did stand for and espouse different outlooks and policies, did represent different social groups, and did articulate a powerful battle for the soul of America that was not without substance. Finally, the persistent cries of fraud attested more, perhaps, to the abilities and power of party organizations than to the full truth of the charges made. Political losers cried fraud as soon as the polls closed, always blaming avaricious organizational imperatives for the denial of the people's will— that is, a victory for the losing party.

Still, because America's political culture retained powerful antiparty sentiments that have never fully died, partisan organizations were often viewed suspiciously even after parties had been firmly established as the basic centerpieces of American political life. A severe critique of parties, partisanship, and the activities of party organizations intensified with the growth of independence and mugwumpery (as well as appearances of increased corruption) from the 1870s onward. This negativism eventually took hold and took its toll. Major economic and social changes, particularly industrialization and urbanization, also affected attitudes toward parties and their ability to function as they had. Nationwide economic interest groups found parties less responsive to their needs than they wished; urban reformers saw in Tammany Hall and other political machines unacceptable levels of corruption. These perceptions had political impact. The late nineteenth century marked the dawn of a new political era, with significant consequences for the practices of partisan politics. Party organizations came increasingly under state regulation. With the rise of a new kind of political boss (first personified by Ohio Republican Mark Hanna), the full realization of the socioeconomic changes by the 1890s, and the weakening of the era's characteristic electoral competitiveness owing to the voter realignment of 1896, the central thrust of party organization began to change. Political bosses and conventions lost their power, parties were no longer the mainstays of American politics. The golden age of American partisan political organization passed.

*See also:* Chester A. Arthur, Democratic National Committee, Election of 1840, Federalist Party, Benjamin F. Hallet, Marcus A. (Mark) Hanna, Andrew Jackson, Abraham Lincoln, Edwin D. Morgan, Franklin Pierce, Thomas C. Platt, Tammany Hall, Martin Van Buren

*Joel H. Silbey*

REFERENCES

Allen, Howard W., and Kay Warren Allen. 1981. "Vote Fraud and Data Validity." In Jerome M. Clubb, William H. Flanigan, and Nancy H. Zingale, eds. *Analyzing Electoral History: A Guide to the Study of American Voting Behavior.* Beverly Hills, CA: Sage.

Basler, Roy P., ed. 1953. *Collected Works of Abraham Lincoln.* New Brunswick, NJ: Rutgers U. Pr.

Benson, Lee. 1961. *The Concept of Jacksonian Democracy: New York as a Test Case.* Princeton: Princeton U. Pr.

Bland, Richard A. 1975. "Politics, Propaganda, and the Public Printing: The Administration Organs, 1829–1849." Ph.D. dissertation, U. of Kentucky.

Burnham, Walter Dean. 1965. "The Changing Shape of the American Political Universe." 59 *American Political Science Review* 7.

Chambers, William N. 1963. *Political Parties in a New Nation.* New York: Oxford U. Pr.

———. 1971. "The Election of 1840." In Arthur M. Schlesinger, Jr., ed. *The History of American Presidential Elections.* Chatham, NJ: Chelsea House.

Chase, James S. 1973. *Emergence of the Presidential Nominating Convention, 1789–1832.* Urbana: U. of Illinois Pr.

Cole, Donald B. 1984. *Martin Van Buren and the American Political System.* Princeton: Princeton U. Pr.

Duncan, Bingham. 1975. *Whitelaw Reid: Journalist, Politician, Diplomat.* Athens: U. of Georgia Pr.

Formisano, Ronald P. 1983. *The Transformation of Political Culture: Massachusetts Parties, 1790s–1840s.* New York: Oxford U. Pr.

Gosnell, Harold F. 1924. *Boss Platt and His New York Machine.* Chicago: U. of Chicago Pr.

Hays, Samuel P. 1957. *The Response to Industrialism: 1885–1914.* Chicago: U. of Chicago Pr.

Hofstadter, Richard. 1969. *The Idea of a Party System: The Rise of Legitimate Opposition in the United States, 1780–1840.* Berkeley: U. of California Pr.

Holt, Michael F. 1978. *The Political Crisis of the 1850s.* New York: Wiley.

Howe, Daniel W. 1979. *The Political Culture of the 1850s.* New York: Wiley.

Jensen, Richard. 1971. *The Winning of the Midwest: Social and Political Conflict, 1888–1896.* Chicago: U. of Chicago Pr.

Josephson, Matthew. 1938. *The Politicos, 1865–1896.* New York: Harcourt, Brace.

Kehl, James A. 1981. *Boss Rule in the Gilded Age: Matt Quay of Pennsylvania.* Pittsburgh: U. of Pittsburgh Pr.

Keller, Morton. 1977. *Affairs of State: Public Life in Late Nineteenth-Century America.* Cambridge: Harvard U. Pr.

King, Preston. 1852. "To Jabez D. Hammon, August 11th." Miscellaneous Papers, New-York Historical Society.

Kleppner, Paul. 1979. *The Third Electoral System, 1853–1892: Parties, Voters, and Political Cultures.* Chapel Hill: U. of North Carolina Pr.

Kruman, Marc A. 1983. *Parties and Politics in North Carolina, 1836–1865.* Baton Rouge: Louisiana State U. Pr.

Leonard, Thomas. 1986. *The Power of the Press: The Birth of American Political Reporting.* New York: Oxford U. Pr.

Luetscher, George. 1903. *Early Political Machinery in the United States.* Philadelphia: U. of Pennsylvania Pr.

McCormick, Richard L. 1981. *From Realignment to Reform: Political Change in New York State, 1893–1910.* Ithaca: Cornell U. Pr.

McCormick, Richard P. 1966. *The Second American Party System: Party Formation in the Jacksonian Era.* Chapel Hill: U. of North Carolina Pr.

———. 1982. *The Presidential Game: The Origins of American Presidential Politics.* New York: Oxford U. Pr.

McGerr, Michael. 1986. *The Decline of Popular Politics: The American North, 1865–1928.* New York: Oxford U. Pr.

McSeveney, Samuel T. 1972. *The Politics of Depression: Political Behavior in the Northeast, 1893–1896.* New York: Oxford U. Pr.

Mandelbaum, Seymour. 1965. *Boss Tweed's New York.* New York: Wiley.

Marcus, Robert D. 1971. *Grand Old Party: Political Structure in the Gilded Age.* New York: Oxford U. Pr.

Mushkat, Jerome. 1971. *Tammany: The Evolution of a Political Machine.* Syracuse: Syracuse U. Pr.

Nichols, Roy P. 1967. *The Invention of the American Political Parties: A Study of Political Improvisation.* New York: Macmillan.

Ranney, Austin. 1975. *Curing the Mischief of Faction: Party Reform in America.* Berkeley: U. of California Pr.

Silbey, Joel H. 1985. *The Partisan Imperative: The Dynamics of American Politics Before the Civil War.* New York: Oxford U. Pr.

Smoger, Gerson Henry. 1982. "Organizing Political Campaigns: A Survey of 19th and 20th Century Trends." Ph.D. dissertation, U. of Pennsylvania.

Stave, Bruce. 1984. *Urban Bosses, Machines and Progressive Reformers.* Malabar, FL: Krieger.

Summers, Mark. 1987. *The Plundering Generation: Corruption and the Crisis of the Union, 1849–1861.* New York: Oxford U. Pr.

Sydnor, Charles S. 1952. *Gentlemen Freeholders: Political Practices in Washington's Virginia.* Chapel Hill: U. of North Carolina Pr.

Thornton, J. Mills. 1978. *Politics and Power in a Slave Society: Alabama, 1800–1860.* Baton Rouge: Louisiana State U. Pr.

Wattenberg, Martin. 1990. *The Decline of American Political Parties, 1952–1988.* Cambridge: Harvard U. Pr.

Wiebe, Robert. 1967. *The Search for Order, 1877–1920.* New York: Hill & Wang.

Wood, Gordon. 1987. "Ideology and the Origins of Liberal America." 44 *William and Mary Quarterly* 628.

## Party Platforms and Platform Writing

National party platforms are statements of party policy adopted by nominating conventions in presidential years. Their purpose is to enunciate the party's policy goals and position on issues in written form. Parties use no set guidelines for the content of the platforms, save for the party's own commitment to address relevant political issues. Platforms vary widely in length, specificity of policy goals, emphasis on policy areas, issue coverage, and accommodation of interests.

The first platform was drafted in 1832 when the National Republican Party composed a series of ten short resolutions avowing their support for Henry Clay, their nominee for President.

These ten resolutions, while not adopted at a party convention, set an example for political parties to represent their intentions through a national platform once party conventions became the standard means of nominating candidates for President and Vice President. The Democratic Party adopted a statement of party principles at its first convention in 1840, while the Whig Party adopted its first platform at convention in 1844. Thereafter, the two major parties have always adopted a platform at their national nominating conventions.

Proponents of responsible parties claim the platforms "indicate how the party stands on . . . interrelated issues that concern various parts of the electorate, . . . offer a coherent program, and provide voters with a proper choice between the alternative policies and programs advanced by the two parties." The platforms function, then, as a basis for rational voting. The voter, informed by the platform of the party goals adopted at convention, is in the best position to make a choice between the policies promoted by each party. This choice relies on the platform's attention to relevant political concerns and on these concerns being communicated by a presidential candidate who supports program initiatives designed to address the issues. These initiatives, in turn, promoted as they are by the party's chief representative, will supposedly attract a majority of adherents and win him the victory. The platform then becomes a governance document being propounded by a victorious candidate.

Writing the platform is the responsibility of an executive committee appointed by the national party committee. For the two major parties, this executive committee includes several members of Congress. In writing the preliminary drafts of the platform, members of the executive committee hold hearings with interest groups and party activists, although these hearings are rarely well attended. The executive committee is assisted by a research staff comprised of Capitol Hill personnel, national party committee staffers, and members of the academic community. The research staff assists in compiling recommendations, formulating language, and, if necessary, negotiating among factions vying for the inclusion of their pet projects in the platform.

Once the platform is written, the Resolutions Committee reviews it at the convention. The Resolutions Committee, made up of convention delegates, may amend the platform and, together with the executive committee, will prepare a final draft. The completed document, as recommended by the Resolutions Committee, is then presented to the full convention for a vote. Along with the vote for adoption, the executive committee chair is formally approved at the opening of the convention. Once recommended by the Resolutions Committee, a platform is rarely, if ever, questioned by the full convention; it is almost always adopted as the party platform.

Resolutions Committee members, before the party rules changes recommended by the O'Hara Commission, have typically been one male and one female delegate from each state and territory represented at the convention. These convention delegates have been given the proposed platform only upon arrival, promoting ignorance on their party and greater influence by the executive committee. Since the adoption of the O'Hara Commission's reforms in 1972, all delegates are sent the executive committee's draft ten days before the convention. The size and composition of the Resolutions Committee also has been expanded. Currently, each state or territory, according to their proportion of the total delegation, is allowed a minimum of one and a maximum of ten delegates on the Resolutions Committee, the size of this committee limited to about 150 members.

While the O'Hara Commission's reforms apply only to the Democratic Party, the Republican National Committee has followed suit by establishing an executive committee early in the election year and conducting regional hearings.

The modern platform is made up of a series of planks dictated by current political concerns on such topics as foreign policy, defense, economic policy, labor, agriculture, resources, social welfare, and civil rights and ethnic policy. These statements either evaluate the party's records and past performance in the particular policy area, or address the party's future programs. While program initiatives—past, present, and future—are elaborated in the platform, the platforms also contain statements of rhetoric and fact unrelated to specific policy areas.

Variation in the platforms can be attributed to the party's current strength. More bargaining among interests will occur when the party is out of power or when preliminary research and hearings are taking place in a competitive primary/caucus season. Incumbent Presidents, standing for reelection, will often dictate a platform that pledges continuity of program initiatives for the following administration. An outgoing President will often bargain with presidential contenders from his own party, yet his influence is considerably less than that of an incumbent President running for reelection. One further source of variation is the actors involved in the platform-writing process who use the platform as a symbolic document for asserting control among factions in the party. For instance, celebrated fights have occurred between party leaders—such as Eisenhower and Taft in 1952, Carter and Kennedy in 1980, and Dukakis and Jackson in 1988—when platform planks that did not meet their expectations were adopted by the convention.

Is the platform fulfilled once the party wins the presidency? While the platform is not followed absolutely, party members in Congress do tend to unite with their President on certain platform pledges. Support for program initiatives is probable without their presence in the platform. Parties tend to differ more widely on policy foci, and candidates may have preexisting dispositions toward a set of issues, such as the Democrats historical support of labor. Platforms are also associated more closely with the presidential candidate than with congressional candidates, and the President may not win a majority in Congress.

Finally, the electorate holds an indirect check on the contents of the platform. Candidates normally anticipate voter reaction in their campaigns, emphasizing what they perceive are voter expectations. The platform, as a campaign document, reflects program initiatives. These program initiatives, also written in anticipation of voter expectations, reflect policy concerns of the electorate. Few people actually read the document, yet the spirit in which it is written promotes voter support.

Party platforms are, then, a series of guideposts for both electoral and governance purposes in presidential election years adopted at the convention by the full delegation. While few people read the document, it is written in anticipation of voter support, thereby reflecting the policy predilections of the masses.

*See also:* Jimmy Carter, Henry Clay, Michael Dukakis, Dwight D. Eisenhower, Jesse Jackson, John F. Kennedy, Presidential Nominating Conventions, William Howard Taft

*Terri Susan Fine*

REFERENCES

Chester, Edward W. 1977. *A Guide to Political Platforms.* Hamden, CT: Archon Books.

Committee on Political Parties, American Political Science Association. 1950. "Toward a More Responsible Two-Party System." 44 *American Political Science Review* Supplement.

Johnson, Donald B. 1978. *National Party Platforms.* Urbana: U. of Illinois Pr.

Monroe, Alan. 1983. "American Party Platforms and Public Opinion." 27 *American Journal of Political Science* 27.

Namenwirth, J. Zvi, and Harold D. Lasswell. 1970. *The Changing Language of American Values: A Computer Study of Selected Party Platforms.* Beverly Hills, CA: Sage.

Ostrogorski, M. 1964. *Democracy and the Organization of Political Parties.* Garden City, NY: Doubleday, Anchor.

Parris, Judith. 1972. *The Convention Problem: Issues in Reform of Presidential Nominating Procedures.* Washington: Brookings.

Pomper, Gerald. 1963. *Nominating the President: The Politics of Convention Choice.* Chicago: Northwestern U. Pr.

———, and Susan Lederman. 1980. *Elections in America: Control and Influence in Democratic Politics.* New York: Longman.

Weinberg, Martha Wagner. 1977. "Writing the Republican Platform." 92 *Political Science Quarterly* 655.

## Party Renewal

This term is used to denote the desirability of stronger parties and a stronger party system in American politics and government. Many writers use the terms "renewal" and "reform" interchangeably, but technically each has a distinctive meaning or at least a distinctive history that sets it apart from the other.

The concept of "party renewal" originated with the Committee for Party Renewal (CPR), which was organized in the mid 1970s by political scientists, led by James MacGregor Burns, who were united in the belief that American political parties should be strengthened as representative and purposeful institutions. The committee chose the term "party renewal" to make clear that its purpose was to revitalize the *existing* party system and, at the same time, to separate itself from earlier academic and political initiatives of a similar sort. The distinctiveness of the term lies in the founding and work of CPR.

The movement for party renewal took shape against a growing academic and popular conviction that political parties had lost much of the muscle and importance that they had once had. David Broder's *The Party's Over* recalls the backdrop of a weakened and weakening party system against which the Committee for Party Renewal was organized. For the most part, proponents of party renewal shared Broder's conclusions on the impaired condition of American parties and his concern about the implications of a diminished party system for the future of politics and democracy in America.

The Committee for Party Renewal also arose in a context of national Democratic Party reform—reform that followed the party's 1968 national convention and focused primarily on the rules by which delegates were to be selected for future Democratic conventions. CPR saw the reform efforts of the Democrats as an opportunity to advance ideas to strengthen the party system and help restore parties to a position of central importance in American politics.

The term "party renewal" was chosen in part to differentiate CPR from the idea of "responsible parties" as urged in the 1950 report, *Toward a More Responsible Two-Party System*, issued by the ten-member Committee on Political Parties of the American Political Science Association. While generally sympathetic to the spirit of that report, organizers of CPR also shared many of the criticisms made of it. At any rate, CPR sought a separate identity most of all so as not to reawaken old controversies within political science.

The CPR's goal was to *renew* the existing parties, not to transform them radically. Where the responsible party advocates had offered a model for a strong party system drawn in part from the British parliamentary party system, the proponents of party renewal took a more pragmatic, more incremental, and less ideological approach. They accepted constitutional and other constraints in American politics that made for a distinctive party system and aimed at renewing the parties so they might be as strong as possible in the American setting.

The term "party renewal" also served to distinguish the Committee for Party Renewal from the ongoing "party reform" within the national Democratic Party. Democratic reform was guided by an ideal of participatory democracy and sought a more open and demographically representative Democratic Party, with more active involvement of party identifiers at all levels of party organization. For the most part, CPR members shared the ideals and objectives of Democratic reforms but feared that the party's narrow focus on procedures alone might ultimately weaken parties further rather than renewing their effectiveness as political institutions.

Unlike party reform, party renewal has not been concerned with just procedural issues but has addressed a broader range of organizational questions and has been more eclectic and less idealistic in its approach. It has also been bipartisan in its organization and been impressed as much by "party building" efforts of the national Republican Party in the 1970s and 1980s as it has by Democratic Party reform.

Party renewal, then, has been guided by certain generally shared principles of strong parties and of a strong party system but has eschewed a single theory of reform as well as a single model for revitalizing the parties. Conceptually, it has been eclectic, pragmatic, and incremental in its approach. Politically, it has been activist, bipartisan, and opportunistic in method, concerned with the vitality of parties at all levels of government and with legislative and judicial actions as well as party rules.

*The Party Renewal Program*

While no single theory or model guides and defines the idea of party renewal, a distinctive perspective on strengthening parties emerges from the declarations made and positions taken by the Committee for Party Renewal. As a program of action, the meaning of party renewal continues to evolve in the work of the Committee, but certain principles backed by specific recommendations for change now seem securely associated with the idea of party renewal and, together, they define its program for strengthening American parties.

1. Parties should be strengthened to secure political democracy within the existing constitutional framework. Like the advocates or responsible parties, proponents of party renewal see political parties as the only broadly based, multi-interested American political organizations that can nominate candidates for office, mobilize popular support behind them, and both organize and give direction to government. Like the responsible parties model, party renewal sees the American constitutional system and political culture as dominated by centrifugal and privatizing forces: the separation of powers, federalism, pluralism, individualism, the suspicion of power, and a negativism toward partisan politics in general and political parties in particular. And like the champions of responsible parties, the friends of party renewal argue that political parties have been a necessary unifying force in the American political system, cutting across the branches and levels of government as well as across voting blocs to aggregate interests, build coalitions, define and enforce programmatic

agendas, and make democracy possible in modern government.

The idea of party renewal thus shares a critique of American parties and of their place in the American political system with the responsible parties model. This perspective separates party renewal from party reform as advanced by the Democrats, where the concern has been almost wholly with democratizing parties internally and not with their more general place or role in the polity at large. It also separates party renewal from party *building* in the Republican Party, where the focus has been primarily on the provision of campaign resources and services the candidates.

Party renewal departs from the idea of responsible parties in its acceptance of the American constitutional framework as setting the conditions within which parties must be strengthened. Party renewal accepts as inevitable that parties will always have to compete with other groups for influence in American politics and that parties will always have to adapt organizationally and operationally to the changing conditions of American politics.

2. Parties should be more important in the political lives of elected officials. Party renewal accepts the candidate-centered character of American elections, but it calls for an expanded and strategically more central role for parties in nominations and campaigns. The goal is not to give political parties absolute control over nominations and campaigns but to create conditions that encourage and enable candidates to rely more on their party in securing nominations, carrying on campaigns, and governing.

Party renewal has urged more extensive use of caucuses and conventions in the selection of party nominees as well as for the adoption of party platforms, preferring preprimary endorsing conventions with thresholds that candidates must meet in order to qualify for the party primary. This process is seen as requiring candidates to campaign for nomination among party organizational activists, providing a qualitative check through peer review, and giving the institutional party greater influence without giving it complete control over nominations.

In campaigns, party renewal understands that candidates have the primary responsibility for their election, but it calls for greater resources and a larger role for parties so that candidates may depend more heavily on the party in their bids for office. CPR has urged restructuring the Federal Election Campaign Act to channel public money to candidates primarily through the parties and to relax restraints on the ability of parties to raise and spend money. Party renewal also believes that the parties themselves should be more active in the recruitment of candidates and in the provision of training, research, expert advice, polling, media, and other necessary campaign services.

Like the responsible parties model, party renewal believes that parties should be instruments of governance. Parties are seen as the one institution that can unite leadership in the different branches and levels of government and direct it toward coherent public policy. Unlike the responsible parties view, however, party renewal does not see party leadership as resting exclusively or predominantly in the executive. It regards the American constitutional system as one of institutions sharing power; thus it acknowledges party leadership in such a system as inevitably collegial in character. To this end, party renewal urges legislative leaders to make maximum use of the party caucus in the conduct of their business and calls upon chief executives to work through their party organization in the conduct of their affairs. And it sees an enhanced role for parties in nominations and campaigns as a key to more effective party leadership in government.

3. Parties should be more important in the political lives of citizens. A democratic politics is grounded in an informed and active citizenry. Party renewal thus shares with party reform a belief in participatory democracy but at the same time does not regard participation as the overriding goal of a democratic politics. While free and active citizenship is seen as essential in a democracy, CPR insists that individual participation must be mixed into the structure of politics in a way that compliments or at least does not undermine political parties, which are also seen as essential in a democracy. Rightly ordered, citi-

zen participation can both inform and check the actions of parties. In turn, parties can mediate popular concerns, translate them into public policy, and be accountable for governance.

Party renewal calls for open and broadly based party organizations at the local level. The local party committee is seen as the foundation for state and national party organization and as a training ground for both party members and potential party candidates. Party renewal urges open and widely publicized local party meetings at which current issues may be discussed and positions taken. It also recommends the use of caucuses open to all party registrants for the purpose of picking convention delegates, endorsing candidates, and adopting platforms. It encourages state party issues or platform conventions as well as state party endorsing conventions.

Two other important functions of the political system—public education and public accountability—are seen by party renewal as central to effective citizenship. More like the responsible parties model than party reform, the renewal perspective believes that parties should play a critical role in each. It calls upon parties to offer a public agenda informed by widespread citizen participation as well as by the experience and expertise of public officials. That agenda both schools voters in the issues and gives them a reasonable choice between alternative courses of action. By endorsing candidates for office, campaigning for their nominees, adopting a platform, and sponsoring candidate debates, parties can and should be a means of public education. And they are the one institution that can be held directly accountable by voters for what government does.

4. Parties should be as free as possible to govern themselves. Political parties are private associations with public responsibilities. The public interest in orderly and honest politics justifies state and federal intrusion upon the activities of political parties in the administration of elections, campaign finance, and voting rights, but party renewal holds that government regulation of parties in these and other areas should be as limited as possible.

Party renewal urges that political parties be free to define their own organization, powers, and procedures; these parties, however, should do so publicly through written charters and by-laws so that all who affiliate with them may know the structure and rules of party governance. The Committee for Party Renewal has endorsed and applauded U.S. Supreme Court decisions applying the First Amendment right of association to parties, decisions that have removed burdensome state regulation of party organization and have in other ways expanded the powers of political parties.

Party renewal also believes that the public interest is best served by state and federal law that complements party self-regulation, not by statutes that substitute for it. It supports requiring voter registration by party, adoption of the party column ballot, and the return to partisan local elections. And it urges that public policy recognize the difference between parties and other political groups. Because parties are more democratic, more egalitarian and majoritarian, party renewal holds that they should be given a privileged position in lawmaking.

Finally, party renewal recognizes and accepts the diversity of the American federal system and the continually changing character of American politics. It believes that political parties need the freedom to build organizations and adopt practices that fit the history, culture, and experience of the different states and that parties require the freedom to adapt as the conditions of politics change. Party renewal is then "contextualist": it recognizes that party building in one state may be different from party building in another. And like party politics itself, party renewal is open-ended and unending.

*The Party Renewal Strategy*

In addition to differences in conception and program, the idea of party renewal also differs in its strategy from those of both responsible parties and party reform. Unlike the idea of responsible parties, party renewal has not been narrowly academic. Party renewal was founded by political scientists and makes regular use of professional meetings in that discipline, but it also has welcomed party officials, campaign activists, political journalists, and others as members. CPR has sought to influence the future of parties directly through legislative, judicial, and other public strategies. Proponents of party renewal have testified before legislative committees, both state and national, as well as party commissions, to support statutory and rules changes to strengthen parties and the party system. They have also sponsored court actions in at least one state, where the Committee for Party Renewal has enjoyed its single greatest success to date, and have joined litigation in others to challenge statutory restrictions on the rights of party members.

Unlike party reform, party renewal has been bipartisan in its orientation and organization. It has sought to speak for the interests of parties and the party system and not narrowly for a particular partisan interest. For the most part, it has endorsed the general thrust of both Democratic Party reform and Republican Party building as two dimensions of party renewal. At the same time, party renewal has gone beyond party reform and party building, as these are understood by the two national parties, to a more general concern with the role of parties in government and in a democratic polity.

The party renewal strategy has thus been principled but pragmatic; incremental, opportunistic, and activist yet broadly concerned. Like America's major parties, party renewal has been coalitional and moderate. It has sought to bring a variety of actors and interests under its banner and to avoid more controversial questions such as whether greater nationalization of power would strengthen parties, whether federal law ought to regulate presidential and congressional elections more extensively, and whether third parties should be encouraged.

The idea of party renewal has itself been shaped in important ways by this strategy. Unlike the idea of responsible parties, which derives from a comprehensive and a priori plan for a strong party system—as well as the ideas of party reform and party building, which are also a priori but much narrower in scope, the concept of party renewal has grown out of a series of specific responses to particular political opportunities (party commissions, congressional hearings) that provided a forum in which to make the case for stronger parties. Insofar as a concept of party renewal exists, it originates in statements, position papers, testimony, and other documents developed by the Committee for Party Renewal in response to targets of opportunity. Recently, the Committee has shown a greater disposition to try to shape events and

not simply react to them, most notably in the case of litigation. This activism has led to a sorting and synthesis of ideas from these somewhat disparate documents into a broader and more coherent idea of party renewal. The idea, however, is in no sense a comprehensive plan for a strong party system as is the concept of responsible parties.

*Conclusion*

The idea of responsible parties shaped a generation of scholars in political science. Yet it was largely ignored by political practitioners and, indeed, parties continued to weaken in the years following its birth. The idea of party reform, in both of its partisan applications, has remade the national parties, but it is unclear that it has strengthened either Democrats or Republicans as democratic institutions linking party voters to party government.

Party renewal has not had the scholarly impact of the responsible parties model, but it has provided an outlet for and perhaps helped to sustain the interests of American political scientists in the health of their party system. It has not enjoyed the political success that party reform has known, but party renewal has at once encouraged these movements and tried to widen their focus to include more general questions of the role of parties in a democratic polity.

Final judgment on the idea of party renewal is impossible because the Committee for Party Renewal remains active, and the idea and its application therefore continue to evolve. Party renewal has helped to keep the question of stronger parties on the academic and public agendas. It may also have helped to prevent parties from becoming any weaker. Finally, party renewal may in its more recent judicial applications be helping to create an environment of law in which parties will be better able to take initiatives to strengthen themselves.

*See also:* Federal Elections Campaign Acts

*Jerome M. Mileur*

REFERENCES

Advisory Commission on Intergovernmental Relations. 1986. *The Transformation in American Politics*. Washington: ACIR.

Broder, David S. 1971. *The Party's Over*. New York: Harper & Row.

Burns, James MacGregor. 1984. *The Power to Lead*. New York: Simon & Schuster.

Committee on Political Parties of the American Political Science Association. 1950. *Toward a More Responsible Two-Party System*. New York: Rinehart.

Fleishman, Joel L., ed. 1982. *The Future of American Political Parties*. Englewood Cliffs, NJ: Prentice-Hall.

Goldwin, Robert A., ed. 1980. *Political Parties in the Eighties*. Washington: American Enterprise Institute.

Kayden, Xandra, and Eddie Mahe, Jr. 1985. *The Party Goes On*. New York: Basic Books.

Lawson, Kay. 1988. "Party Renewal and American Democracy." In Michael R. Beschloss and Thomas E. Cronin, eds. *Essays in Honor of James MacGregor Burns*. Englewood Cliffs, NJ: Prentice-Hall.

Mileur, Jerome M. 1983. "The Committee for Party Renewal." Paper presented at the Annual Meeting of the American Political Science Association, Chicago.

Pomper, Gerald, ed. 1980. *Party Renewal in America*. New York: Praeger.

Price, David E. 1984. *Bringing Back the Parties*. Washington: Congressional Quarterly.

Ranney, Austin. 1975. *Curing the Mischiefs of Faction*. Berkeley: U. of California Pr.

Sabato, Larry J. 1988. *The Party's Just Begun*. Glenview, IL: Scott, Foresman.

## Party Rules in Congress

When the bicentennial One Hundred First Congress convened on January 3, 1989, more than 60 percent of the House and over half the Senate had been elected first during the 1980s. These newer legislators represented a generational shift in terms, for instance, of their perspectives on a variety of issues and their recognition of the potency of media politics. Some of these 1980s Senators were instrumental in electing a new Democratic Majority Leader, George Mitchell of Maine, to replace Robert C. Byrd of West Virginia, who decided not to seek another term in the post. "I do believe we're on the threshold of major change and we'll see a significantly redefined Senate by the end of the decade," said Senator Thomas Daschle (D-S.D.), a supporter of Mitchell's. Senator Daschle was first elected to the Senate as part of the 11-member "Class of '86."

Senator Mitchell's election as Majority Leader took place within the confines of the Democratic Conference and according to party rules and practices that define the procedure when there is more than one candidate vying for a position, as occurred in this case when two other Democrats contested for the post. In Mitchell's case, if no candidate received a majority on the first ballot, then the top two contenders would face off again in a second secret ballot. When Mitchell fell one vote short of a majority, the other two challengers withdrew and the Democratic Conference then elected Mitchell by acclamation.

The selection of party leaders is only one instance in which party rules affect the shape and structure of Congress. Two other areas worthy of exploration are committee organization and floor action. The role and influence of party rules is more visible and dramatic in the House, especially during the 1970s when power was taken from committee chairmen and spread to subcommittees and central party leaders; the operation in that chamber is most important for an understanding of party rules.

### Election of Party Leaders

Party caucuses have been used since the early 1800s to select party leaders. The first known instance of a candidate being nominated by a party caucus for a leadership post occurred in 1811, when Henry Clay was selected by the Whigs as their choice for Speaker. Today, in addition to choosing top party leaders, the caucus or conference (both parties in the Senate and Republicans in the House refer to their party gathering as a conference) authorizes the creation of a variety of party committees. For example, Rule 23 of the House GOP Conference states in part, "The Committee on Policy shall be an advisory committee to the Membership of the House Republican Conference." The Policy Committee suggests action on substantive and procedural matters for GOP members. The Republican Conference Rules for the One Hundred First Congress also establish the hierarchy of its leaders: the Republican leader, the Republican whip, the chairman of the GOP Conference, the chairman of the Committee on Policy, the chairman of the Committee on Research, the vice chairman of the GOP Conference, the secretary of the GOP Conference, and the chairman of the National Republican Congressional Committee.

Who becomes a top party leader represents a major decision for both Democrats and Republicans. Party leaders are strategically positioned to determine what legislation will be subject to floor consideration, whose influence will rise or decline, and what issues are likely to be the subject of debate in the next general election. No one is surprised, then, that many contests occur in caucus or conference over a party's choice of leaders. And those contests are influenced by party rules.

The rules of the House Democratic Caucus, as in the case of the other Capitol Hill parties, outline the procedure when more than two challengers contest for the same party post. "If there are more than two candidates, the nominated candidate receiving the fewest votes on the first and each succeeding ballot shall be eliminated," states Rule 3 of the Democratic Caucus. This rule shapes political strategy. Each candidate, for instance, assesses who will edge out whom on the first or subsequent ballots and then gain the votes of the eliminated candidates. The "low person out" rule influenced the election of Jim Wright, (D-Tex.) as House Majority Leader in December 1976 and paved his way to the speakership.

When Speaker Carl Albert (D-Okla.) announced his retirement from the House at the end of the Ninety-fourth Congress, it was clear that Thomas P. "Tip" O'Neill (D-Mass.) was ready to move unchallenged from his post as Majority Leader to become Speaker. O'Neill's move up the leadership ladder set off a four-way contest for the vacant Majority Leader post among Congressmen Phil Burton (Calif.), Richard Bolling (Mo.), John McFall (Calif.), and Jim Wright, a late entrant into the race. By many press accounts, the real battle was between Burton and Bolling, with Wright a "dark horse" in the contest. On the first ballot, the outcome went this way:

| Burton | 106 votes |
| Bolling | 81 |
| Wright | 77 |
| McFall | 31 |

With McFall out of the race, the other three contenders moved to solidify their own supporters and pick up the backers of McFall. The second ballot, revealed a major surprise—Bolling rather than Wright was eliminated.

| Burton | 107 votes |
| Wright | 95 |
| Bolling | 93 |

Speculation was rife that Burton had arranged for a few of his backers to vote for Wright in order to eliminate Bolling, whom Burton viewed as the stronger challenger. Explained political scientists Bruce Oppenheimer and Robert Peabody:

> The closeness of the Wright-Bolling vote was surprising. A switch of two votes and Bolling would have been in the runoff. Even more confounding was the new Burton total. It was hard to believe that he had increased his total by only one vote. There was speculation that Burton had, in fact, shifted some votes to Wright in order to have a more conservative—and hence weaker—opponent on the final ballot.

Burton denied any vote-switching strategy, but some of Bolling's supporters believed it nonetheless and supported Wright over Burton. On the final ballot, Wright edged Burton by one vote to become the new Majority Leader. Democrats typically elevate their next-in-line officer—from whip to Majority Leader to Speaker. Consequently, Wright became Speaker of the One Hundredth Congress upon the retirement from the House of "Tip" O'Neill. Interestingly, Democrats switched from an appointive (by the Speaker) to an elective whip with the start of the One Hundredth Congress. This party rules change was advocated by many junior Democrats. They wanted a voice in determining which of their partisan colleagues won a place on the pathway that could lead to the speakership.

*Committee Organization: Restrictions on Multiple Chairmanships*

### Background

For much of the twentieth century, powerful committee chairmen, who gained their posts through the inexorable workings of a rigid seniority system, dominated congressional policymaking. The names of Clarence Cannon of Appropriations, Carl Vinson of Armed Services, Howard Smith of Rules, and Wilbur Mills of Ways and Means epitomize the era of committee government, which roughly approximated the period from 1911 and into the early 1970s.

The authority of committee chairmen, frequently dubbed "autocrats" by political commentators, stemmed from a variety of sources, including their absolute control over the hiring and firing of staff, their power to establish subcommittees and designate their chairmen and members, and their undisputed authority over the management and scheduling of the committee's business. A story told by junior Democrat Norman Minetta reveals how one of these chairmen ran his committee.

> After the 1964 election brought in a large new class, the late Harold D. Cooley of North Carolina, then Chairman of the House Agriculture Committee, convened the new Members assigned to his committee, to coach them in proper behavior. Cooley was then a thirty-year veteran of Congress, and very much a gentleman of the old school. His advice went like this: "I hate and detest to hear a new member interrupt a senior member asking a question. You new members will come to realize that, if you

remain silent, the senior members will ask all relevant questions needed to illuminate every point.

As frustration with this kind of elitist behavior soared among liberal Democrats, some of them joined together in 1959 to organize the ad hoc organization the Democratic Study Group (DSG). Procedurally, the DSG wanted to remedy the inequities of the seniority system and change the distribution of internal power in the House. The DSG was aided in its drive for change by the influx of new members into the House, Representatives generally more receptive to change than the senior legislators they replaced. "Like those entering other trades and professions," wrote journalist David Broder, "the House newcomers tend to be men and women impatient with the old ways of doing business; less willing to 'move up the chairs,' waiting silently for years for their turn at a subcommittee chairmanship; less deferential to their elders; and more insistent on grabbing a piece of the action now."

The 1968 election of Republican Richard Nixon to the White House galvanized the DSG into major action on seniority reform. Concerned that conservative committee chairmen might support an expected White House plan to dismantle many social programs, the DSG and other members looked for ways to mobilize and revitalize their party. A broadly supported recommendation was to make regular use of the Democratic Caucus. At the time, the Caucus was largely a dormant entity that met at the start of each Congress to nominate party leaders and then faded away for another two years. The significance of holding regular monthly meetings of the Caucus was underscored by Donald Fraser (Minn.), former head of the DSG. "With the monthly caucuses," he said, "we had regular opportunities to talk about the House reforms. That was the starting point."

That starting point led to a variety of significant party changes that, among other things, infused flexibility into the seniority system and reduced the authority of committee chairmen. The developments of 1969 through 1975 have been fully discussed by LeRoy Rieselbach, who argues that one of their fundamental themes was to "spread the action," diffusing power among subcommittees and junior legislators. A 1971 Caucus rule, for instance, stated that no Democrat could be chairman of more than one legislative subcommittee. The purpose of the rule was to create additional committee leadership opportunities for "have not" members. As political commentator Norman Ornstein explained, three major consequences flowed from the 1971 change: (1) the "reform . . . brought in a maximum of sixteen new subcommittee chairmen; (2) the reform spread power to younger, less senior Members; and (3) the reform improved the lot of non-Southern and liberal Democrats."

In sum, from the late 1960s until the late 1970s, the House Democratic Caucus adopted a series of party rules that, among other things, restricted the authority of committee chairmen, democratized committee assignments and procedures, modified the seniority system, and enhanced the autonomy of subcommittees. One outgrowth of these changes was a restriction on the number of committees and subcommittees that Democrats could chair (Democrats have controlled the House uninterrupted since 1954). Previously, no formal party regulations restricted multiple committee and subcommittee chairmanships.

### Restrictions on Subcommittee Chairmanships

The rules of the Democratic Caucus, rather than the rules of the House, impose a variety of restrictions on the simultaneous holding of chairmanships. Rule 24 (Limitations on Number of Committee Chairmanships) and Rule 29 (Restrictions on Subcommittee Chairmanship) outline the major Democratic chairmanship restrictions and exceptions. The provisions in these rules are also linked to another Caucus rule (17) that classifies House committees into three groupings: exclusive, major, and nonmajor. For example, members who serve on exclusive committees are not to be assigned to other standing committees unless the Caucus waives this requirement. Still another Caucus rule (18) defines how many committees in each category Democrats are permitted to serve on. To give some "feel and flavor" to the origin and politics surrounding some of these developments, here is a portion of Caucus Rule 29 that states, "The chairman of a full committee or select committee with legislative jurisdiction shall not be the chairman of a subcommittee of any other such full committee." (For a comparison of comparable Democratic and Republican rules, see the following chart.)

This particular party rule was adopted during the December 6–9, 1976, early organizational sessions of the Democratic Caucus.

Party Rules in Congress

## SELECTED PARTY RULES COMPARISON: HOUSE DEMOCRATS AND HOUSE REPUBLICANS

### House Democrats

#### Rule 29. Restrictions on Subcommittee Chairmanships

A. No Member shall be chairman of more than one subcommittee of a full committee or select committee with legislative jurisdiction. Provided, however, that the following committees shall be exempt from this provision: House Administration; Standards of Official Conduct; House Recording; and Joint Committees.

B. Members of the Budget Committee shall be eligible for subcommittee chairmanships on such committee without regard to Section A above.

C. The chairman of a full committee or select committee with legislative jurisdiction shall not be the chairman of a subcommittee of any other such full committee.

D. The following committee shall be exempt from paragraph C of this rule: District of Columbia; House Administration; Standards of Official Conduct; House Recording; and Joint Committees.

E. The provisions of paragraphs A and C shall not apply to the subcommittee chairmanships of the Committee on the District of Columbia in the 101st Congress.

### House Republicans

#### Rule 20. Limitations on Subcommittee Ranking Positions

No individual shall serve as Ranking Minority Member of more than one standing, select, or ad hoc Committee and of more than one subcommittee of any standing, select, or ad hoc Committee: provided, however, that upon recommendation of the Committee on Committees and approval of the Conference this provision may be waived.

No individual shall serve as Ranking Minority Member of more than two subcommittees of the standing, select, and ad hoc Committees upon which such Member serves and in no event shall the two be subcommittees of the same Committee: provided, however, that upon the recommendation of the Committee on Committees and the approval of the Conference this provision may be waived.

Source: "Preamble and Rules of the Democratic Caucus," One Hundred First Congress, January 31, 1989, and "The Rules of the Republican Conference of the United States House of Representatives, 101st Congress," December 6, 1988.

Sponsored by DSG chairman Bob Eckhardt of Texas, the Democratic limitation proposal was adopted by voice vote. In a DSG summary of its reform proposals, the group provided the following rationale for the limitation:

Proposal: Prohibit a chairman of a full committee from serving as a subcommittee chairman on another committee. The limitation would not take effect until after the committees have organized for the 95th Congress. Thus, full committee chairmen on non-major committees who chair subcommittees on other non-major committees after organization of the 95th Congress would be exempted from this rule.

Rationale: Existing Caucus rules prohibit Members from chairing subcommittees on two committees yet permit a Member to chair a full committee and a subcommittee on another committee. The proposal would end this illogical exception for full committee chairmen. The proposal would also result in an increase in the number of Members holding subcommittee chairmanships.

No further analysis of the DSG-sponsored rules change appeared in any major newspaper or publication. Instead, press coverage understandably concentrated on such matters as the race for Majority Leader among the aforementioned Burton, Bolling, McFall, and Wright, and the effort (unsuccessful) to make the whip an elective party position.

The new prohibition more than probably represented a continuation of the "spread the action" theme that influenced much Caucus activity during the 1970s. A majority of Democrats, in short, wanted to reduce further the power of committee chairmen and distribute subcommittee chairmanships to Democrats who might not otherwise had an opportunity to head such panels. Many of the newer Democrats, especially the 71 returning from the Class of 1974 (originally 75) and the 47 of the Class of 1976, were strong backers of these changes. Party leaders, too, were generally supportive of Caucus actions designed to weaken the authority of committee chairmen, because they believed the changes would increase their influence in the lawmaking process.

When the Democrats met two years later in their early organizational meetings, they rejected an initiative to weaken committee chairmen even further. Congressman Christopher Dodd (eventually a Senator from Connecticut), who headed a Task Force on House Procedure for the Ninety-fourth Caucus (Democrats elected in 1974), introduced a proposed Caucus rules change to prohibit a full committee chairman from "holding subcommittee chairmanships on that or any other standing, select, permanent select, special, *ad hoc*, or joint committee." Dodd argued "that the change would be in keeping with recent Democratic reforms aimed at distributing power to more members." The Task Force's recommendation was rejected 21 to 85. Numerous full committee chairmen argued against the recommendation. As one chairman stated, if full chairmen could not also chair subcommittees, "You might as well get a clerk to head the committee." Since this 1978 attempt, no efforts in the Caucus have tried to impose further such restrictions on the chairmen of the standing committees.

*Floor Action*

During the past few decades, there has been a rather close tie in several areas that has connected the Democratic Caucus with House floor activities. Of course, the rules of the House, especially revisions from one Congress to the next, are agreed to first by the Democratic Caucus and then approved by the House with party-line voting the invariable practice. The tie between the Caucus and the floor can be highlighted by examining the party steps that tightened the relationship between the Rules Committee and the majority leadership.

Traditionally, the Rules Committee is an agent of the majority leadership because of the panel's strategic scheduling prerogatives. This connection was formalized in 1858 when the Speaker of the House became a member of Rules and later its chair. In 1910 the House removed him from the committee. The panel then operated largely as an independent power, extracting substantive concessions in bills in exchange for "rules," a simple resolution that, if adopted by majority vote of the House, establishes a tailor-made procedure for debating and amending legislation on the House floor. The Committee blocked measures it opposed and advanced those it favored.

As rank-and-file frustration mounted against the Rules Committee, the Democratic Caucus took steps to tighten its top leaders' grip on the panel. In 1973 the Caucus adopted a Democratic Party rule that restricted the panel's authority to grant "closed rules" (prohibiting any and all germane floor amendments). The rule required committee chairmen to provide advance notice in the Congressional Record if they intended to ask Rules for a rule that restricted the floor

amendment process. The party rule also provided a procedure to convene a special Democratic Caucus that could direct the Rules Committee to make germane floor amendments in order despite the contrary preferences of committee chairmen.

In a rare use of this procedure, the Democratic Caucus instructed the majority members of the Rules Committee to permit two floor amendments to the 1974 Oil and Gas Energy Tax Act. One amendment would eliminate retroactively the oil depletion allowance and the other would alter the foreign tax credit used by petroleum companies. Normally, tax measures, which are handled by the Committee on Ways and Means, are considered under closed rules. Ways and Means chairmen have long successfully argued that tax bills are so complicated that chaos would result on the House floor if members were allowed to offer amendments to those measures. A majority of the Democratic Caucus, however, rejected that argument, and as the *Wall Street Journal* noted, "This was the first time the House Democrats used their caucus to prevent [the Ways and Means Chairman] from taking legislation to the floor under a closed rule." This action underscores the possible potential of the Democratic Caucus as an instrument of party policymaking.

In 1975 the Caucus authorized the Speaker to name all of the panel's majority members, subject to Caucus approval, including the chair. (In 1988 Republicans authorized their leader to name the GOP members of Rules to ensure aggressive and articulate challenges to the Democratic-led panel.) The 1975 change effectively transformed Rules into the "Speaker's committee." Later, the Democratic Caucus directed that Rules maintain a disproportionate party ratio—traditionally two to one, but since the early 1980s two to one plus one. In the One Hundred First Congress, nine Democrats and four Republicans sit on Rules.

The cumulative effect of these and other party rules changes has been to strengthen the Speaker's control of the panel and to thus insure that majority party priorities not only receive consideration on the House floor but the same treatment under favorable procedural terms as well. Where Rules was often criticized during the pre-1970s period for blocking or not considering rules for social legislation, such as civil rights bills, the panel today is likely to be castigated (usually by Republicans) for crafting ingenious rules that tilt the procedural playing field to advantage partisan agendas and objectives. For instance, when the House considered a defense authorization bill, the rule structured the floor amendment process so Democratic members could balance antidefense with prodefense votes. Journalist Pat Towell maintains,

> [The rule] ensured that votes on important "anti-Reagan" amendments would be separated by roll calls on less crucial issues, so that moderates and conservatives would be able to cast a "pro-defense" vote following particularly controversial amendments on which the [Democratic] leadership wanted a vote against the administration position.

One GOP House leader became so outraged at such rules that he dubbed them CRAP ("Creative Rule Alteration Procedures"); *Roll Call* reports that Republicans hate the new rules because they "restrict the rights of Members and distort normal legislative procedure beyond all recognition and rationality for narrow partisan purposes." In rebuttal, a Democratic leader wrote that the real Republican complaint "is not to House procedures, but to the policies achieved with those procedures."

Unsurprisingly, the connection between party and floor actions is also evident in the Senate. During the One Hundredth Congress, Senate Democrats made campaign finance reform for Senate general elections a priority. Senate Republicans vehemently opposed the Democratic initiative. They even convened in the GOP Conference to denounce the legislation and to adopt a formal party position against it. The Republican Conference "voted to oppose not just public financing of campaigns . . . but also to oppose any campaign spending limits," said Democratic leader Robert C. Byrd (W.Va.). Byrd strove to break the GOP-led filibuster against the measure. He even forced opponents to carry on an old-fashioned, around-the-clock filibuster in the hope of weakening the GOP-led opposition. In the end, the Senate failed to invoke cloture (the 60-vote procedure for closing off debates) for a record-breaking eighth time. The Democratic leader then pulled the measure from the schedule given the nearly unanimous GOP opposition to it.

## Summary Observations

Change is an "iron law" of politics: the Congress of the 1980s is significantly different in many respects from the Congresses of previous eras. Compared to its 1960s predecessors, for instance, the contemporary Congress is more individualistic, more open, more egalitarian, and more assertive. Not only has an influx of new players come to Congress, but also the legislative playing field itself has undergone some major transformations in part owing to changes in party rules.

The four Capitol Hill parties, especially House Democrats and House Republicans, have evolved an elaborate set of formal procedures to govern party activities. One effect of these developments, as noted earlier, is to recentralize significant authority in the hands of the Speaker. Changes in party and House rules have given today's Speaker more institutional authority than at any time since the era of Speaker Joseph Cannon (R-Ill.) (1903–1911).

Democrats and Republicans continue to advocate revisions in party rules to advance their policy and intraparty objectives. For example, prior to the start of the One Hundred First Congress, Ways and Means chairman Daniel Rostenkowski (D-Ill.) successfully advocated a party rules change to allow the members of the three exclusive committees—Appropriations, Rules, and Ways and Means—to serve on the House Administration Committee. This panel wields important influence over internal House functions (passing on the investigative budgets of the standing committees, for example) and several substantive matters, such as campaign finance reform. Rostenkowski wanted an ally on House Administration to give voice to his concerns on committee funding, campaign finance, and other issues. Speaker Wright also urged that House Administration, like Rules, should be made a "leadership" panel, one that would enable him to name all the panel's members, including the chairman. In short, like the rules of Congress, party rules are regularly adjusted or even waived to meet changing conditions and circumstances. And like some attempts to change Congress's rules, efforts to revamp party rules sometimes reflect efforts to redistribute power.

*See also:* Robert C. Byrd, Joseph Cannon, Henry Clay, Democratic Study Group, George Mitchell, Thomas P. O'Neill, Speaker of the House, James Wright

*Walter J. Oleszek*

REFERENCES

Bach, Stanley, and Steven S. Smith. 1988. *Managing Uncertainty in the House of Representatives*. Washington: Brookings.

Davidson, Roger H., and Walter J. Oleszek. 1989. *Congress and Its Members*. 3rd ed. Washington: Congressional Quarterly.

Ferber, Mark J. 1971. "The Formation of the Democratic Study Group." In Nelson W. Polsby, ed. *Congressional Behavior*. New York: Random House.

Matsunaga, Spark M., and Ping Chen. 1976. *Rulemakers of the House*. Urbana: U. of Illinois Pr.

Mayo, Bernard. 1937. *Henry Clay*. Boston: Houghton Mifflin.

Peabody, Robert L. 1973. *Leadership in Congress*. Boston: Little, Brown.

Rieselbach, LeRoy N. 1978. *Legislative Reform: The Policy Impact*. Lexington, MA: Lexington Books.

Robinson, James A. 1963. *The House Rules Committee*. Indianapolis: Bobbs-Merrill.

Sinclair, Barbara. 1983. *Majority Leadership in the U.S. House*. Baltimore: Johns Hopkins U. Pr.

Smith, Steven S., and Christopher J. Deering. 1984. *Committees in Congress*. Washington: Congressional Quarterly.

## Party Switchers

Almost all elections held for federal and state office in the United States, and many of the elections held for local office, are partisan elections. That is, candidates run as party candidates: they are nominated by political parties, and the party label often appears on the ballot next to their names. This party label carries a meaning. While that meaning may differ from region to region, voters have an instinctive feeling, if not a carefully conceived opinion, of what it means to be a Democrat or a Republican in their community, their state, and their region.

Party labels and party images do not remain constant. At critical periods in American history, political parties have taken stands on major issues—stands that have defined the images of those parties for the citizenry. As an example, in the 1930s the Democratic Party came to be known as the party of the New Deal after Franklin Roosevelt's program in response to the Great Depression. The Republican Party's image was defined by its leaders' responses to Roosevelt's initiatives. At other times party images change more gradually. In the South, where the Democrats held a virtual monopoly on elective office for much of the twentieth century, both parties' images shifted as a result of a series of presidential campaigns in the 1960s and 1970s.

One of the consequences of changes in party image, nationally or in one region, gradually or in response to a critical issue, is that citizens rethink their commitment to the political party they have previously favored. Analyses of partisan realignment explore this process in some detail. Democrats become Republicans; Republicans become Democrats. Some partisans of each party lose their zeal while others become more enthusiastic. Fewer citizens vote straight party tickets.

For public officials elected under a partisan label, rethinking partisan affiliation is a major undertaking. These officeholders owe their nomination, and in some cases their election, to one or the other of the political parties, and to say that they no longer feel tied to that political party could mean to surrendering their office. On the other hand, a declaration of "party switch" might signify recognition that the citizens in their region are changing affiliation and that the elected officeholder is doing so in order to continue to represent those citizens. In either case party switching by elected officeholders, much more rare than switches in party affiliation by those less involved in partisan politics, is a signal that major changes are going on within the political system.

Scholars have looked at party switching by elected officials as a sign that realignments were beginning. Some politicians have clearly switched in recognition of changing party positions. Historically, however, the more common pattern has been for those most closely tied to a party to retain their affiliations but then lose at the ballot box if the electorate has realigned. From 1952 through 1980 only 8 U.S. Representatives or Senators switched party (see Table 1). Party switching by members of Congress was so rare that individuals like Wayne Morse of Oregon or Harry Byrd, Jr., of Virginia were considered to be true mavericks—rare politicians willing to flout accepted ways to gain success.

In the 1980s, however, the Republican Party (especially but not exclusively in the South) has actively sought converts to the GOP side. Six Congressmen switched parties in that decade, all conservative Democrats who became Republicans. The congressional party welcomed the converts, easing the transition by allowing them to retain their seniority and key committee assignments. Presidents Ronald Reagan and George Bush embraced their new copartisans as leaders of a national conversion. While evidence of national partisan realignment is mixed, the Republicans have been successful in convincing large numbers of elected state officials in the South to switch to the GOP. The extent to which this strategy will be successful in extending Republican inroads into the once solidly Democratic South is yet to be determined; but early indications suggest that those who observe

# Table 1

*Party Switchers in Congress (1952–1990)*

| Name | State | House | Direction | Year |
|------|-------|-------|-----------|------|
| Atkinson, Eugene V. | PA | House | D > R | 1981 |
| Byrd, Harry F., Jr. | VA | Senate | D > I | 1970 |
| Gramm, Phil | TX | House | D > R | 1983 |
| Grant, Bill | FL | House | D > R | 1989 |
| Ireland, Andy | FL | House | D > R | 1984 |
| Jarman, John | OK | House | D > R | 1975 |
| Morse, Wayne | OR | Senate | R > I > D | 1952 |
| Peyser, Peter A. | NY | House | R > D | 1976 |
| Reid, Ogden R. | NY | House | R > D | 1972 |
| Reigle, Donald W. | MI | House | R > D | 1973 |
| Robinson, Tommy | OK | House | D > R | 1989 |
| Stump, Bob | AZ | House | D > R | 1981 |
| Thurmond, Strom | SC | Senate | D > R | 1964 |
| Watson, Albert W. | SC | House | D > R | 1965 |

Source: *Congressional Quarterly Almanac, 1952–1989.*

politics should monitor this relatively new phenomenon closely.

*See also:* George Bush, Harry F. Byrd, Jr., New Deal, Ronald Reagan, Franklin D. Roosevelt

L. Sandy Maisel

REFERENCES

Rothenberg, Stuart. 1985. *Party Switchers.* Washington: Institute for Government and Politics.

## Party System in the U.S. House of Representatives

In the twentieth century, national politics increasingly has become the great arena in which most American expectations, interests, and issues sooner or later contend. This is not to say that they always have been resolved or accommodated by political means, only that they have been articulated in the language of politics and refracted through the political process. Such has not always been the case, especially in the United States in the nineteenth century. Yet no one would argue that nineteenth-century concerns were any less divisive or compelling. Americans in the last century, however, did not as frequently turn to the federal government to arbitrate or reconcile their differences. In this century, the United States has undergone a profound change in popular attitudes toward the proper sphere of government. In the same period, America's rise to world power has brought in its wake all the demands on government consequent to international dominance.

The framers of the Constitution clearly intended the House of Representatives to be the most democratic institution in the federal government. The House always has been preter-naturally sensitive to changes, and a major consequence has been an increasingly complicated division of labor. Students of the House can chart its response over time to changes in the wider society by tracing the proliferation of its committees and subcommittees.

Complex divisions of labor, however, generate centrifugal forces that tend to pull organizations apart. Lost in the welter of constituent units—each pursuing its own immediate end—are the general interests of the organization as a whole. To counter this process of Balkanization, strong integrative mechanisms must be developed to hold together what the division of labor would otherwise pull apart. In the House of Representatives, the party system traditionally has served this cohesive purpose. Although neither the Constitution nor the rules of the House mentions them, political parties have acted from the beginning as devices to integrate and rationalize the separate activities of Congressmen.

One of the most striking differences between nineteenth- and twentieth-century Houses of Representatives is the decline in the importance of party strength. A brief glance at the levels of party voting in the House over time will underscore this decline. Likewise, an analysis of the importance of party in the apportioning of committee assignments will reveal a part of what Nelson Polsby has called the "institutionalism of the House of Representatives" (Polsby, 1968, Figure 2).

The decline of party strength in the House of Representatives can be documented by focusing on the components of party strength—interparty divisiveness and intraparty cohesion. The decline of party strength is then treated by summarizing issue dimensions over time. The causes of party decline in the House of Representatives are related to both the exogenous political system, (e.g., electoral changes), and to structural changes in the House itself. The effects of electoral change on House coalitions and thus on party voting is important. Moreover, the effect of internal structural changes on party strength has significance as well. These structural changes are viewed from the perspective of the sanctions available to the leadership to bring dissenting members into line. The consequences of party decline are, of course, multiple and complex. Two major results, however, deserve analysis. The first is the effect of decline upon the party leadership; the second is the consequences of decline on public policymaking.

Any analysis that purports to clarify differences between nineteenth- and twentieth-century Congresses must first decide when the nineteenth century ended and the twentieth began. Different historians with different concerns have marked the turn of the century differently. McKinley's first election, his assassination, the beginning of World War I, even the opening of the New York Armory Show all have been advanced as the real point of transition. About the only year that has almost no advocates is 1900. Here, the most meaningful contention is that the new century began in 1910–1911, with the Sixty-first Congress, which redefined the role of the Speaker.

### The Importance of Party in the House

The emergence of well-articulated party divisions within the House occurred in the Jacksonian era, understandably enough at about the same time that real parties emerged in the electorate. As Ronald Formisano has shown, the earlier organized battles between the Alexander Hamilton and Thomas Jefferson factions in Congress, elite in nature, bore many of the features of later party disputes and clearly foreshadowed the appearance of full-fledged political parties in the next generation. By Jackson's second term, the party system had assumed its characteristic dimensions—party in the electorate, party as organization, and party as government. By the early 1830s, both the Whigs and Democrats had acquired party identifiers throughout all regions of the country. They had established separate and competing local and state organizations. And, Joel Silbey (1967) argues, in the House of Representatives, both voting patterns and internal organization revealed clearly defined party divisions. Moreover, as McCormick (1966) has shown, the parties were intensively competitive across all states. No region was either solidly Democratic or Whig.

The party system has endured despite the periodic disappearance of major parties, despite sectional cleavages, and despite disruptive changes in the nominating mechanism. The American party system is the oldest in the (Western) world. Voting in the U.S. House of Representatives had a pronounced party component long before party was a factor in other national legislatures. Despite the early development of partisan voting in the House, other Western legislative bodies soon surpassed the House in levels of party voting (Lawrence Lowell, 1901). Thus, comparatively low levels of party solidarity distinguish the House from other democratic systems in the modern era. When we argue, consequently, that party strength in the House has declined in the twentieth century, the original point of declension is lower than those typical of European legislatures.

In order to analyze the causes of the decline of party strength in the House of Representatives, party strength needs to be defined more carefully. Table 1 shows the decline in party voting in the House as measured by the percentage of all roll calls in which 50 percent of one party opposed 50 percent of the other. The trend from the heyday of party voting in the 1800–1910 period is definitely downward, with the lowest scores registered in the 1966–1980 period. The 1982 to 1988 scores show an upward movement in the levels of party voting. What remains unclear, however, is what is being measured when votes are aggregated in this manner. Aage Clausen (1973) has shown that votes in the House can be broken down into policy dimensions in any given Congress and that some of the issues consequently exposed have historical continuity. Clausen's work, along with that of Barbara Sinclair, demonstrates the abiding nature of certain issue dimensions at least since the New Deal. They can be arranged under headings that would include civil liberties, government management, social welfare, agricultural assistance, and international involvement. In each of these areas, different coalitions have been at work. Party affiliation, for example, determined voting behavior much more strongly on matters pertaining to government manage-

# Table 1

*Party Voting in the House of Representatives—50th (1887) to 99th (1986) Houses*

| Year Elected | Congress | 50% vs. 50% | Year Elected | Congress | 50% vs. 50% |
|---|---|---|---|---|---|
| 1886 | 50 | 51.1 | 1936 | 75 | 63.9 |
| 1888 | 51 | 78.9 | 1938 | 76 | 71.4 |
| 1890 | 52 | 45.4 | 1940 | 77 | 41.5 |
| 1892 | 53 | 44.8 | 1942 | 78 | 49.4 |
| 1894 | 54 | 68.5 | 1944 | 79 | 48.1 |
| 1896 | 55 | 79.8 | 1946 | 80 | 44.8 |
| 1898 | 56 | 77.2 | 1948 | 81 | 50.9 |
| 1900 | 57 | 67.0 | 1950 | 82 | 64.1 |
| 1902 | 58 | 89.7 | 1952 | 83 | 44.9 |
| 1904 | 59 | 73.5 | 1954 | 84 | 42.3 |
| 1906 | 60 | 57.1 | 1956 | 85 | 49.2 |
| 1908 | 61 | 79.2 | 1958 | 86 | 52.8 |
| 1910 | 62 | 59.5 | 1960 | 87 | 48.8 |
| 1912 | 63 | 61.4 | 1962 | 88 | 51.7 |
| 1914 | 64 | 58.6 | 1964 | 89 | 47.1 |
| 1916 | 65 | 42.7 | 1966 | 90 | 35.8 |
| 1918 | 66 | 44.9 | 1968 | 91 | 29.2 |
| 1920 | 67 | 59.9 | 1970 | 92 | 33.0 |
| 1922 | 68 | 58.7 | 1972 | 93 | 35.7 |
| 1924 | 69 | 43.7 | 1974 | 94 | 42.3 |
| 1926 | 70 | 48.6 | 1976 | 95 | 38.8 |
| 1928 | 71 | 58.2 | 1978 | 96 | 43.5 |
| 1930 | 72 | 57.7 | 1980 | 97 | 35.9 |
| 1932 | 73 | 70.6 | 1982 | 89 | 51.8 |
| 1934 | 74 | 59.9 | 1984 | 99 | 58.6 |

ment than either international involvement or social welfare.

Similar work on nineteenth-century Congresses has shown that the periods from 1850–1876 and 1884–1900 also reveal issues of continuous legislative interest. Party membership does appear to have influenced voting behavior in these earlier periods more profoundly than in the post-New Deal era. Still, some issues of lasting interest clearly were not structured by party. By using rough measures of party cohesion on roll-call votes, analysts can trace a decline in party strength; it is by no means clear, however, how the mix of issue dimensions affected these percentages over time. A more subtle analysis would have to confront the relationship between aggregate voting patterns and issue dimensions. Unfortunately, practical as well as methodological problems impede such an analysis. For the purpose of this article, the imprecise measures presented in Table 1 must serve to annotate the decline of party strength in the House. Although useful as blunt indicators of general trends, these figures mask a complicated pattern of underlying issue dimensions, ones that were

confronted year in and year out by shifting congressional coalitions, not always congruent with party lines.

On the other hand, party affiliation did have some bearing on issue dimension voting, especially in periods of extreme party voting. In periods of weak party voting, it clearly did not. Probably the aggregate measure of party voting roughly reflects the extent to which party structured issue dimension voting at a particular point in time, although the data cannot be broken down more specifically by issue dimension over the entire time series. Two related but distinct components of party voting in Congress—intraparty unity and interparty divisiveness—constitute a second aspect of party strength that should be considered. If, in a given Congress, unity within each party and divisiveness between the two were high, votes tended to follow party lines in a comprehensive fashion. But in another Congress, when unity and divisiveness happened to be low, party affiliation clearly did not structure voting. Two additional combinations of unity and divisiveness are shown in Figure 1.

## Figure 1

DIVISIVENESS

| | | High | Low |
|---|---|---|---|
| U | | Party Structures Voting Comprehensively (A) | Partial Structuring of Voting Consensual (C) |
| N | High | | |
| I | | | |
| T | Low | Partial Structuring of Voting Factional (B) | Party Does Not Structure Voting (D) |
| Y | | | |

When party divisiveness is high but party unity low, party will structure voting on some issues yet not on others. In fact, this is the pattern found by Clausen in the post-New Deal era. If divisiveness is low and party unity high, then party will structure some voting, but also existing will be either a cross-party conflict or a cross-party consensus, such as the conservative coalition of recent years. If we were to rate the combinations by the extent to which party structures voting, the ordering would be A, B, C, and D—from most to least partisan. In the case of the AD diagonal, analysis is relatively straightforward. Party either structures all or most of the voting or none or very little of the voting. Analysis becomes more difficult when one turns to B and C. Here party structuring of the vote falls somewhere between the two extremes. In one case, party structures voting because the parties disagree on some significant subset of issues, while in the other case divisiveness or conflict between parties is low, but intraparty cohesion is high. Thus, in the first case, party divisiveness structures voting even though intraparty cohesion is low; in the second case, however, intraparty cohesiveness structures voting.

Superimposing a Clausen-type dimensional analysis onto the party voting scores shown in Table 1 results in a decline of party strength in the House from cohesive, opposed parties to less cohesive, nondivisive parties. Until the period 1910–1911, party structured voting across a wide spectrum of issue dimensions. Table 2 shows the extent of party structuring of voting patterns on a range of issue dimensions for selected years from 1852 to 1900. Table 3 shows the extent of party structuring of the vote on a range of issue dimensions from selected Congresses since the 1910–1911 period. In Table 1, the results indicate that party correlated with a wider range of issues than is the case for those dimensions shown in Table 2. Even though party never completely structured voting in any pe-

## Table 2

*Average Correlations Between Party and Voting on Known Issue Dimensions for Selected Years in the 19th Century*

| 1853–1871 | Lowest Correlation | Average Correlation | Highest Correlation |
|---|---|---|---|
| **ISSUES** | | | |
| Slavery, Secession, Civil Rights | .41 | .83 | .98 |
| Public Works | .59 | .76 | .91 |
| Railroad/Telegraph Construction | .14 | .43 | .89 |
| Housekeeping | .27 | .78 | .96 |
| Money and Banking | .41 | .80 | .94 |
| Tariff | .02 | .67 | .92 |

| 1890–1900 | Lowest Correlation | Average Correlation | Highest Correlation |
|---|---|---|---|
| **ISSUES** | | | |
| Currency | .21 | .78 | .96 |
| Military Appropriations | .19 | .67 | .94 |
| Tariff | .20 | .81 | .98 |
| Business | .40 | .87 | .98 |
| Public Works | .26 | .39 | .70 |
| Housekeeping | .73 | .91 | .99 |
| Immigration | .26 | .52 | .81 |
| Taxation | .85 | .89 | .92 |

Taken from D. Brady (1982).

# Table 3

*Average Correlations Between Party and Selected Issue Dimensions for Some 20th Century Houses*

| 1925–1938 | Lowest Correlation | Average Correlation | Highest Correlation |
|---|---|---|---|
| **ISSUES** | | | |
| Government Management | .90 | .93 | .96 |
| Agricultural Policy | .09 | .52 | .93 |
| Social Welfare | .78 | .84 | .92 |
| Civil Liberties | .17 | .21 | .46 |
| **1953–1964** | Lowest Correlation | Average Correlation | Highest Correlation |
| **ISSUES** | | | |
| Government Management | .88 | .90 | .96 |
| Agricultural Assistance | .74 | .80 | .92 |
| Social Welfare | .51 | .63 | .83 |
| International Involvement | .05 | .38 | .78 |
| Civil Liberties | .12 | .14 | .22 |

Taken from Barbara Sinclair (1977) and Aage Clausen (1973).

riod, the extent of structuring was greater in the nineteenth century. This evidence corresponds to the decline of party voting shown in Table 1. Thus the partial mapping of issue-dimensional analysis onto the over-time party voting series corroborates the decline of party strength in the U.S. House in the twentieth century. The decline of party strength in the House accelerated after 1938 (see Table 1). This statistical phenomenon reflects the rise of the Conservative Coalition in the Congress. This bloc of southern Democrats and Republicans voting against liberal legislation is by definition antiparty, since elements of one party cross party lines to vote with the opposition. From 1938 until at least the Ronald Reagan era, the Conservative Coalition has been a prominent voting alliance in the U.S. House; however, as David Rohde has shown, southern Democrats increasingly have begun to vote like northern Democrats. Rohde argues that the rise in levels of party voting in the 1982–1988 period results from the increased demographic similarity of the southern Democratic districts to the northern Democratic districts.

In sum, party strength in the U.S. House of Representatives in general has declined, although the Reagan presidency generated a rise in the level of party voting. This decline can be characterized as the movement from highly cohesive and opposed parties to only fairly cohesive and less divisive parties. It means that the extent to which party-structured voting on issue dimensions has dropped over time. The decline in party strength from its nineteenth-century highs began with the revolt against the Speaker in the 1910–1911 period and continued with the rise of cross-party coalitional government in the House. It is important to recognize the existence of low points in party voting.

## Causes of the Decline of Party

The federal arrangement of the American system has produced a fragmented party system. Each of the 50 states has a separate party system. Underlying that system is a pattern of local interests, issues, and voting patterns. At the national level, the American party system is an amalgam of overlapping state, local, and regional interests. The nineteenth-century party system was certainly affected by the federal nature of the American government. Unlike the modern party system, however, partisanship in the last century was stronger in the electorate. Historians' accounts of party strength in the nineteenth century show partisan voting to be important. McCormick on the second party system, Hays (1975) and McKitrick (1975) on the third party system, and the electoral work of Jones and Jensen (1971) clearly demonstrate the importance of party as the major variable accounting for electoral results. The reasons put forward to account for the high levels of partisanship in the last century elections are numerous. They include the use of list voting rather than the Australian ballot, the role of elections as entertainment, and a technological inability to communicate the personal characteristics of candidates to large numbers of voters.

Within the formal party organization, however, elected politicians were able to control the nominating process at every level—local, state, and national—thus providing for a greater degree of party control. The general practice of rotation in office, particularly in the House of Representatives, kept Congressmen from building local sources of support independent of the party organization. The fact that there were no primaries in which members of the same party competed with one another also strengthened the party organization. In sum, a considerable body of evidence suggests that both party in the electorate and party organization were stronger in the nineteenth than in the twentieth century. Whether this stronger partisanship was the result of structural factors or of psychological, behavioral differences is beyond the scope of this analysis. (See Rusk and Converse, 1974.) Suffice it to say that for whatever reasons, party was stronger in the nineteenth than in the twentieth century. If both the electorate and the party organization were strong, a student would expect to find party strength greater in the House. However, the electoral connection between member and constituent has clearly changed.

The most immediate and direct relationship exists between a Congressman and his electorate. Without a plurality of votes, a candidate does not become a Congressman. Thus, if partisan voting has declined over time, some corresponding changes must have taken place in the electoral process. The major change is that in the twentieth century Congressmen are able to control their own fates more easily than their forebears could in the last century. The process of nominating candidates has shifted from the party to the individual. In the first half of the nineteenth century, candidates were rotated by local parties. The famous example of Abraham Lincoln waiting for his turn to run for the House and then serving only one term is a good example of rotation. Until the latter part of the nineteenth century, voting in elections was by party lists rather than by Australian ballot. Both of these mechanisms and what appears to have been a more partisan electorate gave political parties control over candidates. That is, rational candidates considered their electoral fate to be tied to the fate of their party and its presidential candidates, rather than to their own ability to service constituents.

The introduction of the primary as a major nominating vehicle clearly weakened the effect of political parties on the nominating process. As primaries increased in number and media technology became universally available, candidates raised their own money and built their own organizations, which today include pollsters, media managers, and others. The result is that winning candidates are not beholden to party organizations for either their nomination or for their election. Once elected, these Congressmen have increasingly turned to nonpartisan service activities as the major component of their reelectoral success. Members nominated, elected, and reelected under these conditions are not likely to be especially amenable to pressure from party leaders, especially when they see differences between the party leaders' positions and those of their constituents. In sum, the changing American electoral universe has clearly aided the decline of party in the House of Representatives. The decline in partisan identification, the changes in ballot forms, the rise of primaries, and an increased reliance on the electronic media have all increased Congressmen's ability to manage their own electoral fate. Under these conditions, parties as organizations have lost control over nominations and campaigns.

Such was not true of the partisan alignments in the U.S. House of Representatives from roughly 1854 until the period 1910–1911, which pitted the urban industrial North against the more rural South and Border States. This regional alignment was mapped onto the congressional parties, that is, the North was essentially Republican while the South was Democratic. The election of a Democratic majority in the House in 1910 and the subsequent election of Woodrow Wilson in 1912 broke Republican dominance of the North until 1918. From 1920 until the period 1930–1932, the Republicans regained dominance in the North. The Franklin D. Roosevelt landslide in 1932 made the Democrats the dominant party in both the North and South until the 1938 House elections allowed the Republicans to become competitive in the North. The Democratic Party's control of the House from 1930 until today has resulted from of their dominance in northern urban districts combined with their southern contingent. Thus the electoral base of the House Democratic majority from 1938 to at least 1980 has been based on a regional arrangement that was electoral only. The fact that on many issues, especially civil rights (until the late 1960s at least), the Congressmen of these regions disagreed also helped to weaken party strength in the House. Relatively safe in their seats, southern Democrats could count on ultimately rising to positions of power within the committee system. Whether this Dixie dominance rested on the southerners' ability to spend time on Capitol Hill or on the fact that certain elections such as 1946 devastated their northern counterparts makes little difference. The facts are that in the 1938–1980 period southerners held a disproportionate share of committee chairmanships. The northern element of the Democratic Party dominated presidential politics (with 1976 being the only exception), and southerners dominated congressional politics. In short, in the post-1938 period, the Democratic Party in the House was composed of two distinct and often opposed elements, and the consequence of this coalition did not aid party strength in the House. The rise of Republican strength in the South in the Reagan era, however, has brought many conservative districts into the Republican Party fold. This development obviously increases party voting since districts formerly represented by conservative Democrats voting with the Conservative Coalition are now represented by Republicans voting Republican.

### Internal Causes

The major integrative mechanisms in the House over the years have been the congressional parties, especially the majority party. When a congressional party was strong, the House leadership could integrate what the division of labor pulled apart. In an important sense, then, the ability to integrate is a test of party strength. Despite short-term fluctuations, nineteenth-century House leaders had the advantage over their twentieth-century counterparts in this regard. Since 1911, only the three New Deal Congresses (1932–1938) made a point of party strength. From 1938 until 1980, the decline is especially pronounced.

Superior party strength in the nineteenth century stemmed internally from the availability of sanctions to leaders. Kenneth Shepsle makes this point nicely when he argues that legislatures are cooperative games. That is, the stronger the parties' sanctions over members, the higher the level of intraparty cooperation. One reason that European legislatures have high levels of party voting is that their party systems—from local constituencies to party as government—have greater sanctions than do Ameri-

can parties. While levels of party voting in the U.S. House have probably never been as high as they are in European systems, historical analysis shows that the greater the sanctions, the higher the levels of party voting. The greatest sanction available to the congressional leadership has been the power to appoint committees. Party voting in the last century is higher than any period in the post-1915 period with the exception of Roosevelt's first three New Deal Houses. The highest levels of party voting in the history of the House came between 1890 and 1910, when the Speaker had the full complement of floor powers to go with his appointive powers. The Speaker's control of the Rules Committee, his right to recognition on the floor, and his power to count a quorum during the 1890–1910 period increased his ability to discipline dissident members. And Brady and Althoff (1974) have shown that the highest levels of party strength occur in precisely this period.

In the period 1910–1911, a coalition of progressive Republicans and Democrats booted the Speaker off the Rules Committee and broke his stranglehold on committee assignments. With the weakening of the Speaker began the decline of party in the House (see Figure 1). Although Woodrow Wilson was able to work effectively with the Democratic Caucus, the fact that he had to turn to the Caucus at all on important votes underscores the point that the decline of party in the House was already underway. Both party voting and cohesion dropped during Wilson's first term. From Speakers Joseph Cannon through Sam Rayburn down to "Tip" O'Neill, the shift in the internal operation of the House is best described as the movement from authority to bargaining. Speakers Thomas Reed and Cannon were the leaders of their party, and their subordinates (Majority Leader, Whip, etc.) were also committee chairmen. Together they sat like a kind of cabinet government. Cannon's power was extensive enough to permit him to thwart Theodore Roosevelt's legislative package in the Fifty-eighth House. After the Speaker lost the power to appoint committees, the party leadership and the committee leadership diverged. Committee leaders became chieftains with whom the party leaders bargained in order to process and pass legislation. Party leaders since the period 1910–1911 generally have been negotiators and middlemen. Only rarely and under exceptional circumstances have they wielded the kind of power that Reed and Cannon took for granted.

This analysis has shown that from the nineteenth to the twentieth century, changes in the electoral system weakened the connection between party in the electorate, party as organization, and the congressional parties. Internally the loss or sanctions available to the leadership, plus the increasing role of specialization and thus the committee's power, weakened party strength in the House. That these two phenomena are related is not in doubt; however, the state of our knowledge about the specific linkages between these exogenous and endogenous factors is limited. Thus, tying these elements together would involve almost pure speculation. Still, the combination of these factors, however combinatorial, is strongly related to the decline of party strength in the U.S. House of Representatives.

### The Policy Consequences of the Decline of Party

The first and most obvious effect of the decline of party in the House on American public policy is that party leaders, in political scientist V. O. Key's words, are forced into a "ceaseless maneuvering to find majorities." When the "majority" party cannot provide a majority for programs—either the President's or the party leaders'—the result is at best incrementalism and at worst stalemate. The one characteristic common to all periods of major policy change (e.g., Jacksonian reforms, the civil liberties and economic legislation of the 1860s and early 1870s, the New Deal) was the existence of a cohesive majority party and a cohesive opposed minority. In none of these periods have the President and his congressional allies been forced to build and continually rebuild an interparty coalition to enact programs. When party strength is high, policy tends to have direction and consistency. Under conditions of party weakness or political flux, leaders are forced to seek votes and compromise policy in order to form ephemeral majorities. This point could be shown over time given sufficient data. Since such data are lacking, the example will have to stand for the whole in an examination of the process of policy formation first in recent Houses, then in the Reed Houses of the period of 1897–1901 (55th and 56th).

In the contemporary House, the policy process begins in the committees. Individual bills—presidentially sponsored or otherwise—are assigned to the relevant committee or committees. Normally (especially on money bills), the committees are expected to compromise differences between Republicans and Democrats, liberals and conservatives, North and South so that the final product is acceptable to a majority of members. The committee's bill then goes to the House Rules Committee for both clearances to the floor and specific rules governing time, amendments, and so on. The committee system thus determines where work is done, and it clearly shapes policy.

This committee system is separate from the party system in the modern House, where seniority normally determines committee leadership. Throughout most of the post-1910–1911 period, the committee leaders' perspectives differed from those of the party leaders, a problem particularly acute in the post-1938 period. Since 1938, the Democrats have controlled the House for all but four years (1947–1949; 1953–1955), and conservative southern Democrats often chaired important committees. Because many committees were chaired by southerners like Graham Barden (N.C.), Howard Smith (Va.), and George Mahon (Tex.), who were neither national nor presidential Democrats, the House Democratic leadership was often frustrated. Even cursory studies of legislative proposals such as Medicare-Medicaid, aid to elementary and secondary education, and civil rights, will show how committee leaders with different legislative or social views could keep the House party leadership from achieving its desired policy results. The party and committee leadership were from separate and often ideologically opposed power bases, even though they were nominally of the same party. When regular House members could take their cues from either set of leaders, the result was often stalemate. This deadlocked relationship has been further complicated by the recent trend of Republican Presidents and Democratic Houses. In the Reagan era from 1981 through 1988, a conservative President faced a liberal House, and under Speaker James Wright the House had its own agenda.

In contrast, the party and committee system in the 1890–1910 period were blended. The Speaker of the House was chairman of the Rules Committee; the Majority Leader was chairman of the Appropriations Committee; the Majority Whip was chairman of either Judiciary or Ways and Means. The Rules Committee, which had no formal meeting room and consisted of only five members, was subject to the Speaker's call to meet wherever and whenever he chose. The Speaker's unilateral right to appoint committees permitted him to staff the Rules Committee with loyal party men. This capability, in essence, gave him absolute control over the management and timing of all bills. Furthermore, the Speaker could and did use his appointive powers to reward the faithful and to punish the mavericks within his own party. His monopoly on appointments and his formal parliamentary powers assured strong party voting on the floor. The practice of selecting committee chairmen to fill important posts in the party organization further served to blur the distinctions between committee and party. During this era, the Republicans never sought Democratic support for tariff, appropriations, money, and other bills. Rather they alone determined policy direction by writing and enacting legislation over strident, but ineffectual, Democratic opposition. In contrast to the modern House where bills come before the body late in the legislative session, many important bills in the Cannon-Reed era were introduced and passed within the first few days. The passage of the Dingley Tariff early in the special session of the Fifty-fifth House is a classic case in point.

In the heyday of the Speaker-dominated House, the majority congressional party could pass legislation with strong partisan majorities. The Speaker's powers plus a belief in party government were sufficient to ensure these majorities. But this party dominance did not hold true for most of the Houses since the period 1910–1911. Party leaders in the post-1910–1911 period have had to rely on bargaining and compromise to achieve limited policy goals. Their predecessors could rely on authority to carry the day. The contrast in leadership styles between "Czar" Cannon and Sam Rayburn is the difference between authority and bargaining.

This comparison between ideal types of partisan and fragmented congressional policy formation demonstrates the difference between parties which stand for something and those that try to offer all things to all voters. Of course, not all nineteenth-century Houses had strong congressional parties. Nor have all post-1910 Houses had fragmented, indecisive majorities. Franklin Roosevelt's New Deal Houses and Lyndon Johnson's Eighty-ninth House are proof that undiluted policy innovation is possible in the twentieth century. Yet in both these instances party strength was greater than in periods preceding or following them. In general, then, party strength was greater in the nineteenth century than it has been in the twentieth.

One result of this change is clear: public policy formulation in the twentieth century has been more incremental. A congressional policy process dominated by bargaining and compromise virtually assures this slowness. Party leaders who could count on their party's support were freer to examine policy alternatives and innovative solutions: less of their time was necessarily consumed in attempts to build majorities.

*Conclusions*

Party strength was greater before the period 1910–1911 than since. While no one can adduce a complete answer to why this is so, the following reasons seem important: the decline of party identification in the electorate, the rise of primaries as the major nominating mechanism, the concomitant decline in the role of party organizations in nominating candidates, and the development of highly personalized campaign organizations dominated by media and polling technologists. In sum, these factors have helped to create an electoral system in which individual members view their electoral fate as dependent on their own actions rather than those of the local or national party. Members elected under these conditions have fewer incentives than did their nineteenth-century counterparts to vote with their party.

The decline of party as an electoral force in the twentieth century has been paralleled by both a weakening of the party leadership's sanctions over members and a decentralization of policy making to committees and subcommittees. The shift to committees and subcommittees has resulted in an increase in an individual House member's ability to decide on policy matters relevant to his or her constituents. In short, in the twentieth century, parties can use fewer internal incentives (either positive or negative) for members to support the party leaders' positions. In combination with the changed electoral system, the result is a major decline in party strength in the U.S. House of Representatives.

*See also:* Australian Ballot, Individual Speakers of the House, Party Rules in Congress, Speaker of the House

*David W. Brady*
*John Etting*

REFERENCES

Abram, Michael, and Joseph Cooper. 1968. "The Rise of Seniority in the House of Representatives." 1 *Polity* 52.

Anderson, James E. 1979. *Public Policy Making.* New York: Holt, Rinehart, Winston.

Aydelotte, William. 1966. "Parties and Issues in Early Victorian England." 5 *Journal of British Studies* 94.

Benedict, Michael. 1974. *A Compromise of Principle: Congressional Republicans and Reconstruction, 1863–1869*. New York: Karton.

Brady, David. 1973. *Congressional Voting in a Partisan Era*. Lawrence: U. of Kansas Pr.

———. 1978. "Critical Elections, Congressional Parties and Clusters of Policy Change." 8 *British Journal of Political Science* 79.

———. 1980. "Congressional Elections and Clusters of Policy Change in the U.S. House: 1886–1960." In Richard Trilling and Bruce Campbell, eds. *Realignment in American Politics: Toward a Theory*. Austin: U. of Texas Pr.

———. 1982. "Congressional Party Realignment and Transformations of Public Policy in Three Realignment Eras." 26 *American Journal of Political Science* 333.

———, and Phillip Althoff. 1974. "Party Voting in the U.S. House of Representatives, 1890–1910: Elements of a Responsible Party System." 36 *Journal of Politics* 753.

———, and Charles Bullock. 1980. "Is There a Conservative Coalition in the House?" 42 *Journal of Politics* 549.

Burns, James. 1963. *The Deadlock of Democracy: Four Party Politics in America*. Englewood Cliffs, NJ: Prentice-Hall.

Clausen, Aage. 1973. *How Congressmen Decide: A Policy Focus*. New York: St. Martin's.

Chambers, William N., and Walter Dean Burnham, eds. 1975. *The American Party System: Stages of Political Development*. New York: Oxford U. Pr.

Cooper, Joseph. 1961. "Congress and Its Committees." Ph.D. dissertation, Harvard U.

———. 1970. *The Origins of the Standing Committees and the Development of the Modern House*. Houston: Rice U. Publications.

———. 1975. "Strengthening the Congress: An Organizational Analysis." 12 *Harvard Journal of Legislation* 307.

———. 1977. "Congress in Organizational Perspective." In Lawrence C. Dodd and Bruce I. Oppenheimer, eds. *Congress Reconsidered*. New York: Praeger.

———, and David Brady. 1981. "Institutional Context and Leadership Style: The House from Cannon to Rayburn." 75 *American Political Science Review* 411.

———, ———, and Patricia Hurley. 1977. "The Electoral Basis of Party Voting: Patterns and Trends in the U.S. House of Representatives." In Joseph Cooper and Sandy Maisel, eds. *The Impact of the Electoral Process*. Beverly Hills, CA: Sage.

Dodd, Lawrence, and Bruce Oppenheimer, eds. 1981. *Congress Reconsidered*. Washington: Congressional Quarterly.

Fenno, Richard. 1962. "The House Appropriations Committee as a Political System: The Problem of Integration." 56 *American Political Science Review* 310.

———. 1973. *Congressmen in Committees*. Boston: Little, Brown.

———, and Frank Munger. 1962. *National Politics and Federal Aid to Education*. Syracuse: Syracuse U. Pr.

Fiorina, Morris. 1977. *Congress: Keystone of the Washington Establishment*. New Haven: Yale U. Pr.

Formisano, Ronald. 1971. *The Birth of Mass Political Parties: Michigan 1827–1861*. Princeton: Princeton U. Pr.

Ginsberg, Benjamin. 1972. "Critical Elections and the Substance of Party Conflict: 1844–1968." 16 *Midwest Journal of Political Science* 603.

Heclo, Hugh. 1980. *A Government of Strangers*. Washington: Brookings.

Hays, Samuel. 1975. "Political Parties and the Community-Society Continuum." In William N. Chambers and Walter D. Burnham, eds. *The American Party Systems*. New York: Oxford U. Pr.

Huitt, Ralph. 1961. "Democratic Party Leadership in the Senate." 55 *American Political Science Review* 333.

Jensen, Richard. 1971. *The Winning of the Midwest*. Chicago: U. of Chicago Pr.

Jones, Charles O. 1961. "Representation in Congress: The Case of the House Agriculture Committee." 55 *American Political Science Review* 358.

———. 1964. *Party and Policy Making: The House Republican Policy Committee*. New Brunswick: Rutgers U. Pr.

———. 1968. "Joseph G. Cannon and Howard W. Smith: An Essay on the Limits of Leadership in the House of Representatives." 30 *Journal of Politics* 6.

Jones, Stanley. 1964. *The Presidential Election of 1896*. Madison: U. of Wisconsin Pr.

Kernell, Samuel. 1977. "Toward Understanding 19th Century Congressional Careers, Ambition, Competition and Rotation." 21 *American Journal of Political Science* 669.

Key, V. O. 1964. *Politics, Parties and Pressure Group*. 5th ed. New York: Crowell.

Lowell, A. Lawrence. 1901. "The Influence of Party upon Legislation in England and America." *Annual Report, American Historical Association*.

McConachie, Lauros. 1898. *Congressional Committees: A Study of the Origin and Development of Our National and Local Legislative Methods*. New York: Crowell.

McCormick, Richard. 1966. *The Second American Party System: Party Formation in the Jacksonian Era*. Chapel Hill: U. of North Carolina Pr.

McKitrick, Eric. 1975. "Party Politics and the Union and Confederate War Efforts." In William N. Chambers and Walter Dean Burnham, eds. *The American Party Systems*. New York: Oxford U. Pr.

Mayhew, David. 1966. *Party Loyalty Among Congressmen*. Cambridge: Harvard U. Pr.

———. 1974. *The Electoral Connection*. New Haven: Yale U. Pr.

Orfield, Gary. 1975. *Congressional Power: Congress and Social Change*. New York: Harcourt Brace Jovanovich.

Polsby, Nelson. 1968. "The Institutionalization of the U.S. House of Representatives." 62 *American Political Science Review* 144.

———, M. Gallagher, and Barry Rundquist. 1969. "The Growth of the Seniority System in the U.S. House of Representatives." 63 *American Political Science Review* 787.

Rusk, Jerrold, and Phillip Converse. 1974. "Comments in Response to Burnham." 48 *American Political Science Review* 1024.

Silbey, Joel H. 1967. *The Shrine of Party: Congressional Voting Behavior 1841–1852.* Pittsburgh: U. of Pittsburgh Pr.

Sinclair, Barbara. 1977. "Party Realignment and the Transformation of the Political Agenda: The House of Representatives, 1925–1938." 71 *American Political Science Review* 940.

———. 1982. *Congressional Realignment: 1925–1978.* Austin: U. of Texas Pr.

Sorauf, Frank. 1975. "Political Parties and Political Analysis." In William N. Chambers and Walter Dean Burnham, eds. *The American Party Systems.* New York: Oxford U. Pr.

Sundquist, James. 1968. *Politics and Policy: The Eisenhower, Kennedy and Johnson Years.* Washington: Brookings.

———. 1973. *Dynamics of the Party System.* Washington: Brookings.

Wilson, Woodrow. 1885. *Congressional Government.* Cleveland: World Publishing.

## Alice Paul (1885–1977)

Founder of the National Woman's Party. Born to a New Jersey Quaker family, Alice Paul received her A.B. from Swarthmore and graduated from the New York School of Social Work. She later received a Ph.D. from the University of Pennsylvania and an LL.M. from American University. In 1907 Paul traveled to England, where she worked in settlement houses and studied at the London School of Economics. She became involved with the militant tactics of English suffragists Emmeline, Christabel, and Sylvia Pankhurst.

On her return to the United States, Paul joined the National American Woman Suffrage Association (NAWSA) and became an active participant in the suffrage movement. Paul organized a demonstration of 10,000 women's suffrage supporters on the day before Woodrow Wilson's 1913 inauguration in Washington. Following the inauguration, Paul organized the Congressional Union as an arm of the NAWSA.

Paul wanted the Congressional Union to blame the party in power, and especially its leader, Democrat Woodrow Wilson, for denying the vote to women. When the NAWSA rejected the strategy as too radical, Paul left to form her own party, the National Woman's Party (also known simply as the Woman's Party). Under Paul's leadership, the National Woman's Party organized massive demonstrations and arranged a nationwide speaking tour for suffragists.

Hunger strikes were a favored tactic of the NWP. In October 1917, Paul was arrested during a demonstration in front of the White House. Given an especially harsh sentence of seven months in prison, Paul went on a hunger strike and was force-fed daily by prison officials for three weeks. Growing public sympathy, combined with a successful round of court appeals, led to Paul's release.

That Paul's National Woman's Party, as well as the other suffrage organizations, were instrumental in persuading politicians to take women's votes seriously became clear after the 1916 presidential election. In Illinois, one of the states in which women could vote, and the only state that kept voting statistics by gender, Wilson was rejected by women voters by a margin of 2 to 1. The continuing pressure for suffrage ultimately resulted in the passage and ratification in 1920 of the Nineteenth Amendment granting the vote to women nationwide.

Following the suffrage victory, Paul turned her attention to the passage of the Equal Rights Amendment; she remained on the NWP executive committee until 1937. In 1928 she founded the World Party for Equal Rights for Women. Returning from Europe after the outbreak of World War II, Paul again focused her attention on the ERA. She remained an energetic organizer and spokeswoman for equal rights until she suffered a stroke in 1974.

*See also:* National Woman's Party, Woman Suffrage Movement, Woodrow Wilson

*Jeffra Becknell*

REFERENCES

Irwin, Inez Hayes. 1971. *The Story of the Woman's Party.* New York: Harcourt, Brace.

Lunardini, Christine A. 1986. *From Equal Suffrage to Equal Rights: Alice Paul and the National Woman's Party.* New York: New York U. Pr.

## Henry C. Payne (1843–1904)

Republican National Committee chairman for the very brief period of three months. Massachusetts-born Henry Clay Payne was the son of a local Whig public official. At age 20, he moved to Milwaukee, where he achieved considerable success in the insurance business.

Payne's earliest political activities began in 1872 when he helped organize the Milwaukee's Young Men's Republican Club. Payne held the Milwaukee postmastership for ten years (1876–1886) and used it actively as a political base. By 1881 he was head of a Milwaukee "Post Office Clique," enabling him to displace the incumbent state party boss. In 1889 he became president of the Wisconsin Telephone Company and in 1895 president of the Milwaukee Street Railway Company.

Payne served successively as secretary and chairman of the Wisconsin Republican central committee and, after 1888, as Wisconsin national committeeman, and in 1892 declined President Benjamin Harrison's request that he be Republican national chairman. In 1896 Payne was vice chairman of the national committee under Mark Hanna; he strongly favored Theodore Roosevelt for the vacant vice presidential nomination on the William McKinley ticket in 1900 and, still vice chairman, was Chairman Hanna's headquarters manager during the election campaign. When Roosevelt succeeded to the presidency in 1901, he immediately appointed Payne Postmaster General. When Hanna died on February 15, 1904, Payne became acting chairman only to suffer an apoplectic stroke in April.

*See also:* Marcus A. (Mark) Hanna, Benjamin Harrison, Republican National Committee, Theodore Roosevelt

*Ralph M. Goldman*

REFERENCES

Allen, William H. 1901. "The Election of 1900." *Annals of the American Academy of Political and Social Sciences* (January): 53.

Goldman, Ralph M. 1990. *The National Party Chairmen and Committees: Factionalism at the Top.* Armonk, NY: M. E. Sharpe.

Roosevelt, Theodore. Theodore Roosevelt Papers. Library of Congress.

## Peace and Freedom Party

The Peace and Freedom Party (PFP) was the first of several "third" parties to grow out of the "New Left" of the late 1960s and early 1970s. Despite the relative success of the presidential campaigns of Senator Eugene McCarthy (N.Y.) and Senator Robert Kennedy (N.Y.) in the Democratic primaries in 1968, some New Left activists came to the conclusion that only by forming a new party could fundamental change be achieved through the electoral process. That spring, a coalition of white radicals and the Black Panther Party met in Ann Arbor, Michigan, to form the PFP and nominated African-American activist Eldridge Cleaver and Cornell economics professor Douglas Dowd as its presidential and vice presidential candidates respectively.

Cleaver ran a radical campaign, advocating Black nationalism and social revolution. He also claimed that African-Americans had the right to defend themselves against racist policemen. The Cleaver-Dowd ticket was on the ballot in 19 states and won a total of 136,385 votes.

In 1970 the PFP ran 12 candidates for a number of offices in California. After all were soundly defeated, the remaining PFP activists joined the People's Party in 1971.

*See also:* Eldridge Cleaver, Election of 1968, Third Parties in American Elections

*Charles S. Hauss*

## Peace Democrats
*See* Copperheads.

## William Peffer (1831–1914)

The "Father of Populism." After receiving a public school education in Cumberland County, Pennsylvania, William Alfred Peffer farmed, taught school, and practiced law in several states before settling in Kansas in 1870. An ardent Republican, he was elected as a state senator (1874–1876) and presidential elector (1880). But in Kansas, Peffer was known primarily as a newspaper editor. In his influential *Kansas Farmer* (1881–1892), Peffer led the agrarian outcry against railroad abuses, currency contraction, corporate monopolies, speculators, and unresponsive political parties. His editorials always emphasized the necessity for farmers to organize and especially promoted the Farmers' Alliance. He reluctantly broke from the GOP in 1890 to help the Alliance to form the Kansas People's Party. The triumphant new party then elected him United States Senator (1891–1897), making Peffer the first national figure of Populism. Indeed, before the People's Party movement became designated as Populism, it was commonly referred to as Pefferism; and Populists were termed Pefferites or Peffercrats. Peffer chaired the 1891 Cincinnati convention that organized the national People's Party, and polemical books like *The Way Out* (1890) and *The Farmer's Side* (1891), were his own expressions of the early Populist positions on economics and politics. As Senator, Peffer proved tireless in introducing legislation to promote Populist reform demands; politically, he led the antifusion wing of the party and therefore gradually lost his original influence as the Populists increasingly fused with the Democrats. Defeated for reelection in 1897, he returned to journalism and, in 1900, the GOP.

*See also:* People's Party, Railroads

*Peter H. Argersinger*

REFERENCES

Argersinger, Peter H. 1974. *Populism and Politics: William A. Peffer and the People's Party.* Lexington: U. Pr. of Kentucky.

## Thomas J. Pendergast (1872–1945)

The boss of the Kansas City, Missouri, Democratic political machine. An Irish Catholic born in St. Joseph, Missouri, of working-class immigrant parents, Thomas J. Pendergast inherited the machine that his brother Jim had built in low-income areas of Kansas City and then enlarged it. In classic fashion, Tom Pendergast provided jobs and help to the poor, public services for the middle class, contracts and favors to businessmen, and a handsome income for himself. After cementing his hold on Kansas City politics, Pendergast extended his influence into surrounding Jackson County in the 1920s and fostered the career of future President Harry Truman in county politics. Pendergast's machine reached the apogee of its power in the 1930s before falling victim of its own corruption by the end of the decade. After helping to secure Franklin D. Roosevelt's presidential nomination in 1932, Pendergast used the control that Roosevelt gave him of New Deal money and programs to become one of the nation's most powerful political bosses. In 1934 Pendergast helped elect Harry Truman, whose affiliation with the Pendergast machine had not involved him in its graft and fraud, to the U.S. Senate. Soon, however, the Pendergast machine came under federal investigation for illegal election practices, and it suffered a major political defeat in 1938. After Roosevelt withdrew his administration's patronage and Pendergast himself was sentenced in 1939 to 15 months in prison on income tax charges, the machine collapsed. Pendergast never returned to politics after his prison term.

*See also:* Election of 1932, New Deal, Franklin D. Roosevelt, Harry S Truman

*John W. Jeffries*

REFERENCES

Dorsett, Lyle W. 1968. *The Pendergast Machine.* New York: Oxford U. Pr.

## George H. Pendleton (1825–1889)

An Ohio Democratic Congressman, a Senator, a minister to Germany, and an unsuccessful vice presidential and gubernatorial nominee. In 1846 George Hunt Pendleton married the daughter of Francis Scott Key, composer of "The Star Spangled Banner," and he was admitted to the bar the following year. He won election to the Ohio State Senate as a Democrat in 1853, ran unsuccessfully for Congress the following year, but was elected in 1856. During five terms in the U.S. House, Pendleton supported Stephen A. Douglas and the Crittenden Compromise, opposed suspension of habeas corpus during the Civil War, and served on the Judiciary and Ways and Means committees. He was the National Democratic Party's unsuccessful vice presidential nominee in 1864 and was later defeated for reelection to Congress.

After the war Pendleton lost the Ohio gubernatorial election to Rutherford B. Hayes, but he was elected to the U.S. Senate for a single term in 1878. Although reform of the federal civil service had been a political issue for years, it did not become a reality until Pendleton used his position as chairman of the Committee on Civil Service to sponsor what became known popularly as the Pendleton Act. His bill was based on British reform principles incorporated into a draft prepared by the New York Civil Service Reform Association. The bill established a merit system based on competitive examinations, freedom from political interference, and relative job security based on performance. In an era in which Senate nominations were controlled by party leaders, Pendleton's leadership in this effort cost him the Democratic renomination for a second term in the Senate. President Grover Cleveland, however, appointed him minister to Germany, a position he held until his death.

*See also:* Grover Cleveland, Rutherford B. Hayes

*Nicholas C. Burckel*

REFERENCES

Hoogenboom, Ari. 1961. *Outlawing the Spoils: A History of the Civil Service Reform Movement, 1865–1883.* Urbana: U. of Illinois Pr.

Malone, Dumas, ed. 1934. *Dictionary of American Biography.* New York: Scribner's.

Van Riper, Paul P. 1958. *History of the United States Civil Service.* Evanston, IL: Row, Peterson and Company.

## Pendleton Civil Service Act of 1883

This law was the first significant step taken by Congress to restrain the influence of the political spoils system in the federal civil service and to lessen the reliance of parties on the assessment of federal officeholders to finance campaigns.

The spoils system was as old as the Republic, for in the absence of any other personnel system, officers of the executive branch from the President down came to rely on recommendations from members of Congress in making appointments. In time this patronage power formed a central element in the creation and maintenance of political organizations throughout the country, with Senators and Representatives recommending appointees more on the basis of political considerations than fitness for office.

In the post-Civil War period, when the number of offices grew tremendously and the responsibilities of the federal government expanded, reformers pressed for hiring on the basis of merit. Members of Congress deferred decision, torn between the demands of their political organizations and their increasing disenchantment with the unwieldy and time-consuming spoils system. The assassination of James Garfield by a crazed office seeker (Charles Guiteau) galvanized the reform effort, culminating in the passage of the Pendleton Act.

The law created a bipartisan commission to establish competitive examinations for a portion of the service, forbade government employees from soliciting political contributions, and also protected officeholders from forced campaign assessments. Although the original "classified" offices comprised only about a tenth of the service, successive administrations expanded the coverage. Ultimately the act laid the foundation of the modern nonpartisan bureaucracy.

*See also:* James A. Garfield

*Charles W. Calhoun*

REFERENCES

Hoogenboom, Ari. 1961. *Outlawing the Spoils: A History of the Civil Service Reform Movement, 1865–1883.* Urbana: U. of Illinois Pr.

Nelson, William E. 1982. *The Roots of American Bureaucracy, 1830–1900.* Cambridge: Harvard U. Pr.

Sagesar, A. Bower. 1935. *The First Two Decades of the Pendleton Act: A Study of Civil Service Reform.* Lincoln: U. of Nebraska Pr.

Skowronek, Stephen. 1982. *Building a New American State: The Expansion of National Administrative Capacities, 1877–1920.* New York: Cambridge U. Pr.

Smith, Thomas A., et al. 1984. "Politics in the Gilded Age: The Reform of the Spoils System." 4 *Hayes Historical Journal* 4.

## William Pennington (1796–1862)

Speaker of the House of Representatives in the era of the Civil War. William Pennington, Whig governor of New Jersey, was elected Speaker of the U.S. House of Representatives in the Thirty-sixth Congress (1859–1861), his election breaking an eight-week deadlock between sectionally divided Democrats (both pre-Buchanan administration and anti-Lecompton factions), Republican, and Know-Nothing (American) partisans.

Born in Newark, New Jersey, the son of Governor William Sandford Pennington, the young Pennington graduated from Princeton University in 1813. Pennington studied law as a young man, acting as clerk of the United States District Court before his election to the state assembly in 1828. Identifying with the Whig Party, Pennington was elected governor in 1837, winning reelection five times in annual elections. Pennington became involved in the "Broad Seal" War when, as governor, he certified the election of five New Jersey Whig at-large congressional candidates in 1838 following a disputed electoral outcome. The matter was hardly inconsequential as party control of the House on the eve of the Twenty-sixth Congress hinged on the question of the five contested New Jersey seats. Following several days of bitter debate, the House went ahead and organized, electing a compromise candidate to the speakership and three months later seating the New Jersey Democrats. Elected to Congress as a Republican in 1858, Pennington, as an unknown freshman member, was chosen Speaker as a moderate compromise on the forty-fourth ballot when it became apparent that antislavery Republicans would be unable to elect John Sherman of Ohio. Stirred by John Brown's raid at Harper's Ferry, southerners feared the election of nearly any Republican; however, Pennington's election narrowly averted an indescribable holocaust. Pennington's performance as Speaker was undistinguished and ineffectual, particularly as the House was marked by the specter of physical violence.

*See also:* Slavery, Speaker of the House

*Richard C. Burnweit*

REFERENCES

Crenshaw, Ollinger. 1942. "The Speakership Contest of 1859–1860: John Sherman's Election a Cause of Disruption?" 29 *Mississippi Valley Historical Review* 323.

Follett, Mary Parker. 1896. *The Speaker of the House of Representatives.* New York: Longmans, Green.

Nichols, Roy Franklin. 1948. *The Disruption of American Democracy.* New York: Macmillan.

Potter, David M. 1976. In Don E. Fehrenbacher, ed. *The Impending Crisis 1848–1861.* New York: Harper & Row.

## Boies Penrose (1860–1921)

The last of a succession of Pennsylvania Republican political bosses. Boies Penrose's rule over the Republican Party state organization in Pennsylvania extended from the 1860s to the 1920s. Born to a prominent Philadelphia family,

Penrose was educated at Harvard, taking a degree in political economy. As a young lawyer inclined to an independent, reformist approach to politics, Penrose nevertheless aligned himself with the Republican state machine so as to further his political ambitions. Elected to the state assembly in 1884 and to the state senate two years later, Penrose became a lieutenant of state party boss Matthew S. Quay. When Quay forced the retirement of his associate, J. Donald Cameron, from the United States Senate in 1896, he supported Penrose for election to the seat by the Republican-controlled state legislature.

With the death of Quay in 1904, Penrose assumed leadership of the party organization, a vast hierarchy of local political units, the focus of the activities of nearly 25,000 politicians whose patronage needs called for constant supervision. Consequently, in the Senate, Penrose took little interest in national policy questions, though he consistently espoused the protective tariff and took an isolationist stance in foreign affairs. Reelected twice, in 1903 and 1909, by the legislature, and by popular vote in 1914 and 1920, Penrose assumed the leadership of the conservative "Old Guard" faction among Senate Republicans by 1911. As a kingmaker at national party conventions, Penrose is best remembered for his promotion of Senator Warren G. Harding to the presidential nomination in 1920. Dying of cancer and confined to his quarters in Philadelphia, Penrose was not among those present in the famed "smoke-filled room" from which the nominee emerged. Penrose died a pale shadow of burly and intimidating boss who was nicknamed "Big Grizzly." Though stridently criticized for allegedly engaging in corrupt practices, Penrose did not profit personally from his political power.

*See also:* Bosses, Election of 1920, Warren G. Harding, Matthew Quay

*Richard C. Burnweit*

REFERENCES

Bowden, Roger Douglas. 1937. *Boies Penrose: Symbol of an Era.* Freeport, NY: Books for Libraries Press.

Kehl, James A. 1981. *Boss Rule in the Gilded Age: Matt Quay of Pennsylvania.* Pittsburgh: U. of Pittsburgh Pr.

Lukacs, John. 1980. *Philadelphia: Patricians and Philistines 1900–1950.* New York: Farrar, Straus, Giroux.

## People's Party

In response to problems such as falling commodity prices, rising operating costs, and high interest rates for agricultural credit that southern and western farmers confronted in the 1870s and 1880s, the People's Party was formed. The party developed its major pockets of strength in recently settled regions or places undergoing social and economic disorganization. In contrast, the Northeast and Old Northwest developed more diversified agricultural systems and a stronger balance between farming and industry.

As the Southern Farmers' Alliance spread through the South and West between 1887 and 1890, it prepared the way for the new party by contributing to its ideology and leadership. The Alliance made its initial entry into politics in 1890, working through the Democratic Party in the South and independent parties in the West. Over the next two years, the movement for a national party grew, and in 1892 the People's Party held its first national convention at Omaha. Its platform called for the nationalization of the transportation system, the free and unlimited coinage of silver, a flexible national currency, inexpensive loans for farmers, a graduated income tax, laws to discourage large-scale acquisition of land, the direct election of U.S. Senators, the Australian ballot, and the initiative and referendum.

James B. Weaver, the new party's presidential candidate, won slightly more than a million votes and became the first third-party candidate to win electoral votes (22) since the Civil War. In the West the Populists elected ten members of the lower house of Congress, one U.S. Senator, and three governors. But the new party failed to crack the South, where Populists confronted charges of endangering white supremacy by threatening the Democrat's domination. Although the southern Populists did not subscribe to racially egalitarian views, they appealed to Black voters on the grounds of common economic problems and the promise of fair elections.

In states where they won elections, the Populists established impressive reform records. Kansas Populists, for example, enacted railroad and banking regulations, a school text book commission, and a corrupt practices act. When the North Carolina Populists successfully fused with Republicans in 1894, they initiated a reform era in which the fusionists strengthened popular democracy, increased funding for public schools, and worked for a variety of economic reforms.

Despite the records it established in states like Kansas and North Carolina, the People's Party suffered from internal conflicts and confronted the determined opposition of the major parties, each of which expropriated some of its programs. Following the onset of the depression in 1893, the call for free silver became increasingly powerful. The Democrats embraced that issue in their 1896 convention when they nominated William Jennings Bryan for the presidency. The Populists then faced the dilemma of maintaining their distinct identity as a party or of supporting silver by endorsing Bryan. Believing that it would provide the best way to advance reform, the Populists nominated Bryan, after which their party quickly disintegrated.

The People's Party reflected the attempt of rural southerners and westerners to preserve their way of life at a time when they feared that the expansion of industrialization and urbanization threatened agrarianism. Speaking primarily for small, land-owning farmers, the Populists did not win significant support either from tenants or from the most prosperous farmers. The Populists wanted to maintain private property and economic competition among small producers, while demanding that the federal government eliminate monopolies and regulate problems generated by corporate capitalism. Populism represented the last national protest of farmers to the onset of the urban-industrial age.

*See also:* William Jennings Bryan, Election of 1896, Southern Farmers' Alliance, James B. Weaver

*William F. Holmes*

REFERENCES

Argersinger, Peter H. 1974. *Populism and Politics: William Alfred Peffer and the People's Party.* Lexington: U. Pr. of Kentucky.

Destler, Chester McArthur. 1946. *American Radicalism, 1865–1901.* New London: Connecticut College Pr.

Goodwyn, Lawrence. 1976. *Democratic Promise: The Populist Moment in America.* New York: Oxford U. Pr.

Hahn, Steven. 1983. *The Roots of Southern Populism: Yeoman Farmers and the Transformation of the Georgia Upcountry, 1850–1890.* New York: Oxford U. Pr.

Hicks, John D. 1931. *The Populist Revolt: A History of the Farmers' Alliance and the People's Party.* Minneapolis: U. of Minnesota Pr.

Hofstadter, Richard. 1955. *The Age of Reform: From Bryan to F.D.R.* New York: Knopf.

## Claude Pepper (1900–1989)

Leading congressional advocate for the elderly. At his death, Congressman Claude Pepper (D-Fla.) was the oldest member of Congress and one of the most powerful members of the U.S. House of Representatives. In 1983 he assumed the chair of the Rules Committee after having served as chair of the Select Committee on Aging from 1977 to 1983 and of the Select Committee on Crime from 1969 to 1973. Pepper was the only member of the contemporary House of Representatives to have previously served in the Senate. He was a Senator from Florida from 1936 to 1951, having been defeated for renomination in 1950 by George Smathers in what is widely considered to be one of the nastiest campaigns in American history. Pepper, an ardent supporter of Franklin D. Roosevelt's New Deal, led Smathers to call him "Red Pepper" and a "nigger lover," among other names that were even more provocative. However, as the nation's leading spokesman for issues relating to the elderly, Pepper achieved his greatest prominence.

Pepper was born in Alabama, attended the University of Alabama (A.B., 1921) and Harvard University (LL.B., 1924). He settled in Florida, was elected to the state house of representatives in 1929, unsuccessfully sought a Senate seat in 1934, and was finally elected in a special election in 1936. As a Senator, he paid particular attention to foreign affairs. After losing a Senate comeback attempt in 1958, Pepper won a new House seat in the Miami area in 1962 and consistently won more than 60 percent of the vote in subsequent House contests.

As a gesture of respect, Pepper's colleagues always called him "Senator." He maintained an active interest in foreign affairs, especially on questions of the Middle East (his district had a large Jewish population) and on Latin America, where his stance had shifted to the right because of the large Cuban bloc within his constituency. However, after the 1970s Pepper's main concern was with issues relating to the elderly. As the Democratic Party's major spokesman on Social Security, he was a member of the National Commission on Social Security Reform in 1982. He was a major actor in the Congress on such issues as eliminating mandatory retirement for federal workers and lifting the retirement age for private workers, expansion of Medicare to provide long-term care for the elderly, research on arthritis, and mail fraud against the elderly. In 1982, when the Social Security issue was so prominent on the political agenda, Pepper was the most sought-after speaker in the country on behalf of other Democratic candidates. A stirring orator, Pepper appeared with 70 candidates in 25 states in the 1982 elections. In 1983 he was selected to be one of the Democrats who responded to President Ronald Reagan's State of the Union address on national television.

Pepper chose in 1983 to become chair of the Rules Committee, the body that handles most key legislation in the House of Representatives. He succeeded Richard Bolling (D-Mo.) who was a master of legislative strategy, was close to the party leadership, and ran a very tightly controlled committee. Under Pepper, the committee became more consensual among Democratic members and less tied to the party leadership. Pepper received high marks for his handling of internal relations among the committee members, but the reputation of Rules as a power broker waned somewhat. Pepper remained one of the most powerful members of Congress not only because of his key institutional role but also because he successfully mobilized the older Americans who have become a political force in every congressional district.

*See also:* Richard Bolling, Ronald Reagan, Red Scare, Franklin D. Roosevelt

*Eric M. Uslaner*

## Leander H. Perez (1891–1969)

The undisputed political boss of Plaquemines Parish, Louisiana, for nearly half a century. Although his was emblematic of numerous local rural political machines throughout the country, Leander Henry Perez's political organization and statewide influence were surpassed by few. As one of Perez's biographers has noted, "Louisiana politics is traditionally ruthless and highly professional and Perez belonged to the tradition, but he brought to it a particularly aggressive style, unhampered by either subjective or purely moral considerations."

Born in the delta region, Perez attended Tulane Law School, at once becoming active in parish politics. He was initially perceived as a reformer when he was appointed parish judge in 1919. Yet within several years he built an impregnable political machine of his own. By gaining control over the parish's vast oil and mineral deposits through local governing entities and dummy corporations, Perez amassed a personal fortune estimated in the millions, even as most inhabitants of the parish lived in poverty. Indeed, Perez's paternalistic rule owed much to the swampy delta's geographical and social isolation. Elected district attorney for Plaquemines and neighboring St. Bernard Parish in 1924, Perez aligned himself early with Governor Huey P. Long. One of the "Kingfish's" legal strategists in Long's famed 1929 impeachment

trial, Perez routinely supported the Long machine's candidates for state and local offices, usually by providing lopsided electoral margins in his bailiwick. In 1948 Perez broke with the Long faction and bolted from the national Democratic Party in helping to launch the prosegregationist States' Rights Party. In championing the "Dixiecrat" cause, Perez gave vent not only to his opposition to the Democrat's sweeping civil rights plank but also to threatened federal encroachment on Louisiana tidelands oil development. As the civil rights movement progressed, Perez's rhetoric became increasingly inflammatory as he gave leadership to the White Citizens' Councils and advocated violent resistance to civil rights enforcement. Retiring as district attorney in 1960, Perez became president of the newly created Plaquemines Parish Commission Council the following year. During the 1960s Perez was an enthusiastic backer of the presidential candidacies of Alabaman George C. Wallace.

*See also:* States' Rights Party, George Wallace

*Richard C. Burnweit*

REFERENCES

Conaway, James. 1973. *Judge: The Life and Times of Leander Perez.* New York: Knopf.

Jeansonne, Glen. 1977. *Leander Perez: Boss of the Delta.* Baton Rouge: Louisiana State U. Pr.

Sherrill, Robert. 1968. *Gothic Politics in the Deep South: Stars of the New Confederacy.* New York: Grossman.

## Frances Perkins (1882–1965)

First female Cabinet secretary. On March 2, 1933, the *New York Times* editorialized, "Few women in high office have been tested in the fires through which Miss Perkins has passed. Social justice is more than a shibboleth to her; it has been the maxim of her life." This tribute to Frances Perkins marked her appointment as Franklin D. Roosevelt's Secretary of Labor, making her the first woman to serve in a presidential Cabinet. In a long career dedicated to social reform, Perkins played a leading role in the enactment of social welfare legislation first in New York and later in national politics as a member of FDR's Cabinet (1933–1945). In her capacity as Secretary of Labor, Perkins also played an important symbolic and substantive role in a network of New Deal women who worked successfully to open up party politics, particularly the Democratic Party, to the participation of women.

After pursuing graduate studies in sociology and economics at Columbia University and lobbying for the National Consumer League, Perkins was appointed to the New York State Industrial Commission in 1918 by Governor Al Smith, becoming its chairwoman. Her appointment was an indication of new political conditions in the state. New York women won the right to vote in 1918, and Democratic governor Smith was determined to make a significant gesture toward these new female voters by appointing a woman to a position of significance.

Perkins's appointment to the Industrial Commission marked her conversion to the Democratic Party. She came from a family of Republicans who openly admired Theodore Roosevelt. After she was appointed by Smith, a Democratic district leader reported that Perkins was not a registered Democrat, a discovery that caused considerable concern in the Smith partisan administration. At the governor's urging, Perkins agreed to register as a Democrat.

Perkins's apparent indifference to partisanship did not impair her relationship with the prominent Democratic party leader, Mary Dewson. She persuaded Governor-elect Franklin Roosevelt to appoint Perkins as New York State industrial commissioner in 1928; thus, Perkins came to head the largest state department of labor in the country. Dewson also deserved considerable credit for FDR's path-breaking appointment of Perkins as the first woman to serve in a presidential Cabinet after his elevation to the White House in 1932.

Perkins's appointment as Secretary of Labor was of tremendous symbolic importance, signaling greater opportunity for women in party politics and government. Perkins acknowledged that the significance of this appointment for women overcame her reluctance to accept the position in spite of the personal and financial hardship it would cause. As a result of her ardent advocacy of social welfare measures, Perkins was regarded by many as the most "liberal" and progressive of Roosevelt's Cabinet.

The social welfare legislation of the New Deal was also the foundation for a political realignment that strengthened the progressive forces in the Democratic Party and established it as the majority party in American politics, thus ending 70 years of Republican dominance. Perkins, herself, realized that her tenure as labor secretary was was an unusually significant one. As she left the Department of Labor, she told reporters, "I was lucky to live at a time when the United States was ready for social reforms. And I was lucky to live in a period when women

finally got a chance to serve in public life." After her retirement from the Department of Labor, President Harry Truman appointed Perkins to the Civil Service Commission, where she served from 1946 to 1953. After leaving government, Perkins was a highly successful lecturer at Cornell and other universities.

*See also:* Mary Dewson, Franklin D. Roosevelt, Al Smith, Harry S Truman

*Sidney Milkis*

REFERENCES

Martin, George. 1976. *Madam Secretary*. Boston: Houghton Mifflin.

Mohr, Lillian Holmen. 1979. *Frances Perkins: "That Woman in FDR's Cabinet!"* New York: North River Press.

Perkins, Frances. 1946. *The Roosevelt I Knew*. New York: Viking.

Roosevelt, Eleanor, and Lorena Hickock. 1954. *Ladies of Courage*. New York: Putnam's.

Van Riper, Paul. 1958. *History of the United States Civil Service*. Evanston, IL: Row, Peterson.

Ware, Susan. 1958. *Beyond Suffrage: Women in the New Deal*. Cambridge: Harvard U. Pr.

## Esther Peterson (1906– )

Advocate for women's and consumers' rights. Esther Peterson's interest in the labor movement and concern for women workers began in the 1930s while she was teaching at the Bryn Mawr Summer School for Workers in Industry and continued through a series of positions with labor organizations at home and abroad. In 1960, her efforts as acting secretary of the Labor Women's Committee for Kennedy and Lyndon Johnson were rewarded when President John F. Kennedy appointed her director of the U.S. Women's Bureau. She became the highest ranking woman in government when he also made her Assistant Secretary of Labor (1961–1967). Concurrently, she was executive vice chairman of the President's Committee on the Status of Women, a committee that submitted a report in 1963 that profoundly affected women's policy.

In her labor post, she ran regional conferences on the problems of working women, particularly those with dual roles at home and in the workplace and those trying to reenter the labor force. Peterson supported equal pay, child care for working mothers, and extension of the minimum wage. She also insisted that controversial "special labor laws" for women needed to be retained where they protected and revoked where they were discriminatory.

In 1964 President Lyndon B. Johnson added to Peterson's duties when he appointed her special presidential assistant for consumer affairs (1964–1967). In this position, she condemned built-in obsolescence and supported truth in advertising and packaging. After leaving government she continued her consumer activism and served on various committees of the Democratic Party. She was reappointed to her consumer post by President Jimmy Carter and in 1979 became chairman of the Consumer Affairs Council. Since 1980 she has actively pursued these interests outside of government.

*See also:* Jimmy Carter, Lyndon B. Johnson, John F. Kennedy

*Joy A. Scimé*

REFERENCES

Stineman, Esther. 1980. *American Political Women: Contemporary and Historical Profiles.* Littleton, CO: Libraries Unlimited.

## Franklin Pierce (1804–1869)

Fourteenth President of the United States. Historians have not been kind to Franklin Pierce. In Arthur Schlesinger's 1948 "presidential greatness" survey, Pierce was ranked twenty-seventh out of 29 Presidents. His poor performance in the presidency is commonly attributed to personal timidity and vacillation. But the emphasis on these personal inadequacies makes explaining his past successes difficult. Before Pierce was President, his political career had been, according to his biographer Roy Nichols, "phenomenal." He had played a pivotal role during the 1840s in keeping the New Hampshire Democratic Party united. Never defeated for office, Pierce was elected to the state legislature at age 24; at 26 he was speaker; three years later he went to the U.S. House of Representatives; by 36 he was a United States senator; and at 48 he was elected President, the youngest chief executive in U.S. history. These successes (as well as the poor performance of his successor, James Buchanan) suggest that Pierce's difficulties were due, in large part, to the dilemma that slavery posed to the Democratic Party.

After Andrew Jackson's administration, the Democratic Party had defined itself in opposition to hierarchical institutions and privileged minorities. Although the institution of slavery itself had been rationalized in terms of Black inferiority, the Slave Power (i.e., southern domination of national political life) could not be so easily dismissed, even by northern racists. To the radical antibank wing of the Democratic Party, the Slave Power was analogous to the Money Power; both demonstrated that "privilege never restrains its ambition to rule." Pierce thus faced the dilemma of repudiating the egalitarian wing of the party or turning his back on the South.

Pierce aimed to unite the fractured Democrats through rapid territorial expansion. The Democrats had long agreed that territorial expansion was the best way to prevent the centralization of authority that had beset other nations. Cuba, Hawaii, Alaska, the Dominican Republic, and northern Mexico were all viewed by the Pierce administration as legitimate spheres for American expansion. Coupling territorial expansion with Stephen Douglas's doctrine of popular sovereignty, Pierce hoped not only to expand the "sphere of freedom" but also to expunge slavery from congressional debate.

However, the Jacksonian program of territorial expansion and domestic economy, so successful in the past, could no longer mobilize and unify the Democratic faithful. Although Pierce kept faith with Jacksonian policies, the cultural significance of those policies had been transformed by slavery. In the age of Jackson, for example, government subsidies for internal improvements had been anathema to Democrats who viewed such action as unfairly advantaging privileged minorities. By the 1850s, however, Pierce's firm opposition to federal governmental assistance for western economic development was construed by many Democrats as evidence that Pierce was under the thumb of the Slave Power. The kind of presidential actions that had galvanized the Democrats under Jackson now, under Pierce, divided the party.

Pierce never recognized how changing times were making old solutions counterproductive, thus corroborating the limits of his leadership. To identify and channel the direction of cultural change while still living through it is a mark of greatness. That Pierce was not a great President we already know; that others (short of Abraham Lincoln) would have performed better is not so obvious.

*See also:* James Buchanan, Andrew Jackson

*Richard Ellis*

REFERENCES

Ashworth, John. 1986. "The Democratic-Republicans Before the Civil War: Political Ideology and Economic Change." 20 *Journal of American Studies* 375.

Cole, Donald B. 1970. *Jacksonian Democracy in New Hampshire, 1800–1851.* Cambridge: Harvard U. Pr.

Ellis, Richard J., and Aaron Wildavsky. 1988. *Dilemmas of Presidential Leadership from Washington Through Lincoln*. New Brunswick, NJ: Transaction.

Nichols, Roy Franklin. 1958. *Franklin Pierce: Young Hickory of the Granite Hills*. Philadelphia: U. of Pennsylvania Pr.

Skowronek, Stephen. 1984. "Presidential Leadership in Political Time." In Michael Nelson, ed. *The Presidency and the Political System*. Washington: Congressional Quarterly.

## Gifford Pinchot (1865–1946)

Father of the conservation movement in the United States. Educated at Yale (B.A., 1889), Gifford Pinchot then studied at the French Forest School at Nancy. On his return to the United States in late 1890s, Pinchot was the country's first professionally trained forester.

In 1898 Pinchot was appointed chief of the division of forestry in the U.S. Department of Agriculture and, when it became the Forest Service in 1905, its first chief forester. He was an intimate friend and adviser to President Theodore Roosevelt and the guiding genius behind Roosevelt's national conservation movement.

When William Howard Taft succeeded Roosevelt in 1909, Pinchot was asked to stay on; Taft's Secretary of the Interior, with jurisdiction over the public lands, was Richard A. Ballinger. Relations between Pinchot and Ballinger were strained from the outset. They erupted into a spectacular public controversy when Pinchot accused Ballinger of irregularities in the transfer of public lands and, more generally, of betraying Roosevelt's conservation program. Despite Taft's efforts to quiet him, Pinchot kept the matter before the country, and when he took his charges to Congress, in January 1910, Taft fired him.

The Ballinger-Pinchot Affair contributed significantly to a widening rift between Taft and the so-called progressive Republicans. Pinchot and others urged Roosevelt to challenge Taft for the Republican presidential nomination in 1912. When Roosevelt did so and lost, Pinchot became one of the architects of the Bull Moose or Progressive Party under whose banner Roosevelt eventually did run. The resulting split in the Republican Party insured the election of Democrat Woodrow Wilson. Equally important, Roosevelt, Pinchot and their adherents, by leading the Progressives out of the Republican Party, surrendered it to its most conservative element.

Thereafter, Pinchot remained active both in conservation and in politics. Returning to his family's native Pennsylvania, he served two highly regarded terms (1923–1927; 1931–1935) as governor and continued strenuously to promote the cause of conservation.

*See also:* Bull Moose Party, Progressive Party, Theodore Roosevelt, William Howard Taft, Woodrow Wilson

*John F. Coleman*

REFERENCES

Fausold, Martin L. 1961. *Gifford Pinchot: Bull Moose Progressive*. Syracuse: Syracuse U. Pr.

McGeary, M. Nelson. 1960. *Gifford Pinchot: Forester—Politician*. Princeton: Princeton U. Pr.

Pinchot, Gifford. 1947. *Breaking New Ground*. New York: Harcourt, Brace.

## Charles Cotesworth Pinckney (1745–1825)

Federalist leader of the early Republic. No accounting of early American politics and parties is complete without some mention of the Pinckneys. In addition to Charles Cotesworth Pinckney, this aristocratic South Carolina family produced Thomas (his brother) and Charles III (his cousin). All played prominent roles in the formative years of the Republic.

Charles Cotesworth Pinckney made his first impression on the national scene as an officer in George Washington's Continental Army. His hopes for glory were thwarted when the Charleston garrison fell in 1780, and he was interned until 1782. But Washington later took notice of the South Carolinian: the first President always had the highest regard for the men who served under him in the Revolution. He would later call upon many of these old comrades to fill positions in the new national government, deeming their loyalty and reliability beyond reproach.

Pinckney attended the Constitutional Convention in 1787, along with his younger cousin Charles, as a delegate from South Carolina. He said little, but demonstrated strong nationalist sentiments when he did. Perhaps his most noteworthy moment was when he rose to insist that unless the new Constitution took some cognizance of slavery, he could not, on South Carolina's behalf, support it. It was not a noble moment, but Pinckney was only stating openly what many delegates knew to be true—that the price of union in 1787 was accommodation with the "peculiar institution."

Pinckney returned to South Carolina and was elected to its Senate. He was an active supporter of Washington's administration and the Federalist policies that increasingly characterized it.

Pinckney did not always agree with Alexander Hamilton, finding his thinking entirely too British. But his social conservatism and desire for a strong national government to control the "unruly" western farmers made him a committed Federalist. Washington offered Pinckney several important federal offices, but he declined them all until he was named minister to France. In 1800 the Federalists nominated Pinckney as part of a "ticket" in which it was understood that John Adams was to be President and Pinckney Vice President. But the voting system used by the electoral college then required that electors cast two votes for President, one of which had to be for a candidate who was not a resident of the elector's state. This procedure led to an attempt by several South Carolina electors to elevate Pinckney to the presidency; they would vote for Pinckney and Thomas Jefferson. They had calculated (inaccurately as it turned out) that this strategy would give Pinckney and Jefferson an equal number of votes. The Federalist House of Representatives (another miscalculation) would give Pinckney the presidency and squeeze out the hated Adams, whom most southern Federalists distrusted. Pinckney thought the whole maneuver dishonorable and refused to be a part of it.

This incident only reinforced Pinckney's standing among both High Federalists and Adams Federalists. Along with his unquestioned personal honor, this respect and admiration made him the logical candidate of the Federalists in 1804. But the party was already in rapid decline and Jefferson easily won reelection. In 1808 prominent Federalists again put his name forward for President. But Pinckney campaigned hardly at all and, once again, lost decisively. He remained a Federalist until his death, but he never again sought public office.

*See also:* John Adams, Election of 1800, Electoral College, Federalist Party, Alexander Hamilton, Slavery, George Washington

*Glenn A. Phelps*

REFERENCES

Schlesinger, Arthur M., Jr., and Fred L. Israel, eds. 1971. *History of American Presidential Elections, 1789–1968*. Vol. 1. Chatham, NJ: Chelsea House.

Williams, Frances Leigh. 1978. *A Founding Family: The Pinckneys of South Carolina*. New York: Harcourt Brace Jovanovich.

Zahniser, Marvin R. 1967. *Charles Cotesworth Pinckney: Founding Father*. Chapel Hill: U. of North Carolina Pr.

## Hazen S. Pingree (1840–1901)

Leader of the Michigan Republican Party at the turn of the century. Hazen S. Pingree was born in Denmark, Maine, where he was educated before becoming a cobbler and leather cutter—skills that he used after removing to Detroit, Michigan. There he achieved wealth through his successful shoe manufacturing plant. He then turned his energies to politics. As a liberal Republican, he became mayor of Detroit in 1889 and served until 1897. Especially able to win the support of new immigrants, he became an urban reform mayor. His strategy for improving Detroit life was not to tinker with political structures and institutions but to make fundamental social reforms that went to causes of urban grief. Pingree was concerned with the life conditions under which citizens lived, worked, traveled, and spent their leisure time. Thus he took on special interests with gusto, at times using unorthodox methods in order to exercise maximum leverage. He attacked the special interest owners of the telephone, telegraph, electric, and gas companies, as well as those of the transit system, coercing them into lowering their rates. An avid advocate of municipal ownership, Pingree induced transit competition to reduce rates and secured a publicly owned electric company.

Pingree won Michigan's governorship in 1896 and forced a tax on any large corporations who had not previously paid taxes. He also achieved equitable taxation and regulation of corporate and railroad property through a workable system of appraisals. Pingree won national fame for his successes both in Detroit and in Lansing, and his political achievements were completed before and therefore helped usher in the progressive movement.

*See also:* Railroads

*C. David Tompkins*

REFERENCES

Holli, Melvin G. 1969. *Reform in Detroit: Hazen S. Pingree and Urban Politics*. New York.

Starring, Charles S. 1948. "Hazen S. Pingree: Another Forgotten Eagle." 32 *Michigan History* 129.

## Key Pittman (1912–1940)

Nevada Democratic Senator for a quarter of a century. Key Pittman, a Democrat from Nevada, held a seat in the Senate from 1913 until 1940, serving as President *pro tempore* from 1933 on, and chairman of the Senate Foreign Relations Committee in the years before World War II. Born in Mississippi, a descendant of Francis Scott Key (composer of "The Star Spangled Banner"), he attended college in Tennessee and studied law before going west, eventually to the Yukon Territory and Alaska during the gold rush of the 1890s. In 1901 Pittman moved to Nevada. In 1910 he lost a U.S. Senate bid, but in 1912 was chosen Senator by the Nevada legislature. Reelected in 1916 merely by a plurality over Republican and Socialist opponents, he was never seriously challenged again.

Pittman owed political success to his concern for Nevada's major industry—silver. Known as the "silver Senator," he led the western Senators' silver bloc, receiving much credit for laws and international agreements benefiting his constituency. An astute and affable politician in the Democratic Party, Pittman was secretary of the Senate Democratic Caucus under President Woodrow Wilson, secretary of the platform committee at the divided 1924 convention and chairman of that committee in 1928, and the Democratic nominee during the 1920s for Senate President *pro tempore*—a position he held from 1933 until his death. Primarily a party loyalist rather than an ideologue, scholars have categorized Pittman as both a moderate progressive and as a conservative.

During the 1930s Pittman was chairman of the Foreign Relations Committee where he strongly, if erratically, defended Franklin D. Roosevelt's foreign policies against attacks by isolationists. Yet he also supported the Senate's prerogatives against excessive administration claims. Pittman was widely known for his outspoken opposition to Asian and European totalitarianism, often in unpredictable advance of Roosevelt's own diplomacy. He was last reelected only a week before his death.

*See also:* Isolationism in American Politics, Franklin D. Roosevelt

*Eugene S. Larson*

REFERENCES

Glad, Betty. 1986. *Key Pittman: The Tragedy of a Senate Insider*. New York: Columbia U. Pr.

Israel, Fred L. 1963. *Nevada's Key Pittman*. Lincoln: U. of Nebraska Pr.

## Thomas C. Platt (1833–1910)

"Easy Boss" of New York state Republican Party politics from 1888 to 1900. In the words of political historian Richard L. McCormick, "Platt made it a practice to find out where the other leaders would go before he led them there." Local party leaders from throughout the state gathered on Sundays in New York's Fifth Avenue Hotel to attend "Platt's Sunday School," where questions of legislation and patronage

were first aired. During the height of his power in the 1890s, Thomas Collier Platt had little trouble enforcing his will on an acquiescent state government. The interests of business he encouraged through the distribution of contracts and other benefits, and he deflected calls for stronger regulation. Control of party patronage and a steady flow of campaign contributions from businessmen were essential to Platt's operations.

The route to power for the Easy Boss was not an altogether smooth nor uneventful one. Platt first emerged in the 1870s as the ally and confidant of New York's Stalwart Republican boss, Roscoe Conkling. In 1881 he joined Conkling in the U.S. Senate, but within a matter of weeks, they became embroiled with President James Garfield over an appointment to the New York Customs House. Both men resigned from the Senate, expecting the legislature in Albany to reelect them and force the President's hand. But in the aftermath of President Garfield's assassination by a disappointed Stalwart office seeker (Charles Guiteau), the legislature elected other men. Both ex-Senators fell out of power, Conkling permanently and Platt for about six years. By 1888, with Republican fortunes in New York on the upswing, Platt returned to the fray. He helped to nominate and elect Benjamin Harrison to the presidency but broke with Harrison over matters of patronage and Cabinet appointments. In 1898 he began the first of two consecutive terms in the U.S. Senate and in 1900 eased an independent-minded Theodore Roosevelt out of the New York governor's chair and into the vice presidency. Roosevelt's successor in Albany, Benjamin Odell, also dared to defy Platt and thereafter the power of the Easy Boss waned quickly.

*See also:* Bosses, Roscoe Conkling, James Garfield, Benjamin Harrison, Theodore Roosevelt

*John B. Weaver*

REFERENCES

Gosnell, Harold. 1924. *Boss Platt and His New York Machine: A Study of the Political Leadership of Thomas C. Platt, Theodore Roosevelt, and Others*. Chicago: U. of Chicago Pr.

Lang, Louis J., ed. 1910. *The Autobiography of Thomas Collier Platt*. New York: B. W. Dodge.

McCormick, Richard L. 1981. *From Realignment to Reform: Political Change in New York State, 1893–1910*.

## George Washington Plunkitt (1842–1924)

The "Philosopher of Tammany Hall." George Washington Plunkitt was the Democratic ward leader of the Fifteenth Assembly District on

Manhattan's West Side for 50 years and a loyal supporter of every Tammany boss from the infamous William Marcy Tweed to Charles F. Murphy. Born on "Nanny Goat Hill" in what later became a part of Central Park, Plunkitt had little formal education and lived his entire life in the narrow geographic confines of his district, unashamedly enriching himself as a professional politician. One of his proudest boasts was that he briefly held four public offices simultaneously: magistrate, alderman, supervisor, and state senator. Typical of the machine politicians of his time in all ways except his outspokenness, Plunkitt was later characterized by Professor Roy Peel, a student of New York City's political parties, as "[a] minor leader, [a] regimental commander who kept his place in the Tammany organization regardless of external pressures and internal upheavals."

George Washington Plunkitt is thus remembered not because of any extraordinary achievements, but because of his unusual and frank views of the organization politicians of his day from his "office" at Graziano's bootblack stand in the old New York County Court House. These were published by William Riordan of the *New York Evening Post,* as a "Series of Very Plain Talks on Very Practical Politics." In them Plunkitt revealed his fondness of patronage and "honest graft." "If you were on the inside, you did not need to break the law to get rich from politics," Plunkitt said. Wealth was just a matter of using what you knew. "I seen my opportunity and I took it," he observed. His hostilities were to the "curse of civil service reform"; to reformers in politics ("mornin' glories . . . lovely in the mornin' but withered up in a short time"); and to professional politicians from elsewhere—upstate New York Republican "hayseeds" or Brooklyn Democrats—who threatened Tammany's hegemony in the metropolis.

*See also:* Tammany Hall, William M. Tweed

*Gerald Benjamin*

REFERENCES

Riordan, William, with Introduction by Roy V. Peel. 1948. *Plunkitt of Tammany Hall: A Series of Very Plain Talks on Very Practical Politics.* New York: Knopf.

———, with Introduction by Arthur Mann. 1963. *Plunkitt of Tammany Hall: A Series of Very Plain Talks on Very Practical Politics.* New York: Dutton.

## Political Action Committees

So common are references to the "political action committee," and especially to its acronym "PAC," that it is surprising that the term appears nowhere in Congress's legislation about campaign finance. Indeed, in the Federal Election Campaign Act of 1971 and in its 1974 amendments, PACs are variously known as "non-party committees," "separate segregated funds," and "multicandidate committees." In those three phrases, however, we have the materials for a definition of considerable precision.

PACs are, first, committees other than the committees set up by political parties or by candidates for their own campaigns; consequently, they are nonparty committees. Since they cannot use the assets of their parent organizations under federal law (e.g., corporate profits or union dues) and thus must raise funds specifically for political purposes, they are required to maintain segregated funds separate from the ordinary assets of their parent organizations. And to qualify for the contribution limit of $5,000 per candidate per election (as against $1,000 for individuals), they must demonstrate the breadth of operation of a multicandidate committee: they must receive contributions from more than fifty people and make contributions to at least five candidates for federal office.

### Origin and Growth

While the concept of a PAC at the national level evolved in the legislation of the 1970s, PACs began earlier than that. The first was probably the Political Action Committee of the old Congress of Industrial Organizations (CIO); it was established in 1943 to receive and spend money in elections in order to promote the causes of organized labor. The political leaders of the CIO, preeminently Sidney Hillman, thus created and also named a new kind of American political organization in one act of political innovation. When the CIO merged with the American Federation of Labor (AFL) in 1955, the resulting AFL-CIO created its own PAC, called the Committee on Political Education (COPE). COPE was for years the prototypic PAC.

PACs also grew in places other than the labor movement. The American Medical Association's American Medical PAC and the Business-Industry PAC founded by the U.S. Chamber of Commerce were two of the enduring entries from the 1950s and 1960s. The great PAC explosion, however, took place in the 1970s. The first count under the Federal Election Campaign Act (FECA) was 608 at the end of 1974. Just 8 years later, 3,371 PACs had registered under federal law, and the total reached 4,268 by the end of 1988 (Table 1).

The reasons for this PAC boom fall easily into two main categories. It reflects, first, the expansion of *all* group activity in American politics from about the late 1960s. The numbers of interest groups in Washington and the numbers of lobbyists registered with the Congress all increased sharply beginning then. That expansion in turn reflected a number of changes in American politics: the decline of political parties and the consequent vacuum in American politics, the expansion of the agenda of American politics to include new issues of equality and values, and a growing propensity of Americans to organize around and commit themselves to a single issue or a single cluster of issues. A PAC was the political organization of a new politics of specific issues and goals, a politics far more focused and narrow than the sprawling majoritarian politics of the two major parties.

At the same time, the changes during the 1970s in the legal environments of PACs also stimulated their founding and growth. In writing the FECA amendments of 1974, the Congress sought primarily to prevent a repetition of the enormous contributions of individuals to campaigns in 1968 and 1972. Thus, individuals were limited to contributions of $1,000 per candidate per election, while nonparty, multicandidate committees enjoyed the higher limit of $5,000. (Since primary and general elections are separate elections, the limits total $2,000 and $10,000 for a two-year election cycle.) That difference in itself stimulated the development of PACs. But in addition, Congress set an aggregate, overall limit of $25,000 a year on individual contributions without setting any cumulative limit on those of multicandidate committees.

Then in 1976 two additional legal develop-ments gave additional impetus to the growth of PACs. In that year the Supreme Court (in *Buckley v. Valeo*) held the 1974 limits on candidate *spending* unconstitutional even while finding the limits on PAC and individual *contributions* constitutional. Since candidates are free to spend without limits, there are therefore, in effect, no limits on the contributions they might seek from PACs and other sources. In the same year the Federal Election Commission, the agency created by Congress to regulate campaign finance, further stimulated the PAC movement with an advisory opinion on the Sun Oil PAC. While the Congress had earlier authorized the creation of separate, segregated political funds by corporations, unions, and associations, it had not been clear about whether those organizational parents could pay the overhead and administrative costs of their PACs. In the Sun Oil opinion, the FEC said they could.

Although the growth of PACs since the 1970s can be seen in their proliferation, a better indicator is perhaps the sums they contribute to candidates. Since they contribute very little to presidential candidates in the primary season (less than 2 percent of their receipts in 1988), and since they cannot contribute to presidential candidates who accept public funding for their campaigns, the key is their contributions to congressional candidates for seats in Congress. Between 1974 and 1988 those contributions increased from $12.5 million to $155.8 million, more than a twelve-fold increase (Table 2). Even accounting for inflation's rise in the Consumer Price Index, that figure represents an increase of 419 percent in real dollars.

Those total contributions to all congressional candidates do not take the full measure of PAC campaign involvement. Beyond the $155.8 mil-

## Table 1

*Number of PACs Registered with the Federal Election Commission, 1974–1988\**

|  | corporate | labor | association | non-connected | other† | total |
|---|---|---|---|---|---|---|
| 1974 | 89 | 201 | 318 | ** | ** | 608 |
| 1976 | 433 | 224 | 489 | ** | ** | 1,146 |
| 1978 | 785 | 217 | 453 | 162 | 36 | 1,653 |
| 1980 | 1,206 | 297 | 576 | 374 | 98 | 2,551 |
| 1982 | 1,469 | 380 | 649 | 723 | 150 | 3,371 |
| 1984 | 1,682 | 394 | 698 | 1,053 | 182 | 4,009 |
| 1986 | 1,744 | 384 | 745 | 1,077 | 207 | 4,157 |
| 1988 | 1,816 | 354 | 786 | 1,115 | 197 | 4,268 |

\*Data come from FEC press releases; the FEC reports totals twice a year and in the odd-numbered years as well as the even numbered. These data are for December 31 of the even-numbered years.

†These data are for the PACs of cooperatives and corporations without stock.

\*\*In these years totals for these PACs were included with the totals of association PACs.

# Table 2

*PAC Contributions to All Congressional Candidates,\* 1974–1986 (in millions of dollars)*

|      | corporate | labor | association | non-connected | other† | total |
|------|-----------|-------|-------------|---------------|--------|-------|
| 1974 | (breakdowns not available) | | | | | $12.5 |
| 1976 | (breakdowns not available) | | | | | 22.6 |
| 1978 | $9.8 | $10.3 | $11.3 | $2.8 | $1.0 | 35.2 |
| 1980 | 19.2 | 13.2 | 15.9 | 4.9 | 2.0 | 55.2 |
| 1982 | 27.5 | 20.3 | 21.9 | 10.7 | 3.2 | 83.6 |
| 1984 | 35.5 | 24.8 | 26.7 | 14.5 | 3.8 | 105.3 |
| 1986 | 49.4 | 31.0 | 34.4 | 19.4 | 5.3 | 139.4 |
| 1988 | 54.3 | 34.9 | 40.9 | 19.9 | 5.9 | 155.8 |

Source: Adapted from Frank J. Sorauf, *Money in American Elections*, 1988:79; data from FEC Reports.

\*"All Congressional Candidates" includes independent candidates and those of minor parties, as well as those who lose in primaries or otherwise drop out before the general election.

†Includes PACs of cooperatives and corporations without stock.

lion in contributions the PACs made to congressional candidates in 1988, they also gave $9.6 million to political parties. Moreover, they laid out $20.8 million as "independent expenditures," money spent independently of any campaign to urge the election or the defeat of a candidate. In addition, 1988 was a presidential year, and PACs gave $3.4 million to possible presidential candidates in the preconvention stage and then spent $13.6 million in independent expenditures in the general election campaign, most of it to urge the election of George Bush. In sum, then, PACs spent $172.8 million in federal campaigns, $155.8 million of it in direct contributions to candidates for Congress.

Despite their numbers and their robust health, PACs do not monopolize American campaign finance. Their contributions in the 1988 campaign amounted to 31 percent of all the money that congressional candidates received. Candidates for the House got 37 percent of their receipts from PACs, those for the Senate only 23 percent. Despite the successes of PACs, individuals remain the chief source of funds for congressional candidates. In 1988 they contributed 54 percent of those receipts.

## Types and Varieties

The universe of more than 4,000 PACs is enormously varied and complex. The Federal Election Commission's way of categorizing them is the best known; it undergirds Tables 1 and 2. The FEC categories reflect the nature of the parent organization creating the PAC: corporations, labor unions, trade and professional organizations, and so on. Those PACs without parents the FEC calls the "non-connected" PACs.

In the case of two of those categories—corporate and labor—the organizations founding PACs are a comparatively homogeneous group. To be sure, corporations and unions differ in size, and they differ among themselves on specific issues. But they tend to agree on general political ideologies, and so do their PACs. The two other main categories in the FEC system, however, are notoriously diverse. The FEC's category of "trade/membership/health"—usually called "association" or "membership" PACs by others—embraces all manner of membership groups, from the American Medical Association's PAC and that of the American Bar Association to the National Pest Control Association's PAC and the Chocolate Political Action Committee.

The "non-connected" PACs, brought together only by their parentlessness, include a similarly broad range—the National Conservative Political Action Committee, the liberal National Committee for an Effective Congress, the National Right to Life PAC, and the Women's Campaign Fund, for example. Most of them exist to promote an issue or an ideology, but one subvariety, the "personal" or "leadership" PAC, is a case apart. Founded and run by a visible political leader (e.g., Walter Mondale, Tip O'Neill, and George Bush), they make contributions to candidates either to bolster a position of legislative leadership (or a claim to one) or to further the founder's ambitions for higher office (e.g., the presidency).

The logic of the FEC's categories is rooted in the FECA, the chief parts of which Congress wrote in 1974 to create a new order in American campaign finance. That legislation governs the raising of money by PACs (as "separate segregated funds") largely in terms of the components of the parent organization. With some exceptions, that is, corporate PACs can solicit regularly only the corporation's stockholders and its administrative and executive personnel. Labor unions can solicit freely only their members; the same goes for membership associations. Only the PACs without parents may solicit more broadly, as broadly as the whole universe of American citizens, in fact; that freedom makes possible their nationwide, direct mail solicitations.

The distinction between PACs with and without parent organizations, however, has a negative side for the non-connected PACs. Under the FECA as interpreted by the FEC in the Sun Oil decision, parent organizations may pay the indirect, nonpolitical costs of their PACs—the heat, the rent, the staff salaries, the equipment, the postage, and other supplies. (Whatever the parent does not pay, of course, comes from the funds the PAC solicits and receives.) Lacking such a parent, the non-connected PAC must pay its own way. That drawback and the fact that non-connected PACs incur very great fundraising costs in direct mail soliciting forces non-connected PACs to spend a much higher percentage of their receipts for nonpolitical expenses. Some non-connected PACs, in fact, spend no more than 5 percent or 10 percent of their receipts in direct contributions or independent expenditures in campaigns.

Another useful and far simpler way to divide the 4,200 PACs is by size of political assets. In 1988 the PACs making contributions to candidates for federal office gave an average of $48,139, and more than 90 percent of them gave less than $100,000. At the low end of the scale hundreds of PACs gave less than $10,000, often to few more than the required five needed to make them multicandidate committees. And these data do not even include the registered PACs that are inactive in any given election cycle. In the 1985–1986 cycle, in fact, only 3,187 of the 4,157 PACs on file at the FEC made contributions to any candidates for federal office.

On the other hand, some PACs are large and powerful. At the head of the list in 1988, the Realtors PAC gave $3.0 million to 542 federal candidates. The Democratic-Republican Independent Voter Education Committee (DRIVE), a PAC of the Teamsters Union, gave $2.9 million to 425 candidates to finish second, and the American Medical Association PAC ($2.3 million to 474 candidates) came in third. In fact, the 50 most generous PACs contributed a total of $55.7 million in 1986—a stunning 36 percent of the

$155.8 million that all PACs contributed to all federal candidates.

While great quantitative differences separate the big from the little PACs, important *qualitative* differences exist as well. The affluent PACs are the most professional and best staffed; they supply their own information, interview candidates themselves, and carefully inform their contributors about PAC activities. They have larger and more knowledgeable staffs; indeed, some of the largest of them have developed field staffs that assess political possibilities and candidate strength "on location," participating even in the selection and training of candidates. For that reason they are the PACs most likely to make "in-kind" contributions—contributions not of cash, but of campaign goods such as polls, the services of strategists, media and advertising planning, and courses in managing campaigns and being an effective candidate. In short, the 4,200 PACs are most likely to assume an active role in the planning and management of campaigns.

*Decision-Making within the PAC*

PACs are not organizational democracies. In virtually all of them decision-making is highly centralized, and the individuals making the decisions are not responsible in any regular or systematic way to the individuals who give their dollars to the PAC. Moreover, the FECA exerts no pressure toward democracy. On the subject of internal organization, that legislation requires only that the PAC have a name, an address, and a treasurer.

Among the PACs with parent organizations, the parent chooses the officers and staff of the PAC. Corporate CEOs and/or boards most commonly make those decisions for corporate PACs, as do the officers of labor unions and of membership associations. Consequently, the parent organization can set the PAC's policies and direct its decisions; most important, it can integrate the PAC's activities into the parent organization's other political activities, especially its legislative lobbying. Federal statutes place only one major limit on the power of the parent organization: it cannot transfer its assets, its profits, its income from dues to the PAC for it to use in political expenditures. For that purpose the PAC must solicit money into its "separate, segregated fund."

In reality the distribution of authority in the connected PACs is not quite so predictable; some parents do indeed cede a good deal of autonomy to the PAC. In others, conversely, corporate CEOs or powerful association executive directors may make the PAC an extension of their own political vision. PACs of large unions, corporations, and associations often must reconcile the different political views and goals of various interests in the organization—local plants and installations in different parts of the country, state organizations and affiliates in a federated organization, different product divisions in a corporate conglomerate. While they usually do not submit PAC decisions to formal votes of the membership or donors, they cannot overlook their views.

All of that leaves the role of the donors to the PACs both informal and uncertain. Many PACs do inform their donors sedulously of the PAC operations; many also solicit and take seriously donor opinions about PAC operations. For example, PACs commonly make some (often a "few") contributions to candidates for no other reason than the perception that those candidates have support among the PAC donors. But the truth is that very few PAC donors demand a participatory role in the PAC. In the first place, they have made the initial decision to contribute, and their loyalty to the goals of the parent organization has thus been certified. In many PACs with parent organizations, only between 20 percent and 40 percent of the eligible clientele gives to its PAC, and they tend to be the people most in sympathy with the interests of the parent organization. Moreover, some PAC donors may give to PACs in the first place precisely because the "costs" of participation and activity are relatively so low.

Among the non-connected PACs—those without parents—power and authority is another set of questions entirely. In most instances parentless PACs have been established by political entrepreneurs who project a potential political role and a willing body of potential donors; they then found a PAC in response. They or their successors run the PAC they establish, usually filling out boards of directors and staff positions with people of their choice. They fear no control by a parent organization, and their donors are remote from the management of the PAC. Those donors, often solicited by direct mailings, have no reinforcing ties to the PAC through a parent organization, and like the contributors to most direct mail causes, they drop in and out of support easily and often. In fact, a 10 percent response to mail solicitations is a genuine bonanza for such PACs.

## PAC Strategies and Tactics

In one sense a PAC's first strategic decision is the decision to be born. The 3,153 PACs with parent organizations at the end of 1988 were only a fraction of all the PACs that might have been had every corporation, trade union, cooperative, and membership association in the nation chosen to set up a PAC. The central question, then, is why some potential parents create PACs and others do not.

Corporate PACs provide a good and illustrative answer to that question. Only about 1,800 of the 3 million corporations in the United States have PACs, and the most significant characteristic of those who do is their size: for example, more than two-thirds of the country's 200 largest corporations have PACs. Furthermore, the likelihood of a PAC is much greater among corporations whose activities are subject to congressional action—greater, for example, among corporations in oil or other forms of energy, in transportation and communication, in defense contracting, in various aspects of agriculture. On the other hand, some decisions to establish a PAC are attributable to a corporate leader who is willing to shape a political role for the corporation, confident that such a role is proper and useful for it. Among other potential parents of PACs, similar considerations obtain: the large associations, those whose activities concern government, and those with strong political traditions tend to have PACs. Again, those with PACs are in a small minority; the *Encyclopedia of Associations* reports approximately 22,000 nonprofit associations in the United States, while in 1988 the FEC counted only 786 association PACs. The large and centralized national labor unions meet all of the conditions—size, involvement with government action, and political tradition—and virtually all of them have PACs.

Among the non-connected PACs, the decision to found a PAC is in great measure influenced by considerations of the political marketplace. Has someone discovered a need or demand for a PAC? Will the projected clientele contribute funds to the PAC? Is there, in short, a cohesive and responsive group who will respond to direct mail solicitations out there? The PAC without a parent organization has a very real and immediate criterion: the need every two years to raise enough money to pay overhead costs and still provide some additional funds, if only a small percentage of the gross take, for direct political activity.

Almost immediately after birth comes the necessity of decision. And no decisions reveal a PAC's goals and strategies more clearly than its decisions in allocating its political funds to candidates. The goals of PACs fall into four main categories:

Legislative. PACs seek to win access to policymakers, often the powerful ones who occupy positions of party or committee leadership. The indicated strategy, therefore, is contributions to incumbents who occupy positions of power and whose chances of winning reelection are generally impressively high.

Issue-based. PACs seek the triumph of issue positions or even broader political ideologies, and they will, therefore, make contributions to candidates, both incumbents and other challengers, who meet the issue/ideology test, whether it is a test of voting record, party label, or questionnaire responses.

Local or regional. PACs often recognize the importance of the local Congressperson, the local loyalties of their donors, and the need to be a political presence in the communities of which the parent is a part. Those pressures are especially great when the parent organization is federated in structure.

Intraorganizational. PACs must make decisions that protect the organization itself, whether that means contributing in ways that please the donors, the parent organization, or some important person in it. Such a decision may mean supporting candidates simply because some donors support them; most often it means supporting likely winners so that the PAC can claim a record of success in its spending.

Of course, most PACs pursue a mixed strategy that includes more than one of these goals and the strategies that they dictate. The important differences among them are in the varieties of the mix.

If one looks at all PAC contributory decisions, one fact stands out: PACs give overwhelmingly to incumbent candidates. In 1988, for example, almost 76 percent of PAC monies went to incumbents running for reelection to the Congress: 47.1 percent to Democratic incumbents and 28.7 percent to Republicans (Table 3). Indications of ideological contributing also surface in the data for 1988 (and earlier years, too). Labor PACs gave 92.5 percent of their funds to Democrats (Table 3). And while corporate PACs to some extent followed a legislative strategy in dealing with incumbent-challenger races, their ideological heart made them favor Republican candidates markedly in races without incumbents. The other two categories of PACs—association and non-connected—are far more diverse, containing within them PACs of the left, right, and center as well as those of little concern for ideology. An examination of the contribution records of those individual PACs reveals a good many (especially among the non-connected) whose contributions go heavily to candidates of one party or the other.

PAC strategies change with time, however. Those concerned especially about specific issues will increase or decrease their activity as issues affecting them wax or wane in the Congress. Others will react to changing political winds. A number of corporate PACs, for example, rallied behind Republican incumbents in 1982 and 1986 in order to minimize anticipated Republican losses in the Senate. The more experienced and sophisticated the PAC, the more complex and shifting its contributory strategies.

## Table 3

*PAC Contributions to Incumbents, Challengers, and Open-Seat Candidates for Congress by Party Affiliation: 1986\**

| Type of PAC | Incumbent Dem. | Rep. | Challenger Dem. | Rep. | Open Seat Dem. | Rep. |
|---|---|---|---|---|---|---|
| Corporate | 42.7 | 40.2 | 1.6 | 5.3 | 3.4 | 7.0 |
| Labor | 58.6 | 6.9 | 21.2 | 0.2 | 12.7 | 0.7 |
| Association | 46.5 | 35.2 | 3.7 | 3.2 | 4.8 | 6.2 |
| Non-connected | 38.6 | 21.7 | 14.6 | 7.3 | 10.2 | 7.8 |
| All PACs | 47.1 | 28.7 | 8.3 | 3.8 | 6.7 | 5.4 |

*Percentages cumulate horizontally to 100% total; totals may not be exactly 100 because of rounding.

## PACs in the States

A "political action committee" rarely means in the states what it does in the FECA. For example, not very many of the states mimic the federal prohibitions against spending from the treasuries of both corporations and trade unions. Thus in many states, corporations or unions (or both) may not have to go to the trouble of setting up those "separate, segregated funds" that are the core of the PAC under federal law. Moreover, fewer than half of the states have contribution limits that constrain PACs or PAC-like committees.

What we know about PACs in the states suggests that they behave much as do PACs, however differently defined, in congressional elections. In the states as in the nation, they contribute overwhelmingly to incumbent officeholders; PACs everywhere seem to pursue a pragmatic, legislative strategy more than any other. Moreover, in many states PACs account for between 25 percent and 35 percent of the receipts of candidates for the state legislature. The PAC percentage of candidate receipts has also been increasing in the states as it is in congressional campaigns.

To all of this California, the most populous state of all, remains the only documented exception. PAC money accounts for well over half of the receipts of state legislative candidates. That anomaly can be explained away in part, however. The California figures include contributions directly from businesses who can make direct contributions in the state, and there have been no statutory limits on those contributions. Finally, the sheer size of campaign expenditures in California creates a demand for funds far greater than one finds in the other states.

## PAC Power and the Reaction to It

The growth of PACs and their financial strength after 1974, along with the rising costs of campaigning generally, raises the specter of new "fat cats" and new forms of monetary influence in American politics. The issues, especially as they involve PACs, are many, but two stand out: the use of money to influence the outcome of elections and the use of money to influence the making of public policy. In the reformist vernacular these are the issues of "buying" elections and "buying" the Congress.

How much do PACs "buy"? The best evidence is that they do indeed get the "access" that they claim to seek: the opportunities to make their case (or the parent organization's case) with members of Congress, perhaps even just the phone calls returned. As for votes changed by contributions, evidence shows that it happens infrequently. While the campaign contributors as a constituency do command attention, they have not displaced the influence of the voters back home, powerful lobbyists with grass-roots support, the legislative and presidential party, even the personal convictions of the members of Congress.

PAC influence on electoral outcomes is undoubtedly greater. Their overwhelming support of incumbents running for reelection makes it that much harder for challengers to raise the money that they need for effective challenges. PACs thereby add just one more potent advantage to those that incumbents already enjoy in seeking reelection.

The American public, however, is far more alarmed than are scholarly analysts. Public opinion reflects the views dramatized by reformist critics in the media and in public interest groups. Common Cause, the self-styled citizens' lobby, typifies those opinion makers. Founded in the early 1970s as a nonpartisan group to represent certain broad citizen interests, it has long been associated with the reform of American campaign finance. Common Cause was an influential force in the formulation of the 1974 amendments to the FECA, and it has ever since had campaign finance high on its agenda. Its publications feature articles on the subject, and Common Cause regularly makes its conclusions on campaign finance available to American newspapers and electronic media. Indeed, its fundraising campaigns in the 1980s have regularly featured brochures warning that the "Congress is on the auction block. UP FOR GRABS to the highest PAC bidders." The pressure for further reform of American campaign finance has accelerated in the 1980s. Many proposals extend far beyond PACs, but few ignore them. Full public funding for congressional campaigns—with prohibitions against accepting any other money—would exclude PAC contributions along with all others. Partial public funding with matching funds for individual contributions (the model of public funding in the preconvention presidential races) creates an incentive for raising funds from individuals rather than PACs. And the expenditure limits that always accompany public funding proposals would diminish the value of PAC (and all other) contributions simply by reducing the need for them.

Narrower reform options that center on PACs make it clear that one regulatory "agency" has been at hard at work since 1974: inflation. Decreases in the purchasing power of the dollar, measured by rises in the Consumer Price Index, cut the purchasing power of the $5,000 limit to $2,084 by 1988. As for legislative proposals, two have the greatest support: proposals to reduce the PAC contribution limit (e.g., to $3,000), and proposals to limit the sums of PAC money any candidate could accept in a campaign. A proposal embodying both (the Obey-Railsback amendment) with a $3,000 contribution limit and a limit of $70,000 on PAC receipts did pass the House in 1979; a filibuster blocked its consideration in the Senate. Receipt limits, however, are of uncertain constitutionality; the Supreme Court has upheld limits on the contributors of funds, but limits for the candidates receiving these funds have never come before the Court. In 1990 bills passed both the Senate and the House that would have drastically altered the status of PACs. The Senate banned them altogether, and the House reduced the $5,000 contribution limit to $1,000 for PACs that would agree to accept no more than $240 a year from its individual donors. As of late 1990 the two very different bills had not even gone to a conference committee, much less to the two Houses and the President.

Such reform proposals are not without their critics. The PACs themselves, and others too, defend PAC contributions as a form of political activity protected by the First Amendment. Beyond that point critics have more pragmatic concerns. If PACs are prevented from making contributions to candidates by limits on receipts, PACs might well increase their independent spending; some indeed have threatened to do so. Candidates can be held responsible by voters for the way they spend the money they receive; they cannot, however, be held responsible for independent spending on their behalf. Moreover, a limit on PAC receipts or a lower contribution limit will affect PACs differently; the former, for example, would work to the advantage of those PACs able to raise money early in the election cycle and to the disadvantage of those relying on the stimulus of the campaign itself.

See also: AFL-CIO COPE, American Medical Association, *Buckley v. Valeo*, George Bush, Direct Mail, Federal Election Campaign Act of 1971 and Amendments of 1974, Federal Election Commission, Walter Mondale, National Conservative Political Action Committee, National Educational Association,

Thomas O'Neill, Presidential PACs, Ronald Reagan

*Frank J. Sorauf*

REFERENCES

Eismeier, Theodore J., and Philip H. Pollock III. 1985. "An Organizational Analysis of Political Action Committees." 7 *Political Behavior* 192.

———, and ———. 1988. *Business, Money, and the Rise of Corporate PACs in American Elections*. Westport, CT: Quorum.

Epstein, Edwin M. 1980. "Business and Labor Under the Federal Election Campaign Act of 1971." In Michael J. Malbin, ed. *Parties, Interest Groups, and Campaign Finance Laws*. Washington: American Enterprise Institute.

Gopoian, J. David. 1984. "What Makes PACs Tick?" 28 *American Journal of Political Science* 259.

Handler, Edward, and John R. Mulkern. 1982. *Business in Politics: Campaign Strategies of Corporate Political Action Committees*. Lexington, MA: Lexington Books.

Jacobson, Gary C. 1980. *Money in Congressional Elections*. New Haven: Yale U. Pr.

Jones, Ruth S. 1984. "Financing State Elections." In Michael J. Malbin, ed. *Money and Politics in the United States*. Washington: American Enterprise Institute.

Latus, Margaret A. 1984. "Assessing Ideological PACs: From Outrage to Understanding." In Michael J. Malbin, ed. *Money and Politics in the United States*. Washington: American Enterprise Institute.

Masters, Marick F., and Gerald D. Keim. 1985. "Determinants of PAC Participation Among Large Corporations." 47 *Journal of Politics* 1158.

Sabato, Larry J. 1984. *PAC Power: Inside the World of Political Action Committees*. New York: Norton.

Sorauf, Frank J. 1984. "Who's in Charge? Accountability in Political Action Committees." 99 *Political Science Quarterly* 591.

———. 1988. *Money in American Elections*. Glenview, IL: Scott, Foresman.

## Political Consultants in American Democracy

A campaign professional who is engaged primarily in the provision of advice and services (such as polling, media creation and production, and direct-mail fundraising) to candidates, their campaigns, and other political committees is called a political consultant. Broadly the title can adorn almost any paid staffer on even the most minor of campaigns. Usually, however, the label is applied to the relatively small and elite corps of interstate political consultants who usually work on many campaigns simultaneously and have served hundreds of campaigns during their careers. They are the sellers, and often the creators, of advanced campaign technology and technique.

There are basically two kinds of consultants. A *generalist* consultant advises a candidate on most or all phases of his campaign and coordinates most or all aspects of the technology employed by the campaign. A *specialist* consultant concentrates on one or two aspects of the campaign and peddles expertise in one or two technological specialties. While almost all of the early consultants were generalists, most consultants today are specialists (who nevertheless often advertise themselves as generalists).

Whether generalist or specialist, the consultant's primary role is the same: to provide services to campaigns. A consultant is hired to conduct a series of public opinion surveys, or to create a precinct organization, or to orchestrate a direct-mail fundraising effort. The secondary roles played by consultants, however, are sometimes more intriguing and just as substantive as the provision of technological services. Some consultants, for example, play the "expert" role, a position accorded consultants by the campaign staff and the candidate because of their wide experience and masterful reputation. (In many campaigns consultants probably have more influence, and their every word is weighted more carefully, than their actual experience or their degree of involvement with the campaign can justify.) Even though consultants may only visit the campaign once a month or talk with campaign officials weekly, the political professional frequently becomes the grand strategist, designing and supervising the "game plan," orchestrating the press, and selecting the candidate's issues.

*A Brief History of Political Consulting*

Political consultants in one form or another have always been active in American politics, but the campaign professionals of earlier eras were strategists without benefit of the campaign technologies so standard today. Usually, too, consultants were tied to one or a few candidates or perhaps to a state or local party organization. Before consulting became a full-time profession, lawyers were often assigned campaign management chores since they had a flexible work schedule as well as the personal finances and community contacts to do the job properly. The old-time press agent, usually a newspaperman familiar with the locale, was also a crucial and influential figure in a campaign organization. But in most cases these lawyers and press agents were only functionaries when compared to party leaders and organization bosses who wielded far greater authority in political matters.

On a separate track, one supported by the business community, the profession of public relations was developing. Businessmen saw image making as a way to counter a rising tide of business criticism. The federal government followed in close pursuit of public relations professionals, expanding their role considerably during the New Deal. State and local governments, charities, religions, and colleges in succession all saw the "P.R. promise."

Political consultants are clearly direct descendants of the public relations professionals, and the growth of both groups is related to similar phenomena, especially the revolution in mass media communications. Yet political consulting has a genesis all its own. The decline of the political parties has created opportunities for consultants and the tools of their trade. New means of financing campaigns, telling the candidate's story, and getting the candidate's voters to the polls became necessary as the parties' power waned. The new campaign techniques and the development of air travel, television, and the computer combined to give consultants the attributes that candidates desired. The fact that these techniques quickly became too complex for laymen to grasp easily—consultants themselves were forced to specialize to keep up with the changes—and the longstanding American need for, and trust in, experts made professionals that much more attractive. Even if illusionary, the belief that consultants' tricks could somehow bring order out of the chaos of a campaign was enormously reassuring to a candidate. Likewise, rising campaign costs (and expenditure and contribution limitations) have placed a premium on the wise use of every campaign dollar. All of these alterations of the political map seemed powerful arguments for hiring political consultants, who gradually assumed the status of an unquestioned essential for serious campaigns. Everyone now needs consultants if only because everyone else has them.

The consulting movement coalesced first in California. The state's traditionally anemic party system was weakened further in the twentieth century by the addition of new social welfare programs, a broadened civil service system, and a sprawling suburban shift from the central cities matched by the influx of hundreds of thousands of migrants from the East, the Midwest, and the South. An enormous growth in the size of the electorate made organizing difficult (and redistricting an even more wrenching and enveloping process). Finally, California was in the forefront of the popular initiative and referendum movement and had an exceptionally long ballot and a multiplicity of elections.

An initiative campaign showed in fact that modern political consultants could have a major effect. In 1933 the California legislature passed a bill authorizing a flood control and irrigation development in northern California (called the Central Valley Project), which the Pacific Gas and Electric Company (PG&E) believed to be a threat to private power. The utility promptly launched a ballot initiative to reverse the decision. The project's proponents hastily enlisted Clem Whitaker, a Sacramento newsman and press agent, and Leone Smith Baxter, a public relations specialist, to mastermind a campaign to defeat PG&E's initiative. On a limited budget of $39,000, most of which went for radio and newspaper appeals, Whitaker and Baxter managed to save the Central Valley Project.

Not only did PG&E hold no grudge, it actually put Whitaker and Baxter on annual retainer! The two consultants incorporated themselves (as Campaigns, Inc., and later as Whitaker and Baxter Campaigns) and eventually married as well, initiating two decades of smooth sailing for the firm, operating out of San Francisco. The lack of extensive competition enabled Whitaker and Baxter to post a 90 percent success rate in 75 major campaigns. Eventually, rival California consultants (such as Republicans Stuart Spencer and Bill Roberts and Democrats Don Bradley, Joseph Cerrell, and Sanford Weiner) caught up and reduced both Whitaker and Baxter's competitive edge and its win-loss record.

By the early 1950s, political professionals were quite obviously playing an increasingly important part in electoral politics, and four decades later political consultants have become a campaign standard across the United States and not just for major national and statewide contests. State races for lesser offices and U.S. House seats, and elections for local posts and even judicial offices, now usually have the services of one or more consultants. Consultants, moreover, rarely miss an opportunity to expand their domain. The judicial elections in California are a classic illustration. In Orange County a judge seeking another term was defeated in 1940, but no judge lost again until 1978 when *four* were beaten simultaneously. Sitting judges became understandably nervous and sought professional assistance. Joseph Cerrell and Associates, who had never done a judicial campaign until 1978, suddenly found themselves with nine at once. The

agency's candidates, all incumbents up for re-election, made a clean sweep (at $7,500 apiece). Flushed with success, Cerrell sponsored a conference on judicial campaigning in 1979, designed for judges of the superior and municipal courts. For a $100 registration fee a judge would be treated to sessions on topics such as "Campaigning with Dignity: Maintaining the Judicial Image."

The number of consultants has skyrocketed in keeping with the demand for their services. As late as 1960 only a relatively few full-time professionals were in the field, but nearly three decades later there are hundreds—thousands if local advertising agency executives specializing in politics are counted. In addition, they handle a great deal besides candidates' campaigns. Referenda, initiatives, bond issues, and political action committees (PACs) sustain many firms. Some consultants enjoy overseas work in foreign campaigns or specialize in primary and convention nomination battles as well as general elections. Today the average modern professional manages more campaigns in a year than his predecessors did in a lifetime.

### Consultant Services: The New Campaign Technology

Generalist consultants offer an especially wide range of service packages to prospective clients. They will do as much or as little as the campaign organization desires. Some have occasionally done little more than let their name (and, by implication, its successful reputation) be used in a campaign's directory or roster. "Selling our name" is done almost as an endorsement—in exchange for payment, of course.

Specialist consultants usually provide more restrictive services. But those who have been in the business for a long time seem inevitably to diversify their offerings, both because they become more familiar with other technological specialities the longer they are associated with campaigns and because a good deal of additional money is in it and the candidates often request other services. (Having been "sold" on a consultant's product in one area, candidates are often eager to thrust even more responsibility onto a "trusted expert.") Thus established media consultants are quite commonly hired to write a "soup to nuts" campaign plan or to give day-to-day strategy advice. Whether the candidate actually benefits from this sort of arrangement is another question. Some consultants clearly have the background to cover all the bases, but many others learn one specialty well and then offer a series of "add-on" services that are cheap imitations of the work done by competent professionals.

A consultant is undeniably at his best when concentrating on his specialty, and the new campaign technology has become advanced enough in several areas to be well worth employing. Still, the importance of campaign technology to electoral success can easily be overstated (and usually is). Elections, and the choices voters make among candidates, are too complex and involve too many variables to be determined by a single element. In most elections, the new campaign techniques, and the consultants themselves, probably do not make the difference between winning and losing, although they make some difference and in at least a few cases can convincingly be given credit or blame of the margin of victory or defeat. This fact alone would serve to make consultants modestly influential in the conduct of the campaign. But owing in good measure to journalists' "hype" and consultants' own superb sense of self-promotion, the perception is that consultants and technology make the difference in a greater percentage of elections than they are likely to do. This perception among the press and political people simply means that consultants and the new campaign techniques are even more important than their actual electoral effect would justify—more important, certainly, than they deserve to be.

This is not to say that consultants and their technologies are worthless. In general, the new techniques are more effective than many old-fashioned methods. Moreover, consultants and the new techniques can and do influence virtually every significant part of a campaign, and the campaign certainly makes some difference in the outcome of an election. While most voters still make their choices in good part on the basis of party loyalty and many (if not most) have their minds almost made up before the campaign even begins, it is also true that in just about every election as much as a third or even more the electorate is honestly uncommitted or switchable. That number may be growing as the strength of party identification declines. Voter turnout is also variable. Even if persuasive action is fruitless, a campaign's success depends heavily on its ability to stimulate those favorable to it to vote and, alas, to encourage those unfavorable to it to stay at home, mainly through negative

advertising directed almost solely at the opponent's weaknesses.

Technology provides the means to both these ends. New organizational techniques have been developed to stimulate turnout, and a disturbing proportion of the innovative modern media ads is negative. Moreover, for all practical purposes campaigning is now continuous, and voters can be influenced by television, direct mail, and other campaign aids long before the outset of the official campaign season. Some evidence shows that at state as well as national levels, campaign technology is being employed increasingly early.

Still another situation in which campaign technology is especially influential is the primary election, where party identification (absent a preprimary party endorsement) can play no role at all. Many political consultants love to work in primaries, where they believe that relatively low turnouts and a lack of party ties give the new campaign technology its broadest potential use. Finally, campaigns have other functions besides winning, which a European would acknowledge sooner than would an American. Party building for future elections (or candidate building within the personality-centered American system) is a perfectly legitimate and useful campaign goal.

Inevitably, anyone who attempts to assess the effectiveness of modern campaign techniques is humbled by the scarcity of empirical evidence to support any hard conclusions. Compared to the extensive privately supported research in product advertising, there has been little thorough testing of the impact of political media advertisements during campaigns, for example. The impact of any consultant or any technology, then, can usually only be guessed at. No one has the foggiest notion of what percentage of the vote a consultant or a piece of new campaign technology can or does add to a candidate in any given set of circumstances. Campaign observers rarely even have a precise idea of what event or series of events produced the election result. Campaigning remains a complex, unpredictable, and very scientific process, and one may expect (and be grateful) that it always will be.

### Political Consultants in Perspective

Controversy rages over the role and influence of the political consultant in American elections, and properly so. No more significant change in the conduct of campaigns has occurred than the consultant's recent rise to prominence, if not preeminence, during the election season. Political consultants, answerable only to their client-candidates and independent of the political parties, have inflicted severe damage upon the party system and aided the modern triumph of personality cults over party politics in the United States. All the while they have gradually but steadily accumulated great power and influence in a system that is partly their handiwork.

For a group of political elites so prominent and powerful, consultants have been remarkably little investigated and understood. The consultants themselves make the task of separating fact from fiction and image from reality as difficult as possible. They enhance their own images and increase the fees they can command by keeping their campaign techniques as mysterious and bewildering as possible. Most consultants have been intimately involved with politics for decades, and they know better than most elected officials that, in politics, style is closely intertwined with substance. Fame and fortune—not to mention electoral success—come to those who can adjust the mirrors in just the right way and produce sufficient quantities of blue smoke in the public arena.

In using the blue smoke and mirrors of politics to cloud the view of their profession, consultants have found a valuable ally—the working press. Not only do many journalists fail to understand what it is consultants do and how they do it but also those same print and television journalists are responsible in good measure for the glow of expertise and omniscience that surrounds the consultant's every pronouncement. Consultants have become prime and semipermanent sources of information and insight for political reporters, and the election professionals are rewarded with an uncritical press and frequent beatific headlines.

No one reads these headlines more closely than the prospective candidates, and as a consequence virtually no nominee for public office at any level thinks he can survive without a consultant or two. Remarkably, though, if reporters are ignorant of the consultant trade and technology, candidates are far more so. President Gerald Ford, for instance, would admit almost total ignorance of his 1976 direct-mail operation and even decry "junk mail" after leaving the Oval Office, despite the fact that direct solicitations by mail had been one of the most successful aspects of his campaign for the Republican presidential nomination. Many other candidates

have hired media and polling consultants at great cost lacking even a superficial comprehension of their techniques or their real worth, taking on faith what they had read and heard about these election wizards and believing all the while that consultants were essential for victory without knowing whether or why the common wisdom was true. Understandably, candidates lack the specialized training in election technology that their consultants possess and have little time to learn in a demanding pressure-cooker campaign. This leaves the consultant a seemingly indispensable commodity, someone with immense leverage not merely during the election but also after the campaign is over. Few are the politicians who never seek office again, and their relations with consultants are as permanent as their campaigns. Pollster Patrick Caddell and media man Gerald Rafshoon's extraordinary alliance with President Jimmy Carter is by no means exceptional anymore. President Reagan's pollster, Richard Wirthlin, had even greater access to the President and pervasive White House influence than did his predecessor Caddell, for instance.

In the praise being heaped upon the media masters, soothsayers, and direct-mail artists, all sorts of wondrous things are being attributed to them. Actually meeting these political wizards, after preparatory reading of hundreds of articles by awestruck commentators, an observer is inevitably reminded of Dorothy's disappointment when she unmasked the Wizard of Oz. For, despite their clever public posturings, consultants have no potions or crystal balls, and most of them will admit it forthrightly, at least in private. "If I knew the successful formula," conceded one longtime professional, "I would patent it."

It is reassuring (perhaps deceptively so) to hear one of the most widely experienced generalist consultants, Stuart Spencer, insist that "There are good politicians and there are bad politicians, and all the computers and all the research in the world are not going to make the campaign situation any better when bad politicians are involved." Spencer may well be right that consultants cannot turn a sow's ear into a silk purse (although at least a couple of exceptions come to mind). But a less radical transformation at the consultant's hand is possible: a black sheep can become a white one upon application of a little dye, and a corroded silver dollar can be transformed into a shiny one with a chemical and a bit of polish. Consultants and the new campaign technology have not changed the essence of politics, which is still persuasion, still a firm, friendly handshake. But the media of persuasion are no longer the same, and the handshake may be a projection or even an illusion.

Whatever the degree of their electoral influence, consultants (most of them) have talent and enormous experience. I hasten to add that a few well-publicized consultants do not live up even vaguely to their advance billing. As one top professional observed, "The only thing that keeps some of them alive is luck and being in the right place at the right time. They don't really affect anything in a dramatic way because they don't have the political instinct to do it." By and large, however, consultants are hardworking professionals—very bright and capable, politically shrewd and calculating, and impressively articulate. They travel tens of thousands of miles every year, work on campaigns in a dozen or more states simultaneously, and eat, breathe, and live politics. They are no less political junkies than the candidates they serve. For the most part, they are even less concerned with issues, the parties, and the substance of politics than their clients. Consultants are businessmen, not ideologues.

While admired for their abilities and acumen, consultants also suffer an unsavory reputation in some quarters and certainly among the general public, whose distrust of seamy, "smoke-filled-room" political operatives is traditional and enduring. At best consultants are seen as encouraging the natural instincts of plastic politicians. ("Gripp, Grinn, Waffle, & Faykit" is the sign cartoonist Jeff MacNelly hangs outside his fictional consulting firm.) At worst, consultants are denounced as "hustlers" and "con men." Consultants bristle at the slightest mention of any unfavorable press, blaming the criticism on the politicians they work for. As media consultant Michael Kaye expressed it, "People don't like politicians. So no matter how skillfully a political consultant like me does his work, I am a bad guy. I am a packager. I am a manipulator. Now, is it because of what I do, or is it the product that I sell?"

Yet widespread doubt about the work of consultants has a basis more thoughtful than Kaye's analysis suggests. That basis is a deep concern for the health and well-being of the democratic process. What consultants often seem to forget is that their work cannot be evaluated solely within the context of their profession. "Is this artful media?" or "Is this an effective piece of direct mail?" or "Did this action by a political consultant help to elect candidate X?" are legitimate questions and necessary ones for any judgment of a particular consultant's worth. But the ultimate standard by which the profession of political consulting is judged cannot merely be success in electing or defeating candidates. Consultants have much more vital considerations of ethics and democracy to ponder, because electoral politics is the foundation of any democratic society, and important actors in the political sphere must necessarily be the subject of special scrutiny.

While an observer can reasonably conclude that most politicians have been fairly well served by their election professionals, it simply does not follow that the public and the political system have been equal beneficiaries. As the influence of consultants has grown, some very disquieting questions have begun to loom large. Influence peddling, all kinds of financial misconduct, shameful acts of deception and trickery, and improprieties with former clients who are now in public office are only a few of the compromising and unethical practices habitual in far too many consultants' portfolios. At the root of some of the worst offenses is a profit motive unrestrained by ties to party, ideology, or ideals.

As distressing as they are, the ethical concerns fade by comparison to the democratic effects wrought by consultants. Political professionals and their techniques have helped homogenize American politics, added significantly to campaign costs, lengthened campaigns, and narrowed the focus of elections. Consultants have emphasized personality and gimmickry over issues, often exploiting emotional and negative themes rather than encouraging rational discussion. They have sought candidates who fit their technologies more than they matched the requirement of office, and consultants have given an extra boost to candidates who are more skilled at electioneering than governing. They have encouraged candidates' own worst instincts to blow with the prevailing winds of public opinion. Consultants have even consciously increased nonvoting on occasion and meddled in the politics of other countries.

These activities have not occurred in a vacuum. The rules of the political game have been altered dramatically, with consultants clearly benefiting from the changes. The decline of the political parties and the establishment of a radically different system of campaign finance are foremost among the developments that consultants have turned to their advantage. For example, as a direct consequence of the diminution of party strength, an abatement to which consultants have themselves contributed and, in some cases, cheered, consultants have replaced party leaders in key campaign roles.

Yet the power flow from party leaders to political consultants does not have to continue nor must unethical practices remain unchecked. Consultants and their apologists quite naturally can see no system better than the current one, and they will always have a ready excuse for distasteful doings in their profession. But those who lament the recent technological changes in electioneering have only to look to one of the major parties to see the path of renewal that these same new campaign technologies have made possible. A revitalized national and state Republican Party organization, fueled by the marvels that consultants had previously harnessed for themselves and monopolized, has provided the model that can tame consultant abuses and develop a healthier, party-based electoral system in the future.

*Conclusion*

Until this vision of party renewal comes fully to pass, however, the manner in which independent consultants select and elect candidates will be of central importance and of increasing concern. A candidate's adaptability to the new techniques of campaigning, not his competence, has become the standard by which he is judged by political professionals, and this insight has obvious and depressing consequences. One very prominent consultant was unusually frank and reflective in an off-the-record comment he made on his profession:

> As political consultants, we have inadvertently done great damage to the political process, while doing excellent work. We pick people who we, subconsciously or consciously, think are good at using the technologies that we have to offer. In other words, we simply look for good candidates. Whether they become good officeholders is no longer a factor. In fact, we can compensate pretty well for their not being good.

Political consultants and the new campaign technology may be producing a whole generation of officeholders far more skilled in the art of running for office than in the art of governing. Who can forget Robert Redford as a newly elected, media-produced U.S. Senator at the end of the film *The Candidate* pathetically asking his campaign manager, "Now what do I do?" The difficulty today lies not so much with the new techniques, which can be used to reinvigorate the party system, as with consultant-created candidates who think that the packaged campaign answers are the real answers, that the blue smoke and mirrors of politics are the sum and substance of policymaking.

*See also:* Roger Ailes, Douglas Bailey and John Deardourff, Jimmy Carter, Direct Mail, Gerald Ford, Charles Guggenheim, Media and Presidential Campaigns, Joseph Napolitan, Party Identification, Ronald Reagan, Whitaker and Baxter

*Larry J. Sabato*

*REFERENCES*

Agranoff, Robert, ed. 1976. *The New Style in Election Campaigns.* 2nd ed. Boston: Holbook Press.

Kelley, Stanley, Jr. 1956. *Professional Public Relations and Political Power.* Baltimore: Johns Hopkins U. Pr.

Napolitan, Joseph. 1972. *The Election Game and How to Win It.* New York: Doubleday.

Nimmo, Dan. 1970. *The Political Persuaders: The Techniques of Modern Election Campaigns.* Englewood Cliffs, NJ: Prentice-Hall.

Rosenbloom, David. 1973. *The Election Men: Professional Campaign Managers and American Democracy.* New York: Quadrangle.

Sabato, Larry. 1981. *The Rise of Political Consultants: New Ways of Winning Elections.* New York: Basic Books.

## Political Culture and Political Parties

Political culture is a pattern of subjective orientations shared by many individuals within the political system. Political scientist Cynthia Enloe defines culture as "a pattern of fundamental beliefs and values differentiating right from wrong, defining rules for interaction, setting priorities, expectations, and goals." In their 1965 study examining national differences in political culture, Almond and Verba define political culture as the particular distribution of patterns of orientations toward political objects among the nation's citizens. The term "orientations" refers to the psychological aspects (cognitive, affective, and evaluative) of objects and relationships. These objects and relationships include specific roles or structures, incumbents of roles, and particular policies, decisions, and their enforcement. This conceptual framework is further elaborated in terms of the objects of political orientations being the general political system, inputs to and outputs of the political system, and the self. From this conceptual scheme, Almond and Verba make a distinction between participant and subject political cultures.

To Daniel Elazar, political culture is "the particular pattern of orientation to political action in which each political system is imbedded." Comparing the political systems of the American states, Elazar argues that every state has certain dominant traditions of what government ought to do. He believes that three aspects of political culture are influential in structuring the nature of state political systems: a shared set of views about the nature of politics and what government can and should do; the characteristics of those who are active in politics; and the way in which government and politics is carried out by those who are politically active. Although Elazar views the United States as sharing a common political culture, he argues that the national culture is a synthesis of three political subcultures with all three coexisting and perhaps overlapping within the system.

A number of dimensions underlie Elazar's typology of political culture. One is the extent to which government is conceived of as a commonwealth or a marketplace. A second is the expected and approved levels of participation by citizens. Other dimensions include the roles of the bureaucracy and the political parties in the governing process.

Using these three dimensions Elazar posits three types of political culture. An *individualistic* political culture emphasizes utilitarian motives for the organization and operation of government, then, with the political system existing to serve the private marketplace; government serves not the public good but private interests. This individualistic political culture is antibureaucratic, professionalized, and personalistic. A second type of political culture, which Elazar labels *moralistic*, emphasizes a commonwealth conception of the political system. Politics is considered to be a public activity with the goal of attaining the "public good" and advancing the "public interest." In this political culture, citizens share a sense of community and a concern for issues, with government viewed as the instrument for attaining the public good. Political participation is encouraged, and an activistic government is valued. The third type of political culture, the *traditionalist*, Elazar describes as based on ambivalence toward the marketplace and a paternalistic and elitist conception of who should rule and who should benefit from the political system. Government's role is limited to maintaining the status quo, and political power is held by a self-perpetuating group. Social and family ties are most important in determining who should rule, and those outside the elite are expected not to participate in politics. Indeed, few such engage in any political activity. Elazar argues that a state may contain more than one type of political culture, arrayed by regions within a state, or political culture types may overlap within a region. In contrast, Raymond Gastril and Joel Garreau view the United States as made up of distinct cultural regions without overlapping of types within a community or state.

Whether focusing on differences in political culture among geographic areas, or the American states, or nation-states, or ethnic groups, research suggests that such differences do exist and that they have implications for the political party system. What is the relationship between political culture and the political party system? Briefly summarized, the political culture or cultures of a political system or subsystem influence the party system; reactions over time to the party system and the governmental system in which it operates in turn affect patterns of political culture. Political culture is both partially a product of the party system and a significant determinant of the nature of the party system. For example, research by Joel Lieske has tested the utility of the cultural regions schemas of Elazar, Gastril, and Garreau to account for patterns of party identification. Gastril's cultural regions best predicts mean levels of party registration. Controlling for region, considerable variation in the intercorrelations of party registration and ethnic ancestry exist, indicating that cultural region has a significant effect on patterns of party identification.

The patterns of political orientation shape what is expected and permitted in the party system. Thus, political machines could not exist where citizens would not tolerate boss rule and political corruption. In other words, political culture establishes the boundaries within which the party system operates. In turn, however, the activities of parties in recruiting and selecting candidates, the characteristics of those candidates, the policy stands advocated by party officials and the parties' candidates, and the performance of the parties' representatives in elected offices—all affect the orientations of citizens toward the party system. Thus the actions of parties and their members affect political culture, and political culture shapes the nature and activities of the party system.

*See also:* Party Identification

*Margaret M. Conway*

REFERENCES

Almond, Gabriel A., and Sidney Verba. 1965. *The Civic Culture*. Boston: Little, Brown.

Elazar, Daniel J. 1966. *American Federalism: A View from the States*. New York: Crowell.

Enloe, Cynthia H. 1973. *Ethnic Conflict and Political Development*. Boston: Little, Brown.

Garreau, Joel. 1981. *The Nine Nations of North America*. Boston: Houghton Mifflin.

Gastril, Raymond. 1975. *Cultural Regions of the United States*. Seattle: U. of Washington Pr.

Lieske, Joel. 1987. "The Cultural Geography of the American Party System." Presented at the Annual Meeting of the American Political Science Association, Chicago.

Wolfinger, Raymond E. 1972. "Why Political Machines Have Not Withered Away and Other Revisionist Thoughts." 34 *Journal of Politics* 365.

## Political Patronage

Patronage is the allocation of the discretionary favors of government in exchange for political support. Once thought of as consisting only of jobs, patronage includes the vast range of favors awarded by constantly expanding governments whose increased government spending—much of it discretionary—has brought increased opportunities to political supporters. Non-officeholders receive construction contracts, defense contracts, banking and insurance funds, and specialized treatment by the discretionary agencies of government whose power continues to grow. Officeholders, in charge of the machinery of government, have more discretionary power to dispense. In addition to bringing home the dams, post office buildings, military installations, and other programs that make them look good to constituents, they also control the key committee assignments and judicial patronage that smooth their political futures. All these favors cement a politician's loyalty to his party leaders, to whom he is indebted for past favors and from whom he seeks future favors. At the same time, favors help him earn the loyalty of those beneath him in the party structure who are in turn indebted to him for his beneficence.

Patronage powers explain why an incumbent President almost always controls his party's elders; patronage powers also explain why national politics is oriented more to the past than to current movements and more toward conservative than toward innovative programs. In the 1960s, septuagenarians John W. McCormack, the Speaker of the House, and Richard B. Russell, the President *pro tempore* of the Senate, were among the leaders of a congressional system that rewarded longevity with power. Even those members motivated by ideological commitment quickly discover, in the words of the late House Speaker Sam Rayburn of Texas, that "to get along, you have to go along." Rayburn never expected a Congressman to vote against the interests of his constituents, but he often advised members that "anyone should find a way to go along with his leaders 70 percent of the time."

It is sometimes possible for those who seek change through persuasion to bypass the patronage system, and indeed an issue whose time has come may triumph over patronage commitments. Long overdue drug reform legislation championed by the late Senator Estes Kefauver finally reached fruition only after the thalidomide scandal produced a vocal enough public outcry to push the law through its congressional obstacle course. Similarly, political conventions have been stampeded and delegations split by the sheer force of public pressure.

The patronage system thrives as one of the occupational hazards of our democracy. In a land where most people have some degree of freedom of choice, incentives are often required to bestir them to public action or to persuade them to change a course of action. Hence, public officials who do not know how to use patronage are invariable poor administrators, from Governor Lester B. Maddox of Georgia to Mayor John V. Lindsay of New York in his early years in office. Presidents, governors, and mayors without patronage skills usually have great difficulty dealing with their legislatures, which are made up of representatives who are obliged to bring patronage rewards (highways, schools, health stations, jobs) home to their districts. Unable to dispense rewards effectively, these leaders lack tools with which to bargain their own programs into fruition. Many find that they can no longer recruit top-flight administrators who fear the difficulties presented by working with people who do not have the time, energy, or inclination to work hard without the promise of rewards.

The patronage system also ensures that ideology plays a relatively small role in the decisions of government because, as national political conventions indicate, political rhetoric often conceals the hard, cold, unemotional realities of people and their ambitions. Not surprisingly, an ideological approach to politics and government is encouraged by the politicians themselves, who would much rather portray themselves as motivated by principle than by power or personal profit. The ideological approach to government also receives sustenance from a mass media that find it easier, less costly, and infinitely safer to report campaign speeches or depict members of Congress standing toe-to-toe in angry debate on the floor of the House than to learn, for example, why a Congressman changed his vote during a closed meeting of a congressional committee.

Patronage power is a necessary and legitimate extension of the power of elected officials. It is more humane, in one sense, than a meritocracy in which individuals advance solely on merit without regard to years of service or personal loyalties. But it can be cruel too. In Illinois, for example, 10,000 state employees, including the lame, the halt, and some with less than a month to go for their pensions, were dismissed by a new Republican governor, Richard B. Ogilvie, a persistent critic of Mayor Richard Daley's patronage jobs, to firm up his own power base.

The major hazard of patronage, however, is not that it builds political empires or private fortunes but that it encourages public officials to compromise public interest for private gain and to sacrifice the national interest for the needs of their regional constituencies. This process begins with the selection of presidential candidates at national conventions and includes every aspect of public policy and government funding. How much of the defense budget is actually used to protect the country, for example, and how much is allocated for military installations and defense contracts intended to win the support of various legislators who are anxious to obtain more jobs and money for their districts? "I am convinced that defense is only one of the factors that enter into our determinations for defense spending," charged Mississippi Congressman Jamie L. Whitten. "The others are pump priming, spreading the immediate benefits of defense spending, taking care of all services, giving military bases to include all sections." We see the effects in public and congressional insistence on continuing contracts, or operating military bases, even though the need has expired. Patronage may not have been a major factor in the country's initial commitment to Vietnam, but it certainly made withdrawal more difficult.

One wonders how long the Vietnam War would have continued if it had been *against*, and if a reduction in military installations and defense spending enriched rather than impoverished their constituencies and themselves.

To what extent has tax reform been evaded because of the patronage needs of Congressmen and to what extent has pollution been ignored because the polluters had more favors to dispense than did those who opposed pollution? Patronage power also plays a crucial role in determining the quality of the nation's public officials, an interesting balancing act between the forces of obligation and the interests of professionalism. Judicial patronage, by giving politicians the power to determine the caliber of the bench, gives them the power to determine what kinds of decisions will be made. Patronage powers also give politicians the power to determine the quality of law enforcement, one of the more oblique discretionary powers of government. The discretionary aspect of law enforcement surfaces when a new administration vigorously prosecutes public officials who previously enjoyed immunity while their own party controlled the White House.

Patronage vitally affects the nature of national and state legislation, and the quality of life in general, and like other forms of political power, it is used for both public and private interests. Former governor Nelson Rockefeller's threat to withhold "personal favors" from legislators led the New York State Legislature to reverse itself within a few hours and enact a $6 billion slum clearance program, an example of patronage used in the public interest. In contrast, Governor Buford Ellington of Tennessee, a Democrat, acted to benefit private interests when he encouraged the state's six largest banks to endow their favors on legislators in the hopes of shoring up his party's power in the state legislature. The six banks divided up the legislature and made substantial campaign contributions to legislators shortly before the interest rate was increased from 6 percent to 8 percent. Environmental needs could not hope to compete with political considerations when New York's Mayor Lindsay allowed the rezoning of a Queens residential area for commercial uses in order to reinforce his flagging support within the Catholic church (which owned the property in question). "We wanted to do something for the Catholic church," the mayor said, explaining the zoning change, which would have permitted the construction of a shopping center in a section that fronted two schools, a library, a hospital, and a post office. Although the value of the property was greatly enhanced by the zoning change, the quality of life affecting the area's residents was unquestionably imperiled.

Even neighborhood projects, such as parks and traffic lights, seemingly apolitical on the surface, can be used by enterprising politicians to appear as patronage rewards, intended to co-opt the grass-roots voter into the system. The political leader who understands how to use patronage can answer his community's needs by acting as a catalyst, prodding the bureaucracy toward speedily improving his district's services.

Voters who fail to vote their conscience in a general election out of gratitude to a party official for a personal favor or a traffic light or park can hardly be critical of the councilmen, state legislators, or Congressmen who fail to vote their conscience in the legislature but instead go along with their party's leadership out of gratitude for favors they have received and hope to receive. Some argue, however, that a voter who supports a congressional candidate who has expedited the installation of a traffic light is at least acting on the basis of concrete performance, whereas a candidate's position on Vietnam or student uprising may be a good deal less dependable.

The patronage system has a life of its own, developed and expanded over the years to function autonomously, regardless of who is in office or what party controls the legislature. The successful patronage seeker is well aware that government must bank its money, insure its property, and construct office buildings—all on a noncompetitive basis—because bank and insurance rates are fairly uniform and the objective standards for architecture and construction are kept to a minimum.

Government buildings need furniture, stationery, plumbing, heating, wiring, and vending machines that dispense sandwiches, cigarettes, ice cream, and soda—franchises often worth millions of dollars to the recipient of this patronage. When the late Charles Buckley, a Bronx Democratic leader, chaired the House Public Works Committee in Washington, he was also vice president of the Fidelity and Deposit Insurance Company in nearby Maryland. Beneficiaries of Public Works Committee projects were strongly encouraged to buy their own personal insurance from Buckley's company if they wished to continue doing business with the government. Other politicians own construction companies or form corporations to handle the contracts bestowed by government.

Today's patronage opportunities were undreamed of by George Washington Plunkitt,

the turn-of-the-century Tammany ward boss, who defined the difference between what he called "dishonest graft" (blackmail and bribery) and "honest graft" (availing oneself of inside information for personal enrichment). With a verve that does honor to the politicians of his day, Plunkitt noted that he had made a fortune in politics by purchasing real estate with the advance knowledge that a new subway line would soon enhance its value. "I seen my opportunities and I took 'em," boasted Plunkitt, in the best definition to date of honest graft. Although some reformers tend to regard all patronage as "dishonest graft" because it grants benefits on the basis of favoritism and not merit, orthodox politicians consider patronage the pressures and interests on which a democracy rests, well aware that politicians whose patronage is so inflexible that they cannot accommodate new interest groups may soon find themselves displaced. Successful machine politicians rely not only on their ability to satisfy organized local pressure groups but also on their sensitivity to the political desires of the broad base of constituents who are not organized.

Hailed by working politicians in terms of "friendship" and "loyalty," political support takes highly concrete forms when it appears as the quid pro quo for well-placed patronage rewards. The Congressman who is lucky enough to win a new post office for his district may well expect return support in the form of votes at the next election, hefty campaign contributions from contractors constructing the building, or free service at campaign time from party workers grateful for all the new job opportunities offered by a new federal project in their community. Himself the beneficiary of patronage from the executive and legislative leaders who "politically" engineered the passage of the building, the Congressman in turn will be obligated to throw his own "support" resources back into the system; perhaps he will make campaign speeches for the President, sponsor fundraising dinners, or provide other campaign help.

Through these favors, nonpolitical members of a community are co-opted in the politician's quest for his or her own personal advantages, thereby legitimizing self-seeking aspects of political behavior. For although people have many motives for entering political life—loneliness, ideological conviction, the desire to escape an unhappy home life, the need to identify with something greater than themselves—the vast underpinning of both major parties is made up of people who seek practical rewards. Tangible advantages constitute the unifying thread of most successful political practitioners; for whatever reason prompts people to enter politics, if they are to function effectively, they become involved in the chase. Political rewards range from nonmaterial ones, like being picked out of a crowd by a governor or receiving an invitation to a White House dinner or getting appointed to an unsalaried post on an executive commission, to the more tangible rewards, like the easy access to government officials, franchises, legal fees, architect's commissions, contractor's fees, judgeships, and of course nomination for public office.

These favors furnish the backbone of political machines that thrive despite the popular notion that they were rendered obsolete by television and the revolution in communications, which supposedly enable a candidate to bypass party machinery and approach voters directly in the comfort of their living rooms. Anyone who doubts the existence of these machines need only examine the typical ballot and ponder over who selected the judicial and legislative candidates who remain unknown to the average voter. Even so-called charismatic candidates who seem not to need a political machine to win must do business with the machine once they are elected, because these machines still control the state legislatures, city councils, and the judiciary.

The experienced politician has little difficulty in casting bread upon the waters and indeed may view the business of government as one vast bakery. Nearly everyone wants a piece of the action, but some do better than others.

On the national level, these include middle- and upper-class farmers who receive farm subsides; oil drillers who receive oil depletion allowances; airline managers and their users who benefit from federal grants; railroads and shipping firms, which receive subsidies; trucking firms and motorists who receive road subsidies; construction men who receive subsidies to build private housing; suburbanites who write off interest payments on their mortgages as a tax advantage; and veterans who receive federal funds.

Those who would change society—in ways large or small—are advised to pay close attention to the patronage network, a labyrinth that tells far more about how government operates than can be learned from congressional debates and political rhetoric; in fact, patronage practices reveal that cooperation plays a greater role in political life than conflict, the often delusive theme emphasized by the communications media. Political ideology and persuasion can be effective in those relatively rare moments when an idea's hour has come, but their importance has generally been overemphasized. Patronage, on the other hand, which often holds the key to national policy as well as state and city planning, is usually well concealed and generally ignored. Patronage exists because of human nature, offering rewards in a democracy in which men have a choice of conduct. It is both an extension of the electoral process, providing public officials with the tools to govern; and a diminution of the electoral process, robbing legislators of the ability to decide issues solely on the basis of conscience and reason. Finally, patronage is a totally interrelated system, in which franchises granted by municipalities can have profound effects upon the selection of our national leadership and the future of the nation.

### Patronage Opportunities and Political Realities

Even though mayors complain of an increasing political impotence that they attribute to their financial dependence on state and federal government and to the albatross of civil service, the office of mayor emerges as one with vast power. Often equipped with acute instincts for survival, mayors have developed this power by refining the known techniques of political patronage, seeking new routes and rejecting others that seem too limited to be useful. Mayors plead poverty, but city budgets under their jurisdiction have soared to all-time highs, in some cases, mayors can develop into new sources of political support and new areas of obligation.

Like living on love, few politicians can survive in office long on issues alone. Issues are more often used as shortcuts by the "out" party to get in; patronage is used to stay in. In many cases, issues are like patronage, in that the "out" party promises the public certain broad favors, which invariably narrow down to favoring certain groups. No one would question whether school busing or oil depletion allowances constitute an issue or not, yet closer scrutiny reveals that the resolution of these issues inevitably favors one group at the expense of another. Political systems analysts call this deal "the authoritative allocation of values," the power of government to order its priorities to reflect the values of society. In the last analysis, the system hinges on government's tremendous discretionary power inherent in American politics.

Issues, and issue-oriented politics, have sporadic mass appeal, rather than the day-in, day-out appeal that a job or insurance contract or legal referral has for the political professionals. Issue-oriented politicians, therefore, often have a hard time keeping their adherents active in the political arena on a consistent basis.

Consequently, those who attach themselves to issues outside the arena of partisan politics frequently express feelings of political impotence and disenchantment with the democratic process. For without political leverage gained from practicing "the art of obligation," issue-oriented activists often find that they are powerless to change the course of history.

### From the Clubhouse to the Bench

Although reform groups in other parts of the country have been more successful in changing the system of local and statewide judicial selection, in New York, district and country leaders have managed to retain the use of judgeships as a patronage tool of the party and make no secret of how the system works. Before formal nominations are submitted, district leaders who represent a particular judicial area will get together and select the civil court judges who will come from their respective areas. Before agreeing on a slate of nominees, the district leaders engage in an intricate process of bargaining among themselves, and if they can't reach a decision, then the county chairman resolves the dispute, usually by selecting his own candidates. Candidate selection rarely comes to this, however, since the district leaders are reluctant to relinquish their patronage power to the county leader.

On the Supreme Court level, the party hierarchy in a show of democracy runs judicial conventions to nominate the justices. At the convention, county leaders bargain with one another before they alone decide where the judgeships will go.

The real problem with the party-dominated judicial patronage system—and it is the prevailing system nationally—is that the judiciary is compromised by its ties to the political process. How independent can the judiciary be when the judicial decision-makers can hardly be expected to turn against the political system that produced them? Politicians and judges retain close ties with one another, reinforced by ample quantities of courthouse patronage that

grateful judges mete out of the party faithful. Young lawyers still flock to the clubhouses, eager to serve the party in a wide range of menial tasks, accepting as rewards the driblets of refereeships, trusteeships, and guardianships while they wait in hopes of capturing the ultimate prize for political service: the judgeship. By the very nature of the route they took to get to the bench, judges are obligated to party leaders who chose them and party workers who campaigned for them.

### The Judgeship

Of all the jobs now left to the discretion of party leaders, judgeships stand out as the most desirable. Every lawyer wants to be a judge, many politicians admit; witness the high ratio of lawyers involved in the political process. Judgeships are desirable for a variety of reasons. The security afforded by the generous tenure of judgeships offers politicians, scarred from continuous struggles to maintain their power, relatively peaceful retirement professions. A federal judge is appointed for life, while a state supreme court judge in New York, for example, is elected for a period of 14 years, regarded by many as a virtual lifetime appointment. Removed from the fray of political wars, judgeships also offer party veterans the dignity of being part of a high-status profession, a dignity they sorely missed during the long years they wore the label of "politician."

The party also finds judgeships a convenient means of showing publicly how it rewards, through recognition, dominant ethnic and racial groups. Intending to gain support from Black groups, former President Lyndon Johnson appointed the first African-American Supreme Court judge, Justice Thurgood Marshall. President Richard Nixon, in striking contrast, bowed to white southerners of conservative persuasion with his abortive attempt to appoint to the Supreme Court G. Harrold Carswell, a Florida judge who had once made a campaign speech declaring his belief in the doctrine of white supremacy.

If all the candidates seem equally qualified, then often the Justice Department, the President, and the Senators involved will try to choose the man who is identified with a particular ethnic group.

Bitter fights have centered around ethnic considerations, particularly when seats have been held in the past by representatives of minority groups. When Justice Abe Fortas's seat was vacated on the Supreme Court, widespread speculation centered around whether the seat would remain a "Jewish seat," that is, whether a Jew would succeed Fortas.

### Patronage Politics in Congress: The Realities of Representative Government

> In my thirty years of public office, nobody's ever asked me for a favor.
> —Senator Abraham Ribicoff (Democrat-Connecticut)

> I have a constant fight with Portland, but I get most of the projects in Seattle because these fellows have to come back to me for money.
> —Senator Warren Magnuson (Democrat-Washington, and chairman of the Senate Commerce Committee)

The late Sam Rayburn, Speaker of the House longer than any other man, once told freshmen members that a Congressman has two constituencies. "He has his constituents at home, and his colleagues here in the House. To serve his constituents at home, he must also serve his colleagues here in the House." This advice was recalled by D. B. Hardeman, Rayburn's administrative assistant, along with Rayburn's admonition that "To get along, you have to go along. Anybody who tries will find a way to go along with his leaders 60 to 70 percent of the time," the Speaker would say and thereby obtain for his district the dams, defense contracts, tax advantages, architects' fees, model cities, job patronage, and other government largesse that many members say privately are more crucial to their careers than their voting records.

The Speaker's advice is based on mastery of a legislative system that contrasts sharply with the British system, whose classic tradition of representing the national interest was expounded in Burke's famous letter to his constituents back home in Bristol: "Parliament is not a congress of ambassadors from different and hostile interest . . . but parliament is a deliberative assembly of one nation, with one interest, that of the whole; where not local purposes, not local prejudices, ought to guide, but the general good, resulting from the general reason of the whole. You choose a member indeed; but when you have chosen him, he is not a member for Bristol, but he is a member of Parliament."

At the Constitutional Convention, the Founding Fathers chose not to follow the British system but instead to elect representatives of designated districts on the theory that if everyone represented his constituency, then together they would represent the best interests of the nation. A Congressman thus has the constitutional obligation to promote the economic interests in his district. Subsidies to oilmen, homesteaders, railroaders, airlines, shipping interests, colleges, churches, and publications were all begun to promote the national economy. To settle the West, the government gave homesteaders free land, and railroad magnates virtual freedom from government control, just as today the oil industry benefits from generous subsidies on the grounds that the oil supply must be maintained for reasons of national security.

### Yes, But What Have You Done For Me Lately? Constituent Interests and Political Survival

A new, overly ambitious member of the House of Representatives worked especially hard to get a water project for his district. Unexpectedly, he achieved the unheard-of victory of getting the project out of the maze of congressional-executive bureaucracy. A southern committee chairman took the starch out of his victory, however, by suggesting that he had gone about the whole thing in the wrong way. "You never get the whole project," the chairman advised. "You get one mile, and you go home and brag about that, and then you go to the next congress and go for another mile. That way the project is good for five, maybe six terms. You've gone ahead and spent it all in one term, and now you'll have to wait for years for another project." The old-timer was right; and the Congressman was retired by the voters after serving two terms, unable to satisfy their queries of "Yes, but what have you done for me lately?"

The moral of the story is cynical but clear. Ignorant of the inner workings of Congress, the voters often appear insatiable, unpredictable, and ungrateful, regardless of the magnitude of past favors their Representatives have been able to direct their way. The loyalty of an individual constituent, on the other hand, can be bought for a much longer period of time by a lucrative government contract or a secure government job; but Congressmen find that obligating constituents as a group is quite another matter and far more difficult to accomplish. To survive politically, a Congressman must convince the voters—both as individuals and as groups—that he is perennially engaged in doing favors for them; that he is better than his opponents in garnering for his district the benefits of power;

and that he spends the major part of his tenure in office occupied with the business of government advantages. Many members of Congress say privately that bringing home the patronage is more important to their careers than their voting records. Indeed, some Congressmen who are highly respected in Congress are accountably retired by the voters because they have lost contact with their districts and have ignored their patronage obligations.

Doing favors dominates congressional activity at all levels and determines the power configurations of Congress itself. Most Congressmen spend a good part of their day handling favors: special "cases" for their constituents, "issues" for their religion, and favors for conglomerate interests within their districts or states. Individual constituents can expect their Congressman to fight the executive branch's intricate bureaucracy on their behalf by taking their cases before the Veterans Board; expediting loans for them from the Small Business Administration; or perhaps getting them jobs with the post office. Regional and corporate favors include even greater returns—dams, farm subsidies, new federal buildings that attract money and jobs, military bases, defense contracts, purchasing contracts, among other things.

Personal intervention from a Congressman, perhaps the most common (and least expensive politically) form of patronage, pushes a sluggish and unfeeling bureaucracy to provide justice, service, and equity to aggrieved citizens without the clout necessary to produce this reaction on their own. "The congressman is often a glorified messenger boy," explained Congressman Andy Jacobs of Indiana. "His chief function is raising hell if a person is entitled to something and doesn't get it. A call from a congressman will obtain equity."

Congressman do favors for their constituents without erecting the clear-cut bridge of obligations possible with other forms of political patronage. Representatives may never know whether their beneficiaries have voted for them but must bank on the notion that maintaining a perpetually high level of personal-favor activity will inevitably bring them added credit toward their next election. Indeed, many Congressmen owe their long tenure in Congress to the reputation they have carefully developed of attending even to the most minute demands of their constituents while burying themselves in the far reaches of obscurity on issues of national importance. Less consciously, the government provides yet another outlet for congressional favors by perpetuating a relatively poor communications apparatus between itself and the public. Considering this just a normal accompaniment to bureaucratic inertia, Congressmen act as conduits of information, bringing routine answers to aggrieved citizens seeking responses from the government.

### Where the Clubhouse Meets the White House: Presidential Patronage

> If Lyndon found out somebody really wanted something very badly, he would hold it up until he could trade it off for something he really wanted.
>
> —Stewart L. Udall, Secretary of the Interior in the Kennedy and Johnson administrations

> You can't use tact with a congressman. A congressman is a hog. You must take a stick and hit him on the snout.
>
> —A Cabinet member to Henry Adams, in *The Education of Henry Adams*

"You can't keep an organization together without patronage," advised former Tammany leader George Washington Plunkitt. "Men ain't in politics for nothin'. They want to get somethin' out of it." At the peak of his party's organizational pyramid stands the President, ultimately responsible for ensuring that his party's faithful have not entered politics for "nothin'." How well he separates the cream of patronage for the nourishment of the party determines his effectiveness in his loftier, constitutionally protected roles as commander in chief, chief legislator, chief executive, and chief architect of his country's domestic and foreign policy. For the party that elects him and maintains him in power expects the fruits of power to flow its way, to keep alive past relationships founded on mutual obligation. These appointments also determine the President's future effectiveness and the course of national policy.

Balanced against the high expectations of presidential appointments teeter the realities of what concrete forms of patronage are actually under the President's control. In the area of job patronage, for example, his resources are steadily depleting, as civil service "blankets in" more and more categories of federal service, without many allowances to compensate for the attrition of patronage. Whatever their private feeling, Presidents publicly applaud the "blanketing in" process, having learned the public relations value of supporting this policy. New administrations are always surprised to find how little federal job patronage exists, and Presidents must look elsewhere in order to even out their patronage debts. Compared to the governor of Pennsylvania who controls approximately 50,000 jobs, there are only 3,000 patronage jobs open to a new President out of 3 million civilian employees in government.

Although modern Presidents no longer throw everyone out of office to make room for their own supporters as Andrew Jackson did, transition jitters still afflict Washington on the eve of an incoming administration, and even many of those who do have job protection (such as assistants to the assistant deputy secretary) show anxiety, wondering if they will be downgraded or shorn of responsibility by a new layer of government coming into office. Despite all rhetoric to the contrary, all federal job patronage bears a direct relationship to the President's primary obligation to his party, and his entire patronage operation is based on that premise.

The higher the public official, the more vehemently he must protest patronage practices in any form in order to win the respect of the public, whose mental set rests firmly against the realities of American politics. In effect, this forces the politician to pursue a schizoid policy, leaving an enormous gap between theory and practice. If he wants his party to allow him to continue in politics, he must honor his debts and disperse the rewards of government to those who in effect gave him the opportunity to govern; yet if he wants the public to vote for him, he must disclaim any relationship with the tawdry practice of politics as it is.

American patterns of patronage politics sharpen the contrast between the President and his counterparts in totalitarian regimes, since such a large part of his discretionary power is already spoken for when he arrives in office. Bound to the exigencies of political quid pro quo inherent in democratic politics, American political leaders find that their power is checked before they even begin to govern—a factor that renders them less able than dictators to exercise their power arbitrarily.

At times, the President's patronage obligations seem overwhelming. Party leaders stand under the horn of plenty expecting to be showered with jobs, easy access to the White House, federal grants, contracts and franchises as well as substantial White House support at election time. Traditionally, the substantial party contributors—known as "fat cats"—expect their rewards straight from the President in the form of am-

bassadorships, although lately political ambassadorships appear to have dwindled in favor of assigning the posts to career diplomats.

If contributors invest heavily enough to warrant presidential patronage, then they probably cannot afford to leave their own business ventures to accept what by their standards amount to low-paying government jobs. Even so, they expect other forms of White House patronage in return for the patronage they have bestowed on the President in his candidacy. Many contributors welcome what may seem to be nonmaterial types of presidential patronage, such as an appointment to a nonpaying government advisory board, task force, or presidential commission, for these appointments offer wide visibility, free publicity, and lofty status to their beneficiaries, while usually involving very little work. Best of all, appearing on a presidential board makes a man look "plugged in," with channels to all the right contacts in Washington, an image that often materializes into substantial business gains. Many supporters of the President also prefer advisory board appointments because of their generally noncontroversial character. Unlike the appointment of a Supreme Court justice, the public hardly cares who populates these boards, unaware that many of their decisions may affect government spending and the public interest.

Financial supporters may be honored with other minor forms of presidential patronage: an autographed picture of the President; an invitation to a White House dinner or tea or prayer meeting; or a picture taken with the President in the White House Rose Garden, always good for a press release back home. To help him out with these ceremonial patronage obligations to the party, the President frequently uses Cabinet members or the Vice President, who are dispatched on trips throughout the country. Before they arrive, advance men contact party chairmen so that when the dignitary's jet lands, the local leaders can be on hand for pictures, speeches, and all the public relations fanfare so important to the maintenance of the party system.

While ceremonial patronage appears relatively easy to discern, presidential favors that involve preferential treatment (such as delegating contracts, grants, and other material benefits channeled from executive departments) remain obfuscated. Considering it beneath the dignity of the office of chief executive, the President does not often handle his patronage tools directly. Instead, he has built up both formal and informal liaisons, created with the implied function of wielding the potent instruments that control discretionary favors. Once the latter became legitimized, succeeding administrations have allowed their congressional liaison staffs jurisdiction not only over "favors" but also over the content of legislative proposals—a natural quid pro quo with which to follow up congressional favors.

In addition to his own formal liaison staff, the President builds up patronage relationships with selected interest groups, who in turn serve him as extra channels to Capitol Hill, adding their own valuable clout to the President's.

On lower levels of government, lobbies lend their resources to print campaign literature, provide sound trucks, and otherwise help candidates to win elections, always with the expectation that their help will be reciprocated in the future. For cooperative Congressmen with whom they have developed a patronage relationship, lobbies lend their research staff, ostensibly in order to provide understaffed Congressmen with the help they need to "understand" legislation.

Thrust by patronage relationships into an entrepreneurial role between the President and the legislature, many interest groups have developed power comparable to that of party whips—a function our own parties have all but abdicated—bringing recalcitrant members of Congress into line on crucial votes when the President has used up his own and his party's clout with them.

Presidential patronage power over the legislature must be played far more subtly than the patronage games worked out on other levels of government, for the President stands out as the most visible public official, more subject at any time than any other elected official to scandal and public humiliation. For this reason, favors must be traded in the shadows of government, their very success dependent on the loyalty of the participants and, more pragmatically, on their desire to consummate the bargains under consideration.

Few consider patronage politics illegitimate, particularly those circulating around the calm eye of the executive-legislative hurricane. If the game is played right, then the opportunities for political enrichment (not to mention personal enrichment) are unlimited; those who lose either bid different hands or try to reform the system. The game most often boomerangs, however, when the President's expectations grow too great, when he expects more loyalty than he actually gets and places too much stock in his own patronage power. Too many variables affect the successful application of patronage, not the least of which occurs when a Congressman's obligations toward his constituents (and correlatively their expectations and pressures on him) overwhelm both his loyalty and sense of obligation to the President.

### Patronage and Political Change

Although not united by ideology, American political parties are united by patronage, which uses the machinery of government on all levels (federal, state, and local) to enforce party discipline. A recalcitrant official feels the full weight of the organization. If a legislator defies his party's legislative leadership, then his county organization may well give him a primary fight.

In its infinite practicality, co-optation is far more common to American politics than perpetual confrontation, which probably explains why such a wide variety of groups can often operate in direct opposition to each other under the umbrella of the American political system.

Where it counts, the patronage system is secure. Sound planning almost always takes second place to political necessity; and the real rewards of government fall logically to those with the most clout. Reform fails because it comes in an empty vessel. The reformers invariably just want some of the patronage for themselves and rarely leave in their wake concrete programs (e.g., more incentives for civil servants, mandated rational planning for cities, or more stringent competitive bidding procedures for discretionary contracts) to correct the abuses of patronage they fought so hard to remove. When the reformers succeed in gaining some of the patronage for themselves, there remains the nagging question of whether they really represent an improvement over the original patronage dispensers.

Since patronage has deep roots in every branch of legitimate American political life, it is unlikely that real changes can be made without accommodating in some degree to its traditions. Patronage is inevitable because of the existence of the two-party system, pressure groups, the vagaries of constitutional government, the human condition, and the financial exigencies of campaigning. Today the politician finds himself even more indebted to the party than were his predecessors 50 years ago, unless he is fortunate enough to be independently wealthy or endowed with that compelling quality of mass appeal popularly known as charisma. As his campaign expenses expand along with his constituency, he competes for air time and advertising space with the giants of industry, whose lavish budgets were never intended to compare with political expenditures. Inevitably, political obligations increase proportionately as the need for financial support intensifies, a by-product of changing times. Rarely does anyone question the elected official's right to channel back to his supporters whatever refereeships, jobs, and contracts he has managed to retain within the scope of his discretionary power. When political obligations overwhelm decisions, the real dangers of the patronage system flare up to challenge the public good; and all too often, real community needs are sacrificed on the altar of political necessity.

Politicians fear patronage losses more than any other political threat, and they spend a good chunk of their time in office developing what patronage resources they have, while jealously guarding against any incursions into this power.

As a major force in the political system, patronage not only reflects the real power structure but also determines who enters and who succeeds in politics. Lawyers and businessmen dominate the national and state legislatures, because government's rewards suit the legal and business professions. Delegates from the arts, the sciences, skilled and unskilled labor, the medical profession, or the academic world rarely get elected as political representatives; they are forced by the system and by their own inclinations to influence government one step removed from its inner circles.

Political rewards also determine who stays active in politics. Regardless of how he stands on the issues of the day, the Congressman who fails to satisfy his district with military installations, dams, post offices, and the like will have a harder time getting reelected than his colleagues who have mastered the art of obtaining patronage. Even more certain is the unhappy fate of the elective judge—no matter how brilliant his opinions—who fails to send courthouse patronage back to the clubhouse; he will probably receive poor judicial assignments, meet trouble in processing his cases and obtaining clerical help, and most certainly will never regain his party's renomination.

Patronage seems to have a life of its own, ranging from fairly simple favors-such as being able to call the President on the telephone to the more complex rewards that emerge from the maze of military and reclamation budgets. Endemic to democracy, where men have relative freedom of action and the ability to expand their opportunities, patronage also presents many dangers. The most potent danger is the impact of patronage on policy and the exclusion from patronage of those unable to reciprocate support. This means the exclusion of the poor, who cannot contribute financially to politics and whose voter registration lags far behind all other groups and who therefore do not reciprocate through the ballot box; minority groups, whom custom has excluded from traditional rewards; in short, anyone barred by a political system geared to its own maintenance needs. Parceling out rewards on the basis of a political cost-benefits ratio fails in meeting the demands of these groups, whose arbitrary exclusion from the inner world of political decisions has not eliminated them as a very real part of the political process. These groups have real needs that must be answered by government, despite government's traditional patterns of answering public demands on the basis of patronage obligations or political threat.

The real lesson of patronage politics is that those who control patronage invariably control policy. The goal is to harness government's enormous reward powers on behalf of rational planning and on behalf of the public interest.

*See also:* Henry Adams, Bosses, Richard Daley, Andrew Jackson, Lyndon B. Johnson, Estes Kefauver, John V. Lindsay, Richard M. Nixon, George Washington Plunkitt, Sam Rayburn, Nelson Rockefeller, Tammany Hall

*Martin Tolchin*
*Susan J. Tolchin*

## Political Photography in the United States

During the late nineteenth century, the United States underwent a radical change: formally a distended, agrarian culture, it became a corporate, industrial society bound by a capitalist market economy. This new America was characterized by hierarchical structures of authority with control increasingly vested in an expanding federal government; large industrial organizations; and a proliferating number of reform, philanthropic, cultural, and educational associations, all striving to shape events to suit their own purposes.

The putative ability of photography to record exactly, without bias, made it the ideal instrument of persuasion in a culture that assumed that the universe operated according to universal, natural laws understandable to anyone through close investigation. Precise seeing was knowledge; possession of knowledge allowed one to act correctly.

The great photographers of the land west of the Mississippi River all worked at one time or other for the extensive mapping and survey operations mounted by the government in the 1860s and 1870s. Carleton Watkins, Eadweard Muybridge, and Timothy O'Sullivan not only created the public image of the western wilderness but also provided information to Washington on natural resources, wagon and railroad routes, the nature of the native inhabitants, and appropriate sites for military outposts. William Henry Jackson's images of the Yellowstone areas in Montana were directly responsible for the movement in Congress to establish the site as the nation's first national park.

After the turn of the century, landscape photographers often contributed their talents to the expanding environmental movement. From 1930 to his death in 1984, Ansel Adams's polyphonic images of western vistas and public efforts on behalf of the Sierra Club's political agenda contributed heavily to the movement for environmental regulations that peaked in the 1960s and 1970s. Contemporary figures, such as Robert Adams, take a jaundiced view of the impact that American civilization has had on the land and explicitly criticize what they see as rapacious development.

Jacob Riis was the first American to use photography as an instrument for social reform. His lantern slide shows of the stark images that he had made of the inhabitants and living conditions in New York City slums horrified middle-class audiences from 1890 to 1910 and moved them to greater effort toward the rejuvenation of urban areas. Lewis Hine's empathetic photo images of the immigrants at Ellis Island encouraged their acceptance into America, and his later work for the National Child Labor Committee helped to bring about legislation limiting child labor in factories and the mining industry.

The development of the social work profession meant increasingly that it aligned with government to achieve its goals. The most extensive use of photographers on behalf of government social policy occurred during the New Deal of the 1930s. Roy Stryker, head of the photographic unit of the Farm Security Ad-

ministration during the Great Depression, set out to document the persistence of grace and integrity in those most affected by trying economic conditions. Dorothea Lange, Walker Evans, Ben Shahn, and Russell Lee, among many others responded to his admonitions by creating photographic icons of indomitable courage and dignity. Stryker's emphasis on a story, easily grasped, made the photo-essay the dominant mode in American documentary photography in the 1930s.

W. Eugene Smith, Erskine Caldwell, and Margaret Bourke-White, the foremost practitioners of this art, developed the technique into the ideal vehicle for "human interest" stories. Photo-essays, which reduced individuals to indistinguishable Everymans, dominated *Fortune* and *Life* magazines in the 1930s and 1940s. The illustrated story became the perfect vehicle for the popular war photography of the 1940s, a selective and propagandistic enterprise that all too often muted the terrors of the war in favor of maintaining patriotic fervor at a high pitch. Robert Capa, along with Smith, managed to transcend the genre and produce powerful images of combat. In 1955 Edward Steichen, director of photography at the Museum of Modern Art, organized the most ambitious photo-essay ever attempted. "The Family of Man," an act of extraordinary cultural imperialism, reduced the population of the entire world to a limited number of stereotypical roles, all of which accorded with white, western tradition.

By the mid-1950s, however, photography also provided the means for cultural criticism. David Douglas Duncan revealed the horrors of the Korean War. Robert Frank, a friend of Jack Kerouac and an adopted member of the Beats, in 1955 published *The Americans*, a view of the invisible America of the 1950s and a gesture of defiance at the official culture of the photo-essay. Where Frank was largely apolitical, his heirs in the 1960s, such as Danny Lyon, used photography to emphasize dichotomies rather than continuities in American society and to bring political pressure to bear against conditions and policies they abhorred. Bruce Davidson, using the photo-essay, has recorded loneliness and disenfranchisement without diminishing the people who he has caught in his images. Larry Burrows graphically and compassionately pictured the Vietnam War, implicitly criticizing official United States policy in the process.

Photography continues in the last years of the twentieth century to be an arena in which public debate can confront contemporary social and political issues. Efforts to change American policies toward Latin American countries or to secure equal rights for lesbian and gay members of American culture, for example, recall and extend the tradition, originating in the 1890s, of using photographic images as a source of knowledge on which to base reform action.

*J. Fraser Cocks III*

REFERENCES

*Afterimage* [magazine of photography]. Rochester, NY: Visual Studies Workshop.

Fleischauer, Carl, and Beverly W. Brannen, eds. 1988. *Documenting America, 1935–1943*. Berkeley: U. of California Pr.

Green, Jonathan. 1984. *A Critical History of American Photography*. New York: Abrams.

Naef, Weston J., and James N. Wood, eds. 1975. *Era of Exploration, the Rise of Landscape Photography in the American West, 1860–1885*. Boston: (New York Graphic Society) Albright-Knox Gallery/The Metropolitan Museum of Art.

Newhall, Beaumont. 1982. *The History of Photography*. Boston: (New York Graphic Society) The Museum of Modern Art.

## Political Realignment in the Border States

The five Border States considered here are Kentucky, Maryland, Missouri, Oklahoma, and West Virginia. All share a similar pattern of settlement, with early settlers coming from both northern and southern states. Those states in existence during the Civil War also share a history of divided loyalty, which significantly influenced patterns of political conflict from after the Civil War to the New Deal realignment.

All five Border States have shared a pattern of electoral outcomes since 1945. Those electoral consequences cannot be said to reflect realignment (if realignment is defined as major changes in patterns of partisan affiliation and vote-choice patterns that persist across time and across different levels of government). What is evident instead is a two-tiered system of politics in which election outcomes for the more visible offices are especially responsive to candidate characteristics and other short-term electoral forces.

In terms of the proportion of U.S. Senate contests won by Democrats, Democratic victories range from 8 of 17 Senate races in Kentucky since 1945 to 16 of the 17 Senate contests in West Virginia. However, Democratic candidates won all but one Senate election in Kentucky after 1972. This result is in sharp contrast to Oklahoma, where Democrats were victorious in Senate contests from 1945 to 1966; but after that date, Democrats have won only 2 of 7 contests. Whatever the case, the effects of short-term (candidate) characteristics are very evident in these Senate races. Democrats have also been successful in gubernatorial contests in the Border States, winning a minimum of 63 percent since 1945 in all these states. Short-term factors are also influential in these contests, but on the other hand, in Missouri, Republican candidates have won four of the five elections for governor since 1970. Both parties win when their nominees are charismatic, even in the short term.

A different pattern is evident, however, in the outcomes of elections to the state legislatures and U.S. House of Representatives. All states have, with two exceptions, selected national congressional delegations with a majority of Democrats. However, the size of the Democratic majority has declined since 1960 in Tennessee, since 1980 in Missouri, and since 1980 in Kentucky. The positive characteristics of the candidate that contribute to high levels of incumbent reelection in more recent elections undoubtedly help to establish these patterns.

An examination of the results of state legislative contests provides further evidence that realignment really has not occurred in these Border States. Democrats have elected a majority of both state house and senate members in all elections since the mid-1940s in Kentucky, Maryland, Oklahoma, and West Virginia and since the mid-1950s in Missouri. In Oklahoma, the percentage of legislative seats held by Democrats declined slightly beginning in the late 1960s.

In these Border States, the pattern appears to be that of the classic two-tier system suggested by Ladd and Hadley. For less visible offices, partisan identification plays a larger role and patterns of voting similar to those established by the New Deal realignment generally persist. For the more visible offices, short-term factors such as candidate characteristics (including incumbency) and issues greatly influence voter choice. This outcome is most evident in the presidential elections, with Republican candidates enjoying high levels of success in these Border States since 1952. Thus the Democratic Party's presidential candidate has carried Oklahoma only once, Kentucky three times, Missouri four times, and Maryland five times since 1952. In contrast, West Virginia has supported Democratic candidates in seven out of the ten elections between 1952 and 1988.

*See also:* New Deal

*Margaret M. Conway*

REFERENCES

Ladd, Everett Carll, Jr., and Charles D. Hadley. 1978. *Transformations of the American Party System*. 2nd ed. New York: Norton.

## Political Realignment in the New England States

Patterns of party realignment in the New England states offer important insights into the nature of changes that are presently underway in the American party system. Past realignments were generally conceived of as national phenomena tied to national leadership and events. Yet recent trends suggest a more complex process. New studies have documented significant regional shifts in party support occurring in the South and in the Mountain West. Realigning trends in New England, where patterns are decidedly mixed, indicate that the dynamics of state politics may be a critical factor in the realignment process.

The most significant changes have occurred in Vermont and Maine, two traditionally rock-ribbed Republican states where the GOP has lost considerable ground. In Vermont, a realignment in favor of the Democrats has transformed party politics. While Vermonters are still likely to support moderate Republican presidential candidates, in statewide races mixed party control is now the norm. A critical factor in Democratic gains has been marked in-migration of a liberal constituency that activated and energized Democratic Party organizations and produced Democratic victories in local and statewide races. Conversely, the Reagan era with its more ideological brand of Republicanism has actually hurt the traditionally moderate Republican Party in Vermont.

In Maine, two decades of erosion of Republican strength have produced considerable dealignment and significant Democratic gains. Maine is now considered one of the most competitive states in the nation. As in Vermont, voters in Maine are still likely to support Republican presidential candidates, but statewide races also produce mixed results. The legislature in the 1990s is controlled by the Democrats. Republican registration continually declined while the number of Independents increased throughout the 1980s. Candidates can run on an Independent label and the sustained support from voters for these Independent candidates suggests that the dealignment in Maine may have institutionalized a three-way base of voter identification.

In Massachusetts, significant and continuous movement toward the Democratic Party, based on the realignment of the New Deal, puts that state close to a one-party system. The state parties experienced some dealignment or decline in voter support during the early 1970s, when 50 percent of the voters did not affiliate with either party. However, by 1986 voter registration records indicate that while close to 47 percent of the voters were registered Democrats, only 13 percent were affiliated with the Republican Party. Indeed, the significant party divisions in Massachusetts are intraparty struggles within the Democratic Party where the liberal-reform wing of the organization took control in the late 1980s.

New Hampshire remains a solidly Republican state. While some dealignment during the 1960s and 1970s allowed Democrats to win congressional and statewide office, by 1988 party identification indicated strong Republican dominance (47 percent); a sizable portion of Independents (25 percent), however, still constitute a critical margin in any election.

Dealignment is the norm in Connecticut and Rhode Island. Connecticut has experienced significant erosion in Democratic voter support, which presents opportunities for the Republicans. Unaffiliated voters represent about one-third of the states' eligible electorate, and a new nonparty ballot should increase the likelihood of more split-ticket voting in the future. A key factor in dealignment in Connecticut is the moribund character of the old-style, conservative Democratic Party machines that are increasingly unable to address the needs of their potential constituency. Connecticut's Democratic machines are becoming increasingly irrelevant in state politics and policymaking.

Rhode Island presents a similar case. This traditionally Democratic state has experienced massive dealignment during the 1980s, with statewide polls indicating that about 50 percent of the electorate consider themselves Independents. This erosion presented some opportunities for the Republican Party, which did make some notable inroads in statewide offices and the legislature during the early Reagan years. By 1986, however, Democrats—who were still the majority among identifiers—regained control of most of these seats. Lack of strong leadership and scandal in both parties suggest that volatility associated with dealignment will continue to characterize Rhode Island politics in the 1990s.

*See also:* Ronald Reagan, Split-Ticket Voting

*Maureen Moakley*

## Political Realignment in the Southern States

The political realignment in the southern states has been an ongoing process. The last time that the South (defined as the states that composed the Confederacy plus Border States with parallel social, economic, and political characteristics) went solid for the Democratic Party's presidential candidate was 1944. The next presidential election (1948) saw a defection of some southern voters to Senator Strom Thurmond of South Carolina and the States' Rights Democrats. This third party received 39 electoral votes and more than a million popular ballots.

The 1950s were supposedly a return to voting patterns of the past. Dwight Eisenhower and the Republicans swept the country but not the South. During this decade a core of southern states stayed in the Democratic column, the sole contributors to its electoral votes. Moreover, in each election, the Democrats placed a southerner, Senator John J. Sparkman of Alabama (1952), or at least a Senator from a Border State, Estes Kefauver of Kentucky (1956), on the ticket in second place.

It was the 1960s that turned the tide. The 1960 election saw the Democratic Party win a narrow victory. True, the party had a southern Democrat on the ticket in Lyndon B. Johnson, and it did win some southern states. But this election saw defections to Republican Richard Nixon and States' Righter Harry Byrd, Sr., of Virginia. The 1964 race proved to be a critical or realigning election; the Democrats won the battle and their candidates were elected by landslides. But the Republicans had put together a new coalition with its center in the South. The 1964 election nearly reversed the presidential voting patterns of the 1950s. Those southern states that were the basis of the Democrats' sole electoral votes in the 1950s provided Barry Goldwater with his only electoral support in 1964. Four years later—although a third-party candidate, George C. Wallace of Alabama, represented portions of the South—the Republican Party, with a Border State governor (Spiro T. Agnew of Maryland) in the second seat, was not shut out of the South. The fact that no southerner appeared on the Democratic national ticket in 1968 may have contributed to this Republican inroad.

The 1972 election saw the Republicans, with the same Border State governor on the ticket, win by a landslide. Again the Democratic Party neglected the South in both national positions and reaped defeat in southern and Border states. However, 1976 demonstrated what a southerner could do at the helm of the Democratic Party. The Democratic national ticket, led by Jimmy Carter of Georgia, was elected by a narrow margin.

The 1980s put the South back in the Republican column. In 1980, 1984, and 1988, the Republicans ran a southern candidate (George Bush of Texas) on the ticket of either first (1988) or second position (1980 and 1984). While the Democrats also placed a Texan (Lloyd M. Bentsen) on the ticket (Vice President) in 1988, it was not enough to win (although the party did better than in previous outings).

Obviously more was involved than sectional loyalty. Since the foundation of the Democratic Party—an alliance between Thomas Jefferson and Aaron Burr that created a coalition between the South and northeastern states—the South could be counted upon to support the Democrats. Today that certainty has been reversed. Starting with Barry Goldwater, the South has become an ideological supporter of the Republicans.

Senator Goldwater was not the first Republican to espouse the concept that a conservative ideology could loosen the South from the Democrat's grip. Both Senators Robert Taft and William Knowland (conservative leaders within the Republican Party) were not unfriendly to the concept. But it was Goldwater who won the GOP nomination and turned the Republican Party to the ideological right; the South followed. Conservative analyst Kevin Phillips wrote the prescription that as much described the process as suggested how it would work. Richard Scammon and Ben Wattenberg examined the same concept for the Democrats: they suggested going after the "Real Majority" who were increasingly residing in the Sunbelt and voting their pocket books rather than their hearts.

This political realignment did not necessarily take place at the presidential level exclusively. Democrats in Congress such as Strom Thurmond of South Carolina and Phil Gramm of Texas switched parties as they found themselves more comfortable with their ideological rather than traditional brethren. In some states, such as Mississippi, both U.S. Senators were in the Republican fold by the late 1980s, as the voters rather than the officeholders switched political parties or at least voting patterns.

The South still remains probably the most politically alienated section of the nation. This region fought a civil war for its independence. Likewise, its voting patterns often reverse those found outside the area. Rural areas tend to be Democratic and urban areas Republican, while the rest of the nation usually reverses this geographical pattern. But even so, on the national level, the Republican Party can usually count on solid southern backing as long as the Grand Old Party fields a conservative candidate. The Republicans are now working their way down from federal to state to local levels in an area that was once the bedrock of the Democratic Party.

*See also:* Spiro Agnew; Lloyd Bentsen; George Bush; Harry Byrd, Sr.; Jimmy Carter; Dwight D. Eisenhower; Elections of 1960, 1964, 1972, and 1980; Barry Goldwater; William Knowland; Lyndon B. Johnson; William Philip (Phil) Gramm; Richard M. Nixon; Robert A. Taft; Strom Thurmond; George Wallace

*Thomas H. Clapper*

REFERENCES

Bass, Jack, and Walter de Vries. 1976. *The Transformation of Southern Politics: Social Change and Political Consequences Since 1945*. New York: New American Library.

Billington, Monroe Lee. 1975. *The Political South in the Twentieth Century*. New York: Scribner's.

Key, V. O., with Alexander Heard. 1949. *Southern Politics in State and Nation*. New York: Knopf.

Phillips, Kevin P. 1970. *The Emerging Republican Majority*. New York: Anchor Books.

The Ripon Society. 1969. *The Lessons of Victory*. New York: Dial Press.

Scammon, Richard M., and Ben J. Wattenberg. 1970. *The Real Majority*. New York: Coward-McCann.

Sherrill, Robert. 1968. *Gothic Politics in the Deep South: Stars of the New Confederacy*. New York: Grossman.

## Political Realignment in the Western States

Although a distinction must be made between the Mountain West and the Pacific Coast West, realignment has definitely occurred in the western states of the United States since 1945. By realignment is meant major shifts in partisan affiliations and patterns of voter choice. Since the mid-1940s, changes in the patterns of both partisan affiliation and partisan direction of vote choice have occurred, although change has been more extensive in the Mountain West.

In the electoral patterns of the Mountain West (the states of Idaho, Colorado, Montana, Nevada, New Mexico, Wyoming, Utah, and Arizona), there is evidence from patterns both of partisan affiliation apparent in survey data and in electoral outcomes for state and national offices that demonstrates how much realignment has occurred in that region. Democratic Party identification declined, while the proportion of the electorate claiming to be independent increased from the 1960s to the 1980s. Support for Democratic presidential candidates, as measured by proportion of the vote, declined substantially from the 1960s to the 1980s, with declines of lesser magnitude occurring in support of Democratic candidates for Congress.

Voting patterns for state offices in the Mountain West are similar: the proportion of state legislative seats held by Democrats declined. A similar decrease since 1945 in the proportion of statewide offices (other than governor) held by Democrats took place, although a reaction to Watergate is also evident in voting patterns for these offices. Democratic candidates for governor appear to have been exempt from this pattern of depreciation. However, their success may be attributed to popular Democratic candidates rather than state voter support for the Democratic Party. To summarize, a general pattern of decline in voter support for Democratic candidates and a decline in the electoral success of the Democratic Party's candidates occurred in the Mountain West from the 1940s through the 1980s.

One explanation for this pattern of realignment is the region's increasing conservatism on social welfare policies; political scientist Arthur Miller reports that by the mid-1960s, residents of the Mountain States were more conservative on these policy issues than were the residents of any other region of the country. Another explanation might be that the region has experienced considerable in-migration, and those migrants have different characteristics from natives of the region. While those who have migrated are formally better educated than the natives, no one has found a significant difference between the party identification patterns of natives and those of migrants. A second possibility is a generational difference, with the young tending to be more independent or Republican. However, evidence does not support this view, as the decline in Democratic identification has occurred across generations. A third explanation is that the relative importance of political issues has changed or the manner in which the region's residents react to the existing issue agenda has changed. Several different indicators point to a decline in the region's support for an activist federal government.

In the Pacific Coast West (excluding Hawaii and Alaska, which have not been states for the entire period examined), a different pattern occurs, with the evidence supporting a two-tiered theory of electoral outcomes. California, Oregon, and Washington have rarely voted for Democratic presidential candidates since 1948, with the exceptions since 1948 occurring in 1948 (California and Washington), all three states in 1964, 1968 (Oregon and Washington), and 1988 (Oregon and Washington). Democratic candidates for governor have won substantially less than a majority of contests in all three states since 1946. Thus, Democratic candidates for the two major executive offices have been relatively unsuccessful in these three western states after World War II.

Concerning legislative elections, the Democratic proportion of seats held in the U.S. House of Representatives has exceeded 50 percent in California since 1958 and in Washington since 1964, but only rarely since 1948 have Democrats held a majority of House seats from Oregon. While Democratic candidates for the U.S. Senate have been highly successful in Washington, they have won less than one-third of the elections in both California and Oregon since 1948. However, with few exceptions, Democrats have held a majority of seats in both the state house and senate in California and Oregon since 1960 and in Washington since 1945.

Rather than realignment in the Pacific West, the pattern appears to be that the Democratic Party's candidates are successful for less visible offices, and for offices in which candidates do not run statewide, and for offices in which outcomes may in part be determined by the drawing of district lines.

*See also:* Party Identification, Watergate

*Margaret M. Conway*

REFERENCES

Ladd, Everett Carll, Jr., and Charles D. Hadley. 1978. *Transformations of the American Party System.* 2nd ed. New York: Norton.

Miller, Arthur H. 1987. "Public Opinion and Regional Political Realignment." In Peter F. Galderisi, Michael S. Lyons, Randy T. Simmons, and John G. Francis, eds. *The Politics of Realignment.* Boulder, CO: Westview Press.

Stone, Walter J. 1987. "Regional Variation in Partisan Change: Realignment in the Mountain West." In Peter F. Galderisi, Michael S. Lyons, Randy T. Simmons, and John G. Francis, eds. *The Politics of Realignment.* Boulder, CO: Westview Press.

## Politics of Patriotism

In 1916, in the midst of his campaign for the Republican presidential nomination, Theodore Roosevelt proclaimed that he only wanted the support of those "prepared to say that every citizen of this country has got to be pro-United States first, last, and all the time, and not pro-anything else at all." The immediate targets of this thrust were those rival candidates whom Roosevelt accused of pandering to German- and Irish-American voters. Yet all so-called hyphens, whatever their ethnic identity, were targets as well. In making "100 percent Americanism" one of the twin foci of his campaign (his other shibboleth was military preparedness), Roosevelt was helping to invent a style of politics—a politics of patriotism—that would play a part in characterizing U.S. public life for much of the rest of the century. It was a politics that abjured the usual appeals to interests or partisan identification. Instead it proclaimed that an unprecedented threat to the nation's very existence demanded extraordinary measures. This politics appealed to fear. Thus it exacerbated controversies, magnified dangers, and legitimated hysteria as an appropriate response to diversity.

Loyalty was not an altogether new issue in 1916. Indeed, Roosevelt had grown up listening to Republican orators wave the "bloody shirt." Accusations that Democrats lacked devotion to the Union and claims that only Republicans were true patriots had been staples of political rhetoric through the 1880s. What was distinctive about Roosevelt's twentieth-century variant was its explicit linking of the disloyal and the foreign. This connection would become the defining element in the modern politics of patriotism, characterizing not only the 1916 presidential campaign, the wartime prosecutions of socialists and other radicals, and the postwar Red Scare, but also the "American Plan" of anti-unionism conducted by employers through the 1920s and the immigration restriction crusade that culminated in the Johnson-Reed Act of 1924. It was as much a staple of Ku Klux Klan orthodoxy as the doctrine of racial purity. In the 1930s the House Un-American Activities Committee (HUAC) revived this politics of patriotism and laid the groundwork for a second Red Scare in the wake of World War II, a political paranoia that did not burn itself out in the Army-McCarthy hearings of 1954 despite the best efforts of civil libertarians. Instead, the politics of patriotism helped define the status quo against which the New Left of the 1960s emerged.

Theodore Roosevelt's political situation in 1916 also proved paradigmatic of other practitioners of the politics of patriotism. He had split the Republican Party in 1912 thereby interrupting a string of successes that would run from 1896 to 1932. Roosevelt could scarcely expect party professionals to reward him with the nomination, and so he sought to bypass the then-normal process of lining up delegates by demonstrating such massive popular support that the party would have to take him back. For this strategy he needed issues that transcended ordinary partisan loyalty. The call for "100 percent Americanism" was just such an issue. And it has continued to exert a powerful appeal to politicians whose ambitions cannot be satisfied through normal politics. In 1917, for example, New York City mayor John P. Mitchell lost the Republican primary. When he had to seek reelection on a "Fusion" ticket, he decided to campaign against "Turk, Teuton, and Tammany." In 1919 and 1920 U.S. Attorney General A. Mitchell Palmer attached his own presidential ambitions to his success in stamping out radical activities. No Attorney General, it should be emphasized, had ever before used that office as a stepping stone to a presidential nomination.

Not all attempts to exploit the issue came to naught. Massachusetts governor Calvin Coolidge's celebrated refusal to negotiate with Boston police strikers, a strike he portrayed as inspired by un-American sympathies, won him a place on the Republican ticket in 1920. Employers similarly found their portrayal of strikers as Bolsheviki to be an effective way to influence public opinion. The politics of patriotism worked, and it worked well. It was particularly useful when ordinary electoral or bureaucratic politics failed. One of the most striking instances is HUAC, which was created by conservative Democrats and Republicans as a means of harassing those New Deal programs that they could not defeat legislatively. And the Republican Party's decision to give Senator Joseph McCarthy a free hand, despite his notorious inability to back up his charges of Communist activity in the government, makes most sense in the context of the party's stunning defeat in the 1948 presidential contest. So too the ultimate decision by Dwight Eisenhower to refuse to support McCarthy reflects the preference of a victor for ordinary—and predictable—political processes.

See also: Bloody Shirt, Calvin Coolidge, Dwight D. Eisenhower, Elections of 1920 and 1948, House Un-American Activities Committee, Ku Klux Klan, Jo-seph McCarthy, John P. Mitchell, Red Scare, Theodore Roosevelt

*John F. McClymer*

REFERENCES

Coben, Stanley. 1964. "A Study in Nativism: The American Red Scare of 1919–20." 79 *Political Science Quarterly* 52.

Latham, Earl. 1966. *The Communist Conspiracy in Washington: From the New Deal to McCarthy.* Cambridge: Harvard U. Pr.

McClymer, John F. 1980. *War and Welfare: Social Engineering in America, 1890–1925.* Westport, CT: Greenwood.

Murray, Robert K. 1964. *Red Scare: A Study in National Hysteria, 1919–1920.* New York: McGraw-Hill.

## James K. Polk (1795–1849)

The eleventh President of the United States. James Knox Polk was born in North Carolina, began a successful law practice in 1820, and served in the Tennessee legislature from 1823 to 1825, during which time he became Andrew Jackson's friend.

In 1825 Polk entered the House of Representatives where he was to remain for 14 years. He defended the Democratic Party's principles against those of President John Quincy Adams and the National Republicans. When Jackson became President in 1829, Polk assumed the role of key spokesman for the new administration's policies, becoming chairman of the Committee on Ways and Means and leading the movement to destroy the Bank of the United States. After a protracted and bitter battle, involving Polk and Jackson against John Bell and Hugh L. White of Tennessee, Polk became Speaker of the House. He served for four years and faced constant personal attacks. He succeeded, however, by using skill, tact, unremitting toil, and a thorough knowledge of the complex rules of the House.

In the late 1830s, the Whigs seized control of Tennessee politics; in 1839 the Tennessee Democrats responded by persuading Polk to leave Congress and run for governor. He won the race and performed well, but he failed to gain reelection in 1841 and again in 1843. Nevertheless, Polk remained deeply involved in Democratic politics. During the months before the 1844 presidential campaign, Henry Clay was favored as the Whig nominee; the Democrats would almost certainly choose Martin Van Buren. Polk, meanwhile, was being mentioned prominently as the Democrat's candidate for Vice President. However, by the time the conventions met, the situation had changed dramatically.

President John Tyler had tried unsuccessfully to acquire Texas through a treaty of annexation. In the spring of 1844, both Clay and Van Buren wrote public letters opposing annexation because it might lead to war with Mexico and because they wanted the issue killed. Polk, on the other hand, favored both the annexation of Texas and the acquisition of Oregon. Jackson called Polk and other key Democrats to his Tennessee home, concluded that Van Buren could not win, and gave Polk his blessing as the alternative choice for President. At the Democratic National Convention, southerners made it clear that they wanted Texas, that they distrusted Van Buren's attitude toward slavery, and that Van Buren should not be the nominee. As a result, Polk was nominated as a compromise choice on the ninth ballot. The party's platform pledged, among other things, to take all of Texas and Oregon. The Whig convention nominated Henry Clay unanimously, and none of its resolutions even mentioned Texas. A splinter group of Democrats had also nominated Tyler, but he was persuaded to drop out in late August 1844 and to back Polk. James G. Birney, the Liberty Party's candidate, campaigned hard and became a crucial factor in the outcome of the election.

During the campaign, the candidates hurled insults but also discussed a variety of serious issues that divided them, the most important of which were annexation of Texas and the ownership of Oregon. Clay tried to modify his stand on these expansionist issues midway through the campaign, a tactic that only made him look weak in the eyes of many voters. The Democrats, on the other hand, never deviated from their platform pledge. New York was the crucial state, and Birney took enough votes from Clay to cost him the state and the election. In the very close national contest, Polk garnered only 49.6 percent of the popular vote to Clay's 48.1 percent and beat Clay in New York by only slightly more than 5,000 votes. Polk had not secured a popular majority, but President Tyler claimed the election was a mandate to annex Texas. Through a joint resolution of Congress, Tyler laid the groundwork for annexation and, with Polk's acquiescence, began to implement the procedure only a few days before the new President was inaugurated. Texas joined the Union the following December.

Among President Polk's major goals were the legislative acceptance of a lower tariff and an Independent Treasury system, a resolution of the Oregon situation, and the annexation of California. He managed to achieve all of these objectives, which proved to be no easy task. The Democrats who backed Van Buren and John C. Calhoun were upset because Polk's Cabinet selections did not include their factions, and the Whigs showed remarkable unity in fighting the President's policies. At first, Polk seemed to have lost control of his party, but he presented a clear program to Congress and pressured Senators and Representatives relentlessly to adopt it. Moreover, he was helped by the fact that Democrats, on the whole, were still loyal to their party, despite occasional local and sectional lapses.

Although the votes were close, Congress approved both a lower tariff (Walker Tariff, 1846) and the Independent Treasury (1848). Polk, however, failed to hold enough northern Democrats in line to get a graduated price system for the sale of federal public lands. Moreover, a combination of Whigs and northwesterners from both parties enacted a law allowing the use of federal funds to improve rivers and harbors. Polk vetoed this measure, declaring that it violated Democratic principles and that such pork barrel legislation was a source of corruption. Many northern Democrats then accused him of neglecting their needs, while catering to the interests of the South. Nonetheless, by combining political pressure tactics and vetoes, Polk managed to block the basic tenets of the Whig Party's American System, namely a high tariff, a national bank, and state internal improvements at national expense.

Polk's main accomplishments, however, came from diplomacy and war. Through determined effort and bluff, he convinced Britain to accept a compromise settlement that divided the Oregon Territory along the forty-ninth parallel. United States–Mexican relations had long been strained over monetary and Texas boundary claims and over periodic American interest in acquiring California, and perhaps New Mexico, by purchase. When negotiations failed to bring results, the President prepared a war message in May 1846. He was confirmed in his decision when he learned that Mexican troops had crossed the Rio Grande and killed or wounded 16 American troops. Both houses of Congress approved Polk's message overwhelmingly. But as the war dragged on, the Whigs, antislavery advocates, and members of various Democratic factions began combining to defeat certain measures Polk deemed to be essential.

One of the worst episodes of wrangling involved a little-known Pennsylvania Representative, David Wilmot. After meeting with some northern Democrats, who were disgruntled over parts of Polk's foreign, domestic, sectional, and patronage policies, Wilmot started a political storm of long duration and dangerous dimensions. The President had requested $2 million to help negotiate an end to the conflict. Wilmot proposed an amendment that would have prevented slavery from entering any territory the United States might gain from Mexico. The House accepted the proviso, but the Senate refused. This issue, however, would not die and portended future crises for the nation over slavery extension.

After a number of abortive attempts to obtain a peace treaty, Polk sent a minor official and loyal Democrat, Nicholas P. Trist, to negotiate with the Mexican government. The President was angry with Mexico for obstructing the peace process and recalled Trist in October 1847, planning to send a new negotiator with a more severe set of demands. Trist, however, refused to leave, and adhering to the fundamental points of his original instructions, he transacted the Treaty of Guadalupe Hidalgo, which was signed on February 2, 1848. Trist had persuaded Mexican officials to accept the Rio Grande boundary, and to relinquish New Mexico and Upper California, including San Diego. In return, America agreed to pay Mexico $15 million outright and compensate its own citizens for claims they had against Mexico ($3,250,000).

Extremely angry because Trist had defied him and because he wanted more Mexican territory, Polk nevertheless realized that the treaty represented a fair settlement. He also knew that he would have to renew the fighting to get any more land, that the public was weary of the war, that the Whigs also controlled the House and might withhold appropriations for new war-related activities. America might then lose New Mexico and California, and the Democrats could easily go down to defeat in the 1848 election. The President, therefore, decided that he had no other reasonable choice but to submit the treaty to the Senate. During the ratification debates, Whigs continued to object to territorial acquisitions, while some Democrats wanted even more land than the treaty offered. On March 10, 1848, the final vote was 38 to 14 to ratify, and it cut across party and sectional lines.

Polk was a grim, diligent, tough, tenacious, ambitious, often devious and secretive man. He knew what he wanted to accomplish for this nation before he took office, and he gained most of it before he left it. Because of circumstances and certain shortcomings in his personality and political abilities, he never completely controlled the members of his party. He got them to conform often enough, however, to mark him as an extremely effective leader in both foreign and domestic policy. Perhaps his single-mindedness was the most important reason for his immediate successes, but it seems to have hindered his sense of long-range perspective. He could not see or imagine, for example, that the party system and the nation might be endangered by linking the newly acquired Mexican territories with the extension of slavery. He was genuinely convinced that slavery could not exist in New Mexico and California because of their climates. As a result of this simple, narrow view, Polk grossly underestimated the importance southerners placed on their alleged right to transfer the peculiar institution, if they wished to try, and he badly miscalculated the extent to which northerners would go to stop these attempts. As President, Polk had driven himself much too hard, left office exhausted in March 1849, and died only three months later (June 19, 1849) at the age of 54.

*See also:* John Quincy Adams, John Bell, James G. Birney, John C. Calhoun, Henry Clay, Elections of 1844 and 1848, First Bank of the United States, Andrew Jackson, Slavery, Speaker of the House, John Tyler, Martin Van Buren, Hugh L. White, Wilmot Proviso

*Gerald W. Wolff*

REFERENCES

Alexander, Thomas B. 1967. *Sectional Stress and Party Strength: A Study of Roll-Call Voting Patterns in the United States House of Representatives, 1836–1860.* Nashville, TN: Vanderbilt U. Pr.

McCormack, Eugene. 1922. *James K. Polk: A Political Biography.* Berkeley: U. of California Pr.

Nevins, Allan, ed. 1968. *Polk: The Diary of a President, 1845–1849.* New York: Capricorn Books.

Quaife, Milo Milton, ed. 1910. *The Diary of James K. Polk During His Presidency, 1845–1849.* Chicago: A. C. McClurg.

Sellers, Charles Greer. 1957. *James K. Polk, Jacksonian, 1795–1843.* Princeton: Princeton U. Pr.

———. 1966. *James K. Polk, Continentalist, 1843–1846.* Princeton: Princeton U. Pr.

Silbey, Joel H. 1967. *The Shrine of Party: Congressional Voting Behavior, 1841–1852.* Pittsburgh: U. of Pittsburgh Pr.

## Poll Tax

In the early stages of nationhood for the United States, individual states assessed a "head tax" on their residents in order to collect revenue from both holders and nonholders of property. Such a tax, known as a poll tax, allowed for state and local governments to account for their residents more easily, and it was common practice for voting lists in communities to contain the names of those only for whom the town had receipts of payment of property and poll taxes.

As universal white male suffrage became the norm, and as other methods of census and taxation evolved, the use of the poll tax by many states waned. Several states maintained provisions for the poll tax, but few enforced its collection. By the early 1800s, few states collected poll taxes.

Following the Civil War and Reconstruction, however, the political dynamics of the South brought on a resurgence in the use of poll taxes. The dominance of the Democratic Party of the South was being threatened by a coalition of Republicans and Populists who, in some instances, actually seized power in state governments. Poor whites and African-Americans comprised the base of support for Republican and Populist candidates, and Democratic Party leaders sought a means to weaken their opposition parties institutionally.

Poll taxes, in combination with literacy tests and complex registration laws, became the primary methods of excluding poor whites and Blacks from the electoral process. Those who failed to pay poll taxes were excluded from voting, and this prohibition generally resulted in shutting out the poorest individuals. Blacks in particular, who were largely sharecroppers and earned very little cash annually, usually chose not to part with what was nominally a small amount of money but a proportionally large share of their earnings.

Until the 1960s most southern states maintained the payment of the poll tax as a prerequisite to voting. In 1964, with the passage of the Twenty-fourth Amendment outlawing the poll tax as a barrier to participation in federal elections, five southern states (Texas, Arkansas, Alabama, Mississippi, and Virginia) that maintained the poll tax provision were forced to withdraw the use of the tax as a determinant of voting eligibility. The 1965 Voting Rights Act and the 1966 Supreme Court decision in *Harper v. Virginia* reinforced the official opposition of the use of poll taxes as a barrier to participation in any level of the electoral process. These measures effectively wiped out the discriminatory aspects of the poll tax at the state and local level as well.

*See also:* Populism as a Movement and a Party, Reconstruction, Twenty-fourth Amendment, Voting Rights Act of 1965 and Extensions

*Michael Heel*

REFERENCES

Billington, Monroe Lee. 1975. *The Political South in the Twentieth Century.* New York: Scribner's.

Kleppner, Paul. 1982. *Who Voted?* New York: Praeger.

Kousser, J. Morgan. 1974. *The Shaping of Southern Politics.* New Haven: Yale U. Pr.

Ogden, Frederic D. 1958. *The Poll Tax in the South.* Tuscaloosa: U. of Alabama Pr.

Sosna, Morton, 1977. *In Search of the Silent South.* New York: Columbia U. Pr.

## Theodore M. Pomeroy (1824–1905)

Shortest-serving Speaker of the House of Representatives. A graduate of Hamilton College, Theodore Medad Pomeroy studied law with William Henry Seward, entered politics as Cayuga County's district attorney (1851–1856), and served in the state assembly (1857). Elected to Congress from New York in 1860 as a Republican, he gained some fame as an orator while vacillating between the radical and conservative wings of the Republican Party during the war and Reconstruction. When Vice President–elect Schuyler Colfax decided to resign the speakership on March 3, 1869, Pomeroy was elected to fill the vacancy for exactly one day, his last in the House. During the 1870s Pomeroy remained active in Republican politics, becoming mayor of Auburn, New York (1875–1876), temporary chairman of the Republican National Committee (1876), and state senator (1877–1879) before failing in a bid for the governorship (1879).

*See also:* Schuyler Colfax, Republican National Committee, Speaker of the House

*Brooks Donohue Simpson*

REFERENCES

Alexander, DeAlva S. 1909–1923. *A Political History of the State of New York.* 4 vols. New York: Holt, Rinehart, and Winston.

## Populism as a Movement and Party

Since the 1960s, historians of the People's Party of the 1890s, have been highly self-conscious about reconstructing what this party *really* was. Their self-consciousness underscores the first important point that ought to be made about the People's Party: this far-flung coalition, which spanned the South, Midwest, and West; which for a decade strongly influenced congressional, presidential, and state politics; which linked agrarian activists both to rural voters, and, in certain areas, to organizations of laboring men; and which often sought to unite Black and white voters in the South, may be hard for contemporary Americans to understand. Theorists claim—perhaps in response to a renewed appreciation of protest politics that has emerged since the 1960s—that the People's Party (or the Populists, as they were often called) grew out of a highly participatory and communitarian understanding of democratic politics that has been foreign to Americans during most of the twentieth century, when they have tended to be relatively nonpartisan, nonideological, and individualistic in their view of politics.

Even if one discounts the effect that protest in the 1960s and the civil rights movement may have had on redirecting historians' understanding of the People's Party, there is something to this "lost world" view of populism. Third parties in American electoral politics have mostly left a legacy of failure. Yet the sectarian and plainly unpopular character of most American third parties in the last 50 years can invite, and all too often has invited, the false inference that third-party politics in America *always* resembled contemporary third-party politics—marginal to the concerns of most ordinary Americans and often extremist and impractical. The difficulty of accurately reconstructing such important cases of third-party politics as the People's Party is perhaps compounded by the distinctly "candidate-centered" character of those few cases of moderately successful third-party politics that do exist in the twentieth century (e.g., the Robert La Follette, Sr., candidacy of 1924 and the George Wallace candidacy of 1968).

The People's Party was neither sectarian and extremist nor the creature of a single candidate or charismatic politician. Like its immediate predecessor, the Republican Party, which emerged in the 1850s, it grew out of a broad-based and expanding social movement. In the first case the agitation of middle-class abolitionists helped to realign national party politics; in the later case a similar role was played by agrarian ideologues. In both cases agitation and ideas mattered. Populist intellectuals were able conceptually to find connections among post-Civil War commodity price deflation, the reorganization of the monetary system and federal debt management policies, basic American concerns about inequality, and the widespread political corruption of the postbellum decades, and fashioned a sweeping indictment of American society and politics.

Populist agitation led to the formation of a party when the leadership of a large alliance of agrarian interest groups decided to invest in party politics. The party was linked to a vast network of local newspapers and enjoyed a sizable staff of organizers and traveling lecturers and orators. It had an elaborate political program that resulted from a sophisticated analysis of the American political economy. Although American economics was in its infancy, it was developed enough to shape the People's Party's policy proposals. In particular, quantity theory of money was the basis for many Populist proposals. Indeed, the People's Party is an outstanding case of economic analysis shaping party politics.

Even though the People's Party collapsed between 1896 and 1900, its calls for racial equality, reform of the banking system, commodity exchanges, monetary policy, and electoral procedures permanently transformed American political thought. Ironically, however, its emphasis on the quantity theory of money—which was long discredited precisely because it was associated with "radical" populism—has played a role in insulating contemporary monetary policymaking processes from public opinion. Among the most important components of populism was an emphasis on the continuously renewed accountability of the people's representatives. A measure of the enduring relevance of Populist political thought is that it can still cast some light on contemporary issues in American political economy and, in particular, on the role of the Federal Reserve Bank in that political economy. Few cases of American third-party politics can claim an equal legacy.

See also: People's Party, Third Parties in American Elections

*Richard M. Valelly*

REFERENCES

Goodwyn, Lawrence. 1976. *Democratic Promise: The Populist Moment in America*. New York: Oxford U. Pr.

## Populist (People's) Party

A political party that was organized at a convention in July 1892 in Omaha, Nebraska, after earlier attempts by farmers meeting in Ocala, Florida (1890); Cincinnati and Omaha (1891); and St. Louis (early 1892) had failed to produce a new party, the Populist Party was the embodiment of an attitude, a way of looking at life that had been prevalent for almost 20 years, and a general position taken against concentrated economic power. Populism was the reaction of rural people to an agricultural crisis of the late nineteenth century that involved falling profits, monetary deflation, and rising shipping costs.

Populism had a local focus, positing farming people against their apparent opposites—the city, the East Coast, England, or financiers generally. The Populist Party that finally emerged developed out of the National Farmers' Alliance and Industrial Union, from 1877 to 1892, dominated by westerners who founded it and shaped by southerners who built it. The Alliance made attempts to reach out to city workers in the Knights of Labor and to women, whom it enlisted as speakers.

The Populist Party gave the cultural movement of populism, which favored purchasing and merchandizing cooperatives as a way for the subsistence family farm to resist the growing national market, a political focus. The Alliance had earlier backed candidates for state and local offices; the People's Party gave the farmers a national platform.

The Populist Party platform, formulated in the so-called St. Louis demands and endorsed in Omaha, consisted primarily of land, finance, and transportation planks. These included government ownership of the means of communication and transportation—telegraphs, telephones, and railroads; a flexible currency system, with induced inflation through either the issue of greenbacks or the coining of silver at a ratio of 16 to 1, or both; legislation against the monopolization of land purchases, especially by railroads and other corporations; electoral reforms including the direct election of U.S. Senators, the secret ballot, the initiative and referendum, and a single-term for President and Vice President; postal savings banks; a graduated income tax; and the eight-hour day for urban workers. A later proposal, subscribed to at Omaha but not presented in St. Louis, was the "subtreasury" plan allowing farmers to hold nonperishable crops, for which they received government loans, off the market when prices were low.

In 1892 the Populist Party ticket of James B. Weaver, a former Union Army general from Iowa, and James G. Field, an ex-Confederate from Virginia, received 22 electoral votes. This support came from Kansas, Colorado, Nevada, Idaho and one electoral vote each from North Dakota and Oregon. The Weaver-Field ticket

pulled more than one million votes, or approximately 8 percent of the total, the best showing for a new party since the appearance of the Republicans on the national political scene in 1856. Strength in the South, however, proved to be less than anticipated. Nationwide, the Populists probably helped (by splitting the vote) to put both houses of Congress as well as the presidency into Democratic hands for the first time since the Civil War.

In the 1894 congressional elections, hard times reduced the Democratic majority in the Senate and reversed their standing in the House. The Populists benefited, their total vote being approximately 40 percent larger in 1894 than in 1892. They elected six U.S. Senators and seven Congressmen that year.

In 1896 the Populists scheduled their convention after that of the two major parties, assuming that they would be dominated by backers of the gold standard. When the Democrats nominated William Jennings Bryan and the Democratic platform denounced the wealthy and called for stricter federal controls over trusts and railroads, the Populists endorsed Bryan for President. But they selected their own vice presidential candidate, hoping that the Democrats would drop the wealthy Maine banker and shipbuilder Arthur Sewall in favor of the Georgian firebrand, Thomas E. Watson. Bryan accepted the Populist nomination and ignored Watson (who campaigned strenuously). Many Populists consequently voted the Democratic ticket rather than their own, and the party itself virtually dissolved that year in fusion and confusion.

The Populist Party was thereafter effectively absorbed by the Democrats. Although it continued to nominate candidates for President through 1908, its main contribution lay in the eventual acceptance of many of its proposals by the two main political parties. Differences in political cultures hampered the Populists' progress as a party. They were thwarted by the sectional and racial biases after the Civil War, which saw the North identifying with the Republicans and the white South with the Democrats. Class bias also existed against a party that drew its support almost exclusively from farmers. As a mass democratic movement, encompassed in a party, populism did not have a large passive constituency as the mainstream political parties did. Compromises were more difficult to achieve.

*See also:* William Jennings Bryan, National Farmers'

Alliance and Industrial Union, Election of 1896, Populism as a Movement and a Party, Tom Watson, James B. Weaver

*Frederick J. Augustyn, Jr.*

REFERENCES

Durden, Robert Franklin. 1965. *The Climax of Populism: The Election of 1896.* Westport, CT: Greenwood.

Goodwyn, Lawrence. 1976. *Democratic Promise: The Populist Moment in America.* New York: Oxford U. Pr.

———. 1978. *The Populist Moment in America: A Short History of Agrarian Revolt in America.* New York: Oxford U. Pr.

Saloutos, Theodore. 1968. *Populism: Reaction or Reform?* New York: Holt, Rinehart and Winston.

## Adam Clayton Powell, Jr. (1808–1972)

Harlem minister and dominant African-American politician. From the 1930s to the 1950s, the Reverend Adam Clayton Powell, Jr., dominated the Harlem political stage with a dazzling performance that was part Old Testament prophet unmercifully flogging his philistine adversaries, part John the Baptist baptizing his faithful flock with militant leftist ideology, and part unrepentant sinner reveling in the "high life" of New York's cabarets and clubs with sensual singers and Broadway stars.

Powell's was hardly the career one might have expected from the pampered only son of a powerful self-made preacher whose Abyssinian Baptist Church was one of the largest in the country. Thus, it would have come as no surprise when Powell dropped out of City College of New York, earned only a mediocre record at Colgate, and then dropped out of Union Theological Seminary after earning an M.A. from Columbia Teachers College. And it would probably have seemed inevitable when he joined his father's church as an assistant pastor in 1932.

The following year he began to make his own way, and waves, when he organized a meeting of the Committee on the Harlem Hospital, a protest group that included Communists. He continued this alliance with the left through his participation in the "Don't Buy Where You Can't Work" boycott of Blumstein's Department Store in 1934; the strike against the Black weekly, the *Amsterdam News,* in 1935; the National Negro Congress in 1936; and in the coordinating Committee for Employment in 1938. When the Soviet Union allied with Nazi Germany in June 1939, Powell began to withdraw from his "friends in Red Alley." Two years later, however, he sought and received strong Communist Party support for his successful campaign for the New York City Council. This alliance was even stronger when Powell won a congressional seat in 1944, one he retained until his defeat in 1970.

During his long tenure in Washington, D.C., Powell took credit for appointing the first African-American to the United States Naval Academy at Annapolis, attending the first meeting of the nonaligned powers at Bandung, Indonesia, in 1955, and helping to pass the important civil rights legislation of the 1950s and 1960s. In the latter decade his fame had been eclipsed by that of Martin Luther King, Jr., and his image had been tarnished by the House investigation (and ultimate censure) for malfeasance in office. His self-imposed exile in Bimini the last years of his life and the way he flaunted his young mistress there made it easy for the media to discredit this Black man who never ceased calling white capitalist America to account.

*See also:* Civil Rights Legislation and Southern Politics, Martin Luther King, Jr.

*Hal Chase*

## Precinct in Politics

For years, astute political observers have noted that the most intensive campaign work, especially in presidential years, takes place at the grass-roots level. Precinct politics is grass-roots politics. In the United States, cities and counties are divided into precincts or election districts. These precincts are small, manageable (usually neighborhood) areas populated by 200 to 1,000 voters who vote at a common polling place. Approximately 190,000 precincts operate in the United States.

Party organization at the precinct level is the key to electoral success, and the precinct leader or captain plays a crucial role in such organization. Leaders are usually selected either at local party caucuses or in party primary elections, although in some instances, they are appointed by other high-ranking party officials. The leaders' job is to organize the precinct for their party: registering new voters for the party, staying in touch with the precinct to ascertain its basic needs, mobilizing voters on election day, and distributing party rewards to voters (such as patronage jobs) in return for electoral support. Thus, precincts become political battlegrounds for both parties.

In large cities, wards, made up of many precincts, are under the direction of committee persons. The precinct captain works in close conjunction with ward leaders to deliver votes on election day and hold the ward and its precincts for the party after an election. Indeed ward and precinct politics were the basis for the old-style machine politics practiced in cities like Chicago under Mayor Richard Daley, Philadelphia, and New York. Effective ward leaders and precinct captains understood the problems and the needs of the voters in their districts and delivered services and jobs that enabled one party to win entire cities, as the Democrats were wont to capture Chicago under Mayor Daley.

In the past 20 years, high technology has increasingly changed precinct politics. Precincts are now organized by the parties with the aid of a computer, which generates voting lists indicating specific voter preferences for individual candidates and parties. In close presidential election years both parties use this information to identify "swing" precincts that can be captured by either party. These precincts become intense battlegrounds where significant party assets (money, campaign time, advertising) are expended. Any party that captures these "swing" precincts usually reaps the electoral benefits.

*See also:* Richard Daley

*Anthony J. Eksterowicz*

REFERENCES

Patrick, John J., and Richard C. Remy. 1980. *Civics for Americans*. Glenview, IL: Scott, Foresman.

Pious, Richard M. 1986. *American Politics and Government*. New York: McGraw-Hill.

Rakove, Milton. 1975. *Don't Make No Waves . . . Don't Back No Losers*. Bloomington: Indiana U. Pr.

Royko, Mike. 1971. *Boss*. New York: New American Library.

Sorauf, Frank J. 1984. *Party Politics in America*. 5th ed. Boston: Little, Brown.

Tolchin, Martin, and Susan Tolchin. 1972. *To The Victor*. New York: Vintage Books.

## Presidential Debates

In order to permit presidential candidates to give sequential responses to questions posed by a panel of experts, forums, or presidential debates, are held in election years. The debates are broadcast by the three major networks and at no other point in the campaign season do the candidates appear together before a national audience. In this way, the public has its only opportunity to compare how the candidates deal with general policy issues and to evaluate the candidates' responses. The questions are not available to the candidates before the debates; this "newness" tests the candidate's ability to articulate responses to previously undisclosed questions. Televised debates do not adhere to forensic requirements for debate such as the participants being required to take opposite points of view or interact with each other. They do, however, provide an educational service by allowing the public to see how the candidates respond to unprepared questions before a national audience.

Presidential debates were first held in 1960. Both the Democratic and Republican nominees did not choose to debate again until 1976, but all have debated thereafter. Several concerns surround the debates, the most important being sponsorship, campaign finance law, and the commercial television networks.

Section 315 of the Federal Communications Act of 1934 contains the "equal time" provision requiring broadcasters who allowed any political candidate to "use " their station  to allow their opponents "equal time." Congress voted in 1959 to exempt "bona fide" newscasts, news interviews, news documentaries, and on-the-spot coverage of news events from this section. As presidential candidate forums were not covered by the 1959 amendment, an act of Congress suspending Section 315 was necessary if the candidates were to debate. Congress did suspend Section 315 in 1960 but only for that year and only for the presidential campaign, thereby paving the way for John F. Kennedy and Richard Nixon to debate. The commercial television networks sponsored this first set of four one-hour debates. Further suspensions of Section 315 were required until 1975 when the Federal Communications Commission (FCC) exempted presidential debates from the "equal time" provision and then reclassified them as "bona fide" news events provided the story was covered live in its entirety and were sponsored by an organization other than the networks. Through this exemption, an act of Congress became unnecessary for presidential debates to be held.

Besides changes in federal communications law between the first and second series of debates, changes in campaign finance law occurred as well. The 1974 amendments to the Federal Election Campaign Act provided for public financing of presidential campaigns following nomination by a major party. These amendments also required detailed expenditure accounts. The candidates of 1976 were faced with new rules limiting the funding and expenditures of their campaigns. The debates provided, then, a free opportunity for the candidates to communicate to the public on the issues in a national forum. The impetus to debate provided through exemption by the FCC and amendments in 1974 to the Federal Election Campaign Act of 1971 have made the debates an integral part of the presidential selection process.

The networks could no longer sponsor the debates as of 1975. The debates were not intended to benefit one candidate over the other, leaving sponsorship of the debates by a partisan organization impossible. The League of Women Voters Education Fund has sponsored the debates since 1976 and has therefore been responsible for raising the necessary funds for broadcast. In 1987 the Commission on Presidential Debates, co-chaired by the Republican and Democratic national committee chairs, agreed to jointly sponsor the 1988 debates. This decision was made with the view that the proper role of the political parties is to educate the public. The LWV Education Fund claims only a nonpartisan organization can hold an unbiased debate, while the Commission on Presidential Debates claims cosponsorship will promote education, not partisanship. The LWV Education Fund sponsored the debates until 1984. The 1988 debates were sponsored by the Commission on Presidential Debates.

The debate sponsor retains the option of selecting participants. While all candidates invited to debate must agree to participate, bona fide candidacy, determined by the sponsor, is a necessary criterion for invitation. This criterion thus excludes Independent and minor party candidates. Limiting the debates to major party nominees, some minor party candidates have argued, disallows opposing views from being expressed, a purported violation of the fairness doctrine.

Panelists (questioners) are selected from among the journalistic community; the participants select journalists from among the print and broadcast media as well as editors and columnists. From those journalists whom both candidates agree on, a committee, selected by the sponsor, chooses a panel of questioners representing both print and broadcast media.

The debates can occur between Labor Day weekend and election day; however, the majority of debates takes place during the last month of the campaign. Sponsors schedule the debates and determine the date, time, length, and subject covered by each debate. Besides presidential candidates, vice presidential debates have taken place as well; they are regulated by the same criteria as are presidential debates. During the delegate selection ("primary") season, candidates from the same party are allowed to debate, yet the criteria are less rigorous. These debates need not be broadcast nationally on the commercial networks, and the candidates are allowed to interact with each other.

Debates were first held to inform and educate voters, with the expectation that an objective format untainted by prepared, biased campaign rhetoric will assist the voter in making a final choice of candidates. Candidate positions and policy preferences, presented in an environment such as a debate, also prevent the mass media from selectively reporting the issues as they, the media, perceive their importance to be among the electorate. This unique opportunity to view the candidates allows for comprehensive information in the electorate, thereby promoting better educated choice.

Research has shown, however, that presidential debates have little, if any, independent impact on final vote choice. Attitudes toward the candidate and party identification, formed before the debates, are not easily shaken once established. Debates occur in the midst of the campaign season when the voter is being deluged with a multitude of other campaign messages, rendering independent effects of debates difficult to measure. The electoral effects of debates, while minimal, serve to reinforce and polarize a voter's choice, making for a stronger candidate commitment once attachments have been formed. The voter's predilection to view the debates is higher among individuals with stronger partisan attitudes and established candidate choice, promoting polarization among viewers as opposed to establishing support on the sole basis of the debates.

Presidential debates were first held to provide the electorate with a unique opportunity to compare candidate qualities and issue positions through live joint appearances on television. Several million potential voters take advantage of this opportunity, as demonstrated by high Nielsen ratings for all debates, higher than usual for the time slots when the debates are held. While the option to debate remains with the candidates, debates will probably continue to be held in presidential election years simply because they produce an educated and informed public.

*See also:* Elections of 1960 and 1976, Federal Communications Commission, League of Women Voters

*Terri Susan Fine*

REFERENCES

Bishop, George F., Robert G. Meadow, and Marilyn Jackson-Beeck, eds. 1980. *Presidential Debates: Media, Electoral and Policy Perspectives*. New York: Praeger.

Kraus, Sidney, ed. 1962. *The Great Debates: Background, Perspective, Effects*. Bloomington: Indiana U. Pr.

———, ed. 1979. *The Great Debates: Carter vs. Ford, 1976*. Bloomington: Indiana U. Pr.

Lang, Kurt, and Gladys Engel Lang. 1968. *Politics and Television*. Chicago: Quadrangle.

———. 1984. *Politics and Television Re-viewed*. Beverly Hills, CA: Sage.

## Presidential Elections

It is late summer. Delegates to each of the national party conventions have completed their tasks: they have confirmed their respective party's candidates for President and Vice President and ratified a party platform. The candidates are now huddled with their key advisers devising strategy, hiring staff, and gearing up for months of nonstop campaigning.

The potential voters are focused on back-to-school sales, plans for Labor Day picnics, the race for the pennant, and the beginning of the football season. It is another presidential election year. The general election battle is about to begin.

Between now and the second Tuesday in November, presidential candidates and their running mates will travel thousands of miles across the country in search of the magic 270 electoral votes needed to win. What will happen in their quests will be determined by the strengths of their candidacies and the temporal patterns that await them.

### Types of Candidates

Of the many candidate characteristics that have an impact on the campaign, we are most interested in three that reflect their political strength. First, what do the voters think about the way the incumbent President and his party have handled their term in office? Has the administration been able to achieve peace and prosperity? Obviously, the performance of the party that controls the White House has greater impact when the incumbent is a candidate for reelection, but it has some consequences for the party's nominee in any case. Second, what have been the consequences of the nomination contest? Is the nominee at the head of a united party, or has a struggle over the nomination left the party split into antagonistic factions? Third, regardless of the absolute popularity of the major

party candidates, how do they match up with each other? Do they enjoy roughly equal strength among the voters, or is one substantially more popular?

These three considerations can all be measured. The reputation of the incumbent administration is reflected in the Gallup poll approval rating. Nomination contests have been classified as consensual, semiconsensual, and nonconsensual. The relative popularity of the opposing candidates can be measured by the Gallup poll trial heat at the beginning of the campaign. These three measures can then be combined to produce a taxonomy of candidates, and incumbent Presidents can be designated as invincible, optimistic, or endangered. Challengers (or simply candidates in races when no incumbent is running) can be classified as anointed, hopeful, or embattled.

### Invincible Incumbents

The invincibles enter the contest with high marks from both their own party and the voters in general. Since 1948, four incumbent Presidents can be so classified: Dwight D. Eisenhower (1956); Lyndon Johnson (1964); Richard Nixon (1972); and Ronald Reagan (1984). Heading into the convention season of the election year, their approval ratings ranged from 74 percent (Johnson) to 52 percent (Reagan). All four were consensual nominees of their party. Each won renomination without opposition and did so on first ballot with nearly unanimous support.

In addition to enjoying strong approval ratings and easy renomination efforts, these invincible incumbents all began the general election contest leading by at least 10 points in the postconvention trial heat polls. Eisenhower led his opponent by 11 points, Reagan was ahead by 19 points, Nixon outdistanced his rival by 25 points, and Johnson commanded a whopping 36 point lead. The campaign challenge for invincible incumbents is not to *lose* an election that looks as if it has already been won.

### Endangered Incumbents

Endangered incumbents are burdened with political profiles that are the exact opposite of those of their invincible colleagues. As a result, their challenge is to *win* an election that looks as if it has already been lost.

Endangered incumbents enter the race with low approval ratings, but they have won measured support from their party and are tied with or behind their opponents in initial postconvention trial heat polls. Since 1948 three

Presidents have entered the general election contest in the endangered category: Harry Truman (1948), Gerald Ford (1976), and Jimmy Carter (1980).

Before their party's convention, all had approval ratings under 50 percent. Carter was in the worst shape with a 31 percent approval rating, followed by Truman's 39 percent, and Ford's 45 percent. All were semiconsensual nominees. All faced opposition for their party's nomination but still managed to enter the convention in the lead and win on the first ballot.

As the general election began, these endangered incumbents found themselves struggling for voter support. Ford trailed his opponent by 18 points (36 percent to 54 percent), Truman was 11 points behind (37 percent to 48 percent), and Carter was in a dead heat with his challenger (39 percent to 39 percent).

### The Prevalence of Invincible and Endangered Incumbents

Of the seven incumbent Presidents who have sought reelection since 1948, none can be classified as an optimistic (i.e., an incumbent with respectable [around 50 percent] approval ratings, solid but not absolute support from his party, and a status showing that he is slightly ahead or tied with his opponent in the postconvention trial heat polls).

Where are the optimists? Why do incumbents seeking reelection fall into either the invincible or endangered categories? Clearly, if an incumbent in the latter part of his first term has strong approval ratings, a healthy economy, and a stable world situation, a strong challenge to his renomination efforts seems unlikely. Even if the incumbent is not representative of some factions within his party, potential candidates representing those factions do not want to risk their own political capital nor to jeopardize their party's control of the White House by challenging him. For the most part, disgruntled party members will focus instead on trying to ensure that their concerns are addressed by other party leaders or in the party's platform. They will simply bide their time and position their candidates for some future run for the top spot. As a result, the incumbent with strong approval ratings from the voters becomes even stronger politically in the face of little or no opposition to his renomination efforts. With both the voters and his party solidly behind him, he is confident that he can defeat any candidate that the opposition party might nominate.

Of course, the opposite is true for those incumbents who encounter adverse economic conditions or an unstable world situation and, as a result, see their voter support sagging. Instead of rallying around their besieged standard-bearer, rival party activists and other elected leaders search for an alternative presidential candidate. Such alternate aspirants often emerge and try to wrestle away the nomination. If that effort fails, then they and their followers continue to wage battles on the convention floor over platform issues and possible vice presidential choices. This intraparty competition further weakens the political standing of the incumbent. If the opposition party can nominate a strong ticket, then it has an excellent chance of knocking off the endangered incumbent.

### Anointed Challengers

Just as incumbents enter the race from different vantage points, so do challengers. The anointed enjoy enthusiastic party support and have substantial leads over their opponents in the postconvention polls. Since 1948 only one challenger has enjoyed the anointed role: Jimmy Carter (1976). Although not a "classic" consensual nominee of his party, he emerged from the convention as if he had been. The Democratic Party was united. The Carter-Mondale ticket enjoyed widespread party support and was 18 points ahead in postconvention polls. Clearly, this race looked over before it began.

### Hopeful Challengers

Hopeful challengers have to fight for their party's nominations but start their general election efforts in relatively good shape in voter polls. Seven of the candidates during this time period can be so classified: Thomas Dewey (1948), Eisenhower (1952), John F. Kennedy (1960), Nixon twice (1960, 1968), Reagan (1980), Michael Dukakis (1988), and George Bush (1988). Except for Nixon (1960), all were either semiconsensual or nonconsensual nominees. And most were either ahead or tied with their opponents in the postconvention polls. Dewey, Eisenhower, Nixon (1968), and Bush were ahead in their races by 11 percent, 15 percent, 12 percent, and 8 percent, respectively. Nixon (1960), Kennedy, and Reagan entered their general election contests dead even with their opponents. Only Dukakis was behind at the beginning of his fall campaign.

### Embattled Challengers

The embattled challengers may or may not begin the campaign with a divided party. But they face strong opposition in the general election and, as a result, find themselves far behind in the initial trial-heat polls. They seem to be headed for sure defeat. Over the last thirty years, there have been five challengers who fit into the embattled category: Adlai Stevenson twice (1952, 1956), Barry Goldwater (1964), Hubert Humphrey (1968), George McGovern (1972), and Walter Mondale (1984).

All but Stevenson, who was a semiconsensual nominee in his second try, were nonconsensual nominees of their party. They faced stiff opposition for their party's nomination. Even after their respective conventions were held, party unity could not be achieved. And at the start of the general election, the embattled were behind in the polls anywhere from 11 points (Stevenson, 1956) to 36 points (Goldwater).

## The Temporal Pattern

Whatever strengths the candidates bring to the contest, they are all confronted with the same compressed temporal pattern. Unlike nomination politics in which plans are made several years before the convention, all electoral politics is squeezed into the few months between the convention and the general election.

Depending on when the national convention is scheduled, as much as three and a half months or as little as two months may remain between the convention and the general election. One might think that under certain political circumstances campaign strategists could begin preparing for the general election before the convention. This is sometimes true, but the circumstances must be carefully specified.

Obviously, an aspirant who does not have the votes in hand must focus on winning more delegates. And even with enough delegate strength, a candidate cannot always expect a convention that is conflict free. A would-be nominee is faced with numerous delicate and explosive decisions. A platform must be crafted and a running mate must be selected. If the nominee is not a consensual one, then previous challengers and their supporters must be brought on board to build party unity. With so much at risk, careful preparations for the convention are very much in order.

Of course, some invincible incumbents can look forward to their own renomination. In their case, however, the candidates' attention may well be focused on the imperatives of executive politics. If they have foreign or economic crises on their hands, they are going to have to give more attention to the troublesome policy arena than to the relatively distant fall campaign.

This leaves one class of candidate who can use preconvention time for planning the general election campaign: those who can assemble a winning nomination coalition early on and who are themselves free from the responsibilities of the presidency. In recent decades, this would include Nixon in 1968, Carter in 1976, Reagan in 1980, Mondale in 1984, and Bush in 1988. The large number of very recent candidates who have had this opportunity is due to the front loading that has become common in nomination campaigns. With a larger number of delegates being chosen earlier, it is easier to accumulate a majority in time to begin planning for the general election before the convention. The careful selection of vice presidential candidates by Jimmy Carter in 1976 and Walter Mondale in 1984 helped their candidacies as did the extensive strategic planning for Ronald Reagan in 1980 and George Bush in 1988.

Even if candidates are able to launch their campaigns at the conventions (as Reagan and Bush were able to do), general election campaigns must be conducted within tighter time limits than any other. And, as noted above, many candidates must still wait until after the conventions to begin putting their fall campaigns together.

### Organization and Planning

Immediately following their nomination victories, presidential candidates and their staffs are faced with two key strategic questions: who should be selected to fill the top campaign posts; and how should the campaign organization be built at the national, regional, state, and county levels. Although the questions themselves are relatively straightforward, the answers to them are not usually so clear cut.

Frequently, competition is stiff for the top jobs. In 1964 Barry Goldwater had to decide which of two key players in his campaign should serve as national party chair. Faced with a similar problem in 1972, George McGovern actually promised three different supporters that they would head the Democratic Party. Eventually, in each case, party chairpersons were chosen but only after alternative appointments were found for the other contenders.

Along with selecting a national chairperson, the campaign must recruit individuals capable of handling the responsibilities that are associated with the four principal activities that must be carried on by campaign staff: campaign operations, public relations, research, and finance.

The staff needed to run the nationwide organization for the general election campaign is much larger than the staff needed to run a candidate's successive primary campaigns. No longer can staff simply be moved from one state to another. Since the general election is held in every state on the same date, each state needs its own coordinator. Discussing the 1976 Carter campaign organization, campaign manager Hamilton Jordan noted, "Of the 45 to 50 state coordinators (in the general election), only 5 or 6 had been involved in our campaign previously."

Where do the other 40-odd state coordinators come from? Some have been involved in the nomination campaigns of losing aspirants. Some come from other states. Perhaps the most fertile sources of leaders for the state campaigns are the regular party organizations in each state. Wherever the state chairpersons come from, the appointment has to be cleared with the state party organization unless the circumstances are very unusual.

Once the state coordinators have been recruited, local coordinators must be selected. The organization of the campaign committees from national level on down has two consequences. First, a progressively greater overlap unites the presidential campaign committees with the regular party organizations as one moves from the national to the county levels. Second, and more germane to a concern with the temporal pattern of electoral politics, building this organization takes time. Assignments have to be made in research, public relations, and finance as well. Since each leader selects subordinates in consultation with other party leaders, this process goes on sequentially. Finally, the staff must get to know one another and establish working relationships. In general, politicians have found no way to rush the creation of a nationwide campaign organization.

Planning begins as soon as individuals know their responsibilities in the campaign. This planning involves decisions about geographic concentration, positions to be taken on issues, media use, how the candidate is going to be portrayed, how the opposition candidate is to be attacked and by whom, debate strategies, what themes will tie all this effort together, and so on. Some of these strategies may not be worked out in detail in advance, but they have to be decided somehow.

The organization and planning stage is not very visible to the general public. A partial plan may be thrown together overnight, as Joseph Napolitan did once Hubert Humphrey won the Democratic nomination in 1968. Or the plan might be quite comprehensive. The basic Reagan campaign plan in 1980 filled two bulky notebooks, and his backers in fact wrote more than twenty other plans addressing specific circumstances as they arose in the course of the campaign.

How much time a campaign has to work on a plan depends on whether an incumbent is seeking reelection in the race, on the nature of the nomination battle, and on when the parties hold their nomination conventions. Whenever it comes, though, and however thoroughly or hastily it is handled, organization and planning is a necessary prelude to the rest of the campaign.

### Grand Opening

Putting the campaign plans into action and into the public view is the next stage of the general election cycle. This stage—the Grand Opening—includes all activities designed to maintain a front-runner's lead in the polls or to allow an underdog to catch up.

Grand Opening includes the initial major speeches and first campaign swings. This stage of the campaign traditionally started on Labor Day. Democrats often began their campaigns by speaking at a Labor Day rally in Cadillac Square in Detroit. More recently, initial forays have taken place in August. To capitalize on the excitement of having a woman on a major party ticket, and to try to get voters to give the ticket a second look, embattled Walter Mondale and Geraldine Ferraro made a number of August appearances in 1984. And in 1988 earlier strategic planning enabled George Bush to begin a strong line of attack against Michael Dukakis's record during August campaign appearances.

Incumbent Presidents, especially invincible ones, often choose to play "presidential," staying close to the White House during the Grand Opening. Even endangered Gerald Ford followed this pattern in September 1976, when he tried to capitalize on numerous White House Rose Garden appearances. By employing this strategy, Ford hoped to counter his negative approval ratings by highlighting his experience in office and directing the voters' attention to the inexperience of his anointed challenger, Jimmy Carter. Invincible Ronald Reagan, a more confident incumbent with a 15-point lead in the polls, began his 1984 Grand Opening in California, speaking of the buoyant economy and even better things to come in a second term. Reagan hoped this strategy would reinforce the positive attitudes that voters already had about his first term in office.

Whether the grand opening lasts for a few weeks or for most of the campaign season depends on the initial success of this strategy. Even if the hopes of the campaign strategists are not being met, Grand Opening usually lasts for several weeks. It takes at least that long to discover that things are not going well and devise an acceptable substitute course of action.

### Campaign Adjustments

As the campaign moves into high gear, strategists must decide whether to stay with the initial plan to or make minor or major adjustments to it. These modifications occur at different times across campaigns—depending on when those involved determine that some sort of adjustment is needed in order to retain or regain positive momentum in the campaign. Usually, these subsequent adjustments that are made fall into two general categories: strategic adjustment and tactical adjustments.

A strategic adjustment is a serious matter. It suggests that the campaign may be in real difficulty. Such was the case in 1988 when hopeful Michael Dukakis found himself trailing badly in polls taken late in the campaign. His opponent, George Bush, had been successful in painting the Massachusetts governor as a liberal and as being out of step with mainstream America. Dukakis had chosen not to respond directly to Bush's labeling, preferring instead to stick to his convention claim that the 1988 election was not about ideology. This strategy failed miserably and, in the closing days of the campaign, Dukakis abandoned it. In a surprise move at a campaign rally in California, the governor dared not only to mention the "L" word but also to declare that he was a liberal. This late strategic adjustment by the Dukakis campaign was intended to rally the governor's supporters, solidify his standing with traditional Democratic voters, and to move the still large block of undecided voters in his direction.

A strategic adjustment cannot be devised and executed very quickly. It takes time for complaints to work their way up through the campaign structure, and it takes more time for the strategy group to agree that the Grand Opening (in which they have some psychological investment, since they approved it) is not working. In fact, enough time is needed to realize that a strategic adjustment is called for and then to figure out what to do, that not more than one or two real strategic adjustments can occur in a single campaign.

In contrast, a tactical adjustment just requires the campaign to respond to some development. This may be a news bulletin that calls attention to a policy area and therefore suggests placing some emphasis on the candidate's ability to deal with that question. It may be some troubling development within the campaign organization or an untoward statement by the candidate himself, such as Jimmy Carter's personal attack on Ronald Reagan in 1980. A tactical adjustment in this case was needed to counter the negative reaction Carter received for what were viewed as unnecessarily vindictive statements about Governor Reagan.

To counter this "meanness" issue, Carter made an appearance on a Barbara Walters television interview, where he promised to "do the best I can to refrain from any sort of personal relationship with Mr. Reagan so far as criticisms are concerned." This attempted tactical adjustment was not successful because, two days later, President Carter said, "Reagan is not a good man to trust with the affairs of this nation." The suggestion that Governor Reagan was untrustworthy was enough to revive the "meanness" issue in the press.

A tactical adjustment is focused on the original development, is contained in time, and does not involve any general changes in campaign strategy. But, as the above example demonstrates, not all tactical adjustments are successful.

### Debates

Presidential debates can lead to *both* strategic and tactical adjustments. An example of the former occurred in 1980 when endangered incumbent Jimmy Carter found himself trailing in the polls behind hopeful challenger Ronald Reagan. Struggling to pick up voter support, Carter strategists were faced with the decision of whether or not to accept Reagan's late invitation to join him in a one-on-one debate. Previously, Reagan had insisted that Independent candidate John Anderson be included in any presidential debate. Carter objected to appearing with Anderson and refused to debate Reagan unless they were the only two involved.

In late October, the Reagan camp decided to reverse their demand that Anderson be involved and agreed to debate Carter one-on-one. Now the Carter strategists were skeptical whether such a debate, only days before the election, would help their candidate. But how could they refuse when Reagan had met their initial demand to drop Anderson? They could not and they eventually agreed to the debate. The stakes were high. Any misstep by either candidate could prove to be costly because there would be too little time to repair the damages.

Both camps prepared extensively for the debates, but it was Reagan who walked away the more confident candidate. He was able to end the debate by asking voters to decide whether they were better off than they were four years earlier. Carter had no time to make any more strategic adjustments to counter Reagan's strong showing.

As mentioned previously, debates can also lead to tactical adjustments. In the second debate in 1976, Gerald Ford made reference to the absence of Soviet domination in Eastern Europe. The press pounced on this misstatement. The Ford campaign realized that a tactical adjustment was needed. In this case, it included a public statement by the President that he knew there were divisions of Russian troops in Poland and some meetings with ethnic group leaders.

Debates also affect the campaign in two other important ways: they crystallize voter sentiment and punctuate the campaign by providing definitive time periods in which the candidates are compared and evaluated. Of course, these time periods vary since debates do not occur at any set point in every campaign and need not occur at all.

### Time's Up

The curtain has gone up on the Grand Opening, tactical and strategic adjustments have been made, the voters are finally beginning to pay attention to the campaign, but—time's up! One of the ironies of electoral politics is that the period just before the election, when the candidates can command a huge media audience, is also the time when the strategists have the least control over what is happening in the campaign. The meaning of "time's up" is that it is too late to make any more television commercials, too late to buy any more air time, too late to implement any new campaign emphases, too late to do the necessary advance work to prepare more campaign appearances, too late, in sum, to do much more than either carry out the plans that have already been made or try to

## Table 1

*Classes of Campaigns*

Incumbent
Nonincumbent

| | Invincible / Anointed | Optimist / Hopeful | Endangered / Embattled |
|---|---|---|---|
| **Nonincumbent / Anointed** | ///////// | ///////// | *Ford*-Carter '76 |
| **Hopeful** | ///////// | Nixon-Kennedy '60 / Bush-Dukakis '88 | *Truman*-Dewey '48 / *Carter*-Reagan '80 |
| **Embattled** | *Eisenhower*-Stevenson '56 / *Johnson*-Goldwater '64 / *Nixon*-McGovern '72 / *Reagan*-Mondale '84 | *Eisenhower*-Stevenson '52 / *Nixon*-Humphrey '68 | |

Note: All words in italic type refer to incumbents; all words in roman type refer to nonincumbents.

react impulsively, often frantically, to late developments.

*Classes of Campaigns*

Political analysts hypothesize that each campaign has a unique rhythm. But, as we have seen, campaigns feature different types of candidates. Certain things, moreover, tend to happen in each stage of a campaign. Therefore, if we know the candidate pairing for a given campaign (for instance, invincible incumbent against embattled challenger) and the temporal pattern common to all campaigns, we can understand a good deal about the dynamics of any particular campaign.

The eleven most recent campaigns fall into five classes (see Table 1). On four occasions an invincible incumbent has faced an embattled challenger: 1956, 1964, 1972, and 1984. In 1976 an endangered incumbent confronted an anointed challenger, and twice (1948 and 1980) an endangered incumbent has faced a hopeful challenger. In 1952 and 1968 an embattled candidate took on a hopeful candidate. The other two campaigns without an incumbent, 1960 and 1988, have been match-ups between hopeful candidates.

Three classes of campaigns are theoretically impossible. Since an invincible incumbent must enjoy strong approval ratings and be 10 points ahead in the postconvention trial heat, he will face neither an anointed nor a hopeful challenger. For similar reasons, an anointed candidate will never run against a hopeful candidate. The final class would feature an endangered President facing an embattled challenger, or two embattled candidates running against each other. This scenario would require that both parties be in simultaneous disarray, a political situation that has not occurred in recent decades.

### Invincible Incumbent vs. Embattled Challenger

In this class, organization and planning tends to be serene for the incumbent—whether Eisenhower, Johnson, Nixon, or Reagan—but difficult for the challenger. Stevenson, Goldwater, McGovern, and Mondale all had to reunite their parties after arduous nomination contests. The invincible incumbent's Grand Opening strategy remains in place throughout the campaign, needing only tactical adjustments as events require. The incumbent's problem is that important questions (to Nixon about Watergate, for instance) are neglected in the prevailing euphoria. Embattled challengers' campaigns, on the other hand, are marked by

strategic adjustments as they try first one way and then another to gain on the President. Barry Goldwater, for example, moved from principled statements to an attempt to respond to attacks on his competence to handle nuclear arms, to an "override" strategy attacking Johnson, to a final decision to concentrate on small towns and the South. By "time's up," notes of resignation or bitterness dominate the embattled challenger's statements. "I'm going to give you one more warning," said Senator McGovern on November 4, 1972. "If Mr. Nixon is reelected on Tuesday, we may very well have four more years of war." The weary challenger has realized that the task is just too great. The best that any of these four embattled challengers could do was Governor Stevenson's 42 percent of the popular vote in 1956.

### Endangered Incumbent vs. Anointed Challenger

Talking about a "class" that matches an endangered incumbent against an anointed challenger is difficult. Not only is this class a single case, but it happens that the endangered incumbent had a skillfully devised strategy while the anointed challenger's campaign showed many signs of improvisation. The endangered Ford team made very good use of the organization and planning phase, devising an extensive media campaign to encourage voters to perceive Ford as more intelligent and decisive. By the time of the first debate in late September, he had become more popular even outside the South. At this point, Carter made the first of two tactical adjustments, hoping to find some way to hold onto the lead. Even though Ford had had some problems (e.g., a tactical adjustment required by Ford's second debate reference to Eastern Europe), Carter's huge lead had evaporated by the "time's up" stage. The anointed challenger did manage to win, but Ford almost beat him with a skillful campaign. This campaign was marked by a substantial change in voters' preferences, but an anointed challenger with a better campaign plan might have been able to avoid such a serious threat from an endangered incumbent.

### Endangered Incumbent vs. Hopeful Challenger

The two campaigns in which Harry Truman and Jimmy Carter fought to save their presidencies were also marked by substantial changes in voters' preferences. Both endangered incumbents defended themselves by attacking their opponents and emphasizing conflictual themes. Truman did so more consistently, focusing much of his fire on the Republican Party: "that notorious do-nothing Republican Congress has already stuck a pitchfork in the farmer's back." Carter's themes of attack showed up in claims that a Reagan victory would mean "the alienation of black from white, Christian from Jew, rich from poor, and North from South." While Truman spoke of conflict from Grand Opening to election day, challenger Dewey held fast to consensus throughout the campaign: "This great campaign to strengthen and unite our country has meaning far beyond our own shores." Challenger Reagan shifted his themes twice in accordance with his Grand Opening strategy. Another difference between 1948 and 1980 was the absence of strategic adjustments in the Truman and Dewey campaigns, while there were a couple in both the Carter and Reagan campaigns. Close to the end, for example, Reagan decided to call for a one-on-one debate, and Carter decided to accept. In the end, Truman was able to win back enough working-class Independents and Democrats to hold the White House, but double-digit inflation and diplomats held hostage in Iran were too much for Carter to overcome.

### Hopeful Candidate vs. Embattled Candidate

In this class, the two hopeful candidates (Eisenhower, 1952 and Nixon, 1968) were successful. Both of them had better developed campaign plans. The 1952 plan called for attack on the Democratic "mess in Washington," but this vituperation was matched by Eisenhower's own personal moderation, a discretion that reassured voters that a vote for Eisenhower was not a vote to repeal the New Deal. Caught between Wallace and Humphrey in 1968, Nixon took moderate-conservative positions that were sufficiently vague to prevent the loss of votes to either rival. Both Eisenhower and Nixon made tactical adjustments. For example, Eisenhower pledged to go to Korea, and Nixon attacked Humphrey more directly at the end of the campaign when Humphrey began rapidly gaining strength in the East. The strategies of the embattled Democratic candidates, Stevenson and Humphrey, were more improvisational. Humphrey in particular lacked time for an organization and planning phase because of the late, riot-torn Democratic convention. Both also faced the common problem of distancing themselves from unpopular administrations. Stevenson kept his campaign headquarters in Illinois. Humphrey made a strategic adjustment with a bold speech in Salt Lake City indicating how the Vietnamese policy in a Humphrey administration would be different than it had been in a Johnson administration. Humphrey's campaign nearly closed the gap in the last month of the campaign whereas Stevenson's effort had little effect and he lost to Eisenhower by a full 10 percent.

### Hopeful Candidate vs. Hopeful Candidate

The campaigns of 1960 and 1988 had a number of parallels. All of the aspirants had reason to hope—Nixon and Bush as heirs of popular administrations, Kennedy and Dukakis as nominees of the majority party—but none had reason for confidence. In both 1960 and 1988, a central question was how much change the voters wanted. As status quo candidates, Nixon and Bush called for modest change, while out-party candidates Kennedy and Dukakis argued for new departures in policy. The campaigns themselves were marked more by themes than careful expositions of what the candidates would do if elected. Nixon strove to emphasize peace and his own foreign policy experience; Kennedy identified Nixon with Republicanism rather than Eisenhower and spoke of a need to get the country moving again. Dukakis claimed "I'm on your side"; Bush charged that Dukakis was too liberal and was out of the American mainstream. The presidential debates were important in both races. In 1960 they were important because of their novelty and because the contest was so close; in 1988 they facilitated voters' decision-making between two unappealing candidates. There were differences between 1960 and 1988, of course. Many of these could be linked to the much better survey information available in 1988. In 1960, for instance, Nixon adhered to an early campaign pledge to visit every state and spent valuable time just before the election flying to Alaska. In 1988, in contrast, the final appearances of both Bush and Dukakis were dictated by poll information about which states were close. Governor Dukakis made some strategic adjustments in the hope of finding an attractive message, but Nixon, Kennedy, and Bush adhered to their original campaign plans. While there was some voter movement from candidate to candidate, the campaigns had almost net impact. From the initial trial heat to the 50.1 percent to 49.9 percent election, 1960 was a very close campaign. George Bush had an eight-point margin in the post-Labor Day Gallup poll and won the 1988 election with 53.9 percent to Michael Dukakis's 46.1 percent.

*Conclusion*

In short, a continuum runs from a race between an invincible incumbent and an embattled challenger to a race between two hopeful nonincumbents. In the first case, the invincible incumbent has no need to adjust strategies; virtually every embattled challenger makes a few strategic adjustments. When two hopeful nonincumbents run against each other, the race may be very close. In between are contests with mixes of strategic and tactical adjustments and (often) substantial changes in voter preferences. The candidate taxonomy and temporal pattern do not, of course, fully determine what happens in campaigns, but they do provide a means of understanding the major characteristics of presidential contests.

*See also:* Individual presidential and vice presidential candidates, Individual elections

John H. Kessel
Joan E. McLean

*REFERENCES*

Bibby, John F. 1987. *Politics, Parties, and Elections in America.* Chicago: Nelson Hall.

Gallup Poll. 1980. *The Gallup Opinion Index, Report No. 182: Presidential Popularity, A 43 Year Review.* Princeton, NJ: The Gallup Poll.

———. 1980. *The Gallup Opinion Index, Report No. 183: Presidential Candidate Trial Heats, 1936–1980.* Princeton, NJ: The Gallup Poll.

Keech, William R., and Donald R. Matthews. 1977. *The Party's Choice with an Epilogue on the 1976 Nominations.* Washington: Brookings.

Kessel, John H. 1988. *Presidential Campaign Politics: Coalition Strategies and Citizen Response.* 3rd ed. Chicago: Dorsey.

Maisel, Louis Sandy. 1987. *Parties and Elections in America: The Electoral Process.* New York: Random House.

Moore, Jonathan, and Janet Fraser. 1978. *Campaign for President: The Managers Look at '76.* Cambridge: Ballinger.

Wayne, Stephen J. 1988. *The Road to the White House.* 3rd ed. New York: St. Martin's.

White, Theodore H. 1969. *The Making of the President 1968.* New York: Atheneum.

## Presidential Libraries as Research Tools

In 1939 Congress passed legislation establishing the first official presidential library, the Franklin D. Roosevelt Library in Hyde Park, New York. Since that time ten have been authorized; nine are open to the public, and one is in the planning stage.

Beginning with George Washington, tradition dictated that a President's papers are his personal property and Presidents disposed of their papers at will upon leaving office. Washington distinguished between his personal papers and official records; the former were to remain his. Grover Cleveland defined papers this way:

> I regard the papers and documents . . . addressed to me or intended for my use and action unofficial and private, not infrequently confidential, and having reference to the performance of a duty exclusively mine. I consider them in no proper sense as . . . the files of the Department, but as deposited there for my convenience, remaining still completely under my control.

The 1955 Presidential Libraries Act codified this practice of distinguishing between the personal and official records of a presidency. This act had the intention of preserving archival materials that concentrated on certain subjects and periods through the establishment of research centers dispersed around the country and staffed by expert archivists.

The Watergate scandal during Richard Nixon's administration changed the public and legal perception of presidential records. The legal challenges over President Nixon's tape-recorded conversations and other records prompted Congress in December 1974 to pass Public Law 93–526, an act designed to protect Nixon's tape recordings. The accessibility of Nixon's archives is still being contested in the courts. In order to prevent any similar cases in the future, Congress enacted the Presidential Records Act of 1978, which mandated that all presidential records created on or after January 20, 1981, are declared by law to be owned and controlled by the United States and are required to be transferred to the National Archives at the end of the administration. Ronald Reagan was the first President affected by this law.

If a President desires to set up his own library, he selects the site, and private funds must be used for the buildings. The National Archives then staffs and administers the library and makes records accessible to researchers.

The following libraries are now in existence:

Herbert Hoover Library, West Branch, Iowa
Franklin D. Roosevelt Library, Hyde Park,
 New York
Harry S Truman Library, Independence, Missouri
Dwight D. Eisenhower Library, Abilene, Kansas
John F. Kennedy Library, Boston, Massachusetts
Lyndon B. Johnson Library, Austin, Texas
Richard M. Nixon Library, Yorba Linda, California
Gerald R. Ford Library, Ann Arbor, Michigan
Jimmy Carter Library, Atlanta, Georgia

The Ronald Reagan Library (in Simi Valley, California) is in the planning stage and due to open in 1991.

The extant papers of most of the other Presidents before Herbert Hoover are in the Library of Congress, but many papers are also dispersed around the country in repositories such as universities and historical societies as well as in private collections. For instance, the bulk of George Washington's correspondence is in the Library of Congress, but at least 25 other institutions hold some of his papers. And private collectors still acquired Washington correspondence and other documents of his administration on the auction block and through dealers. The papers of John Adams and John Quincy Adams are largely in the Massachusetts Historical Society, but other libraries also have scattered holdings.

Because of the wide geographical dispersion of many of our past Presidents' papers, the presidential libraries are extremely important research tools, primarily because they concentrate most if not all of an administration's records in one location. It is also true that because of the explosion in size of an administration's records, very few private or extrafederal governmental institutions could handle modern presidential records. For instance, the Roosevelt Library in Hyde Park shelves over 16 million manuscripts as well as thousands of other volumes. By the time the papers of Lyndon Johnson's career are collected entirely, his library will house 33 million manuscripts. For John F. Kennedy's shorter political life, the Kennedy Library managed to collect, among other things, over 25 million manuscript pages, 1 million still photographs, and 6.5 million feet of motion picture film. These libraries are also still actively collecting documents of their respective periods.

Most presidential libraries are not limited to the papers of a specific President but also have holdings related to the history and careers of the Presidents and their families. For instance, in 1987 the Roosevelt Library received the papers of Edward J. Flynn, the influential leader of the Bronx, New York, Democratic machine; Flynn was instrumental in Roosevelt's elections and administrations. The Herbert Hoover Library in Iowa holds scores of collections of people connected with Hoover's life and career. The purpose of these libraries is to provide scholars an in-depth view of the era as well as the history of the public and private lives of the Presidents. Their value for the researcher lies in the accumulation and concentration of primary sources in one location.

*See also:* John Adams, John Quincy Adams, Jimmy Carter, Grover Cleveland, Dwight D. Eisenhower, Gerald Ford, Lyndon B. Johnson, John F. Kennedy, Richard M. Nixon, Franklin D. Roosevelt, Harry S Truman, George Washington, Watergate

*Larry E. Sullivan*

REFERENCES

Berman, Larry. 1981. "The Evolution and Value of Presidential Libraries." In Harold C. Relyea, ed. *The Presidency and Information Policy*. New York: Center for the Study of the Presidency; Proceedings 4, No. 1.

Dennis, Ruth. 1978. "Presidential Libraries." In Allen Kent, Harold Lancour, and Jay E. Daily, eds. *Encyclopedia of Library and Information Science*. Vol. 23. New York: Marcel Dekker.

Kahn, Herman. 1959. "The Presidential Library—A New Institution." 50, No. 3 *Special Libraries* 106.

National Archives and Records Administration. 1985. *Presidential Libraries Manual*. Washington: NARA, April 15 (Libraries 1401).

Veit, Fritz. 1987. *Presidential Libraries and Collections*. Westport, CT: Greenwood.

# Presidential Nominating Conventions

Once every four years, in two of the big cities of the United States, the Republican Party and the Democratic Party meet in their national conventions. They meet, first and foremost, because it is a presidential election year and they must nominate their candidates for President and Vice President. That responsibility alone is enough to make the conventions important because a presidential nominating convention is where two people, out of the millions who are theoretically eligible to be President, will be identified as their parties' nominees for the most powerful single office in the world. In less than three months following the conventions, one of those two nominees will be elected President, and in less than six months that person will officially take office.

The conventions accomplish much more than the nomination of the candidate for President and Vice President, however. They carry out other important functions for the party and the polity. Although each convention has a fleeting life span, usually of less than a week, the national get-togethers have been stable features of the American political system almost since its very beginning.

*A Brief History of the Conventions*

The presidential nominating conventions are among the most enduring institutions in American politics. When the Democrats and Republicans meet in their quadrennial national conventions to select a nominee, they are carrying on a tradition that stretches back well over 150 years in American history.

Like the political parties, the national conventions are not provided for in the Constitution. The first two presidential elections were won by George Washington, and there was no contest over his nomination. In Washington's case the Electoral College provided for nomination and election simultaneously. The original concept of the Founders was that the Electoral College would be chosen by the state legislatures, either by popular vote for the electors or by selection by the legislators themselves. The electors would then meet in their state capitols and then cast two ballots each for President, presumably voting from among a list of those eminent citizens with obvious qualifications to be President. Article II provided that the top candidate would become President and the runner-up would become Vice President. (The Twelfth Amendment eventually separated the vote for the offices because of the tie between Thomas Jefferson and Aaron Burr in 1800.) Historian James W. Ceaser has labeled this "the constitutional plan." The plan worked as expected for Washington's two elections; however, even by 1796 the advent of political parties made the original constitutional plan impractical.

In the subsequent early presidential elections (1800–1824) party leaders in Congress got together to make the presidential nominations although these nominations were challenged in some instances by the state legislatures. This process was known as the "Congressional Caucus" system, and it solved the nomination problem reasonably well for this transitional period. However, by 1824, the Caucus was widely criticized for being too narrow and elitist in orientation and for having ignored several popular candidates, most notably Andrew Jackson who was nominated by the Tennessee State Legislature in 1824, the last year that the Congressional Caucus system even attempted to make nominations.

Credit for holding the first-ever national nominating convention is usually given to an obscure third party called the Antimasonic Party, which held a national convention in 1831 to nominate William Wirt. Wirt, a former Attorney General, went on to capture only 7.78 percent of the popular vote; however, the Antimasonic Party not only held the first national convention but also appointed the first

national committee and established other important procedural precedents. The Democratic Party, then under the leadership of President Andrew Jackson, held a national convention in Baltimore in 1832 to nominate Jackson for a second term. The Democrats have held national nominating conventions every four years since 1832.

The Republicans were a new party in American politics when they held their first national convention in 1856 to nominate John C. Frémont. Frémont did not win in 1856; he was beaten by James Buchanan, the Democrat, although Frémont did get more popular votes in 1856 than the Whig-American candidate, former President Millard Fillmore. The Republicans met again in 1860 to nominate Abraham Lincoln who went on to become the sixteenth President of the United States. Lincoln's victory and the Civil War helped established a Republican hegemony over the presidency, one that was broken only by Grover Cleveland and Woodrow Wilson, until Franklin Roosevelt's victories in 1932 and 1936. Roosevelt's New Deal coalition established the Democrats as the majority party in the United States, a majority that lasted well into the modern era. The reign of the Democrats then was broken by consistent Republican presidential victories starting with Richard Nixon in 1968, and (with the single exception of Jimmy Carter's election in 1976) extending through George Bush in 1988. During this long stretch of American history the presidential nomination system was in a state of evolution.

From 1832 through 1968 the national conventions were the preeminent route to the presidential nomination. After the turn of the twentieth century, presidential primaries began to play a role in the nomination system. These primaries were first established legally by Robert La Follette and the Progressives in Wisconsin in 1905 as a means of letting the ordinary voters play a role in selecting the party's presidential nominee. As such, the primaries were an attempt further to democratize the choices of presidential nominees. The primaries also represented a rebellion against some of the excesses and abuses that had grown rampant in the national conventions and the selection of delegates to the conventions. The presidential primaries became very popular between 1912 and 1920, although after 1920 the number of states using the presidential primaries declined somewhat and stabilized in a range of 12 to 17.

From 1920 through 1968 the presidential primaries played some role in the selection of our presidential nominees. Overall, however, primaries have played a secondary role. Estes Kefauver won several primaries in 1952 only to lose the Democratic nomination to Adlai Stevenson, the choice of the party leaders. Certain crucial primaries in key states could be used as a proving ground for the candidate's popular appeal. John F. Kennedy's victories in West Virginia and Wisconsin in 1960 are the best examples of this role. In West Virginia Kennedy proved to the Democratic Party leaders that he could overcome anti-Catholic prejudices and appeal to Protestant voters, and in Wisconsin Kennedy further enhanced his credentials by narrowly defeating Hubert Humphrey from neighboring Minnesota. While the primaries could be important during this era for demonstrating a candidate's popular appeal, the final and most important choices were made by the party leaders in the national conventions. There the party leaders came together to bargain and deliberate over the party's preferred candidates; then they and the rank-and-file delegates voted. For these reasons one scholar has termed the entire era from 1832 through 1968 the "era of brokered conventions." Hubert Humphrey's 1968 nomination to be the Democratic Party's standard-bearer was achieved through the support of Lyndon Johnson and other party leaders and in spite of his failure to enter a single primary that year.

If 1968 was the end of an era in American presidential politics, then 1972 marked the beginning of a new era, one in which the primaries would gain ascendancy in the making of presidential nominations. In 1968 the nation was deeply divided over the Vietnam War and over the aftermath of the civil rights movement. The Democratic Party put on a disastrous convention in Chicago in 1968, one that helped doom the candidacy of Hubert Humphrey against Richard Nixon that year. As a consequence of that convention, the Democrats appointed a party commission to study and reform the rules under which the presidential nominees were selected. This commission, which came to be known as the McGovern-Fraser Commission, promulgated a new set of rules for the 1972 presidential selection process. While those rules did not *require* the use of presidential primaries, state party officials quickly discovered that primaries were the surest route to compliance with the McGovern-Fraser requirements.

In 1972 the number of Democratic primaries jumped to 22 from the 15 held in 1968, and the percentage of delegates chosen in the primaries increased from 40.2 percent to 65.3 percent. The comparable changes for the Republicans were 21 primaries and 56.8 percent of the delegates in 1972 versus 15 primaries and 38.1 percent of the delegates in 1968. Moreover, the mass media attention and focus on the primaries became much more intense. George McGovern was widely perceived to have gained the Democratic Party's nomination because of his victories in certain key primaries. Even though he lost in a landslide to Richard Nixon in the general election in 1972, the lesson of McGovern's primary victories was learned and magnified by the mass media and subsequent candidates.

In 1976 Jimmy Carter further reinforced that lesson. Actually, Carter, then a relatively unknown ex-governor of Georgia, got his first big boost from an unexpected victory in the Iowa caucuses. He then used his "doing better than expected" coverage from Iowa to develop massive press coverage and thus the momentum necessary to win the New Hampshire primary. From these early victories Carter went on to win enough primaries and caucuses to ensure a first-ballot victory and the Democratic nomination in 1976.

By the end of the 1972 and 1976 nominations season, the crucial role of the primaries was well established. A candidate to be successful was required to run in all or most of the primaries and preferably to win some of the early ones—especially New Hampshire, a state that holds the first primary in the nation. Strategic caucus victories—such as the one in Iowa—could also be helpful although such victories were no guarantee of ultimate victory. Even the caucuses took on an aura of mass appeal, with the candidate appeals and media coverage of some of the caucuses becoming much like that afforded the primaries. Since 1972 the United States has nominated its presidential candidates in a mixed system with the primaries being crucial along with certain important caucus/convention states. However, the final and official nomination is made in the national conventions. In short, both stages and steps are necessary and complementary in the contemporary system. Some scholars have termed this most recent system the "era of popular appeal" to denote the necessity of making campaign appeals to the mass voters. The national conventions are themselves critical steps in the nominations process; however, the primaries and caucuses are necessary and even essential prior steps that a successful candidate must negotiate on the long journey to the White House.

## The Functions of the National Conventions

The classic work in the study of national party conventions was by Paul T. David and his associates (1960). In that work the four official functions of the conventions are delineated as the nominating function, the platform-drafting function, the campaign-rally function, and the governing-body function. Furthermore, following and elaborating on the work by David, other scholars have identified other latent functions of the conventions, two of which are the *creation* of a party consensus and the *ratification* of a consensus that may already exist in the party. These are less obvious functions than the more official ones, but they are nevertheless important for the health of the parties, for their competitive positions in the fall campaigns, and for the health of the polity.

## Making the Nomination

First the conventions must make the nomination official. The name of the most likely winner may well emerge from the primary season; however, winning is not official until that person's name is placed in nomination and is confirmed by the roll-call vote. The roll-call vote itself, with the list of the states amplified across the hall, is one of the most dramatic moments of the convention. Even if the probable winner is known beforehand (and no roll call has gone beyond the first ballot since 1952), nevertheless real tension is in the air as the votes mount up toward the crucial victorious number. This is essentially the moment toward which all the candidates' efforts, the countless hours of staff time, and the millions of media words have been directed during the nomination season.

The strategic problem for all the candidates throughout the nomination season is to get that majority of delegates' votes on the first roll call. Nomination is not official after all until 50 percent plus one of the delegates have cast their vote for a single candidate and thus named the party's nominee. Convention week builds toward this event as one of its most climatic moments. The entire nomination process may have gone on for as much as two years before the conventions; however, all of that primary and preprimary season is prologue, and the entire nomination process has pointed toward this last act at the conventions. The candidates want to pass the final test with as much luster added to their personal image and as much support garnered within their parties as possible. Winning the nomination overwhelmingly is the first step in building the momentum necessary for the general election.

No matter how many potential candidates thought about running for President in any single year, and no matter how many started out on the primary trail, only two people will stand alone after the conventions as the official nominees of the Democratic and Republican parties for President of the United States. In addition, the candidate who comes out of the national convention with the most united party and with the best story from convention week has a head start on winning the general election in November. Therefore, the politically important story out of convention week concentrates on how the nominee was chosen rather than how the winner was officially confirmed.

## Making the Vice Presidential Nomination

The vice presidential nominee also has to be chosen as another critical function of the convention. Here the candidate and campaign staff make the choice in most instances, and the convention simply ratifies their choice. Often there are genuine questions about who will be chosen, although in recent elections the candidates have done more careful screening. And some have even announced the names of their choices before the convention starts. In recent elections, the Democrats have engendered a significant amount of interest in and debate over their vice presidential nominees. In 1976 Jimmy Carter spent much of his time between the last state primary and the start of the convention interviewing potential vice presidential candidates. His decision-making process was careful and deliberate, and his choice of Walter Mondale was well received. Mondale had close ties to the traditional New Deal constituency of the Democratic Party and may well have helped Carter win in November.

Mondale tried to repeat the Carter process in 1984. He interviewed numerous potential candidates and finally settled on New York Congresswoman Geraldine Ferraro. While the choice of the first woman to be on the ticket of a major party was the center of intense interest generated in the media, it may not have helped

Mondale's candidacy in November. The much-publicized "gender gap" largely disappeared in November 1984, and women voted for Ronald Reagan at almost the same rates as men. The glare of publicity cast on Ferraro and the long and intense scrutiny the media gave her personal finances and those of her husband may have actually detracted on balance from Mondale's candidacy.

In 1988 intense speculation surrounded the candidacy of Jesse Jackson and his potential for a place on the ticket as Michael Dukakis's running mate. In 1988 Dukakis's handling of the Jesse Jackson candidacy had serious import for his chances for getting strong minority support in November. By the same token, his ultimate choice of Senator Lloyd Bentsen of Texas was an attempt to balance the Democratic ticket both geographically and ideologically as well as adding Bentsen's experience and credentials to complement Dukakis's strength.

In 1988 George Bush probably had two objectives in naming J. Danforth Quayle to be his running mate. First, Quayle was an attempt to reassure the right wing, and especially the Christian Evangelical Right of the Republican Party, since Quayle, a favorite of theirs, took all the right stances on the issues of greatest importance to that strong core constituency in the Republican Party. Bush, who started his career as a moderate Republican, had long been somewhat suspect in the most ardent Republican right-wing circles although his service in the Reagan administration for eight years had allayed some of that suspicion. Nevertheless, naming an acceptable conservative like Quayle could solidify Bush's right-wing base and leave him free to court more moderate forces during the general election. This objective was successfully achieved in November.

The second objective was apparently somewhat more problematic. Bush touted Quayle as his emissary to the younger generation, the baby-boom generation born after World War II who had become the largest demographic age group by 1988. Bush often boasted during the general election of Quayle's ability to represent that younger and more inexperienced generation. (A subtext here was Quayle's supposed appeal to women because of his telegenic good looks, but that strategy was largely abandoned when it appeared to be backfiring.) Bush's appeal to the baby-boom generation was no larger than to the national population as a whole, and some polls showed that Dan Quayle's generation

widely rejected his candidacy. Consequently, the second, more demographic objective went largely unrealized. On balance the polls indicated that the choice of Quayle to be Bush's Vice President was controversial and detracted from Bush's campaign. Nevertheless, it was a decision that did not prove fatal in November.

If it is handled carefully, the vice presidential choice can help to broaden the coalition of the triumphant presidential candidate. In 1980 this broadening of the coalition is essentially what Reagan did by reaching for George Bush as his Vice President, thus placating the "establishment" section of the Republican Party. Carter did the same by naming Mondale and reaching toward the more liberal part of the Democratic Party in 1976. And John Kennedy materially enhanced his probability of carrying Texas and the South and thus winning the general election in 1960 by naming Lyndon Johnson to be his running mate. Johnson had been Kennedy's closest Democratic competition for the presidency in the 1960 nomination season, with Johnson winning the second largest number of delegate votes on the first ballot. The Kennedy, Carter, and Reagan cases are all examples of a presidential nominee successfully using the vice presidential nomination to reach out to the other wing of a divided party.

An opposite example is provided by Barry Goldwater in 1964 when he named New York Congressman William Miller to his ticket. Miller was a relatively unknown conservative who did little to strengthen Goldwater's coalition; in fact, he simply duplicated Goldwater's strength among conservatives. The Goldwater mistake is one that nominees try to avoid in making their vice presidential choice. The naming of the vice presidential candidate has important symbolic and strategic value, and the rational presidential candidate will take those values under careful consideration before a final commitment is made.

### Adoption of the Platform

One of the other important pieces of official business for the convention is the adoption of the party platform. American party platforms are little understood by the public. They are indeed often long winded and rife with glittering generalities. If the party is in power in the White House, the platform typically opens with a review of the many glorious accomplishments of the current administration as well as accolades for the party's past. In these sections the platform is self-congratulatory and filled with hyperbole. If the party is out of power, then the platform presents a contrasting view of the current administration, condemning it for everything awful that has happened and suggesting that the Republic will surely not survive if the rascals are not thrown out. Both parties then offer their prescriptions for the nation's ills and their vision for the future. Included in this prescription are a number of very specific policy and programmatic proposals.

Much in the platforms and the process by which they are written and adopted invites scorn, or at least healthy skepticism, toward them. The past is never as rosy as the party in power paints it, nor is it as tragic as the party out of power believes. Lots of unmistakable political posturing takes place on the platform. Nevertheless, the platforms are important documents and the process of writing and adopting them is an important function of the conventions. The mass media and the American people tend to dismiss platforms out of hand; nevertheless, they do deserve more serious consideration.

First, the platform-writing process began several months before the opening of the convention. The platform committee has held a series of hearings inviting party leaders and interest groups to give testimony on the potential content of the platform. Recently the parties have taken their show on the road, holding platform hearings in a number of diverse cities across the country. These hearings produce voluminous testimony and multiple proposals for addressing the problems confronting the nation.

Long before the convention opens, the platform committee has been at work on drafts of the various sections; and when the convention starts, the platform draft is complete. Only the debate and the adoption stage remain. Sometimes the convention vigorously debates the platform and significant amendments may even be tacked on from the floor. Still, changes are unusual, and such changes as *are* adopted are likely to be incremental adjustments to the work of the platform committee. The entire convention is simply too big and the confusion too great for the convention to act very coherently as a collegial and deliberative body. At best only a few salient issues will receive an airing before the convention.

In essence then the platform is likely to be an instrument of whatever faction of the party is in a dominant position at the time of its writing.

In the party of the President, if he is seeking reelection, the platform is usually under his control. If the out party has a front-runner who has emerged from the primaries, he and his coalition will try to dominate the platform-writing process. Any dominant coalition will try to craft a document that expresses their ideological and programmatic preferences. If they plan carefully enough, they will also look at the platform as a strategic document designed to enhance their prospects for the general election. This strategic view may or may not lead them to want to compromise with other factions within the party.

For example, in 1980 the Reagan conservatives were clearly in charge of their convention. One of the earlier policy commitments that they had made to their supporters was opposition to the Equal Rights Amendment (ERA). Reagan's supporters on the platform committee demanded that the platform omit all references to the ERA. References to the ERA were stricken in spite of the fact that Republican platforms had supported women's rights all the way back to the adoption of the Nineteenth Amendment (1920), giving women the right to vote. Strong protests were lodged by many women's rights supporters; however, the Reagan people's position on the ERA prevailed.

About all the minority faction in a party and convention can do is to offer amendments and to demand a hearing before the convention. Democrat Jesse Jackson's forces in Atlanta adopted this strategy in 1988, for example. Among losing candidates who represent an ideological faction of the party, the public debate may be the major objective anyway since they want publicity for their positions. Often these debates show graphically that the party is split on some matters, and the debate may indicate just how deep the divisions in the party are. The 1968 Democratic National Convention is the classic case in point because that year all of America already knew that the party was split over the Vietnam War. The platform debate engendered an acrimonious exchange over the war between the supporters of Senator Hubert Humphrey and Senator Eugene McCarthy's followers. This floor fight proved to the American public just how deep and bitter the divisions in the Democratic Party had become.

In 1976 incumbent President Gerald Ford should have been in charge of the Republican Party and the convention; on the other hand, many of Ronald Reagan's supporters got onto the platform committee. They forced language into the platform that virtually repudiated much of the Republicans' own foreign policy conducted by Henry Kissinger for both Ford and Nixon. Ford's supporters unhappily and reluctantly acquiesced to this humiliation in the larger interests of party harmony and keeping peace with the Reagan forces.

In 1980 the Democratic convention was dominated by Carter's forces although he had been challenged vigorously in the primaries by Senator Edward Kennedy. Kennedy's faction offered a number of platform amendments that in effect repudiated the Carter administration on jobs, public health care, and foreign policy. In general Carter was able to beat Kennedy on the platform issues although he was forced to give ground on some amendments. This battle also showed how deeply divided the Democrats were in 1980 and how difficult Carter's challenge for the fall campaign would be.

If party factions cannot compromise their differences, then the resulting rift is usually evident in platform debates. If the party cannot heal its differences by the time the convention ends, then its prospects for the general election are much diminished. Thus, the candidates prefer not to have major and open fights over the platform if they can be avoided. Sometimes the platforms adopt the least common denominator on which the various factions can agree, apparently the strategy adopted by the Democrats in 1988. That year the Democrats adopted a platform about 4,500 words long, the shortest in modern history. The Dukakis forces beat the Jackson forces on some issues and compromised with them on others. Both sides professed to be satisfied with the resulting document, although Jackson's forces took some of the issues to the convention floor.

Platforms are important symbolic documents stating the two parties' general position and philosophy plus a wide variety of specific proposals. The two parties ordinarily differ significantly on many of their platform proposals just as their Representatives differ significantly on their votes in Congress. The Republican and Democratic platforms are far from carbon copies of each other in terms of foreign policy, defense policy and spending, and domestic directions such as aid to social security, health care, jobs creation, farm policy, and a variety of other issues. Platforms may not be entirely systematic philosophies or specific blueprints for

programmatic government, but they do deserve serious consideration.

The leading scholar in this field is Gerald Pomper. He and his colleague, Susan Lederman, have done systematic research on the content of the platforms adopted between 1944 and 1976 and the impact of the platforms on subsequent public policy. The platforms are certainly not binding on members of Congress or the President, and they can be ignored as well by other public officeholders. In fact, the nonbinding quality of platforms is one reason that they evoke such skepticism. However, Pomper and Lederman's research indicates that the platforms are more important for the parties and the voters than most people appreciate. In essence Pomper and Lederman argue that the platforms did offer a reasonable number of detailed public policy positions and that these positions differed materially between the two parties. The platforms were also a part of the parties' overall strategies for appealing to the voters in the general election, and the platforms adopted generally advanced those appeals. Finally, the research showed that the parties did take action, once elected to office, to try to redeem a reasonably high percentage of the platform promises. Indeed, almost three-fourths of all platform promises were followed by direct congressional or executive action or by other appropriate steps.

Adopting the platform is one of the most important official functions of the convention, and it is probably more significant an activity than is popularly recognized. The party platform certainly bears a closer relationship to subsequent governmental action than is generally acknowledged.

*The Campaign-Rally Function*

The national conventions are a national political extravaganza. Those planning and participating in the conventions realize that they are first and foremost an opportunity for the parties to celebrate their history and the heroes of their past, to showcase their candidates and their present and future stars, and to appeal to the American people for support in the general elections. Planners regard conventions as exercises in mass persuasion and mass entertainment. The audience are the American voters out there in their homes who must be courted for the November elections. The message centers on the themes of "peace and prosperity" and the party most likely to insure both for the next four years. The mass media, especially television, are the channels through which this pitch is made. Those who plan national conventions regard the entire convention hall as a mammoth television studio. While the center stage is the podium, the entire hall is a backdrop, and often the cameras cut to the floor for interviews and demonstrations or for a simple panning of the crowd searching for colorful hats and signs and interesting faces or delegates listening, talking, or sleeping. The mass media people, who in the modern era now number as many as 15,000 journalists and technicians accredited to any one convention, sometime threaten to overwhelm the whole floor with their sheer numbers. The entire schedule is planned around the television schedule and the desire to put on the best show during prime time. The parties accommodate the media's needs because they understand quite clearly that the journalists are providing the party and their candidates with invaluable air time, print coverage, and access to the voters back home.

The media, in turn, regard the national conventions both as an important story and as an interesting and dramatic political spectacle. Otherwise, they would not devote so many personnel and so much money to convention coverage. It is, after all, a show that occurs only one week every four years; it features political leaders and celebrities from all over the nation, and while some of it is boring, moments of high tension and drama also occur in even the most predictable national convention. (The conventions also occur during the dog days of the summer rerun season in television.) Because of all their news value and entertainment appeal, the national conventions are well covered by the mass media, and the three major networks, between 1960 and 1984, offered "gavel to gavel" (complete) coverage of the national conventions.

In 1984 the networks decided that such coverage was excessive and instead broadcast more limited prime time schedules plus summaries of the daily activities at the conventions. Interruptions of regularly scheduled programs to bring bulletins covering important events as they happened occurred regularly. During convention week the conventions clearly are likely to be the most important news story in the nation, and they are extensively covered by both print and electronic media. The mass media's need for a story complements the parties' needs for favorable news coverage and ultimately for the presentation of their candidates

and their platform. The general election is now really beginning, and the party prospects for November are partially set by the events and tone of the convention. Thus, the conventions are giant campaign rallies, replete with parades, demonstrations, and soaring oratory. In some respects they are the electronic era's equivalent of the torchlight parades and candidate debates of an earlier era, and they may well be the only campaign rally most Americans ever see.

### The Governing-Body Function

The national conventions serve, for one week out of every four years, as the most significant governing body of the national political parties. This exercise in governance is probably the least recognized and least understood official function of the conventions. The national convention delegates are actually meeting to carry on the official business of the national parties. In the intervening three years and fifty-one weeks, this governing body function devolves onto the Democratic National Committee (DNC) and the Republican National Committee (RNC). In addition, the national party chair and the permanent staffs of the DNC and RNC take care of the day-to-day business of the national parties and care for the operation of the two parties' national headquarters in Washington, D.C. Nevertheless, when they are in session the national conventions are the highest official policymaking organs of the national parties.

The national conventions occasionally exercise this authority so as to make significant new policies for the national parties. The Democratic National Convention, though not the Republican, has in recent years delegated some of this authority to other bodies. For instance, the Democratic National Convention in 1968 directed the Democratic National Committee and the national chair to establish a commission to study the rules and to study the delegate selection process and to adopt some changes for the 1972 convention. This resolution led to the establishment of the McGovern-Fraser Commission whose work helped revolutionize the whole presidential selection process. Subsequent Democratic national conventions have each directed the establishment of a commission to study the rules and to recommend changes for the next convention. The national conventions are national party business meetings, where beyond nominating candidates and adopting a platform additional important party business gets dealt with while they are in session.

## Latent Functions of the Conventions

Some experts, following the seminal work of Paul T. David and his associates, have begun to talk about "latent" functions of the conventions. Among these latent functions are the *creation or ratification of a consensus* about the nominees. This consensus is an important consideration for the party's chances in November and for their future in general. Recent conventions have mostly *ratified* a decision that emerged from the primary-caucus season since delegates have simply endorsed the winners of the most support achieved through a combination of primary and caucus/convention victories. If the nominee was evident before the convention gets started, then the party can work on healing old wounds and gearing up for the general election battle. In essence, they can ratify a consensus that already exists or at least one that is emerging by the time of the convention. This is essentially what the Republicans accomplished for George Bush in 1988, although some residual doubt remained in the minds of the supporters' other candidates.

The most obvious example of the consensus ratification function being performed successfully is in the case of the renomination of incumbent Presidents. Eisenhower in 1956, Johnson in 1964, Nixon in 1972, and Reagan in 1984 are the best cases in point. None of these incumbents was seriously challenged in his party, and each was popular at the time of the convention—especially within his own party. Everyone knew who the party's nominee would be. Even if the party had some serious internal strife, the renomination of a popular incumbent President could be a unifying exercise and the party's divisions papered over by them. Eisenhower, Reagan, and Nixon (before Watergate) were unifying symbols in the Republican Party, and they helped dampen the divisions existing among Republicans. The convention could be carefully stage-managed to show the candidate to best advantage and to "position" the candidate for the general election. Naturally this move is by far the most preferable strategic choice for the nominee for November.

If the convention does not have a consensus by the time it starts, then the nominee and his supporters will labor to create a consensus by the end. Ronald Reagan originally faced eight challengers in 1980; by the end of the national convention, however, he was very close to being a consensus choice among the Republicans. On the other hand, Gerald Ford labored mightily to create a consensus on his renomination in the 1976 convention by compromising with Reagan and allowing his delegates to celebrate enthusiastically when Reagan's name was being placed in nomination and otherwise deferring to Reagan on several platform matters. Ford's lack of success in creating a consensus about his nomination then contributed to his defeat in November.

The same problem confronted Carter with Kennedy supporters in the 1980 convention. Neither defeated candidate seemed entirely placated by his successful counterpart's efforts, and both men's support of their party's nominee in the fall campaign was perfunctory. The fact that both cases led to the defeat of incumbent Presidents suggests the importance of healing the party's factional strife before or during the convention. If not consensus, then some kind of *modus vivendi*, some kind of working compromise, must be reached among the factions. Otherwise, the strategic problem is almost insurmountable for the general election. In the modern era only Harry Truman in 1948 has come out of a deeply divided convention to go on to defeat the opposition.

Conventions should be held as much for the strategic purpose of kicking off the general election as for finishing the nomination process. The judicious presidential candidate will regard the conventions in that light and will develop convention strategy with an eye firmly fixed on the general election calendar. One kind of momentum is now coming to an end, and another kind of momentum must be started at this crucial juncture. The candidate whose party is plagued by deep factional strife may have to devote an inordinate amount of attention and effort to securing a first-ballot victory, to the choice of the Vice President, and to the convention as an extraordinarily important objective for the eventual nominee. The general election begins in earnest by the time the convention ends, and by the end of the convention the candidates must position themselves to make as effective an appeal as possible to the wider audience they will face among the general electorate in November. They must keep their own partisans loyal to their candidacy; they try to appeal to more than a majority of Independents if at all possible; and finally they must attract some cross-over voters from the other party if possible. If candidates come out of the national convention with their party reasonably united behind them, and with the image of a reasonably harmonious convention having been held, then they are in a good position for the November general election race.

*Criticism of the Conventions and Possible Change*

The national conventions are an intrinsic component of the overall presidential nomination system, a system that has been subjected to intense scrutiny and considerable criticism since the advent of the new era beginning in 1968. The national conventions have come in for a measure of that criticism, and some have suggested plans for fundamentally changing or even discontinuing the national conventions.

Since 1972 the presidential primaries and the national conventions have been severely criticized. Some critics charge that the primaries have gone too far in reducing the role of party officials and elected public officials and have increased the power of a "presidential elite" (i.e., an unrepresentative group of activists who dominate the primaries and the caucuses). Critics like Jeane Kirkpatrick believe that the conventions should be returned to a more central role in the nominations system, that they should become a "deliberative body" where real decisions are made by the delegates and leaders and where new coalitions can emerge to produce superior candidates from the convention's choices regardless of who won the primaries. These critics, and others, also believe that there is too little "peer review" of the candidates. By that they mean that party officials and public officials (especially members of Congress and governors) know the candidates personally and are in a better position to assess their fitness to be President than are either the delegates or the rank-and-file voters.

One of the manifestations of this strain of criticism has been the advent since 1980 of the "superdelegate" in the Democratic Party: public and party officials (Democratic members of the Senate and of the House of Representatives, and Democratic governors as well as members of the Democratic National Committee and state party chairs) who are given automatic delegate status; they are officially uncommitted to any candidate beforehand and unbound by any primary results. The Republicans have essentially always had superdelegates (although they are not called that) who get their convention seats by way of the state party selections process. The superdelegates plan in the Democratic Party was first promulgated in 1980, when 10 percent of the total delegate seats were reserved for public and party officials, a number raised to 14 percent

four years later. In 1988 the quota for superdelegates was increased again to 15 percent of the total. The superdelegates predominantly backed the winner each year (i.e., Carter in 1980, Mondale in 1984, and Dukakis in 1988). The superdelegate plan was an attempt to introduce more "peer review" or more political insider influence (and elitism if one adopts the views of the critics). Either way, the superdelegates add an element of leadership and elite influence. Superdelegates were especially severely criticized by Jesse Jackson and his followers in 1984 and again in 1988. In addition, Jackson and his forces had little enthusiasm for the lack of "proportional representation" in the selection of many state delegations to the national conventions.

The Democrats used proportional representation rules in 1980, 1984, and 1988; however, they also allowed for several exceptions, which produced "winner-take-all" results at the congressional district level. Under a pure proportional representation system, the percentage of popular votes won by a candidate in each state primary would be directly translated into the same percentage of delegates in the national conventions. Proportional representation systems in the real world never operate with the mathematical precision demanded in the ideal. The question of where to set the flow (i.e., the lowest percentage of popular votes that will get a candidate at least one delegate) is alone enough to distort the results. In most proportional representational systems the rules give the advantage to the candidate who finishes first. Thus, in 1984 and 1988 Jackson's total popular vote in the primaries did not add up to an equal percentage of the national convention delegates. When to that discrepancy was added the fact that most superdelegates supported Mondale in 1984 and Dukakis in 1988, Jackson's criticism of both rules seems understandable.

In a meeting before the opening of the Democratic National Convention in 1988, the Jackson and Dukakis forces agreed to some rules changes for 1992. They will reduce the number of superdelegates by about 40 percent in 1992 and will require proportional representation in all of the states by 1992. This agreement undoubtedly reflected Dukakis's desire to insure party harmony at the national convention and to give Jackson some real victories as a way of insuring the support of Jackson's followers in the general election. His advocacy of these rules changes was consistent with Jackson's overall philosophical objective of shifting power away from the political elites and in the direction of the mass base of the party. In essence, this debate synopsizes the overall struggle over the rules that has gone on in the Democratic Party since 1968.

Other conflicts within both parties reflect on the perceived shortcomings of the national convention and problems inherent to the entire presidential nomination process. One frequently heard criticism is that too much power rests in the hands of the mass media. Media coverage of the primaries has become increasingly important since 1960, and the role of the press in selecting presidential nominees has been subjected to much criticism. Proposals to shorten the campaign season, to limit and control the form and length of political commercials, and to reduce the amounts of money available for political advertising are all attempts to deal with the criticisms raised about the media's role in the primaries and conventions. Most such proposals, in turn, are criticized because of their perceived incompatibility with the First Amendment's guarantees of freedom of speech and press.

Two proposals that have been much debated are variations on the theme of a greater or different role for the presidential primaries. Numerous bills have been introduced in Congress to require either a national primary or to require a series of regional primaries. The national primary concept is relatively simple, and polls consistently show that it is a popular idea with more than a majority of the American people. A national primary would be held on the same day throughout the nation at some time (e.g., July or August of election year) to determine who each party's candidate will be. The analogy would be the way Senators, governors, and others are nominated in the states now. Some such proposals entail a runoff primary if no candidate gets a majority, or as much as 40 percent of the vote in other proposals, on the first round. Some proposals also provide that the parties would then hold a national convention to take care of all of the other official functions such as nominating a vice presidential candidate and adopting a platform. Still other proposals call for the national conventions to be held before the national primary. Whatever the national primary's seeming popular appeal, it has yet to come close to mustering a majority in both houses of Congress.

The regional primary concept is a proposal that has come closer to realization. Senators Walter Mondale and Robert Packwood of Oregon introduced regional primaries bills in the 1970s. Their concept was taken up anew by Senator Alan Dixon of Illinois in 1988. His plan generally calls for the national to be divided into a series of regions, the Northeast, the Midwest, the South, and so on. The states of those regions would then hold primaries on the same day. The order in which the regions would hold their primaries would be determined by lot and would rotate. Supposedly the regional primary would reduce the inordinate impact of such early contests as the Iowa caucuses and the New Hampshire primary. Regional primaries would also allow each geographical region a chance at having a significant impact on the nominations.

One clear step toward the regional primary was taken in 1984 and enhanced in 1988. In 1984 a "Super Tuesday" primary was held in eight states, four of them in the South. In 1988 Super Tuesday was expanded to 20 states where primaries or caucuses were held on the same day. Of these 20, southern states accounted for 11. For this reason the 1988 Super Tuesday elections were often referred to as a "Southern Primary." Several midwestern state officials also debated producing an ad hoc "Midwestern Primary" for either 1988 or 1992. Nevertheless, the 1988 Super Tuesday plan provoked a good deal of criticism. Most vehement were those who said that its objectives of increasing the power of the South in the presidential nomination process and giving an advantage to more moderate candidates in the Democratic Party were not realized.

### Conclusion

Fundamental change in the American electoral system is very difficult to create. Usually basic change results only from serious crises, and other lesser changes are brought about through modest and moderate incremental steps. The American presidential nominating system reflects these fundamental tenets. Basic transitions from one to the next in the four historic eras have resulted from crises of elite legitimacy and mass participation in the electoral system. Not surprisingly these crises focused on the presidency, the most visible and powerful office in the nation. The national conventions are clearly fixtures in the American electoral system. They will probably persist in their basic outline and will only be modified in incremental fashion until the twenty-first century and beyond.

*See also:* Individual presidential and vice presidential candidates, Bosses, Democratic National Committee, Electoral College System, Equal Rights Amendment, Gender Gap, McGovern-Fraser Commission, New Deal Coalition, New Hampshire Primary, Nineteenth Amendment, Republican National Committee, Superdelegates, Vietnam War as a Political Issue, Watergate, Winner-Take-All Systems

*John S. Jackson III*

REFERENCES

Aldrich, John H. 1980. *Before the Convention: Strategies and Choices in Presidential Nomination Campaigns.* Chicago: U. of Chicago Pr.

Barber, James David, ed. 1978. *Race for the Presidency.* Englewood Cliffs, NJ: Prentice-Hall.

Ceaser, James W. 1982. *Reforming the Reforms.* Cambridge, MA: Ballinger.

Cotter, Cornelius, and Bernard Hennessy. 1964. *Politics Without Power.* New York: Atherton.

Crotty, William, and John S. Jackson III. 1985. *Presidential Primaries and Nominations.* Washington: Congressional Quarterly.

David, Paul T., Ralph Goldman, and Richard Bain. 1960. *The Politics of National Party Conventions.* Washington: Brookings.

Davis, James W. 1983. *National Conventions in an Age of Party Reform.* Westport, CT: Greenwood.

Irish, Marian D., and James W. Prothro. 1972. *The Politics of American Democracy.* 5th ed. Englewood Cliffs, NJ: Prentice-Hall.

Kirkpatrick, Jeane J. 1976. *The New Presidential Elite.* New York: Russell Sage.

Marshall, Thomas R. 1981. *Presidential Nominations in a Reform Age.* New York: Praeger.

Miller, Warren E., and M. Kent Jennings. 1986. *Parties in Transition: A Longitudinal Study of Party Elites and Party Supporters.* New York: Russell Sage.

Polsby, Nelson. 1983. *The Consequence of Party Reform.* New York: Oxford U. Pr.

Pomper, Gerald M., and Susan Lederman. 1980. *Elections in America.* 2nd ed. New York: Longman.

Shafer, Byron. 1975. *Quiet Revolution: The Struggle for the Democratic Party and the Shaping of Post-Reform Politics.* New York: Russell Sage.

## Presidential Nominating Politics

An ambitious individual merges his (or, in the future, her) destiny with that of a political party in presidential nominating politics. That much is constant, just as party politics is always a search for power. What varies are the environment of power seeking, the means of power seeking, and the results of power seeking. As these change, the channels of presidential ambition also change.

Beyond individual ambition, the nomination of presidential candidates is one of the major institutions of American politics. As such, it both reflects and affects other American political structures and processes. It is also a different kind of institution, unmentioned in the Constitution. Less tied to legal formalities, the nomination process changes more rapidly, though less obviously, than the overt constitutional system.

The dominant theme in presidential nominating politics is the connection and tension between individual ambition and popular democracy. A single leader will be selected from the millions who belong to a political party. How can this option be accomplished in a continental nation? How can this choice of an ultimate elite be justified in a country dedicated to the equality of all persons? Dealing with these questions involves examining the historical development of presidential nominations, the contemporary process, and possible directions of future change.

### Historical Development

Presidential nominations have evolved through four periods since the onset of American political party competition at the beginning of the nineteenth century. The periods are not always clearly distinct, for change has generally been gradual. The general directions of this evolution have been toward increased participation in the process and toward greater ostensible concern with popular preferences.

The original Constitution had envisaged the nomination of candidates through the Electoral College and the eventual choice of the President in the national House of Representatives. This intention was never realized. The elections of George Washington were unanimous, and the development of parties soon led to various efforts to manipulate the Electoral College for partisan advantage.

The first organized method of presidential nomination was the Congressional Caucus, beginning with the selection of Thomas Jefferson and his Federalist opponents in 1800. To gain the presidency, the emerging political parties needed to unite their efforts. In a large nation with limited means of communication, the caucus of the party's leaders in the Senate and House of Representatives provided a simple means to confer national endorsement and political legitimacy on a single candidate.

The emerging Republican Party successfully used the caucus to nominate and elect Jefferson, James Madison, and James Monroe. By the end of the one-party "Era of Good Feelings," however, the party was fracturing. The Congressional Caucus itself was under attack as an elitist and overcentralized method of selection, out of tune with the emerging populist democracy of the United States. The attack was magnified by the frustrations of four candidates, led by Andrew Jackson, who lost the 1824 nomination of the caucus to William Crawford, the last of the Republican "Virginia Dynasty."

A new system was needed, one that combined mass democracy, federalism, and national party unity. By 1840 the national party convention had been institutionalized, maintaining its formal structure to the present. In its original form, convention delegates were representatives of the state parties and were distributed among these parties in proportion to the electoral votes of their states. Reflecting a decentralized and federalist political structure, the convention was a conclave of autonomous parties. They met every four years to negotiate a compact, whose terms included a party platform, the distribution of patronage and favors and, most vitally, nominees for President and Vice President.

The nineteenth-century party convention was a powerful, decision-making institution. State delegations were united, often in support of their own "favorite son." Even incumbent Presidents could not be certain of victory, and multiple ballots were common, especially in the Democratic Party, which required a two-thirds vote for nomination. Through promises, bargains, and elaborate strategies, the classic convention negotiated nominations as eminent as those of Abraham Lincoln (1860) and Woodrow Wilson (1912) and as deplorable as those of James Buchanan (1856) and Warren Harding (1920).

Over a century, the convention system slowly changed in response to the increasing centralization of the nation and the increasing emphasis on mass democracy. Apportionment of delegates was altered to give greater representation to those states that provided greater support for each party in actual elections. In the Progressive period at the beginning of the twentieth century, direct primary elections came to be used in many states for the selection of delegates, potentially undermining the dominant role of the party organizations. The Democratic Party, in 1936, abolished its requirement of a two-thirds majority, thereby eliminating the veto power of the southern states.

The accumulation of these changes gradually brought the process of presidential nominations into a third period, clearly evident by the significant conventions of 1952. In this period, which ended in 1968, presidential nominations still were made by party elites gathered in the national convention, but their decisions were increasingly affected by outside pressures. Party leaders had always sought to nominate popular candidates, but had relied on their intuition or rough rules of "availability" to gauge the appeal of individuals. Now, three new indicators of popular support became available: television, polls, and primaries.

Television reached half of the nation's households in 1952 and soon became the most used and most trusted source of news for the mass public. This new medium allowed candidates to circumvent party leaders and to bring their campaigns directly to the voters. Furthermore, the obtrusive eye of the television camera reduced the opportunity for private bargaining among politicians. Public opinion polls, a second influence, provided a reliable measure of popular support, one outside the control or the expertise of party leaders. Evidence of the polls' importance could be found in a major scholarly study, which argued that presidential nominations were usually won by the candidate who stood first in opinion polls at the beginning of the presidential year. Third, presidential primaries assumed a new importance after 1952. That year, they contributed both to the withdrawal of Democratic President Harry Truman and to the victory of Republican Dwight Eisenhower.

The new mechanisms limited the autonomy of the nominating conventions. Despite the misgivings of party leaders, John Kennedy won the Democratic nomination in 1960 after waging a personal campaign that used victories in seven primaries to demonstrate the ability of a Catholic to win votes among Protestants. Four years later, in the Republican Party, Barry Goldwater led a successful insurgency of ideological conservatives to wrest control of the party from its traditional moderate establishment.

The fourth and contemporary period in presidential nominating politics began after 1968 when the Democratic Party, divided by the national struggles over civil rights and the Vietnam War, began a series of institutional changes. Every four years since that time, the party has appointed a national commission to revise its rules. Republicans have been far less active, but their party has still been affected by changes in state law initiated by Democrats, by national legislation, and by major constitutional decisions of the U.S. Supreme Court.

### Contemporary Presidential Nominations

In the past, parties nominated candidates; today, candidates win party nominations. The party is no longer a plebeian army that selects a leader from its own ranks. The party has become an arena in which individual gladiators fight one another to gain the applause of the crowd.

The traditional nominating process induced ambitious individuals to create coalitions among established politicians. Candidates emphasized their experience in public office rather than their future policy goals. The nominating process today places more emphasis on the ability of candidates to win direct public support on the basis of their declared issue positions. In the past, the system worked to the advantage of candidates already holding positions of power that could affect convention bargaining. At present, the system works to the advantage of those who have the time and resources to develop a national mass following.

This change is demonstrated by the different character of nominees. Fewer are experienced insiders such as, in 1932, incumbent President Herbert Hoover and New York governor Franklin Roosevelt. Insurgent figures are more likely to be successful, such as Kennedy, Goldwater, Jimmy Carter in 1976, and Ronald Reagan in 1980. Sitting governors of the largest states, once the most likely candidates, are disadvantaged: none was nominated between Adlai Stevenson in 1952 and Michael Dukakis in 1988. The vice presidency, once a target of derision, has become a major source of presidential ambition, most recently exemplified by George Bush in 1988. Incumbent Presidents remain powerful but are now subject to ideological challenges, such as those mounted by Eugene McCarthy in 1968, Reagan in 1976, and Edward Kennedy in 1980.

Contemporary presidential nominations are characteristically marked by the focus on individual candidates and their organizations, the displacement of state party elites by national and media elites, and the importance of strategy and sequencing.

The contemporary stress on individual campaigning has been promoted by the relationships among the three new influences of television, polls, and primaries. By its very nature, television focuses on individuals rather than on abstractions like parties. Polls open the nominating process beyond party leaders, providing regular data on the relative popularity of candidates and on "trial heats" between possible candidates of the major parties. Primaries are the most important legal expression of the focus on individual candidates, for they provide the opportunity for these candidates to win delegates to the national conventions even if party leaders are unsupportive.

These influences interact to magnify their separate effects. Television networks sponsor major opinion polls and conduct national debates among the candidates during the series of primary elections. Candidates' standing in the polls will influence the coverage they receive in the media and affect interpretations of primary votes. Then again, the effects of the primaries are enhanced by mass media coverage and by the tendency of public opinion, as reported in polls, to change in line with primary election outcomes.

In this environment, candidates pursue a simple goal: winning a majority of the delegates to their party's nominating convention. Any such simple goal, however, actually involves many complexities. Although the party nomination is a national decision, it is the cumulative result of decisions reached at local levels through procedures that differ considerably among the states. Furthermore, these state decisions are not independent of one another. Each is affected by earlier decisions in the campaign sequence and by national influences such as the media and polls. Finally, procedures differ between the two major parties.

Some delegates come to the convention *ex officio*, by virtue of the party or public office they hold. In the Democratic Party since 1984, such "superdelegates" constituted about 15 percent of the total body in 1988 but will make up a smaller proportion in the future. A larger number are chosen, most commonly in the smaller states, through caucuses and local meetings open to all party members. In a series of meetings, delegates are selected successively to county or district, state, and national conventions.

Since the onset of party reform in 1968, the largest proportion of delegates are chosen in direct presidential primaries. In 1988 representatives to the national conventions selected through primaries in three-fourths of the states, added up to some two-thirds of all delegates. Twenty years earlier, by contrast, primaries were held in only a third of the states and selected only a minority of the delegates.[1]

Presidential candidates are involved in the selection of delegates, whatever the detailed procedure in a particular state. Legally uncommitted "superdelegates" are solicited for support, and sympathetic activists are urged to attend party caucuses. In the direct primaries, prospective delegates are usually required to declare their candidate preference. In contrast, past party rules permitted, and even encouraged, the selection of uncommitted delegates who were often controlled by party leaders seeking to maintain their maneuverability at the national convention.

This involvement of candidates is facilitated by rules governing the division of delegates. Democratic Party rules forbid the use of "winner-take-all" primaries, instead insisting on some form of proportional division of delegates among the competing candidates. Able to achieve some gain in almost any state, candidates are thereby encouraged to contest most states. Republicans generally allow state parties to make their own rules; the GOP does use the "winner-take-all" system. Most important is California, where the leader in the primary will win the entire delegation of the largest state.

National legislation has also encouraged the individualist trend. In the aftermath of the Watergate scandals, the federal government provided for government subsidy of presidential candidates. Candidates must meet a modest threshold of contributions from private donors.[2] Afterward, the national treasury matches each contribution up to $250, facilitating the entrance of many candidates. The law, moreover, virtually requires involvement in primary elections, because candidates lose their funding if their vote falls below 10 percent in two successive primaries.

Supreme Court interpretation of federal law has had a similar individualist influence. In *Buckley v. Valeo* (1976), the Court declared unconstitutional any limit on a candidate's personal campaign expenditures, but it upheld limits on the total spending of a candidate if that candidate accepted government subsidies. It also upheld limits on contributions, thereby requiring candidates to engage in mass financing of their efforts.

The contemporary system of presidential nominations is a national system, even though it reflects its origins in a decentralized federal party structure. National party rules are binding on state organizations and, according to the Supreme Court, may even override contrary state laws.[3] Financing is provided by the national government, which uses this power of the purse to impose limits both on total spending and on the allocation of expenditures among the states.

This national nominating system also requires skills and expertise different from those of the traditional party convention. When presidential selection came through the creation of a coalition of party leaders, personal and bargaining skills were most important. Today, skills of impersonal communication and effectiveness in influencing mass opinion are emphasized. The dominant advisers in a candidate's entourage are no longer state party "bosses" but opinion pollsters, media specialists, and independent political consultants.

In the modern period, the nominations process goes through a series of stages—from "early days" of multiple candidates to "initial contests" that reduce the field through a "mist clearing" in which attention comes to focus on as few as two or three possibilities. By the final stage (the convention) the nominating decision is likely to be foreclosed.

Following this sequence, individual candidates and their personal organizations develop a national campaign strategy in which the states are not the prizes of political combat but only the tactical sites of battle. Of particular importance are the early contests in Iowa and New Hampshire.

In Iowa, caucuses of party members are held early in February, while New Hampshire holds the first presidential primary one or two weeks later. These contests provide the first opportunity to test electoral sentiment toward the candidates. The winners—or even candidates who exceed earlier expectations—are likely to receive disproportionate attention by the press, by voters in other states, and by financial contributors.

As seen in the campaigns of Carter in 1976, George Bush in 1980, and Gary Hart in 1984, success in these first contests can bring a candidate the important, intangible asset of "momentum." The 1988 experience was somewhat different. The winning candidates in Iowa were unable to capitalize on their victories, but the New Hampshire leaders, George Bush and Michael Dukakis, did go on to win their party nominations. Contests then tend to focus successively on the South, the northern and midwestern industrial states and, in early June, California and New Jersey.

The focus on Iowa and New Hampshire has been criticized as giving undue attention to two unusual states that, especially among Democrats, are unrepresentative of the general party electorate. Clearly the amount of press coverage is disproportionately large in comparison to the number of delegates elected. However, because the number of voters is small, candidates of limited reputation and with limited funds can use these early contests to test their appeal and to broaden the field.

The importance of early success has affected the overall political calendar. Presidential aspirants announce their intentions as long as two years before the election, lengthening the period of the overt campaign. At the same time, many states, seeking to gain more attention from candidates and the media, have advanced the dates of their primaries to the first months of the election year. The result has been the "front-loading" of the process, with more than half of the delegates effectively chosen by the middle of March, typically before voter interest in the presidential nomination develops.

Reflecting these changes, an effort to change nominating strategies was made by southern Democratic state parties in 1988. Twenty states, including the entire South, scheduled their primaries or caucuses for the same date, March 8, "Super Tuesday." By creating a virtual regional primary and a large prize of delegates, they hoped that the victorious candidates would be either from the region or supportive of southern values.

As was the case so often in the past, however, the actual effects of the change were quite different from the intentions of its designers. Only one major southern candidate emerged, but the chief beneficiaries of the system were two liberal northern Democrats, Jesse Jackson and Michael Dukakis. The southern primary had far greater impact among Republicans, assuring the nomination of Vice President Bush.

Earlier beginnings of campaigns also lead to earlier conclusions. No convention since 1952 has required more than a single ballot to choose its presidential candidate. Indeed, the winner of the nomination has been clear in advance of the party meeting in almost all recent cases; in 1988, the two winners were known earlier than at any time in American history.

An old political phenomenon has taken on a new guise. In the traditional convention, candidates close to a majority often sealed their victories by launching a "bandwagon." In the current system, momentum is similarly critical: candidates who do well in early contests can benefit from the accumulation of support after initial primary victories. The effect is particularly likely in multicandidate races, while a contest between only two leading aspirants is more likely to be prolonged.

### Evaluation and Future Directions

The contemporary nominating system has both defenders and critics. More open and more subject to direct popular influence through television, polls and primaries, the process at first seems to accord with American traditions of direct democracy. With over 30 million voters participating in these contests, the selection of presidential nominees appears to rest on a broad popular base. By contrast, selection by party leaders (as in other nations or in the traditional brokered conventions) seems to be undemocratic.

Questions have been raised by political analysts about such assumptions. Voters in primaries have been described as not representative of the total electorate or even of party adherents. They are, instead, more educated and more socially advantaged, and tend to be more extreme in their political views. The result, some argue, is that those nominated have limited appeal to the more moderate voters in the general election.

Critics of contemporary nominating processes are more common. The emphasis on individual campaigning for popular support, exemplified by the spread of primaries, is seen as leading to the domination of conventions by delegates who are inexperienced, unrepresentative of their party rank and file, relatively extreme in their issue positions, and of uncertain loyalty to their parties. The resulting nominees are faulted as "outsiders" with limited electoral appeal. Moreover, their governing skills are often judged inadequate because they have not been adequately assessed through a process of "peer review" by experienced politicians.

More-recent scholarship disputes many of these conclusions. Detailed studies of recent convention delegates conclude that activists remain highly loyal to their party and have considerable political experience. While these new party elites show coherent and distinct ideological positions, they also appear to emphasize electoral success over ideological appeals. Analyses of voting during presidential primaries also shows reasonable popular attention to relevant factors of issues and candidate appraisal.

Continuing efforts to change the presidential nominating system are likely in the future. Longstanding public support exists for a national presidential primary, a position advocated long ago by Woodrow Wilson. In contrast, some support is found for restoration of the powers of the national convention and its imposition of the political tests of "peer review." One means toward both goals would be a preprimary convention, like the ones convened now in many states. Candidates receiving a stated minimum of votes would then contest a single national primary.

Drastic change is unlikely. Major alterations would require support from the very political figures, the parties' presidential nominees, who benefit from the present system. Only a drastic breakdown in the system, such as the unlikely emergence of a new political movement, is likely to induce major innovation. More probable are incremental adaptations, such as an enhanced role for party officials within the present system or more experimentation in methods of delegate selection among state organizations.

National conventions are likely to remain a distinct feature of American politics. They are important, at least, as means of party governance, as a well-publicized and costless national campaign rallies, and as courts of last resort when individual campaigning has not resolved the contest for party leadership. Even with shrunken power, they retain the legitimacy earned over a century and a half. A nation that reveres its formal Constitution will also not lightly discard these informal but traditional institutions.

*See also:* Individual presidential candidates, Bosses, *Buckley v.Valeo*, *Cousins v. Wigoda*, Electoral College System, Federalist Party, Party Platforms and Platform Writing, Political Patronage, Superdelegates, Vietnam War as a Political Issue, Watergate, Winner-Take-All Systems

*Gerald M. Pomper*

## Notes

1 Michigan was the only large state to choose delegates through caucuses in 1988. The difficulties encountered by both parties in that year has already led the legislature to establish a direct primary for the next presidential election.

2 The minimum requirement is $100,000, with at least $5,000 collected from at least 20 states in donations up to $250.

3 *Cousins v. Wigoda*, 419 U.S. 477 (1975); *Democratic Party of U.S. v. La Follette*, 67 L.Ed. 2nd 82 (1981). Also see *Buckley v. Valeo*, 424 U.S. 1 (1976).

## REFERENCES

Abramowitz, Alan I., and Walter J. Stone. 1984. *Nomination Politics*. New York: Praeger.

Adams, William C. 1987. "As New Hampshire Goes. . . ." In Gary Orren and Nelson Polsby, eds. *Media and Momentum*. Chatham, NJ: Chatham House.

Aldrich, John H. 1980. *Before the Convention*. Chicago: U. of Chicago Pr.

Bartels, Larry M. 1987. "Candidate Choice and the Dynamics of the Presidential Nominating Process." 31 *American Journal of Political Science* 1.

———. 1988. *Presidential Primaries and the Dynamics of Public Choice*. Princeton: Princeton U. Pr.

Bryce, James Lord. 1914. *The American Commonwealth*. 3rd ed. New York: Macmillan.

Ceaser, James W. 1979. *Presidential Selection*. Princeton: Princeton U. Pr.

Congressional Quarterly. 1987. "Rules of the Road." 45 *Congressional Quarterly Weekly Report* 1987.

David, Paul, T, Ralph M. Goldman, and Richard C. Bain. 1960. *The Politics of National Party Conventions*. Washington: Brookings.

Hess, Stephen. 1987. "Why Great Men Are Not Chosen Presidents: Lord Bryce Revisited." In James Reichley, ed. *Elections American Style*. Washington: Brookings.

Keech, William R., and Donald R. Matthews. 1976. *The Party's Choice*. Washington: Brookings.

Keeter, Scott, and Cliff Zukin. 1983. *Uninformed Choice*. New York: Praeger.

Kessel, John H. 1988. *Presidential Campaign Politics*. 3rd ed. Homewood, IL: Dorsey.

Kirkpatrick, Jeane. 1976. *The New Presidential Elite*. New York: Russell Sage.

Lengle, James I. 1981. *Representation and Presidential Primaries*. Westport, CT: Greenwood.

Marshall, Thomas R. 1981. *Presidential Nominations in a Reform Age*. New York: Praeger.

McCormick, Richard P. 1982. *The Presidential Game*. New York: Oxford U. Pr.

Miller, Warren E., and M. Kent Jennings. 1986. *Parties in Transition*. New York: Russell Sage.

Polsby, Nelson. 1983. *Consequences of Party Reform*. New York: Oxford U. Pr.

Pomper, Gerald M. 1966. *Nominating the President*. Rev. ed. New York: Norton.

———, with Susan S. Lederman. 1980. *Elections in America*. 2nd ed. New York: Longman.

Price, David E. 1984. *Bringing Back the Parties*. Washington: Congressional Quarterly.

Ranney, Austin. 1972. "Turnout and Representation in Presidential Primary Elections." 66 *American Political Science Review* 21.

Rapoport, Ronald B., Alan I. Abramowitz, and John McGlennon. 1986. *The Life of the Parties*. Lexington: U. Pr. of Kentucky.

Reiter, Howard L. 1985. *Selecting the President*. Philadelphia: U. of Pennsylvania Press.

Rubin, Richard L. 1981. *Press, Party and the Presidency*. New York: Norton.

Sabato, Larry J. 1981. *The Rise of Political Consultants*. New York: Basic Books.

Shafer, Byron. 1983. *Quiet Revolution.* New York: Russell Sage.

Stanley, Harold W., and Charles D. Hadley. 1987. "The Southern Presidential Primary." 17 *Publius* 83.

## Presidential PACs

In 1966 Richard Nixon prepared the way for his 1968 presidential nomination campaign by barnstorming the country on behalf of Republican candidates. The political IOUs he collected provided a foundation for his successful bid for the Republican nomination.

In the wake of the Republican defeat at the polls in 1976, several Republican hopefuls, with their eyes on 1980, adopted Nixon's strategy. The potential candidates, however, added a new element to Nixon's barnstorming. In addition to crisscrossing the country on behalf of other Republicans, they made direct or in-kind contributions to a variety of federal, state, and local candidates and party organizations. The vehicles through which they raised and contributed funds were political action committees (PACs), which until then had been used largely by corporations, labor unions, trade associations, membership groups, and ideological groups to bring their influence to bear on the political process.

Long before the 1980 presidential campaign officially commenced, four Republican hopefuls—Ronald Reagan, George Bush, John Connally, and Robert Dole—formed PACs, ostensibly to raise and spend money on behalf of favored candidates and party committees. The PACs undoubtedly were helpful to the candidates who received support from them, but they also were instrumental in furthering the ambitions of the prospective presidential candidates who sponsored them.

Under the Federal Election Campaign Act (FECA) the PACs were allowed to contribute as much as $5,000 per election to a House or Senate candidate and to give as much to state and local candidates and organizations as applicable state laws permitted. If the PAC sponsors had contributed as individuals, or if their PACs had not qualified as multicandidate committees under the law, they would have been able to contribute no more than $1,000 to each federal candidate per election. Moreover, a supporter of a potential presidential candidate was permitted to contribute a maximum of $1,000 to the candidate once he or she filed for candidacy with the Federal Election Commission (FEC) but could contribute as much as $5,000 to the potential candidate's PAC. Finally, none of the money received and spent by the PACs counted against the overall and individual state spending limits that would apply once those presidential hopefuls who intended to accept public matching funds actually announced their candidacies. Thus, the PACs allowed their sponsors to gain the favor and support of federal, state, and local candidates and state and local party organizations through the direct and in-kind contributions that the PACs made. They permitted the sponsors to travel extensively throughout the country, attracting media attention and increasing their name recognition among party activists and the electorate in general. Finally, they enabled their sponsors to build donor lists that would be useful once their official presidential campaigns began.

In 1981 several potential Democratic candidates for the 1984 presidential nomination followed the lead of their 1980 Republican counterparts and established PACs of their own to fund their preannouncement activities and build their contributor bases. Foremost among them were former Vice President Walter Mondale and Senator Edward M. Kennedy of Massachusetts, then thought to be the front-runners for their party's 1984 nomination. According to FEC reports, during the 1981–1982 election cycle, Kennedy's PAC, the Fund for a Democratic Majority (FDM), raised $2.3 million and spent $2.2 million, only $176,209 of it in contributions to federal candidates. The small portion of funds that the PAC actually contributed to candidates—typical of presidential PACs—indicates that the PAC was not created primarily to influence congressional elections. Following a successful Senate reelection campaign in 1982, Kennedy withdrew from consideration as a presidential candidate. His PAC, however, continued to function. During the 1983–1984 election cycle, the FDM raised about $3.6 million and spent almost $3 million, including $202,925 in contributions to congressional candidates.

Federal Election Commission reports credit Mondale's PAC, the Committee for the Future of America (CFA), with having raised almost $2.2 million during the 1981–1982 election cycle. The committee spent all but $20,000 of what it raised, contributing $228,326 of the total amount to federal candidates. A report issued by the committee itself claimed that the committee had raised and spent slightly more than the FEC records indicate: nearly $2.4 million. The CFA reported having spent 54 percent of its expenditures on fundraising, claiming high fundraising start-up costs. It spent 34 percent on campaign-related activities and 14 percent on overhead. Among campaign-related expenditures listed in the CFA report were travel and logistical assistance for Mondale and his wife, Joan, so they could campaign personally for more than 225 Democratic candidates and organizations; contributions of more than $380,000 to 185 federal, state, and local candidates; advice and research for candidates; and purchase of radio time for broadcasts by Mondale over the 1982 Labor Day weekend as well as production of 55 radio and television spots on social security and unemployment that were distributed free to 33 House candidates and included personalized statements about the candidate by the former Vice President. The CFA continued to operate for a time during 1983 and, according to FEC reports, raised $319,416. The committee was disbanded shortly after Mondale formally announced his intention to seek the Democratic nomination.

In fact Mondale did more than merely copy what potential Republican presidential candidates had done four years earlier. He added a new dimension to presidential PAC fundraising, one that involved the use of "soft money," that is, money raised outside the restraints of federal law but spent on activities intended to influence federal election results. In addition to the CFA, which was registered with the FEC, four state-level PACs were formed to raise and spend money in ways that would be helpful to the prospective presidential candidate. These PACs were able to collect contributions under the laws of the individual states in which the PACs were registered. Often these laws allowed higher individual and PAC contributions than the federal law and permitted contributions from sources that would be prohibited by federal law.

Once the existence of the state-level PACs became a matter of public knowledge, the Mondale presidential campaign issued a memorandum stating that the CFA's four state accounts had received a total of about $395,000: $150,475 in corporate contributions, $160,275 from labor unions, and $84,250 from individuals and groups that had already given the maximum permitted under federal law to the CFA's federal account. Of the total amount, $101,813 was contributed to state and local campaigns. The remainder of the money raised by the state-level PACs was used to cover a portion of such costs as CFA staff salaries and operations allocated to the PACs under a formula that was not disclosed. When issuing the memorandum on the financial activity of the state-level PACs, a Mondale campaign official, formerly a CFA executive director, declared that all four state committees had complied with the campaign contribution, spending, and disclosure requirements of the states and localities in which they were registered.

No other 1984 presidential hopefuls established PACs that achieved the same level of financial activity as those of Kennedy and Mondale. Among Democrats Senator Ernest Hollings of South Carolina established the Citizens for a Competitive America, which, according to the FEC, raised $198,060 in the 1981–1982 election cycle but contributed only $6,000 to federal candidates. Ohio Senator John Glenn's National Council on Public Policy raised $49,826 in 1982 and gave $20,388 to federal candidates.

As the incumbent, President Ronald Reagan had other means of accomplishing the purposes his potential Democratic challengers had sought to achieve by establishing their own PACs. Three Republicans mentioned in press reports as possible presidential candidates in the event that Reagan decided not to seek reelection also established PACs. Senate Majority Leader Howard Baker's Republican Majority Fund (RMF) reported raising $6.4 million during the 1981–1982 and 1983–1984 election cycles and contributing about $871,000 of it directly to federal candidates. Kansas Senator Robert Dole's Campaign America, which Dole had established prior to his 1980 bid for the Republican nomination, continued in operation during Reagan's first term. The PAC raised about $1.5 million from 1981 through 1984 and contributed $560,000 to federal candidates. New York Congressman Jack Kemp's Campaign for Prosperity raised almost $2.4 million during the same period and gave about $321,000 of it to federal candidates.

In preparation for the 1988 presidential nominating contests, several candidates from both parties once again chose PACs as vehicles to prepare their ways in the selection process. Four Republican PACs—those sponsored by Howard Baker, Robert Dole, Jack Kemp, and Lewis Lehrman, who had unsuccessfully sought the governorship of New York in 1982—functioned throughout the 1983–1984 and 1985–1986 cycles. So, too, did the PAC sponsored by Senator Edward Kennedy. Although Vice President George Bush did not initiate his PAC until May 1985, he had used another PAC to fund activities before his official 1980 campaign for the Republican nomination. Democratic candidate Congressman Richard Gephardt of Missouri founded a PAC in 1985 to further his political ambitions, as did Democratic rival Governor Bruce Babbitt of Arizona and Republican hopeful General Alexander Haig, who had served as Ronald Reagan's first Secretary of State. In 1986 Democratic Senator Joseph Biden of Delaware founded a PAC just before his announcement of candidacy.

In early 1986 the FEC issued two advisory opinions on presidential PACs, the first appearing to restrict their range of permissible activities and the second to expand it. In response to a request from Howard Baker's Republican Majority Fund, the FEC ruled five to one that money spent by the RMF to establish steering committees to encourage Baker to seek the nomination would be considered gifts to a testing-the-waters fund that the potential candidate had established and thus could not exceed the $5,000 multicandidate contribution limit. Other activities that would be considered in-kind gifts to the testing fund under the advisory, and thus would be subject to the contribution limit, included travel costs for public appearances by Baker or his representatives at regional party meetings that featured potential 1988 presidential candidates; travel costs for Baker to meet with party leaders in states with early primaries and caucuses; certain RMF administrative expenses; and certain types of newsletter solicitations of contributions. The RMF had sought the advisory in an effort to limit the range of options open to other candidates sponsoring PACs, particularly George Bush, whose PAC already had raised more money than any other presidential PAC. The FEC's response, however, was carefully phrased to restrict the application of the opinion to the activities specifically outlined in the RMF's request.

In March 1986 the commission ruled four to two in response to an advisory opinion request submitted by Bush's Fund for America's Future, permitting the fund to make expenditures to recruit, assist, and donate funds to candidates seeking election as precinct delegates in an August 1986 Michigan GOP contest. The commission concluded that the precinct delegates would not vote directly for national nominating convention delegates but would only choose delegates to the state party's convention. These state delegates would in turn elect national convention delegates. Therefore, such expenditures would not of themselves "constitute contribu-

tions or expenditures for the purpose of influencing the Vice President's or any other candidate's nomination, or election to federal office, nor require allocation to any candidacy for federal office nor trigger any such candidacy." The commission also voted to permit the fund to spend money without attributing it to any candidate's campaign on such activities as travel and appearances by the Vice President, publications and solicitations of funds, and the establishment of steering committees to involve Republican activists in the fund's activities. The commission noted that Bush was not a candidate for office and had not established a testing-the-waters fund.

*See also:* Howard H. Baker, Jr., George Bush, Robert Dole, Election of 1968, Federal Election Commission, Walter Mondale, Richard M. Nixon, Political Action Committees, Ronald Reagan

*Brian A. Haggerty*

REFERENCES

Alexander, Herbert E., with Brian A. Haggerty. 1983. *Financing the 1980 Election.* Lexington, MA: Heath.

———. 1987. *Financing the 1984 Election.* Lexington, MA: Heath.

## Presidential Party Leadership in Congress

Decentralization characterizes the American political system—a reality that creates centrifugal forces afflicting the relationship between the President and Congress. The White House requires a means of countering the natural tendency toward conflict between the executive and legislative branches. The only institution that has the potential to elicit cooperation between both ends of Pennsylvania Avenue on a systematic basis is the political party.

Thus, leading his party in Congress is inevitably one of the most important tasks of the chief executive. No matter what other resources a President may have at his disposal, he remains highly dependent upon his party to move his legislative program. Representatives and Senators of the President's party almost always form the nucleus of coalitions supporting his proposals and provide him, year in and year out, considerably more support than do members of the opposition party.

### The Ties That Bind

Shared party affiliation is more than a superficial characteristic that the President and some members of Congress hold in common. For most Senators and Representatives, shared party affiliation with the President creates a psychological bond, based on personal loyalties or emotional commitment to their party and their party leader; a desire to avoid embarrassing "their" administration, thus hurting their chances for reelection; and a basic distrust of the opposition party—a bond that produces a proclivity for supporting the White House. Of equal importance, this attitude strongly influences the context within which the President attempts to lead his party.

A President may find it easiest to achieve party unity behind his program if his party regains control of one or both houses of Congress at the time of his election. Many new members may feel a sense of gratification for what they perceive as the President's coattails. Moreover, the prospect of exercising the power to govern may provide a catalyst for party loyalty while the loss of power may temporarily demoralize the opposition party.

Reinforcing the pull of party ties and easing the burden of party leadership is policy agreement. Members of the same party typically share many policy preferences, and they often have similar electoral coalitions supporting them and their values.

*Obstacles to Party Unity*

Despite these advantages, all Presidents experience substantial slippage in party cohesion in Congress. Presidents can count on their own party members for support no more than two-thirds of the time, even on key votes. Obstacles to unity often linger within the President's party in Congress, competing with the bonds of party and shared policy preferences. They force him to adopt an activist orientation toward party leadership and to devote his efforts to conversion as much as to mobilization of members of his party.

The primary obstacle to party cohesion in support of the President is the lack of consensus among his party's members on policies, especially if the President is a Democrat. This diversity of views often reflects the diversity of constituencies represented by party members. The frequent defection from support of Democratic Presidents by the southern Democrats, or "boll weevils," is one of the most prominent features of American politics. When constituency opinion and the President's proposals conflict, members of Congress are more likely to vote with their constituencies, to whom they must return for reelection. If the President is not popular in their constituencies, congressional

party members may avoid identifying too closely with the White House, and vice versa.

A shift in the status of party members may present another obstacle to party unity. Just as regaining power may encourage party unity, having to share it may strain intraparty relations. When a party that has had a majority in Congress manages to regain the White House, committee and floor leaders of that party typically will be less influential, because they will be expected to take their lead on major issues from the President. This perceived dependence may cause tensions within the party and make party discipline more difficult.

If the President's party has just regained the presidency but remains a minority in Congress, then its members need to adjust from their past stance as the opposition minority to one of a "governing" minority. This change is not always easily accomplished, however, as Presidents learn upon taking office.

Further difficulties could stem from the fact that the President may not be the natural leader of his party. Indeed, as in the case of Jimmy Carter, the President may have campaigned against the party establishment and not identified with whatever party program existed. Such a new President may arrive in Washington amid an atmosphere of hostility and suspicion that is not conducive to intraparty harmony. Moreover, a President in Carter's situation may be burdened with moving against the tide of his party and its historic practices, rhetoric, and ideology.

*Leading the Party*

The President's relationship with his party's leaders in Congress is a delicate one. Although the leaders are predisposed to support the President's policies and typically work closely with the White House, they are also free to oppose him or lend only symbolic support, which may or may not be effective. Furthermore, party leaders are not in a position to reward or discipline members of Congress on the basis of presidential support.

To create goodwill among congressional party members, the White House provides them with many services and amenities. Although this is to the President's advantage, and may earn him a fair hearing and the benefit of the doubt in some instances, party members consider it their right to receive benefits from the White House and are unlikely to be especially responsive to the President as a result.

Just as the President can lure with the carrot, he can also wield the stick by withholding favors. Yet this measure rarely is taken. Despite the resources available to the President, if members of his party wish to oppose the White House, then the President can do little to stop them. Parties are highly decentralized; national party leaders do not control those aspects of politics that are vital concerns (i.e., nominations and elections) to members of Congress. Members of Congress are largely self-recruited, gain their party's nominations by their own efforts and not the party's, and provide most of the money and organizational support needed for their own elections. Presidents can do little to influence negatively the results of these activities.

*George C. Edwards III*

REFERENCES

Bond, Jon R., and Richard Fleisher. 1990. *The President in the Legislative Arena.* Chicago: U. of Chicago Pr.

Edwards, George C., III. 1986. "The Two Presidencies: A Reevaluation." 14 *American Politics Quarterly* 247.

———. 1989. *At the Margins.* New Haven: Yale U. Pr.

## President's Commission on Campaign Costs

When President John F. Kennedy established the Commission on Campaign Costs in December 1961, he charged its members with recommending able ways to finance presidential general election campaigns and to reduce the costs of running for the presidency. By restricting the commission's jurisdiction to presidential and vice presidential campaigns, Kennedy was pointing an example but not telling Congress how to regulate its own campaigns. Later, when he submitted legislative proposals based on the commission's report, he invited Congress to extend the proposals to all federal offices.

Submitted to the President in April 1962, the commission's unanimous report was heralded by Kennedy at a news conference. Among those who endorsed the report were the chairmen of the Republican and Democratic national committees, former Presidents Harry Truman and Dwight Eisenhower, and Richard Nixon, Adlai Stevenson, and Thomas Dewey—all the living presidential candidates of both major parties in the last quarter century.

The commission stated its belief in a strongly organized and effectively functioning two-party system; in widespread citizen participation in the political system; and in the desirability of voluntary, private action wherever such effort is sufficient to meet electoral needs. The commis-

sion sought to increase public confidence in the ways that campaigns are financed and to instill public respect for the legal system that regulates political finance.

Five of the twelve recommendations in the commission's report were major. They advocated

- That individuals, business, labor unions, and private organizations be encouraged to take part in and to make expenditures for voluntary bipartisan political activities, such as registration and fundraising drives, and that the reasonable costs of such activities be declared deductible for tax purposes;

- That tax incentives be tried for an experimental period extending over two presidential campaigns, allowing either (a) that individual political contributors be given a credit against federal income tax of 50 percent of contributions, up to a maximum of $100 in credits per year; or (b) that contributors be permitted to claim the full amount of their contributions as a deduction from taxable income up to a maximum of $1,000 per tax return per year. The only contributions eligible for these benefits would be gifts to the national committee of a party (on the ballot in ten or more states) or to a single state political committee designated by such a national committee in each state;

- That the unrealistic and unenforceable ceilings on individual contributions and on total expenditures by political committees be abolished, and that an effective system of public disclosure be instituted instead, requiring that the principal sources and uses of money in presidential campaigns be reported to a Registry of Election Finance. The proposed system would have required that periodic reports be submitted by all political parties, committees, candidates, and other campaign groups raising or spending $2,500 or more on behalf of federal candidates, showing a total income and expenditure, and itemizing certain contributions and expenditures;

- That the Congress provide funds for the reasonable and necessary costs of preparing and installing in office new administrations during the transition between the election and inauguration of a new President;

- That a temporary suspension of Section 315 of the Federal Communications Act be enacted, as in 1960, to permit broadcasters to make their facilities available on an equal basis to the nominees of the major political parties for President and Vice President without the legal requirement to do the same for all candidates for those offices.

Taken as a whole, the report presented a model and comprehensive program for reforming the financing of the political system, covering not only federal legislative remedies but also bipartisan activities, certain party practices, and state actions. The purpose was more immediate: to get things moving in the field by establishing a comprehensive program of reform of political finance. To that date, many isolated proposals had been offered, but none was comprehensive or related part-to-part for specific elections. In that sense, the report accomplished its purpose.

In revised form, each of these five proposals was enacted. Yet it took a decade before election reform started, in comprehensive form, with the enactment of the Federal Election Campaign Act of 1971 and the Revenue Act of 1971. These laws went further than the President's Commission suggested by providing a wider series of reforms, including publicly funded presidential campaigns. Nevertheless, the recommendations of the President's Commission on Campaign Costs stand as the beginning of the modern election reform era.

*See also:* Democratic National Committee, Thomas Dewey, Dwight D. Eisenhower, Federal Campaign Act of 1971, John F. Kennedy, Richard M. Nixon, Republican National Committee, Adlai Stevenson II, Harry S Truman

*Herbert E. Alexander*

## President's Commission on Registration and Voting Participation

In 1963 President John F. Kennedy established the President's Commission on Registration and Voting Participation for the purpose of determining reasons for low voter turnout in U.S. elections. Chaired by Richard M. Scammon, Kennedy's director of the Census Bureau, the 11-member commission produced 21 recommendations for the revision of laws and administrative practices that the commission deemed "unreasonable, unfair, and outmoded."

Voter registration reforms included no more than six months' residence for state elections, no more than thirty days' residence for local elections, no residency requirement necessary to cast a vote for President, and simplified absentee registration procedures. Registration should remain open as close to election day as possible.

Proposed changes in voter qualifications included lowering the voting age to 18 and the abolition of literacy tests, this last recommendation drawing the only dissents on the commission. The majority noted the racially discriminatory administration of literacy tests and the ready availability of information sources other than the print media. Dissenters, conversely, opposed discriminatory application of the literacy requirement but argued its validity in ensuring minimal standards of knowledge and understanding.

Other recommendations included declaring election day a half-day legal holiday and keeping polling places open throughout the day until at least 9:00 P.M.

Although addressed to state and local officials, several recommendations were implemented through federal action in response to the civil rights movement emerging at the time of the commission's study and report. Other proposals continue to be debated today.

To combat voluntary nonvoting, the commission advocated register-and-vote campaigns, revision of elementary and secondary school curricula on government, and the spread of effective two-party competition.

*See also:* John F. Kennedy, Literacy Tests

*Douglas I. Hodgkin*

REFERENCES

*Report of the President's Commission on Registration and Voting Participation.* 1963. Washington: Government Printing Office.

## Ivy Baker Priest (1905–1975)

Moderate Republican leader and U.S. Treasurer under President Dwight Eisenhower. Ivy Baker Priest began her political career by helping her mother in efforts to obtain wooden sidewalks for the streets of her childhood home, Bingham, Utah. Both mother and daughter would continue their involvement in politics, with the elder Baker's support in an election becoming highly prized by local candidates.

As a young adult, Ivy Baker Priest joined the Young Republicans in the 1930s. Priest ascended to the presidency of the Utah State Republican Organization where she served from 1934 to 1936 and from 1936 until 1940 she served as director of the Young Republican Western States Organization.

Priest played a great role in the establishment of the first minimum wage law for women working in Utah. In addition, she advocated and envisioned a greater involvement of women in governmental positions, including elective office. Priest herself served as a delegate of the National Committee on Women and, in 1948, attended the national Republican Party convention. Priest also unsuccessfully sought a seat in the U.S. House of Representatives for Utah's Second District in 1950.

After her congressional defeat, Priest continued to be active in Republican politics. She led the "Young Turk" forces that campaigned for Dwight Eisenhower in 1952 before he received the Republican nomination for the presidency. Later in that year, she was appointed assistant in charge of the women's division of the Republican National Committee.

She went on to serve under President Eisenhower as U.S. treasurer. As a consequence of holding that position from 1953 until 1961, her signature appeared on more than $62 billion of paper currency.

Following her stint as a national political figure, Priest was elected treasurer of California, the first woman elected to a statewide office in California. She was reelected to this post in 1970 and served until 1974, when she retired due to ill health.

See also: Dwight D. Eisenhower, Young Republicans

*Reagan Robbins*

REFERENCES

Priest, Ivy Baker. 1958. *Green Grows Ivy*. New York: McGraw-Hill.

## Progressive National Committee

An independent campaign committee established during the 1936 presidential campaign to organize Progressives on behalf of Franklin D. Roosevelt's reelection. Many Progressives supported Roosevelt but wished to remain nonpartisan. Joining the Progressive National Committee enabled them to campaign for Roosevelt without affiliating with the Democratic Party. The committee reflected the President's overall campaign strategy in 1936: to recruit traditionally non-Democratic groups through the formation of several auxiliary and nonparty committees. In 1932 a similar National Progressive League proved successful in promoting Roosevelt's election, and many of those leaders, including Senators Robert M. La Follette, Jr., and George Norris, were members of the Progressive National Committee.

The committee conducted an extensive propaganda campaign through the organization of a large Speakers Bureau and through separate correspondence, publicity, and youth divisions. Speakers delivered major addresses at rallies and over the radio on issues of importance to Progressives such as labor relief, social welfare, agricultural policy, conservation, and the regulation of businesses, banks, and utilities. Nearly 1 million pieces of literature were distributed, while the youth division alone organized committees in many key states and on over 70 college campuses. The committee raised nearly $56,000 to finance their activities, not an inconsiderable sum in Depression-torn 1936.

The Progressive National Committee proved effective in uniting Progressives behind Roosevelt in 1936, and by doing so, it eliminated much of the enthusiasm for a Progressive third-party movement in the immediate future. The committee demonstrated one of the many ways Roosevelt welded together his diverse coalition of supporters.

See also: Election of 1936, Robert La Follette, Jr., George Norris, Franklin D. Roosevelt

*Thomas T. Spencer*

REFERENCES

Feinman, Ronald L. 1981. *Twilight of Progressivism: The Western Republican Senators and the New Deal.* Baltimore: Johns Hopkins U. Pr.

Graham, Otis L., Jr. 1967. *An Encore for Reform.* New York: Oxford U. Pr.

McCoy, Donald R. 1956. "The Progressive National Committee of 1936." 9 *Western Political Quarterly* 454.

Spencer, Thomas T. 1976. "Democratic Auxiliary and Non-Party Groups in the Election of 1936." Ph.D. dissertation, U. of Notre Dame.

## Progressive Party

The genesis for a left-wing third party was the conservative forcing of liberal Vice President Henry Wallace from the Democratic ticket in 1944. Liberals were further dismayed by the anti-Soviet orientation of Harry Truman's administration (e.g., the Truman Doctrine to contain communism abroad) and its initial coolness toward liberal domestic programs and organized labor. The Progressive Citizens of America (PCA) emerged as a coalition of the Congress of Industrial Organizations (CIO) and the Arts, Sciences, and Professions political action committees in 1946, and they drafted Wallace for President in 1948. The PCA had chapters in 25 states and conducted studies and seminars for political workers. The PCA also raised funds and by November was on the ballot in 45 states. The PCA set a record of nearly $3 spent for each vote cast for Wallace, and most of this money came from small contributors collected at paid-admission, voluntary-contribution rallies.

The Progressive Party convention met in Philadelphia on July 23, 1948, and nominated Wallace for President and singing cowboy and Democratic U.S. Senator from Idaho Glen Taylor for Vice President. Among the 3,240 delegates and alternates were many women, Blacks, and young people but few professional politicians. The platform urged world government and understanding between the superpowers and opposed the Marshall Plan, the Truman Doctrine, and racial segregation. The convention's defeat of the Vermont Resolution that stated that the party did not intend to give blanket endorsement to the foreign policy of any nation (such as Russia) led to press charges that the Progressive Party was Communist dominated. The party's chances were hurt as well by Truman's announcement of the Fair Deal, by increasing Soviet intransigence, and by charges that it was splitting the liberal vote. Wallace's party was also hurt by such organizational failures as the absence of a sound machine at the ward and precinct levels, factionalism in some state organizations, the absence of a working labor organization, and ballot accessibility problems.

After electoral defeat in 1948, most liberals including Taylor reestablished their major party ties. Wallace, increasingly disillusioned with Soviet intransigence and leftist Progressive tactics that alienated moderates, resigned from the party after it opposed American entry into the Korean conflict. The party disappeared after its little-known candidates received only 140,023 votes in the 1952 presidential election. The Progressive Party nevertheless receives some credit for Truman's move to the left domestically (the Fair Deal). Wallace also receives praise for risking violence and egg throwers by speaking to integrated audiences in the South.

*See also:* AFL-CIO COPE, Elections of 1944 and 1948, Harry S Truman, Henry Wallace

*Stephen D. Shaffer*

REFERENCES

MacDougall, Curtis D. 1965. *Gideon's Army.* New York: Marzani and Munsell.

Schlesinger, Arthur M., ed. 1971. *History of American Presidential Elections, 1789–1968.* New York: Chelsea House.

Schmidt, Karl. 1960. *Henry A. Wallace: Quixotic Crusade 1948.* Syracuse: Syracuse U. Pr.

Yarnell, Allen. 1974. *Democrats and Progressives: The 1948 Presidential Election as a Test of Postwar Liberalism.* Berkeley: U. of California Pr.

## Progressive Party of Idaho

An example of economic protest politics and state-level radicalism that emerged in jurisdictions outside the Northeast and the South in the 1920s and 1930s, the Progressive Party of Idaho (1920–1928) came into being in part because of the diffusion to Idaho of electoral tactics and protest ideology generated during the rise of the North Dakota Nonpartisan League. An offshoot of the League, the National Nonpartisan League, assigned a minister and former master of the North Dakota State Grange, Ray McKaig, to organize an Idaho Nonpartisan League. As in North Dakota and other states, the Idaho league would "bore from within" one of the regular parties, thus leapfrogging the conservative elements in the party into gubernatorial and legislative power. McKaig's ministry to Idaho was successful enough to launch a League candidate in 1918 for governor, who, running as a Democrat, gained 40 percent of the vote. In response, the 1919 Idaho legislature radically revised Idaho electoral law in order to force the organization of a third party.

In 1920 a League candidate ran as an Independent, winning 20 percent of the vote, and two League candidates ran as Progressive Party candidates for Congress. In 1922, 1924, and 1926, the Progressive Party, now Idaho's second party, vigorously contested statewide elections. But in 1928, shortly before the elections, the Progressive Party disbanded because of a collective decision among the Progressive Party's tiny cadre of competent politicians to fuse with the regular parties and because no talented, middle-level activists seemed able and willing to take their place.

In the 1930s a few remaining Progressive Party activists, hoping to copy the Minnesota Farmer-Labor Party, sought to broker an alliance between Idaho farm and labor leaders. But Idaho Grange and Idaho Federation of Labor leaders declined to invest their resources in an Idaho Farmer-Labor Party.

*See also:* Minnesota Farmer-Labor Party, National Nonpartisan League, North Dakota Nonpartisan League, Progressive Party

*Richard M. Valelly*

REFERENCES

Martin, Boyd A. 1947. *The Direct Primary in Idaho.* Stanford, CA: Stanford U. Pr.

## Progressive Party of Illinois

This political party emerged in 1912 as a reaction to William Howard Taft's renomination for President and died four years later when Theodore Roosevelt declined to become a candidate for President on the national Progressive Party ticket. Insurgent Chicago Republicans formed the nucleus of the Illinois Progressive Party. Its leaders included former political reporter and lawyer Harold L. Ickes; fellow attorney Donald Richberg; Charles R. Crane, wealthy grandson of the founder of the Crane Company; Medill McCormick of the Chicago *Tribune* and his wife, Ruth; Harvard-educated assistant U.S. District Attorney Fletcher Dobyns; and University of Chicago political scientist and city alderman Charles E. Merriam.

At its first state convention in the summer of 1912 the Illinois Progressive Party nominated prominent popular Republican state senator Frank Funk for governor. Although nationally the Progressive Party fared poorly in the general election, in Illinois the party won 24 seats in the lower house of the state legislature where it succeeded in passing a public utilities bill and enacting women's suffrage. Two years later the party nominated Chicago settlement worker and labor organizer Raymond Robins for U.S. Senator. Robins lost and only three party nominees made it to the state legislature. The Illinois party completely collapsed by 1916 when most party leaders followed Roosevelt's lead and returned to the Republican fold, endorsing its presidential nominee, Charles Evans Hughes.

*See also:* Theodore Roosevelt, William Howard Taft

*Nicholas C. Burckel*

REFERENCES

McCarthy, Michael P. 1977. "The Short, Unhappy Life of the Illinois Progressive Party." 6 *Chicago History* 2.

## Progressivism (circa 1890s to 1917)

This reform movement arose in the wake of rapid industrialization and urbanization and was an attempt to bring order to a nearly chaotic society, culminating in major innovation to almost every facet of public and private life in the United States. Progressives sought to improve the political system, the economy, and the standards of day-to-day living, thereby restoring economic competition and equality of opportunity. In the words of progressive Senator Robert M. La Follette, "The supreme issue, involving all the others, is the encroachment of the powerful few upon the rights of the many."

Owing to the somewhat contradictory nature of the various branches within progressivism, controversy continues today over the membership and goals of this extremely diverse movement. It is viewed by some as primarily an urban middle-class operation designed as a kind of protection against being squeezed out of power by an ever-growing working class on the one hand and the increasing power of big business on the other. Others claim the source of the movement to have been the workers themselves, while still others credit business leadership. Progressives have alternately been called altruistic reformers bent on improving the quality of American life (especially for the disadvantaged), and selfish, condescending meddlers bent more on social control than social reform.

Whatever their motivations, progressives tackled any number of the nation's ills, with varying degrees of success. Although progressives accepted industrial capitalism, they were outraged by some of its consequences. Convinced of their ability to improve these conditions, progressives became active in government reform, notably the destruction of political machines in favor of a more genuine democracy. They employed such measures as direct primaries and elections, and the adaptation of the initiative, the referendum, and the recall. As with most movements within progressivism, this transformation of politics and government originated on the local level and only gradually spread into state and federal arenas.

The great trusts, so powerful as to be immune to the discipline of the individual consumer, were attacked and broken down via regulation and tariff reform. A variety of taxation reforms were introduced in an effort to distribute the nation's wealth more evenly. Additional specific legislative achievements encompassed such issues as child labor, industrial working conditions, workers' compensation, and women's suffrage.

Following an era of relatively passive chief executives serving as administrators rather than policy shapers and leaders, progressivism marked the return of such strong, active presidents as Theodore Roosevelt and Woodrow Wilson. It was also characterized by strong faith in the ability and skills of professionals to provide answers to society's ills. Doctors made great strides in public health, while settlement houses arose to provide urban dwellers with education in addition to cultural and social activities.

Educators dramatically improved techniques and standards even as a variety of experts generated economic and business regulations and guidelines.

The end of the progressive movement is as ill defined as its beginnings. Many date its demise to American entry into World War I, marking the diversion of the public's attention from domestic to international concerns. Clearly, in the disillusionment of the war's aftermath, most Americans lost the supreme confidence, optimism, and zeal so vital to the progressive spirit. Progressivism has been viewed by some as an inevitable failure because of its impossibly idealistic and naive beliefs and goals. Others view progressives as casualties of their own success, for having removed the worst of society's excesses, the movement became decreasingly unified and directed. Although greatly fragmented, progressivism persisted in a variety of forms beyond the 1920s, and its emphasis on the responsibility of government is credited as the precursor and foundation for the New Deal of the 1930s.

*See also:* Robert La Follette, New Deal, Theodore Roosevelt, Woodrow Wilson

*Nancy C. Unger*

REFERENCES

Hays, Samuel P. 1967. "Political Parties and the Community-Society Continuum." In William Nisbet Chambers and Walter Dean Burnham, eds. *The American Party Systems: Stages of Political Development.* New York: Oxford U. Pr.

Link, Arthur S., and Richard L. McCormick. 1983. *Progressivism.* Arlington Heights, IL: Harlan Davidson.

McCraw, Thomas. 1974. "The Legacy of the Progressive Era." In Lewis Gould, ed. *The Progressive Era.* Syracuse: Syracuse U. Pr.

# Prohibition

Oklahoma's homegrown storyteller was supposed to have said, "Oklahomans will vote dry as long as they can stagger to the polls to vote." A better verified quotation has the homespun humorist actually saying, "The South [Oklahoma] is dry and will vote dry. That is, everybody that is sober enough to stagger to the polls will." Will Rogers summed up the attitude of many who favored prohibition in public despite their own private behavior. But Will Rogers was wrong. The state of voted itself wet, not once but twice, in 1959 and 1984. And, although Oklahoma offers perhaps the most colorful story of prohibition, controversy over the legal sale of alcohol for drinking certainly is not limited to the Sooner State.

The politics of alcohol consumption has long been an area of intense political interest and fierce local battles. On the national level it is the only issue that not only has resulted in an amendment to the U.S. Constitution but also has suffered the ignominy of having that amendment repealed. On the state level it has swept before it the political future of not only candidates for various offices but also platforms of major parties as well. Herbert Asbury's *The Great Illusion* credits Lyman Beecher with suggesting legal measures to save the drinker in 1826 and General James Appleton of Massachusetts with being the first advocate of national prohibition (rather than temperance) in 1832. While much of the conflict took place within legislative chambers, the transference of the battle to the ballot box was not unusual. Charles Mertz reports that Maine was the first state to adopt a state prohibition law—first by statutory means by the state legislature in 1858; and later in 1884 by constitutional means involving a statewide vote, with 46,972 voting for the measure and 23,811 voting against. But Maine was not the first state to place the measure on a ballot. According to Asbury, prohibition was submitted to the people of Illinois at a special election on June 4, 1855. Abraham Lincoln drafted the original legislation, and Stephen A. Douglas campaigned against it, coupling it with abolitionism. The measure lost in Illinois by approximately 14,000 votes. Even so, in the nineteenth-century American context, prohibition was considered a "progressive" issue along with abolition and woman suffrage.

This coupling of the issue with other emotion-packed agendas caused prohibition to be more than just a stating of preference at the polls. Asbury points to temperance leader Justin Edwards who defined the issue as one of morality and sin, laying the groundwork for temperance to become first a religious issue and then prohibition. The issue lends itself to a natural progression, not only from temperance to prohibition but also from local option to statewide prohibition to amending the national Constitution. As Peter Odegard so carefully documents in his history of the Anti-Saloon League, the issue kept escalating as more and more state action from a higher and higher level of government seemed the only logical solution to making the noble experiment work. Prohibition proved ineffective because alcoholic beverages were always available from the next city, county, state or, eventually, nation. The

American people showed themselves to be resilient to efforts to save their bodies and souls for their own good when that salvation was imposed by a secular government and supported by what was perceived as a vocal but small minority.

Meanwhile, many a vicious battle over prohibition was fought at the polls on the state level. Charles Mertz lists 17 states that adopted prohibition as a constitutional amendment by popular vote between 1858 and 1917. The total popular vote was 1,967,337 for and 1,437,402 against, with the difference between the two sides 529,935 votes. In seven more states citizens voted to adopt the measure between 1917 and 1919. The total popular vote for the period 1917–1919 was 2,937,580 for prohibition and 2,274,863 against with a winning margin of 662,717 (12.7 percent) for the dry forces.

While it took a world war to add prohibition as the Eighteenth Amendment to the U.S. Constitution, scholars generally agree that a major economic depression was necessary to knock it out of the same document. On the way to a national constitutional amendment, the road was paved with states taking the same action after a vote of the people. Should the dry forces lose, they would be back again until their side prevailed. After the repeal of the Eighteenth Amendment, dry states fought a rear guard action with the wets continually forcing the issue to a vote until at last their side prevailed. Thus, for well over a century, the issue of alcoholic beverage and the role of the state in enforcing morals was decided by the people of various states in popular elections. It should be noted that in most cases, the law forbade the sale or transport of the evil brew, not necessarily its consumption.

Oklahoma is a good state to use as a case study. That state saw more than ten statewide votes on the various aspects of prohibition, beginning with statehood when the measure was adopted as part of the state constitution. The number varies depending on how certain issues are considered to be "wet" or not. Proponents of legalizing sales of alcohol failed at the polls time and again until finally, in 1959, these wets won but with only a halfway measure. The 1959 law allowed for the establishment of privately owned package stores. The same day, on a separate question, the electorate voted down a measure allowing county option for the retail sale of liquor by the drink. The promise of revenue for state government was one of the reasons for the eventual success of legal booze in Okla-

homa. But it was not until 1984 that State Question 563 was passed, giving Oklahoma's counties the option to approve or disapprove the retail sale of liquor by the drink. Until 1984 imbibers in theory brought their own alcoholic beverages to private clubs or drank 3.2 (low alcohol) beer in establishments policed by the Tax Commission. While regulations still govern the sale of alcoholic beverage in Oklahoma (retail stores are closed on election days, for example), the state can now be considered officially "wet." As one wit put it, "Before the vote everyone was happy. The drys had the law and the wets had the booze. After the vote, the wets had the law and the booze dried up."

The politics of prohibition, however, played a major role in the political life of Oklahoma. More than one race for governor of Oklahoma was decided on the basis of the candidate's public preference for or against the legalization of alcohol-related practices. Likewise, the fundamentalist churches, especially the Southern Baptists, played a considerable role in state politics as a major pressure and lobbying group. With the wet vote of 1984, commonly accepted wisdom was that their political power had been broken. The winning argument in the 1984 races seems not so much to have been revenue for the state (as in 1959) but for projecting a "modern" image for Oklahoma in the quest for economic development.

See also: Abolition Movement, Anti-Saloon League, Women's Christian Temperance Union

*Thomas H. Clapper*

REFERENCES

Asbury, Herbert. 1950. *The Great Illusion: An Informal History of Prohibition.* Garden City, NY: Doubleday.

Franklin, Jimmie Lewis. 1969. "The Fight for Prohibition in Oklahoma Territory." 49 *Social Science Quarterly* 876.

———. 1971. *Born Sober: Prohibition in Oklahoma, 1907–1959.* Norman: U. of Oklahoma Pr.

Magleby, David B. 1988. "Taking the Initiative: Direct Legislation and Direct Democracy in the 1980s." 21 *PS* 600.

Mertz, Charles. 1931. *The Dry Decade.* New York: Doubleday, Doran.

Moore, W. John. 1988. "Election Day Lawmaking." 20 *National Journal* 2296.

Odegard, Peter H. 1928. *Pressure Politics: The Story of the Anti-Saloon League.* New York: Columbia U. Pr.

Rorabaugh, William H. 1981. *The Alcoholic Republic: An American Tradition.* New York: Oxford U. Pr.

Sterling, Dwayne Wesley. 1965. "The Repeal of Prohibition in Oklahoma." MA thesis, U. of Oklahoma.

Walker, Robert, and Samuel C. Patterson. 1961. "The Political Attitudes of Oklahoma Newspapers: The

Prohibition Issue." 24 *Southwestern Social Science Quarterly* 271.

## Prohibition Party

America's third oldest (and oldest third) political party. Organized around the enduring moral crusade against alcohol, the Prohibition Party's antecedents extend back to independently formed state parties of the 1850s, when the concern over alcohol coincided with opposition to slavery and the rise of the Republican Party. At the end of the Civil War, Prohibitionists turned their full attention to temperance. The first national party convention was held in Chicago in 1869, but its first presidential nominee could only garner a paltry 5,607 votes in 1872. Yet the party's lengthy platform was progressive for its time, including as it did advocacy of universal women's suffrage, civil service reform, and direct election of Senators. Subsequent platforms called for inheritance and income tax legislation, child labor regulations, and pensions for the elderly. The party's high-water year came in 1892, when its presidential candidate received 271,000 votes (2.25 percent).

The party's history can be divided into three periods. From its founding until 1896, the party was dominated by the "broad-gaugers," who emphasized many issues besides temperance; they were more pragmatic in their political approach. Aside from issue diversity, this period was marked by numerous attempts to join forces with the growing Populist Party. Despite many attempts at fusion in several states, the effort ultimately failed because of the Populists' refusal to accept an uncompromising Prohibition plank. The second period was marked by the ascendance of "narrow-gaugers," who stressed adherence to the Prohibition issue alone. The victory of the narrow-gaugers ruptured the party's 1896 convention, and many broad-gaugers (reportedly the majority of the party) joined the Democrats, dropped out of politics, or formed a competing group the National Party (also known as the Free Silver Prohibition Party). Narrow-gauge dominance was also marked by a turn to the political right, fully evident by 1912. During this period, national attention shifted away from the party to axe-wielding Carry Nation, the Women's Christian Temperance Union (WCTU), and the Anti-Saloon League (ASL). Animosity was intense between the Prohibition Party and these organizations, especially because they demonstrated that citizens could be influential in politics without leaving the major parties. Historians generally agree that the Prohibition Party bore no responsibility for the passage of the Eighteenth Amendment. During the Prohibition era, the party occupied itself by working against "wet" candidates and pushing for stronger administration of Prohibition.

The third stage of this evolution, from 1932 to the present, marks the party's return to the Prohibition crusade in the aftermath of the repeal of prohibition in 1933. By the 1950s, the party had built its appeal on distrust of government, advocacy of states' rights, decentralization, and calls for greater free enterprise. Party control thus reverted back to broad-gaugers. In the 1970s and 1980s, the party emphasized nationalism, economic conservatism (e.g., return to the gold standard), and criticisms of national conciliation toward nations like China. Efforts to signal the party's broader interests were reflected in the party's name change in the 1976 and 1980 elections to the New Statesman Party, although consequent voter confusion prompted a return to the original name.

*See also:* Anti-Saloon League, Election of 1976, Populist Party, Prohibition, Slavery, States' Rights Party, Third Parties in American Elections, Women's Christian Temperance Union

*Robert J. Spitzer*

REFERENCES

Blocker, Jack S., Jr. 1976. *Retreat from Reform: The Prohibition Movement in the United States, 1880–1913.* Westport, CT: Greenwood.

Gusfield, Joseph R. 1963. *Symbolic Crusade: Status Politics and the American Temperance Movement.* Urbana: U. of Illinois Pr.

Storms, Roger. 1972. *Partisan Prophets: A History of the Prohibition Party, 1854–1972.* Denver, CO: National Prohibition Foundation.

## Proportional Representation

Proportional representation is used by most democracies to elect their officials. The United States, Great Britain, and a few other former British colonies are the only democracies to rely on plurality elections. Plurality elections are used mostly in conjunction with single-member political districts; one person is elected from a geographic area, such as a U.S. House of Representatives district, and the candidate receiving the most votes wins. Proportional representation often is used in conjunction with multimember districts and party slates. For instance, five Representatives may be elected from one district. If a party receives 40 percent of the vote, then two of its candidates would be elected.

Proportional representation has been used in a few local elections in the U.S, such as city council races where a number of candidates will be selected in at-large elections. Proportional representation is applied by the single transferable vote, or Hare, system. Under this system, voters order their preferences by rank (e.g., first choice, second choice, etc.). A minimum number of votes needed to be elected is established, and candidates receiving more than this number of first place votes are elected. Excess votes for these candidates (i.e., the number of votes received above the minimum needed to be elected) are redistributed according to second place votes. The candidate receiving the fewest first place votes may also be eliminated and the votes for him redistributed according to second place votes. The transferring of votes is continued until the full complement of candidates is chosen.

Since 1900, approximately 25 municipalities, for rather short periods of time, have used proportional representation to select their city councils. Cincinnati, however, used proportional representation for over 30 years (1925–1956). At present only Cambridge, Massachusetts, uses proportional representation for city council elections.

Two semiproportional systems have also been used in the United States. Under "cumulative voting," a voter casts multiple votes. In an election district where three officials are to be elected, a voter would have three votes that he or she could all cast for the same candidate, two for one candidate and one for another, or one vote for each candidate. Cumulative voting was used to elect the Illinois legislature from 1880 to 1980. Another semiproportional method is the limited voting system, in which a voter also has multiple votes to cast but fewer votes than officials to be elected. Limited voting has been used at some time by a half dozen cities, including New York, Boston, Indianapolis, and Philadelphia.

The most publicized use of proportional representation in the United States today is in conjunction with presidential primaries and caucuses. Proportional representation is used to distribute convention delegate seats according to voter preferences. For instance, in the 1984 Massachusetts presidential primary Gary Hart received 39 percent of the vote, Walter Mondale 26 percent, and George McGovern 21 percent. As the result of these vote totals, 47 delegates supporting Hart were chosen, 32 delegates supporting Mondale, and 21 supporting McGovern.

The use of proportional representation in presidential primaries has been controversial. It was recommended by the first two Democratic reform commissions, the McGovern-Fraser and Mikulski commissions, but later commissions weakened this prescription allowing for loophole primaries. Opponents to proportional representation felt that it diluted the strength of a state's delegation at the national convention. Supporters of proportional representation felt that it more accurately reflected voter preferences. Recent arguments have centered on an appropriate cut-off point below which a candidate would receive no convention delegates.

*See also:* Gary Hart, Jesse Jackson, George McGovern, McGovern-Fraser Commission, Walter Mondale

*Barbara Norrander*

REFERENCES

Grofman, Bernard. 1985. "Criteria for Districting: A Social Science Perspective." 33 *UCLA Law Review* 77.

Weaver, Leon. 1986. "The Rise, Decline and Resurrection of Proportional Representation in Local Governments in the United States." In Bernard Grofman and Arend Lijphart, eds. *Electoral Laws and Their Political Consequences.* New York: Agathon.

## William Proxmire (1915– )

Maverick five-term Democratic Senator from Wisconsin. Edward William Proxmire's frugal campaigning and aggressive political style distinguished his career in the United States Senate. Proxmire typically declined campaign contributions, particularly political action committee (PAC) money. His campaign expenditures were exceptionally modest. Accepting no PAC money in either 1976 or 1982, Proxmire spent a total of $697 and $112 respectively. In both contests the Wisconsin Democrat handily defeated his opponent, receiving over 60 percent of the vote.

Much of Proxmire's electoral support likely owed to his high visibility in his home state. He could frequently be found greeting his Wisconsin constituents outside football games or at local industries. He persistently mocked the elite Washington establishment, thus perpetuating an image of solidarity with the people of Wisconsin.

His behavior on Capitol Hill also enhanced his reputation as a bold, energetic, and independent politician. First elected in 1957 to fill the vacant seat caused by the death of Joseph McCarthy, Proxmire quickly shocked fellow Senators, first by accusing Senate Majority Leader

Lyndon Johnson of exercising excessive power and then by filibustering against President Dwight Eisenhower's nominee to the Federal Power Commission. Proxmire also became one of the most fiscally conservative Democrats in federal spending, with the notable exception of dairy price supports. His monthly "golden fleece" award for wasteful federal spending attracted national attention.

Proxmire's political career began in 1950 when he was elected to the Wisconsin State Assembly. He was later unsuccessful in two consecutive campaigns for governor. However, Proxmire gained a reputation for his outspoken criticism of Joseph McCarthy and government incompetence. Proxmire's 1957 Senate victory over the Republican Walter J. Kohler, the man who had twice defeated him for governor, was a stunning upset.

After completing the remainder of McCarthy's term Proxmire was reelected to the United States Senate in 1958 and again in 1964, 1970, 1976, and 1982. He was chair of the Senate Banking, Housing and Urban Affairs Committee, and a member of the Senate Appropriations Committee, and of the Joint Economic Committee. He retired from his Senate seat in 1989.

*See also:* Joseph McCarthy, Political Action Committees

*Paul Haskell Zernicke*

REFERENCES

Clark, Joseph S., et al. 1963. *The Senate Establishment.* New York: Hill and Wang.

Huitt, Ralph K. 1969. "The Outsider in the Senate: An Alternative Role." In Ralph K. Huitt and Robert L. Peabody, eds. *Congress: Two Decades of Analysis.* New York: Harper & Row.

## Joseph Pulitzer (1847–1911)

Journalistic giant who helped instigate the Spanish-American War. Joseph Pulitzer built a newspaper empire that exerted tremendous influence on American politics from the late 1880s until his death. He was born in Hungary and left home at the age of 17 in search of a military adventure, enlisting in the American Union Army in 1864. He joined with Carl Schurz and other Missouri Republicans to form the Liberal Republican Party in 1871, and he became a lifelong Democrat following the defeat of Horace Greeley for President in 1872.

Pulitzer started his empire by buying two failing papers and merging them to form the *St. Louis Post-Dispatch* in 1878. He moved to New York City and bought the *World* in 1883, turning it into one of the leading Democratic voices in the country. Poor health and declining eyesight forced him to run his newspapers through memorandums for much of his life, but he kept tight control over their policies and content. Pulitzer took particular trouble to champion the cause of the workingman and the downtrodden in his newspapers.

The purchase of the *New York Journal* by William Randolph Hearst in 1895 touched off a circulation war between the two publishers, and their competition helped fuel public opinion to start the Spanish-American War. Pulitzer met and befriended Theodore Roosevelt during the 1890s, but the *World* was indicted in 1908 for criminally libeling President Roosevelt and five others. The case was eventually dropped. At his death, Pulitzer endowed the Columbia School of Journalism and the prestigious journalism/writing awards that bear his name.

*See also:* Liberal Republican Party, Theodore Roosevelt

*Richard Digby-Junger*

REFERENCES

Juergens, George. 1966. *Joseph Pulitzer and the New York World.* Princeton: Princeton U. Pr.

Rammelkamp, Julian S. 1967. *Pulitzer's Post-Dispatch, 1878–1883.* Princeton: Princeton U. Pr.

Reynolds, William R. 1950. "Joseph Pulitzer." Ph.D. dissertation, Columbia University.

Swanberg, W. A. 1967. *Pulitzer.* New York: Scribner's.

# Q

## Matthew S. Quay (1833–1904)

United States Senator and Republican "boss" of Pennsylvania. Matthew Stanley Quay played an important role in the presidential election of 1888. Having worked with other party leaders to nominate Benjamin Harrison as the Republican candidate, Quay headed the campaign efforts in his position as chairman of the Republican National Committee. With the aid of strenuous organization and over a million dollars in contributions from businessmen, Harrison carried the doubtful states of New York and Indiana and won in the Electoral College, although he lost the popular vote by a narrow margin. Quay had a cryptic comment afterward: "[Harrison] will never know how close a number of men were compelled to approach the gates of the penitentiary to make him president." This innuendo may suggest actual corruption in the campaign or merely the zealous pursuit of tactics considered acceptable in the Gilded Age.

Quay spent most of his adult life in politics and was respected, if not admired, for his aggressively successful pursuit of power. He skillfully maintained control of Pennsylvania politics from 1887 until 1904 despite incessant opposition from local bosses in Philadelphia and Pittsburgh. As a member of the U.S. Senate, he took a special interest in tariff legislation. He was instrumental in passage of the McKinley Tariff of 1890, but he did not otherwise have a notable legislative career. Quay remained influential in Republican Party matters throughout the 1890s, working closely with Thomas C. Platt of New York and Marcus A. Hanna of Ohio. As a member of the Senate Old Guard he opposed the Progressive tendencies of President Theodore Roosevelt. His short physical stature, coolness under fire, and superb mastery of men and events earned him the title "Napoleon in politics."

*See also:* Election of 1888, Marcus A. (Mark) Hanna, Benjamin Harrison, McKinley Tariff of 1890, Thomas C. Platt, Republican National Committee, Theodore Roosevelt

*John B. Weaver*

REFERENCES

Baumgardner, James L. 1984. "The 1888 Presidential Election: How Corrupt?" 14 *Presidential Studies Quarterly* 416.

Kehl, James. 1981. *Boss Rule in the Gilded Age: Matt Quay of Pennsylvania*. Pittsburgh: U. of Pittsburgh Pr..

McClure, A. K. 1905. *Old Time Notes of Pennsylvania*. Philadelphia: J. C. Winston.

## J. Danforth Quayle (1947– )

The Vice President under George Bush. James Danforth Quayle became an issue in the 1988 presidential campaign. Having sewn up the Republican presidential nomination early, Bush had the luxury of time in choosing his running mate. He narrowed the list of possibilities to five, with Quayle, junior Senator from Indiana, viewed as a long shot. In an effort to generate interest in the Republican National Convention, Bush waited until the convention was in full swing to announce his choice. The late announcement sent the media scrambling for information about this relative unknown. In the following weeks the Quayle nomination became a focus of the campaign.

Quayle was criticized for his lack of experience (two terms as U.S. Representative and elected twice to the U.S. Senate) and questionable intellectual abilities (his academic record was mediocre at best), for advancing in politics and life through his relatives' connections (his father published his home city newspaper and his grandfather published the Indianapolis *Star*, Indiana's major newspaper), and for using his connections to enter the Indiana National Guard to avoid service in Vietnam. The final criticism drew attention to a possible conflict between his conservative, "hawkish," prodefense posture in Congress and his own service record.

In addition to the personal criticism, the Quayle nomination raised other questions. It focused attention on the process by which vice presidential candidates are selected. What did the Quayle choice indicate about George Bush's judgment? Would a person about whom such serious questions had been raised have been nominated by a more party-dominated, less candidate-centered process? It also raised questions about the role of the media in American electoral politics. The media, presented with Bush's choice the day before the nomination was to be ratified by the convention, had to dig quickly to learn all they could about this "unknown." Many in the public, with some help from the Bush-Quayle campaign, began to think that the press pursued the indiscretions in Quayle's past too vigorously. Bush compared the press treatment of Quayle to a "feeding frenzy of bluefish."

Before entering elective politics, Quayle worked in the Indiana attorney general's office and as an administrative assistant to the governor of Indiana He served two not especially distinguished terms in the U.S. House of Representatives before defeating three-term Indiana Senator Birch Bayh in 1980. Quayle earned higher marks in the Senate, however. His major legislative accomplishment was the Job Training Partnership Act, cosponsored with Edward Kennedy (D-Mass.). Despite his reputation for harder work in the Senate, Quayle's celebration as a political lightweight followed him through the campaign, reaching greatest prominence in the vice presidential candidates' debate with Lloyd Bentsen. Quayle, comparing his elective-office experience to that of John F. Kennedy before he entered the White House, left himself open to Bentsen's retort, one that became perhaps the most famous line of the campaign: "Senator, you're no Jack Kennedy."

*See also:* Birch Bayh, Lloyd Bentsen, George Bush

*David J. Hadley*

REFERENCES

Fenno, Richard F., Jr. 1989. *The Making of a Senator: Dan Quayle.* Washington: Congressional Quarterly.

Goldman, Peter, and Tom Mathews. 1989. *The Quest for the Presidency: The 1988 Campaign.* New York: Simon & Schuster.

Nelson, Michael, ed. 1989. *The Elections of 1988.* Washington: Congressional Quarterly.

## Josiah Quincy (1859–1919)

Boston reform politician. Heir to a long family tradition of paternal social concern and political activism, Josiah Quincy was the last Yankee Brahmin to work effectively as an urban reformer in the cockpit of Massachusetts Democratic politics. A graduate of Harvard College (1880) and Harvard Law School (1884), he was determined to apply his patrician talent to public affairs. He entered the political cockpit in 1884 by leading the state's Mugwump bolt from James G. Blaine to Grover Cleveland. Unlike most Mugwumps, he soon became a Democratic Party regular, committed to the politics of public intervention and practical compromise; Quincy moved steadily to the left over the years toward municipal socialism.

Elected to the state legislature in 1886 with support from the Knights of Labor, he promptly sponsored passage of a host of factory regulations, based on English models, which made Massachusetts a leader in the field of labor law. After heading his party's national publicity bureau in the presidential campaign of 1892, he served briefly in Washington as Assistant Secretary of State, distributing State Department patronage to win votes for Cleveland's monetary policies, a task that tagged him in Mugwump eyes as a party spoilsman. In 1895, with strong Irish-American support, he won Boston's mayoralty and launched a breathtaking program of municipal reform, including public baths, a city printing plant run by trade unionists, gymnasium and playground facilities, slum clearance, and city-sponsored projects in the arts. Fabian Socialist Beatrice Webb, visiting Boston in 1898, found Quincy blunt, purposeful, and fascinating—"quite the hero from the pages of a novel." But fiscal problems and mounting opposition from powerful local Democrats, including Martin

Lomasney, who disliked Quincy's "visionary ideas on government," left Quincy by 1900, at age 40, burned out politically. Scorned by skeptics, his "insolvent utopia" created useful precedents for welfare liberals to build on.

*See also*: James G. Blaine, Grover Cleveland, Election of 1892, Mugwumps

*Geoffrey Blodgett*

REFERENCES

Blodgett, Geoffrey. 1965. "Josiah Quincy, Brahmin Democrat." 38 *New England Quarterly* 435.

Tager, Jack, and John W. Ifkovie, eds. 1985. *Massachusetts in the Gilded Age: Selected Essays*. Amherst: U. of Massachusetts Pr.

Webb, Beatrice. 1963. *Beatrice Webb's American Diary, 1898*. David A. Shannon, ed. Madison: U. of Wisconsin Pr.

# R

## Race and Racial Politics

Race has been a central factor in American politics since the earliest days of the American republic. The inclusion of slavery in the Constitution relegated African-Americans to a subordinate position in society and the economy for the first 75 years of American history. While the Civil War constitutional amendments abolished slavery, guaranteed Blacks the equal protection of the laws, and prohibited racial discrimination in elections, these guarantees of racial equality had little lasting impact on the voting rights of African-Americans. By the early 1900s, Blacks were effectively denied the franchise as a result of southern state adoption of racially restrictive electoral laws, involving, for example, the poll tax, literacy tests, and the institutionalization of the "white primary." For much of American history, Blacks were excluded from participation in American elections.

The incorporation of African-Americans into the modern electoral system had its origins in the 1930s and 1940s when Blacks became loyal members of the New Deal coalition. Although President Franklin Roosevelt was not a forceful advocate for Black voting rights, liberal northern Democrats in the Congress pressed steadfastly for federal adoption of anti-poll tax laws. What is more, as a result of the mechanization of southern agriculture, large numbers of African-Americans after World War II migrated from the rural South to the North in search of work. Blacks settled in the urban centers of the North and Midwest, where racial discrimination in elections was less pronounced than in the South, became active in local Democratic Party poli-

tics, and were responsible for providing the margin of victory for the Democrats in the close presidential contests in 1948 and 1960. While northern Blacks faced no legal voting barriers, southern Blacks in the early 1960s were still effectively denied the franchise. In 1964, for instance, only 6.7 percent of voting-age African-Americans were registered to vote in Mississippi.

But in 1965 all of this changed; Blacks in the South were finally guaranteed the right to vote in federal and state elections with passage of the Voting Rights Act of 1965. The national government now had the political authority to disallow state electoral laws and administrative practices that discriminated against African-Americans. In fact, so successful was the Voting Rights Act of 1965 that, by 1984, 66.3 percent of voting-age Blacks were reported as registered to vote as compared to 69.6 percent of voting-age whites. Moreover, the number of Black elected officials increased substantially after 1965. In 1970, for instance, African-American elected officials numbered 1,460 in the United States; by 1985, this number had risen to 6,056.

The incorporation of Blacks into the electoral process and the continuing saliency of racial politics in 1980s had major consequences on the American party system. For one thing, Blacks have remained the most cohesive voting group of the Democratic Party, casting an overwhelming majority of their votes for Democratic office seekers in local, state, and national elections. In 1976 African-Americans provided Jimmy Carter the margin of victory in such crucial states as Missouri, New York, Ohio,

Pennsylvania, and Texas. In 1980 Blacks cast 85 percent of their votes for Carter; in 1984 Blacks cast 87 percent of their votes for Walter Mondale. In congressional and Senate elections, Blacks have voted in much the same way as they have in presidential elections. In fact, in the South, where in some states African-Americans make up as much as 30 percent of the active electorate, the solid Black vote has ensured the Democratic Party's dominance in congressional and Senate elections. Blacks are increasingly seeking congressional seats. In 1986, 38 Blacks (25 Democrats and 13 Republicans) were their party's candidate for House seats, and 23 Blacks, the highest number ever, won congressional contests. In urban elections, the mobilization of the African-American vote has ensured that the Democrats would retain control of most major cities in the United States. Indeed, four of the largest cities in the United States—Los Angeles, New York, Philadelphia, and Detroit—currently have Black mayors. In no small way, Black support for Democratic candidates is one major reason why the Democratic Party has maintained its majority status in congressional, state, and local partisan elections.

African-Americans are increasingly active participants in the Democratic Party organizational and primary politics. While Blacks made up only 5 percent of the delegates at the 1968 Democratic National Convention, they represented 17 percent at the 1988 Democratic National Convention. This substantial increase in the percentage of Black delegates was the result of the McGovern-Fraser reforms that in 1972 established an affirmative action requirement in the delegate selection process; the presidential candidacy of Jesse Jackson also attracted Black delegates. The first major African-American contender for the presidency, Jackson received 17 percent of the Democratic primary vote in 1984 and 29 percent in 1988. In the balloting at the Democratic national conventions, Jackson received the votes of 465.5 delegates (out of 3,922) in 1984, and 1,218.5 delegates (out of 4,162) in 1988. Blacks are now major actors and brokers not only at the mass level but also at the elite level in Democratic Party politics.

The political incorporation of Blacks into the electoral process has had a lasting impact on the American party system. Blacks have replaced white southerners as the most loyal voting bloc in the Democratic Party, resulting in a transformation of major importance that some have identified as a realignment of the American party system, with Blacks expanding and consolidating their strength in the Democratic Party and with white southerners defecting to the Republican Party. This transformation is best demonstrated by the now significant and growing attitudinal differences on racial issues between Republicans and Democrats. Whereas Republicans were the more liberal of the political parties on racial policy issues before 1964, since the mid-1960s Democrats have emerged as the more liberal party on the issue of racial equality. Racial issues, such as school busing, affirmative action, and voting rights, remain some of the most hotly contested and divisive issues on the American political agenda. In fact, racial attitudes figure prominently in the voting behavior of Americans not only in presidential contests but also on ballot issues, such as California's Proposition 13, that do not directly involve race. For all of these reasons, race and racial politics remain central in American elections and in the dynamics of the American party system.

*See also:* Abolition, Jimmy Carter, Elections of 1948 and 1960, Jesse Jackson, McGovern-Fraser Commission, Walter Mondale, New Deal, Franklin D. Roosevelt, Voting Rights Act of 1965 and Extensions

*Richard A. Champagne, Jr.*

REFERENCES

Anon. 1985. *Black Elected Officials.* Washington: Joint Center for Political Studies.

Anon. 1977. *The Black Vote: Election '76.* Washington: Joint Center for Political Studies.

Ball, Howard, and Dale Krane. 1982. *Compromised Compliance: Implementation of the Voting Rights Act of 1965.* Westport, CT: Greenwood.

Bloom, Jack. 1987. *Class, Race, and the Civil Rights Movement.* Bloomington: Indiana U. Pr.

Davis, James. 1983. *National Conventions in an Age of Party Reform.* Westport, CT: Greenwood.

Garrow, David J. 1978. *Protest at Selma.* New Haven: Yale U. Pr.

Henderson, Lenneal. 1987. "Black Politics and American Presidential Elections." In Michael Preston et al., eds. *The New Black Politics.* New York: Longman.

Key, V. O. 1949. *Southern Politics in State and Nation.* New York: Vintage.

Kousser, J. Morgan. 1974. *The Shaping of Southern Politics: Suffrage Restriction and the Establishment of the One-Party South.* New Haven: Yale U. Pr.

Lawson, Steven F. 1985. *In Pursuit of Power: Southern Blacks and Electoral Politics, 1965–1982.* New York: Columbia U. Pr.

Levy, Mark R., and Michael S. Kramer. 1972. *The Ethnic Factor: How America's Minorities Decide Elections.* New York: Simon & Schuster.

Lewinson, Paul. 1932. *Race, Class and Party: A History of Negro Suffrage and White Politics in the South.* New York: Universal Library.

Moon, H. L. 1948. *Balance of Power: The Negro Vote.* Garden City, NY: Doubleday.

Petrocik, John. 1981. *Party Coalitions.* Chicago: U. of Chicago Pr.

Sears, David, et al. 1980. "Self-Interest vs. Symbolic Politics in Policy Attitudes and Presidential Voting." 74 *American Political Science Review* 670–684.

———— and Jack Citrin. 1982. *Tax Revolt: Something for Nothing in California.* Cambridge: Harvard U. Press.

Walters, Ronald W. 1988. *Black Presidential Politics in America.* Albany: State U. of New York Press.

Williams, Linda. 1987. "Black Political Progress in the 1980s: The Electoral Arena." In Michael Preston, et al., eds. *The New Black Politics.* New York: Longman.

Wolfinger, Ray, and Michael G. Hagen. 1985. "Republican Prospects, Southern Comfort." 8 *Public Opinion* 8–13.

Woodward, C. Vann. 1955. *The Strange Career of Jim Crow.* New York: Oxford U. Pr.

## Racial Vote Dilution Cases

The importance of racial vote dilution to parties and elections is obvious; what constitutes unacceptable racial vote dilution is not. Racial vote dilution cases usually involve a voting or districting scheme that otherwise would be acceptable, except that it arguably dilutes the vote of a racial group so as to constitute invidious discrimination in violation of the Fourteenth or Fifteenth amendments or the Voting Rights Act of 1965. Racial vote dilution cases are actually both a subset of apportionment cases and a subset of general racial discrimination cases. Yet the subset has developed a doctrine all its own that does not fit exactly with the doctrinal developments in the broader areas of apportionment and race. For example, the Supreme Court has been much more willing to prohibit vote dilution based on race than dilution based on political ideology. Likewise, in order to demonstrate racial vote dilution, the Court recently has come to allow relatively less rigorous standards of proof than required in some other areas of racial discrimination.

Determining precisely which cases constitute the "racial vote dilution" case is problematic. Nevertheless, the issue is usually separable from other claims of discrimination and has been frequently visited by the Supreme Court. Usually, racial vote dilution cases have involved multimember districting schemes. *Gomillion v. Lightfoot* (1960), frequently considered the starting point for understanding the Court's response to racial vote dilution, is a notable exception. *Gomillion* is particularly interesting to the student of elections because it involved district line drawing before the reapportionment revolution. At issue in *Gomillion* was an Alabama statute that changed the boundaries of Tuskegee from the shape of a square to a 28-sided figure. It had the effect of removing virtually all Blacks from the city limits. The lower courts had upheld the plan contending that the judiciary had no power to overturn the legislature's drawing of municipal boundaries. Justice Felix Frankfurter rejected that argument and declared that the drawing of political boundaries for the purpose of disenfranchising racial minorities was both justiciable and prohibited by the Fifteenth Amendment. Frankfurter took pains to distinguish *Gomillion*, which involved the singling out of a racial minority for discriminatory treatment, from the "political question" of malapportionment, which he fervently argued in *Colegrove v. Green* (1946) was no business of the courts. Frankfurter wrote in *Gomillion* (quoting from an earlier case), "The [Fifteenth] Amendment nullifies sophisticated as well as simple-minded modes of discrimination."

After *Gomillion*, the question has become whether a districting scheme was sophisticated discrimination or a constitutionally or statutorily permissible plan even though racial minorities might continue to lose. As such, most vote dilution cases turn on the facts of a particular situation and therefore involve reviewing the "findings" of a lower court. Though the Court and Congress have enunciated principles to guide lower courts, there is confusion because of the justices' willingness to allow one scheme and not another, even though the two situations seem quite similar. More so than in many areas of law, scholars must examine the entire line of cases rather than the last case to understand what the Court will permit. Likewise, the scholar must examine the Voting Rights Act of 1965, especially Section 2. Amendments to the act affect how earlier cases about vote dilution should be read, especially regarding standards of proof. A detailed exposition by the Court on nonconstitutional issues and what is required to prove invidious discrimination under the act is included in *Thornburg v. Gingles* (1986).

The Supreme Court held early on, and still maintains, that multimember districts are not unconstitutional per se. The Court has acknowledged potential problems with multimember districts and has said that single-member districts are preferred when a lower court designs a redistricting scheme. Legislatures, however, remain free to enact multimember plans so long as they do not infringe upon the one-man, one-vote principle or so long as they do not "operate to dilute or cancel the voting strength of racial or political elements of the voting population." Determining what is sufficient to prove unacceptable dilution is difficult, but both the Court and Congress have stated is that simply because the number of minority Representatives elected is not in proportion to their population in the community is not a justification to require a single-member district(s). Nor is the number of minorities elected over the years sufficient proof. (But see *Thornburg*, which suggests that this failure might be one ingredient that courts consider.) What is most persuasive to the Court in finding dilution is a demonstration that "the political processes leading to nomination and election were not equally open to participation by the group in question—that its members had less opportunity than did other residents in the district to participate in the political processes and to elect legislators of their choice" (*White v. Regester*). What seems to be most important to the Court in making this judgment is the ability to show past discrimination or procedures that might inhibit minorities from securing a nomination, such as candidate slating or the need to receive a majority vote for nomination.

Racial vote dilution cases are fascinating and important, especially for the student of parties and elections. They highlight the complexity of valuing process over outcome. They also quickly unmask the underlying philosophies and understandings of representation, elections, and government held by the justices of the Supreme Court. Surely nothing is more central to the American form of government than the process of election and representation, and judges probably have no special competence in this regard. Their reasoning often seems naive. On the other hand, nowhere were schemes of racial discrimination more disingenuous than those that hid behind electoral processes, and it remained for judges to ferret them out. Racial vote dilution cases have undoubted historical significance, but they are also at the center of contemporary arguments about the role of the judiciary and issues of discrimination.

See also: *Colegrove v. Green*, Fifteenth Amendment, Ideology, *Thornburg v. Gingles*, Voting Rights Act of 1965 and Extensions, *White v. Regester*

H. W. Perry, Jr.

## Radicalism in American Politics

Radicalism, though applicable to either the Far Left or Far Right, generally connotes ultraliberalism, and if defined as advocacy of fundamental or extreme change, it has seldom, if ever, dominated American politics. Yet, close examination reveals three types of radical activity. First, advocates of drastic change have lurked on the electoral fringe since the beginnings of American politics. Second, more orthodox politicians have occasionally embraced novel or unconventional agendas. And third, fears of radicalism, or the exploitation of such fears, have often engendered conservative political reaction.

Legions of radicals, some more successful than others, have dotted American politics. The communalists, feminists, and other reformers of the early nineteenth century, though often compromised by bizarre practitioners, sought basic changes in America's social structure. The abolitionists, led by William L. Garrison, fueled one of the nation's most bitter political struggles. With the onset of industrialization, numerous dissenters appeared, protesting against what they viewed as the growing inequities of American society and suggesting a variety of utopian reforms. Practitioners included Greenbackers, Laborites, Prohibitionists, and to some extent Populists. In the twentieth century, Marxists, convinced that industrial capitalism inevitably fosters class struggle and "wage slavery," have demanded nationalization of the means of production, expansion of the social welfare state, and an end to imperialist practices. Advocates of such reform include Socialists, Communists, some pacifists, and Black militants. In the 1980s, extremist political action committees have taken up new causes, including the environment and animal rights.

Infrequently, mainstream politicians have acted either radically or in ways that elicit charges of radicalism. For instance, during the so-called Radical Reconstruction, Republican Congressmen fundamentally altered the relationship between African-Americans and the state, though subsequent analysis has called the *radical* designation into question. In the 1930s, critics argued that Franklin Roosevelt had embarked on a radical course of action, the New Deal, that would lead to socialism, and in the 1950s and 1960s, opponents leveled similar charges of extremism against civil rights advocates. Yet few mainstream politicians have chosen to embrace Marxism or other Far-Left ideology.

More commonly, conservatives have used fears of radicalism, or of a corresponding insurrection, for political advantage. As early as 1798, Federalists exploited fears of imported social disturbance to pass the repressive Alien and Sedition Acts, a thinly veiled attempt to blunt Republican criticisms. In 1920 A. Mitchell Palmer hoped to parlay his response to the Red Scare into a presidential nomination, and Calvin Coolidge *did* use his reputation for suppressing social unrest to capture the vice presidency. During the 1940s and 1950s, Wisconsin Senator Joseph McCarthy received national prominence for his allegations of subversion in the State Department, and Californian Richard Nixon furthered his political career by helping to convict the alleged communist traitor Alger Hiss of perjury. In all these cases, popular fears of radical subversion, unrest, or violent revolution had a less than solid basis, yet the American electorate has shown a propensity for overreaction to allegations of radicalism. Hence, radicalism has been important as an available enemy for conservative politicians.

*See also:* Calvin Coolidge, Federalists, William Lloyd Garrison, Alger Hiss, Joseph McCarthy, New Deal, Richard M. Nixon, Populists, Prohibition, Red Scare, Franklin D. Roosevelt

*Robert F. Zeidel*

REFERENCES

Buhle, Mari Jo, Paul Buhle, and Dan Georgakas, eds. 1990. *Encyclopedia of the American Left.* New York: Garland.

Diggins, John P. 1973. *The American Left in the Twentieth Century.* New York: Harcourt Brace Jovanovich.

Theoharis, Athan G., and John Stuart Cox. 1988. *The Boss: J. Edgar Hoover and the Great American Inquisition.* Philadelphia: Temple U. Pr.

Warren, Frank A., III. 1966. *Liberals and Communism: The "Red Decade" Revisited.* Bloomington: Indiana U. Pr.

# Railroads

The first big business in the United States, railroads, because of their size and pioneering role in industrialization and because of their interstate character, early on played an active role in the nation's political life. Conversely, railroads often were the targets of rival commercial interests, reformers, and others.

From the outset in the 1820s, the railroad industry required an enormous capital investment and lots of land for its routes. Conse-

quently, to supplement both domestic and foreign private-sector investment, local, state, and federal governments followed the precedents already established for turnpikes and canals and eagerly offered varied, generous subsidies for the rail revolution in transportation.

By mid-century that revolution was well advanced. During the 1850s boom, the nation's trackage doubled to over 30,000 miles, reaching the Mississippi River and linking the Great Lakes with an increasingly integrated national market. Because of an almost unanimous need to expand further west to the Pacific Ocean, the various proposed transcontinental rail routes became a contentious issue in the growing sectional rivalry between the North and South.

That issue was resolved in the 1860s. When the Civil War erupted, Congress and the Abraham Lincoln administration immediately authorized transcontinental lines along northern routes. In 1869 the Union Pacific/Central Pacific road traversed the central plains and the far western mountain ranges to San Francisco, while the Northern Pacific Railway received its charter to build west from Lake Superior to Puget Sound. Until the late nineteenth century, public enthusiasm for railroad building remained at a high price. Consequently, the industry received enormous support, including loans and other forms of aid. Additionally, Congress committed over 175 million acres of public lands, largely in the western states, to the roads (the railroads actually received less, some 131 million acres), while individual state governments contributed another 49 million acres to the industry.

Nonetheless, during the Gilded Age an important countertrend developed. Public opinion began to shift against the railroads as charges of bribery, excessive and discriminatory rates, and general corruption intensified. Massachusetts, Illinois, and other state legislatures responded to shifting popular perceptions by establishing regulatory agencies to correct such abuses. In 1887 the federal government followed the states' initiative by creating the Interstate Commerce Commission to regulate the railroads' behavior.

An important political development underlying passage of that measure and others was the growing antirailroad sentiment among farmers, small merchants, wage earners, and others who registered their dissatisfaction as Grangers, Knights of Labor, the Farmers' Alliances, and a plethora of other dissident groups.

The Populist revolt of the 1890s was the capstone of antirailroad agitation in the nineteenth century. Among their many other demands, the Populists called for government ownership of the now-hated industry. For their part, railroad managers, with their allies in the industrial and financial communities, mobilized all their financial and political resources to defeat the Populist-Democrat coalition, led in 1896 by William Jennings Bryan, the radical "Boy Orator" of the Platte.

During the Progressive era, however, the regulatory impulse persisted, and the railroads' leaders and their opponents continued to seek redress in the national political arena. Theodore Roosevelt's administration launched the most spectacular antitrust litigation of the era when it successfully prosecuted the Northern Securities Company, itself one of the most compelling examples of the general corporate consolidation movement then sweeping American industry. Formed as a holding company in 1901 by rivals James J. Hill and Edward H. Harriman and their banking allies, Northern Securities was immediately the nation's largest railroad organization. (Although the U.S. Supreme Court ordered it dissolved under the Sherman Antitrust Act, Northern Securities proved an important, direct predecessor for the 1970 formation of Burlington Northern, which also combined the Great Northern; Northern Pacific; and Chicago, Burlington & Quincy railroads.)

Controversy continued over the appropriate role of the railroad industry in American life. During World War I, Woodrow Wilson's administration assumed operation of the industry as an integral part of the war effort. Despite popular calls for continued federal operation after 1918, the industry reverted to private control in 1920 as part of the nation's "return to normalcy."

As other forms of transportation (particularly trucking, automobiles, and air travel) developed, the economic role of the railroads declined, as did the intensity of popular political debate over their appropriate behavior. Since the 1960s successive presidential administrations have relaxed antitrust strictures, allowing such giant mergers as the Burlington Northern. With the Staggers Act of 1980 national railroad policy formally entered an era of deregulation. Political controversy has continued to swirl about the industry to the present. However, in the closing years of the twentieth century, it tends to focus upon regional and local issues, such as particular line abandonments and labor disputes. As other forms of transportation have displaced the railroads from their unchallenged, central position in American economic life, they have also diluted national political concerns over the welcomed industry's operation.

W. Thomas White

REFERENCES

Chandler, Alfred D. 1977. *The Visible Hand—The Managerial Revolution in American Business*. Cambridge: Harvard U. Pr.

Cochran, Thomas C. 1953. *Railroad Leaders, 1845–1890: The Business Mind in Action*. Cambridge: Harvard U. Pr.

Hoogenboom, Ari and Olive. 1976. *A History of the ICC: From Panacea to Palliative*. New York: Norton.

Kerr, K. Austin. 1968. *American Railroad Politics, 1914–1920: Rates, Wages, and Efficiency*. Pittsburgh: U. of Pittsburgh Pr.

Kirkland, Edward Chase. 1948. *Men, Cities, and Transportation*. 2 vols. Cambridge: Harvard U. Pr.

Kolko, Gabriel. 1965. *Railroads and Regulation, 1877–1916*. New York: Norton.

Martin, Albro. 1971. *Enterprise Denied: Origins of the Decline of American Railroads, 1897–1917*. New York: Columbia U. Pr.

Saunders, Richard. 1978. *The Railroad Mergers and the Coming of Conrail*. Westport, CT: Greenwood.

## Rainbow Coalition

The National Rainbow Coalition is the organization that supports the Reverend Jesse Jackson's political ambitions, most notable of which were his presidential campaigns in 1984 and 1988.

Like Jackson's candidacy, the Rainbow Coalition's roots lie in the civil rights movement. During the mid-1960s, African-American leaders began seeking ways to institutionalize the support that the civil rights movement had established. In his final book, *Where Do We Go from Here?* (1967), Dr. Martin Luther King, Jr., called on the movement to "embark on social experimentation with their own strengths to generate the kind of power that shapes basic decisions." After the 1968 election that Richard Nixon barely won, it became clear that African-Americans could become an important part of the American electorate and play a major role in determining who won subsequent elections.

In 1971 an African-American national convention was held in Gary, Indiana, attended by over 8,000 delegates. Gary's mayor, Richard Gordon Hatcher, demanded that Blacks receive their share of power in the two major parties; Jackson called for the formation of a "Black Liberation Party"; and Congresswoman Shirley

Chisholm (D-N.Y.) did run in the 1972 Democratic primaries but failed to garner much support from either the elected officials or grass-roots activists who had attended the Gary convention.

For the next decade, the nation heard little discussion of either a new party or a serious African-American presidential candidacy. In 1983 Jackson started a campaign in which he talked about a "rainbow coalition" in which African-Americans, poor whites, and other disenfranchised groups would finally grasp their share of power within the Democratic Party, including ultimately capturing the presidency.

Jesse Jackson had always been a gifted but controversial leader in the civil rights movement, and his candidacy was not greeted with support from many mainline African-American political leaders, who continued to support former Vice President Walter Mondale. Nonetheless, with massive support from grass-roots activists and others, Jackson won 3,282,380 votes (17 percent of the total) in the Democratic primaries and 465.5 of the total 3,923 delegates to the 1984 Democratic National Convention. Jackson ran again in 1988, winning 6,769,019 (29.1 percent) of the primary vote, including substantially more white votes than in 1984, and 1,218.5 of the 4,162 delegates.

Until the end of the 1988 campaign, the Rainbow Coalition itself was seen as little more than the organizational wing of Jackson's personal campaign. However, since 1986 the organization has had a formal structure as the National Rainbow Coalition. At present, it is not known if the Coalition can survive without its charismatic leader. And a debate continues to rage within the African-American community over the proper strategy to follow: either supporting candidates like Jackson who work within the Democratic Party or forming a new party under the Rainbow Coalition or some other banner.

*See also:* Elections of 1984 and 1988, Jesse Jackson, Martin Luther King, Jr., Race and Racial Politics

*Charles S. Hauss*

## Henry T. Rainey (1860–1934)

Democratic Speaker of the House as the New Deal was proposed. Henry Thomas Rainey was a longtime Democrat and member of Congress. He was noted as an advocate of many progressive reforms and as a major supporter of Franklin D. Roosevelt and the New Deal.

Born in Carrollton, Illinois, Rainey attended Knox Academy and Knox College in Galesburg, Illinois, before graduating from Amherst College in 1883 and Union College of Law in Chicago in 1885. He returned to Carrollton to practice law and later became master of the chancery for Greene County. He was first elected to the U.S. House of Representatives in 1902 and served from 1903 until 1921 when he was defeated on the coattails of Warren G. Harding's landslide victory in the 1920 presidential election. Rainey was subsequently returned to Congress two years later and served from 1923 until his death.

A progressive Democrat, Rainey was associated with reform movements both inside and outside of Congress. He sat on the Ways and Means Committee, where he devoted considerable attention to tariffs and taxation. After his return to Congress in 1923, he served as ranking minority member until he assumed the post of Majority Leader when the Democrats gained control of the House in 1931. He was elected Speaker of the House in 1933 when John Nance Garner became Vice President. Rainey's short tenure in that position was highlighted by the help he gave President Roosevelt in shepherding the National Recovery Act and other New Deal legislation through Congress before his death in St. Louis.

*See also:* John Nance Garner, New Deal, Franklin D. Roosevelt, Speaker of the House

*James V. Saturno*

REFERENCES

U.S. Congress. 1936. *Memorial Services*. House Document 74–236, 74th Congress, 1st Sess. Washington: U.S. Government Printing Office.

## Samuel J. Randall (1828–1890)

Democratic Speaker of the House at Reconstruction's end. As time progressed, Samuel Jackson Randall's Pennsylvania brand of fiscal conservatism and support for protectionism found him at variance with many southern and western Democrats who entered the House during and after Reconstruction, a split that led to his ultimate deposition as a party leader.

Randall's father was a prominent Whig politician from Philadelphia, and the younger Randall's upbringing was reflected in his later political career. Samuel entered the House in 1863 from a Philadelphia district; he was reelected continuously until his death. Randall was always an ardent supporter of a high protective tariff, a partiality that explains his continued reelection to the House as a Democrat from a city and state dominated by the Republican Party in the nineteenth century.

Randall's quest for the House speakership began in 1875, when he was narrowly defeated by Michael C. Kerr in a caucus vote for the Democratic Party nomination; Randall was consequentially appointed to chair the Appropriations Committee, a common consolation prize for runners-up in speakership contests at the time. From this position Randall was elected Speaker in the next year, following Kerr's death. As Speaker, Randall used the prerogatives of his office to pursue his own vision of Democratic policy. He used his right of recognition to thwart efforts to bring tariff reductions to the floor, much to the distress of many other Democrats.

Randall was also noted for his attempts to use the rules of the House to guide policy to his liking. He was only moderately successful in this endeavor, failing on several occasions to change House rules to minimize appropriations. For instance, when Randall attempted to change the House rules in 1879 to make it more difficult to consider the omnibus rivers and harbors bill under suspension of the rules, Congressman John Reagan (D-Tex.) successfully led a counterattack that made it even easier to pass water project bills than before. When Randall further attempted to bring all appropriations under even firmer control of the Appropriations Committee in 1880, he was rebuffed, and the House went on to vote to remove agricultural appropriations from the Appropriations Committee's oversight.

Randall's ardent fiscal conservatism and support for protectionism led to his deposition as Speaker in 1883 when the Democrats regained control of the House after a two-year hiatus; instead, the Democrats nominated John G. Carlisle (Kentucky) to be Speaker. In keeping with past practice, Carlisle appointed Randall to chair the Appropriations Committee again. From this position, Randall was able to bottle up legislation of which he disapproved, using the special privileges in the House rules that allowed the Appropriations Committee to report legislation at any time. Partly in retaliation against Randall's behavior, Carlisle led an effort in 1885 to strip the Appropriations Committee of half its spending authority, transferring several appropriations bills to authorizing committees. Later in the same Congress, the Ways and Means Committee singled out a place of Randall-sponsored protectionist legislation for a scathing adverse report. His political fortunes continued to decline in the late 1880s following his unyielding refusal to support President Grover Cleveland's tariff reform efforts.

*See also:* John G. Carlisle, Grover Cleveland, Michael C. Kerr, Speaker of the House

*Charles Stewart III*

## A. Philip Randolph (1889–1979)

African-American social agitator, journalist, labor leader, and civil rights leader. Born in Crescent City, Florida, and raised in Jacksonville, Asa Philip Randolph came to Harlem in 1911 and lived there for the rest of his life.

In 1917 Randolph and his partner, Chandler Owen, launched *The Messenger*, a monthly magazine oriented toward Black socialists; the journal became part of the New Negro movement. Both in its pages and in street-corner speeches in Harlem, Randolph urged Black people to refuse conscription to fight in World War I. As a result he was arrested briefly, but not prosecuted, for treason.

In 1925 Randolph was approached by a group of African-American sleeping car porters who were trying to unionize; they needed a leader who did not work for, and so could not be fired by, the railroads. Randolph agreed to become president, a job he kept until his retirement in 1968. After a long struggle, the Brotherhood of Sleeping Car Porters won a contract with the Pullman Company in 1937.

In 1941 Randolph led the March on Washington Movement, which demanded an end to racial discrimination in defense production. Randolph called off the march when President Franklin Roosevelt issued an executive order banning discrimination and establishing a federal Fair Employment Practices Commission, a concession for which Randolph was criticized by several younger militant Black leaders. Following the war, faced with peacetime conscription into a segregated army, Randolph led a civil disobedience campaign that strongly influenced President Harry Truman's decision to end segregation in the armed forces. In 1963, when the March on Washington finally took place, Randolph, at age 74, played a central role.

In later years Randolph was often criticized by African-American nationalists, but always called for racial unity; he insisted that Malcolm X be included in Harlem Black leadership councils, despite their strong disagreements. In later years he often served as spokesman for united African-American efforts.

Randolph fought racism by white labor leaders for most of his career, but he did receive AFL-

CIO funding for the establishment of the A. Philip Randolph Institute, which he founded in 1963 as a means to unite the African-American and the labor movements.

*See also:* Race and Racial Politics, Franklin D. Roosevelt, Harry S Truman

*John C. Berg*

REFERENCES

Anderson, Jervis. 1973. *A. Philip Randolph: A Biographical Portrait.* New York: Harcourt Brace Jovanovich.

Hanley, Sally. 1989. *A. Philip Randolph.* New York: Chelsea House.

Harris, William H., and Greg LeRoy. 1977. *Keeping the Faith: A. Philip Randolph, Milton P. Webster and the Brotherhood of Sleeping Car Porters, 1925–37.* Urbana: U. of Illinois Pr.

## John Randolph (1773–1833)

Southern secessionist ideologue. John Randolph of Roanoke was a native Virginian of prominent lineage, noted for his eccentric ways, mordant wit, and brilliant oratory. He first won election to the U.S. House of Representatives in 1799. Two years later Randolph's parliamentary skills helped him become chairman of the Committee on Ways and Means and leader of the House Democratic-Republicans. Reelected to the House intermittently until 1829 and serving as President Andrew Jackson's ambassador to Russia from 1830 to 1831 (when poor health forced his return), Randolph was known as a superbly talented but quixotic loner.

Despite moral unease over slavery and laments over the impoverishment of many Virginia landowners, Randolph glorified as uniquely virtuous the tidewater planter class to which he belonged. He openly despised the egalitarian currents of his day as reflecting a misguided worship of "King Numbers," and at Virginia's constitutional convention in 1829 he stood nearly alone against a provision to abolish property qualifications for suffrage. "I am an aristocrat," Randolph once boasted. "I love liberty. I hate equality."

Throughout his career Randolph sought to rally southern sectional consciousness against what he viewed as the danger of a strong federal government controlled by northern business interests. Toward that end he opposed American entry into war with Great Britain in 1812, insisting that such military ventures merely served New England merchants and enlarged national power that might one day be directed against the southern slave system. Similarly he opposed a new charter for the Bank of the United States and a protective tariff (both in 1816), as well as a bill for federally financed internal improvements (in 1817). Each of these measures narrowly passed, and Randolph was among only ten Republican Congressmen who voted against all three bills.

During the 1820s and early 1830s, sectional conflicts over slavery and tariff rates afforded a wider audience for Randolph's warnings. These jeremiads now included repeated prophesies of southern secession as a matter of self-preservation against northern domination. "I look for civil war," he wrote a year before his death. Randolph's defense of states' rights and planter interests helped shape the thinking of John C. Calhoun of South Carolina, who in the 1830s became the foremost apostle of southern nationalism. Yet Randolph's influence was limited by his refusal either to exalt democracy, as most contemporary politicians did, or to join in the growing southern white praise of slavery as a positive good. This Cassandra of the South therefore spoke less for an entire region than for a generation of tidewater aristocrats whose sectional pride adumbrated growing anxieties over their personal and political decline.

*See also:* John C. Calhoun, Andrew Jackson, Secession, Second Bank of the United States

*Robert Weisbrot*

REFERENCES

Adams, Henry. 1882. *John Randolph.* Boston: Houghton Mifflin.

Kirk, Russell. 1964. *John Randolph of Roanoke: A Study in American Politics.* Chicago: Henry Regnery.

Randolph, John. 1834. *Letters of John Randolph to a Younger Relative.* Ed. Theodore Dudley. Philadelphia: Carey, Lea, and Blanchard.

## Jeannette Rankin (1880–1973)

First woman member of Congress. Jeannette Rankin's election in 1916 came at a time when women had the right to vote in Montana and could send a woman to Congress; suffrage at the national level, however, had not been attained. Against the expectations of party leaders in a state controlled by Anaconda Copper Company interests, she defeated seven men for one of the two Republican nominations, with 22,549 votes, as opposed to 15,439 for her closest rival. Her victory was attributed to two factors. First, she was known for her personal and geographically widespread campaign in the at-large district of Montana. (In *Profiles in Courage*, John F. Kennedy admiringly but inaccurately reports that she campaigned on horseback, but in reality, Rankin traveled by car and train.) Second, she received cross-party support from large numbers of Democratic women, including the influential Mrs. John Holt, a major cattle owner in the state. Rankin recognized that Mrs. Holt and others expressly crossed party lines in order to send a woman to represent their interest in Congress. Rankin subsequently introduced the amendment that gave women the right to vote.

Rankin's cross-party support mirrored her political character and the nature of her campaign. Representing Montana at large in the House of Representatives, she had little interest in party labels, claiming, "I never was a Republican. I ran on the Republican ticket." She derived her party affiliation from the traditional loyalties of male family members. Her platform differed significantly from that of the Republican Party. In addition to her position on suffrage, she supported child labor legislation and was committed to keeping the United States out of war in Europe. She was the only member of Congress to vote against both world wars.

A dedicated activist in the causes of women's suffrage and peace, Rankin had links to the National American Woman Suffrage Association and attended the meetings that resulted in the founding of the Women's Peace Party in January 1915. This party sent a delegation that included Jane Adams and Emily Greene Balch to an international meeting of women at the Hague to discuss measures to prevent the spread of war. Women representatives were sent to the chancelleries of the warring powers in an unsuccessful attempt to urge mediated settlement.

Jeannette Rankin was born near Missoula, Montana, of parents who settled when it was still a territory. She graduated from the University of Montana in 1902 and entered the New York School of Philanthropy (now the Columbia School of Social Work) in 1908. She served two terms in the House of Representatives, joining the Sixty-fifth Congress in 1917 and the Seventy-seventh Congress in 1941. In and out of office, she was continuously active in the cause of peace and equality for women. In her nineties, she once again attracted national attention by leading the Jeannette Rankin Brigade, a group of 5,000 women protesting the Vietnam War, in their march on Washington in 1968.

*See also:* National American Woman Suffrage Association, Suffrage

*Victoria A. A. Kamsler*

REFERENCES

Giles, Kevin S. 1980. *Flight of the Dove: The Story of Jeannette Rankin.* Beaverton, OR: Touchstone Press.

Harris, Ted. 1982. *Jeannette Rankin: Suffragist, First Woman Elected to Congress, and Pacifist.* New York: Arno Press.

Josephson, Hannah. 1974. *Jeannette Rankin, First Lady in Congress: A Biography.* Indianapolis: Bobbs-Merrill.

## I. Freeman Rasin (1833–1907)

Leader of the Baltimore City Democratic machine. From 1870 on, Isaac Freeman Rasin formed an alliance with Arthur P. Gorman, leader of the county organization. Gorman went on to serve in the U.S. Senate and acquired a national reputation, while Rasin accepted only modest public offices. Together, however, they dominated post-Reconstruction politics in Maryland.

As was the case in other industrializing cities, Baltimore's growth strained its municipal structures. The Rasin machine provided social services for voters and favors for business. However, relatively few of the traditional foreign-born recipients of urban political favors lived in Baltimore. The organization's base of support came from native citizens in their reaction to the perceived excesses of post-Civil War Republican rule.

I. Freeman Rasin came from an established family on Maryland's Eastern Shore. Educated at Washington College, he entered business in Baltimore and first experienced politics when Know-Nothing gangs terrorized the city. In 1867 he was elected as clerk of the court of common pleas and built the city organization for 18 years. In 1886 he was appointed naval officer of Baltimore by President Grover Cleveland. In 1899 Rasin effected a compromise with the reform elements that preserved his authority in the organization until his death.

*See also:* Grover Cleveland, Arthur P. Gorman

*Karl A. Lamb*

REFERENCES

Crooks, James B. 1976. "Politics and Reform: The Dimensions of Baltimore Progressivism." 71 *Maryland Historical Magazine* 421.

Kent, Frank R. 1968. *The Story of Maryland Politics.* Hatboro, PA: Tradition Press. (Orig. pub. 1911)

Lambert, John R. 1953. *Arthur Pue Gorman.* Baton Rouge: Louisiana State U. Pr.

## John J. Raskob (1879–1950)

Industrialist, political fundraiser, and Democratic National Committee Chairman. Born of poor Alsatian and Irish parents in Lockport, New York, John Jacob Raskob rose to wealth and political prominence through both long hours of work and important acquaintance. Trained in business, he helped participate in the reorganization of E. I. du Pont de Nemours and Company, the gunpowder and chemical company, as secretary to its president, Pierre du Pont; he became its treasurer, finance director, and vice president. Like his colleague, du Pont, Raskob acquired stock in General Motors and reorganized that company, becoming finance director, vice president, and the recognized father of installment buying of automobiles.

Raskob remained involved as a director at both General Motors and du Pont until 1946, but with less influence while he directed his focus to political affairs. In 1919 Raskob became a member of the finance committee of the Association Against the Prohibition Amendment. Not a drinker himself, Raskob opposed Prohibition for what he viewed as its intolerance and fostering of a lack of respect for the law.

Raskob associated in politics with successful Catholic New Yorkers like himself, notably Democratic governor Alfred E. Smith. Smith persuaded the one-time Republican Raskob in 1928 to leave General Motors temporarily to become chairman of the Democratic National Committee. This play was in part an attempt to reassure the business community that the Democrats would not impede prosperity. Raskob's appointment underlined Smith's essentially conservative campaign. Raskob's connections with eastern business, however, did not endear him to southerners and westerners in the Democratic Party, nor did his limited acquaintance with party leaders other than Smith help. Raskob primarily raised campaign funds and built a strong party organization; he was no great original framer of campaign strategy.

At Raskob's suggestion Jouett Shouse, former Congressman from Kentucky, became chairman of the executive committee of the Democratic National Committee after the 1928 defeat. Shouse helped rebuild the party and set up permanent headquarters in Washington, D.C., to monitor the Herbert Hoover administration. Together Raskob and Shouse focused on the repeal of Prohibition, tax cuts, and the five-day workweek.

Raskob opposed Franklin Roosevelt's nomination in 1932, seeking to renominate Smith, then his business associate in the Empire State Building Corporation. But FDR replaced Raskob as DNC chairman in 1932 with James A. Farley.

Raskob's choice as convention chairman (Shouse) was bypassed in favor of Senator Thomas Walsh of Montana. Contemporaries credited Raskob, however, with getting the repeal plank in the Democratic platform.

Basically a Jeffersonian Democrat, Raskob worked with Smith, Shouse, and the du Ponts in August 1934 to form the bipartisan American Liberty League. Its goals were to oppose the New Deal, defend the Constitution, and deny FDR a second term. The DNC paid off a loan to Raskob of $120,000 to sever relations (he himself had written off another loan of $100,000 as a contribution). He in turn funded the League.

Ostensibly inactive in politics after 1936, in the 1940 presidential campaign Raskob wore a "Willkie for President" button, but refused to comment on his switch.

*See also:* Democratic National Committee, James A. Farley, New Deal, Franklin D. Roosevelt, Alfred E. Smith, Thomas Walsh

*Frederick J. Augustyn, Jr.*

REFERENCES

Ingham, John N. 1983. *Biographical Dictionary of American Business Leaders.* Westport, CT: Greenwood.

Wolfskill, George. 1962. *The Revolt of the Conservatives: A History of the American Liberty League, 1934–1940.* Boston: Houghton Mifflin.

## Joseph L. Rauh (1911– )

Democratic liberal activist and co-founder of Americans for Democratic Action. Joseph Louis Rauh graduated from Harvard Law School in 1935, clerked for Supreme Court justices Felix Frankfurter and Benjamin Cardozo, and then served in the Army and other government offices until starting private law practice in 1947. That year he helped found Americans for Democratic Action. Over the years he served as ADA's chairman and vice chairman and at the same time became a force within the Democratic Party, constantly pushing politicians to sponsor liberal legislation, especially civil rights.

In 1948 he organized a successful fight for a strong civil rights plank at the Democratic convention. Throughout the 1950s Rauh kept the civil rights issue before the eyes of lawmakers in Congress and at Democratic conventions. He also criticized the excesses of internal security laws and represented a number of persons accused of Communist ties.

Rauh was part of Minnesota Senator Hubert Humphrey's inner circle of advisers in his 1960 bid for the presidency and worked with

Humphrey in lobbying for the passage of the 1964 Civil Rights Act.

Rauh's activism extended beyond Washington politics. In 1964 he was counsel for the Mississippi Freedom Democratic Party's credentials challenge at the Democratic convention, finally negotiating a compromise that included a promise of reform before 1968.

Rauh backed Eugene McCarthy, another Minnesota Senator, for President in 1967 because of his opposition to the Vietnam War, but in September 1968 he convinced the ADA board to endorse Humphrey after his announcement that he would stop the bombing of North Vietnam.

Even as ADA's influence declined in the 1970s and 1980s, Rauh remained dedicated to civil rights, lobbying against appointees he thought were weak on that issue and supporting liberal candidates nationally.

*See also:* Americans for Democratic Action, Hubert Humphrey, Eugene McCarthy, Mississippi Freedom Democratic Party, Vietnam War as a Political Issue

Mary T. Curtin

REFERENCES

Carson, Clayborne. 1981. *In Struggle: SNCC and the Black Awakening of the 1960s.* Cambridge: Harvard U. Pr.

Gillon, Steven M. 1987. *Politics and Vision: The ADA and American Liberalism, 1947–1985.* New York: Oxford U. Pr.

Hamby, Alonzo. 1978. *Beyond the New Deal.* New York: Columbia U. Pr.

Solberg, Carl. 1983. *Hubert Humphrey:. A Biography.* New York: Norton.

## Samuel T. Rayburn (1882–1961)

"Mr. Sam," the longtime Speaker of the House. Samuel Taliafero Rayburn was the Democratic leader in the House of Representatives, either as Speaker or Minority Leader, for a quarter of the twentieth century. Rayburn's tenure as a legislative leader, from 1937 through 1961, coincided with one of the most fractious periods in the party's history; his leadership style and accomplishments reflected those deep divisions.

Sam Rayburn was born near Kingston, Tennessee, the son of a farmer who moved the family to Fannin County, Texas (in the northeast portion of the state) in 1887. Rayburn entertained political ambitions early in life and found himself elected to the Texas House of Representatives in 1906 at the age of 24. Even in his early political career in Texas, Rayburn showed the traits that would characterize his activity later in Washington: generally populist

in outlook, deeply loyal to personal ties, attentive to political winds in his district, and "moderate" in racial issues (meaning that he was not an ardent segregationist).

In 1912 the House district in which Rayburn resided became vacant owing to the retirement of the incumbent. While only 30 at the time, Rayburn leapt at the opportunity to run for the seat, knowing that this retirement would likely be his only opportunity for election for years to come. Rayburn ran a race in the Democratic primary against seven other men, some of whom also had strong political ties to the congressional district. Relying on his reputation as a "dry" politician and a strong showing in his home and neighboring counties, Rayburn won the nomination with 23 percent of the vote, beating the second-place finisher by fewer than 500 votes. (The weakness of the Republican Party in northeast Texas during this period meant that nomination in the Democratic primary ensured victory in the general election.) Rayburn won most of his subsequent reelection efforts by wide margins, but he did endure substantial primary opposition early in the Great Depression and in 1944.

Rayburn was helped significantly in getting established in his career through the influence of the powerful Texas delegation, whose most powerful member was John Nance Garner. Largely through Garner's sponsorship, Rayburn was appointed to the Interstate and Foreign Commerce Committee in his first term. He immediately became a "work horse" on the committee, helping to craft legislation that created the Federal Trade Commission, regulated railroad securities, and provided disability pensions to World War I veterans. Rayburn was a regular member of Garner's "Bureau of Education," in which senior House members would gather in a small hideaway House office after hours to drink bourbon, exchange political gossip, and socialize selected junior members of the House. (In later years Rayburn would preside over a similar gathering, which he named the "Board of Education.") Rayburn was thus able to combine his network of informal contracts with his rapidly increasing seniority on the Commerce Committee to become an influential member of the House within a very few years of his arrival.

Rayburn's first major opportunities to capture widespread attention for his leadership abilities came during the early years of the New Deal. Rayburn had been John Nance Garner's campaign chairman at the 1932 Democratic convention, playing a key role in convincing Garner to throw his support behind Franklin Roosevelt in exchange for the vice presidential nomination. Returning to the House following the 1932 election, Rayburn found himself elevated to the chair of the Commerce Committee. Rayburn's leadership on the committee was crucial to the passage of several key elements of the New Deal, including the Securities Act of 1932, the Public Utility Holding Company Act, and the Rural Electrification Act of 1936.

Sam Rayburn was elected Speaker of the House in 1940, following the death of Speaker William B. Bankhead. Rayburn had risen to the position of Majority Leader in 1937, following an aborted run for the speakership in that year. Rayburn continued to lead the House Democratic Party until his death, temporarily relinquishing the speakership to Joseph Martin (Massachusetts) only when the Republicans gained control of the House in the Eightieth and Eighty-third Congresses.

Judgments about Rayburn's place in the history of the House must be based on the institutional constraints that he faced during his tenure. Throughout his service as Democratic leader, Rayburn was saddled with the problem of trying to unite the two major regional (and ideological) wings of his party: the northern and southern. The tendency of southerners to come together with Republicans during Rayburn's tenure to form a "Conservative Coalition" gave Rayburn his greatest difficulties. "Mr. Sam" was frequently criticized by northern Democrats for his unwillingness to impose strict party discipline on his fellow southerners, and this dissatisfaction ultimately was institutionalized in the formation of the liberal Democratic Study Group in the late 1950s.

While Rayburn's unwillingness to sanction southerners undoubtedly stemmed in part from his own sympathies with the Conservative Coalition and his skepticism toward many social welfare programs, probably nobody in the House at this time could have successfully imposed strict party discipline on both elements of the Democratic Party. The great heterogeneity among Democrats following the New Deal contrasted with the significant homogeneity of the parties at the turn of the century, when both Democrat and Republican party leaders had been able to impose strict discipline. Had Rayburn enforced stricter discipline, he may have been faced with an outright schism within the Democratic party, yielding even fewer policy

breakthroughs for northerners in the 1940s and 1950s than actually were enacted.

Rayburn finally acceded to northern demands to reform the House Rules Committee following the 1960 election. Ever since the 1930s, the Rules Committee had been the center of Conservative Coalition strength; Rules was numerically dominated by southern Democrats and by Republicans and had been chaired by conservatives for three decades. According to the procedures of the House, practically all legislation had to gain the approval of the Rules Committee before it could be debated on the House floor; the conservative-dominated Rules Committee used this requirement to extract concessions from sponsors of liberal legislation, resulting in the deletion or dilution of provision most objectionable to conservatives. Prompted by liberal Democrats and the newly elected northern Democratic President, John F. Kennedy, Rayburn agreed to challenge the Rules Committee's power by expanding its membership so as to dilute its conservative strength. In a classic political struggle against Rules Committee chair "Judge" Howard W. Smith, Rayburn managed to pass the temporary expansion of the Rules Committee's membership in 1961 on a 217-to-212 vote. Although this victory was the last of Rayburn's major acts as Speaker, it was the first of a series of reforms lasting into the 1970s that made the various subdivisions of the House, especially the leadership, more responsive to the majority of the Democratic Caucus.

*See also:* Lyndon B. Johnson, John F. Kennedy, Majority Party Leadership in Congress, Joseph Martin, Franklin D. Roosevelt, Speaker of the House, Harry S Truman

*Charles Stewart III*

REFERENCES
Dorough, C. Dwight. 1962. *Mr Sam*. New York: Random House.

Hardeman, D. B., and Donald C. Bacon. 1987. *Rayburn: A Biography*. Austin: Texas Monthly Press.

## Henry J. Raymond (1820–1869)

Founder of the *New York Times* and chairman of the Union (Republican) National Committee for Lincoln's reelection. Henry Jarvis Raymond's leadership of his party came at a time when, to indicate their dedication to the preservation of the Union, Lincoln Republicans and War Democrats were frequently united under a Union Party banner. Their uncompromising adversaries were the Radical wing of the Republican Party.

To pave the way for putting a War Democrat, Andrew Johnson, on a Union Party ticket with Abraham Lincoln in 1864, the President and his associates avoided using the Republican Party name. Instead, they renominated Lincoln, added Johnson to the ticket, and chose a "Union national committee" that elected Raymond as its chairman.

Henry J. Raymond arrived in New York City at the age of 20 shortly after graduation from the University of Vermont. He became a power in New York City journalism, sponsored by the famous publisher Horace Greeley. Raymond also entered politics, winning election to the New York State Assembly and becoming speaker of the lower house in 1850. He founded the *New York Times* in 1851 and became lieutenant governor of New York in 1854.

At the first Republican National Convention in Pittsburgh in 1856, Raymond wrote the party's first national platform. In 1861 he was once again elected to the New York Assembly and again chosen speaker. In 1864 Raymond attended the Union National Convention at the head of the New York delegation and became the Union Party national chairman at the end of this convention. He was also elected to the U.S. House of Representatives in the fall elections.

Lincoln's assassination put former Democrat Andrew Johnson into the White House and the Union national chairman into an ambivalent predicament. With the Radical Republicans in control of Congress and embarking upon a harsh Reconstruction plan for the South, President Johnson's managers arranged a midterm national convention in an effort to win a pro-Johnson Congress in 1866. As Union Party chairman, Raymond was obligated to attend. The Radicals used this as a pretext for charging that he had gone over to the opposition party (presumably the Democratic Party) and was therefore subject to expulsion from the Republican chairmanship. A pro-Radical minority on the national committee did vote expulsion, but Raymond never conceded the legality of their action.

*See also:* Horace Greeley, Andrew Johnson, Abraham Lincoln, Republican National Committee, Union Party

*Ralph M. Goldman*

REFERENCES

Goldman, Ralph M. 1990. *The National Party Chairmen and Committees: Factionalism at the Top.* Armonk, NY: M. E. Sharpe.
Simon Cameron Papers. Library of Congress
Abraham Lincoln Papers. Library of Congress

## Kenneth Rayner (1808–1884)

Founder and spokesperson of Know-Nothing Party. Kenneth Rayner of North Carolina enjoyed a long and checkered political career as a Whig, Know-Nothing, and Republican in the South. Voters sent him to the state constitutional convention of 1835, followed by three consecutive terms in the North Carolina House of Commons and three in the U.S. House of Representatives (1839–1844). Rayner earned a reputation as a fiery defender of Whig policies and an ardent supporter of Henry Clay. After his retirement from Congress he served three more terms in the state House of Commons (1846–1852) and one in the state senate (1852–1854). He was presidential elector for Zachary Taylor in 1848.

In 1854 Rayner helped found the national American, or Know-Nothing, Party. A doctrinaire nativist, he became one of the party's preeminent spokesmen. He authored the party's Third (or Union) Degree, an oath that bound members to uphold the Union. A bolting wing of northern Know-Nothings in 1856 nominated him for Vice President on a ticket with Robert F. Stockton. Rayner declined the nomination.

After the firing on Fort Sumter began the Civil War, Rayner served in his state's secession convention. Midway through the war, however, he secretly participated in an abortive peace movement in North Carolina. In 1866 he (anonymously) wrote a laudatory biography of President Andrew Johnson and later became a Republican. The following year Rayner moved to Mississippi, and in 1874 President Ulysses Grant named him to a judgeship on the Alabama Court of Claims. Three years later Rutherford B. Hayes appointed Rayner Solicitor of the Treasury, a post he held until his death.

*See also:* Henry Clay, Ulysses S. Grant, Rutherford B. Hayes, Know-Nothings, Zachary Taylor

*Gregg Cantrell*

REFERENCES

Cantrell, David Gregg. 1988. "The Limits of Southern Dissent: The Lives of Kenneth and John B. Rayner." Ph.D. Dissertation, Department of History, Texas A&M University.

Hamilton, J. G. de Roulhac, ed. 1918. *The Papers of Thomas Ruffin.* 4 vols. Raleigh, NC: State Department of Archives and History.

Rayner Papers. Southern Historical Collection, U. of North Carolina, Chapel Hill.

## Ronald W. Reagan (1911– )

The fortieth President of the United States. Ronald Wilson Reagan changed America.

Reagan spent most of his childhood in the small town of Dixon, Illinois. He entered Eureka College in 1928 where he majored in economics and sociology, earning his B.A. in 1932. He then began a career as a radio sports announcer at a number of radio stations, the most notable being WHO in Des Moines, Iowa.

In 1937, Reagan left Iowa and moved to Hollywood to begin an acting career. Reagan pursued his new profession with enthusiasm, starring in over 50 mostly forgettable movies in the 1940s and 1950s. The most memorable of these were *Knute Rockne: All American* (1940), the story of the famous Notre Dame football coach, and *Kings Row* (1942), the tale of a playboy whose legs are amputated by a deranged physician. In the 1960s Reagan entered the new medium of television and is best remembered for hosting the show "Death Valley Days." While in Hollywood, Reagan served as president of the Screen Actors Guild from 1947 to 1952 and again in 1959.

A Democrat by birth, Reagan supported Franklin Roosevelt and Harry Truman in their presidential campaigns. But he drifted away from the Democratic Party in the 1950s, backing Republican presidential candidate Dwight Eisenhower in 1952 and 1956 over Democrat Adlai E. Stevenson, and Richard Nixon in 1960 against John F. Kennedy. In 1962 Reagan formally changed his party registration from Democrat to Republican.

He was thrust into the national spotlight in 1964 when he made a dramatic appeal on national television on behalf of conservative Republican presidential candidate Barry Goldwater.

Reagan entered active politics in 1966 as the Republican candidate for governor of California. Reagan presented himself to voters as a "citizen politician" and won in a landslide. Four years later he was easily reelected. In 1968 Reagan made an abortive attempt at the Republican presidential nomination won by Richard Nixon. Reagan returned to presidential competition in 1976, challenging Gerald R. Ford for the GOP nomination and losing at the Republican convention by a mere 117 votes out of a total of 2,259 votes cast.

Reagan won the Republican nomination in 1980, easily beating George Bush. Reagan subsequently defeated Democratic candidate Jimmy Carter in a landslide, winning 44 states and 489 electoral votes. Four years later he turned back a challenge from former Democratic Vice President Walter F. Mondale with an even larger win: 49 states and 525 electoral votes—a record.

As President, Ronald Reagan began the so-called "Reagan Revolution," which changed America. In 1981 he signed legislation that reduced federal taxes by 23 percent over three years. Five years later Reagan approved a law that overhauled the federal income tax code. Critics charged that these tax cuts added to the enormous federal budget deficit: during the Reagan presidency, one trillion dollars of additional debt was accumulated—more than all of the Presidents from George Washington to Jimmy Carter combined. But the economic recovery initiated in 1983 lasted longer than any recorded in peacetime America, and it carried with it only a modest rate of inflation.

Another part of the "Reagan Revolution" was a devolution of power from the federal to state and local governments. In 1981 Reagan persuaded Congress to collapse 56 specific federal grants to the states into 9 broader categories called "block grants." Federal guidelines pertaining to other state programs were reduced from 318 pages to 11 pages. According to Reagan the operating principle was clear: "We should use the level of government closest to the community involved for all the public functions it can handle." Reagan called this policy the "New Federalism."

In politics, Ronald Reagan presided over the rejuvenation of the Republican Party. When Reagan launched his campaign for the presidency in 1980, 51 percent of all American voters called themselves Democrats; just 30 percent said they were Republicans. Few had much confidence in the GOP to handle important national problems. But the Republicans experienced a revival during the Reagan years. Differences in party identification narrowed from the gargantuan twenty-one points in 1980 to three to four points in most polls by 1988. The famed New Deal coalition formed by Franklin D. Roosevelt in the 1930s ended, and a new partisan parity took its place. Voters gave Republicans high marks on handling economic and defense issues, while Democrats were favored on matters involving economic redistribution—the "fairness issues." The resultant party parity translated into newfound GOP gains among young voters and white southerners, while Democrats maintained strong support among women and minorities. In electoral terms, Republicans established a presidential majority while Democrats continued their dominance in Congress and in the state legislatures.

In foreign affairs, Ronald Reagan acted as a major agent of change, using the motto "Peace Through Strength." In 1981 he proposed, and Congress passed, the largest peacetime increase in the defense budget. The B-1 bomber, more Midgetman missiles, and additional Trident submarines were built. Congress and the President decided that a 600-ship Navy was required and proceeded to meet the target. Reagan also authorized research on the Strategic Defense Initiative (often called "Star Wars" by its critics)—a protection against the prospect of incoming Soviet nuclear warheads. Finally, Reagan became father to the "Reagan Doctrine"—an American pledge to support insurgent democratic movements against Communist governments, notably in Afghanistan, Angola, and Nicaragua.

Reagan's greatest setback was the discovery that members of his National Security Council sold arms to Iran with some of the proceeds illegally diverted to aid the Nicaraguan Contras. Congress established a select committee to investigate the scandal in 1987; its hearings resulted in a temporary loss of public confidence in Reagan.

As President, Ronald Reagan altered the relationship between the United States and the Soviet Union. In 1987 he and Soviet President Mikhail Gorbachev signed the Intermediate-Range Nuclear Forces (INF) Treaty—the first agreement between the United States and the Soviet Union to reduce the size of each superpower's nuclear arsenal.

Reagan's presidency cannot by measured by deeds alone. Reagan took office at a time of national self-doubt following John F. Kennedy's assassination, the U.S. defeat in Vietnam, the Watergate scandals, Gerald Ford's pardon of Richard Nixon, and Jimmy Carter's malaise. By 1980, 51 percent agreed with the statement, "As the government is now organized and operated, I think it is hopelessly incapable of dealing with all the crucial problems facing the country." Reagan renewed American's self-confidence by reaffirming faith in the values of family, work,

neighborhood, and freedom. By his constant recitation of these shibboleths, Reagan became known as the "Great Communicator," since the effect was to restore pride, patriotism, and hope. By the time Reagan left the presidency, 55 percent rejected the idea that the government was unable to tackle tough problems. Moreover, 78 percent said that Reagan "inspired pride and confidence in America." As a result, Reagan became the first President since Dwight Eisenhower to leave office more popular than when he entered. His last job rating taken by the Gallup Organization showed a 68 percent approval rating, higher than any other departing President who was measured against the yardstick of public polls.

It was Reagan who captured his presidency best. In his Farewell Address, he observed, "We weren't just marking time, we made a difference."

*See also:* George H. W. Bush; Jimmy Carter; Dwight D. Eisenhower; Elections of 1964, 1976, 1980, 1984, and 1988; Gerald R. Ford; Barry Goldwater; John F. Kennedy; Walter F. Mondale; Richard M. Nixon; Franklin D. Roosevelt; Adlai E. Stevenson II; Harry S Truman

*John K. White*

REFERENCES

Barrett, Laurence I. 1983. *Gambling with History: Reagan in the White House.* Garden City, NY: Doubleday.

Blumenthal, Sidney, and Thomas Byrne Edsall, eds. 1988. *The Reagan Legacy.* New York: Pantheon.

Boaz, David, ed. 1988. *Assessing the Reagan Years.* Washington: Cato Institute.

Cannon, Lou. 1982. *Reagan.* New York: Putnam's.

Donaldson, Sam. 1987. *Hold On, Mr. President!* New York: Random House.

Dugger, Ronnie. 1983. *On Reagan: The Man and His Presidency.* New York: McGraw-Hill.

Duke, Paul, ed. 1986. *Beyond Reagan: The Politics of Upheaval.* New York: Warner Books.

Edwards, Anne. 1987. *Early Reagan: The Rise to Power.* New York: Morrow.

Erickson, Paul D. 1985. *Reagan Speaks: The Making of an American Myth.* New York: New York U. Pr.

Goldman, Peter, and Tony Fuller. 1985. *The Quest for the Presidency, 1984.* New York: Bantam Books.

Greider, William. 1981. *The Education of David Stockman and Other Americans.* New York: Dutton.

Henry, William A., III. 1985. *Visions of America: How We Saw the 1984 Election.* Boston: Atlantic Monthly Press.

Jones, Charles O., ed. 1988. *The Reagan Legacy.* Chatham, NJ: Chatham House.

Reagan, Ronald, with Richard G. Huebler. 1965. *Where's the Rest of Me?* New York: Duell, Sloan, and Pearce.

Reeves, Richard. 1985. *The Reagan Detour.* New York: Simon & Schuster.

Regan, Donald T. 1988. *For the Record.* New York: Harcourt Brace Jovanovich

Rogin, Michael. 1987. *Ronald Reagan, the Movie and Other Episodes in Political Demonology.* Berkeley: U. of California Pr.

Stockman, David A. 1986. *The Triumph of Politics: Why the Reagan Revolution Failed.* New York: Harper & Row.

Von Damn, Helene. 1976. *Sincerely, Ronald Reagan.* Ottawa, IL: Green Hill.

White, John Kenneth. 1988. *The New Politics of Old Values.* Hanover, NH: U. Pr. of New England.

Wills, Garry. 1981. *Reagan's America: Innocents At Home.* Garden City, NY: Doubleday.

## Reconstruction

Reconstruction refers to the period following the end of the Civil War when the federal government attempted to reconstruct the Union by reconstructing the governments and economies of those states that had rebelled. Rebel states were occupied by the Union Army, and the reorganization of their governments was overseen by federal governors; rebel state governments were required to adopt reforms before being recognized by Congress; and African-American men were enfranchised, and at the same time, leaders of the secessionist state governments were excluded from politics. Meanwhile the Freedmen's Bureau sought to provide the freed slaves with a new means of livelihood.

Reconstruction was ended by the Wormley Bargain in 1877, a failure in many ways. The old southern elite returned to power. The freed slaves found themselves landless, deprived of political rights and compelled by circumstances to labor as sharecroppers. Franchise restrictions and the one-party Democratic system kept both democracy and progress out of the South for several decades more. The cause of this failure is still the focus of controversy, with some holding that the reconstructionists tried to go too far and others holding that they did not go far enough.

In the first phase, which came to be known as "Presidential Reconstruction," President Abraham Lincoln and then his successor Andrew Johnson established new southern state governments by executive order. Black people were not allowed to vote, and most ex-Confederate officers could qualify by swearing not to rebel in the future. The results horrified the Radical Republicans: "Black Codes" were enacted, establishing a form of contract labor that returned the freedmen to near slavery; anti-Black violence broke out in the South; and 58 former Confederate military and civilian officials were elected to the Thirty-ninth Congress. Congress refused to seat any southern members and launched "Congressional Reconstruction" with passage of the First Reconstruction Act (the first of several) in March 1867, requiring the reorganization of all southern states except Tennessee.

All African-American males age 21 and over were now enfranchised, and property and literacy requirements were removed—a step that expanded the white electorate by approximately 35 percent as well; white southerners now had to swear an "ironclad oath" that they had never voluntarily supported the Confederacy; and southern states were more compelled to ratify the Fourteenth Amendment to the Constitution. The military governors supervised the registration of 1,360,000 voters, of whom 660,000 were white and 700,000 Black, by the end of 1868. This increase compared with 721,000 southern white voters in the election of 1860.

The newly registered voters elected delegates to conventions empowered to draft new state constitutions. Black delegates participated in all of these conventions, although they formed a majority only in South Carolina. White delegates were divided between immigrants from the North and native southerners who had qualified to take the oath. The former were more numerous in Florida, Mississippi, and Virginia; the latter—whose views on racial issues generally differed little from those of other white southerners—were more numerous in Alabama, Arkansas, Georgia, North Carolina, and South Carolina.

The new constitutions were required by Congress to provide for universal male suffrage. In addition, they generally authorized systems of free public education—originally on a racially integrated basis—and for an active state role in welfare and economic development. Petitions by freedmen for redistribution of land—the elusive "forty acres and a mule"—were not taken up.

The inclusion of Black men in the electorate, and the exclusion of at least some ex-Confederates, tipped the political balance in the southern states and in the nation as well. The Union League, effectively an arm of the Radical Republicans, conducted a vast political education campaign among the freedmen. This campaign was short-lived and extended only to the mechanics of voting and to the understanding that the Republican Party had brought emancipation; but it was enough to assure a solid African-American vote for the Republicans.

Many Black Americans won elective office during Reconstruction, including fourteen members of the House of Representatives and two U.S. Senators. (Six more African-American members of Congress served between 1880 and 1901.) This led the conservatives to complain of Black domination or "Africanization"; but in reality African-Americans never won a dominant position in any state and frequently found themselves outvoted by the racists. The highest Black federal representation was eight, including one Senator, in the Forty-fourth Congress (1875–1877), and this total fell back to four in the Forty-fifth Congress, and to one or two for the rest of the nineteenth century.

The reconstructed state governments attempted to organize public schools and promote business. As the federal military presence dwindled, and the Ku Klux Klan, founded in 1865, violently attacked Black and white Radicals, the states also organized militias that included both races.

Not all Radicals were driven solely by principle; the reconstructed governments were also marked by corruption (as were many other American governments of the time). The Radicals' ambitious social programs also strained state treasuries, sometimes driving legislatures to have to enact unpopular new taxes. Conservatives used these problems skillfully to build opposition—often violent—to Radical rule in the South. As the interests of northern Republicans turned to industrial development, the tide began to turn. Blacks were driven from the voting rolls by economic coercion or physical terror, and more and more ex-Confederates won political rehabilitation.

Reconstruction was formally ended in 1877, as part of the compromise that recognized Rutherford B. Hayes as winner of the disputed presidential election of 1876. In fact, however, it had already been ended by Democratic electoral victories in every southern state except South Carolina, Florida, and Louisiana; Reconstruction had ended in Tennessee and Virginia as early as 1869.

The "redeemed" state governments proceeded to institutionalize their victory. The militias were disbanded, leaving African-Americans at the mercy of the Klan. "Jim Crow" laws, mandating racial segregation of public accommodations, were passed throughout the South, and their constitutionality was upheld by the Supreme Court in *Plessy v. Ferguson*. The disenfranchisement of Black voters was reinforced by literacy tests, poll taxes, and other legal subterfuges, and the last Black member of Congress, G. H. White of North Carolina, was defeated in 1900.

The failure of Reconstruction produced a condition of near peonage for most southern African-Americans, who were left as landless sharecroppers with no effective legal or political rights; its failure also produced a condition of stagnation for the whole southern economy. Its political legacy was the one-party Democratic system in the South, in which officeholders were effectively chosen in Democratic primaries by a small percentage of even the white population. Although Black out-migration began to increase at the time of World War I, the political situation remained essentially unchanged until the beginning of the civil rights movement in the mid-1950s.

*See also:* Elections of 1860 and 1876, Fourteenth Amendment, Rutherford B. Hayes, Jim Crow Laws, Andrew Johnson, Ku Klux Klan, Abraham Lincoln, Poll Taxes, Union League of America

*John C. Berg*

REFERENCES

Burgess, John W. 1902. *Reconstruction and the Constitution 1866–1876*. New York: Scribner's.

Du Bois, W. E. B. 1935. *Black Reconstruction in America*. New York: Harcourt Brace.

Dunning, William A. 1904. *Essays on the Civil War and Reconstruction*. New York: Macmillan.

———. 1907. *Reconstruction, Political and Economic 1865–1877*. New York: Harper Brothers.

Foner, Eric. 1988. *Reconstruction: America's Unfinished Revolution 1863–1877*. New York: Harper & Row.

Lynch, John R. 1969. *The Facts of Reconstruction*. New York: Arno Press.

Rabinowitz, Howard N. 1940. *Southern Black Leaders of the Reconstruction Era*. Urbana: U. of Illinois Pr.

Smith, Samuel Denny. 1940. *The Negro in Congress 1870–1901*. Port Washington, NY: Kennikat.

Thornbrough, Emma Lou, ed. 1972. *Black Reconstructionists*. Englewood Cliffs, NJ: Prentice-Hall.

Woodward, C. Vann. 1951. *Origins of the New South, 1877–1914*. Baton Rouge: Louisiana State U. Pr.

———. 1956. *Reunion and Reaction: The Compromise of 1877 and the End of Reconstruction*. 2d ed. Garden City, NY: Doubleday.

## Recruitment and Motivation of Party Activists

Party activists are the leaders and workers at the base of the party organizations. They are the precinct captains, ward chairs, committee members, convention delegates, club actives—the "militants" or "cadres" who presumably fight the party battles in the trenches. They are important because of their roles in organizational maintenance, representation links with the public, and the mobilization of votes. They presumably are closest to the voters and provide the continuity that the party needs in its work in between elections as well as at election time. As the party encounters social change, the activists should be the first to be responsive. The survival of parties depends on the character and activity of these base-level personnel. In an electoral democracy, who these activists are and how they behave in competition with one another are crucial for the system. They should be combative, ideologically distinct, and responsive to their followers. Three questions relevant to an understanding of party activists have persisted in the study of American parties: what incentives lead to the involvement of party activists? to what extent are these motivations sustained? and has the motivational structure of party activism changed in recent years and, if so, with what effects?

The study of the recruitment and motivations of activists can reveal much about the quality and direction of party organizational life. How, through what process, these people get into the organization, why they are attracted to such positions, and the circumstances surrounding their entrance to the party will have implications for party performance. Indeed some controversy does exist on such matters, particularly over whether changing motivational patterns have contributed to party defeat.

A great deal of research has been conducted on the recruitment and motivations of local party activists, the earliest studies dating from the 1930s. An analysis by Harold Gosnell of precinct leaders in Chicago, for example, concluded that economic gain was a dominant incentive for these precinct captains in the Chicago machine. Many had limited educations and came from poor, immigrant families; naturally they aspired to better jobs. After World War II these studies of local party leaders burgeoned, beginning with research in Detroit and Los Angeles in 1956 and followed by many studies in a variety of settings. Several analyzed the motivations of activists in Manhattan, St. Louis, and in many other cities and counties. Later, studies of delegates to state and national conventions added greatly to our knowledge.

From studies of the recruitment of activists gradually emerged a set of observations leading to a "model" of how a person became involved. Socioeconomic status, it was argued, provided the context—certain attitudes that facilitated the development of an interest in partisan politics. And then, an "external push" (by party leaders, other groups, family or friends) finally persuaded people to assume party activist positions. The data suggested that three paths led to involvement: (1) overt recruitment of persons previously socialized to politics; (2) a self-conscious decision by the "self-starter" to become involved, usually after delayed socialization as an adult; and (3) "accidental involvement" of persons who had not been interested previously but who assumed activist responsibilities in the context of social contacts and friendships in the absence of other available personnel.

Two general conclusions resulted from this body of research. One was that recruitment was indeed rather haphazard, particularly because organizational leaders by no means controlled who entered the party, contrary to theories of "oligarchy" and of professional control. A second conclusion showed that as a result of this relatively open recruitment system, the types of activists who joined the party came from different backgrounds and held different perspectives. Some were self-consciously committed to party work for ideological reasons; some were induced to join despite virtually no commitment to causes or issues; some saw the party as opening up a new career; some came into politics as party of a family tradition; some came via activists in other interest groups; and some were genuine loyalists to the party. These differing perspectives undoubtedly had an impact on their performance as party activists.

Discovering specifically why people become activists, as well as why they stay in party work, has been the subject of much research. Considerable agreement emerged from such research, although different interpretations do occur. The differences are basically the result of either the locale or level or time in which the study was conducted. Precinct leaders may differ somewhat from convention delegates; Detroit is not Los Angeles; the 1980 convention is not he same as the one in 1972. Nevertheless, a remarkable confirmation of the findings reported here characterizes most of the studies.

Scholarly research has tended to identify three, sometimes four, basic types of incentives. They are *material* incentives (tangible rewards such as money or jobs or personal career goals); *solidary* incentives (intangible social rewards such as honors and social friendships and the conviviality of politics); and *purposive* incentives (intangible rewards such as satisfaction from achievement of a purpose or working for a policy or cause, including a sense of party loyalty). These types of motivations have been at times linked to types of party organizations. The city machine presumably was primarily material but also included those who had solidary motivations.

The research on motivations used various approaches. Usually, however, survey studies of activists used 11 or 12 specific incentives and asked respondents to indicate whether each was "very important," "somewhat important," or "not important" as a reason for *becoming involved.* The activist was also asked what his or her most important *current satisfaction* from party work was, and what he or she would miss most if required to leave party work *now.* Such data permitted observations, based on recall data, of motives for entrance into party work, as compared to current motivations, thus permitting an assessment of whether motivations had changed during the time that the respondent was a party activist. In later work, panel studies of convention delegates could analyze change over time more directly.

This research has produced a rich set of findings over the years. First, people clearly become party activists for a great variety of reasons. Five motivations seem to dominate as reasons for initially becoming active. These five as revealed in Detroit and Los Angeles studies (both in the 1950s and the 1980s) are shown in Table 1.

A sixth incentive that appears in studies of delegates is "electing particular candidates," important for 70 percent to 80 percent of state conventions delegates and over 90 percent of national convention delegates. This incentive is true of less than one-fourth of the local precinct activists, however.

Material incentives such as "building a career in politics" or "business contacts" are much less relevant in recent studies than in the days of Gosnell's research. We find less than 20 percent reporting such motives. Where "the machine" was, and is, effective, however, such motivations did, and will, prevail.

Clearly, in terms of entrance motivations, party activists have a diverse set of drives, aspirations, and incentives. And their reasons for involvement are overlapping, not mutually exclusive—party loyalty as well as social comradeship. Analysts note, however, that the dominant reasons for *becoming* active are strongly "purposive," tending to be impersonal, philosophical, even ideological. Indeed, when we press these activists in some of these studies to indicate which *one* of these motives was *most* important to them for joining initially, the recollection for over 70 percent is "purposive." This trend is confirmed by the national delegate studies. Also notable in those studies is the high proportion who, when asked about a reason for their decision to become involved in the nominating process, gave responses that emphasized party, policy, and civic duty as well as candidate support.

A continuity over time and a similarity by study and community characterized these patterns of motivations. The differences appear to be marginal, although some variations do exist. In Detroit in 1980 (compared to 1956) respondents revealed somewhat more interest in policy, slightly less in community obligation and social contacts. In Los Angeles, policy concerns remained high. In both cities the importance of party loyalty declined. Yet the five major incentives in 1956 remained the five that ranked highest in 1980 for both Detroit and Los Angeles.

## Table 1

*Local Activists' Motivation for Becoming Active*

| | % saying the motive was "very important" | | | |
| | *Detroit* | | *Los Angeles* | |
| | 1956 | 1980 | 1956 | 1980 |
|---|---|---|---|---|
| Desire to Influence Politics | 58 | 65 | 74 | 71 |
| Feeling of Community Obligations | 65 | 58 | 59 | 50 |
| Party Loyalty | 53 | 38 | 69 | 50 |
| Commitment to Politics as "My Way of Life" | 43 | 50 | 43 | 56 |
| Social Contacts and Friendships | 56 | 41 | 32 | 33 |

# Table 2

*National Convention Delegates' Motivation for Becoming Involved*

| | % saying it was "extremely important" | | | |
| | *Democrats* | | | *Republicans* |
| Reason | 1972 | 1980 | 1972 | 1980 |
|---|---|---|---|---|
| Candidate | 97 | 95 | 94 | 96 |
| Policies | 90 | 82 | 79 | 82 |
| Civic Responsibilities ("Politics is my way of life") | 74 | 78 | 91 | 90 |
| Party Loyalty | 59 | 74 | 90 | 80 |
| Social Contracts (also the fun of politics) | 57 | 72 | 68 | 67 |

What is remarkable is that essentially the same generalization holds for the national delegates from 1972 to 1980. Keeping in mind the strong candidate-centered type of involvement for delegates as distinguishing them from precinct leaders or county committee members, we find great continuity for the five basic motivations. These are remarkably parallel rank orders, signifying continuity in the cultural norms for political motivation for these types of American political elites.

Political analysts have pointed to two types of controversies in this area. One concerns the question of the possible decline of party loyalty. Linked to that is a second concern—whether at a time when activists and delegates become more ideological (or "purposive"), they have less interest in the party per se. The analysis of the 1972 Democratic delegates led Jeane Kirkpatrick to conclude that the emergence of new kinds of activists could lead to the "dismantling of the parties." Subsequent research has demonstrated that this has certainly not been the case. Miller and Jennings's national delegate study data reveal no decline, even a resurgence of party loyalty (see the data presented in Table 2). And other studies have also disconfirmed these early hypothetical concerns, revealing that activists with "purposive" incentives do not necessarily have weak partisanship. The same conclusion emerges from a study of delegates at 11 state conventions in 1980. Some decline in party loyalty may indeed occur at times, but partisanship remains one of the major reasons for involvement.

The concept of "motivational reorientation" has developed to describe the change that takes place in the activist's incentives or satisfaction during his or her period of party work. Several studies have now documented that the activist may be socialized to party organization politics in such a way that the original motivations change—primarily from "purposive" to "solidary" or even to personal career-oriented motivations. Analysts have tried to prove this switch by different methods. In some of these studies, analysts carefully asked how the activist *originally* became interested *and* why he or she originally decided to take a party position. Also asked was what are the *present* basic satisfactions to party work. Also, asked was what the activist would *miss most* if forced to leave party work tomorrow. In this way analysts have been able to discover what the organization really means to the respondent. This method depends on the frankness and correctness of both recollections and of current motives. The level of frankness in the discussion of both early reasons for joining and the current nature of satisfaction has conduced to accepting the disparities between original and current satisfactions as real.

In the early (1956) study of this question of motivational reorientation, political analysts discovered that precinct leaders usually gave some type of purposive explanation for initial involvement, that is, a desire to influence policy (21 percent), community obligations (20 percent), party attachment (13 percent), and so on. Cumulating these responses shows that, while many reasons were advanced as "very important," when pressed for "the best reason," 65 percent gave clearly purposive responses. When the focus was shifted to their explanations for their current satisfaction ("If you had to drop out of political activity tomorrow, what things would you miss the most from such work?"), a different set of responses emerged: social contacts (55 percent), the fun and excitement of politics (10 percent), working for issues and politics (10 percent), moral and philosophical concerns (4 percent), business and personal career interests (1 percent). In addition, 18 percent were fully disillusioned, were not able to indicate any positive satisfactions, and were inclined to leave party work.

If we cumulate responses, we find, both in 1956 and 1980, this pattern for Detroit activists:

## Table 3

*Motivational Reorientation of Detroit Activists*

|  | 1956 | 1980 |
| --- | --- | --- |
| *Entrance Motivation* | | |
| Ideological or Philosophical | 65% | 67% |
| *Current Motivation* | | |
| Ideological or Philosophical | 14 | 28 |
| Difference | -51 | -39 |

Obviously for these activists, some process of resocialization was occurring as a result of their exposure to party work. This exposure and experience resulted in the manifestation of more "solidary" satisfaction and even personal, career, possibly materialistic, motivations when they were queried about what kept them involved. One interpretation is that the party organization was maintained because it provided social recognition, sheer fun of campaigning, and friendships. For many the organization had become primarily a social group. That is not to say that ideology was irrelevant but merely that it was not dominant.

While there is considerable continuity in the motivational basis of party involvement and the sustaining of interest in party work, motivational changes also take place during the activist's career. A panel study of national delegates reveals both phenomena. The study of the 1972 Democratic Party delegates reinterviewed in 1976 and 1980 resulted in evidence not only that change occurred but also that the system maintained itself. Miller and Jennings summarize their findings by asserting that "experience, socialization, or the sheer passage of time produced changes in the perspectives of the 1972 Democratic delegates." Policy concerns were "modified" and attachment to party achieved "greater importance. . . . The amateur's enthusiasm for ideological purity at the expense of party was apparently short-lived."

Research in other countries often reveals differences reflecting the influence of particular cultural norms. Motivation of party activists are

a good example. Motives may be expressed quite differently. In West Germany, for example, 28 percent of the Christian Democratic Union members make explicitly religious references, such as "As a follower of Christ I work for the CDU." Similarly 25 percent of the Social Democrats in Germany state that as union members they should be in the Social Democratic Party (SPD). Further, in some of these countries, extreme parties on "the Left" or "the Right" are much more ideological in motivations than are those in "the Centre." Multiparty systems such as those in the Netherlands, Sweden, and India show greater evidence of ideological commitment as an incentive for entrance into party work than in our system. One major similarity, however, demonstrates strong cross-national uniformity: the decline in ideological motivation, even for extreme parties, during the party career, much as in the United States. In Germany the decline was over 30 percent; in Sweden close to 40 percent; in the Netherlands 40 percent; in India, a decline in ideological perspectives of 48 percent for the Communists and 52 percent for a right-wing party. After a person has been in the party for some time, at least in democratic systems, ideological fervor diminishes and social rewards, as well as the fun of politics, become more important. This finding suggests a basic similarity in the party socialization process across systems.

A requisite for the survival and efficiency of the party organization is the provision of rewards and satisfaction for its working cadres. Parties are relatively open, voluntary groups at the local level in most democratic systems, not usually primarily patronage parties. They consist of many different types who somewhat haphazardly were attracted or recruited to party work. As such they are complex motivational structures. The rewards that people seek differ, therefore, and the organization has to provide them. The very pluralism of the party, the heterogeneity of its activists and their varied aspirations and needs, ironically, may be an advantage rather than a detriment. Ideological objectives can be satisfied for many, but the party is not an exclusively ideological group (many would say, fortunately). Certain personal career opportunities exist for activists, but again, only a minority, fortunately, are involved exclusively for material gain. Social interactions become a major source of satisfaction for many of those who do the hard work of the organization and perform the critical vote mobilization tasks, without necessarily hoping to profit economically or expect instant achievement of policy objectives. Many kinds of activists work in the party, contributing different types of skills, fulfilling different needs, and satisfying quite disparate drives. And thus, while not the most efficient political apparatus, the party in electoral democracies today survives, providing adequate rewards for its activists, maintaining linkages with its support groups, adapting to its own political culture, and, it is hoped, also responding to social change.

*See also:* Bosses, Harold Gosnell

*Samuel J. Edlersveld*

REFERENCES

Bowman, Lewis, and G. R. Boynton. 1966. "Recruitment Patterns Among Local Party Officials." 60 *American Political Science Review* 667.

Clark, Peter, and James Q. Wilson. 1961. "Incentive Systems: Theory of Organizations." 6 *Administrative Science Quarterly* 129.

Conway, M. Margaret, and Frank Feigert. 1968. "Motivation, Incentive Systems and the Political Party Organization." 62 *American Political Science Review* 1159.

Crotty, William, ed. 1986. *Political Parties in Local Areas*. Knoxville: U. of Tennessee Pr.

Eldersveld, Samuel J. 1964. *Political Parties: A Behavioral Analysis*. Chicago: Rand McNally.

———. 1989. *Political Elites in Modern Societies: Empirical Research and Democratic Theory*. Ann Arbor: U. of Michigan Pr.

Gosnell, Harold. 1937. *Machine Politics: Chicago Model*. Chicago: U. of Chicago Pr.

Hirshfield, Robert, Bert Swanson, and Blanche Blank. 1962. "A Profile of Political Activists in Manhattan." 15 *Western Political Quarterly* 489.

Ippolito, Dennis. 1969. "Motivational Reorientation and Change Among Party Activists." 31 *Journal of Politics* 1098.

Kirkpatrick, Jeane. 1978. *Dismantling the Parties*. Washington: American Enterprise Institute.

Marvick, Dwaine. 1980. "Party Organizational Personnel and Electoral Democracy in Los Angeles, 1963–1972." In William Crotty, ed. *The Party Symbol*. San Francisco: Freeman.

Miller, Warren E., and M. Kent Jennings. 1986. *Parties in Transition: A Longitudinal Study of Party Elites and Party Supporters*. New York: Russell Sage.

Rapoport, Ronald B., Alan I. Abramowitz, and John McGlennon. 1986. *The Life of the Parties: Activists in Presidential Politics*. Lexington: U. Pr. of Kentucky.

Wilson, James Q. 1962. *The Amateur Democrat*. Chicago: U. of Chicago Pr.

# Red Scare

The term "Red Scare" refers to a specific event—the antiradical hysteria and repression of 1919 and 1920; but it has also acquired a generic meaning, so that one may speak of the red scare of the late 1940s, or ask whether another red scare might take place.

Radicals faced repression both before and after the Red Scare, but the level of hysteria, the widespread disregard for civil liberties and legal standards, and the sheer quantity of the repression justify singling out this two-year period to have its own name. The Red Scare had three components: repressive state action that broke all limits of constitutional civil liberties or even of logic; extralegal violence, perpetrated both by such organized paramilitary groups as the American Legion and the Ku Klux Klan and by spontaneously gathered lynch mobs; and hysterical outpouring of anti-communist denunciations from the nation's press.

Official repression included the deportation of radicals who were aliens; the trial of native radicals in state courts; and the purging of elected Socialists from legislative bodies. Under the Alien Law of 1918, noncitizens could be deported solely for their political beliefs. Attorney General A. Mitchell Palmer therefore directed his Bureau of Investigation to concentrate on alien radicals, many of whom were arrested in the "Palmer raids." On November 7, 1919, 250 members of the Union of Russian Workers were arrested in coordinated raids in 11 cities; a second raid on January 2, 1920, arrested over 4,000 suspected radicals in 33 cities. United States citizens picked up in these raids were eventually released, but 840 aliens were deported. The number would have been much greater had not Secretary of Labor William B. Wilson and his Assistant Secretary, Louis Post, insisted on some vestige of fair procedure. Palmer sought (but failed to get) a federal criminal anarchy statute to use against native American radicals, but hundreds were prosecuted under state laws and sent to prison purely on the basis of their political views. New York, where the state legislature's Lusk Committee both investigated and prosecuted, was particularly active. Those tried included many of the leaders of the two newly formed Communist parties. New York worried little over civil liberties; when Benjamin Gitlow, a Communist leader, appealed his five- to ten-year sentence on the ground that he had never actually advocated use of violence as charged, the appellate court ruled that, while Communists might not advocate violence, "they are chargeable with knowledge that their aims and ends cannot be accomplished without force, violence and bloodshed, and therefore it is reasonable to construe what they advocate as intending the use of all means essential to the success of their program." Victor Berger, a Socialist member of the U.S. House of Representatives, was expelled from that body by a near unanimous vote and then expelled again after his Milwaukee constituents voted to send him back. Five Socialist members of the New York State Assembly were treated the same way.

Legal repression was supplemented by extralegal violence against radicals, the newly formed American Legion becoming a leader in this activity. The Legion's best-known exploit was the Centralia Massacre in Centralia, Washington, on Armistice Day, 1919; after an armed attack on the Industrial Workers of the World (IWW) hall left three Legionnaires dead, Legion members broke into the jail that night and lynched IWW activist Wesley Everest. Everest was castrated, hanged, and riddled with bullets while hanging; his body, with its neck now a foot long, was then put on public display. The Legion, the Ku Klux Klan, and similar groups disrupted radical meetings and vandalized radical offices across the country.

The nation's newspapers added to the general hysteria throughout 1919 with such headlines as "RED PERIL HERE," "PLAN BLOODY REVOLUTION," and "REDS TRY TO STIR NEGROES TO REVOLT." Exaggerated reports of Bolshevik influence and plans for violence in the unions were widely published. No doubt the press found this role congenial, but it was hardly spontaneous. The newly formed General Intelligence Division (GID) of the Department of Justice's Bureau of Investigation, headed by J. Edgar Hoover, ran a full-scale propaganda campaign, mailing out a steady stream of antiradical press releases, draft editorials, and even cartoons, much of which found its way into print. GID propaganda was particularly active from September 1919 through January 1920.

The mood was set for the Red Scare by parallel upsurges in labor militancy, violent protests, revolutionary political activity, and racial violence. Approximately 25 percent of the industrial working class took part in strikes during 1919. A general strike took place in Seattle in February; the Boston police struck in September; 365,000 steelworkers struck in late September; and 394,000 coal miners struck in November. The IWW, a revolutionary union, led one of these strikes, but its role was often exaggerated by the press.

Other factors that contributed to the Red Scare included a wave of bomb attacks on prominent persons in May and June; law enforcement authorities declared that they had discovered a much larger number of unsuccessful bomb plots. A bomb destroyed the front of the Washington, D.C., residence of Attorney General A. Mitchell Palmer. No one in the Palmer household was injured, but some human remains, together with pieces of violently worded anarchist literature, were discovered on the scene. (The remains were those of a single individual who, according to some reports, had had two left legs; however, no one outside of radical circles seemed to find this anatomical anomaly suspicious.) The Russian Revolution and the founding of two Communist parties that it inspired added to the fear that revolution was imminent. Race riots disturbed 25 cities and towns, with at least 120 people killed, between April and October 1919; and 78 African-Americans were murdered by lynch mobs that year. These racial conflicts too were sometimes portrayed as part of a Bolshevik plot to foment discord.

Some scholars consider the Red Scare an irrational hysteria that gripped the public and its leaders alike; others think it a cynical manipulation of the public's fears so as to achieve such covert political aims as victory at the polls, the weakening of labor unions, and white supremacy. By late 1920 it was over, although repression continued. Congress refused to pass a federal criminal anarchy law, and Palmer's predictions of radical violence on May Day 1920 fell flat. The Red Scare's impact on American ideology was great; its immediate impact on parties and elections was smaller. Palmer, who had hoped to ride the issue into the White House, failed to get the Democratic nomination. President Warren Harding eventually pardoned most of the imprisoned radicals. (Eugene V. Debs ran as the Socialist candidate while still in prison and received 915,302 votes, his highest total ever.) However, the impact on the nascent Communist Party was great; the party was driven underground, lost most of its members, and was rendered ineffective for at least five more years.

*See also:* Victor Berger, Eugene V. Debs, Warren G. Harding, Ku Klux Klan, A. Mitchell Palmer

*John C. Berg*

REFERENCES

Bennett, David Harry. 1988. *The Party of Fear: From Nativist Movements to the New Right in American History.* Chapel Hill: U. of North Carolina Pr.

Brecher, Jeremy. 1974. *Strike!* Greenwich, CT: Fawcett. (Orig. pub. 1972, Straight Arrow Books.)

Colburn, David R. 1973. "Governor Alfred E. Smith and the Red Scare, 1919–1920." 88 *Political Science Quarterly* 423–444.

Foster, William Z. 1968. *History of the Communist Party of the United States*. Westport, CT: Greenwood. (Orig. pub. 1952.)

Howe, Irving, and Lewis Coser. 1974. *The American Communist Party: A Critical History*. 2nd ed. New York: DaCapo Press. (Orig. pub. 1962, Praeger.)

Levin, Murray B. 1971. *Political Hysteria in America: The Democratic Capacity for Repression*. New York: Basic Books.

Murray, Robert K. 1964. *Red Scare: A Study of National Hysteria, 1919–1920*. New York: McGraw-Hill. (Orig. pub. 1955, U. of Minnesota Pr.)

Preston, William, Jr. 1966. *Aliens and Dissenters: Federal Suppression of Radicals, 1903–1933*. New York: Harper & Row. (Orig. pub. 1963, Harvard U. Pr.)

Tuttle, William M., Jr. 1970. *Race Riot: Chicago in the Red Summer of 1919*. New York: Atheneum.

Williams, David 1981. "The Bureau of Investigation and Its Critics, 1919–1921: The Origins of Federal Political Surveillance." 67 *Journal of American History* 560–579.

## B. Carroll Reece (1889–1961)

Post-World War II Chairman of the Republican National Committee. One of 13 children, Brazilla Carroll Reece graduated from Carson-Newman College in Tennessee. An articulate activist in high school and college, he was class valedictorian in both. He got an M.A. in finance from New York University and was a highly decorated infantry officer in World War I.

Returning from Europe in 1919, Reece became director of the School of Commerce, Accounts and Finance at New York University but took a leave of absence in 1920 to run for Congress from the First District of Tennessee. At age 30, he entered Congress and served continuously thereafter. He also became involved in banking. Defeated for reelection only once (1930), Republican Reece became a House expert on economic legislation, particularly in the securities, monopoly, and consumer fields.

In 1939 Reece was elected national committeeman for Tennessee and came to be regarded as the head of the Republican Party in the South. As the candidate of the pro-Robert Taft members of the national committee, Reece defeated the pro-Thomas Dewey candidate for the national chairmanship in 1946 by a vote of 59 to 22.

In the 1946 midterm campaign, Reece popularized the "labor bosses" and anti-Communist themes that continued to be significant themes for many subsequent national campaigns. He also followed Senator Robert A. Taft's lead on most policy and organizational matters. He hoped to become a U.S. Senator from Tennessee in 1948 but was not elected. He was reelected to the House of Representatives in 1950.

*See also:* Robert A. Taft

*Ralph M. Goldman*

## Thomas B. Reed (1839–1902)

One of the most powerful and influential Speakers of the House of Representatives. Thomas Brackett Reed almost single-handedly molded the speakership and House rules into tools for partisan governance in the chamber. His speakership began an era of acute partisanship in the House, one that lasted until the revolt against Speaker Joseph Cannon in the early twentieth century.

Reed was first elected to the House as a Representative from Maine in 1876, and he served continuously until 1899, resigning in protest against President William McKinley's expansionist foreign policy. Reed's espousal of orthodox Republican principles (e.g., "sound money," protectionism, and civil rights) and his long tenure allowed him to rise steadily in the House Republican hierarchy; he became a member of the Rules Committee by 1882 and the Ways and Means Committee by 1884.

Reed was elected Speaker of the House when the Republicans gained control of the chamber in 1889. Extending many of the partisan precedents developed by the Democratic Speaker John G. Carlisle, Reed used his prerogatives as chair and his committee appointment power to ease the way for passage of the Republican program. Reed went beyond Carlisle's efforts, ultimately codifying a series of rules changes that came to be known as the "Reed Rules."

The genesis of the Reed Rules is often traced to events in early 1890 (51st Congress), when the House was considering the contested election case of *Smith v. Jackson*. The Republicans enjoyed only a four-vote majority when the Fifty-first Congress convened, a tiny margin in the resolution of this case of great interest to both parties.

The major tool of minority party obstruction at the time was the "disappearing quorum," by which minority party members, despite their physical presence in the hall of the House, would decline to answer the call of the roll; if the party margin was narrow enough, the absence of just a few majority party members would result in less than a quorum voting. Because the Constitution precludes either chamber of Congress from conducting business in the absence of a quorum, the House would then adjourn. On January 19, 1890, when Charles Crisp (D-Ga.) challenged the consideration of *Smith v. Jackson*, the vote on whether to proceed with its consideration yielded a tally of 161 yeas, 2 nays, and 165 not voting—less than a quorum voting. However, instead of adjourning, Reed ordered that the doors of the House chamber be barred and that the clerk record the names of those Democrats who were physically in the hall but who had failed to answer the previous roll call. The clerk's count indicated that a majority of the House was indeed physically present. Reed ruled that the number of Representatives in the hall of the House, not the number actually voting, determined whether a quorum existed; he then ordered that the consideration of the election case continue.

Democrats, immediately objecting to Reed's tactics, tried to make life difficult for the Speaker for the remainder of the Congress. Despite, or because of, continued Democratic objection to his tactics and interpretation of the House rules, Reed moved to consolidate his control over floor proceedings by changing the House rules to conform with his rulings. The Reed rules, which were passed on February 5, 1890, outlawed dilatory motions, specified that the Speaker could count as present those in the chamber who did not answer the roll call, reduced the quorum of the Committee of the Whole from a quorum of the whole House to 100, authorized the Committee of the Whole to close debate on any section of a bill under consideration, and generally reorganized the order of House business.

When the Democrats regained control of the House in the Fifty-second Congress, they rescinded the Reed Rules. On the other hand, Republicans used delaying tactics to such an advantage that the Democratic majority had to reinstitute many of Reed's innovations at the start of the Fifty-third Congress, also controlled by the Democrats. When the GOP regained control of the House in the Fifty-fourth Congress (1895), with Reed again the Speaker, the Reed Rules were reinstated in full.

Reed's ability to lead the Republican Party with a firm hand and to pursue a strongly partisan policy path in the Fifty-first, Fifty-fourth, and Fifty-fifth Congresses is often attributed to his strong personality. Yet the inability of other Speakers with equally strong personalities to dominate House proceedings to an equal degree (e.g., Samuel Rayburn and Tip O'Neill) suggests that more than personality was involved in Reed's strength. A great part of the parliamentary dominance that Reed seemed to possess, as was true of Speakers David Henderson and Cannon after him, can be explained by the nature of partisan cleavages in the country following Reconstruction. Both parties were fairly homogeneous, with the Republicans centered in the northern cities, the Democrats in southern farms. Because of this relative homogeneity, party leaders were given a free reign by their rank and file to pursue policy with single-minded determination. The system of strong majority party control in the House that Reed initiated and formalized began to disintegrate around the turn of the century, when the bases of the two parties themselves began to dissolve.

*See also:* Joe Cannon, John G. Carlisle, Charles Crisp, David B. Henderson, Sam Rayburn

*Charles Stewart III*

REFERENCES

Galloway, George B. 1962. *History of the House of Representatives*. New York: Crowell.

## George E. Reedy (1917– )

Press Secretary to President Lyndon Johnson. When Pierre Salinger suddenly resigned as Press Secretary to the President of the United States in March 1964, Lyndon Johnson confidently summoned George Edward Reedy to fill the post. Reedy was greatly respected for his keen intellect and political instincts. He also had an experiential background that was well suited to managing President Johnson's relations with the press.

Reedy was executive director of the Senate Democratic Policy Committee during Johnson's tenure as Senate Majority Leader. When Johnson started his term as Vice President, he brought Reedy along to the White House to be his special assistant. Reedy was also appointed to the National Aeronautics and Space Council, which Johnson directed during his vice presidency.

Reedy was born in East Chicago, Indiana, the son of a renowned Chicago newsman. Reedy was a gifted youngster who enrolled in a special program for gifted students at the University of Chicago, earning a B.A. in sociology in 1938, then joining the Washington bureau of United Press International. He enlisted in the Army Air Corps in the summer of 1942. Returning to UPI in 1946, Reedy covered the U.S. Senate. Reedy was so impressed by Johnson's political abilities that he resigned from UPI in 1951 to join Johnson's Senate staff. Contrary to most accounts, only after Johnson helped pass the Civil Rights Act of 1957 did Reedy see Johnson as a potential President.

Disheartened by Johnson's increasingly hostile attitude toward the press, in the Vietnam years, Reedy, citing a need for surgery to correct a painful hammertoe condition, took a leave of absence in the summer of 1965, and then officially resigned as Press Secretary in late spring of 1966. However, he returned to the White House in 1968 as a special consultant to the President on matters of labor-management relations, civil rights, and executive appointments. Reedy then became the Nieman Professor of Journalism at Marquette University.

*See also:* Lyndon B. Johnson

*Paul Haskell Zernicke*

REFERENCES

Goldman, Eric F. 1969. *The Tragedy of Lyndon Johnson.* New York: Knopf.

McPherson, Harry. 1972. *A Political Education.* Boston: Little, Brown.

Reedy, George. 1970. *Twilight of the Presidency.* New York: National Public Library.

## Referenda Voting

A referendum is a procedure whereby a representative body refers a measure to the electorate for its approval. Most often, a measure, if approved by the required majority, then becomes law, although a few referenda are designed to elicit public opinion only and are nonbinding. A referendum may be distinguished from an initiative in which citizens through a petition process initiated a popular vote on a law or constitutional change.

The earliest rationale for referenda lay in the doctrine of the sovereignty of the people; changes in the fundamental organization or operation of a government needed the people's consent, not their representatives'. When Massachusetts in 1778 replaced its colonial charter with a new constitution, it became the first state to hold a popular referendum. By the 1830s, popular approval of state constitutional changes was well established, and through 1985, some 7,965 amendments to constitutions had been voted upon. Only Delaware does not currently permit popular ratification of constitutional changes.

Dissatisfaction with legislators led to new rationales for referenda. In the early nineteenth century, public funds raised through taxation and bond issues were used to finance expanded transportation systems. When escalating debts jeopardized the credit of several states during the panic of 1837, pressure mounted to alter constitutions to make borrowing and taxation laws conditional on voter approval. Rhode Island led the way in 1842, followed by 35 other states to date. Most states have also come to permit local jurisdiction to pass ordinances (such as school levies) that are conditional on voter approval. Some 10,000 to 15,000 of these referenda are estimated to be held annually in the United States.

Also in the nineteenth century, legislators began to use referenda to avoid decision-making on certain controversial issues that threatened party coalitions. Faced with a population growing in its ethic and cultural diversity, they referred value-laden measures (liquor control, gambling restrictions, etc.) to the voters. In 1883 New York authorized the first advisory referendum, on the issue of contract labor in state prisons. In 1898 South Dakota became the first of 26 states to allow voters to initiate legislation or demand a popular referendum on any recently enacted law. The political upheavals of the 1890s had convinced many that traditional political leaders and institutions could not be trusted. Direct democracy, checking legislatures, seemed to be the answer. In the 1960s and 1970s, another period of political upheaval, initiatives again rose in popularity. Political scientist Virginia Graham records some 1,326 initiatives held between 1898 and 1976. Although the issue has come up occasionally in relation to declaring war, Congress has never authorized a national referendum: the idea of a national initiative was considered in the 1970s but dropped.

Because so many referenda on so many different topics have taken place over a wide span of years, study of them as a phenomenon is difficult, and generalization about voting behavior is usually based on severely restricted samples, mostly reflecting the recent past. Rarely if ever have all those voting for candidates in elections also voted on referenda issues. David Magleby reported an average 14 percent to 17 percent drop-off for the period 1970–1982 in three states, a finding similar to that in less extensive studies. Voter initiatives typically had lower drop-offs than legislative submissions. National voter surveys in 1970, 1972, and 1974 indicated that poorer, less-educated voters were less likely to vote on propositions; however, on clearly understood, high-saliency issues, referenda studies show little difference between proposition voters and others at the polls.

Since voters lack cues such as party to suggest how to vote on referenda, many ingenious explanations have arisen to explain referenda outcomes. Betty Zisk, based on studies of four states between 1976 and 1982 and reports of previous studies, discounts several popular mechanistic theories of referenda voting: that voters become more negative as they proceed down the ballot and that they will tend to automatically reject hard-to-comprehend propositions. While historically voters have been more partial to legislative submissions (passing about 60 percent) compared to voter initiatives (passing about 34 percent), the reversal of this trend in several states casts doubt on the notion that voters respond favorably to legislative issues because they believe them to have been weighed more carefully than initiatives.

Voting on relatively unpublicized, largely noncontroversial measures has proved the hardest to explain. Magleby believes that some impulse voting may occur. In other referenda, voting has been found to correlate, at least moderately, with some demographic variable, but the key variable changes with the issue considered. Age, for example, is related to voting on school bonds while race is important in open housing referenda. Party and ideology are more likely to have an effect across issue areas, apparently because voters tend to simplify an issue into one that is explainable in partisan or ideological terms. Zisk delineates a process whereby voters, often influenced by media campaigns or organized canvassing by affected groups, reduce a complex measure to an "easy" one that can be decided on the basis of the voter's core values. In some cases (the death penalty for example), the values are easily applied, and little change in voter perceptions or intentions takes place throughout a campaign or from one campaign to another. In many other cases, however, the campaign itself and especially media efforts determine the values that are triggered. Zisk, in a study of 72 campaigns from 1976 to 1982, found voters changing their initial reactions one-third of the time and the high-spending side in a referendum winning out 78 percent of the time. Nevertheless, it has been difficult historically for special interests through the use of media to enact legislation to benefit themselves; they have been most successful in vetoing legislation harmful to themselves.

Referenda voting, thus, is currently described as a form of expressive or symbolic behavior. While historically since World War II voters have voted conservative on social issues, liberal on economic issues, and inconsistently on environmental issues, this track record may be a poor way to understand the future, as voter attitudes and perceptions change easily with new circumstances and pressures. Originally seen as a check upon representatives and a way to exact popular opinion, referenda now may be seen as more complex phenomena in which voters are pressured and acted upon by interest groups within a general context of their own predispositions and values, much as representatives are. But voters, of course, decide on the basis of much less information than legislators. Whether the safety valve that referenda offer is worth the risk of their calculated manipulation is the central question regarding their future.

*See also:* Ideology

*Phyllis F. Field*

REFERENCES

Butler, David, and Austin Ranney, eds. 1978. *Referendums: A Comparative Study of Practice and Theory.* Washington: American Enterprise Institute.

Graham, Virginia. 1978. *A Compilation of Statewide Initiative Proposals Appearing on Ballots Through 1976.* Washington: Congressional Research Service.

Magleby, David B. 1984. *Direct Legislation: Voting on Ballot Propositions in the United States.* Baltimore: Johns Hopkins U. Pr.

Zimmerman, Joseph F. 1986. *Participatory Democracy: Populism Revived.* New York: Praeger.

Zisk, Betty H. 1987. *Money, Media, and the Grass Roots: State Ballot Issues and the Electoral Process.* Newbury Park, CA: Sage.

## Reform Clubs

Few political institutions have suffered more ambiguity in definition and analysis than the political reform club. Often regarded as organizations that are part of a political movement of "outs" against "ins," of "taking the politics out of politics," of fighting for "good government," the reform club has served a number of functions in the American political arena.

Clubs have served as an organizational forum for the candidacy of maverick politicians and as an entry-level vehicle for potential political activists who perceive themselves as shut out of traditionally organized Democratic and Republican party politics. Reform club organizations have also served as the mechanism for dislodging machine bosses, democratizing the political participatory process, and advancing both general and specific social and economic goals and issues.

In his classic text on club politics in Chicago, New York, and Los Angeles, James Q. Wilson summarized the goals of one post-World War II New York reform club as "the democratization of the party machinery, an improvement in the caliber of party leaders and candidates, and an emphasis on program and principle in attracting both party workers and voters." For Wilson, "the essence of the reform ethic [is] the desire to moralize public life, the effort to rationalize power with law, and the insistence that correct goals will be served only if goals are set and officials selected by correct procedures." The political reform club, then, is often thought to be acting in the public interest as a major instrument for political change and innovation. Reform clubs evolved in reaction to perceived political corruption and an ineptness on the part of traditional political parties to serve these ends.

In contrast to the goals of reform clubs, it is important to note that other forms of the political club have evolved in the United States. In most cases, the form has been that of the auxiliary or "regular" (as distinct from "reform") political club aligned with the traditional party organization. Examples include Democratic and Republican affiliated political youth clubs, veterans' clubs, senior citizen clubs, social clubs, and minority and ethnic clubs.

Regular political clubs have also served as the organizational mechanism for the advancement of individual politicians and party organizations not steeped in the ideals of reform and innovation but rather interested in acquiring power for themselves and for the traditional party organizations. They achieve this goal by winning elections and providing material inducements (jobs, patronage, preferments) to organization members.

Independent political clubs have also evolved as traditional political organizations in communities in which state or local statutes mandate nonpartisan elections, thus preempting the formal and legal existence of Democratic and Republican organizations. While independent political clubs may serve reform goals, this particular manifestation of the political club more often than not ironically supports the traditional maintenance of the roles and goals of party organizations in the guise of nonpartisan political clubs.

Historically, political clubs have been around in the United States since the founding, dating back before the formal establishment of political parties. For example, the Anchor Club, organized around 1799, was an informal political organization supporting the Federalist cause through political activity of a literary nature. Its founders included Pennsylvanian William Clifton, a well-known satirical poet of the time.

An example of both reform and regular political club activity at the local level occurred in 1860 when over 30 political clubs in New Orleans organized to back the candidacy of a number of presidential aspirants, including Democratic presidential hopeful Stephen Douglas. The eventual demise of most of these clubs was attributed to their inability to organize at the precinct level, their incapacity to turn back the national tide in support of Abraham Lincoln, and their incompetence at successfully filling the political gap left by the decline in traditional party organizations in New Orleans

In 1882 Theodore Roosevelt organized one of the first formal political reform clubs in New York City, the City Reform Club of New York. The singular purpose of the club was to mount opposition against the infamous machine politics of Tammany Hall, a regular political club closely tied to the Democratic Party. While relatively ineffective in influencing the outcome of local elections in New York, the City Reform Club's history would influence the activities and strategies of succeeding reform clubs as they evolved in New York City politics.

Twentieth-century reform club activism can best be examined and understood in the context of two reform eras in New York: the "old era" (turn of the century to World War II) and the "new era" (post-World War II to the early 1970s).

The four decades before World War II, the "old" era of reform, were, for the reform clubs, a movement made up of "outs" seeking to be "ins." Analysis by Norman Adler and Blanche Blank, confirming the seminal work by Roy Peel, suggests that "it was an era in which reform hung more on interparty politics than on intraparty politics; an era in which reform was generated by agencies outside the party system—literary muckrakers [and] grand juries," joined by elected officials seeking to replace one party organization with another—the city machine with reform-minded officeholders.

Not surprisingly, representatives of the "out" party in a city or county occasionally formed the backbone of reform movements. Having little to lose, the party out of power would occasionally support the reform effort. However, the era was marked less by long-term reform club activism and more by the temporary organization of reform interests followed by success or failure in the electoral system. If the reform interests were successful, redress of some grievances might take place followed, more often than not, by the eventual disbanding of the reform groups.

In effect, during the "old" reform era, the reform club organization was only minimally institutionalized. During this first half of the twentieth century, mayors like Seth Low, John Purroy Mitchel, and Fiorello LaGuardia formed *temporary* fusion tickets (supported by both Democrat and Republican voters), on their way to electoral victory. The most comprehensive study of this period, as it evolved in New York, can be found in Roy V. Peel's *The Political Clubs of New York*.

The post-World War II era ushered in a period of significant growth and development in reform club activism, particularly in New York City, Chicago, and Los Angeles. For some observers, the post-World War II reform clubs represented a distinct break with traditional party organizations and with regular clubs in terms of membership, ideology, style, and organization, changes particularly clear in New York, where Adler and Blank as well as Wilson found distinct differences between regulars and reformers—distinctions between what Wilson calls "professionals" and "amateurs."

For reform club amateurs, politics was a cause spurred on by their belief in proper and good motives on the part of the politician, widespread political participation by the populous, adherence to democratic values and procedures, and responsiveness on the part of leaders to the demands and expectations of the people.

For the party organization or regular club professional, winning or losing the election is the central goal (public benefit is seen only as a by-product of the electoral victory). For reform club activists, party participation is based on the support of issues. For the regular party organization or club member, the rewards of patronage for the loyal organization followers are the underlying cause for participation. Wilson argues that for the club reformers, principles, not the self-interests of the professionals, are the motive and end of all politics; reform clubs, unlike traditional party organizations and regular political clubs, not only seek to respond to issues but also seek to generate issues.

In Wilson's study of reform clubs in New York, Chicago, and Los Angeles, reformers were responding to very different political environments after World War II.

In New York, the efforts of reform clubs of the 1950s differed from previous attempts to reform the political system. By capturing control of the party machinery, reformers sought to challenge the machine from inside the regular party organization. During the post-World War II years, New York City witnessed significant population changes—an increase in the number of African-Americans, Hispanics, and middle-class whites and the gradual migration out of the city of many members of the traditional white ethnic population base of the machine. Tammany Hall, a conglomeration of regular Democratic clubs in New York City under the general leadership of Carmine DeSapio, was vulnerable to the challenges posed by committed reformers and reform club activists to take over the Democratic party organization.

The post-World War II reform club movement began in earnest in New York in the early 1950s with the rise in power of the Tilden Democratic Club, the Lexington Democratic Club, and the Riverside Democrats. Tammany Hall, under DeSapio's leadership, advocated and instituted some reforms so as to minimize reform club activity. However, many suggested reforms in New York Democratic politics were ignored, including the right of reform club members to review the qualifications of patronage candidates, the removal of judicial appointments from Tammany Hall politics, the adoption of statewide primaries, and the direct election of party leaders. Unlike earlier efforts in 1923 and 1933 to reform the political system from "outside" the party organization, reform club activists by the late 1950s were, in Donald Blaisdell's words, eager to loosen "the grip of Tammany-minded leaders on the party machinery and replac[e] it with control by the party membership itself." By September 1962, reform clubs succeeded in turning DeSapio out as chairman of the Manhattan County Committee and as leader of Tammany Hall. In New York during the 1950s and 1960s, the reform clubs made a significant impact on the political system. They eventually received the support of Mayor Robert Wagner (a former supporter of DeSapio) and were a strong force in the election of Mayor John Lindsay.

Reform clubs in Chicago were faced with an entirely different political environment than that faced by reform clubs in New York City. By the early 1950s, Chicago had probably the strongest big-city party machine in the nation. The reform club amateurs realized that their task was to adapt themselves to the existence of the machine, not try to replace it. For one organization, the Independent Voters of Illinois (IVI), the path was confrontation; for the Democratic Federation of Illinois (DFI), the path was accommodation.

During the 1950s and on into the mid-1970s, both the IVI and the DFI were unsuccessful in accomplishing one of their central goals: party reform. Mayor Richard Daley contributed to the lack of success of these clubs by instigating a number of substantive concessions to "good government" (for example, hiring a reform-minded police commissioner), while at the same time rejecting any procedural changes that might bring about party reform or reduce the impact of a highly sophisticated patronage system. Unlike the New York City reform clubs of the 1950s and 1960s, successful in challenging the regular party organization, Chicago's reform clubs had to content themselves with very limited victories in local political reform.

In California, the weak and ineffectual role of political parties during the post-World War II era fostered a strong reaction by reform clubs to the political environment. At first glance, the California Republican Assembly (CRA) and the California Democratic Council (CDC), two of California's oldest and largest political clubs, appear to represent nothing more than a West Coast version of the regular political club—an auxiliary arm of the organized parties. Closer examination suggests otherwise.

California's election codes until 1959 gave candidates the right to cross-file—that is, to run as both a Republican and a Democrat—when seeking elective office. Cross-filing, along with a recalcitrant Democratic and Republican party leadership unwilling to open up their parties to change or innovation, severely weakened the party organization, reducing the power of the parties to control the nomination process. A political vacuum was created, one eventually filled by political clubs.

During the 1950s, the California clubs (in particular, the CRA and the CDC) were the "work horses" of the political system, providing many of the services—canvassing, fundraising, telephoning—that traditionally fell to party organizations. They also provided an organizational setting in which individuals could enter the political system as activists, unrestricted by the established traditional party organizations seeking to maintain control over party organization and the election apparatus.

While the CRA and the CDC played a number of traditional roles normally carried out by regular party organizations, their reform orientation was evident during the early 1950s. Discussion of policy issues within the clubs distinguished them from machine organizations. The club activists were not motivated by material rewards if for no other reason than that patronage and preferments did not exist. Instead, in return for the support and endorsement of candidates, the reform clubs expected the views of their members on issues, both local and national, to be taken seriously. The California reform clubs provided citizens with an expanded base for political participation. According to several scholars studying the California political system, "in an age of increasingly large government, impersonal bureaucracies, specialized competencies, and techniques of mass persuasion, the CRA and CDC . . . made no small contribution to the democratic process."

The differences between the reform club experiences in New York, Chicago, and Los Angeles underline the difficulties in neatly packaging and labeling the character and structure of the reform club movement in the United States. The clubs that evolved in New York City and its environment after World War II differed significantly in substance, strategy, style, and goals from the reform club movement in Chicago. In turn, the California experience differed significantly from both New York and Chicago.

Given the differences between these three reform club movements in terms of the political environment in which they functioned and in their varying success—or, in the case of Chicago, their lack of success—in reforming the political system, some common threads still run through the club movement during the post-World War II era.

In New York, Chicago, and California, the reform clubs tended to share a common goal of increasing participation in the political process and of opening the political system to greater scrutiny by citizens who wished to involve themselves in politics. In an important sense, most reform clubs tend, in the words of James

Wilson, to "moralize" public life. Reformers want to rationalize power and insist that correct goals will be served only if goals are set and officials selected by correct procedures. While the political reality and environment in each state dictated additional goals for reform clubs, these underlying tenets remained constant.

Beyond the issue of a generally shared set of goals, the attraction of a national presidential candidate, Adlai Stevenson, was instrumental in New York, Chicago, and California, in rallying many reformed-minded Democratic activists to the club movement in the 1950s and early 1960s. For example, the New York Democratic Coalition, which served as the city's "reform holding company" during the early 1950s, reflected, in its membership, the strong attraction of and support for Stevenson, the Democratic Party's presidential standard-bearer in 1952 and 1956. For Coalition members, Adler and Blank argue,

> more than any other figure Stevenson stood for what [they] admired in public life. And what they admired was actually something less than a coherent ideology, something less than a set of platform planks, something less even than a thoroughgoing commitment to be unequivocally against bossism and machines (a position never entirely embraced by Stevenson himself), but rather an ingrained sense of style.

The "style" of Stevenson encompassed subtle matters having to do with the general support of reform conduct and goals as well as support for the underlying political as well as social values of the reformers.

In part, this style was inherited from the New Deal–Fair Deal era and the ongoing work in New York of reform-minded political activists like Eleanor Roosevelt, Herbert Lehman, and Thomas Finletter. Indeed, Tammany Hall's indifference to the Democratic Party's presidential ticket of Stevenson-Kefauver in 1952 (Tammany Hall boss DeSapio's headquarters did not offer very much campaign literature on the presidential race) was a major impetus for the growth of the reform club movement in the Democratic Party in New York City.

The impact of Stevenson on the reform movement in Chicago was no less clear; indeed, he would soon take on the status of the patron saint of reform politics. As in the case of New York, Adlai Stevenson provided the Chicago reformers with a national figure whom they could identify with, a task made easier by their strong sense of loyalty for Stevenson as a former

governor of Illinois. Many members of the DFI had been active in the Stevenson administration in Illinois.

In California, the formation of the California Democratic Council (CDC) in 1953 was stimulated by the political interests of many young political activists attracted to the political process by Stevenson's 1952 presidential campaign. Between 1952 and 1953 the number of Democratic clubs grew from 75 to 175, clubs populated, in good part, by individuals suspicious of traditional politics and politicians and anxious to reform the political process.

In effect, in the 1950s, the significance and impact of the Stevenson presidential campaigns on the growth of the reform club movement cannot be exaggerated. His presence in the national political system instigated the entry and the continued activism of thousands of individuals in the political process; many of these reformers channeled their political activism into local politics once the presidential races had faded into the background.

By the late 1970s the fervor and attachment to reform club movements had slackened considerably. Some exceptions, particularly in California, bucked the tide of apathy. Tom Hayden, a highly visible political activist during the 1960s and early 1970s, organized the California Campaign for Economic Democracy (CCED), which has evolved into an organization with an estimated membership of some 35,000.

Nevertheless, a search of both scholarly and popular journals and magazines published over the past decade reveals relatively little recent research interest in reform club activity. The total number of political clubs has declined over the past 50 years, falling from a high in New York City of 1,177 in the 1930s to fewer than 300 by 1975. That decline has been matched by a diminishing number of reform clubs. In California, the influence of clubs diminished with the end of the ability of candidates to cross-file easily on both the Democratic and Republican tickets. While some scholarly interest in sorting out reform club activity in the state still exists, the data, both in terms of membership figures and operation budgets, is incomplete and difficult to acquire.

For all intents and purposes, by the 1990s, scholarly and journalistic interest in examining the reform club movement in the United States had petered out. Certainly the decline in traditional machine politics in many, if not most, of our large urban centers contributed to a decline in the reform club movement. Reform clubs were, in part, a reaction to machine politics—the Tammany Hall-like organizations that rejected issue politics and discouraged open participation by reform-minded activists. The reform movement during the 1940s and 1950s was, in part, a response to the failure of many party organizations to open their doors to all newcomers. With the demise of the traditional party machine and the steady increase in the use of primary elections to select party candidates, the need for strong, independent, reform clubs has declined.

In cities like Chicago, many of the reformers of the 1950s, 1960s, and 1970s are now active in the party organizations, accounting, to some extent, for the decline in the importance of reform clubs like the Independent Voters of Illinois/Independent Precinct Organization. In effect, the "insider-outsider" distinction so relevant for explaining a great deal of the reform club activity of the 1950s and 1960s has become blurred by a more accessible political system.

No doubt, the significant increase, since the 1950s, in the use of the primary nomination system throughout the United States has also had an impact on the reform club movement. Increasingly, independent and reform-minded candidates can use the primary system to win Democratic and Republic party nominations to a variety of local, state, and federal offices. In effect, access to officeholding through the primary nomination process has made politics and the holding of governmental office more accessible to many would-be reform-minded individuals.

This dirge-like summary should not suggest that either reform politics or the reform club is absolutely dead. However, students of politics now realize that as we enter the twenty-first century, the importance of political reform clubs has almost certainly declined in the competitive world of big-city politics.

*See also:* California Democratic Council, Richard Daley, Carmine DeSapio, Fusion Party in New York City, Fiorello La Guardia, Herbert Lehman, John Lindsay, Seth Low, Eleanor Roosevelt, Theodore Roosevelt, Adlai E. Stevenson, Tammany Hall, Robert F. Wagner, Jr.

*Alan R. Gitelson*

REFERENCES

Adler, Norman M., and Blanche Davis Blank. 1975. *Political Clubs in New York.* New York: Praeger.

Blaisdell, Donald C. 1962. *The Riverside Democrats-Eagleton Institute: Cases in Practical Politics, #18.* New York: McGraw-Hill.

Carney, Francis. 1958. *The Rise of the Democratic Clubs in California.* New York: Henry Holt.

Culver, John H., and John C. Syer. 1980. *Power and Politics in California.* New York: Wiley.

Omens, John, Edmond Costantini, and Louis Weschler. 1970. *California Politics and Parties.* Toronto: Macmillan.

Peel, Roy V. 1968. *The Political Clubs of New York.* New York: Ira S. Friedman.

Straetz, Ralph A., and Frank J. Munger. 1960. *New York Politics.* New York: New York U. Pr.

Wilson, James Q. 1962. *The Amateur Democrat.* Chicago: U. of Chicago Pr.

## Reform of the Presidential Nominating Process

For as long as political parties have nominated presidential candidates, activists have tinkered with the rules. Some reformers are motivated by broad, philosophical approaches to the nominating process, others by a desire to boost the fortunes of particular candidates. The most significant reforms seem to coincide with wider changes in the party system. Whether reform of the rules is the cause or the symptom of these more general changes has been the subject of some controversy.

At the beginning of the Jacksonian era, when mass parties first developed in the United States, the national convention replaced the Congressional Caucus as the chief nominating mechanism. First used by the Antimason Party in 1831 and soon copied by the major parties, the convention gave party elites who were not members of Congress a share of the nominating power. Each state party was given a number of votes proportionate to its votes in the Electoral College and wide leeway as to how it would select its delegates.

The Progressive era of the early twentieth century, when democratization of the parties was the goal, saw two innovations: (1) presidential primaries, in which all voters affiliated with a party could elect delegates to the national conventions or express a preference as to the nominee; and (2) the institution of "bonus votes" by Republicans in 1916 to reward states that voted Republican. The parties had become highly sectionalized, with only a few Republicans in the South. The new reform gave northern state Republican parties extra delegate votes (allocated on the basis of Republican strength in the state) so that southern Republicans would not enjoy too disproportionate a number of delegate seats despite the dearth of Republican voters in their states.

With the New Deal in the 1930s came a gradual weakening of the relatively conservative South in the Democratic Party. The first major rules controversy to ensue was the elimination of the Democrats' requirement that the presidential nominee would need not merely a majority, but two-thirds of the votes, in order to be nominated. The abolition of the two-thirds rule in 1936 was seen as a blow to the South, which lost a possible veto over presidential nominations. In return, the South received a boost in 1944 when the Democrats instituted bonus votes. The refusal of a number of southern Democratic parties to endorse the national Democratic ticket in 1948 led to the "loyalty oath" controversies of the 1950s, when some northern Democrats sought to require all delegates to promise to support the convention's nominees. The emergence of civil rights as a major issue in the 1960s kept the South at the center of convention reforms in 1964 and 1968, with demands by civil rights advocates that Black Democratic delegates from the Deep South be seated at the convention.

### Recent Reform in the Democratic Party

With the persistence of racial conflict and the controversy over the heavy-handed domination of the convention by party elites, the 1968 Democratic National Convention produced a quantum leap in the demand for reform. One source of tension was the "unit rule," a procedure whereby several states' delegations would vote in a winner-take-all fashion, requiring the minority of each delegation to vote the majority's way. In the convention's only victory for liberal reformers, the delegates voted to abolish the unit rule in 1972 and insure that "delegates are elected through . . . procedures open to public participation within the calendar year of the National Convention." More far-reaching was the convention's adoption, without debate or roll-call vote, of a resolution recommending that the national party chairman set up a special committee to "recommend to the Democratic National Committee such improvements as can assure even broader citizen participation in the delegate selection process." At the same time, the Democratic National Committee passed a resolution calling for a Commission on Party Structure "in order that full participation of all Democrats without regard to race, color, creed or national origin may be facilitated by uniform standards for structure and operation."

As a consequence of these various recommendations, Democratic National Chairman Fred Harris, a Senator from Oklahoma, appointed two commissions in February 1969: the Commission on Party Structure and Delegate Selection, chaired by Senator George McGovern of South Dakota; and the Commission on Rules, headed by Congressman James O'Hara of Michigan. The McGovern Commission, which was later chaired by Congressman Donald Fraser of Minnesota after Senator McGovern resigned to run for President at the end of 1970, was concerned mainly with the procedures for selecting delegates, while the O'Hara Commission concentrated on the rules governing procedures at the convention itself.

The McGovern-Fraser Commission produced a series of guidelines, some mandatory and some advisory, for the process of selecting delegates. They can be classified under three headings:

*Fair Play.* Several of the provisions were intended to eliminate some of the ways in which party elites had stacked the process in their favor. Among the mandatory guidelines in this category were those requiring written state rules, including rules for challenging delegate slates; uniform dates and times of delegate selection meetings; prohibition of the automatic designation of delegates merely because of other offices they hold ("ex-officio delegates"); and selection of all delegates in the same calendar year as the convention.

*Fair Representation.* The goal here was to insure that supporters of various candidates, and Democrats in general, would be represented at the convention proportionate to their numbers in the general population. The mandatory guidelines included abolition of the unit rule; selection of at least 75 percent of each state's delegation at a level no higher than the congressional district; and a new apportionment scheme by which each state's representation would be based on a formula weighting population equally with the Democratic vote in the previous presidential election.

*Affirmative Action.* Reacting to the long controversy over the exclusion of African-Americans from many southern delegations, and to similar barriers against women and young people, the Commission mandated that state Democratic parties encourage the representation of those groups in "reasonable relationship" to their presence in the population of the state. Undoubtedly the most controversial of the guidelines, this one was accused by its critics of fostering unofficial "quotas" whereby a specific number of Blacks, women, and young people had to be included in each state's delegation.

The O'Hara Commission's recommendations involved formalizing the rules, streamlining convention proceedings, and making the process fairer to all delegates. For example, clear-cut rules for challenging the credentials of any delegate were established, and a process for randomly assigning seating to state delegations on the convention floor was adopted.

Of the two commissions, the McGovern-Fraser Commission was clearly the more influential, largely because it successfully asserted the power to enforce its "guidelines" and to require the state parties to follow its recommendations. At the 1972 Democratic National Convention, delegates were expelled if they had been chosen by a process out of compliance with the guidelines; among the ejectees was Chicago's powerful mayor, Richard J. Daley. A result was an immediate and ultimately permanent rise in the proportion of delegates who were female, nonwhite, and young. Another major impact was indirect: although the McGovern-Fraser Commission did not recommend that state parties use primaries to select delegates, many states concluded that primaries would be the easiest way to comply with the various guidelines. While in 1968 only 37.5 percent of the delegates to the Democratic National Convention had been selected in primaries, in 1972 that figure shot up to 60.5 percent; since then it has been still higher.

The controversy stirred up by the effects of the McGovern-Fraser Commission led to the establishment of still more reform commissions, setting in motion a seemingly continual series of Democratic reform efforts. The two reform commissions that were engendered by the 1972 Democratic National Convention were the Commission on Delegate Selection and Party Structure (headed by Baltimore City Council member Barbara Mikulski), and the Democratic Charter Commission (led by former North Carolina governor Terry Sanford). Perhaps the most important rule inaugurated by the Mikulski Commission was one requiring that candidates who received more than 10 percent or 15 per-

cent of the vote in a primary or caucus had to receive a share of the national convention delegates proportionate to their share of the votes in the primary or caucus. In other words, if Candidate A receives 40 percent in a primary and Candidate B garners 20 percent, then Candidate A should end up with twice the number of delegates as Candidate B. Known as "proportional representation," this principle carried forward the fair representation goal of the McGovern-Fraser guidelines. On the other hand, the Mikulski Commission loosened some of the other McGovern-Fraser reforms, notably the provisions for affirmative action. To implement the Mikulski Commission's decisions, the party established a Compliance Review Commission.

The Sanford Commission's mandate was unique in that it focused on the national party organs instead of the presidential nominating process. It wrote a party charter that was a kind of constitution for the national Democrats, establishing a judicial council, a finance council, and midterm party conferences to discuss issues. In June 1985, after three such unprecedented conferences in 1974, 1978, and 1982, the party dropped the idea, heeding the argument that these conferences succeeded only in exposing the party's internal divisions to public scrutiny.

After the first post-reform Democratic presidential victory in 1976, the party established a new commission, the Commission on Presidential Nomination and Party Structure, with former Michigan state Democratic chair Morley Winograd at its head; it was the first such commission to perceive as its mandate the reversal of the momentum established by the McGovern-Fraser Commission. No doubt the influence of President Jimmy Carter, who did not want to make it easy for a rival to contest the Democratic presidential nomination in 1980, was a factor. The Winograd reforms included raising the minimum vote in a primary or a caucus that would entitle a candidate to national convention delegates to 20 percent or 25 percent, allowing winner-take-all primary races below the state level, shortening the period (to three months) during which delegates can be chosen, reserving 10 percent of each state's delegation for party leaders and elected officials, and requiring that delegates must vote for the candidate to whom they are pledged. As with the Mikulski rules, the Winograd reforms were overseen by a Compliance Review Commission. Most of these changes, as well as others adopted by the Winograd Commission, were aimed at reversing the Mikulski Commission's emphasis on proportional representation.

Besides the Winograd Commission's reforms, two other significant measures changed the rules for the 1980 convention. One was the Democratic National Committee's decision to require that women comprise half of each state delegation; this rule was adopted for the 1984 convention as well. Second, at the convention itself, the nominee was required to state exactly how his views differed from the party platform.

Three new reform commissions were spawned by the 1980 Democratic National Convention. The main one was the Commission on Presidential Nomination, chaired by Governor James Hunt of North Carolina. Continuing in the spirit of the Winograd Commission, the Hunt Commission aimed to reverse the effects of the McGovern-Fraser and Mikulski commissions more fully. Hunt's people tried to shorten the period during which delegates could be chosen; they undercut proportional representation rules by allowing the front-runner to receive "bonus delegates" and for more types of winner-take-all races to occur; and they increased the proportion of state delegates at the convention who had to be party leaders or elected officials to roughly one-fourth of the delegates.

Also stemming from the 1980 Democratic National Convention was the Platform Accountability Commission, headed by former California Congresswoman Yvonne Brathwaite Burke, National Education Association executive director Terry Herndon, and Mississippi governor William Winter. This group drafted new procedures for the convention's platform committee, but its proposal to establish a Council on Platform Accountability and Implementation, the mission of which was to determine whether or not the party had carried out its platform, was never implemented. The convention also established the Commission on Low and Moderate Income Participation, chaired by Texas Congressman Mickey Leland. As a result of its deliberations, the Democrats added low-income people to their affirmative action target groups and urged state parties to find financial aid to enable such people to participate in party activities.

After the 1984 Democratic National Convention, the Fairness Commission was appointed under the leadership of former South Carolina Democratic state chair Donald Fowler. In March 1986 the Democratic National Committee adopted most of its recommendations for the 1988 national convention: increasing slightly the proportion of delegate slots reserved for party and elected officials, allowing Independents to vote in the Montana and Wisconsin primaries, and reducing to 15 percent the minimum vote in primaries and caucuses that would entitle a candidate to be awarded convention delegates. No doubt future Democratic conventions will produce more reform commissions.

### Recent Reform in the Republican Party

In contrast to the Democrats, the Republicans have done little in recent years to alter how they nominate their presidential candidates. This standpat reaction owes largely to the greater conservatism of the GOP and its emphasis on states' rights; state Republican parties are given great autonomy in writing the rules for delegate selection. On the other hand, because Democratic reforms have sometimes resulted in changes in state law, those changes have dragged the Republicans in their wake. A good example is the dramatic rise in the proportion of Republican delegates chosen in primaries, from 34.3 percent in 1968 to 76.0 percent in 1980.

Like the bitterly divided 1968 Democratic convention, the equally contentious 1964 Republican convention led to a reform effort. A Committee on Convention Reform, headed by a Wisconsin businessman, Robert Pierce, proposed that the 1968 convention be more efficiently organized in order to present a more attractive image to television viewers. But in the words of political scientist William Crotty, "The committee's work had no appreciable effect on the 1968 or later national conventions."

As the Democrats began their major reform effort in 1969, the Republicans established their own reform committee, the Delegates and Organizations (DO) Committee. Chaired by Rosemary Ginn, national committee member from Missouri, its recommendations concentrated on three areas. The first was the efficiency and attractiveness of the convention, including shorter speeches and a study of better ways to present the platform. Second was fair play, including a ban on proxy voting in delegate selection meetings and one on "ex officio" delegates. Finally, the DO Committee made nonbinding recommendations for greater representation of women and young people in delegations. Despite the work of the Committee, the GOP chose not to change its rules in any substantial way for the 1972 convention. That convention overwhelmingly defeated an apportionment formula (proposed by party liberals) that would have increased the representation of the most populous states.

The 1972 convention created another commission, the Rule 29 Committee, which was headed by Congressman William Steiger of Wisconsin. Its mandate was to consider ways to make the party more "open and accessible." Some of its proposals were of the same technical sort that characterized much of the DO Committee's report, while others were exhortations to state parties to bring in more women, minority group members, and young and old people.

In every significant respect, the Republican rules are now what they were decades ago. Unlike the Democrats, for example, the Republicans require no quotas for women on each delegation, nor do they preclude winner-take-all delegate selection processes. No doubt the most important change in the Republican nominating process has been the proliferation of primaries, a change that was more or less forced on the party by external circumstances.

### The Issues

Party reform is a controversial matter. Each rules change is scrutinized by strategists to see whose interests will be adversely affected, and heated debates frequently arise. Within the Democratic Party, the locus of most reform efforts in the past two decades, identifiable factions have emerged to contest these matters; they have also propounded elaborate theories of party organization to support their positions. Their views are worth noting.

Advocates of the McGovern-Fraser and Mikulski reforms argue that a political party should be a relatively permeable institution that represents all demographic and political groups fairly. Fundamentally their perspective is the same as that of the early-twentieth-century Progressive movement, which believed in opening up institutions and then using the electoral process as a means of legitimizing them. These neo-Progressives believe that such procedures as proportional representation and affirmative action are not only desirable in themselves but also will make the Democratic Party stronger by inspiring its members. As the McGovern-Fraser report stated, "Popular control of the Democratic Party is necessary for its survival." Advocates of reform see the long-term consequence as a more open and representative party in which national forces and the rule of law have been strengthened. They also point to empirical studies showing that delegates to state and national conventions in the reform era express deep support for strong parties.

On the other side of the debate are the opponents of reform, who believe that political parties best function as relatively disciplined bodies under the control of an experienced leadership. Only in this way, they argue, can parties most effectively compete with their opponents and perform the functions that parties provide for a political system. A choice between two effectively functioning teams in the general election is a more important form of voter participation than primaries and other intraparty mechanisms. Among the long-term consequences of party reform perceived by the antireformers are the devolution of power to inexperienced and unrepresentative upper-middle-class activists, the increased influence of the mass media and interest groups in primaries, a diminished capacity for governance, and public disaffection from the weakened parties.

### Significance

What is the ultimate significance of all these changes in the rules? This question can be answered in at least three different ways: strategically, systemically, and philosophically.

To candidates and their supporters, mastering the rules has become vitally important, because outcomes of nominating battles can be decided by the rules. Knowing the minutiae of each state's rules can enable a candidate to use them to best advantage. For example, in the New Hampshire primary in 1968 the supporters of Lyndon Johnson ran more candidates for delegate spots than the number of delegates to be elected, while the backers of Eugene McCarthy ran exactly the right number. The Johnson vote was split up among too many candidates, while the McCarthy forces were able to concentrate their support on fewer candidates and thus maximize their delegate strength. Some argue that it was no coincidence that the first Democratic presidential nominee after the reforms began, Senator George McGovern, had been the chair of the most important commission; among the candidates, McGovern best understood the rules. By the same token, his campaign manager, Gary Hart, was to run a strong race 12 years later. The importance of the rules to the outcomes of national conventions has been demonstrated by a number of political scientists, who have shown how different some of those outcomes would have been under different rules.

But strategic considerations are significant only in the short run. Of greater importance is the analysis of the consequences of the reforms for the political system. As noted earlier, uniting both the advocates and the critics of the reforms has been the belief that the reforms have had a major impact on the political parties, the nominating process, and the nature of presidential leadership. Are parties weaker because the role of their leaders has been diminished, or are they stronger because activists now know that they can indeed influence party decisions? Have the parties been opened to the masses, or only to middle-class activists? Is democracy stronger because parties are run more democratically, or weaker because too much power is now wielded by the mass media and interest groups? And is a U.S. President now regarded as more legitimate because he gained office by a more open process, or is he fatally estranged from other party leaders by a nominating process that encourages dog-eat-dog campaign tactics? Those who insist upon any of these positions certainly believe that the reforms did have consequences.

On the other hand, scholars might take a more skeptical approach and ask whether some of those trends would have occurred even had the rules never been adopted. Some have argued, for example, that other western nations with different political systems have seen many of the same changes that the United States has, and therefore the reforms were not necessary to effect these changes. Moreover, some have tried to show that many of these trends began before the reforms were enacted. By this line of reasoning, at most the reforms accelerated developments already in progress.

Finally, these matters touch upon some of the basic issues of democratic theory. How open can political parties be before they cease to function effectively? How hierarchical can these institutions become before they emerge as too remote from their mass membership? What are the appropriate means of insuring the participation of previously underrepresented groups? At what point does the proportional representation of candidates' supporters produce fragmentation of political parties? How important should a party platform be? Answering such questions requires articulating the political theorist's most fundamental beliefs about what democracy means.

Furthermore, party reform requires all of us to face more general issues of reform policy. Is it possible for fallible human intentions to produce improved institutions? Should the fear of unanticipated consequences dissuade reformers from seeking change where change seems needed? Does an inexorable historical tide make such efforts irrelevant? The fascination of such questions, combined with the real stakes in presidential politics, guarantee that reform of the nominating process will continue to enliven American politics for many years to come.

*See also:* Antimasons, Jimmy Carter, Richard J. Daley, Democratic National Committee, Donald Fraser, Fred Harris, James Hunt, Lyndon B. Johnson, George McGovern, McGovern-Fraser Commission, Barbara Mikulski, James O'Hara, Presidential Nominating Conventions, Terry Sanford, Winner-Take-All Systems

*Howard L. Reiter*

*REFERENCES*

Anon. 1970. *Mandate for Reform: A Report of the Commission on Party Structure and Delegate Selection to the Democratic National Committee.* Washington: Democratic National Committee.

Banfield, Edward C. 1980. "Party 'Reform' in Retrospect." In Robert A. Goldwin, ed. *Political Parties in the Eighties.* Washington and Gambier, OH: American Enterprise Institute and Kenyon College.

Bode, Kenneth A., and Carol F. Casey. 1980. "Party Reform: Revisionism Revised." In Robert A. Goldwin, ed. *Political Parties in the Eighties.* Washington and Gambier, OH: American Enterprise Institute and Kenyon College.

Ceaser, James W. 1979. *Presidential Selection: Theory and Development.* Princeton: Princeton U. Pr.

Crotty, William J. 1978. *Decision for the Democrats: Reforming the Party Structure.* Baltimore: Johns Hopkins U. Pr.

———. 1983. *Party Reform.* New York: Longman.

———, and John S. Jackson III. 1985. *Presidential Primaries and Nominations.* Washington: Congressional Quarterly.

David, Paul T., and James W. Ceaser. 1980. *Proportional Representation in Presidential Nominating Politics.* Charlottesville: U. Pr. of Virginia.

Hammond, Thomas H. 1980. "Another Look at the Role of 'The Rules' in the 1972 Democratic Presidential Primaries." 33 *Western Political Quarterly* 50.

Kirkpatrick, Jeane Jordan. 1978. *Dismantling the Parties: Reflections on Party Reform and Party Decomposition.* Washington: American Enterprise Institute.

Lengle, James I., and Bryon Shafer. 1976. "Primary Rules, Political Power, and Social Change." 70 *American Political Science Review* 25.

Miller, Warren E., and M. Kent Jennings. 1986. *Parties in Transition: A Longitudinal Study of Party Elites and Party Supporters.* New York: Russell Sage.

Nakamura, Robert T., and Denis G. Sullivan. 1978. "Party Democracy and Democratic Control." In Walter

Dean Burnham and Martha Wagner Weinberg, eds. *American Politics and Public Policy*. Cambridge: MIT Pr.

Polsby, Nelson W. 1983. *Consequences of Party Reform*. New York: Oxford U. Pr.

Pomper, Gerald M. 1979. "New Rules and New Games in Presidential Nominations." 41 *Journal of Politics* 784.

Rapoport, Ronald B., Alan I. Abramowitz, and John McGlennon, eds. 1986. *The Life of the Parties: Activists in Presidential Politics*. Lexington: U. Pr. of Kentucky.

Reiter, Howard L. 1985. *Selecting the President: The Nominating Process in Transition*. Philadelphia: U. of Pennsylvania Pr.

## Regional Primaries

The process through which the major political parties select their presidential candidates has been under constant scrutiny and criticism for most of this century. Much of the criticism has focused on the fairness of the rules and the representativeness of the process. Thus the Democratic Party eliminated the rules requiring a two-thirds vote to nominate during the Franklin Roosevelt administration; they guaranteed representation on delegate slates for African-Americans during the 1960s; they abandoned the unit rule and insisted on procedural regularity at all stages in the nominating process through a series of reform commissions after the 1968 and subsequent elections. And changes in the Republican Party practices—often required by changes in state laws instigated by the Democrats—have followed suit.

While many political scientists have focused their attention on the nominating rules, other commentators have been concerned about the fairness of the process itself. Nominations are determined by delegates to national nominating conventions. The delegates are selected in the various states (and territories) through processes determined at the state level so long as those processes do not violate national party rules. More specifically, the timing of the delegate selection processes within the states is determined by state law and/or state party rules. The limitations imposed by the national parties set dates before which the process may not begin and by which it must be completed, but within those limitations, state preference prevails.

The scheduling of primaries (and caucuses, although the caucus has received much less attention) has been criticized because it is haphazard and irrational, because it makes the process too long, because it is unfair to the candidates, and because it influences the outcome of the nominating contests in ways un-related to the qualities of the candidates. Critics believe that the New Hampshire primary, traditionally the first in the nation, proves that a very unrepresentative state has undue influence. They have pointed to the obligation for candidates to fly back and forth across the country in order to campaign in areas that have scheduled primaries at the same time, thus wasting time and money. They point to the fact that some states—including some of the most populous states like California, Ohio, and New Jersey—have very little influence because their primaries have been scheduled late in the calendar of primaries, by which time the contests have frequently been settled.

A number of reforms have been proposed to address these complaints. One reform, which retains many of the features of the current system, calls for regional primaries. The states would be divided into groups, by region, with all of the states within a region selecting their delegates at the same time. Variations of this plan, some calling for mandatory regional primaries (e.g., H.R. 4519, introduced into the Congress by Richard Ottinger [D-N.Y.] in 1977) and others for an optional system (e.g., S. 964, introduced by Robert Packwood [R-Ore.] in 1980) have been debated in the Congress, but none has progressed very far in the legislative process. The Supreme Court's ruling in the *La Follette* case, accepting the primacy of party rules, makes it doubtful that a law mandating regional primaries would meet the test of constitutionality.

However, the idea of regional primaries has also appealed to certain party officials. One of the criticisms of the regional primary legislation is that such a plan would give an unfair disadvantage to candidates who were strong in the region holding the first primary; they would be able to capture the momentum that has seemed crucial in many nominating contests. Regional primary legislation has typically solved this problem by calling for the rotation of which region goes first or by ordering the regions through a random selection process. These processes make the system "fair" to different regions over the long run, though they do nothing to change the impact in any one year on any group of candidates.

This very feature led a number of southern leaders to work toward an early southern regional primary, a goal to be achieved not through federal legislation or party rules but through a coordinated effort by state officials at party meetings and in legislative sessions throughout the South. A few southern states did hold a mini-regional primary in 1984; but the effort reached fruition in 1988 when all of the states in the South held their primaries (or caucuses) during the same week.

The goal of the Democrats who devised this strategy was to give support to a southern candidate, putatively a moderate, who would then gain an advantage over liberal candidates from elsewhere in the nation. When the strategy was first implemented, these southern leaders hoped that one of the leading contenders would be a prominent southern politician, such as Georgia Senator Sam Nunn. The ironic result of the 1988 Super Tuesday Southern Primary was that it helped Massachusetts governor Michael Dukakis and the Reverend Jesse Jackson more than it did any of the other candidates. Dukakis was the big winner on that day, because he won in the nonsouthern states that held primaries on the same day (notably Massachusetts and Rhode Island) and because his campaign was so well financed and organized that it did well in selected areas in the South and thus was able to pick up additional delegates. Jackson succeeded because the areas in the South in which black voters are concentrated turned out large numbers of Jackson voters. Albert Gore, the southern candidate in the race, and Richard Gephardt, the moderate Missourian who was still contesting the nomination, did poorly, largely because neither made the kinds of gains the pundits felt they would need to show strength.

In the Republican Party in 1988 the results were not those anticipated either. Conservative opponents of George Bush felt that they would benefit from support in the South, but Bush's campaign was well organized and ready. He beat Pat Robertson and Jack Kemp in the areas where they had to do well. Senator Robert Dole's campaign never got started in the South, so the end result was a crushing Bush victory. The Republican nominating contest ended for all intents and purposes on March 8.

The future of regional primaries is unclear. Advocates often did not like the results. Furthermore, some of the large states (including California) whose primaries are held late in the nominating campaign have decided that they will move their dates forward in order to increase their influence. Thus the strategic rule seems to favor "front-loading" (i.e., holding more primaries early) rather than regionalizing. The schedule of events clearly has had an impact, if an unpredictable one, on results. However, so long as the schedule is wholly determined by local officials, no rational system for improving the process can be implemented.

*See also:* Robert Dole, Michael Dukakis, Richard Gephardt, Jesse Jackson, Jack Kemp, New Hampshire Primary, Marion G. Robertson

*L. Sandy Maisel*

REFERENCES

Ceaser, James W. 1982. *Reforming the Reforms: A Critical Analysis of the Presidential Selection Process.* Cambridge: Ballinger.

Kessel, John H. 1988. *Presidential Campaign Politics.* 3rd ed. Chicago: Dorsey.

Maisel, L. Sandy. 1987. *Parties and Elections in America: The Electoral Process.* New York: Random House.

Orren, Gary R., and Nelson W. Polsby, eds. 1987. *Media and Momentum: The New Hampshire Primary and Nomination Politics.* Chatham, NJ: Chatham House.

## Religion's Impact on Politics

Tension between religion and politics is characteristic of the United States. The tensions between religious groups and the political system are heightened by two unanswered questions: should religious bodies and religious individuals become involved in the life of politics? And, should politics, the state, and the laws of the state be kept totally separate from religious values and principles? These questions and their associated dilemmas derive from differing interpretations of portions of the First Amendment to the Constitution.

At the heart of the matter is the meaning of the "establishment clause." One interpretation argues that the founders intended that the prohibition against establishment should only prevent official recognition of a specific church, as most of the colonies had done before the Revolution. Another interpretation takes Jefferson's call for a "wall of separation between church and state" literally. According to this interpretation, the establishment clause requires strict neutrality among religions and also between religion and no religion; moreover, it requires a tightly sealed division between all activities of government and any possible religious influence. Different interpretations of the Constitution notwithstanding, religion and politics have frequently been tied together in the United States. Historically, religion has played a significant role in politics. In the colonies, Protestant Christianity dominated. Charters of the northeastern colonies and of several early colonial colleges bore the stamp of Puritan Christianity. At that time, exceedingly few Jews or Roman Catholics lived in the colonies. Religious influence in colonial America was pervasive yet not monolithic. Protestant Christianity included religious groups as different as Quakers, Moravians, Anglicans, Congregationalists, Mennonites, and Baptists, but all agreed on the separation of church and state and on several other issues confronting the founding of the state.

Although religious diversity increased up through the Civil War, the big picture changed very little. Protestants dominated and, in general, left politics to politicians. Beginning at the time of the Civil War and continuing until the 1940s, however, immigration of large numbers of Jews and Roman Catholics changed the religious mix in the United States. Although this massive influx did not radically shift the balance away from Protestants, they began to feel their dominance threatened. The Protestant majority responded by trying to slow or stop immigration, by strengthening the emphasis in the public schools on religious education, and by attempting to prohibit the manufacture, sale, and consumption of alcoholic beverages.

Protestant domination declined after World War II. Many of the social changes wrought by overzealous Protestant reformers were overturned, and new secularizing influences made themselves felt. Americans have seen the end of Prohibition, Sunday closing laws repealed, mandatory prayer in public schools declared unconstitutional, nativity scenes on government property challenged, and abortion legalized. Roman Catholics helped elect the first President of their faith in 1960, and they gained federal aid for parochial schools in the 1965 Elementary and Secondary Education Act.

Religiously inspired social and political activism waxed in the 1960s. The civil rights movement, the decade's most powerful instrument of change, was religiously inspired, and many of its leaders were ministers. Liberal Protestant groups and Jews joined in the struggle to eliminate racism and unequal treatment. The war in Vietnam was protested by a number of pacifist religious organizations and individuals and by many others who felt that the war was immoral. Liberal religion's views of politics triumphed as conservative Christianity took a beating in new court decisions and legislation. Considerable change came out of this period, including perhaps most significantly, the legalization of abortion.

By the end of the 1970s, conservative Protestants and Roman Catholics who had lost many battles as new laws overturned old ways, began to reassert themselves politically. By the early 1980s, these conservative groups had made their presence felt as strongly as had liberal religious groups two decades earlier. This impact primarily eventuated from a conservative Protestant resurgence led by evangelicals, the New Religious Right, and their various thinly veiled political organizations such as Moral Majority and Christian Voice.

Today, religion's major impact on politics can be seen in two directions: the individual voter's electoral choices that can be shaped by his or her religious views and the religious bodies and lobbies that act upon legislatures in an attempt to institute their religious program or values. Today, the group most heavily involved in those activities is, broadly defined, the New Religious Right.

Religion plays a not so subtle role by its impact on party identification and on individuals' positions on certain issues. Although not as strong today as it was in earlier eras, religious belief or, more importantly, religious affiliation, helps predict party identification. American Jews identify most heavily with the Democratic Party (74 percent). The majority of Roman Catholics are also Democrats (52 percent), although their affiliation has been declining in recent years possibly owing to cross pressures brought about by a Democratic Party that supports legalized abortion. Protestants are evenly split, with Democrats capturing 44 percent and Republicans 45 percent.

Religious belief again plays a role in helping shape an American's approach to certain issues. Usually social or moral in tone, the issues that are affected by religion include attitudes toward women's rights, civil rights, peace issues such as concerns over foreign intervention, military spending, and of course, abortion. Religious groups of many persuasions have led the way in championing many such issues, politically both left and right, in recent America. Included in this are the Berrigan brothers, members of the Roman Catholic clergy, who in many acts of civil disobedience against the draft, the war in Vietnam, and nuclear weapons infused a sense of religious mission in their political activities. Also included is the Army of God, a group of conservative Protestants who kidnapped a doctor who performed legal abortions.

Although numerous small, mostly liberal Protestant-based peace and disarmament organizations still operate, the bulk of the activity on behalf of religion in the political sphere must certainly now belong to the evangelical movement and to the larger New Religious Right. These groups, bearing self-righteous names such as the Moral Majority, have sought (sometimes successfully) to overturn or replace existing local, state, and federal laws that they believe violate God's plan or that are somehow offensive to them.

*See also:* Moral Majority

*Lisa G. Langenbach*

REFERENCES

Chidester, David. 1988. *Patterns of Power: Religion and Politics in American Culture.* Englewood Cliffs, NJ: Prentice-Hall.

Dunn, Charles W., ed. 1988. *Religion in American Politics.* Washington: Congressional Quarterly.

Noll, Mark A., ed. 1990. *Religion and American Politics: From the Colonial Period to the 1980s.* New York: Oxford U. Pr.

Wald, Kenneth D. 1987. *Religion and Politics in the United States.* New York: St. Martin's.

## Republican Conference

Early in the twentieth century, House and Senate Republicans changed the name of their caucuses to the Republican Conference in order to distance themselves from the connotation of binding power over members' votes. In each Conference, all the members of the Republican Party in the respective chambers choose their leaders and express their views on issues; and thus the Conferences remain the primary bodies of GOP organization and discipline, albeit without real authority over the rank and file.

Caucuses had withered during the years before the Civil War when the Republican Party was beginning. From the mid-1880s until about 1911, strong Republican caucuses made binding decisions and denied choice committee seats to recalcitrant members. In the years between World War I and World War II, party caucuses disintegrated; after World War II, the Republican Conferences were little used. Malcolm Jewell and Samuel Patterson believe that "The leaders preferred to work behind the scenes, without the limitations on their freedom to negotiate and to plan tactics that might be imposed by the caucus." The power of House caucuses has waxed and waned (since their inception), Don Wolfensberger argues, depending on

the relationship of caucuses to the rest of the leadership; the relative power of committee chairmen; Member satisfaction with the status quo, both inside and outside the House; the ability of caucus chairmen and other party leaders to both creatively utilize the caucus while retaining control over it; and the ability of caucuses to tread the fine line between formulating and dictating policy.

In recent years the Republican Party has made greater use of the caucus, partly for a nontraditional reason: the rank-and-file members have sought an increased voice in party decisions. Substantial caucus staffs are another new feature and are largely devoted to public relations.

In the House, the Republican Conference has a chairman, a vice chairman, and a secretary; in the Senate, a chairman and a secretary. House Republicans have Policy, Research, and Campaign committees, and a Committee on Committees, which in turn assigns members to House standing committees. In the Senate, Republicans have Policy, Campaign, Personnel, and Calendar committees, and a Committee on Committees.

Both Conferences meet at the beginning of each biennial session to select their leaders and their staff (party leaders and whips and their assistants), to authenticate standing committee assignments, and to name members to a few party committees. Over the years, attempts to call caucus meetings after the initial ones, primarily to require party loyalty, have proved embarrassing and thus have been avoided. In the 1970s, changes (still in effect) were adopted in both houses, mandating the selection of committee leaders (chairpersons or ranking minority members); in 1971 House Republicans began to vote in the Conference for ranking committee members (after nominations from the Committee on Committees), while in 1973 Senate Republicans did the same (after nominations by the GOP members of each standing committee). Members who have risen to those positions through seniority will not likely be deposed if they retain leadership support.

The Senate Policy Committee now hosts Tuesday luncheons attended by virtually every Republican Senator. The large staffs of the Republican Conference and the Policy Committee provide a wide range of media and communication services. Between the influence of the staff and the interchanges at the weekly luncheons (while there remains nothing resembling a binding vote), continuing communication on strategy—both issues and tactics—reflects and influences a greater partisanship and party antagonism in the Senate.

House Republicans voted in 1975 to open their Conference meetings to the public, but after Ronald Reagan's first election, the doors were closed again. The House Conference now meets with increasing frequency, and meetings may be called at the written request of 50 or more members. Despite its aversion to binding actions, the Conference adopted new rules in the Ninety-ninth and One Hundredth Congresses to move toward increased party unity and discipline, at the instance of restive junior members. For example, "leadership issues" require early and ongoing cooperation between the relevant committees and the leadership as the issue evolves. In 1988 the Conference adopted a more uniform set of party operating rules, and even used the "c" word, providing for Committee Organizing "Caucuses," and Periodic Committee "Caucuses."

*Penny M. Miller*

REFERENCES

Bailey, Christopher J. 1988. *The Republican Party in the U.S. Senate, 1974–1984: Party Change and Institutional Development*. Manchester, UK: Manchester U. Pr.

Clem, Alan L. 1989. *Congress: Powers, Processes and Politics*. Pacific Grove, CA: Brooks/Cole Co.

Galloway, George. 1962. *History of the United States House of Representatives*. New York: Crowell.

Jewell, Malcolm E., and Samuel C. Patterson. 1986. *The Legislative Process in the United States*. 4th ed. New York: Random House.

Jones, Charles O. 1970. *The Minority Party in Congress*. Boston: Little, Brown.

Miller, James A. 1986. *Running in Place: Inside the Senate*. New York: Simon & Schuster.

Ripley, Randall B. 1988. *Congress, Process and Policy*. 4th ed. New York: Norton.

Rogers, Lindsay. 1926. *The American Senate*. New York: Knopf.

Rothman, David J. 1966. *Politics and Power: The United States Senate, 1869–1901*. Cambridge: Harvard U. Pr.

Patterson, Samuel C. 1988. "Party Leadership in the United States Senate." Presented at the University of Nebraska Hendricks Symposium on the United States Senate, Lincoln.

Wolfensberger, Don. 1988. "The Role of Party Caucuses in the U.S. House of Representatives: An Historical Perspective." Presented at the annual meeting of the American Political Science Association, Washington.

## Republican Congressional Campaign Committees (House and Senate)

Both major political parties have maintained committees in each house of Congress to provide technical assistance and financial support to congressional candidates for the past century. For the Republican Party, those committees are the National Republican Congressional Committee (NRCC), which handles House elections, and the National Republican Senatorial Committee (NRSC), which assists senatorial candidates. Membership on each committee is drawn from the GOP membership of the respective chamber, with the chair of the committee serving as a major party official in that chamber.

These committees originated in the era between the Civil War and World War I, when political parties were the principal direct and indirect sources of campaign support; the NRCC was founded in 1866 and the NRSC in 1916. Campaign finance during this period was dominated by party committees, with local committees playing a more significant role than is the case now. The congressional committees, which were and continue to be distinct entities of the Republican National Committee (RNC), were useful because they were removed from direct concern with presidential elections and national party building.

With the passage of the Federal Election Campaign Act (FECA) and its amendments in the 1970s, information about the activity of these committees has become more widely publicized as the quality of that information improved. Data about the contributions to and disbursements of the congressional Republican campaign committees is now periodically published by the Federal Election Commission.

The NRCC spent $1.6 million on behalf of Republican House candidates in 1988, and the NRSC spent $760,488 to assist Republican senatorial candidates; Republican House candidates spent a total of $98.7 million, and Republican Senate candidates a total of $88.1 million in 1988. While these figures suggest that the committees do not play a really significant role in congressional campaign finance, their roles have indeed been critical in certain situations. Moreover, the congressional candidates who stand to gain by their activity have paid close attention to their actions. First, while direct contributions may be relatively small, "indirect expenditures" on behalf of candidates are much larger. Second, these indirect expenditures tend to be used late in the campaign season, providing a key boost to candidates close to election day. Third, while the committees may contribute small amounts overall, strategic spending may make the decisions of the congressional campaign committees critical in certain election campaigns.

In the 1970s the Republican Party generally, and the congressional committees particularly, gained the reputation of being effective both in raising funds and in targeting their spending. Much more so than the Democrats, the Republicans relied on contributions from many small donors whose contributions also helped the GOP to gain an advantage in grass-roots organization. In addition, the Republican committees were reputed to be more strategic in targeting their resources, focusing on open seats and close races.

Given the Republican advantage in fundraising and strategic targeting during the 1970s and early 1980s, many asked whether the Republicans had a "natural" advantage in campaign finance. The answer is unclear. While the fundraising advantage has persisted into the late 1980s, this edge has diminished. The Democratic committees learned from their own mistakes and the Republican gains, and changed their financial strategies. And, for reasons that remain unclear, the Republican advantage in money raised and spent has begun to erode significantly.

*See also:* Federal Election Campaign Act of 1971 and Amendments, Republican National Committee

*Charles Stewart III*

REFERENCES

Alexander, Herbert A. 1972. *Money in Politics*. Washington: Public Affairs Press.

Jacobson, Gary C. 1980. *Money in Congressional Elections*. New Haven: Yale U. Pr.

———. 1985. "The Republican Advantage in Campaign Finance." In John E. Chubb and Paul E. Peterson, eds. *The New Direction in American Politics*. Washington: Brookings.

Overaker, Louise. 1932. *Money in Elections*. New York: Macmillan.

Sorauf, Frank J. 1988. *Money in American Elections*. Glenview, IL: Scott, Foresman.

## Republican Coordinating Committee

A national party policy development panel that functioned from 1965 to 1968. Although the Republicans had created policy panels in the past when they had not controlled the White House, the Coordinating Committee was unique in the following respects: (1) it had broad representation of both elected officials and Republican organizational leaders; (2) its meetings were regular; (3) it employed a professional staff of high quality and maintained a continuity of research activities; (4) its position papers were accepted within the GOP; and (5) it used an institutionalized rather than an ad hoc pattern of operation.

The Committee was initially proposed by the party's congressional leaders, Senator Everett M. Dirksen (Ill.) and Congressman Gerald R. Ford (Mich.) in January 1965 and was backed by the Republican Governors Association, former President Dwight Eisenhower, and the GOP's former presidential nominees. With the support of National Chairman Ray C. Bliss, the Republican National Committee (RNC) agreed to finance and staff the committee.

The Coordinating Committee had a broad membership consisting of former President Eisenhower, four former presidential nominees, seven members of the Senate Republican leadership, nine members of the House Republican leadership, eight Republican governors, six members of the RNC, and a representative of the Republican State Legislators Association. The RNC chairman, Ray C. Bliss, presided.

The Coordinating Committee appointed eight task forces and two study groups composed of representatives from the Congress, governors, and the RNC, along with prominent party leaders and substantive experts. These specialized panels prepared position papers that were reviewed by the full Coordinating Committee before being released to the public. A total of 48 position papers were issued by the Committee between 1965 and 1968. In addition, the Committee also issued a series of brief policy statements designed to attract media attention at each of its meetings. The combined output of the Coordinating Committee provided the basis for the 1968 Republican Party platform.

The Republican Coordinating Committee also functioned as a mechanism through which Chairman Bliss and other leaders worked to develop increased intraparty unity after the divisive 1964 nomination and election campaigns. The Committee was a forum in which intraparty concerns could be discussed informally in the presence of GOP elders and where none of the participants wished to be held responsible for being disruptive or divisive. The Committee operated by consensus and approved its policy statements unanimously.

The Republican Coordinating Committee revived briefly in 1973. Authorized by a September meeting of the RNC, the Committee met at the White House with President Richard Nixon in November. President Nixon, in an effort to rally partisan support for a presidency vitiated by the Watergate scandal, spoke to the group for 40 minutes and pledged full cooperation with the Watergate investigators. Although it issued an ambitious statement of its projected activities, the Republican Coordinating Committee ceased operations after this meeting with Nixon.

*See also:* Ray Bliss, Everett M. Dirksen, Dwight D. Eisenhower, Gerald R. Ford, Richard M. Nixon, Republican National Committee, Watergate

*John F. Bibby*

REFERENCES

Bibby, John F., and Robert J. Huckshorn. 1968. "Out-Party Strategy: Republican National Committee Rebuilding Politics, 1964–1966." In Bernard Cosman and Robert J. Huckshorn, eds. *Republican Politics: The 1964 Campaign and Its Aftermath for the Party.* New York: Praeger.

Lyon, Christopher. 1973. "GOP Revives Policy Unit Independent of the President." *The New York Times.* Nov. 13:1,13.

## Republican National Committee

*The Rules of the Republican Party* calls for the creation of a Republican National Committee (RNC), which is charged with responsibility for the "general management of the Republican party, subject to direction from the national convention." This authorization makes the RNC the official governing body of the party between national conventions. Three basic categories of activity engage the RNC: (1) general party activity—maintenance of the headquarters and staff, public relations, research, fundraising, voter mobilization, and national convention arrangements; (2) candidate assistance—financial, technical, and staff support to Republican candidates; and (3) assistance to state and local GOP organizations.

From an ad hoc organization in the nineteenth century, the Republican National Committee has become institutionalized with a permanent headquarters, a professional staff, substantial financial resources, and an array of programs to advance party goals. As its activities have expanded, its influence has been significantly enhanced, and in the process the Republican Party's national organizations, candidate organizations, and state and local units have become more closely integrated.

### Creation and Gradual Institutionalization

The Republican National Committee's immediate precursor was an ad hoc group of Republican leaders who met in Pittsburgh in February 1856, for the purpose of bringing a new political party into existence. At that meeting, a national executive committee composed of one member from each state and chaired by Edwin D. Morgan, a wealthy New York merchant banker, was created. Meeting at the Willard Hotel in Washington, D.C., on March 27, 1856, the national executive committee issued a formal Call for a national Republican nominating convention in June 1856 in Philadelphia. Issuance of the Call and arrangements for the convention were the only formal acts of the national executive committee.

The Republican National Committee was formally created by the Republican National Convention in Philadelphia at the national nominating convention held in June 1856. Edwin D. Morgan, the chairman of the national executive committee that had issued the convention Call, was elected the RNC's first chairman.

During the post-Civil War era, the RNC functioned mainly as a committee of correspondence composed of party representatives from the states who sought to keep in touch with and maintain the party between presidential elections. During presidential campaigns, the national chairman normally served as the nominee's campaign manager, and subcommittees of the RNC were created to handle such tasks as scheduling speakers and distributing campaign literature.

The committee evolved slowly from an organization in which sketchily differentiated functions were performed by party notables every four years into a continuous operation staffed by professionals. During the chairmanship of Will Hays (1918–1921), continuous year-round staffing of a Washington headquarters was initiated. The RNC did not, however, own a headquarters building until it moved into The Eisenhower Center (310 First Street, S.E., Washington, D.C.) in 1970. The first paid, full-time chairman was John D. M. Hamilton, who was elected in 1936. Paid, full-time chairmen were, however, the exception until the 1970s. The headquarters staff was of modest size—approximately 100 persons in nonpresidential years—during the 1950s and 1960s. It was not until the late 1970s and 1980s that the RNC began regularly operating with a staff of nearly 250 people. With nine organizational divisions each having specific programmatic responsibilities, large professional and clerical staffs, the latest in computer-based technology, routinely complicated bureaucratic procedures, and tight security, the RNC's tastefully decorated headquarters is testimony to the institutionalization of the national Republican Party organization.

## Organization and Structure

### Membership

Although the scope of national committee activities has expanded since the 1950s, the RNC has maintained, except for a brief period between 1952 and 1968, a formal membership based upon the principle of state equality. Since 1968 the national committee has been composed of three members from each state: a national committeeman, a national committeewoman, and the state party chairman. Under rules adopted in 1988, the definition of a state extends not only to the usual 50 states but also to American Samoa, the District of Columbia, Guam, Puerto Rico, and the Virgin Islands. As a result, the RNC has 165 members.

Four methods are used to select for national committeemen and women depending upon state law and state party rules: (1) election in a partisan primary election; (2) selection by a state party convention; (3) selection by a state party central committee; and (4) selection by the state party's delegation to the national convention. The results of the various states' selection processes are ratified by the national convention. National committeemen and women serve four-year terms. State party chairmen automatically become members of the RNC for the length of their tenure in the chairmanship.

The RNC originally consisted of a national committeeman from each state; national committeewomen were added to the committee after ratification of the women's suffrage (Nineteenth) amendment to the Constitution. State chairmen were not members of the committee until a rules change, adopted by the 1952 national convention, gave state chairmen automatic RNC membership if their state (1) cast its electoral votes for the GOP presidential nominee in the last election; or (2) elected a Republican governor; or (3) elected a congressional delegation with a Republican majority. This membership change increased the influence of states with Republican voting strength and worked to the disadvantage of southern states, where the GOP had had little electoral success up to that time. In 1968 all state party chairmen were made automatic members of the RNC. This change was a recognition of the Republican Party's growing electoral and organizational strength in the South. It constituted a reaffirmation of the GOP's confederative organizational structure.

### Officers

The RNC officers include a chairman and a co-chairman (of the opposite sex from the chairman), who are elected by the full committee in January of each odd-numbered year. Party rules require that the chairman and co-chairman "be full-time, paid employees of the national committee" (*The Rules of the Republican Party*, 1988: Rule 23). A secretary and treasurer are also elected by the full committee. In addition, the RNC has eight vice chairmen (one man and one woman chosen by the western, midwestern, northeastern, and southern regional caucuses of RNC members).

The chairman is designated as the committee's chief executive officer and is authorized to appoint a general counsel and chairman of the Republican Finance Committee subject to confirmation by the full RNC.

### Executive Council

Since the RNC is required to meet only twice a year, its Executive Council is authorized to exercise executive and administrative functions of the Committee between RNC meetings. The Council is an eleven-member body composed of three RNC members appointed by the chairman and eight elected by regional caucuses. *Ex officio* members include the chairman, co-chairman, vice chairmen, secretary, treasurer, general counsel, chairman of the Finance Committee, chairman of the State Chairmen's Advisory Committee, the chairman of the Budget Committee, and the president of the National Federation of Republican Women (a long-established party auxiliary organization that operates out of GOP national headquarters).

### Executive Committee

The Executive Committee also serves as an advisory body to the chairman. Its membership reflects the efforts of the RNC to integrate party auxiliaries, key voter groups, and Republican elected officials into the party organization. In addition to the members of the Executive Council, the Executive Committee includes the chairmen of the following party auxiliary organizations: the Young Republican National Federation, College Republican National Committee, National Republican Heritage (ethnic) Councils, Black Republican Council, Republican Hispanic Assembly, Republican Labor Council, and Republicans Abroad. The RNC chairman is also authorized to appoint a representative of Jewish-Americans to the Executive Committee. The RNC has encouraged the formation of associations of Republican elected officials and accorded Executive Committee representation to the Republican leaders of the House and Senate, as well as to the leaders of the following associations: National Conference of Republican Mayors, Republican Governors Association, National Conference of Republican County Officials, National Republican Legislators Association, and National Association of Urban Republican County Chairmen.

## Committees

*The Rules of the Republican Party* requires the creation of a series of committees composed exclusively of RNC members. The responsibilities of these committees are closely related to the RNC's responsibilities for administration of the national convention.

*Committee on Site of the Republican National Convention.* This committee investigates potential convention sites and makes a recommendation to the full RNC concerning the location of the national nominating convention. It is then the responsibility of the full RNC membership to decide upon the national convention site.

*Committee on Arrangements.* Responsible for overseeing the planning and management of the convention, this committee operates through a series of subcommittees responsible for such functions as housing, transportation, security, tickets and badges, and news media.

*Committee on the Call.* Just as the 1856 national executive committee was created to issue the formal Call for a national convention, the RNC continues to perform this function through its Committee on the Call, which prepares the Call for approval by the full RNC.

*Committee on Contests.* The committee reviews disputes over which persons qualify as bona fide convention delegates from the states. Its recommendations are forwarded to the full RNC, which is responsible for preparing a temporary roll of delegates for the convention.

*Standing Committee on Rules.* This committee has the power to review and propose recommendations relating to *The Rules of the Republican Party*. However, neither the Committee on Rules nor the RNC has final authority over these rules. The normal practice for rules changes within the GOP is for the Standing Committee on Rules to propose changes to the full RNC. If approved by the RNC, changes are then forwarded to the Rules Committee of the national convention. Only the national convention,

however, is empowered to makes changes in *The Rules of the Republican Party*.

These procedures make rules changes within the Republican Party relatively difficult; indeed, it is impossible for the RNC to to change national party rules between national conventions, a policy in sharp contrast to the Democrats' practice of permitting the Democratic National Committee (DNC) to approve and implement major changes in national party rules between national conventions.

Republican rules also preclude the possibility of special commissions or committees to reform the rules being appointed by the RNC chairman. Rules review between conventions is the exclusive province of the Standing Committee on Rules. This procedure is designed to prevent the creation of special rules review panels over which the RNC members have little control. Such a panel, the Rule 29 Committee, was created after the 1972 convention. This Committee became highly controversial because of its recommendations to reform state procedures for selecting national convention delegates. To prevent such "runaway" committees in the future, the rules were amended by the 1976 and 1980 conventions to place responsibility for rules review with the RNC's Standing Committee on Rules (on which each state has one representative). This amendment made it impossible within the Republican Party for an ad hoc commission like the Democrats' McGovern-Fraser Commission to propose rules changes and get them adopted.

*Finance Committee.* Unlike the other RNC committees, the chairman and members of the Finance Committee do not have to be formal members of the RNC. The committee chairman is appointed by the RNC chairman, and the committee operates through the Finance Division at RNC headquarters as the fundraising arm of the national committee.

## A Confederate Party Structure

Although the DNC, after a series of rules changes in the 1970s, moved away from its original confederative organizational mode, the RNC has retained its initial confederative character. The position of the RNC within the Republican organizational structure was aptly summarized in Chairman Bill Brock's 1978 report, which opened with the following statement:

> The Republican National Committee [RNC] is the structural heart and soul of the Republican Party. It links a far-flung confederation of . . . state

parties . . . yet it has no charter, permanent constitution, or bylaws—as such. Legally, it is an unincorporated association. It is an organization created and authorized by the Rules adopted at the last preceding National Convention. . . . It operates under these Rules until the next convention convenes and adopts new rules.

*Membership*. Unlike the national convention, where delegates are allocated in accordance with a state's electoral votes and its support for Republican candidates, RNC membership has been based on the principle of state equality. The only exception was a brief period between 1952 and 1968 when state parties were rewarded for electoral success by making their state chairmen RNC members. The composition of the RNC, therefore, stands in distinct contrast to the DNC, which allocates membership among the states based upon a formula that takes into account population and a state's voting record for President.

*Committees*. The RNC's committees further reflect the organization's confederative character. Its most important committee, the Standing Committee on Rules, consists of one member from each state, with each state's RNC delegation empowered to select its representative to the Committee. The Committee on Arrangements is also composed of one RNC member from each state. The composition and selection procedures for the committees on the Call, Contests, and Site also practice a confederative principle. Each of these committees consists of two members from the four regions into which the RNC is divided. Each regional caucus selects its own committee representatives.

*Delegate selection procedures*. Whereas the DNC has become heavily involved in enforcing the national party's elaborate delegate selection procedures upon its state parties, the RNC has not become involved in any significant way in rule enforcement. The RNC's relatively passive role in enforcing national party rules upon state parties reflects a conscious decision to protect the autonomy of state party organizations and the confederative character of the GOP. The rules of the Republican Party are permissive regarding delegate selection procedures and, unlike the Democratic rules, do not bar open primaries, fix a specific time for delegate selection procedures, prohibit winner-take-all primaries, or require equal division between men and women in state delegations. With permissive national party rules governing delegate selection, the RNC has had few occasions to assert its legal authority to bring state delegate selection procedures into conformity with national party rules.

One of the clearest indications of the RNC's determination to retain the GOP's confederative structure occurred in 1975, when it rejected the recommendation of the Rule 29 Committee calling for nonmandatory "positive (affirmative) action" plans of delegate selection on the part of state parties. The RNC's action came amid warnings from RNC members that the proposal by the Rule 29 Committee constituted a threat of party domination from Washington. As Professor Leon D. Epstein has observed, "Rather than do anything deliberate to modify the confederative character of their party, Republicans have seemed intent on preserving it, even while dramatically increasing their national campaign activities."

### The National Chairman

The national chairmanship has changed since World War II from a highly personalized, part-time, unsalaried position to the more well defined role of a professional party manager and spokesperson. The RNC national chairmanship became fully differentiated from federal executive positions during the Eisenhower administration. Although it had been commonplace in the past for the national chairman to serve simultaneously as Postmaster General because of that office's patronage potential, President Dwight Eisenhower was adamant that the RNC chairman would not hold a position in his administration. Nor is it possible any longer for elected officials, such as Representatives and Senators, to serve as national chairmen. Party rules require that the chairman be a full-time, paid employee of the RNC.

### Selection

Although the national chairman is elected formally by the full RNC for a two year term in January of odd-numbered years, the actual selection process varies depending upon whether Republicans control the White House. When the GOP holds the presidency, the national chairman is designated by the President or President-elect and the RNC merely ratifies that choice. Thus President-elect George Bush designated his 1988 campaign manager, Lee Atwater, to be RNC chairman for the term beginning in January 1989. However, when no Republican occupies the White House, a spirited contest for the chairmanship often takes place, as when Bill Brock was elected in 1977 following

Gerald Ford's defeat by Jimmy Carter in the 1976 presidential election.

Earlier in this century, accepted practice allowed for presidential nominees to install a loyalist in the RNC chairmanship immediately following their nomination by the national convention. For example, Eisenhower replaced Guy Galbrielson, a supporter of his opponent for the nomination, with one of his key supporters, Arthur Summerfield, after the 1952 convention. However, as the national chairman has achieved increased stature and support within the GOP because of the services provided by the RNC to state parties and candidates, presidential nominees have found it difficult or imprudent to jettison a national chairman immediately after being nominated. For example, Richard Nixon in 1968 retained Ray C. Bliss, Ronald Reagan in 1980 retained Bill Brock, and George Bush in 1988 retained Frank Fahrenkopf after winning presidential nominations, even though their campaign organizations were reported to want to replace the incumbent national chairmen. Although presidential nominees are no longer apt to replace an incumbent national chairman, they do customarily install a deputy within the RNC, one who is charged with protecting the nominee's interests and handling the RNC's responsibilities for the presidential campaign.

*Leadership styles.* Because the national committee is of a relatively unwieldy size and normally meets only twice a year, the national chairman plays a critical role in determining how the RNC will operate. Traditionally, two basic leadership styles have predominated. One was the speaking chairman, who saw his role as acting as spokesperson on behalf of the party, generating publicity, and criticizing the opposition. Senator Bob Dole (Kansas), who used his often caustic wit to defend the Nixon administration and attack Democrats, exemplified this type of chairman during his tenure (1971–1973). The institutionalization of the RNC with its expanded staff, budget, and programs has meant that increasingly the national chairmen have emphasized their role as organizational leaders. The classic example of a chairman who emphasized party organization building was Ray C. Bliss, a self-described "nuts and bolts chairman," who guided the RNC during its rebuilding years (1965–1969) following the electoral disaster of 1964. More recent chairmen—Bill Brock (1977–1981) and Frank Fahrenkopf (1983–1989)—have similarly emphasized the organi-

zational side of the job, though they have more frequently served as party spokespersons than did Bliss. Only one RNC chairman, George Bush (1973–1974), has ever become President of the United States.

*In-party versus out-party status.* Control of the White House substantially affects the influence of the national chairman and the role of the national committee. National chairmen who have been credited with being the most influential and effective have been those like Bliss and Brock who did not serve with a Republican President. As the most inclusive party organization in the country, the national committee tends to become a focal point of intraparty activity and interest during periods when the party does not hold the presidency. Because they are not subservient to the White House, out-party RNC chairmen have had considerable flexibility in developing GOP strategy and programs. They have been able to exert an independent influence upon the party because they personally campaigned for the chairmanship and developed a core of supporters within the RNC constituency.

When the Republicans have controlled the White House in the years since 1968, the role of the RNC and its chairman has been heavily dependent upon the President and his political operatives on the White House staff. While Richard Nixon was in the White House, the RNC's role as a support mechanism for GOP candidates and state organizations was downplayed; instead the chairman's role as a publicist for the President was emphasized. Unlike Nixon, President Ronald Reagan was highly supportive of the RNC and assisted it generously with fundraising and campaign support. The Reagan political operation was, however, centered in the White House political office with the RNC clearly subservient to the White House. RNC activities reflected the White House priorities. As former chairman Brock (1977–1981) observed, "Once 1980 passed, the party mechanism shifted to one of serving the White House."

White House involvement in RNC affairs frequently makes the job of the national chairman extremely difficult and frustrating. Reagan's first national chairman, Richard Richards (1981–1983) commented candidly about his situation: "It is a tough, tough job to be National Chairman when you have the White House . . . every clerk and secretary in the White House thinks they can do your job better than you can, and they don't even know what you do."

In late 1988, the incoming Bush administration announced that, unlike the Nixon and Reagan administrations, it intended to concentrate its political operations in the RNC and to downgrade the role of the White House political office.

### RNC Activities: From "Politics Without Power" to Heightened Party Centralization and Integration

In 1964, Cornelius Cotter and Bernard Hennessy, the authors of the most authoritative study of national committees, characterized these bodies as "politics without power." Since that time, the RNC has been transformed into an influential participant in electoral politics at not only the national level but at state and local levels as well. RNC politics is no longer "politics without power."

#### Strengthening the Party's Financial Base

The RNC's expanded involvement in electoral politics and its increased intraparty influence has been accomplished in large part because of the strides that it has made in fundraising—particularly fundraising through direct mail solicitations. Direct mail solicitation was begun by the RNC in the early 1960s and expanded during the chairmanship of Ray Bliss (1965–1969). It was not, however, until the chairmanship of Bill Brock in the late 1970s that this program really took off. By 1978 the RNC had amassed a base of 511,638 contributors, 58 percent of whom contributed $25 or less. By the time Brock left the RNC chairmanship after the 1980 elections, the Committee's list of active contributors exceeded 2 million.

Its base of small contributors, augmented by substantial programs for large contributors, has given the RNC a higher level of gross revenues than any other national Republican committee or, for that matter, the DNC. The magnitude of the RNC fundraising operation is shown in the following table that lists gross revenues raised between 1974 and 1988.

With a fundraising capacity unprecedented for an American national political committee, the RNC has been able to expand all three phases of its operations—general party activity, assistance to candidates, and assistance to state and local party units.

#### General Party Activities

A substantial proportion (9 percent in 1987) of the RNC revenues is used for operating expenses maintaining the headquarters, sophisticated equipment, and the staff. An even larger

### RNC Gross Revenues, 1974–1988 (in millions)

| Year | Amount |
| --- | --- |
| 1974 | $ 6.3 |
| 1975 | 8.9 |
| 1976 | 19.0 |
| 1977 | 10.7 |
| 1978 | 14.5 |
| 1979 | 17.1 |
| 1980 | 46.0 |
| 1981 | 32.5 |
| 1982 | 40.0 |
| 1983 | 37.7 |
| 1984 | 62.0 |
| 1985 | 38.0 |
| 1986 | 38.6 |
| 1987 | 30.5 |
| 1988 | 73.5 |

Sources: Xandra Kayden and Eddie Mahe, Jr., *The Party Goes On* (New York: Basic Books, 1985), p. 73; *Chairman's Report*, 1979 through 1988 (Washington, D.C.: Republican National Committee).

overhead expense is the cost of fundraising—31 percent of gross revenues in 1987.

A significant and regularly occurring responsibility of the RNC is handling the arrangements for the national conventions. This task involves a major staff commitment in the months before the convention. The national chairman appoints the convention manager.

Although primarily a organization-building mechanism, the RNC has typically become involved in issue development during periods when the GOP has not controlled the White House. During the 1977–1980 period, for example, Chairman Brock appointed five advisory councils on economic policy, foreign policy, energy, human concerns, and general government composed of 400 political leaders and policy experts. Their reports provided the basis for the 1980 GOP platform. The Republican Coordinating Committee performed similar functions between 1965 and 1968.

The RNC has a large-scale political communications operation with an in-house capacity to produce a steady stream of informational and polemical materials—print, radio, and film—for distribution to both party leaders across the country and to the public. The best known of its advertising efforts was its $9 million television campaign in 1980 using the theme, "Vote Republican for a Change." An integral part of the communications operation has been the political research program, which had a 1988 budget of approximately $1 million. In spring 1988, for example, the RNC began a large-scale opposition research project on Michael Dukakis's record.

The RNC has also been heavily involved in get-out-the-vote drives. It has operated some of these programs directly from Washington, and using computer-based technology, it has also assisted state party organizations in developing Republican voters lists. A further example of its involvement in grass-roots activities was "Operation Open Door" in 1985. This project, designed to encourage Democrats in four target states to change their party registration and involved RNC-funded mailings to 1.2 million households.

### Candidate Assistance

The RNC makes direct contributions to candidates ($2.5 million in 1986 to 350 candidates for Congress, governor, state legislatures, and local offices). The major thrust of its candidate support activities, however, is to provide services either directly to candidates or through state and local party organizations. In the 1980s, the RNC put a lot of money into a joint project with the National Republican Congressional and Senatorial committees to help state parties in target states develop voter lists that could be used in campaigns. In addition, RNC staff provide technical assistance to candidates for all phases of campaigning.

Chairman Bill Brock initiated a special effort to assist state legislative candidates. In 1978 the RNC spent $1.7 million in direct contributions and in candidate assistance operations, an unprecedented level of involvement in state legislative races by a national committee. Since 1978 the RNC has maintained a heavy involvement in state legislative contests. In 1985, for example, it spent $500,000 to support legislative candidates in just one state, New Jersey. In 1988 the RNC contributed $2 million to targeted state legislative races. In 1985 Chairman Frank Fahrenkopf also began in 1985 the "1991 Plan," a joint effort with the National Republican Senatorial and Congressional committees, to recruit and assist state legislative candidates in an effort to have an impact on 1991 congressional and legislative redistricting. A longer term reason for the RNC's increased emphasis on state legislative elections has been its effort to develop a pool of candidates for higher office from among state legislators.

During a presidential campaign, the national committee is authorized under the Federal Election Campaign Act (FECA) to make expenditures on behalf of the presidential nominee ($8.3 million in 1988). The RNC's role in the presidential campaigns, however, is much more extensive than its expenditures authorized under the FECA. The act permits state and local parties to spend without limit for "party building" activities (i.e., get-out-the-vote drives, voter registration, lawn signs, bumper stickers, buttons, and facilities). Since 1980 the national committee has used this provision in the law and its fundraising capacity to channel massive sums of money to state and local party organizations for local "party building" activities designed to support federal campaigns. Analysts estimate that in 1988 the RNC transferred millions of dollars in so-called "soft money" to state and local parties in order to support the presidential campaign. As a consequence of these fund transfers from the national committee to state parties, the state party organizations are playing a more important role in federal election campaigns. They are, moreover, becoming more closely integrated into presidential campaign organizations and RNC operations.

### Assistance to State and Local Parties

Beginning under the chairmanship of Ray Bliss in the late 1960s, the RNC embarked upon a program of providing assistance and training to state party organizations through seminars on political research, campaign management, public relations, and big city operations. Bliss's program designed to get the RNC to function as a major service agency for state parties was expanded by Chairman Brock and his successors during the 1970s and 1980s. For example, between 1977 and 1979, Brock operated a program under which the RNC even paid the salaries of state party organizational directors in an effort to strengthen state organizations.

The RNC has provided direct cash grants to state party organizations and has even initiated a program of grants to local party organizations (e.g., in 1986, 400 key county organizations received a total of $400,000). An extensive program of technical assistance has also been maintained. As noted previously, the RNC has cooperated with the National Republican Senatorial and Congressional committees and state parties in a program to develop voter lists; by 1986 it had compiled more than 60 million voter files in 34 states at a cost of $10 million. In addition, the RNC provides consulting and training services for state parties in the fields of finance, election law compliance, communications, computer science, and campaign management. The national committee's field staff maintains a liaison and provides assistance to state parties on a continuing basis.

### Institutionalization, Nationalization, and Integration

From an organization founded in 1856 with limited functions and an ad hoc style of operation, the Republican National Committee has become highly institutionalized with a permanent headquarters, a large professional staff organized into a series of specialized divisions, and an array of party-building and candidate-support programs. As its resources and activities have expanded, it has also become a major GOP power center that has advanced the nationalization of the Republican Party.

The process of nationalization within the Republican Party has been quite different from that within the Democratic Party. Unlike the Democratic National Committee, the RNC has not asserted control over its state affiliates through rigorous enforcement of national party rules. The RNC has, however, significantly increased its influence within the Republican Party through its programs of cash grants and technical assistance to state and local party organizations and to candidates. Leon Epstein has characterized this process of nationalizing the GOP's campaign effort as analogous to the federal government's grant-in-aid system. Like the federal government, which through the grant system uses state and local governments to achieve national policy objectives, the RNC through its grants of assistance uses state and local parties to achieve its electoral priorities. Just as the federal government's grants enhanced the influence of the national government over state and local governments, so too do the RNC's programs of assistance. Like the federal government's categorical grants, which require state and local governments to follow federal guidelines, the RNC also attaches conditions (albeit highly permissive and flexible guidelines) to the assistance it gives to state parties and candidates.

The flow of resources from the RNC to state parties, a flow that has typified the Republican Party's policy since the late 1970s, stands in sharp contrast with earlier decades. Previously, the intraparty resources flowed in the opposite direction—from the state parties to the national committee. In a state of dependence upon state parties, the RNC lacked the funds to initiate and implement major party-building programs, and it had little leverage and influence over its state affiliates. However, as the RNC developed a potent fundraising capacity of its own and shed its financial dependence upon state parties, its intraparty influence increased. With the RNC engaged in massive transfers of resources to the state parties, it was the state party organizations that were put in a position of dependence.

The post-1960s changes in the intraparty distribution of resources and the increased level of national committee involvement in electoral politics at the national and state/local levels have taken place while the Republicans have adhered strictly to their original confederative organizational structure. With party resources more heavily concentrated in the national organizations than in the past, the Republican National Committee is both an example and an agent of a process of party nationalization that has been evolving in the United States. This process has created a Republican Party that has achieved a high level of intraparty organizational interdependence and integration.

*See also:* Individual chairs of the committee, George H. W. Bush, Democratic National Committee, Direct Mail, Dwight D. Eisenhower, Federal Election Campaign Act and Amendments, Gerald R. Ford, McGovern-Fraser Commission, Richard M. Nixon, Ronald Reagan, Republican Congressional Campaign Committees, Soft Money in Presidential Campaigns, Winner-Take-All Systems, Woman Suffrage Movement

*John F. Bibby*

REFERENCES

Bibby, John F., and Robert J. Huckshorn. 1968. "Out-Party Strategy: Republican National Committee Rebuilding Politics, 1964–66." In Bernard Cosman and Robert J. Huckshorn, eds. *Republican Politics: The 1964 Campaign and Its Aftermath for the Party.* New York: Praeger.

———. 1979. "Political Parties and Federalism: The Republican National Committee Involvement in Gubernatorial and Legislative Elections." 9 *Publius* 229.

———. 1981. "Party Renewal in the National Republican Party." In Gerald M. Pomper, ed. *Party Renewal in America: Theory and Practice.* New York: Praeger.

———. 1986. "Party Trends in 1985: Constrained Advance of the National Party." 16 *Publius* 79.

Burdette, Franklin. 1968. *The Republican Party: A Short History.* Princeton: D. Van Nostrand.

*Chairman's Report.* 1976–1987. Washington: Republican National Committee.

Conway, M. Margaret. 1983. "Republican Party Nationalization, Campaign Activities, and Their Implications for the Party System." 13 *Publius* 1.

Committee for Party Renewal. 1983. *Party Line.* February: 7.

Cotter, Cornelius P., and John F. Bibby. 1980. "Institutional Development of Parties and the Thesis of Party Decline." 95 *Political Science Quarterly* 1.

———, and Bernard Hennessy. 1964. *Politics Without Power: The National Party Committees*. New York: Praeger.

Epstein, Leon D. 1986. *Political Parties in the American Mold*. Madison: U. of Wisconsin Pr.

Herrnson, Paul S. 1988. *Party Campaigning in the 1980s*. Cambridge: Harvard U. Pr.

Huckshorn, Robert J., and John F. Bibby. 1984. "National Party Rules and Delegate Selection in the Republican Party." 16 *PS* 656.

Jacobson, Gary C. 1985. "The Republican Advantage in Campaign Finance." In John E. Chubb and Paul E. Peterson, eds. *The New Directions in American Politics*. Washington: Brookings.

Kayden, Xandra, and Eddie Mahe, Jr. 1985. *The Party Goes On: The Persistence of the Two-Party System in the United States*. New York: Basic Books.

Reichley, A. James. 1985. "The Rise of the National Parties." In John E. Chubb and Paul E. Peterson, eds. *The New Directions in American Politics*. Washington: Brookings.

*The Rules of the Republican Party*. 1988. Adopted by the 1988 Republican National Convention, August 16, 1988, New Orleans, Louisiana.

## Republicanism and the First American Party System

While many issues were left unsettled at the Constitutional Convention of 1787, all of the delegates present agreed that they were creating a "republican" form of government. The meanings that those delegates attached to their republican faiths differed significantly, but at least a few essential components of republican ideology were embraced by virtually everyone at the Convention. At its core the republican consensus was a negative one, embodying the rejection of two important principles that lay at the foundation of the Americans' English heritage—the principles of hereditary monarchy and hereditary aristocracy. The republican alternative to those hereditary norms was "representative democracy," but within that concept lay a multitude of alternative meanings, ranging from direct democracy to a system in which the people's role in the selection and oversight of public officeholders was extremely limited.

The end toward which republican governments were to be directed was the public good. As John Adams noted, "There must be a positive Passion for the Public Good [and] the Public Interest . . . established in the Minds of the People, or there can be no Republican Government, nor any real liberty." In fact, considerable debate split Americans over the best means by which to balance the public good with personal liberty (and, indeed, debate over what the proper doses of those commodities should be), but most of the revolutionary leaders present in the Constitutional Convention had a relatively traditional view of that equation. Reacting to the threat posed by Shays's Rebellion, the delegates wished to create an "energetic" government capable of maintaining the public order in the face of the licentious behavior of the great mass of the citizenry. And, believing in the principle of the "filtration of talent," they created governmental structures—for example, the indirect election of the U.S. Senate and of the chief executive—that gave a broad popular base to the central government and at the same time removed officeholders in certain arms of the government from the direct influence of the passions of the people.

In the dozen years following the adoption of the Constitution in 1788, as the new central government began to operate, the framers' original conception of that Constitution underwent a dramatic transformation. This transformation would significantly alter the structures of many of the essential governmental agencies created by the framers; it would change the relationship between those serving in the government and their constituents; and, most important, it would reshape Americans' understanding of what "republicanism" really meant. The agencies for these dramatic changes were the Republican and Federalist parties, entirely novel entities unimagined by and distasteful to the framers of 1787.

The initial differences over public policy that would lead to the development of institutionalized political parties were provoked by differing conceptions of the meaning of "federalism" as articulated by the Founding Fathers. As the new federal government began to do its job, and as the policies and ideological perspectives of President George Washington's Secretary of the Treasury, Alexander Hamilton, appeared to veer toward a definition of federalism in which the balance of power between the central and the state governments shifted dramatically in favor of the central, opposition within the halls of Congress and, occasionally, within the legislatures of the individual states, began to surface.

The initial core of opposition to Hamilton's policies consisted of those Anti-Federalists who had feared the Constitution's centralizing tendencies from its very inception. Those Anti-Federalists were joined, however, by growing numbers of former Federalists, who had come to recognize that many of the Anti-Federalists' warnings about the powers of the new government were justified. The ranks of former Federalist supporters of the Constitution in the new U.S. Congress were seriously split during the debate over Hamilton's plan calling for the central government not only to fund the continental debt at full value plus interest but also to assume responsibility for the payment of the Revolutionary War debts of the individual states. Opposition to the proposal was particularly strong in the South, and even such staunch nationalists as James Madison came to oppose Hamilton's plan. The grounds for opposition were complex: some opposed the funding proposal because it failed to distinguish between original holders of the continental debt and those speculators who had purchased it subsequently at depreciated prices; nearly all who opposed the assumption of state debts did so on the grounds that it was unconstitutional, believing that to give to the central government the power to meddle in the financial affairs of the individual states would, in the words of Virginia Senator William Grayson, leave the states with little else to do "but to eat, drink, and be merry." Hamilton's proposals ultimately won congressional assent but only after some behind-the-scenes negotiating that guaranteed to southern Congressmen a more southerly location for the nation's capital in the newly created District of Columbia rather than near Philadelphia, as previously planned.

The divisions in Congress over funding and assumption became even sharper in the aftermath of the debate over Hamilton's proposal for a national bank. The bill chartering the First Bank of the United States passed Congress by a nearly two-to-one margin, but opponents of the Hamiltonian plan had raised questions about whether the central government was constitutionally empowered to give a monopoly to a private, profit-making corporation simply because the existence of such a corporation might facilitate the government's financial business. At this point, President Washington issued his well-known request to both his Secretary of Treasury and his Secretary of State, Thomas Jefferson, for opinions on the bank bill's constitutionality. Both Hamilton and Jefferson based their opinions on the "necessary and proper clause" of the Constitution, but each read that clause in a radically different way: Jefferson arguing for a "strict construction" doctrine and

Hamilton for a "broad construction" of those powers necessary and proper to effect the explicitly enumerated powers granted to the Congress.

Jefferson's and Hamilton's opposing interpretations of constitutional doctrine reflected sharply diverging understandings of the meaning of "federalism," and their understandings would in some important respects prefigure the shape of the debate between nationalists and the defenders of state rights for decades to come. Furthermore, and important to note, is that the terms of the debate were still couched in a traditional republican language and within equally traditional understandings of the way governments were supposed to function. It was a debate carried out primarily among well-established members of the political elite, who differed among themselves on how they might best order the affairs of their country. Few people on either side felt any need to resort to appeals beyond the bounds of the national legislature, for they all tended to share a common assumption that the country's political destiny was best left to disinterested, wise, and virtuous leaders like themselves and not to the great mass of the citizens whom they served.

The language that the proponents of each side in the debate used was, quite strikingly, the language of traditional republicanism. Hamiltonian "broad" constructionists argued that payment of the continental and state debts was a matter of "morality and justice"; a failure to honor those financial obligations would be to "render all rights precarious and to introduce a general dissipation and corruption of morals." Hamiltonians defended the national bank in similarly moralistic terms, calling it essential for the defense of the national credit, a "sacred" obligation. Opponents were equally hyperbolic in identifying the "unrepublican" features of Hamilton's plans. Jefferson charged that the "ultimate object of [Hamilton's financial system] is to prepare the way for a change, from the present republican form of government to that of a monarchy," and both he and Madison argued that the bank and the funding and assumption bills would lead toward a "consolidated government" that would sacrifice the public interest to those of the monied aristocracy.

The early debates in Congress over the precise meaning of the new federalist system, however acrimonious they may have been, certainly did not suggest the abandonment of one conception of politics for another. While Madison and

Jefferson were inclined to be increasingly critical of Hamilton's personal motives as well as of the substance of his policies, such personal animus was inseparable from the traditional, elite-dominated political discourse of the age. And as much as Jefferson and Madison may have lamented their defeats at Hamilton's hands, they were nevertheless generally comfortable with the traditional structure within which their contests with Hamilton took place. Nevertheless, in a few years, with the injection of issues of foreign policy and national defense into the political arena, the grounds of debate would shift well beyond the constitutional imperatives of "federalism" to embrace such fundamental issues as the future of America's experiment in independence and the very meaning of revolutionary republicanism itself.

At first glance it would seem puzzling that political divisions over matters of foreign policy would provide the catalyst for the conversion from elite-dominated to mass-based democratic politics in America. The American people in the late eighteenth century were hardly a cosmopolitan lot and they had certainly not kept a close eye on the actions of other nations around the world in the past. Yet the foreign policy issues of the 1790s—and questions of America's proper relationship with the two major European powers, England and France, in particular— would cause the narrowly defined constitutional and sectional divisions in the First and Second Congresses to be transformed into intensely emotional, broadly based popular divisions in the years between 1793 and 1801. The only way to explain the intensity and pervasiveness of the ideological debate generated during that period is to understand the conflict over American foreign policy not merely as a set of diplomatic policy decisions facing the young nation but, more importantly, as a searching debate about the meaning of America's revolutionary experience itself, a debate that would in the final analysis transform the structure of American political life and at the same time alter the definitions that many Americans gave to their republican faith.

In April 1793, with the outbreak of yet another armed conflict between England and France, the newly formed government of the United States found itself, quite against its natural predilection, thrown into the balance of power struggles in Europe. America's revolutionary ally, France, by the terms of the Franco-American treaty of 1778, believed that it had a right to expect substantive aid from the Americans in its struggle against their mutual enemy. George Washington's Secretary of State, Thomas Jefferson, was inclined to agree; while he did not advocate direct military involvement for America, Jefferson did believe that America's diplomatic and spiritual ties to the republican government of revolutionary France at least required some public expression of support for the people of that nation.

Others in the Washington administration had different ideas. Hamilton, arguing forcefully that treaties should remain in force only so long as they served a nation's interest, insisted that the government should "temporarily and provisionally suspend" the Franco-American alliance. Washington, as he did in nearly all of the important decisions during his two administrations, reached an independent judgment on the matter; nevertheless, he took a position much closer to Hamilton's than Jefferson's. The Proclamation of Neutrality of 1793 declared America's intention to conduct itself in a manner "friendly and impartial toward the belligerent powers," but, given the reality of America's well-established economic relationships with England, the Proclamation was justifiably viewed by many as a betrayal both of existing treaty obligations and, more important, of America's commitment to the principles of revolutionary republicanism. For the rest of the decade, in reaction first to the Proclamation of Neutrality, then to the treaty of "amity and commerce" that Federalist John Jay negotiated with Great Britain in 1794, and finally in the repercussions flowing from that treaty in 1797 and 1798 (when France pursued an exceedingly belligerent policy toward American shipping on the high seas) Americans would debate their relationship with those two European powers.

The rhetorical ingredients of that debate suggest that Americans were still a long way from reaching a common understanding about where the logic of their revolutionary republican ideology was taking them. Some of the features of the debate suggest that both the Federalists and the emerging Jeffersonian Republican Party were still working within the same traditional/classical republican framework and drawing on precisely the same themes based on that language for their attacks on their opponents. Both a preoccupation with "virtue" and corruption and an abhorrence of "party" and "faction" infected the debate; Federalists and Republicans alike seemed obsessed with the notion that their opponents had lost their virtue and denounced their adversary's attempts at political organization as a sure sign of the corrosive effects of a lust for power.

Other aspects of the debate suggest that Republicans and Federalists were drawing on different aspects of the same traditional language. The Federalists, committed to the notion that the public good required the restraint of private interests and private passions, condemned the disorderly and self-interested opposition of the Republicans. They were particularly alarmed at the Republicans' attachment to revolutionary France, believing that anarchy, atheism, and the consequent destruction of virtue among that country's citizenry were the inevitable results of excessively popular modes of government. Beginning with the passage of the Alien and Sedition Acts in 1798 and continuing through the election of 1800, the Federalists became even more hysterical in their fear that the combination of Republican loyalty to revolutionary France and the disorderly character of the Republican opposition to government policy at home would lead to anarchy within America. For their part the Republicans tended to draw on the antimonarchical, antiaristocratic aspects of traditional republican language, condemning the Federalists for their close ties with the "monocrats" of England and arguing that their opponents were using their control of the executive branch to install themselves as a permanent, hereditary cabal.

Both the Republican and Federalist languages were what a historian might expect to emerge from political combat anywhere in the Anglo-American world at nearly any time in the eighteenth century, yet indications were that some within the emerging Republican Party had begun to employ a new language—one predicated on a new set of assumptions about the relationship between a government and its citizenry. It is more closely related to what analysts have come to identify as liberal capitalism than to the traditional concerns of classical republicanism. Some Republicans explicitly rejected the Federalists' call for an "energetic" government, claiming that such government accounted for "all those rigid codes of law that have subverted the natural liberties of mankind." Rejecting the classical republican assumption that private interests must be suppressed in the name of the public good, many Republicans came to the conclusion that the collective actions of "free and independent men," unimpeded by the

weight of government regulation and repression, would in themselves result in the greatest public good for the greatest number. Individualistic, utilitarian, and egalitarian, theirs was a doctrine pointing in a very different direction from the one impelling men like John Adams or Alexander Hamilton to call for restraints on personal liberty for the sake of public order.

Students of the period must be careful not to draw too sharp a distinction between Republican and Federalist ideological perspectives, for not all Republicans during the 1790s were not ideologically wedded to "liberalism." Ample evidence points to the fact that many Republicans as well as Federalists were slow to abandon classical republican notions of virtue, disinterestedness, and opposition to party in their rhetorical stances, and some would argue that the economic policies of Hamilton rather than those of Jefferson were in the forefront of the development of liberal capitalism in America. Whatever the ambiguities in the Republicans' and Federalists' own understanding of what they were doing and where they were heading, their actual behavior—first in Congress and ultimately among the electorate at large—was clearly leading them in very new directions.

As early as 1793 opposition leaders like Jefferson and Madison were referring to a "republican interest" in the country, and while they hotly denied charges that they were fomenting a "party spirit" in the country, their actions displayed a self-consciousness of purpose that was hardly in keeping with traditional republican notions of disinterested, elite decision-making. The contradictions between the Republican oppositions' rhetoric and the reality of their organizational efforts is ironic. Clear in both the private correspondence and the public statements of opposition leaders is their rejection of a mass-based, popular party system. Rather, as a minority faction in the national Congress (and likely to remain a minority so long as George Washington continued to lend his considerable prestige to the policies of Hamilton), the Republicans turned to popular appeals to the electorate out of desperation. The methods they used would eventually become the standard devices of political organization throughout America: town and county meetings in which the opinions of the citizenry on American foreign policy were shaped, collected, and mobilized; the self-conscious use of the press to promote the policies and candidates of their party; and, finally, the creation of extragovernmental institutions (congressional nominating caucuses, state and local party committees, legions of precinct workers) to recruit ordinary citizens at the local level into the political process.

The broad outlines of the institutional development of the first American party system are now well established. As indicated above, a growing consciousness of basic constitutional divisions between strict constructionists and broad constructionists appeared as early as the First Congress, but voting in that Congress was strictly factional; moreover, the factional alignments in the First Congress according to broad issues of ideology and national policy were short-lived. The overall levels of agreement among former Federalists and former Anti-Federalists in the First Congress stood only at about 55 percent, just a few percentage points higher than the levels of agreement *between* members of those two camps (49 percent). By contrast, cohesion among the various regional and sectional voting blocs in the First Congress was much more striking and durable.

By the period 1794–1797, however, the transition from factions to parties is clear in the voting behavior of the Representatives to Congress. During those years shifting factional alignments gave way to voting behavior that was much more consistently partisan. More and more often, Congressmen self-consciously identified themselves as either Federalists or Republicans, and levels of voting agreement among members of each of those camps rose to about 75 percent. At this stage in the evolution of parties in Congress, the range of issues capable of producing partisan behavior was still relatively circumscribed, encompassing primarily those issues of economic and foreign policy that touched obviously on the Federalists' and Republicans' differing views of America's future.

During the period 1797–1801 the consistency of party voting in Congress increased markedly; during the two Congresses preceding the presidential election of 1800, party cohesiveness within Federalist and Republican ranks had increased to 85 percent, a level of partisan voting behavior that exceeds even present-day patterns. As an interpreter might expect from these rates of party cohesion, the range of issues affected by partisan voting had widened considerably, including not only questions of foreign policy, economic policy, and constitutional interpretation but also a number of purely "partisan" questions relating to the aggrandizement of

political power within the bureaucratic structures of the executive, legislative, and judicial branches.

These developments have persuaded most students of the period that parties in Congress were well developed by the end of the eighteenth century. Great debate, however, continues over whether a fully developed party system reaching down into the electorate had come into being. Many scholars, pointing to the incomplete character of the party structures at the local level and the persistence of antiparty rhetoric among leaders of both the Federalist and Republican parties, have concluded that while some "party voting" took place in Congress, a full-fledged "party system" did not come into being in America during the 1790s.

To some extent these questions are semantical ones, depending upon the definition of "party," but the heart of the problem is whether the more partisan character of political debate and political organization in the 1790s caused a fundamental transformation in people's conceptions of the political process itself. And the evidence on that question is mixed.

The transformation of American politics was closely tied to two concepts—democracy and nationalism—and both of those concepts came to play an increasingly important role in the political process well before the new government commenced operation in 1789. The forces working for democratization of the political process had been at work in America long before the Revolution, and to some considerable extent the acceptance of a tradition of popular politics was an important precondition to the development of popular political parties. The extent to which democratic styles of politics were accepted varied considerably from region to region; however, and not surprisingly, the extent to which "party" politics filtered down to the electorate at large depended in large measure on the extent to which the various regions had a previous tradition of popular politics.

New York and Philadelphia, for example, had already taken important steps toward a nondeferential, issue-oriented system of politics before the new national government started operation, and when the divisive issues of the 1790s first appeared, the organizers of the Federalist and Republican "interests" mobilized the electorate in support of their respective positions relatively easily. By contrast, the southern states had a long tradition of deferential, elite-dominated politics. As a consequence, while southern

Representatives were among the most aggressive in promoting the Republican interest in Congress during the 1790s, the conduct and content of the political discourse at the local level continued to display many "pre-party" features. While many of the structures of partisan politics (party newspapers, state and county committees) came into being in the southern states, the actual conduct of elections in the South continued to be dominated by traditional factors of personality and prestige.

The change in focus from a provincial to a national politics within America was much less well advanced by the 1790s, but that process was nevertheless underway well before the framers met in Philadelphia to deliberate on a national government. The imperatives of resistance and, finally, of revolution, forced Americans out of a purely provincial view of their political destinies. Indeed, many of the debates of the 1790s—particularly those centering on the strict constructionist/broad constructionist division on constitutional interpretation and those relating to America's relationship with the European powers—were in a significant way extensions of debates begun during the period of the Revolution. Obviously, the creation of a strengthened central government provided a much more clearly focused forum for the resolution of those longstanding questions, and the subsequent emergence of parties in the national Congress would accelerate the tendency to place "national" rather than "local" issues at the center of the political consciousness of Americans. Indeed, one of the ironies of the development of the first American party system is that the principal initiators of that system—the Republican Party—stood unambiguously for the return of power to state and local agencies of government, but the very necessity to organize politically in order to deal with issues coming out of the national Congress would itself tend to direct the popular sensibility toward a "national" rather than a "local" agenda.

As was the case in the democratization of American politics, the nationalization of the political discourse occurred unevenly throughout the country. The residents of America's urban and commercial centers were probably the first to fix their sights firmly on the central government and on issues of national policy as the primary focus of attention, while citizens of the vast expanse of backcountry, stretching from northern New England down into the Carolinas, remained determinedly provincial long after the structures of party organization had been put in place.

The events during the 1790s that did the most to accelerate both the democratization and nationalization of American politics and, indeed, to change radically the way in which Americans regarded their relationship with the government, were the presidential elections of 1796 and 1800. When the Founding Fathers created the Electoral College, they had in mind a system of indirect election whereby virtue and disinterestedness would triumph over passion and interest; but beginning in 1796, and reaching a white-hot fever of partisan vituperation and mobilization in 1800, the leaders of the Federalist and Republican parties directed all of their energies to creating a system in which the role of ordinary voters in the election of the President was direct and immediate. Likewise, the role of the disinterested and virtuous electors envisioned by the framers ended up being reduced to that of mere agents of the will of the party. Although the rhetoric of those elections continued to resonate with traditional themes of personal virtue and disinterested pursuit of the public good, and though leaders of each of the parties continued to preach an antiparty ideology, the extent of popular mobilization around a set of national issues and national symbols that occurred during these elections was absolutely unprecedented.

The role of "party" in American politics reached a temporary high point during the election of 1800. After Jefferson's election and with the subsequent demise of the Federalists, party cohesiveness in Congress would decline markedly during the first two decades of the nineteenth century. The emergence of even more elaborately organized party structures during the period of the second party system would of course reverse that trend, but even during that better-developed phase of party organization, personal, sectional, and purely local considerations would confuse and confound party discipline. Throughout the period of the second party system, and, indeed, throughout all of American political history subsequently, presidential elections have served as the occasions when the efforts of party both in and out of Congress have been most concerted and most effective.

When Thomas Jefferson delivered his inaugural address on the steps of the still-unfinished national capitol in March 1801, he evoked themes that clearly exhibited the mixture of traditional and modern ideas that would guide American politics for the next several decades. The recurrent refrain of his address—his commitment to both "union and republican government"—tended to look backward to the antimonarchical, antiaristocratic heritage of the Revolution. And the most oft-quoted words in the address—"We are all Republicans, we are federalists"—expressed his desire to quell the spirit of "party" that had infected the political debate of the previous decade; though Jefferson's peaceful accession to power in 1801 would do much to establish the tradition of a "loyal opposition" in American politics, even Jefferson himself would continue to manifest an uneasiness about the party system that he had helped bring into being.

But while Jefferson and most other American politicians in the nineteenth century would continue to use the antiparty and antipower language of classical republicanism, the actual conduct of nineteenth-century politics suggests that a very different set of assumptions were at work. The outcome of elections to the Congress and, even more dramatically, to the chief executive's office, would increasingly be determined by concerted, partisan effort by professional politicians rather than by the inherent virtue of individual contestants. The principle of the "filtration of talent," whereby the voice of the people in the selection of public officials was to be muted and refined, was increasingly sacrificed to the practical needs of popular, partisan mobilization. While neither the Federalists nor the Republicans may have intended to give the American electorate such a direct and active role in the selection of public officials, that electorate, once empowered in such fashion, would be reluctant to resume its previous, deferential role. Thomas Jefferson, a well-born and wealthy gentryman born into a society that was wedded to "republican" virtues, probably greeted partisan popular politics with a mixture of anticipation and concern. Andrew Jackson, the product of a different culture in a different age, would embrace the imperatives of democratic partisan politics less equivocally.

*See also:* John Adams, Alien and Sedition Acts, Anti-Federalists, Electoral College System, Federalist Party, First Bank of the United States, Alexander Hamilton, Andrew Jackson, John Jay, Thomas Jefferson, James Madison, George Washington

*Richard Beeman*

*REFERENCES*

Appleby, Joyce. 1984. *Capitalism and the New Social Order: The Republican Vision of the 1790s.* New York: New York U. Pr.

Bailyn, Bernard. 1967. *Ideological Origins of the American Revolution.* Cambridge: Belknap Pr.

Bell, Rudolph M. 1973. *Party and Faction in the House of Representatives.* Westport, CT: Greenwood.

Buel, Richard. 1972. *Securing the Revolution: Ideology in American Politics.* Ithaca, NY: Cornell U. Pr.

Charles, Joseph. 1961. *Origins of the American Party System: Three Essays.* Williamsburg, VA: Institute of Early American History and Culture.

Cunningham, Noble. 1957. *The Jeffersonian Republicans: The Formation of Party Organization, 1789–1801.* Chapel Hill: U. of North Carolina Pr.

Hoadley, John F. 1986. *Origins of American Political Parties, 1789–1803.* Lexington: U. Pr. of Kentucky.

Hofstadter, Richard. 1969. *The Idea of a Party System: The Rise of Legitimate Opposition in the United States, 1780–1840.* Berkeley: U. of California Pr.

Miller, John C. 1960. *The Federalist Era, 1789–1801.* New York: Harpers.

Nichols, Roy F. 1967. *The Invention of Political Parties.* New York: Macmillan.

## Residency Requirements

The length of time a person must live in an area before he or she is eligible to vote is indicated by residency requirements. In the early 1960s, 38 states had residency requirements of one or more years. These lengthy residency requirements disenfranchised people who had recently moved and were particularly unfair to those who moved frequently. Frequent movers tend to be the young and the poor.

The 1970 Voting Rights Act Amendments set a maximum residency requirement of 30 days for voting in presidential elections and required absentee voting procedures for those who failed to meet this deadline. In 1972 the Supreme Court in *Dunn v. Blumstein* restricted the length of residency requirements for other elections. As a result, residency requirements now vary from one day to two months, with most states requiring a 30-day residence. One study concluded that residency requirements no longer have any effect on registration rates.

*See also: Dunn v. Blumstein,* Voting Rights Act of 1965 and Extensions

*Barbara Norrander*

## Responsible Party Debate

Analysts have described three sides to the responsible party "debate": Leon Epstein characterizes one side as enthusiastic "defenders of indigenous institutions"; a second side advocates responsible parties, whether on a British model or otherwise; and a third falls between the first two—favoring stronger parties but accepting as inevitable the limitations of American institutional arrangements.

In 1950 the American Political Science Association (APSA) heard its Committee on Political Parties (chaired by E. E. Schattschneider) call for the transformation of the American party system of that era into one that was more effective, responsible, and democratic. The essential elements of the responsible party doctrine included specific recommendations on (1) how electoral majorities are to be mobilized; (2) how they are to be linked to the government; and (3) how the government is to translate the popular majorities into public policy. Responsible parties link the party-in-electorate, the party organization, and the party-in-government in order to provide coherent policy alternatives. Party discipline is required as well as a coherent program upon which elections are contested. The key to this linkage is the type of parties we have to perform these functions: responsible parties have to state the party programs that they are committed to even if their statements eventuate in defeat at the polls.

Some internal disagreement exists within the responsible parties camp over just how much policy guidance popular majorities can provide to those in government. Schattschneider's view stresses the role of the "opposition" with the public voting for two sets of potential leaders, those in office and those in opposition. This vote is based on the "goodness or badness of the times," and thus it provides only vague policy guidance. The other view (from the 1950 APSA report) is that the public is capable of a more sophisticated level of issue-based and ideological voting. Because they have a choice between parties with different and clearly defined issue and ideological positions, the public is capable of producing a relatively clear policy mandate, which the government is then obligated to translate into actual policy. Regardless of the perceived capacity of the electorate, both sides agree on the need for unified and effective parties. At a minimum, parties must be cohesive enough to translate their platforms into policy and then fight the next election of the basis of their records. The opposition party should then serve as an organized critic of the "in" party.

The APSA report provided a number of specific recommendations to implement this more democratic, responsible, and effective party system. The APSA committee recommended that the parties create a centralized and integrated party organization at the national level that would determine membership criteria for participation in party affairs (e.g., primary voters, seating of delegates at national conventions); institute sanctions against state and local party violations of national party criteria; participate in the recruitment, nomination, and election of congressional candidates; institute sanctions against members of Congress who do not support party positions; and encourage intraparty unity and democracy through the use of primaries.

Recent advocates of responsible parties include Gerald Pomper, who stresses the importance of a coherent ideology and the capacity of the public intelligently to choose among alternatives. A different approach is offered by James MacGregor Burns, who advocates strong parties *and* strong presidential leadership. Burns offers something of an American alternative to the British model with a strong president leading a coherent congressional party.

Those who would defend indigenous American parties against the criticisms of the APSA report and other assorted reformers are not able to offer a neat summary of their position because they are defending an existing system that they believe to be, on the whole, a good one. For the most part, their arguments take the form of a critique of the responsible parties argument based on the constitutional structure. The separation of powers and checks and balances system in the national government are major structural impediments to the realization of some of the basic requirements of the model. The federalized and fragmented nature of our elections for the Congress and the presidency are important political obstacles to attaining the centralized party unity (Ralph Huitt observed that in Congress, party discipline was most likely to be applied when least likely to be effective).

In an essay published in 1961, Edward Banfield provides a positive construction of indigenous American institutions. Party factions, for Banfield, increase the options of party leaders. Rather than being incomplete parties (as compared to European parties), American political parties allow for stable government and continuity between administrations of different parties by allowing for leaders to choose pragmatically between "interests" (e.g., the "profit-minded," the "sectional-minded," and the "nationality-minded") and "principles." The party leader (or "President"), according to Banfield, "could afford to offend some elements of the party on any particular question because there would be enough other elements unaffected (or even gratified) to assure his position. The more fragmented his party, the less attention he would have to pay to any one fragment of it." Both parties would be "fundamentally in agreement" because of the "countless compromises within the parties (each of which would be under the necessity of attracting middle-of-the-road support)." Hence, the type of party desired by this school of thought is one which emphasizes pragmatism over principle and party similarity over party cleavage.

V. O. Key is the most prominent figure occupying the position between the two camps. Key supported stronger parties and stressed the importance of genuine party competition, but he favored neither mass-membership parties nor any other type of European arrangements. Key also believed that responsible parties were not possible because of limitations imposed by indigenous American institutions.

*See also:* V. O. Key, E. E. Schattschneider

*David A. Bositis*

REFERENCES

APSA Committee on Political Parties. 1950. "Toward a More Responsible Party System." 44 *American Political Science Review* Supplement.

Banfield, Edward C. 1961. "In Defense of the American Party System." In Robert A. Goldwin, ed. *Political Parties, U.S.A.* Chicago: Rand McNally.

Burns, James MacGregor. 1963. *The Deadlock of Democracy.* Englewood Cliffs, NJ: Prentice-Hall.

———. 1965. *Presidential Government.* Boston: Houghton Mifflin.

Epstein, Leon D. 1986. *Political Parties in the American Mold.* Madison: U. of Wisconsin Pr.

Goodman, T. William. 1951. "How Much Political Party Centralization Do We Want?" 13 *Journal of Politics* 536.

Huitt, Ralph. 1957. "The Morse Committee Assignment Controversy: A Study in Senate Norms." 51 *American Political Science Review* 313.

Kirkpatrick, Evron M. 1971. "Toward a More Responsible Two-Party System: Political Science, Policy or Pseudo Science?" 65 *American Political Science Review* 965.

Pomper, Gerald. 1971. "Toward a More Responsible Party System? What Again?" 33 *Journal of Politics* 916.

Ranney, Austin. 1951. "Toward a More Responsible Two-Party System: A Commentary." 18 *American Political Science Review* 183.

———. 1954. *The Doctrine of Responsible Party Government.* Urbana: U. of Illinois Pr.

Schattschneider, Elmer E. 1942. *Party Government.* New York: Rinehart.

Turner, Julius. 1951. "Responsible Parties: A Dissent from the Floor." 45 *American Political Science Review* 143.

## Retrospective Voting

The term commonly applied to electoral behavior motivated more by judgments about the past than by expectations for the future is retrospective voting. Obviously, elections affect the future course of the polity, and just as obviously, citizens are moved by promises and prospects. But elections reflect where the polity has been, and citizens are also moved by government achievements and realized conditions. Put most simply, while elections have "prospective" consequences, the citizens who participate in them may not be similarly prospective in their thinking.

Political folk wisdom gives proper credit to the retrospective side of elections, as in the familiar maxim, "incumbents don't lose in times of peace and prosperity." For a time, however, academic specialists paid little attention to the retrospective side of elections. From the mid-1950s through the mid-1970s, the scholarly literature emphasized the prospective. Numerous studies of issue voting and spirited debates about voter rationality and responsibility implicitly cast themselves within a prospective framework: how much did voters know about the policy stands of the contending candidates? Only the occasional dissenter asked what voters could reasonably be expected to know, and further, what they actually needed to know in order for democracy to persist. In the 1980s, however, research rediscovered the retrospective. Scholars have now generated an extensive literature, and the academic portrait of elections has become better balanced.

*Conceptions of Retrospective Voting*

It is one thing to say that elections are partly driven by the past; it is another to specify how that impetus occurs and what aspects of the past are most important. The simplest theory of retrospective voting is that embodied in the traditional notion of "throwing the rascals out." According to this conception, the electorate simply rewards successful politicians with continued tenure in office and punishes unsuccessful ones by turning them out. In his many papers on politics, V. O. Key repeatedly cautioned us not to invest too much policy significance in election results. He argued that

[V]oters may reject what they have known; or they may approve what they have known. They are not likely to be attracted in great numbers by promises of the novel or unknown. Once innovation has occurred they may embrace it, even though they would have, earlier, hesitated to venture forth to welcome it.

Such arguments about the behavior of the electorate are common in the writings of an earlier tradition of American scholars who collectively developed the doctrine of responsible party government. Viewed in this tradition, voters more often offered retrospective judgments rather than providing prospective direction. They were to evaluate the *consequences* of government policies, not choose the policies themselves. Consequently, elections were arenas where popular consent was bestowed or withdrawn, not arenas where the direction of government policy was determined. Not only does such a conception demand relatively little of the voter, but also it legitimates a minimal role for voters as that most conducive to the efficient operation of a mass democracy.

Other conceptions of voting make more demanding assumptions about the citizenry. Of most relevance, Anthony Downs also emphasized the retrospective component in electoral choice, but he departed from the older tradition in two important respects. First, Downs viewed citizens as capable of comparing the policy proposals offered by the contending candidates, not just approving or rejecting the performance of the incumbents. Second, for Downs the purpose of looking at past policies was to achieve a better forecast of future policies; the retrospective was put in the service of the prospective in the Downsian analysis.

Contemporary research supports elements of both the reward-punishment and Downsian theories. The evidence is very strong that voters use the past in forming their expectations about the future, as Downs argued. But the evidence for widespread popular appreciation of specific policy proposals remains thin. What seems most likely is that citizens use realized outcomes, as Key believed, to make inferences about the competence and general goals of the incumbents.

### Retrospective-Prospective, So What?

The most obvious consequence of the distinction between voting as retrospective judgment and voting as prospective choices is in the interpretation of elections. In the pure form of the reward-punishment theory, elections send no policy messages beyond the suggestion that the current incumbents continue whatever they have been doing, or that the new incumbents change whatever the old ones had been doing (or at least, do it more competently). Thus, the message: end the war, end the social unrest, keep the economy growing, lower the misery index, four more years. Such a message does not contain any policy recommendations as to how those outcomes are to be realized.

In contrast, the Downsian theory invests elections with policy significance; the incumbents' victory is a direct expression of a popular preference for their proposals relative to that of the competition. The contemporary synthesis discounts the importance of elections in offering specific policy guidance, but it affirms the forward-looking perspective of the citizenry.

An illustration might be the 1980 election. An incumbent President (Jimmy Carter) was soundly defeated by a fairly extreme candidate (Ronald Reagan) of the country's putative minority party. For many political commentators the election results heralded a sea change in American public opinion—the end of liberalism, a turn to the right, the resurgence of conservatism. Such interpretations naturally were more common in Republican/conservative circles, but more than a few Democratic commentators feared that their adversaries were correct. When the data became available, however, academic analysts overwhelmingly rejected this portrait of the 1980 outcome. The voting was far more a rejection of Jimmy Carter than an endorsement of Ronald Reagan. Voters were expressing dissatisfaction with the poor state of the economy and America's international embarrassment in Iran more than they were embracing supply-side economics or the New Right social agenda.

The same example shows the importance of election interpretations. During the period that the "sea change" interpretation was widely accepted, President Reagan was able to bend Congress to his will and work major changes in American public policy. As perceptions of a Republican electoral revolution faded, however, Reagan ceased to be a larger-than-life figure, and the normal politics of bargaining and compromise reasserted itself. What Reagan chose to attempt, and the success of what he attempted, depended at least in part on a reading of the election returns as a prospective mandate rather than a retrospective rejection.

### Economic Retrospective Voting

The lion's share of the 1980s research on retrospective voting focuses on *economic* retrospective voting. Several characteristics of economic issues make them ideal vehicles for retrospective voting. First, economics is widely viewed as important; next to national defense and internal order, economic prosperity is probably seen as the most important responsibility of modern governments. Second, there is a broad consensus on end states: low unemployment, low inflation, low taxes, balanced budgets, and high growth are all widely regarded as good. Third, economists describe numerous policy alternatives, many of them highly technical and difficult to explain to nonexperts and most of them matters of considerable disagreement among the experts. Thus, many voters understandably consider only overall conditions and presume that existing policies are good if conditions are good and bad if conditions are bad.

Innumerable statistical studies suggest that something of this sort clearly goes on, in presidential elections at least. Indeed, some argue that most of what happened in the 1980 and 1984 presidential elections can be understood purely as a reflection of voter reactions to the state of the economy. The evidence for congressional elections is much weaker and more controversial. Contemporary congressional incumbents to a considerable degree have managed to escape the responsibility for economic ups and downs.

Macrorelationships, however, are generally consistent with numerous microlevel behavioral processes. We know that economic conditions affect presidential elections, but the precise nature of that reaction remains a matter of much dispute. On its face the evidence that voters react to changes in their *personal* economic status seems weak, but Douglas Rivers claims that the strength of the relationship is underestimated by standard methods of analysis. On its face the evidence that voters react to changes in *national* economic conditions seems strong, but Gerald Kramer maintains that the strength of the relationship is overestimated by standard methods of analysis. Personal and national are not completely independent, of course, and levels (e.g., the group) between the personal and national require further exploration. But whatever research ultimately shows, the degree to which voters are narrowly self-interested or more societally conscious ("sociotropic"), is only a detail within the general theory of retrospective voting, though a detail that takes on some

importance because it affects the interpretation of election outcomes.

The empirical study of economic retrospective voting has raised a number of other interesting questions. How do voters judge economic conditions, and how do they forecast future conditions? How accurate are their judgments and forecasts? Little is known about this subject, but Pamela Conover and her associates report that retrospective judgments are more accurate than prospective forecasts (certainly a plausible finding given the level of disagreement among professional economists engaged in forecasting) and that inflation forecasts are less accurate than unemployment forecasts. Thus, unless economic conditions are at the extremes of good or bad, considerable latitude exists for candidates to put a different "spin" on the same objective reality. Of course, at the aggregate level some of the different spins would be expected to cancel out.

Another interesting question concerns responsibility for economic conditions. Several studies suggest that the impact of economic conditions is constrained by the strong ethic of self-reliance or individualism that characterizes the American political culture. Some significant fraction of the electorate does not translate changes in economic well-being into political action, believing that such ups and downs are less the result of government action than the outcome of their personal life choices. A clear reflection of this contingent connection occurs in the political debate over the fixing of responsibility for good and bad conditions. Incumbents wish to take credit for the good and avoid responsibility for the bad; challengers allege the opposite. Much of their struggle will center around their resulting attempts to fix credit and blame.

Generations of politicians have correctly seen that aggregate economic conditions play a major role in the presidential voting. But the way in which economic conditions are translated into individual voting decisions, the relation between perception and reality, and the degree to which the relationship is politically manipulable are matters that remain on the research agenda, as is the question of economic effects on elections other than for the presidency.

### Retrospective Voting and Democracy

Retrospective voting is an important form of political behavior, but how well does it serve American democracy? Many political activists are unsatisfied with the notion that voters do not pay close attention to issue debates and the precise policy stands advocated by the candidates but instead base their votes on past performance and developments. One typical defense of retrospective voting is offered by Key:

> The prospects for the future may generally tend less to engage the voter or to govern his actions. Those prospects tend to be hazy, uncertain, problematic. Voters may respond most assuredly to what they have seen, heard, experienced. Forecasts, promises, predicted disaster, or pie in the sky may be less moving.

In essence this defense suggests that issue-oriented activists are only deluding themselves when they pay close attention to policy debates. Lyndon Johnson promised that "Asian boys will fight Asian wars." Richard Nixon, the Republican cold warrior, imposed wage and price controls and established relations with "Red" China. Ronald Reagan promised to balance the budget. Problems change, circumstances change, candidates lie, knowledge advances—for all sorts of reasons what government ends up doing may have little to do with what elected officials advocated in a campaign conducted several years previously. Voting on the basis of experience may actually use a more dependable kind of knowledge than that embodied in a campaign's position papers.

A second traditional defense of retrospective voting is even stronger. Not only is retrospective voting a reasonable course of behavior for ordinary voters in a complex, uncertain world, but it is also a course of behavior that has desirable systemic consequences. Knowing that they will be held to account at some future time, politicians have incentives to anticipate the problems that arise so that they receive a favorable judgment at that time. Rather than be constrained by specific platform promises, elected officials are free to innovate, to adapt to changing conditions, in a word, to lead, because they will be judged on the bottom line, not on their specific actions.

Generations of scholars have found arguments like these compelling, but modern conditions make the first all the more reasonable, while at the same time seriously undercutting the second. With the breakdown of party allegiances and the development of an entrepreneurial "every-man-for-himself" style in the campaign arena and in government, politics has become more complex and more confusing. Voters have more reason than ever to base deci-

sions on experience rather than on alternatives such as ads with high production values. But while the decline of party makes retrospective voting more justified than ever from the citizen's standpoint, the obscured lines of political responsibility detract from its favorable systemic consequences.

Key and his forerunners who developed the argument that retrospective voting and anticipated reactions would stimulate creative leadership and responsible government presumed the existence of corporate entities—political parties—that would be the locus of responsibility. In candidate-centered politics, however, individual officeholders repeatedly deny culpability for the larger actions of government. Presidents complain about recalcitrant Congresses, who in turn charge Presidents with failures of leadership. Elected officials blame unelected judges, who lash back at irresponsible politicians. Governors blame the federal government, while federal officials say the states must do more to help themselves. Local, state, and national elections are held at different times, citizens vote for the person not the party; and coattails are largely a thing of the past. It has become next to impossible for voters to make sensible attributions of responsibility for major national problems.

Difficult as this situation is, the current condition of divided government makes it still worse. When the Republicans control the presidency and Democrats the Congress, each party naturally blames the other for any problems. Worse yet, each party has an electoral incentive to contribute to the other's failure. Like many of our other theories, the theory of retrospective voting was not developed with contingencies like these in mind.

*See also:* Jimmy Carter, Election of 1980, Lyndon B. Johnson, V. O. Key, Richard M. Nixon, Ronald Reagan

*Morris P. Fiorina*

REFERENCES

Brody, Richard A., and Paul M. Sniderman. 1977. "From Life Space to Polling Place: The Relevance of Personal Concerns for Voting Behavior." 7 *British Journal of Political Science* 337.

Campbell, Angus, Philip E. Converse, Warren E. Miller, and Donald E. Stokes. 1960. *The American Voter.* New York: Wiley.

Conover, Pamela Johnston, Stanley Feldman, and Kathleen Knight. 1987. "The Personal and Political Underpinnings of Economic Forecasts." 31 *American Journal of Political Science* 559.

Downs, Anthony. 1957. *An Economic Theory of Democracy.* New York: Harper & Row.

Feldman, Stanley. 1982. "Economic Self-Interest and Political Behavior." 26 *American Journal of Political Science* 446.

Fiorina, Morris P. 1981. *Retrospective Voting in American National Elections*. New Haven: Yale U. Pr.

Frantzich, Stephen E. 1989. *Political Parties in the Technological Age*. New York: Longman.

Key, V. O., Jr. 1966. *The Responsible Electorate*. New York: Vintage.

Kiewiet, D. Roderick, and Douglas Rivers. 1985. "The Economic Basis of Reagan's Appeal." In John E. Chubb and Paul E. Peterson, eds. *The New Direction in American Politics*. Washington: Brookings.

Kinder, Donald R., and D. Roderick Kiewiet. 1979. "Economic Grievances and Political Behavior: The Role of Personal Discontents and Collective Judgments in Congressional Voting." 23 *American Journal of Political Science* 495.

Kramer, Gerald H. 1983. "The Ecological Fallacy Revisited: Aggregate-Versus Individual-Level Findings on Economics and Elections and Sociotropic Voting." 77 *American Political Science Review* 92.

Loomis, Burdett. 1988. *The New American Politician*. New York: Basic Books.

Nye, Norman H., Sidney Verba, and John R. Petrocik. 1976. *The Changing American Voter*. Cambridge: Harvard U. Pr.

Ranney, Austin. 1954. *The Doctrine of Responsible Party Government*. Urbana: U. of Illinois Pr.

Rivers, Douglas. 1990. "Microeconomics and Macropolitics: A Solution to the Kramer Problem." 84 *American Political Science Review*.

Schattschneider, E. E. 1960. *The Semisovereign People*. 1975. Hinsdale, IL: Dryden.

## Walter P. Reuther (1907–1970)

The "conscience of the American labor movement." Walter Philip Reuther saw trade unions as catalysts for economic and social justice rather than as mere bargaining agents. He was born in Wheeling, West Virginia, the son of an emigré Socialist involved in trade union activities. Reuther grew up to become the most influential union leader (president of the United Automobile Workers [UAW]) in America's most important industry during that industry's most prosperous times (1946–1970). Embued with an early belief in the benefits of a partnership between government, labor, and industry, as embodied in a welfare state, the young and idealistic Reuther joined the Socialist Party. He campaigned for Norman Thomas in 1932 and was discharged in 1933 from the Ford plant in Detroit for union activities. Unable to find employment elsewhere, Reuther went with his brother Victor on a three-year bicycle tour of Germany, the Soviet Union, India, and Japan. He spent 16 months of that time working in the Gorki automobile plant built by Ford for the Soviet government.

Returning to Detroit in 1935, Reuther led the first major strike in that city's auto industry in December 1936. By 1937 he was a full-time union organizer because his union work prevented him from getting a job anywhere. Reuther joined the UAW at its beginning in 1935; in 1936 he became a member of its executive board; in 1942 he was elected first vice president; and from 1946 to 1970 Reuther was president.

Reuther supported Franklin Roosevelt's presidential bids in 1936, 1940, and 1944. He endorsed Governor Frank Murphy of Michigan in 1938 in his unsuccessful attempt at reelection. Reuther drifted away from the Socialists, many of whom remained his friends and supporters, and resigned from the party in 1940. He backed a no-strike pledge during the war and served on several government boards, including the Office of Production Management and the War Manpower Commission. Reuther led the UAW in a 133-day postwar strike (1945–1946) against General Motors, achieving an "escalator clause" that tied wages to a cost-of-living index established in Washington. This triumph garnered him support in the union against the Communist-backed faction. Reuther used this support after his 1947 reelection as UAW president to expel the Communists, thereby consolidating his power.

In 1948 Reuther originally favored Justice William O. Douglas for President, but he eventually backed Harry Truman. He opposed the "progressive" left-wing Henry Wallace that year, although Reuther was not totally against organizing a third party, and helped to found the liberal, anti-Communist Americans for Democratic Action.

An assassination attempt by an unknown assailant in April 1948 left Reuther partially paralyzed, but his incapacity did not lessen his ardor for social causes. As president of the Congress of Industrial Organizations (CIO) from 1952 to 1955, succeeding Philip Murray, he led that organization into a partnership with the American Federation of Labor (AFL) in 1955. Reuther strongly supported John Kennedy in 1960, but he quarreled with George Meany over whether he or Meany should approve the administration's labor appointments. Meany vetoed Ambassador Adlai Stevenson's selection of Reuther as a delegate to the United Nations in 1961 and successfully opposed Reuther's choice in 1962 for Under Secretary of Labor. A long-time member of the NAACP, Reuther led the UAW in support of the August 1963 March on Washington, was the only labor representative to speak there, and denounced the AFL-CIO's failure to endorse the march.

An ardent supporter of Lyndon Johnson in 1964 and a confidant of the President, Reuther eventually moved away from his initial support of the Vietnam War. He did not, however, lead his union into the antiwar movement in the same way that he had rallied it to the civil rights cause. Reuther withheld support from any one of the competing Democratic presidential candidates in 1968, although he opposed the Republicans on economic issues. In 1968 Reuther withdrew his union from the AFL-CIO because of his continuing disagreements with Meany. In 1969, together with the Teamsters, the UAW organized the Alliance for Labor Action, a socially oriented federation. Reuther's last official act before dying in an airplane crash in Michigan in May 1970 was to condemn the American incursion into Cambodia.

*See also:* Lyndon B. Johnson, John F. Kennedy, National Association for the Advancement of Colored People, United Nations, Vietnam War as a Political Issue, Henry Wallace

*Frederick J. Augustyn, Jr.*

REFERENCES

Cormier, Frank, and William J. Eaton. 1970. *Reuther.* Englewood Cliffs, NJ: Prentice-Hall.

Dubofsky, Melvyn, and Warren Van Tine, eds. 1987. *Labor Leaders in America.* Urbana: U. of Illinois Pr.

Fink, Gary M., ed. 1984. *Biographical Dictionary of American Labor.* Westport, CT: Greenwood.

Gould, Jean, and Lorena Hickok. 1972. *Walter Reuther: Labor's Rugged Individualist.* New York: Dodd, Mead.

Reuther, Victor. 1976. *The Brothers Reuther and the Story of the UAW: A Memoir.* Boston: Houghton Mifflin.

## Revenue Act of 1971

Approved by Congress on December 9, 1971, and signed into law by President Richard Nixon on December 10, the Revenue Act of 1971 (Public Law 92–178), along with the Federal Election Campaign Act of 1971, laid the foundation for the modern system of presidential campaign finance. The act created the Presidential Election Campaign Fund, a separate account in the U.S. Treasury, and established a voluntary checkoff provision on individual federal income tax returns that allowed individuals to designate one dollar of their tax payments (or two dollars for married couples filing jointly) to the fund. Monies from the fund would be used to provide public subsidies to the campaigns of presidential candidates who met certain eligibility requirements. The act also provided for a system of federal income tax credits for political contri-

butions to candidates for federal, state, and local office, and to some political committees, including national, state, and local committees of a national political party.

The Revenue Act revived the tax checkoff and campaign fund provisions of the 1966 Presidential Election Campaign Fund Act, which was adopted as an amendment sponsored by Senator Russell Long to the Foreign Investors Tax Act of 1966 (Public Law 89–809). This legislation was effectively terminated before becoming operative in 1967. In response to escalating campaign costs and a widespread perception that the Republican Party's financial superiority would restrict the Democratic presidential nominee to an inadequate campaign in 1972, the Congress reenacted this proposal in an altered form in 1971, following a bitter partisan debate dominated by the approaching presidential election. To avoid a threatened veto by President Nixon, implementation of the tax checkoff provision was delayed until the 1972 tax year, thus postponing the collection of revenues until 1973 and making the law's public subsidy program effective only for the 1976 presidential campaign.

As enacted, the act allowed a taxpayer to earmark a checkoff contribution to the candidate of a specified party or direct that it be placed in a nonpartisan general account. Individuals who gave a financial contribution to a candidate for federal, state, or local office could claim a federal income tax credit for 50 percent of their contribution, up to a maximum of $12.50 on a single return and $25 on a joint return. Alternatively, a political contributor could claim a tax deduction for the full amount of any contributions, up to a maximum of $50 on an individual return and $100 on a joint return.

The act also established the requirements for determining public subsidies to presidential general election campaigns in accordance with the provisions of the Federal Election Campaign Act of 1971. Presidential candidates were eligible to receive subsidies from the Presidential Election Campaign Fund if they agreed to abide by the act's statutory restrictions. The principal restrictions were that the candidate adhere to an overall spending limit of 15 cents multiplied by the voting-age population of the United States and, for major party candidates (defined as those whose party received more than 25 percent of the popular vote in the previous presidential election), that they refused to accept contributions beyond the public subsidy. These candidates were eligible for a grant equal to the overall spending limit. Minor party candidates (defined as those whose party received between 5 percent and 25 percent of the popular vote in the previous presidential election) were eligible for a fraction of the major party grant based on the party's vote in the previous election compared with the average vote received by the major parties. Candidates of new parties or of minor parties who reached the eligibility threshold in the current election were entitled to post-election subsidies based on their share of the vote compared with the average vote for the major party candidates. If the balance in the fund was insufficient for the full costs allowed under the law, funds would be distributed to the candidates on a prorated basis. The act granted the Comptroller General the responsibility of certifying payments from the fund, receiving and publishing disclosure reports, and enforcing the law.

Since its adoption the act has been amended a number of times. In a 1973 amendment to legislation continuing a temporary debt ceiling, Congress made two changes to the checkoff provision to simplify its implementation and promote public participation: the option of earmarking the contribution to a specific party was repealed, and the Internal Revenue Service was directed to place the checkoff in a visible location on tax forms. The allowable tax credit for political contributions was increased to $25 on an individual return and $50 on a joint return by the Tariff Schedules Amendments of 1975, doubled again by the Revenue Act of 1978, and repealed by the Tax Reform Act of 1986. The tax deductions allowed under the law were doubled under the 1974 Federal Election Campaign Act Amendments and repealed by the Revenue Act of 1978. The public financing program and the statutory provisions governing the Presidential Election Campaign Fund have undergone a number of modifications as a result of the 1974 Federal Campaign Act Amendments, the subsequent amendments of 1976 and 1979, and legislation concerning the public financing of national nomination conventions (Public Law 98–355). The thrust of these legislative amendments has been to expand the public subsidy program to include presidential primaries and nominating conventions and to alter the formula for determining general election subsidies.

See also: Check-offs, Federal Election Campaign Act of 1971 and Amendments, Richard M. Nixon, Revenue Act of 1978

*Anthony J. Corrado*

REFERENCES

Adamany, David W., and George E. Agree. 1975. *Political Money: A Strategy for Campaign Financing in America.* Baltimore: Johns Hopkins U. Pr.

Alexander, Herbert E. 1976. *Financing the 1972 Election.* Lexington, MA: Lexington Books.

———. *Financing Politics: Money, Elections, and Political Reform.* 3rd ed. Washington: Congressional Quarterly.

Cantor, Joseph E. 1985. *The Presidential Election Campaign Fund and Tax Checkoff.* Washington: Congressional Research Service.

———. 1987. *Campaign Financing in Federal Elections: A Guide to the Law and Its Operation.* Washington: Congressional Research Service.

Congressional Quarterly, Inc. 1982. *Dollar Politics.* 3rd ed. Washington: Congressional Quarterly.

## Revenue Act of 1978

Approved by Congress on October 15, 1978, and signed into law by President Jimmy Carter on November 6, the Revenue Act of 1978 (Public Law 95–600) altered the tax deductions and credits for political contributions established by the Revenue Act of 1971 as modified by the Tariff Schedules Amendments of 1975. It eliminated the deduction for political giving and doubled the maximum tax credit to $50 on an individual return and $100 on a joint return. The credit was later repealed by the Tax Reform Act of 1986.

This change in the tax provisions for political contributions was adopted as a minor amendment to an $18.7 billion tax relief bill designed to offset social security and other tax increases anticipated for 1979. It was formed by a House-Senate compromise that sought to maintain an incentive for political giving while simplifying taxes and reducing the overall amount of the tax cut to meet administration budget objectives. The initial bill approved by the House repealed the deduction and retained the credit in order to provide some tax simplification, reduce tax liabilities, and maintain an incentive for political participation. The Senate amended the bill to retain the deduction and double the maximum tax credit in order "to further expand individual participation in the electoral process" by encouraging contributions. But members of the committee agreed to repeal the deduction if the House would accept the increase in the credit. The conference committee adopted this suggestion and included it in the bill that became law. The amendment helped to reduce the overall amount of the tax package by increasing tax revenues by a projected $3 million annually.

*See also:* Revenue Act of 1971

*Anthony J. Corrado*

REFERENCES

Cantor, Joseph E. 1986. *Campaign Financing in Federal Elections: A Guide to the Law and Its Operation.* Washington: Congressional Research Service.

*Congressional Quarterly 1978 Almanac.* 1979. "Congress Approves $18.7 Billion Tax Cut." Washington: Congressional Quarterly.

United States Congress. House of Representatives. 1978. *Conference Report. Revenue Act of 1978.* Hse. Rept. 95–1800. 95th Cong., 2nd Sess.

———. ———. Committee on Ways and Means. 1978. *Revenue Act of 1978.* H. Rept. 95–1445. 95th Cong., 2nd Sess. Washington: U.S. Government Printing Office.

———. Senate. Committee on Finance. 1978. *Revenue Act of 1978.* Sen. Rept. 95–1263. 95th Cong., 2nd Sess.

## Reynolds v. Sims
377 U.S. 533 (1964)

This Supreme Court case resulted from an apportionment dispute in Alabama. That southern state had experienced significant population growth and movement since a 1900 districting statute, but it had not reapportioned state legislative districts to reflect these demographic changes. As a result, areas with substantially equal populations in 1960 often had substantially diverse levels of representation. Generally the urban areas of the state had grown more than the rural areas, and city dwellers were most disadvantaged by the system. Some revised apportionment plans had been considered by the state legislature, but none was acceptable to the Alabama Federal District Court or the Supreme Court.

Chief Justice Earl Warren presented the opinion of the Supreme Court. The Supreme Court decided that this apportionment case was more like *Baker v. Carr* than the more recent *Gray v. Sanders;* the case accordingly forced a determination of the basic standards and applicable guidelines for implementing the Court's decision in *Baker v. Carr.*

The Supreme Court asserted that it did not doubt the inherent discrimination and irrationality of Alabama's apportionment statute. The question, said the Court, was whether any constitutionally cognizable principles that would justify departures from the basic standard of equality among voters existed in the apportionment of seats in state legislatures. The Court asserted the the discrimination in Alabama was easily demonstrable mathematically, and the right to vote of residents of one part of the state

was simply not the same as that of individuals living in a favored part of the state.

The Court believed that diluting the weight of votes because of place of residence impaired basic constitutional rights under the Fourteenth Amendment just as much as did discrimination based on factors such as race or economic status. Because of this dilution of the voting strength of identifiable voters, the Alabama apportionment plan was unconstitutional. The Court said that the equal protection clause required a state to make an honest and good-faith effort to construct districts, in both houses of its legislature, as nearly equal in population as possible. Minor divergences from equal population, however, might be justified when based on legitimate considerations of a rational state policy. No circumstances were found, however, to justify the continuance of the Alabama system. The Court also suggested the standardization of decennial reapportionment, with changes in districts following to the results of each census.

Justice John Harlan dissented, arguing that he detected no violation of anyone's constitutional rights and that the legislative history of the equal protection clause showed that it was not intended to be used to reject the apportionment plans of state legislatures.

*See also: Baker v. Carr, Gray v. Sanders*

*Scott Cameron*

## John J. Rhodes (1916– )

Republican House Minority Leader from 1973 to 1980. As an ally of Barry Goldwater, John Jacob Rhodes ran for attorney general of Arizona in 1950. He lost, but two years later he became the first Republican ever to be elected to the U.S. House from the Grand Canyon state. In 1961 he became chairman of the newly created Subcommittee on Special Projects of the House Republican Policy Committee. The subcommittee tried to develop long-range party policy through their research on key issues. In 1965 House Republicans elected Rhodes chairman of the Policy Committee, where he strove to give the GOP a more positive image in the wake of the Goldwater defeat.

In 1973, when Gerald Ford became Vice President, Rhodes succeeded him as House Minority Leader. He faced big problems. First, Watergate had put all Republicans on the defensive. Second, the 1974 elections ended in a net loss of 48 GOP House seats. Third, House Democrats were becoming so much more assertive that Rhodes charged that they were abusing their procedural power; Democrats responded that they were carrying out majority rule. Fourth, some young Republicans argued that he had failed to adopt a creative and confrontational leadership style.

Frustrated, Rhodes gave up his leadership post in 1980. He retired from Congress two years later.

See also: Gerald R. Ford, Barry Goldwater, Minority Party Leadership in Congress, Watergate

*John J. Pitney, Jr.*

REFERENCES

Jones, Charles O. 1970. *The Minority Party in Congress.* Boston: Little, Brown.

Rhodes, John J. 1976. *The Futile System: How to Unchain Congress and Make the System Work Again.* McLean, VA: EPM.

## Richard Richards (1932– )

Republican National Committee chairman at the beginning of the Reagan administration. Immediately following his renowned efforts as campaign coordinator of the Ronald Reagan–George Bush campaign in the western United States in their 1980 bid for the nation's two highest offices, Richard Richards was elected chairman of the Republican National Committee. Richards, born in Ogden, Utah, was the son of a sign painter. He served in the U.S. Army from 1952 until 1955. Richards enrolled in the College of Law at the University of Utah and first became active in Republican politics there. He joined the state's Young Republican Organization and was eventually elected chairman.

Richards's involvement with the party led to his election as the chairman of the Utah Republican Party. In addition, Richards worked for a year in Washington, D.C., as administrative assistant to Congressman Laurance J. Burton, also of Utah, from 1963 to 1964. Richards was a delegate to the Republican National Convention in 1968, 1972, 1976, and 1980.

During these years of working in the Republican Party, Richards gained recognition for his organizational capacity and for the emphasis and importance he placed upon grass-roots politics.

Richards became a national figure immediately following his campaign coordinator assignment when he was elected the chairman of the Republican National Committee (RNC) under President Reagan in January 1981. He served the national Republican Party in this capacity from 1981 until 1983 and, in this role, demonstrated a talent for raising money for Republi-

can candidates. In fact, in Richards's first year the RNC raised approximately $32 million, nearly twice the previous record of $17 million for a nonelection year.

See also: Ronald Reagan, Republican National Committee

*Reagan Robbins*

## Right to Life Party

This New York–based party is a single-issue minor party devoted to the abolition of abortion. The Right to Life Party's (RTLP) antecedents trace back to a study group of Merrick, Long Island, housewives. During the New York State Legislature's consideration of a more liberal abortion law in 1969, the formerly apolitical study group became involved in an unsuccessful effort to defeat the law. Subsequent enactment of a liberalized law in New York in 1970, coupled with the Supreme Court's ruling in *Roe v. Wade* (1973) removing most state restrictions on abortion, accelerated the interest of these suburban women in the abortion issue.

Leaders date the formation of their party to 1970, when they attempted to run two candidates for Congress. In 1976 they worked actively for the Conservative Party nominee for the U.S. Senate, Barbara Keating. Her 16 percent showing encouraged right to life activists.

In 1976 party leader Ellen McCormack ran a single-issue campaign as a candidate in the Democratic Party's presidential primaries, garnering 238,000 votes in 18 primary states and acquiring 22 convention delegates. Despite what some considered a promising showing by a political unknown, this right to life group opted out of major party channels and in 1978 succeeded in placing Mary Jane Tobin, a party founder, on the ballot as a gubernatorial candidate in New York (McCormack ran for lieutenant governor). Right to life leaders had decided that working within the major parties was fruitless, since neither was perceived as responsive to the right to life concern. In the election, Tobin received 130,193 votes (2.6 percent)—more than the New York Liberal Party's candidate. The significance of her showing extended far beyond the seemingly small vote total. According to New York law, a political party obtains official ballot status by running a gubernatorial candidate who receives at least 50,000 votes. Parties reaching this threshold have an automatic line on the ballot until the next gubernatorial election (parties are rank ordered on the ballot according to gubernatorial vote total). For the

RTLP, winning a ballot line represented a major victory. First, it meant that the party's anti-abortion position would be an automatic part of the ballot landscape in New York. Second, it meant that the party could engage in important bargaining with candidates for office through a unique feature of state law—the cross-endorsement rule. According to this provision, parties may nominate candidates already endorsed by other parties. The votes for a candidate from all lines are then added together. Natural political insecurity combines with competitive politics in the state to produce a situation in which most office seekers are anxious to appear on as many ballot lines as possible. The RTLP has used its ballot line to bargain with candidates by offering the line in exchange for support for the anti-abortion position and by threatening to run its own candidates with the hope of siphoning votes away from enemies.

In 1979 the party claimed to have endorsed over 600 candidates running for office in the state. In 1980 RTLP endorsed McCormack for President, despite some sentiment within the party that it should have endorsed Ronald Reagan. She appeared on the ballot in three states (N.Y., N.J., Ky.), receiving 32,327 votes. In 1984, after an intense intraparty struggle, the RTLP decided not to endorse anyone for President. Reagan was rejected because of the feeling that his opposition to abortion was insufficiently enthusiastic. This position illustrated the singlemindedness and inflexibility of the RTLP on abortion. Indeed, it has feuded with other right to life groups because of their perceived willingness to engage in bargaining and compromise.

The RTLP has been heavily involved in New York state politics. Although the stated preference of its leaders has been to endorse major party candidates for Congress, for the state legislature, and for local offices, it has not hesitated to run its own candidates. In fact, most of the candidates it endorses run solely on the RTLP line. The RTLP's zenith year was 1980, when it endorsed candidates in more than three-fourths of all races for Congress, state senate, and state assembly (the average vote on the RTLP line for major party candidates for these races was about 3.5 percent; for candidates running without a major party endorsement, it was about 2.4 percent). The party's most visible symbolic victory was its endorsement of successful Republican Senate nominee Alphonse D'Amato. His vote total on the RTLP line exceeded his overall margin of victory, thereby fostering the RTLP claim that it had elected D'Amato. In every year since 1980, however, the number of RTLP candidates and endorsements has progressively declined, as has their vote percent (in 1986, less than a third of congressional and state legislative races included RTLP-endorsed candidates, and their average vote percentages fell over 1 percent from 1980). Voter enrollment in the RTLP topped out at about 22,000 in 1985.

The decline of RTLP fortunes is attributable to several circumstances: (1) the RTLP's emphasis on single-issue purity over conventional political norms of bargaining and compromise; (2) consequent alienation of many right to life sympathizers, including candidates for office who began to view the RTLP endorsement as more stigma than benefit; (3) the relative political liberality of state politics; and (4) the absence of any concrete political victories in New York.

A study of the leaders and members of the RTLP revealed that many in both categories were formerly uninvolved in politics but were activated by their strong feelings against abortion. Even among those whose only involvement with the party is enrollment, 75 percent reported engaging in abortion-related political acts beyond voting, such as attending protest meetings. The study also found among identifiers high levels of political awareness and efficacy, yet high levels of cynicism toward government. The vast majority are either Catholic or fundamentalist Protestant. In general, the measured social and attitudinal characteristics of RTLP identifiers and leaders conform closely to studies of other "New Right" groups motivated by social-issue concerns.

The future of the RTLP suggests no dramatic turnaround. The dominance of the concern for issue purity over expanding the party's base has sharply limited its growth potential. Its survival in the 1980s is attributable in large measure to New York's electoral rules, which have the effect of giving minor parties some basis for bargaining despite the continued dominance of the major parties.

*See also:* Ellen McCormack, Ronald Reagan, Mary Jane Tobin

*Robert J. Spitzer*

REFERENCES

Spitzer, Robert J. 1987. *The Right to Life Movement and Third Party Politics*. Westport, CT: Greenwood.

## William H. Riker (1920– )

Academic political theorist. Widely known in international social science circles as one of the early developers of formal (or positive or rational choice) political theory, William H. Riker is the author of several works on the subject. Among the most prominent applications of the rational choice technology are the subjects of parties, voting, and elections.

One of the first game-theoretic ideas in political science is Riker's *Theory of Political Coalitions* (1962). In contrast to Downs's (1957) treatment of parties as exogenously given "teams" of activists, Riker conceives of parties as arising endogenously as coalitions out of the structure of competition, the rules of participation, and, most importantly, the manner in which rewards are distributed. His famous Size Principle suggests a dynamic of party behavior—namely, the inevitability of oversized coalitions to pare themselves down to smaller size. That is, a coalition that is larger than is necessary to win whatever is at stake (an office, the right to organize a government, etc.) cannot sustain itself for long.

Riker's theory of rational political participation appears in a widely cited 1968 paper. According to this theory, a prospective participant is conceived of principally as a rational calculator of costs and benefits. In mass political settings, the instrumental benefits of participation (in particular, the difference in outcome that could be produced by the participation discounted by the often infinitesimal likelihood that such participation will in fact make this difference) are typically far outweighed by participation costs (the latter including the cost of informing oneself, deciding among the alternatives, and implementing the decision by going to the polling place). The deduction from this approach is that participation and turnout in mass elections will be small to nonexistent, a prediction not in accordance with empirical evidence on mass political behavior. Riker and Peter Ordeshook, consequently, amend the benefit-cost calculus with a consideration of the fact that voting is not merely an investment but also a form of consumption. The latter ranges from sheer entertainment value to a sense of citizen duty. This amended formulation is more notably in accord with common sense and empirical regularities than the stark benefit-cost calculus of the economists.

In two recent books, Riker develops ideas about how parties compete strategically. Not only do they engage in strategic "position-taking" on exogenously given issue dimensions, but also they engage in the practice of creating new issues. Indeed, in this later work, Riker develops a second dynamic of party competition, namely, that losing coalitions search for new issues in their office-seeking behavior in order to split up an existing governing coalition. This second dynamic has the salutary effect of rescuing political "losers" from the ash heap of history by identifying them as important agents of political change. As Riker notes, "This new and wholly political interpretation differs sharply from economic interpretations, interpretations in terms of ideology, and such ad hoc interpretations as the notion of critical elections."

*Kenneth Shepsle*

REFERENCES

Downs, Anthony. 1957. *An Economic Theory of Democracy*. New York: Harper & Row.

Riker, William H. 1962. *A Theory of Political Coalitions*. New Haven: Yale U. Pr.

———. 1982. *Liberalism Against Populism: A Confrontation Between the Theory of Democracy and the Theory of Social Choice*. San Francisco: Freeman.

———. 1986. *The Art of Political Manipulation*. New Haven: Yale U. Pr.

———, and Peter C. Ordeshook. 1968. "A Theory of the Calculus of Voting." 62 *American Political Science Review* 25.

## Ripon Society

An organization that represents the moderate-to-liberal wing of the Republican Party. The Ripon Society's major purpose is disseminating ideas and debating issues through magazines, books, op-ed articles, and seminars. Its leading publication is the *Ripon Forum*, a magazine containing moderate Republican opinion and commentary. *A Newer World: The Progressive Republican Vision of America*, published in 1988, ended a fifteen-year hiatus for the Society in book publishing.

The Ripon Society was founded in 1962 by a group of Harvard University and Massachusetts Institute of Technology graduate students with the aim of influencing the Republican Party to adopt more liberal positions. The Society supported Nelson Rockefeller's bids for the presidency in 1964 and 1968 and George Bush's bid in 1980. The Ripon Society opposed the nomination of Ronald Reagan in 1980.

The Ripon Society adopted its name from the city of Ripon, Wisconsin, which claims to be the birthplace of the Republican Party. James Leach (R-Iowa) has been Ripon Society chairman since 1981. In recent years, the Society has honored George Bush, women in the Republican Party, and the Senate Republican leadership with Republican of the Year Awards, and Robert Packwood with the Jacob Javits Excellence in Public Service Award.

See also: George H. W. Bush, Ronald Reagan, Nelson Rockefeller

*Barbara Norrander*

### Ripon Society v. National Republican Party
525 F. 2d 567 (1975)

By rejecting a challenge to the formula that apportioned delegates to the Republican National Convention, this case reconfirmed the authority of political parties to govern their internal affairs, already firmly established in *Cousins v. Wigoda* (1975). As previously determined in *Bode v. National Democratic Party* (1971), the one-person, one-vote rule that applied to elections to the U.S. House, to state legislatures, and to local governing bodies did not apply to party organizations.

At issue was the Republican formula for the 1976 convention, one that has remained in effect since then. That rule awards bonus delegates to a state that supported the party's nominees in the previous general election. In addition to a base of three delegates for each electoral vote, a state carried by the presidential ticket, according to historian James Davis, won "four and a half delegates plus 60 percent of the state's electoral vote total, rounded upward if necessary; one delegate for each GOP senator elected; a maximum of one delegate for states going Republican for governor; and one delegate for states electing a House delegation at least half Republican." This formula obviously favored conservative interests located in small and southern states.

The Ripon Society, a group of moderate and liberal young Republicans, had sought unsuccessfully at the 1972 Republican National Convention to apportion delegations according to population and Republican voting strength. In December 1972 they challenged the formula in district court; there the uniform bonus system was declared unconstitutional, but the proportional-bonus aspect was allowed. After both sides appealed the case, a three-judge appeals court sustained the Ripon Society on both counts. However, the full appeals court for the District of Columbia reversed the three-judge panel by a nine-to-one vote. The United States Supreme Court refused certiorari in February 1976 (424

U.S. 933), thereby allowing the lower court ruling to remain intact.

The lower court essentially reaffirmed *Cousins*, arguing that courts should not lightly interfere with the internal processes of political parties, for "it is the essence of the First Amendment rights, which the parties exercise, that they make their own contrary (and rational) judgments without interference from the courts."

"The Equal Protection Clause does not impose the same one person, one vote rule upon all elected and decision-making bodies." Such a rule depends upon the purposes of the body. As an organization seeking control of the government, the party's rights of freedom of association are at stake. Therefore, an assessment of whether equal protection is satisfied must determine whether "the representational scheme and each of its elements rationally advance some legitimate interest of the party in winning elections or otherwise achieving its political goals."

The Court found that a rational case could be made for the victory bonus system, aimed as it was toward orienting party policies to win particular states and to provide incentives to state organizations to carry their states. The proportional dimensions of the presidential bonus recognized that large states are more important than small ones in achieving victory. The uniform bonuses for other offices recognized the uniform importance of winning the positions of Senator and governor.

Voting rights, therefore, are offset by a political party's First Amendment rights to choose a rational formula to advance legitimate party interests. In the context of strong competition between the parties for the presidency, voting rights are preserved in the general election.

See also: Bode v. National Democratic Party, Cousins v. Wigoda, Ripon Society

*Douglas I. Hodgkin*

REFERENCES

Davis, James W. 1983. *National Conventions in an Age of Party Reform*. Westport, CT: Greenwood.

### Thomas Ritchie (1778–1854)

Influential Democratic-Republican journalist. Thomas Ritchie had close ties with Thomas Jefferson and the Republican Party and maintained his influence in national politics until the time of the Compromise of 1850. Ritchie was one of the key foundations upon which the Democratic-Republican dominance of the Dynasty era was built, within the nation and the commonwealth. He was born in Tappahannock, Virginia, where his education was supervised by his cousin, Spenser Roane, one of Virginia's leading jurists and a sophisticated and outspoken advocate of the Virginia school of agrarian state rights republicanism. Ritchie then became a teacher, a profession that fostered his lifetime support for public education and education for women, both of which had meager constituencies in the Virginia of his day.

Ritchie ended up pursuing his intellectual and pedagogical interests by opening a bookstore in Richmond, and it was there that Jefferson, Roane, and their colleagues found him a likely candidate to start the Democratic-Republican paper that they believed Federalist Richmond badly needed in 1803. Accordingly, Ritchie became the editor of the frankly partisan Richmond *Enquirer*, which began publication in 1804. The *Enquirer* quickly became the leading newspaper in the state as well as the most authoritative source of Democratic-Republican doctrine in the nation throughout the Dynasty years.

Ritchie was accused of being a member of the "Richmond Junto," the self-appointed committee that was believed to run Virginia politics during the first three decades of the nineteenth century. Although evidence about the Junto's existence and operation remains questionable to this day, Ritchie, Roane, and their colleagues were certainly men who exerted enormous influence over both doctrine and policy. Nevertheless, Ritchie never seemed to hesitate to take an independent stand when it suited him. He was a forthright supporter of state constitutional reform, manhood suffrage, and even the abolition of slavery after Nat Turner's Rebellion. Ritchie was always more of an editor than a political operator and more of a Virginian than a national figure. His most important national contribution was probably the key role he played in forming the Virginia–New York coalition that assured Andrew Jackson's election in 1828. Ritchie and Martin Van Buren formed a strong personal bond that was crucial in the formation and continued survival of what would become the Democratic Party.

Throughout most of his career Ritchie steadfastly resisted invitations to go to Washington, D.C., to edit a national paper. When he finally succumbed to the offers in 1845, his earlier reluctance was vindicated. His Virginia approach was not a success on the national level. Nevertheless, Ritchie remained an important voice in national political affairs until after

the Compromise of 1850. His was a fascinating and distinguished career that spanned the period between the Revolution and the Civil War with an active thoroughness enjoyed by few.

*Kathryn A. Malone*

## Frank L. Rizzo (1920– )

Colorful and controversial Philadelphia politician. Frank Lazarro Rizzo served as mayor of Philadelphia from 1972 to 1979. Rizzo rose to public prominence as a police officer in the city, joining the force as a patrolman in 1940 and climbing from the ranks to become police commissioner in 1967. He had a reputation for toughness throughout his police career, and he capitalized on this image in his pursuit of the mayoralty in 1971. With the support of the city's Democratic political organization, headed by Peter Camiel and the incumbent Democratic mayor, James H. J. Tate, Rizzo defeated William Green, Jr., and Hardy Williams in the primary. In the general election, he overwhelmed the patrician Republican Thatcher Longstreth. Shortly after taking office, however, Rizzo became embroiled in a public dispute with Democrat Peter Camiel over Rizzo's support for President Richard Nixon's reelection in 1972 and the distribution of patronage within the city. When both men made criminal accusations, each took a lie detector test at the suggestion of a local newspaper, but only Camiel "passed."

In 1978 Rizzo mounted a drive to amend the city charter so as to allow him to run for a third term, but on November 8, 1978, he lost the vote by a two-to-one margin, with most African-Americans and Independents opposing him. Rizzo again sought the mayor's office in 1986, this time as a Republican. With the endorsement of William Meehan, the chairman of the Republican Party, Rizzo defeated John Egan, also a Democrat turned Republican in the primary, but he narrowly lost to the incumbent, Wilson Goode, in the general election. Rizzo has remained politically active; he was named by Vice President George Bush to head his presidential campaign in the city in 1988. He later ran unsuccessfully for mayor as a Republican.

*See also:* William Green

*Thomas J. Baldino*

REFERENCES

Daughen, Joseph R., and Peter Binzen. 1977. *The Cop Who Would Be King: Mayor Frank Rizzo*. Boston: Little, Brown.

Featherman, Sandra, and William L. Rosenberg. 1979. *Jews, Blacks, and Ethnics: The 1978 "White Vote"*

*Charter Campaign in Philadelphia.* New York: American Jewish Committee.

Hamilton, Fred J. 1973. *Rizzo.* New York: Viking.

## C. Wesley Roberts (1903–1975)

Republican National Committee chairman for a brief period in 1953. Born into a Kansas newspaper family, Charles Wesley Roberts attended Kansas State College as a journalism major, and became coeditor and copublisher, together with his father and a brother, of three weekly newspapers. Ten years later Roberts became active in Republican Party affairs as the manager of an unsuccessful gubernatorial campaign. The following year he became executive secretary of the Republican state committee and, from 1939 to 1943, served as secretary to Governor Payne Ratner.

During World War II, Roberts served as a major in the Marine Corps. His first postwar political position was as publicity director of the Kansas State Highway Commission. From 1947 to 1950, he was Republican state chairman.

When Arthur Summerfield assumed the Republican national chairmanship in 1952, he recruited Roberts as director of organization. Upon Summerfield's resignation, a five-member nominating committee considered only Roberts on grounds that he was a leading Republican in nominee Dwight Eisenhower's home state. Within a month of his election as national chairman, a group of hostile Kansas state legislators brought charges against Roberts for evading the Kansas Lobbying Act. Roberts resigned from the chairmanship and returned to his newspaper and insurance businesses.

*See also:* Dwight D. Eisenhower, Republican National Committee, Arthur Summerfield

*Ralph M. Goldman*

REFERENCES

Goldman, Ralph M. 1990. *The National Party Chairmen and Committees: Factionalism at the Top.* Armonk, NY: M. E. Sharpe.

## Marion G. (Pat) Robertson (1930– )

Evangelical telecaster turned Republican politician. Marion Gordon (Pat) Robertson is a popular religious broadcaster, who in 1988 ran unsuccessfully for the Republican presidential nomination. Son of a United States Senator from Virginia, Pat Robertson graduated from Yale Law School and entered business briefly, but when that failed his thoughts turned to the ministry. After his "born-again" experience in 1956 he began training for the Baptist ministry, and while still a student he "spoke in tongues," a vital experience for charismatic Christians. Ordained a Baptist preacher, he opened the nation's first Christian television stations and with his skills built his Christian Broadcasting Network, one of the first cable companies, into a communications empire.

Robertson gradually entered politics. As host of the "700 Club," his religious talk show, he often commented on political affairs, especially after the Watergate scandal intensified his interest in politics. In 1976 he supported Democrat Jimmy Carter, who, like Robertson, was a Southern Baptist. In 1980, disappointed with Carter's policies, he backed Republican Ronald Reagan. In 1984 he switched to the Republican Party, and by 1986 he established the Freedom Council, a political organization for charismatic Christians. With polls showing that one-third of Americans call themselves "born-again" Christians, his potential base was considerable. Despite collecting over 3 million signatures on petitions supporting his candidacy, raising $6 million by the spring of 1988, a strong showing in Michigan, and a surprise second-place finish over George Bush in Iowa, Robertson's presidential bid collapsed quickly after a poor showing on Super Tuesday in the South. Scandals among TV evangelists hurt Robertson's image, and he never had much appeal beyond his charismatic Christian base. A majority of evangelicals voted for other candidates. Robertson's candidacy symbolized the outrage that conservative Christians felt toward America's permissive society, resentments encouraged earlier by George Wallace and Ronald Reagan.

*See also:* Jimmy Carter, Election of 1988, Evangelicals, Ronald Reagan, George Wallace

*Douglas Carl Abrams*

REFERENCES

Donovan, John B. 1988. *Pat Robertson.* New York: Macmillan.

Harrell, David Edwin, Jr. 1987. *Pat Robertson.* New York: Harper & Row.

## Joseph T. Robinson (1872–1937)

Four-term Democratic U.S. Senator from Arkansas. Joseph Taylor Robinson was Democratic floor leader in the Senate (1922–1933 as Minority Leader, 1933–1937 as Majority Leader) during the New Deal and the Democratic candidate for Vice President in 1928, running with Governor Alfred E. Smith of New York.

Robinson was reared in modest circumstances in rural Arkansas. He studied law at the University of Arkansas and began practice in 1894, winning election to the general assembly the following year. In 1903 Robinson was elected to the U.S. House of Representatives where he served for five terms. In 1912 he became Arkansas' governor, only to resign some two months after he took office as he was elected U.S. Senator by the legislature. A staunch supporter of the policies of President Woodrow Wilson, Robinson fought for ratification of the treaty creating the League of Nations. Having won the respect of party leaders for his effective legislative skills, he was elected successor to Senate Democratic leader Oscar W. Underwood in 1922.

Robinson's selection as Smith's 1928 running mate was designed to counter opposition to Smith, the "wet," urban, Catholic Tammany politician, with a candidate who was a "dry," rural, Protestant, southern conservative. Indeed, Robinson was the first southerner to appear on a national ticket since the Civil War. With the election of Franklin D. Roosevelt and a Democratic Senate majority in 1932, Robinson, as Senate Majority Leader, assumed a key role in handling all administration bills. Robinson's leadership of the controversial "court-packing" Judiciary Re-organization bill (1937) marked the Arkansas Senator's most difficult legislative battle. Promised the first Supreme Court vacancy Roosevelt would fill, Robinson died from a heart attack in the midst of forging a court reform compromise. An able parliamentarian, Robinson enhanced the position of Senate Majority Leader to become "the President's man" in the Senate, a role that his successors would henceforth be expected to maintain.

*See also:* League of Nations, New Deal, Franklin D. Roosevelt, Alfred E. Smith, Oscar Underwood, Woodrow Wilson

*Richard C. Burnweit*

REFERENCES

Alsop, Joseph, and Turner Catledge. 1938. *The 168 Days*. Garden City, NY: Doubleday.

Patterson, James T. 1967. *Congressional Conservatism and the New Deal: The Growth of the Conservative Coalition in Congress, 1933–1939*. Lexington: U. Pr. of Kentucky.

Weller, Cecil Edward, Jr. 1986. "Joseph Taylor Robinson: Keystone of Franklin D. Roosevelt's Supreme Court 'Packing Plan.'" 7 *Southern Historian* 23.

## Nelson A. Rockefeller (1908–1979)

Forty-ninth governor of New York and the forty-third Vice President of the United States. The third of six children in the third generation of one of America's wealthiest and most famous families, Nelson Aldrich Rockefeller, a lifetime Republican, spent his early career in national government in foreign and domestic policy posts to which he was appointed by Presidents Franklin D. Roosevelt, a Democrat, and Dwight D. Eisenhower, a Republican. Convinced as a result of these experiences that real governmental power could only be had through winning elective office, and ambitious for the presidency, Rockefeller returned to New York, served as chairman of a temporary commission to prepare for an abortive state constitutional convention and then in 1958 successfully challenged Averell Harriman, the incumbent Democratic governor.

Much was at stake in this election in New York. Harriman too wanted to be President, and his great wealth—Harriman was heir to the New York Central Railroad fortune—neutralized money as a campaign issue in this "battle of millionaires." Almost a generation younger than his opponent, the underdog Rockefeller campaigned in the progressive tradition of Governors Charles Evans Hughes and Tom Dewey before him, taking liberal positions on social issues, pushing for conservative fiscal stands, and lambasting "bossism" and the "Tammany machine." He won by more than half a million votes in 1958 and then went on to capture the governorship three more times. By the time he resigned at the end of his fifteenth year in 1973, Rockefeller had served New York as governor longer that anyone in more than a century and a half. Though criticized for excessive spending, he was widely rated for his achievements in the state as one of the greatest American governors in the twentieth century.

But Rockefeller could not work the political magic on the national scene that he could in the Empire State. Probably *the* spokesman for the GOP's eastern progressive wing, Rockefeller was the victim of the shift in his party's center to the South and West and its increased dominance by ideologically conservative activists. Additionally, his hopes were damaged by personal choices—his divorce and remarriage in 1964—and by a seeming unwillingness to seek the presidency with the same fervor and commitment that he had the governorship.

Unable to stop Richard Nixon for the GOP presidential nomination in 1960, and hampered by a campaign pledge to serve his full four-year term as governor, Rockefeller settled for dictating much of the platform in the "Fifth Avenue Compact," only to earn considerable intraparty enmity following the Republican loss in that year. Booed by passionately hostile delegates to the 1964 GOP convention, a spectacle dramatically captured on national television, Rockefeller's defeat was powerfully symbolic of the party's turning away from a broad-based, ideologically diverse national coalition.

A masterful campaigner, Rockefeller was able to square the political circle in New York, retaining suburban and rural Republican support while simultaneously attracting labor backing and large numbers of minority and ethnic voters in Democratic New York City. Indeed, against Arthur Goldberg in 1970, he actually carried the metropolis. His campaigns, extraordinarily well financed from family resources, were candidate-rather than party-centered and meticulously organized. They were notable for innovative uses of polling and for direct mail and media advertising. Some of the brief television spots used in the hotly contested 1966 campaign, ads in which the Rockefeller record was dramatized but the beleaguered and unpopular governor never appeared, are now recalled as classics of the genre.

After a brief period as a private citizen following his resignation from the governorship in 1973, Nelson Rockefeller became the second appointed Vice President under the provisions of the Twenty-fifth Amendment to the U.S. Constitution. He was selected for this position by Gerald Ford, himself appointed, and after arduous hearings in both the Senate and House of Representatives, Rockefeller became part of the only national administration in American history entirely headed by nonelected officials. Fearful of the effects of Rockefeller's presence on his ticket in the conservative South and West, President Ford asked him to step down in 1976, a decision Ford later said he regretted. Rockefeller did so, returning to the state he had transformed, where he died of a massive heart attack in 1979.

See also: Thomas Dewey, Dwight D. Eisenhower, Gerald Ford, Richard M. Nixon, Tammany Hall

*Gerald Benjamin*

REFERENCES

Benjamin, Gerald, and T. Norman Hurd, eds. 1984. *Rockefeller in Retrospect.* Albany: Rockefeller Inst. of Government.

Collier, Peter, and Horowitz, David. 1976. *The Rockefellers: An American Dynasty.* New York: Holt, Rinehart and Winston.

Connery, Robert, and Gerald Benjamin. 1979. *Rockefeller of New York.* New York: Oxford U. Pr.

——, and ——, eds. 1974. *Governing New York: The Rockefeller Years.* New York: Academy of Political Science.

Kramer, Michael, and Sam Roberts. 1976. *I Never Wanted to Be Vice President of Anything.* New York: Basic Books.

McClelland, Peter D., and Alan L. Magdovitz. 1981. *Crisis in the Making: The Political Economy of N.Y.S. Since 1945.* New York: Cambridge.

Persico, Joseph. 1983. *The Imperial Rockefeller.* New York: Simon & Schuster.

Underwood, James, and William L. Daniels. 1982. *Governor Rockefeller in New York: The Apex of Pragmatic Liberalism in the U.S.* Westport, CT: Greenwood.

### Rogers v. Lodge
458 U.S. 613 (1984)

This case upheld the decision of a federal district court and court of appeals that the Burke County, Georgia, at-large election system used to select the five county commissioners was discriminatory against Blacks. Lower courts had found that the system had been maintained for discriminatory purposes. As a remedy the district court ordered that the county be divided into five districts. The Supreme Court found that the lower court had used the proper standards for determining discrimination, and since the lower court's findings of fact were not clearly erroneous, the Court would not question the findings.

No Black had ever been elected to the county board of commissioners even though Blacks made up a substantial majority of Burke County's population. This fact alone did not justify the ruling, but evidence suggesting that those in power were able to ignore the concerns of the racial minorities seemed to be dispositive.

Like all modern multimember district cases, *Rogers* turns upon the findings of the lower court. *Rogers* is of particular interest, however, when compared with other cases in which the Court was unwilling to find racial discrimination. Casual observers have difficulty distinguishing the facts that make one system acceptable and another not. *Rogers* has relevance only when read in the context of other multimember district cases. To determine current standards of proof, *Thornburg v. Gingles* is more instructive. *Rogers* does seem to further the notion, however, that what really troubles the Court is barring access rather than result.

See also: Thornburg v. Gingles

H. W. Perry, Jr.

## George W. Romney (1907– )

Prominent industrialist and three-term governor of Michigan. George Wilckey Romney achieved national prominence as the leading candidate for the 1968 Republican presidential nomination. Following his landslide reelection as governor in November 1966, polls rated Romney a favorite over President Lyndon Johnson and considerably stronger than any other GOP contender. His front-runner status continued through August 1967 when he withdrew his support for the Vietnam War, asserting that his previous support was the result of "brainwashing" by the Johnson administration. While the term had been used metaphorically, it engendered headlines, political cartoons, and Gridiron Club satiric verse. Romney quickly slipped in the polls, propelling Richard Nixon to the lead. Several weeks before the New Hampshire primary, Romney withdrew as a candidate, urging fellow moderate Republicans to select a popular candidate as an alternative to Nixon. Following Nixon's election in 1968, Romney was appointed Secretary of Housing and Urban Development, a post he held until 1974.

Romney was born in Mexico, a fact that raised an issue of constitutional eligibility: "No person except a natural-born citizen . . . shall be eligible to the office of President" (Article II, Section I, Paragraph 4). The law firm of Sullivan & Cromwell concluded that his birth to United States citizens met the test. The birthplace issue had been previously considered in the case of the potential presidential nominations of Franklin Roosevelt, Jr., and Christian Herter.

Leaving Mexico at age five, Romney was raised in Idaho and Utah. Following studies at George Washington University, Romney advanced in corporate positions eventually to be recruited in 1950 by Nash-Kelvinator Corporation (later American Motors) as vice president. He became president in 1954 and successfully revitalized the company, introducing America's first "compact" car. In 1960 he spearheaded a campaign to rewrite Michigan's constitution, a task ultimately completed in 1963. Romney was elected Michigan's governor in 1962, 1964, and 1966.

George Romney's support of the moderate element of his party stemmed from his support of civil rights and his strong exception to the involvement of the John Birch Society in the Republican Party.

See also: Election of 1968, New Hampshire Primary, Vietnam War as a Political Issue

W. Mitt Romney

## Eleanor Roosevelt (1884–1962)

Most important American woman of the twentieth century. Anna Eleanor Roosevelt was an advocate of social reform and a participant in Democratic women's politics in the 1920s and 1930s, typifying the new roles and aspirations of female political activists in the post-suffrage era. As First Lady in her husband President Franklin Roosevelt's administration, she redefined the office, transforming this position into a national platform for the interests of women, minorities, and the young. In her later years she continued to pursue the goals of democracy and social justice through her political activities and appointed offices.

The first child of Elliott and Anna (Hall) Roosevelt, Eleanor seemed destined to enjoy a quiet, private life with all the benefits of class and privilege that characterized the Victorian world of New York's upper-class society. But before she was ten, both of her parents had died, as had her younger brother; and she and her second brother, Hall, were left to the detached care of their stern maternal grandmother. At the age of 15 Eleanor was sent to Allenswood, a London finishing school, where she came under the influence of Marie Souvestre, the French headmistress. Under Mlle. Souvestre's personal tutelage, Eleanor flourished emotionally and intellectually. She developed a sensitivity to social issues and, upon her return to New York, undertook settlement house work and joined the National Consumer's League, which was committed to securing health and safety legislation for workers, especially women. This early involvement in social reform activities and her marriage to distant cousin Franklin Delano Roosevelt in 1905 were the sources of her later political activism.

Eleanor Roosevelt's early experience in Democratic Party politics was hardly auspicious. Her activities were dependent on her husband's growing political career, and she gamely devoted herself to the duties of a politician's wife. While Franklin served as Assistant Secretary of the Navy during World War I, Eleanor developed her organizational skills and her interest in social reform by coordinating activities at Washington's Union Station canteen, working with the Red

Cross and leading a drive to improve conditions at St. Elizabeth's Hospital. But her participation in the 1920 presidential campaign was limited to a month-long trip as the vice presidential candidate's wife. She was so unknown to the public that one newspaper mistakenly identified a picture of another woman cropped from a Roosevelt family photograph as the candidate's wife.

Roosevelt expanded her political activities after the 1920 campaign. Her increased activism was spurred by her discovery in 1918 of her husband's affair with Lucy Mercer, an episode that ended all hope of finding personal fulfillment in marriage, and by her husband's polio, which led Louis Howe, Roosevelt's political mentor, to encourage Eleanor to serve as her husband's surrogate in politics and public life. In 1921 she joined the League of Women Voters, where she learned to draft and analyze legislation, and in 1922 she became active in the Women's Trade Union League, a group concerned with securing maximum hours and minimum wage laws for women. At this time, she also began to engage in partisan organizational activities and devoted the next six years to the Women's Division of the New York State Democratic Committee. Beginning with the women of Duchess County, she organized all but five counties for the Democrats in New York State by 1924. In that year she also chaired a platform subcommittee on women's issues at the Democratic National Convention.

The turning point in Roosevelt's political career came in 1928 when she became the head of the Women's Committee for Democratic presidential candidate Al Smith. In this capacity, she organized and administered party appeals to women, minorities, and independent voters. During her husband's tenure as governor of New York, she refrained from engaging in partisan political activities, but she kept on building a political network and speaking out in support of social reforms. In support of Franklin's candidacy in the 1932 election, she coordinated the activities of the Women's Division of the Democratic National Committee, working with Molly Dewson to mobilize thousands of women precinct workers. After the election she played a key role in convincing her husband and party chairman James Farley to make the Women's Division a permanent operation and persuaded Molly Dewson to become its director. Through Dewson's efforts and Eleanor's support, the Women's Division became an important part of

national party operations, organizing more than 60,000 women precinct workers in the 1936 campaign and securing, for the first time, equal representation of women on the Democratic platform committee.

As First Lady, Eleanor Roosevelt transformed the office into a unique instrument for promoting political participation by women and social reform. She relied on her own political skills and access to the President to make the most of the opportunities afforded by the New Deal. She worked tirelessly to secure appointments for women in Washington and in state relief agencies; she used her press conferences and public appearances to highlight the needs of the dispossessed, especially those who lacked influence in Washington such as unemployed women, minorities, and the young. Her efforts were instrumental in improving the benefits offered to women and minorities through such agencies as the Federal Emergency Relief Administration, the Civil Works Administration, and the National Youth Administration. At a time when the President was dependent on the political support of southern Democrats for the passage of legislation, she actively promoted the cause of civil rights and the needs of Blacks. Her willingness to assist minorities and her uncompromising support of federal antilynching laws, fair employment practices, and the integration of the armed forces were crucial to the realignment of African-American voters during the 1930s and 1940s. Although often criticized and at times thwarted by the practical concerns of the President or members of his administration, throughout her husband's presidency Eleanor maintained her efforts to achieve reforms that would advance her notions of democracy and social justice.

By 1940 the First Lady had become an independent force in the Democratic Party, as evidenced by her role in the selection of Henry Wallace as the vice presidential candidate. While the convention was willing to accept an unprecedented third term for the President, it sought to decide the vice presidential nomination on its own. By all accounts, her hurried flight to Chicago and speech to the delegates calmed the convention and saved the Wallace nomination. Long before 1945, she was prepared to undertake her own political career.

After President Roosevelt's death, Eleanor continued to be the most effective woman in American politics. Her commitment to human rights and international cooperation led President Harry Truman to appoint her as a United States delegate to the United Nations. There she served as the principal architect of the 1948 Declaration of Human Rights. In 1947 she had refused to support the newly formed Progressive Party because of its platform of accommodation toward the Soviet Union. Instead she led the movement to establish Americans for Democratic Action, a group supporting social reform at home and Truman's anti-Communist foreign policy.

In the 1950s, Roosevelt remained a powerful figure. She spoke out against McCarthyism, maintained her support for Black civil rights, and continued to mobilize public opinion for international cooperation. She resigned her position at the United Nations when Dwight Eisenhower became President in 1953, but she remained active in Democratic politics. She campaigned vigorously for her friend Adlai Stevenson in 1952 and 1956. In 1960 she preferred Stevenson to John Kennedy but warmed to Kennedy as his New Frontier revived the spirit of reform in federal policymaking. In December 1961, Kennedy appointed Roosevelt to her last official position, as chair of his Committee on the Status of Women. It was an appropriate end to an illustrious career for she, more than any other, exemplified the political independence and personal autonomy that become the abiding themes of the women's movement in the post-suffrage era.

*See also:* Americans for Democratic Action; Molly Dewson; Elections of 1920, 1932, 1952, and 1960; James Farley; John F. Kennedy; League of Women Voters; McCarthyism; New Deal; Franklin D. Roosevelt; Alfred E. Smith; Adlai Stevenson II; Harry S Truman; United Nations; Henry Wallace

*Anthony J. Corrado*

REFERENCES

Hareven, Tamara K. 1975. *Eleanor Roosevelt: An American Conscience.* New York: Da Capo.

Hoff-Wilson, Joan, and Marjorie Lightman, eds. 1984. *Without Precedent: The Life and Career of Eleanor Roosevelt.* Bloomington: Indiana U. Pr.

Lash, Joseph P. 1971. *Eleanor and Franklin.* New York: Norton.

———. 1972. *Eleanor: The Years Alone.* New York: Norton.

Roosevelt, Eleanor. 1937. *This Is My Story.* New York: Harper.

———. 1949. *This I Remember.* New York: Harper.

———. 1958. *On My Own.* New York: Harper.

Ware, Susan. 1981. *Beyond Suffrage: Women in the New Deal.* Cambridge: Harvard U. Pr.

## Franklin Delano Roosevelt (1882–1945)

Leader of the United States in the Great Depression and World War II. Franklin D. Roosevelt, the fifth cousin of President Theodore Roosevelt, was born in Hyde Park, New York, attended Harvard University (where he was later elected to Phi Beta Kappa) and Columbia Law School. In 1905 he married his fifth cousin once removed, Eleanor Roosevelt. In 1910 he was elected to the New York state senate and then reelected in 1912. Roosevelt served as Assistant Secretary of the Navy from 1913 to 1920, and was the Democratic vice presidential nominee in 1920. Partially paralyzed by polio in 1921, he sought to rehabilitate himself at Warm Springs, Georgia. In 1924 and 1928 he made the presidential nominating speech for Alfred Smith at the Democratic convention. Elected governor of New York State in 1928, he was reelected in a landslide in 1930. As governor he stressed planning in the areas of an efficient statewide highway network, land use and population studies, and conservation of natural resources and park development, as well as state aid for relief and unemployment insurance. Roosevelt was elected President as a Democrat in 1932 (after being nominated on the fourth ballot) and was reelected three consecutive times. Labeled an "active-positive" by political scientist James David Barber because of his activism, flexibility, and enjoyment of the presidency, FDR is regarded by historians as one of the few "Great Presidents."

Roosevelt was elected President because of public dissatisfaction with incumbent Republican Herbert Hoover's reluctance to allow the federal government to help people cope with the Great Depression. Though Roosevelt promised a balanced budget, he also pledged a New Deal for the people, one that prominently included unemployment relief and public works projects. Roosevelt's New Deal programs involved a dramatic increase in federal governmental intervention in the economy, and they clearly associated the Democratic Party in the public mind with liberal domestic programs. In addition to relief programs, the New Deal included increased government regulation of business practices and permanent reforms in the economic system, such as government protection of collective bargaining and implementation of the social security retirement system.

Roosevelt's New Deal helped convert the Democratic Party from a minority party based largely in the South to a majority party with wide national support. Reflecting this broadening support, the 1936 Democratic convention eliminated the two-thirds rule that had previously given the South veto power over the presidential nomination. In addition to white southerners and Catholics who had always voted for Democrats, Roosevelt's New Deal coalition attracted groups that benefited from his liberal domestic programs: blue collar workers, lower-income citizens including Blacks, and intellectuals and Jews who favored a liberal political philosophy. Since the 1930s more Americans have psychologically identified with the Democratic Party than with the Republican Party, and Democrats have usually controlled Congress.

Roosevelt rejected Thomas Jefferson's philosophy of minimal government in favor of a government that would be active in all areas in which it could do a better job than the private sector, seeking the greater good for the greater number of Americans. Roosevelt sought to combat the Depression by increasing the purchasing power of groups like farmers and wage earners through New Deal programs. He also urged "social justice" by means of a progressive income tax that would raise the standards of low income families. Initially a supporter of government partnership with business in a self-regulated economy, by 1935 he broke with business, used class rhetoric, and promoted government regulation of business. Roosevelt felt that his support for domestic reform programs was essentially conservative, since it provided protection against rapid and unwise changes originating with revolution or radicalism. He was not without opposition by 1937; Vice President John Nance Garner of Texas led a bipartisan bloc of Republicans and southern Democratic Congressmen called the "conservative coalition" in an effort to halt the creation of any additional New Deal programs.

While Roosevelt had the backing of the Dutchess County Democratic organization when he was first elected in 1910, as a legislator he became an adversary of the state Democratic organization led by Tammany Hall. His defeat for the Democratic U.S. Senate nomination in 1914 by a Tammany Hall candidate led him to move toward an understanding with the organization, which welcomed him because of his strength in Republican upstate New York. As governor, he named Edward Flynn, the Bronx party boss, as secretary of state, and used patronage to rebuild the county party organizations

in upstate New York. As President, FDR's patronage appointments were coordinated through Postmaster General James Farley, former chairman of the national Democratic Party, who required that job applicants have the approval of their local party committeemen. Roosevelt generally stayed out of his party's primary elections, except in 1938 when he unsuccessfully sought to "purge" a few conservative Democratic Congressmen. By 1939 he had abandoned his effort to promote fidelity to domestic liberalism because of the need for party unity in the face of developing world war.

Despite being a party man, he admitted to voting Republican in several Dutchess County elections because of the need to "clean house" or because the Republican was the "better man." He also had urged Democratic state party leaders to support "just and wise" legislation regardless of which party had offered it. Roosevelt was said to dream of more ideologically consistent parties with the liberals of both existing parties joining together to oppose both parties' conservatives. As late as 1944 he fantasized joining with Wendell Willkie to build a liberal party free of the conservative South, but the deaths of both men ended these plans.

*See also:* Thomas Dewey, Elections of 1920 and 1932, James Farley, Edward Flynn, John Nance Garner, Herbert Hoover, New Deal, New Deal Coalition, Eleanor Roosevelt, Theodore Roosevelt, Alfred E. Smith, Tammany Hall, Harry S Truman, Henry Wallace, Wendell Willkie

*Stephen D. Shaffer*

REFERENCES

Barber, James David. 1985. *The Presidential Character.* Englewood Cliffs, NJ: Prentice-Hall.

Greer, Thomas. 1958. *What Roosevelt Thought: The Social and Political Ideas of Franklin D. Roosevelt.* East Lansing: Michigan State U. Pr.

Ladd, Everett C., and Charles D. Hadley. 1978. *Transformations of the American Party System.* 2nd ed. New York: Norton.

Schlesinger, Arthur M. 1960. *The Politics of Upheaval.* Boston: Houghton Mifflin.

Sundquist, James. 1973. *Dynamics of the Party System.* Washington: Brookings.

Tugwell, Rexford. 1972. *In Search of Roosevelt.* Cambridge: Harvard U. Pr.

## Theodore Roosevelt (1858–1919)

Reform activist President of the U.S. The twenty-sixth President of the United States (1901–1909), Theodore Roosevelt was born in New York City. He overcame ill health as a child to lead a robust adult life as a naturalist, explorer, rancher, historian, soldier, and politician.

He served as a New York assemblyman, failed in his 1886 campaign to become mayor of New York City, was appointed U.S. Civil Service commissioner in 1889, and became president of the New York City Board of Police Commissioners in 1895.

President William McKinley appointed "Teddy" Assistant Secretary of the Navy in 1897, a post he resigned the next year to lead his volunteer cavalry regiment, the Rough Riders, during the Spanish-American War. His military record helped him capture the New York governorship in 1898. After McKinley's first Vice President, Garret A. Hobart, died, Roosevelt was persuaded by Thomas C. Platt and a unanimous Republican convention to accept the position. He became President in 1901, after McKinley was assassinated. At 42 years of age, Roosevelt holds the record as the youngest President in American history.

Although historians differ on the exact nature of his political ideology, Roosevelt considered himself a conservative Republican who represented traditional middle-class values. He maneuvered his career between populist politicians, such as William Jennings Bryan and Robert La Follette, and ultraconservative businessmen and members of Congress, such as the Speaker of the House, Joseph G. Cannon.

Roosevelt was a reformer who was willing to work with the conservative wing of the Republican Party. As President, he started slowly to avoid a split in his party. After he secured the confidence of the public and of several members of Congress, Roosevelt tried unsuccessfully to obtain legislation to regulate corporations. Nevertheless, his activity was rewarded with mass popularity, and the Republican convention in Chicago unanimously nominated him for President in 1904, even though a conservative was selected as his Vice President. The 1904 campaign was a landslide for Roosevelt and the Republicans in both houses of Congress. He became the first Vice President in American history to be elected President on his own after succession to the office upon the death of his predecessor.

Roosevelt grew more progressive after his landslide victory, but he still avoided a break with the most reactionary members of the party. Conservative by nature, he feared big government, so he advocated a Square Deal to regulate corporate monopolies in order to assure a competitive free enterprise system. He established the Department of Commerce and Labor with the first Jewish secretary in a presidential Cabinet. Roosevelt earned a substantial record in the conservation of natural resources and various administrative improvements. He was the first American chief executive to use presidential commissions, to establish a White House press room, and to receive the Nobel Peace Prize (1905, for his role in ending the Russo-Japanese War). He pursued a vigorous foreign policy, including the construction of the Panama Canal.

Roosevelt stuck to his 1904 promise not to break precedent and seek another term in 1908. Instead he selected William Howard Taft, his Secretary of War, as the GOP candidate. After Taft offended Republican progressives, Roosevelt returned to politics to try to capture the 1912 Republican nomination. Although he won several primary victories, Roosevelt found the convention controlled by Taft conservatives. In response, he formed the Progressive (Bull Moose) Party. Although winning almost 30 percent of the popular vote and 88 electoral votes, Roosevelt was defeated by Woodrow Wilson. Taft came in third.

In 1916 Roosevelt rejected another third-party effort in favor of campaigning for the Republican candidate Charles Evans Hughes. While in the Oval Office, he had worked behind the scenes to get Hughes elected as the Progressive governor of New York, even though Roosevelt's extreme prowar views hurt Hughes's campaign in 1916. Roosevelt's "stewardship" approach to presidential power, which asserted that the chief executive could do anything not specifically forbidden by the Constitution or statute, serves as the twentieth-century model for an activist presidency. Polls of presidential experts consistently rank Theodore Roosevelt as one of the top seven presidents in American history.

*See also:* William Jennings Bryan, Bull Moose Party, Joseph G. Cannon, Elections of 1896 and 1912, Charles Evans Hughes, Robert La Follette, William McKinley, Thomas C. Platt, Progressive Party, William Howard Taft, Woodrow Wilson

*William D. Pederson*

REFERENCES

Harbaugh, William H. 1975. *The Life and Times of Theodore Roosevelt*. New York: Oxford U. Pr.

Morris, Edmund. 1979. *The Rise of Theodore Roosevelt*. New York: Coward, McCann and Geoghegan.

Nathan, Meyer. 1968. "Theodore Roosevelt and the 1916 Election." 5 *Rocky Mountain Social Science Journal* 64.

Pederson, William D., and Ann M. McLaurin, eds. 1987. *The Rating Game in American Politics*. New York: Irvington.

———. 1991. "Theodore Roosevelt as a Model of Mental and Physical Fitness." In Natalie A. Naylor, ed. *Theodore Roosevelt and the Birth of Modern America.* Westport, CT: Greenwood Press.

Schwengel, Fred. 1987. *The Republican Party.* Washington: Acropolis Books.

## Elihu Root (1845–1938)

Nobel Prize-winning Secretary of State. Elihu Root appeared at a critical juncture in the growth of industrialization in America, offering outspoken support for conservative tradition in both domestic and international affairs. Anti-imperialists, progressives, muckrakers, and pacifists pictured Elihu Root as an iron-willed corporate lawyer who fought constitutional change and social experimentation; upheld colonialism, militarism, and laissez faire; and always somehow managed to identify principles with party loyalty.

A graduate of Hamilton College and the City College of New York Law School, Root was criticized for serving as counsel to William M. Tweed of the infamous Tammany Hall. Seemingly inured to the social evils of the day, Root established his reputation as a highly successful corporate lawyer, dedicated to helping American business firms circumvent tax increases, regulation, and antitrust legislation.

As Secretary of State under Presidents William McKinley and Theodore Roosevelt (1899–1904), Root formulated U.S. colonial policies in Puerto Rico and the Philippines, regimes that would last until 1917 and 1913 respectively. He also modernized the U.S. Army and authored much of the Platt Amendment authorizing the United States to intervene in Cuba to preserve Cuba's independence.

As Secretary of State (1905–1909), Root received the 1912 Nobel Prize for his contributions to the peace in the western hemisphere, for his dedication to the causes of international arbitration, for his defense of the sanctity of treaties, and for his earlier establishment of an "enlightened" colonial system.

From 1909 to 1915 Republican Root served New York in the United States Senate, but, as an ingrained conservative in the age of progressivism, he found service there the least successful part of his public career. In late 1916, as a private citizen, Root supported the immediate entry of the United States into the war against Germany. Following the war Root served as adviser on the covenant of the League of Nations and counsel for the League to the advisory commission of international justice that convened at The Hague in 1920. His last act in public service was as a delegate to Geneva in 1929 to revise statutes of the Permanent Court of International Justice.

*See also:* League of Nations, William McKinley, Theodore Roosevelt, Tammany Hall, William M. Tweed

*Nancy C. Unger*

REFERENCES

Jessup, Philip C. 1938. *Elihu Root.* New York: Dodd, Mead.

Leopold, Richard W. 1954. *Elihu Root and the Conservative Tradition.* Boston: Little, Brown.

## Elmo Roper (1900–1981)

Political pollster. Together with George Gallup and Archibald Crossley, Elmo Roper was one of the fathers of political polling. Roper's path to public opinion research was, however, an unusual one. Roper was born in Iowa and attended the University of Minnesota and the University in Edinburgh before failing in the jewelry business. His great discovery was that retailer reactions to new products were a much better predictor of product marketability than were the expert judgments of home office personnel. Richardson Wood, of the J. Walter Thompson advertising agency, was impressed with Roper's technique and introduced him to Paul Cherington, professor of marketing at the Harvard Business School. The three formed a marketing research firm, Cherington, Roper, and Wood, in 1934. Wood left in 1935, and in 1937, with Cherington's departure, the firm became Elmo Roper, Incorporated.

Roper's breakthrough into political polling came in 1935, when *Fortune Magazine* hired the firm to do a quarterly marketing survey aimed at the business community. Roper saw the potential of a political survey in 1936 to show the effectiveness the marketing techniques (relatively small quota samples) that his firm had been using. Roper's survey forecast Franklin Roosevelt's support at 61.7 percent, only 1 percent from the actual result (compared with Gallup's and Crossley's 7 percent error). In 1940, and again in 1944, Roper came within 1 percent. Only in 1948, when he announced in September that Thomas Dewey was so far ahead that further polling would be useless, were his results far off.

Roper's interest in public opinion went well beyond simply making election predictions, which he saw as "socially useless." In particular, he was interested in exploring areas of public ignorance in order to aid in public education. Roper believed that "objective" researchers should still involve themselves in public policy matters, and he did. During World War II, he served with the Office of Production Management and the Office of Facts and Figures; he eventually became director for both the Office of Coordinator of Information and the Office of Strategic Services. After the war, as a member of the board of directors of the Fund for the Republic, he was instrumental in securing financial support for Samuel Stouffer's *Communism, Conformity, and Civil Liberties*. He also founded the Roper Research Center to make commercial research data widely available.

*See also:* George Gallup, Franklin D. Roosevelt

*Ronald B. Rapoport*

REFERENCES

Converse, Jean. 1987. *Survey Research in the United States*. Berkeley, CA: University of California Press.

Roper, Elmo. 1957. *You and Your Leaders*. New York: William Morrow.

## J. Henry Roraback (1870–1937)

Leader of the Connecticut Republican Party. John Henry Roraback was born in Sheffield, Massachusetts, and attended high school in Great Barrington. Lacking funds for law school, Roraback read the law privately and began law practice in tiny North Canaan, Connecticut, in 1892.

From that small Connecticut town, Roraback built a Republican machine as powerful as any urban Democratic organization. At age 21, he was named North Canaan's Republican chairman; in 1898 he won a seat on the Republican State Central Committee where he served for two years. In 1901 he was hired as a railroad lobbyist. By 1905 he organized the Berkshire Power Company. Two years later he formed the Connecticut Light and Power Company, the eventual nucleus of his financial empire.

In 1912 Roraback unseated Michael H. Kenealy as chairman of the Republican State Central Committee by a single vote. Immediately, Roraback began building his political machine by linking the Republican-dominated small towns with Connecticut's utility and manufacturing industries, businesses that gave Roraback the money needed to finance his campaigns. In return, the state government would be solicitous of their interests.

The result was to install Roraback as de facto political leader of Connecticut. He denied renomination to two Republican governors who incurred his disfavor. Roraback's power extended to the state legislature where he determined who would occupy the leadership posts and committee chairs. When the legislature was in session, Roraback would reside at a stately Hartford hotel. At the conclusion of each legislative day, a stack of pending bills would be brought to Roraback who would subsequently decide how his Republican legislators would vote.

Roraback also played a part in GOP presidential politics. He was a member of the Republican National Committee from 1920 and served as a vice chairman from 1922 until his death. Roraback attended every Republican National Convention from 1908 to 1936, where he was a powerful voice in the selection of GOP presidential candidates.

The coming of the New Deal was presaged in Connecticut with the strong showing of Democratic presidential candidate Alfred E. Smith in 1928, followed two years later by the election of Democrat Wilbur L. Cross to the governorship. But Republicans continued to dominate in the legislature—especially in a state house of representatives gerrymandered to favor the GOP. Roraback continued to be a major figure in Connecticut politics, aligning himself closely with Governor Cross, until his suicide.

*See also:* Wilbur L. Cross, Republican National Committee

*John K. White*

REFERENCES

Goldman, Ralph M. 1990. *The National Party Chairmen and Committees: Factionalism at the Top*. Armonk, NY: M. E. Sharpe.

Lieberman, Joseph I. 1966. *The Power Broker: A Biography of John M. Bailey, Modern Political Boss*. Boston: Houghton Mifflin.

Lockard, Duane. 1959. *New England State Politics*. Princeton: Princeton U. Pr.

## Rosario v. Rockefeller
### 410 U.S. 752 (1973)

The state of New York has a closed system of primary elections. In order to prevent voters sympathetic to one party from voting in the other party's primary so as to select a weak candidate from that party—a practice called "party raiding"—New York restricts the ability of its citizens to participate in party primaries. Under New York law, a voter must enroll in the political party of his choice at least 30 days before the general election in order to vote in the next party primary. The cutoff date for enrollment and registration occurs approximately eight to eleven months before a primary election. The Supreme Court upheld this durational affiliation requirement in *Rosario v. Rockefeller*.

The constitutionality of New York's delayed-enrollment scheme was challenged by a group of residents who had attained voting age in 1971 before the October 2, 1971, cutoff date for registration and party enrollment. Because these individuals registered and enrolled in a party in December 1971, their party enrollment could not become effective until after the November 1972 general election. They were, therefore, ineligible to vote in the June 1972 presidential primary election.

These residents brought suit, alleging that New York's election law deprived them of their right to vote in the 1972 presidential primary and abridged their First and Fourteenth Amendment rights to associate with the party of their choice. They argued that the time period between the enrollment deadline and the next primary election was unreasonably long and that New York's interest in preventing party raiding was not compelling enough to warrant such a severe restriction on the franchise.

The district court agreed and granted the plaintiffs the declaratory relief sought. The court of appeals for the Second Circuit reversed, holding that the delayed-enrollment scheme was a constitutional deterrent against party raiding. The Supreme Court, in a five-to-four decision, affirmed the judgment of the court of appeals.

In his majority opinion, Justice Potter Stewart, who was joined by Chief Justice Warren Burger and Justices Byron White, Harry Blackmun, and William Rehnquist, argued that New York's election law neither disenfranchised the petitioners nor violated their First and Fourteenth Amendment rights to associate with the political party of their choice because "the statute merely imposed a time deadline." He pointed out that the petitioners could have enrolled prior to the cutoff date but "chose not to." Therefore, "their own failure to take timely steps to effect their enrollment" caused their disenfranchisement.

The majority acknowledged that the time period between the enrollment deadline and the next primary election was "lengthy." The Court held, however, that preventing party raiding and preserving the integrity of the electoral process were legitimate state goals. The delayed-enrollment scheme was reasonably tied to those goals because a voter who had to enroll in a party before the general election was unlikely to register in the party he intended to vote against in the general election.

In his dissent, Justice Lewis Powell, who was joined by Justices William Douglas, William Brennan, and Thurgood Marshall, argued that because the New York statute place restrictions on the fundamental constitutional rights of suffrage and free association, it should be subject to strict scrutiny. While he recognized that preventing party raiding was a legitimate state goal, he believed that the state's interest was not compelling because most voters who declare or change party affiliation do not do so with the intent to raid a primary. Moreover, Justice Powell argued, the state's interest could be protected through less severe measures. Because raiding tends to occur just before a primary is scheduled, a more reasonable deadline of 30 to 60 days before the primary would simultaneously protect the period most vulnerable to raiding activity and the availability of the franchise.

*See also:* Suffrage

*Robin Bye Wolpert*

REFERENCES

Lewy, Glen S. 1973. "The Right to Vote and Restrictions on Crossover Primaries." 40 *University of Chicago Law Review* 636.

Taslitz, Neal. 1974. "*Rosario v. Rockefeller* and *Kusper v. Pontikes*—Voters and Other Strangers." 23 *DePaul Law Review* 838.

Tribe, Laurence. 1988. *American Constitutional Law*, second edition. New York: The Foundation Press.

## Alex Rose (1898–1976)

Co-founder and leader of the New York–based Liberal Party. Until his death, Alex Rose was a pivotal figure in New York City, state, and national politics for five decades. Born Olesh Royz in Warsaw, Poland, Rose was a tanner's son. At age 15, he was sent to America to pursue a career in medicine. With the outbreak of World War I, Rose became a sewing machine operator and a Zionist labor movement activist. In 1918 he enlisted in the Jewish Legion of the British Expeditionary Force that fought in Palestine.

In the 1920s he rose in the ranks of the hat union. In 1936 he helped form the American Labor Party (ALP), created to provide a progressive electoral alternative to the Tammany-dominated Democratic Party as a means of lending support to Franklin Roosevelt and the New Deal. Increasingly harsh intraparty strife between old line Socialists and Communists led Rose and his associates to bolt the ALP to form the Liberal Party in 1946. Rose became president of the United Hatters, Cap and Millinery Workers International Union in 1950, holding that post until 1976.

As head of the small Liberal Party, Rose orchestrated or facilitated several political upsets, including the nomination of Averill Harriman for governor in 1954, the reelection of Robert F. Wagner, Jr. as New York City mayor in 1961 (rescuing Wagner from political oblivion after Tammany Democrats tried to deny him renomination), the reelection of John Lindsay as mayor in 1969 solely on the Liberal line, and the nomination and election of long shot Hugh Carey for governor in 1974. Rose, always ideologically radical, was nevertheless respected for his practical political skills and uncanny ability to pick winners in electoral contests.

See also: American Labor Party, Liberal Party of New York, John Lindsay, Franklin D. Roosevelt, Robert F. Wagner, Jr.

*Robert J. Spitzer*

## Victor Rosewater (1871–1940)

Journalist, economist, and man of world affairs. Victor Rosewater was born of a German Jewish family in Omaha, Nebraska. His parents had emigrated to the United States from Bohemia in 1854, settled in Cleveland, and changed their name from Rosewasser. Rosewater attended Johns Hopkins and Columbia universities, graduating in 1891. He also received his M.A. (1892) and Ph.D. (1893) from Columbia with a dissertation on municipal finance.

Rosewater returned to Omaha to work on the editorial staff of the *Omaha Bee*, an influential newspaper founded by his father in 1871. He became its managing editor in 1895, editor in 1906, and editor and publisher in 1917. In 1920 Rosewater sold the newspaper.

Always active in public affairs, Rosewater lectured in municipal finance at the University of Nebraska (1896–1897) and at the University of Wisconsin (1904). He was a member of the National Civic Federation and of the Nebraska State Commission on Workmen's Compensation in 1911. By 1908 newspaper editor Rosewater had an important influence on the Nebraska Republican Party as a strong supporter of Theodore Roosevelt, and especially of Roosevelt's conservation program. In that year, he was elected a member of the Republican National Committee (RNC) and also served as a delegate to the White House Conference on the Conservation of Natural Resources. He remained on the RNC until 1912 and was its chairman during the early days of the Republican convention of 1912. In that position, the short, weak-voiced, and unprepossessing Rosewater played a major role in the struggle between the William Howard Taft and Roosevelt forces.

Rosewater had begun work as early as 1907 in behalf of Taft's nomination, knowing that Taft was Roosevelt's choice at that time. In 1908 Rosewater was director of publicity in the West for the Taft campaign; William Jennings Bryan won his home state, Nebraska, in that year's presidential election, however. As Roosevelt and Taft parted ways, Rosewater remained with Taft, partly because the Roosevelt forces in Nebraska were joined with the allies of Senator Robert La Follette, a Progressive who Rosewater disliked.

As chairman of the national committee at the Chicago convention, Rosewater's rulings facilitated the election of Taft's candidate, Senator Elihu Root, as temporary chairman of the convention; precipitated the walkout of Roosevelt's delegates; and led to Taft's renomination on the first ballot. By the time of the convention, Rosewater had been defeated for reelection as national committeeman from Nebraska by emerging Progressive Party forces. He returned to his civic and editorial work in Omaha, watching Nebraska go for Woodrow Wilson in the 1912 general election. In 1916 Rosewater became a member of the advisory committee of the RNC. But his active role in party politics was over.

See also: William Jennings Bryan, Election of 1912, Robert La Follette, Republican National Committee, Theodore Roosevelt, Elihu Root, William Howard Taft

*Frederick J. Augustyn, Jr.*

### REFERENCES

Goldman, Ralph M. 1990. *The National Party Chairmen and Committees: Factionalism at the Top.* Armonk, NY: M. E. Sharpe.

## Runoff Primaries

Ten southern and Border States, as well as cities and counties across the nation, nominate candidates for public office using a majority rather than a plurality rule. Under the majority system, a successful candidate must get an absolute majority in the first primary election. If no one attracts at least 50 percent of the vote, the top two candidates face each other in a second, or "runoff," primary—a feature often called the "dual primary system." States employing the runoff include Alabama, Arkansas,

Florida, Georgia, Louisiana (which has a unique open-primary rule, followed by a nonpartisan second primary that serves as the general election), Oklahoma, Mississippi, North Carolina, South Carolina, and Texas. From 1937 to 1947, Utah also used this procedure. Arizona and South Dakota also have provisions for the runoff. While South Dakota has never used its runoff, in 1990 the Arizona gubernatorial race resulted in no majority winner in the general election, and, thus, for the first time in American history, a runoff general election was held in 1991.

The runoff method of election began to be practiced soon after the turn of the century, following the demise of the Republican Party in the South. In the absence of serious two-party competition, the Democratic primary became the only battle ground for would-be office-holders. Owing to the crowded list of candidates on the primary ballot, a relatively small fraction of the vote might well constitute a plurality. The leader of an ideologically extreme political bloc might poll the most votes and win an election, even though most of the electorate may have preferred any of the other alternative candidates. Democratic Party officials throughout the South established the runoff to insure that nominees for public office had indeed gained the support of a majority of the voters in their constituencies.

In the 1980s the runoff procedure became a subject of controversy. In his first bid for the Democratic presidential nomination in 1984, Jesse Jackson, an African-American minister and political activist, castigated the dual-primary system as a major barrier to the electoral success of minority candidates. Among the examples cited by the Reverend Jackson was a 1982 election in the Second District of North Carolina. In June of that year, H. M. (Mickey) Michaux, Jr., a popular Black candidate for Congress who had previously served as a state legislator and United States attorney, won the first primary by a 44.5 percent margin. Trailing him were two white candidates with, respectively, 32.7 percent and 22.8 percent of the vote. Had the contest ended there, Michaux might have gone on to win the general election and become the first Black Congressman from his district since 1898. In the runoff primary, however, white voters rallied around the remaining white candidate and defeated Michaux, 53.6 percent to 46.4 percent. Citing this and other setbacks for African-American politicians, Jackson recurrently used this rallying cry in his presidential campaign

speeches of 1984: "We must end the second primary before it ends us."

On the other hand, other observers of American elections—several of whom were sympathetic to Jackson's vision of Black electoral successes—thought that abolition of the runoff might be a cure worse than the disease. "Nominations in one-round, wide-open Southern primaries might send dozens of Black Congressmen to Washington by thin pluralities," wrote historian Theodore H. White (1984), "but it would also give enormous opportunities to Republicans to put down strong regional grassroots wherever whites fear blacks and seek alternatives." The end result of abandoning the runoff would be more Republicans in office and, ironically, legislatures less sympathetic to issues of significance to African-Americans.

Moreover, suggested other commentators, the second primary might actually benefit the nomination chances for some minority candidates. Former Georgia state senator and national Black leader Julian Bond has stated that "[the runoff] actually discriminates against the numerical minority, black or white, in elections in which there is a racial polarization." Similarly, Harold W. Stanley, a political scientist, has observed that, in some situations, without a second primary African-American candidates might "split the black vote and allow a white candidate to gain a plurality nomination" (1985). In two major court cases challenging the runoff provision, one in New York City (Butts, 1985) and another in Arkansas (Whitman, 1988), presiding judges have found in favor of the dual-primary system and rejected (at the appellate level in New York) charges of discrimination brought by African-American plaintiffs.

See also: Julian Bond

*Loch K. Johnson*

REFERENCES

Bullock, Charles S., III, and Loch K. Johnson. 1991. *Runoff Elections in the United States.* Knoxville: U. of Tennessee Pr.

*Butts v. City of New York.* 1985. United States Court of Appeals for the Second Circuit, New York, Docket No. 85–7670.

Ewing, Cortez A. M. 1953; 1980. *Primary Elections in the South: A Study in Uniparty Politics.* Norman: U. of Oklahoma Pr.

Stanley, Harold W. 1985. "The Runoff: The Case for Retention." 18 *PS* 231.

*Whitfield v. Democratic Party of the State of Arkansas.* 1988. United States District Court, Eastern District of Arkansas, Docket No. H–C–86–47.

## William A. Rusher (1923– )

Influential conservative political strategist. A liberal Republican by upbringing and education, William Allen Rusher moved to the right in the mid-1950s because of his enthusiasm for Whittaker Chambers's *Witness* (1952) and in reaction to the turmoil of the Joseph McCarthy years (Rusher served as a special counsel to the Senate Internal Security Subcommittee, 1956–1957). In 1957 he became the publisher of the conservative Republican *National Review* and, with William F. Buckley, worked to close the gap between conservative intellectual thought and effective political action.

In 1961 Rusher was particularly incensed by Richard Nixon's famous "sellout on Fifth Avenue" platform concessions to the liberal Nelson Rockefeller that alienated the conservatives in the Republican Party. Rusher, Congressman John Ashbrook, and political scientist F. Clifton White launched the "Draft Goldwater Movement." Determined to nominate a conservative for President in 1964, Rusher, Ashbrook, and White gathered together 23 like-minded conservatives and began the process of building a grass-roots organization that would assume control of the Republican Party and secure the nomination of conservative Barry Goldwater. Rusher's principal contribution to the movement came in a 1963 article in *National Review*, "Crossroads for the GOP"; here he outlined the electoral strategy for a Goldwater victory. In 1975, in his book *The Making of the New Majority*, Rusher argued for the formation of a new political party comprised of economic and social conservatives. While this new party never materialized, the concept of a broad-based appeal to conservatives of both parties was successfully employed by Ronald Reagan in his 1980 presidential campaign.

*See also:* William F. Buckley, Whittaker Chambers, Elections of 1964 and 1980, Barry Goldwater, Richard M. Nixon, Ronald Reagan, Nelson A. Rockefeller, F. Clinton White

*David B. Raymond*

REFERENCES

Nash, George H. 1976. *The Conservative Intellectual Movement in America; Since 1945.* New York: Basic Books.

Rusher, William A. 1968. *Special Counsel.* New Rochelle, NY: Arlington House.

———. 1975. *The Making of the New Majority Party.* New York: Sheed and Ward.

———. 1984. *The Rise of the Right.* New York: Morrow.

White, Clifton F. 1967. *Suite 3505: The Story of the Draft Goldwater Movement.* New Rochelle, NY: Arlington House.

## Richard B. Russell (1897–1971)

Powerful U.S. Senator from Georgia. On the occasion of Richard Russell's death, the *Washington Post* wrote, "In a real sense, he was the closest thing remaining to the embodiment of the Senate of old, the keeper and the symbol of the tradition, mores and tone that gave the place its stature throughout most of the history of the republic." As chairman of two important Senate committees, first Armed Services, and then Appropriations, and as a leader of the southern Democratic block, Russell proved to be a friend of the New Deal and a powerful force for increased military spending (though he initially opposed American involvement in Southeast Asia). Russell was perhaps best known as a conservative leader of southern resistance to civil rights legislation, engineering some of the Senate's most protracted anti-civil rights filibusters.

Russell entered the U.S. Senate in 1932, having already served as speaker of the Georgia House of Representatives (at the age of 30) and governor of the state. His climb up the Senate seniority ladder culminated with his selection as chairman of the Armed Services Committee in 1951. In 1953 Russell's colleagues demonstrated their respect for his leadership, and appreciation for his electoral security, by selecting him to chair the committee of inquiry created to investigate President Harry Truman's controversial recall of General Douglas MacArthur from Korea. He stepped down from Armed Services in 1969 as the undisputed champion of American military might, but he retained the chairmanship of the powerful Appropriations Committee.

Russell was the archetype of the southern Senator, hailing from a one-party state whose whites-only politics virtually guaranteed re-election and long seniority. The seniority, of course, brought him great power and influence in national affairs. In the 1960s, with Russell as chairman of Armed Services in the Senate and Congressman Carl Vinson as chairman of Armed Services in the House, military affairs in Congress were reduced to, in the words of one commentator, "whispered conversations between Georgians."

Richard Russell's dominance in the Senate was unquestioned; George Reedy claims that "with Russell's blessing, almost any measure could pass the Senate. Against his determined opposition, it was doomed." He was, however, unable to use his Senate power as a springboard to national office, twice (1948 and 1952) mounting dismally unsuccessful campaigns for the Democratic presidential nomination. At his death, he was President *pro tempore* of the Senate.

*See also:* New Deal

*Tom A. Kazee*

REFERENCES

Kearns, Doris. 1976. *Lyndon Johnson and the American Dream.* New York: Signet.

Reedy, George E. 1986. *The U.S. Senate.* New York: Mentor.

White, William S. 1957. *Citadel: The Story of the U.S. Senate.* New York: Harper & Row.

## Bayard Rustin (1910–1987)

Civil rights activist. Born in West Chester, Pennsylvania, Bayard Rustin devoted his life to the pursuit of civil rights. He went to prison as a conscientious objector to World War II (Rustin was a dedicated pacifist) and studied Gandhi's ideas of "nonviolent direct action." Despite his early association with the Young Communist League in New York City and a conviction for homosexual activity, he played a leading role in the struggles for Black equality.

In the 1940s Rustin worked for the Fellowship of Reconciliation (FOR), where he helped organize the Congress of Racial Equality (CORE). In 1941 he assisted in A. Philip Randolph's "March on Washington Movement," which contributed to Franklin Roosevelt's decision to issue antidiscrimination Executive Order 8802. At CORE, Rustin participated in the "Journey of Reconciliation," a movement intended to demonstrate the persistence of discrimination in interstate commerce.

He began his association with Dr. Martin Luther King, Jr., in 1956. During Alabama's Montgomery bus boycott, Rustin, the recent executive secretary of the War Resister's League, urged King's adoption of nonviolent tactics. Shortly thereafter, he organized a meeting at which the Southern Christian Leadership Conference (SCLC) emerged, and later, as part of the SCLC's Research Committee, he advised King on contemporary politics.

Rustin continued to work for civil rights during the 1960s and 1970s. In 1963, as deputy director, he coordinated the March on Washington, the fulfillment of Randolph's two-decade-long dream. To alleviate the social and economic inequities that plagued African-Americans, Rustin ardently stressed the need for a leftist coalition working through the federal government, belief that led this lifelong pacifist to support the Vietnam War rather than break openly with President Lyndon Johnson. After 1964 Rustin directed the A. Philip Randolph Institute, which promoted racial equality and peace, job training, voter registration, and coordination among liberals.

*See also:* Lyndon B. Johnson, Martin Luther King, Jr., A. Philip Randolph, Vietnam War as a Political Issue

*Robert F. Zeidel*

REFERENCES

Fairclough, Adam. 1987. *To Redeem the Soul of America: The Southern Christian Leadership Conference and Martin Luther King, Jr.* Athens: U. of Georgia Pr.

Garrow, David J. 1986. *Bearing the Cross: Martin Luther King, Jr., and the Southern Christian Leadership Conference.* New York: Morrow.

Viorst, Milton. 1979. *Fire in the Streets: America in the 1960s.* New York: Simon & Schuster.

# S

## Dwight M. Sabin (1843–1902)

U.S. Senator from Minnesota and chair of the Republican National Committee. Dwight May Sabin was born on a stockbreeding farm in LaSalle County, Illinois, the youngest son of Horace C. and Maria Sabin who had migrated in 1834 from Connecticut and returned there in 1857. Dwight attended Phillips Academy at Andover, Massachusetts, served three months in the Union Army in 1863, and worked in lumbering and on the family farm. In 1868 he moved to Stillwater, Minnesota, where he became a successful lumberman, eventually diversifying into the manufacture of railroad cars and agriculture machinery and amassing a large fortune. Adopting his father's Republicanism, he served in the Minnesota Senate from 1872 to 1875 and was elected to the lower house in 1878 and 1881. He defeated an overconfident Republican incumbent, William Windom, for the U.S. Senate seat in 1883. A regular national convention delegate since 1872, he succeeded Marshall Jewell as chair of the Republican National Committee in 1882, but, as an avowed Chester Arthur supporter, he resigned his post when James G. Blaine became the Republican nominee in 1884. In the Senate he served as chair of the committee on railroads and on the committee on Indian affairs. William D. Washburn defeated him for the Republican senatorial nomination at the end of his first term.

See also: Chester A. Arthur, James G. Blaine, Marshall Jewell, Republican National Committee

*Phyllis F. Field*

REFERENCES

Falwell, William Watts. 1926. *A History of Minnesota.* Saint Paul: Minnesota Historical Soc.

Goldman, Ralph M. 1990. *The National Party Chairmen and Committees: Factionalism at the Top.* Armonk, NY: M. E. Sharpe.

## Everett Sanders (1882–1950)

Republican Congressman from Indiana and GOP leader. Everett Sanders was Republican national chairman (1932 to 1934) during and after President Herbert Hoover's unsuccessful reelection campaign in 1932. Sanders was born and raised in Indiana, where his father was a farmer and a Baptist preacher. After Indiana State Normal School, Sanders taught school for a brief period before continuing his education at Indiana University. He practiced law at Terre Haute, between 1907 and 1917, building a large clientele as well as a political following. In an upset victory against a longtime Democratic incumbent, Sanders won the Fifth District seat in the House of Representatives in 1917 and served continuously until 1925.

Sanders became a member of the powerful House Steering Committee and held other influential positions during his years in Congress. At the end of his fourth term, he announced that he did not intend to run again, but he did manage the speakers bureau for the 1924 Calvin Coolidge presidential campaign. That service changed his plans to return to his law practice; President Coolidge invited him to become presidential secretary, a position through which Presidents kept a hand on party matters. Sanders was presidential secretary from 1925 to 1929.

Sanders then joined the law firm of James W. Good, who was Herbert Hoover's principal adviser on midwestern political affairs. When Good died, Sanders took over this political obligation. In 1932, hoping to have the Coolidge following represented in his campaign for President, Hoover sought the former President's recommendations for the national party chairmanship. Coolidge named Sanders, and Hoover concurred.

In the national chairmanship, Sanders was blamed by many Republican leaders for Hoover's defeat, leading to dozens of postelection demands for his resignation. During a hospitalization in 1934 he did resign for reasons of illness.

*See also:* Calvin Coolidge, Herbert Hoover

*Ralph M. Goldman*

REFERENCES

Latham, Edward C. 1960. *Meet Calvin Coolidge.* Brattleboro, VT: Stephen Greene Press.

Goldman, Ralph M. 1990. *The National Party Chairmen and Committees: Factionalism at the Top.* Armonk, NY: M. E. Sharpe.

## Terry Sanford (1917– )

Educator, officeholder, and party activist. Terry Sanford, Democratic governor of and U.S. Senator from North Carolina, was a longtime advocate of strong party organization. In the 1980s he criticized the "participatory disorder" through which Americans pick their President and warned, "The danger of democracy is . . . that we somehow bring ourselves to believe that the democracy of the town hall can be extended to nationwide decisions." His central contribution to Democratic Party procedures came when he chaired the Charter Commission from 1973 to 1974. Popularly known as the Sanford Commission, its task was to propose a new charter on national party processes to a 1974 midterm party conference. The commission largely endorsed the work of the McGovern-Fraser, O'Hara, and Mikulski commissions on delegate selection and convention rules. Sanford was also the first director of the Center for National Policy (formerly the Center for Democratic Policy), a think tank with close party and congressional ties designed to formulate policy alternatives for the 1980s.

As governor of North Carolina from 1961 to 1965, Sanford was one of the first of a new breed of progressive southern Democrats. He was a strong advocate of civil rights and invented what today would be called industrial policy by upgrading public education as a means of luring high-tech industry to North Carolina's Research Triangle Park. Sanford was president of Duke University from 1969 to 1985, but he remained active in national party politics, making two somewhat limited runs at the White House in 1972 and 1976. In 1986 he was elected to the U.S. Senate in a surprise victory over incumbent James Broyhill, who had been appointed to serve the last year of John East's term.

*See also:* McGovern-Fraser Commission, Sanford Commission

*David T. Canon*

REFERENCES

Democratic National Committee. 1974. *Official Proceedings of the 1974 Conference on Democratic Party Organization and Policy.* Washington: Democratic National Committee.

Sanford, Terry. 1966. *But What About the People?* New York: Harper & Row.

———. 1967. *Storm Over the States.* New York: McGraw-Hill.

———. 1976. *The Schools That Fear Built: Segregationist Academics in the South.* Washington: Acropolis Books.

———. 1981. *The Dangers of Democracy.* New York: Westview.

———. 1983. *The Interest Rate Dilemma.* New York: KCG Productions.

Talmadge, Samuel R. 1964. *The New Day.* Zebulon, NC: Record Publ. Co.

## Sanford Commission

The Democratic Party Charter or "Sanford" Commission (1972–1974), named after its chair, Terry Sanford, drafted the body of national party law that permanently authorizes the Democratic National Committee (DNC). The Republican National Committee (RNC), by contrast, exists solely by virtue of rules adopted at each quadrennial Republican National Convention. The Commission was authorized by the 1972 Democratic National Convention. National party reform had been part of the 1968 reform mandate, but both the McGovern-Fraser and the O'Hara commissions were preoccupied with the more pressing issues of presidential selection and convention modernization. Both reform commissions claimed jurisdiction; ultimately, a jointly drafted charter was presented to the party in May—far too late for consideration by the 1972 convention. Jean Westwood, DNC chair, appointed Terry Sanford, then the president of Duke University and former governor of North Carolina as the commission chair. Sanford, a moderate unassociated with reform, was acceptable to all party factions.

Unlike the Mikulski Commission, whose mandate had been to revise an existing set of procedures, the Sanford Commission was authorized to create something wholly new: a code of national party law. The stakes were high, and several antireform party factions sought to use the Sanford Commission to gut the McGovern-Fraser reforms. After the defeat of McGovern, Chairwoman Westwood was replaced by Robert Strauss (in December 1972); he initially viewed the reform faction as only an epiphenomenon of 1972. The conservative bargaining position of labor (notably the AFL-CIO's George Meany and Al Barkan) and its newly formed ally, the Coalition for a Democratic Majority, was thus strengthened. The Commission was composed of 164 members, an unwieldy number that probably magnified the influence of organized factions.

The first decision of consequence was to hold a Mid-Term Party Conference as authorized by the 1972 convention. Under pressure from party leaders and conservatives, the conference was scheduled in Kansas City for December 1974 and limited to consideration of the charter provisions. The Sanford Commission adopted an unofficial draft of its proposed charter, with final resolution of such relatively uncontroversial issues as whether midterm conferences should be required or optional, the establishment of a judicial council, and the tenure of the DNC chair held over for a meeting in mid-August. In the interim, with the "blessing and support of the national chairman and his staff," the AFL-CIO leaders, despite their already strong presence on the Sanford Commission, began replacing commission members unable to attend the August session with appointees hostile to reform. With their strength ensured, the restorationists not only noted the liberal alternatives to the tabled charter provisions but also sought to reverse significant McGovern-Fraser reforms included in the draft charter.

The restorationists first attacked the Mikulski compromise on affirmative action for minorities and women. The compromise was designed to replace the quota concept, and the restorationists sought to limit its applicability simply to delegate selection rather than to all party affairs, then to replace the phrase "insure representation" with "encourage participation." This maneuver angered African-Americans and women who felt that the Mikulski compromise had already significantly weakened their gains under McGovern-Fraser. At an impasse, the Commission proposed four options and left the issue for the December conference to resolve. The restorationists then proposed to void the major procedural McGovern-Fraser/Mikulski reforms by removing the requirement that delegates be selected during the election year and by moving the ban on the unit rule and winner-take-all primaries from the charter to the more easily amended by-laws. (The charter may be amended only by a majority of the national convention or a two-thirds supermajority of the DNC.) Reform supporters, led by Blacks, walked out, forcing Sanford to adjourn the meeting for lack of a quorum and leaving these issues unresolved. The response to the attack by the restorationists demonstrated the strength of the reform forces, bringing Strauss, who strongly wished to unify the party, to the recognition that the Democratic Party's center had shifted, a realization reinforced by an endorsement of the Mikulski proposals by Democratic governors shortly after the 1974 Democratic landslides. Don Fraser, a Commission member, emerged as a key strategist for the reform bloc. Strauss personally intervened: meeting with Commission members and reform supporters after the August meeting, securing the endorsement of Chicago's mayor, Richard Daley, and chairing both the Charter Conference (yielding only to Sanford during the charter debate) and the 52-member Rules Committee.

The result was a major defeat for labor and the restorationists. The Charter, adopted on December 7, 1974, reaffirmed the McGovern-Fraser procedural reforms and the Mikulski affirmative action compromise, which was to be applied to all party affairs as well as to delegate selection. Women achieved an exemption for equal division from the ban on quotas. The state parties, now required to adopt written party by-laws, were required to file them with the DNC within 30 days of ratification. Party midterm conferences were made optional, and provisions were made for national finance organizations and judicial and National Education and Training Councils. The DNC, enlarged to 350 members, was required to prepare an annual public report and empowered to elect the DNC Executive Committee. All meetings of national Democratic Party committees and conferences were open to the public. In the face of a most serious challenge posed by the restorationists, the Democratic Party Charter was able to institutionalize the major achievements of the party reform era.

*Denise L. Baer*

REFERENCES

Crotty, William J. 1977. *Political Reform and the American Experiment*. New York: Harper & Row.

———. 1978. *Decision for the Democrats*. Baltimore: Johns Hopkins U. Pr.

———. 1983. *Party Reform*. New York: Longman.

## Scandals and Scandalizing

Scandals are, above all, important in politics as weapons—weapons to attack another faction, party, group, or leadership. The scandalization/defamation directed against Thomas Hutchinson, who held a series of official posts in Massachusetts in the 1760s and 1770s, ultimately that of royal governor, found its way into the Declaration of Independence in 1776. This slander was designed and executed by such zealous ideologues as James Otis, Jr., and Samuel Adams, but historians have found little truth in the accusations against Hutchinson or, for that matter, against the British cabinet and George III.

Probably no other campaign of scandalization in American history has been equally epoch making; however, it had such parallels as (1) the Popish Plot of the 1680s in England and its sequel, the allegation that the legitimate heir to the British throne, the so-called "Old Pretender," was a changeling, smuggled into the delivery room on a warming pan—all leading to the Glorious Revolution of 1689 and the firm establishment of parliamentary government in Britain; and (2) the stories, true and false, told about Czar Nicholas II and his Court before the Russian Revolution of 1917.

Scandal mongering in the American colonies led to acceptance of the notion that George III, actually one of the mildest monarchs of his age, was an unprincipled tyrant; and it played a part in forcing many whose natural inclinations were moderate (such as Benjamin Franklin) to align themselves with the revolutionary cause. Much American history has subsequently been influenced by these colonial scandals. In 1919 and 1946 consequent attitudes played a part in American eagerness to break up the old colonial empires, sometimes contrary to the national interests of the United States. They have also restimulated from time to time a foolish, knee-jerk sympathy among American Progressives for self-styled democratic revolutionaries, from the Hungarian Kossuth on down to China's Mao and Cuba's Castro.

Creative oversimplification, not to say distortion, is more characteristic of political scandalization than the candid concern for facts that Thomas Jefferson claimed in the Declaration. However, on some occasions, the truth of a situation did appear damning (e.g., in the investigation in the late 1940s led by Richard Nixon of Alger Hiss and other Stalinist fellow travelers in the federal bureaucracy). But even here, campaign orators (such as Nixon himself) engaged in the non sequitur that because a few fellow travelers had been discovered in the bureaucracy, many more must be harbored there.

The limited and credible findings of Nixon as investigator and the naive innocence of many American officials in the 1940s, confronted with Stalinist efforts at infiltration, did not go far enough for opponents of Harry Truman and Adlai Stevenson. Nixon's discoveries were less dramatic than the farrago of charges raised by Senator Joseph McCarthy against scores of people, many of the claims false or irrelevant. McCarthy not infrequently supplemented charges of treason with a hint that some of the traitors were homosexual. In so doing he appealed not only to Slavic-Americans, who justifiably wanted an explanation of why and how the United States had abandoned their homelands, but also to a number of other working-class Americans, who, typically, suspected upper-class intellectuals of "unnatural" sexual proclivities. These two themes, if they were not as helpful as they seemed to Republican candidates, were encouraged by leaders like Senator Robert Taft who once told McCarthy to "go to it." Ironically, liberal Americans, venerating Jeffersonian democracy, lambasted McCarthy as illiberal and un-American, even though the Senator was using techniques and styles that Jefferson and others had employed successfully from 1763 to 1776.

The scandalizer finds it easier to start with a substratum of truth and to build upon it an edifice of fancy. Because effective scandals activate a good many people who are normally not politically oriented, explanation in terms of the complexity of great power politics and the naiveté of American officials about Stalinist aims and ambitions, among other things, would have been confusing in the extreme to many who were impressed by McCarthy's charges against Democratic policies from 1943 to 1952.

A simple explanation of a distressing phenomenon is a large part of the psychological value of much scandalizing. For instance, albeit amazing to modern or southern ears, during the Civil War Abraham Lincoln was regarded as unduly prosouthern and proslavery. The explanation given, and sometimes believed, was that his wife, Mary, was a southern sympathizer since she had relatives who fought for the South. The latter was true, but her pro-South leanings were improbable and, if true, had no influence on the President or anybody else of political importance. Had the Civil War been lost, there was material for a "stab in the back" legend.

At a more physical level, Woodrow Wilson in the last months of his presidency was physiologically unable to perform his full duties. No credible explanation was publicly given. Business was carried on in a somewhat hole-in-corner fashion to conceal the President's incapacity. Opponents floated a story that Wilson was suffering the terminal stages of syphilis. This scandal was probably more damaging to Wilson's Democratic associates, possibly even to the League of Nations that he fathered, than to some less emotion laden pathology such as an actual stroke would have been. The more partisan Republicans latched on to the idea and publicized it through an oral "poison squad."

These memorable scandals involve issues in which the survival of a polity or a regime was at stake. Most scandals, on the other hand, are more limited in scope. No hard-and-fast line can be drawn, to be sure, between major scandals and minor ones; it could be argued that *the* major tempest in Washington during the Jackson administration was actually of political importance. At any rate, Cabinet wives and administration spouses refused to call on the wife of the Secretary of War, Peggy O'Neill Eaton. She supposedly had had an affair with John Eaton while married to someone else. The President was outraged or pretended to be (some think he orchestrated the scandal himself for political purposes); ultimately the Cabinet and the Vice President, John Calhoun, were led to resign. (One importance of the scandal is said to be that Calhoun became again a Representative of South Carolina and strengthened all the sectional tendencies in that state leading ultimately to secession. Had he remained a truly national figure, secession would not have occurred!)

From the Ulysses Grant administration (1869) on, numerous scandals have centered on issues of corruption, alleged corruption, and abuse of office. Many of them have been ably interpreted by a great student of local corruption, Lincoln Steffens: "The real explanation and villain in the Fall of Man was not Eve, not Adam, not the serpent, not the devil, but the apple." Where much is to be gained, and the prospect of getting away with dishonesty is good, some prominent people will try their luck; and some of them will be exposed. It is not, however, generally basic moral or political significance that leads some of these potential scandals to be deadly and others to be shrugged off. A high proportion of such Washington scandals are similar to Hollywood scandals. If they seem to be entertaining enough to play well, and if they can be used to show the unsympathetic character of someone who deserves to be undermined (Richard Nixon, for instance), then scandals will become matters of public indignation. A political historian finds it relatively easy to imagine Franklin D. Roosevelt or John F. Kennedy engaging in activities similar to the earlier stages of Watergate. Indeed, Roosevelt's neutrality-busting dealings with Winston Churchill before the outbreak of World War II might well be seen as a much worse abuse of power than anything connected with Watergate—except that in this event FDR was proven right; and Nixon was of course wrong. Roosevelt, however, surely would have, and Kennedy probably would have played the resulting firestorm very differently.

Washington scandals also resemble Hollywood scandals in another important respect; a fair number of Americans (and probably citizens of other nations) enjoy the role of the "inside dopester" and of being able to tell others the inside dope, what is "really going on." The tendency also overlaps another common phenomenon; a significant number of persons are envious and jealous of people more prominent than they. They express such envy by inventing or spreading scandals about the prominent. This scandal-mongering action preoccupies employees, secretaries, assistants, and less-distinguished colleagues.

A common contention nowadays is that the media create scandals. This argument is not on the whole true; the media do, however, disseminate scandals for two reasons: (1) there is an audience for scandals among the public, because of the envy and malice just referred to, and also because of curiosity and the desire to get the inside dope; and (2) many media people regard it as their sacred duty to expose wrongdoing wherever it occurs.

Much more active in the creation of scandals in the last few years have been prosecutors (especially federal prosecutors) who develop, sometimes on flimsy grounds, doubtful charges against officials. One such case is the indictment of Ronald Reagan's Secretary of Labor William Donovan, doing, as a businessman in the construction industry, what any reasonable person would have done to reconcile the conflict between federal laws and requirements and the practical necessities of a situation. He thereby violated (or appeared to violate) federal law, although we have no reason to suppose he did any harm in so doing. In fact the jury found him not guilty; but he had to spend two years, millions of dollars, and enormous worry and energy defending himself. Similarly, the U.S. District Attorney's office in Baltimore charged Marvin Mandel, arguably the ablest governor that Maryland ever had, with something so complex and esoteric that many of those actively interested in politics in Maryland at the time could not and do not yet understand the charges. Among them was one that Mandel had violated the federal mail-fraud laws by permitting transcripts of his press conferences to be sent to the University of Maryland libraries. Mandel was found guilty and served a prison term; when the decision was subsequently reversed, he went back to serve three or four hours at the end of his original term as governor.

In these cases, and in many others, most citizens and many fellow professionals regarded charges as proof of wrongdoing; further public service would probably be closed to either man. In a masterful account of actions by federal prosecutors against state and local officials, Arthur Maass has demonstrated that cases such as Mandel's have happened in a good many jurisdictions, reflecting the varying and capricious notions of federal prosecutors about political morality.

What is regarded as a scandal is subject to the idiosyncrasies of time, place, and constituency; in other words, scandal is a matter of fashion. The major explanation for the defeat of a previously respected and popular U.S. Senator in Massachusetts in 1946 was gossip about his alleged homosexuality: but in the mid-1980s, two Congressmen and some state legislators, who had publicly acknowledged their homosexuality, were reelected in the same state. In Minnesota peccadillos so minor they would never have been mentioned in West Virginia have become serious campaign issues. In the 1830s, whether or not to shun the wife of a Cabinet member because her earlier career had not been clearly chaste provoked a storm: if such an unlikely thing were to occur during the George Bush administration of the 1990s, it would at most provide material for stand-up comics! Similar great variations makes it totally impossible to consider here the record of scandals and scandalizations in different states, municipalities, or counties (things that would have been shocking indeed in Montgomery County, Maryland, in the 1950s would have been commonplace in Charles or Allegany counties, then, in that same state). Given this disparity, what is generally regarded in a specific political culture as natural or even respectable may suddenly become the subject of serious condemnation when metropolitan or national attention is devoted to the matter—for example most practicing Maryland politicians and political activists did in fact take for granted the kind of thing that Governor, and later Vice President, Spiro Agnew did as governor until the national press and federal prosecutors focused on his continuing the same practices as Vice President. Agnew had to resign his national office for reasons still cloudy to the politicians of Maryland.

*See also:* Samuel Adams, Spiro Agnew, John C. Calhoun, Ulysses S. Grant, Alger Hiss, Andrew Jackson, John F. Kennedy, League of Nations, Abraham Lincoln, Joseph McCarthy, Richard M. Nixon, Franklin D. Roosevelt, Adlai Stevenson II, Robert Taft, Harry S Truman, Watergate, Woodrow Wilson

*Lewis A. Dexter*

REFERENCES

Bailyn, Bernard. 1974. *The Ordeal of Thomas Hutchinson.* Cambridge: Harvard U. Pr.

Bryant, Arthur. 1948. *Samuel Pepys: The Years of Peril.* London: Collins.

Dexter, Lewis A. 1982. "What If Joseph McCarthy Had Not Been a U.S. Senator in 1950–5? and/or What If There Had Been a Serious Responsible Senator with Gifts as Great as McCarthy's for Publicity Who Had Preempted the Communism-in-Government Issue?" In Nelson Polsby, ed. *What If.* Lexington, MA: Stephen Greene.

Dexter, Lewis A. 1970. *Elite and Specialized Interviewing.* Evanston, IL: Northwestern U. Pr.

———, and David Braybrooke. 1991. "Corruption." In *Encyclopedia of Ethics.* New York: Garland.

———, and David M. White, eds. 1964. *People, Society, and Mass Communications.* New York: Free Press.

Hollander, Paul. 1981. *Political Pilgrims.* New York: Oxford U. Pr.

Levin, Jack, and Arnold Arnluke. 1987. *Gossip: The Inside Story.* New York: Plenum Press.

Minnigerode, Meade. 1926. "Peggy Eaton." *Some American Ladies.* New York: Putnam's.

Resnow, Ralph, and Gary A. Fine. 1976. *Rumor and Gossip: A Social Psychology of Hearsay.* New York: Elsevier.

Riesman, David, et al. 1950. *The Lonely Crowd: A Study of the Changing American Character.* New Haven: Yale U. Pr.

Weinstein, Allen. 1978. *Perjury: The Hiss-Chambers Case.* New York: Knopf.

## E. E. Schattschneider (1892–1971)

Author of several books on interest groups and the American political party system. Elmer E. Schattschneider's *Politics, Pressures, and the Tariff* (1935) was influential in shaping the "group approach" to the study of politics. In *Party Government* (1940), he argued for the importance of parties, best captured in his thesis "that the political parties created democracy and that modern democracy is unthinkable save in terms of the parties." His Committee on Political Parties of the American Political Science Association (APSA) issued an influential report, *Toward a More Responsible Two-Party System* (1950), that proposed reforms in American government and parties in order to enhance discipline and accountability. Returning to an analysis of groups in *The Semisovereign People* (1960), he is best remembered for the observations that "the flaw in the pluralist heaven is that the heavenly chorus sings with a strong upper-class accent," that the American system is especially hospitable to rule by narrow interests, and that vigorous party competition serves as the best check on those special interests.

Schattschneider earned his B.A. in 1915 from the University of Wisconsin, his M.A. from the University of Pittsburgh in 1927, and his Ph.D. from Columbia University in 1935. He taught at Senior High School at Butler, Pennsylvania, from 1919 to 1926; at Columbia, 1927 to 1930; at the New Jersey College for Women, 1929 to 1930; and at Wesleyan University, 1930 to 1960. In Connecticut, he served on the Middletown City Council, State Board of Mediation and Arbitration, and State Board of Pardons. He was vice president of APSA in 1953 and president from 1956 to 1957.

*Douglas I. Hodgkin*

REFERENCES

American Political Science Association, Committee on Political Parties. 1950. *Toward a More Responsible Two-Party System.* New York: Rinehart.

Schattschneider, E. E. 1935. *Politics, Pressures, and the Tariff.* New York: Prentice-Hall.

———. 1942. *Party Government.* New York: Rinehart.

———. 1960. *The Semisovereign People.* New York: Holt, Rinehart and Winston.

## Augustus Schell (1812–1884)

Wealthy New York financier and Democratic Party leader. Augustus Schell served as chairman of the Democratic National Committee (1872–1876) when the Democratic National Convention endorsed the nominee of the Liberal Republican Party, Horace Greeley, in 1872. Schell and Republican editor Greeley had cooperated in their post–Civil War advocacy of speedy reincorporation of the South into the Union. The two men were part of the effort to get Jefferson Davis, the imprisoned president of the Confederacy, released on bail.

Schell, an attorney and the most famous of four brothers prominent in New York City financial circles, became a New York City Democratic Party district leader by the 1840s. A spokesman for New York's "Hard Schell" faction (economic conservatives willing to tolerate the institution of slavery), Schell was Tammany's 1852 candidate for governor, served as Democratic state chairman (1853–1856), and became a collector of the port of New York for his energetic work in the James Buchanan campaign.

When Horatio Seymour, the Democrats' 1868 presidential nominee, became disenchanted with the poor campaign effort of the national committee, he asked his campaign manager to establish the Order of the Union Democracy to supplement the party's efforts. Samuel Tilden became "Chief" of these campaign clubs and Schell "Vice Chief." In the course of these activities, Schell extended his good relations with southern Democrats.

In 1872 the leadership of the Democratic Party hoped to take advantage of a split in the Republican Party by endorsing, sight unseen, any ticket nominated by the new Liberal Republican Party. When the Liberal nominee unexpectedly turned out to be Horace Greeley—a Republican foe of long standing—Democrats, chagrined and confused, reluctantly kept their pledge to endorse. Anticipating Greeley's preference for Schell as his campaign chairman, the New York Democratic state convention chose Schell as its representative on the national committee, where he was elected national chairman. Schell's energetic coordination of the Democratic and Liberal Republican campaign organizations brought many Liberals into the Democratic Party permanently and facilitated the postwar reconciliation between northern and southern Democrats.

*See also:* Jefferson Davis, Horace Greeley, Liberal Republican Party, Horatio Seymour, Tammany Hall, Samuel Tilden

*Ralph M. Goldman*

REFERENCES

Bigelow, John. 1908. *Letters and Literary Memorials of Samuel J. Tilden.* 2 vols. New York: Harper.

Schell, Francis. 1885. *Memoir of Augustus Schell.* New York: Privately printed.

## Phyllis S. Schlafly (1924– )

Antifeminist leader of the anti-ERA movement. Known for her role as organizer of "Stop ERA" and of the conservative Eagle Forum, New Right activist Phyllis Stewart Schlafly has helped redraw the boundaries of party and ideological allegiance regarding the Equal Rights Amendment. Her anti-ERA movement became the center of a new coalition of the radical right, religious activists, and the "Silent Majority," involving many previously apolitical people in the political process. Schlafly's campaign against ratification of the ERA actually did little to change general levels of support for the amendment among the population at large. However, her efforts brought about a striking reversal of party support and a polarization of party activists.

When the Equal Rights Amendment was introduced in 1923, its strongest opponents included labor unions, progressive organizations, and many prominent Democrats. These liberals believed that "equal rights" would dismantle special protective legislation for women and children, which, in the absence of a strong working-class movement, provided for more humane working conditions. In 1940 the ERA appeared in the Republican Party's platform, and the Democrats finally included it in 1944, despite strong labor opposition. Throughout the 1950s and early 1960s the Republican Party was pro-ERA; Democratic opinion was mixed. Labor opposition finally dissipated with the passage of Title VII of the Civil Rights Act of 1964, which prohibited job discrimination on the basis of sex and was interpreted to extend protections to men rather than deny them to women. The 1970s saw polarization among activists on the issue, as the focus of debate switched from abstract rights to concrete changes in the role of women. The general language of the amendment was associated with controversial issues such as abortion and the draft for women. Stop ERA worked to portray the amendment as antifamily in its consequences. By 1980 party lines had completely switched. The Republican

platform and presidential candidate opposed ERA; the Democrats supported it. By changing the terms of the debate and concentrating resistance in a relatively small number of states, Stop ERA successfully blocked the amendment. In June 1982 the ratification deadline ran out, with only 35 of the needed 38 states having ratified. Paradoxically, Schlafly's campaign to defeat the Equal Rights Amendment provides evidence of women's ability to master interest-group politics while attempting to create and preserve limitations on the extent of women's citizenship.

Phyllis Schlafly was born Phyllis MacAlpin Stewart in St. Louis. Her father was a sales engineer for Westinghouse, who lost his job in the Great Depression; her mother, who had two college degrees, took on the support of the family. Schlafly paid her way through college at Washington University, by working a 48-hour-a-week night shift in a munitions plant. She graduated Phi Beta Kappa and won a fellowship to Radcliffe, earning a master's degree in government at the age of 20. She worked in Washington, D.C., for a congressional research organization for one year and then returned to St. Louis where she was hired by Claude Bakewell, a young Republican lawyer, to run his successful campaign for the House of Representatives.

After marrying Fred Schlafly, she herself ran for Congress in 1952 (she was known as the "powder-puff candidate") and again in 1970. Her campaign slogan in her second House race ("A woman's place is in the House. The House of Representatives.") was nearly identical to that of the ardently feminist Bella Abzug. Schlafly lost both races. She has written nine books; the first was *A Choice Not an Echo* in support of Senator Barry Goldwater's presidential campaign, published in 1964 by a company that she established. Others include the antifeminist tract *The Power of the Positive Woman* and five books on national defense. *Kissinger on the Couch* was an 800-page denunciation of Richard Nixon's former Secretary of State and his policy of détente. After Schlafly was named to Ronald Reagan's Defense Policy Advisory Group during his first presidential campaign in 1980, she requested that he make her Secretary of Defense.

A John Birch Society member, Schlafly launched the Stop ERA movement, founded the Eagle Forum, began publishing the monthly Phyllis Schlafly report (circulation 356,000), wrote a syndicated column in 100 newspapers, and at 51, when her youngest child was 11, entered Washington University's Law School, where she graduated twenty-fourth out of 207. In addition to these interests, Schlafly has become known for her controversial stands on sexual harassment (not a problem because "men hardly ever ask sexual favors of women from whom the certain answer is no") and Social Security ("Well, it's a free country. But if people decide not to have children they should be forced to sign a piece of paper saying that they will forfeit Social Security benefits"). In speaking engagements, her favorite opening line remains, "I would like to thank my husband Fred for letting me come today."

See also: Bella Abzug, Eagle Forum, Barry Goldwater, Ronald Reagan

*Victoria A. A. Kamsler*

REFERENCES

Felsenthal, Carol. 1981. *The Sweetheart of the Silent Majority: The Biography of Phyllis Schlafly.* Garden City, NY: Doubleday.

Mansbridge, Jane. 1986. *Why We Lost the ERA.* Chicago: U. of Chicago Pr.

## John G. Schmitz (1930– )

Conservative Congressman and third-party presidential candidate. In 1968 the American Independent Party, led by Alabama governor George Wallace, was on the ballot in every state of the Union. In the race for President, Wallace's party garnered 42 electoral votes and over 9 million popular votes. In the next presidential election, John Schmitz became the American Independent Party's 1972 nominee following an attempt on the life of Governor Wallace. Schmitz, however, was unable to duplicate the success that Wallace achieved in 1968. He was on the ballot in fewer than 40 states and while he received over 1 million votes, much of his popular support came as a protest against Richard Nixon and George McGovern, the candidates fielded by the Republican and Democratic parties.

Before he began his public service, Schmitz taught history, philosophy, and political science at Santa Ana College in California. Schmitz also began his political career in California as a Republican, having been elected to serve in the California State Senate in 1964 and 1966. He went on to serve the U.S. House of Representatives in the Ninety-first and Ninety-second Congresses. Soon after his defeat in the 1972 primary for reelection to Congress, Schmitz was called upon to become a third-party candidate for the nation's highest office.

Schmitz became a member of the John Birch Society, an organization that, he believed, recognized and worked against the evil of communism and was dedicated to the preservation of American values. A main theme of his presidential campaign was additional assistance by the United States Government to this country's Communist enemies. Schmitz charged that the U.S. Government, primarily through trade, had been instrumental in fostering technical and military advancements by the Soviet Union.

See also: American Independent Party, George McGovern, Richard M. Nixon, George Wallace

*Reagan Robbins*

REFERENCES

Frady, Marshall. 1973. "The American Independent Party." In Arthur M. Schlesinger, Jr., ed. *History of U.S. Political Parties: The Politics of Change.* New York: Chelsea House.

Huckshorn, Robert J. 1984. *Political Parties in America.* Monterey, CA: Brooks/Cole.

Schmitz, John G. 1974. *Stranger in the Arena.* Santa Ana, CA: Rayline Printing.

Smallwood, Frank. 1983. *The Other Candidates: Third Parties in Presidential Elections.* Hanover, NH: U. Pr. of New England.

## Carl Schurz (1829–1906)

Foremost German-American politician of the nineteenth century, Carl Schurz was born in Liblar, Prussia. While a student leader at the University of Bonn during the 1848 revolution, he won fame by his dramatic rescue of his teacher, Gottfried Kinkel, from Spandau prison following the revolution's collapse. Unable to be safely active in European politics, Schurz came to America in 1852. His recent bride, Margarethe Meyer, provided financial security while he honed his journalistic skills, studied law, and analyzed American politics.

Attracted by its antislavery position, he became a Republican Party organizer; Schurz soon became a highly valued campaign orator and writer for German audiences, although some immigrants rejected his anticlericalism and his radical ideas. President Abraham Lincoln rewarded him for his support in 1861 with the Spanish ministry, but Schurz resigned in less than a year to remain closer to the struggle over slavery. Appointed a brigadier general and subsequently promoted to major general, he served courageously but without much success in the Civil War. President Andrew Johnson sent him to report on southern conditions after the war but suppressed his report, which called for Black suffrage, until Congress forced him to release it.

Keynote speaker at the Republican convention in 1868, Schurz built on his growing fame and strong ethnic support in Missouri to win election to the Senate in 1869. With suffrage for African-American males safely enacted, he went on to make civil service reform his cause. Disappointed with President Ulysses Grant, he helped found the Liberal Republican Party in 1872 and presided over its first convention. Despite Schurz's disloyalty, President Rutherford Hayes appointed him in 1877 as Secretary of the Interior, where he was successful in implementing a merit system. He also favored aid to Native Americans and conservation. Increasingly independent of regular party leaders, he moved to the sidelines, wrote for important political journals in several states, presided over the National and New York Civil Service Reform leagues, and led a final crusade against imperialism at the turn of the century.

*See also:* Anti-Imperialist League, Ulysses S. Grant, Rutherford B. Hayes, Andrew Johnson, Liberal Republican Party, Abraham Lincoln, Mugwumps

*Phyllis F. Field*

REFERENCES

Fuess, Claude M. 1932. *Carl Schurz, Reformer (1829–1906)*. New York: Dodd, Mead.

Trefousse, Hans L. 1982. *Carl Schurz, A Biography.* Knoxville: U. of Tennessee Pr.

## Hugh D. Scott, Jr. (1900– )

Republican U.S. Senate Minority Leader. Hugh Doggett Scott, Jr., was elected to the U.S. House of Representatives from Philadelphia in 1940 and 1942. After wartime naval service, he returned to the House in 1946. As a GOP urban liberal, he chaired the Republican National Committee during the Thomas Dewey campaign of 1948 and backed Dwight Eisenhower's nomination in 1952. In 1958 Scott went on to the Senate, a seat he barely held in the 1964 Lyndon Johnson Democratic landslide. During that year, he helped spearhead the unsuccessful "Stop Goldwater" movement in the GOP.

After Everett Dirksen died in 1969, Scott defeated Howard Baker of Tennessee for the post of Minority Leader. (Ironically, in light of his later reputation as a moderate, Baker was the conservatives' choice.) As Minority Leader, Scott defended President Richard Nixon's foreign and defense policies. On domestic issues, he sometimes broke ranks. He opposed the conservative Nixon civil rights policy and voted against the Supreme Court nomination of the putative reactionary Clement Haynsworth. Although Scott originally belittled Watergate allegations as

trivial, he worked in the summer of 1974 to persuade Nixon to resign.

In 1975 he announced that he would not seek another term. In 1976 Scott faced allegations about receiving improper campaign contributions from Gulf Oil, but the Senate Ethics Committee decided not to take action against him.

*See also:* Howard Baker, Thomas Dewey, Everett Dirksen, Dwight Eisenhower, Barry Goldwater, Minority Party Leadership in Congress, Richard M. Nixon, Republican National Committee, Watergate

*John J. Pitney, Jr.*

REFERENCES

Bailey, Christopher J. 1988. *The Republican Party in the U.S. Senate 1974–1984: Party Change and Institutional Development.* New York: St. Martin's.

Barone, Michael. 1990. *Our Country: The Shaping of America from Roosevelt to Reagan.* New York: Free Press.

Woodward, Bob, and Carl Bernstein. 1976. *The Final Days.* New York: Avon.

## Winfield Scott (1786–1866)

Whig candidate for President in 1852. His candidacy marking another Whig attempt to win the presidency by nominating a general, Winfield Scott had had as illustrious a military career as his Whig predecessor, Zachary Taylor, and better civil qualifications. A war hero since 1812 and a Whig Party veteran, Scott had been seen as a presidential possibility for over a decade. In 1852, however, the Whig Party proved to be too sharply divided and Scott too inept a candidate. The Democrats and Franklin Pierce triumphed.

At the 1852 Whig convention, southern slave owners clashed with the northerners who had opposed the elaborate Compromise of 1850. The proslavery forces won the platform fight, forcing an endorsement of states' rights and of the Compromise. But on the fifty-third ballot, the antislavery forces won the nominating brawl. In an unprecedented telegram to the convention, the antislavery Scott knuckled under to accept the convention's proslavery terms. Other northern Whigs supported the candidate while "spitting upon the platform," in Horace Greeley's memorable phrase.

During the campaign, the egotistical Scott—known as "Old Fuss and Feathers"—could not maintain the candidate's then-traditional silence. Using an inspection of a military hospital site in Kentucky as an excuse, the general stumped. Even many Whigs winced at his transparent appeals: Scott, one friend admitted, "acts like a god and talks like a fool." Guffawing

Democrats chided Scott for demeaning both his rank and the presidency. The Democrat Franklin Pierce's decisive victory illustrated the advisability of silence as well as the Whigs' weakened condition. After his defeat, the Virginia-born Scott continued serving his country, remaining loyal to the Union during the Civil War.

*See also:* Franklin Pierce, Slavery, Zachary Taylor

*Gil Troy*

REFERENCES

Elliott, Charles Winslow. 1937. *Winfield Scott: The Soldier and the Man.* New York: Macmillan.

Potter, David M. 1976. "The Impending Crisis, 1848–1861." In Henry Steele Commager and Richard B. Morris, eds. *The New American Nation Series.* New York: Harper & Row.

Randall, J. G., and David Donald. 1969. *The Civil War and Reconstruction.* Rev. ed. Boston: Little, Brown.

Smith, Arthur D. Howden. 1937. *Old Fuss and Feathers: The Life and Exploits of Lt.-General Winfield Scott.* New York: Greystone.

## William W. Scranton (1917– )

Republican Pennsylvania governor and presidential contender. William Warren Scranton was the Republican governor of Pennsylvania from 1963 to 1967. The Scranton family has a long and distinguished history in Pennsylvania, particularly in the northeastern region where a city bears the family name. Following service in World War II, Scranton graduated from Yale University. In 1959 he went to work as a press assistant for Secretary of State John Foster Dulles. In 1960 Scranton ran for Congress, and in a closely contested election, he defeated the Tenth District's popular Democratic incumbent. A liberal on civil rights, a conservative on fiscal policy, and an internationalist on foreign affairs, Scranton was very much an independent Republican during his one term in the House.

In 1962, when he was approached by the Pennsylvania's Republican leaders about running for governor, he initially declined. But when President Dwight Eisenhower repeated the request, and a divisive primary battle loomed between Senator Hugh Scott and Judge Robert Woodside, Scranton consented. He defeated Democrat Richardson Dilworth, the mayor of Philadelphia and the endorsed candidate of incumbent governor David L. Lawrence, by some 400,000 votes. In June 1964 Nelson Rockefeller's decision to drop out of the race for the Republican presidential nomination left liberal and moderate Republicans without a candidate. After some hesitation, Scranton entered the contest but lost to conservative Barry Goldwater 883 to 214 votes on the first ballot at the GOP convention in July. Since leaving elected office, Scranton has served on numerous appointed commissions, one such being the President's Commission on Campus Unrest.

*See also:* Richardson Dilworth, Dwight D. Eisenhower, Barry Goldwater, David L. Lawrence, Nelson Rockefeller, Hugh Scott

*Thomas J. Baldino*

REFERENCES

Alderfer, Harrold F. 1976. *William Warren Scranton: Pennsylvania Governor, 1963–1967.* Mechanicsburg, PA: Local Government Service.

Wolf, George D. 1981. *William Warren Scranton: Pennsylvania Statesman.* University Park: Pennsylvania State U. Pr.

## Secession

From the ratification of the Constitution until the Civil War, many Americans accepted the theoretical right of a state to secede from the Union on constitutional or revolutionary grounds. The country, however, achieved little consensus on what grievances might in fact justify actual use of this right. It was potentially so disruptive of normal political life that until the escalation of sectional conflict over slavery, secession usually remained a subject for theoretical discussion and Fourth of July oratory rather than practical politics. The rise of political parties concerned with the formation of national coalitions to win control of the federal government and the presidency normally tended to discourage serious consideration of secession, as the concept by its nature was destructive of such coalitions and of party unity. In a competitive two-party system the identification of a party with secessionist tendencies gave its rival the opportunity to make charges of disruptive particularism and lack of patriotism. When it was possible, most party leaders were ready to relegate secession to theoretical claims like those of the Virginia and Kentucky resolutions of 1798 and 1799 and its serious advocacy to political outcasts like Aaron Burr. From time to time, however, the issue did intrude upon major party politics.

The Democratic-Republican Party—with a decided southern orientation and a firm control of the federal government from 1800 to 1820—was able to neutralize earlier secessionist tendencies among some of its followers. The Federalists, on the other hand, paid a high price for the activities of a small but highly visible secessionist minority. In the face of repeated electoral defeat and growing resentment with the War of 1812, some New England Federalists such as Timothy Pickering advocated drastic revisions of the Constitution and, failing this, separation from the Union. Party moderates were able to defeat the extremists at the Hartford Convention of 1814 and thus reject secessionist resolutions. The Federalist Party was, however, stigmatized as secessionist and disloyal by their Republican rivals. The Federalist's were in serious decline in any case, but the largely underserved secessionist label precluded a revival and practically insured their final demise.

In 1820 the crisis over admission of Missouri as a slave state for the first time established a close connection between southern defense of slavery from northern interference and threats of southern secession. The Missouri Compromise was to a large extent a response to the danger that these threats raised not only to Democratic-Republican Party organizations but to the Union itself. The development of the "second party system" of Whigs and Democrats as highly competitive national parties in the 1830s tended to remove secession temporarily from the center of active political discussion. Secession was relegated to the activities of relatively small minorities in both the North and South, vocal regionalists who distrusted the desire or ability of the national parties to uphold their particular sectional interests.

John Calhoun has often been called "the father of secession," but while he became profoundly hostile to national parties and desired new constitutional arrangement to guarantee southern rights he was also devoted to his own version of the Union. Calhoun's sectional, antiparty activities may well have contributed to the ultimate victory of secession but such was not his intent. In the North, some abolitionists not only saw little chance of converting either major party but also became convinced that the federal government and the Constitution were so tied to the "slave power" that they advocated "no union with slaveholders" and the secession of the free states. Neither of the abolitionist parties, the Free Soil Party and Liberty Party, adopted this secessionist position, but these party politicians and the whole abolitionist movement were severely damaged by charges of disloyalty and incitement to civil war.

In the 1840s the explosive issue of the expansion of slavery or its restriction in the territories seemed to many southerners to involve both their material interests and honor and encouraged them to reexamine secession as an ultimate weapon in sectional conflict. Southern Whigs and Democrats were faced with the possibility of a regional "southern rights" party if they appeared to be insufficiently militant in defense of slavery. The result was that southern leaders like Jefferson Davis and Robert Toombs began to stress the possibility of secession in order to force concessions from the North in general and from the northern wing of their own party in particular. Increasingly they tended to designate certain events or legislation as so unacceptable that they would have to consider secession. Enactment of the Wilmot Proviso, refusal to admit a new slave state, weakening of the Fugitive Slave Law, or interference with the domestic slave trade were some of these test cases. Few of these party leaders were as yet really anti-unionists, and the degree to which their threats were sincere statements of position, political rhetoric, or calculated sectional brinkmanship is difficult to determine; until 1860 the threats were never put to the test. The immediate result was a series of compromises that won at least token victories for southern rights and saved the national parties from inroads by real southern "fire-eaters" or northern Free Soilers. However, serious danger lay in the fact that secessionist rhetoric seemed to get results and became a part of normal southern politics. The North saw growing resentment against an aggressive "slave power" and a feeling that as secession in the South never seemed to become a reality, it was a bluff designed to intimidate northern politicians and voters. The Republican Party emerged in part on the supposition that the North needed a party to stand up to the "slave power" and to call the secessionists' bluff.

The major sectional crisis from 1848 to 1850 over lands acquired from Mexico was temporarily resolved by the famous Compromise of 1850, but the American polity saw the first appearance of a significant number of overt secessionists who genuinely rejected both the national political parties and the Union. Men like William Yancey of Alabama and Richard Barnwell Rett of South Carolina now promoted southern secession not as a bargaining device but out of a desire to block compromise and create a separate southern republic. Their rejection of the Compromise of 1850 temporarily disrupted party organizations in the South where Southern Rights tickets battled Constitutional

Union parties pledged to support the Compromise. The Constitutional Unionist strength came primarily from Whigs, but it also drew many votes from former Democrats. Their victory in the crucial states of Georgia and Mississippi insured compromise and the rejection of secession. Southern voters then largely returned to their former Whig or Democratic loyalties, but they returned with a greater recognition of secession as an acceptable reality of politics and more qualifications to their commitment to the Union.

After 1850 most southern politicians, while not favoring leaving the Union, tended to evaluate that more according to what conditions might make secession desirable or even inevitable. Southern rights advocates assumed a much larger role in the Democratic Party while Whigs and Constitutional Unionists tended to show their commitment to the South by declarations and platforms that listed those numerous contingencies that would force these southerners to reconsider their support of the Union. The bitter dispute over Kansas/Nebraska and the rise of the sectional, free-soil Republican Party confronted the South with the problem of a major party in which it would have little membership and no leverage. Fearing the loss of control over the federal government, many southern spokesmen responded with a new criterion that would activate the fuse of secession in the election of a Republican President. Ominously this resolution transferred the decision from the compromise-oriented world of professional politicians in Congress to the less manageable one of the electorate.

In the 1856 presidential election, talk of secession in the event of a Republican victory was a significant factor in James Buchanan's success in drawing enough votes in the free states to secure the presidency. In 1860 the crumbling party system produced four presidential candidates, none of whom ran as a secessionist. The Republicans, partly as a matter of tactics and partly out of conviction, tended to play down the danger of secession as a mere bluff created to defeat Abraham Lincoln. Some southern Democrats had deliberately split their party in the hope that this rift would lead to a secession crisis, but John Breckinridge, the southern Democratic candidate, ran as the only man who could satisfy the South within the Union. Only the northern Democrat Stephen Douglas campaigned as if he recognized secession as a real threat. After the Republicans won state elections in October, Douglas toured the South in a desperate effort to convince southerners that secession was treason and the North that the threat was real and immediate. The disoriented politicians and shattered party system were unable to find another compromise or even to effectively warn the voters that a real secession crisis had come.

Lincoln's election set in motion a secessionist movement that created a new, improvised political alignment in the southern states where Immediate Secessionists competed with Cooperationists for delegates to state conventions. A determined and articulate Immediate Secessionist Party was able to take seven states out of the Union in a little over ten weeks from November 1860 to February 1861. In spite of the fact that they constituted a significant minority even in the lower South and a probable majority in the upper South, the Cooperationists appeared divided and unsure of themselves. The Immediate Secessionists owed much of their success to the fact that in most southern states they were in firm control of the dominant Democratic Party organizations and with them the state governments. Voting on secession did not always follow former party lines, but Cooperationists drew the bulk of their support from former Whigs and Constitutional Unionists who had a much weaker organization. In an age when party loyalty was deep and enduring, the Immediate Secessionist base among Democrats was probably decisive. The Cooperationists polled a significant vote, but few of them were unconditional Union men; some were secessionists who wished to wait until all the southern states could act together rather than individually. Others desired a last effort to obtain major concessions from the North, while many were conservatives who distrusted the fire eaters and populist Democrats who often led the Immediate Secession movement.

The success of the Temporary Cooperationists in the upper South and their sizable vote even in the Gulf States misled many northerners (including Abraham Lincoln) into the hope and belief that secession was a temporary panic and that soon a silent Union majority would reassert itself. Lincoln, as the head of a party that had always denounced secessionist threats as a form of a political blackmail, built his policy on avoiding both concessions and coercion and waiting for the rise of a rival southern unionism. This continued misunderstanding of secession by northern leaders through the winter of 1860–1861 prevented any effective response.

The precarious loyalty of Constitutional Unionists and Conditional Unionists rested on the hope of concessions that the Republicans would never make and on the avoidance of any outbreak of violence. When Confederate guns opened fire on Fort Sumter, Cooperation and Conditional Unionism ceased to be a political force and four more states left the Union.

Secession completed and made permanent the breakdown of the "second party system" of two major parties with nearly equal strength in both North and South. In the 1850s this system had been clearly in a state of rapid change owing to tensions aroused by sectional and ethnic rivalries, but even as late as the 1860 election the outcome of this process was uncertain. The actual secession of 13 states then finally precluded a number of alternatives still possible before the winter of 1860–1861. The Republicans were denied the possibility of evolving into a more moderate, less purely sectional party as a number of their leaders like Francis Blair, William Seward, and Thurlow Weed had expected. The divided Democrats lost the chance to unite their party in opposition and to stage a decisive comeback in the 1864 election. The Constitutional Unionists were denied the possible role of a conservative party with support in both sections.

The election of 1860 gave the Republicans the presidency, but their opponents had a majority of about 10 votes in the Senate and 21 in the House. Under normal conditions the Republicans had little hope of organizing the new Congress or of enacting their program. Secession drastically changed this situation as the long-dominant southern wing of the Democratic Party went South and left a demoralized remnant of only 43 northern Democratic Congressmen and ten Senators. The Republicans now controlled all committees and had substantial majorities to pass not only their war and antislavery measures but also their extensive economic program of railway, tariff, and currency legislation that some historians have called a second American revolution. The unprecedented opportunity that secession gave the Republicans enabled a new and unstable coalition to consolidate itself as the "party of the Union," which much of the northern electorate for generations regarded as the grand embodiment of patriotism and economic growth. A number of prominent Democrats like William Stanton, Benjamin Butler, and John Logan became Unionists in 1861 and then Radical Republicans. Secession

may not have created the Republican Party, but secession made it the dominant party in America for 50 years.

That same secession brought disaster to the Democratic Party. The fact that the party survived and even remained highly competitive in about half the northern states during the war years indicates the commitment of nineteenth-century voters to traditional party loyalties. It was, however, only in 1874 that the Democrats again achieved a majority in the House of Representatives and ten years after that before they could elect even a minority President.

The party system created by secession and Civil War was, unlike its predecessor, highly sectional: the Republicans dominated much of the North and West while the Democrats were based on the solid South and on certain ethnic groups in northern cities. Secession was dead as a viable theory and as a political alternative after 1865, but its impact on the party system continued for at least a century.

*See also:* Abolition Movement, John Breckinridge, James Buchanan, Benjamin Butler, John C. Calhoun, Constitutional Union Party, Jefferson Davis, Stephen A. Douglas, Elections of 1856 and 1860, Free Soil Party, Liberty Party, Abraham Lincoln, John Logan, Missouri Compromise, Slavery, Robert Toombs, Thurlow Weed

*Harold B. Raymond*

REFERENCES

Cooper, William. 1978. *The South and the Politics of Slavery, 1828–1856.* Baton Rouge: Louisiana State U. Pr.

————. 1983. *Liberty and Slavery: Southern Politics to 1860.* New York: Knopf.

Fahrenbacher, Don E. 1980. *The South and Three Sectional Crises.* Baton Rouge: Louisiana State U. Pr.

Klappner, Paul. 1979. *The Third Electoral System, 1853–1892.* Chapel Hill: U. of North Carolina Pr.

Nevins, Alan. 1947. *The Ordeal of the Union.* New York: Scribner's.

Nichols, Ray. 1947. *The Disruption of the American Democracy.* New York: Macmillan.

Potter, David. 1976. *The Impending Crisis 1848–1861.* New York: Yale U. Pr.

Sibley, Joel. 1977. *A Respectable Minority: The Democratic Party in the Civil War Era.* New York: Norton.

## Second Bank of the United States

Against the advice of President James Madison, a divided Republican Party allowed the Bank of the United States, charged with guaranteeing a sound currency and promoting commerce, to close. During the War of 1812, however, public finance became extremely disorganized, and state banks sometimes suspended specie payments. A chastened Congress then chartered the Second Bank of the United States in 1816. And the Supreme Court subsequently upheld its constitutionality under the necessary and proper clause (*McCulloch v. Maryland*, 1819).

During Andrew Jackson's presidency, the bank became a major issue. In 1829 Jackson raised the question of its constitutionality, claiming that the bank had not fostered a sound or uniform currency, a charge that was simply untrue. The bank's charter was scheduled to expire in 1836, and Jackson did not want it renewed. Hoping to save the bank and embarrass Jackson during an election, bank president Nicholas Biddle requested renewal in 1832. When the bill passed Congress, Jackson vetoed it. His veto message used faulty economics and claimed that the bank fulfilled no necessary function, gave special privileges to rich stockholders, endangered democracy, and invaded states' rights.

The "Bank War" proved to be the primary issue of the 1832 campaign. To oppose Jackson's antibank Democrats, the National Republicans chose Henry Clay, who believed that the public favored recharter. Clay failed to understand that the bank, by regulating money markets and preventing inflation of state bank notes, had made enemies among debtors, businessmen, and some state bankers; Jackson proceeded to carry 16 of 24 states. After his reelection, Jackson withdrew federal deposits from the bank, and its charter expired without renewal in 1836.

*See also:* Henry Clay, First Bank of the United States, Andrew Jackson, James Madison

*Sue Patrick*

REFERENCES

Curtis, James C. 1976. *Andrew Jackson and the Search for Vindication.* Boston: Little, Brown.

Govan, Thomas P. 1959. *Nicholas Biddle: Nationalist and Public Banker, 1786–1844.* Chicago: U. of Chicago Pr.

Hammond, Bray. 1957. *Banks and Politics in America from the Revolution to the Civil War.* Princeton: Princeton U. Pr.

Latner, Richard B. 1979. *The Presidency of Andrew Jackson: White House Politics, 1829–1837.* Athens: U. of Georgia Pr.

McFaul, John M. 1972. *The Politics of Jacksonian Finance.* Ithaca: Cornell U. Pr.

Pessen, Edward. 1969. *Jacksonian America: Society, Personality, and Politics.* Homewood, IL: Dorsey.

Remini, Robert V. 1967. *Andrew Jackson and the Bank War.* New York: Norton.

## Theodore Sedgwick (1746–1813)

Early Federalist leader in the U.S. House of Representatives. A wealthy member of the Massachusetts gentry who was related by marriage to most of the important families in New England, Theodore Sedgwick believed that his social standing obligated him to participate in public affairs—a principle that dominated the course of his adult life. He was active in Whig politics before the Revolution but was initially reluctant to support independence. Most attribute his caution to his lifelong fear of democracy and disorder, conditions he believed would undermine the established social order. Nevertheless, he served in the Massachusetts legislature for most of the 1780s.

Sedgwick was an early supporter of the federal Constitution and was a delegate to the Massachusetts ratifying convention. He was elected to the first four U.S. Congresses and aligned himself with the faction that would become the Federalists. Sedgwick served briefly in the Senate and returned to the House in 1799 to serve as Speaker. His election as Speaker was a bit of a surprise because of his imperious and partisan nature. By then the Federalists had split into two bigger factions—those who supported President John Adams and those who supported Alexander Hamilton. Sedgwick was one of the few men who was trusted by both wings of the party. Thus, when the Republicans tried to exploit the dissension among the Federalists in order to elect their own Speaker, the Federalists united (albeit temporarily) to choose Sedgwick.

He left Congress after the Republican electoral triumph of Thomas Jefferson in 1800. Like many of the "old federalists" he withdrew in horror from national politics and focused on salvaging Federalist principles at the local level. From 1802 until his death he served on the Massachusetts Supreme Court.

*See also:* John Adams, Federalists, Alexander Hamilton, Thomas Jefferson, Speaker of the House

*Glenn A. Phelps*

REFERENCES

Fischer, David Hackett. 1965. *The Revolution of American Conservatism: The Federalist Party in the Era of Jeffersonian Democracy.* New York: Harper & Row.

Furlong, Patrick J. 1967. "John Rutledge, Jr., and the Election of a Speaker of the House in 1799." 24 *William and Mary Quarterly* 432.

Welch, Richard E. 1965. *Theodore Sedgwick, Federalist: A Political Portrait.* Middletown, CT: Wesleyan U. Pr.

# Pete Seeger (1919– )

Political folksinger. As a songwriter and performer, Pete Seeger has contributed enormously to the music of social movement politics in America. Pete Seeger's youth was spent in a family devoted to academe, radical politics, and government service. He attended Harvard University for two years (1936–1938) and then sought a career in journalism before turning to folk music.

In the early 1940s, Seeger helped to form the Almanac Singers. Returning from Army service in World War II, he headed People's Songs, Incorporated, and published *People's Songs Bulletin*. In 1948 the increasingly left-oriented Seeger campaigned for Henry Wallace. Later he was to become a member of the Weavers, a singing group whose left-leaning politics did not preclude massive commercial success (e.g., "Tzena, Tzena," and "Goodnight Irene") in the early 1950s (nor did popularity preclude the Weavers from being blacklisted by anti-Communist activists). Seeger's own prominence and his radical, left-wing political past led eventually to his being subpoenaed in 1955 by the House Committee on Un-American Activities (HUAC). He subsequently was cited for contempt of Congress for failing to respond to HUAC's satisfaction. Although sentenced to prison in 1961, Seeger later saw his conviction overturned.

The 1960s found Seeger's musical talents (adapting, for example, "We Shall Overcome") dedicated initially to aiding the civil rights movement. Later his performances and music ("Waist Deep in the Big Muddy," for instance) were mobilized toward ending American involvement in the Vietnam War. In the late 1960s Seeger turned his energies toward environmental concerns. Most notable in this respect was his effort to construct the sloop *Clearwater* as a platform for promoting a cleaner Hudson River.

Seeger's musical roots are American. His vision, however, was to use music as a means for social change and thus harmony within and across boundaries of class, race, or nationality. In "Where Have All the Flowers Gone?" the lyric asks, "Oh, when will they ever learn?" As a modern troubadour, Pete Seeger worked to educate and thereby to make the world a kinder and gentler place.

*See also:* Vietnam War as a Political Issue, Henry Wallace

*Charles Longley*

REFERENCES

Dunaway, David King. 1981. *How Can I Keep from Singing: Pete Seeger*. New York: McGraw-Hill.

## Senate Democratic Policy Committee

Formed in 1947, the Senate Democratic Policy Committee and its Republican counterpart were envisioned by their creators as agents for transforming the broad goals of their respective parties into specific legislative proposals. In practice, however, the committee has developed quite differently.

The Democratic Policy Committee is chaired by the floor leader, who also chairs the Democratic Party's caucus and the Steering Committee, which makes committee assignments. The whip and caucus secretary serve as ex officio members, as does the President *pro tempore* of the Senate when the Democrats hold a majority. The floor leader appoints the six other committee members, who continue to serve as long as they remain in the Senate. The committee staff assists the chairman in carrying out leadership responsibilities.

Lyndon B. Johnson was the first Democratic floor leader to exploit the resources of the Policy Committee. From 1953 to 1961, he made it an extension of his own powerful leadership style. Under Mike Mansfield (1961–1977), the committee debated policy issues and made recommendations on party positions and the scheduling of floor proceedings. In recent years the Policy Committee has played a less influential role. Robert Byrd, Democratic floor leader from 1977 to 1988, did not rely on the committee for assistance in scheduling while the Democrats were the majority party. Byrd allowed two vacancies on the committee to remain open, one from 1983 and the other from 1985, until his resignation. Byrd's successor, George Mitchell of Maine, has begun a process of reinvigorating the Policy Committee using collegial negotiations as a means of cementing his support within the party.

*See also:* Robert C. Byrd, Lyndon B. Johnson, Mike Mansfield, George Mitchell, Senate Republican Policy Committee

*John A. Clark*

REFERENCES

Bone, Hugh A. 1958. *Party Committees and National Politics*. Seattle: U. of Washington Pr.

## Senate Republican Policy Committee

The Senate Republican Policy Committee was created by statute in 1946 and organized in

1947. The Senate version of the Legislative Reorganization Bill of 1946 recommended policy committees for each party in both houses of Congress. The House deleted these provisions, but the Senate allotted funds for its own policy committees in a supplemental appropriations bill.

The chairman of the Republican Policy Committee is elected by the GOP Conference, composed of all Republican Senators. In the early days of the committee, Chairman Robert A. Taft acted as the principal spokesman for the Republicans on domestic issues. Other chairmen have proved to be less influential. The first Policy Committee had nine members; since then it has grown to include nearly half of the Republican delegation on several occasions, with 22 members since 1983. The actual size of the committee is determined by the Republican Conference; the conference selects some members of the conference, while others qualify because of elected positions in the leadership.

Because of its size, the Policy Committee functions best as a communications vehicle for the leadership. When the GOP is in the minority, the committee recommends policy positions to the floor leader and to the conference. Unlike its Democratic counterpart, the Republican Policy Committee has not scheduled bills for floor action when the party controls the Senate; that duty is handled by the floor leader.

*See also:* Senate Democratic Policy Committee, Robert A. Taft

*John A. Clark*

REFERENCES

Bone, Hugh A. 1958. *Party Committees and National Politics.* Seattle: U. of Washington Pr.

## Seneca Falls Convention

Representing the formal beginning of an organized movement for women's rights in the United States, the Seneca Falls Convention was held in July 1848. The Declaration of Sentiments and Resolutions growing out of the Convention provides one of the most important articulations of the goals of the early American feminist movement.

The meeting was held in Wesleyan Chapel in Seneca Falls, New York, then the home of Elizabeth Cady Stanton. It was attended by approximately 300 people, including 40 men. Lucretia Mott and Elizabeth Cady Stanton were the chief organizers of the Convention, and both women played a major role in drafting the resolutions debated and passed at the meeting. Stanton and Mott had attended the 1840 World Anti-Slavery Convention held in London at which women were denied seats as delegates. At the London meeting, Stanton and Mott spent considerable time discussing the problems facing women in America.

The major document emerging from the Seneca Falls Convention was its Declaration of Sentiments and Resolutions. This set of resolutions was intentionally patterned after the Declaration of Independence, insisting that "We hold these truths to be self-evident: that all men and women are created equal." Much of the Declaration of Sentiments is a litany of the "repeated injuries and usurpations on the part of man toward woman, having in direct object the establishment of an absolute tyranny over her." While the opening remarks on the purpose of the Convention were made by Lucretia Mott, John Mott, her husband, was made chair of the meeting. Other men such as Frederick Douglass, who spoke in favor of giving women the franchise, participated in the Conference. After considerable discussion, delegates decided that men would be allowed to sign the Declaration.

These resolutions were discussed and adopted without undue controversy except for the one concerning universal women's suffrage. This resolution demanding the franchise for women was viewed by many of both genders, both at Seneca Falls and in subsequent meetings, as being too radical. Other resolutions dealt with general civil and social rights of women such as education and legal status. The religious rights of women were also addressed in a resolution attacking male-oriented interpretations of the scriptures.

Along with the passage of the Married Women's Property Act of New York in the same year, the Seneca Falls Convention served to galvanize the early feminist movement. Despite the negative publicity generated by the Seneca Falls meetings, other conventions were held over the next several years in New York, Ohio, Massachusetts, and Pennsylvania.

*See also:* Frederick Douglass, Elizabeth Cady Stanton, Suffrage

*Susan L. Roberts*

REFERENCES

Gurko, Miriam. 1974. *The Ladies of Seneca Falls: The Birth of the Woman's Rights Movement.* New York: Macmillan.

Schneir, Miriam, ed. 1969. *Woman's Rights Conventions: Seneca Falls & Rochester, 1848.* New York: Arno and The New York Times.

———. 1972. *Feminism: The Essential Historical Writings*. New York: Random House.

## Seniority System

A mechanism in the U.S. Congress for selecting committee leaders, the seniority system's sole criterion for selection was length of service, or seniority, on a particular committee. Members of the majority party with the most seniority became chairmen, while their counterparts in the minority party became ranking members.

In the Senate, the seniority system emerged in the Democratic Party before the Civil War, but the scarcity of elected party members between 1861 and 1879 prevented seniority from becoming a hard and fast rule of selection during that period. Notwithstanding, violations in seniority have occurred only occasionally in either party since 1879. The decentralized nature of the Senate created a demand for an automatic decision rule on committee leadership. Although Senate Republicans formally abandoned a mandatory seniority system in 1973, the Democrats following in 1975, seniority remains the most important factor in the selection process.

The seniority system arrived in the House of Representatives around 1920. Before its inception, appointments were left to the discretion of the Speaker. Although seniority did have some impact, selection of committee chairs was more likely to reflect either the interests of a cohesive party or of the Speaker's personal power. Membership turnover in the House was so great that seniority was not a useful measure of specialization or merit. As congressional career patterns changed, members began to demand rewards for extended lengths of service. The Speaker's arbitrary powers of appointment, for example, were removed during the "overthrow" of Joseph Cannon of Illinois in 1910 and 1911. Within a few years the seniority system was firmly entrenched in the House.

Much of the control over the legislative process that had formerly belonged to the Speaker was transferred to committee chairs following the revolt against Cannon. But while the Speaker was elected by the entire membership, chairs of committees were chosen automatically according to seniority. Though automatic, the seniority system was far from neutral. It favored members from electorally "safe," uncompetitive districts, often conservative southern Democrats. These conservative chairmen, with the support of Republicans and other southern Democrats, were able to block civil rights and liberal social legislation for many years.

By the 1960s, the composition of the Democratic Party in the House had changed. Younger, more liberal members made up a larger portion of the party, but southerners continued to retain control of the most powerful committees. Clearly, an unresponsive seniority system was lagging behind changes in the makeup of the congressional Democrats. Junior members became increasingly frustrated as their legislative initiatives were stifled in committee.

In 1971 House Democrats and Republicans officially ended the seniority system. They notified their respective committees on committees that seniority need not be the only criterion allowed in the nomination of committee chairs and ranking members; subsequently, all nominations were subject to approval by the entire party memberships. These and other reforms in the early 1970s were designed to reduce the power of committee chairmen, and indeed, three chairmen in 1975 and one in 1985 were removed from their posts by the Democratic Caucus.

The seniority system originally developed when Congress needed a politically noncontroversial procedure for selecting committee leaders. Since its demise, some committee chairmen have been forced to modify their behavior at the risk of losing their positions. Seniority is no longer the sole factor involved in the selection process, even though it continues to be observed in most cases.

*See also:* Joseph G. Cannon

*John A. Clark*

REFERENCES

Abram, Michael, and Joseph Cooper. 1968. "The Rise of Seniority in the House of Representatives." 1 *Polity* 52.

Hinckley, Barbara. 1971. *The Seniority System in Congress*. Bloomington: Indiana U. Pr.

Polsby, Nelson W., Miriam Gallaher, and Barry Spencer Rundquist. 1969. "The Growth of the Seniority System in the U.S. House of Representatives." 63 *American Political Science Review* 787.

## William H. Seward (1801–1872)

Adviser to Presidents Abraham Lincoln and Andrew Johnson. At the 1860 Republican National Convention presidential candidate William Henry Seward won a plurality of delegate votes on the first two ballots. Owing to the opposition of a coalition of antireformers (mostly former Know-Nothings and ex-Jacksonian Democrats), however, Seward lost the nomination to Abraham Lincoln, who became President the following March. As Secretary of State and closest official adviser in both the Lincoln and Andrew Johnson administrations, Seward maneuvered skillfully and successfully to keep foreign nations from intervening in the Civil War on the side of the southern Confederacy, persuaded the French peaceably to evacuate Mexico in 1867, and negotiated more international agreements than had all of his predecessors combined, among them the treaty purchasing Alaska. He also laid the groundwork for the celebrated Alabama Claims arbitration settlement, a resolution that helped to change traditional Anglo-American enmity to rapprochement.

A graduate of Union College, Seward was the first Whig governor of New York (1839–1843). Notable for his educational and prison reform measures, he was also a leading advocate of peaceful manifest destiny and a national spokesman for universal human rights. Appealing (as had the Founding Fathers) to a "higher law" than the man-made enactments that protected human oppression, Seward broke with the Whig Party majority over the Compromise of 1850 and as a U.S. Senator led the reformers who opposed the further extension of slavery into the western territories during the decade of the 1850s. His purpose was to prevent the "irrepressible conflict" from erupting into civil war, while at the same time insisting on an end to the aggrandizements of the slaveholders.

In retirement after 1869, Seward made a notable round-the-world tour. Following an abortive attempt to complete his memoirs, and still suffering from the effects of an assassin's vicious attack on the night Lincoln was killed, Seward died at his home in Auburn, New York.

*See also:* Andrew Johnson, Know-Nothings, Abraham Lincoln

*Norman B. Ferris*

REFERENCES

Baker, George E. 1884. *The Works of William H. Seward.* Boston: Houghton Mifflin.

Bancroft, Frederic. 1900. *The Life of William H. Seward.* New York: Harper.

Ferris, Norman B. 1985. "William H. Seward and the Faith of a Nation." In *Traditions and Values: American Diplomacy, 1790–1865.* Lanham, MD: U. Pr. of America.

Lothrop, Thornton K. 1899. *William Henry Seward.* Boston: Houghton Mifflin.

Seward, Frederick W. 1877. *Autobiography of William H. Seward, from 1801 to 1834, with a Memoir of His Life and Selections from His Letters from 1831 to 1846.* New York: D. Appleton.

———. 1891. *Seward at Washington, as Senator and Secretary of State.* New York: Derby and Miller.

Van Deusen, Glyndon. 1967. *William Henry Seward.* New York: Oxford U. Pr.

## Horatio Seymour (1810–1886)

Unsuccessful Democratic presidential candidate in 1868. Horatio Seymour was born in Pompey Hill, New York, to the family of a prosperous businessman and Democratic Party politician. Seymour received his formal education at local academies in New York and Connecticut. Although admitted to the bar in 1832, he never opened a law practice.

Instead, Seymour embarked on a political career, holding the offices of military secretary to New York's Governor William L. Marcy (1833–1839), Democratic state assemblyman (1841, 1844–1845), mayor of Utica (1842), and finally governor of the state (1852, 1862–1864). Controversy over his veto of a prohibition law contributed heavily to his failure at reelection as governor in 1855. During Seymour's second term, he warmly supported the Union effort in the Civil War but opposed Abraham Lincoln's policies of emancipation of the slaves and military conscription. Despite Seymour's firm handling of draft riots in New York City, he narrowly lost his bid for reelection in 1864 as a result of the heavily Republican vote cast by the state's soldiers.

In 1868 Seymour presided over a deeply divided Democratic National Convention whose delegates selected the genuinely reluctant New Yorker to head their ticket. A greenback ("cheap Money") platform and a running mate, Francis Blair of Missouri, who had encouraged southern resistance to Reconstruction, seriously handicapped the Democrats' chances among moderate northern voters. The Republicans also had the advantage of Ulysses S. Grant's popularity as a military hero and their party's control over most southern state governments. Although defeated handily in the electoral college by Grant, Seymour received 47 percent of the popular vote nationwide and a majority in the supposedly Republican South. Seymour thereafter took up the life of a gentleman farmer and shunned public office.

*See also:* Election of 1868, Ulysses S. Grant, Abraham Lincoln, William L. Marcy, Prohibition

*John R. McKivigan*

REFERENCES

Mitchell, Stewart. 1938. *Horatio Seymour of New York.* Cambridge: Harvard U. Pr.

Silbey, Joel H. 1977. *A Respectable Minority: The Democratic Party in the Civil War Era, 1860–1868.* New York: Norton.

Wall, Alexander J. 1929. *A Sketch of the Life of Horatio Seymour, 1810–1866.* New York: New York Historical Society.

## Milton J. Shapp (1912– )

Self-made millionaire turned political reformer. Milton Jerrold Shapp was governor of Pennsylvania from 1971 to 1978. During the 1950s, Shapp founded Jerrold Electronics and made it a leader in the field of cable television technology. But he also was interested in politics, and in 1960 Shapp supported John F. Kennedy as a delegate from Pennsylvania to the Democratic convention. Following Kennedy's election, Shapp served as a consultant to a number of agencies, including the Peace Corps and the Department of Commerce.

In 1964 he considered running for the Senate, but as he was opposed by Pennsylvania's Democratic Party leaders, Shapp withdrew. He challenged the organization Democrats in 1966, running in the Democratic gubernatorial primary and defeating Robert Casey, a party-endorsed candidate. He lost the general election to Republican Raymond Shafer.

Continuing his independent political activities in 1968, he again split with his party's leaders at the national convention by supporting Eugene McCarthy's bid for the presidency. During his 1970 gubernatorial campaign, Shapp again defeated Robert Casey in the primary, and this time he beat Republican Raymond J. Broderick in the general election, becoming the first Jewish governor in the state's history. As governor, Shapp brought fiscal stability to Pennsylvania through budget cutting and a flat rate income tax.

A new state constitution adopted in 1968 allowed Shapp to become the first governor to succeed himself, and in 1974 he narrowly defeated Republican Drew Lewis, despite allegations of corruption within the Shapp administration. Though Shapp's last term saw several notable achievements, scandals plagued key figures in his administration, leaving his political reputation a checkered legacy.

*See also:* Eugene McCarthy

*Thomas J. Baldino*

REFERENCES

Weber, Michael P. 1988. *Don't Call Me Boss: David L. Lawrence, Pittsburgh's Renaissance Mayor.* Pittsburgh: U. of Pittsburgh Pr.

## Clement L. Shaver (1867–1954)

Democratic National Committee chairman from 1924 to 1928. Clement Lawrence Shaver became active in Democratic politics quite early. While still in his mid-twenties, he went to Washington as a protégé of West Virginia Congressman William L. Wilson. Employed as a clerk in the United States Weather Bureau, he also studied law at what later became George Washington University, was admitted to the bar in West Virginia in 1899, and practiced law without partners until his retirement in 1942. In later years, Shaver acquired several business interests, including farming, stock raising, and the sale of coal and timber lands.

Shaver served three terms in the West Virginia House of Representatives, once as floor leader. He was chairman of the Democratic state central committee from 1912 to 1920, managing a successful gubernatorial and two successful senatorial campaigns. In West Virginia, he was familiarly known as "Shaver the Sphinx" for his Calvin Coolidge–like reluctance to talk.

Shaver and presidential candidate John W. Davis came to know each other as Democratic county chairmen in the same congressional district. It was Shaver's firm conviction from the very first that Davis had the qualifications to be President "if people ever got to know him." Davis had the opportunity when he was nominated on the one hundred third ballot as the compromise nominee of the 1924 Democratic National Convention.

As soon as he was elected Democratic national chairman, Shaver announced plans for creating a special campaign advisory committee of his predecessors in the chairmanship and for bringing into the campaign all the managers of the preconvention candidates. Shaver was unable to compose either of these groups. In fact, the divisions that so deeply split the convention carried over directly into the campaign and beyond. Factional maneuvers dominated his otherwise uneventful tenure.

*See also:* Calvin Coolidge, John W. Davis, Woodrow Wilson

*Ralph M. Goldman*

REFERENCES

Goldman, Ralph M. 1990. *The National Party Chairmen and Committees: Factionalism at the Top.* Armonk, NY: M. E. Sharpe.

## James S. Sherman (1855–1912)

U.S. Vice President in 1908. Long involved in Republican Party politics, James "Sunny Jim" Schoolcraft Sherman served one term (1908–1912) as William Howard Taft's Vice President. Renominated in 1912, Sherman succumbed to illness before the general election.

Sherman was raised in a politically active family: his father, Richard, served in the New York legislature, clerked in the U.S. House of Representatives, and later headed New York's game and fish commission. A graduate of Hamilton College (N.Y.) in 1878, James Sherman subsequently earned an LL.B. there in 1880.

In 1884 Sherman won election as mayor of the normally Democratic Utica. Two years later he was elected to Congress where he represented his upstate New York district for over twenty years, incurring only a one-term defeat. Sherman's somewhat undistinguished congressional tenure was marked by a particular interest in the affairs of Native Americans; he chaired the Indian Affairs Committee for 12 years. Probably most notable was Sherman's role of a parliamentary tactician in the House. As a member of the Rules Committee, "Sunny Jim" was a confidant of Speakers Thomas Reed, David Henderson, and, especially, Joseph Cannon.

In 1908 Sherman was chosen by the Republican National Convention delegates to balance the Theodore Roosevelt–directed presidential nomination of William H. Taft. Four years later, although suffering from ill health, Sherman reluctantly accepted the vice presidential renomination and again joined Taft on the GOP ticket. Sherman was the first vice presidential candidate to receive successive nominations. Illness, however, largely precluded his participation in the campaign, and Sherman died in October 1912. He was replaced as the vice presidential nominee by Nicholas Butler in what was to be a losing Republican effort.

*See also:* Nicholas Butler, Joseph G. Cannon, David Henderson, Thomas Reed, Theodore Roosevelt, William Howard Taft

*Charles Longley*

## John Sherman (1823–1900)

Ohio Republican legislator, Cabinet officer, and presidential contender. The political career of John Sherman coincided with the birth of the Republican Party and its growth during the Civil War, Reconstruction, and late-nineteenth-century eras. A moderate on race and Reconstruction, and later identified with the Half-Breed Republicans, Sherman always remained close to the center of party ideology, often played a mediating role between opposing viewpoints, and left his stamp on many legislative achievements, especially in financial matters. Yet his highest goal, the White House, constantly eluded him. Three times he sought his party's nomination for the presidency, but for various reasons each try was unsuccessful.

A native and lifelong resident of Ohio, John Sherman inherited a family tradition of Federalist and Whig party politics and was in the first group of Republicans elected to Congress in 1854. After serving in the House of Representatives for six years, and missing an opportunity to become Speaker only because of the intensifying sectional conflict, Sherman entered the Senate in 1861, just as the Civil War commenced. Less conspicuous in that conflict than his illustrious brother, General William T. Sherman, Ohio's new Senator concentrated on financial questions, helping to shape wartime legislation on currency, banking, and taxation. After the Civil War John Sherman opposed the immediate withdrawal of the greenbacks from circulation and after several years of indecision helped the Republicans in Congress to unite on a plan of gradual resumption of specie payments. Leaving the Senate in 1877 to become Secretary of the Treasury under Rutherford B. Hayes, Sherman presided over the return to a gold-backed currency in 1879. The next year he entered the presidential race, using the patronage powers of his Cabinet post to build up support but to no avail. Ironically, Sherman's selection of fellow-Ohioan James A. Garfield as the man to nominate him only helped to put Garfield in the spotlight, and on the thirty-fifth ballot the convention chose Garfield as its candidate.

Sherman returned to the Senate in 1881 and served there until 1897, when he closed out his political career as William McKinley's first Secretary of State. He had some interest in the 1884 presidential nomination, but James G. Blaine was the early and overwhelming choice of Republicans that year. In 1888, after Blaine had firmly taken himself out of the race, Sherman made his last and most determined bid. Sherman refused to withdraw his name even after he obviously lacked sufficient support to win, a stubborn tactic that helped to prolong the convention for a time, until Benjamin Harrison was finally nominated. In both 1880 and 1888 Sherman became embittered toward friends who had putatively betrayed his interests. A closer examination of the facts reveals that Sherman's austere personality, the stands that he had taken on various controversial issues, and his lack of a Civil War military record were more important drawbacks. Respected by most Republicans for his ability, experience, and party loyalty, he nevertheless lacked the devotion and admiration attracted by other leaders of his era.

*See also:* James G. Blaine, James A. Garfield, Benjamin Harrison, Rutherford B. Hayes, William McKinley, Stalwarts (and Half-Breeds)

*John B. Weaver*

REFERENCES

Burton, Theodore. 1906. *John Sherman.* Boston: Houghton Mifflin.

Marcus, Robert D. 1971. *Grand Old Party: Political Structure in the Gilded Age, 1880–1896.* New York: Oxford U. Pr.

Sherman, John. 1895. *John Sherman's Recollections of Forty Years in the House, Senate, and Cabinet.* Chicago: Werner.

## Sherman Antitrust Act

The Sherman Antitrust Act of 1890 represented the first important step by the federal government to come to grips with the rising political issue of antimonopolism. A venerable motif in American politics dating back at least to the age of Andrew Jackson, antimonopolism reached a crescendo in the late nineteenth century as Americans grew anxious over burgeoning giant corporations with seemingly unlimited economic power and allegedly concomitant political power. At first denounced primarily in the rhetoric of farmer and labor organizations and third parties such as the Greenbackers, these business trusts and other combinations had by the mid-1880s become a serious political problem. Major party politicians feared losing support to splinter groups, but they also felt genuine economic qualms over these great concentrations of capital. In 1888 both the Republican and Democratic platforms promised relief from trusts.

That year the Republicans won both Congress and the presidency, and the Sherman Antitrust Act was one of several important laws passed with GOP support. Originally introduced by Ohio Senator John Sherman in 1888, the proposal underwent considerable change until its final 1890 version outlawed combinations "in restraint of trade or commerce" but did not specifically ban trusts in production—a flaw soon pointed out by the Supreme Court. Despite this weakness, the Sherman law was a path-breaking attempt to deal with monopolies at the federal level. Nonetheless, in the congressional elections that soon followed its passage, the "progressive" Sherman Act could not outweigh the unpopularity of several other measures by the Republicans, including the McKinley Tariff Act, and the GOP suffered a devastating defeat.

*See also:* John Sherman, Trusts

*Charles W. Calhoun*

REFERENCES

Letwin, William. 1955. "Congress and the Sherman Antitrust Law: 1887–1890." 23 *University of Chicago Law Review* 221.

———. 1965. *Law and Economic Policy in America: The Evolution of the Sherman Anti-Trust Act.* New York: Random House.

Thorelli, Hans B. 1955. *The Federal Anti-Trust Policy: Origins of an American Tradition.* Baltimore: Johns Hopkins U. Pr.

## Sherman Silver Purchase Act

Passed in 1890, the Sherman Silver Purchase Act's greatest impact on politics came three years later with the bitter fight over its repeal, a political struggle that put the currency issue at center stage and shattered the Democratic Party.

Currency agitation recurred frequently throughout the economically volatile post-Civil War decades. A compromise passed during Republican President Benjamin Harrison's administration, the Sherman Silver Purchase Act temporarily mollified silverites by calling for government purchase of virtually all the country's silver production with Silver Certificates; anti-inflationists grudgingly accepted the Sherman Act since it averted free coinage and made the certificates redeemable in gold as well as silver, thereby preserving gold as the ultimate basis of money in the United States.

Early in Grover Cleveland's second term, the panic of 1893 and the onset of depression led the administration to press for repeal of the law. Since the Treasury Department had regularly redeemed Silver Certificates in gold, the Sherman law contributed to the severe drain on gold accompanying the depression. Cleveland believed repeal would do much to restore business confidence, but he faced strong opposition from silver interests in Congress, especially the Senate, which witnessed a rancorous two-month struggle during which Cleveland steadfastly refused to compromise.

Repeal proved a Pyrrhic victory; it did little to boost the economy, it further alienated the silver wing of the Democratic Party, and it helped make currency a paramount political issue. The Democrats lost heavily in the 1894 House elections. William Jennings Bryan, a leader against repeal, captured the Democratic presidential nomination in 1896 and rode the free-silver issue hard, only to suffer a resounding defeat at the hands of William McKinley.

*See also:* William Jennings Bryan, Benjamin Harrison, William McKinley

*Charles W. Calhoun*

REFERENCES

Hollingsworth, J. Rogers. 1963. *The Whirligig of Politics: The Democracy of Cleveland and Bryan.* Chicago: U. of Chicago Pr.

Nevins, Allan. 1932. *Grover Cleveland: A Study in Courage.* New York: Dodd, Mead.

Socolofsky, Homer E., and Allan B. Spetter. 1987. *The Presidency of Benjamin Harrison.* Lawrence: U. Pr. of Kansas.

Welch, Richard E., Jr. 1988. *The Presidencies of Grover Cleveland.* Lawrence: U. Pr. of Kansas.

Williams, R. Hal. 1978. *Years of Decision: American Politics in the 1890s.* New York: Wiley.

## R. Sargent Shriver (1915– )

Democratic Party activist and vice presidential candidate in 1972. Director of the Office of Economic Opportunity (OEO) from 1964 to 1968 and then ambassador to France until 1970, Robert Sargent Shriver earned a law degree from Yale University, served in the Navy during World War II, managed the Merchandise Mart in Chicago, and married Eunice Kennedy, the sister of President John Kennedy. He first entered politics on the Chicago Board of Education, did campaign liaison for John Kennedy's presidential race in the 1960, and then directed the new Peace Corps until 1966 and the OEO from 1964. He was asked to design both the Peace Corps and the OEO to eliminate poverty rapidly, but he also had to placate those who feared an independent poverty bureaucracy; his worthwhile solution was to intensify participation of the poor and of local politicians in the Community Action Program. Funding cutbacks caused by the Vietnam War, the excessive expectations of most Americans, and a disorganized profusion of projects engendered strong criticism from all sides, including other federal agencies. Poverty was not defeated, OEO administration was sometimes inept, and the new agency was operating for a weak bureaucratic position. Conservatives attacked the chaotic organization, and the poor proved angrily ungrateful.

Following his posting to Paris, Shriver ran in 1972 as the vice presidential candidate on George McGovern's ticket, but both proved too liberal for the country, which gave Richard Nixon re-election by a landslide. The OEO may have lost the War on Poverty, but it did set up the Job Corps for teenagers and Volunteers In Service to America (VISTA) to help alleviate poverty in Appalachia. Unfortunately for the Democrats, the OEO was used by their opponents as a prime example of liberal waste, even though it never cost more than $4 billion a year; this public perception of mismanagement helped create a more conservative consensus in the 1970s.

*See also:* John F. Kennedy, George McGovern, Richard M. Nixon, Vietnam War as a Political Issue

*Jeremy R. T. Lewis*

REFERENCES

Collier, Peter. 1984. *The Kennedys: An American Drama.* New York: Summit Books.

Davis, John H. 1984. *The Kennedys: Dynasty and Disaster.* New York: McGraw-Hill.

Ginzberg, Eli, and Robert M. Solow, eds. 1974. *The Great Society: Lessons for the Future.* New York: Basic Books.

Redman, Coates. 1986. *Come As You Are: The Peace Corps Story.* San Diego: Harcourt Brace Jovanovich.

## Leon Shull (1913– )

National spokesman for liberal causes. Leon Shull was the national director of the liberal political action group Americans for Democratic Action (ADA) from 1964 to 1985, and, from 1951 to 1963, he was executive director of the Southeast Pennsylvania Chapter of the ADA. When the Democratic Party nominated Senator John Sparkman of Alabama to be Adlai Stevenson's running mate in 1952, Shull was a prominent proponent for a more forceful condemnation of Sparkman's civil rights record in the ADA's endorsement of the Democratic ticket.

In the 1960s, a rift over U.S. involvement in Vietnam developed between the ADA's traditional elements, led by Gus Tyler, and the reformers, under Allard Lowenstein. While Shull sought to reconcile these factions, antiwar sentiment was widespread in the ADA. As a result, Shull and the ADA reaffirmed their endorsement of Eugene McCarthy's antiwar candidacy even at the 1968 Democratic convention that nominated Hubert Humphrey.

As late as the 1980s, Shull was defending the use of government as an agent of change. Under his leadership, the ADA opposed "Reaganomics" vigorously and pushed for "economic democracy" and national economic planning. Shull's pragmatism in economic affairs clearly had a limit, and with Ronald Reagan's laissez faire admiration for big business, that limit was reached.

*See also:* Americans for Democratic Action, Hubert Humphrey, Allard Lowenstein, Eugene McCarthy, Adlai E. Stevenson II, Vietnam War as a Political Issue

*Samuel F. Mitchell*

REFERENCES

Gillon, Steven M. 1987. *Politics and Vision: The ADA and American Liberalism, 1947–1985.* New York: Oxford U. Pr.

Shull, Leon. 1975. *Hard Core Liberals: A Sociological Analysis of the Philadelphia Americans for Democratic Action.* Cambridge: Schenkman.

## Silver Republicans

Although his nomination for the presidency was supported by business interests within the Republican Party, William McKinley's congressional record on the issue of the free coinage of silver was considered ambiguous. At the Republican National Convention in St. Louis in 1896, Senator Henry M. Teller of Colorado attempted to take advantage of this ambiguity by proposing a revised currency plank in the Republican platform. This plank maintained that the GOP favored the use of both gold and silver as equal standards and would thus attempt to secure the free coinage of silver at a ratio of 16 to 1. Teller's proposal was resoundingly rejected by a vote of 818 1/2 to 105 1/2. Deciding to continue the fight, Teller left the hall accompanied by 33 other pro-silver delegates, mostly from South Dakota, Idaho, and Montana.

A Silver Republican Party was hastily organized by Senator Teller and returned to hold their convention in St. Louis in July at the same time the Populists did. To their surprise, the Silverites exercised almost no influence at all on the Populist gathering; in fact, their representatives were refused any rights on the floor of the Populist convention. At their own convention, the Silver Republicans had to satisfy themselves with echoing the Democrats and Populists by nominating William Jennings Bryan by acclamation. Their platform, however, was not as far-reaching as those of Bryan's other supporters, consisting of the single silver plank already rejected by the Republicans.

After Bryan's defeat in the election of 1896, the Silver Republicans briefly continued their tenuous existence. They even held a second convention in Kansas City in July 1900, where they supported Bryan's second presidential bid.

*See also:* William Jennings Bryan, William McKinley

*James V. Saturno*

REFERENCES

Mayer, George H. 1964. *The Republican Party.* New York: Oxford U. Pr.

Nash, Howard P., Jr. 1959. *Third Parties in American Politics.* Washington: Public Affairs Press.

## Furnifold M. Simmons (1854–1940)

North Carolina lawyer, political organizer, and U.S. Senator. Born on a farm in eastern North Carolina, Furnifold McLendel Simmons graduated from Trinity College (1873) and then practiced law until 1901. Soon after his graduation, he became active in Democratic politics. He was elected to Congress in 1886 but two years later was defeated by an African-American Republican. In 1892, when he was chosen chairman of the Democratic State Executive Committee, Simmons developed a very successful county-by-county organization. Democratic election victories earned him an appointment as collector of Internal Revenue for the Eastern District of North Carolina. After the Democrats lost the elections of 1894 and 1896 to a combination of Republicans and Populists, Simmons was recalled to the chairmanship of the party in 1898.

Retaining the chairmanship until 1907, Simmons built up an organization called by his enemies the "Simmons machine." Simmons himself thought of this organization simply as "Friends" who turned to him for political advice, particularly in gubernatorial elections. In 1898 and 1900 Simmons managed virulent and successful white-supremacy campaigns designed to unite all white men behind the argument that Republican victory meant "Negro domination." The Democrats elected majorities in both houses of the North Carolina legislature. In 1900 the goals also included electing a Democratic governor and preventing future Republican victories by disfranchising Black voters. In this campaign, Charles B. Aycock was elected governor and the state adopted a constitutional amendment that imposed a literacy test for voting and grandfathered the voting status of white males. Moreover, white registrars were given great power to determine who was eligible to vote.

After its success in the election of 1900, a grateful Democratic Party nominated Simmons in the first statewide senatorial primary held in North Carolina, and the legislature elected him U.S. Senator in 1901, an office that he held for the next 30 years. Only in 1912 and 1930 was he opposed in the Democratic primary. In the Senate, he served on the Committee on Commerce (1906–1931), chaired the Finance Committee (1913–1919) and was partly responsible for developing the policies that financed the U.S. war effort during World War I. From 1919 to 1931, he was ranking Democrat on the Finance Committee with a reputation as a knowledgeable, hardworking public servant.

In 1928 conservative southerner Simmons refused to support the "wet," Roman Catholic, urban Alfred E. Smith as the Democratic presidential nominee. Instead, Simmons put together an anti-Smith organization that enlisted enough Democratic voters, when combined with the state's Republicans, to carry North Carolina for Herbert Hoover.

Smith's defeat, celebrated by Simmons as a victory, proved to be a deathblow to Simmons's career. His organization in North Carolina was already breaking down in the mid-1920s; young Democrats were otherwise minded. His "Friends" were old, tired, or dead. And in 1928, he committed the cardinal political sin: he bolted. The end came in the Democratic senatorial primary of 1930, when, in a record turnout, the 76-year-old Senator carried only 16 of 100 counties, and Josiah W. Bailey defeated him by 70,000 votes.

*See also:* Herbert Hoover

*Richard L. Watson, Jr.*

REFERENCES

Anderson, Eric. 1981. *Race and Politics in North Carolina, 1872–1901: The Black Second.* Baton Rouge: Louisiana State U. Pr.

Edmonds, Helen G. 1951. *The Negro and Fusion Politics in North Carolina, 1894–1901.* Chapel Hill: U. of North Carolina Pr.

Escott, Paul D. 1985. *Many Excellent People: Power and Privilege in North Carolina, 1850–1900.* Chapel Hill: U. of North Carolina Pr.

Puryear, Elmer. 1962. *Democratic Party Dissension in North Carolina, 1928–1936.* Chapel Hill: U. of North Carolina Pr.

Rippy, J. Fred, ed. 1936. *F. M. Simmons, Statesman of the New South: Memoirs and Addresses.* Durham, NC: Duke U. Pr.

## Jerry Simpson (1842–1905)

"Sockless Jerry," a Populist political agitator. Jerry Simpson, a Populist Congressman, was born in New Brunswick, Canada. After working as a sailor on the Great Lakes for two decades, he settled in Kansas in 1878, first as a farmer, then as a miller, a rancher, and marshal of Medicine Lodge, Kansas. Always interested in radical opposition politics, Simpson ran unsuccessfully for the legislature as a Greenbacker in 1886 and as a Union Labor candidate in 1888. In 1890 he helped organize the People's Party in Kansas and was its nominee for Congress from south-western Kansas. Although self-educated, Simpson had a sharp wit, and his folksy political style made him an effective prophet of the Populist message of economic and political reform to his largely rural audiences. The "sockless" sobriquet derived from a misguided Republican attempt to ridicule that style.

Simpson was elected to the U.S. House of Representatives (with Democratic support) in 1890, 1892, and 1896. In Congress, he led the Populist delegation but introduced few bills and largely limited his speaking to the repartee in which he was unexcelled. Politically, he was a leader of the fusion wing of the People's Party, recognizing that he needed Democratic support in his own district and convinced that only Democratic-Populist cooperation would achieve national success. His tactics to promote fusion (and himself) often infuriated other Populists. After his 1898 defeat for reelection to the House, he published a scurrilous newspaper, *Jerry Simpson's Bayonet*, for two years and then became a land agent for the Santa Fe Railroad. Sockless Jerry, like many other Populist firebrands, eventually faded into obscurity.

*See also:* Greenback Party, People's Party

*Peter H. Argersinger*

REFERENCES

Bicha, Karel Denis. 1967. "Jerry Simpson: Populist Without Principle." 54 *Journal of American History* 291.

Diggs, Annie L. 1908. *The Story of Jerry Simpson.* Wichita, KS: Jane Simpson.

## Upton B. Sinclair (1878–1968)

Renowned muckraking novelist and propagandist for Socialist Party causes. Upton Beall Sinclair ran as the Democratic candidate for governor of California in 1934 at the helm of the grass-roots End Poverty in California (EPIC) movement. Born in Baltimore, Maryland, into a family torn by alcoholism and poverty, the young Sinclair developed a social conscience clearly reflected a vast literary output that addressed a wide range of societal and economic injustices. With the publication of *The Jungle* (1907), a novel that unleashed a storm of indignation against the inhumane and unsanitary conditions he uncovered in the meatpacking industry, Sinclair won wide acclaim as a social reformer. Eventually based in California, Sinclair occasionally participated in social protest strikes and ran several times as a token Socialist candidate for Congress and for the governorship in the 1920s.

In 1933 Sinclair changed his party registration to Democratic and again declared his candidacy for governor. Espousing a platform that promised to supplant capitalism partially with "production for use," Sinclair set off a crusade among the masses of the Depression weary, backed by over 800 flourishing EPIC clubs. Sinclair's candidacy sent shock waves through the state's Democratic Party organization that was backing the candidacy of George Creel. Sinclair easily defeated Creel in the primary. In the general election, Sinclair was opposed by an incumbent reactionary Republican, Frank F. Merriam, and the Commonwealth-Progressive Party nominee, Raymond L. Haight. In the vicious campaign that followed, conservative California economic interests mounted a $10 million drive that attacked Sinclair personally and charged that EPIC would lead to a Communist takeover. Deserted by the Franklin Roosevelt administration and hurt by the Haight candidacy (which drew support from the Democratic Party's loyalist northern base), Sinclair got 879,537 votes to Merriam's 1,138,620 and Haight's 302,519. The EPIC movement, which disintegrated when Sinclair returned to writing, nonetheless contributed to the surge of majority Democratic voter registration in the state and brought new leadership to the party through its sponsorship of the state and legislative candidacies of such individuals as future governor Culbert L. Olson and U.S. Senator Sheridan Downey. More broadly, Sinclair and EPIC championed many of the then-radical concepts eventually embodied in Roosevelt's Second New Deal, such as Social Security and the Works Progress Administration. When he died in 1968, Sinclair had written some 90 books and remained a prophetic yet controversial figure to the end.

*See also:* Socialist Party of America

*Richard C. Burnweit*

REFERENCES

Burke, Robert E. 1953. *Olson's New Deal for California.* Berkeley: U. of California Pr.

Delmatier, Royce D., Clarence F. McIntosh, and Earl G. Waters. 1970. *The Rumble of California Politics 1848–1970.* New York: Wiley.

Harris, Leon. 1975. *Upton Sinclair: American Rebel.* New York: Crowell.

Phillips, Herbert L. 1968. *Big Wayward Girl: An Informal Political History of California.* Garden City, NY: Doubleday.

Rogin, Michael P., and John L. Shover. 1970. *Political Change in California: Critical Elections and Social Movements, 1890–1966.* Westport, CT: Greenwood.

Sinclair, Upton. 1934. *I, Governor of California and How I Ended Poverty.* Los Angeles: Upton Sinclair. Privately published.

———. 1935. *I, Candidate for Governor, and How I Got Licked.* Pasadena, CA: Privately published.

———. 1962. *Autobiography of Upton Sinclair.* New York: Harcourt, Brace and World.

## Single-Member Districts

A district in which a single candidate is elected to represent constituents in that geographical area. Voters are limited to casting one vote and selecting one representative in single-member districts. In contrast, a multimember district is one from which multiple candidates are elected to represent voters within the district's geographical confines. Voters can cast as many votes as seats are up for election. At-large elections are frequently treated as a special category of multimember districts, a practice usually confined to local municipal, county, or school board contests. The entire municipality, county, or school district is treated as a singular district from which multiple representatives are elected to the governing body.

Advocates of single-member districts, also referred to as wards, view as their major attributes (1) simplicity to the voters thereby increasing voter registration and turnout rates; (2) greater accessibility of officeholders to voters, making officeholders more responsive and accountable to their constituents; (3) greater representation of diverse geographical areas; (4) reduction in campaign costs for candidates seeking election and a reduction in the advantage of "interest groups with large bankrolls"; and (5) greater representation of minorities (partisan, racial, ethnic).

Edward Banfield and James Wilson, critics of single-member districts (and, therefore, proponents of multimember districts), argue that wards (1) increase "the tendency for the [legislative body] to proceed by a process of trading . . . and to do nothing when advantageous trades cannot be arranged"; (2) reduce the equity of public policy decisions by promoting decisions based on an equal share of resources for each district without regard to need; (3) encourage parochialism in decision-making to the detriment of the collective, or public at-large; (4) reduce campaign costs only temporarily; (5) increase voter participation rates only initially; (6) reduce the effectiveness of representatives from districts where minorities dominate if they are not part of the governing majority coalition; and (7) restrict the ability of residentially dispersed minorities to coalesce, or bloc vote, with one another.

At one time, multimember state legislative districts were quite common. Before 1980 one-third of all state legislative lower house seats and one-sixth of all state senate seats were chosen in this manner. But litigation initiated against multimember districts by racial, ethnic, and partisan minorities subsequently restricted their use.

Among U.S. cities, 11.6 percent elect their council members from single-member districts; 64 percent elect from at-large (multimember) districts. The trend over the past ten years has been away from each of these practices toward a combination, or mixed, electoral configuration. Under a mixed system, some of the council members are elected at large; the remainder are elected from single-member districts. Mixed systems are especially popular in multiracial communities where one minority group is residentially concentrated, but others are residentially dispersed. The concentrated group benefits from the single-member districts whereas the dispersed group benefits from the at-large (multimember) positions.

Single-member, or ward-based, districts are treated as part of an unreformed local governmental system, a characterization similarly assigned to strong mayor-council governments and partisan elections. Unreformed systems are associated with older, larger cities in the Northeast and Midwest. Multimember, or at-large, districts are regarded as components of reformed local governmental systems, along with the commission and council-manager forms of government and nonpartisan elections. The reformed system emerged out of the Progressive era in response to the corruption associated with big-city bosses and ward politics. It was designed to depoliticize government and promote a citywide approach to municipal problems.

In recent years minorities have attacked reformed systems as discriminatory. Specifically, racial minorities have argued that multimember districts dilute their ability to participate in the political process and elect candidates of their own choice in violation of the equal protection clause of the Fourteenth Amendment and the federal Voting Rights Act. As a consequence, most recent scholarly research has focused on the relative impact of single-member and multimember systems on minority officeholders.

Single-member district systems have generally been found to produce more minority officeholders, particularly where the group is sufficiently large, residentially concentrated, and politically cohesive. Single-member district systems have not been found to promote the election of women to office; women candidates are more successful under multimember districts. Single-member district systems have also not been found to promote the election of racial and language minorities where the minority group is small, geographically dispersed, and politically splintered.

*See also:* Voting Rights Act of 1965 and Extensions

*Susan A. MacManus*

REFERENCES

Banfield, Edward C., and James Q. Wilson. 1963. *City Politics.* Cambridge: Harvard U. Pr.

Browning, Rufus P., Dale Rogers Marshall, and David H. Tabb. 1984. *Protest Is Not Enough: The Struggle of Blacks and Hispanics for Equality in Urban Politics.* Berkeley: U. of California Pr.

Bullock, Charles S., III, and Susan A. MacManus. 1990. "Structural Features of Municipalities and the Incidences of Hispanic Council Members." 71 *Social Science Quarterly* (December).

———, and———. 1991. "Municipal Electoral Structure and the Election of Councilwomen." 53 *Journal of Politics* (February).

Darcy, R., Susan Welch, and Janet Clark. 1987. *Women, Elections, and Representation.* New York: Longman.

Davidson, Chandler, ed. 1984. *Minority Vote Dilution.* Washington: Howard U. Pr.

Engstrom, Richard L., and Michael D. McDonald. 1981. "The Election of Blacks to City Councils: Clarifying the Impact of Electoral Arrangements on the Seats Population Relationships." 75 *American Political Science Review* 344.

Heilig, Peggy, and Robert J. Mundt. 1984. *Your Voice at City Hall.* Albany: State U. of New York Pr.

Karnig, Albert K. 1976. "Black Representation on City Councils: The Impact of District Elections and Socioeconomic Factors." 12 *Urban Affairs Quarterly* 223.

———. 1979. "Black Resources and City Council Representation." 41 *Journal of Politics* 134.

———, and Oliver Walter. 1976. "Election of Women to City Councils." 56 *Social Science Quarterly* 605.

———, and Susan Welch. 1979. "Sex and Ethnic Differences in Municipal Representation." 60 *Social Science Quarterly* 465.

———. 1980. *Black Representation and Urban Policy.* Chicago: U. of Chicago Pr.

———. 1982. "Electoral Structure and Black Representation on City Councils." 63 *Social Science Quarterly* 99.

MacManus, Susan A. 1985. "Mixed Electoral Systems: The Newest Reform Structure." 74 *National Civic Review* 484.

———. 1987. "City Council Election Procedures and Minority Representation: Are They Related?" 67 *Social Science Quarterly* 133.

Renner, Tari. 1988. "Municipal Election Processes: The Impact on Minority Representation," in *The Municipal Year Book 1988*. Washington: International City Management Association.

Robinson, Theodore, and Thomas R. Dye. 1978. "Reformism and Black Representation on City Councils." 59 *Social Science Quarterly* 133.

Taebel, Delbert. 1978. "Minority Representation on City Councils." 59 *Social Science Quarterly* 142.

Thernstrom, Abigail M. 1987. *Whose Vote Counts? Affirmative Action and Minority Voting Rights*. Cambridge: Harvard U. Pr.

Vedlitz, Arnold, and Charles A. Johnson. 1982. "Community Racial Segregation, Electoral Structures, and Minority Representation." 63 *Social Science Quarterly* 729.

Welch, Susan. 1990. "The Impact of At-Large Elections on the Representation of Blacks and Hispanics." 52 *Journal of Politics* 1050.

## Slavery

Slavery was a significant influence in American politics from the founding of the Republic until the Civil War. All Americans prided themselves on their personal liberty, but southerners, in close contact with slavery as a necessary evil or a positive good, were united in the conviction that any outside interference with their peculiar and sensitive labor system was an intolerable threat to their liberty. The protection of southern rights, therefore, was the most basic obligation of political parties.

Virginia's James Madison wrote that "the institution of slavery and its consequences was the line of demarcation" in the Constitutional Convention of 1787. Southerners made it clear that any federal government empowered to interfere with slavery in the states was a barrier to the Union. The Constitution represented a compromise that did not specifically mention slavery but protected it with a fugitive slave law, the three-fifths clause, and postponed any congressional action on the Atlantic slave trade until 1808. In the South much of the debate on ratification was centered on whether the Constitution sufficiently protected slavery from outside interference.

The development of a two-party, Federalist-Republican rivalry (1796–1816) again shows the influence of slavery in politics. Both parties deliberately avoided a clear stand on this disruptive issue, but neither could hide the fact that it had some of its origins in sectional rivalry. Thomas Jefferson and Madison consistently maintained that Congress had no power over slavery in the states, and their followers made much of the fact that their leaders were slaveholders. The Republican Party piled up overwhelming majorities in the slave states in every presidential election from 1796 to 1816. Northern Federalists, complaining that slaveholders dominated the government, articulated most of the arguments against slavery; but out of concern of their southern wing and their hierarchical view of society, the Federalists never adopted a formal antislavery program. The dominance of the national government and the party system gave ample protection to their "peculiar institutions." This complacency was shattered by the dramatic reappearance of slavery as a divisive issue in the question of its extension to Missouri in 1820. Republican Party unity was shattered as northern Congressmen voted solidly for the restriction of slavery, and southerners launched an all-out defense. Party discipline and fears for the Union resulted in compromise but raised serious doubts about the ability of the party system to deal with sectional tensions. For a time southerners believed that they had found a new champion in Andrew Jackson, a slaveholder and advocate of local liberties. His two presidential contests with John Quincy Adams in 1824 and 1828 divided partly along sectional lines.

The emergence in the 1830s of a highly competitive two-party system was based on a variety of issues, among which slavery played a significant if not always welcome role. The natural inclination of both Whigs and Democrats was to try to ignore, stifle, or compromise disruptive sectional conflicts over slavery. As Martin Van Buren put it, "party attachment . . . provided a complete antidote to sectional prejudice by producing contrary sentiments." This adjustment was, however, maintained only with great difficulty. The southern Whigs began out of growing fear that the Democratic Party was not a reliable guardian of southern rights against a new and a more militant wave of abolitionist agitation. Jackson's aggressive assertion of federal authority in the nullification crisis of 1832 and the Democratic nomination of a northern machine politician, Martin Van Buren, in the 1836 presidential election, convinced some southerners that an alternative southern party was necessary. Nationally the Whigs were a loose coalition of traditionalist economic interests, social conservatives, and strict constitutionalists, but in the South they began as avowed champions of security of slavery. In 1836, Hugh

White, a regional Whig candidate, polled 49.3 percent of the vote and carried two states largely on the basis of being a southern slaveholder. In the North, Whig candidates William Henry Harrison and Daniel Webster endeavored to avoid the slavery issue.

In the South both Whigs and Democrats were judged not only according to this influencing support of the South's right to exclusive control of slavery but also according to their ability to persuade the northern wing of their parties to accept this arrangement. Failure to achieve this consensus on slavery invariably brought charges of sacrificing principle to partisan advantage and the spoils of office. A similar though less formidable pressure existed in parts of the free states, where Whig or Democratic Congressmen had to show that they were not becoming "dough faces" or minions of the slave power. The strength of the national parties and the importance of other issues is indicated by the fact that for nearly 20 years both Whigs and Democrats maintained national ties and effective party organizations in both sections. Only a few northern Congressmen, notably John Quincy Adams and Joshua Giddings, were able to follow lonely careers as persistent critics of slavery. In the South, John Calhoun's efforts to replace national parties with a united region and political maneuvering with constitutional guarantees of slavery won little support outside South Carolina.

Antislavery men were sufficiently frustrated by the major parties to undertake the formation of their own political organizations. The Liberty Party, launched in 1840, was never able to poll more than 3 percent of the presidential vote while its successor, the Free Soil Party, won 13 percent in 1848 only by a dubious alliance with Democrat Martin Van Buren. In 1852, when the dissident Democrats returned to the fold, the Free Soil vote fell to 4 percent. Clearly, most voters were unwilling to abandon strong party loyalty in order to cast votes for a one-issue third party. This ideology does not, however, explain the full significance of the antislavery parties. The national and local balance between Whigs and Democrats was often so close that the loss of a few thousand votes could be crucial. Scholars of the presidency argue that 18,000 Liberty Party votes in New York and Michigan cost Henry Clay the presidency in 1844 and that the Free Soil vote in Ohio denied Lewis Cass victory in 1848. Whether their hypotheses are true remains uncertain, but major party

leaders had to constantly worry about such possibilities. The two outstanding Whig leaders, Henry Clay and Daniel Webster, saw their perennial quest of the presidency undermined by their own futile efforts to satisfy antislavery "Conscience Whigs" and southern slaveholders.

The major parties might have continued to avoid or at least mitigate the slavery controversy had it not become entangled with territorial expansion. Between 1840 and 1848, the annexation of Texas and success in the Mexican War opened a vast new area to contention and upset the potential balance of free and slave states. This potential for expansion tended to shift the slavery issue from one of philanthropic interference in the states where slavery had full constitutional protection to the territories where the claims for slavery expansion of "free soil" involved the material and social goals of numerous voters. In 1846, the Wilmot Proviso, calling for the exclusion of slavery from all territory acquired from Mexico, became a test of sectional loyalties. No slave state Congressman of either party could accept this challenge to southern rights, yet both Whigs and Democrats in the North were under growing pressure to "preserve the territories for freedom."

Both parties sought a formula that would effect a compromise between the territorial issue and their desire to preserve their party's national unity. For a time the Democrats were held together by the ambiguous doctrine of popular sovereignty. The Whigs, who acknowledged more antislavery sentiment among their northern followers, first futilely tried a policy of no annexation at all and then nominated a southern slaveholder with no know political commitments. Zachary Taylor was elected President but soon outraged southern Whigs by favoring admission of California and New Mexico as free states. Taylor's death and the Compromise of 1850 gave the Whigs a brief reprieve, but in 1852 their share of the presidential vote in the slave states fell from 52 percent to 45 percent. State and local elections in the South were even more disastrous, and by 1853 only 14 of 65 southern Congressmen were Whigs. The Kansas-Nebraska bill completely divided the Whigs along sectional lines, with northern Whigs moving into the Know-Nothing, Free Soil, or Republican parties. In the South, former Whigs endeavored to build an opposition party based on southern rights and union. As the American and then the Constitutional Union Party, they won 43 percent and 38 percent of the presidential vote in the slave states but had virtually no appeal in the North where these parties polled 10 percent in 1856 and 1 percent in 1860.

For a short time the likely successor to the Whigs as a national party seemed to be the American or "Know-Nothing" Party. This nativist organization did not owe its spectacular success in the elections of 1854 and 1855 to the slavery issue, but its rapid decline as a national party a year later was also closely related to the dispute over slavery in the territories. In the northern states American Party voters often combined nativism with other issues (notably free soil) while in the South the party was largely a refuge for former Whigs seeking an opposition party to compete with the Democrats as champions of slavery and southern rights. In local elections the "Know-Nothings" could build coalitions on various issues, but at the national level they were completely unable to overcome the divisive effect of sectional conflict. In 1856 the party's convention split wide open when northern delegates walked out rather than endorse the Kansas-Nebraska Act. Know-Nothing voters then shifted in considerable numbers to the Republican Party in the North and became Democrats or Constitutional Unionists in the South.

Historians have explained the spectacular rise of the Republicans in terms of various issues, economic interests, and ethnic rivalries. All of these forces went into building the party at the crucial local level where it was indeed a coalition, but the force that held it together and made it the dominate party in the free states was its commitment to preserve free society and the territories from the encroachments of the "slave power." As an openly sectional party, the Republicans, unlike the other parties, found the slavery issue not a source of weakness and disruption but a source of unity. They had some hope of appealing to poor southern whites and building strength in the slave states, but failure to do so did not preclude victory in the electoral college. In 1860 the Republicans won control of all but one of the northern states and elected Abraham Lincoln President with 54 percent of the popular vote in the free states but only a plurality of 39.9 percent nationally. The slavery issue had finally destroyed the old bisectional national party system and created a new one primarily based on sectional rivalry.

The slavery issue and the political crisis of the 1850s did not destroy the Democratic Party in the way it did the Whigs, but it created serious sectional conflicts within it. The traditional Jacksonians, midwestern "butternuts" of southern heritage, and Catholic emigrants who made up much of the Democratic electoral support were much less susceptible to antislavery agitation than were the Whig constituencies. The party leaders were at times able to satisfy the demands of their southern wing for support of slavery and southern rights with only a minimal loss of northern voters to the Republicans or Know-Nothings, but the continuing debate over slavery expansion placed northern Democrats in an increasingly difficult situation. Party discipline persuaded most northern Democratic Congressmen to cast reluctant votes for the Kansas-Nebraska bill, but disaster followed in the election of 1854 when 70 out of 91 of them lost their seats. The National Democratic administration and Democratic members of Congress fell more and more under southern domination so that in 1859 southerners held 69 of the 101 Democratic seats in the House and 28 out of 38 of the party's Senators were from the slave states. To survive in state and local elections, northern Democrats had to oppose what voters perceived as extreme proslavery legislation such as the Lecompton Constitution for Kansas and a federal slave code for the territories. This resistance convinced their southern allies that Stephen Douglas and northern Democrats had violated the unwritten sectional compact that held the party together and were little better than free soilers. By 1860 many southerners despaired of the National Democratic organization as a reliable defender of slavery and were determined to field a presidential ticket and platform pledged to southern rights even at the cost of splitting the party. For the northern wing, Stephen Douglas and popular sovereignty were the only hope against Republican charges that they were subservient to the "slave power." The result was deadlock, three different Democratic conventions, and two Democratic presidential tickets.

The election of 1860 was in effect two sectional elections. In the southern states John Breckinridge (D) and John Bell (Constitutional Union) ran a close race centered on which men could best protect slavery, but collectively they polled only 10 percent of the vote in the free states. In the North, Abraham Lincoln (R) and Stephen Douglas (D) competed over their party's claims to secure the territories for freedom, but they secured only 12 percent of the southern votes. All four candidates claimed that they were for the Union, but the slavery issue had finally disrupted not only the party system stem but also the nation.

Secession and Civil War did not immediately remove the slavery question from politics. Northern Democrats were divided on support for a war for union conducted by a Republican administration but were united in fierce opposition to Lincoln's Emancipation Proclamation. Some historians have attributed the heavy Republican losses in the 1862 congressional elections to this issue. In 1864 Lincoln ran on a platform advocating a constitutional amendment to end slavery, while the Democrats proclaimed that interference with slavery had perverted a war for the Union into an abolitionist revolution. Lincoln's substantial electoral majority followed by the victory of Union arms finally removed the issue of slavery but not the issue of race from American politics.

*See also:* John Quincy Adams, John Bell, John Breckinridge, John C. Calhoun, Henry Clay, Constitutional Union Party, Stephen A. Douglas, Free Soil Party, William Henry Harrison, Andrew Jackson, Kansas-Nebraska Act, Know-Nothings, Liberty Party, Abraham Lincoln, Secession, Zachary Taylor, Three-Fifths Compromise, Martin Van Buren, Daniel Webster, Wilmot Proviso

*Harold B. Raymond*

REFERENCES

Cooper, William, Jr. 1978. *The South and the Politics of Slavery 1828–1856*. Baton Rouge: Louisiana State U. Pr.

Cooper, William, Jr. 1983. *Liberty and Slavery: Southern Politics to 1860*. New York: Knopf.

Gienapp, William. 1987. *The Origins of the Republican Party 1852–1856*. New York: Oxford U. Pr.

Holt, Michael. 1978. *The Political Crisis of the 1850s*. New York: Wiley.

Kleppner, Paul. 1979. *The Third Electoral System 1853–1892: Parties, Voters and Political Culture*. Chapel Hill: U. of North Carolina Pr.

McCormick, Richard. 1966. *The Second American Party System, Party Formation in the Jacksonian Era*. New York: Norton.

Remini, Robert. 1959. *Martin Van Buren and the Making of the Democratic Party*. New York: Columbia U. Pr.

Robinson, Donald. 1971. *Slavery and the Structure of American Politics 1765–1820*. Lexington: U. Pr. of Kentucky.

## John Slidell (1793–1871)

Louisiana secessionist Senator. Born in New York and graduated from Columbia College, John Slidell established his legal practice in New Orleans, where he served as a United States district attorney. In his candidacies for a seat in the U.S. House of Representatives, he was defeated in 1828 but elected in 1843. He lost races for the U.S. Senate in 1834 and 1849 but was elected in 1853 and 1859. He withdraw from the Senate in 1861 when Louisiana seceded from the Union.

Slidell became particularly active in Democratic presidential politics as a supporter of James Polk's Secretary of State, James Buchanan, who really had been running for President since 1844. The 1852 national convention deadlocked on the candidacies of Lewis Cass, Stephen A. Douglas, and Buchanan, finally nominating a compromise, Franklin Pierce, on the forty-ninth ballot. The Buchanan forces, led by Slidell, took credit for retiring Cass and blocking Douglas.

For the 1856 national convention, Slidell had organization and strategy securely in place. Buchanan was nominated on the sixteenth ballot when his principal opponent, Senator Douglas, conceded, and Slidell became the prime mover in the Buchanan campaign, personally taking over the major Democratic newspaper, the Washington *Union*. As the principal fundraiser, he engaged the Republicans in a "Wall Street War." When Buchanan was elected, Slidell controlled the bulk of the presidential patronage.

When the constitutional convention of the Kansas Territory drafted the Lecompton Constitution protecting slave property despite a popular referendum that opposed slavery in the territory, President Buchanan and Senator Slidell supported congressional acceptance of the constitution. Territorial governor Robert J. Walker resigned in protest, and Senator Douglas condemned the Buchanan administration.

Slidell led the opposition to Douglas in the 1860 Democratic National Convention and the defection of the southern delegations. Previously moderate on the issue of southern secession from the Union, Slidell was now an extreme, "Ultra," supporter. During the Civil War, he served as a Confederate commissioner to Europe, seeking recognition and loans for the Confederacy. He never returned to the United States, spending the rest of his life in Paris and London.

*See also:* James Buchanan, Lewis Cass, Stephen A. Douglas, Franklin Pierce, James K. Polk

*Ralph M. Goldman*

REFERENCES

Crenshaw, Ollinger. 1945. *The Slave States in the Presidential Election of 1860*. Baltimore: Johns Hopkins U. Pr.

Moore, John Bassett, ed. 1900–1911. *The Works of James Buchanan*. Philadelphia: Lippincott.

Sears, Louis M. 1925. *John Slidell*. Durham, NC: Duke U. Pr.

## David A. Smalley (1809–1877)

Early chairman of the Democratic National Committee. Boyhood schoolmate and lifelong friend of Senator Stephen A. Douglas, David Allen Smalley served as Democratic National Committee chairman (1856–1860) in part as a conciliatory gesture to Douglas, the "Little Giant." At the 1852 Democratic National Convention, Smalley was a convention vice president and a representative of the squatter sovereignty doctrine during the writing of the platform. Although his Vermont delegation voted for Douglas on 48 ballots, his active participation in Franklin Pierce's campaign was rewarded by appointment as a collector of customs.

The son of a Vermont surgeon, Smalley practiced law in Jerico, Vermont. In 1836, when he moved to Burlington, Smalley was still an ardent Jacksonian. In 1842 he won election as a Democratic state senator from a normally Whig county. Later, he divided his time between his lucrative practice and the chairmanship of the Democratic state committee.

At the national convention of 1856, Smalley again led the Vermont delegation in support of Douglas until the Illinois Senator conceded the nomination to James Buchanan. Smalley, speaking for Douglas and on behalf of reconciliation on the slavery issue, then urged the convention to give a southerner second place on the ticket.

As the most experienced campaigner among the three carry-over members from the previous national committee, Smalley was a logical choice for national chairman, particularly in view of his reputation for "remarkable powers of organization." He was expected to and did perform vigorously in the conduct of the campaign.

President Buchanan appointed him a United States district attorney in 1857, an office he held until his death. Smalley became an ardent War Democrat, famous for his 1860 charge to the United States Circuit Court in New York that the acts of the secessionists were "high treason."

*See also:* James Buchanan, Democratic National Committee, Stephen A. Douglas

*Ralph M. Goldman*

REFERENCES

Carleton, Hiram. 1903. *Genealogical and Family History in the State of Vermont*. New York: Lewis Publishing.

Goldman, Ralph M. 1990. *The National Party Chairmen and Committees: Factionalism at the Top*. Armonk, NY: M. E. Sharpe.

Nevins, Allan. 1947. *Ordeal of the Union*. 2 vols. New York: Scribner's.

Nichols, Roy Franklin. 1931. *Franklin Pierce: Young Hickory of the Granite Hills*. Philadelphia: U. of Pennsylvania Pr.

———. 1948. *The Disruption of American Democracy*. New York: Macmillan.

## Eleanor C. Smeal (1939– )

Feminist political activist and former president of the National Organization for Women. Eleanor Cutri Smeal received her B.A. from Duke University in 1961 and an M.A. in political science from the University of Florida two years later. In 1963 she married Charles R. Smeal, a metallurgist. She joined the National Organization for Women (NOW) in 1971, helping start a local chapter in the Pittsburgh area. Active in the local chapter of the League of Women Voters, Smeal reportedly was introduced to feminist literature by her husband during a recuperation from a slipped disk in 1969.

After serving on the national board of directors of NOW (1973–1977), Smeal was elected NOW president in 1977 and reelected to two successive terms, the maximum allowed by NOW's by-laws. Smeal was billed as a full-time homemaker during her first tenure as NOW president. She was instrumental in NOW's ascendancy as leader of efforts to ratify the Equal Rights Amendment (ERA), to the exclusion of NOW's activity on other issues. After supporting Judy Goldsmith for NOW president in 1983, Smeal worked briefly as a political consultant for the Democratic National Committee, producing a widely circulated report on the gender gap, part of which was later published in her book, *How and Why Women Will Elect the Next President* (1984). Stressing her graduate course work in political science and her political expertise, Smeal also produced and marketed a political newsletter, *The Eleanor Smeal Report*, during this period.

In 1985 Smeal was elected president of NOW in a bitter and divisive campaign during which she charged that NOW's million dollar debt and membership decline following the 1983 ERA defeat were due to Goldsmith's pragmatic coalitional-leadership style. Arguing that NOW should "go back to the streets," Smeal advocated ratification of the ERA and organized several abortion rights rallies. Smeal did not seek reelection in 1987, announcing instead a campaign for the "Feminization of Power," a traveling convention-style tour staged in major cities. At these rallies women are exhorted to offer themselves for public office in mass meetings led by Smeal and other celebrities. While the Feminization of Power campaign does not fund women candidates, the tour is subsidized by the Fund for a Feminist Majority, a nonmembership organization.

*See also:* League of Women Voters, National Organization for Women

Denise L. Baer

REFERENCES

Smeal, Eleanor C. 1984. *How and Why Women Will Elect the Next President.* New York: Harper & Row.

## Al Smith (1873–1944)

"The Happy Warrior." The first Roman Catholic to be nominated by a major party for President of the United States, Alfred Emanuel Smith was born the son of Irish immigrants. At age 12, in the shadow of New York City's Brooklyn Bridge, he went to work as a day laborer in the Fulton Fish Market.

At a very young age, Smith took an active interest in Democratic Party politics. His first political job was as a clerk in the office of the commissioner of jurors in 1895. A few years later, he won a seat in the New York State Assembly where he served for 12 years. During his tenure he served as chairman of the powerful Assembly Ways and Means Committee, and in 1913 he was elected assembly speaker.

In 1918 Smith was elected governor. He served a total of eight years; he lost once in the Republican landslide of 1920 but was reelected in 1922, 1924, and 1926. In 1928, he was succeeded by his political ally Franklin D. Roosevelt.

As governor, Smith instituted major reforms in state government. He established an executive budget, which he called "the biggest reform in the manner and method of the state doing business that has been so far suggested." Smith also campaigned successfully for bond referenda that authorized the reconstruction of state institutions and capital facilities, the development of the state's park and parkway system, and railroad grade-crossing elimination.

Smith sought the Democratic presidential nomination in 1920 and 1924, but he encountered stiff opposition from Democrats in the South and West. For all that, Smith won the Democratic nod in 1928. Among those supporting him was Franklin D. Roosevelt, the unsuccessful 1920 Democratic vice presidential candidate. Roosevelt dubbed Smith "the happy warrior," a label that stuck.

Smith's victory at the 1928 Democratic convention was more than a personal triumph; it signified acceptance at last of the group of which he was a member. The *New Republic* observed, "For the first time a representative of the unpedigreed, foreign-born, city-bred, many-tongued recent arrivals on the American scene has knocked on the door and aspired seriously to the presidency seat in the national council chamber."

Smith's Catholicism was a key factor in his loss to Republican Herbert Hoover; a majority of American Protestants believed that Smith would defer to the wishes of the Pope in his policies. But his religion also helped his party; Smith won the overwhelming support of Catholic immigration, many of whom were first-time voters. In sample Irish areas of Boston, Providence, and Hartford—cities with large Catholic populations—Smith received 91 percent, 71 percent, and 60 percent of the vote respectively.

Smith not only captured the votes of many Catholic immigrants but cemented their loyalties as well. In southern New England's major cities, for example, Smith drew crowds that outnumbered those who welcomed the popular flier Charles Lindbergh home in 1920. In Boston, 750,000 supporters greeted Smith; in Hartford, 100,000; in Providence, 40,000. Smith later wrote of his Boston reception, "So intense was the feeling, so large the throng, that at times I feared for the safety of Mrs. Smith riding with me in the automobile."

Most of the Catholic immigrants who voted for Smith in 1928 went on to side with Democratic presidential candidate Franklin Roosevelt four years later. Roosevelt had succeeded Smith as governor of New York in 1929, and Smith, who initially ran against FDR for the 1932 Democratic presidential nomination, supported him after Roosevelt became the party's choice.

But Smith broke his longstanding alliance with Roosevelt over the New Deal. Together with Herbert Hoover, John W. Davis, and William Randolph Hearst, Smith joined the Liberty League—an anti-New Deal organization formed in 1934. The League opposed "the caprice of bureaucracy" and the "tyranny of autocratic power." Two years later, Smith supported the Republican candidate for President, Alfred M. Landon. In 1940 he backed Republican Wendell L. Willkie.

The New Deal embittered Smith, and he died ostracized from his party. Nevertheless, Smith began a party realignment that culminated with Franklin Roosevelt's reelection as President in 1936.

*See also:* John W. Davis, William Randolph Hearst, Herbert Hoover, Alfred M. Landon, Liberty Party, New Deal, Franklin D. Roosevelt, Wendell L. Willkie

*John K. White*

REFERENCES

Burner, David. 1968. *The Politics of Provincialism: The Democratic Party in Transition, 1918–1932.* New York: Knopf.

Handlin, Oscar. 1958. *Al Smith and His America.* Boston: Little, Brown.

Huthmacher, J. Joseph. 1967. *A Nation of Newcomers: Ethnic Minorities in American History.* New York: Delacorte.

Kerke, Robert P. 1989. "The State of the Executive Budget." In Peter W. Colby and John K. White, eds. *New York State Today: Politics, Government and Public Policy.* Albany: State U. of New York Pr.

Lorant, Stefan. 1951. *The Presidency.* New York: Macmillan.

Moscow, Warren. 1948. *Politics in the Empire State.* New York: Knopf.

Silva, Ruth. 1962. *Rum, Religion and Votes: 1928 Reexamined.* University Park: Pennsylvania State U. Pr.

Smith, Alfred E. 1929. *Up to Now: An Autobiography.* New York: Viking.

White, John Kenneth. 1983. *The Fractured Election: Political Parties and Social Change in Southern New England.* Hanover, NH: U. Pr. of New England.

## Gerrit Smith (1797–1874)

Abolitionist, philanthropist, temperance advocate, and leader of the Liberty Party. Gerrit Smith ran for President in 1848, 1856, and 1860 and was elected to Congress in 1852. Smith was born in Utica, New York, the son of a wealthy landowner. He believed in Christian reform through individual voluntary action and abhorred slavery because it prevented such action. He founded and led the Church of Peterboro, a nonsectarian community church devoted to antislavery preaching.

Smith was a political abolitionist. Like the ex-slave Frederick Douglass, whose opinions he may have influenced, he believed that the Constitution could be given an antislavery interpretation and that political action against slavery on the national level was therefore permissible. He helped found the Liberty Party in 1840 but left it to start the Liberty League when the party's majority chose to unite with the Free Soilers. He ran for President as the League's candidate against Whig Zachary Taylor in 1848 on a platform of emancipation throughout the country, receiving 2,545 votes, all in New York.

In 1852 Smith was sent to Congress by a broad antislavery coalition. He served for one year, making 400 pages of speeches (which he later published), and then resigned. Smith continued to call for immediate emancipation, running for President again in 1856 and 1860, but he received little support. After the Civil War began, he supported the Republicans and continued to do so for the rest of his life (except in the late 1860s when he attempted to found a national prohibition party).

Philanthropist Smith gave away at least $8 million during his lifetime. He supported abolitionist and temperance organizations, churches, and individuals who appealed to him. His financial support was of great help to many leaders of the antislavery movement, including John Brown, whose raid at Harper's Ferry he supported secretly. Smith committed himself briefly to the Utica State Lunatic Asylum after the failure of Brown's raid, where he was treated for exhaustion and depression, but he then returned to public life and philanthropic activity.

*See also:* Abolition Movement, Frederick Douglass, Free Soilers, Liberty League, Liberty Party, Zachary Taylor

*John C. Berg*

REFERENCES

Friedman, Lawrence J. *Gregarious Saints: Self and Community in American Abolitionism, 1830–1870.* New York: Cambridge U. Pr.

Harlow, Ralph. 1939. *Gerrit Smith, Philanthropist and Reformer.* New York: Henry Holt.

Kraut, Alan M. 1979. "The Forgotten Reformers: A Profile of Third Party Abolitionists in Antebellum New York." In Lewis Perry and Michael Fellman, eds. *Antislavery Reconsidered: New Perspectives on the Abolitionists.* Baton Rouge: Louisiana State U. Pr.

McKivigan, John R., and Madeleine L. McKivigan. 1984. "'He Stands Like Jupiter': The Autobiography of Gerrit Smith." 65 *New York History* 189.

Sewell, Richard H. 1976. *Ballots for Freedom: Antislavery Politics in the United States, 1837–1860.* New York: Oxford U. Pr.

Smith, Gerrit. 1855. *Speeches of Gerrit Smith in Congress.* New York: Mason.

Sorin, Gerald. 1971. *The New York Abolitionists: A Case Study of Political Radicalism.* Westport, CT: Greenwood.

## Howard W. Smith (1883–1976)

Influential congressional opponent of civil rights. Elected to the U.S. House of Representatives in 1930, where he served until 1967, Howard Worth Smith was born in Virginia, graduated from Bethel Military Academy in Virginia, and received a law degree from the University of Virginia. He served as the commonwealth's attorney of Alexandria, judge of the corporation court in Alexandria, and judge of the Sixteenth Judicial Circuit of Virginia.

A politician of great skill, Judge Smith became an important cog in Senator Harry F. Byrd, Sr.'s Virginia Democratic political machine. He also achieved national prominence as chairman of the powerful Rules Committee.

As a Congressman, Smith authored the Smith Act, which required alien registration and punishment for Communists advocating the overthrow of the government. He cosponsored the Smith-Connally Wartime Act, outlawing strikes in defense industries. He opposed extension of federal power to the states, social welfare programs, and civil rights legislation. Indeed, Judge Smith refused to support the Democratic Party's presidential nominees in both 1960 and 1964, angering many Virginia Democrats.

His most important battles were over civil rights legislation. As chairman of the House Rules Committee, he consistently refused to release such legislation for floor debate. Two developments eventually diminished Smith's political power. First, in the early 1960s the membership of the House Rules Committee was expanded from 12 to 15, giving House liberals a slight majority. Second, in 1964 a 21-day rule, which permitted legislative committee chairs to bypass the Rules Committee and thereby facilitated the release of Johnson administration–sponsored legislation from Rules, was adopted.

By the mid-1960s a confluence of events contributed to Judge Smith's political demise. Smith's failure to support his party's presidential nominees, his inability or unwillingness to obtain federal benefits for his district, a sharp increase in Black voter registration in his district, the effects of congressional redistricting leading to a more moderate political outlook for his district, and the presence of an effective "liberal" challenger, George C. Rawlings, all combined to end Judge Smith's political career with a defeat in the Democratic primary in 1966. Ironically, Rawlings was defeated by Republican William L. Scott in the general election campaign.

*See also:* Harry F. Byrd, Sr., Communism as a Political Issue, Lyndon B. Johnson

*Anthony J. Eksterowicz*

REFERENCES

Dierenfield, Bruce J. 1981. "Conservative Outrage: The Defeat in 1966 of Representative Howard W. Smith of Virginia." 89 *The Virginia Magazine of History and Biography.*

## Margaret Chase Smith (1897– )

Leading Senate critic of the demagogue Joseph McCarthy. In Maine she was referred to simply as "our Maggie." Margaret Chase Smith represented Maine for 32 years in the Congress, 8 in the House of Representatives and 24 in the Senate. During that time she was recognized nationally not only because she was one of the few women in national life, not only because of the distinctive rose that graced her desk daily, but also because she was an articulate and outspoken advocate on important national issues.

Margaret Chase was born in Skowhegan, Maine. In 1929 she married Clyde Smith, a successful businessman and an active Republican. Smith was elected to Congress in 1936 and, as was not unusual in the days of limited staff, his wife served as his chief assistant. In 1940, when her husband died, Smith succeeded him in the House, achieving her seat in the same manner as did most women before the 1970s.

After serving eight years in the House, Smith decided to seek election to the Senate. Ignored by many party regulars in the primary, Smith won the Republican nomination, then tantamount to election in Maine. Her victory in 1948 made her the first woman ever elected to the United States Senate.

Smith achieved national acclaim on June 1, 1950, for her "Declaration of Conscience," which criticized fellow-Republican Joseph McCarthy for his unwarranted attacks on government employees and elected officials whom he claimed were part of an international Communist conspiracy. She was the first Republican to take on McCarthy publicly, a courageous stand that won the respect of her party and the nation. Throughout her career Maggie Smith worked hard at her job. She made a practice of never missing a roll-call vote in the Senate. A moderate, she became an expert on military affairs, serving as the ranking Republican on the Senate Armed Service and Space committees. Though she was concerned about equal treatment of women in the military, Smith never considered herself part of the feminist movement. However, her place in the history of women in politics is secure as she was the first woman to have her name placed in nomination at one of the major party's national conventions.

Margaret Chase Smith lost her bid to serve a fifth term in the Senate when she was defeated by Democratic Congressman William Hathaway in 1972. Hathaway made an issue of Smith's age, but he never criticized her integrity or the quality of her service to the people of Maine. Smith returned to her native Skowhegan, delivering a large number of public addresses and working actively on her papers housed in a library that bears her name.

*See also:* Joseph McCarthy

*Kenneth P. Hayes*

## Mary Louise Smith (1914– )

First woman to chair the Republican National Committee. Mary Louise Smith was nominated to succeed George Bush as leader of the Republican National Committee in September 1974 and sought to rebuild the party after the Watergate scandal with grass-roots seminars and the appointment of more women. She became the first woman to organize and call to order the national convention of a major party in the United States. While associated with the Gerald Ford wing of the GOP, Smith was known primarily as a party loyalist. She has served as a Ronald Reagan appointee to the U.S. Civil Rights Commission and a member of several United Nations special delegations in the 1970s. Smith is at present the vice chair of the "Republican Mainstream Committee," a progressive organization.

A trained social worker in Iowa, Smith began her involvement with the Republican Party as a volunteer campaign worker in the early 1950s. Subsequently, she was elected precinct committeewoman, county vice chairman, and Iowa's Republican national committeewoman (1964–1984). She served as an alternate delegate in 1964 and has been a delegate to each Republican National Convention from 1968 to 1984, regularly participating as a member of the Convention Arrangements Committee and as a member of the Platform Committee in 1968 and 1972. She attended in 1988 as an officer of the convention.

Smith has been active on several Republican Party reform committees: serving as a member of the "Eisenhower" Committee (Special Committee of the RNC on convention reforms) and as vice chairman of the Rule 29 Committee. Active in the Iowa Federation of Republican Women, she is also a founding member of the Iowa Women's Political Caucus, a member of the advisory board of the National Women's Political Caucus (NWPC), and a member of the board of Planned Parenthood of Mid-Iowa. At the 1988 Republican convention, Smith, describing herself as a "feminist," moderated a forum on the gender gap sponsored by the Ripon Society and the Republican Task Force of the NWPC. Smith's outspoken support of civil rights resulted in her ouster from the Republican-appointed Civil Rights Commission. First appointed as a commissioner in 1981 and serving as the commission's vice chair from 1982 to 1983, Smith and Jill Ruckleshaus were not reappointed as expected to a reorganized commission.

Smith is widely respected by activists in both parties. In 1972 she was a member of the Bipartisan Committee to Study Methods of Financing Quadrennial National Nominating Conventions; in 1980 she was a member of a bipartisan delegation of the American Political Foundation to study European political parties in Lisbon, Madrid, and Paris. She continues an active speaking career and has participated in academic conferences on political parties and presidential nominations.

*See also:* George H. W. Bush, National Women's Political Caucus, Ronald Reagan, Ripon Society

*Denise L. Baer*

## Samuel Smith (1752–1839)

Jeffersonian Republican political panjandrum. A formidable Republican Party leader in Congress, Samuel Smith's support of many of Thomas Jefferson's presidential initiatives contributed to their passage, and his opposition to James Madison's administration contributed to many of its political failures. Born in Carlisle, Pennsylvania, Smith was educated in Baltimore's public schools and graduated from Princeton University. He was a hero in the Revolutionary War and the War of 1812 and for decades held high posts in Maryland's militia. Smith served in the Maryland House of Delegates (1790–1792), the U.S. House (1793–1803 and 1816–1822), and the U.S. Senate (1803–1815 and 1822–1833). He was also mayor of Baltimore from 1835 to 1838.

Although in the early 1800s congressional party leaders were informally designated, they wielded significant influence. As a Republican leader in both houses, Smith did not always support the Jefferson administration (1801–1809); nonetheless, he helped ensure adoption of such key administration measures as repeal of the Judiciary Act of 1801, passage of the Embargo Act of 1807, and passage of the First and Second Enforcement acts.

During Madison's presidency (1809–1817), Smith was often the backbone of Senate Republican opposition; for example, he forced Madison to withdraw his original candidate for Secretary of State in favor of Smith's brother, Robert Smith; delayed the administration's fiscal and military measures; and defeated Madison's efforts to recharter the Bank of the United States.

*See also:* First Bank of the United States, Thomas Jefferson, James Madison

*Elaine K. Swift*

REFERENCES

Cassell, Frank A. 1971. *Merchant Congressman in the Young Republic: Samuel Smith of Maryland, 1752–1839.* Madison: U. of Wisconsin Pr.

Pancake, J. S. 1972. *Samuel Smith and the Politics of Business.* University: U. of Alabama Pr.

## Smith v. Allwright
### 321 U.S. 649 (1944)

This Supreme Court case overruled *Grovey v. Townsend* (295 U.S. 45 (1935)), which had upheld the right of a political party to decide in convention to exclude Black voters. Texas statutes required that the Democratic Party hold primary elections. In turn the party at a state convention adopted a rule that restricted party membership and primary voting rights to white citizens otherwise qualified to vote.

The party's lawyers argued that the Democratic Party was a private voluntary association entitled to determine who was a member and who could vote in its primaries. The Court decided however, that the Democratic Party was performing functions delegated by the state. The state mandated the selection of convention delegates by party primary and required nomination in the state party convention for printing on the ballot as the party candidate. "[T]his statutory system for the selection of party nominees for inclusion on the general election ballot makes the party which is required to follow these legislative directions an agency of the State in so far as it determines the participants in a primary election." Since the state is thus responsible for the actions of the party, constitutional obligations apply and racial discrimination in the primary election process was prohibited.

It long seemed that the application of constitutional standards regarding election fraud (as in *United States v. Classic*) and racial equality as in the white primary cases (including *Terry v. Adams* and others in addition to *Smith v. Allwright*, challenging whites-only primaries)

implied that party primaries were public rather than private events and generally subject to state and federal regulation. More recently the Court seems to be saying that such an interpretation of the white primary cases is much too broad. Instead the white primary cases appear to mean that the power or obligation of the government to secure racial equality in political affairs overrides the right of association of the political parties. The question then becomes one of determining the scope of the area in which the equal protection requirements override the right of association.

*See also: United States v. Classic*

*Stephen E. Gottlieb*

REFERENCES

*O'Brien v. Brown,* 409 U.S. 1 (1972)

*Tashjian v. Republican Party,* 107 U.S. 544 (1986)

*United States v. Classic,* 313 U.S. 299 (1941)

## Social Democratic Party (1898–1901)

A short-lived political party that represented the views of turn-of-the-century reformers who accepted industrialization but rejected the accompanying class struggles by attracting working-class voters, the Social Democrats believed that they could transform the capitalist United States into a Socialist republic. The Social Democratic Party (SDP) included some of America's most prominent Socialists, and it later merged with rivals and fellow travelers to form a more durable Socialist Party.

The SDP began with the efforts of Eugene V. Debs, Victor Berger, and others in the aftermath of the abortive Pullman strike of 1894 and the defeat of William Jennings Bryan in 1896 to unite the fragmented American Left. At the July 1897 meeting of the American Railway Union, delegates created a new alliance, the Social Democracy of America (SDA). Fraught by schism from its inception, SDA sought to combine Debs's utopian goals with Berger's call for political action. Still after a volatile 1898 convention, the political activists, including Debs, bolted to form the Social Democratic Party.

The Social Democrats intended to end the struggle between workers and owners through cooperative control of production, but until this change occurred, the Social Democrats advocated specific reforms intended to better the lives of the laboring class. The party called for the nationalization of large cooperations and municipal ownership of public utilities. Workers could bring about this lofty goal, and thereby insure the equitable distribution of society's wealth, by electing SDP candidates. Realizing that their agenda would take time, Social Democrats also supported specific (often decidedly middle-class) reforms, including reduced hours of labor, standard rates for the transportation of farm products, and public credit for community projects. The party also wanted to improve American morality through temperance, restriction of divorce, prohibition of prostitution, and equal rights for women.

The Social Democrats attained only limited success, with farm and labor issues often dividing the party faithful. For instance, deciding the SDP's proper position on trade unionism yielded considerable disagreement. Still, the SDP fielded local slates of candidates and achieved a few victories, particularly in Haverhill, Massachusetts. The party grew, and by 1900 it had 4,636 members in 226 branches and the support of 25 newspapers. Eugene Debs had an even larger national constituency. At the 1900 SDP convention, Debs received the party's nomination for President, and after initial reluctance, he embarked on an ambitious campaign. These heroic efforts did not engender much success; Debs received fewer than 100,000 votes, less than 1 percent of the those cast, from isolated pockets of support.

The poor election results did not discourage SDP stalwarts. Debs saw the campaign as a beginning, not an end. He believed that socialism often carried a negative connotation and that Social Democrats must therefore increase their efforts to educate voters. Defeat convinced the SDP rank and file that the party must unify its divergent elements and end internecine squabbles between its leaders. Toward this end, at an Indianapolis, Indiana, convention in 1901, delegates representing the SDP and other Socialist factions agreed to form a new coalition, the Socialist Party of America.

*See also:* William Jennings Bryan, Eugene V. Debs

*Robert F. Zeidel*

REFERENCES

Kipnis, Ira. 1952. *The American Socialist Movement, 1897–1912.* New York: Columbia U. Pr.

Salvatore, Nick. 1982. *Eugene V. Debs: Citizen and Socialist.* Urbana: U. of Illinois Pr.

Shannon, David A. 1955. *The Socialist Party of America.* New York: Macmillan.

## Socialism in American Politics

Socialists have long occupied the American political Left. First, they embodied the hopes of those who wished to replace capitalism with a cooperative state. In the early twentieth century, both they and their critics believed that socialism offered a serious challenge to laissez faire capitalism. The ideology attracted large numbers of immigrants, particularly Jews, but also many natives. Later, after the movement's decline in the 1930s, Socialist candidates served as alternatives for those unhappy with major party candidates. Because American Socialists by and large rejected revolution and sought reform through the political process, they achieved a certain acceptability and enjoyed a certain degree of success in the United States.

The first Socialist groups predated the onset of industrialization, though not all ventured into politics. For example, in 1825 Robert Owen established the short-lived communitarian settlement at New Harmony, Indiana, and during the 1820s Thomas Skidmore advocated periodic redistribution of wealth. Concomitant with the growth of corporate capitalism was the proliferation of Socialist movements. In 1872 Karl Marx moved the First International to New York, a ploy that engendered the Socialist Labor Party (SLP), led by Daniel De Leon. And in 1898, a rival group, including Eugene V. Debs, created the Social Democratic Party (SDP). In 1901 the SDP, a splinter faction of the SLP, and other groups coalesced to form the Socialist Party of America (SPA). Only the purist Socialist Laborites and a few "Fabian Socialists" remained outside the SPA, and in 1919, its far left split off to form the Communist Party.

The Social Democrats have fielded presidential tickets throughout the twentieth century, but none ever attracted as much as 10 percent of the popular vote or carried a single state. Debs dominated the party's first two decades, seeking the presidency four times. In 1912 he received 6 percent of the popular vote, the highest ever by an avowed left-wing candidate, and in 1920, while in prison, he received 913,644 votes, the highest numerical total. The SPA endorsed Robert M. La Follette's Independent (Progressive) candidacy in 1924, but thereafter, for the next 20 years, Norman Thomas carried the Socialist banner. Thomas received a high of 881,951 votes, but even in the depths of the Great Depression, he could garner only 2 percent of the popular vote. The SPA declined rapidly after 1948 and did not have a presidential candidate from 1960 to 1972. In 1976 Frank P. Zeidler revitalized the tradition, and in 1980, a virtual unknown, David McReynolds, drew 7,000 votes.

Between 1900 and 1960, Socialists did manage to win a variety of local elections. Victor Berger of Wisconsin, among others, served in the U.S. Congress, and numerous Socialists won seats in state legislatures. Berkeley, California; Butte, Montana; and Flint, Michigan, for example, had Socialist administrations; in 1912 Socialists held over 1,200 offices in 340 communities. Some of their greatest success occurred in Milwaukee, Berger's home city. Three Socialists served as mayor, including Frank Zeidler, who retired in 1960, and others successfully ran for the common council, the county board, and the school board. Though the Milwaukee Socialists provided honest, efficient government and implemented various types of municipal ownership, Marxist critics dubbed the locals "sewer socialists" because of their concern for practical matters and willingness to work with other reformers.

*See also:* Victor Berger, Communist Party, Eugene V. Debs, Daniel De Leon, Robert M. La Follette, Social Democratic Party, Socialist Labor Party, Socialist Party of America

*Robert F. Zeidel*

REFERENCES

Buhle, Mari Ju, Paul Buhle, and Dan Georgakas, eds. 1990. *Encyclopedia of the American Left*. New York: Garland.

Egbert, Donald D., and Stow Persons, eds. 1952. *Socialism and American Life*. 2 vols. Princeton: Princeton U. Pr.

Shannon, David A. 1955. *The Socialist Party of America: A History*. New York: Macmillan.

Stave, Bruce M., ed. 1975. *Socialism and the Cities*. Port Washington, NY: Kennikat.

## Socialist Labor Party

Formed in 1877 by a disparate group of Socialists associated with the First International, the Socialist Labor Party (SLP) became an important nineteenth-century political arm of the nascent American Socialist movement. The SLP suffered early on from internal squabbles among its largely German-American leadership. This factionalism ceased in 1890 with Daniel De Leon's entry into the party. A doctrinaire Marxist, De Leon took control of the SLP and transformed it into a top-down, centrally organized party espousing revolution. De Leon remained the SLP's leader until his death in 1914. He failed, however, to make the SLP competitive against the more popular electoral Socialist party, the Socialist Party of America (SPA).

De Leon was an uncompromising leader, and his insistence upon keeping the SLP a revolutionary party met with opposition both within his party and the trade union movement. Having failed in its audacious attempt to control the American Federation of Labor (AFL) in the mid-1890s, the SLP leadership divided on the question of its policy toward trade unions. De Leon favored creating dual Socialist unions to rival established AFL craft unions; Morris Hillquit and the moderate "kangaroo" faction argued for boring from within existing unions. Hillquit and the minority wing broke with De Leon and joined Eugene Debs and Victor Berger in founding the SPA in 1901. Later, the SLP attempted to control the syndicalist Industrial Workers of the World (IWW), but De Leon and other SLP members of the IWW were expelled from the union in 1908 for their political dogmatism.

The SLP's great challenge came from the SPA. Unlike the SLP, the SPA participated in electoral politics, a tactic that proved successful in such diverse regions as Milwaukee, Schenectady, New York City, and Oklahoma. Eugene V. Debs's highly visible presidential campaigns also drew support for the SPA. The SPA was much more open to divergent Socialist and radical points of view; this flexibility made it, not the SLP, the principal voice of twentieth-century American socialism. SLP continues, remaining a Marxist splinter sect.

*See also:* Eugene V. Debs, Daniel De Leon, Morris Hillquit, Socialist Party of America

*John Walsh*

## Socialist Party of America

Founded in 1901, the Socialist Party of America (SPA) became the only mass-based American party of the Left in the twentieth century. During the pre-World War I period, its prime, the SPA was a heterogeneous coalition of political and labor organizations, classes, and Socialist points of view. This heterogeneity freed the SPA from the doctrinaire narrowness that so often characterized other leftist parties but created divisions among American Socialists over electoral tactics, union support, and revolution. As a result of internal division, state suppression, and a conservative postwar political climate, the SPA never regained its pre-success.

Initial party membership was less than 10,000. But with able administration, an activist party press, and the leadership of Eugene V. Debs, notably in the presidential campaign of 1908 when he toured 33 states in the famed "red special" train, the party's number grew to a high of 118,000 in 1912. In the election of that year, Debs received 900,000 votes, or 6 percent of the total cast. He matched this number in 1920; with an enlarged electorate, however, his vote represented only 3.5 percent of the total.

An extensive Socialist press assisted the party's rapid prewar rise. The SPA could claim the support at one time of some 323 newspapers, published at varying intervals and in several languages. The most important national Socialist publications included *The Appeal to Reason*, the *International Socialist Review*, and *The Masses*, edited by Max Eastman and Floyd Dell. In 1913 combined Socialist circulation peaked at an estimated 2 million readers.

SPA candidates won an impressive number of local and state public offices. In 1911 and 1912 the SPA held some 1,200 positions in 344 municipalities; of that total, 79 Socialist mayors were elected in 24 states, serving, among others, the cities of Schenectady, New York; Berkeley, California; Flint and Kalamazoo, Michigan; and Rockaway, New Jersey. Victor Berger became the first Socialist elected to Congress, representing Milwaukee in the lower house. Meyer London followed suit in 1916, holding a seat from New York City through 1922.

Although the SPA enrolled no transcendent theoretician who could adapt socialism to the American environment, the articulation of various Socialist viewpoints did largely account for the diverse nature of the SPA's supporters. First, the SPA drew great support from the residue of agrarian radicalism in the Midwest. Second, the relatively conservative social gospel movement, led by Walter Rauschenbusch, attracted several progressive reformers to the SPA and guided George Lunn's agenda as mayor of Schenectady. Victor Berger's moderate gradualism, modeled after the famous German Socialist critic of Marx, Eduard Bernstein, proved successful in Milwaukee, particularly among German-Americans. Eugene V. Debs, who favored a harder line than Berger, especially concerning the use of unions, had a universal appeal. Born in Terre Haute, Indiana, Debs showed that socialism was not solely a foreign importation. He continued to attract public support even during his jail sentences and after the SPA split asunder in 1920.

The two groups that founded the SPA—the Independent Labor Party headed by Berger and Debs and the splinter "kangaroo" wing of the Socialist Labor Party under Morris Hillquit— brought to the SPA a commitment to forge lasting alliances with existing trade unions. The SPA never achieved this goal, thereby denying to its partisans the crucial labor base that was so important to English and German socialism in the same era. The "kangaroo" wing departed the Socialist Labor Party after its sectarian leader, Daniel De Leon, advocated a policy of "dual unionism"—the creation of Socialist trade unions to run parallel to the conservative American Federation of Labor (AFL); Hillquit favored rapprochement with the AFL. The SPA continued Hillquit's position and strove to bore from within the AFL, but AFL head Samuel Gompers steered the union away from Socialist entanglement and toward an informal attachment to the Democratic Party. The industrial unionist and syndicalist Industrial Workers of the World (IWW), the only overarching organized labor alternative to the AFL, disavowed the parliamentarianism and gradualism of the SPA and favored direct industrial action coordinated by the union alone. The IWW's leader, Bill Haywood, was also a member of the SPA, but his extreme syndicalist politics divided the party and ultimately caused his expulsion in 1913. Failing entente with the AFL and having repudiated the IWW, the SPA was left with no significant union base.

Analysts posit several reasons for the SPA's failure, ranging from internal disputes to problems engendered by the electoral system to wider theoretical notions suggesting socialism's incompatibility with American political culture. In 1919, bickering over an ill-conceived Bolshevik cry for immediate revolution split the Socialists in three: Louis Frenna and other Socialist Foreign Language Federation leaders created the American Communist Party in response to the Bolsheviks; a largely American-born group of Socialists formed a rival Communist Labor Party; and the rest, a majority, remained with the SPA. In the 1930s a similar crisis occurred over whether to include Trotskyites in the party.

External forces also deterred SPA growth. The SPA opposed World War I and suffered government suppression as a result; Eugene V. Debs and Victor Berger, for example, were jailed during the war. Abetting this decline were the difficulties that the federal electoral laws and a long-standing two-party system create for any third party. Success for the SPA required that it distinguish itself from progressive elements in the established parties; but the SPA had to appear within the dominant political culture. With Debs as leader, the SPA showed that it did have a truly American base; however, the increasing prominence of radical Foreign Language Federations espousing revolution suggested what Daniel Bell calls American socialism's "other worldliness."

American social conditions did indeed detract from the SPA's appeal. The widespread ownership of private property, the opportunities provided by a just-closed frontier, and the appearance, if not always the reality, of social mobility channeled laborers' political beliefs toward a more conservative capitalistic line. Unlike Europe where hard-fought democratic reforms created national and class identities, all adult white laborers possessed full suffrage in America before the SPA's founding. Finally, no one great cause appeared to unite the American working class, and, although the SPA tried, it could not generate an alternative political culture based on socialism.

*See also:* Victor Berger, Communist Labor Party, Communist Party, Eugene V. Debs, Daniel De Leon, Morris Hillquit

*John Walsh*

REFERENCES

Bell, Daniel. 1960. *The End of Ideology: On the Exhaustion of Political Ideas in the Fifties*. New York: Free Press.

———. 1967. *Marxian Socialism in the United States*. Princeton: Princeton U. Pr.

Cantor, M. 1978. *The Divided Left: American Radicalism, 1900–1975*. New York: Hill and Wang.

Destler, C. M. 1946. *American Radicalism, 1865–1901*. New London: Connecticut Col. Pr.

Dubofsky, M. 1969. *We Shall Be All: A History of the IWW*. Chicago: Quadrangle Books.

Hendrickson, K. E. 1975. "Tribune of the People: George R. Lunn and the Rise and Fall of Christian Socialism in Schenectady." In B. M. Stave, ed. *Socialism and the Cities*. Port Washington, NY: Kennikat.

Karson, M. 1958. *American Labor Unions and Politics 1900–1918*. Carbondale: Southern Illinois U. Pr.

Kipnis, I. 1952. *The Socialist Movement, 1897–1912*. New York: Columbia U. Pr.

Laslett, J. H. M. 1970. *Labor and the Left. A Study of Socialist and Radical Influences in the American Labor Movement, 1881–1924*. New York: Basic Books.

Lipset, S. M. 1977. "'American Exceptionalism' in North American Perspective." In E. M. Adams, ed. *The Idea of America*. Cambridge: Ballinger.

———. 1977. "Why No Socialism in the United States?" In S. Bialer and S. Sluzar, eds. *Sources of Contemporary Radicalism*. Boulder, CO: Westview.

———. 1983. "Radicalism or Reformism: The Sources of Working-Class Politics." 77 *American Political Science Review* 1.

Miller, S. 1973. *Victor Berger and the Promise Constructive Socialism*. Westport, CT: Greenwood.

Perlman, S. 1928. *A Theory of the Labor Movement*. New York: Macmillan.

Salvatore, N. 1982. *Eugene V. Debs. Citizen and Socialist*. Urbana: U. of Illinois Pr.

Shannon, D. A. 1955. *The Socialist Party of America, A History*. Chicago: Quadrangle Books.

Weinstein, J. 1967. *The Decline of Socialism in America 1912–1925*. New York: Monthly Review of Books.

———. 1975. *Ambiguous Legacy: The Left in American Politics*. New York: New Viewpoints.

## Socialist Workers Party

Formed in December 1937 by James P. Cannon, Max Shachtman, and James Burnham, the Socialist Workers Party (SWP) became for a very brief time the focal point of the anti-Stalinist, revolutionary Left in America. From its inception the SWP was avowedly Trotskyite in its orientation, indeed gaining the support of Leon Trotsky himself. The party drew many of its initial members from those purged by the Communist Party of America in 1929 for left-wing criticisms of the Soviet Union. The SWP aimed to achieve proletariat revolution at home, and, under the guidance of the Fourth International, true Socialist transformation worldwide, without the emergence of the crippling bureaucracies that Trotsky believed characterized the Stalin-led Communist retreat from revolution in the Soviet Union.

Throughout its existence, the SWP remained a doctrinaire sect of a miniscule size, never exceeding more than a few thousand members. Factional disputes on points of arcane dogma diminished the party's overall coherence. Just two years after its founding, a major schism emerged between James Cannon, on the one hand, and Max Shachtman and James Burnham on the other, over the so-called Russian Question. Cannon, following Trotsky, argued that although Stalin's regime was "degraded," the basis existed in the Soviet Union for a true Socialist society. Shachtman and Burnham saw no hope in Soviet Russia and left the SWP to found the Workers Party (WP) in 1940. Another major factional dispute broke out in 1953 pitting Cannon against Bert Cochran and George Clarke over the Fourth International's call for Trotskyite to work within all existing Socialist and Communist parties. This dispute led to yet another internal SWP purge.

World War II posed a significant problem for SWP, as it did for radicals in general. No slaves to tactical consistence, the Communist Party called for a cessation of all revolutionary activity until fascism was defeated. The SWP, however, followed a more complex and precarious path, supporting the war effort, while at the same time working toward "true" proletarian democracy in the West. Several SWP members were jailed under the Smith Act. The war did not spur worldwide revolution, as Trotsky had hoped, nor has the shape of postwar international relations resembled Trotsky's vision. Remaining a committed opponent of western democracy, the SWP continued to be the most strident critic of Soviet expansionism among revolutionary Left parties. Despite renewed interest in Trotsky in the 1960s, the SWP in the 1990s proved to be no nearer its goals of socialism at home and permanent revolution abroad than it was at its founding in 1937.

*See also:* Communist Party of America, Socialist Party of America

*John Walsh*

## Soft Money in Presidential Campaigns

Since enactment of the 1974 Federal Election Campaign Act Amendments, presidential candidates and their contributors have devised several means of circumventing the law's contribution and expenditure limits. Among those means, "soft money"—money raised outside the restraints of federal law but spent on activities intended to influence federal election results—has assumed a role of substantial importance, particularly in general election campaigns, thereby arousing considerable controversy.

Although soft money is used to avoid Federal Election Campaign Act (FECA) limits, interpretations of the law by the Federal Election Commission (FEC) and amendments to the FECA enacted in 1979 have actually encouraged its use. Before enactment of the 1979 amendments, the FEC permitted those party committees financing activity in connection with both federal and nonfederal elections to establish separate federal and nonfederal accounts. The FEC also permitted party committees to allocate administrative expenses between the two types of accounts in proportion to the amount of money spent on federal and nonfederal elections or on another "reasonable basis." Subsequent advisory opinions permitted additional expenditures to be allocated between party committee federal and nonfederal accounts, including expenditures for voter registration and turnout drives conducted by state and local parties.

In 1979, in an effort to foster the grass-roots political activity that was missing from the 1976 presidential general election campaign—the first to be publicly funded—Congress passed amendments to the FECA allowing state and local party organizations to conduct specified activities that could benefit federal candidates without the payments made for those activities being considered contributions or expenditures under the FECA. Among the exempted activities were preparation and distribution of slate cards, sample ballots, or other printed listings of three or more candidates for public office for which an election is held in the state; preparation and distribution of grass-roots campaign materials such as pins, bumper stickers, and yard signs for use in connection with volunteer activities on behalf of candidates; conduct of voter registration and turnout drives on behalf of the parties' presidential and vice presidential candidates.

In the case of all three types of exempted activity, only that portion of the costs allocable to federal candidates must be paid out of contributions subject to FECA limits. The remainder may be paid from funds raised under applicable state laws, which, unlike federal law, often permit corporate and/or union political contributions and give freer rein to individual and political action committee contributions than federal law does. The 1979 law, then, extended the principle of allocation to activities that bear directly on publicly funded presidential general election campaigns and lifted spending limits on state and local party committees paying for such activities.

In the 1980 general election campaign, the Republican National Committee (RNC), working in tandem with the Ronald Reagan–George Bush campaign organization, effectively co-opted the mechanism that had been set in place by the 1979 FECA Amendments specifically to encourage grass-roots activity in presidential and other federal election campaigns. The RNC raised some $9 million from individuals and corporations, a bonanza that was then split up among those states where such contributions to party committees were permitted and where spending for voter identification and turnout drives would have the greatest benefit. When money raised for the presidential ticket by state and local parties was combined with the money raised nationally and channeled to individual states, the total spent by state and local party committees on behalf of the Reagan-Bush ticket reached $15 million. The national Democratic Party, slower to recognize the possibilities afforded by the 1979 amendments, raised only about $1.3 million at the national level—largely from unions and individuals—and then also channeled it to those state and local party committees permitted to accept it. An additional $2.7 million was raised and spent by state and local party committees from their own sources.

In 1984 the RNC and presidential campaign operatives raised about $5.6 million in soft money and passed it along directly to state party committees that could accept and use it in ways to benefit the Republican ticket. Individual state party committees raised and spent an additional $5 million on exempt activities. The Democratic National Committee and the Walter Mondale–Geraldine Ferraro campaign combined raised about $6 million in soft money, most of which was deposited first in national committee nonfederal accounts. Some of this money was subsequently transferred to states to be used for voter registration and turnout.

The use of soft money in presidential and other campaigns has generated criticism among several observers of campaign finance, who claim it makes a mockery of the campaign law's contribution and expenditure limits. In February 1988 the FEC published a notice of inquiry seeking comments on possible revisions of its regulations dealing with allocation of expenditures—including expenditures for exempt party activities—between federal and nonfederal accounts of party committees.

*See also:* Federal Election Campaign Act of 1974 and Amendments, Federal Election Commission, Political Action Committees

Brian A. Haggerty

REFERENCES

Alexander, Herbert E. 1986. *"Soft Money" and Campaign Financing.* Washington: Public Affairs Council.

———, with Brian A. Haggerty. 1983. *Financing the 1980 Election.* Lexington, MA: Heath.

———, and ———. 1987. *Financing the 1984 Election.* Lexington, MA: Heath.

Freeberg, Ellen M., and Ellen S. Miller. 1987. *Public Policy and Foundations: The Role of Politicians in Public Charities.* Washington: Center for Responsive Politics.

Lindstrom, Peter, and Ellen Miller. 1985. *Money and Politics: Soft Money—A Loophole for the '80s.* Washington: Center for Responsive Politics.

## Sore Loser Laws

Laws that prevent candidates who lose in party primaries from running as independents in general elections have been adopted in slightly over half the states. This prohibition tries to forestall the continuation of internal factional struggles beyond the primary, and it certainly reduces the number of names on the ballot.

Independent or third-party candidates may still qualify for the ballot through alternate procedures.

These sore loser laws became an issue during John Anderson's attempt to qualify for the general election ballot during his 1980 presidential campaign. Because he did attempt to remove his name from primary ballots or because of ambiguity in the application of sore loser laws to presidential primaries, he managed to overcome this hurdle in all states.

The Supreme Court did uphold California's sore loser law in 1974 (*Storer v. Brown*). While exclusion of candidates from the ballot appears to be undemocratic, the Court went along with the state's desire to enable the parties to play a role in winnowing the number of candidates at successive stages of the process. Voters, then, will have clear-cut choices, and the winner in the general election will have sufficient support to govern effectively.

The existence of sore loser laws in a state reinforces the presumption that almost all candidates will seek office by contesting the party primaries. In an era of candidate-centered campaigning, such laws protect the parties from excessive fragmentation and prevent the distortion of general election outcomes that might otherwise be caused by disgruntled candidates.

*See also:* John Anderson, *Storer v. Brown*

Douglas I. Hodgkin

REFERENCES

Price, David E. 1984. *Bringing Back the Parties.* Washington: Congressional Quarterly.

## Southern Farmers' Alliance

Founded as a stockman's association in 1874, the Southern Farmers' Alliance (SFA) became a strong farmers' organization in the mid-1880s when it spread throughout the cotton-growing regions of Texas. To small, land-owning farmers it offered the hope of improving their status by means of cooperatives through which they could buy goods at reduced prices and sell crops on a bulk basis for higher prices. Between 1887 and 1890 the Alliance spread throughout the nation, but its major strength centered in the South and the western plains. With membership open to men and women, it attempted to revitalize rural culture by combining the features of an evangelical church, a fraternal lodge, and a school.

As members became more aware that the cooperatives alone could not relieve economic distress, they turned to politics. At its national meeting in 1889, the SFA adopted a platform calling for the abolition of the weak banking system, the establishment of a flexible currency, the free and unlimited coinage of silver, the nationalization of railroads, and laws to discourage large-scale engrossment of land.

In 1890 the Alliance entered politics by forging alliances with the Democratic Party in the South and independent parties in the West. Although the SFA enjoyed some electoral success in both sections, Alliance-dominated legislatures in the South still failed to enact promised reforms. That failure, combined with the collapse of the cooperatives in face of falling cotton prices in 1891, contributed to the order's rapid demise. The SFA played an important role in preparing many of its members to become Populists. When the People's Party appeared in 1892, it derived much of its ideology, organizational structure, and leadership from the Southern Farmers' Alliance.

*See also:* National Farmers' Alliance and Industrial Union, People's Party, Populist (People's) Party

*William F. Holmes*

REFERENCES

Barnes, Donna A. 1984. *Farmers in Rebellion: The Rise and Fall of the Southern Alliance and People's Party in Texas*. Austin: U. of Texas Pr.

Holmes, William F. 1984. "The Southern Farmers' Alliance and the Georgia Senatorial Election of 1890." 50 *Journal of Southern History* 197.

Mitchell, Theodore R. 1987. *Political Education in the Southern Farmers' Alliance, 1887–1900*. Madison: U. of Wisconsin Pr.

Schwartz, Michael. 1976. *Radical Protest and Social Structure: The Southern Farmers' Alliance and Cotton Tenancy, 1880–1890*. New York: Academic Press.

Steelman, Lala Carr. 1985. *The North Carolina Farmers' Alliance: A Political History, 1887–1893*. Greenville, NC: East Carolina U. Pr.

## Southern Politics

Politically the South has been the nation's most distinctive region. Southern political uniqueness, like much of its economic and social distinctiveness, is traceable to the Civil War. Losing the Civil War, the freeing and enfranchising of African-Americans and the affiliation of Black voters with the Republican Party pushed white southerners toward the Democratic Party.

Democratic dominance was never really unchallenged, however, until the turn of the century. The end of the Populist insurgency, which was accompanied by Black disfranchisement, left the Democratic hegemony intact, save for a few GOP enclaves in the Appalachian highlands. While the realignment of the 1890s left much of the country in the control of one or another single party, the South was unique in the intensity and the persistence of Democratic control. For decades Republicans not only never won, but they rarely fielded candidates.

The Democratic Party, whose members ranged from the ideological heirs of the Populists to the most conservative representatives of the business community, was often fragmented. During the second quarter of the twentieth century, Georgia, Louisiana, and Virginia had well-established bifactional Democratic politics. The other eight states of the Confederacy had multifactional politics in which followings tended to be personal and short-lived.

Until the 1970s, the tenure of most southern governors was limited to four years. The frequency with which the governor's chair came open contributed to multicandidate campaigns for top state offices. Open congressional seats, although infrequent, attracted multiple candidates. As a consequence of the large candidate fields and the absence of a Republican opponent in the general election, most southern states adopted a runoff primary to insure that a small plurality of the electorate could not suffice to elect.

In the 1990s, seven southern states and Oklahoma require majority support for nomination; in North Carolina, nominees must poll 40 percent of the vote. Louisiana has a unique open primary in which Democrats and Republicans compete together. If no candidates receives a majority on the first ballot, the top two vote-getters meet in a runoff. Candidates who poll a majority in the initial balloting are elected. Most Louisiana runoffs involve two Democrats, with gubernatorial runoffs being the one situation likely to have a Democrat and a Republican facing each other in this second round of balloting.

Campaign styles, as well as electoral structure, were influenced by one-party dominance. One way to attract attention in the crowded primary fields was to make personalities, not issues, the focus of the campaigns. Rhetoric as hot as Cajun cooking and behavior intended to entertain the rustic voters at the branchheads and crossroads of the rural South characterized southern campaigns almost until a generation ago. In addition to demagoguery, several of these colorful politicians were touched by scandal but rarely convicted. Some, like former Georgia governor Eugene Talmadge, turned scandal to their advantage. When opponents charged

Talmadge with misuse of state funds, he stirred the passions of his supporters by telling them "Yeah, it's true. I stole, but I stole for you, the dirt farmers!"

In the issueless context in which most of these campaigns were conducted, candidates' strongest supporters were often their "friends and neighbors." Each candidate ran strongest in the region of the state from which he or she came, where he or she had gone to school, or where there were relatives. For example, Alabama's populist governor, Jim Folsom, had two bases of overwhelming support: the area around Elba where he grew up and the area around Cullman where he had sold insurance.

For generations the bond uniting southern politicians of various styles and from different parts of their states was a public commitment to white supremacy. African-Americans were driven from the political arena after a series of elections in which their votes were manipulated by competing white powerbrokers. Around the turn of the century, when disenfranchisement took place, Blacks still were the majority in many rural areas of the South, and, until denied the ballot, Blacks were still being elected to a range of offices that included the U.S. House.

African-Americans were disfranchised through the adoption of literacy and understanding tests, the white primary, and the poll tax. Despite exemptions such as the grandfather clause that were intended to permit illiterate whites to register, the lower classes of both races were in fact eliminated from the electorate. The constricted electorate facilitated manipulation by rural political bosses. Their influence was particularly great in Georgia where nominations for statewide and congressional positions required not a majority of the popular vote but a majority of the county unit vote.

Failure to reapportion state legislatures allowed the rural Black Belt to exercise undue influence. The potential for African-American rule in these areas, should Blacks be allowed to vote, made these legislators adamantly opposed to any efforts to extend political or economic rights to minority citizens.

Changes beginning in the 1950s and accelerating in the 1970s have eliminated much of southern distinctiveness. In response to its northern Black constituents, the national Democratic Party called for civil rights legislation. Once the northern wing of the party breached the tacit understanding that civil rights would not be an issue, conservative southerners

had less reason to remain Democrats. In 1952 Dwight Eisenhower carried four of the six Rim South states, and his coattails brought Republicans to Congress from North Carolina and Virginia.

Conservative presidential candidate Barry Goldwater's nomination triggered further changes in 1964. That year the first Republicans in modern times were elected to Congress from the Deep South, while southern Blacks moved massively into the Democratic Party. In areas having a sizable African-American vote, Democratic nominees are now less conservative, with Republicans dominating the right end of the spectrum.

As party competition has supplanted the Democratic primary and runoff as the locus of candidate choice, the down-home idiosyncratic colorfulness of the candidates and their friends' and neighbors' ties have become less significant. Southern elections are now more like those in the rest of the country with pollsters, media consultants, and direct mail experts playing important roles.

As the GOP has matured in the South, the distribution of partisan success there also has become more like that in other regions. Convergence has been greatest at the presidential level where, according to Earl and Merle Black "on the average, the post-Great Society presidential elections have produced the smallest difference between the South and the rest of the nation ever observed since the end of Reconstruction."

*See also:* Direct Mail, Barry Goldwater, Poll Tax, Eugene Talmadge

*Charles S. Bullock III*

REFERENCES

Anderson, William. 1975. *The Wild Man from Sugar Creek*. Baton Rouge: Louisiana State U. Pr.

Bullock, Charles S., III. 1988. "The South in Congress: Power and Policy." In James F. Lea, ed. *Contemporary Southern Politics*. Baton Rouge: Louisiana State U. Pr.

Grafton, Carl, and Anne Permaloff. 1985. *Big Mules and Branchheads*. Athens: U. of Georgia Pr.

Key, V. O., Jr. 1949. *Southern Politics in State and Nation*. New York: Knopf.

Kousser, J. Morgan. 1974. *The Shaping of Southern Politics*. New Haven: Yale U. Pr.

Parker, Joseph B. 1988. "New-Style Campaign Politics: Madison Avenue Comes to Dixie." In James F. Lea, ed. *Contemporary Southern Politics*. Baton Rouge: Louisiana State U. Pr.

## Harrison E. Spangler (1879–1965)

Short-term chair of the Republican National Committee. Harrison Earl Spangler was the son of a farmer-politician, born on an Iowa farm. He served as a private in the Spanish-American War, studied law at the University of Iowa, got his degree in 1905, and joined a firm in Cedar Rapids in 1907.

A doorbell-ringing Republican, Spangler worked his way up through the precinct and county organizations in Iowa. By 1930 he was chairman of the Republican State Central Committee and, in 1931, a national committeeman, a position he held until 1952. Spangler was a member of the executive committee of the national committee in 1932.

Kansas Republicans were the only winning Republican organization in the nation in 1932 and felt justified in taking initiatives in national party affairs. They proposed that a Republican grass-roots convention be held in the Midwest as a first step in reviving the national party. Iowa state chairman Spangler was asked to help. Some 6,000 delegates from ten midwestern states gathered in Springfield, Illinois, in June 1935, generating much rank-and-file and press enthusiasm. Spangler was charged with sustaining the initiative, and he carried it forward by inaugurating Grass Roots clubs, encouraging Young Republican clubs, and endorsing women's organizations.

Following the defeat of Wendell Willkie in the presidential race of 1940, the search for a chairman became a choice between a Willkie internationalist or a Robert A. Taft isolationist. Spangler proved to be the compromise.

As national chairman, Spangler created a 49-member Post-War Advisory Council to write a "realistic peacetime program for American progress"—that is, a draft platform for the 1944 Republican National Convention. The document and related organizational activities at national headquarters paved the way for a well-run convention in 1944. Spangler's successor, Herbert Brownell, Jr., retained him as general counsel to the national committee for the ensuing four years.

*See also:* Herbert Brownell, Jr., Robert A. Taft, Wendell Willkie

*Ralph M. Goldman*

REFERENCES

Goldman, Ralph M. 1990. *The National Party Chairmen and Committees: Factionalism at the Top.* Armonk, NY: M. E. Sharpe.

Johnson, Donald B. 1960. *The Republican Party and Wendell Willkie.* Urbana: U. of Illinois Pr.

## John Sparkman (1899–1985)

Alabama's man in Washington for more than four decades. John Sparkman began his political career in 1936 when he won a seat in the U.S. House of Representatives as a New Dealer. In 1946 he prevailed in a special election to fill John H. Bankhead's unexpired Senate seat at the same time achieving reelection to the House. Sparkman thus became the only person in history to be elected to both chambers at the same time. The same year, he headed the Democratic National Committee's Speakers' Bureau. In this position, he kept abreast of political developments and potential problems for the party. One such problem was the Dixiecrat Revolt in 1948. Dixiecrats were conservative southern Democrats in mutiny against the liberal civil rights policy of their party's majority.

Sparkman and Senator Lister Hill led the fight against the Dixiecrats in Alabama by urging the state's voters to support the Democratic presidential nominee, Harry S Truman, instead of the Dixiecrats' nominee, Strom Thurmond. However, the Dixiecrats managed to insure that no Alabama presidential electors were pledged to Truman, so Alabamians could not vote for him. Sparkman's failure to outmaneuver the Dixiecrats did not in fact hurt him politically; he won a full term to the Senate in 1948 with 84 percent of the vote.

To insure the South's return to the national Democratic Party in the 1952 election, presidential nominee Adlai E. Stevenson asked Sparkman to be his running mate. Dwight D. Eisenhower defeated the Stevenson-Sparkman ticket, but Sparkman's presence facilitated Alabama's return to the national party. He was reelected to the Senate four more times and retired in 1978 to end the longest career of any Alabamian in the U.S. Senate.

*See also:* Elections of 1948 and 1952, Adlai E. Stevenson II, Strom Thurmond, Harry S Truman

*Henry J. Walker, Jr.*

REFERENCES

Barnard, William D. 1974. *Dixiecrats and Democrats: Alabama Politics, 1942–1950.* University: U. of Alabama Pr.

Grafton, Carl, and Anne Permaloff. 1985. *Big Mules and Branchheads: James E. Folsom and Political Power in Alabama.* Athens: U. of Georgia Pr.

Sims, George E. 1985. *The Little Man's Big Friend: James E. Folsom in Alabama Politics, 1946–1958.* University: U. of Alabama Pr.

Van Der Veer Hamilton, Virginia. 1987. *Lister Hill: Statesman from the South.* Chapel Hill: U. of North Carolina Pr.

## Speaker of the House

The Speaker of the United States House of Representatives is one of four federal officials designated by the Constitution. His constitutional role as the presiding officer of the "people's branch" of the Congress carries with it the obligation to be fair and impartial in enforcing the rules of the House, and to be forceful and dignified in defending the rights and privileges of the House with respect to the President, the Senate, and the courts. Third in line of succession to the presidency, the Speaker is often said to hold the second most powerful office under the Constitution. Such power as the speakership possesses, however, derives as much from the Speaker's political role as from his constitutional duties.

The American speakership traces its origin to the same position in the British House of Commons. Today the speaker of the Commons is a nonpartisan presiding officer. But in the seventeenth century when the American colonies were established, the speaker of the Commons was deeply involved in the political struggles of the day, and it was that highly politicized version of the speakership that was transported across the Atlantic by the colonists. While not much is known about the colonial speakership, it was in all likelihood a highly political position, and the Founders would certainly have expected the speakership of the United States House of Representatives to be a political as well as a parliamentary office.

And so it has been. Frederick C. Muhlenberg of Pennsylvania (1789–1791; 1793–1795) was elected Speaker of the First Congress with Federalist support. From then on, Speakers of the House have been deeply involved in national political issues, and the speakership has been shaped by the evolution of the American political system. During the early years of the Republic the federal government was relatively weak and inconsequential. With the development of political parties, partisan pressures on the speakership increased. Still, until the 1830s the speakership was not essentially a party position. One indication of this was the role that Henry Clay of Kentucky played as Speaker (1811–1814; 1815–1820; 1823–1825). Clay was elected to the speakership in 1810 on his first day of service in the House. He remained Speaker (with a couple of short interruptions) until 1824 when he became Secretary of State in the John Quincy Adams administration. Every time that Clay, a Democratic-Republican at the time, sought the speakership he was elected by an overwhelming vote, even winning the support of members associated with the Federalist opposition. The "Western Star" was a great national leader as Speaker, as Secretary of State, and as a United States Senator. He remains the only Speaker of the House to have loomed larger than the office itself.

Other antebellum Speakers were less illustrious than Henry Clay, and in fact the antebellum speakership was usually a very weak institution. During the Andrew Jackson administration the political party system crystallized, with the Whig Party emerging in opposition to Jackson Democrats. While Speakers at this time were more likely to represent party interests, the political parties were themselves weak, and the speakership could not be strong. The weakness of the political parties during what has been called America's "second party system" probably owed to the infirmity of the antebellum state. The two decades before the Civil War were marked by increasing sectional controversy over slavery and its extension into the territories in the West. The fundamental schisms in the polity shattered the party system, and many small fringe parties emerged, of which the Free Soilers and Know-Nothings were the most famous.

Operating in the midst of a fragmented political system, the speakership of the House was marked by high turnover. Of the 48 men who have served as Speaker, 12 served between 1834 and 1860. Only two Speakers during this period served for two successive Congresses. Although marked by tenures of short duration, the speakership was defined by important powers that were made more significant because of the controversy over slavery. Speakers had the power to appoint committees and the right of floor recognition; this authority meant that the party controlling the chair could very likely control the House agenda. Ironically, so important were these powers that the struggle for the speakership often forced candidates to make commitments about committee appointments and policy issues in advance of being elected. The result was a speakership that was in form powerful but in fact incapable of governing the House.

The decade before the Civil War witnessed the denouement of the speakership. On several occasions, the House was paralyzed by protracted speakership elections; on two occasions, the House had to use the plurality rule when no candidate could win a majority. In 1860, on the eve of the Civil War, the House eventually elected a complete newcomer, William Pennington of New Jersey (1860–1861), to the chair. Pennington and Henry Clay were the only two newcomers ever elected as Speaker, but in Clay's case the choice owed to his great popularity, while Pennington was elected because he was a nonentity.

Even if the antebellum speakership was weak, several of the antebellum Speakers were very competent. Henry Clay was the only antebellum Speaker to have shaped the office to his own interest and was the greatest among them. But Andrew Stevenson of Virginia (1827–1834), James K. Polk of Tennessee (1835–1839), Robert Winthrop of Massachusetts (1847–1849), Howell Cobb of Georgia (1849–1851), and Nathaniel Banks of Massachusetts (1855–1857) were also effective Speakers of the antebellum era.

After the Civil War a new era in American politics brought with it a new rendition of the speakership. Unlike its prewar predecessor, this new speakership marked its primary tendency in the steady accumulation of centralized power in the House. In the midst of a two-party system that was at first dominated by Republicans but later relatively competitive, the speakership became a very powerful office under the rules of the House. Sectional conflict did not disappear with the end of the war, and after the South returned to full participation in the government, it resisted the attempts of the Radical Republicans to impose a political order hostile to southern culture. One of the techniques employed in the House was obstructionism, the use of rules and procedures to delay business and then to defeat legislation. Two of the most common practices were the use of dilatory motions and the disappearing quorum. The former could take the form of motions to adjourn, useless quorum calls, motions to read in-full the previous days journal, or frivolous amendments. Quorums disappeared when members who were physically present would refuse to respond to their names. The Democratic minority pioneered the use of these tactics in resisting "force" bills designed to enforce voting rights for African-Americans in the South; but in the years after 1873 the Republicans too often availed themselves of obstructive tactics when in the minority.

While this trend was under way, Speakers were getting more powerful. They retained the power to make committee appointments and came increasingly to control the floor agenda. As the nation embarked on a prolonged period of nationalization and industrialization, the legislative agenda of the House became much more crowded, and the principal means for controlling it was the Speaker's power of floor recognition. In the 1870s Republican Speaker James G. Blaine of Maine (1869–1875) developed the practice of using a "Speaker's list" of members seeking floor recognition. Speakers had always had the right to ask, "for what purpose does the gentleman rise?" Blaine asked members to come to him for prior clearance for floor recognition, and if the Speaker did not approve of the purpose, then the member would fail recognition.

Even the use of a list was inadequate to the business of the House, however, in considering major pieces of legislation; the House really needed a way of structuring and limiting debate. To this end the House evolved the practice of designing separate rules for each bill that came to the floor. At first floor rules were designed by the Speaker and a committee that he would appoint. In 1880 the House undertook a major reform of its procedures under the leadership of Democratic Speaker Samuel J. Randall of Pennsylvania (1876–1881); chief among the results was the creation of a standing Rules Committee, appointed and chaired by the Speaker. This development meant that the Speaker could now control all committee assignments, floor recognition, and the terms under which all legislation would be debated.

The stage was set for an all-encompassing speakership, but across its path lay "obstructionism." In 1890 the back of obstruction was broken by one of the House's great Speakers, Thomas B. Reed, Republican of Maine (1889–1891; 1895–1899). "Czar" Reed had vowed that he would defeat obstructionism or resign the speakership. When the Fifty-first Congress convened in 1890, he delayed presenting a new code of rules to the House until all disputed election cases had been settled. Operating under general parliamentary law, Reed choose to count a quorum when the Democrats refused to answer the roll call in a disputed election case. Amid pandemonium in the House, Reed calmly insisted on the principle that members physically present could not be constitutionally absent, and when the House codified that principle in the rules of the Fifty-first Congress, the most important form of obstructionism was dead. When the Democrats returned to power in the Fifty-second Congress, they revived the old rules. Reed, however, used those rules to block the

House until finally the Democrats conceded that the Reed Rules would become permanent.

With a highly centralized speakership, and obstructionism a thing of the past, little stood in the way of legislative despotism. From 1901 to 1910 Joseph G. "Uncle Joe" Cannon, Republican of Illinois, ruled the House with an iron hand. One member, asked by a constituent for a copy of the rules of the House, sent along a picture of Uncle Joe instead. Under Cannon, the House rules were the Speaker's will. In controlling the agenda of the House, Cannon was able to control the agenda of the government. Even so popular a President as Theodore Roosevelt was forced to bargain with Cannon, and usually Uncle Joe got his way.

The political significance of Cannonism lay less in the Speaker's powers than in the ends for which they were used. Unlike the 1890s, when the Republicans were solidly entrenched as the nation's governing majority, by the first decade of the twentieth century, the Republican Party was divided from within by the schism between its "stalwart" and "progressive" wings. Roosevelt led the progressives, Joe Cannon and Senator Nelson Aldrich of Rhode Island stood for the stalwarts. By using their control over congressional procedures to block progressive legislation, especially tariff reform, Cannon and Aldrich placed themselves between rock-hard supporters within their congressional caucuses and the growing strength of progressivism in the country at large.

In 1910 the House revolted against Cannon when progressive Republican George Norris of Nebraska led a fight to take control of the Rules Committee away from the Speaker. The House eventually voted to reconstitute the Rules Committee and make the Speaker ineligible to serve on it. In one of the most dramatic moments in the history of the lower chamber, Cannon conceded defeat and offered to vacate the chair so that the House could elect a new Speaker. History has treated Uncle Joe more harshly than he deserves. He was a homespun and good-humored man who had the personal affection of many of the same members of the House who opposed his policies. Most of the insurgent Republicans who had voted to strip him of his powers refused to rob him of his post, and Cannon stood reaffirmed, if not vindicated, before the House. The voters, however, were less kind to him in the 1912 election, and he was swept out of office for only the second time in his 50-year career. Reelected to the House in 1914, he remained there until his retirement in 1924. Joe Cannon served his country and district for 46 years and was one of the most influential Speakers in the history of the House.

The revolution of 1910 broke the back of the speakership, just as the adoption of the Reed Rules had broken the back of obstructionism 20 years before. But politics involves power, and power would not disappear simply because one loci had been dismantled. During the 50 years after the revolt against Cannon a new system of internal governance came to dominate the House, a process by which the Speaker became first among several feudal barons, the committee chairmen, who together controlled the legislative agenda. When the Democrats took control of the House in 1912, they decided to further reduce the powers of the speakership. The authority to make Democratic committee appointments was transferred to the Democratic members of the Ways and Means Committee, the chairman of which also served as Democratic floor leader. Speaker Champ Clark of Missouri supported the diminution of his own power in order to make the House a more democratic institution.

But the changes in the rules did not lead to greater democracy in the House. Instead, the standing committees and their chairmen played an ever-increasing role in controlling the House's business. On both the Democratic and Republican sides, adherence to the seniority principle led to the entrenchment of an elite at the head of the committee lists, a practice especially significant in the Democratic Party because the Democrats' seniority roster was top-heavy with southern conservatives. The Republicans controlled the House for only two Congresses after 1932, and this long period of Democratic hegemony shaped the House in the image of the party's caucus. Between 1932 and 1961 that image reflected the dominance of the solid South.

The Speakers of the House during its feudal era were often weak. When the Republicans were in power in the 1920s Nicholas Longworth of Ohio (1925–1930) was an assertive yet popular Speaker, but Longworth had the benefit of a solid partisan majority. His friend and successor, John Nance Garner of Texas (1931–1932) was a strong leader who was limited by a very narrow partisan majority. During the 1930s, Franklin D. Roosevelt dealt with a series of weak Democratic Speakers, men who had been nurtured in the tradition of deference to committees and who, as Speaker, were loath to challenge the power of the baronial committee chairs. One of those barons, Sam Rayburn of Texas, was among the most influential of the Depression-era chairmen. Under his leadership, the House Interstate and Foreign Commerce Committee passed several pieces of major regulatory legislation during FDR's first administration. Rayburn was one of several Texas committee titans at that time, and the very power of the rest of the Texas delegation prevented him from winning a place in the party's leadership until 1937. From 1937 to 1941 he served as Democratic floor leader, and when Speaker William Bankhead of Alabama (1937–1941) passed away, Sam Rayburn became Speaker of the House.

Rayburn was the House's longest-serving Speaker, and during his later years he became a figure of legend. Although his power derived wholly from his position, his public image eventually transcended his station; starting as Mr. Speaker, he became Mr. Sam. As leader of the Democrats from 1941 until his death in 1961, he was the central figure in the House's feudal power structure, first among equals, the broker of the powerbrokers. Rayburn had fewer powers than such powerful Speakers of the past as Cannon, Reed, Blaine, and Clay; yet his influence in the House was as central to its system of governance than as theirs had been before. It simply operated on a different principle. Whereas the czars of old had been able to control the business of the House through personal popularity, the force of partisan majorities, and aggressive use of formal powers, Rayburn shaped the congressional agenda by working hand-in-hand with the House committee chairmen.

Often, this arrangement meant that Rayburn had to accede to his chairmen's preferences, but he had little reason to oppose them since normally his views were not much different from theirs. Rayburn's speakership was reactive in many respects, accommodative in others. He was forced to react to the initiatives of a presidency that Roosevelt had made strong, and he was forced to accommodate the demands of committee chairmen who he could seek to persuade but could not command. His ability to operate in this environment for two decades owed in large part to the fact that he had shaped it himself. The feudal milieu was ideally suited to Rayburn's temperament, position, and beliefs.

But among the circumstances that permitted Rayburn to be so effective as Speaker was the fact that the nation was willing to tolerate the the conservative agenda of the congressional power structure. By the late 1950s, the tide of reform pressed against the shoals of committee governance. The House Rules Committee had evolved from its origins in the revolt against Cannon to become a powerful and independent force in controlling the congressional agenda. It was dominated by a coalition of conservative Democrats and Republican led in 1961 by Virginia Democrat "Judge" Howard Smith. With the election of John F. Kennedy in 1960, liberals moved to break the back of the Rules Committee by packing it with more liberal members. In the last great fight of his career, Rayburn was successful in winning a narrow victory over Smith that permitted the Speaker to gain working control of the Rules Committee. Eight months later, Rayburn died, passing from the scene just as the great torrent of reform was about to break.

In the years since Rayburn's death, the House has entered a new era in its evolution, and the speakership has changed dramatically from the office that Rayburn so honorably held. The speakership of John W. McCormack (1962–1970) witnessed the beginning of the reform movement, as liberals in the House pressed for institutional reforms as a means to enact progressive legislation. The House reforms of the late 1960s and early 1970s were marked by two conflicting directions. One tendency was toward democratization and the diffusion of power: the liberal Democrats who led the reform movement believed that the dominance of southern conservative committee chairmen had impeded the enactment of progressive legislation and were determined to undermine the power of the barons. The other tendency was toward a stronger speakership. Members recognized that the House could not function efficiently unless the Speaker could manage its business effectively, and such utility required that the powers of the speakership be enhanced.

The tendency toward diffusion led the House to strip from the committee chairs much of their control over their committees; in their place numerous subcommittees were given independent powers. The tendency toward centralization led House Democrats to give to their Speaker the power to control the Rules Committee and the power to make committee assignments through the Democratic Steering and Policy Committee, which the Speaker chairs. The Democratic Caucus also retained the right to accept or reject the Steering and Policy Committee's nominations of committee chairmen.

Most of these changes came about during the tenure of Speaker Carl Albert, Democrat of Oklahoma (1971–1976). Albert's tenure was the most difficult and controversial of the twentieth century, as the Congress and the country were shaken by the Vietnam War, controversy over school busing and other social issues, and the Watergate crisis. The Speaker of the House is constitutionally third in line of succession to the presidency, and on two occasions Speaker Albert stood "a heartbeat away" from the White House. These major political conflicts and the reform movement inside the House combined to make the Albert speakership a difficult one.

Speaker Albert had served in the House leadership since he was appointed as Democratic Whip by Sam Rayburn in 1955. As Majority Leader under Speaker John McCormack from 1961 to 1970, he had helped marshal Lyndon Johnson's Great Society through the House. His effectiveness as a legislative leader had depended importantly on his ability to work with both the senior southern conservatives, and the younger liberal reformers who were out to unseat them. In this respect, Albert was well suited to facilitate the transition from the old order to the new, but he could not easily assume the leadership of the reform movement itself. As a result, Albert's tenure witnessed the anomaly of a greatly strengthened speakership nurtured by a Speaker whose position inhibited the aggressive use of the new-found powers at his disposal. The Albert legacy to the House was a speakership that had recaptured much of the formal power that had been stripped away in the aftermath of the revolt against Cannon. His successor, Thomas P. (Tip) O'Neill, Jr., of Massachusetts (1977–1987), was the beneficiary.

Tip O'Neill was among the most colorful of American Speakers. His five-term speakership was one of the longest in American history. O'Neill's Irish verve lent itself well to the democratic culture in the House that evolved during the 1960s and 1970s. As Speaker he sought to include many Democrats in various leadership activities. One of O'Neill's favorite devices was the use of task forces to press for enactment of individual bills. Under O'Neill's leadership, the Democratic Party's Steering and Policy Committee became more active, and its Whip organization enlarged.

Still, O'Neill was not greatly interested in the details of legislation, usually deferring to the committee system when it came to substance. Now, however, the committees were no longer the key venues; their subcommittees, numbering over 150 in all, made the key decisions on legislation. With the decline in the power of the full committees, members no longer felt much of an obligation to defer to them when legislation was brought to the floor. As a result, control of floor action became more important. The Republican minority became adept at fashioning troublesome amendments and substitutes, and the Democratic leadership had to worry about protecting its members. At the same time, O'Neill made increasing use of the power of "multiple referral" (another innovation of the Albert speakership), a feature that meant that on many major bills several committees and subcommittees had pieces of the action. All of these maneuvers combine to make the Speaker's job of regulating floor action very difficult and serve to explain O'Neill's inclusive methods.

Actually, Tip O'Neill had two speakerships, not just one. The speakership of the House is usually a reactive office, and the main force to which it often reacts is the presidency. When a Speaker and a President are of the same party, the Speaker will ordinarily accept an obligation to support the President's policies; when the two are of opposing parties, the Speaker will assume the role of loyal opposition. During Jimmy Carter's presidency, Tip O'Neill was cast in the role of administration supporter on Capitol Hill, even if Carter's policies were too conservative for O'Neill. When, in 1980, Ronald Reagan swept into the White House and the Republicans took control of the Senate, Tip O'Neill became the nation's leading elected Democrat and was a vocal opponent of the Reagan administration.

For a Speaker of the House to have become so publicly visible was very unusual. In O'Neill's case, his high profile as the nemesis of the Reagan revolution was made more prominent because of his Irish persona and larger-than-life appearance. Tip O'Neill came to symbolize all that was best and worst in Democratic liberalism and in the process became the best known Speaker in American history.

In the later part of the twentieth century the speakership of the House regained much of the power and prestige that it had lost when Uncle Joe Cannon was toppled from power; but the House of Representatives and the political system at large had changed in fundamental ways, and even a speakership clothed in some of the powers of old could not easily play so dominant a role. The fundamental fact about the House has always been that its members come from independently elected and geographically defined districts. By the last decade of the century, those members were also independent of national, state, or local party organizations and were essentially autonomous political entrepreneurs whose electoral fate lay largely in their own hands.

In dealing with this large community of mavericks, a good Speaker has to seek in various ways to further his own ends. Speaker's must communicate, conciliate, cajole, and occasionally coerce. The powers at their disposal are substantial, but they are only effective if used at the right time and for the right purpose. A Speaker who uses his powers arbitrarily, systematically, and punitively is likely to jeopardize his position. In the end, the principal obligation of the Speaker of the House is to facilitate its action on the public agenda. The House of Representatives is and must be a deliberative institution within which public dialogue on the nation's weal continuously takes place. The Speaker of the House is the leader of his party and will ordinarily seek to enact its program. But the enactment of the party program is itself only a means to an end, and the larger end of politics is the formation of consensus on the legitimacy of these policies that the Congress enacts.

In this context, then, the controversial speakership by Jim Wright (1987–1989) must be considered. Speaker Wright possessed many of the qualities that members of the House have often desired in their Speaker. Wright's manner was forceful, his mind keen, and his grasp of public policy sophisticated. In his first term as Speaker, he ventured into new terrain, such as his involvement in the negotiations over a peace plan for Central America. He often used his control over the Rules Committee to fashion restrictive rules for floor consideration of major bills, and he was apparently indifferent to the minority Republicans and their leadership. At the same time, Wright was willing to call publicly for new revenues to address the budget deficit, and he pushed relentlessly for the enactment of initiatives in public works, highway construction, aid to the homeless, and trade legislation.

In seeking to drive the House in the direction of his preferred policies, Jim Wright eventually undermined the comity that is necessary for the House to function well. Major legislative victories in the One Hundredth Congress led to bitter acrimony in the One Hundred First. The enmity Wright earned among Republicans was not counterbalanced by affection in the Democratic Caucus. When Speaker Wright made himself vulnerable to charges of ethical impropriety, he was forced to resign the speakership. The real cause of his resignation was not the ethics charges themselves; Wright was forced to resign because he had conducted the speakership in a way that was at odds with the political culture of the House and the values of its members. This lesson was not lost on his successor, Thomas Foley of Washington, who has sought to manage the House in a more conciliatory fashion.

Whether the Speaker of the House be an institutional facilitator in the mode of Carl Albert, a public symbol as Tip O'Neill became, a hard-driving partisan as Jim Wright sought to be, or an institutional therapist like Tom Foley, the speakership itself will play a significant role in the political system, more important than at any time since the turn of the century. The country has become more difficult to govern, just as the government has become more difficult to control. The Speaker of the House has more to do with how well the Congress functions than any other single person. A Speaker cannot do it alone, because his powers are not plenary; but a Speaker who does not put the powers at his disposal to their best effect will not fulfill the obligations of office. Today the government needs a Speaker who is both wise and assertive in the use of the powers of the office—assertive enough to lead and wise enough to know how.

*See also:* Individual Speakers, Presidents, and political parties; Majority Party Leadership in Congress; George Norris; Vietnam War as a Political Issue; Watergate

*Ronald M. Peters, Jr.*

REFERENCES

Bolling, Richard. 1964. *House Out of Order.* New York: Dutton.

———. 1968. *Power in the House.* New York: Dutton.

Brown, George Rothwell. 1922. *Leadership of Congress.* New York: Arno Press.

Cheney, Lynne, and Richard Cheney. 1983. *Kings of the Hill.* New York: Continuum.

Chiu, Chang-Wei. 1928. *The Speaker of the House of Representatives Since 1896.* New York: Columbia U. Pr.

Cooper, Joseph, and David Brady. 1981. "Institutional Context and Leadership Style: The House from

Cannon to Rayburn." 75 *American Political Science Review* 411.

Dasent, Arthur Irwin. 1911. *The Speakers of the House of Commons*. New York: Burt Franklin.

Follett, Mary Parker. 1904. *The Speaker of the House*. New York: Longmans, Green.

Hasbrook, Paul Dewitt. 1927. *Party Government in the House of Representatives*. New York: Macmillan.

Kennon, Donald. 1984. *The Speakers of the U.S. House of Representatives: A Bibliography 1789–1984*. Baltimore: Johns Hopkins U. Pr.

Peabody, Robert. 1976. *Leadership in Congress*. Boston: Little, Brown.

Peters, Ronald M., Jr. 1990. *The American Speakership*. Baltimore: Johns Hopkins U. Pr.

Ripley, Randall. 1967. *Party Leaders in the House of Representatives*. Washington: Brookings.

Sinclair, Barbara. 1983. *Majority Party Leadership in the U.S. House*. Baltimore: Johns Hopkins U. Pr.

## Specie Resumption Act

The Public Credit Act of 1869 provided for resumption of specie (precious metal) payments, which had halted during the Civil War, at the earliest possible date. The Coinage Act of 1873, which demonetized silver, guaranteed that resumption would occur with gold as the specie basis, but the depression of 1873 made specie resumption politically more difficult.

In 1875 Senator John Sherman (R-Ohio) wrote a bill requiring that resumption of specie payments begin on January 1, 1897. In addition Sherman's bill allowed the Treasury Department to redeem fractional paper currency in silver, repealed the charge for coining gold, removed limitations on bank note issues, and set a $300 million lower limit on greenbacks. Sherman designed his bill to unite Republican soft and hard money factions, and it passed Congress on a nearly straight party vote. President Ulysses Grant signed this Specie Resumption Act.

During the period 1876–1878, when many in Congress sought to repeal the measure, repeal became politically entangled with parallel monetary bills favoring free silver and greenback expansion. In 1876 the House passed a measure to repeal resumption; most Democrats and midwestern Republicans were in favor, with other Republicans and gold Democrats opposed. This bill died in the Senate because of Sherman's opposition. In 1877 the House once again tried to repeal resumption with party members split. Senate Republicans and Democrats finally united on a proposal that would not disturb resumption but would freeze total greenback circulation at $346 million; this bill became law in 1878. Specie resumption began on schedule after the Treasury Department accumulated a substantial reserve of gold.

*See also:* Ulysses S. Grant, Greenbacks, John Sherman

Sue C. Patrick

REFERENCES

Nugent, Walter T. K. 1968. *Money and American Society, 1865–1880*. New York: Free Press.

Unger, Irwin. 1964. *The Greenback Era: A Social and Political History of American Finance, 1865–1879*. Princeton: Princeton U. Pr.

## Split-Ticket Voting

When voters cast their ballots for candidates of two or more political parties for different offices in the same election, split-ticket voting occurs. This pattern contrasts with voting a straight ticket, when voters cast ballots for candidates of only one party. Split-ticket voting is a key symptom of the relative decline of voter loyalty to political parties, since many voters no longer rely on the party label to guide their voting decisions. Successive surveys from the 1950s to the 1980s chart a progressive rise in split-ticket voting among voters regardless of the strength of their partisan identification (although those who consider themselves strong Democrats or Republicans split their tickets less often than Independents). An important consequence of split-ticket voting is split outcomes, whereby the same geographical areas will support candidates from different parties for different offices. At the national level, this paradigm has resulted in partial or complete Democratic Party control of the House of Representatives for 36 of 38 years from 1952 to 1990, yet Republican Party control of the presidency for 26 of those same years. Rises in split-ticket voting often precede major political upheavals as well, as was true in the 1890s and 1920s.

The rise in split-ticket voting is at least partly the consequence of declining partisan allegiances, but it is also related to the way in which voters are presented choices. Studies have demonstrated that split-ticket voting can be encouraged or discouraged according to how candidates and parties are arrayed on the ballot. The party-column ballot, which arrays candidate names according to political party (party labels appear at the top of the ballot, with offices usually appearing in the far left column) encourages straight-ticket voting. The office-block ballot, on the other hand, reverses this arrangement by placing party labels along the left margin, and offices at the top, thereby emphasizing individual choices for each office. Split-ticket voting is also less likely when the ballot form provides voters an opportunity to vote for a party's entire slate either by pressing a single lever or by checking a single box.

Split-ticket voting was virtually impossible in American elections before the twentieth century. Up until that time, each political party prepared its own ballot, listing only the candidates of that party. Voters would then obtain the party ballot of their choice from "party hawkers" who would peddle them on the street on election day; the voters would then bring the ballots to the polling place. In an effort to stem voter fraud, the secret or Australian ballot was introduced in the 1890s. This method of voting introduced state controls over the election process, made voting a private act (voter preferences could readily be discerned under the old system), and incorporated all recognized candidates on a single ballot, thereby prompting a rise in split-ticket voting. According to one study, only about 5 percent of the electorate voted a split ticket in 1900; in the 1980s, over half the electorate did. Split-ticket voting occurs with greatest frequency in state and local elections.

See also: Australian Ballot, Party Identification

*Robert J. Spitzer*

REFERENCES

Hill, David B., and Norman R. Luttbeg. 1983. *Trends in American Electoral Behavior*. Itasca, IL: F. E. Peacock.

Rusk, Jerrold G. 1970. "The Effect of the Australian Ballot Reform on Split Ticket Voting: 1876–1908." 64 *American Political Science Review* 1220.

## Benjamin M. Spock (1903– )

Child-rearing expert turned antiwar activist. An internationally renowned expert on children for over four decades, Benjamin McLane Spock has also received attention for his political activism. Spock was the first individual to be trained as both a pediatrician and a psychiatrist, and he drew upon his professional preparation to produce *The Complete Book of Baby and Child Care*. First published in 1946, this book has greatly influenced the child-rearing practices of post-World War II parents. Rather than the rigidity and discipline emphasized by its predecessors, Spock's book stressed flexibility and affection in child nurture and provided answers to many basic parenting questions that were not addressed in other works. Since its publication, his book has sold more than 30 million copies, second in sales only to the Bible.

It was not until the 1960s that Dr. Spock became actively and publicly involved in politics. According to Spock, the catalyst for this involvement was the 1962 decision of President John F. Kennedy to resume nuclear testing in order to maintain strategic superiority over the Soviet Union. In response, Spock joined the National Committee for a Sane Nuclear Policy (SANE). He announced his membership with an advertisement in major newspapers, cautioning that renewed testing would lead to a bilateral nuclear arms buildup that would increase the possibility of a nuclear accident or conflict. Relating his concerns to his vocation, Spock warned of the dangers of radioactive contamination of the food supply, particularly milk, and the consequences for children.

The Vietnam War continued Spock's radicalization. Having campaigned for Lyndon Johnson, Spock opposed his administration's intensification of the war. The doctor became a leading figure in the peace movement and was arrested and convicted in 1968 for violating selective service laws by urging draft-aged males to refuse conscription; his conviction was overturned in 1969. Spock was also accused of contributing to the radical nature of students in the 1960s and early 1970s because of his permissive theory of child rearing. In 1972 Spock ran for the presidency as a candidate of the People's Party. In 1981 he was arrested outside of the White House protesting President Ronald Reagan's budget and its potential effect on children and families. He remains active in the peace and antinuclear movements, having established the Benjamin Spock Center For Peace in 1982.

See also: Lyndon B. Johnson, John F. Kennedy, Nuclear Freeze Movement, People's Party, Ronald Reagan, Vietnam War as a Political Issue

*Susan L. Roberts*

REFERENCES

Bloom, Lynn Z. 1972. *Doctor Spock: Biography of a Conservative Radical*. Indianapolis: Bobbs-Merrill.

Michalek, Irene R. 1972. *When Mercy Seasons Justice: The Spock Trial*. Boston: Branden Press.

## Robert Squier (1934– )

Democratic Party media strategist. A former film producer for public television, Robert Squier was active in the 1968 presidential campaign of Hubert Humphrey. The shows that Squier helped produce for the campaign intentionally showed Vice President Humphrey responding to provocative questions asked by the audience. These ads were designed to develop a contrast with the more tightly controlled format used by Republican nominee Richard Nixon. Squier was active in the unsuccessful campaign of Senator Edmund Muskie (D-Maine) for the 1972 Democratic presidential nomination. He also had relatively minor roles in the 1976 and 1980 presidential campaigns of Jimmy Carter (D).

However, Squier's reputation as an innovative media producer rests largely on his work in campaigns for governor and the United States Senate. For instance, Squier helped a long-shot candidate, Florida state senator Bob Graham (D), win the governorship. The commercials that showed Graham working in various occupations, such as a garbage collector, helped him rise from obscurity. He went on to serve two terms as governor and then won a seat in the U.S. Senate.

Squier also handled Mississippian William Winter (D) in a 1979 campaign for Democratic nomination for governor. Winter was running against a woman, who was the sitting lieutenant governor, but he emphasized in one Squier-produced television spot that "the governor is commander in chief of the National Guard. . . . The Guard is the first line of national defense." Political observers believe the spot took advantage of the electorate's biased perception that female politicians lack toughness. Winter won the race.

A rare mishap by Squier occurred in Missouri's 1986 U.S. Senate race, where his client, Lieutenant Governor Harriet Woods, started her advertising campaign by appearing with a "crying farmer" in a spot attacking her opponent. The spot backfired, and Squier left the campaign in mid-summer.

*See also:* Jimmy Carter, Hubert H. Humphrey, Edmund S. Muskie, Richard M. Nixon

*Steve Lilienthal*

REFERENCES

Diamond, Edwin, and Steven Bates. 1984. *The Spot: The Rise of Political Advertising on Television.* Cambridge: MIT Pr.

## Neil O. Staebler (1905– )

Michigan leader in political party renewal and election reform. Neil Staebler was a political fundraiser whose interests in the regulation of political finance, in party building, and in encouraging students and young people to participate in politics were paramount.

Staebler's businesses enabled him to devote many years to Democratic politics and public service. He served for more than a decade as chairman of the Michigan Democratic State Central Committee (1950–1961) and, for almost as many years, as a member of the Democratic National Committee from Michigan. Following redistricting, he ran for a seat in the U.S. House of Representatives in a one-time at-large district and served in the Eighty-eighth Congress.

Staebler was a founding member of the Federal Election Commission from 1975 to 1978, and he helped to establish that body. For 16 years Staebler served on the board of trustees of the Citizens' Research Foundation, a private-sector, university-based organization in the same field as the FEC; he was chairman of CRF for seven years.

Staebler has taught courses at several universities. He is the author of *The Campaign Finance Revolution* (1979) and co-author of *How to Argue with a Conservative.*

*See also:* Federal Election Commission

*Herbert E. Alexander*

## Stages of Party Development

The history of the major political parties in the United States can be described in terms of five principal stages.

### The Early Parties, 1790s–1824

The first parties were formed after the Constitution was adopted and the government was underway. Generated by the debate over the issues that engaged Congress and the President—the government's assumption of the war debt, the creation of an excise tax, and the establishment of a national bank—the parties provided the new administration with its most visible sources of support and opposition. Those who stood to benefit from the policies adopted by Washington and his Secretary of the Treasury, Alexander Hamilton (merchants manufacturers, bankers, creditors, and speculators), became Federalists and backed the administration. Those who were disadvantaged (small farmers, laborers, debtors, and generally the poorer members of the society) became Republicans and opposed it.

The early parties were not broad-based organizations; they lacked grass-roots support. Parties were composed primarily of elected officials and others who desired public office. Of the two most prominent early parties, the Federalists had the narrower base. Unable and seemingly unwilling to broaden their appeal, they declined rapidly as a competitive force. In contrast, the Republicans, blessed with a succession of prestigious presidential candidates—the so-called Virginia Dynasty of Jefferson, Madison, and Monroe—were able to coalesce their supporters and give their party a national appeal. The Republicans became the majority party by 1800 and the only national party by 1820.

## The Sectionalization of Parties, 1828–1854

By the mid-1820s, however, the Republicans had become a victim of their own success. Without a rival to compete against, they split into feuding factions. In the election of 1824 two dominant groups emerged: one, the National Republicans, supported John Quincy Adams; the other, the Democratic-Republicans, backed Andrew Jackson. After presidential candidate Jackson was defeated by a vote in the House of Representatives in 1824, he organized a broad-based political coalition and won the 1828 election by a substantial margin.

Jackson built his support in the West and South primarily by appealing to small farmers and newly enfranchised voters; in the East he was supported by Catholics and new immigrants. His opposition, the Whig Party (which developed largely in reaction to Jackson) was composed of the wealthier farmers from the South and West, commercial interests from the East, and antislavery advocates in the Northeast and Appalachia. The Whig Party held itself together in national campaigns by running popular military heroes as candidates.

The policies of the new parties reflected these bases of support. The Democrats supported a rural, agrarian society, one in which the national government had a limited role. The Whigs envisioned a more heavily industrialized society with a stronger central government. They were divided on the slavery question, one that eventually resulted in the Whigs' disintegration.

## The Civil War and Its Aftermath, 1856–1896

The Civil War and the issues generating it led to a schism within the Democratic Party and the collapse of the Whigs as a political entity. The Democrats split over slavery into a northern and southern faction, with each running its own candidates for President in 1860. The Whigs also lost their southern support over slavery and suffered defections in the North primarily out of the fear that newly arrived immigrants would take jobs away from American labor.

In 1854 a new party, the Republicans, was organized. Composed primarily of white laborers and small framers who feared the expansion of slavery in the West, of abolitionists who opposed all forms of slavery, and of entrepreneurs who trumpeted the glories of free enterprise and private ownership, the party ran its first presidential candidate in 1856. John C. Frémont received 40 percent of the vote even though he was not even on the ballots in a number of southern states. With the Democrats divided and the Whigs in disarray, the Republican candidate, Abraham Lincoln, won in 1860 with only 39.8 percent of the total popular vote.

## The Republican Era, 1896–1928

The parties were reasonably competitive at the national level until the end of the nineteenth century. Then a recession in 1893 during a Democratic administration led to a realignment of political forces, with the Republicans gaining adherents in the Northeast and Midwest from many urban ethnic groups other than Irish Catholics and from organized labor. Although the Democrats lost support in the industrial centers, they increased it in the grain-producing states of the prairie and the silver mining states of the Rockies largely on the basis of a free-silver policy advocated by their three-time presidential candidate, William Jennings Bryan. The South remained staunchly Democratic.

The Republican Party dominated national politics until the 1930s. During this period Republicans controlled Congress for all but six years and the White House for all but eight. In the 1920s, however, the flow of new immigrants, combined with unpopular Republican policies, particularly Prohibition, led the urban ethnic groups to return to the Democratic Party. In 1928, for the first time, the Democrats won a majority in the large cities.

## The Democratic Era, 1932–1980s

In the 1932 election the Republicans found themselves in the unfortunate position of campaigning as the incumbent party during one of the greatest economic depressions in the nation's history. They suffered accordingly. The Democrats maintained and expanded their support among white southerners, Catholics, and the urban working class. By 1936 Depression-devastated African-Americans had abandoned the party of Lincoln for the party of economic recovery, the Democrats. Jews, attracted by President Franklin Roosevelt's liberalism and his anti-Nazi foreign policy, shifted to the Democrats. Although the Republican Party retained its hold on northern Protestants, the Democrats made inroads among this group as well, particularly among those in the lower economic group. The electorate was thus divided, as never before, along economic class lines, with the less prosperous more Democratic and the more prosperous more Republican. The exception was the South where voters, regardless of their socioeconomic status, voted for Democrats.

Since the realignment in the 1930s, the party coalitions have become weaker, but they have not completely disintegrated. Although the Democrats continue to dominate the states and the House of Representatives, the Republicans have increased their vote at the presidential level.

The most significant and enduring shift between the major party coalitions during this period has been the defection of southern white Protestants to the Republican column at the national level. Catholic support for the Democratic Party has also waned. Jewish voters, however, have remained loyal to the Democrats, and certain racial minorities have become more Democratic. Since the civil rights legislation of the 1960s, African-Americans have increased their support of Democratic candidates; Hispanics have also tended to vote heavily Democratic.

Northern white Protestants remain the backbone of the Republican Party, but southern whites, Catholic, and labor union families—the core of the Democrat's New Deal coalition—now compose about one-half of the Republican vote in recent presidential elections. Additionally, some minority groups such as Asian-Americans and Cuban-Americans now vote regularly with the Republicans. White evangelical Protestants, potentially 15 percent to 20 percent of the total electorate, have also joined the Republican ranks.

Scholars are divided over whether a realignment of the parties has occurred or is occurring. One school of thought maintains that realignment is taking place, with the Republicans the likely beneficiaries. Others, however, contend that a dealignment has occurred with partisan affiliation declining and Independents increasing. What seems clear is that the New Deal coalitions have weakened and shifted to the point that the fifth stage of party development has probably been completed.

See *also:* Individual parties and candidates, Democratic Republicans, Federalist Party, John C. Frémont, Partisan Coalitions in the Electorate

*Stephen J. Wayne*

## Stalwarts (and Half-Breeds)

The terms "Stalwart" and "Half-Breed" designate two factions within the Republican Party during the 1870s and 1880s, cliques whose antagonism crested at the national convention in 1880 and in the first months of James A. Garfield's administration. At the convention the Stalwarts backed Ulysses S. Grant for a third term, while their opponents favored James G. Blaine or, to a lesser extent, John Sherman. After a stalemate lasting 35 ballots, the convention turned to a dark horse, Garfield, who was more closely identified with the Half-Breed faction.

As President, Garfield appointed James G. Blaine as his Secretary of State. Blaine, who was the leader of the Half-Breeds, showered Garfield with patronage advice. This brought trouble for the President, especially in the Stalwart bastion of New York, whose U.S. Senators, Roscoe Conkling and Thomas Platt, particularly resented the appointment of William H. Robertson to the customs collectorship. A bitter battle ended with Robertson's confirmation and Conkling and Platt's petulant resignations from the Senate. Garfield's assassination by a deranged office seeker claiming to be a Stalwart helped to seal that faction's disrepute.

Generally speaking, the Stalwarts exhibited greater internal cohesion than the Half-Breeds, but neither faction established a hierarchical structure or machinery to pursue well-defined aims. Each label stood more for a set of attitudes than for an identifiable organization. Traditional historical accounts date the origin of the groupings to the intense hatred that developed between Conkling and Blaine while the two served together in the House in the late 1860s. In this view, Republican factionalism fed upon this personal rivalry and soon became simply a contest for the spoils of office.

More recent scholars assign an ideological dimension to the differences between Stalwarts and Half-Breeds, though recognizing that these coteries were not polar opposites. Stalwarts believed that the key to future victories for the Republicans lay in keeping alive the issues growing out of the Union triumph in the Civil War. Essentially backward looking, they favored a strong southern policy. Their contempt for Rutherford B. Hayes's "Miss Nancy" policy toward the South led them to fight for Grant's return to the White House. They argued for sterner measures to protect southern Republicans, both Black and white, from Democratic "outrages." Indeed, over half the Stalwarts who backed Grant in the 1880 convention represented states in the solidly Democratic South, and most of the remainder hailed from heavily Democratic northern districts. Facing severe struggles in Democratic strongholds, Stalwarts believed the party's survival dependent upon disciplined organization and tried-and-true issues.

Under Blaine's leadership, Half-Breeds sought to reorient the GOP toward the future. The near disaster of the Hayes election in 1876 caused them to deemphasize the "Bloody Shirt" and to stress instead economic concerns, including calls for sound currency, tariff protection, and the dispensing of various kinds of government largesse. Blaine's nomination in 1884 over ex-Stalwart Chester Arthur sealed the Half-Breed takeover of the party. Although Blaine lost to Grover Cleveland, Cleveland's successor Benjamin Harrison and a Republican Congress enacted much of the Half-Breed program into law.

*See also:* Chester A. Arthur, James G. Blaine, Bloody Shirt, Grover Cleveland, Roscoe Conkling, James A. Garfield, Ulysses S. Grant, Benjamin Harrison, Rutherford B. Hayes, Thomas C. Platt, John Sherman

*Charles W. Calhoun*

REFERENCES

Jordan, David M. 1971. *Roscoe Conkling of New York: Voice in the Senate.* Ithaca: Cornell U. Pr.

Muzzey, David S. 1934. *James G. Blaine: A Political Idol of Other Days.* New York: Dodd, Mead.

Peskin, Allan. 1978. *Garfield.* Kent, OH: Kent State U. Pr.

———. 1984. "Who Were the Stalwarts? Who Were Their Rivals? Republican Factions in the Gilded Age." 99 *Political Science Quarterly* 703.

Welch, Richard E., Jr. 1971. *George Frisbie Hoar and the Half Breed Republicans.* Cambridge: Harvard U. Pr.

## Edwin M. Stanton (1814–1869)

Speaker, organizer, and party manager for Ohio Democrats. As a radical Jacksonian, Edwin McMasters Stanton was a firm supporter of Martin Van Buren and followed him into the Free Soil Party in 1848. He soon returned to the Democrats but then renounced active politics for a distinguished legal practice in Pittsburgh and Washington.

In 1860 Stanton was appointed Attorney General by President James Buchanan. In that post, he advocated a firm stand against secession both to the President and secretly to the Republican leaders. A "war Democrat," Stanton had a reputation for honesty and industry that persuaded President Abraham Lincoln to make him Secretary of War in January 1862. With harsh, ruthless efficiency he made a major contribution to the military success of the Union.

Convinced that victory in the war was dependent on the retention of Lincoln and the Republicans in power, Stanton used the vast influence and patronage of the War Department to this end. In state and congressional elections in 1862 and 1863 and even more in Lincoln's reelection campaign in 1864, he furloughed soldiers to vote and generals to campaign. Political assessments of cash were levied on departmental clerks, munitions workers were pressured for money, and provost marshals were used to harass "disloyal" elements. Stanton also exercised considerable influence in selecting Republican candidates in several states. He was an "organizer of victory" not only for the Union armies but also for the Republican Party. Common dedication to a hard war and a harsh reconstruction united Stanton with the Radical Republicans and involved him in bitter conflict with President Andrew Johnson. He actively promoted Johnson's impeachment, and when impeachment failed, he resigned in 1868. Firmly rejecting suggestions for his own candidacy, Stanton supported General Ulysses S. Grant in the 1868 presidential election.

*See also:* Free Soil Party, Ulysses S. Grant, Andrew Johnson, Abraham Lincoln

*Harold B. Raymond*

REFERENCES

Hendrick, Burton. 1946. *Lincoln's War Cabinet.* New York: Doubleday.

Pratt, Fletcher. 1953. *Stanton: Lincoln's Secretary of War.* New York: Norton.

Thomas, Benjamin E. 1962. *Stanton: The Life and Times of Lincoln's Secretary of War.* New York: Knopf.

## Elizabeth Cady Stanton (1815–1902)

Nineteenth-century crusader for women's rights. Elizabeth Cady Stanton was instrumental in formulating the women's rights movement's strategy and articulating its needs. Stanton began her public career as an abolitionist and remained faithful to that cause, but she chose instead to dedicate herself to women's rights. To that end, she helped to organize the 1848 Seneca Falls Convention at which women outlined their grievances and, at her urging, demanded the right to vote. This challenge brought her into conflict with reformers who believed rights needed first to be achieved for the freedmen, and with the Republican Party, which considered Black rights a vital means to solidify victory over the South. The disagreement came to a head when Stanton tried to include women's suffrage in the Fourteenth Amendment. After the Republicans successfully opposed this maneuver, she and her coworker, Susan B. Anthony, turned to the 1867 Kansas campaign to convince them of its popularity. The Republicans continued to oppose women's suffrage, instead supporting Black male suffrage. This encouraged Stanton and Anthony to appeal to Democrats and enlist the aid of the Copperhead, George F. Train. His white supremist arguments on behalf of women's suffrage further angered reformers. The defeat of both referenda ended any lingering attempts to link women's suffrage with suffrage for African-Americans.

Stanton petitioned, campaigned, and published the *Revolution* on behalf of the cause. She and Anthony attempted an alliance with the National Labor Union in 1868. They not only encountered the opposition and hostility of working men but also were unable to convince working women that the vote would improve their economic status. While the effort exposed Stanton to the needs of workers, its failure encouraged her to rely on white middle-class women.

Stanton's split with the reformers was completed when she and Anthony unsuccessfully demanded that the Republican-supported Fifteenth Amendment include women. They opposed the amendment as written and challenged the credentials of the Republicans as the party of reform. Stanton concluded that suffrage could only be successful as an autonomous movement of women. To that end, she helped to create, and became president of, the National Woman Suffrage Association in 1869. Opponents formed the American Woman Suffrage Association. When, at her urging, Senator Aaron A. Sargent of California introduced a women's suffrage amendment in 1878, she testified on its behalf in congressional hearings. She also tried to test the constitutionality of the local laws by trying unsuccessfully to vote on several occasions.

Unlike Anthony, Stanton believed the movement should ally as a strong independent force with other political groups supporting radical change. In the early 1890s, she was enthusiastic about the Populists and by the end of the decade, she was expressing sympathy for the growing Socialist movement.

While Stanton continued to work for the vote, she considered it a vital part of a much larger program of women's emancipation, including an end to economic discrimination and more liberal divorce and property laws. Her writings and speeches became a staple of feminist thinking, and she urged women to challenge and question any limitation whether imposed by tradition, church, or state.

After relinquishing the presidency of the newly united National American Woman Suffrage Association in 1892, she devoted her last years to a critical analysis of organized religion.

*See also:* Abolition Movement, Susan B. Anthony, Copperheads, Fifteenth Amendment, National American Woman Suffrage Association, Suffrage, Woman Suffrage Movement

*Joy A. Scimé*

REFERENCES

DuBois, Ellen C. 1978. *Feminism and Suffrage: The Emergence of an Independent Women's Movement in America, 1848–1869.* Ithaca: Cornell U. Pr.

———. 1981. *Elizabeth Cady Stanton, Susan B. Anthony: Correspondence, Writings, Speeches.* New York: Schocken Books.

Griffith, Elisabeth. 1984. *In Her Own Right: The Life of Elizabeth Cady Stanton.* New York: Oxford U. Pr.

James, Edward T., Janet Wilson James, and Paul S. Boyer. 1971. *Notable American Women 1607–1950.* Cambridge: Belknap Press.

## State-Level Radicalism

A type of party politics that appeared in several state jurisdictions outside the Northeast and the South, state-level radicalism flourished between 1916 and 1941. Its politicians proved capable of mounting statewide campaigns, of electing members of Congress, and of electing governors. Because it was a politics of coalition and of economic protest, it sought to join farmers, workers, and small businessmen behind policy ideas that prescribed government action to reduce market hazards for these three categories of producers. The 1920s and 1930s saw several examples of this type of party politics, including quite successful organizations, like the Minnesota Farmer-Labor Party (1918–1944), and brief, "movement" organizations, such as End Poverty in California (1934).

America's experience with state-level radicalism was not unique. Relatively "new" nations with federal systems, former colonies of England, with large agricultural economic sectors as well as industrialized sectors have had analogous experiences. "Province-level radicalism" emerged in Canada; out of it grew the New Democratic Party. The development of Australia's party system developed in a similar way.

State-level radicalism was stronger, more common, and more significant for national and state-level public policy in America than most earlier literature on American party politics has suggested. When the "national realignment" perspective on American party politics grew up in the 1950s, mainly in response to the New Deal's impact on American politics, it deflected attention from state-level radicalism by emphasizing the periodic diffusion of balanced, two-party competition throughout American jurisdictions as a central tendency in American party politics. But implicit in the national realignment perspective was the idea that American party politics has often been typologically diverse and, at the electoral level, behaviorally diverse. Implicit in any theory of central tendencies is an emphasis on diversity. In this vein of appreciating diversity as well as central tendency in American party and electoral politics, observers have been reconsidering state-level radicalism: its emergence, its policy impact, and the logic of its disappearance as a type of party politics.

Among the more important conditions for the emergence of state-level radicalism was the greater political decentralization of America before the New Deal. Between 1916 and 1926, state-level radicalism was diffused from North Dakota, where the Nonpartisan League was born, through north central, northwestern, and southwestern states. But by 1926 the first wave in the diffusion of state-level radicalism had left only one self-sustaining organization, the Minnesota Farmer-Labor Party.

State-level radicalism made some difference to national agendas and national policymaking during the 1920s, helping to set the stage for Robert La Follette, Sr.'s 1924 presidential campaign and playing a significant role in the organization of La Follette's campaign itself. La Follette's performance in 1924, in turn, played a role in stimulating a reform of agricultural policy in the late 1920s (i.e., the adoption of a surplus purchase policy), and in a reform of industrial relations (i.e., the Railway Labor Act of 1926).

At the state level, the influence during the 1920s of "contagion from the left," to use Maurice Duverger's term, was strong in some states, notably North Dakota, South Dakota, and Minnesota. In these three states, at any rate, "contagion from the left" led to banking, electoral law, and tax reform, and to more regulation of labor markets and public utilities.

The unusually strong revival of the Minnesota Farmer-Labor Party in the 1930s contributed to the establishment of the Wisconsin Progressive Party. The Minnesota Farmer-Labor Party and the Wisconsin Progressive Party were very activist during their periods of dominance. They changed labor law and systems of collective bargaining in the two states; they moved to make the tax systems of these two states more progressive and to increase the incidence of corporate taxation; they acted, relatedly, to lighten the tax load on farmers and urban homeowners; they sought to insulate small business and country bankers from competition with larger organizations; and they sought to slow the rate of mortgage foreclosure on farms.

At the national level, the Farmer-Labor and Progressive delegations in Congress had some influence on the formulation of foreign policy, farm policy, unemployment insurance policy, youth employment policy, and old age insurance policy. Also, between 1934 and 1938 these delegations pursued a strategy of building a national third party by staking out positions to the left of the New Deal.

But the most important national policy legacy of state-level radicalism during the 1930s resulted from litigation. Through successful defense of the Minnesota Mortgage Moratorium Act before the Supreme Court, the Minnesota Farmer-Labor Party was able to achieve lasting legitimacy for presidential and gubernatorial efforts on behalf of redistributive welfare measures.

Yet by helping to legitimate the general thrust of New Deal policies the Minnesota Farmer-Labor Party's leaders only strengthened the kinds of political structures that eventually constrained them and their counterparts in Wisconsin. Successful implementation of New Deal policies changed the interest group politics of rural and industrial society. The Agricultural Adjustment Act strengthened a conservative organization, the Farm Bureau. The Wagner Act helped to deepen the split between the American Federation of Labor and the Committee for Industrial Organization. These changes made it much harder for Farmer-Labor and Progressive politicians to keep their coalitions together. As the public became more aware of interventionist, macroeconomic management, possibilities for periodic discontent with a new welfare state grew. Sharp dissatisfaction emerged during the Roosevelt Recession of 1937. By 1938 Farmer-Labor and Progressive organizations were badly weakened, never fully to recover. Eventually both organizations disappeared in the 1940s.

The development of the national political economy in the 1930s destroyed once prospering state-level organizations.

*See also:* AFL-CIO COPE, Robert La Follette, Minnesota Farmer-Labor Party, Nonpartisan League, Wisconsin Progressive Party

*Richard M. Valelly*

REFERENCES

Valelly, Richard M. 1989. *Radicalism in the States: The Minnesota Farmer-Labor Party and the American Political Economy.* Chicago: U. of Chicago Pr.

## State Party Committees

The formal structure of contemporary American state party organizations was fixed with the rise of the convention system of nominating Presidents in 1832. With some variations among the states, the caucus, committee, and convention structure is intact 150 years later. European scholars grudgingly acknowledged the advanced standing of American party organization in the nineteenth century, making reference to the party machines that operated under the guise of the traditional structures. Led by a new breed of party managers, the parties preceded business corporations and government agencies in achieving hierarchical ordering of constituent units, in fielding disciplined cadres of workers in large numbers, and in acquiring and employing large resources toward organizational goals.

Although the old forms persisted, an accretion of circumstances—including the Australian ballot, the primary, and New Deal intrusions on party functions—had sapped the strength of the party machines by the 1950s. New means of communication and transport, the introduction of new skills and ways of organizing and servicing campaigns, and the movement of interest groups and nonparty candidate-support groups into campaign roles changed the relations of candidates and parties. This erosion of old ways and intrusion of new forces, especially when accompanied by shifts in voter attitudes toward political parties, led to a period of scholarly uncertainty of the consequences. This uncertainty gave way to a widespread perception of party decline.

Some of the signs also showed that the changes in process might not have an entirely negative impact. Party organizations at the state level were the source of financial support for the national parties, and this structure suggested at least some organized capacity for replenishment of resources by the state parties. Hesitant signs of incubating bureaucracy were present in the institution of paid professional leadership in some parties. And competitiveness, often linked by scholars to strengthening of party organization, was increasing.

One deterrent to recognition that the parties might be entering a new stage of organization building was the shift of research focus from institutional studies of politics to survey research on the attitudes and behaviors of the presidential electorate. With the neglect of systematic cross-sectional observation of party organizations and the availability of national-level survey data over time, scholars and journalists increasingly accepted survey data on the partisanship of the electorate as indicators of the state of parties, including party organization. Conventional wisdom that parties as organizations were increasingly inactive and irrelevant lessened the sense of need or of interest to study party organizations, and theories of electoral politics developed in the decades prior to the 1990s, omitted party organization.

In the late 1960s and early 1970s some political scientists discerned signs of a stronger organizational infrastructure at the state party level than were generally acknowledged. This insight led scholars to devise measures to permit assessment of state party organizations. Lack of resources and of relevant data sets put a premium on improvisation and somewhat limited the usefulness of the resulting composite measures. In 1976 Huckshorn's seminal study of state party chairs confirmed these impressions and, more importantly, the feasibility of collecting systematic cross-sectional data to cast light on the condition of the party organizations. State party organizations had been rediscovered. Subsequent investigation confirmed that the fate of the political machine did not predict the future for party organizations, which, since the 1950s, have increased in organizational and programmatic strength and become more effectively articulated into national networks of constituent units.

*Origins, Persistence, and Change*

State party committees developed within a decade of creation of the convention system for nominating Presidents. In his study of party formation in the 24 states admitted to the Union by 1824, Richard McCormick concludes that by 1836 every state but South Carolina either had a two-party system or the "basic outlines . . . had been delineated." By the election of 1840 Whig and Democratic party machinery was in place in every state, voters responded to partisan appeals, and the party alignments were similar for state and national offices

Party structures were needed at the national level to schedule and issue the call for delegates to the quadrennial national nominating conventions. State party committees were needed to receive the call and managed the delegate-selection process. Both the national and state parties had roles in the conduct of the presidential campaign. These imperatives did not produce an instant network of state party committees. As McCormick points out, "Parties did not 'emerge,' neither did they 'form,' rather they were formed by astute and energetic politicians" and their management became the concern of "men from many ranks and callings" attracted to "tangible rewards in the form of patronage and prestige" for making party management a vocation.

Some state parties emerging in the era of this second party system preceded large-scale business enterprise in taking on the characteristics of sophisticated organizations, hierarchically structured and led. Clifton Yearley has shown that party organizations in the late nineteenth century continued to grow in size more rapidly than other forms of organized endeavor, wielding resources exceeded only by the largest corporations. Having removed control of the presidential selection process from "a patrician class" and having put it in the hands of party managers, this new organizational vehicle for mobilizing social and political energies proceeded to transcend the constitutional separation of powers. The party machines at state and local levels bridged public and private spheres and ranged across branches of government to deliver services that were beyond the capacity of weak and ineffectual governments. Equivalent levels of government could not achieve the organizational capacity and discipline of the parties, which proceeded to treat government as an extractive industry, levying assessments on candidates and officeholders and imposing spending and taxing programs that accomplished crude redistributive ends.

By the end of the nineteenth century, state-level electoral competition between the Republican and Democratic party successors to the antebellum second-party system had waned. State electorates were offered fewer and fewer opportunities to make choices between two parties with real prospects of alternating in office.

E. E. Schattschneider estimates that only one-seventh of the population in 1904 lived in states "in which parties contested the elections on relatively equal terms," and by 1920 this had fallen to one-ninth. Twenty years after the New Deal realignment of 1932, signs of the era of the one-party states were still plentiful. In the mid-1950s only 22 states had, in Malcolm Jewell's words, "at least a semblance of an effective two-party system" measured by absence of one party control of governor and both legislative chambers for as many as 16 of the preceding 20 years. McCormick has linked the strength of early state party structures to electoral competitiveness, an association that colored V.O. Key's and Schattschneider's analyses for more recent eras. Absence of effective two-party competition was thought to be associated with reduced inducements to build minority party organization and with an organizationally weak or factionalized dominant party. It is probably not coincidence that the use of the primary to nominate candidates (upon which Key fastened blame for decline of party organization) was introduced in a period of widespread one-party rule.

The nineteenth-century structure of caucuses, committees, and conventions was present and sufficiently used in the 1950s, and the party machines and bosses still sufficiently visible, particularly at the city and county level, to encourage the impression that the old order prevailed. In at least one state, Indiana, the ruling party retained power to impose assessments on patronage appointees and to subcontract at least one function of government to party organization leaders (core). But after World War II change was percolating through the political system. This was recognized by Harry Truman's White House aide, Clark Clifford, who warned the President of the need to adapt the 1948 campaign accordingly:

> The one particular upon which all politicians agree is that the leadership of the Democratic organization is moribund. . . . Those alert party machines which, beginning with 1932, turned out such huge majorities in the big cities for the Democratic ticket have all through the years of their victories been steadily deteriorating underneath—until in 1944 the Democratic organization found itself rivaled, in terms of money and workers, and exceeded in alertness and enthusiasm by the PAC.
>
> Everywhere the professionals are in profound collapse.
>
> Hague and Kelley admit publicly they are through as political bosses of the first magni-

tude. They have left no one in their places; their organizations are shot through with incompetence. There are a few signs of revival in New York under Mayor O'Dwyer but hardly enough to justify any optimism. In Ohio the regular organization wars with former Governor Lausche. Jim Curley, still Boston's greatest vote getter, fills his cell with threats of smashing the party in Massachusetts—and no one doubts for a minute that he can do it. Pennsylvania is torn between Lawrence and Joe Guffey and every time Lawrence gets some Federal patronage to dispense, Guffey sings the praises of Henry Wallace as publicly as possible. The California quarrel is so dramatic it needs no comment. In worse or less degree, the situation is the same in most of the states.

A subsequent study of the 1948 campaign offered corroborating evidence. David, Moos, and Goldman discovered that "very few of the state political conventions of 1952 were within the grip of a recognized political boss." Schattschneider observed that this finding

> when put with the evidence of erosion of the local machines suggests that a profound change in the character of the party system has already taken place. It involves a shift in the locus of power within the party system; indeed, it involves a changed concept of power itself. Considering the central role played by the local boss in the literature of American politics it now seems likely that the whole body of traditional propositions descriptive of the political system must be revised.

Clearly, the parties were in transition, but toward what? At the system level, party realignment, which had been a reiterative theme in the 1920s, reemerged in some interpretations of the developing trend; for the party organizations the most persuasive diagnoses were cast in terms of party decline, but with some dissenting voices and with scattered counter indications. Key (1956) discerned an "almost . . . complete absence of functioning state-wide [party] organization," claiming further that "while no consensus of the state of state central committees is available, the general impression that most of them are virtually dead is probably not far wrong." This view persisted for nearly two decades. But a contrary impression may be gained from Schattschneider's assessment:

> The major parties are now the most highly competitive large-scale organizations in American society, more competitive than business (which usually competes marginally) or the churches or the labor unions. The area and scale of party competition have been expanded greatly

by the extension of the two-party system and by the establishment of the conditions for a much more rapid alternation of the parties in power. Competition on this scale provides powerful incentives for organization. It tends strongly to draw all political organizations, i.e., the pressure groups, Congress, etc., into the vortex of party conflict.

Alexander Heard's study of 1950s-era party finance found sufficient levels of fund transfers between party committees and sufficient evidence of national party reliance upon state parties for funding to suggest the presence of supporting party organizational infrastructure in the states. A hoard of otherwise inaccessible data spread throughout the text and footnotes of Heard's book reinforces this impression.

The demise of the machine and the boss were prelude to development of bureaucracies at state party headquarters on the model of the national party committees. Schattschneider may well have been right in believing, that increasing electoral competitiveness—the challenge of large-scale entry into the arena of electoral campaigns by groups that parties perceived as rivals—contributed to such development. But these events were occurring at a time when the study of parties as organizations was slipping into eclipse.

### The Quest for Concept and Theory

Perhaps because it was so authoritatively known that the parties were in decline, interest in research on party organizations also declined, giving way in the 1950s to emphasis on individual voter attitudes and behaviors, guided by social-psychological models and survey methods (Natchez).

As it moved into the national sample survey of voters in the 1952 presidential election, the Center for Political Studies (CPS) proposed "to study the impact of the activities of the major parties on the population." The authors of The Voter Decides later acknowledged this was the "objective least adequately dealt with" in their 1952 election study. The party identification chapter opens with assurance that the "internal organization . . . techniques, and activities" of parties had been much studied over the years. The CPS emphasis, therefore, would be "to analyze the perceptions, evaluations and actions of those who identify with them." The CPS party identification variable gained acceptance as an indicator of the general condition of the American political party, including party organization, on the implicit premise—suited to membership parties—that level of affiliative support is a predictor of level of party, and party organizational, strength. This premise as fully obviated need for systematic research on the state party organizations as did Anthony Down's theory.

In his seminal analysis Downs joined party and the electorate in symbiotic relationship. Voters require candidates and cues to assist the process of choice, and parties require votes in order to win office. But Downs defined a party as "teams of candidates" and outlined processes of party decision-making that permitted no role for party organizations. Moreover, in subsequent theory building, party organization fell between the conceptual cracks.

Little wonder that Frank Sorauf (1963) expressed concern about the absence of "'party' as an organized recruiter and elector of candidates . . . in many of the recent excellent studies of American voting and electoral politics." He warned that "the ability to win elections has become virtually the only measure of party functioning," with the consequence that party is perceived as a "momentary electoral coalition," not as a political organization.

Three works of modern political science attempt systematically to build theories pertinent to party organization. The first, the 1950 American Political Science Association (APSA) report, presents a model of "responsible parties," chiefly important because it states norms of performance for the American national party system and details a program for party change. The second, by Samuel Eldersveld, emerges from a study of political parties in Michigan's Wayne County (Detroit) and is guided by a sociological conceptualization of party organization that emphasizes the fluidity of interpersonal and subcoalitional relationships. The third and the most rigorously systematic theory relevant to party organization is the body of work created by Joseph Schlesinger. In a succession of restatements since 1965, this endeavor has evolved from a theory of party structure to a more embrasive theory of party.

Developed under the guiding hand of E. E. Schattschneider, the 1950 report of the APSA Committee on Political Parties features a prescriptive model that reminded some readers of textbook descriptions of British parliamentary politics. The APSA model not only incorporates party organization as an element but also burdens party with the job of fusing constitutionally separated powers, thus bringing to mind the power politics of the party machines of the nineteenth century. Responsible parties should offer to the electorate clearly alternative sets of policy proposals, catalyzing an electoral decision in the form of a mandate. Structures and processes for enforcing party discipline within government should then enable the ruling party to perform on the mandate so granted. Democratic political scientists on his White House and national committee staffs interested President Harry Truman in some of the APSA's proposed innovations, and in the late 1950s the report inspired some of Paul Butler's innovations as chairman of the Democratic National Committee (Roberts). The "responsible party" model embodies scholarly preconceptions about the desired character of parties that continue to influence political theorists but are unlikely to reshape the system.

Suited to and generalized from the local party structure in the Detroit area, Eldersveld's conceptualization of party structure is nonbureaucratic—open, informal, and personalized; it is depicted in terms that evoke a sense of evanescence. Party has been reduced to a "proliferation of ruling group[s] and the diffusion of power prerogatives and power exercise." With skill and insight Eldersveld conveys a sense of the kaleidoscopic reality of Detroit party politics. Probably as a consequence of its unique virtues, Eldersveld's study has not been replicated. The depiction of autonomous "strata commands" and relations among party units based upon "mutual deference" is undoubtedly faithful to the parties of the early 1960s, but the parties of the 1980s are moving from it.

Schlesinger began to assemble the major elements of a theory of party, beginning with his work on party organization in 1965 and moving on to the structure of political opportunities in 1966. He later explicated a formal theory, with the third major element of party system in place, in 1985. Schlesinger's work constitutes the richest contribution to a theory of party in American political science. For an article on American state party organizations, or for a researcher focusing on the traditional party organizations, however, the theory, while suggestive, cannot be taken as guide. Only to the limited extent that a traditional party organization controls access to or plays "a part in the attainment of" a desirable office can it be considered a "real organization."

Schlesinger's theory, which is founded upon office seeking and in which office seekers are central, rejects any presumptive claim to relevance for the formal structure of party organization. He abstracts from the matrix of formal and informal structures and processes those clusters of organized action that are in pursuit of office and denominates them "nuclear" or "multinuclear" party. The distinction is based upon the pursuit of a single office or the organized effort to coordinate a number of such campaigns for office. Nuclear and multinuclear party organizations operate within the interstices of the organizational forms and processes associated with the major parties and cut across their office-seeking functions. Schlesinger's two types of party structure are shaped by and responsive to the political opportunities that comprise "the rules for attaining" offices "and general patterns of behavior surrounding their attainment."

Schlesinger acknowledges that the general character of this structure is "laid out in the various constitutions and electoral laws" of the states. Thus the inclusion of blueprints for interrelated party committee structures in state election codes may leave a door open for eventual accommodation of Schlesinger's conceptual party and the traditional party organizations. The nuclear party might then be forthrightly recognized as candidate campaign organizations (mandated by statute at the federal level and increasingly at the state level). National and state party committees are increasingly assuming multinuclear functions.

But a formal incorporation of the regular committee structures into the theory would not suffice. For Schlesinger's theory to facilitate empirical research on party relationships to office seeking in contemporary America, it would have to recognize (a) the array of organizational forms relevant to office seeking; and (b) the ambivalence underlying candidate-party organization relationships. The first will be touched upon in a succeeding section. Schlesinger's theory strongly hints at party organization-candidate relationships that are free of conflict of interest. Yet Gary Jacobson points out that "the collective interests of a party do not coincide with the individual interests for each of its candidates. The party's optimal distribution of campaign resources will not be optimal for every candidate, and vice versa." In the words of Jewell and Olson, parties and candidates in fact "take a pragmatic, even manipulative, view to-

ward each other," as the one pursues a possibly structurally skewed perception of the collective interest, and the other focuses upon individual pursuit of ambition.

Thus students of American party organization find themselves in about the circumstance outlined by the Social Science Research Council's Committee on Political Behavior in 1955. In a widely noted memorandum, the SSRC called attention to the "paucity of theory" in the field of state parties and politics, concluding that "comparative work in this field will probably have to proceed on the basis of some very simple, crude propositions of a broadly functional character."

*Rediscovering Party Organizations*

Emergence of a magnet field of theory-guided inquiry can have a preemptive impact within a discipline, focusing scholarly attention and resources available for research. As the attendant process of generating new data and theory attracts a new generation of scholars and as new data sets become readily available for secondary analysis, interest and effective capacity for research in cognate fields may be diminished or impoverished. Research on voting carried on by the Center for Political Studies may have contributed in this manner to the diminution of systematic research on state party organizations. After decades devoid of systematic cross-sectional research, party organization became an academic wasteland. Indeed, academic perceptions of the trend for party organizations were contrary to the course of party development by the early 1970s. Consider Wilson's impression that

> [t]he political party, at least in the United States, is a conspicuous exception to the general tendency for society to become increasingly organized, rationalized, and bureaucratized. Parties, as organizations, have become, if anything, weaker rather than stronger; present party organizations have shown little sign of becoming bureaucratized.

Early signs of renewed scholarly concern for systematic comparison of state party organizations were Ronald Weber's and David Olson's attempts to construct measures that would permit a rating of parties across the states according to their organizational strength. Shortly thereafter, Huckshorn's research on state party chairs, based on interviews with all 100 state chairs, demonstrated that the parties were alive and more or less well. A subsequent investigation—the Party Transformation Study—revealed a long-term trend toward enhanced strength of party organizations at the state level between 1960 and 1980. This profile showed that parties were becoming more bureaucratically complex, stronger and more stable in their financing, and stronger in their programs for party building and for assisting candidates. In 1983 and 1984 the Advisory Commission on Intergovernmental Relations conducted a survey of state party chairs or executive directors that confirmed for those years the earlier findings (Conlan). By the 1980s party organization at the local, state, and national levels had obtruded on scholarly awareness to the point of rediscovery.

*Dimensions of State Party Organization*

Organizationally strong state parties command resources, employ full-time leadership and staff, and conduct programs to build the party and win election. Functionally strong party organizations employ the resources of money, staff, and program to influence the selection of candidates, to enrich those candidates' campaigns for office, and to mobilize support for the party as symbol and votes for party candidates. Strong state parties also relate in constructive ways to other units of party, to partisans in public office, and to such sources of campaign resources as political action committees (PACs) and interest groups. This description suggests that strong party organizations will be found in competitive party systems. Insofar as the cumulation of changing patterns of state party competitiveness leads to a national realignment, state party organizations may be active as promoting or retarding agents. Recent studies permit assessment of some dimensions of party organizational and functional strength and of the relationships between elements of both.

Describing state party organizations and documenting change in the elements of organi-zational strength over time is a relatively simple matter in comparison to efforts to determine the consequences of party organizational strength, according to Bernard Hennessy, for "other characteristics of the party system or the polity in general." And since documenting the characteristics of such organizations is logically prior to the more problematic issue of their relationship to the functional strength of parties we begin with description.

Drawing upon Party Transformation Study data, David Price constructed a table that demonstrates the dramatic change in state party budget resources from 1961 to 1979: Compensating for inflation by adjusting the definition of "marginal," "medium," and "high" for the two years 1961 and 1979, the proportion of state party organizations reporting medium and high budgets increased from 31 percent to 69 percent over the period of nearly two decades, and the proportion of marginally budgeted state parties declined form 69 percent to 31 percent. "Stable, regularized, and adequate financing is required to support a party headquarters operation. Unpredictable funding impedes continuous operation and organizational planning," Gibson reasoned in 1983. Data collected from 53 parties in 27 states in 1978 and 1979 showed that the average budget was $340,667 and the median $210,000. For these parties, the smallest budget was $14,000 and the largest $2.5 million. Just over one-quarter of the parties had a budget of less than $100,000. Finally some 41 percent of the income making up these budgets was drawn from "regular" sources (e.g., direct mail, dues, state subsidies, and programs such as "Dollars for Democrats").

By the beginning of the 1960s, the transition toward professional leadership and a stable and accessible headquarters had begun among state parties. William Prendergast has reported that seven Republican state chairs were full-time paid

## Table 1

*Comparison of State Party Budgets, 1961 and 1979*

| Percentage of Organizations in Each Category | 1961 | | 1979 |
|---|---|---|---|
| Marginal (0–$50,000) | 69% | (0–$100,000) | 31% |
| Medium ($50,001–$150,000) | 19% | ($100,001–$300,000) | 43% |
| High (more than $150,000) | 12% | (more than $300,000) | 26% |
| Sample size | 67 | | 68 |
| Mean | $64,924 | | $292,038 |
| Median | $37,950 | | $193,803 |

party executives and 36 of the state committees maintained a permanent headquarters with at least one paid professional staff member. Daniel Ogden reported that 4 state Democratic parties were led by full-time paid chairs, 14 had a full-time paid executive director, and an additional 7 employed full-time professional staff. By the late 1970s only 15.1 percent of the reporting state Democratic parties and 6.1 percent of the state Republican parties lacked full-time paid leadership. The mean size of staff increased from 2.3 to 4.5 for the Democratic and from 4.5 to 7.0 for the Republican state parties between the early 1960s and the late 1970s.

We know that at least some state party organizations employed professional staff as early as the 1920s (Dewson), and Heard indicates state party organization staffing during the 1950s. Employing a somewhat broad definition of professional party staff, Roland Ebel surveyed 104 state and territorial party chairs in 1960, receiving 94 responses and the names of 167 professional "party staff." When separately surveyed, 89 percent of the 74 responding staff members reported that they worked full time and only 3 percent worked exclusively during campaign times. Ebel went on to score and rank order the state parties according to degree of professionalization. Thus subsequent recall by state party chairs of professional staffing in the early 1960s and a gradual increase in staffing by both parties in the succeeding decades are substantiated by earlier studies.

When they are assigned values on a scale of 0 to 1.000, 53 percent of the 90 state parties surveyed in the period 1975–1980 could be called organizationally strong or moderately strong, while 47 percent came off as weak or moderately weak (Table 2). The preponderant placement for each party fell somewhere in the middle—moderately strong for the Republicans, moderately weak for the Democrats. Table 2 is consistent with the prevalent impression among political scientists like Sorauf (1980): "Republicans find it easier to build centralized, cohesive parties than do the Democrats." But although interparty disparities persisted in the 1960s and 1970s, Bibby et al. have shown that regional disparities in organizational strength within each party declined in the 1970s.

## Functional Effectiveness of State Party Organizations

Organizationally robust state parties should function as prime movers, influencing candidate selection, playing important roles in election campaigns, and cooperating with the party's elected public officials. They may also be expected to relate to other units of party organization and to nonparty groups active in electoral politics. From a systemic perspective, the state party organizations should be forces for realigning and counterrealigning shifts in patterns of interparty competition.

For the most part research on state party organizations has yielded results that are only sketchy and suggestive on these topics. That is to say, the quantity and quality of present inquiry point to an agenda for research in the decades ahead rather than presenting a definitive picture of the performance of contemporary state party organizations. The agenda includes "some very simple, crude propositions" of theoretical significance in the spirit of the Social Science Research Council prescription of 1985.

## Electoral Significance

Party control of the selection of candidates is high on the list of every prescription for "responsible" parties. Key's (1956) analysis of the relationship between the infectious spread of the primary method of nomination and the weakening of party organization in the states

## Table 2

*Organizational Strength of Democratic and Republican State Parties, 1975–1980*

| Number of parties | Republican | Democratic | Total |
| --- | --- | --- | --- |
| Party organizational strength score | | | |
| .750–1.000 (Strong) | 8 | 2 | 10 |
| .500–.749 (Moderately strong) | 27 | 11 | 38 |
| .250–.499 (Moderately weak) | 9 | 26 | 35 |
| .000–.249 (Weak) | 1 | 6 | 7 |
| Totals | 45 | 45 | 90 |

has become a basic tenet of American political science. Moreover, despite the growing strength of party organizations, their role in the recruitment of candidates has declined rather than increased in the decades since Key's research. A sustained record of nominating governors-to-be by primary totals ranging from 80 percent to 100 percent of the vote may reasonably be taken to suggest the presence of strong nominating structures in any state. Sarah Morehouse found that 20 states placed within this range when the winning gubernatorial primary vote was averaged for the period 1956 through 1978; furthermore, preprimary endorsing was practiced in 17 of these states in 1980. She contended that "it is in the [endorsing] states . . . that the party leaders and workers can groom candidates and count on nominating them for state-wide office." Nominating strength denotes "strong party" for Morehouse, but the association of party organizational strength with recruitment and strong primary votes remain items on the agenda for future research.

A modest start has been made toward exploring the significance of party organizational strength for the gubernatorial vote, but here too the field for inquiry is relatively fresh. Increments in the strength of state party organizations in 32 nonsouthern states have been shown to correlate strongly and significantly to increments in the party's "normal" vote for governor.

V. O. Key's (1956) theoretical association of "a normal electoral division hovering around or moving toward the 50–50 point" as a stimulus to party organizational strength ("reconstruction of party organization") was formulated in an era of consolidation of the New Deal realignment, when party competitiveness was increasing at a sluggish pace in the states outside the South. Using a "measure of organizational strength of state political parties" cumulated from county-level party strength, Patterson and Caldeira found a strong relationship between strength and interparty competitiveness. As a component in a four-variable model, party strength had a "powerful impact on partisan competition," second only to education. This finding is consistent with a dynamic model in which equilibrating changes in the strength of the two-party organization in a state could affect electoral success and competitiveness and, when generalized to 50 states, could reinforce or counter dealigning or realigning trends. The way is thus opened to bring state party organization into theories of electoral realignment.

On the basis of his study of electoral change in 18 formerly Republican states from 1932 to 1970, Gary Greenhalgh gained the impression that the realignment "along Democratic lines in a number of the states had to await the emergence of a liberal, activist leadership clique . . . who wrested control of the state Democratic party from the conservatives in their states." It may also be that the contribution of party organization to realignment processes is multiphased, with national or local intervention creating minority party strength that is then directed to electoral goals and affects interparty competition. When this heightening of minority party organizational strength occurs, it prods the majority party into developing higher levels of organization and stimulating additional programmatic activity.

*Linkage with Officeholders*

According to Key (1960), the "interplay [that] occurs between mass opinion and government" involves intermediating activities by numerous structures including political parties. Key thought American parties were poorly equipped to link people with their political leaders. In the broadest sense, an empirical model for examining the linkage activities of parties must emphasize the intermediating aspect, allowing for communication between party and government that in turn becomes the basis for communication between party and the public. Illustrative instances of such linkage can be documented at the national level: for example, Lyndon Johnson involved the Democratic National Committee in mobilizing support for elements of the Great Society program in Congress; he also used the DNC to solicit the help of party elites and Democratic elected officials to mobilize public support. But the record is bare of broad, systematic empirical studies of this scope at the state or national levels.

Examining the reciprocal relationships between state party organizations and governors, although touching upon only one part of the sphere that Key had in mind, could point the way to broader studies. Recent inquiry into linkage between party organizations and both governors and legislators in 27 states suggests that organizational strength contributes to party linkage with officeholders but with differences between the parties. For the Republicans, strength is associated with higher levels of linkage with governors and legislators. Democratic linkage to legislators and to governors is inversely related. With more limited resources than the Republicans in the late 1970s, the state Democratic parties appear pressed to emphasize one or the other (Cotter et al., 1984: Ch. 6).

### Relations Between Party Units and with Nonparty Groups

Within a federal system of multilayered jurisdictions, development of patterned relationships among varying echelons of the party organization is to be expected. Such expectations appeared farfetched in the immediate post-World War II decades when the Democratic Party was a loose confederation of rebellious state units. But the era of party "reform" has transformed the Democrats into a national party of state constituent units. In the Republican Party, the formally autonomous state organizations are bound to the national party by service and funding. Regional and national associations of state party chairs serve as vehicles for lateral integration, and with all party chairs in each party becoming members of the national committees by 1972, national-state relationships strengthened. Caucuses of state party chairs have become important forces in national party affairs. In many states the county chairs of one or both parties are organized and able to act in concert to protect their interests at the state level.

Modern state party organizations are likely to accept some leadership direction from the national party, and integrative relationships between the two levels of party might reasonably be expected to strengthen the state headquarters. A 27-state analysis indicates that "state-national party integration does seem to strengthen Democratic state party organizations" but shows no impact upon the Republican organizations in the states (Huckshorn et al.). The Democratic finding is particularly significant in light of the heavy emphasis upon the enforcement of party rule in the Democratic national-state relationship. By the period studied (1975–1980) Republican state parties had been the recipients of national GOP aid in the form of money, service, and staffing for some years, and the state parties had established high levels of organizational strength. This point invites the surmise that integration may already have influenced the strength levels of Republican state parties in the early 1970s with such success that the national/state relationship is no longer significant toward the end of the decade.

Existence of national networks of constituent party organizations encourages the expectation that organizationally strong state parties will have highly interpretive relations with their local party units. The alternative perspective of fragmented parties is consistent with the pattern of integrative relationships actuated from the bottom, which Heard found in the 1950s. Both expectations are satisfied in initial efforts to explore relations between state and local party organizations. For the Republican parties, one study argues, "levels of integration ... are largely a function of variability in the strength of state party organizations, whereas levels of integration within Democratic parties are largely a function of variability in the strength of local party organizations." These divergent patterns may be explained by the greater urban focus of the Democratic Party.

State legislative party structures analogous to the campaign committees in the U.S. Congress emerged and became increasingly visible in the 1980s. State party financing of legislative campaigns increased in the second half of the 1970s after an earlier decline, and 80 percent of the state organizations reported legislative candidate recruitment effort in the period 1975–1980. In the early 1980s, either Republican or Democratic legislative leaders and caucuses in 24 states raised campaign funds for legislative candidates. In 12 states, Jewell reports, such fundraising appeared "to have a significant impact on legislative elections," and all four legislative parties were active in fundraising in most of these states. Jewell (1986) goes on to declare that "there is some evidence, however fragmentary, of such fund-raising activity" by legislative party leadership in 32 states. The relationships between the two national party committees and the campaign committees in the House and Senate, which have become close over the years, suggest the possible development of similar patterns in the states. And the probable differences among the states makes comparative inquiry the more appropriate. Such inquiries will make it necessary to distinguish carefully the concepts of linkage between the state parties and legislators and the concepts of integration between state parties and legislative campaign structures.

Emergence of the profession of political public relations and of vendors of specialized campaign services was recognized in the 1950s (Kelley, Heard). A then-novel organizational form, the political action committee (PAC) has grown exponentially in the 1970s and 1980s to become a third force in electoral politics, beyond parties and candidates. State party organizations are accustomed to working with nonparty groups. A study of party chairs in 27 states showed Republican chairs focusing heavily on fundraising and Democrats upon volunteers and service in their relations with such groups. The spectrum of Democratic sources of aid was much broader than that for Republicans, and Democratic chairs cited over twice as many sources of aid as did Republicans. PACs have by no means entirely swept away the traditional array of groups accustomed to working with the parties. But some of those groups now act at least in part through PACs, and the conglomeration of PACs has changed the organizational landscape of politics. The state party organizations undoubtedly will adjust.

According to a 1984 compilation by the Interstate Bureau of Regulation, nonfederal PACs that are registered and more or less active in the 41 states that register PACs and release PAC lists number 8,500. The proliferation of nonfederal PACs combined with an estimate by the California Commission on Campaign Financing (1985) estimate that business and labor PAC contributions comprised 59 percent of state assembly candidates' funds in 1984 make clear the need to include state-party–PAC relations in future studies.

### Conclusion

American political parties have simply not displayed a commitment to goals that would transform society, nor have they sought to shape their partisans' cultural, social, and material values, missions more characteristic of the social democratic and Socialist parties of Europe. The American parties' history of pragmatic concern to field candidates and win votes as conditions of officeholding is well documented. In earlier phases of party history, the chief purpose of office winning was more clearly and directly entrepreneurial—spoils, jobs, assessments, services with which to bind voters, other resources for the party and its organizational elite. Parties sufficiently well organized to meet these standards emerged as from chrysalis in rhythm with the electoral cycle. As late as the 1950s the entrepreneurial party continued to be the model for successful parties in the United States.

With the evident decline of "boss" party leadership by the 1950s, yet at a time when the pattern of future party development was not

prefigured in events, American state parties seemed to have become empty shells. Declining partisanship in the electorate, increasing candidate independence in seeking party nominations and organizing general election campaigns, growth rather than atrophy of primaries, expanding state and national statutory intervention in party and campaign affairs, the proliferation of nonparty groups asserting independent roles in election campaigns have presaged steady and dramatic erosion of party and party organizational strength. But the reverse seems to have happened. State parties that were autonomous to the point of denying their national presidential candidate a position on the ballot under the party name in four states in 1948 were in the 1980s constituent units of a network of party organizations accepting the authority of national (Democratic) party rule. The state party organizations in the 1980s were stronger, by bureaucratic and program measures and in their lateral and hierarchical relationships, than at any time in the twentieth century. The state chairs of each party gather in national associations and at national committee meetings to discuss mutual experiences, problems, successes, and failures. And they meet to develop strategies for getting more of what they want from their national committee in whose headquarters they have an office and staff.

What does all this activity signify? Robert Michels, a pioneer in the systematic study of political parties, warned that as parties become more organizationally strong "[m]echanism becomes an end in itself. . . . Thus, from a means, organization becomes an end." Have the two networks of interactive party organizations—local-state-national—become ends rather than means? Are the participatory concerns of the two parties contrasting so starkly to the entrepreneurial parties of old lessening interparty competitiveness? Are the parties becoming merely frolicsome conclaves, opportunities for social interaction? None of these fears appears warranted.

Party networks reinforce the strength of the individual units to field programs relevant to office winning and electoral competitiveness. The state parties draw important resources from electorally active nonparty groups. The parties sometimes contract for the services of firms selling fundraising, polling, and other necessary skills, often bringing the vendors and candidates together. The state party organizations relate to governors and legislators. The state party organizations now seem to have the capacity to be intermediating bodies, subordinating means to ends as they attempt to ally to control government and policy. Yet the extent to which that capacity is realized need not be relegated to speculation. It is feasible to break that question into a series of empirical questions in the expectation that research may produce reasonably confident answers.

*See also:* Individual state party leaders, Australian Ballot, Bosses, Clark Clifford, Democratic National Committee, V. O. Key, Robert Michels, Political Action Committees, Responsible Party Debate, E. E. Schattschneider, State Party Leaders

*Cornelius P. Cotter*

REFERENCES

American Political Science Association, Committee on Political Parties. 1950. *Toward a More Responsible Two-Party System.* New York: Rinehart.

Bryce, James (Viscount). 1909. *The American Commonwealth.* New York: Macmillan.

California Commission on Campaign Financing. 1985. *The New Gold Rush: Financing California's Legislative Campaigns.* 2 vols. Los Angeles: Center for Responsive Government.

Campbell, Angus, Gerald Gurin, and Warren E. Miller. 1954. *The Voter Decides.* Evanston, IL: Row, Peterson.

Chase, James S. 1973. *Emergence of the Presidential Nominating Convention, 1789–1832.* Urbana: U. of Illinois Pr.

Clifford, Clark. 1947. "Memorandum for the President. November 19, 1947." Clifford Papers, Box 21. Independence, MO: Harry S Truman Presidential Library.

Conlan, Timothy, Ann Martino, and Robert Dilger. 1984. *State Parties in the 1980s. Intergovernmental Perspective.* Washington: U.S. Advisory Commission on Intergovernmental Relations.

Core, J. Manfred. 1964. *1964 Report of Indiana State Democratic Central Committee.* White House Central Files, Ex PL 7, Box 122. Austin: Lyndon Baines Johnson Presidential Library.

Cotter, Cornelius P., James L. Gibson, John F. Bibby, and Robert J. Huckshorn. 1984. *Party Organizations in American Politics.* Pittsburgh: U. of Pittsburgh Pr.

Crotty, William. 1978. *Decision for the Democrats: Reforming the Party Structure.* Baltimore: Johns Hopkins U. Pr.

———, ed. 1986. *Political Parties in Local Areas.* Knoxville: U. of Tennessee Pr.

David, Paul T., Malcolm Moos, and Ralph M. Goldman. 1954. *Presidential Nominating Politics in 1952.* 5 vols. Baltimore: Johns Hopkins U. Pr.

Dewson, Mary W. 1949. *An Aide to the End.* Unpublished memoir. Hyde Park, NY: Franklin D. Roosevelt Presidential Library, Dewson papers; Cambridge, MA: Schlesinger Library, Radcliffe College.

Downs, Anthony. 1957. *An Economic Theory of Democracy.* New York: Harper & Row.

Ebel, Roland H. 1960. "The Role of the Professional Staff in American State Parties." Ph.D. dissertation, Michigan State U.

Eldersveld, Samuel J. 1964. *Political Parties: A Behavioral Analysis.* Chicago: Rand McNally.

Gibson, James L., Cornelius P. Cotter, John F. Bibby, and Robert J. Huckshorn. 1983. "Assessing Party Organizational Strength." 27 *American Journal of Political Science* 193.

———, ———, ———, and ———. 1985. "Whither the Local Parties? A Cross Sectional and Longitudinal Analysis of the Strength of Party Organizations." 29 *American Journal of Political Science* 139.

Heard, Alexander. 1960. *The Costs of Democracy.* Chapel Hill: U. of North Carolina Pr.

Herrnson, Paul S. 1988. *Party Campaigning in the 1980s.* Cambridge: Harvard U. Pr.

Hofferbert, Richard I. 1972. "State and Community Policy Studies: A Review of Comparative Input-Output Analyses." In James A. Robinson, ed. *Political Science Annual.* Indianapolis: Bobbs-Merrill.

Huckshorn, Robert J. 1976. *Party Leadership in the States.* Amherst: U. of Massachusetts Pr.

———, James L. Gibson, Cornelius P. Cotter, and John F. Bibby. 1986. "Party Integration and Party Organizational Strength." 48 *Journal of Politics* 977.

Interstate Bureau of Regulation. 1984. *State Political Action Legislation and Regulations.* Westport, CT: Quorum Books.

Jacobson, Gary C. 1985–1986. "Party Organization and Distribution of Campaign Resources: Republicans and Democrats in 1982." 100 *Political Science Quarterly* 604.

James, Judson. 1974. *American Political Parties in Transition.* New York: Harper.

Jewell, Malcolm E. 1955. "Party Voting in American State Legislatures." 49 *American Political Science Review* 773.

———, and David M. Olson. 1988. *American State Political Parties and Elections.* 3rd ed. Chicago: Dorsey.

Kayden, Xandra, and Eddie Mahe, Jr. 1985. *The Party Goes On.* New York: Basic Books.

Kelley, Stanley, Jr. 1956. *Professional Public Relations and Political Power.* Baltimore: Johns Hopkins U. Pr.

Key, V. O., Jr. 1949. *Southern Politics in State and Nation.* New York: Knopf.

———. 1956. *American State Politics: An Introduction.* New York: Knopf.

———. 1961. *Public Opinion and American Democracy.* New York: Knopf.

Kirkpatrick, Evron M. 1971. "Toward a More Responsible Two-Party System: Political Science, or Pseudo-Science?" 65 *American Political Science Review* 965–990.

Mayhew, David R. 1986. *Placing Parties in American Politics.* Princeton: Princeton U. Pr.

McCormick, Richard P. 1966. *The Second American Party System: Party Formation in the Jacksonian Era.* Chapel Hill: U. of North Carolina Pr.

Michels, Robert. 1949. *Political Parties.* Glencoe, IL: Free Press.

Natchez, Peter B. 1985. *Images of Voting/Visions of Democracy.* New York: Basic Books.

Olson, David M. 1971. "Attributes of State Political Parties: An Exploration of Theory and Data." In James A. Riedel, ed. *New Perspectives in State and Local Politics.* Waltham, MA: Xerox Publishing.

Ostrogorski, Moisei. 1902. *Democracy and the Organization of Political Parties, Vol. II: The United States.* New York: Macmillan.

Patterson, Samuel C., and Gregory Caldeira. 1984. "The Etiology of Partisan Competition." 78 *American Political Science Review* 691.

Price, David E. 1984. *Bringing Back the Parties.* Washington: Congressional Quarterly.

Roberts, George C. 1987. *Paul M. Butler: Hoosier Politician and National Political Leader.* Lanham, MD: U. Pr. of America.

Schattschneider, E. E. 1956. "United States: The Functional Approach to Party Government." In Sigmund Neumann, ed. *Modern Political Parties: Approaches to Comparative Politics.* Chicago: U. of Chicago Pr.

Schlesinger, Joseph A. 1965. "Political Party Organization." In James G. March, ed. *Handbook of Organizations.* Chicago: Rand McNally.

——. 1966. *Ambition and Politics: Political Careers in the United States.* Chicago: Rand McNally.

——. 1984. "On the Theory of Party Organization." 46 *Journal of Politics* 369–400.

——. 1985. "The New American Political Party." 79 *American Political Science Review* 1152.

Shafer, Byron E. 1983. *Quiet Revolution: The Struggle for the Democratic Party and the Shaping of Post-Reform Politics.* New York: Russell Sage.

Skowronek, Stephen. 1982. *Building a New American State: The Expansion of National Administrative Capacities, 1877–1920.* New York: Cambridge U. Pr.

Sorauf, Frank J. 1963. *Party and Representation: Legislative Politics in Pennsylvania.* New York: Atherton Press.

——. 1980. *Party Politics in America.* 4th ed. Boston: Little, Brown.

Sundquist, James. L. 1983. *Dynamics of the Party System.* 2nd ed. Washington: Brookings.

U.S. Advisory Commission on Intergovernmental Relations. 1986. *The Transformation in American Politics: Implications for Federalism.* Washington: ACIR.

Ware, Alan. 1985. *The Breakdown of Democratic Party Organization, 1940–1980.* Oxford, UK: Clarendon Press.

Wilson, James Q. 1962. *The Amateur Democrat.* Chicago: U. of Chicago Pr.

——. 1973. *Political Organizations.* New York: Basic Books.

Yearley, Clifton K. 1970. *The Money Machines: The Breakdown and Reform of Governmental and Party Finance in the North, 1860–1920.* Albany: State U. of New York Pr.

## State Party Leaders

In the past, the state party chair was viewed as an unimportant office occupied by an obscure politician serving at the will of powerful elected officials. These chairs have seldom been noticed by the public and have usually not been noticed by the public and have usually not been recognizable to any but a small group of party activists. Until recently, the state party chairs performed one of two functions: officiating as liaison between the governor and the party when it is in power or serving as a focal point for a party name but lacking party units united under a party name but lacking the unifying force necessary to be a central party entity. Since the 1960s, however, substantial changes in the functions, role, and leadership of the state party have occurred.

Most political scientists now believe that state party organizations and their officers have become indispensable units in the infrastructure of an increasingly more significant party system. State parties are an important link between the local and the national parties and, as such, provide more focus for stronger and more effective leadership.

*The Emergence of State Party Organization*

During the last quarter century, state party organizations have emerged from obscurity. Since 1956, when political scientist V. O. Key, Jr., noted "almost a complete absence of functioning state-wide organization(s)" to the present, considerable growth and sophistication has characterized state parties, and a remarkable increase has occurred in the volume of literature devoted to studies of state parties. Yet few people know much about state party organizations and their leaders, who have almost always been overshadowed by national party leaders. National political leaders are more visible because what they do is subject to scrutiny by more people, and they also have far better opportunities to publicize themselves because of their more ready access to the national media. Furthermore, national parties have been better financed, thereby permitting them a more wide ranging and sophisticated public relations effort.

In the past 25 years, however, state party organizations have themselves began to attract attention. Most state parties have full-time chairpersons who are often assisted by full-time professional executive directors. They are more likely to have permanent, fully staffed headquarters almost always located in the capital city. Fundraising is becoming more sophisticated and public relations more innovative. Although progress has been uneven from state to state, almost general growth and the emergence of other strong signs of vitality has enhanced the influence of state party leaders.

Each of the two major parties has a state central committee headed by a state chairperson in all 50 states. The "policy" body of the party is the central committee, the members of which are selected in a number of ways, their composition often provided by state law or party rules. Some central committees are apportioned: one member per specified number of party voters per district. Others have *ex officio* members who belong by virtue of their tenure in some other office. Congressional, county, legislative, city, and precinct committees are often represented by delegates or members selected by smaller party units. Some of these committees are small in size, while others can have dozens, even hundreds, of members. The state committee is responsible for electing a state chairperson in 73 percent of the parties; chairpersons in the remaining 27 percent are elected by the state convention. Most are elected to two-year terms, but because turnover is great, the average chairperson's tenure is between two and three years.

A mid-1970s study of party chairs found that they were overwhelmingly males in their mid-40s and that 75 percent were college graduates, with over half holding graduate degrees. Most were professional persons or business and management executives. Sixty-eight percent were Protestant, 20 percent Catholic, and 3 percent Jewish of those whose religious affiliation could be identified. Over 60 percent had served as county, city or other local party chairpersons, and 50 percent had served on the state party committee (sometimes a requirement for election to the chair). Seventeen percent, however, had never held a party position before their election as the state leader. A substantial number has held public office: 26 percent at the city, county, and local level; 28 percent as members of the state legislature; 4 percent in state executive branch positions; and 2 percent at the national executive or congressional levels. These characteristics are about the same for those elected to state chair positions as they are for other groups of political elites.

State party chairpersons have traditionally been discussed in the context of whether their own political party was in or out of power (i.e., the party holding the governor's office). For the party in power the mission of the chairperson or other party leaders is clear: they are the servants of the governor in office and, in most cases, responsible for or acquiescent in his or her election. The state chairperson's role in the state party, however, is never a simple reflection of the policies of the governor.

## The Chairperson's Roles

State chairpersons today play three distinct roles, depending upon the political milieu in which they find themselves. Some serve as political agents of an incumbent governor, and their power and influence derives from that governor. Usually the governor has been responsible for their election to the chair of the party; often a manager or important figure in the governor's campaign will get the office. These chairpersons rarely exercise real control over the party machinery but serve instead as the governor's representative to and means of control of the party. Such political agents often lack a personal following, and aside from their loyalty to the governor, they may not rate the party's leadership post very highly among their political responsibilities. Depending upon state, some agents are in the front lines fighting the governor's battles, while others toil in obscurity, operating behind the scenes and doing what they are told.

A second type of party chairperson is the in-party independent: one who serves the party controlled by the governor, but who is also a legitimately elected leader who achieved office through his or her own efforts and, in some instances, despite the governor's opposition. Some of these individuals were elected to the office as agents of a gubernatorial candidate who later lost; nevertheless, circumstance permitted them to retain the office and cast them in a more independent role. They occupy their position because their party won the highest office in the state but with a candidate other than the one with whom they originally affiliated. Others occupy places of power in the party in their own right; they have campaigned for and won the office on their own. Sometimes the winning candidates for governor simply permitted the party to make its own choice, while in other cases the election of party chair antedated the election of the governor, thus removing some gubernatorial control over the party office. In a few states, party chairpersons may have a long tradition of political independence, some of them holding office through the terms of more than one governor.

Finally, the third type of state party chairperson is the out-party independent who presides over an organization that does not control the governorship. Out-party chairs are often elected from their own political base, although some may be the personal choice of a defeated gubernatorial candidate who retained office after the election. For many years most southern Republican state chairs were out-party independents. The out-party independents are often recognized as real party leaders, especially when their party holds few statewide offices.

The scope of power and activities of state party chairpersons is bounded by tradition, law, and rules. Even so, the type of chair and the way in which the duties of that office are carried out is in control of the governorship. Those who see themselves as political agents are dedicated to serving the governor in his role as party leader. Those who serve as in-party independents are usually "organizational" leaders, leaving the "political" leadership to the governor. And out-party independents are often the real leaders of the party, exercising political power in their own right.

Recent research has confirmed that state party organizations are becoming stronger, with increased capabilities in party building, candidate recruitment, and campaign service. These added responsibilities have made it even more essential that the state party organizations be headed by capable and energetic leaders. This is the case because the modern state chairperson has four important intraparty responsibilities that are dependent on the existence of an effective party organization.

### Responsibilities of the Chairperson

First of all, the chair has a responsibility to maintain a working relationship with the local or grass-roots units of the organization. Since many political scientists believe that the principal strength of the parties lies with the county organizations, the state party must certainly be strong and well led if the local units are to receive the kind of leadership needed to build an effective political organization. Theirs is not always an easy relationship. Both the state and county units are competing for money from the same sources; they both represent different constituencies with conflicting demands generating built-in tensions. Only a masterly party leader can bridge the gap and unify the warring factions. Many are unable to do it, but recent research suggests that more party leaders recognize the importance of cohesiveness and are devoting substantial efforts to these relationships.

The second intraparty responsibility of the state party leader is to maintain an effective working relationship with the elected governing body of the party—usually the state central committee. These governing bodies are elected in a variety of ways as defined in state law or party rules. They may be composed of ex officio members, serving by virtue of their election to some other post or by other party governance units, such as the party primary, caucus, or convention. State committees range in size from a few members to several hundreds. Regardless of how selected, the state chairpersons must determine how the committee will be used, that is, how best to make the executive committee serve the needs of the party. That determination is often resolved by the chair's relationship with the committee and whether or not the party controls the governorship.

A relatively new enterprise for state parties is the necessity to assist elected officials with both substantive and political aid. This one, the third intraparty responsibility, has been particularly helpful to the party's legislators, but aid has in some states been used more broadly than that. Basically, this new responsibility involves a lobbying role for the party leadership since party leaders are responsible for setting policy goals if the party is out of power or for supporting the governor's policies if it is in power. Furthermore, in some highly structured parties, the state leaders may feel some responsibility for seeing that the party platform is adopted.

Finally, the last responsibility is to maintain the state headquarters. Virtually all of the state parties now operate a headquarters of some kind, usually in the state capital. Clear since the 1960s has been a mandate to serve the administrative needs of the statewide party units, by means of at least a minimal staff; that requires administration, funding, a recruitment structure, and day-to-day services. The rapid growth of competitive two-party states in recent years (and the simultaneous growth of political technology) has made the need for a state party headquarters more obvious; such changes have required that the leadership take a more pronounced role.

The extent of the chairperson's role is determined by the degree of professionalism permitted by the level of organizational bureaucratization. Over 90 percent of the state parties have either a full-time paid chairperson or a full-time paid executive director, a development representing remarkable growth since the early 1960s when the movement to more professional party organizations began. Another ingredient in the level of bureaucratization is the stability of tenure among the chairs. The most stable party had only two chairs between 1960 and 1980 while the least stable had 12. Almost half of the state parties had an average tenure for professional staff of two years or less.

Finally, the third dimension of professionalism is the extent of autonomy of the state chair from the state central committee. In one recent study, responses to a series of questions designed to elicit a measure of the degree of independence showed that almost 70 percent of these leaders were relatively independent of control by the committee.

Clearly, state party units are more complex than has been thought. Most maintain a party headquarters, provide substantial organizational resources, and exhibit some degree of bureaucratization. These are measures of just how far state party organizations have come in recent years, and they are signs as well of the growth in responsibility and power of the state chairpersons.

Also clear, however, is the intricate connection between the state organizational apparatus, including the chairpersons, and the elected state officeholders. In a study of political parties in the 1980s, the Advisory Commission on Intergovernmental Relations (ACIR) found that 87 percent of the party leaders surveyed thought that elected officials should become more involved in party affairs. Most did maintain, however, that elected officials were more involved with party leaders than had been true in the past. A majority of party chairs, in fact, suggested that their gubernatorial, congressional, and state legislative officeholders were "very" or "somewhat" active in the affairs of the party. This level of activity illustrates the necessity for the modern state party leader to maintain at least a minimal level of integration. The increased activity may well reflect the increased levels of financial, staff, and technical support being furnished by the party organizations to the candidates and officeholders.

### The State Party Committee

The 100 state committees in the 50 states are widely varied. Chief differences in composition depend upon the party unit from which the state central committee members are chosen and the way in which they are chosen. State central committee members are selected in two ways. In nine states members are selected by the voters, usually in primary elections. Obviously, this method severely limits the ability of state party leaders to set their own direction for the party. Twenty-seven states, on the other hand,

require that committee members be elected by delegates to the state, congressional district, or county conventions, or by committee members at those different levels. Among strong party advocates, this "inner-circle" system is far superior since it gives the leadership, operating through the official apparatus, control over the membership of the central committee. Fourteen states have no regulation at all by statute, leaving the manner of selection to party rules.

The duties of state committees, aside from electing or supporting the state chair, are varied. The committees are often responsible for organizing and calling party conventions at periodic intervals usually provided by law. They are sometimes responsible for writing a party platform, although this chore is most often left to the state convention. In some states they have direct responsibilities in the selection of delegates to the national convention, and they are often instrumental in the raising and spending of campaign funds. Whatever their role, the members of the state committees are usually influential in the party and occupy positions in its leadership. Even if the chairperson owes the central committee no allegiance, he or she must be concerned with maintaining a working relationship with the committee members in order to maximize the party's role.

### Developing Party Support

Party organization, in order to survive, must develop reliable bases of support; and in order to do that, they must cultivate a constituency by making themselves useful. Two types of program developments can assist in building a constituency: institutional support activities and candidate-directed activities. Much of the institutional support is directed toward sustaining the organization itself, while support for candidates is often more focused on a particular kind of candidate (those, say, running for the state legislature) and is exclusionary in the sense that these services are not available to the party at large. Both types of program development, however, are designed to provide services and to build constituencies. They provide the party with a *raison d'être*.

Five types of party activity are in the category of institutional support: (1) fundraising; (2) electoral mobilization programs; (3) public opinion polling for the party at large; (4) issue leadership; and (5) publication of a newsletter. From the perspective of the party chair, fundraising is a major responsibility both in terms of the amount of money raised and the diversity of sources from which it comes. Diversification stabilizes the party's income and insulates the party from the vagaries of a single source of money. Most state parties derive most of their income from major fundraising events, direct mail, and large contributions. In each case, the chairperson, working with an executive director or a finance chair, is responsible for the effort. Virtually all other party activities are dependent on the success of fundraising.

Electoral mobilization programs are quite common among state party organizations with over two-thirds of them operating ongoing voter identification, registration, and get-out-the-vote drives. These programs have grown remarkable in the past 20 years, some of the initiative coming from the national party organizations and some from the greater sophistication of the state parties and their chairpersons.

Public opinion polling is not as widespread, but over half the state party chairs regularly conduct routine polls either throughout the year or during the election season. Access to regular polls is dependent on the availability of money to pay for them. Even so, most chairs recognize the importance of polling to the accomplishment of their mission and, even if unable to afford it now, have polling as a principal goal.

Nearly half of the state parties devote considerable attention to the development of the state platform, and half are involved in the development of campaign issues. Almost a third of the parties claim to develop issues independently of candidates. One study in the 1970s showed that development of specific political issues strongly reflected the judgment of the state chair as to the party's position.

Finally, what might be viewed as a relatively trivial component of institutional support activity—the publication of a party newsletter—is in fact a major vehicle for communicating with party constituent groups and for maintaining the political strength of the chairperson. Over two-thirds of state parties publish newsletters, thus providing those party chairs with a ready avenue of communication and political education.

A second kind of programmatic activity focuses more specifically on candidates themselves and includes five principal components: (1) financial contributions to candidates; (2) provision of services to candidates; (3) involvement in the recruitment of candidates; (4) involvement in the selection of conventional delegates; and (5) preprimary endorsements. These kinds of activities build an important clientele for both the party and its leadership as well as contributing to the party's chances for successful campaigns to win office. Thus, the party organization benefits from contributing to an important party constituency, and the individual candidate's campaign benefits from the assistance of the party without feeling threatened by the organization.

The average state party in the late 1970s contributed money to candidates for an average two of the following offices: governor, state constitutional officers, U.S. House, U.S. Senate, and state legislature. Although contributions of parties to candidates have declined slightly, such a decline may reflect a redistribution of the resources to different candidates as well as recognition that some statewide campaigns for major office require strong independent fundraising efforts that produce such large sums that party money can be used for other purposes.

The second component of candidate-directed activity is the services provided to candidates. In a recent study of state party organizations party officers identified nine types of services: (1) advertising and media assistance; (2) accounting/compliance assistance; (3) polling; (4) research; (5) registration/voter identification/turnout; (6) staff assistance; (7) literature/phones/direct mail; (8) fundraising; and (9) seminars on campaign techniques. Relatively few parties assisted candidates with fundraising, but almost all conducted one or more seminars or campaign workshops, and the other seven activities have become common among many state parties.

Recruitment of candidates has always been a difficult task for parties, but a majority of state parties (usually led by the state chairperson) recruit for state and local offices, usually at the state legislative level. State parties rarely recruit candidates for top state offices, a practice that has become more common only in one-party areas than in developing two-party systems. Some evidence shows that the level of recruitment activity has declined since the 1960s, but state parties may simply have changed priorities from statewide offices to state legislative district races. Even so, candidate recruitment remains an important candidate-directed activity of the state party leadership, and the chairperson is usually responsible for its success or failure.

State parties are sometimes positioned so that they can influence the selection of delegates to the national party conventions, especially after national convention delegates became proxies for presidential candidates. Nevertheless, only 12 percent of the state chairs claimed any ability to influence the selection of delegates, while 46 percent specifically disclaim such an influence.

Finally, the most significant way in which parties can attempt to further the causes of specific candidates is through the preprimary endorsement. Half the parties acknowledge endorsing candidates, 28 percent formally and 22 percent informally. In almost every campaign setting, the endorsement of the party provides an important voting cue to primary participants and is widely sought by candidates.

A review of the data on programmatic activities suggests that party organizations have become substantially more active during the last two decades. Using the two available collections of data (Advisory Commission on Intergovernmental Relations; Huckshorn), comparisons of state parties in the late 1970s to those in the early 1960s clearly show that today's parties are more likely to be involved in voter mobilization programs, public opinion polling, servicing candidates, and producing newsletters. Little change has taken place in the development of issues and in providing financial contributions to candidates. The number of parties engaged in preprimary endorsements has increased slightly, but both recruitment of candidates and efforts to influence the selection of national convention delegates have declined. In general, state parties today have more programmatic capacity than they did in earlier years, and this greater level of activity and service has increased the role of the state chairperson.

## National Party Influence on State Leaders

In 1968 the Republican National Committee was expanded to include all of the state chairpersons as voting members. In 1972 the Democratic National Committee, as a part of a major reorganization and restructuring, was also expanded to include all of the state chairs as well as the highest ranking state party officer of the other gender. The addition of the chairpersons to the two national committees had a profound effect on their activities and behavior because it brought a high level of practical experience to the bodies. Both parties also support state chairpersons' associations, which meet regularly

and, depending on the leadership, are active in party affairs, policy planning, and other intraparty activities. On occasion each of the associations has been effective in bringing the views of the state parties to bear on the national party apparatus.

## Conclusion

American political parties have shown remarkable endurance and adaptability in the face of a rapidly changing political environment. A good deal of evidence shows increased party organizational strength at the national level and in a great many states. The success of the party organizations that have proven to be most enduring has often been attributable to an imaginative and flexible leadership committed to the support of traditional party activities balanced by the use of innovative new techniques that have become available in recent years—that is, party organizations are only as good and as strong as their leadership and their activists.

*See also:* Individual state party leaders, County Party Organizations, Democratic National Committee, Republican National Committee, State Party Committees

*Robert J. Huckshorn*

REFERENCES

Advisory Commission on Intergovernmental Relations. 1986. *The Transformation in American Politics.* Washington: ACIR.

Cotter, Cornelius P., James L. Gibson, John F. Bibby, and Robert J. Huckshorn. 1989. *Party Organizations in American Politics.* Pittsburgh: U. of Pittsburgh Pr.

Gray, Virginia, Herbert Jacob, and Robert B. Albritton. 1990. *Politics in the American States: A Comparative Analysis.* 5th edition. Glenview, IL: Scott Foresman/Little, Brown.

Huckshorn, Robert J. 1976. *Party Leadership in the States.* Amherst: U. of Massachusetts Pr.

Jewell, Malcolm E., and David M. Olson. 1988. *Political Parties and Elections in the American States.* Chicago: Dorsey.

Key. V. O., Jr. 1956. *American State Politics: An Introduction.* New York: Knopf.

# State Party Nominating Systems

The selection of candidates for public office is certainly the most vital function of a political party. In the United States, however, this function has increasingly been taken over by the voters in primary elections. The direct primary, more than any other feature of the American party system, has served to weaken state and local party organizations and contributed to the rise of a highly individualistic, candidate-centered style of politics.

During the early nineteenth century, party nominations for most state offices in the United States were controlled by caucuses made up of each party's (the Democratic-Republicans and Federalists) members in the state legislature, sometimes supplemented by delegates elected from legislative districts that were then being represented by the opposing party. Similarly, presidential nominations were controlled by the members of each party's congressional caucus. During the 1820s, however, this system came under increasing criticism, especially by supporters of Andrew Jackson, as narrow and elitist. By 1832 the congressional caucus had been replaced by a national nominating convention made up of delegates from each state. Many of the state parties also changed their procedures for selecting candidates from the legislative caucus to a state party convention.

The nominating convention, made up of delegates either elected directly by local party organizations or chosen at county conventions, remained the dominant method of selecting candidates for statewide office until the early twentieth century. By the 1890s, however, the convention system itself had come under attack for its proclivity to perpetuate the power of party bosses. After the end of Reconstruction, one-party domination became the prevalent political pattern in many states. With the Democratic Party dominant in the South and the Republicans prevailing in much of the rest of the country, rarely did real competition show up in elections. Nomination by the dominant party was tantamount to election, and the nomination process was often controlled by a small group of party leaders.

The direct primary was seen by reformers as a tool to break the power of these party leaders. Of course, reformers were not always motivated entirely by disinterested concern with good government. Many of the progressive reformers, like Robert La Follette of Wisconsin, saw the direct primary as a means to achieve power for themselves. In 1903 Wisconsin adopted the first statewide direct primary law, although a number of southern states had used primaries previously. By 1917 a majority of states had adopted the direct primary as the method of nominating candidates for most statewide offices.

Today, the direct primary is used in every state (Connecticut in 1955 was the last state to abandon a pure convention system). However, considerable variation characterizes the methods by which primaries are conducted among the 50 states. These variations have important consequences for the role played by party leaders and organizations in the nomination process. In some states, party leaders and organizations retain considerable influence in the selection of candidates; in others, the parties have become little more than passive spectators in the nomination process.

### Mixed Convention and Primary Systems

In several states, party conventions still play an important role in the nomination process. Virginia law allows each party to select either a primary or a convention to nominate candidates for state offices. In recent years, both major parties have nominated candidates for statewide office in Virginia by convention rather than in a primary election. Eight states (Connecticut, Colorado, Delaware, New Mexico, New York, North Dakota, Rhode Island, and Utah) provide for preprimary endorsements under state law, and in one state (Massachusetts), party rules governing endorsements have been accepted as legally binding by the state courts. In three other states (Minnesota, Wisconsin, and Illinois) at least one party makes informal preprimary endorsements at its state convention.

The effects of preprimary endorsements on the nomination process vary considerably. In some states a candidate must receive a minimum percentage of votes at the party convention in order to obtain a place on the ballot. If only one candidate receives the required number of votes, then that candidate is nominated without a primary. In other states, a candidate who does not receive the required number of votes at the party convention may qualify for the primary ballot by bringing in a certain number of signatures on petitions. However, the candidate who receives the largest number of votes at the state convention may also receive the top position on the primary ballot.

"Legal" endorsements appear to be quite effective. Between 1960 and 1986 according to Malcolm Jewell and David Olson, 57 percent of candidates receiving "legal" endorsements had no primary opposition. In contrast, only 28 percent of candidates receiving informal endorsements were unopposed, and only 20 percent of all northern primaries were uncontested during this period. When they had opposition in the primary, endorsed candidates were victorious in about three-fourths of the contests. Candidates receiving "legal" endorsements enjoyed only a slightly higher rate of success than those receiving informal endorsements.

Based on this evidence, the major advantage of a preprimary endorsement appears to be in discouraging primary opposition. If an endorsed candidate does face opposition in the primary, party endorsement does not guarantee success. However, an endorsed candidate usually has several advantages over any challengers. Along with the top line on the primary ballot, endorsees generally receive financial and organizational assistance from the state party and more favorable media coverage. A party endorsement may also help a candidate to raise money and recruit volunteer workers.

Despite these advantages, many candidates have successfully challenged party endorsements in recent primary elections. In fact, party endorsements appear to make little or no difference to primary voters; most voters either do not know which candidate has been endorsed or do not care. A candidate who is denied the party endorsement can always use the time-honored technique of campaigning against the "party bosses." Rudy Perpich in Minnesota, Edward King in Massachusetts, and Mario Cuomo in New York all won governorships after successfully challenging candidates endorsed by their own parties.

While preprimary endorsements do not always guarantee nomination to a candidate, the endorsing convention may have other benefits for a state party. By giving activists an opportunity to participate in selecting candidates, the party convention may help to stimulate the development of local party organizations. The use of a nominating convention can also help a party to avoid the expense and divisiveness of a primary election. In 1981, after years of bitterly contested primaries and losses in the general election, the Virginia Democratic Party shifted from a primary to a nominating convention to choose its candidates for statewide office; the Democrats proceeded to sweep all three major statewide offices. Four years later, the Democrats again used a nominating convention and again elected all of their major statewide candidates.

## Types of Primary Elections

In most of the states, the primary election is the only method of selecting candidates for public office. However, the rules governing the conduct of primary elections vary considerably from state to state. The most important differences among state primaries involve the re-

quirements for voting in the primary. In states with "closed" primaries, a voter must be registered with a party in order to vote in that party's primary; in states with "open" primaries, party registration is not required and any registered voter may participate in a party's primary.

Twenty-five states currently require voters to be registered with a party in order to vote in that party's primary election. However, eight of these states allow voters to enroll or change their registration on the day of the primary. In addition, two states require party registration but allow voters registered as Independents to participate in either party's primary. In the states that require party registration before a voter can participate in a primary, the cutoff date for changing one's registration varies from less than two months to almost a full year before the date of the primary.

Twenty-two states currently use an open primary to nominate candidates for state offices. Voters are free to participate in either party's primary, although 11 states require that voters publicly choose the party primary in which they wish to vote. In nine states, voters are able to choose a party in the privacy of the voting booth. Two states, Washington and Alaska, utilize a system known as the "blanket primary": a voter can participate in both parties' primaries for different offices at the same time. Finally, the state of Louisiana uses a nonpartisan primary election. The names of all Democratic and Republican candidates appear on the same primary ballot. If a candidate receives a majority of the vote in the primary election, then that candidate is elected; if no candidate receives a majority, then a runoff election is held between the top two vote-getters in the primary, regardless of their party affiliation.

In addition to the distinction between open and closed primaries, another important characteristic of a state's primary system is the presence or absence of a runoff requirement. Eleven states currently use a runoff primary. These include all of the states of the old Confederacy except Tennessee, along with the Border State of Oklahoma. Until recently, of course, nomination in a Democratic primary was tantamount to election in all of these states. Under the runoff system, if no candidate receives a majority of the vote in the first primary, a runoff election is held between the two leading candidates.

The argument for the runoff primary is that a candidate who receives a minority of the vote in a multicandidate field should not automatically receive a party's nomination. In the runoff primary, a candidate must demonstrate their acceptability to a majority of primary voters. However, in recent years the runoff primary has come under attack from civil rights groups who charge that its real purpose is to prevent African-Americans from being nominated.

*Voter Turnout in Primary Elections*

Voter turnout in U.S. primary elections is generally low. According to Jewell and Olson, between 1960 and 1986, an average of about 30 percent of the voting-age population turned out in gubernatorial primary elections even when both parties had contested races. Turnout in primary elections was generally higher in states with open primaries and closely contested races and lower in states with closed primaries and one-sided races. Even under the most favorable conditions, however, voter turnout rarely exceeds two-fifths of the voting-age population.

In states in which one party enjoys a dominant position, a much larger turnout usually characterizes the dominant party's primary than the minority party's primary. An even larger number of voters may turn out in the majority party's primary than in the general election, a phenomenon most common in the South where, until recently, the winner of the Democratic primary was almost assured of being elected. However, as two party competition has trickled down from presidential to state and local elections, contested Republican primaries have become much more common in the South, and turnout in southern Republican primaries has been gradually increasing relative to turnout in southern Democratic primaries.

Studies of voter participation in primary elections have generally found that voting in primaries is influenced by the same factors that influence voting in general elections. Voters tend to be older, better educated, and more affluent than nonvoters. In addition, the influence of partisanship on turnout may be even stronger in primaries than in general elections. Voters who consider themselves Independents or who identify only slightly with a party are less likely to take an interest in an intraparty contest than voters who identify strongly with that party. In states with closed primaries, Independents are not permitted to vote in a party's primary unless they choose to register with that party. The result is that strong partisans make up a disproportionate share of the electorate in primary elections.

Given the relatively low turnout in most primaries, primary voters might not be said accurately to reflect the views of all of a party's supporters in the electorate. However, a study of primary voters in Wisconsin did not find any consistent ideological bias among primary voters—Democratic primary voters were not consistently more liberal than Democratic identifiers and Republican primary voters were not consistently more conservative than Republican identifiers in the electorate. The ideological composition of the primary electorate probably depends on the types of candidates who are running in a particular primary.

While voters in party primaries do not necessarily hold more extreme views than do party supporters in the electorate, they tend to have more extreme views than do voters in the general election. Democratic primary voters are generally more liberal than the electorate as a whole, and Republican primary voters are generally more conservative than the electorate as a whole. In 1980, for example, according to a national survey conducted by the Center for Political Studies (CPS) at the University of Michigan, the average Democratic primary voter placed herself at 3.9 on a one-to-seven scale, with one the most liberal and seven the most conservative position; conversely, the average Republican primary voter placed herself at 4.9. The average voter in the general election came out at 4.3 on the same scale. (These scores exclude about one-third of the respondents in the survey who could not place themselves on the liberal-conservative scale.) While the question in the CPS survey asked about presidential primary elections, the results for voters in state primary elections would probably be similar.

Because of the ideological composition of the Democratic and Republican primary electorates, liberal Democrats and conservative Republicans generally have an advantage over moderates in primary elections. The candidate who wins the primary, therefore, is not necessarily the candidate with the broadest electoral appeal. This situation can lead to problems in November, especially for the minority party, which must appeal to independent voters and supporters of the majority party in order to win the general election.

*Consequences of Primary Laws*

States with open primaries generate a great deal of concern about the frequency and significance of crossover voting or "raiding" by the opposition party. In the case of "raiding," supporters of one party deliberately sabotage the opposing party's primary by voting for the weakest candidate. To be successful, such a raid would probably have to be planned and well publicized in advance, but any such action would invite condemnation by the media as well as retaliation by the victimized party. No concrete evidence of such organized raiding has been uncovered. Of course, individual voters may possibly engage in raiding without any central planning or direction. To affect the outcome of an election, however, such behavior would have to be widespread, and raiders would have to have a high level of agreement about who would be the weakest opposition candidate. These conditions would be very difficult to satisfy. In a study of voters in an open gubernatorial primary election Alan Abramowitz and his associates found that 10 percent of the voters in the Democratic primary planned to vote for the Republican candidate in the general election, regardless of who won the primary. However, evidence of strategic voting among this group was lacking—most of them voted for the more conservative Democrat in the primary, and he was generally regarded by Republican Party leaders as a stronger general election candidate than was his opponent. Such strategy is hardly useful.

While raiding appears to be rare or nonexistent, crossover voting does occur with some regularity in open primaries. Even in states with closed primaries, nothing prevents a voter from registering with the opposing party in order to vote in its primary. Steven Finkel and Howard Scarrow found that about 5 percent of voters in closed primary states were registered with a party different from the one they identified with. In open primaries, crossover voters and Independents probably comprise a large proportion of all voters, especially when only one party has a contested primary. According to a CBS News–New York Times exit poll, only 52 percent of the voters in the 1988 Wisconsin Democratic presidential primary considered themselves Democrats; 32 percent of these voters called themselves Independents, and 14 percent thought of themselves as Republicans. In contrast, a CBS News–New York Times exit poll in New York, a state with a closed primary, found that 80 percent of those voting in the Democratic primary were Democratic identifiers; only 14 percent of these voters were Independents, while 6 percent considered themselves Republicans or expressed no party preference.

Independents and crossover voters appear to be motivated primarily by attraction to a particular candidate in the primary. In some cases, the candidate preferences of crossover voters and Independents differ from those of partisans. Therefore, Independents and crossover voters can indeed alter the outcome of a primary. In 1972, for example, James Lengle found that George Wallace's victory in the Michigan Democratic presidential primary was aided by large numbers of Republicans who crossed over to vote in the Democratic primary because Richard Nixon had no serious opposition in the Republican presidential primary. Similarly, in 1984 Ronald Reagan faced no opposition for the Republican presidential nomination, so many Independents and Republicans chose to vote in Democratic presidential primaries. According to Larry Bartels, these Independents and Republican crossover voters tended to favor Gary Hart over Walter Mondale, who received his strongest backing from regular Democratic partisans.

Very little research has been done on the extent or consequences of crossover voting in state primary elections. In a 1982 survey in Michigan, a state with an open primary, Malcolm Jewell reports that almost half of the primary voters switched back and forth between parties depending on the candidates and issues in the primary rather than voting consistently in one party's primary. Surveys of primary voters in Wisconsin, the birthplace of the open primary, found that crossover voters generally constituted less than 10 percent of the electorate in state primaries compared with an average of about 20 percent in presidential primaries; however, a large proportion of the voters in state primary elections were Independents.

In the South, where open primaries predominate, turnout in the Democratic primary often greatly exceeds the vote for Democratic candidates in the general election, while the Republican vote in November is usually several times larger than the turnout in the Republican primary. This pattern suggests that, despite the development of two-party competition in the region, many southern Republicans and Independents continue to vote in Democratic primary elections. The presence of these independents and crossover voters in the Democratic primary may be an important element in the survival of conservative Democratic officeholders. As Republican primaries in the South become more competitive, we would expect more

Republican and Independent voters to be drawn into these contests, possibly leaving some conservative Democratic officeholders in a precarious position in the Democratic primary.

## Competition in Primary Elections

The goal of the progressive reformers who instituted the direct primary was to transfer control of the nomination process from party bosses to the public. In practice, however, popular control of party nominations is often frustrated by a lack of meaningful competition in primary elections. In 1978, Craig Grau's survey of state legislative primaries in 14 states found that 53 percent of the Democratic primaries and 83 percent of the Republican primaries went uncontested. Although competition is more common in primaries for major statewide offices, between 1960 and 1986 about one-fourth of all gubernatorial primaries in the United States were not contested. The likelihood of a contested primary increases if a primary takes place in the dominant party, if no incumbent is in the race, and if no candidate gets a preprimary endorsement.

Even if a primary is contested, competition may not be meaningful; one candidate often enjoys an overwhelming advantage in the primary because of familiarity or financial resources. This imbalance is most likely to occur when an incumbent is running. According to recent calculations, between 1956 and 1984, only 48 percent of all contested gubernatorial primary elections outside the South were decided by a margin of less than 20 percentage points. During this same period, only 24 percent of all contested primaries involving incumbents were decided by a margin of less than 20 percentage points, and only a handful of incumbent governors was defeated in primaries.

The mass media have been playing an increasingly prominent role in statewide primary elections. In primaries, just as in general elections, candidates rely heavily on television to get their message across to the electorate. Media development has, in turn, greatly increased the cost of primary campaigns. As a result, a telegenic appearance and personal wealth have become increasingly important assets for candidates seeking statewide office. In recent years a number of candidates with little or no political experience but with great personal wealth—men like John Y. Brown in Kentucky and Lewis Lehrman in New York—have successfully sought gubernatorial nominations. In the future we will probably see more wealthy and mediagenic political amateurs running in primary elections.

## Conclusions: The Nominating Process and the Party System

The direct primary is a unique feature of the American party system. In no other democracy are voters given the right to designate party candidates. Party conventions are still used in several states to endorse and occasionally to nominate candidates. In most states, however, party leaders and organizations are passive spectators rather than active participants in the nominating process. Candidates who want to be nominated must appeal directly to the voters through the mass media, probably the single most important explanation for the decentralized, individualistic style of politics that has developed in the United States since the end of World War II.

The implications of the direct primary for American politics extend beyond political campaigns to the policymaking process itself. Candidates who feel little or no obligation to party leaders or organizations for their selection also feel little or no obligation to work with and support the party in office. Therefore, the ability of the parties to provide a source of cohesion within the legislature and between the executive and legislative branches of government has been diminished. Coalition building has become a more complex and difficult task.

*See also:* Blanket Primaries, Caucuses, Closed Primary, Crossover Voting, Robert M. La Follette, Open Primary, Politics of Presidential Nominations, Runoff Primaries, Voter Turnout in Primaries

*Alan I. Abramowitz*

### REFERENCES

Abramowitz, Alan I., John J. McGlennon, and Ronald B. Rapoport. 1981. "A Note on Strategic Voting in a Primary Election." 43 *Journal of Politics* 899.

Adamany, David. 1976. "Cross-Over Voting and the Democratic Party's Reform Rules." 70 *American Political Science Review* 536.

Bartels, Larry M. 1988. *Presidential Primaries and the Dynamics of Public Choice.* Princeton: Princeton U. Pr.

Black, Merle, and Earl Black. 1982. "The Growth of Contested Republican Primaries in the American South, 1960–1980." In Laurence W. Moreland, Tod A. Baker, and Robert P. Steed, eds. *Contemporary Southern Political Attitudes and Behavior.* New York: Praeger.

Finkel, Steven E., and Howard A. Scarrow. 1985. "Party Identification and Party Enrollment: The Difference and the Consequence." 47 *Journal of Politics* 620.

Grau, Craig H. 1981. "Competition in State Legislative Primaries." 6 *Legislative Studies Quarterly* 35.

Hedlund, Ronald D., Meredith W. Watts, and David M. Hedge. 1982. "Voting in an Open Primary." 10 *American Politics Quarterly* 197.

Jewell, Malcolm E. 1984. *Parties and Primaries: Nominating State Governors.* New York: Praeger.

———, and David M. Olson. 1988. *Political Parties and Elections in American States.* 3rd ed. Chicago: Dorsey.

Kenney, Patrick J. 1983. "Explaining Turnout in Gubernatorial Primaries." 11 *American Politics Quarterly* 315.

Key, V. O., Jr. 1964. *Politics, Parties, and Pressure Groups.* 5th ed. New York: Crowell.

Lengle, James I. 1981. *Representation and Presidential Primaries.* Westport, CT: Greenwood.

Ranney, Austin. 1968. "The Representativeness of Primary Elections." 12 *Midwest Journal of Political Science* 224.

———. 1972. "Turnout and Representation in Presidential Primary Elections." 66 *American Political Science Review* 21.

———, and Leon Epstein. 1966. "The Two Electorates: Voters and Non-Voters in a Wisconsin Primary." 28 *Journal of Politics* 598.

## State Regulation of Political Parties

American political parties have been so heavily regulated during most of the twentieth century that their supervision appears to be a natural condition. Yet in other democratic nations, parties are not regulated in the same way or to the same degree. For example, European parties elsewhere retain organizational control over the selection of their nominees for elective public office, subject at most to legal provisions for fairness and honesty rather than to statutorily mandated direct primaries of the kind administered by most American state governments. In this respect, other democratic nations treat parties as private associations.

So indeed had the United States until late in the nineteenth century, when states began significantly to intervene in what had been internal party matters. Then, during the progressive decades after 1900, most states firmly established the regulatory framework still so largely in place. State laws vary greatly, but they most often require that party nominees be chosen by voters in state-managed direct primaries. Many laws also specify, sometimes in ways now evidently unconstitutional, the composition, selection method, and duties of party committees. In these respects, American parties look like statutory creations, even quasi-governmental agencies. By having public roles along with private associational roles, parties resemble privately owned public utilities that are also heavily regulated.

In regulating parties, national legislation is tangential. The most nearly direct national regulations flow from congressional legislation dealing with campaign finance in federal elections; here parties—national and to some extent state parties—are subject to restrictions, as are candidates, nonparty committees, and individual contributors. Otherwise, Congress has not only left the regulation of state parties almost entirely to the states, but it has also abstained from the general regulation of national party committees. Thus, national parties as such are hardly regulated at all though they are affected by state regulation of all those state parties that together are the components of each major national party. More significant than Congress as a national government actor in this area is the U.S. Supreme Court, since it has imposed constitutional standards that states and their parties must meet—when, for example, these bodies determine a voter's eligibility in primary elections.

To explain the dominance of states in regulating parties, it is only necessary to note that the regulation relates to elections and that the conduct of elections has, under the U.S. Constitution, been largely left to the states. For national as well as for state offices, states have enjoyed considerable latitude within the limits imposed by federally guaranteed voting rights and by certain uniform national provisions (as to election dates, for example). The limits have become a little narrower recently, but states continue to exercise most of their traditional power over elections. Certainly, their power was largely unencumbered in the early decades of the twentieth century when states extended their control of elections to include the regulation of parties involved in those elections. The most specific justification for that extension was the legal recognition of parties that followed from the adoption, in the late nineteenth century, of a state-provided ballot listing party nominees. Perhaps states would have regulated parties anyway, as some had tried to do even before they provided the ballot, but the state's claim to determine the process by which the party label was won became more compelling once that label was officially recognized.

Understanding party regulation as an extension of state power over elections, however, does not itself explain why American parties are so much more heavily regulated than parties in other democratic nations. Many other nations also put party labels on official ballots, and in any event governmental power over elections (be it national or state power) could elsewhere have been legally extended as fully it has been in the United States. Why only in America? Distinctive historical circumstances provide a large part of the answer. American party organizations became large and powerful in response to the early existence of a mass electorate, a development that took place several decades before its modern European counterparts came into being. Indeed, during most of the nineteenth century, American parties were widely regarded as the most highly developed in the world. But that did not mean that they were always admired by high-minded people, in the United States or abroad.

Instead, by the late nineteenth century, American parties struck many observers as both too powerful and infamously corrupt. Their strength rested heavily on patronage, widely available in the form of government jobs for party workers during a century when such jobs almost always lacked the protection of subsequent civil service laws. State and especially local party leaders, called bosses, headed patronage-built organizations, called machines, and wielded great political power often without holding elective office themselves. They seemed to choose the elected officials through their control of the internal party nominating process and by their organizational success in subsequently mobilizing the electorate (or, as frequently alleged, by stealing ballots, bribing voters, and stuffing the ballot box). In some places too, the party machines, while depending on the votes of the economically disadvantaged, were closely tied to particular business interests believed to be corruptly favored by governmental action.

In short, American parties had a bad name among good-government advocates of the late nineteenth and early twentieth centuries. They were not primarily ideological or programmatic, in the style of the new European parties, and they were certainly not organized to reform the political system. Rather, the Republican and Democratic parties—frequently either one or the other in a given jurisdiction—were themselves principal institutional features of the system. Reforming them looked essential if government were to become honest, efficient, and truly responsive to the public good.

Early efforts to reform parties from inside had largely failed. Not only were the two major parties thought unlikely to reform themselves,

but also they seemed too well established to be superseded by a new party. State regulation of Republicans and Democrats looked more feasible, but motivations for doing so varied a good deal. No doubt, many reformers disliked not merely the bosses themselves, but they were also reacting against the mass American electorate. Bourgeois reformers worried especially about immigrants in large cities, who supported the bosses in return for favors and political consideration.

But other political housecleaners, even the middle-class ones, sought popular support for democratizing agendas. Championing progressivism, in the first few decades of the twentieth century, they advocated the regulation of parties along with the regulation of those business interests that they treated as supporters and manipulators of party machines. Preeminent among the progressive reformers was Robert La Follette in Wisconsin, but progressivism characterized the particularly stringent party-regulatory legislation of most upper midwestern states and of several western states. Reform in most northeastern states was less strongly anti-organizational, but it too reflected some of the same progressive outlook. Southern states, however, responded to different interests as they established primary elections for the dominant Democratic Party from which African-Americans were to be excluded.

The progressivism responsible for party regulation can be linked to an older American tradition of political openness at odds with the kind of organizational control exercised by the city machines or, for that matter, by *any* strong party even if composed of ideological activists. In accord with that tradition, American parties developed not as dues-paying membership organizations but as amorphous aggregates of a party's regular voters. All such voters were believed to have a right to participate in party affairs and, in particular, to select party nominees for elective office. In the nineteenth century, without state-run direct primaries, party voters were supposed to be able to participate through party caucuses or even through party-conducted primaries. At certain times and places, fairly large numbers attended these party events. Commonly, however, party meetings were effectively controlled by a handful of leaders and their immediate followers. Control by insiders, also evident at party conventions, often seemed highly manipulative if not actually corrupt. At the very least, organizational practice did not meet the American democratic ideal, the short-comings most egregious where one party was historically so dominant as to be virtually certain of electing its nominees. Then, as was the case in many American constituencies in 1900 (and even later), most voters played no effective role at all. Only a few organizational leaders determined nominees, whose election was a foregone conclusion. Unsurprisingly, therefore, the regulatory movement that produced the direct primary was especially strong in one-party states.

The essence of the progressive legislation was to define party as a statutory entity composed of its voters, thus following the traditional American conception. Those defined by the state as party voters then had the legal right to participate in those party affairs that the state managed as part of its election machinery—primary nominating contests and often also the choice of certain party officials. Not all states defined party voters in the same way. About 20 states, including the largest, now require enrollment in a particular party at a date before a primary election, arranging for party enrollment much as they do for voter registration itself. State officials actually record party "membership," a truly extraordinary service if parties are thought to be private associations. Although most other states require only that voters declare their party at the primary in order to participate in party candidate selection, that action also involves election officials before whom party declarations are made. The state's official "service" for parties is of a different nature in the minority of states that have neither party enrollment nor party declaration requirements, allowing choice of party to be made in the secrecy of the voting booth; but the "open" primaries in these states are nonetheless government-provided elections for parties as are the "closed" primaries.

From an organizational standpoint, the state is hardly performing a service for parties by running these parties' primaries since leaders and activists are thus deprived of their control over nominations. Understandably, traditional party organizations opposed direct primaries along with many other state regulations. How, then, were progressive reforms enacted by state legislatures composed of Republicans and Democrats? One answer is that some legislators were not responsive to the traditional party organizations; though elected under Republican or Democratic labels, they were often opposed to an established machine either in principle or because they belonged to a faction that expected to benefit from reform, particularly of the nominating process. Another answer is that even legislators who liked political machines found it politically expedient, in some places, to enact regulatory reforms when progressivism was most popular. In doing so, however, they could be expected to develop legislation in a form least unfavorable to organizational interests. The closed primary is certainly one such form, and it is found mostly in states whose traditional party organizations remained strong during most of the first half of the twentieth century.

With or without the closed primary, regulatory legislation includes advantages for major parties that should be considered along with the burdens. The most obvious is privileged ballot access. To be qualified for a place on official ballots, a party usually needs only to have polled a certain portion of votes at a previous election. From the start, Republicans and Democrats qualified in most states, but many minor parties and all new parties had to do so by petitions frequently requiring substantial numbers of signatures. In other ways, too, the states have institutionalized the major parties—for instance, by giving them roles in appointing election officials and in having their committees perform certain statutory tasks. Altogether, the Republican and Democratic parties are treated as a de facto electoral duopoly that enjoys a privileged position under state regulation. The two-party system thus looks like the political equivalent of a natural monopoly in the economic sphere. Plainly, however, such treatment is now subject to constitutional limits. The Supreme Court has declared that states cannot impose unreasonably high barriers to ballot access by new parties.

Increasingly, too, the federal courts have begun to examine critically the way state regulations of major parties impinge on associational freedom. Thus, the Supreme Court invalidated California legislation that prohibited official governing bodies of political parties from endorsing or opposing candidates in primary elections, in *Eu v. San Francisco Democratic Committee* (1989), which decision also invalidated the state's specifications for the organization and composition of those governing bodies.

From one angle, the impingement on freedom is clear not only when a state restricts what a party may do in a campaign, or how party committees may be organized, but also when it prescribes how a party's nominees are to be chosen. Yet only since the 1970s have state powers in these areas been seriously challenged in the federal courts. For almost three-quarters of a century, after a few early challenges in state courts, the constitutionality of virtually all of the state regulatory legislation on parties was evidently taken for granted. When originally enacted during the Progressive era, regulatory legislation could not then have been effectively challenged under the Constitution because the First Amendment had not yet been judicially incorporated into the Fourteenth Amendment and applied to the states. Even that incorporation, when it occurred, did not explicitly involve freedom of association until after mid-century. Then the leading case concerned the National Association for the Advancement of Colored People (NAACP) rather than a political party.

That political parties could successfully invoke similar constitutional rights against state regulation remained in doubt until the 1970s and 1980s. States could claim that they dealt with entities legislatively created for election purposes—that is, statutory parties of voters who choose nominees for public office. Any organizational apparatus representing a party of this kind—even with its conventions, meetings, and activist following—seemed nevertheless a state agency that the state could arguably regulate even to the extent of prohibiting it from engaging in certain campaign activities in which other groups legally engage.

Nothing about such regulation, however, kept Republicans or Democrats from forming private, nonstatutory associations of their own, calling them parties, and undertaking the activities forbidden to the statutory parties. That, in fact, is what party activists did for a time in Wisconsin and California. Few states, however, persisted in so stringent a regulation of their statutory parties as to force the creation of extra-legal parties, and California's prohibition of official party endorsement in primaries has now been ruled unconstitutional (as noted above).

More significant in the 1990s is the controversy over direct-primary laws. If the party whose primary the state conducts is a private association entitled to freedom of association, then how can the state rather than the party itself determine who votes in that primary? Or, for that matter, how can the state decide that the party nominees should be chosen in a primary rather than in a convention if the party organization should want a convention? These questions, when raised in the 1970s and 1980s, were more novel than challenges to other state regulations because of the mid-century treatment of primaries as state elections. In *Smith v. Allwright* (1944), the Court had held that a primary involved state authority even when statutes left the primary to be conducted by party officers and according to party rules. Here and in *Terry v. Adams* (1953), a case that extended the doctrine to an association within a party, the Court was invalidating "white primaries" that were meant to keep African-Americans from voting in the most meaningful elections. To frustrate such efforts to evade the impact of the Fifteenth Amendment, the Court had to treat what were ostensibly intraparty elections as if they were state elections. A few decades later, confronting different issues, the Court finds no contradiction in regarding primaries as party affairs, at least for some rule-making purposes. The justices started doing so in two decisions—*Cousins v. Wigoda* (1975) and *Democratic Party of the U.S. v. Wisconsin ex rel La Follette* (1981)—that upheld national party claims against state regulation of the selection of delegates to national party conventions. Then in *Tashjian v. Republican Party of Connecticut* (1986), the Court held that a state could not constitutionally prohibit unaffiliated electors from voting in the primary of a party whose organization wanted unaffiliated electors to cast ballots along with enrolled Republicans. The decision was carefully limited to the narrow issue at hand, and the validity of other aspects of primary laws remains to be tested.

However constitutionally uncertain, most state party regulation remained in force at least through the 1980s. Though legislation changes from time to time in response to causes other than those following from judicial decisions, states did not broadly retreat from handling parties as if they were quasi-public agencies. Such treatment is institutionalized by some states in their constitutions, not merely in statutes. Wherever found, the regulatory provisions of the 50 states are hard to summarize; their variety does not readily fit a simple comprehensible classification. Nevertheless, an unusually full and useful description is presented in a report by the Advisory Commission on Inter governmental Relations (1986), a good starting point for anyone wanting to know which states (as of the mid-1980s) regulate which aspects of party organizations and activities, and how they do so. The report's description is the source for what follows here by way of a much briefer effort to illustrate the scope of state regulation.

The first of two broad regulatory categories concerns party structure. Thirty-six states mandate the selection of state central party committees, nine of them mandating selection by primary voters and the other 27 states mandating selection by party officials (themselves often selected by primary voters). Most states also specify whether elected public officials are to be excluded or included on state central committees. About half the states mandate meeting dates and regulate internal rules and procedures for these committees. The pattern for local party committees is roughly similar, and in at least one respect state regulation is even more usual since all but five states regulate some aspect of the internal rules, procedures, and activities of local party committees. Summarizing its account of state regulation of state and local party organization in this first category, the Advisory Commission classified 19 states as heavy regulators, 17 as moderate regulators, and only 14 as light regulators. To be sure, much of this organizational regulation may now be successfully challenged on the same grounds that the U.S. Supreme Court used to invalidate California's statutory provisions for internal party structure in *Eu v. San Francisco Democratic Committee* (1989).

The second category of regulation consists of laws governing the role of state and local party organizations in the electoral process. Regulation in this respect has already been observed to flow from the widespread but not universal use of the state-mandated direct primary that deprives party organizations themselves of the power to bestow the party label. The deprivation is lessened in a few states by laws that formally recognize the preprimary endorsements of party organizations, accompanied by privileged access to the primary ballot. Such regulatory provisions are pro-party in much the same sense as the more frequent statutory requirements of party enrollment for voting in primary elections; they are meant to help party organizations win primaries for their candidates once primaries are substituted for conventions in the nominating process. Another kind of pro-party regulation is the "sore loser" law. It prohibits candidates who have contested but failed to win a party primary from running in the general election under another label. Slightly more than half the states have such a law. Still one additional pro-party election statute ought to be mentioned: the provision in 21 states for straight-ticket voting by pulling a single party lever or by marking a single party box.

The several pro-party provisions of regulatory statutes presumably reflect the partisan interests of those legislators responsible for their enactment. They also represent the views of most political scientists who champion strong parties and who are now especially devoted to measures that lessen the organizational disadvantages of the direct primary. Indeed, political scientists may more often be overtly critical of the direct primary itself than are legislators and other public officeholders who have succeeded in winning primary elections and who thus have a stake in the system. Even pro-party political scientists, however, regard the abolition of the direct primary as politically unfeasible. Hence, they join party-oriented politicians in favoring regulations that will promote organizational strength as much as possible within the context established by the direct primary. In other words, pro-party political scientists do not always oppose state regulations. The "right kind" of regulation—party enrollment as a condition for voting in a party primary, for example—may be favored even though it involves a state-imposed and a state-administered definition of party membership.

Recently, the pro-party posture in relation to state regulation has become identified with a judicial doctrine that seeks to reconcile the state's right to specify the nature of party privileges with a claim that parties should be free from regulations that they do not want. The doctrine is evident in the arguments supporting the Supreme Court's decision, in *Tashjian*, that Connecticut's closed-primary statute had to yield to the Republican Party rule allowing unaffiliated electors to vote in certain Republican primaries. Though the Court's opinion did not indicate that it would uphold any other kind of party rule, or party rules generally, against state statutes, the advocates of party rights could be expected to invoke the doctrine of freedom of association whenever a party wants either a more open or a more closed primary than state law stipulates or when a party wants to nominate its candidates by convention rather than by primary. "Party" here, as in Connecticut, is the statutorily identified organization of elected committees and convention delegates. For that kind of organization to exercise power in determining rules for party nominations would not be unprecedented, even in twentieth-century America. A few states (notably in the South) have long allowed parties to specify certain eligibility requirements for their primary voters and even to decide whether they want to nominate by primary or by convention. Though these practices may seem merely residual and exceptional, it is now entirely possible that the Supreme Court will so broadly apply freedom of association that states would have to accommodate each party's own preferences with respect to the nominating process.

Even the unlikely establishment of so far-reaching a judicial doctrine should not be assumed to lead to actual changes in the conduct of direct primaries or in many other aspects of state regulation of political parties. After all, few parties may want to change, or find it expedient to change, the most significant statutory rules in their states. Existing major parties, especially their elected public officeholders, probably have stakes in whatever primary system exists, and their voters are accustomed to that same system. Like much of the rest of the regulatory legislation, the direct primary is a well-established institutional feature of American politics. Certain obviously onerous regulations, on the other hand, are more likely to be challenged, as both Republican and Democratic party committees challenged California's unusually severe prohibition against party organizational activity in primary contests. Judicial success in that instance is not itself a radical accomplishment. No more than two other states had recently imposed such a prohibition, and, as observed earlier, the California statute had not prevented extra-legal organizations of Republicans and Democrats from endorsing and campaigning for candidates in primary elections. The advantages of campaigning through the statutory party, available in most states, do not seem overwhelming since organizational leaders may often be inhibited by political calculations from taking overtly active roles in primary contests. Nor is it clear that parties will find large advantages in following California's parties by constitutionally freeing themselves from the statutory specifications concerning internal structures that are, admittedly, imposed in many states.

In other words, the currently limited strength of party organizations might not be greatly increased by judicial deregulation. And a thoroughgoing deregulation, by courts or legislatures, could be electorally disadvantageous to the established major parties. Suppose that parties were treated as purely private associations entitled to no ballot listing beyond what individual candidates perhaps wished to put beside their names. Primary elections, if held, would merely be competitions between individual candidates, as in nonpartisan contests. Parties, like other groups, could then merely endorse and campaign for candidates, but they would have no special statutory recognition. Thus, Republicans and Democrats would be deinstitutionalized, or privatized, much as they are in other nations, raising an open question on whether the established American parties would prosper in such a newly created deregulated environment.

*See also: Cousins v. Wigoda*, Fifteenth Amendment, Robert M. La Follette, National Association for the Advancement of Colored People, *Smith v. Allwright*, Sore Loser Laws, *Tashjian v. Republican Party*

Leon D. Epstein

REFERENCES

Advisory Commission on Intergovernmental Relations. 1986. *The Transformation in American Politics: Implications for Federalism*. Washington: ACIR.

## States' Rights Party

By the early 1940s, many southern Democrats became increasingly concerned about the liberal direction of the national Democratic Party in support of African-Americans and organized labor. These conservative southerners supported Roosevelt in 1944 only after he had dumped liberal Vice President Henry A. Wallace from the ticket. After becoming President in 1945, Harry Truman proceeded to court disillusioned liberals, labor, and Blacks with the Fair Deal, the Taft-Hartley Act veto, and civil rights measures emanating from his Committee on Civil Rights, reasoning that the increasingly alienated South had nowhere to go and would remain safely Democratic.

Disillusioned Southern Democrats met in Jackson, Mississippi, in May 1948 at a conference of States' Rights Democrats; they urged the national Democratic Party to repudiate civil rights programs and endorse states' rights. Truman's forces at the national convention sought to appease the South merely by reiterating the party's vague platform plank on civil rights from 1944, but the convention's liberal forces, led by Minneapolis mayor Hubert Humphrey, succeeded in adopting a strong plank supporting specific civil rights measures. The Mississippi delegation and half of the Alabama delegation walked out of the convention in protest.

On July 17 in Birmingham about 6,000 southern delegates, calling themselves the real Democratic Party, met as States' Rights Democrats or Dixiecrats. They nominated the governors Strom Thurmond of South Carolina as President and Fielding Wright of Mississippi as Vice President. The candidates accepted their nominations at a second convention in Houston on August 11. The Dixiecrats carried only Alabama, Mississippi, South Carolina, and Louisiana in November, the only states where the Democratic state central committees had listed Thurmond and Wright on the ballots as the official Democratic Party presidential nominees.

The Dixiecrat movement clearly demonstrated the political distinctiveness of the South, its preoccupation with maintaining the racial status quo, and its willingness to support alternatives to the national Democratic Party. In addition to opposing federal civil rights measures, the Dixiecrats also opposed increased federal power, centralization, and paternalism espoused by the national Democratic Party. The Dixiecrats hoped either to throw the election into the House of Representatives where they could bargain over civil rights or to show how indispensable southern support was for Democratic Party presidential victories with the defeat of Truman. Yet many Southern Democrats supported Truman, especially in areas with fewer Blacks and where race was a less salient issue. These Truman loyalists feared loss of federal projects and patronage and a Democratic Party split that would only help the Republicans. Truman's victory also took wind from the Dixiecrats' sails. The States' Rights Party faded after 1948.

*See also:* Civil Rights Legislation and Southern Politics, Hubert Humphrey, Franklin D. Roosevelt, Strom Thurmond, Harry S Truman, Henry A. Wallace, Fielding Wright

*Stephen D. Shaffer*

REFERENCES

Barnard, William. 1974. *Dixiecrats and Democrats: Alabama Politics, 1942–1950.* Tuscaloosa: U. of Alabama Pr.

Garson, Robert. 1974. *The Democratic Party and the Politics of Sectionalism, 1941–1948.* Baton Rouge: Louisiana State U. Pr.

Tindall, George. 1972. *The Disruption of the Solid South.* Athens: U. of Georgia Pr.

Turner, Julius, and Edward Schneier. 1970. *Party and Constituency: Pressures on Congress.* Baltimore: Johns Hopkins U. Pr.

## Gloria Steinem (1934– )

Feminist founder of *Ms.* magazine. Gloria Steinem epitomized the image of what it was to be a feminist in the 1970s—single, successful, and savvy. She was the founding editor of *Ms.* magazine in 1972; by the mid-1970s, 500,000 readers were buying *Ms.* monthly to read articles such as "Can Women Love Women?" and "Down with Sexist Upbringing." A staunch supporter of a women's right to choose an abortion, Steinem co-founded Voters for Choice, an independent political committee to support the election of pro-choice members to Congress. She also steadfastly supported the inclusion of lesbian rights among feminist concerns, a stance that marked her in some circles as an advocate of what was called sexual politics.

Steinem was born the daughter of a resort owner and former newspaperwoman whose own mother had been president of the Ohio Women's Suffrage Association. At Smith College Steinem majored in government and graduated in 1956 with high honors and a fellowship to India where she witnessed the effects of dire poverty. By 1960 she was a free-lance writer in New York; her first by-lined article, "The Moral Disarmament of Betty Co-Ed," was an article about the sexual revolution. In 1963 she worked as a Playboy Bunny and wrote about the job in an exposé about the working conditions of women at the club. In 1983 she published *Outrageous Acts and Everyday Rebellions*, an anthology of two decades of her writings.

Steinem also embraced politics, initially as a campaign volunteer, then as a writer; her "The City Politic" column in *New York* magazine, which she started writing in 1968, made her one of the first female political commentators. For her column she spent time with a radical women's group called The Redstockings, an experience that opened her to talking about her own abortion. "Suddenly, I was no longer learning intellectually what was wrong," she later said, "I knew."

Armed with a purpose, Steinem poured her energies into the women's movement. Aside from founding *Ms.* magazine, the first publication owned, operated, and edited by women and devoted to feminist issues, Steinem went on the lecture circuit promoting issues such as the Equal Rights Amendment and the pro-choice position. She encountered resistance and audiences that did not share her views. "If we just explain to everybody how unjust this is," she once said, "They will want to fix it."

But that was not to be. The ERA campaign lost in the state houses and radical feminism began to lose its luster as traditional values and consumerism intruded. In an interview with *Esquire* magazine in 1984 Steinem debunked a myth that she had helped create: "No feminist ever said we should be superwoman. No one has any right to expect us to be."

*Melissa Ludtke*

REFERENCES

———. 1984. "Gloria at 50." Gala Celebration program, Waldorf-Astoria Anon./, New York

## John C. Stennis (1901– )

Six-term Democratic Senator from Mississippi. The Senate tenure of Mississippi Democrat John Cornelius Stennis ranks as second longest on record, slightly behind that of the late Arizona Democrat Carl Hayden, who served from 1927 to 1969. Stennis entered the Senate in November 1947 after winning special election to fill the unexpired term of the deceased Senator Theodore G. Bilbo. Before retiring in January 1989, Stennis had won reelection six times with minimal opposition; his lowest share of the vote was 64 percent in 1982 against a strong Republican challenge.

Honoring his integrity that transcended party lines, the Senate unanimously elected him President *pro tempore* in January 1987. Stennis served on the Armed Services Committee for four decades and as chairman from 1969 to 1981. Placed on the Appropriations Committee in the 1950s, he became chairman in 1987. The first Democratic Senator to call for censure of the reckless Red-baiter Senator Joseph R. McCarthy in 1954, Stennis served as first chairman of the Senate Ethics Committee upon its creation in 1965. Always an advocate of a strong defense posture, Stennis led in the successful passage of the controversial War Powers Act in 1973, despite strong presidential opposition. Although Stennis joined other southerners in opposing civil rights legislation in earlier years, he voted to extend the Voting Rights Act in 1982 and endorsed Black Democrat Mike Espy's successful bid in 1986 to represent Mississippi's Second District in the House. Of 78 recorded votes on which President Ronald Reagan took a position in 1987, Stennis's support score was 47 percent—the same as Georgia Democrat Sam Nunn's but much lower than Mississippi Republican Thad Cochran's 73 percent. Indicative of bipartisan admiration, President Reagan joined others in honoring Stennis on June 23, 1988, in an event called "Celebration of a Legend," where he announced that a nuclear powered aircraft carrier would be named for the Mississippi Democrat.

*See also:* Theodore G. Bilbo, Carl Hayden, Joseph R. McCarthy, Voting Rights Act of 1965 and Extensions

*Thomas N. Boschert*

REFERENCES

Abney, Glenn F. 1968. *Mississippi Election Statistics, 1900–1967.* University, MS: Bureau of Governmental Research.

Benenson, Bob. 1987. "Stennis, Evans Retire." 45 *Congressional Quarterly Weekly Report* 2698.

Billington, Monroe Lee. 1984. *Southern Politics since the Civil War.* Malabar, FL: Krieger.

Calmes, Jacqueline. 1987. "Chairman Stennis: Sharing the Workload." 45 *Congressional Quarterly Weekly Report* 1178.

Lamis, Alexander P. 1984. *The Two-Party South.* New York: Oxford U. Pr.

Towell, Pat. 1987. "Sen. Stennis Dodges Effort to Honor Him." 45 *Congressional Quarterly Weekly Report* 2993.

## Alexander H. Stephens (1812–1883)

Vice President of the Confederate States of America. Alexander Hamilton Stephens struggled throughout his life to reconcile his devotion to constitutional principles with the political realities of serving the South's best interests, often finding himself out of step with the movement for southern independence in peace and war. Graduating from Franklin College (later the University of Georgia) in 1832, he became a lawyer and politician, serving in the state legislature from 1836 to 1842 as a Whig. A member of the House of Representatives from 1843 to 1859, Stephens became an increasingly strident defender of slavery and the abstract constitutionality of secession; nevertheless, he advised moderation as a practical matter, supporting the formation of the Union Party in Georgia in the aftermath of the Compromise of 1850. Shifting from Whig to Democratic ranks in the aftermath of his failure to secure the election of Daniel Webster in 1852, Stephens became increasingly convinced that southern interests would best be served by remaining within the Union, and he argued against secession in the absence of overt acts of northern aggression.

An outspoken opponent of secession in 1860, Stephens nevertheless followed the verdict of Georgia for disunion and soon found himself catapulted into prominence. One of the drafters of the Confederate constitution of the Confederate States of America, he was elected vice president of the new republic in February 1861. But Stephens soon found himself at odds with CSA president Jefferson Davis on a score of issues ranging form states' rights to civil liberties, eventually charging that Davis was perpetuating the very wrongs once used to justify secession. He undertook several peace initiatives, most notably the Hampton Roads Conference of February 1865, as he continued to oppose Davis's prosecution of the war.

Captured by Union troops in May 1865 and imprisoned at Fort Warren in Boston, Stephens was eventually released the following October. An avowed supporter of President Andrew Johnson's plans for Reconstruction, he was elected U.S. Senator from Georgia, although the Senate refused to seat him; the following year he attended the National Union Convention in support of Johnson. His resistance to Republican Reconstruction was coupled to his continuing efforts to defend the legality of secession in his two-volume *A Constitutional View of the Late War Between the States*. In his declining years he continued to be active in Democratic politics as a newspaper editor, member of the U.S. House of Representatives (1873–1882), and governor of Georgia (1882–1883).

*See also:* Jefferson Davis, Secession, Daniel Webster

*Brooks Donohue Simpson*

REFERENCES

Howe, Daniel Walker. 1979. "Alexander Stephens and the Failure of Southern Whiggery." In Daniel Walker Howe, ed. *The Political Culture of the American Whigs*. Chicago: U. of Chicago Pr.

Phillips, Ulrich B., ed. 1911. *The Correspondence of Robert E. Toombs, Alexander H. Stephens, and Howell Cobb*. Washington: American Historical Association.

Schott, Thomas E. 1988. *Alexander H. Stephens of Georgia: A Biography*. Baton Rouge: Louisiana State U. Pr.

Stephens, Alexander H. 1868, 1870. *A Constitutional View of the Late War Between the States*. 2 vols. Philadelphia: National Publishing Co.

Von Abele, Rudolph. 1946. *Alexander H. Stephens: A Biography*. New York: Knopf.

## Thaddeus Stevens (1792–1868)

Dominant Radical Republican leader of the Civil War and Reconstruction House of Representatives. Thaddeus Stevens was an uncompromising opponent of slavery and secession throughout his career. Born into impoverished conditions in frontier Vermont, Stevens, a clubfooted and sickly child, was educated by a determined, widowed mother. Stevens graduated from Dartmouth College in 1814 and subsequently studied law, commencing practice in Gettysburg, Pennsylvania. His defense of runaway slaves won him notoriety as an advocate of abolition, and in 1831 he aligned with the Anti-Masonic Party, winning a seat in the Pennsylvania legislature two years later. Stevens's defense of the free school system in the state, his support for the protective tariff, and his resolution calling for the abolition of slavery won him wide acclaim throughout Pennsylvania. Elected to the U.S. House of Representatives in 1848 as a Whig, Stevens, in denouncing the Compromise of 1850 and the Fugitive Slave Act, assumed a preeminent leadership role among the little band of free-soil advocates in that chamber.

Disenchanted with the moderation of the Whigs in Congress, Stevens left the House in 1853, though he participated in the formation of the Republican (Peoples') Party in Lancaster County, Pennsylvania, in 1855. In 1858 he was reelected to Congress, where because of his mastery of parliamentary strategy and his sardonic oratorical prowess, his influence surpassed that of the Speaker. As George Mayer, historian of the GOP, has noted, "Few dared to tangle with Stevens in debate, and he alternately ridiculed and frightened challengers into submission." Elected chairman of the Ways and Means Committee in 1861, and of the newly formed Appropriations Committee in 1865, Stevens wielded vast authority over all revenue matters and most legislation affecting prosecution of the war.

Objecting to President Abraham Lincoln's mild Reconstruction policies, Stevens believed that the rebellious southern states had placed themselves beyond the protection of the Constitution and should revert to territorial status at the war's end, in turn preventing the return of southern (and Democratic) representatives sufficient to challenge Republican control of Congress. Further, early in the war Stevens called for the immediate emancipation of the slaves, the provision of a slave army, and confiscation of rebel property, all of which Lincoln opposed on political grounds.

When President Andrew Johnson sought to carry out Lincoln's Reconstruction policies, Stevens, as the leading House member serving on the Joint Committee on Reconstruction, responded with harsh and vindictive opposition to Johnson's actions. In 1866 under Stevens's whip, Congress passed the Freedmen's Bureau Bill and the Civil Rights Bill over the President's veto and set forth a punitive Fourteenth Amendment requiring full Black suffrage that itself became a major issue between the President and the Radical Republican congressional leaders in the 1866 fall elections. Emboldened by the Republicans' electoral victory of 1866, Stevens and the Radicals imposed military Reconstruction upon the South and promulgated the Fifteenth Amendment. When Johnson defied Congress' Tenure of Office Act in removing Secretary of War Edwin M. Stanton, Stevens brought an impeachment resolution against the President on February 22, 1868. Though mortally ill, Stevens assisted in managing the case against Johnson and, deeply disappointed with its outcome, died shortly after the President's acquittal. A believer in the equality of man, Stevens was buried in a biracial cemetery in his words on the tombstone "illustrat[ing], in my death the principles which I advocated through a long life."

As the architect of congressional Reconstruction, Stevens has been alternatively praised or vilified for establishing postwar Republican rule throughout the national government and securing conditions conducive to long-term northern capitalist expansion and political predominance. Given his extreme prescriptions for Reconstruction, Stevens's true motivations and the extent of his actual influence in the House will continue to stir scholarly debate.

*See also:* Fifteenth Amendment, Andrew Johnson, Abraham Lincoln, Reconstruction, Edwin M. Stanton

*Richard C. Burnweit*

REFERENCES

Benedict, Michael Les. 1974. *A Compromise of Principle: Congressional Republicans and Reconstruction 1863–1869.* New York: Norton.

Bogue, Allan G. 1989. *The Congressman's Civil War.* Cambridge: Cambridge U. Pr.

Brodie, Fawn M. 1959. *Thaddeus Stevens: Scourge of the South.* New York: Norton.

Current, Richard Nelson. 1942. *Old Thad Stevens: A Story of Ambition.* Westport, CT: Greenwood.

Mayer, George H. 1967. *The Republican Party, 1854–1966.* New York: Oxford U. Pr.

Williams, T. Harry. 1965. *Lincoln and the Radicals.* Madison: U. of Wisconsin Pr.

## Adlai E. Stevenson (1835–1914)

Turn-of-the-century Illinois Democratic politician and vice president under Grover Cleveland. A Democratic loyalist who worked to bridge factional differences in his party, Adlai Ewing Stevenson was born in Kentucky, the son of a planter. He attended Centre College in Kentucky for two years, studied law in Illinois, and was admitted to the bar in 1858. Opening an office in Metamora, Illinois, he became active in Democratic politics. Stevenson campaigned for Steven A. Douglas against Abraham Lincoln in 1858 and 1860 and served as a George McClellan elector in 1864. Appointed master in chancery (1860–1864), he then won election as a State's attorney (1865–1869). In the election of 1874, Stevenson won a congressional seat in a normally Republican district, lost it in 1876, and regained it in 1878 through appeals to Greenbackers. He thus became identified with the Democrats' soft-money, low-tariff elements, whom the national party needed to placate. In 1885 President Grover Cleveland appointed Stevenson first assistant postmaster. In an era of increased debate over civil service reform, "Adlai and his Axe" hewed down 40,000 Republican postmasters accused of partisanship by Democrats. An angry Republican Senate rejected his appointment as justice of the Supreme Court of the District of Columbia when Cleveland left office in 1889. In 1892 Stevenson headed Illinois' delegation to the Democratic convention and won the vice presidential nomination to balance the eastern hard-money Cleveland. Stevenson was William Jennings Bryan's running mate in 1900 and ran unsuccessfully for governor of Illinois in 1908 at the age of 73. He died in Chicago.

*Phyllis F. Field*

REFERENCES

Cook, J. W. 1915. "The Life and Labors of Hon. Adlai Ewing Stevenson." 8 *Journal of the Illinois State Historical Society* 209.

Schlup, Leonard. 1977. "Grover Cleveland and His 1892 Running Mate." 2 *Studies in History and Society* 60.

————. 1979. "Democratic Talleyrand: Adlai Stevenson and Politics in the Gilded Age and Progressive Era." 78 *South Atlantic Quarterly* 182.

————. 1979. "Vice-President Stevenson and the Politics of Accommodation." 7 *Journal of Political Science* 30.

## Adlai E. Stevenson II (1900–1965)

Twice an unsuccessful Democratic candidate for President of the United States. Adlai Ewing Stevenson is best remembered as one of the premier political speakers and writers of the twentieth century. Stevenson, born in Los Angeles, grandson of Grover Cleveland's Vice President and father of a U.S. Senator from Illinois, both of whom shared his name, had an archetypal establishmentarian education:

Choate, Princeton, Harvard and (after being recalled to Chicago for family concerns) Northwestern law schools. He practiced law in Chicago but moved to Washington with other idealistic New Deal attorneys in 1933. After government service he returned to Chicago; however, he retained his Washington ties and his interest in international affairs, and these made him a solid candidate for wartime posts as special assistant first to Secretary of the Navy Frank Knox and then to Secretary of State Edward Stettinius.

After World War II, Stevenson was a major player in the establishment of the United Nations, heading the U.S. "preparatory" commission for the U.N. and then serving as senior adviser to the American delegation to the first U.N. General Assembly. When he went home to Illinois, Stevenson was tapped as Democratic "Boss" Jake Arvey's choice for governor. He won a landslide victory over the scandal-plagued Republicans and earned the reputation as an effective, progressive leader of his state's government.

On the eve of the 1952 election, Democratic President Harry Truman's popularity in the polls dipped to 25 percent; Americans blamed Truman for the debilitating Korean War. While the preconvention stage of the nominating process made Truman's unpopularity clear and led to his announcement that he would not seek reelection, no obvious successor emerged. Stevenson was the object of the last genuine draft, when the Democratic convention turned to him as the party nominee. He led a surprisingly eloquent campaign against Dwight Eisenhower, the Republican nominee whose popularity from his days as supreme commander of Allied forces during World War II made him, for all practical purposes, unbeatable. New Deal and Fair Deal liberalism fell before a wave of reaction to 20 years of unbroken Democratic control of the White House and blame for "Communism, Corruption, and Korea." Eisenhower won 55 percent of the popular vote, carrying 39 states and the Electoral College.

During the first Eisenhower term Stevenson kept his political fences well mended. The party turned to him again in 1956; but his second campaign, notable for its call for an end to atmospheric testing of atomic weapons, was even less successful than his first. In 1956 Ike won 58 percent of the popular vote and the electoral votes of 41 states.

After his second defeat Stevenson seemed happy to return to the practice of law, to punditry, and to tending his Illinois farm. His reputation as a man of fairness, sincerity, insight, and humor emerged from two presidential campaigns not just untarnished but with added luster. He was particularly the hero of the idealistic young, who revered his opposition to the Red-baiting demagoguery of Wisconsin Republican Senator Joseph McCarthy. "My definition of a free society," Stevenson wrote, "is a society where it's safe to be unpopular."

Stevenson's last political hurrah was yet another draft effort, led by thousands of fervent liberal Democrats who felt he should have a real chance at the presidency after Eisenhower's second term ended in 1960. The preconvention campaigns of Senators John Kennedy (D-Mass.), Hubert Humphrey (D-Minn.), Stuart Symington (D-Mo.), and Lyndon Johnson (D-Tex.) did not dissuade Stevenson admirers, like former First Lady Eleanor Roosevelt, from hoping that the convention would turn again to the party's former standard-bearer. In a moving speech that brought the convention to its feet at a frenzied pitch, Minnesota Senator Eugene McCarthy placed Stevenson's name in nomination: "Do not reject this man who made us all proud to be Democrats. Do not leave this prophet without honor in his own party." But, while Stevenson might have won the delegates' hearts, Senator Kennedy had won their political allegiance and was nominated on the first ballot and elected in November 1960.

As President-elect, Kennedy had the difficult task of deciding on a role for Stevenson in his administration. Kennedy wanted to dominate the foreign policy arena and feared that Stevenson, as Secretary of State, would be too prominent. As a result he tapped Stevenson for the lesser post of United States Ambassador to the United Nations, though he raised that position to Cabinet rank. At the U.N., Stevenson played an important role in the crisis-filled early 1960s, gaining most visibility by confronting the Russians in the Security Council at the height of the Cuban missile crisis with pictorial evidence of offensive missiles in Cuba. While Stevenson was not part of Kennedy's "Irish mafia" and never became a confidante of the President, he remained a commanding presence at the U.N. until his death.

Stevenson's career inspired a generation of intellectual liberals who marveled at his intelligence, suffered his losses with him, and bemoaned the fact that the nation never benefited to the fullest extent from his talents. But old pols remember Stevenson as well, recalling his practical political humor as the candidate who claimed that the Republicans' slogan really was, "Throw the rascals in."

*See also:* Jacob Arvey, Dwight D. Eisenhower, Hubert H. Humphrey, Lyndon B. Johnson, John F. Kennedy, Eugene McCarthy, Joseph McCarthy, Eleanor Roosevelt, Stuart Symington, Harry S Truman

*Charles W. Bassett*

REFERENCES

Martin, John B. 1977. *Adlai Stevenson and the World.* Garden City, NY: Doubleday.

Stevenson, Adlai E. 1972–1979. *The Papers of Adlai E. Stevenson.* Boston: Little, Brown.

White, Theodore H. 1961. *The Making of the President 1960.* New York: Atheneum.

## Adlai E. Stevenson III (1930– )

Scion of a well-known Illinois political family. Adlai Ewing Stevenson III achieved his own prominence as a United States Senator and two-time gubernatorial candidate. "Adlai III" originally entered state Democratic politics as a reformer wary of the Chicago organization. Like his father before him, Stevenson eventually reached an accommodation with the regulars and was elected to the U.S. Senate in 1970. He served ten years there as a quiet but conscientious lawmaker of liberal orientation. A smashing vote-getter with a famous name and reputation for probity, he was often talked of as a possible national candidate. It was, therefore, a surprise to many when he declined to run for reelection in 1980, with the suggestion that he found the work of the Senate boring.

Stevenson was back in the political arena within two years, however, as a candidate for governor of Illinois. Despite a lackluster campaign, he came within 5,000 votes of defeating two-term incumbent James R. Thompson. Private life claimed Stevenson once more, but at the last minute he decided to take on Thompson again in 1986. The Democratic primary destroyed this campaign before it got going. Taking advantage of voter apathy and ignorance, two followers of the politically daffy Lyndon LaRouche managed to win places on the Stevenson-led ticket as nominees for lieutenant governor and secretary of state. Stevenson then sought to distance himself from LaRouche associates by formally renouncing the Democratic nomination. He reemerged as the candidate of a makeshift party called Illinois Solidarity. The end result was another Stevenson defeat, this time by a large margin.

*See also:* Lyndon LaRouche

*John R. Schmidt*

## Andrew Stevenson (1784–1857)

First Democratic Speaker of the U.S. House of Representatives. Andrew Stevenson of Kentucky served the longest continuous speakership in the nineteenth century. Elected to the chair four consecutive times, Stevenson was Speaker from 1827 to 1834.

Stevenson was born in Culpepper County, Virginia, the son of a planter. An alumnus of the College of William and Mary, he became a successful Richmond lawyer and began his public service in 1809 when he was elected to the Virginia House of Delegates. He served there for most of the next twelve years and for three years was its speaker (1812–1815). He was twice defeated for election to the U.S. House by John Tyler, who later became the nation's tenth President. After Tyler's departure from the House, Stevenson began service in 1821.

He was first elected to the speakership in 1827 after midterm losses had cost President John Quincy Adams his majority in the House. Stevenson defeated John W. Taylor of New York, the Speaker of the previous House, 104 to 94 on the first ballot. His three reelections in 1829, 1831, and 1833 were relatively easy first-ballot victories.

Stevenson was not a legislative innovator. His close friendship with President Andrew Jackson limited his role to pushing the legislative program of the President. Jackson benefited greatly from Stevenson's speakership; it allowed him to use the House to fend off criticism from the less compliant Senate, which was guided by two of his rivals, Henry Clay and Daniel Webster.

Jackson appointed Stevenson as minister to Great Britain in 1836, two years after Stevenson had left the House. He served in that capacity until 1841 when he returned to Virginia and left public life to return to planting.

*See also:* John Quincy Adams, Henry Clay, Andrew Jackson, John W. Taylor, John Tyler, Daniel Webster

*Garrison Nelson*

REFERENCES

Smith, William Henry. 1971. *Speakers of the House of Representatives of the United States.* New York: AMS Press.

Wayland, Francis Fry. 1949. *Andrew Stevenson, Democrat and Diplomat, 1785–1857.* Philadelphia: U. of Pennsylvania Pr.

## Henry L. Stimson (1867–1950)

Patrician Cabinet officer under four U.S. Presidents. Secretary of War under William Howard Taft (1911–1913), Secretary of State under Herbert Hoover (1929–1933), and Secretary of War under Franklin D. Roosevelt and Harry S Truman (1940–1945), Henry Lewis Stimson was one of the most distinguished public servants in twentieth-century American government. Born in New York of a family with roots going back to seventeenth-century Massachusetts, Stimson was educated at Phillips Academy (Andover), Yale College, and Harvard Law School. He became an important Wall Street lawyer with wide contacts in the nation's financial and corporate world, but he had as well an abiding and ultimately preeminent interest in government service, obvious skill in public administration, and a mounting concern about advancing American aims and interests in world affairs.

Though active for some years in Republican Party politics (he ran unsuccessfully for governor of New York in 1910), Stimson found his niche in appointive office rather than electoral politics. His most important public service came in the Hoover and Franklin D. Roosevelt administrations. As Hoover's Secretary of State, Stimson dealt especially with international financial problems, arms control, and the Japanese invasion of Manchuria. In June 1940, President Roosevelt's desire for a strong, bipartisan Cabinet as the war approached (as did FDR's 1940 "third-term" presidential election) led him to press Stimson into service as Secretary of War. Stimson oversaw the mobilization of the World War II U.S. Army, figured in key diplomatic as well as military decisions, brought into government such men as Robert Lovett and John McCloy, who would continue as important "establishment" public servants in the postwar era, and played a central role under Roosevelt and Truman in the development and employment of the atomic bomb.

*See also:* Herbert Hoover, Franklin D. Roosevelt, Harry S Truman

*John W. Jeffries*

REFERENCES

Morison, Elting E. 1960. *Turmoil and Tradition.* Boston: Houghton Mifflin.

Stimson, Henry L. 1948. *On Active Service in Peace and War.* New York: Harper.

## Lucy Stone (1818–1893)

Advocate of female equality and African-American freedom. Growing up in a Massachusetts Congregationalist farm family, Lucy Stone strained against the bonds of female subordination enforced by her father and her church. Her attraction to the antislavery movement aligned her in her youth with the extreme views of the radical abolitionist William Lloyd Garrison. In 1843, at age 25, she entered Oberlin College, an Ohio outpost of interracial and coeducational higher learning. Her growing oratorical talent, though denied expression at Oberlin, won her a job after graduation as a lecturer for Garrison's American Antislavery Society. Braving often hostile crowds, she spoke widely for both Black and female emancipation, and in 1852 she campaigned for the election of the upstate New York abolitionist Gerrit Smith to Congress. In 1855 she married Henry Browne Blackwell, in a ceremony that asserted the ideal legal equality of husband and wife. As a further statement of autonomy she thereafter kept her own name.

The birth of her only child, Alice Stone Blackwell, temporarily removed her from the reform circuit, but soon after the Civil War she resumed active suffrage agitation. Disappointment over their failure to win Republican Party support for female enfranchisement through a federal constitutional amendment led to factional disputes among Stone and other suffragists. Stone strove to advance the cause of women's rights through tactics more socially moderate than those of rival feminists like Susan B. Anthony and Elizabeth Cady Stanton. Affirming loyalty to the Republican Party, Stone parted company with the more radical Anthony and Stanton, and in 1869 she organized the American Woman Suffrage Association to secure the vote for women in state and municipal elections. In 1872 she and her husband became editors of the weekly *Woman's Journal*, based in Boston, and turned it into the country's foremost suffrage newspaper. Its editorial stance balanced steady commitment to women's rights with relatively conservative attitudes toward labor unions, strikes, monetary reform, and divorce.

In the presidential election campaign of 1884 Stone fiercely attacked the Democratic presidential candidate Grover Cleveland for his loose personal morality in fathering an illegitimate son. The longstanding breach between her American Woman Suffrage Association and the National Woman Suffrage Association led by Anthony and Stanton was finally closed in 1890 with an organizational merger producing the National American Woman Suffrage Association. This resolution of hostilities was interpreted in retrospect as a recognition that Stone's policies of social moderation for the suffrage movement had finally prevailed at the end of her career.

See also: Abolition Movement, Susan B. Anthony, William Lloyd Garrison, National American Woman Suffrage Association, Gerrit Smith, Elizabeth Cady Stanton, Suffrage

Geoffrey Blodgett

REFERENCES

Blackwell, Alice Stone. 1930. *Lucy Stone: Pioneer of Woman's Rights*. Boston: Little, Brown.

Flexner, Eleanor. 1959. *Century of Struggle: The Woman's Rights Movement in the United States*. Cambridge: Harvard U. Pr.

Hays, Elinor Rice. 1961. *Morning Star: A Biography of Lucy Stone, 1818–1893*. New York: Harcourt, Brace & World.

Wheeler, Leslie, ed. 1981. *Loving Warriors: Selected Letters by Lucy Stone and Henry B. Blackwell, 1853 to 1893*. New York: Dial.

## Storer v. Brown

415 U.S. 724 (1974)

In 1972, the California Elections Code refused ballot position to any Independent candidate for elective public office if he voted in the immediately preceding primary or if he had a registered affiliation with a qualified political party at any time within one year prior to the immediately preceding primary election. In addition, the Independent candidate also had to file nomination papers signed by more than 5 percent of the entire vote cast in the preceding general election in the area for which the candidate sought to run. Further, the signatures had to be obtained during a 24-day period following the primary and ending 60 days prior to the general election, and none of the signatures could be gathered from persons who voted during the primary election.

Prior to the 1972 elections, the appellants Storer, Frommhagen, Hall, and Tyner, along with certain of their supporters, filed their actions to have relevant sections of the elections code declared unconstitutional on the grounds that the laws infringed on rights guaranteed by the First and Fourteenth amendments and by adding qualifications for the office of United States Congressman, contrary to Article I of the Constitution. Storer and Frommhagen each sought ballots status as Independent candidates for Congress. Hall and Tyner claimed the right to

ballot position as Independent candidates for President and Vice President of the United States. They were members of the Communist Party, and that party had not qualified for ballot position in California.

The United States Supreme Court affirmed the judgment of the lower court by refusing to grant relief to Storer and Frommhagen with respect to the 1972 general election. Both men were registered Democrats until early in 1972. This affiliation with a qualified political party within a year prior to the 1972 primary disqualified both men under California law, and the Supreme Court ruled that California was not prohibited by the United States Constitution from enforcing that provision against both these men. Citing *Williams v. Rhodes* [393 U.S. 23 (1968)], the Court held that although the citizens of a state are free to associate with one of the two major political parties, to participate in the nomination of their chosen party's candidates for public office, and then to cast their ballots in the general election, the state must also provide feasible means for other political parties and other candidates to appear on the general election ballot. The appellants relied heavily on *Williams v. Rhodes* by asserting that substantial burdens on the right to vote or to associate for political purposes are constitutionally suspect and invalid under the First and Fourteenth amendments and under the equal protection clause unless those burdensome provisions are essential to serve a compelling state interest.

After reviewing the California requirement that the Independent candidate be unaffiliated with a political party for a year before the primary, the Supreme Court determined that the law was expressive of a general state policy aimed at maintaining the integrity of the various routes to the ballot. Moreover, the Court acknowledged the long experience of California in permitting candidates to run in the primaries of more than one party (only in 1959 had California forbade the cross-filing practice). The Court sanctioned California's efforts to protect the direct primary process by refusing to recognize Independent candidates who did not make early plans to leave a party and take the alternative course to the ballot.

The Supreme Court came to a different conclusion with respect to Hall and Tyner. The Court ordered further proceedings in the district court to examine the extent of the signature-gathering obligation imposed on Independent candidates for President and Vice President under California law. Standing alone, gathering 325,000 signatures in 24 days did not appear to be an impossible burden. However, the Court weighted the practical implications of the law, particularly whether the available pool is so diminished in size by the disqualification of those who voted in the primary that the 325,000 signature requirement, to be satisfied in 24 days, stood as too great a burden on the Independent candidates for the offices of President and Vice President. The Supreme Court could not find a sufficient state interest for California to impose such a burden.

See also: Communist Party of the United States, Fourteenth Amendment, *Williams v. Rhodes*

*Scott McDermott*

## Robert S. Strauss (1918– )

Powerful Democratic behind-the-scenes political mover and shaker. Robert Schwarz (Bob) Strauss was born and raised in Texas, the elder son of a Jewish dry goods merchant. He went to the University of Texas (LL.B. 1941) and became active in Democratic politics, especially in association with his classmate, the future Texas governor, John B. Connally. From 1941 to 1945 Strauss was a special agent of the FBI. After the war he formed the Dallas law firm of Akin, Gump, Strauss, Hauer and Feld. The firm prospered, and Strauss in due course also became owner of broadcasting properties and real estate. The firm's offices in Dallas and Washington (much augmented in the 1970s and 1980s) have remained his base of operations.

Strauss's political career ladder has been inside the Democratic Party: Democratic National Committee member from Texas (1968–1970); member, executive committee, Democratic National Committee (1969–1977); treasurer of the party (1970–1972); and party national chairman (1972–1977). He was appointed ambassador and special trade representative by President Jimmy Carter in 1977, and from 1979 to 1981 he was Carter's personal representative for Middle East negotiations.

Since the late 1960s, Strauss has been a significant figure in the behind-the-scenes world of Washington politics. His friendships are bipartisan, in spite of his strong ties to the Democratic Party apparatus, and include important members of the American business and legal communities. He has the reputation of being able to express unwelcome truths with charm and persuasiveness, a useful quality when difficult negotiations are afoot. For relaxation

he plays poker and goes to the races. His friends attest to his high-minded idealism, which he advances, as well as disguises, in tough talk about political realities and down-home, good-old-boy rhetoric. Journalists find him irresistibly entertaining and only the most mean-spirited contrarians among them insist that self-promotion as well as public spiritedness enters into his high-energy, boredom-avoiding, busy round of life. Strauss disarmingly pleads nolo contendere to the charge, pointing out that a high profile can also be a resource in Washington.

See also: Jimmy Carter, John B. Connolly, Democratic National Committee

*Nelson W. Polsby*

## Student Nonviolent Coordinating Committee

Emerging from the southern African-American sit-in campaigns of 1960, the Student Nonviolent Coordinating Committee, or SNCC (pronounced Snick), later helped open up the Democratic Party to fuller southern Black participation. SNCC evolved from a conference convened in April 1960 in Raleigh, North Carolina, by Ella Baker, a radical aide to Martin Luther King, Jr. The conference drew delegates mainly from the southern Black colleges. Remaining independent of older civil rights leaders but inspired by King's Gandhian and Christian tenets, SNCC delegates extolled nonviolence as a spiritual ideal as well as a tactic for confronting injustice. They also called for a "Beloved Community" in which all races would live in harmony.

Eventually the most militant of the major civil rights groups, SNCC sustained the interracial freedom rides after white violence had nearly ended them in May 1961. SNCC also organized previously quiescent Black communities in the Deep South, a strategy that sometimes helped competing civil rights groups press their own reform agenda. SNCC's groundwork in Selma, Alabama, enabled the Southern Christian Leadership Conference of Martin Luther King, Jr., to mobilize demonstrations that drew national coverage and spurred passage of the strong Voting Rights Act in August 1965.

Activists working for or closely allied with SNCC helped form the Mississippi Freedom Democratic Party in 1964 as an integrated alternative to the white regular Democrats. At the Democratic National Convention in August 1964, the Freedom Democrats received, but rejected, a token concession of two nonvoting delegate posts. Their challenge to Mississippi's regular Democrats contributed, however, to the inclusion of African-Americans in every southern delegation to the 1968 Democratic National Convention.

SNCC's disillusionment with mainstream politics led it to denounce American intervention in Vietnam and to foster all-Black political organizations. The "Lowndes County Freedom Organization" in Alabama, later known as the Black Panther Party, tried vainly to oust the regular Democrats in 1966 in elections marred by fraudulent ballot counting. In June 1966 SNCC's chairman Stokely Carmichael demanded "Black Power," a slogan that denoted African-American solidarity but connoted separatism and even revolution. By 1967 Carmichael's successor, H. Rap Brown, alienated SNCC's remaining white liberal supporters by calling for ghetto riots and violent overthrow of the social order as racist, imperialist, and corrupt. By then SNCC had only a few dozen workers, a growing number of them informers in the pay of FBI director J. Edgar Hoover.

SNCC disbanded in the early 1970s amid federal repression, internal feuding, and a conservative backlash that SNCC's own radicalism had helped fuel. Some former SNCC activists nonetheless penetrated mainstream politics, including Julian Bond, a Georgia state legislator from 1965 to 1986, and John Lewis, who won election to the Atlanta City Council in 1982 and to the U.S. Congress in 1986. SNCC's most enduring legacy remains its grass-roots organizing among southern Blacks in the early 1960s, which speeded the dismantling of racial barriers to voting and government service.

See also: Julian Bond, H. (Rap) Brown, Stokely Carmichael, Martin Luther King, Jr., John R. Lewis, Vietnam War as a Political Issue, Voting Rights Act of 1965 and Extensions

*Robert S. Weisbrot*

REFERENCES

Carson, Clayborne. 1981. *In Struggle: SNCC and the Black Awakening of the 1960's*. Cambridge: Harvard U. Pr.

Forman, James. 1985. *The Making of Black Revolutionaries*. Washington: Open Hand.

Sellers, Cleveland. 1973. *The Rivers of No Return: The Autobiography of a Black Militant and the Life and Death of SNCC*. New York: Morrow.

Zinn, Howard. 1965. *SNCC: The New Abolitionists*. 2nd ed. Boston: Beacon.

## Students for a Democratic Society

The most important and most controversial New Left organization of the late 1960s and the 1970s, Students for a Democratic Society (SDS) was formed in 1959 as the youth wing of the social-democratic League for Industrial Democracy. In 1962, 59 delegates approved what came to be known as the Port Huron Statement, a document largely written by Tom Hayden advocating sweeping social reform and participatory democracy. For the next three years, SDS engaged in a variety of locally based programs designed to build support for reforms that went beyond what President Lyndon Johnson had proposed in his "war on poverty."

By 1965, SDS had come to focus almost all of its attention on the rapidly escalating war in Vietnam. SDS activists were in the forefront of all major protest movements against the war and the draft. By 1968, SDS was organized on some 150 American campuses and claimed nearly 100,000 members. In 1970 it played a major role in organizing the protests following the Ohio National Guard's fatal shooting of four students at Kent State University during antiwar protest demonstrations.

As the war dragged on and peaceful protest methods showed few signs of bringing it to an end, SDS began to fragment. Many militant members turned to Marxism, others to the anarchistic values and methods of the "hippie" and "yippie" movements, and still others to violence, forming what came to be known as the Weathermen, a group responsible for a series of bombings and robberies in the early 1970s. Meanwhile, more moderate SDS members turned to conventional politics, supporting either Democrat George McGovern or a number of third-party candidates in 1972. By that time, the remaining factions in SDS were all underground, and the organization had for all intents and purposes gone out of existence.

See also: Lyndon B. Johnson, George McGovern, Vietnam War as a Political Issue

*Charles S. Hauss*

REFERENCES

Flacks, Richard. 1988. *Making History*. New York: Columbia U. Pr.

Hale, Dennis, and Mitchell Cohen. 1967. *The New Student Left*. Boston: Beacon.

Sale, Kirkpatrick. 1973. *SDS*. New York: Vintage.

## Suffrage

The framers of the Constitution struggled with the problems of participation and representation. In theory they favored a government of, by, and for the people. In practice, however, they feared that the narrowly self-interested behavior of the people could lead to a tyranny of the majority.

To prevent such a tyranny, they could have restricted suffrage. Imposing such restrictions, however, would not have been consistent with the principles of political rights articulated in the Declaration of Independence or the preamble to the Constitution. Restriction, moreover would have placed the ratification of the Constitution in jeopardy. Instead, the framers took another tack, designing a system to represent different constituencies: the nation (President/Vice President), the states (Senate), and the people (House of Representatives). Moreover, the framers avoided the divisive issues of who would be eligible to vote and how that voting would be conducted by initially vesting the responsibility for resolving these questions with the individual states but retaining for the Congress the authority to legislate on these matters if it so chose.

Thus, states were free to restrict suffrage, and most did. Many required property ownership as a condition of voting. This requirement effectively disenfranchised women, racial minorities, and those under a certain age who did not own property. Some states imposed an additional requirement—a belief in God, a Christian God.

By the 1830s most states had eliminated property and religious restrictions. The Fifteenth Amendment, ratified in 1870, removed race and color as qualifications for voting. In theory, this enabled all Black males to vote. In practice, it enfranchised those in the North and Border States but not those in the South. A series of institutional devices such as the poll tax, literacy tests, and restrictive primaries in which only Caucasians could participate (white primaries), combined effectively with social pressure to prevent African-Americans from voting in the South for another 100 years.

In the twentieth century, the passage of the Nineteenth, Twenty-fourth, and Twenty-sixth amendments continued to expand the voting-age population. In 1920 women received the right to vote; in 1964 the collection of a poll tax was prohibited in national elections; in 1971 suffrage was extended to all citizens 18 years of age and older. Previously, each state had established its own minimum age.

Moreover, the Supreme Court and Congress began to eliminate the legal and institutional barriers to voting. In 1944 the Court outlawed

the white primary (in *Smith v. Allwright*, 321 U.S. 649). In the mid-1960s, Congress—by its passage of the Civil Rights Act (1964) and the Voting Rights Act (1965)—banned literacy tests in federal elections for all citizens who had at least a sixth-grade education in an American school. Where less than 50 percent of the population was registered to vote, federal officials were sent to help facilitate registration. No longer was long and costly litigation necessary to ensure the right to vote. Amendments to the Voting Rights Act have also reduced the residence requirement for presidential elections to a maximum of 30 days.

The expansion of suffrage has produced more voters, but enlarging the electorate has also meant that a smaller percentage of that electorate actually votes. Newly enfranchised voters tend to cast ballots less regularly than those who have previously enjoyed the right to vote.

Registration procedures still act as an impediment to voting. These procedures vary from state to state. The period during which people may register, the places where they have to go to do so, and even the hours when registration may occur are controlled by state law. Naturally, the harder the states make it to register, the smaller the vote they can expect. This is a particular problem for a mobile society such as that of the United States. With one-third of the population moving on an average of every two years, the need to reregister in order to vote effectively decreases the size of the vote. Two political scientists, Raymond E. Wolfinger and Steven J. Rosenstone, estimated that turnout could be increased by as much as 9 percent by making modest adjustments in these laws that would ease registration procedures.

Concern has been voiced about the relatively low turnout of voters in the United States as compared with other democratic countries. If the percentage of eligible voters in the United States who actually vote is compared to that of 21 other democratic countries located primarily in Western Europe, then the United States ranks twentieth; if, however, the percentage of registered voters who actually vote is the basis for comparison, then the United States fares better, ranking eleventh out of 24. And unlike many other countries, the United States does not impose penalties on those who fail to register and vote, nor does it have a national system for automatic registration. Legislation to create such a system was proposed but not enacted in the One Hundred First Congress.

The difference between the proportion of registered voters who actually cast ballots (about 80 percent) and the proportion of all eligible voters (including those who are not registered) who do so (50.15 percent in 1988) suggests that registration procedures remain a major obstacle to higher voter turnout in the United States.

See also: V. O. Key, Literacy Tests, Poll Tax, *Smith v. Allwright*, Twenty-fourth Amendment, Twenty-sixth Amendment, Voter Turnout, Voting Rights Act of 1965 and Extensions

*Stephen J. Wayne*

REFERENCES

Key, V. O., Jr. 1958. *Politics, Parties, and Pressure Groups.* New York: Crowell.

Squire, Peverill, Raymond E. Wolfinger, and David P. Glass. 1987. "Residential Mobility and Voter Turnout." 81 *American Political Science Review* 45.

Wayne, Stephen J. 1992. *The Road to the White House.* 4th ed. New York: St. Martin's.

Wolfinger, Raymond E., and Steven J. Rosenstone. 1980. *Who Votes?* New Haven: Yale U. Pr.

## Arthur E. Summerfield (1899–1972)

Eisenhower's Postmaster General. Arthur Ellsworth Summerfield was born in Michigan, completed his formal schooling at the end of the seventh grade, and at age 13, started working in a Chevrolet plant. Summerfield later sold real estate, lost substantial assets in the stock market crash of 1929, then formed the Summerfield Oil Company as a distributor for Pure Oil. In 1930 he became the Chevrolet dealer for Flint, Michigan, and in time, he was reputed as having the largest Chevrolet dealership in the world.

Simultaneously, Summerfield carried on a career in Michigan Republican politics. In 1942, he sought, but failed to receive, the party's nomination for Michigan secretary of state. In 1943 he was appointed chairman of the finance committee of the state central committee. At the end of an intense factional contest in 1944, he was elected national committeeman and re-elected in 1948. In recognition of his fundraising skills, in 1946 he became regional vice chairman of the Republican national finance committee for the northern central states.

During the postelection efforts to have Thomas E. Dewey's colleague Hugh D. Scott, Jr., vacate the national committee chairmanship, Summerfield, considered a middle-of-the-roader in the Robert Taft–Thomas Dewey competition for control of the national organization, was made chairman of the national committee's strategy committee to coordinate the 1950 mid-term elections. As head of the Michigan delegation to the 1952 national convention, his delegation's votes started the bandwagon's swing to Eisenhower.

Summerfield accepted the national party chairmanship for the duration of the election campaign only. During this brief tenure, he was able to establish a coordinating board to guide the work of the two congressional campaign committees and the national committee. From 1953 to 1960, Summerfield served as Postmaster General.

See also: Thomas E. Dewey, Dwight D. Eisenhower, Republican National Committee, Hugh D. Scott, Jr.

*Ralph M. Goldman*

REFERENCES

Goldman, Ralph M. 1990. *The National Party Chairmen and Committees: Factionalism at the Top.* Armonk, NY: M. E. Sharpe.

## Charles Sumner (1811–1874)

Outspoken abolitionist U.S. Senator from Massachusetts. As chairman of the Senate Foreign Relations Committee from 1861 to 1871, Charles Sumner was in a notable position to influence U.S. foreign policy during a crucial period of history. Instead, isolated from his colleagues by a domineering, intolerant attitude as well as a penchant for wild invective—qualities rarely overcome by his eloquence and sincerity—Sumner contributed little to the nation's progress. During the Civil War he claimed that the citizens of the Confederate States (inhabitants of "conquered provinces") had lost their constitutional rights. This doctrine helped to provoke a series of disputes between congressional radicals and President Andrew Johnson that resulted in Johnson's impeachment.

Early in the Ulysses Grant administration, Sumner sabotaged the President's plan to acquire Santo Domingo. His insistence on "indirect damages" incurred by the United States because of British assistance to the South during the Civil War almost torpedoed the Geneva arbitration agreement of 1872. At Grant's insistence, Sumner had already been ousted from his Foreign Relations Committee chairmanship, his only important service in that post having been to provide crucial support for Senate approval of the Alaska purchase treaty in 1867.

Born in Boston, Sumner graduated from Harvard College and its law school and became a leading abolitionist lecturer and publicist. Elected to the U.S. Senate in 1851 by a coalition of Massachusetts Democrats and Free Soil Party members, he soon became notorious for his merciless verbal assaults upon southern slaveholders. In 1856, caned at his Senate desk by a South Carolinian, he suffered such serious lingering trauma that he was unable to resume his Senate seat on a regular basis for three and a half years.

*See also:* Free Soil Party, Ulysses S. Grant, Andrew Johnson

*Norman B. Ferris*

REFERENCES

Donald, David. 1960. *Charles Sumner and the Coming of the Civil War.* New York: Knopf.

———. 1970. *Charles Sumner and the Rights of Man.* New York: Knopf.

Ferris, Norman. 1987. "Charles Sumner." In Frank N. Magill, ed. *Great Lives from History. American Series.* Pasadena, CA: Salem Press.

Pierce, Edward L. 1877–1893. *Memoirs and Letters of Charles Sumner.* Boston: Roberts Bros.

Storey, Moorfield. 1900. *Charles Sumner.* Boston: Houghton Mifflin.

Sumner, Charles. 1969. *Complete Works.* New York: Negro Universities Press.

## SUN PAC

The Federal Election Commission (FEC) on November 18, 1975, issued the SUN PAC advisory opinion, which had its most profound impact in clarifying whether and how corporations could establish political action committees (PACs). This FEC decision also shaped subsequent regulation of corporate and labor political activity. Sun Oil Company sought rulings on whether it was permitted (1) to establish, administer, and solicit voluntary contributions to a separate political committee that would give contributions to candidates (SUN PAC); and (2) to establish a payroll deduction plan through which donors would designate the recipients of contributions (SUN EPA).

In 1974 at the urging of organized labor, Congress had amended the Federal Election Campaign Act (FECA) to permit government contractors to establish and maintain political action committees. Some unions feared that their manpower training and development agreements with the government made their PACs vulnerable to challenge. Labor later regretted this success, for corporate PACs proliferated as a result of the SUN PAC decision.

The FEC, in a 4-to-2 decision, ruled that Sun Oil and, by extension, other corporations (1) could use corporate funds to establish, administer, and solicit funds for both types of political committees so long as they remained as separate segregated funds; (2) could make political contributions and expenditures through their PACs so long as the funds are voluntary contributions to the PAC; (3) could solicit both stockholders and employees of the corporation while abiding by certain guidelines to avoid coercion; and (4) could establish multiple PACs with separate contribution and expenditure limits.

Many corporations quickly established PACs, more than doubling the number of PACs within a few months. Organized labor and the dissenters were also concerned that the ruling destroyed Congress's intended balance between corporations and unions, for unions were restricted to soliciting only their members, while the SUN PAC decision permitted corporations to solicit all employees as well as stockholders. Moreover, while a firm could use the payroll checkoff to collect contributions, the Taft-Hartley Act prohibited unions from using this method.

In 1976 congressional Democrats sought to rectify the imbalance. The new amendments to the FECA restricted corporate PACs to soliciting only stockholders, administrators, and their families; and union PACs could solicit only union members and their families. However, twice a year each was allowed to solicit by mail through an independent third party those not included in these restrictions. Organized labor won the right to use payroll deduction plans among members if the company PAC used that method. Finally, all of a corporation's or an international union's political committees would be considered a single PAC for contribution purposes.

Despite these reversals of some of SUN PAC's holdings, the prime impact of the ruling, the clarification of the FECA's provisions for corporate and labor participation in politics through the PAC mechanism, remains its most significant legacy.

*See also:* Check-offs, Federal Election Campaign Act of 1974, Federal Election Commission, Political Action Committees

*Douglas I. Hodgkin*

REFERENCES

Cantor, Joseph E. 1984. *Political Action Committees: Their Evolution, Growth and,* [sic] *Implications for the Political System.* Washington: Congressional Research Service.

Epstein, Edwin M. 1979. "The Emergence of Political Action Committees." In Herbert E. Alexander, ed. *Political Finance.* Beverly Hills, CA: Sage.

Federal Election Commission. 1975. Advisory Opinion 1975–23. *Federal Register.*

## Superdelegates

Following the election of 1980, Democratic Party officials formed a new review commission to recommend changes in the party's presidential nomination process. Whereas Democratic leaders and insiders had traditionally chosen the presidential nominee, reforms in the selection process since 1968 broadened participation in the selection procedure, thus deemphasizing the influence of highly partisan regulars and opening the process to party members who have a less direct stake and perhaps less knowledge of potential candidates. While primaries and caucuses had made the selection of the nominee more democratic, Democratic leaders argued that nominees chosen under this process were less-experienced outsiders and generally poorer candidates than their prereform counterparts had been.

One of the recommendations of the Hunt Commission was the introduction of "superdelegates" into the nomination process. Beginning in 1984 the Democratic Party leadership allocated some 566 delegate slots for congressional and state party members, officially selected as uncommitted delegates. This measure was designed to reinstate some of the influence that leaders had lost during the reforms of the late 1960s and early 1970s and to allow Democratic regulars to break deadlocks among candidates vying for the nomination or reinforce support for a particular candidate. In addition, party leaders hoped that the superdelegates would reverse the trend toward nominating outsiders that the reforms had actually encouraged. Voting as a bloc, superdelegates would in theory constitute the largest delegation at the 1984 and 1988 conventions and hold the balance of power.

In fact, superdelegates have not been able to act as powerbrokers, mostly because few superdelegates preserve their uncommitted status all the way to the party convention. In 1984 the House caucus of superdelegates indicated in a straw poll that no less than 50 percent would support Walter Mondale at the convention. This declaration came months before the convention. Mondale could count on similar support among Senate superdelegates and among state party officials. While at the end of the primary and caucus season Mondale had not yet secured enough delegate votes to claim victory, the candidate won nomination through personal contact with individuals, rather than bargaining with any single delegation. Mondale cer-tainly could not have won the nomination without his wide support from superdelegates, but by having pledged their support early in the campaign, superdelegates lost much of their influence before the convention—the arena where their influence should have been greatest.

Likewise in 1988, superdelegates played an insubstantial role at the Democratic convention. Governor Michael Dukakis managed to secure a majority of delegates throughout the primary and caucus season, and some of his delegate strength also came from superdelegates expressing their support long before the convention. The Reverend Jesse Jackson made a late appeal when, on the basis that superdelegates were officially uncommitted at the convention, he encouraged superdelegates to vote in accordance to voting percentages expressed in primaries and caucuses. In the end, Jackson lost both this argument and the nomination, although some change in the role that superdelegates will play at the 1992 convention has been adopted.

*See also:* Michael Dukakis, Jesse Jackson, Walter F. Mondale

*Michael Heel*

REFERENCES

Cook, Rhodes. 1983. "Party Rules Change: Superdelegates May Pick Next Democratic Nominee." In James Lengle and Byron Shafer, eds. *Presidential Politics: Readings on Nominations and Elections*. New York: St. Martin's.

Walker, Jack L. 1984. "The Presidency and the Nominating System." In Michael Nelson, ed. *The Presidency and the Political System*. Washington: Congressional Quarterly.

## Surge and Decline

The phenomenon known as "surge and decline" is an effort to explain the presidential party's loss of seats in the subsequent midterm election. The pattern of midterm losses for the President's party has been remarkably consistent. With the exception of 1902, when Republicans gained nine seats but lost the majority because of new seats following the 1900 census, and 1934, when the Democrats gained nine seats, the President's party has always lost seats in the House of Representatives. Such losses are not quite as predictable in the Senate, but they remain significant. Since the turn of the century, the size of these midterm losses has ranged from a high of seventy-five House seats lost by the Republicans in 1922 to a low of four House seats lost by the Democrats in 1962. While no one can argue with the regularity of these losses, scholars explain their cause differently.

The term "surge and decline" was popularized by Angus Campbell in the 1960s to describe fluctuations in turnout and partisanship in national and midterm elections. Campbell hypothesized that midterm losses were directly related to the differences between "high-stimulus" or presidential elections and "low-stimulus" or midterm elections and subsequent levels of turnout. Until the mid-1970s, Campbell's theory of surge and decline remained the dominant explanation for midterm losses.

Discussion of the theory of surge and decline is closely related to the analysis of "coattail" voting and the impact of national forces on state and local elections. The theory of the coattail effect posits that the attraction of the winning presidential candidate picks up a number of congressional seats that the President's party might not ordinarily capture. The conventional theory of surge and decline is that the strong stimulation of a presidential election artificially inflates the success of the President's party at the congressional level. With the absence of coattails and a lower turnout, midterm losses for the President's party represent a return to more normal voting patterns.

Another explanation for midterm losses for the President's party focuses on midterm elections as referendum. Edward Tufte's economic voting theory argues that midterm elections reflect voting on public perceptions of the President and the administration's management of the economy. Tufte's theory also seeks to explain the magnitude of the midterm losses, suggesting that a change in the President's approval rating is related to the national midterm congressional vote.

One of the latest variations on theories interpreting midterm losses by the President's party is R. S. Erikson's "presidential penalty" theory. This explanation assumes negative voting on the part of the electorate toward the President's party regardless of presidential popularity or performance. The presidential penalty theorists criticize previous theories of surge and decline, arguing that midterm outcomes vary quite widely and that popular as well as unpopular Presidents suffer losses.

Given a Congress that continues to emphasize constituency cues in voting and continues to enjoy the advantage of incumbency, a more complete understanding of the pattern of surge and decline is becoming increasingly important.

*Susan L. Roberts*

REFERENCES

Campbell, Angus. 1960. "Surge and Decline: A Study of Electoral Change." 24 *Public Opinion Quarterly* 397.

Erikson, Robert S. 1988. "The Puzzle of Midterm Loss." 50 *Journal of Politics* 1011.

Ferejohn, John A., and Randall L. Calvert. 1984. "Presidential Coattails in Historical Perspective." 28 *American Journal of Political Science* 127.

Jacobson, Gary C., and Samuel Kernell. 1981. *Strategy and Choice in Congressional Elections.* New Haven: Yale U. Pr.

Tufte, Edward R. 1975. "Determinants of the Outcomes of Midterm Congressional Elections." 69 *American Political Science Review* 812–826.

## Survey Research Center

Founded in 1946 at the University of Michigan as part of the Institute of Social Research under the leadership of Rensis Likert and Angus Campbell, the Survey Research Center (SRC) pioneered large-scale academic survey research. The SRC has carried out an impressive array of studies of social, psychological, economic, and political phenomena, and it conducts research relating to survey methods. It also provides interdisciplinary graduate training in all aspects of survey methods.

Building on earlier work at the National Opinion Research Center (founded at the University of Denver before moving to the University of Chicago), the Bureau of Applied Social Research at Columbia University, and the U.S. Government, the SRC was organized around three major programs concerned respectively with economic behavior, human relations, and political behavior. Of particular importance to students of political parties is the work of Angus Campbell and his colleagues in the political behavior program. Beginning with a relatively small national study of the 1948 election, the SRC began an extraordinary series of studies of the American electorate that continues today under the rubric of the National Election Study. The 1952 election brought the first large-scale SRC study of the American electorate and resulted in *The Voter Decides* (by Angus Campbell, Gerald Gurin and Warren Miller). The center then mounted a second national survey of the American electorate in 1956, and produced *The American Voter* (Campbell and Miller were joined in this project by Philip Converse and Donald Stokes). *The American Voter* effectively set the agenda of electoral research for the next generation and remains essential reading in the field of electoral behavior.

In addition to its many contributions to the different fields of social science, the SRC has for years offered an annual summer institute in survey research methodology. Courses cover all aspects of survey research from design and sampling, to instrumentation, to analysis of survey data. Survey methods are applied to problems of business, public health, education, government, and the social sciences. The SRC, through its research and educational programs, deserves credit for helping to lead the way toward a recognition that "big science" is possible and beneficial in the social sciences. The impressive work of the Survey Research Center at Michigan has helped stimulate the development of dozens of survey research centers at universities throughout the world.

*Walter J. Stone*

## Swing Ratio

How popular votes are translated into legislative seats is a question of both practical and theoretical importance. The swing ratio indicates the expected change in the percentage of U.S. House seats held by a party that would be produced by a one percentage point shift in the popular vote for the party's congressional candidates. The swing ratio for recent congressional elections has been estimated at approximately 2.0, meaning that a one percentage point increase (or decrease) in the Democratic share of the vote will produce a two percentage point increase (or decrease) in the Democratic share of U.S. House seats.

Estimates of the swing ratio are produced in two different ways. Most commonly, the swing ratio has been arrived at through a linear regression of the relationship between votes and seats over a set of elections. Although some have criticized the use of a linear relationship, the method produces a reasonably good fit and yields coefficients that are easily interpreted. Alternatively, the swing ratio can be determined by examining the distribution of the vote across House districts for any given election. A swing ratio of 2.0 implies that each party is within one percentage point of victory in about 2 percent of the seats. Thus a shift of one point in the vote, if distributed evenly across all districts, would alter the outcome in 2 percent of the races. Reassuringly, both methods yield quite similar results.

The current swing ratio is small by historical standards. The late nineteenth century displayed a swing ratio of more than double the current one. The declining swing ratio is viewed as undesirable by some analysts, who see the current situation as one marked by insulation of congressional incumbents from national forces, separation of congressional election results from presidential outcomes, and inability of popular mood swings to be translated into legislative majorities.

*Charles L. Prysby*

REFERENCES

Jacobson, Gary C. 1987. *The Politics of Congressional Elections*. Boston: Little, Brown.

Tufte, Edward. 1973. "The Relationship Between Seats and Votes in Two-Party Systems." 68 *American Political Science Review* 211.

## Stuart Symington (1901–1989)

Four-term Democratic Senator from Missouri. Graduating from Yale in 1923, (William) Stuart Symington quickly established himself as a bright and inventive businessman. In 1938 he took over a failing company, Emerson Electric Manufacturing, and turned it around. Despite Symington's support of Republican presidential candidates in 1940 and 1944, President Harry Truman recruited him in 1945 to chair the Surplus Property Board. In 1946 Truman appointed him the first Secretary of the Air Force, a post that he held until 1951 when Truman asked him to lead the Reconstruction Finance Corporation. In 1952 Symington mounted his Senate campaign, defeating J. E. Taylor, Truman's preference, in the Democratic primary and besting Republican James P. Kem in the general election.

In the Senate he developed a reputation as an expert on defense issues, particularly those involving the Air Force. At the Democratic convention in 1956, Symington first considered running as a dark horse candidate for President but decided against this course. He did try for the presidency in 1960, and although he had Truman's support, Symington faced the reality of a crowded field in which he had little name recognition outside of Missouri. When his candidacy failed, Symington continued his career in the Senate, where he was an early and vocal critic of America's Vietnam policy. He retired from the Senate in 1976. His son James Wadsworth Symington was Democratic Congressman from Missouri from 1969 to 1977.

*See also:* Harry S Truman

*Thomas J. Baldino*

REFERENCES

Wellman, Paul I. 1960. *Stuart Symington: Portrait of a Man with a Mission*. Garden City, NY: Doubleday.

White, Theodore H. 1961. *The Making of the President 1960*. New York: Signet Books.

# T

## Robert A. Taft (1889–1953)

Ohio legislator known as "Mr. Republican." A U.S. Senator from 1939 until his death, Robert Alphonso Taft was the son of U.S. President William Howard Taft (1912–1916). He became well known for his conservative, isolationist, anti-New Deal policy stands.

Taft was elected chairman of the Republican Policy Committee in the Senate when it was formed in 1947. He used this position to become the national Republican spokesman on domestic issues, while Senate Minority Leader Arthur Vandenberg took the lead on foreign policy.

After unsuccessful runs for the Republican presidential nomination in 1940 and 1948, Taft mounted an intensive third campaign in 1952. He and Dwight Eisenhower were deadlocked going into the GOP convention in July. The initial roll call showed Taft trailing by the slim margin of 595 to 500, with 604 delegates needed for the nomination, but Eisenhower was selected on the first ballot after votes shifted in his favor. Despite his disappointment at losing the nomination, Taft campaigned for Eisenhower before the general election.

Taft was elected Majority Leader when the Republican-controlled Senate convened in 1953. He immediately became one of the Eisenhower administration's staunchest supporters in Congress. His support was short-lived, however, as he was diagnosed with cancer in May. Taft resigned the majority leadership on June 10 and died on July 31.

His son, Robert Taft, Jr., represented Ohio in the U.S. House of Representatives and the U.S. Senate in the 1960s and 1970s.

*See also:* Dwight D. Eisenhower, Majority Party Leadership in Congress, Minority Party Leadership in Congress, Robert Taft, Jr., William Howard Taft, Arthur Vandenberg

*John A. Clark*

REFERENCES

Patterson, James T. 1972. *Mr. Republican: A Biography of Robert A. Taft.* Boston: Houghton Mifflin.

## Robert Taft, Jr. (1917– )

One of many Ohio political Tafts. A descendant of the most notable political family in Ohio, Robert Taft, Jr.'s father was an Ohio Senator, who was known as "Mr. Republican" in the early 1950s. His grandfather was William Howard Taft, President of the United States and Chief Justice of the Supreme Court. His son, Robert A. Taft III, was the Republican candidate for lieutenant governor in Ohio in 1986.

A lawyer by profession, Taft was elected to the Ohio House of Representatives in 1955, two years after his father's death. He remained there until 1962, serving as majority leader for the last two years. He was elected to the U.S. House in 1962 as an at-large representative from Ohio, due to delays in redistricting. Two years later, he came within 17,000 votes of replacing an incumbent Senator, Stephen M. Young. Taft returned to Congress in 1967 and remained there for two terms. In that time he served as chairman of the Republican Conference Research Committee in the House.

Taft ran for the Senate again in 1970. He beat Governor James A. Rhodes by a scant 5,270 votes in the Republican primary and then narrowly defeated Howard Metzenbaum in the general election. Metzenbaum won a rematch in 1976 to end Taft's Senate career.

As a Senator, Taft was known to be less conservative than his father. He practiced law in Cincinnati and Washington following his defeat.

*See also:* Robert A. Taft, William Howard Taft

*John A. Clark*

## William Howard Taft (1857–1930)

Twenty-seventh President of the United States and Chief Justice of the U.S. Supreme Court. William Howard Taft was a reluctant trailblazer in both the 1908 and 1912 presidential campaigns. As Solicitor General, a federal judge, the first civil governor of the Philippines, and Theodore Roosevelt's Secretary of War, Taft became known as an intelligent, fair-minded conservative. When Roosevelt decided not to run for President in 1908, he designated Taft as his heir.

Taft entered national politics reluctantly; he would much have preferred a seat on the Supreme Court. It "is awful to be made afraid of one's shadow," as most campaigners are, Taft maintained. After his nomination by the Republicans in 1908, Taft anticipated a subdued, traditional campaign from his front porch in Cincinnati.

Taft's serenity, however, was soon shattered. The Democrats nominated the fiery William Jennings Bryan for a third time. Although initially intending to remain passive, by mid-September Bryan was stumping. Republicans began to doubt their strength, especially in the West, where the conservative Taft was considered a poor substitute for cowboy President Roosevelt. Swayed by the westerners and by an anxious Roosevelt, Taft took to the stump. Thus, for the first time in American history, both major party nominees campaigned actively and openly.

Although Taft regarded the campaign as "one of the most uncomfortable four months of my life," he won handily. The rambunctious Teddy Roosevelt went off hunting in Africa, while President Taft went about governing in Washington. But Roosevelt soon found Taft too conservative and his own retirement too restful. By 1912 Roosevelt was lambasting his old friend and protégé for selling out to the Republican "Old Guard." The Republican Party was deciding, Roosevelt believed, whether to be "the party of the plain people" or "the party of privilege and of special interest." Roosevelt declared himself a Progressive.

A Progressive reform, the direct primaries, offered the one opportunity for Roosevelt to recapture the Republican Party. By 1912 a dozen states allowed voters to elect delegates to the national convention directly. For the first time, a popular preconvention campaign was possible.

Taft himself was probably the last person in America to believe that Roosevelt would run against him, observers half-joked. Roosevelt's campaign forced the languid Taft to become the first sitting President to stump for his own renomination. Throughout the spring, the two old friends battled in the Republican primaries. "The spectacle presented by the fierce fight for the nomination . . . should bring a blush of shame to the cheek of every American," the *New York Times* tut-tutted. Roosevelt won Republican hearts, taking most of the primaries; Taft, however, won the Republican nomination. A GOP "steamroller" of bosses and officeholders renominated the incumbent at Chicago. Roosevelt stormed out, eventually running as the Progressive (Bull Moose) Party's nominee.

Satisfied with stopping Roosevelt's bid for the Republican nomination and determined to maintain some dignity, Taft resigned himself to a fall defeat. The Democrat Woodrow Wilson eked out a victory in the three-way race. After his defeat, Taft taught law at Yale. In 1921 he fulfilled his true ambition—Warren Harding appointed Taft Chief Justice of the Supreme Court, and he served in that capacity until his death.

*See also:* William Jennings Bryan, Warren G. Harding, Theodore Roosevelt, Woodrow Wilson

*Gil Troy*

REFERENCES

Manners, William. 1969. *TR and Will: A Friendship That Split the Republican Party.* New York: Harcourt, Brace & World.

Pringle, Henry F. 1939. *The Life and Times of William Howard Taft: A Biography.* 2 vols. New York: Farrar & Rinehart.

Taft, William H. 1909. *Political Issues and Outlooks: Speeches Delivered Between August, 1908, and February, 1909.* New York: Doubleday, Page.

Youngman, Elmer H., ed. 1913. *Progressive Principles by Theodore Roosevelt: Selections from Addresses Made During the Presidential Campaign of 1912.* New York: Progressive National Service.

## Thomas Taggart (1856–1929)

Four-decade leader of Indiana's Democratic Party. One of the leading politicians in Indiana for nearly 40 years, Thomas Taggart was a Democrat in a predominantly Republican state.

Although his terms in public office were fleeting, his leadership in the Indiana Democratic Party put him in a position to have influence in national politics.

Taggart became known in Indiana politics in 1886, when he was elected Marion County (Indianapolis) auditor in a period in which few Democrats would even consider contending for the post. He was made county Democratic chairman in 1888, the same year that Marion County voted for Grover Cleveland against Benjamin Harrison, the first time the county had gone Democratic since 1856. This feat, along with Taggart's reelection as county auditor in 1890, catapulted him into prominence among the state Democratic Party. He was chosen chairman of the Indiana Democratic Party from 1892 to 1894, and was elected mayor of Indianapolis in 1895, an office he held until 1901. Taggart served on the Democratic National Committee from 1900 to 1912 and was its chairman between 1900 and 1908.

His burning ambition for many of these years was to serve in the U.S. Senate. Taggart failed to receive the Democratic nomination in 1910 but was appointed to the Senate in 1916 to fill the vacancy caused by the death of Benjamin Shively. Taggart's service in the Senate was short-lived, as he lost the special election to fill the remainder of Shively's term by a narrow margin to the Republican James Watson. Taggart's attempt to unseat Watson in the regular election of 1920 failed by a more substantial margin.

As a national party official, Taggart was instrumental in charting the course of many key events of his era. The high point of his prominence came in 1904, when he directed the losing presidential campaign of Alton Parker. He was instrumental in the 1912 campaign, turning the Indiana delegation to Woodrow Wilson at a strategic moment. He was a supporter of James Cox in 1920, while strongly supporting dark horse candidates from Indiana in 1924 and 1928, Senator Samuel Ralston and banker Evans Woolen.

*See also:* Grover Cleveland, James Cox, Democratic National Committee, Benjamin Harrison, Woodrow Wilson

*Charles Stewart III*

REFERENCES

Goldman, Ralph M. 1990. *The National Party Chairmen and Committees: Factionalism at the Top.* Armonk, NY: M. E. Sharpe.

## Eugene Talmadge (1884–1946)

Georgia Democratic leader. An astute Georgia politician, Eugene Talmadge used the state's unique electoral system to gain some rather significant political power that he used to oppose the New Deal. In 1932 he won the governorship with a minority of popular votes, a victory made possible because of Georgia's county-unit electoral system in which the 8 most populated counties had 4 unit votes each and the smallest 121 counties had 2 unit votes each. With his rural support, Talmadge easily won the majority of county-unit votes and was reelected in 1934.

As Georgia's governor, Talmadge attacked the New Deal as socialistic and wasteful. Further in 1936 with the backing of large corporations and Huey Long's anti-FDR supporters, he organized a "Grass Roots Convention" in Macon, Georgia, to oppose Franklin D. Roosevelt's reelection. The convention was a failure, producing no presidential candidate and no future plans. Some historians believe that if Huey Long had survived assassination, the convention would have nominated Long for President and Talmadge for Vice President.

In the 1938 Senate race between Talmadge, Lawrence Camp, and incumbent Walter F. George, Roosevelt asked Georgians to defeat George because of his opposition to the New Deal. Most Georgians did not approve of FDR's intervention and returned George to the Senate. Without Roosevelt's interference, Talmadge would have probably won the race. Talmadge returned to the governor's chair in 1942 and was reelected in 1946 with a minority of popular votes but died before taking office.

*See also:* Walter F. George, Huey Long, New Deal, Franklin D. Roosevelt

*Henry J. Walker, Jr.*

REFERENCES

Anderson, William. 1985. *The Wild Man from Sugar Creek: The Political Career of Eugene Talmadge.* Baton Rouge: Louisiana State U. Pr.

Cobb, James C. 1954. "Not Gone, But Forgotten: Eugene Talmadge and the 1938 Purge Campaign." 38 *Georgia Historical Quarterly* 226.

Henson, Allen Lumpkin. 1945. *Red Galluses: A Story of Georgian Politics.* Boston: House of Edinboro Publishers.

Key, V. O., Jr. 1949. *Southern Politics in State and Nation.* New York: Knopf.

Michie, Allen H., and Frank Ryhlick. 1939. *Dixie Demagogues.* New York: Vanguard.

# Tammany Hall

Perhaps more than any other symbol, Tammany Hall came to embody machine government in the United States. Originally called the Society of Saint Tammany, after a legendary Delaware Indian chief, Tammany Hall was founded in 1789 in New York City. Its initial interests involved performing works of charity and promoting patriotism in the new nation. On patriotic holidays, for example, Tammany braves donned feathers and war paint and whooped their way along the city streets.

All of the original founders were artisans, tradesmen, and bankers—not politicians. Society members were classified as hunters, warriors, and Sachems (chiefs). A Grand Sachem presided over the organization, and its clubhouse was called "the Wigwam." But with the rise of political parties in the United States, Tammany acquired a distinctly partisan character. Elected governor of New York in 1817, De Witt Clinton was instrumental in transforming the formerly benevolent Tammany organization into a subgroup of the Democratic-Republican Party. Forty years later, Tammany had become an absolute subsidiary of the Democratic Party.

In 1854 Fernando Wood became the first Tammany-Democratic mayor of New York City. Ties between the Tammany and the Democrats grew even stronger; in 1860 William Marcy Tweed was elected chairman of the Democratic Party Central Committee for New York County, and three years later he was named Grand Sachem of Tammany. Tweed's selection as Grand Sachem cemented the linkages between Tammany and the Democratic Party.

Waves of immigrants—first from Ireland and later from eastern, central, and southern Europe—provided Tammany with a pool of potential voters. Many of these new Americans were "have-nots" who needed everything: jobs, food, and help in finding their way in a strange country. New York State proved unwilling to provide much help. Until 1931, New York law forbade the use of public funds to support anyone outside a public institution—only the poorhouse was a legitimate source of help. But if someone temporarily out of work could receive no help from the state, Tammany Hall was there to lend a hand with money or a temporary job (such as shoveling snow or digging a ditch for the gas company). Tammany also provided Thanksgiving and Christmas baskets and sponsored neighborhood picnics—often the only outing many could attend.

What Tammany asked for in return was loyalty on election day. And the devotion that Tammany received was so great that it transformed New York City into a virtual one-party Democratic area—a legacy that lasts to this day. Tammany's domination in the city enhanced its antipathy against Republican-controlled upstate New York. George Washington Plunkitt, a powerful figure in the Tammany organization, once typically derided the Republican upstate legislators as "hayseeds."

As time passed, Tammany Hall became synonymous with corruption. Plunkitt, in a set of famous interviews in the early 1900s with William L. Riordan of the *New York Evening Post*, attempted to justify the organization's practices. Plunkitt created a distinction between "honest" and "dishonest" graft: honest graft involves having knowledge about a forthcoming municipal project, be it the construction of a bridge or a new road, and acting upon it; dishonest graft is outright stealing from the public treasury. Plunkitt, who became a millionaire through the use of "honest graft," said of it and himself, "I seen my opportunities and I took 'em."

The corruption associated with Tammany Hall spawned a new breed of politician—the New York City reformer. Old pol Plunkitt called them "morning glories," noting that while they might win an occasional battle, Tammany still kept winning the war. History was on Plunkitt's side when he made those remarks at the turn of the century. From 1854 to 1934 Tammany controlled city hall for 70 of these 80 years. But the passage of time spawned a group of reformers who collectively were some of the most powerful enemies ever arrayed against a political organization. These included Franklin D. Roosevelt, who had been opposed by Tammany since his entry into politics in 1910; Herbert H. Lehman, Roosevelt's successor as New York governor; and Fiorello La Guardia, the feisty New York mayor who finally wrested control of the city from Tammany.

As governor, Roosevelt repealed the law prohibiting the state from aiding those temporarily in need. This relief deprived Tammany of some of its patronage power. As President, FDR's New Deal further bureaucratized government assistance and reduced the influence of political parties in providing aid to the poor. The result was the eventual destruction of the big-city machines. Meanwhile, Roosevelt's successor as governor, Lehman, starved the organization of state patronage while he was in office.

But it was the 12-year reign of Fiorello La Guardia that rendered Tammany Hall virtually powerless. La Guardia's election in 1933 signaled the beginning of another reform administration. But unlike his predecessors, La Guardia was no "morning glory," winning reelection twice more for a total of 12 years in office. Political commentator Warren Moscow writes that "No one before La Guardia had ever figured on a reform administration succeeding itself, and while the machines had been able to stand his first four years in office, with their carry-over appointees, the last eight years were ruinous." City posts came to be occupied by professionals who held lengthy, fixed terms of office. For example, a magistrate's term was ten years. Thus, La Guardia institutionalized the civil service.

Things became so bad for Tammany that it was forced to rely on the patronage of the judges it had selected, a ploy that proved insufficient. In 1943 the bank foreclosed the mortgage to its Wigwam, and Tammany Hall became defunct.

*See also:* De Witt Clinton, Fiorello La Guardia, Herbert H. Lehman, George Washington Plunkitt, Franklin D. Roosevelt, William M. Tweed

*John K. White*

REFERENCES

Moscow, Warren. 1948. *Politics in the Empire State.* New York: Knopf.

Riordan, William L. 1963. *Plunkitt of Tammany Hall.* New York: Dutton.

## Ida M. Tarbell (1857–1944)

Muckraking journalist of the early twentieth century. Ida Minerva Tarbell brought a mood of almost extravagant earnest ethical concern to her investigations into the business practices of her day. Growing up in western Pennsylvania, where booming oil fields were coming under the monopolistic grip of John D. Rockefeller, prepared her psychologically for her most famous work, *The History of the Standard Oil Company* (1904). A graduate of Allegheny College, Tarbell spent eight years working for the *Chautauquan* and three more in Paris before joining the staff of the socially caustic *McClure's* magazine in 1894. Her meticulous critique of Rockefeller's empire was serialized in *McClure's*, as were her earlier writings on Napoleon and Abraham Lincoln. In 1906 Tarbell left *McClure's* for the *American Magazine*, where she wrote extensively on the role of tariff protection in promoting monopoly. After 1915 she became a

fixture on the lecture circuit and remained a prolific free-lance writer for the next 20 years.

The limits of Tarbell's reformist zeal showed in her skepticism about the woman suffrage movement and in her admiration for modernizing industrialists like Henry Ford, Elbert Gary, and Owen D. Young, in whose careers she detected evidence of farsighted social responsibility. Tarbell's political heroes included Grover Cleveland as well as Theodore Roosevelt and Woodrow Wilson. She shared some of the post-World War I disenchantment with democratic politics, and she was one of many Americans to be momentarily impressed by Benito Mussolini, whom she interviewed in 1926. The New Deal's early efforts at economic reorganization also won her sympathy. Though she was not a profound political analyst, Ida Tarbell's sensitive, moderate perceptions made her an influential communicator of mainstream progressive attitudes to her generation.

*See also:* Grover Cleveland, Theodore Roosevelt, Woodrow Wilson, Woman Suffrage

*Geoffrey Blodgett*

REFERENCES

Brady, Kathleen. 1989. *Ida Tarbell: Portrait of a Muckraker.* Pittsburgh: U. of Pittsburgh Pr.

Chalmers, David M. 1964. *The Social and Political Ideas of the Muckrakers.* New York: Citadel Press.

Tarbell, Ida M. 1939. *All in the Day's Work.* New York: Macmillan.

Wilson, Harold S. 1970. *"McClure's Magazine" and the Muckrakers.* Princeton: Princeton U. Pr.

## Tariffs and Trade

Once the subject of heated party debate and intense party rivalry, the tariff in American history has declined in importance as a partisan political issue over the last half-century. Only in the 1980s has protectionism reassumed a political importance in national economic and trade policies that rivals levels of interest before the 1930s.

The first nationally protective legislation of the United States Congress, the Tariff Act of 1789, originated in the nation's search for revenue in the aftermath of independence. The protection of nascent economic production was also an immediate objective of tariff legislation, and it was in the definition of trade efficacy that duties assumed prominence in party contentions. The War of 1812 helped to entrench sectional divisions over tariff policy as politicians began to plan for the economic growth of the United States with a new urgency. While the industrializing North favored protection, political leaders in the southern states decried tariffs in the same way that the South opposed all federal government tactics to develop the northern economy.

The nullification crisis of 1832, in which South Carolina bitterly abrogated federal tariff legislation, was the first in the South's antecedents to secession. As a result of the dispute, regional divisions over protection hardened. Both Democrats and Whigs nevertheless understood that party unity would depend on subsuming the tariff issue in national, multiregional contests. For this reason and for the problems of the Mexican War and secession, the tariff was important, but it was not an issue at the center of elections and partisan politics in the years leading up to the Civil War.

In the final decades of the nineteenth century, regional interests remained the basis of political decision-making and revisions of tariff legislation. The Democratic Party maintained a tradition favoring low tariffs, but Democrats were fractured on the issue, with political alliances and regional allegiances taking precedence over party affiliation in national debate. The complexity of intraparty divisions often forced the tariff to a secondary status in party platforms and priorities. As they had before the Civil War, Democrats united and concentrated on the more pressing issues of monetary reform and the cyclical financial crises. At important congressional votes Democrats from the most industrialized states sometimes broke party ranks in support of Republican Party protectionism.

Partisan debate on the tariff reached a zenith at the end of the century. Democratic President Grover Cleveland made decreased protectionism a vital part of his 1888 election platform, but Republican domination in both houses of Congress led to the passage of the fiercely protectionist McKinley Tariff Act of 1890. The Dingley Tariff in 1897 reinforced the ties among protectionism as a political issue, Republican Party strength, and the political power of the Northeast and growing industrial sections of the Midwest. Republican Party strength in the 1890s assured the highest import duties in nineteenth-century American history.

During the first three decades of the new century, conflict over the tariff centered about four legislative turning points: the Payne-Aldrich Tariff, the Underwood Tariff, the Fordney-McCumber Tariff, and the Tariff Act of 1930. After a decade without significant reform,

popular associations of protectionism with a newly perceived national menace, the trust, led both major parties to advocate a new evaluation of duties on imported goods. The Payne-Aldrich Tariff of 1909 was to have offered important duty reductions, more closely reflecting the needs of all Americans and not simply those of the vilified corporate combinations. Republican protectionist amendments to the legislation, however, prevented the expected outcome.

Real change finally came with the Underwood Tariff legislation of 1913 and the establishment of free entry for an assortment of previously protected items including many manufactured goods. Underwood's legislation was the first in half a century to effect significant decreases in duties. The election victory of Woodrow Wilson and his vociferous role in support of tariff reform had accentuated a popular belief that the Republican election loss of 1912 represented a rejection of high duties. The Democrats' platform had denounced the tariff as a major cause of the unequal distribution of wealth in the United States and had described farmers and workers as suffering victims of these duties.

As in the past, partisan politics and electoral reversals would continue to form the basis for change. Republican House and Senate electoral triumphs in 1918 led to the passage of the Fordney Emergency Tariff in 1921 and the more lasting Fordney-McCumber Tariff of 1922. Unlike early sectional determinants of the tariff as a political issue, by the early 1920s the principal concerns of Republican protectionism were support for the ailing agriculture sector and measures designed to counter a resurgence of postwar German productivity. The Democrats were stalwart in their opposition describing Fordney-McCumber in the party's 1924 presidential platform as dishonest.

By the late 1920s, corporate backers of the Republican party were a forceful influence behind the renewed strength of the Smoot-Hawley Tariff of 1930. President Herbert Hoover strongly supported appeals from hundreds of interest groups for more protection, but the Republican project ended disastrously. With the passage of Smoot-Hawley, immediate international trade retaliation undercut world commerce and brought about the onset of depression.

Often credited with a causal role in the Great Depression, the Tariff Act of 1930 was the final product of the traditional party-based protectionist disputes. The subsequent determination of appropriate tariff levels was subject to a professionalization in many areas of American government, one that would eliminate partisanship as the basis for decisions. The experience of worldwide retaliation to the Smoot-Hawley legislation led the United States Government to pursue a tariff policy of international treaties and bilateral agreements in the 1930s and 1940s. The American wartime experience and the American role in the rebuilding of Europe suggested to many that the most productive route in foreign trade policy was in reaching amiable agreements with other nations.

By the mid-1940s the United States had adhered to the General Agreement on Tariffs and Trade (GATT), had concluded bilateral trade accords with 27 nations, and had slashed tariffs on imported goods by more than 40 percent. Beginning in the final years of World War II, and increasingly in the late 1940s and 1950s, Republican politicians began supporting liberal trade legislation. Democratic Party domination in government during the 1950s and 1960s continued Franklin Roosevelt's emphasis on negotiating external agreements. Where opposition to freer trade arose, it represented industry or regionally based parochial objections, such as those voiced by the powerful lumber and wood lobby from the northwestern states. President John F. Kennedy, in a radical step away from the long history of American government conservatism in trade, advocated an end to tariff barriers internationally in a 1962 message to Congress.

With the economic crisis of the early 1970s came renewed calls for protectionist legislation from sectors of the Democratic Party, with the support of organized labor. It was not, however, until the early 1980s that party politics and the issue of the tariff became intertwined again in a parallel to the protectionist debates of the early 1900s. The Republican administration of President Ronald Reagan won election in 1980 and reelection in 1984 stressing freedom from government strictures in domestic and foreign economic policies. As a feature of this policy, the President acted to end tariffs as an impediment to the free flow of international trade.

In the nation's most ambitious effort in history at bilateral tariff reduction, the United States entered into negotiations in the late 1980s with Canada for an all-encompassing free trade agreement. Party alignments over the tariff had become secondary as Reagan pressed for bipartisan support of the free trade agreement. It was a crucial triumph of President Reagan's redefinition of the Republican Party's economic agenda and a strong statement on the unity of purpose of both parties, when the Senate gave overwhelming final approval to the United States–Canada Free Trade Agreement in September 1988, with all tariffs between the two nations slated for elimination by 1998.

*See also:* Grover Cleveland, Herbert Hoover, John F. Kennedy, Ronald Reagan, Franklin D. Roosevelt

*David Sheinin*

REFERENCES

Ashley, Percy. 1970 (orig. 1904). *Modern Tariff History: Germany, United States, France.* New York: Howard Fertig.

Baker, Richard Cleveland. 1941. *The Tariff Under Roosevelt and Taft.* Hastings: Democrat Printing Co.

Baldwin, Robert E. 1985. *The Political Economy of U.S. Import Policy.* Cambridge: MIT Pr.

Bauer, Raymond A., Ithiel de Sola Pool, and Lewis Anthony Dexter. 1972. *American Business and Public Policy.* Chicago: Aldine, Atherton.

Cohen, Stephen D. 1977. *The Making of United States International Economic Policy.* New York: Praeger.

Curtis, Thomas B., and John Robert Vastine, Jr. 1971. *The Kennedy Round and the Future of American Trade.* New York: Praeger.

Destler, I. M. 1986. *American Trade Politics: System Under Stress.* Washington: Institute for International Economics.

Fried, Edward R., Frank Stone, and Philip H. Trezise, eds. 1987. *Building a Canadian-American Free Trade Area.* Washington: Brookings.

Johnson, Emory R. 1915. *History of Foreign and Domestic Commerce of the United States.* Washington: Carnegie Institution.

Kaufman, Burton I. 1982. *Trade and Aid: Eisenhower's Foreign Economic Policy, 1953–1961.* Baltimore: Johns Hopkins U. Pr.

Lake, David A. 1988. *Power, Protection, and Free Trade.* Ithaca: Cornell U. Pr.

Olson, Robert K. 1987. *U.S. Foreign Policy and the New International Economic Order.* Boulder, CO: Westview.

Pincus, Jonathan J. 1977. *Pressure Groups and Politics in Antebellum Tariffs.* New York: Columbia U. Pr.

## Tashjian v. Republican Party
### 479 U.S. 208 (1986)

The U.S. Supreme Court held that the state of Connecticut could not constitutionally prevent unaffiliated electoral registrants from voting in a state-conducted Republican primary election when the Republican Party of Connecticut wanted to allow such registrants, along with Republican registrants, to cast ballots in its primary in *Tashjian v. Republican Party of Connecticut.* A party rule thus prevailed against the restrictions of the state's closed-primary law.

If the result here should appear at odds with the presumed constitutionality of state primary laws during most of this century, then it can nevertheless be said to follow from Supreme Court opinions, in the previous decade, upholding party rights derived from guarantees of freedom of association under the First and Fourteenth amendments. The most relevant of those opinions, *Cousins v. Wigoda* (1975) and *Democratic Party of the U.S. v. Wisconsin ex rel La Follette* (1981), upheld national party challenges to state laws affecting the choice of presidential nominating convention delegates. In *Tashjian*, a state party challenged a law providing primary elections for state and congressional offices. To be sure, the Connecticut Republican Party did not challenge the power of the state to require a primary in statutorily defined circumstances, but only the law's provision that excluded unaffiliated voters when a party wanted to allow them to cast primary ballots.

Yet in asking the Court to decide in its favor with respect to the specific provision, the Republican challenge might be thought implicitly to suggest that a party should have the constitutional right to decide for itself how to nominate its candidates—even without any primary if it so chose. However logical, no such far-reaching doctrine was reflected in the Court's opinion. On the contrary, the decision in *Tashjian* was sharply limited to the provision directly challenged. The Court even said that its holding did not necessarily mean that a party could successfully challenge other state regulations of primary voting qualifications, such as statutory prohibitions against enrolled members of one party voting in another party's primary. Hence, without subsequently successful constitutional challenges, *Tashjian* does no more than force some 20 closed-primary states to allow unaffiliated registrants to vote in the primary of a party that wants them. Some of these states responded in the first year or so after the decision by enacting enabling legislation or by appropriate administrative action but not always in conjunction with a party request for the change. In the four largest closed-primary states—California, New York, Pennsylvania, and Florida—no legal response to *Tashjian* occurred in 1987. In a few states, notably North Carolina, the minority Republican Party followed the Connecticut Republican precedent in opening its primary to unaffiliated registrants though they are a much smaller proportion of the electorate than Connecticut's one-third.

Whether minority parties in still more states will move in the same direction is uncertain, and so is the possibility that majority parties would eventually find it expedient to do likewise.

Probably more significant is whether *Tashjian* will lead to other successful constitutional challenges to state primary laws, perhaps against open primaries by parties that want them closed or abolished altogether. Projecting any such judicial victories is problematic given the language of the opinion and also the bare five-to-four majority of aging justices sustaining the opinion in 1986.

*See also:* Closed Primary, *Cousins v. Wigoda, Democratic Party of the U.S. v. Wisconsin,* Fourteenth Amendment, State Regulation of Parties

*Leon D. Epstein*

## John W. Taylor (1784–1854)

Abolitionist Speaker of the U.S. House of Representatives. Active in New York state politics, John W. Taylor was first elected to the House of Representatives in 1812, serving until 1833. Only a moderate antislavery advocate, he was nonetheless seen in the South as an especially bitter foe of southern interests. His opposition to the three-fifths clause in the Constitution led him to second James Tallmadge's amendment to the Missouri bill in 1819, which would have prohibited the further introduction of slavery into Missouri and liberated the children of slave parents there at the age of 25. Taylor then introduced a similar amendment to the Arkansas Territorial bill, but he was again unable to secure its passage. On the Missouri question, he defended the constitutionality of the Tallmadge Amendment, arguing that the power of Congress to admit states gave it the right to prescribe conditions on that admission. In 1820 he was elected to complete Henry Clay's term as Speaker of the House. In his new "nonpartisan" position, he disengaged himself from the Missouri debates and allowed Clay a free hand in working out the Missouri Compromise (including the rejection of the Tallmadge Amendment).

During the administration of John Quincy Adams, Taylor was again elected Speaker in 1825 as representative of the President's partisans. Distrusted in the South, he was unable to bring strong leadership of discipline in a House that saw the Jacksonian Democrats succeed in blocking the Adams legislative program. A supporter of Henry Clay in organizing the national Republican Party, Taylor was defeated in the

Speaker's election in the next Congress. In 1832 he lost his seat in Congress because of the opposition of the Martin Van Buren Democrats. Taylor remained politically active in New York until 1843 when he retired to Ohio.

*See also:* John Quincy Adams, Henry Clay, Jacksonian Democrats, Andrew Stevenson

*Frederick J. Blue*

REFERENCES

Bemis, Samuel G. 1956. *John Quincy Adams and the Union.* New York: Knopf.

Dangerfield, George. 1952. *The Era of Good Feelings.* New York: Harcourt, Brace & World.

———. 1965. *The Awakening of American Nationalism, 1815–1828.* New York: Harper & Row.

Hargreaves, Mary W. M. 1985. *The Presidency of John Quincy Adams.* Lawrence: U. Pr. of Kansas.

Moore, Glover. 1953. *The Missouri Compromise, 1819–1821.* Lexington: U. of Kentucky Pr.

## Zachary Taylor (1784–1850)

"Old Rough and Ready," the twelfth President of the United States. Zachary Taylor served as commander of the Army of Occupation on the Mexican Border, as an Indian-fighter, and in the War of 1812 before being elected President of the United States in 1848. Major General Taylor was an ideal candidate for either party. His Mexican War victories at Palo Alto and Resaca de la Palma in May 1846 prompted both Whigs and Democrats to nominate the general. "Convention be damned," an impatient Kentuckian yelled after Taylor's victory at Buena Vista in February 1847, "I tell ye General Taylor is going to be elected by spontaneous combustion." Taylor preferred the Whig Party, yet his mating dance with the Whigs was complicated, the resulting marriage, strained.

From his military-tent-turned-campaign-headquarters, Old Rough and Ready unleashed a barrage of contradictory letters about the nomination. He professed disinterest in politics; he had never voted in any presidential election. But how could he defy the people's wishes? If forced, he would consent to be "President of the nation, and not of a party." Whigs now had to choose between party regularity and a popular candidate, between principles and success.

Taylor had his own choice to make and began playing the party game. In a letter of April 22, 1848, Taylor attempted to quell Whig doubts. "I AM A WHIG, but not an ultra Whig," he said, distancing himself from party domination. Taylor's popularity and his professions of party loyalty clinched his nomination by the Whigs. Northerners appreciated his silence on the sla-

very-extension question; southerners assumed the slaveholding general's support for their peculiar institution. With no definable platform, the Whig ticket was an elaborate evasion testifying to deep divisions in the Whig Party. Henry Clay, the symbol of traditional Whig virtue, smarted from defeat, wishing out loud that he too could "slay a Mexican."

After his nomination, Taylor tried to avoid public statements. But many of his private letters, often containing professions of nonpartisanship, were reprinted. Democrats attacked General "Mum" as a candidate of "No avowed principle," while Whig regulars resented the general's disdain for party politics. Taylor's second Allison letter in September 1848 reaffirmed his devotion to the Whigs, arguing that "good Whig doctrine" demanded nonpartisanship. In a close election, with Lewis Cass's Democratic effort crippled by Martin Van Buren's Free Soil Party in the crucial swing state of New York, Taylor triumphed. To Whig managers like Thurlow Weed, the election "vindicated the wisdom of General Taylor's nomination." But to purists like Horace Greeley, 1848 marked "the triumph of General Taylor, not of our principles." Greeley declared it a Pyrrhic victory; Whigs were "at once triumphant and undone."

As President, Taylor pleased northern Whigs and angered southerners by refusing to promote the extension of slavery into the territories. He died suddenly during the struggle over the Compromise of 1850. He was the last Whig President.

*See also:* Lewis Cass, Free Soil Party, Horace Greeley, Mexican War, Martin Van Buren, Thurlow Weed

*Gil Troy*

REFERENCES

Bauer, K. Jack. 1985. *Zachary Taylor: Soldier, Planter, Statesman of the Old Southwest.* Baton Rouge: Louisiana State U. Pr.

Dyer, Brainerd. 1946. "Zachary Taylor." In Fred C. Cole and Wendell H. Stephenson, eds. *Southern Biography Series.* Baton Rouge: Louisiana State U. Pr.

Greeley, Horace. 1869. *Recollections of a Busy Life.* New York: J. B. Ford.

Peterson, Merrill D. 1987. *The Great Triumvirate: Webster, Clay and Calhoun.* New York: Oxford U. Pr.

Potter, David M. 1976. "The Impending Crisis, 1848–1861." In Henry Steele Commager and Richard B. Morris, eds. *The New American Nation Series.* New York: Harper & Row.

Rayback, Joseph G. 1970. *Free Soil: The Election of 1848.* Lexington: U. Pr. of Kentucky.

Weed, Harriet A., and Thurlow Weed Barnes. 1883–1884. *Life of Thurlow Weed, Including His Autobiography and a Memoir.* 2 vols. Boston: Houghton Mifflin.

## Teapot Dome

The Teapot Dome scandals evolved from the lease of naval oil reserve lands to private oil developers Harry Sinclair and Edward Doheney. In 1922, Progressives, who were suspicious of the anticonservationist orientation of the Warren Harding administration, stirred up a Senate investigation, which was headed by Senator Thomas Walsh. This committee received testimony that the oil developers had given or "loaned" Secretary of the Interior Albert Fall (who had granted the leases) about $400,000. By early 1924 Teapot Dome and other investigations of the Harding administration seemed likely to dominate the presidential election; however, in February Democratic hopes of turning the corruption issue into electoral victory were severely damaged. Doheney testified that he had employed four former members of Woodrow Wilson's Cabinet, including the 1924 Democratic presidential front-runner, William Gibbs McAdoo. No improper motive was demonstrated, but this testimony tended to make oil money bipartisan and blurred the corruption issue. McAdoo's loss of credibility as a reform candidate encouraged New York governor Alfred E. Smith to challenge McAdoo seriously for the nomination and contributed to a bitter Democratic convention that divided the party over "oil, whiskey, and religion." Teapot Dome encouraged Progressives to reject both major parties as corrupt and to launch the third-party candidacy of Robert La Follette. The Republicans were aided by the death of President Harding before the scandal broke and by his replacement with the uninvolved but shrewd Calvin Coolidge who seemed the embodiment of simple puritanical virtues. The Teapot Dome leases were eventually canceled and Fall convicted, but trials and investigations (which went on for years) had little further political impact. Some historians claim the disillusionment of many Progressives by the scandals ultimately contributed to the rise of the New Deal coalition.

*See also:* Calvin Coolidge, Robert La Follette, William G. McAdoo, Progressive Party, Alfred E. Smith

*Harold B. Raymond*

REFERENCES

Adams, Samuel H. 1939. *The Incredible Era: The Life and Times of Warren Gamaliel Harding.* Boston: Houghton Mifflin.

Allen, Lee N. 1963. "The McAdoo Campaign for the Presidential Nomination in 1924." 24 *Journal of Southern History* 211.

Bates, Leonard J. 1955. "The Teapot Dome Scandal and the Election of 1924." 60 *American Historical Review* 302.

———. 1963. *The Origins of Teapot Dome: Progressives, Parties and Petroleum 1909–1921.* Urbana: U. of Illinois Pr.

Burner, David T. 1968. *The Politics of Provincialism: The Democratic Party in Transition, 1918–1932.* New York: Knopf.

Bush, Francis X. 1954. *Enemies of the State.* New York: Bobbs-Merrill.

Ise, John. 1928. *United States Oil Policy.* New Haven: Yale U. Pr.

McCoy, Donald. 1967. *Calvin Coolidge: The Quiet President.* New York: Macmillan.

Murray, Robert K. 1969. *The Harding Era: Warren G. Harding and His Administration.* Minneapolis: U. of Minn. Pr.

Naggle, Burl. 1962. *Teapot Dome, Oil and Politics in the 1920s.* Baton Rouge: Louisiana State U. Pr.

Russell, Francis. 1968. *The Shadow of Blooming Grove: Warren G. Harding in His Times.* New York: McGraw-Hill.

White, William Allan. 1940. *A Puritan in Babylon: The Story of Calvin Coolidge.* Boston: Macmillan.

## Telethons

Marathon television events used to raise money have been called telethons. Sometimes used as a device to raise political money, the Democratic Party held four annual TV telethons from 1972 to 1975, featuring entertainers, political spots, and direct appeals for money. Following the 1968 presidential election, the Democratic National Committee (DNC) had accumulated a debt of $9.3 million that it had not retired by 1972. DNC treasurer Robert Strauss asked John Y. Brown for fundraising schemes, and the telethon idea emerged. In addition to raising money, the purposes of the telethons were to make fundraising more democratic by relying on many small contributions, to help unify the party, and to increase the participation of average citizens in party activities. State-national Democratic Party ties were strengthened because, after the 1972 effort, states got back from the national committee a percentage of the profits raised in each state. Table 1 below summarizes the fundraising efforts.

Although the telethons succeeded in raising money from large numbers of small contributions (the mean contribution was about $12), those who contributed represented an elite population, insofar as they were highly educated, had high incomes, were political activists, and voted as highly partisan liberal Democrats. The drop in contributions after the 1975 effort—

# Table 1

*The Democratic National Telethons; Dates, Themes, Duration, Network Affiliations, Net Profit, and Initial Audience*

| Date of Telethon | Theme of Telethon | Duration in Hours (in Any One Time Zone) | Television Network Affiliation | Total Net Profit (Net Receipts Minus Production Costs) | % of Television Households Watching During First Hour[a] |
|---|---|---|---|---|---|
| 1972 Telethon, July 8–9, 1972 | "Save the Two-Party System" | 19 hrs. | ABC | $1,900,000[b] | NA |
| 1973 Telethon, Sept. 15–16, 1973 | "America Goes Public" | 8 hrs. | NBC | $1,941,978 | 6.8% |
| 1974 Telethon, June 29–30, 1974 | "Answer America" | 21 hrs. | CBS | $2,847,833 | 12.9% |
| 1975 Telethon, July 26–27, 1975 | "Tune in America" | 21 hrs. | ABC | $ 909,771 | 5.7% |

[a]Data supplied by the A. C. Nielsen Company. The 6.8 percent represents 4,500,000 households, the 12.6 percent represents 8,540,000 households, and the 5.7 percent represents 3,900,000 households. Cumulative watching data is only available for the 1974 telethon. For that year's effort the Nielsen Company estimates that approximately 40 percent of television households watched at least some of the telethon. For the same year a Roper poll (74–8) found that 22 percent of the population eighteen years and older claimed to have seen some of the telethon.
[b]Profit and loss statements are not available for the 1972 telethon. Therefore this figure represents an estimate from newspaper sources and interviews with the telethon staff.

Source: Ellwood and Spitzer.

attributed to the fact that 1975 was an "off" political year, that the contributor pool may have been exhausted, that viewership was declining, and the Watergate/anti-Nixon backlash was subsiding—led to the termination of the telethons. Organizational complexity and rising TV production costs have discouraged similar efforts. Telethons continue to be effective, however, in charity drives and television evangelical fundraising efforts.

*See also:* Democratic National Committee, Robert Strauss, Watergate

*Robert J. Spitzer*

REFERENCES

Ellwood, John W., and Robert J. Spitzer. 1979. "The Democratic National Telethons: Their Successes and Failures." 41 *Journal of Politics* 828.

Schramm, Wilbur, and Richard F. Carter. 1959. "Effectiveness of a Political Telethon." 23 *Public Opinion Quarterly* 125.

## Television Advertising and Politics

In the 1950s many politicians expressed apprehension and even disdain about using television advertising to communicate their message to the voters. However, the money that today's candidate for major political office allocates for television advertising is frequently the single largest expense in the campaign budget.

Naturally, the fact that candidates place such reliance on television advertising often draws criticism from the academia, the news media, and even politicians who consider spot commercials to be a costly and superficial method of communication. Not only have these critics expressed concern that politicians' use of television advertising has accelerated the decline of a once strong two-party system but also that widespread use of negative commercials has served to increase voter cynicism. Worries also have been sounded that candidates could be so skillfully packaged that inexperienced and unethical candidates would be foisted upon an unsuspecting electorate. But the experience of more than three decades of exposure to televised political advertising has led observers to conclude that the reservations held by critics have at least some truth but frequently could apply to the preelectorate political era as well.

Voters in the United States received their first serious look at political advertising on television in the 1952 presidential campaign. Both sides employed advertising experts, but the better-funded Republican candidate, Dwight Eisenhower, mounted the superior effort. Such noted advertising experts as Bernard Duffy and Rosser Reeves played key roles in the planning and execution of Eisenhower's advertising campaign. The general was shown in a series of spots explaining his views to questions posed by the voters. During the filming, Eisenhower reportedly muttered his disillusionment "that an old soldier should come to this." The Democratic nominee Governor Adlai Stevenson (D-

Ill.) warned that the voters did not want "politics and the presidency to become the plaything other high-pressure men, of the ghostwriters, of the public relations men." However, Eisenhower won a landslide victory.

Four years later, Stevenson mounted an even more lavish advertising campaign to try to be competitive with President Eisenhower. Once again, the Republican candidate won, but television advertising became a firmly established fixture of presidential campaigns.

Generally, television advertising by politicians has not served to strengthen the two-party system. However, factors such as the increased affluence and mobility of the American public, the civil service system, the lessening of ethnocultural distinctions, and the use of government to deliver services that the old political boss once provided have played just as important roles in diminishing party loyalty. Certainly, television advertising does tend to focus on promoting candidates more graphically on their personal qualities and on their stands on issues than it does on their party affiliation. And candidates have used and will continue to use advertising to run against the party organization's choice in a primary.

However, television advertising has provided candidates with a strong vehicle to deliver a message in areas where their party's organization is weak. Furthermore, political parties have used generic advertising in this decade to try to influence the climate of public opinion. In 1980 the national Republican Party enjoyed success with its "Vote Republican for a Change" campaign.

The political bosses who once wielded great power in elections have become all but extinct. Their demise coincided with the rise of independent political media consultants, who usually work for the candidates of one party and understand politics and advertising.

Some journalists have represented the better-known consultants as crafty manipulators of public opinion, and undiscerning critics seized upon Joe McGinniss's *The Selling of the President 1968* as providing confirmation of their belief that candidates could be packaged and sold to a naive American public. Yet McGinniss wrote an insider's book about the advertising campaign designed to make former Vice President Richard Nixon (R) a more appealing candidate and concluded that the effort "collapsed beneath the weight of Nixon's grayness." Vice President Hubert Humphrey, a naturally outgoing candidate, ran a less noticeably slick advertising campaign that showed him to be a warm and open politician.

Nixon survived a fast Humphrey close, but the lesson learned was that the candidate's true personality and abilities cannot be disguised for long by advertising. The news media's coverage of the candidate represents an independent variable that can limit the influence of advertising. Furthermore, an opponent is likely to be waging his or her own television campaign that can challenge the candidate's claims. A candidate's slick advertising may mask incompetence, but once in office the candidate must perform up to the voters' expectations or else face defeat at the polls.

Negative television advertising has frequently been employed by political campaigns, and new production techniques allow a candidate to answer an attack spot quickly with a commercial that contains a counchargearge. Consultants argue that such tactics are the equivalent of debates and thus inform voters about issues. Voters, the consultants say, may cite disapproval of negative appeals when asked by pollsters but tend to take the information they learn from attack spots into account when deciding how to cast their vote. Critics of negative advertising maintain that such tactics have only deepened the public's cynicism about politicians and the electoral process.

Yet negative appeals have frequently played a prominent role in American politics. For instance, even before television was invented the Democrats mounted a public relations offensive against President Herbert Hoover and his inability to cope with the Depression.

Earlier in this century, the party bosses and their patronage-based politics still had clout despite the efforts of reformers. But, as media consultant Charles Guggenheim has astutely pointed out, the problems of organizational politics have been "traded off" and replaced by the perplexing questions that television advertising and media politics pose to the students of the democratic process.

*See also:* Dwight D. Eisenhower, Charles Guggenheim, Herbert Hoover, Hubert H. Humphrey, Negative Advertising, Richard M. Nixon

*Steve Lilienthal*

REFERENCES

Diamond, Edwin, and Stephen Bates. 1984. *The Spot: The Rise of Political Advertising.* Cambridge: MIT Pr.

McGinniss, Joe. 1968. *The Selling of the President 1968.* New York: Trident.

## Temperance and Prohibition

What exactly are the differences between temperance and prohibition? According to Norman Clark, "Temperance became a social movement in American history when large numbers of citizens began to urge an individual discipline—usually the avoidance of ardent spirits—to protect individual health and family well-being. Prohibition, on the other hand, became a social and political movement when large numbers of voters began to demand that the collective disciplines of the state and federal government be employed to halt the traffic in all intoxicating beverages." And there rests the difference. As a social movement, temperance was a matter of individual conscience. As a political movement, prohibition meant the intervention of the government (whether local, state, or national) in order to save the individual from his own weaknesses.

Fully understanding the problem involves the context of its time and this country. The use of alcoholic beverages in early America was widespread, accepted, and even expected. Alcohol had many benefits on the frontier that might not seem evident within another period of history. One of its advantages was that "liquid lightning" was more easily transported than the raw materials that composed it. One of the first threats to our young republic was the so-called "Whiskey Rebellion" when farmers staged more than a lively protest over the high federal excise tax on whiskey, much as there had been on tea in Boston Harbor some two decades earlier. While tea has taken its place in history, whiskey and other alcoholic beverages have continued to be a social problem and a political issue. This is not because there was no representation involved in the taxation of alcoholic beverages but rather its consumption remained a major economic, social, and moral problem— a problem that eventually became a political issue.

The social problem led to reaction. Granted, local laws usually punished excesses, but this legal severity did not stop intemperance from being seen both at home and abroad as a kind of American national curse. The evil seemed obvious to any who would observe and, at first, so did the solution. Temperance was an individual decision, perhaps reinforced by community, family, or peer pressure, but nonetheless, temperance was a decision enforced by conscience rather than by the authority of the government. While the Temperance movement became increasingly popular during the period both before and immediately after the American Civil War, it laid the foundations for its own successor, the Prohibition movement. For example, President Rutherford B. Hayes was a member of the Sons of Temperance and while President, his wife was known as "Lemonade Lucy" for refusing to serve intoxicating beverages in the White House. Yet Hayes, as with many early temperance men, opposed prohibition.

Beginning in localities, prohibition spread to include entire states and finally, the nation. Its logic was inescapable. As long as intoxicating beverages were available across the adjacent local/county/state/national boundary, the experiment would fail. The primary insurance of prohibition's success was to be certain that booze was not available merely by crossing a political boundary. The fact that alcohol was accessible either by smuggling or illegal manufacture within political borders would eventually kill prohibition.

It was not just the consumption of alcohol that the prohibitionists tried to stop. After all, consumption as such was not illegal. It was the public consumption in a saloon that the prohibitionist sought to ban. It was the saloon and its attendant evils that so outraged many temperance leaders that prohibition became favored, and its goal was not so much to dry up America as to close down the saloon. It was no accident that the leading organization promoting prohibition was the Anti-Saloon League. The League was aided by a number of favorable circumstances including the general skill with which its leaders operated in the political arena and the self-defeating tactics of their opposition. If the saloon was beyond redemption, then its political supporters were just as inept and ineffective. Guided by unenlightened perceptions of the most narrow of self-interests, the saloon and alcoholic beverage industry did almost as much harm to their own cause as did their opponents.

Much has been written about the successful pressure politics that led to the Eighteenth Amendment making the United States a dry country. Odegard is still cited in scholarly literature and quoted concerning the development and powers of special interests. Less has been written about the Prohibition Party. From 1884 through 1896, the Prohibition Party might have held the balance of power had our Presidents been selected by popular rather than electoral vote. During this period the Prohibition Party never received fewer than 150,000 votes, a considerable number in a close race when one considers the total popular vote cast for President was usually fewer than 15 million. In 1888 the Prohibition Party managed to come in third, with the Union Labor Party in fourth place. This diffusion was partially the problem of the Prohibition Party during this era. The electoral field featured other minor parties and, with the exception of 1888, the dry forces usually came in fourth behind the Greenback Party, or the People's Party or the National Democrats (not to be confused with the regular Democratic Party that ran William Jennings Bryan in that election). The Prohibition Party, nevertheless, has nominated a presidential candidate in every presidential election since 1872, and it is the minor political party with the longest life in American history despite the fact it never won a single electoral vote. Organized in 1869, it has remained a steady if now-declining feature of American partisan politics.

If nothing else, the history of the Prohibition Party demonstrates the superior strategy of interest group versus partisan politics when dealing with a single issue rather than a coalition or collection of positions. Interest group politics infiltrated and effectively gained influence in both major parties regarding prohibition. It was an issue that seemed to rise above mere partisanship, something that made it attractive to reformers and do-gooders. Even so, the Republican Party seemed to be the favorite of the prohibitionists and vice versa while the Democrats were (at least once) called the party of "Rum, Romanism and Rebellion."

This image of progress and reform was one that followed the movement up until the actual imposition of prohibition. Before the Civil War temperance was associated with abolitionism and other reform movements. As Timberlake has demonstrated, the prohibitionist urge was part of the progressive movement in America, including the call for women's suffrage, free coinage of silver, direct election of the President and U.S. Senators, and the initiative and referendum. After the Civil War, those who did not dare to advocate the vote for themselves felt free to campaign for prohibition. From Carry Nation to Frances E. Willard, the temperance/prohibition campaign had the strong involvement and support of women. Again, Carry Nation only attacked the open saloon that provided alcoholic beverages in defiance of the law. Also, it was not a coincidence that one of the strongest dry organizations was the Woman's Christian Temperance Union. Feminism and sobriety became fused in an interlocking social movement.

However, the prohibition movement had its dark side. In the North and Midwest it was also part of the nativist movement—anti-immigrant, anti-Catholic, and anti-urban. In the South, part of its appeal was anti-Black—a method of controlling the Black population under the guise of protecting whites. Thus, while claiming to reflect some of the most reform-minded aspects of the progressive movement, the prohibition movement also produced some of the less desirable effects of populism. And, should anyone forget, despite its goals, its methods (as practiced by the Anti-Saloon League) were at least as corrupt and devious as those of its opponents. Finally, a major result of the movement's success in legally requiring the American citizen to abstain from public purchase of alcoholic beverage was the rise of organized crime.

*See also:* Anti-Saloon League, William Jennings Bryan, Greenback Party, Rutherford B. Hayes, People's Party, Populism, Prohibition Party, Third Parties in American Elections

*Thomas H. Clapper*

REFERENCES

Asbury, Herbert. 1950. *The Great Illusion: An Informal History of Prohibition.* Garden City, NY: Doubleday.

Cashman, Sean Dennis. 1981. *Prohibition: The Lie of the Land.* New York: Free Press.

Clark, Norman H. 1984. "Prohibition and Temperance." In Jack P. Greene, ed. *Encyclopedia of American Political History.* New York: Scribner's.

Franklin, Jimmie Lewis. 1971. *Born Sober: Prohibition in Oklahoma, 1907–1959.* Norman: U. of Oklahoma Pr.

Furnas, J. C. 1965. *The Life and Times of the Late Demon Rum.* New York: Capricorn Books.

Gusfield, Joseph R. 1963. *Symbolic Crusade: Status Politics and the American Temperance Movement.* Urbana: U. of Illinois Pr.

Kleppner, Paul. 1973. "The Greenback and Prohibitionist Party." In Arthur M. Schlesinger, Jr., ed. *History of U.S. Political Parties, 1860–1910: The Gilded Age of Politics.* New York: Chelsea House.

Kobler, John Allen. 1973. *Ardent Spirits: The Rise and Fall of Prohibition.* New York: Putnam's.

Lender, Mark Edward. 1984. *Dictionary of American Temperance Biography: From Temperance Reform to Alcohol Research, the 1600s to the 1980s.* Westport, CT: Greenwood.

Mertz, Charles. 1931. *The Dry Decade.* New York: Doubleday, Doran.

Odegard, Peter H. 1928. *Pressure Politics: The Story of the Anti-Saloon League.* New York: Columbia U. Pr.

Sinclair, Andrew. 1962. *Prohibition: The Era of Excess.* Boston: Little, Brown.

Timberlake, James H. 1963. *Prohibition and the Progressive Movement, 1900–1920.* Cambridge: Harvard U. Pr.

Tyrrell, Ian R. 1979. *Sobering Up: From Temperance to Prohibition in Antebellum America, 1800–1860.* Westport, CT: Greenwood.

## Third Parties in American Elections

Few subjects so excite the passions of political activists and scholars alike as political parties and candidates for the presidency who contend outside the structure of the two major parties through third parties. They have long been considered spoilers, reactionary, vengeful, destabilizing, and even—in the heyday of anti-socialism and anti-communism—treasonous. Third parties are bent only on undoing the delicate balance of basic American political institutions and its pragmatic approach to politics, it is argued. By drawing away votes from the major parties, they may prevent the election of a President by a true majority, not to mention the mischief they can cause in the Electoral College in a close presidential contest. They introduce foreign ideas and receive publicity in an election in far greater proportion than their numbers and ideas justify.

Those who look not at the personalities involved or specific third-party beliefs—which by conventional standards of their day can seem quite radical indeed, from antislavery in the mid-nineteenth century, to communism in the early twentieth century, to segregation in the late 1960s—see them in a different light. The dominant view among political scientists is that third parties function in the American electoral arena to vent those minority views that cannot find a home in consensus and compromise-oriented major parties. Sometimes these views appeal to only a tiny segment of society or are short-lived. At other times they eventually move center stage in society. Yet in a nation that prides itself on the free exchange of ideas, as unpalatable as that often may be, third parties keep alive the exchange of ideas in the all-important electoral arena. They may prick the conscience, provoke debate on sensitive topics, and raise heretical thoughts, but by doing so they compel public debate. In times of transition, they also serve as "stepping-stones" as blocs of voters move from one to the other of the major parties over the course of two or more elections. Contrary to their stereotype, on a couple of occasions they have even occupied the center (John Anderson in 1980, the Constitutional Union Party of 1860) rather than the extremes of the political spectrum.

In enumerating the fundamental conditions of a democratic society, political theorists include the right to vote, the right of free expression, the right of political association, and the right to compete freely and equitably for elective office—that is, the right to run for office and/or form any number of third political parties. This last is at the core of the pluralist view of democracy and the cornerstone of the American political thought so well articulated by James Madison. Only with each of these rights in place can the views of the electorate meaningfully be translated into public policy, the heart of the representative democratic process. Giovanni Satori goes so far as to say that the willingness of a society to tolerate even the most "anti-system" parties is a litmus test of its political strength, its stability, and its commitment to democracy.

Less on principle than on pragmatic grounds, third parties can be viewed as the safety valve of the American electoral process. Without the opportunity to vent their hostility, anger, or extreme beliefs within the electoral arena, third-party supporters might, on the one hand, invade and undermine one of the major parties, or on the other, take their causes underground as clandestine and extralegal movements. This argument, of course, turns on its head the more conventional view that third parties are *destabilizing* because they bring to the surface issues that cannot readily be addressed within the political arena. Instead, the safety valvers assert that it is better to air views about racism, nuclear power, class conflicts, or whatever else within the electoral arena, than to suppress them and channel the energies of their advocates into even more destructive activities outside of it.

The debate over third parties thus touches some of the more sensitive nerves of the American electoral system on who can participate in the electoral arena and by what means, and their fate hinges on how the competing views are balanced. As will be seen, in practice, pure democratic theory has not proved compelling in American politics, though in recent years some of the legal constraints on third parties established over the course of the twentieth century have been lifted. Since the beginning of the Republic, third parties have not been placed on anything near equal footing with the two dominant parties, but neither have they been unequivocally prohibited. It is fair to say, viewed across the 200-year American experiment in democratic elections, that third parties have neither realized their theoretical potential as channels of access and power for minorities and dissident groups nor wreaked the havoc to the political process so feared by many.

Most contemporary scholars favor a broader role for third parties in the American electoral arena, though one far short of a European type multiparty system. While their influence can great and varied, evidence of third parties undermining the electoral process simply does not exist. This scholarly consensus flows also from the commitment of political scientists to a more open electoral process, one in keeping with broad democratic principles. As a rule, therefore, they would shift the burden of proof to those who would seek to curtail third-party activity.

Finally, a rich case study literature on American third parties is growing, with virtually every third party chronicled: Joseph G. Rayback, *Free Soil: The Election of 1848* (1970); John D. Hicks, *The Populist Revolt: A History of the Farmers' Alliance and the People's Party* (1961); James Weinstein, *The Decline of Socialism in America, 1912–1925* (1969); Jody Carlson, *George C. Wallace and the Politics of Powerlessness* (1981), and many, many more. While these are fascinating in detail and provide a rich and colorful history, the purpose here is to sketch out broad themes and the implications of third parties for the electoral process in general.

### Third Parties in a Two-Party System

Much can be said for studying the crags and crannies of the moon up close. Yet to know the moon in its fullness requires understanding it in relation to the earth, the sun, and the solar system. Likewise, much can be learned by examining third parties in their own right, but a full appreciation necessitates an understanding of their position within America's two-party electoral system—a system that is the product of the constitutional framework, the institutional arrangements of elections as they have evolved over time, and the fundamental values and beliefs of Americans.

*Fundamental Values.* Some American historians argue that political conflict in the United States has seldom been waged over irreconcilable class, religious, ethnic, or like conflicts. For 200 years, few disagreements have been allowed to escalate into fundamental challenges to the Constitution, the governmental framework, the regulated but largely free-enterprise market economy, and the patterns of social status. Instead, politics is most often concerned with divisions over secondary issues that are susceptible to negotiation and compromise, thus allowing diverse voters to come together in America's characteristically large, coalitional major political parties. This has been possible, according to Louis Hartz in his classic *The Liberal Tradition in America*, both because America never experienced the permanent divisiveness of the feudal structure and religious cleavages of older European societies and because the United States formed around a shared set of egalitarian beliefs and constitutional principles. Politics, then, has been more of a give-and-take affair over the moderate middle ground. This moderation has been not only a virtue of the American experience, according to Herbert Agar, but also "the price of union."

When divisive political issues have arisen, they have fitted into a natural dualism and thus into two competing parties. The effect over time has been to reinforce the strong cultural belief in the naturalness and appropriateness of the two sides of an issue and a two-party approach to politics. This thesis, maintained by the eminent political scientist V. O. Key, Jr., is given support in initial division over the adoption of the Constitution, followed by the Federalist-Jeffersonian alignment throughout the formative stages of the party system. In turn came the split between North and South in the mid-nineteenth century, and then later and into the twentieth century it was reflected in urban-rural, labor-management, social class, and most recently Sunbelt-Frostbelt divisions.

Once patterns of politics and expectations are established they are hard to refashion, clearly the case with two-partyism. A new party invariably has difficulty overcoming well-established party attachments and voting habits and the built-in edge that this political tradition gives candidates of the major parties.

*Institutional Arrangements.* Most political scientists today believe that this system might change if the institutional arrangements of the electoral system did not channel candidates and voters into a two-party alignment. The central element in two-partyism is the winner-take-all arrangement in the electoral arena. Awarding office to the candidate with the most votes (by plurality) in a geographically based electoral district—that is, within a single-member district—assures that only one can be the victor. Thus those who coalesce into a majority-seeking party coalition to gain victory are "rewarded," while those who fail to do so are "penalized." Compared to European proportional systems of elections, which awards elective offices according to the proportion of popular vote received by a party in the general election, evidence shows that single-member districts are heavily biased against third parties.

This effect has given rise to the oft-heard and popular campaign appeal by major parties that to vote for a third party is to "waste" one's vote; without much chance of winning a majority of the votes, the third party inevitably comes up empty-handed. This axiom is usually accompanied by the dire warning that for a voter to cast his or her ballot for the third-party candidate, and by doing so denying it to the majority party closest to the voter's sympathies, could possibly enable the least preferred candidate to win the election. In the significant third-party efforts of both 1968 and 1980, where good survey data is available on the preferences of voters before the election and then their actual vote, ample evidence reveals that the wasted vote argument was used quite effectively by the major parties against third-party contenders: the Republicans against George Wallace in 1968, and the Democrats against John Anderson in 1980.

No reason necessitates the fact that the two coalitional parties that would evolve within each of many single-member districts spread across the United States—for instance, within each of the 50 states—would take on the same party labels and work together nationally, but they do. This cooperation results from the need to form national party coalitions in competition for the presidency and the control of Congress. Taken together, single-member districts and the elections for the President and Congress are the most important institutional factors in channeling competition into two major-party coalitions.

*Direct Primaries.* The system of direct primaries within the Democratic and Republican parties developed first during the early-twentieth-century Progressive era and, revitalized over the past two decades, helps maintain the two-party monopoly. Primaries were introduced to enable dissenters and challengers to reigning party leaders who might otherwise leave the party to express themselves through intraparty electoral contests. The theoretical rationale was that party primaries made for a more open, democratic, and participatory internal party processes. Pragmatic thinking was that follow-ing the primary contests all the members of the party could be called on to unite behind the majority's choice of a candidate in facing the common enemy (the other major party) in the general election.

*Access to the Ballot.* Clearly major cultural and institutional reasons have contributed to the formation and perpetuation of a two-party system. Other, equally important, though not as encompassing features of the electoral system, whatever their intended purpose, have served to severely discourage third parties. The most obvious are the rules governing access to the ballot.

If election laws banned access to the ballot to all but the Democratic and Republican parties, their partisan bias would be obvious, and their repeal would probably become a burning constitutional issue. Historians cite no evidence that maintenance of the two reigning parties has been their sole aim. Rather, ballot laws were initiated either to eliminate the widespread corrupt election practices of the late nineteenth and early twentieth centuries and to keep voter choice to a reasonable number. Not only would a long list of candidates cause confusion, but also elections could then be won by very small pluralities of votes—a rather undemocratic outcome. Thus, various filing dates, petitions, and so forth are placed in the path of all contenders for public office in each of the 50 states. Those placed before new and third parties, however, are usually much more severe than those before the two major parties.

Government officials do have an obligation to keep the number of contenders within tolerable limits. But what is tolerable? Are three, four, a dozen or more candidates acceptable, or is it in the public interest to limit the number to two? Moreover, to what extent are constitutional rights jeopardized when, as has often been the case, election laws place extraordinary burdens in the paths of third parties?

Historically government had little to do with administering elections and thus affecting the number of party contenders. Before the Civil War, elections were largely left to the political parties themselves. Any group that wanted to compete for office could do so by printing and distributing its own ballot. The growth of corrupt political machines after the war and rise of a professional middle class in the United States precipitated widespread demand for nonpartisan and publicly administered elections. The response was an almost complete conversion to the secret ballot in the decade of the 1890s—copied from the Australians—with elections conducted and regulated by public officials in each of the states. Adoption of the Australian ballot was a major step in eliminating election fraud, voter intimidation, and ballot-box stuffing. But the change had its downside since those in government were also partisans of the Democratic and Republican parties, and these officials have often appeared to use their authority to curb all but their own cohort under the guise of protecting the electoral system.

*The Pendulum Swings.* Under the early forms of the Australian ballot, third parties could qualify for a position with relative ease. In reaction to the "Bull Moose" Party of Teddy Roosevelt in 1912, a faction that bolted from the Republicans only after Roosevelt did not win his party's nomination, and the rise of Socialist and labor parties in the teens and early 1920s, numerous ballot regulations sought to hinder all third parties. The change was so dramatic that by 1924 the Progressive Party of that year, headed by Robert La Follette, found state ballot laws "almost insuperable obstacles to a new party." The Progressives were frustrated by being denied the use of a single party label across all the states—in California it was forced to appear under the Socialist column—sometimes facing extensive petition and registration requirements, and, in Ohio, being denied party poll watchers at election booths.

In reaction to the spread of socialism and communism abroad and then again after World War II, in the late 1930s and 1940s states adopted loyalty oath requirements for candidates, banned any party that "advocated the overthrow of government by force of violence" (i.e., the Communist Party), and harassed and restricted most all parties on the left. Some even tried to prevent Henry Wallace and his Progressive Party from getting on the ballot in 1948 because of his alleged Communist sympathies. In addition to all the usual problems of ballot access, the most troubling for Henry Wallace—given his late start—was the various early filing deadlines. California required third parties to declare themselves in March and 14 other states by July 1, before either of the major parties had decided upon their candidates. The States' Right Party of 1948, the southern anti-integration wing of the Democratic Party, ran into comparable trouble attempting to get on the ballot in the southern states.

Little had changed by the time the American Independent Party, led by George Wallace, burst upon the scene in 1968. Third parties could get on the ballot through petition in three-quarters of the states, but in many the deadlines remained early and/or the number of supporting signatures required was high. Sixty percent of the states still had on their books rules barring Communist or subversive parties. After securing 3 million signatures—a number equal to 4 percent of the votes cast in the general election of 1968—running under six different party labels, and waging several major court challenges, Wallace's AIP did eventually get on the ballots of all 50 states, though that success required a substantial drain on its resources.

Nineteen sixty-eight signaled a major turning point for the legal standing of third parties. In the case of *Williams v. Rhodes*, for the first time the Supreme Court took the position that third parties had First Amendment protections of speech and association and that the states, despite their responsibility for conducting elections, could not do so to the exclusion of third parties. In striking down Ohio's ballot law, the Court argued that the goal of structuring elections so as to produce a majority victory must be balanced against the rights of third parties to contest elections. In light of this and the other court victories achieved by the AIP, Frank Sorauf, one of the most highly respected observers of American political parties, was able to assert that "the Wallace campaign of 1968 can be viewed as a triumph over virtually all the obstacles that state laws place in the way of minor parties."

While the constitutional principal established by *Rhodes* is eminently important for third parties, opinion on its effect remains divided. To begin with, despite several rulings since, the Court has refused to specify in concrete terms the balance between the states' "compelling interest" in placing restrictions in the path of third parties and the constitutional rights of those parties. Moreover, in practice, many obstacles remain. In considering the experience of the most recent significant third-party effort, that by John Anderson in 1980, Frank Smallwood sees ballot access as still a major hurdle. While Anderson eventually got on the ballot of all the states and the District of Columbia, approximately a million petition signatures had to be gathered—from a low of 155 in Washington to over 100,000 in California—with substantially different rules and formulas from one state to the next, draining enormous time and energy away from the campaign. Thus, while it is clear that the Court has come down squarely against a two-party monopoly, how accessible the ballot must be remains vague.

*Campaign Finance.* All third parties believe that they have been woefully underfunded in their bid for office. This inference may be accurate, but it is also a truism of politics for nearly all candidates running for almost every public office in the land. More appropriately, the relevant issue is whether third parties are underfunded relative to the major party contenders. Though precise records have been maintained only in recent years, the best estimates of campaign expenditures since the turn of the century suggest a mixed picture. The Bull Moose Party of 1912 stands out as the best funded among third parties, with campaign expenditures equal to 60 percent of the average of the two major parties; for the Progressives of 1948 it was 47 percent; for the AIP in 1968, 39 percent; and for John Anderson in 1980, 49 percent. Most of the third parties on the left and all the smaller minor parties have not done nearly so well. For example, the Socialist Party, at its height in 1908, had expenditures equal to only 8 percent of the major parties, and for the Progressives of 1924 it was only 9 percent.

The disparity with the majors has meant that third parties have never been able to field the kind of national campaign organization—and today, media-oriented campaign—comparable to the Democrats and Republicans. This feature should not come as a surprise given the much longer time the major parties have had to cultivate funding sources. Moreover, just as many Americans are hesitant to vote for third parties for fear of wasting their vote, so too are they hesitant to contribute to parties that really do not stand a chance of winning.

A more serious matter in an age of publicly funded major party presidential elections is that third parties are now very much at a disadvantage not simply because of their inherent difficulties in raising money but because of their unequal treatment under federal law. In reaction to years of escalating campaign costs and finally the fundraising scandals surrounding the Richard Nixon campaign of 1972, Congress finally acted. In adopting the Federal Election Campaign Act of 1974, Congress said in effect to presidential candidates of the two major parties, forswear private sources of funding and all the appearances of conflict of interest this

entails and the federal government will provide full campaign funding as well as underwrite your national party convention. The same law provides no up-front money for third parties unless they have demonstrated significant vote-getting ability in the previous presidential election or after they have received more than 5 percent of the popular vote.

The effect of the law on third parties was evident in 1980, when in addition to the half-dozen or so very small parties that contest every election, both John Anderson (as Independent) and Ed Clark (as Libertarian) ran substantial third-party campaigns. Like all candidates, under the new law they were prohibited from accepting large contributions (more than $1,000 from individuals and $5,000 from organized committees), but they were denied the large infusion of public monies to off set this constraint awarded during the campaign to the major parties. While they spent much of their time soliciting contributions, the major party contenders were campaigning. Although Anderson did qualify for $4.2 million in retroactive federal funds after receiving 6.6 percent of the popular vote, the money did him little good after the votes were counted. Clark, who raised over $3 million on his own and received a little more than 1 percent of the popular vote, received no federal funds at all. Frank Smallwood's interviews with all the third-party contenders in 1980 and his analysis of the election shows clearly that the law places the federal government in the position of financially underwriting the two-party monopoly of American politics while offering virtually nothing to third parties.

### Theories of Third-Party Voting

What makes third parties so fascinating to scholars is that by all rights they should not appear, let alone attract any significant proportion of votes. Yet they have in one in five presidential elections: 8 percent of the popular presidential vote for the Antimason Party in 1832, 10 percent for the Free Soilers in 1848, 21 percent for the American Party in 1856, 13 percent for the Constitutional Union Party and 18 percent for the Breckinridge (southern) Democrats in 1860, 8.5 percent for the Populists in 1892, 27 percent for Teddy Roosevelt's Bull Moose Party and 6 percent for the Socialists in 1912, 16.5 percent for the Progressives of 1924, 13.5 percent for the American Independent Party in 1968, and 6.5 percent for John Anderson in 1980.

### Single-Factor Theories

*Economic Depression.* A single factor, the depression stage of the economic cycle, has often been described as the crucial cause of third parties. The groups affected first and most acutely, the less prosperous yet politically sensitive farmers and industrial workers, flock to the protest banners of parties like the Populists, Progressives, and Laborites. This thesis is born out by Rosenstone, Behr, and Lazarus's recent empirical analysis, which shows that economic conditions of the agricultural sector correlate with third party voting, especially in the late nineteenth century. As the economy plummets into a depression and hardship spreads widely, one or both of the major parties shift attention to economic issues and propose remedial action. Hence, the argument goes, following the initial thrust of third parties, major parties undermine their cause.

But several of the third parties that emerged before the late-nineteenth-century era of rapid industrial growth defy such generalization. It is equally difficult to explain the significant third-party drives of the post-World War II era solely or mainly as responses to performance of the economy. In effect, the economic protests thesis is helpful but of limited use in developing an overall pattern of third parties, particularly those that have emerged out of intense social, racial, and foreign policy controversies.

*Political Ambition.* Third parties are often described as largely the product of major-party politicians whose ambitions are thwarted. And in actuality the third-party efforts that have received the greatest number of popular votes were all led by major-party politicians prominent at the state or national level before their third-party bid. The 1924 Progressive candidate, Senator Robert M. La Follette, for example, had been a leader of the reform wing of the Republican Party in Wisconsin and nationally for two decades before his third-party campaign. Similarly, George Wallace served as the Democratic governor of Alabama before and after his third-party candidacy in 1968. John Anderson was a Republican Congressman from Illinois for two decades before leading the independent National Unity campaign in 1980; likewise his running mate for Vice President, Patrick Lucey, was a respected Democrat and former Wisconsin governor. Moreover, three of the most promi-

nent third-party contenders—Martin Van Buren in 1848, Millard Fillmore in 1856, and Theodore Roosevelt in 1912—had formerly been President of the United States under the banner of one of the major parties. A clear relationship exists between having a nationally prestigious candidate at the head of the ticket and a significant third-party vote.

To find that third parties do best with nationally known political figures at the head of the ticket, however, only begs the question of when and why such figures bolt from the major parties. Ambition alone seems an insufficient answer. Politicians of ambition and fame can always be found within the major parties, with many anxiously awaiting the chance to serve as standard-bearer of one of the major parties. Few end up being called, and the great number of ambitious politicians who hold positions of statewide and national leadership might well create many significant third parties in every election if personal ambition is the crucial factor involved. Likewise, if ambition is the key, why did Henry Wallace fail to generate widespread voter support in 1948? As Vice President under Franklin Roosevelt and as Cabinet officer under two Presidents, Wallace was widely known and had demonstrated his drive for high office. Moreover, he championed the cause of farmers and industrial workers, the two constituencies that most often have supported third parties; these voters could easily have given him more than his 2.4 percent of the popular vote.

The personal ambition of leaders is surely an important element in the composition of third parties. Without a candidate and an army of dedicated workers, third-party votes would never materialize. Successful third-party efforts, however, appear to depend on conditions beyond the leader's control. Hence, the zeal of a man like George Wallace would have been of little consequence without the expanding civil rights movement and racial divisiveness of the 1960s.

*Steppingstones.* Sweeping realignments within the two-party system, precipitated by social and political upheavals that render old party alliances untenable, provide fertile ground for third parties. As the literature on party realignments makes clear, on those rare instances when new issues are imposed on the political agenda, they can severely disrupt the traditional major-party coalitions. Disaffected groups, while prepared to break from their old party coalition, nevertheless are hesitant to coalesce with their longstanding adversaries in the other major party and thus are open to appeal from other quarters. Proponents of the realignment thesis understand the appearance of third parties as a response to the need of these disaffected transitional groups. Usually after one election has passed, the alternate major party actively courts the disaffected group and wins its confidence, spelling doom for the third party.

In the 1960s when the United States was undergoing unprecedented social and political upheavals, some observers saw a realignment of forces between the major parties. The American Independent Party was therefore interpreted as the refuge in the realignment shuffle of conservative Democrats, particularly in the South, en route to an ultimate merger with the Republican Party. Likewise, the Free Soil Party of 1848 and several third parties of the 1850s can be seen as steppingstones for groups alienated from one of the major parties during that major period of realignment.

Another opportunity for third parties during the realignment process can come about because of disillusionment and disaffection with both of the major parties as an alignment system unravels, should the major parties fail to reform around one or more new issues and win the strong loyalty of the voters. The general disaffection from both major parties following the demise of the New Deal coalition in the 1960s continuing throughout the 1970s, combined with dissatisfaction by groups within both major party 1980 candidates, appears to have provided the opening for John Anderson's National Unity campaign. Anderson wed the social welfare and civil rights posture of the Democrats with the deregulation and market economy of the Republicans into a hybrid middle course—a juxtaposition of positions that appealed to middle-class voters of 1980 but one that was impossible, given their traditional stands, for either of the major parties to embrace.

These examples suggest the importance of the realignment process to understanding the rise of third-party voting. The elections of 1912 and 1924 on the other hand, saw significant third parties that arose when no fundamental realignment was underway. Conversely, the most far-reaching realignment of the twentieth century—the reshuffling of loyalties that formed the New Deal era—failed to produce significant third-party voting. Like the depression and political ambition theories, then, realignments provide insight to some third parties but are only a partial explanation. Each may be necessary, but by itself each is insufficient.

### Spatial Voting Theory

Building on these approaches, contemporary scholars have developed a theory of third-party voting lodged not so much in the specifics of social and political events or political ambitions per se, but on how certain events create abnormal distributions of voter preferences and how, in turn, the major parties respond by either incorporating them or leaving the field open to third parties. Significant third-party voting can best be understood, in other words, only in light of abnormalities in the operating of the two-party system.

In normal times and working within the framework of the two-party monopoly, a number of political groups are all attempting to become part of a winning major-party coalition. Given the need to gather a majority of voters in the context of diverse interests, the most viable strategy for major party candidates, as Downs has argued, is to move to the center on issues, rather than appealing to the extremes. If it is to succeed, E. E. Schattschneider believes, a major party "must be supported by a great variety of interests sufficiently tolerant of each other to collaborate, held together by compromise and concession, and the discovery of certain common interests." Its managers must realize that they "need not," or more appropriately cannot, "meet every demand by every interest." Under certain circumstances, however, moving to the center may not be the best strategy. To do so makes sense only when opinions are arrayed in a normal bell-shaped distribution or when they are almost equally distributed. For example, given two parties, $A$ and $B$, and a bell-shaped distribution of opinion on an issue as depicted in Figure 1, competition for the most voters compels both parties to seek the middle ground or point $AB$. Given this logic, the major parties are seen as nothing more than Tweedledum and Tweedledee on most issues. If candidate $A$, for instance, were to take position $A1$, then candidate $B$ would be free to take position $B1$, and under the assumption that voters will support the party closest to themselves, $B$ can expect to win with the votes of well over a majority of the electorate. Thus, under most circumstances, fighting for the center is the only viable strategy for both major parties.

## Figure 1

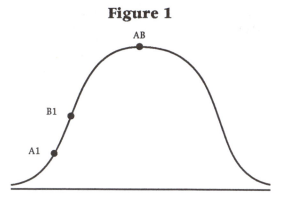

The same is true when opinions are more or less equally divided as shown in Figure 2. Any move away from the center by one party leaves an opportunity to fill the void between itself and the first party, thus winning the support of a majority of voters.

## Figure 2

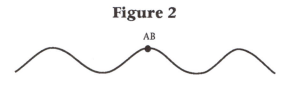

These two customary patterns of public opinion can be accommodated within the framework of two-party politics. The split in public opinion that occurs when views on fundamental issues polarize is not so easily resolved. With voters solidifying into two fairly equal and distinctive camps, moderation is replaced by conflict and confrontation. In these instances of intense political crisis the two parties, Robert Dahl believes, "each striving to retain the support of the extremists on its flanks, will only exacerbate a conflict."

In this context the existing political parties must either change their strategies or lose ground to new and more aggressive parties; the fence straddlers, mollifiers, and compromisers invariably lose to dogmatic, aggressive zealots. That is, neither major party can afford to take the center position, *AB*. If both major parties opt for the same side of the issue as is depicted in Figure 3, they risk leaving the opposing view, one that appeals to roughly half of the electorate, to a third party to exploit. If the divisive issue dominates the election, then the third party would be an almost certain winner in a

three-party contest. Each major party can therefore be expected to move to the side of the issue most compatible with its traditional leaning, becoming an avid champion rather than a middle-of-the-roader. For example, if the electorate split into two fairly equal groups on a divisive economic issue, as for example during the New Deal, the Democratic Party can be expected to shift to a more liberal position, say, to *B1*, and the Republicans to a more conservative stance, *A1*. In this case politics would probably not remain low-keyed, moderate, or compromise-oriented, but, nonetheless, the contest could be expected to remain two-party.

## Figure 3

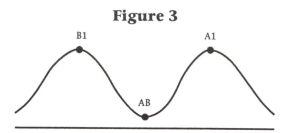

A variation on the bipolar distribution that provides an opening for third parties is a largely bipolar split with a notable number of voters left in the middle. With both major parties moving to the extremes to hold on to their largest constituencies, the opportunity arises for a third party to claim the center ground. Though this situation has seldom occurred in practice, it does fit the case of the success of the Constitutional Union Party just before the Civil War.

Finally, when a vast majority of the electorate is at one extreme and an intense minority at the other, the major parties are again unable to take the centrist position, *AB* (see Figure 4). The presence of intense conflict demands that the parties choose sides. But when a large majority of the electorate falls to one side of the issue, neither major party is likely to champion the opposite view. Thus the two compete for the

## Figure 4

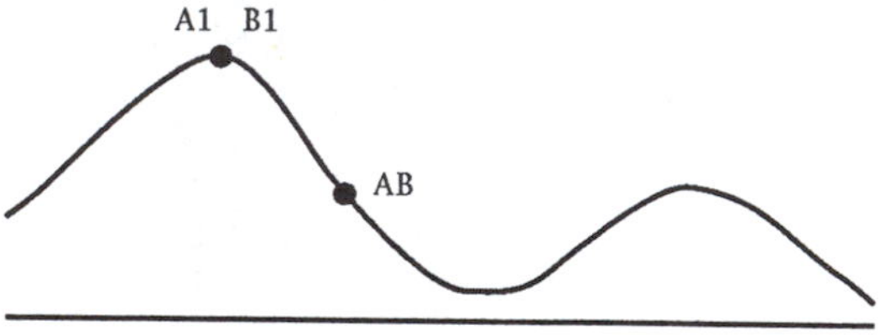

votes of the vast majority, seeking the middle range of the majority side of the conflict (position *A1B1*, Figure 4). In this situation a third party quite logically emerges to champion the intense and estranged minority as did the American Independent Party in 1968, Populists in 1892, and Free Soilers in 1848.

In sum, at least three conditions are necessary for a significant third party to emerge in a presidential election in the American two-party system. Most important is a departure from the usual bell-shaped or evenly spread distribution of public opinion on the major issues of the day. This deviation usually occurs in a period of intense social and political controversy that results in an estranged minority separated from the much larger majority opinion, such as in 1832, 1848, 1892, 1912 (especially with respect to the Socialist vote), 1924, and 1968. A modified bipolar distribution of opinion can also open the way for a centrists' third party such as with the Constitutional Unionists of 1860 or possibly even the vote for John Anderson in 1980, but this centrism has not often occurred. Second, the minority position must be either rejected or shunned by both major parties, alienating the minority. Finally, a politician or political group willing to exploit the situation by initiating a new party must step forward.

Moreover, the conditions appear to be cumulative; each is necessary for the next to operate. Except in a period of social and political crisis or the turmoil that can occur during a realignment of the major parties, politically active minorities are usually absorbed by the major parties. And, if the major parties take opposite positions on controversial issues, little leeway remains for a third party. Lastly, lacking an intense minority abandoned by both of the major parties, few politicians of repute will venture out to lead a third-party effort.

### The Withering of Third Parties

Perhaps more predictable than the emergence of significant third parties is their seemingly inevitable demise. While parties such as the Prohibitionists, Socialist Laborites, and Libertarians have had long histories, no third party that has garnered significant popular votes in a presidential election has returned again to better its initial success. The consistent decline owes principally to two factors: the major parties' efforts to adopt its rhetoric if not its position on issues following the strong showing of a third party and the inevitable lesson learned by the third party candidates of the insurmountable obstacles they face competing within a system designed to foster only two parties. Consequently, by the following election, the third-party constituency has a choice between an already defeated "extremist" third party with little hope of victory and a major party more sympathetic to its cause.

Once the major parties begin to undermine their positions on one or two divisive issues, the third party is at a distinct disadvantage. The major parties have the organizational resources, deep-rooted party attachments, a moderate and reasonable image, and access to policymaking needed to deliver on campaign promises. They offer the hope of patronage and other rewards to the party activists. And the fervor aroused by the third party when it initially entered the two-party system is difficult to sustain.

Third parties also lose ground because of shifts in public concern. As a political crisis runs its course and its intensity subsides, the prospects for maintaining voter support for the third party diminishes. Thus a third party that in one election gains attention with a highly visible and divisive issue may find itself irrelevant and ignored by most voters four years hence.

George Wallace appreciated the difficulties of running a second time and in 1972 refused to head the American Independent Party, instead entering the Democratic Party primaries (only to have his career cut short by an attempted assassin's bullet). John Anderson, when asked shortly after the 1980 election if he would mount a third-party challenge in 1984, was quite conscious that his prospects would depend more on the Democratic and Republican response to his initial bid and to the then mood of the electorate, than to anything he would be able to say or do:

> I'm not going to do it if it appears to be a vain, quixotic thing that is really not supported by a ground swell of real enthusiasm. However, if I feel that there really is a vacuum in the political arena, that the Democrats are just coming up with old solutions and Republicans are going to continue the course they've been following, yes, the option is obviously open and there.

Of course, circumstances had indeed changed, and by 1984 John Anderson had faded from the scene, leaving the field to the Democrats and Republicans facing off in their conventional two-party contest.

## Impacts on the Political System

*Program Adoption.* While few third-party candidates have ever seriously expected to win a presidential election, most believed that by raising issues and by demonstrating popular support at the polls, they could affect the course of public policy. They have had mixed success. Immigration was not halted in the 1850s in response to the demands of the nativist American Party, nor were railroads, telegraph, and telephone industries nationalized following the strong showing of the Populist Party in 1892. The Calvin Coolidge and Herbert Hoover administrations did not make the sweeping reforms in the industrial system called for by the 1924 Progressives. After decades of campaigning, the Socialist Party has yet to achieve its essential objectives.

Although third parties' programs may not be implemented directly or immediately, many of their ideas eventually have been incorporated into the programs of major parties and translated into public policy. The slavery restriction and internal improvements themes of the Free Soil Party of 1848 and 1852 were sized by the Republican Party of 1856, and both became public policy under the Republican administrations of the 1860s. Progressive taxation, regulation of railroads, child labor laws, and social insurance were ideas introduced into the political dialogue by Socialists, Farmer-Laborites, Progressives, and Populists. The major portion of the New Deal programs of Franklin Roosevelt have been traced directly to the Progressive platforms of the preceding decades. More recently, the Richard Nixon administration was accused of placating the American Independent constituency after winning office in 1968 by postponing school desegregation deadlines, curtailing civil rights activities of the Justice Department, and appointing racially conservative judges to the federal courts.

Third parties have been especially prominent in battles over suffrage and election reform. Long before such ideas were accepted by the major parties, the Populists, Progressives, and Socialists were stumping for the direct election of United States Senators, women's suffrage, the recall and referendum, primary elections, and corrupt practices legislation. On most of these issues, however, the connection between third-party activity and the adoption of programs is neither direct nor pervasive. Like most third-party programs, their adoption depended on factors often beyond the control of the party first to advocate them.

*Thwarting Majority Will.* One of the longstanding fears of third parties is that they can prevent a majority of votes (50 percent plus one) from going to any single candidate in an election, in which case the victory would simply go to the candidate with the most votes—the plurality winner. This possibility can be eliminated, of course, by restricting the election to two parties. But how serious is the problem and what would be the price of eliminating it in terms of the rights of voters to organize and candidates to offer themselves to the voters?

The question of where third parties have prevented majorities from forming as well as denying victory to one of the major parties in presidential elections divides into a question of the contest for popular votes and another of the contest in the Electoral College where the President is actually selected. The answer to the latter question is an emphatic no. In all elections with significant third-party votes, one of the major parties has carried a majority of the Electoral College. Never has a third party either played the role of kingmaker in the Electoral College by throwing its votes to one of the major parties or forced a contingent election in the House of Representatives.

However, third parties have prevented the formation of popular majorities on a number of occasions, and they have also affected the outcome of elections by drawing off popular votes disproportionately from one of the major parties, leaving victory to the other. In a number of those presidential elections, restricting competition to the two traditional parties might have produced different outcomes. To begin with, despite the significant third-party challenger in 1832, 1924, and 1980, the elections were carried by more than 50 percent of the popular vote; thus even if all of John Anderson's votes in 1980 had gone to the Democratic Party, Ronald Reagan would still have won. The elections of 1848, 1856, 1860, 1892, 1912, and 1968 were won with a plurality of popular votes, and the outcome might have changed if the significant third-party challenge had somehow been excluded.

Whether these elections were won by the candidate who would have received a majority vote in a two-way contest had the third party been removed is a far more difficult question to answer. No conclusive evidence identifies the voters' second or third preferences among the candidates, since only their first choice is recorded on the ballot. Even if this data were available, the strategies of the major parties would probably have differed had there been no third party. Moreover, popular votes are filtered through the Electoral College, which reflects shifts in state choices and only indirectly in the national popular vote, thus compounding the problem of estimating the actual impact of third parties on the outcome of bygone elections.

Some evidence from public opinion polls does exist on the second preference of third-party voters in the 1968 election, and it suggests that the Republicans would have carried the election by an even greater margin if George Wallace was denied a position on the ballot. Such data is not available for earlier contests, and trying to second-guess what voters would have done in a two-way contest is really too speculative.

*Democratic Practice.* From the point of view of democratic theory, program success or failure per se is not so important. Indeed, political scientists have found no evidence that two-party systems perform any better than multiparty systems of government.

Third parties are defended most often on other grounds: they raise and dramatize new and sensitive issues, they can increase interest in politics and the public policy process, and they provide voters with an alternative choice in the voting booth. Finally, they serve as the only effective check within the electoral arena on the two-party monopoly. In other words, the standards are those of an open and free electoral process that places the burden of proof on those who would restrict third parties, more so than already provided by the barriers built into single-member electoral districts and national presidential and congressional elections.

### Issues for Further Inquiry

Scholarly interest in third parties has moved from traditional concerns with a single campaign to the single-factor theories of third-party voting to a multifactor general theory of significant third-party voting. Additionally, the hurdles confronting a third party have been laid out in a series of stages and multiple paths, and recent third-party voting patterns have been modeled quantitatively. Taken together a rather full picture of third parties in the electoral arena emerges, though surely the opportunity is there to expand and reinterpret the available data. Remaining, in addition, are two areas that can greatly benefit from further inquiry.

The virtual consensus among observers that third parties serve a valuable democratic function in the electoral arena and American politics in general has led to numerous proposals for lifting some of the more onerous constraints on them, though falling short of calling for the overturn of the Constitution and the single-member district form of election. These range from proposals for a nationally uniform and easily accessible ballot law to more equitable access for all parties on the national media, including third party participation in nationally televised presidential debates, to revision of the Federal Election Campaign Act lessening its burden on third parties. Possibly even more far-reaching is the suggestion that New York State's ballot law, under which third parties both thrive yet contribute to major party coalitions, be adopted nationwide. Robert Spitzer has become a most vocal proponent of this approach. While each of these ideas merits consideration and would probably enable more and/or stronger third parties to compete in elections, the exact nature of their effect not only on third parties but on the major parties as well is sorely in need of investigation.

Also in need of examination is the extent to which secular trends will of themselves facilitate the rise of third parties. As noted, the legal climate has changed since the *Rhodes* decision of 1968 making the ballot much more accessible to third parties. To the extent to that the courts continue to protect the rights of third parties, one of their historical barriers will be appreciably lifted. Second, the traditional pattern of political socialization whereby parents passed on to their children partisan identification has been replaced largely by media learning and cues from the nightly news. To the extent that partisan loyalty formerly transcended campaigns and candidates, third parties, especially start-up parties, found it difficult to make inroads into the electorate. In a media age, however, where partisanship has become far less relevant than media exposure, third parties may find their task much easier. Third, some students of political realignments now believe that the old New Deal alignment that began to collapse in the 1960s is not going to be replaced by a new and enduring alignment of Democratic and Republican partisans; it is predicted to simply bounce along from election to election in a permanent stage of "dealignment." The resulting party factionalization and voter disaffection combined with a more educated and issue-oriented electorate appears to account for the upswing in third-party voting in the elections between 1968 and 1980. This trend may well continue. Lastly, in a media age, the prospects of an overnight media-created personality looms as never before. Should attention be heaped upon a third-party contender (or a major-party loyalist who sees the media potential if he or she were to become a third-party contender), the prospects for garnering a significant vote outside the two major parties increases appreciably. Indeed, a hint of this came in the early stages of the 1980 campaign as John Anderson became the darling of the media. These trends need to be examined and where critical incorporated into our understanding of third parties.

Observers have no reason to believe that the basic structure of two-partyism in the United States will be changing dramatically. But with a loosening of the legal constraints on third parties and the continuing evolution of a more media-oriented, issue-oriented, educated, and volatile electorate, third-party voting may nevertheless become more commonplace in American elections.

*See also:* Individual parties and candidates, Australian Ballot, Electoral College System, Federal Election Campaign Act of 1974, V. O. Key, Single-Member Districts, *Williams v. Rhodes*, Winner-Take-All Systems, Woman Suffrage Movement

*Daniel A. Mazmanian*

REFERENCES

Agar, Herbert. 1966. *The Price of Union.* 2nd ed. Boston: Houghton Mifflin.

Bone, Hugh H. 1943. "Small Political Parties Casualties of War." 32 *National Municipal Review* 524.

Burnham, Walter Dean. 1970. *Critical Elections and the Mainsprings of American Politics.* New York: Norton.

Carlson, Jody. 1981. *George C. Wallace and the Politics of Powerlessness.* New Brunswick, NJ: Transaction Books.

Dahl, Robert A. 1956. *A Preface to Democratic Theory.* Chicago: U. of Chicago Pr.

Downs, Anthony. 1957. *An Economic Theory of Democracy.* New York: Harper & Row.

Evans, Eldon C. 1917. *A History of the Australian Ballot System in the Unites States.* Chicago: U. of Chicago Pr.

Hartz, Louis. 1955. *The Liberal Tradition in America.* New York: Harcourt, Brace and World.

Hicks, John D. 1961. *The Populist Revolt: A History of the Farmers' Alliance and the People's Party.* Lincoln: U. of Nebraska Pr.

Iyengar, Shanto, and Donald R. Kinder. 1987. *News That Matters: Television and American Opinion.* Chicago: U. of Chicago Pr.

Katz, Richard S. 1980. *A Theory of Parties and Electoral Systems.* Baltimore: Johns Hopkins U. Pr.

Key, V. O., Jr. 1964. *Politics, Parties, and Pressure Groups.* 5th ed. New York: Crowell.

Ladd, Everett C., Jr. 1982. *Where Have All the Voters Gone?* New York: Norton.

Mackay, Kenneth C. 1966. *The Progressive Movement of 1924.* New York: Octagon Books.

Mazmanian, Daniel A. 1974. *Third Parties in Presidential Elections.* Washington: Brookings.

Panetta, Leon E., and Peter Gall. 1971. *Bring Us Together: The Nixon Team and the Civil Rights Retreat.* Philadelphia: Lippincott.

Phillips, Kevin P. 1969. *The Emerging Republican Majority.* New York: Doubleday.

Powell, Bingham G. 1981. "Party Systems and Political System Performance." 75 *American Political Science Review* 861.

Rae, Douglas W. 1967. *The Political Consequences of Electoral Laws.* New Haven: Yale U. Pr.

Ranney, Austin. 1983. *Channels of Power: The Impact of Television on American Politics.* New York: Basic Books.

Rayback, Joseph G. 1970. *Free Soil: The Election of 1848.* Lexington: U. Pr. of Kentucky.

Ricker, William H. 1962. *The Theory of Political Coalitions.* New Haven: Yale U. Pr.

Rosenstone, Steven J., Roy L. Behr, and Edward H. Lazarus. 1984. *Third Parties in America: Citizen Response to Major Party Failure.* Princeton: Princeton U. Pr.

Satori, Giovanni. 1976. *Parties and Party Systems: A Framework for Analysis.* Cambridge: Cambridge U. Pr.

Schattschneider, E. E. 1942. *Party Government.* New York: Rinehart.

Schmidt, Karl M. 1960. *Henry Wallace: Quixotic Crusade 1948.* Syracuse: Syracuse U. Pr.

Smallwood, Frank. 1984. *The Other Candidates: Third Parties in Presidential Elections.* Hanover, NH: U. Pr. of New England.

Sorauf, Frank. 1980. *Political Parties in America.* 4th ed. Boston: Little, Brown.

Spitzer, Robert J. 1987. *The Right to Life Movement and Third Party Politics.* Westport, CT: Greenwood.

Stedman, Murray S. and Susan W. 1950. *Discontent at the Polls.* New York: Columbia U. Pr.

Sundquist, James L. 1983. *Dynamics of the Party System: Alignment and Realignment of Political Parties in the United States.* Rev. ed. Washington: Brookings.

Weinstein, James. 1969. *The Decline of Socialism in America, 1912–1925.* New York: Vintage.

Wiseheart, Malcolm B., Jr. 1969. "Constitutional Law: Third Political Parties as Second Class Citizens." 21 *University of Florida Law Review* 701.

## Norman M. Thomas (1884–1968)

Six-time presidential candidate of the Socialist Party of America. The son and grandson of Presbyterian pastors, Norman Mattoon Thomas was a Presbyterian minister as a young adult and later became a Christian socialist and pacifist. Inclined toward radicalism by his experiences in a poor immigrant parish in New York and by his reading of Walter Rauschenbusch and other Social Gospel writers, Thomas joined the Socialist Party in 1918 because of his antiwar views.

Thomas's intellect, character, and oratorical skills quickly made him a Socialist Party leader and by 1928 its presidential nominee. The best showing made by Thomas and the post-Eugene Debs Socialist Party came in 1932, when Thomas won nearly 900,000 votes—yet that was just 2 percent of the total vote in the midst of the Great Depression. As factionalism and the New Deal bled away Socialist strength during the remainder of the 1930s, Thomas proposed that the party abandon electoral politics, and he became increasingly involved in antiwar activity by the end of the decade. After World War II, Thomas, now more a reformer than a radical, continued to urge the Socialist Party to focus on education rather than elections and to work for such broad causes as peace, economic reform, civil rights, and civil liberties. By the time Thomas died the Socialist Party had essentially adopted that course.

*See also:* Eugene V. Debs, Socialist Party of America

*John W. Jeffries*

REFERENCES

Johnpoll, Bernard K. 1970. *Pacifist's Progress: Norman Thomas and the Demise of American Socialism.* New York: Quadrangle.

Swanberg, W. A. 1976. *Norman Thomas: The Last Idealist.* New York: Scribner's.

## William ("Big Bill") H. Thompson (1867–1944)

Three-time Republican mayor of Chicago. William ("Big Bill the Builder") Hale Thompson was one of the most controversial politicians in Chicago's history. Thompson was a master of political invective who countered critics with scathing personal vilification. Big, brash and full of braggadocio, he was a formidable campaigner. Thompson, however, was always more than a political showman. Although never able to develop a strong precinct organization, he was adept at Republican coalition building during a period when Chicago's ethnic composition was in political flux. Thompson shrewdly exploited the social and political tensions of the 1920s.

Initially, in 1915, this son of wealth campaigned on a "good government" platform. World War I provided him with an opportunity to court a large but isolated German constituency. Thereafter, Thompson shifted from middle-class reform to ethnic factional politics,

capitalized on Chicago's broad opposition to Prohibition, and won a substantial following in the African-American community. Thompson also reigned over what is called Chicago's golden age of public works, a period of vast public expansion not without opportunities for some graft.

A series of scandals thwarted Thompson's third consecutive nomination in 1923, but Big Bill returned to city hall in 1927 for a tumultuous third term. In 1931 he tried again, but the factional strife he had helped foster had left the Republican organization a shambles. Further, the pall of the Depression hung over the city, while spoils politics and an incredible problem of organized crime revolved around Thompson. This 1931 election is considered a watershed in Chicago politics. The victory of Anton Cermak began a Democratic domination of Chicago government that has lasted over a half-century.

*See also:* Anton Cermak

*Gene D. L. Jones*

## Thornburg v. Gingles
478 U.S. 30 (1986)

This Supreme Court case held that certain multimember state legislative districts in North Carolina impaired the ability of Black voters to elect representatives of their choice in violation of Section 2 of the Voting Rights Act. *Thornburg* is particularly important because it is an exposition of how dilutions of racial voting can be proven under Section 2 of the Voting Rights Act.

Earlier, the Court had held in *Mobile v. Bolden* (446 U.S. 55 (1980)) that disproportionate effects alone were not sufficient to claim unconstitutional race dilution; discriminatory intent had to be shown. *Bolden* was a constitutional ruling, not a Voting Rights Act case; but in *Bolden*, Section 2 of the Act was seen as adding no more protection than was already provided by the Fifteenth Amendment; therefore, *Bolden's* standards of proof had relevance for Voting Rights Act cases. Critics claimed that *Bolden* left little guidance as to how discriminatory intent might be proved, and many thought that proving intent was too stringent a standard for discrimination cases involving voting. Largely as a result of *Bolden*, Congress amended Section 2 of the Voting Rights Act. *Thornburg* gives a detailed post-amendment statutory interpretation. Essentially, the amended version of Section 2, especially as construed in *Thornburg*, makes it easier to prove discrimination.

Section 2(b) of the Voting Rights Act, as amended, allowed "the totality of circumstances" as evidence of discrimination; and it stated that "the extent to which members of a protected class have been elected to office in the State or political subdivision is one circumstance which may be considered: *Provided*, That nothing in this section establishes a right to have members of a protected class elected in numbers equal to their proportion in the population" (42 USC Sec. 1973). Writing for a majority, Justice William Brennan gave a very detailed analysis of what constitutes proper evidence of a violation of Section 2. To find a multimember district unacceptable, the plaintiffs must demonstrate that "a bloc voting majority must *usually* be able to defeat candidates supported by a politically cohesive, geographically insular minority group." Therefore, "if difficulty in electing [minorities] and white bloc voting are not proven, minority voters have not established that the multimember structure interferes with their ability to elect their preferred candidates." Justice Brennan then discussed in detail, usually for the majority but not always, how to determine racially polarized voting and the degree of bloc voting that is legally significant, among other things.

Multimember state legislative districts are still allowed, but *Thornburg* has made them more vulnerable to attacks on the basis of racial vote dilution.

*See also:* Fifteenth Amendment, *Mobile v. Bolden*, Voting Rights Act of 1965 and Extensions

*H. W. Perry, Jr.*

## Three-Fifths Compromise

"Representatives and direct Taxes shall be apportioned among the several States . . . according to their respective Numbers which shall be determined by adding to the whole Number of free Persons . . . three-fifths of all other Persons." This famous part of Article I, Section 2 of the United States Constitution giving southern slaveholders partial representation in Congress for their slave population was approved with relatively little resistance in the ratification struggle of the late 1780s. But it would become one of the most controversial parts of the Constitution as sectionalism deepened.

The three-fifths concept was first proposed in the Confederation Congress in 1783 in an effort to apportion taxes according to population rather than land values. During the convention of 1787, it was tied to representation in the House of Representatives by James Wilson of Pennsylvania. Prolonged debate followed before the compromise was approved on July 12. The fact that the three-fifths clause thus acknowledged slavery and rewarded slave owners with substantially more power in Congress received little attention in the state ratification conventions, although James Madison felt it necessary to defend it in *Federalist* Number 54.

Northern resistance to the compromise heightened in the nineteenth century. With the direct tax provision never having been invoked, the opposition cited increasing southern power in Congress. The Federalist Hartford Convention in 1814 called for its repeal as part of the attack on Virginia Republican domination of the government. More seriously, northerners charged in the Missouri debates of 1819 to 1821 that slave state representation in the House had been increased by at least 15 seats owing to the provision. The admission of Missouri, another slave state, would merely add to the discrepancy.

After 1830, abolitionist attacks, led by the radical William Lloyd Garrison wing, cited the three-fifths clause as one of several parts of the Constitution that made it a proslavery document. The clause remained a focal point of the abolition crusade until the Thirteenth Amendment abolished slavery itself and the Fourteenth Amendment established a new method of apportioning representatives.

*See also:* Abolition Movement, James Madison, Missouri Compromise, Slavery

*Frederick J. Blue*

REFERENCES

Finkleman, Paul. 1981. *An Imperfect Union: Slavery, Federalism and Comity.* Chapel Hill: U. of North Carolina Pr.

Fiske, John. 1988. *The Critical Period of American History, 1783–1789.* Boston: Houghton Mifflin.

Gerteis, Louis S. 1987. *Morality and Utility in American Anti-slavery Reform.* Chapel Hill: U. of North Carolina Pr.

Wiecek, William. 1977. *The Sources of Antislavery Constitutionalism in America, 1760–1848.* Ithaca: Cornell U. Pr.

## Strom Thurmond (1902– )

Quintessential twentieth-century southern politician. Strom Thurmond was born in the politically active town of Edgefield, South Carolina, and was elected state senator in 1933 and circuit judge in 1938. He became governor in 1947 after campaigning against the state's political establishment. Thurmond became a leading spokesman for southern Democratic dissidents after President Harry Truman began advocating greater civil rights for African-Americans in 1948; he was the presidential nominee of the States' Rights Party that year. As governor, Thurmond had supported progressive measures like better educational opportunities, but he argued that racial matters were best handled through gradual change on the state and local levels rather than intervention by the federal government. His conservative political philosophy stressed individual initiative and talent, which guaranteed inequality because of the unequal distribution of talents among people.

In 1954 Thurmond became the only U.S. Senator ever to be elected in a write-in campaign, arguing that the state Democratic executive committee should have called a special election after the death of the incumbent instead of appointing their own choice to run unopposed in November. Senate Democrats welcomed the rebel South Carolinian into the Democratic Caucus, since they needed his vote to control the Senate. As promised, Thurmond resigned his seat in 1956, permitting the people to vote in a special election (he ran without opposition) to send him back to Washington. In the Senate, Thurmond was the author of the Southern Manifesto declaring the South's legal resistance to school desegregation, and he set a filibuster record of 24 hours and 18 minutes in opposition to the 1957 Civil Rights Act. His consistently conservative philosophy on economic, racial, and defense issues often led to conflicts with the John Kennedy administration in the early 1960s.

As early as 1961 Thurmond had expressed support for an ideological realignment of the two parties. After Republicans nominated conservative Barry Goldwater for President in 1964 and Democratic President Lyndon Johnson pursued liberal policies and chose Hubert Humphrey as his running mate, Thurmond announced his support for Goldwater and his conversion to the Republican Party. He accused the national Democratic Party of being controlled by minorities, unions, political bosses, and liberals like Humphrey and Robert Kennedy. Republican Senate leader Everett Dirksen promised that Thurmond could keep his Senate seniority accumulated as a Democrat. Campaigning across the South for Goldwater, Thurmond's efforts may have helped a Republican presidential candidate carry South Carolina for the first time since Reconstruction. Re-

taining a conservative voting record in the Senate of the 1970s and 1980s, Thurmond also placed increased stress on constituency service, even appealing to his Black constituents (in 1971 Thurmond was the first southern Senator to hire a Black professional staff member). Thurmond was reelected to the Senate at the age of 88 in 1990.

*See also:* Everett Dirksen, Barry Goldwater, Hubert H. Humphrey, Lyndon B. Johnson, Robert F. Kennedy, States' Rights Party, Harry S Truman

*Stephen D. Shaffer*

REFERENCES

Garson, Robert. 1974. *The Democratic Party and the Politics of Sectionalism, 1941–1948.* Baton Rouge: Louisiana State U. Pr.

Lachicotte, Alberta. 1967. *Rebel Senator, Strom Thurmond of South Carolina.* New York: Devin-Adair.

## Samuel J. Tilden (1814–1886)

Unsuccessful candidate in the celebrated disputed presidential election of 1876. Samuel Jones Tilden was born in New Lebanon, New York, attended Yale briefly, and earned a law degree from New York University. Contacts with Martin Van Buren and other prominent Democrats, gained through his successful farmer father, spurred political interests and boosted his law practice in New York City. His appointment as corporation counsel of New York in 1843 was an early step in his eventual amassing of a large fortune. Typically a Democratic organizer, propagandist, and adviser rather than an officeholder, Tilden served only a single term in the state legislature (1846) where he assisted Governor Silas Wright in working out a compromise to end manorial estates in eastern New York.

As the growing split among Democrats over slavery and other issues weakened his party, Tilden, who began as an antiextensionist, became increasingly conservative on slavery. He strongly opposed Abraham Lincoln in 1860, remained aloof from the Civil War, and then managed Horatio Seymour's campaign against Ulysses Grant in 1868. Sensing a growing public dissatisfaction with corruption, Tilden, as New York state party chair (1866–1876) purged the Democrats of the Tweed Ring, providing valuable assistance to prosecutors. In 1874, benefiting from his "clean" image, Tilden won the gubernatorial nomination and defeated incumbent John A. Dix in the closely divided state.

Angling for an 1876 presidential nomination, Tilden vigorously, though unproductively, chased after fraudulent contractors ("The Canal

Ring") on the Erie Canal. The contrast to Grant's scandal-ridden administration won him the chance to oppose Republican Rutherford B. Hayes in 1876. Massive voter frauds in Louisiana, Florida, and South Carolina left the vote count in those states in dispute. Tilden's acquiescence to an electoral commission on these southern elections cost him when it awarded all of the disputed votes to Hayes. Tilden lost by one vote in the Electoral College (185 to 184), despite having received 250,000 more popular votes than Hayes. Tilden's final public act was to leave his large fortune to found the New York Public Library.

*See also:* Election of 1876, Electoral College System, Ulysses S. Grant, Rutherford B. Hayes, Horatio Seymour, William M. Tweed

*Phyllis F. Field*

REFERENCES
Bigelow, John. 1895. *The Life of Samuel J. Tilden.* New York: Harper.
Flick, Alexander C. 1939. *Samuel Jones Tilden.* New York: Dodd, Mead.

## Benjamin R. Tillman (1847–1918)

"Pitchfork Ben," charismatic political leader of southern farmers. Benjamin Ryan Tillman created a revolution in South Carolina politics with the support of the state's farmers. In 1889 disgruntled farmers wrested control of the Democratic Party from the Bourbon Democrats, who had ruled South Carolina since the end of Reconstruction, and nominated Tillman for governor. Angered by these usurpers, arch conservatives bolted the party and nominated Alexander C. Haskell for governor at their impromptu Peace and Harmony Convention; Tillman, however, easily won the election. With his reelection in 1892 and the election of Tillmanites to the state legislature and the U.S. Congress, Tillman's revolution was complete.

Tillman soon turned his attention to national politics. In 1893 he marshaled a combination of southern and western Democrats against Grover Cleveland's eastern Democrats on the issue of free silver. The next year, he was elected to the Senate, promising to stick Cleveland in the ribs with his pitchfork (hence earning himself the nickname "Pitchfork Ben") if the President failed to support free silver. In 1896 Tillman wanted to be the Democratic presidential nominee. He made the longest speech at the Democratic National Convention, but the party chose the relatively moderate William Jennings Bryan over the tough-talking agrarian.

Tillman won reelection to the Senate in 1900, 1906, and 1912. Despite this success, his influence in South Carolina's politics increasingly declined.

*See also:* William Jennings Bryan, Grover Cleveland, Tillman Act of 1907

*Henry J. Walker, Jr.*

REFERENCES
Carlton, David. 1982. *Mill and Town in South Carolina: 1880–1920.* Baton Rouge: Louisiana State U. Pr.
Simkins, Francis Butler. 1926. *The Tillman Movement in South Carolina.* Gloucester, MA: Peter Smith.
———. 1944. *Pitchfork Ben Tillman: South Carolinian.* Baton Rouge: Louisiana State U. Pr.
Woodward, C. Vann. 1951. *Origins of the New South: 1877–1913.* Baton Rouge: Louisiana State U. Pr.

## Tillman Act of 1907

Lavish contributions to political candidates by major corporations at the end of the nineteenth century reached levels that alarmed progressive government reformers. At the national level, the Republican presidential crusades of 1896 and 1900 saw Mark Hanna raise unparalleled amounts of money for the William McKinley campaigns. In various states, specific corporations with particular interests in governmental policy, railroads being the chief example, dominated the political process. Conversely, muckrakers in the press and civic organizations, such as the National Publicity Bill Organization, sought legislation regulating campaign finance. These calls for reform reached a fever pitch during the 1904 campaign, when Democrats claimed that Republican national chairman George B. Courtelyou, who had served as Secretary of Commerce and Labor before assuming party leadership, was financing the entire Republican campaign from corporate gifts.

While the partisan criticism did not affect the successful election of Theodore Roosevelt, echoes of that criticism and further revelations in which corporations admitted giving extremely large sums to the Republican campaign led a humbler President Roosevelt to include a call for campaign finance reform in his annual messages to Congress in 1905 and 1906. Earlier a bill to restrict corporate gifts to campaigns had been championed by New Hampshire Republican William E. Chandler, who eventually was defeated in a bid for reelection, largely owing to the influence of the Boston and Maine Railroad in his state. Though out of office, Chandler still longed for campaign reform as retribution for his defeat. He convinced Democratic Senator

Benjamin R. "Pitchfork Ben" Tillman from South Carolina, a friend from his days in the Senate, to reintroduce the legislation he had sponsored some years earlier. Tillman was no political saint, but he had Populist blood in his veins.

The campaign finance reform bill might well have died had not Tillman personally and indignantly continued to press for investigations of corporate wrongdoing. Finally, after the 1906 congressional elections, in which the Republicans lost less than one-third of the 92 seats they had gained in 1904, the majority felt they could safely appease the growing public sentiment that some action had to be taken. The Tillman Act of 1907 (34 Stat. 864), which passed in the first days of the new Congress, prohibited contributions by corporations and national banks to federal political campaigns. The limitation on who can give to a political campaign (and on how much certain types of individuals can give) has been one of the main themes of campaign finance reform from the time of the passage of this first major legislative effort to regulate campaign financing until the present.

*See also:* George B. Courtelyou, Marcus A. (Mark) Hanna, Theodore Roosevelt, Benjamin Tillman

*L. Sandy Maisel*

REFERENCES

Alexander, Herbert E. 1984. *Financing Politics: Money, Elections, and Political Reform.* 3rd ed. Washington: Congressional Quarterly.

Mutch, Robert E. 1988. *Campaigns, Congress, and Courts: The Making of Federal Campaign Finance Law.* Westport, CT: Praeger.

## Titular Head of Party

An anomaly of the United States party system is the lack of a formal organizational status for the "titular" leaders of the presidential wing of the national parties. The President and his most recently defeated opponent are formal members of their party only to the extent that they have enrolled at registration time, made a financial contribution, or have been elected to a party committee in a primary or by a caucus. Incumbency in the presidency or recent service as the party's presidential nominee carries no special formal status. This system contrasts to the usual arrangement in parliamentary organizations in which the prime minister and the leader of the opposition are the official and governmentally supported heads of their respective parties.

The President and the defeated out-party nominee are official party leaders in title only, drawing whatever influence they have informally from resources that may be available to them. Since the President has very substantial resources, such as governmental office, patronage, public attention, and staff, his titular party leadership status is encompassed by his formal power. As a consequence, the rubric of titular leader is most often applied to the recently defeated presidential nominee. Title, according to the comment of Senator Richard Russell of Georgia in 1953, means "title without authority." Adlai E. Stevenson, the person to whom Russell referred, also had something to say on the subject.

In our country this role is an ambiguous one. . . . [T]he titular head has no clear and defined authority within his party. He has no party office, no staff, no funds, nor is there any system of consultation whereby he may be advised of party policy and through which he may help shape that policy. . . . Yet he is generally deemed the leading spokesman of his party. And he has—or so it seemed to me—an obligation to help wipe out the inevitable deficit accumulated by his party during a losing campaign and also to do what he can to revise, reorganize and rebuild the party.

In the course of United States party history, a few defeated presidential nominees have succeeded in being assertive titular leaders: Martin Van Buren, Henry Clay, William Jennings Bryan, and Adlai E. Stevenson II.

Americans have heard relatively little public or academic debate about the implications of a titular leadership status. For example, the ambiguity of titular leadership may in part enable an out-party to set aside without major internal disruption its defeated leader as it searches for a more electable one. On the other hand, without a leader who serves as the out-party's official single spokesperson, the party may speak with many and conflicting voices, thereby causing confusion in the policymaking process.

*See also:* William Jennings Bryan, Henry Clay, Richard B. Russell, Adlai E. Stevenson II, Martin Van Buren

*Ralph M. Goldman*

REFERENCES

Goldman, Ralph M. 1969. "Titular Leadership of the Presidential Parties." In Aaron Wildavsky, ed. *The Presidency.* Boston: Little, Brown.

———. 1990. *The National Party Chairmen and Committees: Factionalism at the Top.* Armonk, NY: M. E. Sharpe.

## Mary Jane Tobin (1931– )

Co-founder of New York's Right to Life Party. A Merrick, New York, housewife who, along with Ellen McCormack, formed the New York–based Right to Life Party (RTLP) in the late 1960s, Mary Jane Tobin participated in a book discussion group with other Long Island housewives. In 1969 they became involved in politics by attempting to block the passage of a liberal abortion law in New York. In 1978, at the age of 47, Tobin was the RTLP's candidate for governor (McCormack ran for lieutenant governor). On a budget of $63,870 (half of which was devoted to television advertising), she received 130,193 votes (2.6 percent), enough to give the party the number four line on the New York State ballot (official state recognition for a party is based on its gubernatorial vote).

Tobin is a retired nurse and the mother of three, married to a corporate executive. She is a Roman Catholic and former Democrat. Tobin continues to be a key party leader and has worked successfully to defeat efforts within the RTLP to broaden the party's appeal. Some dissident party members complain that the RTLP structure and rules are weighted in such a way as to give the Long Island faction disproportionately greater control over official affairs. For example, Tobin and other leaders succeeded in beating back efforts to have the party endorse Ronald Reagan for President in 1980 and 1984 (the party endorsed McCormack for President in 1980, and no one in 1984), as the leaders felt that Reagan's stand against abortion was insufficiently tough.

*See also:* Ellen McCormack, Ronald Reagan, Right to Life Party

*Robert T. Spitzer*

REFERENCES

Spitzer, Robert J. 1987. *The Right to Life Movement and Third Party Politics.* Westport, CT: Greenwood.

## Alexis de Tocqueville (1805–1859)

French chronicler of post-Revolutionary America. Most observers will maintain that Alexis de Tocqueville has few, if any, rivals as an analyst of the strengths and weaknesses of liberal democracy in America. A European aristocrat, Tocqueville's admiration for democracy was tempered by a keen sense of the grandeur of the old order and the potentially fatal weaknesses inherent in the new.

At age 21, Tocqueville, with Gustave de Beaumont, toured North America from May 1831 to February 1832 to study American penitentiaries. The first volume of *Democracy in America*, the book he wrote after his visit, was an immediate success; it was published in 1835 and the second volume in 1840. He served in the Chamber of Deputies from 1839 to 1851, and for five months in 1849 as minister of foreign affairs. Retiring from public life in 1851, Tocqueville later produced *The Old Regime and the French Revolution.*

Tocqueville's practical aim as a scholar was to provide a "new political science" for "a world itself quite new." The extension of democracy was, in Tocqueville's eyes, inevitable. The question was how to encourage its better, liberal form and how to ward off its worst tendencies—individual selfishness, envy, isolation, and the sacrifice of freedom. In America he found the lesson Europe needed on how to keep democracy liberal.

The character of a regime, for Tocqueville, was determined less by geographical and historical conditions than by laws; customs and mores, however, were most important of all. The essence of democracy was not a broad electoral franchise but an equality of social conditions: divided inheritances and the freedom to compete animated the material ambitions of all, creating vast energy and widespread well-being. Democracy eliminated extremes, the greatness of the few and the misery of the many. Power was broken up and dispersed. But untempered by countervailing institutions, democracy could lead to an ever narrower and more frenetic egoism and isolation.

The democratic principle of equality worked pervasively. Statesman and parties of great principles were replaced by small men and parties of petty interests. Institutions intermediate between the individual and society as a whole tended to dissolve, leaving anxious conformists and building an ever more powerful and oppressive majority opinion. The final danger was that fatigue and envy would lead men to trade their liberty for the despotic equality provided by a paternalistic state.

The pathology of democracy can be warded off, according to Tocqueville, by promoting institutions and mores that do not deny self-interest but elevate, broaden, and enlighten it, thereby creating active and self-confident citizens.

Among the institutions that support liberty in America are the power of religion, respect for law and rights, and active citizenship supported by local self-government and especially administrative decentralization. Also important were popular juries that diffuse the spirit of legalism, stable family life, and the enlightened self-interest of individuals freely associating with others for projects of local improvement.

See also: Isolationism in American Politics

Stephen Macedo

REFERENCES

de Tocqueville, Alexis. 1955. *The Old Regime and the French Revolution*. Trans. Stuart Gilbert. Garden City, NY: Doubleday.

———. 1969. *Democracy in America*. Ed. J. P. Mayer, trans. George Lawrence. Garden City, NY: Doubleday.

———. 1971. *Recollections*. Eds. J. P. Mayer and A. P. Kerr, trans. George Lawrence. Garden City, NY: Doubleday.

## Robert A. Toombs (1810–1885)

Co-founder of the Constitutional Union Party. A wealthy planter and prosperous lawyer, Robert Augustus Toombs was elected to the Georgia legislature (1837–1840) and to Congress (1844–1850) as a conservative Whig and conditional Unionist. The growing sectional crisis and his own impetuous temperament at times led him into extremist rhetoric, but he strongly supported the Compromise of 1850 barring slavery from California. With Alexander Stephens and Democrat Howell Cobb, Toombs formed the Constitutional Union Party, which won the crucial support of Georgia for the Compromise. In 1851 Toombs was elected to the United States Senate and reluctantly became a Democrat when the Constitutional Union Party and the Compromise failed to take root nationally. The rise of the Republicans drove him toward the extreme proslavery position. After the election of Abraham Lincoln he broke with his old friend Stephens and campaigned successfully for the immediate secession of Georgia.

Toombs was elected to the provisional Confederate Congress, but his hopes for the presidency were destroyed by his rivalry with Cobb and his own reputation for intemperance. He was appointed Secretary of State but resigned after five months in frustration over President Jefferson Davis's domination of the Cabinet. He then secured a commission as a brigadier general while retaining his congressional seat. As a soldier, Toombs was often insubordinate and always critical of "West Point stupidity." He had one heroic and crucial defensive stand at the battle of Antietam but resigned his commission when he was not promoted. He became a bitter states' rights critic of the Davis administration but failed to secure election to the Senate in 1863. After the war, Toombs refused to apply for pardon but exercised considerable influence in restoring Georgia to Democratic rule. He dominated the Georgia Constitutional Convention of 1877 as an agrarian opponent of corporations and business-oriented advocates of a "new South."

See also: Howell Cobb, Jefferson Davis, Abraham Lincoln, Secession, Alexander Stephens

Harold B. Raymond

REFERENCES

Montgomery, Horace. 1944. *Cracker Parties*. Baton Rouge: Louisiana State U. Pr.

Thompson, William Y. 1966. *Robert Toombs of Georgia*. Baton Rouge: Louisiana State U. Pr.

## Tories (Toryism)

Our understanding of Toryism in the United States has often been clouded by the fact that history is usually perceived through the eyes of the victor. This orthodox view suggests that the patriots were interested in American liberty and independence and that, by opposing the patriots during the Revolution, Tories stood for aristocracy, privilege, and British domination.

Modern scholarship has suggested a much more complex picture of American Toryism. First, a distinction must be made between pre-Revolutionary Tories and Revolutionary Tories. For many decades before the Revolution, most American colonies saw a protracted political struggle between the state legislatures and the state governors. Those who supported the governors were often part of a "court" party (more of a faction, really) while those who supported the legislature saw themselves as the "country" party. In this sense, the American political universe looked much like the British model. The "country" faction called themselves Whigs, while the "court" faction called themselves Tories.

In America, Tories were more inclined to support the governor's prerogatives, often because they held appointive office ("placemen") or because the governor's policies benefited their interests. They were social conservatives fearful that only royal authority could maintain civilized virtues in a rough-and-tumble New World. Many were Anglicans or other religionists who desired either an established church or protection of their religious beliefs by the Crown. Some were simply Englishmen unable to shake their loyalties to the home country. The royal governors, rather than the more locally minded legislatures, represented England to them. Interestingly, many Tories were outspoken in their defense of liberty, but their perception of liberty was based on their status as Englishmen under the English Constitution. By 1775, however, the patriots were defending liberties that were already considerably more expansive than these.

The Revolutionary War changed the political tapestry dramatically. No longer was the battle a conflict between American legislatures and American governors representing the Crown. Now the conflict was between independent American states and British authority. Some Whigs who had supported American interests before the war either could not accept the violence of the rebellion (many were religious pacifists) or could not sever their umbilical to the Crown and thus became Loyalists. Some Tories found that their political and social conservatism was too deeply rooted in American soil to permit them to bear arms against their countrymen. Some of these former Tories joined the struggle for independence; some tried to sit out the war quietly. In short, once the war began, a Tory was one who opposed independence. Other factors became secondary.

A Tory party never existed in America; Tories, scattered over the thirteen colonies, never shared a common political agenda. They never existed as an ongoing political institution with a core of leaders and supporters. They lacked any of the communications networks common to modern political parties. Toryism was a state of mind. It was a particularly European vision of society— deeply communitarian, deferential, organic, and conservative—that after the Revolution was no longer to play a significant role in American politics.

*Glenn A. Phelps*

REFERENCES

Labaree, Leonard W. 1948. *Conservatism in Early American History.* Ithaca: Cornell U. Pr.

Murrin, John M. 1980. "The Great Inversion, or Court Versus Country." In J. G. A. Pocock, ed. *Three British Revolutions: 1641,`1688, 1776.* Princeton: Princeton U. Pr.

Nelson, William H. 1964. *The American Tory.* Boston: Beacon.

## John G. Tower (1925–1991)

U.S. Senator, arms negotiator, and defense industry consultant. John Goodwin Tower is better known for a position he did not hold than for one he did. On March 10, 1989, the United States Senate defeated President George Bush's nomination of John Tower for Secretary of Defense. Tower's defeat placed him among only seven other Cabinet nominees rejected by the Senate in its 200-year history.

John Tower was born in Houston, Texas, received a B.A. from Southwestern University in 1948, and an M.A. in political science from Southern Methodist University in 1953. Between 1951 and 1961, Tower taught political science at Midwestern State University.

In May 1961, Republican Tower was elected to fill the Texas senatorial vacancy caused by the resignation of Lyndon Baines Johnson, when Johnson became Vice President. Tower was the first Republican Senator from Texas since Reconstruction. He was reelected in 1966, 1972, and 1978.

In the Senate, Tower served on the Committee on Armed Services, among others. He served as Armed Services chairman from 1981 to 1984. During the Ronald Reagan administration, Tower was instrumental in securing congressional approval of increased spending for the military.

Following his retirement from the Senate, Tower served as U.S. negotiator on long-range missiles at the Nuclear Arms Talks in Geneva. He also chaired a defense industry consulting firm. In 1987 President Reagan appointed Tower to chair the Iran-Contra Commission, investigating the unauthorized sale of weapons to Iran and the diversion of funds to "Contra" forces fighting the Sandinista government of Nicaragua.

In December 1988, President-elect Bush nominated Tower to be Secretary of Defense. Bush and Tower were fellow Texans, and Tower had supported Bush's candidacy ardently. While Washington initially anticipated that Tower's nomination would be approved easily, troublesome reports concerning Tower's behavior soon led to a national debate over the former Senator's fitness to head the critical Department of Defense.

Between December 1988 and March 1989, the debate focused on Tower's "womanizing" and drinking. The FBI conducted both a background check and a separate investigation in which agents asked more than 100 people about Tower's drinking. In addition, Tower's critics raised conflict of interest concerns stemming from his receipt of $750,000 in fees from major defense contractors between 1986 and 1988.

By the time his confirmation hearings were held, Tower's personal life had become public. Tower was questioned extensively on the subject of drinking by members of the Senate Armed Services Committee. He admitted that he drank excessively in the 1970s but denied having a drinking problem.

When his nomination came to the vote, the committee rejected Tower along strictly partisan lines. The Senators who voted against Tower stated that the evidence of Tower's drinking persuaded them that he was not fit to hold as critical a position as Secretary of Defense. The Republican Senators, dismissing the allegations as innuendo, focused on Tower's expertise and his years of excellent service.

Despite the vote of the committee, Tower could have been confirmed by the Senate as a whole. To succeed, the administration needed yea votes from at least five Democrats, not to mention a number of skeptical Republicans. Although the Bush administration fought hard for the President's choice, Tower's nomination was defeated in the full Senate by a 53-to-47 margin. Three Democrats, Christopher Dodd, Lloyd Bentsen, and Howell Heflin, voted for Tower, while Nancy Kassebaum was the sole Republican to vote against him.

See also: Lloyd Bentsen, George H. W. Bush, Lyndon B. Johnson

*Jeffra Becknell*

## A. C. Townley (1880–1959)

Archetypal political entrepreneur. Arthur Charles Townley, a successful farmer ruined by the business cycle in agriculture, saw a "market" for a certain type of politics among the cash crop farmers of the Northwest and Southwest. He established two great protest organizations— the North Dakota Nonpartisan League and the National Nonpartisan League—to tap this market.

The business cycle played a key role in shattering Townley's second career. The 1921–1923 recession killed off Townley's organizational creations. In 1922 Townley began a third career, founding a marketing cooperative, the National Producers Alliance, but abandoned it to become a wildcat oil driller.

In 1929 Townley founded the American Temperance League, advocating federal control of liquor sales. In 1930 he unsuccessfully tried for Congress in western North Dakota against an old Nonpartisan Leaguer, running on a platform of Prohibition's repeal. In 1933, in the depth of the Great Depression, Townley regained some influence in what was left of the old Nonpartisan League. North Dakota governor William Langer sent him to Washington to push, without success, a plan of massive federal loans for cooperative factories and industries in rural regions. In the late 1940s and early 1950s

Townley became virulently anti-Communist. In 1956, after television came to North Dakota, he tried a red-baiting campaign for the U.S. Senate against Quentin N. Burdick (D) but got fewer than 1,000 votes. Before he could embark on yet another career, Townley died.

See also: William Langer, National Nonpartisan League, North Dakota Nonpartisan League

*Richard M. Valelly*

REFERENCES

Morlan, Robert L. 1985. *Political Prairie Fire: The Nonpartisan League, 1915–1922*. St. Paul: Minnesota Historical Soc.

Remele, Larry. 1981. "Power to the People: The Nonpartisan League." In Thomas W. Howard, ed. *The North Dakota Political Tradition*. Ames: Iowa State U. Pr.

## Francis E. Townsend (1867–1960)

Political reformer of the Great Depression. Born in Livingston County, Illinois, Francis Everett Townsend graduated from Omaha Medical College in 1903 and moved to Belle Fourche, South Dakota, to practice medicine. Because of poor health, he moved to Long Beach, California, in 1920. In 1933 he lost his job as an assistant county health officer because of a change in county administrations. Unemployed and 66 years old, Townsend became alarmed at the flight of the poverty-stricken elderly during the Great Depression.

In September 1933 Townsend announced his proposal that the federal government provide each American over the age of 60 with a pension of $150 a month. This figure was soon increased to $200 a month. Each recipient of this pension would be required to spend all of this amount by the end of each month. Townsend assumed that his policy would not only support the elderly but would also create jobs for younger Americans as consumption and, thus, business activity sharply increased. This pension program would be funded by a national sales tax.

In January 1934 Townsend and his real estate associate, Robert E. Clements, established an organization to publicize the plan, calling it Old-Age Revolving Pensions (OARP). Throughout 1934 and 1935, Clements quickly and skillfully publicized and organized the Townsend movement throughout the United States. By 1935 nearly 500,000 paid memberships in the Townsend clubs made the organization a political enterprise to be dealt with.

In January 1935 Townsend persuaded California Congressman John S. McGroarty to submit a pension bill based on his plan to the

House of Representatives. Townsend's bill eventually died in the House. In August 1935 Congress passed and President Franklin Roosevelt signed the Social Security Act, thereby deflating the appeal of the Townsend movement. Furthermore, congressional investigations of Clements's questionable accounting practices and probable embezzlement of contributions and dues tarnished OARP's public image. Because of his refusal to continue testifying before Congress, Townsend was cited for contempt and found guilty but was pardoned by President Roosevelt. He gave his organization's endorsement to Father Charles Coughlin's Union Party in the 1936 presidential election, but the Townsend plan will remain one of the "radical" propositions characteristic of the desperately needy of the Great Depression of the 1930s.

*See also:* Charles Coughlin, New Deal, Franklin D. Roosevelt, Union Party

*Sean J. Savage*

REFERENCES

Bennett, David H. 1969. *Demagogues in the Depression: American Radicals and the Union Party, 1932–1936.* New Brunswick, NJ: Rutgers U. Pr.

Swing, Raymond. 1935. *Forerunners of American Fascism.* New York: J. Messner.

Townsend, Francis E. 1943. *New Horizons: An Autobiography.* Chicago: J. L. Stewart.

## Townsend Plan

A pension proposal formulated and promoted by Dr. Francis E. Townsend from 1933 until 1936. According to the Townsend Plan, the federal government would pay a pension of $200 a month to every person over the age of 60 provided that the entire amount be spent before the beginning of the next month. The Townsend Plan assumed that this rapid circulation of money and sharp increase in consumption would stimulate economic recovery and generate jobs for younger, unemployed Americans. The pensions were to be financed by a national sales tax.

The 66-year-old Townsend first proposed this pension plan in September 1933 in a letter written to the *Long Beach Press Telegram*, and he was impressed by the favorable response to his proposal among Long Beach's elderly residents. On January 1, 1934, he and a real estate associate, Robert E. Clements, established a nonprofit organization to publicize and organize a movement for the Townsend Plan. They named it Old-Age Revolving Pensions (OARP). One year later, Townsend clubs had been organized throughout

the United States, and paid memberships numbered nearly 500,000. OARP began to publish a newspaper, the *Townsend National Weekly*, to promote the Townsend movement. Membership dues and contributions were collected throughout the nation and sent to OARP.

In January 1935 Townsend persuaded Congressman John S. McGroarty of California to submit a bill to the House of Representatives to enact the Townsend Plan. Congress defeated the bill without even a roll-call vote. Although several more Townsend bills were submitted to Congress, the prospect of the Townsend Plan becoming a federal program quickly faded for basically two reasons. First, Congress passed and President Franklin D. Roosevelt signed the Social Security Act in August 1935. This enactment of federal old-age pensions, however modest compared to Townsend's proposed pensions, mitigated the grievances of the elderly as well as the attraction of the Townsend Plan. Second, the integrity and public image of OARP were tarnished by intensive, highly publicized congressional investigations of OARP's finances. Clements had used questionable accounting practices and had apparently embezzled funds from a movement that he cynically referred to as a "racket." Clements resigned from OARP and his testimony led Congress to aggressively question the subpoenaed Townsend. After Townsend refused to continue testifying, he was cited for contempt of Congress and found guilty but was pardoned by President Roosevelt.

The Reverend Gerald L. K. Smith appeared to fill Clements's position in OARP. As a close political operative of Huey Long, Smith had organized Long's Share Our Wealth clubs throughout the United States. Smith sought to forge a close political alliance with Long's Share Our Wealth movement and Father Charles Coughlin's National Union for Social Justice. Out of Coughlin's movement, the Union Party was founded; and William Lemke, a North Dakota Congressman, was nominated as its candidate for President in the 1936 election. Although Townsend was determined to keep his organization independent, Smith persuaded him to publicly endorse the Lemke candidacy. The Union Party's campaign was a disaster. It was weakened and burdened by the discord and bickering among Coughlin, Smith, Townsend, and Lemke as well as Coughlin's harsh, bitter, personal invectives against Roosevelt.

Even though Townsend's support of the Union Party was somewhat muted and ambivalent, the public's loose association of him with Coughlin and the priest's vitriolic diatribes against the popular FDR fragmented Townsend's national following. After the 1936 landslide re-election of President Roosevelt, the Townsend movement was virtually dead. The *Townsend National Weekly* newspaper, however, continued to be published until the early 1940s.

See also: William Lemke, Huey Long, Francis E. Townsend, Union Party

*Sean J. Savage*

REFERENCES

Bennett, David H. 1969. *Demagogues in the Depression: American Radicals and the Union Party 1932–1936.* New Brunswick, NJ: Rutgers U. Pr.

Swing, Raymond. 1935. *Forerunners of American Fascism.* New York: J. Messner.

Townsend, Francis E. 1943. *New Horizons: An Autobiography.* Chicago: J. L. Stewart.

## Transnational Parties

Political party movements become transnational when they develop supranational organizations that cooperate in a variety of ways across national boundaries. The membership of the major transnational parties consists of national parties, observer groups, and individual persons.

Transnational parties meet most of the attributes of all political parties. They are organizations that have as their principal goal the placing of their avowed representatives into governmental offices. Their organization is formal—that is, officers are elected, headquarters are maintained, membership is defined, and rules of operation are enunciated. Numerous related activities include the declaration of manifestoes or platforms proposing programs of public policy, the reaffirmation of shared political values, and the distribution of patronage when available. Transnational parties also make nominations for supranational offices, engage in election campaigns, create coalitions of interest groups, and mobilize rank-and-file supporters.

The transnational parties are commonly referred to as "internationals." The most prominent ones include the Socialist International, the Christian Democratic International, the Liberal International, and the Conservative International. No longer formally organized is the Communist International (Comintern), replaced to a large degree by the International Department of the Communist Party of the Soviet Union. The formal names of the major democratic transnationals are the International Socialist Conference, the Christian Democratic World Union, the World Liberal Union, and the International Democrat Union. The Republican Party of the United States is a member of the Conservative International. The Democratic Party, through its National Democratic Institute for International Affairs, is an observer member of the Liberal International.

*Communist Internationals*

The best known and oldest of the transnational parties have been the Marxist internationals. The Communists particularly see theirs as precursor of a world political system in the Marxist-Leninist mold.

Founded as the International Working Men's Association in 1848, the original Marxist movement was called the First International by 1864. During the decade that followed, the International organized trade unions and party affiliates in several countries, disbanding, however, in 1877. In 1889 a coalition of trade unions, reformist Marxist parties, and revolutionary groups merged to become the Second, or Socialist Worker's, International, which reached into 23 countries by the time World War I forced it to disband.

The Bolshevik Revolution of 1917 in Russia created the first entirely Communist-controlled government. In 1919, Lenin, rejecting the parliamentarian and gradualist approach of the Socialist Second International, founded the Third International, that is, the Communist International (Comintern). The Comintern program was explicit and determined: the creation of a Communist world-state; the violent overthrow of established capitalist regimes; the replacement of these regimes with "dictatorships of the proletariat," that is, Communist Party oligarchies; the use of subversion, espionage, united fronts, and other Marxist-Leninist tactics in the pursuit of these objectives.

The Comintern was dissolved in 1943 as a gesture to the Allies fighting the common battle against the Axis. In 1947, however, a Communist Information Bureau (Cominform) was established by representatives of Communist parties in nine countries of Europe.

Shortly after World War I and again during the McCarthy era in the early 1950s, the open campaign of the Comintern worldwide generated "Red scares" that made anticommunism a significant theme in U.S. party politics. The very term "internationals" and "Comintern" conjured up images of subversion, espionage, treason, "boring from within," and the overthrow of American institutions.

During the four decades following World War II, the world Communist movement experienced fluctuating fortunes. Tito of Yugoslavia was expelled from the Cominform in 1948 for advocating "separate roads" to socialism. A decade later a breach between the Soviet and Chinese parties initiated an era of Sino-Soviet tension, which waxes and wanes into the 1990s. In 1956 the Cominform was disbanded at the same time that unsuccessful liberalizing uprisings were taking place in Poland and Hungary. In 1957 the Soviet Union attempted to reestablish the International or some equivalent but to no avail. By 1960 Maoism (a Chinese variant of Communism) became a leading force in the Third World. By 1975 Eurocommunists in Italy and France were distancing themselves from Moscow-centered programs.

To deal with this growing polycentrism, the Communist Party of the Soviet Union (CPSU) established in its International Department country and regional desks for most of the countries in the world. Moscow also gave support to the World Peace Council, its principal "front" organization. Communist parties have operated in 96 countries, with a claimed party membership of 90 million. The largest memberships, as of 1987, were in China (44,000,000), the Soviet Union (18,500,000), and Romania (3,557,000), followed by North Korea, East Germany, Yugoslavia, Poland, Czechoslovakia, Italy, and Bulgaria. However, their doctrinal variety—Titoists, Maoists, Trotskyites, Eurocommunists, and others—is testimony of the factionalism that has recently existed in the movement.

An entirely new era in the Communist movement was inaugurated with the advent of the Gorbachev era in the Soviet Union and the 1989 dismantling of the Berlin Wall. Most Communist regimes have been rejected in Eastern European countries, so some Communist parties are now calling themselves Socialist.

## Socialist International

Although the Socialist International regards itself as the direct successor of the Second, or Socialist Worker's, International, a wholly new organization was inaugurated after World War II. Specifically, on March 5, 1945, at the invitation of the British Labor Party, the First Conference of Social Democratic Parties, with 13 parties represented, gathered in London to plan the founding of a new international. By 1951 a new Socialist International came into being.

According to recent count, the Socialist International claims a membership of 47 national parties, 15 consultative parties, 3 fraternal organizations (e.g., the International Union of Socialist Youth), and 8 associated organizations. There are 22 Socialist parties in Western Europe, another 11 in Latin America, 5 in Asia, 3 in the Middle East, 3 in Africa, and 3 in North America. World headquarters are in London.

Historically, most Social Democrats and Laborites have advocated nonviolent change within the context of parliamentary systems; most as well have been staunch in their opposition to totalitarian political methods. Some Socialists have from time to time preferred collaboration and "united fronts" with all fellow-Marxists, on the dubious assumption that governmental power could be shared and that shared power might even serve as a moderating force among the more revolutionary factions. This expectation continues to be a source of dispute among Socialists. In the early years of the present revival, a major concern of Socialist parties was containment of the spread of communism.

In 1969, under the leadership of Chancellor Willy Brandt, West Germany adopted an Ostpolitik strategy of rapprochement with the Soviet Union and Eastern Europe. This policy weakened the anti-Communist stance of German Socialists and carried over into Brandt's leadership of the Socialist International in the 1970s, during which a kind of détente prevailed between Socialists and Communists. In most recent practice, the Socialist International has favored firmness in dealings with Eurocommunists, but it has engaged in united fronts with Communists in the Third World.

## Christian Democratic International

Christian democracy emerged in the nineteenth century as an antagonist of liberalism. Christian Democrats also opposed the centralizing tendencies of nineteenth-century nation-states. The movement was steeped in its Catholic theological origins and was more active in local than in national politics. After World War II, however, these parties set aside their Catholic emphases, gathered members elected to governmental office throughout Europe, began to gain influence in Latin America, and gave substantial attention to the task of transnational organization.

First efforts at international Christian Democratic cooperation were initiated by Don Luigi Sturzo as early as 1919, shortly after the founding of the Italian People's Party. The First International Congress of People's Parties was held in Paris in December 1925. Successive congresses were held during the 1920s and 1930s. In 1936 Sturzo once again took up his campaign to create a transnational Christian Democratic party. By 1940 an International Democrat Union was organized and included many European governments-in-exile. In July 1947 an international congress established the International Union of Christian Democrats. Principal headquarters are in Brussels.

Today, Christian Democrats have a World Union and three regional organizations, one each in Western Europe, Central Europe, and the Americas. Some Christian Democratic parties are much more conservative than others and have become associated with the Conservative International, that is, the International Democrat Union.

## Liberal International

Liberals were the major ideological force in Europe during the nineteenth century, representative of commercial and industrial interests in particular. International conferences of liberals made their first appearance in 1910 but not until April 1947 did liberals take steps toward transnational organization. On April 14, 1947, representatives of 19 liberal parties and groups, mainly European, signed a Liberal Manifesto in Oxford, England; this agreement became the basic document of the World Liberal Union, or Liberal International. Headquarters were established in London.

The International was predominantly European in its membership and policy concerns until the Canadian Liberal Party joined in the early 1970s. Thereafter, the leadership of the Liberal International began to focus on issues from a global rather than a Eurocentric perspective and also began to reach out to organized liberals on other continents. Nineteenth-century ideological doctrines were either dropped or modernized by a Declaration of Oxford in 1967 and the Liberal Appeal of 1981.

In the mid-1980s, Democratic Party leaders in the United States, particularly those associated with the National Democratic Institute for International Affairs (NDI), became interested in the work of the democratic internationals. A delegation of NDI officials attended the congress of the Liberal International in Madrid in October 1985. In June 1986 NDI again sent observers to meetings of the Liberals. Soon after, NDI applied for and received observer membership in the Liberal International. On October 2, 1986, former Vice President Walter Mondale, acting in his capacity as chairman of the National Democratic Institute, led a delegation of eight to the annual congress of the Liberal International in Hamburg to accept membership.

## Conservative International

The most recently constituted transnational is the International Democrat Union (IDU), an outgrowth of the European Democrat Union (EDU) and the Pacific Democrat Union (PDU).

In 1982 Vice President George Bush attended the annual congress of the European Democrat Union in Munich. The EDU is made up of Conservative and several Christian Democratic parties. Vice President Bush was accompanied by Republican Party chairman Frank Fahrenkopf. Fahrenkopf was aware of transnational parties in his role as an officer of the bipartisan American Political Foundation, a position he held in association with Democratic national chairman Charles Manatt. The Foundation was dedicated to improving transnational communication among political party leaders in all democratic countries.

In June 1982 Vice President Bush took the initiative in bringing Japanese, Australian, Canadian, and U.S. conservatives together to establish the Pacific Democrat Union. In 1983 delegates from the EDU and the PDU met in London to found the International Democrat Union. Bush then arranged to host the first annual congress of the newly formed Conservative International at the 1984 Republican National Convention in Dallas. A second conference was held in Washington in July 1985, attended by 250 officials of approximately 40 political parties worldwide. The IDU claims a membership of 29 national parties.

## Activities of Transnational Parties

The democratic transnational parties engage in several kinds of activities typical of pluralist parties, including the following.

1. *Election of party leaders to public offices.* This activity was pursued for the first time supranationally in the first three direct elections of representatives to the European Parliament in 1979, 1984, and 1989. Most of the transnationals ran coordinated

campaigns throughout Western Europe. Election effort has also taken the form of assistance to colleagues seeking national office in countries other than their own (e.g., the Socialist International helping Socialists in Portugal and Spain and the Christian Democrats helping their colleagues in Venezuela and El Salvador).

2. *Coordination of transnational party programs.* This has been most evident in the manifestoes and other programmatic declarations produced by transnational party congresses. Despite widely held myths about the ideological purity of the transnational parties, intense intraparty debates over the specific content of party manifestoes and declarations often enliven discussions of programs.

On a day-to-day basis, policymaking by regional transnational parties may be observed, for example, in the work of the Party Groups serving the membership of the European Parliament. Each major European transnational party represented in the Parliament—Socialists, Christian Democrats, Liberals, Conservatives, Greens—has its own caucus-like organization whose staff prepares research and policy studies and draft declarations on the issues before the European Parliament.

3. *Development of global party organization.* Each of the major transnational parties has operated at its own organizational pace. The Communists have been the most systematic, providing training and other resources to party cadres in countries throughout the world. Running a close second in organizational experience and success are the Socialists, somewhat constrained by their tactics of peaceful change and national self-determination. Christian Democrats have been particularly successful organizationally in Europe and Latin America. Conservatives have also accomplished a great deal in their first half-dozen years. Liberals, burdened by minority status and a penchant for independence, have taken the longest to mobilize their transnational membership.

4. *Supranational centers of operation.* Transnational parties, like other evolving organizations, have acquired formality and vitality as a consequence of such regular activities as annual party congresses, the maintenance of world headquarters, periodical publications, the sponsorship of research and study institutes, cooperation in legislative assemblies, and active propaganda campaigns. The centers of these transnational activities vary in formality from the well-organized Party Groups in the European Parliament to the informal collegial consultations at the United Nations. Transnational party representatives are in evidence in a number of supranational and regional organizations, often collaborating with each other on an informal basis.

5. *Cooperation among transnational parties.* The leaders of the democratic transnational parties share certain political goals, the principal of which is the spread and success of democratic institutions throughout the world. With over 100 totalitarian or authoritarian political regimes extant in the world, spreading democracy requires not only ideological rhetoric but also substantial cooperation among practicing democrats. For this reason, the presidents of three transnationals—Christian Democrats, Liberals, and Social Democrats—met together for the first time in Rome on April 10, 1984, to discuss their common interests. The meeting produced the first joint statement ever issued by the transnationals.

The statement, titled "Common Appeal on Latin America," applauded democratic developments then occurring in Latin America, inviting democratic forces to link up with one or another of the (then) three major transnational parties. The statement was so well received in Latin America that the officers of the three transnationals, despite their fundamental difference on most issues, were encouraged to make another joint statement in 1986. The new International Democrat Union joined the group of three. After consultation with the United Nations Fund for Population Affairs, the secretaries-general of the four transnational parties declared their common concern for the many problems being created by unbridled population growth in many parts of the world. It has been suggested that the four transnationals form a Commission of Democratic Transnational Parties to serve as a "mentor organization" for the Central American democratization process.

## Involvement of United States Parties

Substantial reasons exist for expecting increased American participation in transnational party affairs. Understanding political events in many parts of the world is increasingly difficult if the role of the transnational parties is ignored. In the case of El Salvador, for example, the Socialist International and the Christian Democratic International have been deeply involved in the politics of that unhappy and war-torn community.

Another reason for United States party involvement is the dramatic growth since World War II in the number and reach of transnational nongovernmental organizations (NGOs). NGOs are in effect transnational pressure groups. Well over 3,000 NGOs exist and have substantial memberships, many with important memberships in the United States. Hundreds are registered with such supranational bodies as the United Nations and the European Commission. They include international trade unions, international chambers of commerce, and other NGOs of almost every type: religious, professional, scientific, academic, humanitarian, agricultural, and many others. U.S. influence in world affairs is likely to be greatly enhanced by international coalitions of NGOs put together and led by transnational parties.

Finally, transnational parties provide opportunities and means for global civic education in the values and open processes of democratic politics, an activity for which United States parties are particularly adept. Because secrecy and democracy do not go well together, U.S. parties can participate in protecting and promoting an open world politics.

See also: George H. W. Bush, Frank Fahrenkopf, Charles Manatt, Walter F. Mondale, United Nations

*Ralph M. Goldman*

REFERENCES

Goldman, Ralph M. 1983. *Transnational Parties: Organizing the World's Precincts.* Lanham, MD: University Pr. of America.

———. 1990. *From Warfare to Party Politics: The Critical Transition to Civilian Control.* Syracuse: Syracuse U. Pr.

## Harry S Truman

"Give 'em hell, Harry," the thirty-third President of the United States. Born in Lamar, Missouri, Harry Truman believed that party organizations were important in the seizure and application of political power. As an organization man who had started his political career with local precinct activity, he strongly believed in party regularity and unity. Despite being promoted for the U.S. Senate in 1934 by Tom Pendergast's Kansas City Democratic Party machine, Truman generally continued the independent judgment and concern for government efficiency that he had shown as a county judge. In a successful but close 1940 reelection bid, Truman gained additional expertise in the exercise of partisan political power, as he forged an alliance with organized labor and with the Democratic leader of St. Louis. His wartime chairmanship of a Special Committee to Investigate the National Defense Program led to national recognition of his concern for honesty and efficiency in government. In 1944 Franklin D. Roosevelt successfully appealed to Truman's sense of party loyalty and desire for party unity during a time of war in getting him to accept the vice presidency; at Roosevelt's death, he became President in 1945.

The Republicans with a slogan of "Had Enough?" regained control of Congress in the 1946 election during a time of public dissatisfaction with economic and foreign conditions. Truman's subsequently announced Fair Deal was a proposed extension of the liberal philosophy of the New Deal into health insurance, civil rights, housing, and other domestic areas, and constituted a short-term strategy for reelection as well as a long-term proposed reform in the political system. While a conservative coalition of southern Democrats and Republicans effectively killed the Fair Deal, Congress' original consideration of these liberal programs set the stage for their eventual enactment in subsequent Democratic presidential administrations.

Despite his low popularity and the widespread expectation of his general election defeat, machine politicians in the Democratic National Committee lined up enough delegates to allow Truman to receive the 1948 Democratic presidential nomination. Senate Majority Leader Alben Barkley's rousing keynote address attacking the Republican Party led to his selection as Vice President. Truman then shifted public attention from his own troubles by attacking the Republican-controlled "do-nothing Eightieth Congress."

In the general election campaign, Truman stressed partisan considerations by associating the Republican Party with "special interests" like the rich and big business and by reminding voters of Democratic support for the New Deal and local projects provided by the Democratic presidential administration. An aggressive Democratic National Committee revitalized various demoralized party organizations across the nation, while organized labor strongly supported Truman and the rest of his party's ticket. Truman's reelection and the Democrats' control of Congress demonstrated that the New Deal Democratic coalition, consisting of labor, African-Americans, Jews, farmers, and lower income people was not merely associated with FDR but had become the majority political coalition in America.

Fearing conservative congressional Republican control of domestic and foreign policy under a Dwight Eisenhower administration and distrusting political reformers like Tennessee Senator Estes Kefauver, Truman urged Illinois governor Adlai E. Stevenson to accept the 1952 Democratic presidential nomination. Stevenson subsequently had to dissociate himself from the unpopular Truman administration.

Throughout his political career, Truman regarded himself as a Jeffersonian Democrat concerned about the "common man" and constantly adapting to modern conditions. As an admirer of "liberal" Presidents, he wanted to ensure that government was run for the benefit of all of the people rather than the special interests who had the "inside track." Truman believed that Republicans balanced budgets mechanically, while he was concerned over the "human budget" and felt that Democrats promoted a fairer distribution of the nation's prosperity. Believing in the convention system and organization politics, Truman felt that a presidential primary would be too expensive and strenuous on candidates and envisioned modern campaign advertising as "big lie" techniques.

*See also:* Alben Barkley, Dwight D. Eisenhower, Tom Pendergast, Franklin D. Roosevelt, Adlai E. Stevenson II

*Stephen D. Shaffer*

REFERENCES

Gosnell, Harold. 1980. *Truman's Crises: A Political Biography of Harry S Truman*. Westport, CT: Greenwood.

Hartmann, Susan. 1971. *Truman and the 80th Congress*. Columbia: U. of Missouri Pr.

McCoy, Donald. 1984. *The Presidency of Harry S Truman*. Lawrence: U. Pr. of Kansas.

Miller, Merle. 1974. *Plain Speaking: An Oral Biography of Harry S Truman*. New York: Berkley.

Phillips, Cabell. 1966. *The Truman Presidency: The History of a Triumphant Succession*. New York: Macmillan.

Truman, Harry S. 1956. *Years of Trial and Hope, Memoirs*, Vol. 2. New York: New American Library.

Truman, Margaret. 1973. *Harry S Truman*. New York: Morrow.

## Jonathan Trumbull, Jr. (1740–1809)

Post-Revolutionary War governor of Connecticut. Born in Lebanon, Connecticut, the second son of his Connecticut governor father, Jonathan Trumbull, Jr., graduated from Harvard in 1759 and, after holding various local offices in Lebanon, was elected to the general assembly in 1774. Trumbull's nationalism and Federalism were grounded in his wartime experiences. In 1775 the Continental Congress appointed him paymaster for the northern armies. Trumbull then served as comptroller of the treasury, only to replace Alexander Hamilton as General George Washington's secretary. Years of attempting to feed, clothe, and equip an army in order to win the war, all with little or no support from a weak central government, hardened Trumbull's conservative values. He was one of many senior army officers active in the nationalist movement of the early 1780s, and he threw all of his political weight behind the federal constitution.

Trumbull was elected to the First, Second, and Third Congresses, and he served as Speaker in the Second. Both in the House and in the Senate (to which he was elected in 1794), Trumbull was prominent among the hard core of Federalists who supported Alexander Hamilton's fiscal plans. He resigned from national office in 1796 to become deputy governor of Connecticut, and he held the governorship from 1797 for 12 years until his death. Under his leadership, Connecticut became the last bastion of Federalism, holding out against Republican forces and policies that Trumbull viewed as subversive and dangerous to the Republic. In 1809 the aging Trumbull defied President James Madison's order to call out the state militia to enforce the embargo, arguing that such action would be unconstitutional.

*See also:* Alexander Hamilton, James Madison, George Washington

*Simon P. Newman*

REFERENCES

Fischer, David Hackett. 1965. *The Revolution of American Conservatism: The Federalist Period in the Era of Jeffersonian Democracy*. New York: Harper & Row.

Ifkovic, John W. 1977. *Connecticut's Nationalist Revolutionary: Jonathan Trumbull, Junior*. Hartford: The American Revolution Bicentennial Commission of Connecticut.

Shipton, Clifford K. 1873. *Sibley's Harvard Graduates*. Boston: Massachusetts Historical Society.

Trumbull, John. 1809. *Biographical Sketch of the Character of Governor Trumbull*. Hartford, CT: Hudson and Goodwin.

## Lyman Trumbull (1813–1896)

Civil War-era Illinois U.S. Senator. Lyman Trumbull played a key role in sectional politics during the Civil War era. He moved in and out of political parties, seemingly driven more by conscience than by political expediency. During his long career he was successively a Democrat, a Republican, a Liberal Republican, and then once again a Democrat; he ended his career in the 1890s with a brief flirtation with populism. His most important role was in the United States during the critical period 1855 to 1873.

Born in Colchester, Connecticut, Trumbull moved to Illinois in the 1830s and quickly established himself in Democratic politics. He served in several state posts including justice of the Supreme Court before his election to the U.S. Senate in 1855. In winning the Senate seat as an antislavery Democrat, he not only defeated the Democratic incumbent but also the Whig candidate, Abraham Lincoln.

Trumbull's Senate career was characterized by controversy, as he first battled Stephen A. Douglas in opposition to popular sovereignty over slavery in the territories. During the Civil War he was both supporter and critic of President Lincoln. A constitutionalist, he resisted what he considered to be Lincoln's arbitrary arrest policy. Late in the war, he was instrumental in Senate passage of the Thirteenth Amendment, abolishing slavery.

During the Andrew Johnson administration, Trumbull broke with his Republican colleagues and voted to acquit the President of impeachment charges. In 1872 he joined the Liberal Republicans and was denied reelection to the Senate the following year. By 1876 he had returned to the Democratic fold and four years later ran unsuccessfully for governor of Illinois. Finally, in 1894, he drafted a platform for Chicago Populists. To this legal-minded official, political principle rather than expedience was the driving force in his many party switches.

*See also:* Stephen A. Douglas, Andrew Johnson, Liberal Republicans, Abraham Lincoln, Populist (People's) Party

*Frederick J. Blue*

REFERENCES

Benedict, Michael Les. 1973. *The Impeachment and Trial of Andrew Johnson.* New York: Norton.

Bowers, Claude G. 1929. *The Tragic Era: The Revolution After Lincoln.* Cambridge: Riverside Pr.

Roshe, Ralph J. 1979. *His Own Counsel: The Life and Times of Lyman Trumbull.* Reno: U. of Nevada Pr.

White, Horace. 1913. *The Life of Lyman Trumbull.* Boston: Houghton Mifflin.

## Truncated Parties

A truncated party refers to an elite organization divorced from a mass base. Political scientist Kay Lawson introduced the term "truncated" party to distinguish between traditional conceptions of party predicated on the existence of "a relatively durable social formation . . . which links leaders at the centers of government to a significant popular following in the political arena and its local enclaves" through symbols of party identification and loyalty, linking them with newer conceptions of party based upon the decline in party identification among the electorate. American parties have usually been classified as "cadre" parties—electorally oriented episodic organization of political notables lacking an enrolled membership yet still supported by voters with an attachment to the party. The truncated party takes the cadre concept one step further: truncated parties lack even the symbols of party identification and attachment.

Rational choice theorists have always argued that the party concept must admit that voters as ordinary citizens have a rational incentive to participate. Several contemporary theorists, citing the development of permanent party organizations with full-time staff, have proposed new empirically based definitions of party predicated on the notion of a truncated party system. Theorists like Paul Herrnson have proposed the "party-as-broker" model stressing the role of party staff in mediating between candidates and groups providing campaign resources; similarly, Christopher Arterton suggests a "PAC model" of parties in which parties are there primarily to channel interest group donations to candidates. Stephen Frantzich, citing innovation theory, stresses the organizational evolution of parties into "service-vendors." Some scholars, like Walter Dean Burnham who classifies the contemporary system as an "interregnum era" based on the tandem appearance of partisan decomposition and electoral volatility with increased elite organization, decry the development of the "permanent campaign." Denise Baer and David Bositis, on the other hand, have stressed the role of social movements in linking elites and masses in their critique of the limitations of the "truncated party" solution to contradictions in contemporary party theory.

*See also:* Party Identification

*Denise L. Baer*

REFERENCES

Arterton, G. Christopher. 1982. "Political Money and Political Strength." In Joel L. Fleishman, ed. *The Future of American Political Parties*. Englewood Cliffs, NJ: Prentice-Hall.

Baer, Denise L., and David A. Bositis. 1988. *Elite Cadres and Party Coalitions: Representing the Public in Party Politics*. Westport, CT: Greenwood.

Blumenthal, Sidney. 1982. *The Permanent Campaign*. New York: Touchstone.

Burnham, Walter Dean. 1985. "The 1984 Election and the Future of American Politics." In Ellis Sandoz and Cecil V. Crabb, Jr., eds. *Election 84*. New York: Mentor.

Chambers, William N. 1967. *An Economic Theory of Democracy*. New York: Harper & Row.

Frantzich, Stephen E. 1989. *Political Parties in the Technological Age*. New York: Longman.

Herrnson, Paul. 1988. *Party Campaigning in the 1980s*. Cambridge: Harvard U. Pr.

Lawson, Kay. 1978. "Constitutional Change and Party Development in France, Nigeria, and United States." In Louis Maisel and Joseph Cooper, eds. *Political Parties: Development and Decay*. Beverly Hills, CA: Sage.

Schlesinger, Joseph. 1984. "On the Theory of Party Organization." 46 *Journal of Politics* 369.

## Trusts

The issue of trusts and their regulation by government was a dominant political theme during the Populist-Progressive era, from the late nineteenth century into the early twentieth century. Although trusts were a specific organizational arrangement for businesses, in the popular mind "trusts" were any combination of firms in a given industry created to increase corporate profits and reduce competition. The move toward business concentration following the Civil War spawned a reaction among those adversely affected by it. Midwestern and southern Populists, reflecting rural values, denounced first the large railroads and then the cartels or pools that controlled prices. Opposition to the beef, whiskey, tobacco, and sugar cartels particularly affected farmers. But the entire nation was affected by the consolidation mania resulting in the nation's first real trust—Standard Oil in 1882 under John D. Rockefeller—and later the creation of International Harvester, United States Steel, and others. By 1900 over 300 trusts had a capitalization in excess of $7 billion. The largest 2 percent of manufacturers produced nearly 50 percent of all manufactured goods.

Economic panics in 1893 and 1907 increased public concern over the impact of trusts. The power of the trusts not only influenced economic developments but also drew the attention of politicians. The high water mark of national Populist reaction was the nomination of William Jennings Bryan in 1896 by the Democrats after his stirring "Cross of Gold" speech. Populists, in a separate convention, also nominated Bryan. Ostensibly the major issue was the gold standard, but in a larger sense the presidential campaign revolved around the role of government in business; Democrats favored a more active role, and Republicans under William McKinley resisted the growth of government.

Although states made some attempts to control the power of railroads and the growth of trusts, Congress did not create the Interstate Commerce Commission until 1887 and did not pass its first antitrust legislation until 1890. The Sherman Antitrust Act defined and outlawed combinations in restraint of trade. President Theodore Roosevelt used the act to prosecute the trusts aggressively, helping to earn his trust-busting reputation. The Supreme Court's invocation of the "rule of reason," however, meant that only "unreasonable" restraint of trade was outlawed under the Sherman Act. Despite antitrust prosecutions under Roosevelt and William Howard Taft, the weak Clayton Antitrust Act of 1914 was the only other major antitrust legislation adopted during the period.

Two Progressive era Presidents represented different governmental responses to business consolidation. Both Theodore Roosevelt and Woodrow Wilson articulated their positions on the trusts in the 1912 presidential campaign. Progressive Roosevelt, influenced by Herbert Croly, espoused a sweeping "New Nationalism" that recognized corporations and bigness, but called for strong federal governmental regulation. Democrat Wilson campaigned for a "New Freedom" that sought to protect the small entrepreneur by opposing bigness and, therefore, the formation of trusts. After his election, however, Wilson moved gradually toward regulation rather than trust busting as a method for dealing with growing corporate power and influence. Wilson used the findings of the Pujo Commission popularized by Louis D. Brandeis in *Other People's Money*, to attack the "money monopoly"—the banks. His regulatory efforts resulted in the Federal Reserve Act of 1913 and the Federal Trade Commission Act of 1914.

*See also:* Louis D. Brandeis, William Jennings Bryan, Herbert Croly, William McKinley, Theodore Roosevelt, Sherman Antitrust Act, William Howard Taft, Woodrow Wilson

*Nicholas C. Burckel*

REFERENCES

Chandler, Alfred D., Jr. 1977. *The Visible Hand: The Managerial Revolution in American Business*. Cambridge: Belknap Press.

Lamoreaux, Naomi R. 1985. *The Great Merger Movement in American Business, 1895–1904*. New York: Cambridge U. Pr.

McCraw, Thomas K. 1984. *Prophets of Regulation: Charles Francis Adams, Louis D. Brandeis, James M. Landis, and Alfred E. Kahn*. Cambridge: Belknap Press.

## Rexford G. Tugwell (1891–1979)

Member of Franklin D. Roosevelt's "Brains Trust." Rexford Guy Tugwell helped plan the early New Deal and served in Roosevelt's first-term administration. Tugwell was born and raised in upper New York State and earned his bachelor's, master's, and doctoral degrees from the University of Pennsylvania's Wharton School of Finance and Commerce. A noted agricultural economist as a member of the Columbia University faculty in the 1920s, Tugwell became part of the unofficial cabinet, the "Brains Trust," that advised Roosevelt during the 1932 campaign and then helped design the initial New Deal programs. He was closely involved with the Agricultural Adjustment Administration, served as Assistant and then Under Secretary of Agriculture, and in May 1935 became head of the Resettlement Administration, which sought to help marginal farmers. Tugwell also acted as a general policy adviser to President Roosevelt. Self-assured and assertive, he articulated ideas of government economic planning and controls with roots in institutional economics and New Nationalist progressivism. To Tugwell, the New Deal did not go nearly far enough toward a centrally controlled economy nor did it implement the far-reaching planning and reform he advocated. He left the administration after Roosevelt's first term but remained on good personal terms with FDR. Tugwell later served a number of public and academic posts and was the author of nearly three dozen books.

See also: New Deal, Franklin D. Roosevelt

*John W. Jeffries*

REFERENCES

Sternsher, Bernard. 1964. *Rexford Tugwell and the New Deal*. New Brunswick, NJ: Rutgers U. Pr.

Tugwell, Rexford G. 1967. *The Brains Trust*. New York: Viking.

## Joseph P. Tumulty (1879–1954)

Confidant of Woodrow Wilson. Joseph Patrick Tumulty was probably the only person who remained close to Woodrow Wilson throughout the President's political career. Tumulty grew up in Jersey City, New Jersey, where he practiced law and became involved in local Democratic Party politics. Elected to the New Jersey Assembly in 1906, he emerged as a leader of the insurgent faction and as a strong supporter of Wilson during his 1910 gubernatorial campaign. After Wilson's triumph, Tumulty became his personal secretary, managing the governor's office and dispensing patronage so as to advance Wilson's legislative agenda in New Jersey.

With Wilson's election to the presidency in November 1912, Tumulty moved to the White House. Deeply devoted to Wilson and his political program, Tumulty was a loyal friend and trusted adviser. He guarded access to Wilson's office, dealt on a day-to-day basis with politicians and reporters, dispensed patronage and plotted political strategy, carefully studied public opinion, and in many states sought to mediate quarrels within the Democratic Party. A warm and gregarious man, Tumulty helped to compensate for the President's solitary academic habits.

Wilson's confidence in Tumulty gradually declined, and in November 1916 he tried to dismiss his longtime secretary. Tumulty's impassioned protest, however, weakened Wilson's resolve, and Joe Tumulty stayed on until the end of Wilson's presidency. After America's entry into World War I, Tumulty became an expert on the domestic aspects of war and peacemaking, regaining much of the President's trust.

Worried about the deteriorating position of the Democratic Party, Tumulty tried, without much success, to shift the President's attention to domestic developments. The Senate's rejection of the Treaty of Versailles and the rout of the Democratic Party in the 1920 elections were a dismal conclusion to Tumulty's otherwise remarkably successful career. Finally out of power, Tumulty pursued a lucrative law practice in Washington and followed closely Democratic Party politics. He supported Alfred E. Smith for the nomination in 1924 and 1928, but he was never close to Franklin D. Roosevelt and felt much ambivalence toward the New Deal. Tumulty always remained faithful to the Wilsonian legacy, believing until the end of his life that, as Woodrow Wilson's personal secretary, he had "lived in the presence of a great man."

See also: New Deal, Franklin D. Roosevelt, Alfred E. Smith, Woodrow Wilson

*Charles E. Neu*

REFERENCES

Blum, John M. 1951. *Joe Tumulty and the Wilson Era.* Boston: Houghton Mifflin.

Link, Arthur S. 1956. *Wilson: The New Freedom.* Princeton: Princeton U. Pr.

Tumulty, Joseph P. 1921. *Woodrow Wilson As I Know Him.* Garden City, NY: Doubleday.

## William M. Tweed (1823–1878)

Boss of New York City's Tammany Machine. William Marcy Tweed, the leader of the Tweed Ring, was the most powerful politician in New York City in the late 1860s. Beginning with his downfall in 1871, his name has come to symbolize both political bossism and municipal corruption.

Tweed was the foreman of a volunteer fire company, an alderman, a congressman, and a member of the board of education before being elected to the New York County Board of Supervisors in 1857. He remained a county supervisor until 1870 and simultaneously served as deputy street commissioner (1864–1870), chairman of the Tammany Hall General Committee (1863–1871), state senator (1867–1871), grand sachem of the Tammany Society (1869–1871), and Superintendent of Public Works (1870–1871).

By simultaneously occupying offices in the Democratic Party and in county, city, and state government, Tweed was able to centralize power in his own hands. Boss Tweed's influence was never really institutional, however, but personal. Rather than occupying the top position in a hierarchical organization, Tweed was the central figure in a shifting network of officeholders. Exercising no authority over the members of this "ring," Tweed had to direct a steady flow of payoffs to his associates in order to secure their cooperation. The chief source of these payoffs were kickbacks by contractors who overbilled for the goods and services that they sold to the city.

The Tweed Ring was overthrown after the *New York Times* published documents revealing massive corruption under its auspices. Cartoonist Thomas Nast's caricatures of a bloated and epicene Tweed also helped to discredit the Boss. Estimates of the amount stolen exceeded $40 million. Tweed was arrested in October 1871, convicted in 1873 for failure to properly audit city bills, and died in prison.

*See also:* Bosses, Urban Political Machines, Tammany Hall

*Martin Shefter*

REFERENCES

Callow, Alexander. 1966. *The Tweed Ring.* New York: Oxford U. Pr.

Hershkowitz, Leo. 1977. *Tweed's New York: Another Look.* Garden City, NY: Doubleday.

Mandelbaum, Seymour. 1965. *Boss Tweed's New York.* New York: Wiley.

## Tweed Ring

Dominating the politics of New York City from 1868 to 1871, the Tweed Ring controlled the first modern urban political machine. Its basis of power was Tammany Hall, the leading faction of the local Democratic Party; the Tweed Ring molded Tammany into the successful organization that would control the Democratic Party and city government for years to come. At its pinnacle the Tweed Ring exercised tremendous power; its demise, however, came in the face of the usual charges of extreme corruption and graft.

William M. Tweed was Tammany's first undisputed boss. Entering politics in his twenties and finding considerable success in electoral politics, Tweed captured the two prime positions in the city's Democratic politics; he was chairman of the General Committee of Tammany and grand sachem (leader) of Tammany at age 40. The other prominent individuals in the Tweed Ring were A. Oakey "O.K." Hall, mayor of New York from 1869 to 1872; city chamberlain Peter B. "Brains" Sweeny; and city comptroller Richard "Slippery Dick" Connolly. In a city ripe for leadership and coordination, the Ring found ample opportunity to establish itself.

Mid-nineteenth-century New York City, like other urban areas, was straining under the demands of a rapidly growing urban population. By 1870 a full 44 percent of the city's population was foreign born, predominantly German and Irish. The Tweed Ring was able to court this immigrant population, relatively homogeneous by the standards of the diverse ethnic populations later in the century, with the promise of material resources in exchange for political support. Not only did Tweed use the pool of patronage positions that has become closely associated with the operation of urban machines, but he also established his own public welfare program providing aid to the poor and a system of public assistance to religious institutions, especially the Roman Catholic church of which many immigrant poor were members.

The Ring also relied upon local political leaders to maintain dominance over Democratic politics in New York City. Under Tweed's control, Tammany established a tightly organized ward and election district club network. To maintain allegiance of local leaders in this decentralized arrangement, the Tweed Ring reportedly resorted to large-scale graft. The support of public officials was secured by returning to them a percentage of official revenue. Thus, the Tweed Ring created a strong bond between itself and its bases of support.

The Tweed Ring guided Tammany to overwhelming electoral success. Yet accounts of the Ring's growth and maintenance are clearly overshadowed by those of its rapid and dramatic decline. Reaching its height of power in 1870, by the summer of 1871 its downfall had begun. The *New York Times* published accounts of the Tweed Ring's corrupt practices, and *Harper's Weekly* carried a series of cartoons by Thomas Nast in which Boss Tweed and his associates were portrayed as vulgar and self-serving. Both exposés generated public concern while arrests of Ring members, including Tweed himself, also precipitated increasingly heavy Tammany losses at the polls. Boss Tweed was reelected as the city's Superintendent of Public Works, but his associates in the Ring faltered in the election. Eventually Tweed would serve time following conviction on felony charges. He died in prison in 1878.

The intricate network of political support created by the Tweed Ring was not sufficient to fend off its rapid and permanent demise. Tammany Hall, however, suffered only a temporary setback and eventually regained its position of dominance in the politics of New York City.

*See also:* Thomas Nast, Tammany Hall, William M. Tweed

*Barbara Trish*

REFERENCES

Allswang, John M. 1986. *Bosses, Machines, and Urban Voters*. Baltimore: Johns Hopkins U. Pr.

Zink, Harold. 1930. *City Bosses in the United States*. Durham, NC: Duke U. Pr.

## Twelfth Amendment

Ratified in 1804, this amendment to the U.S. Constitution specifies the process by which the President and Vice President are elected. Under the procedure, as originally defined by the Constitution, each elector in the Electoral College casts two votes in the presidential election. The candidate receiving the largest number of electoral votes served as President, and the candidate receiving the second largest number of votes in the Electoral College performed the duties of Vice President. In the event that no person received a majority of the votes or in the case of a tie vote, the election would be decided by the House of Representatives.

For the first two national elections, this system worked satisfactorily, but inherent weaknesses appeared by the third election. Competing political parties had come into existence at this time, and George Washington, who retired after his second term, was the only politician who could have commanded the support of the entire nation. Observers noted that a tie vote between two candidates could easily take place, thereby throwing the election into the House of Representatives for a decision. Because of the top two total vote selection criteria, the initial election system also could prevent the President and Vice President from being of the same political party. Additionally, some of the electors who feared a tie vote, might not use their second vote. Thus, by trying to insure the election of their candidate for the presidency, they permitted the opposition's candidate to secure the vice presidency.

This eventually first manifested itself in the 1796 election when John Adams, a Federalist, and Thomas Jefferson, a Democratic-Republican, became President and Vice President, respectively. In the 1800 election, further complications arose when the Electoral College—primarily through intrigue and miscalculation—cast 73 votes apiece for Thomas Jefferson and Aaron Burr, thereby forcing the election into the House. Not until the thirty-sixth ballot, and after much political haggling, was Jefferson elected President. To alleviate this constitutional fault, the Twelfth Amendment stipulated that electors cast separate ballots for President and Vice President, with the candidate receiving a majority of the vote for each office winning election. In the event that no candidate receives a majority of the vote, then the House will elect the President or the Senate will vote for the Vice President. Only twice since the adoption of the Twelfth Amendment has the election of the President or Vice President been relegated to Congress: in the 1824 election, when a House vote resolved an indecisive ballot in the electoral college by placing John Quincy Adams in the White House; and in the 1836 election, when the Senate decided an electoral vote with no majority candidate by choosing Richard M. Johnson as Vice President.

*See also:* John Adams, Aaron Burr, Electoral College System, Thomas Jefferson, Richard M. Johnson, George Washington

*Hal T. Shelton*

## Twenty-fourth Amendment

On January 23, 1964, South Dakota became the thirty-eighth state (fulfilling the three-fourths majority requirement) to ratify the Twenty-fourth Amendment, thereby instituting a constitutional act prohibiting the use of the poll tax as a prerequisite to voting in federal elections. While the new amendment modified laws only in the five southern states of Texas, Arkansas, Mississippi, Alabama, and Virginia, the debate and controversy surrounding the poll tax issue brought in broader social and constitutional issues.

The poll tax itself had evoked protest from civil rights leaders throughout the mid-twentieth century. Poll taxes were most common in southern states, where they were used as a political tool to disfranchise African-American voters. Proponents of the poll tax argued that nothing was unconstitutional about requiring all citizens to pay a "head tax"; this point in fact was not the issue. At the heart of the debate was the payment of the poll tax as a determinant of an individual's eligibility to vote. Thus, the context of the tax, rather than the tax itself, was the focus of concern.

Ironically, the passage of the Twenty-fourth Amendment itself would not eliminate the use of the poll tax to bar individuals from voting in some elections. States' rights advocates argued that any amendment restricting a state's power to run its own elections would be unconstitutional; hence, the restrictive language of the Twenty-fourth Amendment covered only federal elections. Ratification of the Twenty-fourth Amendment was largely symbolic, as the use of the poll tax in state and local elections was still permissible in 1964.

Despite the theoretically small impact that the Twenty-fourth Amendment appeared to have, the social climate of the times that permitted passage of the constitutional addition also encouraged other major changes in voting rights accorded to Blacks and poor whites. The Voting Rights Act of 1965 outlawed the use of literacy tests as a determinant of voters' eligibility, and also mandated federal action to register voters in those states where registration was less than 50 percent of those eligible to vote. On the judicial side, in 1966 the Supreme Court in *Harper v. Virginia* ruled that poll taxes used as prerequisites to voting were counter to the equal protection clause of the Constitution.

The practical effects of the Twenty-fourth Amendment's passage are uncertain in magnitude. Registration and participation of African-American voters in the South was increasing before 1964, and because the amendment's ratification came so close to the passage of the Voting Rights Act and the *Harper* decision, an isolated assessment of the benefits derived from the Twenty-fourth Amendment alone is difficult. However, the fact that Black turnout in the South increased from 12.7 percent in the period 1952–1960 to 53.6 percent in the period 1964–1980 is an indication that the liberalization of laws and practices associated with voting greatly increased the "re-franchisement" of African-Americans in the South. The passage of the Twenty-fourth Amendment certainly began this liberalization process.

*See also: Harper v. Virginia,* Poll Tax, Voting Rights Act of 1965 and Extensions

*Michael Heel*

REFERENCES

Billington, Monroe Lee. 1975. *The Political South in the Twentieth Century.* New York: Scribner's.

Kleppner, Paul. 1982. *Who Voted?* New York: Praeger.

Kousser, J. Morgan. 1974. *The Shaping of Southern Politics.* New Haven: Yale U. Pr.

Sosna, Morton. 1977. *In Search of the Silent South.* New York: Columbia U. Pr.

## Twenty-sixth Amendment

In 1971 the right to vote in all elections was extended to all citizens 18 years of age by the Twenty-sixth Amendment to the U.S. Constitution. During the 1960s, student and other activists in the "new left" argued that people between 18 and 21 were eligible to be drafted to fight in Vietnam but were not allowed to participate in the process of choosing the leaders who would be making public policy. By 1970, that case had effectively been made, and Congress passed the Voting Rights Amendments of 1970, which purported to lower the voting age to 18.

Later that year, however, the Supreme Court in *Oregon v. Mitchell* upheld the 1970 amendments to the degree that they pertained to federal elections. But because the Constitution gave the states the basic right to determine who had the right to vote in nonfederal elections, subject to the provisions of the Fourteenth and Seventeenth amendments, the Court held the 1970 amendments unconstitutional to the degree that they infringed on those states' rights.

The decision threatened to disrupt the 1972 elections, in all likelihood requiring a cumbersome and expensive dual system in which some people would be able to vote in federal, but not state, races. Therefore, on March 23, 1971, Congress sent to the states the proposed Twenty-sixth Amendment. In record time (167 days), the amendment was ratified by the required 38 states.

The amendment enfranchised about 11 million Americans who otherwise would not have been able to participate in the 1972 elections. It has not, however, made much of an impact, since public opinion surveys and other research suggest that young people are less likely to vote than their elders; and when they do vote, few differences separate the young from the old.

*See also: Oregon v. Mitchell*

*Charles S. Hauss*

## Two-Thirds Rule in Democratic Convention

Adopted by the Democratic National Convention in 1832, the two-thirds rule initially stated "that each State be entitled in the nomination to be made of the candidate for the Vice Presidency to a number of votes equal to the number which they will be entitled in the Electoral Colleges . . . and that two-thirds of the whole number of the votes in the convention shall be necessary to constitute a choice."

The rule traces its antecedents to the first party convention ever held—that of the Antimason Party in 1832. That convention's Committee on Business recommended that the chosen candidates had to receive "the votes of three-fourths of all the members present." Thus, more than a simple majority of the delegates was required for nomination.

Meeting at their first convention in 1832, the Democrats adopted a variant of the Antimason rule. At the insistence of President Andrew Jackson, Democrats invoked the two-thirds requirement. Jackson wanted to remove Vice President John C. Calhoun from the Democratic ticket after the two had a falling out, involving, among other matters, the supposed "nullification" rights of the southern states. The two-thirds rule guaranteed the nomination of the man Jackson wanted to succeed Calhoun, Martin Van Buren.

A majority of delegates at the 1835 Democratic convention favored retaining the rule. As was the case earlier, this procedural vote insured the nomination of Martin Van Buren—this time for President. Jackson was instrumental in keeping the rule, since having served two terms he wanted to retire, and he wanted to have Vice President Van Buren succeed him as President. Ironically, when Van Buren sought the presidency again in 1844, the two-thirds rule killed his chances, as the South deemed him unacceptable.

The rule persisted for 104 years after its adoption in 1832, largely at the insistence of the South. The two-thirds rule effectively gave southerners a veto power over prospective Democratic presidential nominees. For example, in 1912 the rule blocked the nomination of Champ Clark, the Speaker of the U.S. House of Representatives, who was unable to obtain the necessary southern backing. In 1924 the Democratic National Convention took a record 103 roll calls until John W. Davis mustered the required two-thirds vote.

Franklin D. Roosevelt, long opposed to the two-thirds rule, successfully fought for its repeal at the 1936 Democratic National Convention. Among those leading the fight for repeal was the son of one of its victims, Senator Bennett Clark of Missouri. Southerners vehemently argued for the rule's continuance. But finally a compromise was agreed to whereby states at future Democratic conventions would not be represented according to their populations but according to the number of Democratic votes cast in elections. With that, the two-thirds rule passed into the history books.

*See also:* Antimasons, John C. Calhoun, James (Champ) Clark, John W. Davis, Andrew Jackson, Franklin D. Roosevelt, Martin Van Buren

*John K. White*

REFERENCES

David, Paul T., Ralph M. Goldman, and Richard C. Bain. 1960. *The Politics of National Party Conventions.* Washington: Brookings.

Lorant, Stefan. 1951. *The Presidency.* New York: Macmillan.

## Millard E. Tydings (1890–1961)

Conservative, segregationist U.S. Senator and victim of McCarthyism. A lawyer and Democratic U.S. Senator from Maryland and a debonair, austere, witty conservative, Millard Evelyn Tydings is known for two political battles. The first was as a states' rights advocate and opponent of Franklin D. Roosevelt's court-packing scheme and work relief programs in 1938. The second was as a defender of honesty and integrity in 1950 as the head of a special Senate Foreign Relations Committee investigating Senator Joseph McCarthy's charges of Communist conspiracy in the State Department. Both FDR and McCarthy personally campaigned against Tydings in Maryland, in the senatorial primary and in the general elections respectively. McCarthy succeeded where FDR had failed in handing Tydings his first electoral defeat.

Before his four terms in the U.S. Senate (1927–1951), Tydings worked briefly as a civil engineer and then as an attorney. He served as a member of the Maryland House of Delegates (1915–1917); in Europe with the American Expeditionary Force; as speaker of the Maryland House of Delegates (1919–1921); as state senator (1921–1923); and two terms in the U.S. Congress (1923–1927). Tydings was chairman of the Senate Armed Services Committee and a member of the Senate Foreign Relations Committee and of the Joint Committee on Atomic Energy.

Tydings was one of the foremost anti–New Deal southern Democrats in the U.S. Senate. *The Christian Science Monitor* in September 1945 judged Tydings, Walter George of Georgia, and Harry Byrd of Virginia as leaders of the conservative southern wing of the Democratic Party.

After he easily survived FDR's attempted purge in 1938, Tydings continued to oppose the President's foreign and domestic policy. An ardent fiscal conservative, Tydings in November 1940 called for widening the income tax base so that taxpayers lower on the scale would pay more to alleviate the federal deficit. In 1941 he voted against the extension of the draft law that he had supported in 1940; he generally opposed what he regarded as excessive American generosity in Lend-Lease provisions; and he opposed government involvement in business.

Among Tydings's legislative accomplishments were the Tydings-McDuffie Act of 1934, which promised the Philippines independence in 1946, and his role in the establishment of the position of Secretary of Defense.

Tydings opposed a third term for FDR and received a smattering of votes (9) himself at the 1940 Democratic convention (to 946 for FDR, 72 for James Farley, and 61 for John Nance Garner). Tydings seconded Farley's motion to make FDR's nomination unanimous, however. In 1944 Tydings was mentioned by anti–New Deal Democrats as a possible leader of a convention fight against a fourth term for FDR, possibly involving a third-party revolt. Tydings, de-

murred, however, having already received Democratic National Committee assistance in his May primary fight. Tydings ran ahead of the national ticket in Maryland that year by 29,000 votes, despite little support from labor and Black voters.

A committed segregationist, Tydings nevertheless supported Harry Truman in 1948, although in the Senate he endorsed Republican proposals for budget cuts. His last great battle arose in 1950 out of Tydings's denunciation of Senator McCarthy on the Senate floor. McCarthy's charges, Tydings alleged, were "without an ounce of truth" and amounted to "a fraud, a hoax, and a deceit." Charged by Senator William Jenner with conducting a whitewash of treason, Tydings was forced to throw himself completely into a bitter reelection struggle. The campaign was marked by a contrived composite photograph circulated by the supporters of his opponent, John Marshall Butler, ostensibly depicting Tydings in conversation with the American Communist Earl Browder. Perhaps by drawing excessive attention to this fraud, Tydings, the perennial critic of national Democratic administrations, was defeated, ironically as a defender of the increasingly unpopular Truman administration. Although endorsed by Americans for Democratic Action that year, Tydings drew meager support from liberal voters. Butler also courted the Black vote with some success, and Tydings narrowly lost by 40,000 votes. His attempt at a comeback against Butler in 1956 was cut short after he won a closely contested primary, when Tydings resigned as Democratic Senate nominee for reasons of health.

*See also:* James Farley, John Nance Garner, Walter George, Joseph McCarthy, Franklin D. Roosevelt, Harry S Truman

*Frederick J. Augustyn, Jr.*

REFERENCES

Walsh, Richard, and William Lloyd Fox, eds. 1983. *Maryland: A History.* Annapolis, MD: Hall of Records Commission, Department of General Services.

## John Tyler (1790–1862)

Tenth President of the United States. Few now remember John Tyler, except perhaps as the latter half of the famous 1840 campaign slogan, "Tippecanoe and Tyler Too." This ignorance is unfortunate, for John Tyler undertook a novel, if unsuccessful, effort to govern the nation without the support of either of the two established political parties.

The election of William Henry Harrison in 1840 gave the Whig Party—an amalgam of hierarchical and individualist cultures—control of the White House for the first time. Unfortunately for the ill-starred Whigs, Harrison died one month after assuming office, making Tyler, an ex-Democrat, the President. Tyler was a Virginia states' rights politician whose primary political interest was in limiting the size and scope of the federal government. In the 1828 election, he had supported Andrew Jackson over John Quincy Adams, primarily because of his distrust of Adams's support for a strong central government. Though suspicious of Jackson's commitment to increasing public participation in government, Tyler was impressed enough by Jackson's opposition to federally sponsored internal improvements and the national bank to back Jackson's reelection effort.

After Jackson's reelection, Tyler became increasingly disenchanted with Old Hickory. Jackson's confrontational response to the South Carolina nullifiers in 1832 convinced Tyler that active presidential leadership would inevitably produce an active federal government. "What interest is safe," Tyler wondered, "if the unbridled will of the majority is to have sway." The egalitarian preference for majoritarianism, Tyler decided, was incompatible with his individualistic concern for self-regulation.

Although Tyler joined the Whigs in censuring Jackson, he was no believer in the Whig plan for reestablishing a national bank. Twice in the summer of 1841 the Whig-controlled Congress passed bills to establish a national bank, and twice President Tyler vetoed them. Tyler's vetoes caused an uproar within the Whig Party. All but one member of the Cabinet resigned, and Tyler was read out of the Whig Party. In an effort to reconstruct a governing coalition, Tyler presented a proposal for a "Board of Exchequer," a proposal that was aimed at former Jackson supporters who, like himself, had been repelled by Jackson's egalitarianism and those Whigs, particularly southern ones, who wanted a more limited role for federal institutions than was envisioned by the Whig Party.

It was a bold strategy with an appealing logic. After all, agreement over individualism linked the Democratic and Whig parties. Despite initial interest in the Exchequer plan, however, Tyler was unable to shake loose enough Democrats and Whigs from their party moorings to pass the plan. By the end of 1842, Tyler had only two supporters in the Senate and six in the House. The President's failure stemmed from impediments inherent in the existing two-party system. Individualists on both sides were unwilling to defect because to weaken one's own party risked allowing the opposition to gain control. Individualists in the Democratic Party—an amalgam of individualism and egalitarianism—were afraid to defect to Tyler because this move could allow the hierarchical Whigs to triumph and reinstate a national bank, and individualistic Whigs hesitated to defect for fear that desertion would strengthen the Democratic Party and usher in a return to radical antibank policies.

Having failed to establish a new party on the basis of banking and finance, Tyler turned next to territorial expansion to rehabilitate his political fortunes. In the spring of 1843, Tyler began to push the annexation of Texas to the top of the national agenda. With the leading candidates of both major parties (Martin Van Buren and Henry Clay) opposed to the idea, Tyler calculated that annexation, by fomenting divisions within the two parties, would allow him to attract the individualist center that had eluded him in the banking controversy. Unfortunately for Tyler, the Democrats, by nominating James Polk (a vigorous proponent of annexation) instead of Van Buren, took over Tyler's main issue, forcing him to withdraw from the presidential race. Although Tyler had failed to create a new party, he had started a shift within the Democratic Party toward a group with a more individualistic and less egalitarian hue. The result was that Tyler, like many of his followers, felt comfortable returning to the Democratic fold.

*See also:* John Quincy Adams, Henry Clay, William Henry Harrison, Andrew Jackson, James K. Polk, Martin Van Buren

*Richard Ellis*

REFERENCES

Ellis, Richard J., and Aaron Wildavsky. 1988. *Dilemmas of Presidential Leadership from Washington Through Lincoln.* New Brunswick, NJ: Transaction.

Friedman, Jean E. 1976. *The Revolt of the Conservative Democrats: An Essay on American Political Culture and Political Development, 1837–1844.* Ann Arbor, MI: UMI Research Pr.

Lambert, Oscar Doane. 1936. *Presidential Politics in the United States, 1841–1844.* Durham, NC: Duke U. Pr.

Morgan, Robert J. 1954. *A Whig Embattled: The Presidency Under John Tyler.* Lincoln: U. of Nebraska Pr.

Seager, Robert, II. 1963. *And Tyler Too: A Biography of John & Julia Gardiner Tyler.* New York: McGraw-Hill.

# U

## Morris K. Udall (1922– )

Outspoken proponent of organizational and legislative reform. Morris King Udall has been a longtime Democratic member of Congress and was an aspirant for his party's presidential nomination in 1976. Udall was born in St. Johns, Arizona. His father (Levi Stewart Udall) was a chief justice of the Arizona Supreme Court. Udall enrolled at the University of Arizona in 1940, and after two years he interrupted study there to enter the armed forces, serving as an officer in a special services branch for those partially handicapped. (A childhood accident had resulted in the loss of one eye.)

Discharged from the military in 1946, Udall returned to the University of Arizona Law School, played one season of professional basketball for the original Denver Nuggets, completed his law degree in 1949, and subsequently began a private law practice in Tucson with his older brother Stewart.

In 1952 Udall was elected prosecuting attorney for Pima County. In 1954, while Stewart won election to Congress, Morris Udall failed in his bid for election to the Arizona Superior Court. Six years later he failed to succeed his father on the state's supreme court. When Stewart Udall resigned from Congress to become Secretary of the Interior in the John Kennedy administration, the younger Udall won a special election in May 1961 (by 1 percent) and entered the House of Representatives at age 39. Although compiling a solidly liberal voting record, Udall generally has carried his district by comfortable margins.

"Mo" Udall's tenure in Congress has been marked by several stages. After less than four terms, Udall in 1969 contested the reappointment of aged John McCormack as Speaker of the House, running in a symbolic assault on the Old Guard and reflecting disenchantment with the traditional folkways of Congress. Even though pledging to "step aside" if chosen, Udall was soundly trounced. Two years later Udall seriously sought designation as Majority Leader. Again he was defeated in the party caucus. In both instances Udall was seen as a threat to the "get along, go along" dictum of the seniority system. Not surprisingly, Udall later assumed a major role in orchestrating the House's internal reforms of the 1970s. He was, as well, an early proponent of campaign finance and voter registration reform.

Although thwarted in his efforts to achieve a leadership position, Udall developed a reputation for serious and sustained legislative commitment. As chair of the Interior Committee, Udall was particularly effective in the environmental field: strip mine control (1977), Alaska land development (1980), nuclear waste management (1982), and federal wilderness protection (1984). Udall also was involved in reforming the postal service and pay scales for federal employees. An alternating chairman of the Office of Technology Assessment, in 1985 he assumed as well a junior seat on the Foreign Affairs Committee. The early "maverick" thus became an established, dogged, and artful legislator fulfilling what was to him "the job of the Congressman."

In 1976 Udall sought the Democratic presidential nomination, but his was a campaign marked by numerous second-place finishes and an eventual loss to Jimmy Carter. Four years later, Udall endorsed Edward Kennedy's ill-fated nomination challenge to Carter. Despite twice opposing his party's top candidate, Udall nonetheless maintained the respect of his fellow partisans. Any further interest in higher national office was effectively ended in the early 1980s when Congressman Udall was diagnosed as having Parkinson's disease.

Morris Udall's public record is characterized generally by a commitment to organizational reform, electoral democratization, and legislation aimed at achieving "collective goods." Long and widely recognized as an astute and richly humorous observer of political life, Udall's more than quarter-century of service in Congress locates him among that body's most notable and effective members.

*See also:* Jimmy Carter, Edward M. Kennedy, John McCormack

*Charles Longley*

REFERENCES

Udall, Morris. 1972. *Education of a Congressman.* New York: Bobbs-Merrill.

———, and Donald Tracheron. 1966. *The Job of the Congressman.* New York: Bobbs-Merrill.

## Oscar W. Underwood (1862–1929)

First Democrat after Henry Clay to lead his party in both houses of the Congress. Oscar Wilder Underwood was elected to the House of Representatives from the Birmingham, Alabama, district in 1894 and served there until 1915, when he began two terms in the Senate. Through hard work, personal warmth, a mastery of the rules, and a willingness to compromise, Underwood gradually emerged as one of the leading Democrats in the House. When the Democrats won control of that body in 1910, he became the party's floor leader and also chairman of the powerful Ways and Means Committee. Underwood proved effective in uniting House Democrats and in championing tariff reform and in 1912 was a serious contender for the Democratic presidential nomination.

After Woodrow Wilson's election, Underwood cooperated with the President in carrying out his legislative program. In 1913 he helped to push the Underwood Tariff and the Federal Reserve Act through the Congress. Although Underwood had little interest in reform beyond these two measures, he continued to cooperate with the Wilson administration, supporting a wide variety of domestic measures

and Wilson's position in the fight over ratification of the Treaty of Versailles.

By 1920 Underwood had lost touch with many popular currents in state and national politics. His opposition to prohibition, labor unions, woman's suffrage, and the Ku Klux Klan, weakened his position both in Alabama and in the national Democratic Party.

Resigning his minority leadership in 1924, Underwood once again sought the Democratic nomination for the presidency. However, he won only the Alabama primary, and even after the long convention deadlock between William Gibbs McAdoo and Alfred E. Smith resulted in both withdrawing their candidacies, Underwood lost out as the compromise candidate to John W. Davis. He declined to run for reelection in 1926, sensing that he would face a difficult challenge in the Democratic primary, and retired to Woodlawn, his estate near Washington. As his career drew to a close, Underwood grew disillusioned with the American political sense, forgetting his own pragmatism as a congressional leader and decrying the drift of the nation away from the principles of the Constitution.

*See also:* William G. McAdoo, Alfred E. Smith, Woodrow Wilson

*Charles E. Neu*

REFERENCES

Johnson, Evans C. 1980. *Oscar W. Underwood: A Political Biography.* Baton Rouge: Louisiana State U. Pr.

Underwood, Oscar W. 1928. *Drifting Sands of Party Politics.* New York: The Century Company.

## Union League of America

Allied with the Republican Party during the Civil War era, the Union League of America, also known as the Loyal League, was a secret political society. The organization achieved its main significance when it became the primary means by which southern Blacks were mobilized once they received the franchise.

The Union League was founded during the Civil War as a northern social club supporting the war effort. (It shared common origins with the modern patrician clubs of the same name.) The League employed a ritual resembling that of the masons, but it was explicitly partisan in character, obliging members to vote for loyal candidates for office. By 1864 the group had a substantial mass following and played a significant role in the reelection of President Abraham Lincoln. At the direction of the League's longtime president, James M. Edmunds, the League spread into the southern states immediately after the war. It became the primary vehicle for "Unionist" opinion among white yeomen in the mountain regions.

With the implementation of military Reconstruction in 1867, the Republican Party faced the task of mobilizing thousands of newly enfranchised southern freedmen. The Union League seemed appropriate for this purpose because its clandestine character minimized outside intimidation. Funded by the Republican Party, scores of organizers spread through the southern states, initiating freedmen into the order. The response of the freedmen was dramatic, as hundreds of thousands joined the Union League within months. The organization became a major force within the southern Republican Party, becoming the nucleus of "Radical" factions in several states.

At the grass-roots level, however, the Union League movement took on a wider mission than simply the political maneuverings of a partisan club. League meetings were the scene of agrarian revolts, protesting authoritarian holdovers from slavery on the plantations. Talk of land redistribution, or "Forty Acres and a Mule," circulated freely in council meetings. League mobilization helped undermine efforts by landowners to maintain coercive methods of plantation discipline. In the cotton regions, for example, the League was integrally involved in the breakdown of gang labor and centralized management and the emergence of decentralized tenant farming as the paradigm form of plantation production.

By the late 1860s the organization was in decline throughout the South. Having successfully brought African-American voters into the party, Republican leaders saw little further use for the organization and ceased funding it. Further, the rise of the Ku Klux Klan and similar terrorist organizations attacked the League at the local level. The national body survived until the 1890s as a "paper organization," but with little significance after its heyday during Reconstruction. Despite the rapid repression of the League in the South, it initiated a pattern of Black support for the Republican Party that lasted for over half a century.

*See also:* Abraham Lincoln

*Michael W. Fitzgerald*

REFERENCES

Fitzgerald, Michael W. 1989. *The Union League Movement in the Deep South: Politics and Agricultural Change During Reconstruction.* Baton Rouge: Louisiana State U. Pr.

Gibson, Guy James. 1957. "Lincoln's League: The Union League Movement During the Civil War." Ph.D. dissertation, University of Illinois at Urbana.

## Union Party

In any nascent, still somewhat unknown political party, the unexpected death of a talented and highly charismatic leader would probably engender factionalism, disarray, an incapacity to attract political money, and poor electoral performance. The record of the Union Party's performance in the 1936 elections illustrates this general truth about political parties. As will become clear below, however, the Union Party's history also suggests the partially contingent nature of the New Deal's success.

The bullets with which Dr. Carl Weiss felled Senator Huey Long of Louisiana at the state capitol in Baton Rouge in 1935 also effectively killed the third-party movement that Long intended to lead in the 1936 elections. Long had developed a "Share Our Wealth" movement that clearly worried President Franklin Roosevelt and his political advisers. Long's assassination obviously improved the Democratic Party's already strong chances in 1936.

After Long's death, some of his allies put together a third party anyway—the Union Party. Organizationally it consisted of little more than a coalition of three men: Father Charles E. Coughlin of Michigan, the popular radio priest whose ideas mixed obsession with monetary policy with a soupçon of anti-Semitism and Roman Catholic social justice doctrine; the Reverend Gerald L. K. Smith, a former Long assistant who took over the "Share Our Wealth" movement; and Dr. Francis Townsend, a California physician whose advocacy of very generous old age income security allowances played a key role in the development of American social security policy. These ideologues sought to appeal not only to their own followers but also to the ordinary, hard-pressed people that the flamboyant Long most likely would have attracted. They ran a competent and in some ways admirable politician, Republican Congressman William Lemke of North Dakota. But the funds raised for Lemke's presidential effort amounted to roughly what it costs today to run a single state legislative campaign in a medium-sized industrial state. Lemke had trouble with his backers, and he had trouble getting on the ballot in many states. He gained less than 2 percent of the national popular vote, failing to carry any states.

Yet a closer look at the Union Party's record reveals suggestive—although probably no more than suggestive—evidence about the threat that Huey Long might have posed to the New Deal had he lived to run his presidential campaign. Long may well have carried states in the South. Lemke's strength in North Dakota and Minnesota (13.4 percent and 6.6 percent respectively) were clearly votes for Lemke, but he also ran ahead of his national average in several other midwestern states; Long might have developed strength in these states. Finally, the data on the congressional campaigns of 1936 indicate that the Union Party enjoyed unusual local strength in Rhode Island, Massachusetts, New York, and parts of Michigan. Long might have been able to construct a national, and possibly formidable, coalition.

The Union Party's history thus not only illustrates the importance of accident and leadership in party politics but also continues to suggest the partially contingent nature of the New Deal's success and consolidation.

*See also:* Charles E. Coughlin, William Lemke, Huey Long, Franklin D. Roosevelt, Francis Townsend

*Richard M. Valelly*

REFERENCES

Rosenstone, Steven J., Roy L. Behr, and Edward H. Lazarus. 1984. *Third Parties in America: Citizen Response to Major Party Failure.* Princeton: Princeton U. Pr.

## Union Party (1860s)

Formed early in the Civil War by Republicans seeking to broaden the base of political support for their party and the war effort, the Union Party welcomed pro-war Democrats into the new organization, using it first to maintain power in closely contested state elections and then to secure the reelection of Abraham Lincoln.

The Union Party appeared first in Ohio in 1861 when both Democrats and Republicans feared that they could not win with the usual party labels. Nominating David Tod, a War Democrat for governor, the Union Party was controlled by Republican leaders but received sufficient votes from Democrats to defeat the regular Democratic nominee. In 1862, in a successful effort to retain control of the U.S. Congress, the Union Party strategy was used in other closely contested northern states, although wherever the Republicans were more secure (as in New England), they were much less willing to share power with Democrats. Throughout the North, the more radical Republicans frequently resisted welcoming Democrats into their ranks.

Major victories for the Union Party in 1863 included John Brough's election as governor of Ohio over Clement Vallandigham and Andrew Curtin's as governor in Pennsylvania. In 1864 Republicans held a national Union convention to renominate Lincoln in an effort to show the bipartisan nature of the party. As a further appeal to dissatisfied Democrats, the Union Party nominated Democrat Andrew Johnson for Vice President.

With the death of President Lincoln and the growing division between Andrew Johnson and Congress in 1865, the Union Party coalition gradually broke apart. Unionists did hold a convention in Philadelphia in 1866, but by then most Republicans had left Johnson's Cabinet, and northern voters were increasingly antagonized by the President's Reconstruction policies. By the fall elections, old party labels had been restored as Republicans increased their control of Congress. The Union Party, a wartime strategy, could not survive the restoration of the Union itself.

*See also:* Andrew Johnson, Abraham Lincoln, Clement Vallandigham

*Frederick J. Blue*

REFERENCES

Burdette, Franklin L. 1972. *The Republican Party: A Short History.* New York: D. Van Nostrand.

Hyman, Harold. 1971. "The Election of 1864." In Arthur M. Schlesinger, Jr., and Fred L. Israel, eds. *History of American Presidential Elections, 1789–1968.* 4 vols. New York: Chelsea House.

McPherson, James M. 1982. *Ordeal by Fire: The Civil War and Reconstruction.* New York: Knopf.

Mayer, George H. 1964. *The Republican Party, 1854–1964.* New York: Oxford U. Pr.

Trefousse, Hans. 1973. "The Republican Party, 1854–1864." In Arthur M. Schlesinger, Jr., ed. *History of United States Political Parties.* 4 vols. New York: Chelsea House.

## Unit Rule

The unit rule was one of the main procedures that the first Democratic-Republican Party national convention adopted when it met in Baltimore in 1832. Following the precedent of the first national party convention, held by the Antimasons in 1831, the Democrats also based each state's portion of delegates on its Electoral College representation, let each state determine its method for selecting national delegates, required a special majority (two-thirds rule) for nomination and created a national committee to handle party affairs between elections. A persuasive factor in adopting the unit rule was that some states in 1832 sent more delegates than they were entitled to. The rule consequently prevented a chaotic fragmentation of votes, although the decision to use the unit rule was left to each state. State delegations using the unit rule allowed a simple majority within the delegation to commit the entire delegation to the majority's choice.

Both the unit rule and the two-thirds majority proved cumbersome for the Democrats. Wisely, the Republican Party, formed in the 1850s, never adopted either standard. In part, the two-thirds rule was justified as a logical corollary to the unit rule. Under the unit rule it was hypothetically possible that without the two-thirds standard less than an actual majority of all delegates could choose the party nominee. This anomaly could happen if states following the unit rule bound their delegations to the same candidate (*X*) by narrow majorities within each delegation, and non–unit rule states recorded large majorities for candidates other than *X*. But if states required a two-thirds majority, then this possible impact of the unit rule was lessened. Ironically, this connection between the two rules was not considered when the two-thirds rule was dropped by the Democrats at the 1936 convention.

In a more general vein, the unit rule, once in place, was defended on the grounds that it increased the power of small states; prospective party nominees could win the entire delegate strength from such states rather than merely the number of delegates who were personally persuaded to support a candidate. Of course, large states used the rule as well. Since votes under the unit rule were ordinarily taken in caucus, the rule also aided state parties in concealing internal partisan splits that could be embarrassing or exacerbated by public disclosure.

Use of the unit rule was often provocative and attempts were made to modify or eliminate it, at least in 1860 and 1884, and the groundwork for its extinction was done in the 1964 Democratic convention. It was formally abolished in 1968. That decision at the much maligned convention in Chicago was instigated by the combined forces of Senator Eugene McCarthy of Minnesota and Senator George McGovern of South Dakota, who had inherited the leadership of delegates committed to Senator Robert F. Kennedy, assassinated two months before the convention. By 1968 only 11 southern and Border States used the unit rule, dramatically personified by the large Texas delegation led by Governor John Connally, a longtime confidant of President Lyndon Johnson. Abolition of the rule was part of the McCarthy-McGovern appeal for an "open" convention. Since Vice President Hubert Humphrey had long advocated more democracy and reform of obstructive party rules, a substantial majority of delegates was prepared to drop the unit rule, although the action was bitterly opposed by Connally and others. Implementation of this was subsequently stressed in *Mandate for Reform* (1970), the Report on Selection to the Democratic National Committee, prepared by the so-called McGovern-Fraser Commission.

The 1968 convention did not address a logical consequence of its repeal of the unit rule: the winner-take-all presidential primaries. Arithmetically, these primaries could be less defensible than the unit rule in caucus states. For example, Robert Kennedy won the 1968 California Democratic presidential primary with less than 50 percent of the votes but was awarded 100 percent of California's delegates. When the illogicality of these primaries was initially posed, the national party relied upon the state parties and legislatures to bring about remedies. That did not always follow, and at the 1972 convention, the Humphrey forces were at first successful in challenging McGovern's claim to all of the delegates from the California primary. Although the McGovern majority in the full convention overturned that Humphrey protest, directives were made to prohibit such winner-take-all primaries in the future. By the 1976 convention, the issue had been resolved.

*See also:* Antimasons, John B. Connally, Hubert H. Humphrey, Lyndon B. Johnson, Robert F. Kennedy, Eugene McCarthy, George McGovern, McGovern-Fraser Commission, Winner-Take-All Systems

*Thomas P. Wolf*

REFERENCES

Becker, Carl. 1899. "The Unit Rule in National Nominating Conventions." 5 *American Historical Review* 64.

Casey, Carol F. 1980. "The National Democratic Party." In Gerald M. Pomper, ed. *Party Renewal in America*. New York: Praeger.

Chase, James S. 1973. *Emergence of the Presidential Nominating Convention, 1789–1832.* Urbana: U. of Illinois Pr.

Crotty, William J. 1978. *Decision for the Democrats: Reforming the Party Structure.* Baltimore: Johns Hopkins U. Pr.

David, Paul T., Ralph M. Goldman, and Richard C. Bain. 1960. *The Politics of the National Party Conventions.* Washington: Brookings.

Goldman, Ralph M. 1979. *Search for Consensus: The Story of the Democratic Party*. Philadelphia: Temple U. Pr.

Lengle, James I., and Byron Shafer. 1976. "Primary Rules, Political Power, and Social Change." 70 *American Political Science Review* 25.

Shafer, Byron. 1983. *Quiet Revolution: The Struggle for the Democratic Party and the Shaping of Post-Reform Politics*. New York: Russell Sage.

Wekkin, Gary D. 1984. "Nation-State Party Relations: The Democrats' New Federal Structure." 99 *Political Science Quarterly* 45.

## Unit Rule, Abolition of

A provision that awarded all of the delegate votes from a given political jurisdiction to the candidate who won a majority of them, in some states, this rule was only in effect at the national conventions, but in others (e.g., Texas), the unit rule held at all stages of the delegate selection process. The unit rule in effect created winner-take-all primaries, conventions, and caucuses, becoming a significant issue for the Democrats in part because of sectional divisions within the more heterogeneous party. It was not an issue for the Republican Party; the Republicans had a different body of party law, and their history did not include the sectional divisions that characterized the other major party.

Many in the Democratic Party objected to the unit rule since it clearly diminished the representation of minority points of view. Front-runners benefited from the unit rule as did sectional, as opposed to national, candidates. Since the unit rule was primarily used in southern and Border States (in the prereform era these were bastions of Democratic strength), it was thought that the unit rule prior to 1972 provided for a "southern veto" of Democratic nominees who were unacceptable to the party leaders from that region.

The unit rule was abolished by the Democratic Party when the McGovern-Fraser reforms were implemented in 1972. Despite the many subsequent modifications of the McGovern-Fraser reforms, the abolition of the unit rule has been upheld.

Jeane Kirkpatrick, a member of the Winograd Commission, which reformed Democratic rules during the Carter administration, and later a member of the Reagan administration, has been critical of the unit rule because she believes it has contributed to the creation of factions rather than majorities within the Democratic Party.

*See also:* McGovern-Fraser Commission, Unit Rule, Winograd Commission

*David A. Bositis*

REFERENCES

Baer, Denise L., and David A. Bositis. 1988. *Elite Cadres and Party Coalitions*. Westport, CT: Greenwood.

Crotty, William J. 1983. *Party Reform*. New York: Longman.

Kirkpatrick, Jeane J. 1978. *Dismantling the Parties*. Washington: American Enterprise Institute.

Shafer, Byron E. 1983. *The Quiet Revolution*. New York: Russell Sage.

## United Democrats of Congress

An informal group in the U.S. House of Representatives, the United Democrats of Congress (UDC) was active from 1973 to 1984 (92nd–98th Congresses). The moderate-to-conservative caucus members, from all geographic areas, viewed themselves as mainstream Democrats who, after the liberal George McGovern's presidential candidacy in 1972, organized to reassert their influence. The UDC constitution dedicated the group to "provide that the policies and actions of the Democratic party both locally and nationally accurately and adequately reflect the moderate and divergent philosophy of Democrats." The group worked on leadership elections within the congressional party, appointments to House committees, the issue positions of the executive, and the rules, procedures, and platform of the national party.

This informal party caucus operated as an intraparty group within the congressional party to affect party rules and organization and policy outcomes. It drafted proposals for Democratic Caucus rules changes and sought to influence Democratic leaders on issue votes and House procedures. The group also worked to build floor voting coalitions on, for example, tax reform and synthetic fuels legislation. During Jimmy Carter's presidency, the UDC met regularly with administration officials, and occasionally with the President himself, for off-the-record discussion of issues.

Unlike most other congressional caucuses, the UDC also was active at the national party level. Members worked with the Democrat Party's Winograd Commission on delegate selection, were active in supporting the inclusion of moderate planks in the party platform, and opened a UDC office at the party conventions.

*See also:* Jimmy Carter, George McGovern, Winograd Commission

*Susan Webb Hammond*

REFERENCES

Hammond, Susan Webb. 1989. "Congressional Caucuses in the Policy Process." In Lawrence C. Dodd and

Bruce I. Oppenheimer, eds. *Congress Recondidered.* 4th ed. Washington: Congressional Quarterly.

———, Daniel P. Mulhollan, and Arthur G. Stevens, Jr. 1985. "Congressional Caucuses and Agenda Setting." 38 *Western Political Quarterly* 582.

Loomis, Burdett A. 1981. "Congressional Caucuses and the Politics of Representation." In Lawrence C. Dodd and Bruce I. Oppenheimer, eds. *Congress Reconsidered.* 2d ed. Washington: Congressional Quarterly.

## United Jewish Organizations v. Carey
### 430 U.S. 144 (1977)

This case had no majority opinion from the Supreme Court, making a summary of its holdings difficult. Fundamentally, however, the Court held that states may use racial criteria for districting when trying to comply with Section 5 of the Voting Rights Act. Use of such criteria does not violate either the Fourteenth or Fifteenth Amendment. Without a majority opinion, and given that the holding was limited to the particular situation, the breadth of the ruling is questionable. However, *UJO* is important because, had the Court's judgment gone the other way and denied the ability to use racial criteria, it might have had major implications for the effectiveness of the Voting Rights Act and for congressional power generally to enforce the Fourteenth and Fifteenth amendments.

Section 5 of the Voting Rights Act required that any state or political subdivision covered by the Act must submit any change in a legislative apportionment scheme to the U.S. Attorney General (or to a court) for approval; and the state or political subdivision must demonstrate that the changes have neither the purpose nor effect of abridging the right to vote on the basis of race or color. New York failed such a demonstration with regard to some state legislative districts in Kings County when it submitted its 1972 reapportionment plan. The state revised the plan as it affected the particular districts and resubmitted it to the Attorney General in May 1974. In order to meet what were perceived to be the Attorney General's objections, the 1974 plan did not change the number of districts with nonwhite majorities, but it did alter the size of the nonwhite majorities. In the two Kings County districts that had the smallest nonwhite majorities, 61 percent and 52 percent, the size of the nonwhite majority was increased to 65 percent and 67.5 percent.

The Williamsburgh area, home to about 30,000 Hasidic Jews, was affected by the changes. The 1972 plan placed the Hasidic community entirely in one assembly district (61 percent nonwhite) and one senate district (37 percent nonwhite). The revised 1974 plan split the community between two senate and two assembly districts. The petitioners (UJO) argued that (1) use of racial criteria in districting and apportionment is never permissible; (2) even if there could be race-conscious drawing of lines to remedy effects of unconstitutional apportionment, there were no findings here that would require or justify white voters being reassigned to increase the size of Black majorities; (3) use of a "racial quota" in redistricting is never acceptable; (4) use of a 65 percent nonwhite racial quota was unconstitutional. Justice Byron White, who wrote the opinion announcing the judgment of the Court, dismissed the first three claims fairly quickly, citing previous cases involving the Voting Rights Act, especially *South Carolina v. Katzenbach* (383 U.S. 301), *Beer v. U.S.* (425 U.S. 130), and *City of Richmond v. U.S.* (422 U.S. 358). According to Justice White, "neither the Fourteenth nor Fifteenth Amendment mandates any per se rule against using racial factors in districting and apportionment . . . [and] the permissible use of racial criteria is not confined to eliminating the effects of past discriminatory districting or apportionment." He also argued that to comply with Section 5, the state must decide how substantial majorities must be, and a reapportionment "cannot violate the Fourteenth or Fifteenth Amendment merely because a State uses specific numerical quotas in establishing a certain number of black majority districts."

Justice White went on to argue (with fewer justices joining him in this part of the argument) that New York had the right to redraw the districts whether or not it was authorized to do so by the Voting Rights Act. He noted that the plan "represented no racial slur or stigma with respect to whites. . . . [T]here was no fencing out of the white population from participation in the political processes of the county, and the plan did not minimize or unfairly cancel out white voting strength."

*See also:* Fifteenth Amendment, Voting Rights Act of 1965 and Extensions

*H. W. Perry, Jr.*

## United Labor Party

Organized concurrently with the labor-agrarian coherence and a growing social unrest in the 1870s and 1880s, the United Labor Party (ULP) championed the concerns of working people. The party often supported Greenback candidates and usually attracted disenchanted Democrats. Between 1868 and 1888, various farmer-labor parties, though seldom a major force in national contests, elected or supported numerous local candidates and called attention to issues either spurned, ignored, or straddled by the major parties. Though Democrats and Republicans dominated Gilded Age politics, United Labor and similar coalitions did offer alternatives for the discontented.

The ULP achieved moderate success in New York and Illinois. The party backed single-taxer Henry George in the 1886 New York City mayoral race, helping him to a second-place finish, almost 8,000 votes ahead of the Republican nominee, Theodore Roosevelt. George and his supporters then campaigned for New York Secretary of State, but George received only a few thousand more votes than he had at the municipal level. At Chicago, in 1887, the ULP ran a slate of labor candidates, including an iron molder for mayor, and elected one alderman. Even these limited successes proved to be difficult, in part because of the popular confusion of labor activists with "anarchists."

The ULP reached its zenith in 1888. It held a sparsely attended convention (simultaneously with that of the Union Labor Party), which the national committee chairman described as more of a conference, at Cincinnati in May. The ULP's platform combined chastisement of existing political and economic institutions with advocacy of specific reforms. "We denounce the Democratic and Republican parties as hopelessly and shamelessly corrupt," the delegates declared, ". . . unworthy of the suffrage of those who do not live upon public plunder." The laborites castigated the system that permitted monopoly, compelled men to pay for the "common bounties of nature," and produced depravity, low wages, depression, and class conflict.

To combat these maladies, the ULP proposed taxation of property based on use instead of location, abolition of all taxes on industry, nationalization of railroads and telegraphs, reorganization of the nation's financial system, reduction of workers' hours, adoption of the Australian ballot, and prohibition of child and convict labor. The party also called for sanitary inspection of tenements and factories, common benefit and use of all values that arise from "the growth of society," an end to the "abuse of conspiracy laws," and reform of the judicial system. In support of these reforms, ULP asked

for the cooperation of all who sought "to establish justice, to preserve liberty, to extend the spirit of fraternity, and to elevate humanity."

The United Labor convention nominated Robert H. Cowdrey of Illinois and William H. T. Wakefield of Kansas for President and Vice President, respectively. In August, representatives meeting at Chicago futilely tried to combine Union Labor and United Labor parties. The ULP refused to cooperate, and its ticket received few votes in the national election, perhaps owing to a splintered constituency or to duplicity on the part of managers who worked for the Republicans. The ULP subsequently disappeared, but many of its "planks" reappeared in the 1892 People's Party platform.

*See also:* Australian Ballot, Greenback Party, Theodore Roosevelt, Suffrage

*Robert F. Zeidel*

REFERENCES

Fine, Nathan. 1928. *Labor and Farmer Parties in the United States, 1828–1928.* New York: Rand School of Social Science.

Haynes, Fred E. 1916. *Third Party Movements Since the Civil War.* Iowa City: State Historical Society of Iowa.

Keller, Morton. 1977. *Affairs of State: Public Life in Late Nineteenth-Century America.* Cambridge: Harvard U. Pr.

Stanwood, Edward. 1898. *A History of the Presidency from 1788 to 1897.* Boston: Houghton Mifflin.

## United Nations

The origin of the United Nations during World War II provides an early example of modern bipartisan foreign policymaking. Following World War I, bitter partisan squabbling between Senate Republicans and Democratic President Woodrow Wilson had helped keep America from membership in the League of Nations. Republicans on the whole continued to spurn Wilsonian internationalism during the interwar period. But after the attack on Pearl Harbor discredited isolationism, political necessity and changed global realities moved many Republicans to call for a formal international organization, the focus of which increasingly centered on a permanent United Nations. In 1942 both a Republican congressional caucus and the GOP's national committee urged American cooperation with other nations to preserve postwar peace. Former Republican presidential candidate Wendell Willkie publicized internationalism with his 1943 book, *One World.* In the 1943 Mackinac Declaration, GOP leaders approved "post-war co-operative organization among sovereign nations." That same year congressional Republicans supported the Connally and Fulbright resolutions, both of which called for a formal postwar international structure. In line with the GOP's traditional conservative nationalism, Republicans qualified these endorsements by insisting that American membership in the United Nations preserve national sovereignty and constitutional processes.

Anxious to avoid Wilson's mistakes, the administration of Franklin D. Roosevelt sought Republican cooperation when organizing the U.N. and defining American membership in it. Throughout World War II, Secretary of State Cordell Hull held bipartisan consultations on postwar international organization. Senator Arthur H. Vandenberg of Michigan emerged during these meetings as the most influential Republican on the issue. In 1944 Hull appointed a top GOP official to the American delegation to the Dumbarton Oaks Conference, which began planning for the U.N. Bolstered by overwhelming public support, the foreign policy planks of both parties in 1944 called for an international organization. At negotiations between Hull and John Foster Dulles, adviser to Republican presidential candidate Thomas E. Dewey, both sides agreed that the U.N. would not be discussed as a partisan issue throughout the 1944 presidential campaign. It was the first such arrangement in American history.

The 1944 election was nonetheless a referendum on international organization. Conservative Republicans supported the proposition that the American delegate to the U.N. would not be allowed to approve deployment of U.S. armed forces unless Congress gave its assent. In October 1944 GOP Senator Joseph Ball, a fervent internationalist who had seconded Dewey's nomination, challenged the Republican candidate to denounce this reservation. Dewey declined, contending that his agreement with Hull prevented specific comment. When Roosevelt called for allowing the American delegate wide discretion within constitutional limits, Ball endorsed the President and thereby helped the Democratic ticket capture independent-voting internationalists in November. Moreover, on election day a number of Republican and Democratic isolationists lost congressional seats while internationalists scored gains.

The following spring Vandenberg played a significant role at the U.N. charter conference at San Francisco, particularly in safeguarding American freedom of action. All but two Re-

publican Senators approved the U.N. charter in July 1945. The partisan wrangling of 1919 and 1920 was on the whole avoided, the GOP committed itself to the U.N., and the organization has since never become a serious election issue.

*See also:* Thomas E. Dewey, John Foster Dulles, Cordell Hull, Isolationism in American Politics, League of Nations, Franklin D. Roosevelt, Arthur H. Vandenberg, Wendell Willkie, Woodrow Wilson

*Jeffery C. Livingston*

REFERENCES

Campbell, Thomas M. 1973. *Masquerade Peace: America's UN Policy, 1944–1945*. Tallahassee: Florida State U. Pr.

Darilek, Richard E. 1976. *A Loyal Opposition in Time of War: The Republican Party and the Politics of Foreign Policy from Pearl Harbor to Yalta*. Westport, CT: Greenwood.

Divine, Robert A. 1967. *Second Chance: The Triumph of Internationalism in America During World War II*. New York: Atheneum.

———. 1974. *Foreign Policy and U.S. Presidential Elections, 1940–1948*. New York: New Viewpoints.

Westerfield, H. Bradford. 1955. *Foreign Policy and Party Politics: Pearl Harbor to Korea*. New Haven: Yale U. Pr.

## United States v. Classic
### 313 U.S. 299 (1941)

This Supreme Court case sustained indictments in federal prosecutions in Louisiana for election fraud for willfully altering and falsely counting and certifying primary election ballots for the Democratic nomination to Congress. The federal statute under which defendants were prosecuted made it a crime to conspire to injure any person in the exercise of rights "secured by the Constitution" or to deprive any person of rights "protected by the Constitution" under color of law. The primary was required and defined by Louisiana law. The Democratic Party was arguably a private voluntary association. The problem, therefore, was to determine in what sense federal constitutional guarantees were violated by this misuse of the state primary machinery for the Democratic Party primary.

Initially *United States v. Classic* was understood as holding that political parties are public organizations rather than private associations. The state's obligation to prevent discrimination within them thus appeared to be a more general subordination of parties to constitutional and statutory commands. That view appeared to support the extensive regulation of the nomination process and party organization by state statutes. As the Court has begun to revive the associational rights of political parties, *Classic* (and the white primary cases, particularly *Smith v. Allwright* and *Terry v. Adams*) have come to stand for a special duty of the government to intervene with respect to political participation of racial minorities and other suspect classes. *O'Brien v. Brown* distinguished the white primary cases as dealing with invidious racial discrimination. More recently in *Tashjian v. Republican Party*, the Court reinterpreted *Classic* and the white primary cases as implying that private rights must be honored except in the face of compelling public interests. Therefore, some have interpreted the white primary cases and *Classic* to mean that the power or obligation of the government to defeat fraud and secure racial equality in political affairs overrides the right of association of the political parties. The question then becomes one of determining the scope of the area in which the equal protection requirements override the right of association.

See also: *O'Brien v. Brown, Smith v. Allwright, Tashjian v. Republican Party*

Stephen E. Gottlieb

REFERENCES

Brest. 1982. "State Action and Liberal Theory." 130 *University of Pennsylvania Law Review* 1296.

Tribe, Laurence H. 1988. *American Constitutional Law.* Mineola, NY: Foundation Press.

## United States v. O'Brien
### 391 U.S. 367 (1968)

This Supreme Court case held that, despite First Amendment implications, a person could be punished for burning a draft card because the government had legitimate and important interests in prohibiting the destruction of draft cards. The incidental restrictions on the First Amendment are no greater than what is necessary for furtherance of the government's interest.

On March 31, 1966, David O'Brien burned his draft card on the steps of the South Boston Courthouse. He claimed he did it "so that other people would reevaluate their positions with the Selective Service, with the armed forces, and reevaluate their place in the culture of today, to hopefully consider my position." O'Brien was convicted under a federal statute that had been amended in 1965 by Congress so that "an offense was committed by any person 'who forges, alters, knowingly destroys, knowingly mutilates, or in any manner charges any such certificate.'" O'Brien argued that the amendment was enacted to abridge free speech; he also suggested that it served no legitimate legislative purpose.

In an opinion written by Chief Justice Earl Warren, the Court rejected O'Brien's arguments. Aside from the societal importance of the case at the time, it stood as an important precedent for when speech could be curtailed; and it helped further a "speech/conduct" distinction. The Court acknowledged the "speech" aspects of O'Brien's behavior, but it was willing to draw the line because of the perceived governmental interest and the perception that burdening such conduct did not inhibit speech in an unconstitutional way.

Though the precedential value of *O'Brien* is questionable, it is a particularly interesting case for political scientists. Not only does it address the interesting issues involving speech and governmental interests, but it is also an example of a case in which societal factors weigh heavily on the law. Whether or not it is "surprising" that Earl Warren would write such an opinion, the deference of the Court to the Congress at this time on this subject is fodder for debates over the role of the Court in issues perceived to pertain to war efforts.

H. W. Perry, Jr.

## Jesse M. Unruh (1922– )

California political wheeler-dealer. Jesse Marvin Unruh was perhaps the most powerful figure in the California Democratic Party in the 1960s. Unruh was elected to the California Assembly in 1954 and was elevated to speaker in 1961, serving in that post until 1968. His domination of the Democratic Party and his reputed practice of "boss" politics during this era led his rivals to give him the title "Big Daddy." His influence, however, led to his appointment as John F. Kennedy's southern California campaign manager during the 1960 presidential election campaign. Though Richard Nixon carried California on election day, Kennedy fared well in Unruh's southern end of the state, carrying Los Angeles County by a considerable margin. For his services, Unruh was able to have great weight in patronage during the Kennedy administration; but then he saw his national influence decline during the Johnson years.

From 1965 to 1967 Unruh generally supported Lyndon Johnson's Vietnam policy. A turnaround occurred, however, when Unruh privately urged Robert F. Kennedy to seek the Democratic nomination in early January 1968, before the Tet Offensive in Vietnam seriously undermined Johnson's credibility. Then in 1968 he became the first major national politician to announce his support for Robert F. Kennedy for the presidential nomination and he assumed the role of Kennedy's California campaign manager. RFK won the California primary in June, but then disaster struck. While at the celebration party with Unruh, the young candidate was assassinated by Sirhan B. Sirhan.

In August 1968, at the troubled Democratic convention in Chicago, Unruh tried unsuccessfully to create a movement to draft Edward Kennedy for the presidency; failing in that effort, he gave his support to peace candidate Eugene McCarthy. After the Democratic defeat, Unruh again focused his attention on California politics, unsuccessfully challenging Republican incumbent Ronald Reagan in the 1970 gubernatorial contest. At that point, Unruh became a less active participant in politics, launching a new career as professor at several institutions.

*See also:* Edward M. Kennedy, John F. Kennedy, Robert F. Kennedy, Eugene McCarthy, Richard M. Nixon, Ronald Reagan

*Jeffrey G. Mauck*

REFERENCES

Cannon, Lou. 1969. *Ronnie and Jesse: A Political Odyssey.* New York: Putnam's.

## Urban Interests' Influence on National Policy

The decade of the 1930s began a fundamental change in the relationship between the nation's cities and the federal government. Before the New Deal, analysts could not really speak of a national urban policy. For all that, the actual impact of the New Deal on the nation's cities was relatively small. Still, it was a start. During the two decades following World War II, the federal government's involvement in the cities expanded with the adoption of the Urban Renewal program and the Public Housing program. Even with these programs, however, the actual federal impact on the nation's cities continued to be relatively small. It was not until the 1960s, with the enactment of "the Great Society," that the federal government became heavily involved in trying to solve urban problems. This decade brought the creation of the Department of Housing and Urban Development, the first federal department devoted to urban affairs. In addition, Lyndon Johnson's Great Society greatly expanded the jurisdiction of the Department of Health, Education and Welfare (later divided into the Department of Health and Human Services and the Department of Education). During the decades of the 1970s and 1980s, the role of the federal government in urban affairs continued, although it was significantly changed from that created during the 1960s.

The participation of the federal government in the field of urban policy meant that city governments were quick to discover that they had a significant stake in the authorizations, appropriations, and administrative decisions being made in Washington. The growing importance of federal programs meant that leaders in city government increasingly looked toward Washington rather than to their own state capitals for assistance. In order to push their claims in the federal government, some of the larger cities opened offices in Washington, employing full-time staff to lobby the federal government to expand urban programs. In addition, mayors of the nation's largest cities used the U.S. Conference of Mayors to dramatize the pressing need of the nation's cities and to goad the federal government into action.

Moreover, most cities became directly involved with those federal agencies that administered national urban policies, primarily because of the increase in federal grant-in-aid programs. These programs allocated funds to city governments to solve local problems identified as important by the federal government. Grant-in-aid programs—providing funds either directly to the cities or by passing funds through the states—produced a dramatic change in the urban fiscal condition. Many city governments became heavily dependent on the availability of federal monies, which were uncertain because of the unpredictability of appropriations decisions made in Congress as well as the great deal of discretion enjoyed by the agencies implementing grant programs. Furthermore, many grant programs were highly competitive as cities competed with one another for federal funds. The competitive nature of the search for federal grants introduced great uncertainty into the financial planning of city governments.

Local governments, by now heavily dependent on the flow of federal money, often turned to their representatives in Congress to intervene on their behalf. As the national government's involvement with cities expanded, these Representatives and Senators found that they were expected to facilitate and promote the flow of federal funds to their urban constituencies. Re-election-oriented members of Congress from urban areas, who may have previously defined their primary political role as sponsoring or supporting legislation based on the interests of their urban constituents, discovered that the increased involvement of the federal government in urban affairs led them to become more directly involved in the administration of federal urban policy. Members from urban areas and their staffs increasingly had to become conduits between the urban government and the federal agencies. The result was a decentralized policymaking subsystem made up of donors (federal bureaucrats), recipients (state and local governments), and middlemen (elected members of Congress and their staffs).

While the federal government's involvement with urban problems continued during the 1970s and 1980s, the specific nature of the relationship between the federal government and the cities has changed. Dissatisfaction on the part of big-city mayors with the uncertainty surrounding the grant-in-aid process in conjunction with the dissatisfaction of conservatives opposed to the expanding role of the federal bureaucracy led the Richard Nixon administration (1969–1974) to propose changes in the way in which federal funds would be allocated to state and local areas. These new programs (e.g., the General Revenue Sharing and the Community Development Block Grant programs) were designed to make the allocation of funds to cities more predictable and less subject to federal control by reducing the discretion enjoyed by federal agencies. Under these programs, the federal government provided funds to states and cities based on predetermined formulas. Even though these changes were designed to reduce federal discretion in the allocation of funds, the fact that programs such as the Community Development Block Grant Program continued to require the submission of a complicated application before cities could receive their "entitlement funds" meant that the "middleman" role played by members of Congress was still necessary. In addition, a large number of federal programs servicing the cities still operated as discretionary grant programs.

During the Ronald Reagan administration (1981–1989), severe cutbacks in federal funds for domestic programs (mandated by budgetary decisions adopted in 1981) resulted in slowing down the flow of federal funds to urban areas. Furthermore, the fiscal limitations imposed by massive budget deficit in the 1980s prevented any major new federal spending initiatives aimed at the cities. As a result, city governments have been forced to find alternative sources of funds.

Therefore, the decade of the 1980s represented a return to a more limited federal role. However, the relationship between the federal government and the cities, started during the 1930s and greatly expanded during the 1960s, while undoubtedly different, still continues.

*See also:* Lyndon B. Johnson, Richard M. Nixon, Ronald Reagan

*Richard Fleisher*

REFERENCES

Fiorina, Morris P. 1977. *Congress: Keystone of the Washington Establishment.* New Haven: Yale U. Pr.

Gelfand, Mark I. 1975. *A Nation of Cities: The Federal Government and Urban America, 1933–1965.* New York: Oxford U. Pr.

Hale, George E., and Marian Lief Palley. 1981. *The Politics of Federal Grants.* Washington: Congressional Quarterly.

Judd, Dennis R., and Francis N. Kopel. 1978. "The Search for National Urban Policy from Kennedy to Carter." In Theodore J. Lowi and Alan Stone, eds. *Nationalizing Government: Public Policies in America.* Beverly Hills, CA: Sage.

Kantor, Paul, with Stephen David. 1988. *The Dependent City: The Changing Political Economy of Urban America.* Glenview, IL: Scott, Foresman.

## Urban Political Machines

Representing one of the most colorful chapters in the history of American politics, the machine, as it was usually referred to, epitomizes the best and worst of the political parties. The urban political machine was best in the sense that the machine provided the flexibility and adaptability for the nation's political system to adjust to fundamental economic and demographic changes during the nineteenth century (industrialization, immigration, urbanization) that radically transformed the American nation; and it provided the basis for a minority party—normally the Democrats during this era—to build its base and eventually to compete effectively with the dominant party, the Republicans. The inclusiveness, adjustment to mass suffrage, and the mobilization of new and competing electorates provided alternative choices and helped serve the democratic ends of a more representative and accountable party and political system.

When the localized politics of the urban machines were eventually tied to national-level party concerns and candidates—manifested in the presidential bid of machine-product Governor Alfred E. Smith of New York in 1928, which forged a nationwide coalition of the cities, the South, labor unions and working-class people, and the small farmer—the consequence was a critical realignment of American politics that resulted in the New Deal Party System and the dominance of the Democrats nationally from the 1930s to the present. Curiously, the New Deal itself and the social programs it spawned, along with the enmity of political figures like Franklin Roosevelt, Fiorello La Guardia, and reform governors at the state level, contributed to the end of the machine's glory days.

The machine performed a service in acculturating and assimilating immigrants, located most prominently in the major industrial cities of the Northeast and Midwest, into the American mainstream. These newcomers were the Irish, Poles, Jews, Germans, Czechs, Italians, Swedes, and, in the machine's later stages and with less certainty or success, African-Americans. This group migrated from the South in the post-Depression years to work in the steel plants and automobile assembly plants of the North.

Less admirable, and the object of constant attack from critics, was the corruption, favoritism, patronage, and other abuses of public office associated with the machine and its leaders. The antimachine reformers—themselves mostly middle-class to upper-middle-class professionals and earlier immigrants well removed from the entry-level social status of the ethnics who formed the machine's base—constantly railed against the thievery and lax moral and ethical standards that it associated with the machine and those who supported it. The reformers called for a basic change in government structure and in the operations of city government, including the introduction of "good government" principles of economy and efficiency of operation combined with an emphasis on minimal governmental activity and responsibility. The Progressive era reformers wanted to apply their conception of business-like assumptions to local politics. And they were to prove largely successful.

In fact, the machine may have fulfilled its functions all too well. As the ethnic groups that provided the base of the machine's support progressed economically, they became less dependent on the political largesse of the local boss. The waves of immigration that fed the nineteenth century's need for cheap and unskilled industrial labor abated; the government began to supply on a general basis the social benefits once given on a personalized and particularistic basis by the machine; and the poor who had lived in the slums and ethnic ghettoes, those most dependent on machine help, moved up the social ladder and, in the process, relocated to the suburbs. As these events took place, the days of the machine drew to a close.

The machine era is not as far in the past as some Americans might assume. The period laid the basis for the modern party system, and it is worth remembering that many machines persisted well into the post-World War II years. Some machines—or their remnants—continue to operate in urban areas (most notably in Chicago) to this day. As late as 1950, the Committee on Political Parties of the American Political Science Association reported in *Toward a More Responsible Two-Party System* that the United States still suffered from a parochial, localized, and issueless machine politics, even in the postwar years. The call in the report for a "responsible" party system based on the presentation in campaigns and implementation once in office of policy positions of national relevance was offered as contrast to the limited, shortsighted, and corrupt approaches identified with the machine.

The era of the machine was then both an unusually boisterous one in American politics and one of the most significant for understanding the operations, the contributions, and most importantly, the adaptability of the party system in the United States to the political and social demands that shape its being.

This article offers a definition of the machine and a fundamental analysis of its contributions; it traces in broad strokes the history of the political machine and identifies the distinguishing characteristics of its operations and then provides a discussion of the major reasons for its decline.

The machine aspect of American politics is the most written about, the best recorded, and the most romanticized in U.S. political history. Not to be ignored is the fact that the machine rose to fulfill social and political needs that were inadequately handled by other governmental or private agencies. The machines' long-run contributions were as real as their readily apparent venality and corruption. The costs of machine government were high, but the services provided were essential to the development of the contemporary party system and, even more significantly, to the assimilation, or socialization, if you will, of new groups into an expanding national culture and consciousness.

*Defining a Political Machine*

A political machine was a party organization

led by a political leader or boss, with a reasonable cohesive and unified (for American parties) organizational structure. It controlled nominations for public office within its areas of jurisdiction, usually the local level (city, county, or rural area, although a statewide political machine, while rare, was not unknown), and it controlled the operations of local government, including the awarding of patronage jobs, city services, contracts, and preferential treatment for favored groups and individuals.

The machine's operations were often extralegal and at times corrupt. Its aim was to wield political power and then to use this power for personal and group profit. An exchange theory analogy can be used to explain the machine's approach. The voter's support was given in exchange for rewards (i.e., services, jobs, symbolic gratifications) provided by the machine. To be able to give the rewards, the machine had to control the local government. The machine was built on the support of groups in the city's electorate that it represented. These groups were usually ethnic groups living in the major urban areas of, in particular (but not exclusively), the Northeast and the industrial cities of the Midwest and Great Lakes states.

The machine offered symbolic rewards and recognitions as well as jobs and other tangible benefits and assisted in the acculturation to American society for newly arrived immigrant groups. The machine and its local ward leaders and precinct workers often acted as brokers, or intermediaries, between the immigrants and the government, the courts, the police, and other official agencies such as naturalization officers, tax collectors, and city inspectors. In return the machine received the votes of the people it represented. The consistent, unquestioning electoral support of these groups allowed the machine to operate city governments with relative impunity, often unchecked and unaccountable to any public agency or constituency. This extraordinary power eventually led to the abuses of office that finally contributed to the machine's decline.

The calculus was simple enough. The machine and its leaders wanted political power. Political power led to personal wealth. To gain power, the machine needed to control public office by determining who the candidates were and by assuring them a loyal and predictable vote in elections. In return, the quid pro quo was that the machine provided services and tangible, material rewards on a personal basis to those who supported it.

The reward system was particularistic and personal, and it emphasized material gains. For this reason, machine politics has been called conservative, nonideological, and nonprogrammatic. This lack of any purposive political program is one of the major criticisms directed at the machine in the previously mentioned report of the American Political Science Association. A good deal of truth inheres in these designations.

The machine did not directly challenge the class or social divisions or the economic system or government forms found in American society. It accepted the basic political and economic principles underlying a liberal democratic structure within a capitalist economic system. The machine contented itself with trying to get for itself, its leaders, and its clientele groups a share of the action—a piece of the American dream.

Still, in a way often overlooked and basically unanticipated and unacknowledged by its leaders, the machine was an innovative and even revolutionary force in American politics. It contributed, for practical rather than ideological reasons, to a concept of positive government, one that weighed in on the side of the least advantaged in American society. The fruition of the machine ethos in this regard was the New Deal of Franklin Roosevelt and its commitment of political resources to assist those most in need. The degree of commitment and the level of support for redistributive policies has varied in successive administrations and by political party since the inception of the New Deal, but the basic conception of the positive role of government while challenged has not been reversed.

The machine was a personalized, service-oriented political institution that was ripe for much of the romanticizing and myth making found in novels and films (for example, Edwin O'Connor's *The Last Hurrah*, 1956) as well as for sympathetic depictions in the social science literature. The system was almost feudal in its operation, depending on kinship ties (Irish helping Irish, Poles helping Poles, and so on), an informal but clearly understood reciprocal reward structure (votes equal power equal services), and a personal web of obligations that served to tie subject to master in a never-ending series of mutual exchanges.

In many respects also, the machine was a self-contained, well-bounded ecopolitical system. It operated most effectively in a concentrated geographical area among people with shared views, backgrounds, and political expectations (the political "ethos" that Edward Banfield and James Wilson and others refer to). As times changed and the boundaries of the system expanded, it failed to adapt effectively. The geographical dispersion of populations, the changing social status of its core supporters, and a redefined role for the national government all had their impact, as did changes in technology and in the increasing availability of information through a more depersonalized and accessible media. All these developments were to contribute to the machine's difficulties. Its inability to accommodate itself to a changing political climate led to its decline in all areas and to its demise in most.

Key phrases to use in describing the machine then would include power-oriented; profit-motivated; service-based; clientelistic; patronage- and job-oriented; particularistic and parochial in its concerns; pragmatic and nonideological in policy matters; materialistic; personalized; and, in many if not most cases, corrupt.

### The Social Role of the Machine

The political machine operated at many different levels. At one level was its role within and contributions to the broader society of which it was a part. In this context, the sociologist, Robert Merton, has identified the functions served by the machine for the broader social and political system. These functions can be "manifest," obvious, easily identified, and recognized by all who participate in or observe them. Or they can be, and often are, "latent," unintended, and usually unrecognized consequences of activities in which the machine engaged. Employing this concept then, the functions performed by the machine for the American system are virtually uncountable.

The political machine helped acculturate generations of immigrants into American society. It figuratively and literally met people at their boats, helped them settle in ethnic neighborhoods, provided them with gift baskets of food or clothing or coal for heating at Christmas and Thanksgiving (a tradition still practiced in some ward organizations in the city of Chicago), occasionally got them jobs, and acted as an intermediary with government agencies. The political machine gave these newcomers a political voice and, over time, a helping hand in moving up in American society.

In the process, the form of acculturation that the machine emphasized clearly provided benefits to the governing system. The machine never questioned the underlying assumptions of American society. Indeed, the machine provided an outlet for social frustrations and a way to adapt to an unfamiliar and often threatening environment, thus providing a legitimating force on behalf of the government and a strong alternative to potential violence and to radical political movements. In effect, the machine, with all its faults, helped manage and direct conflict and change within the accepted political arena. It deemphasized class conflict and helped raise its supporters to middle-class status. The machine fostered support for the governing system among the poor and the recently arrived by presenting a benign and supportive face to government bureaucracy.

The political machine helped overcome the fractionalization of government and the decentralization of power and authority inherent in American political structures. The government of the United States uses a system emphasizing separation of power and a federal alignment of authorities with shared power. This arrangement is reflected at successively lower levels of government, from national to state, county, and local jurisdictions and including even special election and tax districts (school, parks, judicial, legislative, recreational, water, conservation, land regulatory, among others). Coherent political action can be difficult to achieve. The machine, at one level, provided a sense of direction and a decisionmaking structure that helped government to work.

It expanded the conception of the role of government, involving it more broadly on a social welfare basis in the affairs of individuals and in using government as a lever on behalf of society's less fortunate. It helped the nation adjust to a number of transformations that took place during the extraordinary growth experienced in the nineteenth century: the implementation of mass suffrage and the other by-products of the radical democratic movement of the Andrew Jackson years and its aftermath, the expansion of the nation westward, the influx of large numbers of immigrants, and the changeover from a rural country with an agrarian base to an urban one with an industrial one.

The political machine was selective in those it chose to help, and the cost was often high.

But it played a significant role in the political development of the American nation, one not fully appreciated until its declining days.

### The Machine as Service Agency

Theorizing about the machine and its impact is one thing; describing its operations is quite another. Operationally, the activities engaged in by the machine and those who worked on its behalf were specific, people related, and primarily materialistic, tied to immediate needs and involving personal rewards. The machine was the major social service agency for the poor in the urban areas before the introduction of the welfare state with the New Deal. Its only competition came from limited and privately financed charitable organizations and from early social work experiments such as Jane Addams's Hull House in Chicago. Local government had always restricted itself basically to limited management activities and to police and safety functions. Yet the contest between machine and private agency was hardly equal; the social engineering efforts of the day had severely limited outreach. The machine, on the other hand, could reach into any ward in the city, providing the services needed to meet the challenges of living in the primitive conditions present in many cities during the nineteenth century.

In addition to the assimilation and social and economic adjustment functions provided for its ethnic base, the machine met the needs of many in the business community for a quick and sympathetic response to their problems. The implementation or enforcement of zoning codes could be adjusted; public services (electric power, transit lines, sewage disposal, water delivery) could be franchised; construction permits, building code exemptions, and the licensing of professional and business concerns could be expedited; city contracts awarded; ordinances selectively enforced or ignored; roads paved or upgraded; and civic services (water, sewerage, police and fire protection) provided—all, of course, for a price—to meet a businessman's need to compete. In some cities, just about everything was for sale. In Chicago, during the 1890s, certain aldermen (the "Grey Wolves" as they were called) were accused of selling the very streets of the city at minimal prices to a private developer to build transit lines. Another example from the same city, approximately three-quarters of a century later, shows how the machine can use its governing powers, in this case powers of eminent domain and condem-

nation, to close a street in the downtown area and then sell it to a private corporation for development. In this case, the corporation was Sears Roebuck, and the result was the construction of the Sears Tower, the world's tallest office building.

This second instance was considered good business in that it induced a major company to remain in the city, providing jobs and creating wealth (although Sears, with new tax breaks, relocated to the suburbs two decades later). The enormous building programs that preceded and followed the Sears project—superhighways; public buildings; colleges and universities; water filtration plants and drainage canals; harbor developments and river improvements; construction of the world's largest airport; new libraries, fire, and police stations; public parks and forest preserves; the construction of massive public housing complexes, exposition halls, and trade centers, cultural and sports complexes—illustrate how the modern machine of Chicago's Richard Daley worked to provide the access to money, patronage jobs, and kickbacks as well as business and popular support that formed the core of the machine's existence. The difference between the Daley machine and others that preceded it was that its actions in these areas were generally acclaimed by the business community, builders, civic leaders, the media, and many social scientists as a model of what a machine—or any forward-looking, business-oriented administration—could do within the context of contemporary politics.

The machine could also benefit small- and medium-sized businesses through such awards of insurance, road service, and building contracts; legal fees; and the placement of public funds in banks or through bonding agencies. In Chicago, as an example, it is a rare alderman or ward leader who does not maintain a law office, own an insurance firm, run a security service, or operate some other small business positioned to benefit from public largesse.

Also noteworthy in this context was the need of criminal elements for machine cooperation to shield their activities—extortion, bookmaking, prostitution, drug running, racketeering—from official sanctions. Organized crime became associated in varying degrees with the machines in many urban areas; racketeers could pay handsomely for the services they wanted, and many machine leaders were more than willing to comply.

### The Machine as Vote Mobilizer

A third activity of the machine, directly related to the services that it supplied to its constituents, was the mobilization of votes to win elections. The businesses provided the money, the machine and its allies—the trade and, especially, city workers' unions and organized crime in some cities—provided the manpower. The ward and precinct leaders—that is, the ones who wished to hold onto their jobs—turned out the machine vote on election days. Machine control of election activities may not have been as difficult as it might seem. As indicated, many people depended on the machine for jobs and selective benefits. In Chicago, the Daley machine was estimated to have between 30,000 and 50,000 patronage jobs at its disposal at any given time in city and county government and through access to friends in private enterprise. If numbers of this magnitude are subdivided by the 50 wards in the city, the incentives for individuals and the families dependent on these incomes to see the machine succeed in elections is formidable. It has been shown, not surprisingly, that in another machine city (Gary, Indiana), the areas with the greatest patronage concentrations vote more heavily for machine candidates.

Turning out the vote did not end the machine's activities. The machine controlled every aspect of the electoral process, from writing the laws governing the elections, certifying who could vote, registering voters, and counting the ballots to deciding—through electoral commissions it appointed or judges it nominated and elected to office—any disputes that might arise over procedures or outcomes. The election judges, the police who maintained order at the polling places, the printers who supplied the ballots, the election boards and court officials who ruled on disputed ballots and election fraud practices, all were directly controlled by the machine. Add to the sympathetic election officials such practices as repeat voting, ballot stuffing, voting by inhabitants of graveyards, the registration of voters from empty lots or abandoned buildings, vote buying, padded registration rolls, and the voting of those who had moved from the area and no one could be surprised that the machine seldom if ever lost an election of consequence (this means primarily local elections; statewide, congressional, and presidential elections were often of secondary importance).

Perhaps the most marked illustration of a machine's power to deliver the vote in modern times came in an election of national consequence—the presidential election of 1960. A belief (encouraged both by the machine itself and the losing candidate, Richard M. Nixon) has it that the Daley machine held out its vote until the downstate Illinois Republican totals were in. The machine then delivered just enough votes in Cook County to give Illinois and the presidential victory to John Kennedy in one of the closest contests in American history. The role the machine played received extra credibility when the new President invited the Daley family to be his first overnight guests in the White House.

### Working for the Machine

In this regard, taking a look at machine operations from the perspective of the local precinct worker might prove worthwhile. Chicago under the Daley machine can serve as an example. Often a "payroller" (that is, someone paid for a job on the public payroll for which he/she seldom if ever showed up), the party worker's real assignment was to keep in close touch with the voters in his area. This liaison often meant door-to-door canvassing between elections as well as during campaigns, serving as an intermediary in such matters as getting trees pruned, sidewalks and streets paved, free trash cans delivered (a tradition in Chicago), or in acquiring other public services and in resolving disputes with city agencies. In addition, the party worker was expected to spend several nights a month in the ward headquarters and to attend all ward-level candidate rallies. In return, the machine took care of the worker, providing a job and an income—the more indispensable the worker, the better the job—as a city roof, water, safety, or electrical inspector; a sanitation worker; a policeman; a janitor; a security guard; an insurance adjustor; a clerk in the assessor's or recorder's office or their equivalents; and, for the more successful, a smooth path to public office. The party work expected of the precinct captain in some machine's such as Chicago's was demanding; the rewards, however, were substantial.

Overall, the system functioned reasonably well. Most people associated with the machine benefited directly in some manner, many quite tangibly. Few personally or directly lost anything; the cost was picked up by the public treasury.

*The Rise of the Urban Machine*

The rise of the machine was in direct response to fundamental changes in the development of the nation. Many of these have been mentioned, but they deserve brief review.

The election of Andrew Jackson as President in 1828 ushered in a new era of mass democracy, one that in its provisions for an expanded mass suffrage helped establish the political climate that made the machine possible. Before this period, politics had been elitist with the vote restricted by property and wealth as well as by race and sex.

The second contribution to machine politics was economic. The increasing industrialization of the country created the need for cheap labor to work in the factories and to lay the tracks for the railroads during the nation's westward expansion. A constant demand for large quantities of unskilled immigrant labor resulted. As much as they were disliked by the Americans who had preceded them and their culture, language, and even morality stereotyped and ridiculed, the nineteenth century's rapid economic expansion depended on immigrants.

Third, then, is the social changes brought on by the mass immigration that took place between the 1830s and 1921, when it was effectively curtailed through new immigration laws. The Irish, Germans, Scandinavians, Italians, and other southern Europeans came to the United States in successive waves. The Irish, Italians, and Jews from various Eastern European countries and, more selectively, the Germans and the English settled in the developing cities of the Northeast and, as the nineteenth century evolved, the industrial cities of the Midwest.

Not all groups took with equal facility to politics. The Irish, possibly because they had immigrated in heavy numbers early, spoke the language, had a general familiarity with the system, enjoyed a strong sense of ethnic identity and a solid community base built around the Catholic Church, had an immediate and lasting effect on the development of the machine. Many of the early machine leaders were Irish, and well into the twentieth century, despite changing ethnic constituencies, the Irish remained firmly in political control of many cities.

Fourth, and directly related to both industrialization and mass immigration, was the rise of the city. At the time the Constitution was adopted, the United States was 95 percent rural; the nation's five largest cities had estimated populations between 16,000 and 40,000. The cities began to grow in the decades immediately preceding the Civil War. In the last half of the nineteenth century, urban populations outgrew rural areas by a three-to-one ratio. By 1920 and the close of mass immigration, the United States had completed the shift from a dominantly rural nation to one with a majority of the population living in urban areas. The city, of course, provided the social, geographical, and political base for the machine.

Finally, as indicated earlier, a need emerged for a centralized and positive governing authority in a political system that before the advent of the machine had emphasized decentralized, localized, and fractionalized decision-making and public agencies with limited responsibilities. The demand for a more responsive government, one more attuned to the concerns of ethnics and business interests in a period of rapid economic expansion, provided an opening that the machine was quick to fill.

A particular configuration of economic, social, and political forces then created the unique historical conditions that gave rise to a new conception of government. The new political demands created the environment that gave birth to the machine. Seen in this context, the machine was a creature of its time and a particular stage in the political evolution of the nation.

*Types of Machines*

As indicated, most of the major political machines were located in the urban areas of the Northeast and upper Midwest. The Progressive movement that dominated much of the political thinking at the turn of the century was particularly antimachine and, more broadly, antipolitical party and antipolitics. Many of the Midwest, Plains, Mountain, and Far West states that were settled in the heyday of the Progressive era enacted stringent limitations on both party activities and on organizations that made normal political party operations, much less machine practices, difficult. The extremes may be found in states like California and Wisconsin that effectively crippled formal party development.

Machine operations and characteristics varied widely. Cities with major political machines included New York City and Albany; Chicago; Gary, Indiana; Jersey City, Hoboken, and Newark in New Jersey; Pittsburgh and Philadelphia; Boston; Cleveland, Toledo, and Cincinnati in Ohio; Memphis; and on the West Coast, San

Francisco. The complete list is, of course, much longer. These machines were often identified with their leaders and their political styles, ranging from the vengeful and petty "Boss" Crump of Memphis to the respected Republican Boss Cox of Cincinnati; from the genial and charismatic James Michael Curley of Boston to the dour, meticulously organized, and efficient Richard J. Daley in Chicago; and from the generally ethical Charles F. Murphy of New York's Tammany Hall and Martin Lomasney of Boston to the corrupt and mob-dominated operations of Frank Hague in Jersey City. The diversity in operations and leadership styles belies any simple description as to how they operated.

Possibly the most famous of machines is that of Tammany Hall in New York City. A brief sketch of its life cycle provides one model of machine operations. Tammany Hall was originally founded as a fraternal organization at about the same time that George Washington was being sworn in for his first term as President. Initially a social club, Tammany became more political as the years passed, eventually emerging as the dominant party organization in Manhattan. Its fortunes and its reputation fluctuated with those of its leaders: "Boss" (William Marcy) Tweed, Charles Murphy, and Richard Croker were among the more prominent. Tammany Hall flourished from the 1870s to the 1930s when it began to experience a series of reversals that were to eventually destroy it.

Tammany Hall's corruption in the latter half of the nineteenth century was legendary. As examples, the Tweed Ring is estimated to have skimmed off some $100 million in graft in one three-year period alone. Up to 90 percent of the cost of some public buildings was attributed to corruption. Some Tammany leaders became millionaires. One (Croker) eventually went to jail, a rare occurrence for a boss. Still, the organization remained powerful, controlling political offices in New York City and constituting a force in state and national elections. Tammany—and Murphy protégé—Alfred E. Smith served a distinguished term as governor of New York and ran as the Democratic candidate for President in 1928. Tammany also supported (although reluctantly) Smith's successor as governor and a later Democratic presidential nominee, Franklin D. Roosevelt.

Roosevelt, while elected with machine support nationwide, really did not depend on an urban ethnic base; he was not sympathetic to

the corruption and abuses of machine operations. FDR eventually assisted in the formation in New York City of a labor-based, antimachine political group in the mid-1930s, the Liberal Party, to support New Deal policies and to contest with Tammany for political control. Roosevelt's antipathy coincided with the election of a Fusion candidate running on an antimachine platform, Fiorello La Guardia, to the mayor's office. La Guardia served from 1933 to 1945 and spent much of his considerable political power undermining the machine and destroying its patronage base. Along with other opponents, he helped start local reform clubs as an alternative to the machine's ward organizations. These reform clubs endorsed and ran their own candidates for political office. Yet Tammany lingered on under leaders such as Carmine DeSapio until the 1960s when its own corruption and continuing ties to organized crime (in addition to a changing political environment) combined to deprive it of whatever influence it still retained.

Tammany Hall is not representative of all of the urban machines. Each had its own political history, and each responded to a different mix of social and economic forces. Taken together, however, the political machine dominated the politics of the latter nineteenth century and many lasted well into the twentieth century, some operating in one form or another up to recent times. The post-New Deal era, however, has been notably unsympathetic to machine operations.

### The Decline of the Machine

Most political machines were corrupt to some degree. As time and public attitudes changed, toleration for machine graft diminished. "We saw our chances and we took them," according to Tammany leader William Plunkitt, who made a distinction between "honest" graft and "dishonest" graft. "Honest" graft included selective awarding of contracts, jobs, legal fees and the like, and profiteering from insider information (as for example in land acquisitions and contract bidding). "Dishonest" graft would be the bid rigging, kickbacks, bribes, and the payoffs from criminal activities that were patently illegal. According to Plunkitt, "honest" graft was acceptable; "dishonest" graft was not.

It is unlikely that most machines made such a fine distinction. These categories of kinds of graft were clearly spurious. On the other hand, all machines were corrupt to varying degrees.

They were in business for profit, and they all stole in one manner or another from the public treasury. As their corrupt practices received more attention—through the cartoons of Thomas Nast in the nineteenth century and later through the angry and sensationalistic exposés of "muckraking" journalists like Lincoln Steffens (*Shame of the Cities*, 1900) around the turn of the century—and as public tolerance for both the machine and its corrupt practices decreased, the beginning of the end had set in.

The Progressive movement of the early twentieth century was a response to machine abuses. It advanced measures intended to cripple the machine and destroy the power of the boss. While progressivism did not accomplish such ends immediately, it did hurt the machine and, not incidentally, political parties more generally, and it did permanently reshape the environment in which the machine operated and the context in which local politics in the future would be conducted.

Progressive era reforms were advocated by middle-class and upper-middle-class business, professional, intellectual, and publishing interests not directly benefited by machine operations. These groups advocated standards of official behavior distinctly different from those of the machine, stressing objective professional competence and public service motivations for those who served in government. Decision-making was to be based on business-like principles of efficiency and economy in government.

To achieve such ends, the Progressives advocated a series of structural reforms in political institutions, preferring not to deal with the social conditions and social reforms needed to address the problems that gave rise to the machine. The Progressives advocated the direct primary to break the machine's hold on political nominations. They endorsed the short ballot, both to centralize authority and accountability and to lessen the information burden for the prospective voter. They lobbied for civil service exams and procedures and merit appointments to eliminate patronage. Progressives espoused stringent campaign law and restrictive party statutes to control political receipts and expenditures and to limit party organization and activities. At-large (rather than district or ward) elections, which were supposed to dilute the power of ethnic groups, combined with nonpartisan electoral systems that actually prohibited political party activity, are standard now in the majority of American cities (three-fourths of those over 25,000 in population have nonpartisan elections). Progressives championed proportional representation, the city manager and city council forms of government, initiative, referendum, and recall provisions, the Australian (secret) ballot, and the reorganization of urban and state governments to increase service delivery and decrease political control. The broad public administration movement and good government groups such as the National Municipal League (established in 1894) intended to professionalize public service grew out of this movement.

Another factor leading to the decline of the machine was the limits put on immigration. By 1921 the last of the great waves of immigration, bringing millions of southern and eastern Europeans to the United States, had virtually ended, depriving the machine of its traditional base of support. The new immigrants—African-Americans, who came north seeking jobs in the automobile and steel factories during the Depression and after World War II, Hispanics, and, to a lesser degree, Asians—did not integrate well into machine operations. In fact, these newcomers were often perceived of as a threat to the machine and its leaders. In effect, the machine stopped growing and adapting. Steven Erie has recently argued that the machine never served other groups as well as it did its original Irish constituents. As its client groups moved up to middle-class status and out to the suburbs, the machine's base contracted, and it died.

The rewards that the machine could offer began to pale in comparison with what the welfare state could supply nationally and apolitically on the basis of demonstrated need. The machine had always had a limited appeal to an emerging middle class. The postindustrial period, accordingly, has not been hospitable to a continued machine presence.

All of these ingredients combined to decrease the influence of the machine. Basically, time had run out. The machine was a product of a particular historical era and set of social conditions. When the nation changed, the machine was not able to operate effectively in an environment in which its political base had eroded and the rewards it could offer were less significant. Public attitudes and political structures changed; the machine could not compete effectively in the new political environment. With its operations curtailed by law, economics, and social change, the machine became something of a historical curiosity.

## The Pros and Cons of the Machine

Americans' general perception of the machine, perhaps understandably, has been negative. Assessing the machine and its operations, Alex Gottfried has written,

> The political, social, economic, and financial costs of corrupt machines are incalculable but enormous, whatever their inevitability or functional utility. The cost in terms of the "degradation of the democratic dogma" cannot be measured. Tens of millions of Americans have developed cynical attitudes toward the myths of our political system. . . . The low prestige of politics and politicians is another result, since it has served to keep many potentially able people away from the public arena. The civil service has been degraded. The United States lagged fifty years behind European countries in adopting public welfare and social insurance programs. The physical city and the quality of life therein have deteriorated. Few cities have been specifically planned, and thus lack parks, beaches, and other public amenities. Inadequate schools, inadequate fire protection, inadequate and/or brutal police service, the development of slums, lack of minimum standards for housing, neglect of tenements, rent gouging, lack of consumer protection, wholly inadequate hospital and public health services, almost total lack of protective labor legislation, and long delays in legislation for the protection of women and children—all have been caused by rapacious machines.

Political analysts find an element of truth in each of these indictments, although some wonder if other, broader social forces in the United States did not contribute significantly to the conditions attributed to the machine.

Other observers argue that in the post-machine era, government may become more fragmented, aloof, and inaccessible than ever before. These critics maintain that the reforms advocated by the Progressives have a decided bias toward upper-middle-class interests and values and that cities adopting Progressive reforms may be less responsive to minority interests and less likely to engage in public spending. The research on these questions to date has been inconclusive. Certainly, nonpartisan elections have resulted in low turnouts, poorly mobilized and informed electorates, insulated officeholders, and, more arguably, a political upper-middle class and Republican Party bias in the vote.

The relevance of debating the achievements or costs of machine politics may be limited. Yet an understanding of the machine and its operations does help in understanding contemporary politics, where we are and how we arrived at what we have. But for Americans with a limited historical perspective, it may also be sufficient to remember that the machine was a product of an era and its evolution. Its rise and demise, strengths and weaknesses, formed an integral part of the social and economic drama that have combined to produce the American experience.

*See also:* Australian Ballot, James Cox, Edward Crump, James Michael Curley, Richard J. Daley, Carmine DeSapio, Fusion Party in New York City, Frank Hague, Andrew Jackson, John F. Kennedy, Fiorello La Guardia, Liberal Party, Martin Lomasney, Charles F. Murphy, Thomas Nast, Richard M. Nixon, Franklin D. Roosevelt, Alfred E. Smith, Tammany Hall, William M. Tweed

*William Crotty*

## REFERENCES

Adrian, Charles, and Oliver Williams. 1959. "The Insulation of Local Politics Under the Nonpartisan Ballot." 53 *American Political Science Review* 1052.

Allswang, John M. 1971. *A House for All Peoples.* Lexington: U. Pr. of Kentucky.

———. 1978. *The New Deal and American Politics: A Study in Political Change.* New York: Wiley.

———. 1986. *Bosses, Machines, and Urban Voters.* Baltimore: Johns Hopkins U. Pr.

American Political Science Association. 1950. *Toward a More Responsible Two-Party System.* Washington: American Political Science Association.

Andersen, Kristi. 1979. *The Creation of a Democratic Majority 1928–1936.* Chicago: U. of Chicago Pr.

Banfield, Edward C. 1961. *Political Influence.* New York: Free Press.

———, and James Q. Wilson. 1963. *City Politics.* New York: Vintage.

Binkley, Wilfred E. 1971. *American Political Parties: Their Natural History.* New York: Knopf.

Bridges, Amy. 1984. *A City in the Republic.* Cambridge: Harvard U. Pr.

Browning, Rufus, Dale Rogers Marshall, and David Tabb. 1984. *Protest Is Not Enough.* Berkeley: U. of California Pr.

Buenker, John D. 1973. *Urban Liberalism and Progressive Reform.* New York: Scribner's.

Callow, Alexander B., Jr. 1970. *The Tweed Ring.* New York: Oxford U. Pr.

———, ed. 1976. *The City Boss in America.* New York: Oxford U. Pr.

Connors, Richard J. 1971. *A Cycle of Power: The Career of Jersey City Mayor Frank Hague.* Metuchen, NJ: Scarecrow Press.

Costikyan, Edward N. 1966. *Behind Closed Doors.* New York: Harcourt, Brace & World.

Crotty, William J. 1986. "Local Parties in Chicago: The Machine in Transition." In William Crotty, ed. *Political Parties in Local Areas.* Knoxville: U. of Tennessee Pr.

Curley, James Michael. 1957. *I'd Do It Again.* Englewood Cliffs, NJ: Prentice-Hall.

Cutright, Phillips. 1963. "Measuring the Impact of Local Party Activity on General Election Vote." 27 *Public Opinion Quarterly* 372.

Dorsett, Lyle W. 1968. *The Pendergast Machine*. New York: Oxford U. Pr.

——. 1977. *Franklin D. Roosevelt and the City Bosses*. Port Washington, NY: Kennikat.

Ebner, Michael H., and Eugene M. Tobin, eds. 1977. *The Age of Urban Reform*. Port Washington, NY: Kennikat.

Erie, Steven P. 1988. *Rainbow's End: Irish-Americans and the Dilemmas of Urban Machine Politics, 1840–1985*. Berkeley: U. of California Pr.

Eulau, Heinz, and Kenneth Prewitt. 1973. *Labyrinths of Democracy: Adaptations, Linkages, Representation, and Policies in Urban Politics*. Indianapolis: Bobbs-Merrill.

Flynn, Edward J. 1947. *You're the Boss*. New York: Viking.

Gardiner, John A., and David J. Olson, eds. 1974. *Theft of the City*. Bloomington: Indiana U. Pr.

Glazer, Nathan, and Daniel P. Moynihan. 1970. *Beyond the Melting Pot*. Cambridge: Harvard U. Pr.

Gosnell, Harold F. 1937. *Machine Politics: Chicago Model*. Chicago: U. of Chicago Pr.

Gottfried, Alex. 1962. *Boss Cermak of Chicago*. Seattle: U. of Washington Pr.

Gove, Samuel K., and Louis H. Masotti, eds. 1982. *After Daley: Chicago Politics in Transition*. Urbana: U. of Illinois Pr.

Green, Paul M., and Melvin G. Holli, eds. 1987. *The Mayors: The Chicago Political Tradition*. Carbondale: Southern Illinois U. Pr.

Guterbock, Thomas M. 1980. *Machine Politics in Transition: Party and Community in Chicago*. Chicago: U. of Chicago Pr.

Handlin, Oscar. 1951. *The Uprooted*. New York: Grosset & Dunlap.

——. 1958. *Al Smith and His America*. Boston: Little, Brown.

Hawley, Willis D. 1973. *Nonpartisan Elections and the Case for Party Politics*. New York: Wiley.

Heidenheimer, Arnold J., ed. 1970. *Political Corruption: Readings in Comparative Analysis*. New York: Holt, Rinehart & Winston.

Hershkowitz, Leo. 1978. *Tweed's New York: Another Look*. Garden City, NY: Anchor Books.

Hicks, John D. 1960. *Republican Ascendancy 1921–1933*. New York: Harper & Row.

Higham, John. 1972. *Strangers in the Land*. New York: Atheneum.

Hofstadter, Richard. 1959. *The Age of Reform*. New York: Knopf.

Holli, Melvin G. 1969. *Reform in Detroit: Hazen S. Pingree and Urban Politics*. New York: Oxford U. Pr.

——, and Paul M. Green, eds. 1984. *The Making of the Mayor: Chicago 1983*. Grand Rapids, MI: Eerdmans.

Jones, Bryan D. 1985. *Governing Buildings and Building Government*. University: U. of Alabama Pr.

Key, V. O. 1959. "Secular Realignment and the Party System." 21 *Journal of Politics* 198.

Kleppner, Paul. 1985. *Chicago Divided: The Making of a Black Mayor*. DeKalb: Northern Illinois U. Pr.

Ladd, Everett C., Jr. 1970. *American Political Parties: Social Change and Political Response*. New York: Norton.

——, and Charles Hadley. 1975. *Transformations of the American Party System*. New York: Norton.

La Guardia, Fiorello H. 1948. *The Making of an Insurgent: An Autobiography 1882–1919*. New York: Capricorn Books.

Lee, Eugene. 1960. *The Politics of Nonpartisanship*. Berkeley: U. of California Pr.

Lowi, Theodore J. 1964. *At the Pleasure of the Mayor*. Glencoe, IL: Free Press.

Lubell, Samuel. 1951. *The Future of American Politics*. New York: Harper.

Mandelbaum, Seymour J. 1965. *Boss Tweed's New York*. New York: Wiley.

Mann, Arthur. 1965. *La Guardia Comes to Power. 1933*. Philadelphia: Lippincott.

Merton, Robert K. 1957. *Social Theory and Social Structure*. Glencoe, IL: Free Press.

Meyers, Gustavus. 1937. *The History of Tammany Hall*. New York: Modern Library.

Miller, William D. 1964. *Mr. Crump of Memphis*. Baton Rouge: Louisiana State U. Pr.

Miller, Zane L. 1968. *Cox's Cincinnati*. New York: Oxford U. Pr.

Morgan, David, and John Pelissero. 1980. "Urban Policy: Does Political Structure Matter?" 75 *American Political Science Review* 722.

Mushkat, Jerome. 1971. *Tammany: The Evolution of a Machine, 1789–1865*. Syracuse: Syracuse U. Pr.

Nixon, Richard M. 1962. *Six Crises*. Garden City, NY: Doubleday.

O'Connor, Edwin. 1956. *The Last Hurrah*. New York: Bantam Books.

O'Connor, Len. 1975. *Clout: Mayor Daley and His City*. Chicago: Henry Regnery.

——. 1977. *Requiem: The Decline and Demise of Mayor Daley and His Era*. Chicago: Contemporary Books.

Ostrogorski, M. 1921. *Democracy and the American Party System*. New York: Macmillan.

Parenti, Michael. 1967. "Ethnic Politics and the Persistence of Ethnic Identification." 61 *American Political Science Review* 717.

Peel, Roy V. 1935. *The Political Clubs of New York City*. New York: Putnam's.

Pinderhughes, Dianne. 1987. *Race and Ethnicity in Chicago Politics: A Reexamination of Pluralist Theory*. Urbana: U. of Illinois Pr.

Rakove, Milton. 1975. *Don't Make No Waves . . . Don't Back No Losers*. Bloomington: Indiana U. Pr.

——. 1979. *We Don't Want Nobody Sent*. Bloomington: Indiana U. Pr.

Riordan, William L. 1963. *Plunkitt of Tammany Hall*. New York: Dutton.

Robinson, Frank S. 1977. *Machine Politics: A Study of Albany's O'Connells*. New Brunswick, NJ: Transaction Books.

Rossi, Peter H., and Philips Cutright. 1961. "The Impact of Party Organization in an Industrial Setting." In Morris Janowitz, ed. *Community Political Systems*. Glencoe, IL: Free Press.

Royko, Mike. 1971. *Boss: Richard J. Daley of Chicago*. New York: Signet.

Salter, J. T. 1935. *Boss Rule: Portraits in City Politics*. New York: McGraw-Hill.

Scott, James C. 1972. *Comparative Political Corruption*. Englewood Cliffs, NJ: Prentice-Hall.

Shannon, William V. 1963. *The American Irish*. New York: Macmillan.

Shefter, Martin. 1976. "The Emergence of the Machine: An Alternative View." In Willis D. Hawley and Michael Lipsky, eds. *Theoretical Perspectives on Urban Politics*. Englewood Cliffs, NJ: Prentice-Hall.

———. 1978. "The Electoral Foundations of the Political Machine: New York City, 1884–1897." In Joel H. Sibley, Allan G. Bogue, and William H. Flanigan, eds. *The History of American Electoral Behavior*. Princeton: Princeton U. Pr.

Steffens, Lincoln. 1960. *The Shame of the City*. New York: Hill and Wang.

Sundquist, James. 1973. *Dynamics of the Party System*. Washington: Brookings.

Tarr, Joel Arthur. 1971. *A Study in Boss Politics: William Lorimer of Chicago*. Urbana: U. of Illinois Pr.

Tolchin, Martin, and Susan Tolchin. 1972. *To the Victor*. New York: Vintage.

Tucker, David M. 1981. *Memphis Since Crump: Bossism, Blacks, and Civic Reformers, 1948–1968*. Knoxville: U. of Tennessee Pr.

Walton, Hanes, Jr. 1972. *Black Politics: A Theoretical and Structural Analysis*. Philadelphia: Lippincott.

Welch, Susan, and Timothy Bledsoe. 1986. "The Partisan Consequences of Nonpartisan Elections and the Changing Nature of Urban Politics." 30 *American Journal of Political Science* 128.

Wendt, Lloyd, and Herman Kogan. 1971. *Bosses of Lusty Chicago*. Bloomington: Indiana U. Pr.

Wilson, James Q. 1960. *Negro Politics: The Search for Political Leadership*. Glencoe, IL: Free Press.

Wolfinger, Raymond E. 1972. "Why Political Machines Have Not Withered Away and Other Revisionist Thoughts." 34 *Journal of Politics* 365.

Zink, Harold. 1930. *City Bosses in the United States*. Durham, NC: Duke U. Pr.

# V

## Clement L. Vallandigham (1820–1871)

Conservative opponent of abolitionists. A Jacksonian Democrat suspicious of eastern economic interests and Yankee social meddling, Clement Laird Vallandigham's ideal remained, "the Union as it was forty years ago." Despite lifelong residence in Ohio, he took great pride in his family's southern heritage. Vallandigham entered Ohio politics as a member of the "Miami" faction, a group that believed that the economic interests of the Northwest were neglected. He served in the Ohio legislature from 1845 to 1847 and after two unsuccessful campaigns, he was finally elected to Congress in 1856. Vallandigham held the very marginal Third Congressional District until 1862 when gerrymandering and Republican charges of disloyalty finally defeated him.

In Ohio and then in Washington, Vallandigham was a bitter opponent of abolitionists and Republicans. He interviewed the wounded John Brown in 1859 and became convinced that Brown was part of a vast Republican conspiracy to take over the government. In the 1860 election Vallandigham was secretary of the national committee that supported Stephen A. Douglas. He was one of 44 Congressmen who refused to vote for a resolution stating that Abraham Lincoln's election was not grounds for secession. The departure of southern Congressmen in 1861 left him a member of a tiny Democratic minority of whom many were War Democrats. Vallandigham voted against almost every war measure and sought ways to restore an effective opposition. The Lincoln administration's restrictions on civil liberty, the emancipation proclamation, and the coercive military draft convinced him that a war begun for the Union had been preserved to "universal political and social revolution."

Vallandigham led the "purists" who embarrassed more pragmatic "legitimist" Democrats by their insistence that vindication of principles was more important than electoral victory. In 1863 he sought to dramatize his faltering campaign for governor of Ohio by a calculated defiance of Union General Ambrose Burnside's proclamation against speeches undermining the war effort. On May 1, Vallandigham made a speech in which he called the war "wicked, cruel and unnecessary"; he was promptly tried by a military commission and sentenced to imprisonment. The incident created a storm of protest on constitutional grounds, which Lincoln tried to resolve by banishing Vallandigham to the Confederacy. After a brief stay in the South, he was able to reach Canada and conduct his campaign from Windsor, Ontario. His "martyrdom" won Vallandigham the Democratic gubernatorial nomination but enabled the Republicans to turn the election into a referendum on loyalty in which the Democrats won only 39 percent of the civilian and 6 percent of the soldier vote.

In 1863 Vallandigham became commander of the Sons of Liberty, a semisecret antiwar society that Republicans claimed was a widespread conspiracy for treason and armed revolt. Revisionist historians have largely refuted these charges and have shown that Vallandigham was not really very active in the organization. He always publicly advocated only constitutional resistance and loyalty to "the Union as it was," but in Richmond and Canada he hinted to Confederate officials that if they could hold out, a separate Northwest Confederacy and a negotiated peace were possible.

Vallandigham virtually wrote the 1864 national Democratic platform including a strong peace plank, but he had reluctantly to accept General George McClellan's nomination. His repeated efforts to keep the general from repudiating the peace plank were unsuccessful. After the war Vallandigham sought new issues and hoped for a party realignment. He was influential at the National Union Convention in 1866 but in the interests of harmony remained behind the scenes. In 1868 he supported the candidacy of Salmon Chase but failed to revive his own Ohio political career when his bid for Democratic support for the Senate and a campaign for Congress both failed.

*See also:* Abolition Movement, John Brown, Salmon Chase, Stephen A. Douglas, Gerrymandering, Jacksonian Democracy, Abraham Lincoln

*Harold B. Raymond*

REFERENCES

Klement, Frank L. 1970. *The Limits of Dissent: Clement L. Vallandigham and the Civil War.* Lexington: U. Pr. of Kentucky.

Nichols, Roy. 1948. *The Disruption of American Democracy.* New York: Macmillan.

Paludan, Phillip S. 1988. *A People's Contest: The Union and the Civil War.* New York: Harper & Row.

Silbey, Joel. 1977. *A Respectable Minority: The Democratic Party in the Civil War Era.* New York: Norton.

# Martin Van Buren (1782–1862)

Eighth President of the United States. Martin Van Buren played a key role in building and defending a political system based on mass participation, sectional dependence, and the idea of a permanent opposition to promote the general welfare. Born in Kinderhook, New York, Van Buren became a law clerk in New York City for William P. Van Ness in 1801. After Van Buren's return to Kinderhook two years later, he opened his own legal practice and participated in politics as the defender of the Clinton-Livingston factions, in opposition to Aaron Burr. Van Buren soon acquired a reputation as a shrewd political tactician and was elected to the state senate in 1812. He began to develop a number of alliances and quickly emerged as a serious rival to De Witt Clinton, New York's foremost Republican leader.

In 1816 Van Buren won reelection to the state senate and was also chosen as attorney general of the state. But he opposed certain aspects of Clinton's canal bill, and when Clinton was elected governor in 1817, he removed Van Buren as attorney general. Nevertheless, Van Buren's prestige continued to grow. He led a legislative faction known as the Bucktails, and with this power base he won election to the U.S. Senate in 1821. Yet he continued his deep interest in state politics and headed the influential Albany Regency that protected his position at home in New York.

In 1823 Van Buren attempted to renew the old alliance of southern and New York Republicans. In particular, he managed the northern wing of a coalition that supported William H. Crawford of Georgia for President. During the election campaign, however, Crawford suffered a stroke. When no candidate won a majority of the electoral votes, the House of Representatives selected John Quincy Adams as the next President.

Van Buren increasingly opposed the policies of the Adams administration, and he finally decided to support Andrew Jackson, who had lost the presidential election of 1824 despite polling the most popular and electoral votes. Van Buren, who believed that a free government needed political parties, repeatedly propounded his theme of combining southern planters and northern Republicans in an alliance to prevent conflict between the slave and free states. In 1827 Van Buren won reelection to the Senate, but the next year he resigned his seat to run for governor of New York. He believed that this campaign would allow him to generate more support in New York for Jackson's 1828 presidential campaign. After Jackson won the presidency, Van Buren accepted a position as Secretary of State.

Van Buren proved to be able and energetic in foreign affairs, and he also continued to advise Jackson on a wide range of domestic matters. In August 1831 Van Buren resigned his Cabinet position, only to have Jackson appoint him as minister to Great Britain. But Vice President John C. Calhoun, Van Buren's archenemy, led the opposition in the Senate that refused by one vote to confirm his appointment.

In May 1832, however, Van Buren triumphed over Calhoun when the New Yorker accepted the Democratic vice presidential nomination as Jackson's running mate, thus becoming the heir apparent after Jackson's reelection. Indeed, in 1835 the Democratic National Convention unanimously endorsed Van Buren for the presidency. In his presidential campaign he re-affirmed Jackson's opposition to the Bank of the United States and restated his defense of slavery where it already existed. In the election Van Buren won a large majority of the electoral vote against the Whig Party's regional candidates. Soon, however, the panic of 1837 sent the country into an economic depression. In response, Van Buren refused to change his basic hard-money policy, and he continued to oppose the national government's expansion of credit. Instead, he advocated the establishment of the Independent Treasury system.

The depression was clearly the reason that the Whig candidate, William H. Harrison, defeated Van Buren in the presidential election of 1840. After his defeat, Van Buren continued to take an active interest in politics. He hoped to win the Democratic Party's nomination in 1844. Southern opposition prevented this victory, and by 1848 Van Buren split with the Democrats over the extension of slavery into the territories. He became a representative of "free-soil" (antislavery) Democrats in New York. He was also the Free Soil Party's candidate for President in 1848, but he won only 10 percent of the popular vote and no electoral votes.

By 1852 Van Buren had returned to the Democratic Party hoping that the slavery issue could be resolved peacefully. With secession and the Civil War, he was a supporter of Union activists in New York.

*See also:* John Quincy Adams, Aaron Burr, John C. Calhoun, De Witt Clinton, William H. Crawford, William Henry Harrison, Andrew Jackson

*Steven E. Siry*

REFERENCES

Cole, Donald B. 1984. *Martin Van Buren and the American Political System.* Princeton: Princeton U. Pr.

Niven, John. 1983. *Martin Van Buren: The Romantic Age of American Politics.* New York: Oxford U. Pr.

Wilson, Major. 1984. *The Presidency of Martin Van Buren.* Lawrence: U. Pr. of Kansas.

## Arthur H. Vandenberg (1884–1951)

Republican Senate leader on foreign affairs. Arthur Hendrick Vandenberg, born and reared in Grand Rapids, Michigan, attended local schools and one year at the Law Department of the University of Michigan before becoming editor of the *Grand Rapids Herald* at age 22. He served as publisher until 1928 when he was first appointed and then elected to the U.S. Senate as a Republican. Vandenberg immediately began serving on the Senate Foreign Relations Com-

mittee where he espoused isolationism but voted for the World Court. His major achievements were to sponsor a bill providing for automatic decennial reapportionment after each census and an amendment to the Glass-Steagall banking bill in 1933 providing for the Federal Deposit Insurance Corporation, which eventually became a permanent federal agency. A supporter of President Herbert Hoover and critic of President Franklin Roosevelt, Vandenberg opposed much of the New Deal as a moderate conservative. He supported isolationist legislation and opposed American involvement in World War II until the attack on Pearl Harbor.

Vandenberg, however, abandoned isolationism during the war, supported the UNRRA (United Nations Relief and Rehabilitation Administration), and the Connally resolution providing for adherence to a postwar international peace-keeping organization. Then, at the 1945 Mackinac Conference on Republican policy, he helped convince his party to support international organization. Rescued from political oblivion by his January 10, 1945, speech supporting the United Nations Organization, Vandenberg was appointed a delegate to the United Nations Conference on International Organization by President Roosevelt to write the U.N. Charter, for which he subsequently helped win approval in the Senate. A good friend of President Harry Truman, Vandenberg was appointed a delegate to the United Nations and to the Paris Conference of Foreign Ministers to write the postwar peace treaties. Active in writing the legislation establishing the Atomic Energy Commission, he was easily reelected with only token opposition in 1946 Republican landslide and became chairman of the Senate Foreign Relations Committee.

An advocate to close cooperation between the legislative and executive branches of government as well as both parties, he became a champion of bipartisan foreign policy. His leadership of the Foreign Relations Committee produced unanimous votes in favor of the Aid to Greece and Turkey proposal, approval for the Marshall Plan for economic assistance to a war-devastated and starving Europe, and the Rio Treaty of Mutual Assistance with Latin American Countries. Especially close to Secretary of State George C. Marshall and his Under Secretary, Robert A. Lovett, Vandenberg produced the Vandenberg Resolution with Lovett's assistance, placing the Senate on record favoring a mutual assistance pact for the defense of Europe. Enacted overwhelmingly, the Vandenberg Resolution paved the way for the North Atlantic Treaty Organization, supplemented by the Military Assistance Program, which created the Western Alliance to defend against Russian aggression.

Although continuing to defend bipartisan foreign policy, he was deeply disappointed by Thomas E. Dewey's defeat in the 1948 presidential election, during which President Truman had so bitterly denounced Congress despite Vandenberg's efforts to insure that Congress enacted the President's entire foreign policy program. When the Democrats regained control of the Senate in 1949, Vandenberg lost his Foreign Relations chairmanship, and bipartisanship began to fall apart after Dean Acheson's appointment as Secretary of State. Vandenberg became very ill in late 1949, only once to return to his beloved Senate before his death.

*See also:* Dean Acheson, Thomas E. Dewey, Herbert Hoover, Franklin D. Roosevelt, Harry S Truman, United Nations

*C. David Tompkins*

REFERENCES

Tompkins, C. David. 1970. *Arthur H. Vandenberg: The Evolution of a Modern Republican, 1884–1945*. East Lansing: Michigan State U. Pr.

Vandenberg, Arthur H., Jr., ed. 1952. *Private Papers of Senator Vandenberg*.

## James K. Vardaman (1861–1930)

Flamboyant turn-of-the-century Mississippi politician. Pandering to the racial prejudices and economic woes of poor white farmers and holding them spellbound for hours with oratorical flourish and rabble-rousing zeal, Democrat James Kimble Vardaman of Mississippi became one of the more flamboyant southern politicians of the early twentieth century. An imposing six footer, Vardaman wore his dark hair down to his shoulders. Called "The White Chief" by admirers, he dressed in a white suit, wore white boots, and campaigned on a flatbed wagon pulled by a team of white oxen. On the stump Vardaman railed against bankers and large corporate interests and called for repeal of the Fifteenth Amendment on voting rights. Using crude and coarse tactics, he raised fears about the rape of white women by Black men and took special displeasure with President Theodore Roosevelt's association with Booker T. Washington and Republican patronage policy.

Early in life Vardaman alternated as lawyer, newspaper editor, cotton planter, state legislator, and officer in the Spanish-American War. Unsuccessful in two attempts to secure the gubernatorial nomination at the state Democratic convention, Vardaman won Mississippi's highest office in the first statewide direct primary election in 1903. He accomplished moderate progressive reforms as governor (1904–1908) without the taint of corruption of personal misbehavior. In a close contest for the U.S. Senate in 1907, popular Congressman John Sharp Williams, Democratic Minority Leader of the U.S. House, defeated Vardaman. In this intense election, which drew national attention, William Randolph Hearst's papers supported Vardaman while others favored Williams. Vardaman failed again in 1910, when the Mississippi legislature chose the aristocratic LeRoy Percy instead to fill a U.S. Senate vacancy. Pitted against Percy before the voters in 1911, Vardaman won handily and served in Washington from 1913 to 1919.

As U.S. Senator, Vardaman frequently opposed President Woodrow Wilson's policies and usually voted on national issues as did the maverick Senator Robert La Follette (R-Wisc.). An avowed opponent of U.S. entry in World War I, Vardaman failed to regain his seat in 1918. Defeated in a final attempt for the Senate in 1922 and in bad health, he retired from public life.

Always an admirer of William Jennings Bryan, Vardaman never tried to force a political machine in the factional politics of Mississippi's one-party system. However, his blatant racial diatribes against African-Americans overshadow any progressive liberalism reflected in his political ledger.

*See also:* William Jennings Bryan, Fifteenth Amendment, William Randolph Hearst, Robert La Follette, Theodore Roosevelt, Booker T. Washington, Woodrow Wilson

*Thomas N. Boschert*

REFERENCES

Holmes, William F. 1970. *The White Chief James Kimble Vardaman*. Baton Rouge: Louisiana State U. Pr.

Key, V. O., Jr. 1984. *Southern Politics in State and Nation*. New York: Knopf.

Kirwan, Albert D. 1951. *Revolt of the Rednecks, Mississippi Politics: 1876–1925*. Lexington: U. Pr. of Kentucky.

Kousser, J. Morgan. 1974. *The Shaping of Southern Politics*. New Haven: Yale U. Pr.

McMillan, Neil R. 1989. *Dark Journey: Black Mississippians in the Age of Jim Crow*. Urbana: U. of Illinois Pr.

Osborn, George Coleman. 1981. *James Kimble Vardaman: Southern Commoner*. Jackson, MS: Hederman Bros.

Percy, William Alexander. 1941. *Lanterns on the Levee*. New York: Knopf.

## Vare Brothers Machine

The Vare Brothers—George A., Edwin H., and William S.—led a Republican machine based in the river wards of Philadelphia (those below South Street that comprised the Third Congressional District) from approximately 1900 to 1933. And during the last 15 of those years, they controlled the Republican organization throughout the city. At the turn of the twentieth century, the Philadelphia Republican machine was headed by state insurance commissioner Israel Durham, a friend of the Vares. The Republican machine was a typical one for its time, maintaining its support through patronage and the manipulation of city contracts. Unsurprisingly, many of these contracts went to the Vare Brothers Construction Company.

The Vare Brothers machine established itself as a force within the city when, after years of Democratic dominance, it captured South Philadelphia for the Republicans in the congressional elections of 1900. The Vares initially worked closely with Durham and Bois Penrose, U.S. Senator and leader of the Pennsylvania Republican Party, to ensure Republican hegemony in the city.

When Durham retired in 1907, the city's leadership was divided between state senator James P. ("Sunny Jim") McNichol, a protégé of Penrose, and the Vares. "While each faction regarded the other with suspicion, both defended the organization against outside opposition, and they usually limited their rivalry to municipal contracts and other spoils," wrote political scientist Lloyd Abernethy.

William Vare's effort to become Philadelphia's mayor in 1911 split the Republican organization. Penrose and McNichol supported George H. Earle, who won the primary, but this strategy allowed Rudolf Blankenburg, a reform Republican, to win the general election.

Penrose's death in 1921 cleared the way for the Vare machine to take absolute control of the Republican organization. While William Vare was successful in his effort (in Vare's words) to "force" Herbert Hoover's nomination at the Republican convention in 1928, he was less successful in his personal drive for the Senate in 1926 and in his relations with Republican state leaders like Joseph R. Brundy, Andrew Mellon, and Gifford Pinchot. Heavy losses by the Vare machine in the elections of 1933 caused a revolt within the Republican organization in which Joseph Grundy and Joseph N. Pew, Jr., assumed

the party's leadership, marking the end of the Vare era in Philadelphia.

*See also:* Herbert Hoover, Andrew Mellon

*Thomas J. Baldino*

REFERENCES

Abernethy, Lloyd M. 1982. "Progressivism, 1905–1919." In Russell F. Weigley, ed. *Philadelphia: A 300-Year History.* New York: Norton.

Saltar, John T. 1935. *Boss Rule: Portraits in City Politics.* New York: McGraw-Hill.

Vare, William S. 1933. *My Forty Years in Politics.* Philadelphia: Roland Swain.

## Joseph B. Varnum (1751–1821)

Early Massachusetts leader of the Congress. Joseph Bradley Varnum was the second of the eight Speakers of the U.S. House to come from Massachusetts. Varnum was a Democratic-Republican and a supporter of President Thomas Jefferson.

Varnum was born in Dracut, Massachusetts, a largely self-taught farmer and Revolutionary War veteran who began political life in the Massachusetts House of Representatives in 1780. He served also in the state senate until his election to the U.S. House in 1795. He served in the House from 1795 to 1811 when he was elected by the Massachusetts legislature to serve in the U.S. Senate.

He was first elected Speaker in 1807 when Speaker Nathaniel Macon (Dem.-Rep.–N.C.) chose not to appear at the balloting. Macon had served as Speaker in the three previous Congresses (1801–1807) but had angered President Jefferson by not replacing John Randolph of Roanoke (Dem.-Rep.–Va.) as chairman of the Ways and Means Committee. Randolph and his fellow Virginian had feuded on a number of issues, and Macon's unwillingness to replace Randolph cost him the President's support and, eventually, the speakership.

Varnum served as Speaker for two Congresses (1807–1811) and pleased the Jeffersonians by quickly replacing Randolph. In his first election he captured 59 votes on the first ballot, easily outdistancing his two closest rivals by 42 votes each. Two years later in 1809, Macon sought a comeback and forced the issue to a second ballot where Varnum prevailed 65 to 45.

In his Senate career, Varnum earned most of his praise chairing the Military Affairs Committee during the War of 1812. He was defeated for reelection to the U.S. Senate and returned to Massachusetts where he served in the state senate until his death.

See also: Thomas Jefferson, Nathaniel Macon, John Randolph

*Garrison Nelson*

REFERENCES

Smith, William Henry. 1971. *Speakers of the House of Representatives of the United States.* New York: AMS Press.

## Vietnam War as a Political Issue

American involvement in Vietnam, culminating in the deployment of more than half a million U.S. soldiers in Southeast Asia during the late 1960s, proved disastrous for the nation's diplomacy and its social peace. The U.S. military commitment stemmed from two developments in the late 1940s: a Communist-led revolution against French colonial rule in Vietnam; and the exacerbation of cold war politics, which led the United States to dismiss overtures by the left-wing Vietnamese rebels and instead to support France, a key Western ally. By 1954 the United States was funding nearly 80 percent of the French war effort in Indo-China, and President Dwight D. Eisenhower repeatedly warned the skeptical that a Communist takeover in Vietnam would destabilize nearby Asian governments, toppling them like "dominoes."

In July 1954, after the French had suffered a decisive defeat, the U.S. helped to secure accords to Geneva that temporarily preserved French rule in southern Vietnam while ceding northern Vietnam to the Communists. The U.S. gradually replaced French influence in the south, helping an autocratic but pro-Western ruler, Ngo Dinh Diem, to establish a permanent anti-Communist state. President Eisenhower approved Diem's rejection of elections to reunite Vietnam (as originally mandated at Geneva for 1956), for fear that the North Vietnamese Communist leader, Ho Chi Minh, would win 80 percent of the vote. Despite American aid totaling more than a billion dollars, by 1961 Diem's repressive regime had spawned a broad range of anti-Diem insurgent groups that included the powerful Communist-led National Liberation Front.

For President John F. Kennedy, whose 1960 election campaign had promised forceful leadership to contain communism anywhere in the world, the conflict in Vietnam posed a deepening crisis. Unwilling to let Diem's regime fall to the Communist-controlled National Liberation Front but wary of involving the U.S. openly in an Asian land war, Kennedy increased the presence of U.S. military "advisers" to 16,000. As Diem's position nonetheless continued to deteriorate and as Diem resisted American pres-

sure for social reforms that would build broad support, Kennedy reluctantly sanctioned a generals' coup. With CIA aid, the plotters toppled South Vietnamese President Diem on November 1, 1963; the generals then had Diem murdered. Yet by the time President Kennedy was assassinated three weeks later, the U.S. still had no coherent policy on the Vietnamese war.

During the 1964 presidential election campaign, Kennedy's successor, Lyndon Johnson, early clothed his Vietnam policy in bipartisan congressional support. On August 7, 1964, he secured a resolution (by a vote of 88 to 2 in the Senate and 416 to 0 in the House) mandating military action after a putative North Vietnamese attack on the U.S. destroyer *Maddox* in the Tonkin Gulf near North Vietnam and a doubtful second incident two days later. Although the Republican nominee, Senator Barry Goldwater, urged even stronger action, including the bombing of North Vietnam, Johnson won a landslide victory in part by assuring voters that he would not send "American boys" to fight in Asia.

Johnson soon abandoned his campaign assurances on Vietnam, impelled by the continued weakness of the South Vietnamese government, a belief that American credibility was at stake in a global struggle against communism, and fear that loss of South Vietnam to Communist guerillas would discredit his administration and polarize the nation. Treating the 1964 "Tonkin Gulf" resolution as an open-ended endorsement of his bellicose policies, Johnson ordered the first sustained American bombing of North Vietnam in February 1965 (Operation "Rolling Thunder"), and in March he sent two Marine battalions to defend the Danang airfield—the first official U.S. combat troops in South Vietnam. The American military presence escalated to nearly 200,000 troops by December 1965, to nearly 400,000 in 1966, and to nearly half a million in 1967.

President Johnson's stated strategy in the war—to win "the hearts and minds" of the Vietnamese people—proved an early casualty of both U.S. and South Vietnamese government policies. American B-52 raids on North Vietnam reinforced that nation's war resolve; while in the South, tactical air strikes, artillery fire, and the use of napalm and chemical defoliants against suspected Communist enclaves devastated the countryside, created most of the country's 4 million refugees (some 25 percent of the population), and stirred sympathy for Communist guerillas. Equally unpopular was the American-directed strategic hamlet program begun by the Kennedy administration, a tactic that forcibly removed peasants from their ancestral homelands and relocated them in barbed-wire enclosures built to insulate them from the Communists. A succession of military and civilian regimes in South Vietnam meanwhile proved more adept at courting U.S. leadership than in attracting indigenous popular support.

The administration's failure either to achieve a rapid victory or even to clearly define victory led to growing antiwar protests throughout the U.S. that shattered Lyndon Johnson's foreign policy consensus and his presidency. On January 31, 1968, the Communists (heavily augmented since 1965 by regular units of the North Vietnamese Army) launched an offensive during the Tet lunar holiday that, although repulsed with heavy losses, belied the Johnson administration's claims of an imminent end to the war. In February and March 1968, Senator Eugene McCarthy of Minnesota and Senator Robert Kennedy of New York attracted solid support as antiwar candidates in early Democratic presidential primaries. As approval of President Johnson's war leadership plummeted, he announced on March 31 a temporary bombing halt in order to promote peace talks and then added that he would not seek another term as President. In the fall presidential election, the Republican nominee, Richard Nixon, who had promised a rapid but honorable end to the war (without giving details), won narrowly over his Democratic opponent, Vice President Hubert Humphrey, who was damaged by his ties to Johnson's foreign policy.

In early 1969 President Nixon began phased withdrawals of U.S. troops, and later that year he stated, in a broad policy shift, that the U.S. now expected allied nations to shoulder a greater share of the military burden for their own defense. Still aiming to repel the Vietnamese Communists, Nixon ordered the secret bombing of Communist sanctuaries in neighboring Cambodia in March 1969; and on April 30, 1970, he ordered an "incursion" into Cambodia to destroy those sanctuaries. This belligerent action, regarded as illegal by antiwar activists, sparked protests that closed down 400 American colleges and universities, though the antiwar movement quieted as American soldiers continued to leave Vietnam (only a few thousand combat troops remained by the end of Nixon's first term). In the 1972 presidential election

Nixon easily defeated an antiwar candidate, South Dakota's Democratic Senator George McGovern. On January 27, 1973, Nixon's Secretary of State, Henry Kissinger, and the North Vietnamese diplomat Le Duc Tho signed a treaty in Paris that provided for withdrawal of remaining U.S. soldiers, release of all U.S. prisoners of war, and a cease-fire between North and South Vietnamese soldiers. Renewed fighting among the Vietnamese tempted Nixon to revive the American combat role, but public opinion clearly contradicted this course. Congress further constrained the administration's hawkish impulses by passing a War Powers Act in 1973 that limited presidential deployment of military forces in the absence of congressional approval and by requiring an end to bombing missions in Cambodia by August 14, 1973. Early in 1975 the South Vietnamese government began to collapse in the face of Communist assaults, but Congress refused a plea by Nixon's successor, President Gerald Ford, for $700 million in emergency aid. In April, Communist forces entered Saigon, shortly after Communists had taken power in Cambodia.

The war in Vietnam cost the United States 58,000 lives, 270,000 wounded, and $150 billion; while the Vietnamese on both sides suffered 4 million killed or wounded. The war also undermined a 20-year-old U.S. consensus in foreign affairs, as Americans reconsidered the practicality, if not the core wisdom, of intervention to contain communism anywhere, under any circumstances, and at any cost in manpower and resources. The ensuing contraction of U.S. military spending and commitments, lowered morale in the armed forces, heightened public cynicism about the purposes of American military actions, sharpened mistrust of presidential leadership, and polarization of public opinion in foreign policy are all unintended legacies that endured well after the end of America's role in Vietnam.

*See also:* Dwight D. Eisenhower; Elections of 1960, 1964, 1965, and 1972; Gerald R. Ford; Barry Goldwater; Lyndon B. Johnson; John F. Kennedy; Robert F. Kennedy; Eugene McCarthy; George McGovern; Richard M. Nixon

*Robert S. Weisbrot*

REFERENCES

Fulbright, J. William, ed. 1966. *The Vietnam Hearings.* New York: Vintage.

Gelb, Leslie H., and Richard K. Betts. 1979. *The Irony of Vietnam: The System Worked.* Washington: Brookings.

Gravel, Mike, ed. 1971. *The Pentagon Papers.* 5 vols. Boston: Beacon.

Karnow, Stanley. 1984. *Vietnam: A History.* New York: Penguin.

Lewy, Guenter. 1978. *America in Vietnam.* New York: Oxford U. Pr.

Santoli, Al, ed. 1976. *Everything We Had: An Oral History of the Vietnam War by Thirty-Three American Soldiers Who Fought It.* New York: McGraw-Hill.

## John Volpe (1908– )

Road-building governor of Massachusetts. In 1960, becoming the first Italian Catholic to be nominated for governor of Massachusetts, John Volpe, that same year, was the only Republican to win statewide office in the Bay State. Volpe successfully completed his two-year term as governor of Massachusetts in 1963, having lost by less than 3,000 votes in his bid for reelection in 1962. In 1964 and 1968, however, Volpe sought and recaptured the office of governor.

As a boy, Volpe apprenticed with a plasterer and worked as a hod carrier before starting his own construction business. In 1948 Volpe entered Massachusetts politics and in 1950 became the deputy chairman of the Republican State Committee.

In 1953 Volpe's knowledge of construction and of transportation issues landed him an appointment as the Massachusetts commissioner of Public Works. At this post Volpe started the largest highway building program the state had ever known. By 1956 the now well known Volpe received an appointment from President Dwight Eisenhower as interim federal highway administrator.

In 1968 Spiro Agnew narrowly beat out Volpe as the vice presidential running mate to Richard Nixon. In 1969 Volpe resigned the governorship of Massachusetts at President Nixon's behest to accept the post of Secretary of Transportation.

As Secretary, Volpe sought to stop disruptive transportation projects in favor of revamping mass transit systems. As a means of reducing highway fatalities, Volpe championed the cause of equipping cars with air bags. A final accomplishment was the inclusion of several African-Americans in high positions within Volpe's department.

In 1973, when Nixon restructured his Cabinet, Volpe was given the post of ambassador to Italy. Ironically, Volpe had been denied this post 20 years previously by the Eisenhower administration.

*See also:* Spiro Agnew

*Reagan Robbins*

*REFERENCES*

Kilgore, Kathleen. 1987. *John Volpe: The Life of an Immigrant's Son.* Dublin, NH: Yankee Books.

## Voter Turnout

Voter turnout is defined as the fraction comparing the number of people who voted in an election to the number of people who were eligible to vote. In recent presidential elections turnout rates have varied between 50 percent and 55 percent.

People who vote in elections are considerably different from those who do not vote. The most distinctive characteristic of voters is that they tend to be better educated than nonvoters. Education leads to participation by creating the attitude that it is one's civic duty to vote. Education also leads to increased interest in politics and instills the necessary skills to overcome the bureaucratic aspects of voting, such as complying with registration requirements.

The second most distinctive aspect about voters is that they tend to be older than nonvoters. Young adults are less likely to vote because they move frequently, requiring registration before they can become eligible to vote. Young adults who do not attend college also tend to be less interested in politics, know less about politics, and follow politics less carefully in the news than do older adults of similar educational backgrounds. Young adults who attend college, however, do not rate lower on these motivational factors and vote at higher rates.

In recent elections women and men have been voting at the same rate. In the past, women were less likely to vote because of lingering effects of women's later enfranchisement. Women were not legally eligible to vote until the Nineteenth Amendment was ratified in 1920. Because many women reared before this date were conditioned to believe that politics was not something with which they should be concerned, some of these women did not vote even after they became legally eligible to do so. By the 1970s, however, most of these women were no longer in the electorate. Instead, women who came of age after 1920 comprised the female element of the voting electorate and were just as likely to vote as men.

African-Americans historically were less likely to vote than whites. Much of this reluctance owed to discrimination in the South, where poll taxes and literacy tests were used to disenfranchise Black voters. Once these legal restrictions were removed in the 1960s, African-American participation rates rose. Blacks continue to vote at a rate about 5 percent lower than whites, but this gap may be due to Blacks generally having less education and lower socioeconomic status than whites. Race does not turn out to be a factor in voting turnout when educational and economic backgrounds are held constant.

A few other individual characteristics are related to turnout. Hispanics vote at a rate one-half that of whites. Catholics and Jews are more likely to vote than Protestants. Finally, Democrats and Republicans are more likely to vote than independents. Democrats and Republicans care more who wins the election, and they have an easier time deciding for whom to vote. Both these factors lead them to vote more often.

Turnout historically has been lower in southern states. Through the 1960s intimidation and legal restrictions were used to prevent African-Americans from voting, lowering turnout rates. Southern women also seemed to retain a more traditional view toward voting: women's voting rates lagged behind men's voting rates for a longer period in the South. Finally, southerners have traditionally been poorer and less well educated than northerners and, therefore, less likely to vote. As these three factors changed in the 1960s and 1970s southern state turnout rates have been catching up with northern state rates.

Registration laws as well affect turnout rates. These laws were instituted during the Progressive era in an attempt to remove corruption from the election process. However, registration requirements set up an additional hurdle that had to be met before voting. In some states, this hurdle could be quite high, requiring registration at only one county office within a limited period of time. In the most lenient states, voters can register through the mail or at the polls on election day. One study concluded that the most stringent set of registration requirements reduces turnout by 9 percent.

Turnout rates have declined since 1960 despite the easing of registration laws and an increase in the educational level of the American public. Both these trends should have led to a higher turnout. Two circumstances seem to be responsible for the decline in turnout. The first is a simple demographic trend—the baby boomers, the large number of children born between 1946 and 1964, came of age during this time period. Young adults now comprised a considerably larger proportion of the voting-age population, and as is typical of all generations of young people, they are less likely to vote than their elders. The second reason for the decline in turnout since 1960 centers on changes in political attitudes. More Americans began to distrust their government in this era. They were prepared to believe that politicians and the government would not be responsive to their needs or listen to their opinions. Therefore, they concluded, voting served no purpose. Additionally, fewer and fewer individuals were identifying themselves as Democrats or Republicans at this time. More people thought of themselves as independents, and independents are less likely to vote.

Turnout rates in the United States are significantly lower than in other democracies. Turnout rates over the last 40 years averaged 95 percent in Australia, 93 percent in Italy, 77 percent in Great Britain, and 73 percent in Japan, but only 58 percent in the United States. Some of the reasons for lower turnout in the United States owe to legal differences. In other countries, the government takes steps to insure that all of its citizens are registered to vote. In the United States, individual initiative is required for registration. Other democracies also make it easier to vote by holding elections on weekends or holidays. The second ingredient explaining lower turnout rates in the United States is the lack of a political party specifically addressing the concerns of the lower class. European democracies often have socialistic parties that spend considerable energy in mobilizing less-educated, working-class individuals. Additionally, religious or ethnic parties mobilize their constituencies. Parties in the United States are not as directly linked with specific groups, so this mobilization process does not normally occur. As a result, turnout rates are lower in the United States and the voting electorate is comprised to a significant extent of middle-class citizens.

*Barbara Norrander*

REFERENCES

Asher, Herbert B. 1988. *Presidential Elections and American Politics: Voters, Candidates, and Campaigns Since 1952.* Chicago: Dorsey.

Flanigan, William H., and Nancy H. Zingale. 1987. *Political Behavior of the American Electorate.* Boston: Allyn and Bacon.

Wolfinger, Raymond E., and Steven J. Rosenstone. 1980. *Who Votes.* New Haven: Yale U. Pr.

## Voter Turnout in Primaries

Voter turnout in primaries—those elections held to nominate candidates for the Democratic and Republican parties—is lower than turnout in general elections, during which the Republican candidate competes against the Democratic candidate. As such, one of the major concerns over primary turnout is whether those who do bother to vote represent accurately those who choose not to vote.

Turnout in presidential primaries averages about one-third of the eligible electorate. Yet primary voters constitute one-half of the electorate for the general election, because turnout rates in the general election are also fairly low at about 50 percent. Since the presidential primary electorate comprises a sizable proportion of the presidential electorate, few differences exist between the two electorate groups. Presidential primary voters are only slightly better educated; they are older and more strongly partisan. They are not more ideologically extreme.

Turnout rates in presidential primaries are affected by the nature of the race. When more candidates are competing, turnout is higher. When candidates spend more time in a state, turnout is higher. If the ballot is more complicated, in that voters have to pick and choose among a long list of delegates, turnout is lower. Many other primary rules obtain, with a great deal of variation among which states use which rules. For instance, some states legally bind delegates to vote at the convention for the candidate under whose name they were elected. Some states use proportional representation to allocate delegates to match preference primary results. Other states use winner-take-all rules. Finally, different methods are used to place candidates' names on the ballot. While some studies have found that some of these rules will influence turnout rates, one study points out that most voters do not know which rules are used in their states. As such, these rules cannot have a direct impact on turnout rates. However, some of these rules have small, indirect effects on turnout rates, because these rules influence where candidates compete and how vigorously they compete. These two factors, as stated previously, do affect turnout rates.

Turnout in gubernatorial primaries is about 30 percent, with turnout rates higher in the South and West than in the East or Midwest. Turnout appears to be higher in open primary states and where the race is more closely contested. Turnout is also higher in states in which parties do not endorse candidates before the primary is held.

Primaries historically have been very important in the South, where the winner of the Democratic Party primary was assured of winning the general election, since the Republican Party was very weak in these states. At times, turnout in southern Democratic primaries would be higher than turnout in the general election. Southern primaries, however, are becoming more like primaries in other states as politics in the South becomes more like other states. Turnout has been declining in Democratic primaries but not increasing in Republican primaries. As a result, turnout in southern primaries is decreasing.

As is true of presidential primary voters, gubernatorial primary voters tend to be strong partisans. Again, no consistent evidence demonstrates that gubernatorial primary voters are more liberal or more conservative than nonvoters. Finally, gubernatorial primary voters tend to be better educated, to have a higher socioeconomic status, and to be more interested and more knowledgeable about politics than other voters.

*See also:* Open Primary, Winner-Take-All Systems

*Barbara Norrander*

REFERENCES

Geer, John G. 1989. *Nominating Presidents*. Westport, CT: Greenwood Press.

Jewell, Malcolm E., and David M. Olson. 1988. *Political Parties and Election in American States*. Chicago: Dorsey.

Norrander, Barbara, and Gregg W. Smith. 1985. "Type of Contest, Candidate Strategy and Turnout in Presidential Primaries." 13 *American Politics Quarterly* 28.

———. 1986. "Selective Participation: Presidential Primary Voters as a Subset of General Election Voters." 14 *American Politics Quarterly* 35.

## Voting Rights Act of 1965 and Extensions

Intended to guarantee the full exercise of the franchise to Blacks and other minorities, the Voting Rights Act of 1965 must be seen as one of the most successful pieces of political legislation in recent history. It led both immediately and in the two decades since its passage to dramatic growth in Black registration and Black voter turnout and even more dramatic increases in the number of Black elected officials. It has also had significant consequences for improving Hispanic representation and some limited but important consequences for Native American representation in the Southwest as well.

From a policy perspective the Voting Rights Act has six key components:

1. 1965 provisions abolishing literacy tests. This barrier, customarily enforced with a double standard for whites and Blacks, was a key party to the post-Reconstruction elimination of Black suffrage in the South.

2. 1965 provisions prohibiting the use of any device that would impose unreasonable financial hardships on persons of limited means as a prerequisite for voting.

3. 1965 provisions permitting the Justice Department to dispatch federal marshals as observers or registrars in parts of the South to end the denial of the right to vote for Blacks. The protective cloak to the federal government was especially important in the 1960s when Black registration in some areas of the South was virtually nil and harassment and intimidation of Blacks seeking to exercise the franchise was commonplace.

4. 1965 provisions requiring jurisdictions covered by Section 5 of the act to submit *any* proposed change in their election provisions at *every* level of government to the Department of Justice for preclearance, thus ensuring that the proposed change would not have the effect or purpose of abridging the right to vote. Initially, the only covered jurisdictions were in the South, but in 1975 coverage was extended to include all or part of 22 other states, including, for example, New York and Colorado. As of 1989, the act covers 16 states in whole or part. The preclearance requirement became important in reapportionment during the 1970s when it led to the substantial elimination of multimember district plans in southern legislatures. Earlier, these districts often had been used to submerge pockets of Black population large enough to form the core of single-member districts. In states such as South Carolina and Mississippi this change (in conjunction with Black registration gains) dramatically increased the number of Black legislators.

5. 1975 provisions requiring the use of bilingual ballots in jurisdictions with greater than 5 percent population whose native language was not English. These provisions have had their primary impact in Hispanic concentrations in both the Northeast and the Southwest.

6. 1982 amendments (Section 2) that everywhere in the U.S. prohibited the use of any electoral device that would have the purpose or effect of diluting minority voting strength at all levels of government. Section 5 preclearance requirements had affected only *changes* in election procedures; thus current discriminatory practices could be continued even if they could not be initiated. Section 5, moreover, had affected only some states. Although the amended Section 2 provisions did not have the prohibitory bite of Section 5, with its Justice Department preclearance requirements, they were potentially of even greater importance—especially in ending the discriminatory use of at-large elections. In 1980 over 60 percent of all U.S. cities elected some (in most cases all) of their council persons at large, and the most well substantiated propositions in political science demonstrate that, in jurisdictions with substantial minority populations, at-large elections tend to depress levels of minority electoral success.

In the 1960s the most important provisions of the Voting Rights Act were seen as those that protected the rights of Blacks in the South to register and vote. In the 1970s Hispanics and other groups were given the protection of the act, and the Section 5 preclearance provisions became those that were seen as having the real force. After the 1982 amendments to the act, the new language of Section 2 became the basis of most voting rights lawsuits. Like the ramification of the Court's decisions in *Brown v. Board of Education* and *Baker v. Carr*, it has taken the subsequent decades for the full scope and consequences of the Voting Rights Act to become clear.

The Voting Rights Act passed 333 to 85 in 1965, despite the strong opposition of southern Democrats. Together with the Civil Rights Act of 1964 and the Immigration Reform Bill of 1965, it is one of the cornerstones of contemporary race relations in the United States. Its provisions have been challenged but held to be constitutional by the U.S. Supreme Court, and its coverage has been interpreted by federal courts as extending to all aspects of election organization, including annexations, locations of voting booths, and choice of electoral systems. Thus, the act has come to cover far more than simple denial of the franchise.

In particular, the use of multimember districts (the polar type of which is an at-large election) will be held in violation of Section 2 of the Voting Rights Act if (1) within the multimember district, a compact contiguous minority population is large enough to form the basis for at least one majority-minority district if single-member districts were to be drawn; (2) voting in the jurisdiction is polarized along racial or linguistic lines; and (3) the minority community demonstrates cohesive voting behavior, and the candidates whom it supports lose with sufficient frequency so as to deny to minority members an equal opportunity to elect candidates of choice. The exact meaning of these conditions is spelled out in more detail in the *Thornburg v. Gingles* (106 S. Ct. 2752), which is now the leading case on the meaning of the Section 2 standard.

The Section 5 preclearance provisions put the burden on covered jurisdictions to demonstrate that changes do not have discriminatory effects or purpose. Thus, the usual "innocent until proven guilty" standard is seemingly inverted. As a result of Section 5's preclearance powers in the South and elsewhere, the Justice Department has direct authority over local and state statutes and administrative procedures—a remarkable tilt in federal-state relations that both proponents and opponents of the Voting Rights Act liken to a "Second Reconstruction," especially since the Justice Department often relies on Black informants within the community to provide it with information about the probable consequences of any submitted changes.

The role of the Justice Department in enforcing the Voting Rights Act is highly controversial. On the one hand, liberal critics of the Justice Department's administration of Section 5, like Howard Ball and his associates, claim that "negotiated compliance leads the Justice Department to defer unduly to local authorities—at the expense of minority voting rights." Other critics charge inadequate policing of the preclearance provisions, permitting states to implement changes in election procedures without undergoing preclearance. Still other critics like Bullock accept that Justice Department enforcement of the act (especially in the 1980s under President Ronald Reagan) has been lax and that some preclearance decisions, like the department's 1982 acceptance of a plan splitting New Orleans' Black population into two congressional districts, have been reached on political grounds. On the other hand, in remarkable contrast, analysts like Abigail Thernstrom contend that the Justice Department has sometimes displayed a "get-the-racist-bastards approach" toward its internal review of preclearance sub-missions that is inappropriate to its quasi-judicial role. Moreover, Thernstrom claims that "the Republican administration of Ronald Reagan had pressed as diligently in [enforcement] as its predecessors."

Because the Voting Rights Act does not stipulate specific tests for vote dilution, the meaning of that concept has been the topic of continuous case-by-case adjudication, while at the same time there has been an ongoing evolution of administrative standards within the Voting Rights Section of the Justice Department. The interpretation of the act has involved a remarkable sequence of negotiations, leading perhaps to a kind of "reflective equilibrium," in which social scientists' courtroom testimony in voting rights cases in the late 1960s and 1970s influenced judicial interpretation of the statute. This development in turn set the stage for further social science testimony in the 1980s on the proper interpretation of terms such as "racially polarized voting," which finally became the basis for subsequent court decisions. The process has been at work from the first successful vote dilution case heard by the Supreme Court, *White v. Regester* (412 U.S. 755 (1973)), through *Thornburg* (1986).

Because of the group nature of vote dilution claims, the evidentiary standards in voting rights cases differ sharply from those in other tort cases outside the civil rights area—instead of proof of particular discriminatory acts against particular individuals there is the need to demonstrate a complex statistical pattern of "social facts." In the short run, such evidence poses problems of interpretation for both attorneys and judges. In the long run it may possibly give rise to a "new jurisprudence appropriate for the activist state" of the sort discussed by Bruce Ackerman.

*See also: Baker v. Carr*, Literacy Tests, Ronald Reagan, Single-Member Districts, *Thornburg v. Gingles*, *White v. Regester*

*Bernard Grofman*

REFERENCES

Ackerman, Bruce A. 1983. *Reconstructing American Law.* Cambridge: Harvard U. Pr.

Ball, Howard. 1984. "The View from Georgia and Mississippi: Local Attorneys' Appraisal of the 1965 Voting Rights Act." In Chandler Davidson, ed. *Minority Vote Dilution.* Washington: Howard U. Pr.

———, Dale Krane, and Thomas P. Lauth. 1982. *Compromised Compliance and Implementation of the 1965 Voting Rights Act.* Westport, CT: Greenwood.

Brown, Raymond, and Duane McMahon. 1983. *The State of Voting Rights in Georgia in 1982.* Atlanta: Southern Regional Council.

Davidson, Chandler, ed. 1984. *Minority Vote Dilution.* Washington: Howard U. Pr.

———, and George Korbel. 1981. "At-Large Elections and Minority-Group Representation: A Re-Examination of Historical and Contemporary Evidence." 43 *Journal of Politics* 4.

Engstrom, Richard L., and Michael D. McDonald. 1986. "The Effect of At-Large Versus District Elections on Racial Representation in U.S. Municipalities." In Bernard Grofman and Arend Lijphart, eds. *Electoral Laws and Their Political Consequences.* New York: Praeger.

———. 1987. "Quantitative Evidence in Vote Dilution Litigation, Part II: Minority Coalitions and Multivariate Analysis." 19 *The Urban Lawyer* 1.

Grofman, Bernard. 1982. "Alternatives to Single-Member Plurality Districts: Legal and Empirical Issues." 9 *Policy Studies Journal* Special Issue (3). Reprinted in Bernard Grofman, Arend Lijphart, Robert McKay and Howard Scarrow, eds. *Representation and Redistricting Issues.* Lexington, MA: Lexington Books.

———. 1985. "Criteria for Districting: A Social Science Perspective." 33 *UCLA Law Review* 1.

Jacobs, Paul W., II, and Timothy G. O'Rourke. 1986. "Racial Polarization in Vote Dilution Cases Under Section 2 of the Voting Rights Act. The Impact of *Thornburg v. Gingles.*" 3 *Journal of Law and Politics.*

Karlin, Pamela, and Reyton McCrary. 1988. "Book Review: Without Far and Without Research: Abigail Thernstrom on the Voting Rights Act." *Journal of Law and Politics.*

Marshall, Dale Rogers. 1981. "Review of Black Representation and Urban Policy." 75 *American Political Science Review* 1046.

Parker, Frank R. 1983. "Racial Gerrymandering and Legislative Reapportionment." In Chandler Davidson, ed. *Minority Vote Dilution.* Washington: Howard U. Pr.

Thernstrom, Abigail. 1987. *Whose Vote Counts? Affirmative Action and Minority Voting Rights.* Cambridge: Harvard U. Pr.

# W

## Benjamin F. Wade (1800–1878)

A leader of the Radical Republican faction in Congress during the Civil War and Reconstruction. Benjamin Franklin Wade was one of the authors of the Wade-Davis Manifesto that called for legislative as opposed to executive control of the reconstruction of the Union.

Born into a large, impoverished New England farm family, Wade received scant education as a child. Resettling in the Ohio Western Reserve in 1821, he labored at various jobs, eventually taking up the practice of law. Coarse in speech and given to a bluff, vituperative manner, Wade won election to the Ohio state senate in 1837 and 1841 as an opponent of the fugitive slave law. Uncompromising in his antislavery stance, Wade was elected to the U.S. Senate in 1851 by a Whig in Free Soil Party coalition. A Republican from 1856 and one of the most belligerent of Unionist leaders during the Civil War, Wade headed the Joint Committee on the Conduct of the War, and investigatory body that spurred the Abraham Lincoln administration to pursue a more vigorous military policy and served as a propaganda agency for instilling patriotic fervor among civilians. In sponsoring the Wade-Davis Bill, with Congressman Henry Winter Davis of Maryland, which was passed by Congress (July 2, 1864) and pocket vetoed by President Lincoln, Wade sought to secure congressional control over Reconstruction and to require stringent conditions for readmission of the rebellious southern states. After Lincoln's death, new President Andrew Johnson attempted to implement Lincoln's mild Reconstruction policy. Wade, with other radicals in both houses of Congress, was prepared, after December 1865, to resort to almost any extremity, including impeachment of the President, to assure predominance of the congressional policy. Elected President *pro tempore* of the Senate in 1867, and consequently Johnson's successor in the event of his removal from office, Wade was ultimately thwarted by Johnson's acquittal and his own defeat for reelection to the Senate in 1868.

*See also:* Henry Davis, Free Soil Party, Andrew Johnson

*Richard C. Burnweit*

REFERENCES

Benedict, Michael Les. 1977. *A Compromise of Principle: Congressional Republicans and Reconstruction 1863–1869.* New York: Norton.

Bogue, Allan G. 1981. *The Earnest Men: Republicans of the Civil War Senate.* Ithaca: Cornell U. Pr.

Trefousse, Hans L. 1963. *Benjamin Franklin Wade: Radical Republican from Ohio.* New York: Twayne.

Williams, T. Harry. 1965. *Lincoln and the Radicals.* Madison: U. of Wisconsin Pr.

## Robert F. Wagner, Jr. (1910–1991)

Democratic mayor of New York City from 1954 to 1965. Robert Ferdinand Wagner, Jr., was born in New York City, the son of U.S. Senator Robert F. Wagner. The young Wagner received a private school education and graduated from Yale in 1933 and the Yale Law School in 1937. His rise in Democratic politics assured by his father's ties to the Tammany political machine, Wagner was elected to the state assembly in 1937 and served until he joined the Army at the outbreak of war in 1942. Returning as a lieutenant colonel in 1945, Wagner was appointed by Mayor William O'Dwyer to several city commissions.

In 1949 Wagner was elected president of the borough of Manhattan as the Democratic-Liberal candidate. Selected by Tammany leader Carmine G. DeSapio to oppose incumbent Mayor Vincent R. Impelliteri in 1953, Wagner was elected mayor and subsequently reelected in 1957. Wagner's tenure as mayor was marked by significant civil service reforms and his appointment of nationally recognized experts to key administrative posts. Additionally, the city made substantial progress in slum clearance, increasing the size of the police department, and tighter budgetary control. In his 1961 reelection bid, Wagner broke with DeSapio and the regular Democratic Party organization in joining ranks with the reform club movement, known as the Committee for Democratic Voters, led by former U.S. Senator Herbert H. Lehman and Eleanor Roosevelt. Campaigning against "bossism," Wagner handily won reelection and led the reformers' successful takeover of the Tammany organization. During Wagner's final term, the city was beset by increasing crime and racial tension and a series of protracted strikes. In 1965 Wagner declined to seek a fourth term. After leaving office, he was unsuccessful in subsequent attempts to regain the mayoralty.

*See also:* Carmine DeSapio, Herbert H. Lehman, Eleanor Roosevelt, Robert F. Wagner, Sr.

*Richard C. Burnweit*

REFERENCES

Costikyan, Edward N. 1966. *Behind Closed Doors: Politics in the Public Interest.* New York: Harcourt, Brace and World.

Moscow, Warren. 1967. *What Have You Done for Me Lately?: The Ins and Outs of New York City Politics.* Englewood Cliffs, NJ: Prentice-Hall.

———. 1971. *The Last of the Big Time Bosses: The Life and Times of Carmine DeSapio and the Rise and Fall of Tammany Hall.* New York: Stein and Day.

## Robert F. Wagner, Sr. (1877–1953)

Democratic United States Senator from New York from 1927 to 1949. Robert Ferdinand Wagner, Sr., is remembered as a pioneering figure in the formulation of federal labor policy as well as authoring landmark legislation in public works, welfare, and housing.

A German immigrant to the United States at the age of eight, Wagner experienced firsthand the frightful living conditions that many of his legislative efforts ultimately sought to rectify. Educated at City College of New York, Wagner graduated from New York Law School in 1900. As a young lawyer, he joined the local Democratic Tammany Club and was elected to the

state assembly in 1905 and to the state senate in 1909. In the legislature, in league with Alfred E. Smith, then assembly speaker, Wagner promoted a socially conscious legislative program with the blessing of Tammany's liberal boss Charles F. Murphy. As chair of the State Factory Investigating Committee (1911–1915), Wagner secured the enactment of some 56 workplace protection laws.

In 1919 Wagner was elected to the New York Supreme Court. Elected to the U.S. Senate in 1927, Wagner specialized in labor issues well in advance of the Great Depression. With the onset of the New Deal, as chairman of the National Labor Board under the National Industrial Recovery Act (NIRA), Wagner fought to secure the rights of workers to organize and bargain collectively. When the NIRA was declared unconstitutional, Wagner proposed and indeed prodded the Franklin Roosevelt administration into accepting the more coercive National Labor Relations Act, ever after known as the Wagner Act (1935). Moreover, Wagner spearheaded efforts to extend the scope of federal government involvement in public welfare and economic planning with passage of the Social Security Act (1935), the Wagner-Steagall Housing Act (1937), and the landmark Full Employment Act (1946). At his retirement in 1949, the New York Senator left behind a legacy of progressive legislation that few of his colleagues could equal.

*See also:* Charles F. Murphy, Alfred E. Smith, Tammany Hall

*Richard C. Burnweit*

REFERENCES

Bailey, Stephen Kemp. 1968. *Congress Makes a Law: The Story Behind the Employment Act of 1946.* New York: Columbia U. Pr.

Bernstein, Barton J. 1968. "The New Deal: The Conservative Achievements of a Liberal Reform." In Barton J. Berstein, ed. *Towards a New Past: Dissenting Essays in American History.* New York: Pantheon.

Berstein, Irving. 1960. *The Lean Years: A History of the American Worker, 1920–1933.* Boston: Houghton Mifflin.

———. 1970. *Turbulent Years: A History of the American Worker, 1933–1941.* Boston: Houghton Mifflin.

Huthmacher, J. Joseph. 1968. *Senator Robert F. Wagner and the Rise of Urban Liberalism.* New York: Atheneum.

Leuchtenburg, William E. 1963. *Franklin D. Roosevelt and the New Deal 1932–1940.* New York: Harper & Row.

Nevins, Allan. 1963. *Herbert H. Lehman and His Era.* New York: Scribner's.

Patterson, James T. 1967. *Congressional Conservatism and the New Deal: The Growth of the Conservative*

*Coalition in Congress, 1933–1939.* Lexington: U. Pr. of Kentucky.

Schlesinger, Arthur M., Jr. 1957–1960. *The Age of Roosevelt.* 3 vols. Boston: Houghton Mifflin.

Vittoz, Stanley. 1987. *New Deal Labor Policy and the American Industrial Economy.* Chapel Hill: U. of North Carolina Pr.

## Daniel Walker (1922– )

Antimachine governor of Illinois. A controversial report and a well-publicized "state walk" brought Daniel Walker national fame, the governorship of Illinois, and fleeting vision of the White House. The Annapolis graduate had originally planned a naval career but switched to law and liberal Democratic politics. Eventually, he became an executive at Montgomery Ward.

Walker first achieved political prominence as the editor of a government-commissioned study of the violence surrounding the 1968 Democratic National Convention in Chicago. The "Walker Report" placed heavy blame for the disturbances on the local police, a conclusion that did not endear the author to Chicago's Mayor Richard J. Daley. Shortly thereafter, Walker declared himself an antimachine Democratic candidate for governor of Illinois in the 1972 election.

He decided to take his message to the people by walking the length of the state, a technique pioneered by Lawton Chiles in Florida. Walker's campaign clearly caught the public fancy. He first upset the popular lieutenant governor, Paul Simon, in the Democratic primary and then won the general election over the heavily favored Republican incumbent, Richard Ogilvie. As governor, Walker pursued a policy of tight budgeting and controlled taxation. This penurious administration once again brought him into conflict with the Chicago organization, and his four years in office proved contentious. Early in his term, Walker had been talked of as a possible presidential candidate. But in 1976, he was defeated in the Democratic primary by the Daley-backed candidate. Walker then entered private business. He encountered severe legal difficulties and in 1987 was sentenced to prison for bank fraud.

*See also:* Richard J. Daley

*John R. Schmidt*

REFERENCES

Walker, Daniel. 1984. *Dan Walker Memoir.* Springfield, IL: Oral History Office, Sangamon State U.

———, ed. 1968. *Rights in Conflict: The Walker Report.* New York: Bantam Books.

## Frank C. Walker (1886–1959)

Democratic Party leader under Franklin Roosevelt. Frank Comerford Walker was treasurer of the Democratic Party from August 1932 to January 1934, Postmaster General from September 1940 to June 1944, and Democratic National Committee chairman from January 1943 to January 1944. Born in Plymouth, Pennsylvania, Walker grew up in Montana. A practicing Roman Catholic, he received a law degree from the University of Notre Dame in 1909, practiced law in Montana, and progressed rapidly from an appointment as deputy prosecuting attorney to election to the Montana House of Representatives. Moving to New York City in 1924, Walker soon proved successful in both law and politics, and through Roosevelt confidant Henry Morgenthau, he became an active supporter of Franklin Roosevelt's presidential candidacy in 1932. He was named treasurer of the Democratic Party in 1932, and following Roosevelt's election, he was appointed executive secretary of the Executive Council, a committee established to coordinate the large number of New Deal agencies. Later he became executive director of the National Emergency Council, which supplanted the Executive Council.

Walker proved more than a run-of-the-mill New Deal bureaucrat. He advised Roosevelt on political matters and on issues of importance to Catholic Americans. In 1935 he left the administration to pursue private business, but he continued to act as a political adviser to the President. In 1940 Walker succeeded James A. Farley as Postmaster General. In 1943 he replaced Edward J. Flynn as head of the Democratic National Committee. Walker continued to be a loyal supporter of Roosevelt until the President's death in April 1945.

*See also:* Democratic National Committee, James A. Farley, Edward J. Flynn, Franklin D. Roosevelt

*Thomas T. Spencer*

REFERENCES

Goldman, Ralph M. 1990. *The National Party Chairmen and Committees: Factionalism at the Top.* Armonk, NY: M. E. Sharpe.

Simon, Paul L. 1965. "Frank Walker, New Dealer." Ph.D. dissertation, U. of Notre Dame.

## James J. Walker (1881–1946)

Dapper, flamboyant 1920s mayor of New York City. James John Walker was a Tammany Hall Democrat and the mayor of New York City from 1925 until 1932. At first resisting the urgings of his father, an Irish immigrant and Tammany politician, to enter politics, Jimmy Walker graduated from New York Law School in 1904 but spent a number of years in Tin Pan Alley writing lyrics to popular songs. Then after a stint as a Tammany district captain under his father, Walker served in the state legislature from 1909 to 1925, the last four years as Democratic senate leader. His magnetic personality and his loyalty to the organization led Tammany's chieftains to tap him as their candidate for mayor of New York in 1925. Elected easily and then reelected even more handsomely, the charming and dapper "Beau James" seemed to symbolize Jazz Age New York.

Leaving most of the work to others, Walker—known as the "Night Mayor"—was associated more with sports, nightlife, and bally-hoo than with the real if relatively modest accomplishments of his administration. By the early 1930s, visibility and popularity had become notoriety and disgrace. Frequently absent on vacations abroad and involved in a tabloid-publicized extramarital affair with an actress, Walker was brought down by the investigation of Judge Samuel Seabury into Tammany corruption and Walker's graft-ridden administration and suspicious personal finances. After the intervention of Governor Franklin D. Roosevelt, whose presidential candidacy put FDR in the ticklish situation of needing to support the investigation without alienating Tammany Hall, Walker resigned on September 1, 1932. Followed by Fiorello La Guardia's far different three-term reform mayoralty, a distinctive era of New York life and politics was over, as was Walker's political career.

*See also:* Fiorello La Guardia, Franklin D. Roosevelt, Tammany Hall

*John W. Jeffries*

REFERENCES

Walsh, George. 1974. *Gentleman Jimmy Walker*. New York: Praeger.

## Robert J. Walker (1801–1869)

Pre-Civil War Jacksonian Democrat. Robert John Walker, United States Senator from Mississippi, confidant of President John Tyler, Secretary of the Treasury under President James K. Polk, and governor of the Kansas Territory by appointment of President James Buchanan, was a dominant figure in national politics from the 1830s to the 1850s. Often referred to as "the Wizard of Mississippi," Walker had few equals as a political broker. His chairmanship of the

Democratic Party's central committee in Washington in 1844 has led some historians to refer to him as the first chairman of the first party national committee. However, only two-thirds of the states were represented on the central committee; subsequent national committees required representation of all states.

Robert J. Walker was born to politics, educated for politics, and married into a political family. His father was a justice of the Pennsylvania Supreme Court. His wife belonged to the Bache-Dallas political dynasties of Pennsylvania. Walker graduated from the University of Pennsylvania at the age of 18, worked as a surveyor while studying law, and began his legal practice in Pittsburgh in 1822. Four years later he joined his brother's law office in Mississippi.

An ardent Jacksonian even before he moved to Mississippi, by 1832 Walker had put together a relatively modern state political machine and became the undisputed leader of the Jackson party. In a spectacular campaign, he won a seat in the United States Senate in 1836. By 1838 he was recognized as the spokesman for the Southwest of that day.

After he began his second term in the Senate in 1841, Walker became a confidante of President Tyler, who was dedicated to the defeat of nationalism and centralization as represented by Whig Henry Clay and Democrat Martin Van Buren. Tyler's key ally in this enterprise of dispersion was Senator Walker. In the Democratic Party, Walker led the faction that favored the annexation of Texas and opposed former President Van Buren's renomination. Walker's strategy at the 1844 national convention resulted in the nomination of James K. Polk, the first "dark horse" nominee for President. Walker next became chairman of the 15-member central committee that was responsible for managing Polk's campaign.

In the Polk administration, Walker hoped to be appointed Secretary of State but settled for the Treasury. Walker's influence in Congress reached new heights during this period. Passage of a Walker Tariff Bill was instrumental in pressing the British to settle the dispute over the boundary between Oregon and Canada.

Confronted with the difficult issue of slavery in the Kansas Territory, President Buchanan asked Walker to take on the territorial governorship. When Buchanan later supported the controversial proslavery Lecompton Constitution for the new state, Walker resigned and condemned the administration. He returned to a lucrative law practice, continued his efforts to prevent a split in the Democratic Party over the slavery issue, and during the Civil War, helped the Treasury Department sell bonds abroad to support the Union war effort.

*See also:* James Buchanan, Henry Clay, James K. Polk, Slavery, John Tyler, Martin Van Buren

*Ralph M. Goldman*

REFERENCES

Brown, George W. 1902. *Reminiscences of Governor R. J. Walker*. Rockford, IL: Privately printed by the author.

Dodd, William E. 1914. "Robert J. Walker, Imperialist." An address given at Randolph-Macon Women's College, April 15, 1914. Library of Congress.

James K. Polk Papers. Library of Congress.

Robert J. Walker Papers. Library of Congress.

## George C. Wallace (1919– )

Antidesegregation governor of Alabama and four-time presidential contender. George Corley Wallace campaigned heavily against desegregation throughout much of his political career. Wallace was born on an Alabama farm, flew combat missions over Japan, and worked his way through the University of Alabama law school by boxing professionally, winning the state's Golden Gloves championship twice. In 1953 he was elected circuit judge, earning the title of the "Fighting Judge" for opposing federal Civil Rights Commission rulings.

He lost the governor's race in 1958 to a militant segregationist, leading to his vow never to be "out-segged" again. He won the governorship in 1962 on a states' rights platform and then "stood in the schoolhouse door" as promised, first to bar two African-American students from the University of Alabama and then to prevent desegregation of the Alabama public schools. President John Kennedy had to federalize the National Guard both times to integrate these educational institutions.

Wallace ran in Democratic presidential primaries in 1964, faring well until he withdrew following the Republican nomination of conservative Barry Goldwater. Governor Wallace used troopers to block Martin Luther King, Jr.'s 1965 Selma civil rights marches, forcing President Lyndon Johnson to federalize the Guard. Because he was barred by state law from succeeding himself in 1966, his wife Lurleen ran as his surrogate and won four more years for Wallace as de facto governor.

In 1968 Wallace ran for President on the American Independent Party ticket in all 50 states, winning five southern states and 13.6 percent of the vote. He undercut President Richard Nixon's conservative support by outflanking him on segregation and law and order. In 1969 a national American Independent Party was formed, though Wallace declined to head it officially. He opposed the Nixon administration's busing program to desegregate schools and the withdrawals of American troops from Vietnam.

Wallace returned to racial appeals (and Ku Klux Klan support) to win the Alabama governorship again in 1970 from incumbent Albert Brewer who appealed to the "future" (i.e., the "bloc vote" of Blacks). The Nixon administration had put Wallace on their enemies list, funded his opponent, and ordered an IRS investigation of Wallace's tax returns. In 1971 he blocked busing for racial balance and in 1972 ran in Democratic presidential primaries, strongly opposing crime, taxes, and busing. The Democratic National Committee chair and the president of the AFL-CIO disowned him, but he won the Florida primary with 42 percent, came in second in Wisconsin and Pennsylvania, won Indiana with 40 percent, and took Alabama, Tennessee, and North Carolina as expected. He was shot and paralyzed while campaigning in Maryland, whose primary he won as he did Michigan's. George McGovern clinched the nomination with a win in California, and Wallace remained neutral, in the general election, pleading ill health.

Wallace's gubernatorial reelection in 1974 with 64 percent of the primary vote included a quarter of the African-American votes, the result of his newly conciliatory rhetoric. His populist appeal to workingmen was wearing thin, however, because of Alabama's lack of welfare and labor legislation, penurious spending for education, and widespread corruption.

Wallace ran for the Democratic presidential nomination in 1976, highlighting issues like crime and taxation, since race seemed to be receding in importance. Without protest rhetoric, he lost the Florida and North Carolina primaries to the unknown Jimmy Carter of Georgia, a reformist candidate. These unexpected defeats precipitated his withdrawal and eventually his retirement when his governor's term expired in 1978. Wallace had never formed a lasting coalition or realignment, but he had forced both major parties to compete hard for the South and to back off on busing for racially balanced schools.

See also: American Independent Party, Jimmy Carter, Barry Goldwater, Ku Klux Klan

Jeremy R. T. Lewis

REFERENCES

Crass, Philip. 1976. *The Wallace Factor*. New York: Mason/Charter.

Frady, Marshall. 1968. *Wallace*. New York: World Publishing Company.

Greenshaw, Wayne. 1976. *Watch Out for George Wallace*. Englewood Cliffs, NJ: Prentice-Hall.

Wills, Garry. 1970. *Nixon Agonistes: The Crisis of the Self-made Man*. Boston: Houghton Mifflin.

## Henry A. Wallace (1888–1965)

Franklin Roosevelt's Vice President turned Truman opponent. Born in Iowa of Scotch-Irish background and influenced by his religious patriarchal grandfather, Uncle Henry, Henry Agard Wallace graduated from Iowa State College in 1910 and became a renowned agricultural scientist. As Secretary of Agriculture in the Franklin Roosevelt administration, Wallace became a leading New Dealer while also showing a pragmatic willingness to compromise with conservatives on agricultural issues. Initially an independent Republican, he became a Democrat in 1936 and vigorously attacked the GOP presidential candidate, Alf Landon. His internationalist orientation won him the vice presidency in 1941, though conservatives forced him off the ticket in 1944. President Harry Truman fired Wallace from his next position as commerce secretary in 1946 after Wallace made a speech critical of Truman's "get tough" policy toward Russia.

Wallace initially preferred working within the Democratic Party to make it a "progressive" force, but after announcement of the Truman Doctrine and Truman's military aid request for the right-wing governments of Greece and Turkey, Wallace increasingly felt that there were insignificant policy differences between the two major parties. After a brief stint as editor of *The New Republic* magazine, he became the Progressive Party candidate for President in 1948. When broad popular support failed to materialize, Communist sympathizers (Wallace refused to repudiate them) gained greater influence over the Progressive Party. Wallace's candidacy was hurt by the climate of postwar reaction, the 1948 Communist coup in Czechoslovakia, the Berlin blockade, and the return of labor and Blacks to Truman's Democratic candidacy. Wallace received only 2.4 percent of the popular vote, no electoral votes, and his party failed to influence the outcomes of any congressional races.

While a few have considered Wallace a prophet for expressing concern that Truman's foreign policy would lead America to support numerous corrupt, albeit anti-Communist, dictatorships across the world, others have felt that he was a simplistic idealist who refused to recognize Soviet aggression. While maintaining his support for the United Nations and lobbying for generous economic aid to developing nations, in later years he recanted his sympathetic orientation toward Russia.

See also: Alfred Landon, Progressive Party, Franklin D. Roosevelt, Harry S Truman

Stephen D. Shaffer

REFERENCES

Lord, Russel. 1947. *The Wallaces of Iowa*. Boston: Houghton Mifflin.

Markowitz, Norman. 1973. *The Rise and Fall of the People's Century: Henry A. Wallace and American Liberalism, 1941–1948*. New York: Free Press.

Schapsmeier, Edward, and Frederick Schapsmeier. 1968. *Henry A. Wallace of Iowa: The Agrarian Years, 1910–1940*. Ames: Iowa State U. Pr.

———. 1970. *Prophet in Politics: Henry A. Wallace and the War Years, 1940–1965*. Ames: Iowa State U. Pr.

Schmidt, Karl. 1960. *Henry A. Wallace: Quixotic Crusade 1948*. Syracuse, NY: Syracuse U. Pr.

Walton, Richard. 1976. *Henry Wallace, Harry Truman, and the Cold War*. New York: Viking.

## Thomas J. Walsh (1859–1933)

United States Senator from Montana and investigator of Teapot Dome scandal. The son of Irish immigrants, Thomas James Walsh was born in Two Rivers, Wisconsin, attended public schools there, but was largely self-educated. At the age of 16 he began teaching school and became principal of the high school at Sturgeon Bay, Wisconsin. Walsh received an LL.B. in 1884 from the University of Wisconsin, from which he later received an advanced law degree. He married his first wife, Elinor Cameron McClemonts, and practiced law with his brother in Dakota Territory until 1890 when he established an office in Helena, Montana.

In Montana, Walsh specialized in litigation against the state's principal mining and railroad companies, while earning a statewide reputation as an honest, pro-labor attorney. He entered public life in 1906 as an unsuccessful Democratic candidate for Congress, and in 1911, owing largely to the efforts of the hostile Anaconda Company, he was denied a seat in the United States Senate. In 1912, however, Walsh defeated progressive Republican Joseph M. Dixon and entered the Senate, where he served with distinction from 1913 to 1933.

During that time, he developed a close relationship with Woodrow Wilson and was the incumbent President's western campaign manager in 1916. In the Senate, Walsh advocated a wide range of progressive measures, including women's suffrage, enactment of the child-labor amendment, and protection of farm organizations and trade unions from the Sherman Antitrust Act. He supported the League of Nations, the World Court, and arms limitations, and in 1916 he led the fight to confirm the nomination of the liberal labor lawyer Louis D. Brandeis to the Supreme Court.

Walsh gained national popular attention because of his leadership in the investigation of the Teapot Dome and Elk Hills oil scandals that rocked the Warren Harding administration in 1923. The following year he served as chair of a deeply divided Democratic National Convention but declined the vice presidential nomination proffered by presidential candidate John W. Davis. He also was named chair of the Democrats' 1932 convention, which nominated Franklin D. Roosevelt for President. After the fall elections, Roosevelt appointed Walsh Attorney General. Thomas J. Walsh died suddenly while on his way to Washington to attend the Roosevelt inauguration ceremonies.

*See also:* Louis D. Brandeis, John W. Davis, Joseph M. Dixon, Warren G. Harding, League of Nations, Franklin D. Roosevelt, Sherman Antitrust Act, Teapot Dome, Woodrow Wilson, Woman Suffrage Movement

*W. Thomas White*

REFERENCES

Bates, J. Leonard. 1963. *The Origins of Teapot Dome.* Urbana: U. of Illinois Pr.

———. 1966. *Tom Walsh in Dakota Territory.* Urbana: U. of Illinois Pr.

———. 1974. "Politics and Ideology: Thomas J. Walsh and the Rise of Populism." 65 *Pacific Northwest Quarterly* 49.

———. 1974. "Watergate and Teapot Dome." 73 *South Atlantic Quarterly* 145.

Carter, Paul A. 1964. "The Other Catholic Candidate: The 1928 Presidential Bid of Thomas J. Walsh." 55 *Pacific Northwest Quarterly* 1.

O'Keane, Josephine. 1955. *Thomas J. Walsh: A Senator from Montana.* Francestown, NH: M. Jones Co.

Stratton, David H. 1974. "Two Western Senators and Teapot Dome: Thomas J. Walsh and Albert B. Fall." 65 *Pacific Northwest Quarterly* 57.

Tucker, Ray Thomas, and Frederick R. Barkley. 1932. *Sons of the Wild Jackass.* Boston: L. C. Page.

## Marcus L. Ward (1812–1884)

Radical Republican chair of the post-Civil War Union (Republican) National Committee. Marcus Lawrence Ward was elected to the chairmanship of his party's national committee by the vote of less than half the committee's full membership, an action of dubious legality. Ward, a moderate, had accepted the Radical argument that his predecessor, Henry J. Raymond, had betrayed the Republican Party by attending a pro-Andrew Johnson midterm convention.

A New Jersey candle manufacturer, Ward entered active politics at age 43 as the Republicans were organizing their new party in his state. By the time the Civil War broke out, Ward was head of the party's state organization and on friendly terms with Abraham Lincoln. Shortly thereafter he won national prominence for his establishment of a veterans aid service.

Ward ran unsuccessfully for governor in 1863 but was elected in 1865. A year later, the Democrat who opposed him in the gubernatorial race led a New Jersey delegation into a pro-Johnson midterm convention. Since President Andrew Johnson had been a War Democrat before he joined Abraham Lincoln on a Union Party ticket, the pro-Johnson incident prompted Ward to join the Radical efforts to recapture the Republican National Committee and party.

Radicals arranged for a meeting of the "Union Executive Committee" in September 1866 to determine what action ought to be taken against Chairman Raymond for attaching himself to the presumed opposition (pro-Johnson) party. The Radicals were happy to fill the chairmanship with Ward, a convinced and outspoken Republican moderate.

Ward remained as chairman until the 1868 "Union Republican" National Convention that nominated Ulysses S. Grant. He returned to his manufacturing interests thereafter, serving a term in the House of Representatives from 1873 to 1875.

*See also:* Ulysses S. Grant, Andrew Johnson, Abraham Lincoln, Henry J. Raymond, Union Party

*Ralph M. Goldman*

REFERENCES

Marcus L. Ward Papers. New Jersey Historical Society.

## Earl Warren (1891–1974)

California Republican officeholder and later Chief Justice of the United States Supreme Court. Born in Los Angeles, Earl Warren had a long and distinguished career in public affairs. Eight times a candidate for political office, he was the dominant figure in California politics for two decades. A law school graduate of the University of California, Warren's career took off as a three-term district attorney (1925–1939) for Alameda County and as attorney general of California (1939–1943).

For his outstanding service, Warren received the Republican nomination in the gubernatorial election of 1942 and defeated the incumbent Democratic governor, Culbert L. Olson, by some 300,000 votes. A genial, liberal Republican who enjoyed bipartisan support, Warren compiled a progressive record that was blemished only by his participation in the war-hysteria-induced evacuation of 110,000 Japanese-Americans from the West Coast during World War II. Owing to California's tradition of "cross-filing," Warren secured both the Republican and Democratic nominations in 1946 and easily won a second term by capturing 98 percent of the vote. In the meantime, his ability to balance budgets while expanding social services in the state attracted national attention.

Twice in contention for the Republican presidential nomination (1948, 1952), Warren became the vice presidential running mate of the lackluster Thomas E. Dewey in 1948 and suffered his only political defeat in that election. In 1950 Warren won a third consecutive term as California governor, soundly crushing Democrat James Roosevelt (Franklin's son) with 2,344,542 votes to Roosevelt's 1,333,856. Accepting President Dwight D. Eisenhower's appointment as Chief Justice of the U.S. Supreme Court, Warren resigned the California governorship in 1953. Over the next 16 years, he guided the Court toward landmark decisions on civil rights, legislative apportionment, and criminal procedure. He led the Court during one of its most "political" eras, as decisions reached during his tenure structured much of the nation's political agenda. From his retirement in 1969 until his death in 1974, Warren maintained a much lower profile, speaking out on Court reform but not substantive issues.

*See also:* Thomas E. Dewey, Dwight D. Eisenhower

*Karl E. Valois*

REFERENCES

Harvey, Richard B. 1969. *Earl Warren: Governor of California.* New York: Exposition Press.

Katcher, Leo. 1967. *Earl Warren: A Political Biography.* New York: McGraw-Hill.

Warren, Earl. 1977. *The Memoirs of Earl Warren.* Garden City, NY: Doubleday.

Weaver, John D. 1967. *Warren: The Man, the Court, the Era.* Boston: Little, Brown.

White, G. Edward. 1982. *Earl Warren: A Public Life.* New York: Oxford U. Pr.

## Washington Benevolent Society

Attempting to popularize and strengthen the Federalist Party, the Washington Benevolent Society in the early nineteenth century promoted Federalist ideas, attacked the doctrines of the Republican Party, and contributed to the process of political democratization. In response to Thomas Jefferson's embargo prohibiting all exports, a group of New York City Federalist merchants under the direction of Isaac Sebring, Gulian C. Verplanck, and Richard Varick founded the Washington Benevolent Society in early 1808. The organization attempted to imitate the success of the Republican-sponsored Tammany Society. Thus, it held quarterly or monthly secret meetings designed to create a fraternal atmosphere among the members. In addition, the Washington Benevolent Society sponsored elaborate and well-orchestrated public gatherings that celebrated independence, commerce, and national unity. The War of 1812, unpopular among Federalists, got its lumps as well.

The Washington Benevolent Society idea rapidly spread from New York City into western New York State and eastward into New England. By 1812 it had reached southward to Maryland and as far west as Ohio. Altogether observers counted at least 298 branches, and there were probably many more. As in New York City, the founders of the other branches were usually young Federalists attempting to compete with the Republican organizations.

Although some of the branches participated in humanitarian work, they were primarily concerned with politics. Whether directly or indirectly involved in nominating candidates and supervising campaigns, the resources of the Washington Benevolent Society were at the disposal of the Federalist Party. But the political effectiveness of the Society is an open question.

The expansion of the Society ended as the Federalist Party declined in the aftermath of the "treasonous" Federalist Hartford Convention; the Treaty of Ghent, which honorably ended the War of 1812; and the Battle of New Orleans, a great American military victory over the British in January 1815. Nevertheless, some of the branches remained active for many years. The one in Philadelphia continued to meet until the mid-1830s. Most, however, were gone by 1824, when the Jacksonian ascendency began.

See also: Federalist Party

Steven E. Siry

REFERENCES

Fischer, David Hackett. 1965. *The Revolution of American Conservatism: The Federalist Party in the Era of Jeffersonian Democracy*. New York: Harper & Row.

Kass, Alvin. 1965. *Politics in New York State, 1800–1830*. Syracuse, NY: Syracuse U. Pr.

## Booker T. Washington (1856–1915)

Turn-of-the-century African-American political power. One of the most successful "bosses" in an era dominated by such politicians, Booker T. Washington's "Tuskegee Machine" was national in scope whereas those of his contemporaries were only local or statewide.

The three major sources of Washington's power lay in the white community. The first of these was the white press that seized upon the content of his famous 1895 Atlanta address and promoted it and him as *the* leader of the African-American community until his death. In that address, Washington emphasized the Protestant work ethic of education, self-help, cleanliness, hard work, punctuality, and thrift with the added advice to remain in the South and forego agitation for political and social equality and justice in favor of gaining "the little green ballot." For example, "The opportunity to earn a dollar in a factory just now is worth infinitely more than the opportunity to spend a dollar in an opera-house." This statement and his most famous one—"In all things that are purely social we can be as separate as the fingers, yet one as the hand in all things essential to mutual progress"—were public endorsements of segregation and a major constituent in the applause that whites gave him in his Atlanta appearance and the support they gave him later. A White House dinner with President Theodore Roosevelt in October 1901 was the most important source of Washington's power. In return for endorsing Roosevelt's administration and nomination for President in 1904, Washington gained a strong voice in federal Black political appointments nationwide.

The Tuskegee Machine's other source of power was white philanthropy to Black schools, especially Black colleges. Through his close ties with Andrew Carnegie, the General Education Board established by John D. Rockefeller, Sr., in 1903, and others, Washington influenced the flow of funds to higher education for African-Americans.

Through his leadership of the National Negro Business League with its nationwide local branches and its annual summer conventions, Washington developed an institutional framework through which he rewarded his supporters, punished his detractors, and gathered information. One such detractor, Dr. W. E. B. Du Bois, rallied the opposition to the Tuskegee Machine with his attack on Washington in *The Souls of Black Folk* in 1903.

In 1906 Washington lost significant numbers of supporters when he failed to denounce the Atlanta race riots and Roosevelt's dishonorable discharge of all the African-American men in three companies of the 24th U.S. Infantry who allegedly used violence to retaliate against a racist attack on one of their comrades in Brownsville, Texas. Defections increased when Washington failed to speak out against the rising tide of mob attacks and lynchings such as the one in Springfield, Illinois, in 1908. The Tuskegee Machine was weakened further by the establishment of the NAACP in 1910. Its final disintegration might not have taken place, however, had Washington made more people aware of his "secret life."

Beginning in the 1890s, Washington began secretly funding legal suits and lobbying efforts that sought to overturn or defeat segregation, disfranchisement, and peonage (involuntary servitude for debt). His efforts in the first two areas failed, but those in the Alonzo Bailey case led to the overturning of the Alabama peonage law in 1911. With Virginia-born Woodrow Wilson's election the following year and his appointment of fellow southern white Democrats to his Cabinet, the Tuskegee Machine lost the major source of its power. Even the little green ballots of Rockefeller's General Education Board did not equal the ear of Presidents, and the political magic of the Wizard of Tuskegee waned until his death.

See also: W. E. B. Du Bois, National Association for the Advancement of Colored People, Theodore Roosevelt, Woodrow Wilson

Hal Chase

REFERENCES

Daniel, Pete. 1972. *The Shadow of Slavery: Peonage in the South 1901–1969*. Urbana: U. of Illinois Pr.

Du Bois, W. E. B. 1903. "Of Mr. Booker T. Washington and Others." In *The Souls of Black Folk*. New York: New American Library.

Harlan, Louis R. 1972. *Booker T. Washington Papers*. 13 vols. Urbana: U. of Illinois Pr.

Meier, August. 1963. *Negro Thought in America 1880–1915: Racial Ideologies in the Age of Booker T. Washington*. Ann Arbor: U. of Michigan Pr.

Spencer, Samuel R. 1955. *Booker T. Washington and the Negro's Place in American Life*. Boston: Little, Brown.

## George Washington (1732–1799)

"Father of his country," first President of the United States. Some irony attends the inclusion of George Washington in a reference work about American political parties. Few figures from the founding era were more opposed to parties and factions than was Washington. When, in his Farewell Address, he railed against the "baneful effects of the spirit of party," he was reflecting a view he had held even before his presidency. Yet despite his antiparty beliefs Washington was a central figure in the rise of partisanship in American politics.

Before the Revolutionary War, about all that could be said about Washington's political sentiments was that he supported the Revolution. His appointment as commander of the Continental Army, however, considerably sharpened his political personality. He was confronted by the obstinacy of the state governments, the weakness of the national Congress, and the specter of a cabal he believed was dedicated to undermining his authority. Thus, out of practical experience, he became a committed nationalist and was sought out by others, notably Robert Morris and James Madison, to support efforts to reform the central government and increase its powers.

After he resigned as commander, he continued his quiet support of the nationalists. As conditions in the new nation deteriorated (at least in his eyes) he corresponded widely with a circle of political friends. When the Constitutional Convention was called, these friends urged the reluctant Washington to attend. His own high regard for his reputation made him reticent about making a potentially quixotic effort. But the nationalists needed him, and Madison finally convinced him to attend. Even with Washington's support, the nationalists did not achieve everything on their agenda. But Washington was convinced that the new Constitution was a great improvement over the old order. In the ratification struggle and the subsequent elections for the new Congress, Washington fairly bubbled over the election of federalists and railed at the occasional successes of "malignant" and "unprincipled" antifederalists.

George Washington did not view these activities as partisan. His political ideology was a variant of classical republicanism. According to this view, something called the public interest was identifiably different from selfish and parochial interests. The virtuous man could only attain fame and glory by pursuing this public good. Harmony, not conflict; unity, not diversity characterized the classical republican view of society. Washington, therefore, envisioned American politics as one in which everyone shared a common purpose and common vision of the good life. Temporary disagreements over specific policies were acceptable. But permanent factions or parties, differing fundamentally in their views of the public interest and competing for the trappings of power, were inconsistent with republicanism. Indeed, he perceived them as unpatriotic.

Washington tried to prevent the rise of parties after his election to the presidency. He believed that the primary causes of faction were sectionalism and personalism. Washington attempted to overcome these potential sources of disruption in two ways. First, he made a point of distributing important federal offices to people from all 13 states. His personal notes show that he was constantly reminding himself to balance his appointments geographically. Second, he often tried to attract (though not always with success) prominent figures from other political camps, hoping to co-opt them into his administration. His first Cabinet (Alexander Hamilton, Henry Knox, Thomas Jefferson, Edmund Randolph) reflects this tactic.

For a time this strategy worked. But Hamilton and other Federalists (as they would come to be known) and a faction led first by Madison and later by Jefferson clearly had different visions of what the new republic should be like. As specific policies emerged and were debated in Congress, those differences sharpened even further. Washington pleaded with Hamilton and Jefferson to restrain their passions and work for the common good, but in 1793 Jefferson stepped down and any chance at maintaining a common vision of the national interest was lost.

Washington was greatly disturbed by these developments and threatened to resign after his first term. Madison, Hamilton, and Jefferson all pleaded with him to stay on, perhaps sensing that Washington was the only person capable of holding the new government together. Washington consented, but he later regretted his decision bitterly. Most scholars believe that by 1796 American politics was represented by two coherent, cohesive factions—the Federalists and the Jeffersonian Republicans. By that time Washington's own partisan preferences were clear. He had, in fact, always been a Federalist. His social conservatism and economic nationalism made him so. There was no ignoring the fact that he had never opposed any major initiative of Hamilton and his allies, but he had balked at a number of important Republican claims. While Washington continued to try to masquerade his partisanship, the Jeffersonian opposition, not surprisingly, made the Old Soldier an object of increasingly personal ridicule, especially through its newspapers.

By the end of his second term partisan lines were firmly drawn. Washington's vision of a unified national government embarked on a common purpose was shattered. To some, it was a dream grounded in unreality at the very outset; factionalism had always been a common part of American colonial life. It was not likely to recede simply because of a new Constitution. Indeed, some see Washington's antipartyism as something much more like one-partyism, in which opposition is perceived as inherently illegitimate and a threat to the Constitution.

Washington's legacy to American political parties is that he gave them critical breathing space. Had the first President openly sided with one faction at the outset of the new government, American politics might have developed quite differently. By publicly restraining his own doubts about opposition factions in the new Republic, Washington allowed American politics to adapt to and absorb parties as legitimate elements in our constitutional system. Madison warned about the dangers of faction in *Federalist* Number 10; he noted that they could either be suppressed or dispersed. When the Alien and Sedition Acts were enacted in 1798 (actions that Washington endorsed) Americans no longer believed that everyone who opposed the government was unpatriotic. This attempt at suppressing a political faction was ultimately unsuccessful. But the attempt might have succeeded in 1791. In the final analysis, American political parties owe much to Washington, the antiparty President.

*See also:* Alien and Sedition Acts, Federalist Party

*Glenn A. Phelps*

REFERENCES

Flexner, James T. 1972. *George Washington*. 4 vols. Boston: Little, Brown.

Ketcham, Ralph. 1984. *Presidents Above Party: The First American Presidency, 1789–1829*. Chapel Hill: U. of North Carolina Pr.

Phelps, Glenn A. 1989. "George Washington and the Paradox of Party." 19 *Presidential Studies Quarterly* 733.

Rakove, Jack N. 1979. *The Beginnings of National Politics: An Interpretive History of the Continental Congress*. New York: Knopf.

## Harold Washington (1922–1987)

First African-American mayor of Chicago. Harold Washington led the Chicago Black community to a historic political victory over the Democratic machine, only to die suddenly in the year of his greatest triumph. A former state legislator and incumbent Congressman, Washington ran for mayor in 1983. As was the case in many other cities, the Democratic Party organization in Chicago became the voice and vehicle of white resistance to Black political empowerment. While formally endorsing Washington, the Chicago machine's leaders worked hard to elect his Republican opponent. Meanwhile, national Democratic leaders came to Washington's aid. Washington won the election, the beneficiaries of a huge Black turnout and a share of white liberal and Hispanic voters.

Washington's narrow mayoral victory did not bring him full power. His African-American and white liberal allies controlled only 21 of Chicago's 50 council seats. A court-ordered reapportionment in 1986 led to the election of four new Black and Hispanic legislators. For the remainder of his first term, Washington was able to break a 25 to 25 tie vote in the council, giving him the barest of governing majorities.

Washington's minority-reform coalition won its greatest victories in 1987 as Washington gained reelection and his council base expanded. His candidate for chairman of the Cook County Democratic Party was selected. But Washington's sudden, fatal heart attack that November set off a series of chaotic events that cost his coalition control of the city.

By 1989 Richard M. Daley, son of the late longtime Chicago boss, had won the mayoralty. However, the minority-oriented appointments of the new mayor confirmed the long-term impact of Washington and his movement.

*See also:* Richard J. Daley

*Raphael J. Sonenshein*

REFERENCES

Kleppner, Paul. 1985. *Chicago Divided: The Making of a Black Mayor*. DeKalb: Northern Illinois U. Pr.

O'Laughlin, John. 1980. "The Election of Black Mayors." 70 *Annals of the Association of American Geographers* 353.

Preston, Michael B. 1987. "The Election of Harold Washington: An Examination of the SES Model in the 1983 Chicago Mayoral Election." In Michael B. Preston, Lenneal J. Henderson, Jr., and Paul L. Puryear, eds. *The New Black Politics: The Search for Political Power*. 2nd ed. New York: Longman.

Starks, Robert T., and Michael B. Preston. 1990. "Harold Washington and the Politics of Reform in Chicago: 1983–1987." In Rufus Browning, Dale Rogers Marshall, and David Tabb, eds. *Racial Politics in American Cities*. New York: Longman.

## Watergate

The Watergate complex of apartments, offices, and shops near the Potomac River in Washington, D.C., gave its name to that series of events and investigations that revealed the existence of a private political espionage organization operating out of the White House. The ensuing scandal caused Richard M. Nixon, thirty-seventh President of the United States, to resign his office.

Watergate consisted of two separate conspiracies. The espionage organization was the first. Formulated after the 1971 publication of *The Pentagon Papers*, classified (but routine) documents relating to the conduct of the Vietnam War, the espionage group was called the Plumbers; its purpose was to "stop leaks." The Plumbers' mission was expanded to include sabotage of the Democratic Party in order to discredit its leading contenders for the 1972 presidential nomination. The Democrats had eventually nominated Senator George McGovern, whom Republican President Nixon regarded as the candidate easiest to beat. Nevertheless, the espionage plot continued, and some of its clandestine operation came to public view on June 17, 1972, when five men were arrested for breaking into the Watergate headquarters of the Democratic National Committee. Their purpose was to replace a defective "bug" (listening device) earlier planted in a telephone.

The second Watergate conspiracy was directed from the White House itself. It was designed to cover up the involvement of Nixon administration officials in the first conspiracy. One of the men arrested for the break-in was a security director of the Committee for the Reelection of the President, Nixon's main campaign group. But presidential spokesmen derided the Watergate episode as a "third-rate burglary," the silence of those arrested was purchased, and no White House staff members were officially implicated. In the November election, Nixon carried every state but Massachusetts, winning 61 percent of the vote.

Nonetheless, Washington district judge John J. Sirica suspected that the full truth had not been told at the trial, and two young reporters from the *Washington Post*, Carl Bernstein and Bob Woodward, followed the story doggedly. Disturbed by the allegations of fraud, illegal contributions, and other crimes interfering with the electoral process, the U.S. Senate established a Select (special) Committee to investigate the charges, chaired by Senator Sam J. Ervin of North Carolina. Televised hearings of the Ervin Committee lasted through the summer of 1973. The star witness was John Dean, the White House counsel, who implicated former Attorney General John Mitchell, White House Chief of Staff H. R. Haldeman, and John D. Ehrlichman, Nixon's domestic affairs assistant, rather than become the scapegoat himself. The nation began to get a picture of the extent of Republican intervention in the Democratic election campaign and the possible connection between campaign contributions and government policy.

On July 16, presidential aide Alexander Butterfield told the Ervin Committee about a secret tape-recording system in the President's Oval Office in the White House. Speculation then centered on the content of those tapes and whether Nixon would provide them. The compelling question, repeatedly phrased by Tennessee Senator Howard Baker, was, "What did the President know, and when did he know it?" By September, the Ervin Committee hearings ended, profoundly affecting public attitudes toward Richard Nixon and his administration.

The Nixon Justice Department then was forced to appoint a special prosecutor in the case (Archibald Cox), who demanded specific tapes. Nixon refused, claiming the right of executive privilege. Nixon then ordered Attorney General Elliot Richardson to discharge Cox. On Saturday, October 20, 1973, rather than complying, Richardson resigned; he had promised Congress, he said, to protect Cox's independence. Richardson's assistant, William D. Ruckelshaus, also refused to discharge Cox, and he was fired. Finally, Robert Bork, the new Acting Attorney General, fired Cox, and Texas attorney Leon Jaworski was eventually appointed as special prosecutor. The incident became famous as "the Saturday Night Massacre."

Jaworski asked for still other tapes, then went to court when Nixon refused his request. Judge Sirica ruled that the President was bound to produce evidence required by a court of law, unless national security would be compromised. The White House appealed this ruling, and the Supreme Court agreed to hear the case without prior consideration by an intermediate court. On July 24, 1974, with Justice William Rehnquist (who had recently served Nixon) not participating, the Court ruled unanimously in the case of *U.S. v. Nixon* that the concept of executive privilege does not allow a President to deny evidence of a possible crime to a court.

Meanwhile, the Committee on the Judiciary of the House of Representatives conducted ten weeks of hearings on the more specialized question of whether Richard Nixon had committed such "high crimes and misdemeanors" that he should be impeached. Like Sam Ervin, Judiciary chairman Peter Rodino patiently accumulated data from and about lesser political figures that inexorably pointed to involvement by the Oval Office. The kangaroo court procedures of the committee that had considered the impeachment of President Andrew Johnson a century earlier were carefully avoided. On the decision day for *U.S. v. Nixon*, Rodino's committee met to debate proposed articles of impeachment. On July 27, 29, and 30, 1974, three specific articles were approved.

In complying with the Supreme Court decision, the White House on August 5 released three new transcripts. They showed that, as early as June 23, 1972, Nixon had known of the Watergate break-in and helped plan the cover-up. Richard Nixon had conspired to obstruct justice.

Senator Barry Goldwater led the House and Senate Republican Minority Leaders in telling Nixon that he would be both impeached and convicted. On June 8, 1974, President Nixon announced his resignation. Nixon's victorious 1972 running mate, Spiro Agnew, had resigned in October 1973 as a part of a bargain with the Justice Department over possible charges of extortion and bribery. Gerald R. Ford became the President.

The response of Congress to Watergate was to provide for the public funding of presidential campaigns and to further regulate the use of money in elections. A more subtle impact occurred in the American public itself. Although the constitutional system functioned to resolve the crisis, the amount of trust placed by the American people in their political leaders declined. In the 1976 campaign, Jimmy Carter made a simple promise: he would never lie. Before Watergate, presidential candidates had never considered such a promise necessary or even relevant.

*See also:* Spiro Agnew, Howard Baker, Committee to the Reelect the President, Democratic National Committee, Election of 1972 and 1976, Gerald R. Ford, George McGovern, John Mitchell, Richard M. Nixon

*Karl A. Lamb*

REFERENCES

Bernstein, Carl, and Bob Woodward. 1974. *All the President's Men*. New York: Simon & Schuster.

Drew, Elizabeth. 1974. *Washington Journal: The Events of 1973–1974*. New York: Random House.

Ervin, Sam J., Jr. 1980. *The Whole Truth: The Watergate Conspiracy*. New York: Random House.

Fields, Howard. 1978. *High Crimes and Misdemeanors*. New York: Norton.

White, Theodore H. 1975. *Breach of Faith: The Fall of Richard Nixon*. New York: Atheneum.

## James E. Watson (1863–1948)

Indiana Republican legislator who served as U.S. Senate Majority Leader. Born at Winchester, Indiana, James Eli Watson grew up, as one observer put it, with "but limited opportunities of associating with Democrats, if he had any such inclinations." A graduate of DePauw University, he studied law and was admitted to the bar in 1886. First elected to the U.S. House of Representatives in 1894, he unsuccessfully sought renomination two years later. Reelected in 1898, he served in the House during the Fifty-sixth through the Sixtieth Congresses (1899–1909).

Watson resumed his law practice following an unsuccessful bid for the governor's office in 1908, but he remained actively involved in Republican affairs. A compelling orator, he presided over many Republican state conventions during the first quarter of the twentieth century and was repeatedly a delegate to the Republican national conventions. Following the death of Senator Benjamin F. Shively in 1916, Watson was elected to fill the vacancy. He was returned to the Senate in 1920 and 1926, an exemplar of conservative Old Guard Republicanism during the "Prosperity Decade." Soundly defeated in the Franklin Roosevelt landslide of 1932, Watson retired to the practice of law in Washington, D.C.

*Robert G. Barrows*

REFERENCES

Seeds, Russel M. 1899. *History of the Republican Party of Indiana*. Indianapolis: Indiana History Company.

Taylor, Charles W. 1895. *Biographical Sketches and Review of the Bench and Bar of Indiana*. Indianapolis, IN: Bench and Bar Publishing Company.

Trissal, Francis M. 1922, 1923. *Public Men of Indiana: A Political History*. 2 vols. Hammond, IN: W. B. Conkey Company.

## Tom Watson (1856–1922)

People's Party advocate of populist programs. Born on a plantation three miles south of Thomson, Georgia, Thomas E. Watson spent his youth in poverty following his father's financial ruin after the Civil War. In 1872 he entered Mercer University, joined the bar in 1875, and became a noted criminal defense lawyer. In 1882 he won a seat in the lower house of the state legislature on the Democratic ticket. As a legislator, Watson made himself unpopular with the Democratic establishment by attacking the convict lease system and corporate power and by advocating the protection of tenant farmers' property from seizure by landlords. Watson did not run for reelection.

In 1888 Watson supported the antitariff Grover Cleveland for the presidency, but he soon became captivated by the National Farmers' Alliance and Industrial Union. In 1890 he ran for Congress in Georgia's Tenth District as a Democrat who championed the "radical" St. Louis demands of the Farmers' Alliance. Upon his election, Watson became an ardent spokesman for the "cheap money" Alliance cause. In 1891 he joined the People's Party and actively sought the vote of African-Americans. Fraudulent voting practices helped deny him reelection the next year as well as in his congressional bid in 1894. Two years later, the People's Party nominated Tom Watson for Vice President. During the campaign, he ardently opposed fusion with the Democratic Party. After defeat of the People's Party, Watson became a political recluse and a vitriolic critic of Blacks, Catholics, and Jews. In 1904 and 1908, the Populists, now desperate for candidates, nominated him for the presidency.

Watson returned to the Democratic Party in 1910 but bolted to support Theodore Roosevelt's Progressive Party two years later. In 1920 he successfully ran for the United States Senate from Georgia on the Democratic ticket. He served without distinction and earned a reputation for belligerency. Chronic asthma attacks weakened Watson's health during the summer of 1922, and he died soon after of a cerebral hemorrhage.

*See also:* Grover Cleveland, Election of 1896, National Farmers' Alliance and Industrial Union, People's Party, Progressive Party, Theodore Roosevelt

*R. Douglas Hurt*

REFERENCES

Durden, Robert F. 1965. *The Climax of Populism: The Election of 1896.* Lexington: U. Pr. of Kentucky.

Shaw, Barton C. 1984. *The Wool-Hat Boys: Georgia's Populist Party.* Baton Rouge: Louisiana State U. Pr.

Woodward, C. Vann. 1973. *Tom Watson: Agrarian Rebel.* Savannah, GA: Beehive Press.

## James B. Weaver (1833–1912)

Twice the presidential nominee of third parties. James Baird Weaver was born in Dayton, Ohio. Educated in public schools and the Cincinnati Law School, he began practicing law in Iowa in 1856. Weaver's heroic military service in the Civil War earned him a general's rank and a promising start to a political career in Iowa. But while he easily won election to minor offices, Iowa's Republican bosses denied Weaver nominations for Congress (1874) and for governor (1875). These rebuffs, combined with his growing opposition to Republican financial policies, led Weaver to join the Greenback Party. Although favoring inflation, he was not a financial radical and attacked the "money power" as much for its corruption of the political process as for its financial manipulations. Weaver won the Greenback presidential nomination in 1880, capturing 308,000 popular votes, and was elected to Congress from Iowa on the Greenback ticket in 1878, 1884, and 1886.

Thereafter, Weaver pursued monetary and political reform by working with the Farmers' Alliance and helping launch the People's Party. He received the Populist presidential nomination in 1892, summarized his principles in an earnest campaign book, *A Call to Action*, and won 22 electoral and more than a million popular votes. Weaver next tirelessly accepted the mission of promoting fusion between Populists and silver inflationists within the major parties. His sometimes ruthless machinations set the stage for William Jennings Bryan's unsuccessful fusion campaign of 1896, which ended in the virtual destruction of the People's Party, perceived as too radical by most Americans east of the Mississippi. Weaver then drifted into the Democratic Party, his political career ending weakly as mayor of Colfax, Iowa.

*See also:* William Jennings Bryan; Elections of 1880, 1892, and 1896; National Farmers' Alliance and Industrial Union, Greenback Party; People's Party

*Peter H. Argersinger*

REFERENCES

Colbert, Thomas B. 1978. "Political Fusion in Iowa: The Election of James B. Weaver to Congress in 1878." 20 *Arizona and the West* 25.

Haynes, Fred E. 1919. *James Baird Weaver.* Des Moines: State Historical Society of Iowa.

# Daniel Webster (1782–1852)

Foremost political orator of the pre-Civil War period. Daniel Webster played a preeminent role in American politics from the War of 1812 to the middle of the nineteenth century. First elected to the House of Representatives as a Federalist in 1812, he represented New Hampshire for two terms (1813–1817). After moving to Massachusetts in 1816, he won election to the House, serving from 1823 to 1827. In 1827 he moved to the United States Senate, where his two terms (1827–1841, 1845–1850) were interrupted by service as Secretary of State under William Henry Harrison and John Tyler (1841–1843). In 1850 he resigned his Senate seat once more to accept Millard Fillmore's offer of a second term as Secretary of State, a position he held until his death in 1852. A perennially unsuccessful presidential prospect, Webster won only one nomination for the office, as one of three Whig candidates who lost out to Martin Van Buren in 1826. Military heroes William Henry Harrison, Zachary Taylor, and Winfield Scott blocked his path to the Whig nomination in 1840, 1848, and 1852, respectively.

Originally a Federalist, Webster was one of the founders of the Whig Party in the 1830s. While he found himself in opposition to President Andrew Jackson over the rechartering the Second Bank of the United States, he embraced Whiggery wholeheartedly only after his efforts to form an alliance with the Jackson administration collapsed after the nullification crisis. Reflecting the changing economic interests of his constituents from shipping and commerce to manufacturing, he not only dropped his early opposition to tariff legislation but also became an ardent advocate of protectionism in addition to sponsoring federally supported economic development. Nor were his contributions limited to party politics. As the counsel for the winning side in several critical Supreme Court cases, including *Dartmouth College v. Woodward*, *McCulloch v. Maryland*, and *Gibbons v. Ogden*, he played a key role in shaping the nationalistic and prodevelopment policies of the Marshall Court.

Webster is perhaps best remembered for his talents as an orator. Two speeches in particular stand out: the "Second Reply to Hayne" in 1830 and his address on March 7, 1850, in support of compromise efforts. Not only did his orations make him famous, but they also provided him with an opportunity to advance his political ambitions. Profoundly uncomfortable with the popular politics of Jacksonian America, with its emphasis on party organizations, its celebration of egalitarianism and the common man, and its erosion of a world based on order, ability, and deference, Webster through his oratory hoped to circumvent the party organizations by establishing a direct and powerful tie with the people. By assuming the role of the "Defender of the Constitution," he hoped to establish himself as the preeminent authority and interpreter of that revered document, no small prize when one recalls that most political debate was couched in constitutional terms. Perhaps worship for the document could be transformed into support for the political ambitions of its stalwart defender.

Ultimately Webster's career floundered upon the issue of slavery, because its divisive nature threatened the nationalism upon which Webster had staked his political fortunes. The Massachusetts Senator had first gained widespread national prominence and support with his opposition to southern efforts to define state supremacy and nullification. Mildly antislavery during most of his political career, he refrained from associating himself too closely with staunch abolitionists like Charles Francis Adams and William Henry Seward. During Taylor's administration, however, Webster believed that the 1852 Whig nomination would be his if he could curry southern favor; hoist upon his own petard, his conciliatory efforts during the debates over the Compromise of 1850 alienated many of his northern supporters. In the end, Webster failed to gain sufficient support for his last bid at the White House, while his actions lent credence to charges that he was an opportunist more concerned with personal ambition than with the public good.

*See also:* Charles Francis Adams, Election of 1852, Federalist Party, William Henry Harrison, Andrew Jackson, Winfield Scott, Second Bank of the United States, William Henry Seward, Slavery, Zachary Taylor, John Tyler, Martin Van Buren

*Brooks Donohue Simpson*

REFERENCES

Bartlett, Irving H. 1978. *Daniel Webster*. New York: Norton.

Baxter, Maurice. 1984. *One and Inseparable: Daniel Webster and the Union*. Cambridge: Harvard U. Pr.

Brown, Norman D. 1969. *Daniel Webster and the Politics of Availability*. Athens: U. of Georgia Pr.

Current, Richard N. 1955. *Daniel Webster and the Rise of National Conservatism*. Boston: Little, Brown.

Dalzell, Robert F., Jr. 1973. *Daniel Webster and the Trial of American Nationalism.* Boston: Houghton Mifflin.

Howe, Daniel Walker. 1979. *The Political Culture of the American Whigs.* Chicago: U. of Chicago Pr.

Nathans, Sydney. 1973. *Daniel Webster & Jacksonian Democracy.* Baltimore: Johns Hopkins U. Pr.

Peterson, Merrill D. 1987. *The Great Triumvirate: Webster, Clay, and Calhoun.* New York: Oxford U. Pr.

Wiltse, Charles W., et al., eds. 1974–. *The Papers of Daniel Webster.* 14 vols. in 4 series. Hanover, NH: Dartmouth Col. Pr.

## Wednesday Group

An informal party caucus in the House of Representatives founded in 1963 by moderate-to-liberal Republicans (such as John Lindsay and Charles Goodell, both of New York), the Wednesday Group's purpose is to develop legislative proposals and influence the policy agenda and approach of the congressional party. Unlike other informal caucuses, membership in this intraparty group is by invitation. Members represent diverse geographic regions and committees. In recent years, ideological diversity has increased as more conservative Republicans have joined the group.

The caucus serves an important information exchange function and is one of the few congressional subunits to conduct long-range research. Research reports and the regular Wednesday meetings of members to discuss pending committee and floor activities serve an "early warning" function.

The Wednesday Group has been influential in placing issues on governmental agendas and in defining the parameters of debate. Its report in the 1970s on an all-volunteer U.S. army increased the visibility of that issue, and a U.S.–China trade report in January 1979 was used by both Republicans and Democrats during floor debate and vote. In recent Congresses the Wednesday Group sought to identify directions for Republican policy in the 1980s. It conducted "agenda studies" on military and defense policy; energy and the environment; and social policy, including civil rights, welfare, and child care. In some instances members developed legislation on these issues.

One of the few informal caucuses to have its own office, the Wednesday Group operates with a staff of three or four aides. A parallel but more informally organized Senate Wednesday Group of moderate Republican Senators exists primarily to exchange information.

*See also:* John Lindsay, Charles Goodell

*Susan Webb Hammond*

REFERENCES

Elliott, John M. 1974. "Communication and Small Groups in Congress: The Case of Republicans in the House of Representatives." Ph.D. dissertation, Johns Hopkins University.

Groennings, Sven. 1973. "The Clubs in Congress: The House Wednesday Group." In Sven Groennings and Jonathan P. Hawley, eds. *To Be a Congressman: The Promise and the Power.* Washington: Acropolis Books.

Hammond, Susan Webb, Daniel P. Mulhollan, and Arthur G. Stevens, Jr. 1985. "Congressional Caucuses and Agenda Setting." 38 *Western Political Quarterly* 582.

———. 1989. "Congressional Caucuses in the Policy Process." In Lawrence C. Dodd and Bruce I. Oppenheimer, eds. *Congress Reconsidered.* 4th ed. Washington: Congressional Quarterly.

Loomis, Burdett A. 1981. "Congressional Caucuses and the Politics of Representation." In Lawrence C. Dodd and Bruce I. Oppenheimer, eds. *Congress Reconsidered.* 2nd ed. Washington: Congressional Quarterly.

## Thurlow Weed (1797–1882)

Early "boss" of New York's Whig Party. More than any other man, Thurlow Weed made the "boss" a reality of American politics. He was born and lived his entire life in New York State, apprenticing in the printing trade as a child. His savvy, ambition, and gift for managing men helped him land a lobbying position at the Albany state capitol in 1824. Once there, Weed displayed a unique skill at merging warring political factions into cohesive, successful coalitions. He also met and befriended lawyer William H. Seward in 1824, and the pair remained close political allies throughout the rest of their careers.

In 1826 Weed capitalized on Antimasonic excitement to develop his own base of political power. He established the *Albany Evening Journal* in 1830 and made it one of the leading political organs of the newly formed Whig Party. Following the recession of 1837, Weed guided the Whigs into state office, helping Seward win election as governor. In 1838 Weed and Seward began a business partnership with the young Horace Greeley. Weed became a figure of national political importance during the 1840s as every Whig presidential candidate courted his support. Weed successfully engineered the presidential victories of William Henry Harrison in 1840 and Zachary Taylor in 1848. He supported his old friend Seward for President in 1860, but his candidate narrowly lost the new Republican Party's nomination to Abraham Lincoln. Seward, however, was named to the

Cabinet, and Weed served as an adviser to Lincoln.

Weed's political stock began to decline in the 1850s when, archetypically for political bosses, he had to answer for numerous questionable business dealings. He spent his final years in political disrepute but not before he had spawned a new generation of New York bosses including Roscoe Conkling and William M. Tweed.

*See also:* Roscoe Conkling, Horace Greeley, William Henry Harrison, Abraham Lincoln, William H. Seward, Zachary Taylor, William M. Tweed

*Richard Digby-Junger*

REFERENCES

Badasty, Gerald J. 1983. "The New York State Political Press and Antimasonry." 64 *New York History* 261.

Hazelton, Gerry Whiting. n.d., circa 1870. "Essay on Thurlow Weed." Madison, WI: Unpublished manuscript, Area Research Center, University of Wisconsin, Milwaukee.

Payne, George Henry. 1929. *History of Journalism in the United States.* New York: Appleton.

Van Deusen, Glyndon Garlock. 1947. *Thurlow Weed, Wizard of the Lobby.* Boston: Little, Brown.

## Fred Wertheimer (1939– )

Brooklyn-born Fredric Michael Wertheimer is the youngest (along with John Gardner and David Cohen) of the leaders giving energy and direction to Common Cause, the nonprofit, nonpartisan, predominantly liberal Washington interest group. He was educated at the University of Michigan (B.A., 1959) and Harvard Law School (1962), and has worked for Common Cause since 1971 and been its president since 1981. Since 1969 he has been married to National Public Radio news broadcaster Linda Wertheimer.

If John Gardner was the architect and David Cohen the philosopher of Common Cause, then Fred Wertheimer is the crusader. A skilled and aggressive debater, easily aroused to indignation, he can be found out front whenever Common Cause adopts a policy position. This aggressiveness frequently causes his adversaries to underestimate Wertheimer's reflectiveness and his personal fair-mindedness, and he is sometimes seen as a hard-liner for whatever the line is. Wertheimer is a tireless campaigner with a great flair for phrasemaking, and his political effectiveness is not underestimated. His commitment is solidly grounded in a pure-hearted devotion to liberal principles and complete personal integrity, mingled with a rather low opinion of the motivating forces that animate political life in the United States.

*See also:* David Cohen, Common Cause, John Gardner

*Nelson W. Polsby*

REFERENCES

McFarland, Andrew S. 1984. *Common Cause: Lobbying in the Public Interest.* Chatham, NJ: Chatham House.

## Wesberry v. Sanders
### 376 U.S. 1 (1964)

In *Wesberry v. Sanders*, the Supreme Court determined that unduly imbalanced congressional districts within a state were unconstitutional. Justice Hugo Black, writing for a majority of the Court, stated that the principle of equal worth for each vote in a state was "a fundamental idea of democratic government" and a "principle tenaciously fought for and established at the Constitutional Convention." In his opinion Black summarized the decision holding of the Court and the Court's reasoning, writing, "We say that, construed in its historical context the command of Art. I, Sec. 2, that Representatives be chosen by the 'People of the several States' means that as nearly as is practicable one man's vote in a congressional election is to be worth as much as another's." Thus, the Court ruled that as nearly as practicable congressional districts within a state must have equal populations.

Justice John Harlan dissented in the *Wesberry* case on two grounds. First, he argued that the Constitution left to the states the determination of how they would apportion their allotted seats in the House of Representatives. Harlan noted that Article I, Section 2 of the Constitution explicitly allowed the states to set the voting standards for congressional elections by making the standards the same as those for suffrage in elections for the lowest legislative house in each of the states.

Second, Harlan argued that "the supervisory power of Congress is exclusive" regarding elections. Thus, even if the Court were disturbed by Congress's failure to redistrict according to population, Harlan believed that the Court had no jurisdiction to overturn the districting plan in question.

Nevertheless, the Court did overturn the Alabama plan in question where the maximum percentage of deviation was over 140 percent. Since then, it has used the same reasoning to overturn other plans with smaller deviations from the norm, with the invalidated deviations running as low as 0.7 percent in *Karcher v. Daggett*.

*See also: Karcher v. Daggett*

*Keith Barnett*

## Jean Westwood (1923– )

First woman to chair the Democratic National Committee. Jean Westwood has been continuously active in Democratic Party politics for over 30 years. A Utah native, Westwood, a freelance writer and partner in the Westwood Mink Ranch, attended the University of Utah and San Diego State University. In 1974 she moved to Arizona following an accident in which her husband Richard Westwood became temporarily paralyzed, forcing Jean Westwood to withdraw as a candidate for an open U.S. Senate seat.

In the 1950s and 1960s, Westwood ran many minor campaigns in Utah and played major roles in the campaigns of Governors Calvin Rampton and Scott Mattheson, Senator Frank Moss, Congressman David King (on whose staff she served for two years), and Congressman Wayne Owens. In 1964 and 1968, she ran the Utah presidential campaigns of Lyndon Johnson and Hubert Humphrey. In 1971, Westwood was appointed as national co-chair of the McGovern campaign (with John Douglas and later, DNC chair Lawrence O'Brien), eventually serving as McGovern's campaign director for 14 western states. In 1975 she became campaign director for the presidential campaign of North Carolina's ex-governor Terry Sanford, in return for his agreement to chair the Charter Commission of the Democratic Party at her request as DNC chair. After Sanford subsequently withdrew from the race, Westwood worked for the Morris Udall campaign. In 1980 she co-chaired the Ted Kennedy campaign in Arizona, and in 1984, the Gary Hart campaign. She has been an adviser and active participant in every campaign of Arizona's Bruce Babbitt, from attorney general to his 1988 presidential campaign. During Governor Babbitt's nine-year tenure in office, she was a member of his five-person "kitchen cabinet" and served as a member and co-chair of the advisory board of the Office of Economic Development (later, the Arizona Department of Commerce). Westwood has also participated in the campaigns of Congressman Udall, Senator Dennis De Concini, Phoenix mayor Terry Goddard, and Navajo chief Peterson Zah, and she served as co-chair of the Draft Rose cam-

paign for Governor Rose Moffard. Cynics claim that Westwood has a rather mediocre record as a prognosticator of successful office seekers, but she has made hosts of friends among western Democrats for her loyalty and hard work.

Jean Westwood has been a delegate to each of the Democratic midterm conventions and to the nominating conventions from 1964 to 1984 (after suffering a stroke, she was unable to attend in 1984), serving on the 1968 platform and the rules committees in 1972, 1976, and 1978. She chaired the Arizona delegation in 1976 and co-chaired it in 1980. She was the Utah Democratic national committeewoman from 1965 to 1976, serving on the executive committee of the DNC from 1965 to 1972. In her tenure on the DNC, Westwood served as a key strategist and leader of the liberal forces during the early years of party reform.

At the 1972 Democratic convention, Westwood served as the McGovern representative on the rules and credentials committees and managed the California challenge. Westwood marshaled a floor coalition supporting the rules committee proposals mandating the Party Charter Commission, a new reform commission and the appointment of the commission chairs before the election. Elected as DNC chair at the conclusion of the convention— the first woman to serve in that capacity— Westwood was challenged by Robert Strauss after the McGovern defeat. Westwood won reelection to the DNC chair in December 1972 by three votes under an agreement with four of those voting that she would then resign. She, rather than Strauss (elected chair subsequently), appointed the chairs and members of the Mikulski and the Sanford Commissions. Strauss enlarged both commissions, appointing Westwood to the Charter Commission where she served as executive committee member and treasurer.

*See also:* Democratic National Committee; Elections of 1964, 1968, and 1980; Hubert H. Humphrey; Lyndon B. Johnson; Edward M. Kennedy; George McGovern; Barbara Mikulski; Lawrence O'Brien; Terry Sanford; Robert Strauss; Morris Udall

*Denise L. Baer*

REFERENCES

Westwood, Jean M. 1974. "The Political Status of Women—1974." 20 *Wisconsin Academy Review* 2.

———. 1989. "The Navajo Nation Elects a Chairman: The *Real* Americans and the *Realpolitik*." In Larry J. Sabato, ed. *Campaigns and Elections: A Reader in Modern American Politics*. Glenview, IL: Scott, Foresman.

## Burton K. Wheeler (1882–1975)

Progressive Democratic U.S. Senator from Montana. Burton Kendall Wheeler was born in Hudson, Massachusetts, and after graduation from Hudson High School in 1900, he worked briefly as a stenographer in Boston. Moving to the Midwest, Wheeler received his LL.B. from the University of Michigan in 1905 and began practicing law in Butte, Montana, the same year. He quickly distinguished himself by winning a number of important damage suits against railroad and mining companies operating in the state.

Wheeler's political career began in 1910 when he was elected as a Democrat to the Montana House of Representatives. A supporter of Progressive causes and fellow Progressive Senator Thomas J. Walsh, Wheeler was appointed United States District Attorney for Montana by Woodrow Wilson, serving in that capacity from 1913 until his resignation in 1918. In 1920 he ran unsuccessfully for governor in a brutal contest, but two years later, Wheeler was elected to the United States Senate where he served until 1947.

In the Senate, Wheeler immediately aligned himself with the Progressive farm bloc and sponsored various reforms, including federal relief for farmers, the soldiers' bonus, repeal of the Esch-Cummins railroad law (the 1920 Transportation Act that returned the operation of railroads to the private sector), and American diplomatic recognition of the Soviet Union. He captured national attention for his role, with fellow Montana Senator Walsh, in prosecuting the famous Teapot Dome and Elk Hills oil scandals of the 1920s, which forced the subsequent resignation of Warren Harding's Attorney General, Harry M. Daugherty. In 1924 he bolted the Democratic Party and campaigned as Senator Robert M. La Follette's vice presidential running mate on an independent ticket sponsored by the Congress for Progressive Political Action. Together, they polled nearly 5 million popular votes as a protest against the conservative candidates of the two established parties.

Subsequently, Wheeler became an important supporter of the New Deal in the early 1930s, sponsoring legislation such as the Wheeler-Howard Act that reformed federal Indian policy, railroad labor reforms, regulation of utilities, and other measures. He broke with Franklin Roosevelt in 1937 over the "court packing" controversy and became a leading voice for isolationism, or nonintervention in European affairs in the late 1930s. He was defeated for reelection in 1946, losing to Republican Zales Ecton, whereupon he resumed practicing law in Washington, D.C.

*See also:* Harry M. Daugherty, Warren G. Harding, Robert M. La Follette, Franklin D. Roosevelt, Teapot Dome, Thomas J. Walsh, Woodrow Wilson

*W. Thomas White*

REFERENCES

Burke, Robert E. 1986. "A Friendship in Adversity: Burton K. Wheeler and Hiram W. Johnson." 36 *Montana, The Magazine of Western History* 12.

Griffith, Robert. 1979. "Old Progressives and the Cold War." 66 *Journal of American History* 334.

Malone, Michael P. 1973. "Montana Politics and the New Deal." In Malone and Richard B. Roeder, eds. *Montana's Past: Selected Essays.* Missoula: University of Montana.

———, and Richard B. Roeder. 1976. *Montana: A History of Two Centuries.* Seattle: U. of Washington Pr.

Noggle, Burl. 1965. *Teapot Dome: Oil and Politics in the 1920s.* New York: Norton.

Ruetten, Richard T. 1963. "Showdown in Montana, 1938: Burton Wheeler's Role in the Defeat of Jerry O'Connell." 54 *Pacific Northwest Quarterly* 19.

———. 1968. "Senator Burton K. Wheeler and Insurgency in the 1920s." In Gene M. Gressley, ed. *The American West: A Reorientation.* Laramie: U. of Wyoming Pr.

———. 1977. "Burton K. Wheeler and the Montana Connection." 27 *Montana, The Magazine of Western History* 2.

Spritzer, Donald E. 1973. "Senators in Conflict." 23 *Montana, The Magazine of Western History* 16.

Tucker, Ray Thomas, and Frederick R. Barkley. 1932. *Sons of the Wild Jackass.* Boston: L. C. Page & Co.

Wheeler, Burton K., and Paul F. Healy. 1962. *Yankee from the West: The Candid, Turbulent Life Story of the Yankee-Born U.S. Senator from Montana.* Garden City, NY: Doubleday.

## Whiskey Ring

During and following the Civil War, rumors were rife of efforts to defraud the federal government through the establishment of a "whiskey ring": distillers who paid off federal revenue officials in exchange for abatement of excise taxes on distilled liquors and spirits. In 1874 Secretary of the Treasury Benjamin H. Bristow's systematic investigation of the ring uncovered enormous fraud and corruption, resulting in the indictment of three government officials in St. Louis; many claimed that the payoffs were channeled into the coffers of the Republican Party. Perhaps most alarming were allegations that implicated President Ulysses Grant's private secretary, Orville E. Babcock, in the conspiracy. Babcock was charged with obstructing the administration's plans to capture and prosecute the ring members. The investigation turned lurid with reports that Babcock had not only accepted gifts but also the companionship of a young lady known only as "Sylph."

Declaring "Let no guilty man escape," Grant initially favored the thorough investigation and vigorous prosecution of all implicated. Eventually he became persuaded, not without justification, that Bristow was using the investigation to enhance his chances for the Republican presidential nomination in 1876. Unwisely dismissing the allegations against Babcock as manufactured political propaganda, Grant came to his former aide's defense. With both sides maneuvering for political advantage, justice suffered. Efforts to implicate Grant failed miserably; moreover, his impassioned defense of his private secretary was critical in gaining Babcock's acquittal. But Babcock's questionable behavior had aroused the President's suspicions, and uncertain about where the truth lay, he replaced Babcock as private secretary. Bristow resigned after the conclusion of the trial; anti-Grant Republicans, mostly survivors of the Liberal Republican debacle of 1872, advocated Bristow's candidacy for President in 1876 as the representative of reform.

Historians now judge Babcock guilty as charged, but contemporary opinion was more mixed. Despite his implication in several more scandals, Babcock was retained as superintendent of lighthouses by the reform-minded Rutherford B. Hayes. Nor does the scandal appear to have had a significant impact on the fall election campaign, as Bristow's 1876 presidential ambitions died with Hayes's nomination as the Republican standard-bearer. Invoking "executive privilege," Bristow refused to testify about his conversations with the President despite Grant's express wish that he do so, a decision that cast suspicion upon Bristow's motivation in pursuing the scandal.

*See also:* Election of 1876, Ulysses S. Grant, Rutherford B. Hayes, Liberal Republicans

*Brooks Donohue Simpson*

REFERENCES

Hesseltine, William Best. 1935. *Ulysses S. Grant: Politician.* New York: Dodd, Mead.

McDonald, John. 1880. *Secrets of the Great Whiskey Ring.* Chicago, IL: Belford, Clarke & Co.

Webb, Ross A. 1969. *Benjamin Helm Bristow: Border State Politician.* Lexington: U. Pr. of Kentucky.

Woodward, C. Vann, ed. 1974. *Responses of the Presidents to Charges of Misconduct.* New York: Dell Publishing.

## Whitaker and Baxter

Pioneers in campaign public relations. Clem Whitaker, Sr. (1899–1961) and Leone Smith Baxter (Whitaker) (1913– ), the "mom-and-pop team" who, according to Theodore White, "invented the profession [of campaign consultant] in the 1930s," became accomplished at applying the techniques of public relations to political campaigns. Called upon to assist in the adoption of a 1933 referendum to develop water resources in California's Central Valley, Whitaker was joined by Baxter, then manager of the Redding, California, Chamber of Commerce. Both had experience as reporters, and Whitaker had operated a statewide news bureau from Sacramento and lobbied there as well. Their joint enterprise, Campaigns, Incorporated, perhaps the first campaign management firm, proved to be immediately successful. They promptly created the Clem Whitaker Advertising Agency and the California Feature Service, a clipping service that sent editorials and other features to smaller California newspapers. The ad agency handled advertising for Campaigns, Incorporated; the clipping service, although largely benign in content, promoted a point of view sympathetic to that espoused by Whitaker and Baxter.

Crucial to the prosperity of the firm were two factors: the criteria used in managing campaigns and the distinctive political climate of California. Whitaker and Baxter were selective in accepting clients; they helped only on issues compatible with their own generally conservative philosophy and worked with candidates of a similar persuasion, almost all of them Republicans. After accepting a client, they promptly secluded themselves to draft a "plan of campaign" based upon 50 procedures (rules) that they had formulated early on. Then they developed a counterstrategy that was likely to be used by opponents. These documents, including a budget, were presented to the client. If the client accepted their program, Whitaker and Baxter assumed complete control of the campaign. The client's only responsibilities were to meet the budget and be available for duties as laid out in the plan.

Whitaker and Baxter operated on the assumption that they took on only accepted and commendable issues and sound candidates; if these were properly presented to the public, they reasoned, victory was certain. The key ingredient was effective communications, especially with voters. Often, their plan was widely circulated; so opponents as well as sympathizers could know its contents, for example, they developed a plan to defeat President Harry Truman's national health insurance proposal.

When the firm began, California was especially hospitable to a public relations approach to campaigning. Two decades before, California Progressives, led by Hiram Johnson, had laid the groundwork for undermining conventional party legislative politics by adopting cross-filing, the initiative, and the referendum. Cross-filing diluted party identification and loyalty; initiative and referendum facilitated bypassing or overruling legislative decision-making and gubernatorial leadership. Whitaker and Baxter preferred appealing directly to the electorate—an approach that resolved an issue for several years—rather than legislative lobbying, which might have to be repeated year after year, if only because of legislative turnover.

In 1958, when rival campaign agencies had already emerged in California and the techniques pioneered by the firm were spreading across the nation, the two founders sold the firm to Whitaker's son, Clem, Jr., and two associates. At that time, the original partners, who had been husband and wife for several years, organized Whitaker and Baxter, International, to represent clients on the national and international scenes. By the 1980s the firm under Clem, Jr., no longer accepted partisan campaigns and offered services directed to various facets of government in all 50 states and in the nation's capital.

*Thomas P. Wolf*

REFERENCES

Agranoff, Robert, ed. 1972. *The New Style in Election Campaigns.* Boston: Holbrook.

Baxter, Leone. 1950. "Public Relations Precocious Baby." 6 *Public Relations Journal* 18.

Kelley, Stanley, Jr. 1956. *Professional Public Relations and Political Power.* Baltimore: Johns Hopkins U. Pr.

———. 1960. *Political Campaigning: Problems in Creating an Informed Electorate.* Washington: Brookings.

Nimmo, Dan. 1970. *The Political Persuaders: The Techniques of Modern Election Campaigns.* Englewood Cliffs, NJ: Prentice-Hall.

Pitchell, Robert J. 1958. "The Influence of Professional Campaign Firms in Partisan Elections in California." 11 *Western Political Quarterly* 278.

Rosenbloom, David Lee. 1973. *The Election Men: Professional Campaign Managers and American Democracy.* New York: Quadrangle.

Sabato, Larry J. 1981. *The Rise of Political Consultants: New Ways of Winning Elections.* New York: Basic Books.

Whitaker, Clem. 1946. "Public Relations of Election Campaigns." 2 *Public Relations Journal* 7.

———. 1950. "Professional Political Campaign Management." 6 *Public Relations Journal* 19.

———, and Leone Baxter. 1955. "Election Year Coming Up!" 11 *Public Relations Journal* 11.

———. 1956. "Campaign Blunders Can Change History." 12 *Public Relations Journal* 4.

White, Theodore H. 1982. *America in Search of Itself: The Making of the President, 1956–1980.* New York: Harper & Row.

## Whitcomb v. Chavis
### 403 U.S. 124 (1971)

This Supreme Court case held that multimember districting schemes are not unconstitutional per se, nor is a districting plan unconstitutional because it has a disproportionate effect on a racial minority. The Court held that if the proportion of minorities elected is smaller than their numbers in the population, this does not prove invidious discrimination. Moreover, Congress has since amended the Voting Rights Act in such a way to ease the proof of racial discrimination.

Indiana had several multimember districts from which two or more legislators were elected at large. Some of the appellees argued that multimember districts should be held unconstitutional per se because with bloc voting, legislators would overrepresent their constituents. Overrepresentation could also be proven by a mathematical theory. Writing for the Court, Justice Byron White noted that he did not quarrel with the mathematics but that the "position remains a theoretical one . . . and does 'not take into account any political or other factors which might affect the actual voting power of the residents, which might include party affiliation, race, previous voting characteristics or any other factors which go into the entire political voting situation.'" The Court seemed to leave open the possibility that multimember districts may in themselves some day be found unconstitutional, but they have never yet so ruled.

In a different line of attack, appellee Patrick Chavis and others argued that Indiana's apportionment scheme "invidiously diluted the force and effect of the vote of Negroes and poor persons living within certain Marion County [Indianapolis] census tracts" but with single member districting "the ghetto area would elect three members of the house and one senator, whereas under the present districting voters in the area 'have almost no political force or control over legislators because the effect of their vote is canceled out by other contrary interest groups' in Marion County."

Appellant Edgar D. Whitcomb, governor of Indiana, argued that "Marion County's problems were countywide and that its delegation could better represent the various interests in the county if elected at large and responsible to the county as a whole rather than being elected in single-member districts and thus fragmented by parochial interests and jealousies."

Ruling against Chavis, the Court held that purposeful discrimination does not exist, "the fact that the number of ghetto residents who were legislators was not in proportion to ghetto population [does not] satisfactorily prove invidious discrimination absent evidence and findings that ghetto residents had less opportunity than did other Marion County residents to participate in the political processes and to elect legislators of their choice."

Justice White went on to suggest that in a winner-take-all system, some people may be habitually unrepresented. "[G]uaranteeing one racial group representation is not easily contained. It is expressive of the more general proposition that any group with distinctive interests must be represented in legislative halls if it is numerous enough to command at least one seat and represents a majority living in an area sufficiently compact to constitute a single member district. This approach would make it difficult to reject claims of Democrats, Republicans, or member of any political organization . . . who in one year or another, or year after year, are submerged."

*H. W. Perry, Jr.*

## F. Clifton White (1918– )

Architect of Barry Goldwater's 1964 nomination strategy. Born in Leonardsville, New York, and raised in the suburbs of New York City, [Frederick] Clifton White attended Colgate University, where he majored in social science. He had a distinguished war record as an Army Air Corps bomber pilot.

White's long career in politics began with an unsuccessful Republican primary bid for a seat in the House of Representatives. He continued in Republican politics, actively working in the presidential campaigns of Thomas E. Dewey in 1948 and Dwight D. Eisenhower in 1952. White was active in organizing young Republicans, serving effectively as their national chairman. He continued his political activity in state and national politics as a public relations counselor between 1955 and 1960. In 1958 he managed the primary campaign of Walter Mahoney, who

lost the Republican gubernatorial nomination to Nelson A. Rockefeller. In 1960 White became the coordinator of the Citizens for Nixon-Lodge Committee.

After a bitter Nixon-Lodge defeat, White became disenchanted with the Republican Party. Like many other conservative political advisers and strategists within the party, White believed that Richard Nixon failed to offer the voters a definite choice. Soon after the 1960 Nixon defeat, White and other conservative Republicans began to form an organization that was designated to seize immediate control of the Republican Party for their conservative cause. White believed that early organization of conservative party members would deny the liberal Republican Rockefeller the presidential nomination in 1964.

In October 1961, White, Congressman John Ashbrook (R-Ohio), and 20 other friends and professional colleagues from across the nation met in Chicago for the first time to organize their conservative crusade. Senator Barry Goldwater (R-Ariz.), the Republican Party's most outspoken conservative, was their choice for the nomination. In November 1961 White met with Goldwater for the first time. Goldwater refused to commit himself to the White group, but neither did he denounce it. Throughout the next two years, Goldwater continued this ambivalence. He was determined to maintain his freedom of choice. Goldwater believed he owed nothing the White organization, since it was formed without his knowledge or consent.

In February 1963 the White group announced a Draft Goldwater Committee, with White as the national director. When he finally did announce his candidacy, Goldwater would entrust his campaign only to his trusted Arizona friends. White was asked to play only a minor role—director of field operations. Later he headed the Citizens for Goldwater/Miller.

Despite his demotion, White had a significant effect on the Goldwater campaign. His efforts at grass-roots organization paid large dividends. Goldwater volunteers infiltrated delegate meetings at precinct, municipal, and county levels throughout the country. While Goldwater lost the New Hampshire primary, delegates were assembled throughout the rest of the nation. By the time Goldwater won in California, the race was over, and he won the nomination on the first ballot.

After Goldwater was overwhelmingly defeated in the November election, White returned to New York and the public relations business until

1967. He then began work in the 1968 presidential campaign of Governor Ronald Reagan (R-Calif.). By the time of the 1968 convention, Richard Nixon had an insurmountable lead, and the former Vice President soundly defeated Reagan.

Soon after the convention, White managed the campaign for U.S. Senator of New York conservative James L. Buckley. Although Buckley was defeated in the campaign, he did succeed in amassing a large number of votes. This strong showing helped him in 1970, when White managed Buckley to a successful campaign for the Untied States Senate.

In the years that followed, White continued to be active in conservative and "regular" Republican politics. In 1972 he was a member of Nixon's Committee to Re-elect the President. In 1976 he was an adviser to the Gerald Ford Committee. In 1980 he reunited with Ronald Reagan, became a senior adviser for the Reagan-Bush presidential campaign, and was Ronald Reagan's political director at the Republican National Convention. After the Reagan victory in 1980, White became a member of the President-elect's transition team. Subsequently, White formed the International Foundation for Electoral Systems, a clearinghouse for democratic processes in other countries.

White believes that the Reagan victories may have created hidden costs for the Republican Party. "As a result of Ronald Reagan's almost total dominance of the political scene from 1966, he has denied movement to leadership to almost a whole generation of Republican leaders." White became involved in the George Bush campaign, but he does not believe that "Bush can become a leader of the conservative movement."

*Christopher Rogers*

## George White (1872–1953)

Chair of the Democratic National Committee from 1920 to 1921. George White was born in Elmira, New York, schooled in Pennsylvania, and earned his degree from Princeton University in 1895, where he was a student in two of Woodrow Wilson's classes. He eventually settled in Marietta, Ohio, made some money in the oil production industry, and as a Democrat, won election to the Ohio House of Representatives. His election from a predominantly Republican district earned him a statewide reputation as an effective campaigner.

White served in the Ohio legislature from 1905 to 1908, where he became a leader of the prohibition forces. In 1910 and 1912, he was elected to the U.S. Congress, where he became a close friend of Congressman James M. Cox, succeeding him on the Ways and Means Committee when Cox successfully ran for governor of Ohio. White and Cordell Hull of Tennessee were the two most popular members of the House of Representatives.

As the 1920 presidential year approached, Governor Cox asked Ohio national committeeman Edmund H. Moore to manage his preconvention campaign, with George White assisting. The Cox candidacy was one of the best organized in an otherwise factionalized year in the Democratic Party. A stalemate at the national convention was anticipated and, in fact, occurred.

Cox, Moore, and White were an ideal combination for advancing a compromise candidacy. Cox was a Democratic "winner," having been elected several times in a predominantly Republican state. Moore was a "manager's manager," having close associations with several of the party's most powerful state bosses. White, as a former Princeton student, was a friend of President Wilson, a dry, and a popular member of the House of Representatives. Cox was nominated on the forty-fourth ballot.

After Cox's defeat in the election, under hostile pressure from the supporters of William Gibbs McAdoo, White resigned from the national chairmanship. He also was eager to prepare himself to run for governor of Ohio, which he eventually did in 1930, serving for two terms.

*See also:* James M. Cox, Cordell Hull, William G. McAdoo, Woodrow Wilson

*Ralph M. Goldman*

REFERENCES

Goodman, T. William. 1950. "The Presidential Campaign of 1920." Ph.D. dissertation, Ohio State University.

## Hugh Lawson White (1773–1840)

Whig presidential candidate against Martin Van Buren. Tennessean Hugh Lawson White's political career followed a rather typical pattern for a member of the post-Revolutionary generation. White settled in Knoxville in 1796 to practice law. From 1801 to 1824 he continuously held a variety of state legislative and judicial positions in Tennessee. When Andrew Jackson resigned from the United States Senate in 1824, White was elected to replace him and served in that position until he resigned in a conflict with the state legislature over the Independent Treasury in 1839.

In general, White's views reflected republican ideology and were in line with those of Jackson who twice considered him for Cabinet positions. He gradually parted ways with the Old Hero over the succession of Van Buren and charted his own independent course as President *pro tempore* of the Senate. Although he was nominated by the Alabama legislature, White's presidential bid grew out of the political infighting between the James Polk and John Bell factions in Tennessee. Most of these southerners who opposed Van Buren turned to White as the region's anti-administration candidate. He won 36 percent of the popular vote in 9 of the 12 slave states and the 26 electoral votes of Georgia and Tennessee. Although he received the votes of southern Whigs and would later endorse Henry Clay for the 1840 nomination, White really did not think of himself as a Whig, nor was he part of a plot to throw the 1836 election into the House of Representatives as many Democrats feared.

*William G. Shade*

REFERENCES

Gresham, Laura P. 1944. "The Public Career of Hugh Lawson White." 3 *Tennessee Historical Quarterly* 291.
Sellers, Charles. 1957. *James K. Polk: Jacksonian*. Princeton, NJ: Princeton U. Pr.

## John White (1802–1845)

One of five single-term Speakers of the U.S. House of Representatives in the 1840s. John White of Kentucky gained his start in state politics as a loyal soldier in the organization of Senator Henry Clay. Born near Cumberland Gap, Kentucky, White was a country lawyer but was not particularly well educated. He served one term in the Kentucky House of Representatives in 1832 before moving to the U.S. House. He was elected as a Whig and served from 1835 to 1845.

He was elected Speaker in 1841, defeating Democrat John W. Jones of Virginia on the first ballot by a vote of 121 to 84. White was renominated by the Whigs in 1843, but the party's losses in the midterm election cost him his speakership. He lost that contest in a rematch with Jones, 59 to 128. He returned to the Whig's back benches for the remainder of that term.

Perhaps the most notable aspect of his life occurred after he had delivered an eloquent and impassioned speech in the House. Because White was not known for such eloquence, his colleagues were suspicious about the origin of the speech. When it was discovered to have been plagiarized from one given by the dishonored Aaron Burr, the former Vice President who had killed Alexander Hamilton and who had been tried for treason, the highly mortified White shot himself to death, seven months after he had left the House.

*See also:* Aaron Burr, Henry Clay, Alexander Hamilton

*Garrison Nelson*

REFERENCES

Smith, William Henry. 1971. *Speakers of the House of Representatives of the United States*. New York: AMS Press.

## John C. White (1925– )

Chairman of the Democratic National Committee under President Jimmy Carter. John C. White, a moderate from Texas, replaced former Maine governor Kenneth M. Curtis, who served less than a year as chairman of the Democratic National Committee. (Curtis had resigned because of troubles with Carter over party direction and other party matters.)

White was 53 years old in 1978 when he took over as head of the Democratic National Committee. He was a survivor of 25 years in the rough and tumble world of Texas politics and had risen through the ranks as a loyal and dedicated Democrat. White served as commissioner of agriculture for 14 terms in Texas and had been serving as Assistant Secretary of Agriculture when he was chosen by Carter to replace Curtis. He also was attractive because of his history of strict party loyalty and his lack of enemies.

John White was chairman of the Democratic National Committee for less than three years. During his tenure as chairman he tried to strengthen the Democratic financial situation and improve the nominating process. White, however, lost his chairmanship in 1980 as a direct result of Carter's defeat. He had been a strong supporter of Carter throughout the 1980 nominating primaries, a partisanship that put him into disfavor with other powerful Democrats who then called for his resignation. He was ousted soon after the 1980 election and was succeeded by Charles Manatt.

*See also:* Kenneth M. Curtis, Democratic National Committee, Election of 1980, Charles Manatt

*Mary Ann McHugh*

## Kevin H. White (1929– )

Mayor of Boston for 16 turbulent years. Kevin Hagan White was elected mayor of Boston in 1967, after serving for two years as an assistant district attorney and seven years as Massachusetts secretary of state. Although he originally appeared to be a rising star in both Massachusetts and national politics, White never managed to advance beyond Boston City Hall.

The scion of a politically prominent Boston family, Kevin White seemed bred for public life. His Irish Catholic heritage and his Brahmin education at Tabor Academy and Williams College, in combination with his telegenic appearance, often evoked comparison with the Kennedys—a resemblance that, to White's dismay, would never fully materialize. White was defeated in his 1970 bid to become governor, and although a leading contender for the 1972 Democratic vice presidential nomination, he lost out to Sargent Shriver (whose Kennedy connections were more specific).

In his 1967 mayoral campaign, White promised to address concerns that Boston had been ignoring the neighborhoods while concentrating upon the revitalization of downtown. His ensuing outreach programs and expansion of access to city services were widely acclaimed. Though he carried the reform banner for a while, over time White established a formidable, patronage-based political machine that carried him through any electoral challenges and municipal crises that arose. White managed to weather the explosive conflict over busing for racial integration of Boston's schools, as well as the fiscal disaster wrought by a ballot initiative that slashed property taxes. Eventually his machine collapsed when key operatives became embroiled in scandal. Although never directly implicated in any wrongdoing, in 1983 Kevin White announced that he would not seek a fifth term as mayor. He now teaches at Boston University.

*See also:* Election of 1972, R. Sargent Shriver

*William P. Corbett*

REFERENCES

Higgins, George V. 1984. *Style Versus Substance: Boston, Kevin White & the Politics of Illusion.* New York: Macmillan.

Lukas, J. Anthony. 1985. *Common Ground: A Turbulent Decade in the Lives of Three American Families.* New York: Knopf.

## Theodore H. White (1915–1986)

Chronicler of presidential elections. Beginning with *The Making of the President 1960,* "Teddy" White transformed the art of campaign journalism in the United States. That book, a Pulitzer Prize winner, and the series of others that he wrote on the next three presidential elections gave readers a sense of the drama of campaigns and an insider's perspective on the personalities and events that were instrumental in nominating and electing American Presidents in the post-Eisenhower era.

White, a native of Boston and a graduate of Boston Latin and Harvard (1938), began his career as a foreign correspondent, first in Asia and then in Europe. Before concentrating on presidential campaigns, he wrote novels (e.g., *The View from the Fortieth Floor*) and worked for the *The Reporter* and *Collier's.* With the demise of *Collier's* in 1956, White operated free-lance for the rest of his career.

As early as 1954, White was covering elections, but it was his account of the 1960 presidential race—which had culminated in Senator John F. Kennedy's narrow win over Vice President Richard M. Nixon—that raised White's writing to the apex of his craft. Election day itself was only the capstone of his reportorial edifice. The foundations of his approach lay in the early days of the nominating processes. Using these he constructed vivid descriptions of the prospective nominees' strengths, flaws, and strategies, and the political milieux of the states in which they competed. A self-professed storyteller rather than an abstract analyst, White in his presidential series employed a lyrical style, quite metaphoric, and replete with frequent allusions to events and figures from the past and other cultures. No one before had recounted presidential contests in such rich prose.

White was both a witness to and, in part, a source of seismic changes in the nominating processes that occurred in the 1960s and 1970s. He was not pleased with the increased intrusion of the media, especially the electronic media, into campaigns. He saw campaign coverage expand from a handful of reporters in 1956 to almost 2,000 by 1980. Ironically, his own work was a principal stimulus to this increased media attention to presidential recruitment. White was also perturbed by the "absurd" growth of presidential primaries (*America in Search of Itself*).

After the success of his first campaign book, White also served as an election commentator for CBS-TV. His final three books were broad assessments of Richard Nixon's role in history, White's own life and times, and the politics of 1956 to 1980.

*See also:* Election of 1960, John F. Kennedy, Richard M. Nixon

*Thomas P. Wolf*

REFERENCES

Calloway, John D., et al., eds. 1988. *Campaigning on Cue*. Chicago. William Benton Fellowship Conference, U. of Chicago.

White, Theodore H. 1961. *The Making of the President 1960*. New York: Atheneum.

———. 1965. *The Making of the President, 1964*. New York: Atheneum.

———. 1969. *The Making of the President, 1968*. New York: Atheneum.

———. 1973. *The Making of the President, 1972*. New York: Atheneum.

———. 1975. *Breach of Faith: The Fall of Richard Nixon*. New York: Atheneum.

———. 1978. *In Search of History: A Personal Adventure*. New York: Harper & Row.

———. 1982. *America in Search of Itself: The Making of the President, 1956–1980*. New York: Harper & Row.

## Wallace H. White (1877–1952)

Longtime Republican U.S. Senator and Congressman from Maine. Born in Lewiston, Maine, into a politically prominent Maine family, Wallace Humphrey White, Jr., attended Bowdoin College, and as a young man he served as secretary to his grandfather, Senator William P. Frye, the President *pro tempore* of the Senate. White studied law and established practice in the District of Columbia and Lewiston, Maine, in 1903. In 1916 he was elected to the U.S. House of Representatives, where he served on the Merchant Marine and Fisheries Committee (he eventually became chairman). White's interest in radio technology led him to sponsor legislation that, over a period of years, resulted in the creation of the Federal Communications Commission. As a member of the Senate from 1931, White had a major part in writing the landmark 1934 Communications Act.

In the Senate White served on the Foreign Relations and Interstate and Foreign Commerce committees, where he espoused undeviating loyalty to conservative Republican principles. Known, in his own words, as a "quiet backstage negotiator, not a debater on the floor," White assumed the minority floor leadership during the illness of Senator Charles L. McNary in 1944 and was elected to the position permanently on McNary's death in 1945. Self-effacing in the presence of more politically powerful Senate Republicans like Robert A. Taft, the de facto Republican leader on domestic policy, and Arthur H. Vandenberg, who dominated foreign policy issues, White, as the nominal leader, was apparently acceptable to both the Old Guard conservatives and the contingent of restive younger Republican Senators eager to recast the party's negative image. He retired in 1948.

*See also:* William P. Frye, Charles L. McNary, Robert A. Taft, Arthur H. Vandenberg

*Richard C. Burnweit*

## William Allen White (1868–1944)

Journalist, newspaper publisher, and author. William Allen White played a central role in the Progressive reform movement of the early twentieth century. Born in Emporia, Kansas, White began his career as journalist in 1891. Four years later with a borrowed $3,000, White purchased his hometown newspaper, the *Emporia Gazette*, providing him with a lifelong forum for his political ideas. Always a Republican, White gained national attention in 1896 with his editorial, "What's the Matter with Kansas?" It blamed the economic decline of Kansas on the radical programs of the state's Populist Party and implied that the Democratic/Populist presidential nominee, William Jennings Bryan, was similarly radical.

Despite these conservative Republican roots, White's later friendship with Theodore Roosevelt and various Kansas political leaders converted him to the cause of political reform in the early 1900s. Thereafter, he became an ardent Progressive, writing for the muckraking magazine *McClure's*, working for Progressive Republican political candidates, including Roosevelt and Robert La Follette, and eventually bolting the GOP in 1912 to support the Bull Moose Party. During the 1920s White attempted, with little success, to encourage Republican Presidents like Warren Harding and Calvin Coolidge to support Progressive policies. Although he supported Franklin D. Roosevelt's early reforms, seeing them as extensions of the Progressives' reform agenda, White remained suspicious of the New Deal's centralization of power in the national government and thus never supported FDR personally. With the approach of World War II, White lent his support of the internationalist cause by heading the national Committee to Defend America by Aiding the Allies.

Throughout most of his life White never wavered from his Progressive beliefs, supporting a wide variety of middle-class, moderate reforms in order to protect the democratic, capitalistic state in America. He was a dedicated and popular journalist as well, whose editorial voice echoed far beyond the Flint Hills of Emporia.

*See also:* William Jennings Bryan, Bull Moose Party, Calvin Coolidge, Warren G. Harding, Robert La Follette, Populist (People's) Party

John W. Malsberger

REFERENCES

Jernigan, E. Jay. 1983. *William Allen White*. Boston: Twayne.

Johnson, Walter. 1947. *William Allen White's America*. New York: Henry Holt.

Tuttle, William M., Jr. 1970. "Aid-to-the-Allies-Short-of-War Versus American Intervention, 1940: A Reappraisal of William Allen White's Leadership." 56 *Journal of American History* 840.

White, William Allen. 1946. *The Autobiography of William Allen White*. New York: Macmillan.

## White v. Regester

412 U.S. 755 (1973)

In this case the Supreme Court for the first time struck down multimember districts on constitutional grounds. (Multimember districts are not unconstitutional per se, however, as was shown in *Whitcomb v. Chavis*.) The Supreme Court unanimously upheld the district court's order to disestablish the multimember districts in Dallas and Bexar counties, Texas, because they had been found to discriminate invidiously against cognizable racial or ethnic groups. A nonunanimous Court, however, reversed one part of the lower court's opinion that had found a maximum variation of 9.9 percent between House districts as unacceptable.

Two years earlier, *Whitcomb v. Chavis* had upheld a multimember district in Indiana and had established that finding a multimember district unconstitutional put the burden of proof on the plaintiff to "produce evidence to support findings that the political processes leading to nomination and election were not equally open to participation by the group in question—that its members had less opportunity than did other residents in the district to participate in the political process and to elect legislators of their choice."

In *White*, the Supreme Court agreed with the district court's findings that the plaintiffs had met this burden in both Dallas and Bexar counties. Writing for the Court, Justice Byron White was not specific as to how and what parts of the evidence met the burden, but he concluded that the findings were sufficient to sustain the judgment. The district court had earlier noted the history of official racial discrimination in Texas. It also cited rules requiring a majority vote to win primaries and a "so-called 'place' rule limiting candidacy for legislative office from a multimember district to a specified 'place' on the ticket, [resulting in] a head-to-head contest for each position."

In Dallas County, a white-dominated organization, the Dallas Committee for Responsible Government (DCRG) was found effectively to control the slating of Democratic Party candidates. Moreover, as recently as three years earlier, the DCRG had relied upon "racial campaign tactics in white precincts to defeat candidates who had the overwhelming support of the black community." The district court also noted that only two Blacks had served in the Dallas delegation since Reconstruction. *Whitcomb*, on the other hand, demonstrated that such a fact in and of itself would not prove invidious discrimination. Nevertheless, the district court concluded that "the black community has been effectively excluded from participation in the Democratic primary selection process, and was therefore generally not permitted to enter the political process in a reliable and meaningful manner."

With regard to Bexar County (San Antonio), the district court noted that Mexican-Americans in Texas "had long 'suffered from, and continue to suffer from, the results and effects of invidious discrimination and treatment in the fields of education, employment, economics, health, politics and others.' . . . The typical Mexican-American suffers a cultural and language barrier that makes his participation in community processes extremely difficult, particularly . . . with respect to the political life of Bexar County. [A] cultural incompatibility . . . conjoined with the poll tax and the most restrictive voter registration procedures in the nation have operated to effectively deny Mexican-Americans access to the political processes in Texas even longer than the Blacks were formally denied access by the white primary.'" The district court saw the residual impact of these barriers as low voter registration and only two Mexican-Americans ever having served in the legislature from the barrio of Bexar County. Based on "the totality of the circumstances" the district court concluded that single-member districts were required to remedy the effects of past and present discrimination.

Regarding the issue of disparity in the size of districts, the largest total variation between the most underrepresented and overrepresented districts was 9.9 percent; the average deviation from the ideal being 1.82 percent. Twenty-three districts were overrepresented or underrepresented by more than 3 percent, and three by more than 5 percent. The majority opinion by Justice White stated that in previous cases the Court had not held "that any deviations from absolute equality, however small, must be justified to the satisfaction of the judiciary to avoid invalidation under the Equal Protection Clause . . . we do not consider relatively minor population deviations among state legislative districts to substantially dilute the weight of individual votes in the larger districts so as to deprive individuals in these districts of fair and effective representation." Justice White also noted that "state reapportionment statutes are not subject to the same strict standards applicable to reapportionment of congressional seats."

*See also:* Racial Vote Dilution Cases, *Whitcomb v. Chavis*

*H. W. Perry, Jr.*

## L. Douglas Wilder (1931– )

The first modern African American elected as a state's governor. Lawrence Douglas Wilder was born in the segregated Church Hill section of Richmond, Virginia, just a short distance from the State Capitol in which he would make political history. Wilder was educated in Richmond schools and graduated from Virginia Union University. After service in the Korean War, which was Wilder's first experience in an integrated environment, he went on to Howard University Law School in Washington, D. C., because no law school in Virginia was open to African-Americans at that time. He returned to Richmond to begin a lucrative practice of criminal law.

In 1969 Wilder entered politics, winning a seat in the State Senate from Richmond. The first Black politician elected to the Virginia legislature in this century, Wilder's campaign was made possible because the popular incumbent ran for lieutenant governor; he won in part because, in heavily racial voting, two conservative white candidates split the white vote. Wilder's 16 years in the state senate were marked first by prominent leadership on civil rights (though as a younger man he had never participated in a single civil rights demonstration) and then by a gradual moderation. Throughout his tenure, however, he was never shy about confronting Virginia's political establishment. In 1982, for example, he threatened to run as an an independent against the United States Senate nominee preferred by Governor Charles Robb. The perspective nominee had to withdraw as

his candidacy would have been doomed by an African-American on the ballot running as an independent. Governor Robb as angered; Wilder's perceived power increased.

In 1985 Wilder ran successfully for lieutenant governor, becoming the first African American to hold statewide office in the South since Reconstruction. His campaign, run on a financial shoestring, is legendary in Virginia; he literally drove to and campaigned in every town in the commonwealth. The lieutenant governor's job in Virginia is largely ceremonial, but the prominence he obtained by winning office served him well as he sought to succeed Gerald L. Bailes, who was prohibited from seeking reelection by Virginia's "one term and out" law.

Race was a prominent, but not determinant, issue in the 1989 gubernatorial contest. Wilder campaigned hard on his opposition to banning abortions; observers say that issue, more than race, had an impact on the result. Wilder did not draw as many votes from many conservative white areas of the state as did his running mate. As has been the case in other states in which African-Americans ran against white opponents, poll results, even exit polls, consistently showed Wilder garnering more votes than he actually received. The clear implication is that some voters do not cast their ballots for African American candidates even when they tell pollsters that they do.

Wilder's victory places him at the forefront of national politics. Unlike Jesse Jackson, he has demonstrated that he can poll white votes and win elections. Although not as well known as Jackson, immediately after his election speculation began that Wilder would find a place on the Democratic national ticket as early as 1992.

*See also:* Jesse Jackson, Race and Racial Politics

*L. Sandy Maisel*

## David T. Wilentz (1894–1988)

Democratic political boss in New Jersey. Any account of politics and political parties in New Jersey during the twentieth century would have to consider the role of David Theodore Wilentz, one of the most powerful political bosses in a state where, until the early 1970s, bosses and strong party organizations essentially controlled local politics, the legislature, and the statewide nomination process. Wilentz, for all that, did not fit the stereotype of the boss. While he was a shrewd and savvy politician who controlled the powerful Middlesex County Democratic machine for over a half-century, he was also an educated and articulate attorney, who was known for his legal brilliance in court and for his commitment and loyalty to the members of his organization. Even opponents admitted that the breadth of his political concerns went well beyond the narrower interests of his own political organization. As one old-timer noted, "He was the boss with the brains."

Born in Lithuania, his family settled a year later in Perth Amboy, in Middlesex County, where Wilentz lived all his life. After serving in the Army during World War I, he completed his law degree and was appointed city attorney for Perth Amboy. In his early twenties he became involved in Democratic organizational politics in Middlesex, challenging the traditional Republican control of the county. By 1928 having developed a coalition of ethnic enclaves and blue-collar workers, he built a powerful political machine that remained invincible for half a century. In 1934, through the influence of Frank Hague, his political boss confrere, Wilentz was appointed state attorney general. During the decade that he served, he attracted statewide attention for his flair, brilliance, and leadership; at this time he achieved national notoriety for his role as prosecutor in the famous Lindbergh kidnapping trial (a role that revisionist historians have subsequently denigrated, criticizing Wilentz for his part in courtroom sensationalism and "cooking" the evidence).

But his more notable achievements were in his role as a political leader in New Jersey. Throughout his career, he managed to combine an interest in the maintenance of his political organization with an informed concern with modern political issues that were facing a state where patronage and traditional party politics were becoming obsolete. He recruited and groomed generations of capable legislators, and in an era when gubernatorial nominations were the fiats of a handful of party elites, Wilentz enlisted outstanding Democratic candidates for that post. Until late in his long career he maintained a keen interest in and provided encouragement to Democratic legislators and governors who were attempting to resolve difficult political policy issues like the income tax and home rule—issues that might have offended his constituency. A man of great charm, humor, and intelligence, he left his mark on Democratic voters and party workers in Middlesex County and elected policymakers throughout the state.

*See also:* Frank Hague

*Maureen Moakley*

## William R. Willcox (1863–1940)

New York Republican politician. National chairman of the Republican Party from 1916 to 1918, William Russell Willcox was Charles Evans Hughes's "personal choice," following consultation with former President Theodore Roosevelt; Hughes was hoping to bring as many Roosevelt Progressives as possible back into the Republican Party in 1916. Willcox was 53 years old at the time, having been raised on a farm and educated at the University of Rochester and Columbia Law School. He practiced law in New York City, and in keeping with the popular organizational theories of the day, he belonged to the Efficiency Society of New York and was its president for a time. Willcox's first public appointment was as commissioner of parks in 1902.

Willcox was long involved with both Republicans Theodore Roosevelt and Charles Evans Hughes. In 1905 President Roosevelt appointed him postmaster of New York City. Willcox was also a leading member of an organization called "The Hughes Alliance," established to help Hughes win the gubernatorial nomination over the objections of the regular Republican organizational leadership. Willcox controlled a great deal of patronage in New York City.

Willcox was in private law practice at the time of his election as national party chairman. Hughes's relationship with the Republican National Committee in 1916 was reminiscent of his with the New York party organization eight years earlier, involving a national organization to campaign independently of the national committee. Willcox's experience in the New York situation and his friendship with both Roosevelt and Hughes made him a logical choice for the chairmanship. Hughes's narrow defeat in the election led to severe recrimination about Willcox's management of the campaign and to demands that he retire from the national chairmanship.

*See also:* Charles Evans Hughes, Theodore Roosevelt

*Ralph M. Goldman*

REFERENCES

Nicholas Murray Butler Papers. Columbia University.

Goldman, Ralph M. 1990. *The National Party Chairmen and Committees: Factionalism at the Top.* Armonk, NY: M. E. Sharpe.

Greenlee, Howard S. 1950. "The Republican Party in Division and Reunion, 1913–1920." Ph.D. dissertation, University of Chicago.

## G. Mennen Williams (1911–1989)

Liberal Michigan Democratic governor. Born in Detroit, Michigan, in 1911, [Gerhard] Mennen Williams was called "Soapy" by Michigan voters and politicians because of the shaving cream products firm (the Mennen Company) owned by his mother's family. He got a B.A. from Princeton University in 1932 and his law degree from the University of Michigan in 1936. From 1936 to 1937, he served as a board member of Michigan's Social Security Administration. As a protégé of Michigan's liberal Democratic governor, Frank Murphy, Williams was appointed assistant attorney general of Michigan in 1937 and served until 1938. From 1939 until 1948 with the exception of his wartime service in the Navy, Williams held a series of federal positions in the Justice Department and in the Office of Price Administration.

As an activist politician, Williams came back to Michigan determined to reorganize and revitalize the state's Democratic Party as a consistently liberal, reformist organization that would be closely allied with Michigan's labor unions, especially the United Auto Workers (UAW) under the leadership of Walter Reuther. Williams was first elected Michigan's governor in 1948 and was reelected five times, serving in this office until 1961. As governor, Williams focused on effecting reforms in civil rights, mental health services, public education, and the state's tax base. With his trademark bow ties and boyish grin, he made frequent appearances in regional and national media.

Williams took an active role in national politics. He was a member of the Democratic National Committee from 1954 until 1961. During the John Kennedy and Lyndon Johnson administrations, he served as Secretary of State for African Affairs and then as U.S. ambassador to the Philippines. From 1971 to 1983, he held a seat as a justice of the Michigan Supreme Court. In 1983 Williams was appointed chief justice of this court.

*See also:* Lyndon B. Johnson, John F. Kennedy, Frank Murphy

*Sean J. Savage*

REFERENCES

Buffa, Dudley W. 1984. *Union Power and American Democracy: The UAW and the Democratic Party 1935–1972.* Ann Arbor: U. of Michigan Pr.

Fenton, John H. 1966. *Midwest Politics.* New York: Holt, Rinehart, and Winston.

Selcraig, James Truett. 1982. *The Red Scare in the Midwest, 1945–1955: A State and Local Study.* Ann Arbor, MI: UMI Research Pr.

## Hosea Williams (1926– )

Controversial civil rights leader. A controversial and politicized African-American leader of the civil rights movement since the early 1960s, the Reverend Hosea Williams was born in Attapulgus, Georgia. He received a degree in chemistry from Morris Brown College and was employed as a research chemist from 1952 to 1963. During those same years, he also became a minister and an active member of the Southern Christian Leadership Conference (SCLC) headed by Dr. Martin Luther King, Jr. Williams held a number of offices in the SCLC, including special adviser to Dr. King, political action coordinator, and national executive director, a position he held from 1969 to 1971 and again from 1977 to 1979, when he was removed by the SCLC's board in a battle over his choice of strategies. Some conflict also characterized his position in the SCLC and his duties as a member of the Georgia House of Representatives.

Williams was one of the strongest supporters of direct action among SCLC leaders. Following Dr. King's death in 1968, he led the SCLC to consider questions of poverty as well as race, a strategy that led him to organize the Poor Peoples Union of America in 1973. In 1975 Black Media, Incorporated, named him Civil Rights Leader of the Year. Williams was also one of the first civil rights leaders to enter electoral politics. In 1972 he lost a primary for the Democratic nomination to the United States Senate from Georgia. In 1973 he lost the Democratic primary for mayor of Atlanta.

In 1974 he was elected to the Georgia House of Representatives and has been returned to office in every election since then. In 1984 he entered the primary for his United States congressional seat but won only 29 percent of the vote even though the district was 65 percent African-American.

Williams's political career has been marked by controversy. In 1976 he was one of the few civil rights leaders to oppose Jimmy Carter, claiming that as governor, Carter had not done enough to help Georgia's African-Americans. In 1980 Williams endorsed Ronald Reagan, again faulting President Carter's civil rights record.

*See also:* Jimmy Carter, Martin Luther King, Jr., Ronald Reagan

*Charles S. Hauss*

## Williams v. Rhodes
### 393 U.S. 23 (1968)

In 1968 the Ohio American Independent Party (AIP) and the Socialist Labor Party both brought suit to challenge the validity of Ohio election laws on the ground that they denied these parties, and the voters who might wish to vote for them, the equal protection of the laws, guaranteed against state abridgment by the equal protection clause of the Fourteenth Amendment. These two parties asserted that Ohio election laws had made it virtually impossible for a new political party, even though it had hundreds of thousands of members, or an old party, which had a very small number of members, to be placed on the state ballot to choose electors pledged to particular candidates for President and Vice President of the United States.

Specifically, the Ohio Revised Code required a new party to obtain petitions signed by qualified electors totaling 15 percent of the number of ballots cast in the last preceding gubernatorial election. This burdensome requirement, together with other restrictive provisions of the Code, made qualifying on the ballot nearly impossible for any except the Republican and Democratic parties. The two traditional parties faced substantially smaller burdens because they were allowed to retain their positions on the ballot simply by obtaining 10 percent of the votes in the last gubernatorial election; neither were they required to obtain any signature petitions. A three-judge district court ruled these restrictive Ohio election laws unconstitutional but refused to grant the Ohio American Independent Party and the Socialist Labor Party the full relief they had sought; therefore, both parties appealed to the United States Supreme Court.

The Ohio American Independent Party was formed in January 1968 by Ohio supporters of former Governor George C. Wallace of Alabama. During the following six months a campaign was conducted to secure signatures on petitions to give the party a place on the ballot. Over 450,000 signatures were eventually obtained—significantly more than the 15 percent (433,100 signatures) required by Ohio law. However, the secretary of the state of Ohio informed the AIP that it would not be given a place on the ballot because it had failed to present the signatures by a February 7, 1968, deadline imposed by state election laws. Having demonstrated its numerical strength, the AIP argued that the early deadline for filing petitions, together with other onerous provisions, denied the party and certain Ohio voters equal protection of the laws. The three-judge district court unanimously agreed with this contention and ruled that the state must be required to provide a space for write-in votes. A majority of the district court refused to hold, however, that the American Independent Party's name must be printed on the ballot, on the ground that Wallace and his adherents had filed their suit too late to allow the Ohio legislature an opportunity to remedy the law in time for the presidential balloting. The appellants then moved before Justice Potter Stewart, circuit justice for the Sixth Circuit, for an injunction that would order the AIP's candidates to be put on the ballot pending appeal. Justice Stewart granted the injunction.

Before the Supreme Court, Ohio argued that it had absolute power to put any burdens it pleased on the selection of electors because of Article 2, Section 1 of the Constitution, providing that "Each State shall appoint, in such Manner as the Legislature thereof may direct, a Number of Electors . . ." to choose a President and Vice President. The Court indeed conceded that this section does grant extensive power to the states to pass laws regulating the selection of electors. However, the Court also recognized that these powers are always subject to the limitation that they may not be exercised in a way that violates other specific provisions of the Constitution. The Court declared that no state can pass a law regulating elections that violates the Fourteenth Amendment's command that "No State shall . . . deny any person . . . the equal protection of the laws." The Ohio election laws placed burdens on two different, although overlapping, equal protection rights—the right of individuals to associate for the advancement of political beliefs, and the right of qualified voters, regardless of their political persuasion, to cast their votes effectively. The Court reaffirmed the precious nature of the right to associate for the advancement of political goals and the right of each voter to vote for a candidate of his or her choice. The right to form a party for the advancement of political goals means little if a party can be kept off the election ballot and thus denied a commensurate opportunity to win votes. So also, the right to vote is heavily burdened if that vote may be cast for only one of two parties at a time when other parties are clamoring for a place on the ballot.

Ohio argued that a state may validly promote a two-party system in order to encourage compromise and political stability. The Court disagreed saying that the Ohio system did not merely favor a "two-party system"; it favored two particular parties—the Republicans and the Democrats—and in effect tended to give them a complete monopoly in the election proceedings. In addition, Ohio expressed the concern that if three or more parties are on the ballot, then it is possible that no one party would obtain 50 percent of the vote, and the runner-up might have been preferred to the plurality winner by a majority of the voters.

The Court was not persuaded. Ohio had failed to show a "compelling interest" that justified imposing such heavy burdens on the right to vote and to associate. The Court ordered that Governor Wallace's name remain on the ballot.

*See also:* Socialist Labor Party, George C. Wallace

*Scott McDermott*

## Wendell L. Willkie (1892–1944)

Republican presidential nominee in 1940. Wendell Lewis Willkie was born a small-town boy in Elwood, Indiana, and rose to become a corporate lawyer and president of a utility company. He initially achieved prominence by opposing public power projects like the Tennessee Valley Authority and attacking the antibusiness excesses of Franklin D. Roosevelt's New Deal.

Willkie's nomination on the sixth ballot by the Republican Party for President in 1940 demonstrated the efficacy of a public relations campaign led by the print media to influence public opinion and attract convention delegates. That nomination also illustrated the power of "amateurs," who established Willkie clubs across the country, bombarded convention delegates with supportive literature (and chanted "We Want Willkie" from the convention galleries), and then during the general election set up a presidential campaign effort that paralleled the campaigns for other offices and caused tension with the Republican Party organization.

The nomination in 1940 of Willkie, who had been a Jeffersonian Democrat as late as 1938, was the first of a string of victories for the eastern "liberal" establishment part of the Republican Party. It signaled the minority Republican Party's acceptance of the central domestic programs of the New Deal. It also rejected the traditional isolationism of the GOP in favor of emerging bipartisanship in foreign policy, centered on active support for the embattled democracy of Britain (Republicans acted as the "Loyal Opposition" party under Willkie). Willkie was also a strong supporter of civil rights and the civil liberties of politically unpopular groups.

The nomination of a business leader who had been relatively unknown to the public only three months before the GOP convention reflected the dearth of strong competing candidates and of public officials at the convention, in part owing to the repeated Democratic landslides of the 1930s. Moreover, FDR was breaking all traditions by running for a third term as President. The developing war in Europe reduced support for the candidacies of the inexperienced Thomas Dewey and the isolationist Robert Taft. Willkie's attractive personal characteristics also helped him: he came across as warm, approachable, forthright, dynamic, and eloquent. His uncompromising adherence to principles, however, hurt his subsequent ability to unify and lead the Republican Party.

Willkie's losing effort in 1940 still won him 45 percent of the popular vote and the electoral votes of ten states (especially in the isolationist farm belt), an enormous improvement over the party's showing in the two previous presidential elections. He lost because of the popularity of Roosevelt and his New Deal program, because of the ominous international situation especially in Europe and because of persistent class voting and Republican weakness among the middle and lower classes. Citing the importance of the European war, Roosevelt had conducted a White House Rose Garden campaign, quite subdued until the last two weeks before the election, when he began to blast traditional Republican opposition to his New Deal programs.

Supporting higher taxes during the 1944 Republican nomination contest, Willkie withdrew after defeat in the Wisconsin primary; he lost because Republican voters reacted against his vigorous and persistent attacks on traditional conservative Republican policies and leaders. Before his death, he urged the realignment of the parties along pure ideological lines.

*See also:* Thomas E. Dewey, Franklin D. Roosevelt, Robert A. Taft

*Stephen D. Shaffer*

REFERENCES

Barnard, Ellsworth. 1966. *Wendell Willkie: Fighter for Freedom.* Marquette: Northern Michigan U. Pr.

Dillon, Mary Earhart. 1952. *Wendell Willkie, 1892–1944.* Philadelphia: Lippincott.

Johnson, Donald Bruce. 1960. *The Republican Party and Wendell Willkie*. Urbana: U. of Illinois Pr.

Keech, William R., and Donald R. Matthews. 1977. *The Party's Choice*. Washington: Brookings.

Neal, Steve. 1984. *Dark Horse: A Biography of Wendell Willkie*. Garden City, NY: Doubleday.

Schlesinger, Arthur M., Jr., ed. 1971. *History of American Presidential Elections, 1789–1968*. New York: Chelsea House.

## David Wilmot (1814–1868)

Author of the Wilmot Proviso. A Pennsylvania lawyer and politician of ordinary ability, David Wilmot, during the 1830s, supported Andrew Jackson and the Democratic Party, and in 1844 he helped Martin Van Buren gain the Pennsylvania Democratic convention's endorsement for President. That same year, Wilmot was elected to the House of Representatives from a district that had a consistent habit of choosing Democrats.

When he first arrived in Washington, Wilmot found himself allied with those northern Democrats who were accusing President James K. Polk of ignoring the growing needs of the North and of showing favoritism toward the demands of the South. Nevertheless, Wilmot, temporarily at any rate, backed the administration's policies, including the Walker Tariff, whose greatly reduced rates were universally unpopular among the rest of the Pennsylvania delegation.

However, Wilmot eventually came to believe that the South was becoming too aggressive and powerful for the nation's good. More specifically, he worried that if land in the Southwest were acquired as a result of the Mexican War, southerners might attempt to move their slaves to it. Wilmot was opposed to the extension of slavery, but he was not an abolitionist and did not believe in racial equality. On August 8, 1846, Polk asked the House for $2 million to help attain a peace treaty with Mexico. Wilmot, after conferring with several northern Democrats, decided to offer an amendment (the Wilmot Proviso) to the appropriations bill; his amendment banned slavery from any territory that might be subsequently wrenched from Mexico's grasp. On several occasions, the House approved Wilmot's proviso, but the Senate always rejected it. The Polk administration was adamantly opposed to this measure and finally converted enough northern Democrats to its position to get the amendment dropped from the bill.

Wilmot contributed little of political substance during his other two terms in the House,

but he had become a nationally known figure because of his Proviso. In 1848 he broke with the Van Buren Democrats and became a member of the Free Soil Party. By 1850, Democrats loyal to James Buchanan were dominant in Pennsylvania, and they damaged Wilmot's candidacy so badly that he decided not to run for office again.

Wilmot became a leader in the formation of the Republican Party, and many historians have mistakenly claimed that he was an early Republican candidate for governor of Pennsylvania. He supported Abraham Lincoln in 1860 but declined the offer of a Cabinet position. Wilmot really wanted to become a United States Senator, and he was able to fill out Simon Cameron's term (1861–1863) when Cameron became Secretary of War. As a Senator, he backed Lincoln's policies consistently and saw the basic principle of his Proviso become the law of the land on June 19, 1862. He was not reelected to the Senate because Democrats had gained a majority in the Pennsylvania legislature, but Lincoln named him judge of the federal court of claims. As a judge, he turned in only a mediocre performance before his death.

*See also:* Abolition Movement, James Buchanan, Simon Cameron, Election of 1844, Free Soil Party, Andrew Jackson, Abraham Lincoln, James K. Polk, Martin Van Buren, Wilmot Proviso

*Gerald W. Wolff*

REFERENCES

Going, Charles Buxton. 1924. *David Wilmot, Free Soiler: A Biography of the Great Advocate of the Wilmot Proviso*. New York: Appleton.

Morrison, Chaplain W. 1967. *Democratic Politics and Sectionalism: The Wilmot Proviso Controversy*. Chapel Hill: U. of North Carolina Pr.

## Wilmot Proviso

Although its origins and results were both complex and far-reaching, as written, the Wilmot Proviso was a simple, straightforward statement. In the summer of 1846, President James K. Polk asked Congress to appropriate $2 million to help him negotiate a finish to the Mexican War, which had only begun in May 1846. Subsequently, in August, a Pennsylvania Democrat and first-term Representative named David Wilmot offered an amendment to the bill that the President had requested. This proviso provided for the exclusion of slavery from any territory taken from Mexico as a result of the war.

At any rate, the House passed the Proviso package (eventually, several times). The coalition that won its success involved various northern factions, who saw moral, political, and economic advantages in supporting it. Both Whigs and Democrats, representing the Northwest, were angry with Polk for vetoing a bill to improve rivers and harbors in their section. Some northern Democratic Congressmen, moreover, were still upset with the southerners in their party, whom they blamed for defeating Martin Van Buren's bid for the 1844 presidential nomination. Beyond these factions, more than a few northeastern Representatives bore considerable ill will toward both President Polk and southern Democrats for backing the Walker Tariff (1846), which eliminated the principle of protectionism. Similarly, many northwestern Congressmen excoriated Polk and southerners in general for tamely accepting only a portion of the slaveless Oregon Territory, while eagerly entering a war to seize all of the territory of Texas where slavery was allowed. Thus, these disparate northern groups, displaying a wide array of motives and interests, decided to coalesce around the potentially explosive slavery extension issue in an effort to inflict some pain on Polk and the South.

When the Wilmot Proviso was first put to a vote in the House, every northern Whig approved it, as did every northern Democrat, save four. On the other hand, all the southern Democrats and all except two southern Whigs voted against it. The Senate, however, left for vacation in 1846 without dealing with the issue. At the next session in February 1847, the Proviso was once more attached to an appropriations bill, this time for $3 million. The northern Representatives decided again to stick together and push the measure through against solid southern opposition. The Senate, however, responded by passing the appropriation without the Proviso. This time the House acquiesced but only because Polk managed to persuade a few northern Democrats to accept it. The bitter struggle over the extension of slavery into the territories, however, created many immediate political problems and produced devastating, long-range consequences.

The Wilmot Proviso quickly became a major issue in the South. In February 1847, Senator John C. Calhoun of South Carolina introduced a series of stinging anti-Proviso resolutions based on his states' rights interpretation of the Constitution. On the other hand, in the North all but one state legislature passed resolutions supporting the Proviso, and northern political candidates, newspapers, and public meetings all rallied to the Proviso's defense. In the Senate, Daniel Webster of Massachusetts maintained that Congress had constitutionally blocked slavery in the Louisiana Purchase Territory by passing the Missouri Compromise of 1820 and could repeat the process again by adopting the Wilmot Proviso.

In the Twenty-ninth and Thirtieth Congresses, these opposing interpretations of the Proviso affected party unity profoundly. The Democratic majorities in the Senate and House could no longer muster consistent unity, and crucial bills to support the war effort in Mexico were stymied. Northern Democrats could not make up their minds whether to oppose the Proviso, as their Democratic President Polk insisted, or to support it, as their constituents increasingly demanded. Southern Democrats and Whigs, for their part, portrayed Wilmot and his supporters, unwaveringly, as dangerous fanatics, while northern Whigs tended to back the Proviso solidly. Leaders, in both parties, who deplored the growing sectionalism in their organizations, tried to placate their membership and to get newspapers to play down the Proviso issue.

But once the slavery extension issue was in the open, it was difficult to quell and demanded imaginative solutions to save the party system and perhaps the nation. In 1847 and 1848, some politicians suggested that Congress could be taken out of the picture by allowing the new areas to skip the territorial stage and enter the Union immediately as states. Others wanted the Supreme Court to decide whether slavery could exist legally in the territories. Neither of these views won approval, and as other bills involving territorial slavery were introduced, the North-South split became even more pronounced (although on issues unrelated to slavery extension), but party lines continued to hold.

For the 1848 election, the Democrats wound up picking Lewis Cass of Michigan as their candidate; he was the father of popular sovereignty and openly opposed the Wilmot Proviso. The southern Democrats, however, after all the efforts to please them, did not trust Cass and withheld complete and enthusiastic support. The southern Whigs also promoted sectionalism by emphasizing the fact that their party's candidate, Zachary Taylor, was from the South and owned slaves. In this way, they hoped to woo southern Democrats to their side and thus divide the Democrats along North-South lines, while still maintaining Whig unity. While all of this maneuvering was taking place, a coalition of mostly Democratic northerners did indeed form the Free Soil Party in 1848, nominated Martin Van Buren, concentrated on promoting the Wilmot Proviso, and did rather well at the polls. Nonetheless, some traditional politicians in both parties tried mightily to blunt the obvious rise in North-South sectionalism in this election and, at this point, seemed to meet with some immediate success.

Sectionalists, however, would not be silenced, and the issue of slavery in the territories provided their major incentive. This problem had to be settled soon with some sort of policy, and the new Whig President, Zachary Taylor, realized it. Congress, however, made no move to organize the territories in 1849. As a result, debate over the extension of slavery continued with increasing bitterness, and adherents of sectional unity, such as Calhoun, began to believe that they had some chance of "reforming" the parties along sectional lines.

One possible solution to the territorial slavery problem would have been to extend the Missouri Compromise line dividing slave from free states to the Pacific Ocean. Polk, himself, had favored this plan. For one thing, it had worked well in the Louisiana Purchase Territory since 1820. If the line had been pushed to the West Coast, then it would have divided New Mexico and California approximately in half; slavery would be excluded north of it but would have been welcomed south of the line. Some antislavery advocates even favored this idea, because they believed that these new western lands were unconducive to slavery. Most northerners who opposed slavery, however, objected to the plan on the grounds that the South might someday convince the United States to take land in Central America or the Caribbean. As a result, because of these fears, this device never acquired enough northern votes to pass.

Another possible answer would have been to adopt a method first proposed by ex-Democratic presidential candidate Lewis Cass in the late 1840s, namely popular sovereignty. This theory asserted that the people of a territory, through their legislatures, not Congress, should decide whether slavery should be legal there. Congress' role should be confined to establishing governments in the territories, and it should never pass restrictive legislation, such as the Wilmot Proviso.

By 1850, Congress had no way of avoiding the problem of organizing the territories, and the doctrine of popular sovereignty played a major role in creating the famous compromise. Within a year or so, parties once again reasserted their primacy in Congress. However, if parties and their power did not die easily in the 1850s, the Kansas-Nebraska Act of 1854, which featured popular sovereignty, did damage them badly. It strained the Democratic Party badly, ultimately ruined the Whigs, and led to the creation of the northern Republican Party. In 1857, Calhoun's position on slavery extension seemed to be vindicated in the Dred Scott decision striking down a version of popular sovereignty. But while southern Democrats joyously accepted it, their northern colleagues clung to popular sovereignty. In 1860 the Democratic Party finally split along North-South lines over the issue of slavery in the territories and nominated two candidates: John Breckinridge (South) and Stephen Douglas (North). As a result, the last viable national party disintegrated into sectional division, helping to clear the way for a civil war. The Wilmot Proviso began as a political gambit, but it planted a virulent sectional cancer that wrecked the party system and ceased only in the wake of a protracted and deadly conflict.

See also: John Breckinridge; John C. Calhoun; Lewis Cass; Stephen A. Douglas; Elections of 1844, 1848, and 1860; Free Soil Party; Kansas-Nebraska Act of 1854; Mexican War; Missouri Compromise; James K. Polk; Zachary Taylor; Martin Van Buren; David Wilmot

*Gerald W. Wolff*

REFERENCES

Alexander, Thomas B. 1967. *Sectional Stress and Party Strength: A Study of Roll-Call Voting Patterns in the United States House of Representatives, 1836–1860.* Nashville, TN: Vanderbilt U. Pr.

Going, Charles Buxton. 1924. *David Wilmot, Free Soiler: A Biography of the Great Advocate of the Wilmot Proviso.* New York: Appleton.

Morrison, Chaplain W. 1967. *Democratic Politics and Sectionalism: The Wilmot Proviso Controversy.* Chapel Hill: U. of North Carolina Pr.

Silbey, Joel H. 1967. *The Shrine of Party: Congressional Voting Behavior, 1841–1852.* Pittsburgh: U. of Pittsburgh Pr.

## Henry Wilson (1812–1875)

Whig, Free Soil, and Know-Nothing politician. Early poverty in New Hampshire and a desperate struggle for self-education (he taught school for a time) and economic advancement gave Henry Wilson a lifelong desire for recognition and public office. This combined with a naturally conciliatory temperament led him into frequent political deals, changes of party, and inevitable charges of demagoguery. He was, however, sincerely and consistently dedicated to advancing freedom and the common man.

From 1840 to 1848, he served in the Massachusetts legislature as an antislavery "Conscience Whig." Disgusted with the nomination of the opinionless Zachary Taylor in 1848, Wilson left the Whigs as soft on slavery and helped found the Free Soil Party. During the next decade he shifted from one coalition or party to another in search for a suitable vehicle for his own ambition and his passionate crusade against the "slave power" in Washington and the Cotton Whig oligarchies of Massachusetts. He engineered the coalition that elected Charles Sumner to the United States Senate from Massachusetts in 1851 but was himself defeated in three bids for governor of Massachusetts, first as a Free Soiler and then as a Republican. Wilson attached himself to the Know-Nothing (American) Party in 1855 and managed to be elected to the Senate. In 1856 he was one of the antislavery men who broke with the Know-Nothings to become an ardent promoter of John Frémont's Republican candidacy for President.

From 1856 to 1872, Wilson was a Radical Republican Senator and during the Civil War, an able chairman of the military affairs committee. Although a strong supporter of African-American suffrage and reform, Wilson remained a Republican Party stalwart and conciliator rather than joining the revolt against President Ulysses Grant. In 1872 he won a hotly contested nomination as Grant's Vice President, and in spite of failing health he continued to cherish presidential ambitions and egalitarian ideals until his death while still in office.

*See also:* Conscience Whig, Election of 1872, Know-Nothings, Slavery, Charles Sumner, Zachary Taylor

*Harold B. Raymond*

REFERENCES

Baum, Dale. *The Civil War Party System.* Chapel Hill: U. of North Carolina Pr.

Brauer, Kinley. 1967. *Cotton Versus Conscience.* Lexington: U. Pr. of Kentucky.

Gienapp, William. 1987. *Origins of the Republican Party.* New York: Oxford U. Pr.

McKay, Eduard. 1971. *Henry Wilson, Practical Radical.* Port Washington, NY: Kennikat.

## Woodrow Wilson (1856–1924)

Progressive Democratic President of the United States. Beginning with the election of William McKinley in 1896 and ending with the election of Franklin Roosevelt in 1932, only one Democrat—Woodrow Wilson—interrupted Republican Party dominance of the presidency. During Wilson's two terms (1913 to 1921), America wrestled with the obligations and pressures of a newly emergent great power. At home, Progressives battled with conservatives over the proper role of government in regulating the economy and providing for the social welfare. In foreign affairs, after a prolonged but ultimately unsuccessful attempt to remain neutral in the face of the Great War in Europe, America fought to create a peace that would "make the world safe for democracy."

[Thomas] Woodrow Wilson was born in Staunton, Virginia. He attended Davidson College, Princeton University, and the University of Virginia law school. After an unsuccessful attempt to establish a law practice, Wilson earned a Ph.D. in history and political science at Johns Hopkins University. His doctoral dissertation, a classic study of the power of committees in Congress, was published in 1885 as *Congressional Government.*

Wilson later taught at Bryn Mawr College and at Wesleyan and Princeton universities, eventually being selected as Princeton's president in 1902, initiating variously successful educational reforms and engaging powerful members of Princeton's faculty over the development of a graduate school. The graduate school struggle, which Wilson lost, led to his resignation in 1910.

Wilson's reforms brought him to the attention of George Harvey, editor of the conservative *Harper's Weekly,* and James Smith, Jr., who, as boss of the New Jersey Democratic machine, was looking for a gubernatorial nominee. Smith had no love for reformers, but Wilson—whose father had railed against the "black Republican" Abraham Lincoln—was a reformer with a southern conservative background.

Wilson won the gubernatorial election handily and immediately moved into the ranks of contenders for the 1912 Democratic presidential nomination. At the convention, the Democrats—eager for power after capturing a 55-seat majority in the House of Representatives in the 1910 midterm elections—struggled to choose between Wilson and House Speaker Champ Clark. A leader in the early balloting,

Clark was not able to muster the two-thirds majority then required for nomination. Wilson won on the forty-sixth ballot; in the words of historian Arthur Link, "no man in the history of American politics had such a spectacular and rapid rise to political prominence."

On the Republican side, Theodore Roosevelt, having embraced the reform agenda of the Progressives, took on incumbent President William Howard Taft and the Old Guard conservatives for the GOP presidential nomination. Roosevelt was popular—he even won the presidential primary in Taft's own Ohio—but the convention was controlled by Republican conservatives. The beaten Roosevelt and a diverse collection of social reformers then met in Chicago to create the Progressive Party. After adopting what Link calls "the most significant platform since the Populist platform of 1892," the Progressives nominated Roosevelt (who said he felt like a bull moose) for President, and California governor Hiram W. Johnson for Vice President.

This split in the Republican Party ensured Wilson's election in November. Although he won only 42 percent of the popular vote, Wilson's 435 electoral votes overwhelmed Roosevelt (27 percent, 88 electoral votes) and Taft (23 percent, 8 electoral votes). Interestingly enough, nearly 1 million voters—about 6 percent of the electorate—voted for Socialist Eugene V. Debs. In Congress, the Democrats secured majorities of 73 seats in the House and six in the Senate.

An admirer of the British model of party government, Wilson used patronage, calls for party discipline, and the absence of charismatic Democrats in Congress to create majorities in support of his policy agenda. Congress passed the Federal Reserve Act, created the Federal Trade Commission, and confirmed Wilson's nomination of liberal Louis Brandeis for the U.S. Supreme Court. Calling himself a "progressive with the brakes on," Wilson accelerated his commitment to reform only as the 1916 election neared. Needing to win Progressive (and Socialist) votes to stay in the White House, Wilson pushed rural credit, workmen's compensation, and child labor laws through the House and Senate—all in 1916. Wilson also doggedly avoided involvement in the spreading conflict in Europe; "he kept us out of war" became the rallying cry for Democrats in the campaign of 1916.

The Republicans, united again, nominated Supreme Court justice Charles Evans Hughes for President. The remnants of the Progressive Party tried to renominate Teddy Roosevelt, but he declined, and that party disbanded two weeks after their convention. In the campaign, Hughes struggled to attract the votes of Progressive Republicans without alienating the GOP's conservative base. His difficulties were exacerbated by the bellicosity of Roosevelt, who traveled the country and condemned Wilson for being "pushed around" by the likes of Mexican rebel leader Francisco "Pancho" Villa.

Despite his problems, Hughes came within 23 electoral votes of winning (277 to 254). Wilson received 51.7 percent of the popular vote, although the Democrats lost three seats in the Senate and twenty-one seats in the House. In fact, the Democrats were able to form a working majority in the Sixty-fifth Congress only by enlisting the support of two Progressives, one Prohibitionist, one Socialist, and one Independent.

American involvement in World War I and Wilson's personal efforts to negotiate "peace without victory" dominated his second term. In an address to a joint session of Congress on January 8, 1918, Wilson outlined Fourteen Points to be used to end the war. "Open covenants . . . openly arrived at," freedom of the seas, arms reductions, and creation of a League of Nations, among other provisions, were included.

Wilson traveled to the Paris Peace Conference to help put together the Treaty of Versailles, but his political position at home had eroded. The GOP had won majorities in both the House and the Senate in the 1918 midterm elections, and Republicans and members of the Senate criticized their virtual exclusion from the U.S. delegation in Paris. Isolationists—known as "irreconcilables"—firmly opposed the League, and another group of Senators, led by Republican Henry Cabot Lodge, refused to ratify the treaty unless "reservations" were attached. An uncompromising Wilson took his internationalist case to the American people; but he collapsed while on a tour of the Midwest and West and later suffered a paralytic stroke in October 1919 in Washington. Wilson, who rarely left his bed for the remainder of his term, watched as his treaty, and his dream of the United States joining the League of Nations, was defeated in the Senate.

Hope for resurrection of United States participation in the League ended with the 1920 presidential election, in which James M. Cox and the Democrats (and a platform endorsing the League) were soundly defeated by Warren G. Harding and the Republicans. Wilson's last public speech, on Armistice Day 1923, sounded a familiar tone of decisiveness and moralism. Referring to those who had opposed him, Wilson remarked, "I have seen fools resist Providence before and I have seen their destruction, as will come upon these again—utter destruction and contempt. That we shall prevail is as sure as God reigns."

*See also:* Louis Brandeis, James B. (Champ) Clark, James M. Cox, Election of 1912, Eugene V. Debs, League of Nations, Henry Cabot Lodge, Theodore Roosevelt, William Howard Taft

*Tom A. Kazee*

REFERENCES

Bailey, Thomas A. 1966. *Presidential Greatness: The Image and the Man from George Washington to the Present.* New York: Appleton-Century.

Blum, John Morton. 1980. *The Progressive Presidents.* New York: Norton.

Garraty, John A. 1956. *Woodrow Wilson.* New York: Harper & Row.

Link, Arthur S. 1947–1965. *Wilson.* 5 vols. Princeton: Princeton U. Pr.

———. 1954. *Woodrow Wilson and the Progressive Era: 1910–1917.* New York: Harper & Row.

———. 1979. *Woodrow Wilson: Revolution, War, and Peace.* Arlington Heights, IL: AHM Publishing.

Mulder, John M. 1978. *Woodrow Wilson: The Years of Preparation.* Princeton: Princeton U. Pr.

## Window Concept

The "Window" refers to the Democratic Party's attempts to place limits on the length of the primary and caucus season for the selection of national convention delegates. The term "window" is an analogy to the window of opportunity in time that the space program has to launch missions in order to reach their prescribed orbit successfully. The first application of this concept was the requirement beginning in 1972 that all processes affecting delegate selection had to occur within the calendar year of the convention. Beginning in 1980, the "window" for scheduling these contests was set between the second Tuesday in March and the second Tuesday of June of the election year. Special exemptions were granted to the New Hampshire primary and for the Iowa, Maine, and Minnesota caucuses. States seeking greater influence and media attention had been moving their contests earlier and earlier in the calendar year, a strategy that resulted in even earlier scheduling of the Iowa and New Hampshire dates; their state statutes required them to be "first" in the nation.

This irregularity was the major issue receiving public attention in the deliberations of the Commission on Presidential Nomination chaired by Governor James B. Hunt of North Carolina in 1981 and 1982. To have required states like Iowa and New Hampshire to conform would have risked defiance from state parties protective of their traditional early status. Rural partisans argued that early small state contests encouraged both grass-roots campaigning and party building there.

Because the Republican Party has no window, a few state parties have held early caucuses. The most notorious was Michigan's election of Republican precinct delegates in August 1986 as the first step in the selection of 1988 national convention delegates. Still, the problem seems to bother Democrats more than Republicans.

*See also:* Elections of 1972 and 1980, James B. Hunt, New Hampshire Primary

*Douglas I. Hodgkin*

REFERENCES

Price, David E. 1984. *Bringing Back the Parties.* Washington: Congressional Quarterly.

## Winner-Take-All Systems

In this type of election, the person who receives most of the votes is awarded all of the benefits. Two striking examples of this in U.S. politics are the Electoral College and presidential primaries.

Voters who go to the polls in November cast a vote for the Democratic, Republican, or third-party candidate for President. However, the U.S. Constitution mandates that this vote is not really a vote for the presidential candidate but a vote for a slate of electors who support that candidate. These electors cast the actual votes for a state and determine who will be the next President.

Currently all states except Maine (discussed below) apply the winner-take-all principle for selecting electors. Whichever presidential candidate receives the most popular votes in a state sees all his electors selected. Even if the presidential candidate receiving the most votes does not receive a majority of the vote, the candidate acquires the loyalty of all of the state's electors.

The Constitution does not require that winner-take-all rules be used in the selection of electors. Proportional representation could be used; that is, a presidential candidate receiving 40 percent of the popular vote in a state would receive 40 percent of the electors or district rules could be used. Alternatively, several election districts, most likely those coinciding with congressional districts, could be created in a state. Each district would select one of the state's electors, while two electors would be elected at large. The popular vote in each district would determine which elector would be chosen. As different candidates may win in different congressional districts, electors chosen from a state may support different candidates. Michigan in 1892 chose and Maine since 1972 has chosen their electors by the district method.

The winner-take-all aspect of the Electoral College system tends to disadvantage most third-party or independent candidates for President. A third-party candidate could win 30 percent of the nationwide popular vote yet receive no Electoral College votes because he failed to receive the most vote in any one state. Third-party candidates whose strengths are concentrated in a few states, such as George Wallace in 1968, are not as disadvantaged by the electoral college.

Winner-take-all provisions have also been used in presidential primaries. Again, voters cast ballots for one set of candidates, this time the candidates running for the presidential nomination of the Democratic or Republican party. Actually, however, they are selecting another group of people, the national party convention delegates, who will make the real decisions on the party's presidential nomination. With winner-take-all rules, whichever presidential candidate receives the most votes in a state garners all the convention delegates.

Winner-take-all rules seem especially inequitable in conjunction with presidential primaries in which three or more candidates are frequently competing. With the more numerous candidates, first-place candidates often do not receive a majority of the votes nor do they receive significantly more votes than second-place candidates. Because of these perceived biases in winner-take-all provisions, Democratic reformers in the McGovern-Fraser Commission recommended and those in the Mikulski Commission managed to prohibit winner-take-all rules in Democratic primaries. Subsequent commissions, however, have weakened this provision, allowing for loophole primaries. Winner-take-all rules can still be used in Republican Party primaries.

*See also:* Election of 1968, Electoral College System, McGovern-Fraser Commission, George Wallace

*Barbara Norrander*

## Winograd Commission

The Winograd Commission, chaired by Michigan State Democratic chair Morley Winograd, was originally appointed in 1975 by Robert Strauss, chair of the Democratic National Committee (DNC), as the Commission on the Role and Future of Presidential Primaries. The commission's ostensible purpose was to address the problems of state parties and the proliferation of primaries that was an unintended consequence of the original McGovern-Fraser reforms. The appointment of Winograd, a little-known state party chairman (and *not* an elected official) who was close to the AFL-CIO, fueled expectations that the commission would review party reform more generally. Its low profile, its limited mandate, and the irregularity of its authorization by the national chair and not the national convention undermined its legitimacy; unable to clarify its role, the first Winograd Commission suspended work pending the outcome of the 1976 campaign. With Jimmy Carter the certain nominee, the 1976 Democratic National Convention sanctioned the Winograd Commission with an expanded mandate under the new name of the Commission of Presidential Nomination and Party Structure. Its membership was enlarged, with the balance of additional members to be appointed by the incoming Carter administration.

The 55-member Winograd Commission was thus divided into three major groups: about one-third were those directly appointed by the White House, another third were restorationists (labor, party regulars, and the Coalition for a Democratic Majority [Jeane Kirkpatrick, Austin Ranney]), and the last third were either reform supporters (Donald Fraser, John Quinn) or else those who had no firm views on reform issues. The White House appointees, whose major concern was the forthcoming Carter reelection campaign, and the restorationists, who wished to limit the influence of issue activists, clearly shared converging interests.

The Winograd Commission completed its work in 1978. Its recommendations were reviewed and revised by the DNC, as well as by an unusually active Compliance Review Commission (CRC) appointed by DNC chair John C. White (a Carter nominee) to oversee implementation of the rules. Two changes were uncontroversial: in accordance with a charter amendment adopted by the 1976 convention, the commission required that affirmative action programs contain "specific goals and timetables," and the commission (under 1976 convention directive) interpreted the "fair reflection" language to ban direct-election ("loophole") primaries (with the exception of those in single-member districts). The commission defeated a proposal calling for equal division of delegates by gender (31 to 23), but that was later reinstated by the DNC. Other Winograd Commission innovations include a ban on open primaries and the institution of the bound delegate rule (binding pledged delegates on their first ballot vote, a provision that was challenged by the Edward Kennedy forces at the 1980 convention). The Coalition for a Democratic Majority achieved one of its major aims in the Winograd provision for a 10 percent add-on (based on the state allocation) of at-large delegates to be appointed by the state parties. Although pledged, the add-on delegate slots were reserved for state party and public officials and served as a precursor for the "superdelegates."

The remainder of the Winograd provisions were designed to benefit Carter's candidacy. First, the Winograd Commission established a three month "window" (from the second Tuesday in March to the second Tuesday in June), during which primaries and caucuses could be held thus shortening the length of the campaign (although five exemptions were granted by the CRC). Candidates were required to file 55 days before a primary or caucus (later altered by the DNC to extend from 30 to 90 days). The procedures for candidate approval of prospective delegates were also refined. Finally, the commission proposed an escalating minimum "threshold" necessary for delegates to be allocated to presidential hopefuls rising from 15 percent to 20 percent to 25 percent of the voters in primary and caucus as a minimum needed to qualify for our delegates at all with the minimum rising as the process continued toward to convention. The threshold provision was revised by both the DNC and the CRC, with the final interpretation requiring a 15 percent threshold in the case of two candidates. The procedures for delegate allocation became so complicated that considerable assistance from the DNC-controlled CRC was required. One issue left unresolved—despite the interest of a majority of the commission members—was the initial mandate to curb the proliferation of primaries, leading commission member Donald Fraser to conclude that "the work of the commission was diverted to rewriting the rules in order to protect the incumbent."

*See also:* Jimmy Carter, Coalition for a Democratic Majority, Democratic National Committee, Election of 1976, Donald Fraser, Edward M. Kennedy, Jeane Kirkpatrick, McGovern-Fraser Commission, Superdelegates, John C. White

*Denise L. Baer*

REFERENCES

Crotty, William J. 1983. *Party Reform.* New York: Longman.

Kirkpatrick, Jeane. 1978. *Dismantling the Parties: Reflections of Party Reform and Party Decomposition.* Washington: American Enterprise Institute.

Price, David E. 1984. *Bringing Back the Parties.* Washington: Congressional Quarterly.

## Robert C. Winthrop (1809–1894)

"Cotton Whig" legislator from Massachusetts. Entry into politics as a Whig was almost a hereditary right and duty for Robert Charles Winthrop owing to his ancestry and to his ties to the Boston aristocracy. Contemporaries described him as "the perfection of prudence and respectability and as neither great nor strong . . . a man of decencies, decorums and proprieties." He belonged to the Whig faction headed by Abbot Lawrence, later known as "Cotton Whigs," followers of Henry Clay and hostile to both antislavery radicalism and the ambitions of Daniel Webster.

Winthrop was elected to the Massachusetts legislature, serving from 1835 to 1840, and to the Congress, serving from 1840 to 1850, where he served one term as Speaker of the House (1847–1849). Like most Massachusetts Whigs, he disliked slavery and opposed the annexation of Texas. He refused, however, to carry this opposition to the point at which it might endanger the Union, legitimate party ties with southern Whigs, and legislation favorable to the prosperity of Massachusetts industry. As an almost perfect embodiment of "Cotton Whig" moderation and the faction's most prominent national officeholder, Winthrop became the target of savage criticism from antislavery "Conscience Whigs." In Congress they combined with southern extremists nearly to block his election as Speaker and in 1849 succeeded in defeating his bid for reelection to that office.

For some time Winthrop was groomed as the ultimate successor to Webster in the Senate and in 1850 was appointed to finish his term. The next year, however, a coalition of Free Soilers and Democrats in the Massachusetts legislature replaced him with his bitter critic, the caustic abolitionist Charles Sumner. As a supporter of compromise, peace, and union, Winthrop's political career was destroyed by the secession crisis. He rejected invitations to join the Republicans and supported the American and Constitutional Union candidates. Winthrop lobbied for the Crittendon Compromise but never again held public office.

*See also:* Henry Clay, Conscience Whigs, Cotton Whigs, Free Soil Party, Charles Sumner, Daniel Webster

*Harold B. Raymond*

REFERENCES

Brauer, Kinley. 1967. *Cotton Versus Conscience: Massachusetts Whig Politics and Southern Expansion, 1843–48.* Lexington: U. Pr. of Kentucky.

Donald, David. 1960. *Charles Sumner and the Coming of the Civil War.* New York: Knopf.

O'Conner, Thomas. 1918. *Lords of the Loom, the Cotton Whigs and the Coming of the Civil War.* New York: Scribner's.

Winthrop, Robert C. 1852–1886. *Addresses and Speeches on Various Occasions.* Boston: Little, Brown.

## William Wirt (1772–1834)

Prominent Attorney General of the United States and Antimason presidential candidate. Born in Bladensburg, Maryland, William Wirt became a part of Jeffersonian Republican legal circles by 1800. He attained early visibility with his forceful arguments against Aaron Burr in the treason trial of 1807. Wirt also gained literary recognition with his successful "The Letters of the British Spy" (1803), his moral and literary essays *The Old Batchelor* (1814), and the overlaudatory and romantic *Sketches of the Life and Character of Patrick Henry* (1817).

The advent of the James Monroe presidency meant that Wirt had to abandon further literary pursuits and become totally involved in legal and political affairs. Appointed Attorney General in 1817, he held the office for 12 years through the Monroe and John Quincy Adams presidencies. He played an important role in the critical Supreme Court decisions *McCulloch v. Maryland* (1819), *Dartmouth College v. Woodward* (1819), and *Gibbons V. Ogden* (1824). Assuming an office that had kept few records of previous decisions, he instituted a system of record keeping that established a body of legal precedent for future attorney generals. Perhaps his best known role as an attorney came after leaving government service with his defense of the Cherokee Indians against the efforts of Georgia and the Andrew Jackson administration to remove the tribe. Wirt lost, but heroically!

Wirt's enmity toward Jackson led him to a disastrous foray into presidential politics in 1832. The reluctant candidate of the Antimasonic Party, he had hoped that third-party advocates would combine with National Republicans against Jackson. When that strategy failed to develop, Wirt did no campaigning and finished a distant third behind Jackson and Henry Clay, carrying only Vermont. He continued his private legal practice in Baltimore until his death.

*See also:* Antimasons, Aaron Burr, Henry Clay, Election of 1832, National Republicans

*Frederick J. Blue*

REFERENCES

Boles, John B. 1971. *A Guide to the Microfilm Edition of the William Wirt Papers.* Baltimore, MD: Historical Soc.

Hargreaves, Mary W. M. 1985. *The Presidency of John Quincy Adams.* Lawrence: U. Pr. of Kansas.

Kennedy, John P. 1849. *Memoirs of the Life of William Wirt.* Philadelphia: Lea and Blanchard.

Vaughn, William P. 1983. *The Antimasonic Party in the United States, 1826–1843.* Lexington: U. Pr. of Kentucky.

White, Leonard. 1951. *The Jeffersonians: A Study of Administrative History, 1801–1829.* New York: Macmillan.

## Richard B. Wirthlin (1931– )

Ronald Reagan's pollster and campaign strategist. Richard Bitner Wirthlin is a pioneer in the field of political research. Wirthlin was born in Salt Lake City and got B.A. and M.A. degrees from the University of Utah. Later he earned his Ph.D. in economics at the University of California at Berkeley and then joined the economics faculty at Brigham Young University. Wirthlin left academia in 1969 to form his own polling and strategic communications firm, Decision/Making/Information. In 1987 Decision/Making/Information changed its name to Wirthlin Group.

Wirthlin began political polling in 1964, helping a friend in his race for Utah governor. His first major national race came in 1968 when he served as Barry Goldwater's Senate campaign poll taker. The same year he made his entry into presidential politics when he conducted a poll for then California governor Ronald Reagan. Since then, Wirthlin has been the pollster and principal strategist for all of Reagan's campaigns, including his reelection bid for governor of California in 1970, his unsuccessful effort in 1976 to wrest the Republican presidential nomination from Gerald R. Ford, and his landslide presidential victories of 1980 and 1984.

As Reagan's pollster, Wirthlin developed new and important survey research measures. In 1968 he initiated "tracking"—the continuous monitoring of the course of a campaign—and a sophisticated geo-demographic targeting scheme. Two years later, while taking surveys for Reagan's gubernatorial campaign, he applied the techniques of economic modeling to politics. Although not perfect, such modeling of political behavior showed promise. He also developed forecasting techniques at the state level to generate estimates of the electoral vote count. Wirthlin refined these techniques in a "Political Information System" (PINS) for Reagan's 1980 presidential campaign. PINS—while providing accurate, coordinated, and timely strategic information to the campaign—also accurately forecast the election outcome. Wirthlin used PINS to predict Reagan's reelection in 1984.

As pollster to the President, Wirthlin refined a technique called "speech pulse." A small group of voters were asked to react to key phrases in presidential speeches using a hand-held device. Phrases that received very positive responses were dubbed "resonators," and were repeated in subsequent Reagan addresses.

Wirthlin's innovations have led to recognition by his peers. In 1981 he was named Adman of the Year by *Advertising Age*, the first poll taker so named. Many officeholders have sought his services. In 1981 one-half of all Republican U.S. Senators were Wirthlin clients.

*See also:* Elections of 1980 and 1984, Gerald R. Ford, Barry Goldwater, Ronald Reagan

*John K. White*

REFERENCES

Honomichl, Jack J. 1986. *Honomichl on Marketing Research*. Lincolnwood, IL: NTC Business Books.

Mayer, Jane, and Doyle McManus. 1988. *Landslide: The Unmaking of the President, 1984–1988*. Boston: Houghton Mifflin.

Perry, Roland. 1984. *Hidden Power: The Programming of the President*. New York: Beaufort Books.

White, John Kenneth. 1988. *The New Politics of Old Values*. Hanover, NH: U. Pr. of New England.

## Wisconsin Progressive Party

The key role played by Robert La Follette, Jr., and Philip La Follette in the formation in 1934 of the Wisconsin Progressive Party (1934–1946) speaks volumes about the initial fragility of the New Deal. In 1934 intelligent, practicing politicians—the heirs, in the case of the La Follettes, to a successful state political dynasty—could and did seriously believe that the New Deal's future was quite open. They strongly suspected that in 1936 a national third-party movement might well capitalize on discontent with the New Deal's supposedly palliative measures. The plausibility of this perception seems hard to fathom only if one assumes the inevitability of the New Deal's success.

The Progressive Party was patterned in large part after the Minnesota Farmer-Labor Party (1918–1944): indeed its founders considered naming their organization the Wisconsin Farmer-Labor Party. The left wing of the founding convention represented such forces as the Wisconsin Federation of Labor, radical farmers, and the Milwaukee Socialists. Eventually these forces grouped themselves into an organization that became known as the Farmer-Labor Progressive Federation. It was this constituency that was interested in a Wisconsin Farmer-Labor Party. But the founders opted for a label already familiar to the Wisconsin electorate. In rational terms, they opted for lower "transactions costs" with the Wisconsin electorate.

Until 1934 the La Follettes headed a liberal faction within the Wisconsin Republican Party known as "the Progressives." How well organized this faction was can be gauged from the ease with which the La Follettes and their local supporters switched to a new party and succeeded in electoral settings as third-party politicians, albeit with a familiar label.

Philip La Follette lost the Wisconsin governorship after a single term to a Democrat in 1932. But as a Progressive he won reelection in 1934 and 1936. The 1936 election was the height of the Progressive Party's electoral strength; it gained the Progressives solid control of the Wisconsin congressional delegation and it also gained control, if by a very thin margin, of the Wisconsin legislature. Although a bitter session, the 1937 legislative session led to a "little TVA," the Wisconsin Development Authority, a "little Wagner Act," and higher relief spending, among other measures. But in 1938 the Progressive Party broke apart and steadily lost strength until it closed shop in 1946. It did elect a governor in 1942, but he died before he could take office. In any case, he had plans for merging the Progressives and the Republicans.

The Progressive Party disintegrated in part because of Philip La Follette's somewhat bizarre effort in 1938 to create a national third party. Furthermore, the New Deal's intervention into Wisconsin's economy and society weakened the Progressive coalition in the same ways that the

New Deal weakened the Minnesota Farmer-Labor coalition. Although there is no strong evidence that Franklin Roosevelt intended the defeats of the Wisconsin and Minnesota third-party forces, he nonetheless took great satisfaction in those conquests.

*See also:* Philip La Follette, Robert M. La Follette, Jr., Minnesota Farmer-Labor Party

*Richard M. Valelly*

REFERENCES

Backstrom, Charles Herbert. 1956. "The Progressive Party of Wisconsin, 1934–1946." Ph.D. dissertation, University of Wisconsin.

Miller, John E. 1982. *Governor Philip F. La Follette: The Wisconsin Progressives and the New Deal.* Columbia: U. of Missouri Pr.

Rogin, Michael Paul. 1967. *The Intellectuals and McCarthy: The Radical Specter.* Cambridge: MIT Pr.

## Woman Suffrage Movement

The American political tradition, with its rich rhetoric of sovereignty, representation, and individual rights, denied that women had a right to vote. Until 1848 the denial rested on a consensus of silence. Beginning in that year, when Elizabeth Cady Stanton prevailed on a woman's rights meeting at Seneca Falls, New York, to come out for women's right to the franchise, politicians had to justify the exclusion of women from the body politic. At first the reasons had a tidy simplicity. Despite a commitment to "individualism," patriarchal attitudes lingered. "Individual" was taken to mean the head of a family, and through that head, women enjoyed virtual representation. The economic foundations of patriarchal politics remained. Indeed the states had only recently abandoned property qualifications that white heads of families had to meet in order to vote. When woman's claim to a right to vote was met with jokes about who would tend the hearth if women left home for the polls, the humor barely disguised men's inability to regard the sexes as alike in anything. Home life, along with the racial caste system, preserved strong vestiges of hierarchy in a nation still working out the ramifications of republicanism.

That simple but basic dilemma persisted as a constant personal issue and a pervasive cultural conflict. But the woman suffrage question moved to new terrain over the next 72 years, until ratification of the Nineteenth Amendment gave women the vote in 1920. During the Civil War, the meaning of U.S. citizenship emerged as a central political issue in the wake of emancipation of slaves, and women were able to make their claim for political rights as part of that debate. From Reconstruction onward, justifications for denying votes to women were drawn from American political discourse. They were expressed in terms of opportunities at the next election, of the extent of federal power, of the rights of states, of winning southern support, of holding urban voters, and of whether to expand or contract the electorate.

From the perspective of suffragists, this connection with national politics promised a more efficient resolution of their complaint, a clean enactment of law rather than the drawn-out changing of minds. Yet suffragists lacked the coinage that changed laws, and legislative action proved very difficult to achieve. The strategic possibilities open to suffragists changed not only with the platforms and behavior of politicians but also with their own steadily growing acceptance among women and their persistence as a presence in American politics. At no time in their protracted experiment with indirect influence on the political process did they have the help of a political party. Only in the very last years of the contest, when Woodrow Wilson came to their aid, did a powerful political figure stand by them and deliver his best. The major parties failed women as did the political culture. The fragmented and contradictory ways that Americans wrestled with political and economic inequities left suffragists isolated from other democratic movements. The record of support for woman suffrage from third parties is nearly as dismal as it was from the major parties. To the third parties (the Populists, for instance), some other alliance mattered more, usually the dream of gaining strength in southern states. Suffragists became willing participants in this politics of narrow self-interest. When they won their amendment in 1920, they walked away from the reality that most African-American women, sister suffragists since 1848, had won nothing at all. Those women had to fight on for 45 more years, until passage of the Voting Rights Act of 1965 assured them the vote.

At its inception the woman's rights movement derived a political strategy from the antislavery movement with which its supporters uniformly identified. Among William Lloyd Garrison abolitionists, women had gained near equality of action and opportunity, while that radical group's antielectoral methods allowed women full participation in reform. The movement's understanding of sexual equality derived from the particular analysis women made of their situation but found expression through the egalitarianism defined by abolitionists. Avoiding reference to the Constitution because of its implication in slavery, women relied on the Declaration of Independence as a text on perfect equality. Like Garrisonians they pursued change through moral suasion, trying to create a public educated to their own ideals. Political abolitionists perforce excluded women by relying on the ballot, yet their reasoning and their vision also shaped the immediate political experience of many woman's rights advocates. The inclusion of suffrage among the demands issued at Seneca Falls in 1848 thus spoke to an audience who valued the ballot for its uses as much as it expressed a symbolic capstone to the basic elements of civil equality.

Suffrage did not, however, emerge as the central element of reform during the antebellum years. It may have expressed the supreme equality of law, but suffrage took its place among many other reforms designed to eliminate women's legal disadvantages, while legal equality itself took its place beside a wide range of social and economic goals to achieve equal opportunity. In practice this sweeping program meant that activists were as likely to be agitating for access to education as for legal reform. And when lobbying state legislatures, they were as likely to press for change in laws of custody and property as for their enfranchisement.

The Civil War transformed the political culture from which suffragists drew their inspiration. At the start of the war woman's rights workers pulled back from confrontation over their own legal disabilities to redirect themselves as female abolitionists into national politics. They were carried into unprecedented roles by the transition of the antislavery movement from an extraparliamentary moral reform to a radical caucus of the party in power. For example, the Women's Loyal National League, headed by Susan B. Anthony and Stanton, took the lead in pressing Congress for a law to emancipate slaves. The campaign also led women through a critical change in expectations for the federal government once slavery had ended. Like Black politicians and abolitionists, the leading female politicians lost their fear of a southern-dominated national government and saw hope for equality through federal legislation.

Not until the Republican Party rejected universal suffrage was there need for a woman suffrage movement. Universal suffragists, men and women alike, campaigned in 1866 and 1867 to rid state laws of racial and sexual disenfranchisement and to frame a federal amendment that would protect a national, impartial right to vote. However, Republican leaders settled instead on the enfranchisement of African-American men. The ramifications of this situation for woman suffragism were tragic. Not only were woman's rights pitted against the rights of freedmen, but they were also categorically denied by careful use of the word "male" in provisions of the Fourteenth Amendment regarding congressional representation and, later, in the Fifteenth Amendment's specificity about not abridging rights on account of race and previous condition of servitude.

Woman suffragists divided among themselves in this crisis. One group stayed with the Republican Party. To them the proposed amendments were a necessary, if disappointing, solution to the immediate vulnerability of freedmen. When they formed the American Woman Suffrage Association (AWSA) in 1869, under the leadership of Lucy Stone and Henry Blackwell, suffragists envisaged a political movement that would work with Republicans and welcome male allies into its councils. In selecting tactics, Stone accepted Republican advice that suffragists prove the existence of a demand for suffrage by winning the right under state laws. The other major group of suffragists, under the leadership of Stanton and Anthony, took an independent course and campaigned against the amendments. They looked to build a political force expressing women's self-interest, independent of parties and men. They tried their hands at playing Democrats off against Republicans with some appalling consequences as they consorted with notorious racists who favored woman suffrage. They did, however, have some luck in identifying congressional supporters. Disregarding Republican caution, their National Woman Suffrage Association (NWSA) proposed a sixteenth amendment in 1869.

But not even Stanton and Anthony wholly abandoned Republican alliances during this period. Within the GOP the battles over Reconstruction were not over, and the chance to influence federal decisions remained promising. Two strategies developed, one judicial and one political. Francis and Virginia Minor, Republican suffragists in St. Louis, urged women to attempt to register to vote and file suit if their rights were denied. The Minors argued that the combined effect of the Fourteenth and Fifteenth amendments was to guarantee federal protection for voting rights as an essential element of national citizenship. Between 1868 and 1874 women followed their advice in dozens of towns from the District of Columbia to Washington Territory, and in several places they succeeded in voting. Virginia Minor herself was denied registration, and her case started through the courts.

Simultaneously Victoria Woodhull and Representative Benjamin Butler opened up a political front. Woodhull urged Congress at the end of 1870 to pass a declaratory act that would enfranchise women. Making an argument similar to the one advanced by the Minors, she emphasized that the federal government had included voting rights within the definition of national citizenship and committed itself to protect the rights of citizens against their abridgement by states. Reference to race in the Fifteenth Amendment was, by this argument, merely suggestive of forbidden discrimination and not an exclusive statement of entitlement. An act of Congress would complete what the Constitution now clearly intended.

The NWSA encouraged women to vote while it also directed a political campaign toward obtaining the declaratory act. The fact that powerful Republicans denied the claims of the Minors and Woodhull was immediately evident. John Bingham launched the counteroffensive with the majority report of the House Judiciary Committee against Woodhull's memorial. He denied that the Fourteenth and Fifteenth amendments changed the relations between state and federal governments or defined national citizenship. Although suffragists circulated Butler's able minority report to the House supporting their claim, Bingham's report reflected the party's dominant position. At the 1872 political conventions, suffragists appealed for planks in party platforms. The regular Republicans offered what suffragists called a "splinter," an expression of thanks for women's devotion to the cause of freedom and support for their progress toward "wider fields of usefulness." In the euphoria of the moment when a national party's platform mentioned women for the first time, suffragists campaigned for Ulysses S. Grant and were financed in their effort with party funds.

Susan B. Anthony's campaign contributions included voting for Grant and the Republican congressional ticket at Rochester, New York. She was promptly arrested by federal marshalls for illegal voting under the terms of the Enforcement Act of 1870. In a trial coordinated closely by Republican Roscoe Conkling, the narrowest interpretations of the Fourteenth and Fifteenth amendments were advanced to convict her. Undaunted, the NWSA continued to argue the case for national citizenship and a declaratory act until 1875 when the Supreme Court decided *Minor v. Happersett*, Virginia Minor's case against a St. Louis election official. In its most important decision on woman suffrage and a major step in the retreat from Radical Reconstruction, the Court rejected the claim that voting rights derived from the rights of citizenship and acknowledged no rights to suffrage that arose from the Constitution.

*Minor v. Happersett* was a critical moment in the history of the franchise. The voting rights of freedmen in the South were thenceforth sustained only by the slim reed of the Fifteenth Amendment, and the Court soon let stand various state restrictions on Blacks' right to vote. At the same time, the Court's decision isolated the vision of Radical Reconstruction outside mainstream politics where only radicals, woman suffragists among them, would keep alive the ideal of "national protection for national citizens." Not even woman suffragists themselves could stand united behind that phrase. The AWSA demurred from rousing its members to support a new federal amendment in 1876 on the grounds that voting rights were referred by the Constitution to the states.

Over the next 20 years no major party advanced principles on which suffragists could hope to hang their cause, and no third party endorsed suffrage to act as a lever against the major parties. What strength suffragists showed came from their work organizing women and from a few friends in key places. The NWSA clung to the goal of national citizenship. Marking centennials of the American Revolution, suffragists highlighted the contradictions in a nation that denied its women the very rights it rebelled to attain—women refused to pay taxes, women threw tea in Boston Harbor, women promulgated a new "woman's Declaration of Independence." With public attention turned in their direction, they mounted an elaborate campaign of petitions, hearings, and lobbying to win congressional support for a sixteenth amendment. In 1878 Senator Aaron Sargent introduced the amendment, which the Senate referred to the unfriendly Committee on Privileges and Elections. During the summer of 1880 the NWSA gathered some 10,000 signatures to prove to the political conventions that women wanted to vote. At Chicago they assembled hundreds of women to buttonhole Republican delegates; smaller groups lobbied at the Democratic and Greenback-Labor conventions. When the parties failed to support the cause, they went directly to the candidates. By 1882 senatorial suffragist sympathizers managed to create a Select Committee on Woman Suffrage, and the House followed suit. Both committees reported favorably on the bill.

Meanwhile, the AWSA pursued its state suffrage strategy. The possibility of incremental gains and the reality of nearly constant agitation did educate vast numbers of voters and women. Better than the NWSA federal strategy, state campaigns put a premium on building strong local associations and allowed greater engagement in suffrage work to the rank and file. Although the AWSA accommodated the Republican Party's wish to postpone a federal amendment, they gained no advantage in the states. No state granted suffrage to women before 1890, although the territories of Wyoming, Utah, and Washington did so. State referenda failed in Kansas in 1867, Michigan in 1874, Colorado in 1877, Nebraska in 1882, Oregon in 1884, Rhode Island in 1887, Washington in 1889, and South Dakota in 1890. To that number of defeats might be added countless campaigns to place referenda on ballots and to prompt state constitutional conventions to act. The AWSA could claim some progress in winning limited suffrage—local option, school, and municipal suffrage. In theory these gains could be used to pyramid the political power of women until congressional delegations elected by women would grant national suffrage. But in nineteenth-century practice, the few voting women failed to hold politicians accountable to the cause.

Both national associations benefited from alliances with new constituencies of women, particularly with the Woman's Christian Temperance Union (WCTU). Frances Willard, head of the WCTU, had always hoped for fusion between her evangelical crusaders and proponents of political rights, and by 1879 she had prevailed on her members to allow state locals to endorse suffrage. Susan B. Anthony courted the WCTU's membership because it comprised the largest and most powerful force of women in the country. The WCTU brought vast resources, a strong local base, and personal fervor on a scale that suffragists had never approached,

and temperance women had a strong southern membership.

Seeds of serious trouble were planted even while suffragists seemed to make progress in the 1880s. In Congress the consequences of post-Reconstruction reconciliation loomed to block the federal amendment. House suffragist sympathizers could not sustain support after 1882, and the bill received adverse reports in the next two Congresses. The Select Committee on Woman Suffrage moved more steadily and brought the amendment to a vote in 1887. Some 26 Senators absented themselves while the remaining body defeated the measure by a margin of two to one. Twenty-two of the 34 negative votes came from the Solid South. When James A. Garfield and Susan B. Anthony had argued in 1880 about Republican support for suffrage, Anthony had seen this trend on the horizon and scolded Garfield for his capitulation. In a private letter to him Anthony wrote, "The Republican party did run well for a season in the 'line of liberty.' But, alas, since 1870, its Congressional enactments, majority reports, Supreme Court Decisions, and now its Presidential platform, show a retrograde movement, (not only for woman, but for men of color) limiting the power of the National Government in the protection of United States Citizens against the injustice of the States."

Although Anthony's position suggested that suffragists had sustained an ethos of republicanism and an ideal of democracy through a period of national reaction, their alliance with temperance women seemed to contradict that mission. These newcomers to the cause did not share the heritage of Reconstruction. They rejected natural rights as a basis for women's politics and claimed not equality with men but superiority to them. They aspired to vote because the ballot would serve as a weapon to protect their own moral standard, not because, in Anthony's phrase, the ballot was "the right protective of all other rights."

By the end of the 1880s the suffrage movement distinguished itself neither as a symbol of democracy nor as a vital political force. This lack of clarity complicated the problem of finding allies. When the People's Party considered its platform during preliminary meetings through 1891, woman suffrage could not win acceptance despite the importance of women in the movement and the cooperation already established between Frances Willard and many principals of the Populist movement. Suffragists were blocked from two directions. If the People's Party endorsed woman suffrage, the South would be lost to their influence, or so the leaders reasoned. At the same time, the Populists regarded woman suffrage as a moral rather than a political question. Along with prohibition, suffrage might be a virtuous addition to the platform, but it was politically tangential. Populists were unable to connect their own political and economic agenda and the enfranchisement of half the people.

In 1890 the aging leaders of the American and National associations decided to merge their groups into a National American Woman Suffrage Association (NAWSA). The rivalries and differences born of Reconstruction came to an end in order to clear the way for a younger generation of leaders. A case can be made that the merger finished the campaign for a federal amendment. The AWSA's strong state associations, reinforced by ambivalence even in the NWSA, pushed the national group to the background. Anthony could not even prevail on the membership to retain her practice of yearly meetings in Washington to keep the amendment alive in Congress. In the new association, state campaigns took precedence, and members wanted annual meetings to serve as regional propaganda. But to place blame for the demise of a federal campaign on the NAWSA is to ignore Congress, where suffrage had fewer friends in the 1890s than at any time since the war. After 1887 the amendment had stayed alive until 1896 by heroic but fruitless effort. Reports to the Senate were favorable in 1889 and 1893 but came without recommendation in 1890 and 1896; the House committee favored the measure in 1890 and opposed it in 1894. With that faltering record the matter rested for nearly 20 years. The mounting disfranchisement of southern African-Americans and the North's tolerance of this violation of the Fourteenth and Fifteenth amendments precluded serious consideration of federal action to enfranchise women.

A few western victories followed the AWSA-NWSA merger—Colorado (1893), Idaho, and Utah (both 1896)—and sharpened suffragists' focus on states, but that wave also receded. No additional states enfranchised women until 1910. State political parties showed greater willingness than national ones to endorse the cause: Kansas Populists, California Republicans and Populists, all the major parties of Colorado, to name a few. But by and large political parties

ignored the movement rather than opposed it through the lull between 1896 and 1910. In that vacuum powerful interest groups came to the fore. In the South, opponents stirred fear of enfranchising Black women. In the North, resistance rose from the liquor industry and urban machines. These groups exploited a condition that suffragists themselves had created—their identification with Protestant nativism and middle-class morality. To liquor interests women personified temperance, and because temperance pitted itself against Catholicism, immigrants, and working-class subcultures, the industry had a considerable base susceptible to its political manipulation. The liquor industry also had money that it poured into state antisuffrage campaigns. To urban machines, the women represented reform, or "municipal housekeeping." Many of the same cultural and class divisions between suffragists and urban voters also opened the way for machines to define suffrage as against their own interests.

Against tougher opposition, the NAWSA pitted new political prowess. Carrie Chapman Catt emerged in the 1890s as the leader who understood both the need for tighter local structure and for national coordination of state action. State associations, previously auxiliaries in name, became so in fact as the NAWSA detailed their responsibilities for organizing from precinct to legislature and reserved to the national convention the decision about which states merited serious campaigns. Victories in Colorado and Idaho had validated the new style. And even in California, where suffragists lost a referendum in 1896, the campaign set new standards for women's participation and for saturation of the electorate. Although Catt herself resigned as NAWSA president in 1905, the Washington State victory in 1910 showed all the earmarks of a Catt campaign—massive mobilization, canny maneuvers around the opposition, and vigilance until the last ballot was counted. Bureaucracy updated the suffrage movement, but it hardly solved its problems. Neither Catt nor her successor, Anna Howard Shaw, established alliances that would provide suffragists with the power they needed to win.

Nonetheless, suffragism attracted new support during the very years when the movement lost momentum. And from new supporters came new ideas. The South finally began to move. The NAWSA took its annual meeting to Atlanta in 1895 and by 1903, all states in the region boasted suffrage associations. Although white-only societies were tolerated and states' rights became official policy in 1903, African-American women also gravitated to the movement. Newly organized into national federations, Black women saw in the suffrage movement not only the means to empower themselves but also the only political force concerned with expanding voting rights and thus, implicitly at least, asserting the importance of the ballot for all citizens. White southerners and African-Americans with their distinct and contradictory interests, each representing political communities whose values they brought into the suffrage movement, were extreme examples of a new trend. Other new groups included society women, immigrant women, wage earners, trade unionists, Socialists, professional women, and the new urban progressives. United on a single-issue platform, suffragists increasingly shared no other common political values or traditions.

If national coordination and leadership were to continue, the NAWSA's tactics had to take into account distinct political subcultures. The new groups wanted a voice in defining both the purposes of voting and the conduct of the movement. Jane Addams typified the new recruit to national leadership, as her Chicago constituency was typical of the new rank and file. She wielded considerable political power in Chicago and Illinois in the 1890s before coming to the suffrage movement, and she was fast developing her own idea of urban politics and the responsibilities of the state. Addams had constituencies among immigrant and laboring women around Hull House and among college students and philanthropists for whom she was already a heroine. With ample opportunity to initiate propaganda for suffrage, people like Addams needed the latitude to act within a coordinated framework.

Just such local power bases were the key to breaking away from the old methods of the suffrage movement. In Boston, New York, Chicago, and Philadelphia, second- and third-generation suffragists founded new societies, confident that their generation could set new directions. Like Harriot Stanton Blatch's League of Self-Supporting Women in New York, these groups categorized the diversity of suffragists to make use of common experiences and cultures. By 1910 most large cities boasted a choice of suffrage clubs, and in New York the clubs coordinated their efforts through an Interurban Council. Out of grass-roots initiative came new tactics too—open-air meetings, parades, automobile tours, and anything that would attract an audience and the press with its novelty as well as its message.

The leader who captured the imagination of the restless suffragists was Alice Paul, a new recruit with several years experience among British suffragists who decided to make suffrage her full-time job in 1912. As her first American contribution, she revived the proposal for a federal amendment, and by March 1914 she had pushed it to a vote in both the Senate and the House. Though she started out as a committee head within the NAWSA, the older leadership drove her out, and from 1913 she led rival organizations, the Congressional Union for Woman Suffrage and later, the National Woman's Party. Paul's British experience informed her strategy and tactics. Democrats in power, she reasoned, should be held accountable for their inaction and opposition to woman suffrage. Especially in states where they already voted, women should campaign against Democrats until prosuffragists in the Democratic Party prevailed. Her tactics were public and militant, designed to put the party in ever more awkward positions.

State suffrage continued to be the goal of the NAWSA. After the 1910 victory in Washington, the results of further campaigns were mixed. California gave women the vote in 1911, but of six state campaigns in 1912, only three succeeded. While Paul argued that a renewed federal campaign offered greater efficiency than unpredictable, repetitive state campaigns, the NAWSA faced southern opposition in its own membership and feared confrontation with Congress. In 1914 Republicans proposed a suffrage amendment that referred the matter to states, and the NAWSA endorsed it. Both amendments came before Congress in March 1914, and suffragists worked against each other in the debate that followed. From that low point, the NAWSA began to make concessions both to the livelier constituency that Paul represented and to the more hopeful political climate.

Carrie Chapman Catt returned to the NAWSA presidency in 1916, and although she and Alice Paul simply could not cooperate, Catt's implementation of a coherent strategy made it possible for the two groups to work in parallel. State campaigns took on greater value within a framework of congressional strategy. The campaigns of 1915 aimed to break the solid East by winning suffrage in New York, New Jersey, Pennsylvania, or Massachusetts. When all four elections were lost, Catt began right away to rebuild the movement in New York for 1917. That time women won, and the victory could be attributed to a new combination of factors. Not only had suffragists gained support from many ethnic voters and from the Socialist Party, but also Tammany Hall and the machine Democrats had decided not to join the antisuffrage forces. At the federal level such a victory changed minds, votes, and the numbers of representatives elected by women.

In their 1916 platforms Republicans and Democrats endorsed woman suffrage as good policy but steered clear of the federal amendment. To get leadership, the suffragists needed Woodrow Wilson. The NAWSA befriended him and worked closely with Cabinet officers, their wives, and women of the Wilson family. The Congressional Union for Woman Suffrage confronted him. Nothing short of endorsing woman suffrage would still their outspoken opposition to his administration. This combination of politeness and militance finally moved Wilson. In 1917 militant suffragists were arrested in the District of Columbia, jailed in secret without access to lawyers, and force-fed when they protested their treatment by fasting. The press, the public, and many politicians were outraged by the events. Slowly Wilson came to believe what had happened to the protestors and what the effects had been on public opinion. The nonmilitants were at hand to help him make the right decision, and he declared woman suffrage to be not only good legislation but also a necessary war measure.

The remaining political obstacles did not fall at once. By associating suffrage with the war, Wilson could at least turn Congress's full attention to the matter. But a Democratic President still faced the powerful opposition of southerners in his own party. At the same time the archenemy of suffrage in the Senate was Republican Henry Cabot Lodge, whose views on suffrage were no more representative of his party than Wilson's were. When voting began in 1918 it was regions more than parties that governed the results. The House voted first, on January 10, 1918, and passed the amendment by the two-thirds required. Despite Wilson's endorsement of the measure, Democrats divided, 104 against to 102 for passage, while Republicans carried it by voting strongly in favor. The Senate delayed a vote until September, when Wilson took bolder steps by addressing the body during debate on the measure. Sixty-two Senators supported the amendment, but Lodge managed to field 34 votes in opposition. Opposition came from the same quarters in both houses: the Northeast and the South. In the House, the South joined Massachusetts, Pennsylvania, New Jersey, and Ohio. In the Senate its allies were the New England Republicans and a scattered group of ardent states' rightists, several from states where women already voted.

By targeting four Democratic Senators in the 1918 election, suffragists defeated two and made their election contests very close for the others. With that example of their growing power, they tried one more time to gain Senate passage during the Sixty-fifth Congress. They were stronger but still one vote shy of victory. It remained for the Sixty-sixth Congress to carry the amendment. The House voted overwhelmingly in favor, and with telegraphic lobbying by Wilson from Paris, the measure squeaked through the Senate.

Ratification occurred in August 1920. The NAWSA remained fully mobilized to the end, following detailed plans laid out on the basis of their experience with the various state legislatures and governors in the past. Their lobbying skills were the best. Suffragists had not, however, won the South. With Wilson's help they had momentarily overwhelmed the obstacle of states' rights, but it remained a force among their own members as well as a crushing influence in national politics. By attaching the federal amendment to the national emergency of war, they had no need to revive the tradition that a federal amendment represented a principle about national citizenship.

Elections in 1920 revealed the cost of that change. The Nineteenth Amendment, no stronger than the Fifteenth, could not overcome barriers intended to deny voting rights to African-Americans. An estimated 5 million women could not exercise their newly won right. The exclusion was not complete. In an odd twist of history, some white suffragists boycotted the election to protest federal usurpation of state control over voting laws, while Black women went to the polls. Some states simply harassed women when they tried to register and a persistent Black voter could prevail. But the problem worsened, and the numbers of disfranchised Black women climbed during the decade. Black leadership and some white suffragists responded to the new discrimination immediately in the hope that the League of Women Voters (successor to the NAWSA) and the National Woman's Party would see a need to complete the job of enfranchisement. At annual meetings of both groups in 1921, proposals were made that Congress establish a commission to investigate enforcement of the Nineteenth Amendment. In the League the debate prompted southern whites to walk out, and the leadership decided that a strong League took precedence over equal rights. The National Woman's Party also failed to support the call for investigations. In a perverse application of their strict egalitarian faith, party members reasoned that Black women disfranchised on account of race had attained sexual equality with Black men.

Black suffragists at work between 1920 and 1965 could rarely afford to focus solely on the right to vote when basic legal protections and economic justice eluded them as well. Clearing the way to suffrage remained, nonetheless, an item of immense importance on a complex agenda for change.

*See also:* Abolition Movement, Susan B. Anthony, Benjamin Butler, Carrie Chapman Catt, Fifteenth Amendment, Ulysses S. Grant, League of Women Voters, Henry Cabot Lodge, National American Woman Suffrage Association, National Woman's Party, Alice Paul, People's Party, Populist (People's) Party, Slavery, Socialist Party of America, Elizabeth Cady Stanton, Lucy Stone, Tammany Hall, Voting Rights Act of 1965 and Extensions, Woodrow Wilson, Women's Christian Temperance Union, Victoria Woodhull

*Ann D. Gordon*

REFERENCES

Berry, Mary Frances. 1986. *Why the ERA Failed: Politics, Women's Rights, and the Amending Process of the Constitution.* Bloomington: Indiana U. Pr.

Buhle, Mari Jo, and Paul Buhle, eds. 1978. *The Concise History of Woman Suffrage: Selections from the Classic Work of Stanton, Anthony, Gage, and Harper.* Urbana: U. of Illinois Pr.

DuBois, Ellen Carol. 1978. *The Emergence of an Independent Women's Movement in America, 1848–1869.* Ithaca: Cornell U. Pr.

———. 1987. "Outgrowing the Compact of the Fathers. Equal Rights, Woman Suffrage, and United States Constitution, 1820–1878." 74 *Journal of American History* 836–862.

Flexner, Eleanor. 1975. *Century of Struggle: The Woman's Rights Movement in the United States.* Cambridge: Belknap Press.

Foner, Eric. 1987. "Rights and the Constitution in Black Life During the Civil War and Reconstruction." 74 *Journal of American History* 863.

Holton, Sandra Stanley. 1986. *Feminism and Democracy: Women's Suffrage and Reform Politics in Britain, 1900–1918.* New York: Cambridge U. Pr.

Lunardini, Christine A. 1986. *From Equal Suffrage to Equal Rights: Alice Paul and the National Woman's Party, 1910–1928.* New York: New York U. Pr.

Stanton, Elizabeth Cady, Susan B. Anthony, and Matilda Joslyn Gage. 1881–1886. *History of Woman Suffrage.* 3 vols. New York: Fowler and Wells.

## Woman's Christian Temperance Union

The Woman's Christian Temperance Union (WCTU) was established in 1874 by Annie Wittenmyer to transform a local temperance movement based on moral suasion into a national campaign for laws controlling the sale and consumption of alcohol. The organization was run solely by women who found it attractive because it appealed to them in their roles as keepers of the home. Ironically, the WCTU extended women's sphere of action while operating on the basis of their traditional domestic role, a fact most evident when Frances Willard became president in 1879. She turned the goal of temperance into a campaign for total social reform, arguing that injustice caused alcoholism. Willard also supported the extension of women's rights (equality in marriage and divorce) so that women would not be economically dependent on men. Claiming that they could not protect their home without a voice in public affairs, she encouraged members to support the suffrage movement. By doing so, she attracted conservative women, who would not ordinarily be drawn to progressive ideas, into innovative social action. These efforts also encouraged the liquor industry to finance opposition to suffrage.

In 1880 the organization established the Home Protection Party, which merged with the Prohibition Party in 1882 to form the Prohibition Home Protection Party. Their National Prohibition Party ran presidential candidates (1884–present), costing Republican James Blaine the election in 1884 and achieving their highest vote in 1892 (271,000 or 2.3 percent). After Willard's death in 1898, the WCTU joined with the Anti-Saloon League to elect supporters and acquire a prohibition amendment. The short-lived experience with the Eighteenth Amendment, accounted a failure by most, left them undaunted, and they continue their efforts to the present day.

*See also:* Anti-Saloon League, James G. Blaine

*Joy A. Scimé*

REFERENCES

Earhart, Mary. 1944. *Frances Willard: From Prayer to Politics.* Chicago: U. of Chicago Pr.

Gusfield, Joseph R. 1963. *Symbolic Crusade: Status Politics and the American Temperance Movement.* Urbana: U. of Illinois Pr.

Knight, Virginia C. 1976. "Women and the Temperance Movement." 70 *Current History* 201–203.

Kobler, John. 1973. *Ardent Spirits: The Rise and Fall of Prohibition.* New York: Putnam.

## Women's Equity Action League

One of the many organizations that emerged out of the new feminist movement of the 1960s, the Women's Equity Action League (WEAL) was created when Elizabeth Boyer and others expressed opposition to the "radical" platform of the National Organization for Women. Claiming that the organization was too militant, especially regarding abortion and homosexual rights, and its goals too diffuse, Boyer and her cohort withdrew and formed WEAL. They established goals that aimed to achieve equality and improvement of women's status through education, legislation, and litigation. Their specific projects were chosen to meet the immediate needs of their professional membership. Because many were lawyers, they focused on class action cases to establish precedent.

Early in its history, Bernice Sandler, chair of the Action Committee for Federal Compliance in Education, devised a plan to challenge discrimination in higher education. She saw the potential of Executive Order 11375 issued by President Lyndon B. Johnson in 1968 to forbid discrimination in federal contracts. In January 1970, WEAL requested an immediate class action and compliance review of all institutions holding federal contracts. The organization filed specific charges against educational institutions including the entire state university systems of California, Florida, and New Jersey. In October, it filed a class action suit against all medical schools. Within two years, 100 reports were prepared that documented sex discrimination. The action not only confirmed the problem as a legitimate one, but it also led to Title IX of the 1972 Higher Education Act that specifically prohibited discrimination on the basis of sex at all levels of education.

In 1972 WEAL established its national office in Washington, D.C., and created the WEAL Educational and Legal Defense Fund. The Fund supported legal costs for selected sex discrimination cases and enforcement of laws and financed information kits on laws, regulations, and the filing of complaints. A fund called SPRINT was established to bring sexual equality to sports.

Over the years, WEAL has joined coalitions with other women's groups and taken part in commissions on human rights and the status of women. The organization's interests have focused on the education and economic status of women and include efforts to end discrimination in tax laws, social security, and insurance policies. It has supported the protection of rights in hiring and promotion, flexible work hours, tax credits for child care, and the abolishment of sex-typed employment. WEAL also investigates discrimination in the military.

The group maintains a legislative division that monitors Congress, provides witnesses and research to congressional hearings, and lobbies for specific legislation. It not only acts as an advocate at all levels of government but also as a watchdog for the enforcement of laws. WEAL's work helped to achieve the 1974 Equal Credit Opportunity Act; the Pregnancy Disability Act of 1978, which later became an amendment to Title VII of the 1964 Civil Rights Act; and the Women's Equity Educational Act. Its membership remains committed to the achievement of reform through pragmatic means.

*See also:* National Organization for Women

*Joy A. Scimé*

REFERENCES

Cummings, Bernice, and Victoria Schuck, eds. 1979. *Women Organizing: An Anthology.* Metuchen, NJ: Scarecrow.

Gelb, Joyce, and Marian Lief Palley. 1982. *Women and Public Policies.* Princeton: Princeton U. Pr.

Tuttle, Lisa. 1986. *Encyclopedia of Feminism.* New York: Facts on File.

Wandersee, Winifred. 1988. *On the Move: American Women in the 1970s.* Boston: Twayne.

Williamson, Jane, Diane Winston, and Wanda Wooten. 1979. *Women's Action Almanac.* New York: Morrow.

## Women's Peace Party

Begun in 1915 in response to the war in Europe, the Women's Peace Party (WPP) marked the transition of the traditional peace movement in the United States, becoming a vehicle for broad economic, social, and political change. The WPP departed from earlier peace organizations that were premised upon maintenance of order and stability. Instead, while seeking peace, the WPP pursued domestic reform and political radicalism.

The WPP was an outgrowth of the Women's Peace Parade of August 29, 1914, in New York City. The parade was organized by Fanny Garrison Villard, the 70-year-old daughter of the abolitionist William Lloyd Garrison. Approximately 1,500 women in mourning dress marched silently down Fifth Avenue behind a peace flag. While those organizing the parade did not have a specific agenda, they did desire to express the right of women to oppose war. The parade was significant, however, in that it attracted veteran female activists to the peace movement—suffrage workers, social reformers, and labor leaders.

In January 1915, a party organizing convention in Washington, D.C., attracted such activists as Jane Addams, Carrie Chapman Catt, Charlotte Perkins Gilman, and Harriot Stanton Blatch. The organization that emerged, historian Roland Marchand claims, was based on "the solidarity of all women in an instinctive but rational opposition to war." The platform of the WPP welded the goals of peace and suffrage, arguing that women's political participation would significantly enhance the prospects for peace in the world. The WPP also called for democratic control of foreign policy, the elimination of the economic causes of war, and nationalization of armament factories.

The party's president was Jane Addams, the Quaker suffragist. Primarily an urban movement, the WPP had chapters in Boston, New York, San Francisco, Chicago, Philadelphia, and St. Louis. Ambitious in its pursuit of peace, a WPP delegation attended an International Congress of Women at The Hague in April 1915 in hopes of securing an independent diplomatic means to end the war.

By 1916 and 1917, the strength and influence of the WPP had waned. The increasing sympathy for the Entente, the breaking of diplomatic relations with Germany, and eventual entry into the conflict, did little to increase the appeal of the WPP's opposition to military preparedness and demands for new peace initiatives. In this atmosphere, suffragists began to distance themselves from the WPP, disavowing peace activities as threatening to undermine their cause. With numerous state referenda approaching, Carrie Chapman Catt, president of the National American Woman Suffrage Association, resigned her position in the WPP and ceased to appear at its functions.

The WPP continued to exist after the United States entered the war, but its antiwar activity ceased. After the armistice, it resumed activities and participated in the Women's International Congress in Zurich in 1919. Later in 1919, the WPP became the American arm of the Women's International League for Peace and Freedom, a group that still existed during the Vietnam War.

*See also:* Carrie Chapman Catt, William Lloyd Garrison, National American Woman's Suffrage Association

*Susan L. Roberts*

REFERENCES

Marchand, C. Roland. 1972. *The American Peace Movement and Social Reform, 1898–1918*. Princeton: Princeton U. Pr.

Steinson, Barbara J. 1982. *American Women's Activism in World War I*. New York: Garland.

## Fernando Wood (1812–1881)

First of the modern Tammany Hall political bosses. During the Civil War, Fernando Wood was a leader of the Democratic Party's peace faction, unflatteringly known as the Copperheads. During 1839 and 1840 he was chairman of the young men's committee of Tammany Hall, leading to his election to a term in the U.S. Congress from 1841 to 1843. He devoted the period from 1844 to 1850 to making money as a successful merchant.

During the 1840s, immigration was swelling New York City as well as the political activity of the Society of Saint Tammany (Tammany Hall). Tammany was increasingly coterminous with the city's Democratic Party organization. As were other Democrats in New York State, Tammany was split between Barnburners (strictly opposed to slavery) and Hunkers (tolerant of the institution of slavery). Carefully exploiting the factional differences, Wood emerged as Tammany's nominee for mayor in 1850, only to be defeated in the election.

After 1850 some Barnburners who had bolted the party in 1848 to support former President Martin Van Buren returned to join with certain Hunker elements to become the Softshell faction. The Hardshells were those who refused to readmit the Barnburners. In Tammany Hall, the factions literally fought pitched battles to gain control of the hall and the city government. The Softshells gained the upper hand, received most of the local patronage from the Franklin Pierce administration, and, in 1854, elected the mayor and, as the first of the Tammany bosses, launched as corrupt an administration as the city had yet seen.

When Tammany reformers under the leadership of Samuel J. Tilden defeated Wood's reelection, Wood departed to form his own Mozart Hall organization, which helped elect him mayor again in 1859. In 1858 Wood contributed substantial funds to the senatorial campaign of Stephen A. Douglas in Illinois over the objection of the James Buchanan forces. He later tried to bring together a fusion of the Douglas and John Breckinridge slates after the 1860 national conventions.

Once the Civil War began, Wood became the eastern leader of the Peace Democrats, thus aligning himself with Clement L. Vallandigham of Ohio, the midwestern leader. At one point, Mayor Wood proposed that New York City declare itself a "free city," taking itself and its lucrative port revenues out of the Union. Wood was elected to the House of Representatives for the 1863–1865 term and, subsequently, over the period from 1867 to 1881.

*See also:* Barnburners, James Buchanan, Copperheads, Steven A. Douglas, Hunkers, Peace Democrats, Tammany Hall, Samuel Tilden, Clement L. Vallandigham, Martin Van Buren

*Ralph M. Goldman*

REFERENCES

Myers, Gustavus. 1901. *The History of Tammany Hall.* New York: Published by the author.

Werner, M. R. 1932. *Tammany Hall.* Garden City, NY: Garden City Publishing.

## Leonard Wood (1860–1927)

U.S. Army general and Republican presidential contender. Leonard Wood represents the prototypical victim of the "smoke-filled room" of early-twentieth-century American politics, and his failure to get the Republican Party nomination for President in 1920, despite having led on each of the first five ballots, accurately reflects upon the nominating system of his time.

Unlike today, when performance in the primary season is tantamount to party nomination, in Wood's day primaries were usually empty affairs. Hence, although he collected nearly five times as many primary votes as did actual party nominee (and eventual President) Warren Harding, Wood met with defeat on the convention's tenth roll call.

Unfortunately for Wood, California Senator Hiram Johnson, one of three other major Republican candidates, split the party's Progressive wing, thus blocking Wood from attaining the 493 votes needed to nominate. A strong-willed Progressive from New Hampshire, Wood never stood a legitimate chance with party chieftains once the proceedings moved from the floor of the Chicago convention hall into the legendary "smoke-filled room." There, history has it, the GOP's conservative leaders deliberated throughout the night, ultimately deciding upon Harding, who was certain to go along with their program, as a compromise choice.

Many of Wood's greatest accomplishments occurred two decades earlier when, as military governor of U.S.-occupied Cuba, he played the leading role in inaugurating a new school system, expanding public works projects, introducing municipal government, and reforming the prisons—all in just two-and-a-half years on the island.

A Harvard medical school graduate, former Army surgeon, and Medal of Honor recipient, Wood later served as major general of the regular Army, governor general of the Philippines, and, for a brief period, as chief of staff. Fort Leonard Wood in Missouri is named in his honor.

*See also:* Election of 1920, Warren G. Harding, Hiram Johnson

*Geoffrey H. Simon*

REFERENCES

Goldinger, Carolyn, ed. 1987. *Presidential Elections Since 1789.* Washington: Congressional Quarterly.

Hagedorn, Herman. 1931. *Leonard Wood.* New York: Harper & Row.

Lane, Jack. 1978. *Armed Progressive: General Leonard Wood.* San Raphael, CA: Presidio Press.

Socha, Evamarie, ed. 1987. *National Party Conventions: 1831–1984.* Washington: Congressional Quarterly.

Wayne, Stephen J. 1984. *The Road to the White House: The Politics of Presidential Elections.* New York: St. Martin's.

## Leonard F. Woodcock (1911– )

Labor leader and diplomat. Born in Providence, Rhode Island, to a British immigrant family, Leonard Freel Woodcock attended British schools while his father was interred in Germany during World War I after going there to seek employment in 1914. Woodcock returned to the United States in 1926 and attended Wayne State University and the Walsh Institute of Accountancy in Detroit. He turned to machine assembly, joined a plant union that became the United Automobile Workers Union (UAW) in the late 1930s, and rose in its ranks. He was staff representative to the UAW (1940–1946), regional director in Michigan (1947–1955), vice president responsible for General Motors and aerospace divisions (1955–1970), and president of the UAW upon the death of his mentor and predecessor Walter Reuther.

The executive board of the union appointed Woodcock to succeed Reuther in May 1970 when Douglas Fraser, another vice president, withdrew from contention. The UAW was then the second largest and perhaps the most socially conscious union in America. As vice president in charge of GM, Woodcock, a longtime member of the American Civil Liberties Union, the Urban League, and the NAACP, had won the first clause barring racial discrimination in employment among that company's UAW workers. President John Kennedy had once offered him sub-Cabinet and ambassadorial positions, all of which Woodcock refused. In 1968, after Robert Kennedy announced his candidacy for the presidency, Woodcock rallied to his support, as did others of the UAW's secondary leadership. The more cautious Reuther chose not to lean toward any one of the Democratic contenders.

In his first press conference after his selection as UAW president, Woodcock stood by Reuther's agenda, condemning the Vietnam War. Thereafter, he went to Atlanta to participate in a "march against repression" led by the Southern Christian Leadership Conference and to a United Nations–sponsored conference on environmental pollution. A low-keyed, less exuberant speaker than Reuther, Woodcock maintained that the chief role of the UAW was to serve its members and secondarily to foster the good of society as a whole. He continued the union's active involvement in Democratic politics after his election by the general membership in 1972.

After his endorsement of Jimmy Carter in 1976, Woodcock was appointed chief American liaison officer to Peking (1977–1979). After the establishment of formal diplomatic relations, Woodcock became the first American ambassador to the People's Republic of China (1979–1981). Since 1981 he has been an adjunct professor at the University of Michigan.

*See also:* American Civil Liberties Union, Election of 1976, John F. Kennedy, Robert F. Kennedy, National Association for the Advancement of Colored People, United Nations, Vietnam War as a Political Issue

*Frederick J. Augustyn, Jr.*

REFERENCES

Cormier, Frank, and William J. Eaton. 1970. *Reuther.* Englewood Cliffs, NJ: Prentice-Hall.

Fink, Gary M., ed. 1984. *Biographical Dictionary of American Labor.* Westport, CT: Greenwood.

## Victoria Woodhull (1838–1927)

Radical feminist. Victoria Woodhull's stormy career repeatedly violated the boundaries of conventional thought and behavior that defined the woman's sphere in Gilded Age America. An Ohio-born daughter of eccentric backcountry drifters, Woodhull experienced mystic visions from early childhood and grew up in an aura of spiritualist possibilities. Her maturing personal ambition survived an early marriage, motherhood, and divorce. Adventurous and beautiful,

she attracted a sequence of male admirers who introduced her to a broad range of utopian reform causes.

In 1868 she moved her entourage to New York City. There, she and her sister, Tennessee Claflin, befriended Cornelius Vanderbilt, who helped launch them on a brief, bizarre career in stock market speculation. Next Woodhull turned to politics. Converted by the radical thinker Stephen Pearl Andrews to his vision of Pantarchy—a perfect state of free thought and free love among free individuals—she declared herself a candidate for President in 1870. A newspaper, *Woodhull & Claflin's Weekly*, promoted her cause, which now intersected with the woman suffrage movement. In 1871 she appeared before a congressional committee to demand immediate recognition of women's voting rights, and she entered into momentary alliance with Susan B. Anthony. After breaking with Anthony, Woodhull had herself nominated for President by her Equal Rights Party in 1872. But her decision to expose the sensational Beecher-Tilton adultery case (Henry Ward Beecher was a prominent Congregationalist minister, Mrs. Tilton the wife of one of his colleagues) in her newspaper landed her in jail on election day, charged with passing obscenity through the mails. Though acquitted, she found that her career as an exponent of female self-determination had peaked. In 1877 she moved with her sister to England, where they both married into respectable affluence.

*See also:* Susan B. Anthony, Women's Suffrage

*Geoffrey Blodgett*

REFERENCES

Johnston, Johanna. 1967. *Mrs. Satan: The Incredible Saga of Victoria C. Woodhull.* New York: Putnam's.

Sachs, Emanie. 1928. *"The Terrible Siren": Victoria Woodhull, 1838–1927.* New York: Harper.

Smith, Page. 1970. *Daughters of the Promised Land: Women in American History.* Boston: Little, Brown.

Stern, Madeleine, ed. 1974. *The Victoria Woodhull Reader.* Weston, MA: M&S Press.

## Hubert Work (1860–1942)

Republican politician in the 1920s. Hubert Work won his M.D. from the University of Pennsylvania and, after he established his medical practice, became involved in Colorado Republican Party affairs. He attended the national convention of 1908 as a delegate-at-large from Colorado, was elected Republican state chairman in 1912, and served as national committeeman from 1913 until his appointment to the Post Office Department. At the outbreak of World War I, Work volunteered for service in the Army's Medical Corps.

In 1922, when Will Hays resigned as national chairman and Postmaster General to accept the presidency of the Motion Picture Producers and Distributors of America, he enthusiastically recommended to President Harding that Dr. Work become Postmaster General. Work had administrative talents comparable to those of Hays. He reduced the deficit of the Post Office Department from $81 million in 1921 to $24 million in 1923 without any increase in postal rates.

When the crooked Albert B. Fall resigned as Secretary of the Interior in 1923, President Harding asked Work to take on the difficult task of cleaning up the scandal-ridden department. President Calvin Coolidge kept him on as Secretary of the Interior. When Herbert Hoover announced that he would make the race for the presidential nomination in 1928, Work was the first member of the Cabinet to declare his support.

The national committee was particularly interested in influencing Hoover's choice of a national chairman and created a Special Committee of Twenty-four to advise the nominee. The recommendation was Secretary of the Interior Work. Work encountered many personality conflicts during the management of the campaign and quietly reduced his participation. President Hoover subsequently offered Work the ambassadorship to Japan in 1929, but Work decided to return to his medical practice.

*See also:* Calvin Coolidge, William Hays, Herbert Hoover, Republican National Committee

*Ralph M. Goldman*

REFERENCES

Hoover, Herbert. 1952. *The Cabinet and the Presidency, 1920–1933: The Memoirs of Herbert Hoover.* New York: Macmillan.

## Fielding L. Wright (1895–1956)

Vociferous advocate of racial segregation. A Mississippi state legislator from the conservative and aristocratic Delta region, house speaker, lieutenant governor, and governor, Fielding Lewis Wright was selected as the vice presidential candidate for the States' Rights Party in 1948.

In his January 1948 inaugural address, Wright attacked President Harry Truman's civil rights commission, calling its proposals antisouthern and accusing national Democratic leaders of taking the South for granted. At the February Southern Governors' Conference, he urged immediate dissociation from the Democratic Party and sought a meeting of "true Democrats" in Jackson, Mississippi. After that Jackson meeting, Wright became honorary chairman of a People's Committee of Loyal States' Rights Jeffersonian Democrats, which engaged in fundraising and publicizing of the southern cause.

In May over 1,000 states' rights Democrats met in Jackson, with South Carolina governor Strom Thurmond as its keynote speaker, and made plans to meet in Birmingham, Alabama, after the Democratic National Convention. In late June the Mississippi state Democratic convention selected Wright as a national Democratic convention delegate and instructed all delegates to walk out of the convention if Truman was nominated.

The Birmingham States' Rights convention in July selected as its nominees the only two southern governors in attendance—Thurmond as President and Wright as Vice President. Its platform stressed states' rights as embodied in the Tenth Amendment to the Constitution. The candidates accepted the nomination at a states' rights rally in Houston, Texas in August. During the campaign, Wright cited Thomas Jefferson's support for states' rights and attacked the increasing centralization of power in Washington as a prelude to totalitarianism. The party carried only four southern states in which Thurmond and Wright were listed on the ballot as the official Democratic Party nominees.

*See also:* Election of 1948, States' Rights Party, Strom Thurmond, Harry S Truman

*Stephen D. Shaffer*

REFERENCES

Garson, Robert. 1974. *The Democratic Party and the Politics of Sectionalism, 1941–1948.* Baton Rouge: Louisiana State U. Pr.

Hilliard, Elbert Riley. 1959. "A Biography of Fielding Wright: Mississippi's Mr. State Rights." M.A. thesis, Mississippi State University.

Sumners, Cecil L. 1980. *The Governors of Mississippi.* Gretna, LA: Pelican.

## James C. Wright (1922– )

First Speaker of the U.S. House of Representatives forced to resign in mid-session. Jim Wright became Speaker of the U.S. House of Representatives at a time when partisanship in the U.S. Congress was reaching modern highs and at a time when the Speaker's office was regaining much of its past political strength. Ironically, despite (or because of) the expansion of the

Speaker's powers in the 1980s, Jim Wright found himself embroiled in ethical questions about his financial dealings.

James Claude Wright, Jr., was born in Fort Worth, and after serving in the Army Air Corps during World War II, he returned to Texas, where he began his political career as a member of the Texas House of Representatives following the 1946 election. He was denied renomination to his seat two years later but reentered politics in 1950 when he was elected mayor of Weatherford, a small town near Fort Worth. Wright used his position as mayor as a base in the contest for the U.S. House of Representatives from the Twelfth Congressional District of Texas in 1954; and Wright won his House seat by defeating the incumbent in the 1954 Democratic primary by a surprisingly comfortable margin. He was rarely opposed in future Democratic primaries, his closest general election occurring in 1980 when he garnered only 60 percent of the vote.

In 1961 Wright ran to fill Lyndon Johnson's unexpired Senate term. The nonpartisan primary featured 71 declared candidates, and Wright finished third, failing by 20,000 votes (of 1 million cast) to reach the runoff. The winner of the subsequent runoff, John Tower, was Texas's first Republican Senator since Reconstruction. Wright continued to entertain senatorial ambitions, entering the regular 1966 senatorial election to challenge Tower. Because Wright was able to raise only $48,000 of the $500,000 he believed necessary to wage a credible campaign, he was forced to abandon the race.

Wright's Senate candidacies in the 1960s produced a great irony about his subsequent career. On the one hand, his failure to raise necessary campaign funds in 1966 and the ability of his major opponents in 1961 and 1966 to get tremendous sums from business interests made Wright an opponent of "fat cat" campaign contributions and a supporter of campaign finance reform. On the other hand, the debt that he incurred in these Senate races also encouraged him to pay more attention to raising funds for his election campaigns and to pursue outside business interests.

In the initial years of his House career Wright developed a reputation as one who paid close attention to his Texas constituency, staking out positions in favor of a large defense establishment and western water projects. Beginning in 1955 Wright began service on the House Public Works Committee. He became an active champion of Texas water projects, including one particularly controversial project that transformed Fort Worth into a seaport. Had Wright not been elected Majority Leader after the 1976 congressional election, he would have become the chairman of the Public Works Committee instead.

Moreover, Wright was a constituently strong defender of the U.S. military and defense efforts. During the 1960s and early 1970s he was a determined supporter of the Vietnam War. Throughout his House service Wright demonstrated strong support for various military aircraft, especially those manufactured by General Dynamics, which had a plant close to his district.

Although Wright staked out positions in favor of a strong national defense and plentiful public works programs, he was also noted for being one of the few consistently pro-labor southern Democrats. Throughout his career he showed himself to be one of the most liberal southern Democrats, a stance that put him in the middle of the House Democratic Party. Wright's moderate ideas aided his rise within the ranks of House Democrats in the 1970s and 1980s.

Jim Wright was elected House Majority Leader following the 1976 congressional election in one of the classic leadership races in the history of the House. Wright faced a formidable field of three other aspirants to succeed Tip O'Neill (Mass.). John J. McFall (Calif.) had previously been the Democratic Whip and under emerging precedent could have expected to become party leader. Yet McFall had been implicated in the "Koreagate" scandal earlier in 1976, and many rank-and-file Democrats believed that he would be a liability as the chief spokesman for the party in the House. Both John Burton (Calif.) and Richard Bolling (Mo.), his other opponents, were noted liberal reformers, though of different political generations.

Wright was aided in his 1976 race for the majority leadership by two factors: northern liberals split their initial support between Bolling and Burton; and certain big-city delegations, notably Chicago and Philadelphia, reportedly supported Wright. Three ballots of the Democratic Caucus were necessary to narrow down the field to a head-to-head duel between Wright and Burton. Wright won by one vote (148–147). (Some speculated that Burton's supporters had thrown their votes to Wright on the second ballot, hoping to set up a final contest between Burton and Wright and avoid a final confrontation between Burton and Bolling. Burton denied using this strategy.)

Wright spent his entire tenure as Majority Leader shoring up his political support within the party and planning his ultimate ascent to the speakership. Thus when it became known that O'Neill would retire after the 1986 election, Wright was able to announce in January 1985—two years before the speakership election—that he already had commitments from a majority of Democrats. Wright was chosen by the Democrats for the House speakership by acclamation after rumors that he would be challenged by Illinois' Dan Rostenkowski proved groundless.

As Speaker, Wright continued the heightened partisanship that had characterized much of O'Neill's speakership. Because Wright was closer to the center of the Democratic Party than O'Neill, he was perhaps even better able to bring conservative Democrats along with the party leadership. Wright announced a program at the beginning of 1987 that was meant to be a response to the conservative legacy of Ronald Reagan, and he was largely successful in promoting it in the House. As the 1988 election approached, Wright supported efforts by Democrats to craft a Democratic alternative to President Reagan's programs and to get them passed by the House, usually accompanied by howls from House Republicans.

The best known of Wright's efforts to build a partisan counter to Ronald Reagan's policy initiatives was his plan for a resolution to military tensions in Central America. Frustrated with what he perceived to be an unwillingness of many top administration officials to assist a peace initiative that had been suggested by Central American leaders, Wright launched his own negotiation sessions with Nicaraguan president Daniel Ortega and Nicaraguan cardinal Miguel Obando y Bravo in November 1987. Once these meetings became known, administration officials and Republican members of Congress accused Wright of unconstitutionally meddling in foreign policy. Eventually the controversy died down, with Wright reaching an accord with the administration over the U.S. Government's approach to negotiations in the region. But congressional Republicans clearly resented Wright's efforts and frequently used them as evidence that Wright was leading the Democrats on a path of congressional usurpation of executive powers; Wright later traced his own downfall directly to this episode.

Wright resigned the speakership and his House membership in the middle of 1989 amid allegations that he had profited unethically from a series of financial involvements with a Fort Worth developer, George Mallick, and from a scheme to circumvent limitations on outside income through a special deal to publish Wright's book *Reflections of a Public Man*. The allegations against Wright were investigated by the House Committee on Standards of Official Conduct (Ethics Committee), which released a critical report on Wright's financial dealings in April 1989. Although Wright initially attempted to fight the allegations, he eventually announced his retirement from the speakership. Because the Democratic Majority Leader, Tony Coelho, was also embroiled in ethical problems of his own, Wright was eventually succeeded in the speakership by House Majority Whip Thomas Foley.

*See also:* Richard Bolling, Tony Coelho, Thomas Foley, Lyndon B. Johnson, Thomas P. O'Neill, Ronald Reagan, Speaker of the House, John Tower

*Charles Stewart III*

# XYZ

## XYZ Affair

In the fall of 1797, John Marshall, Charles Cotesworth Pinckney, and Elbridge Gerry were sent by President John Adams to France to negotiate a treaty of amity and commerce. The treaty was necessary because of the crisis in Franco-American relations caused by French reaction to the Jay Treaty. The French minister of Foreign Relations, Charles-Maurice de Talleyrand-Périgord, insisted that an American loan and a bribe be made before any talks began. The American ministers refused, and when the correspondence on this shady dealing was made public in the spring of 1798, it resulted in such a surge of national pride that Adams and the Federalists gained greatly in the ensuing elections and were raised to their apex in popularity, much to the dismay of Thomas Jefferson and the Democratic-Republicans.

Marshall and Pinckney arrived in revolution-ridden Paris on September 27, 1797, and were joined there by Gerry on October 4. Soon thereafter, the American ministers learned that the French Directory had been offended by remarks President Adams had made on May 16 during a special session of Congress and that they would not be received officially until they had placated the Directory with both a bribe and a loan. The price was steep, a bribe of about $250,000 and a loan of $12 million. The Americans did offer to return to America and receive further instructions if France would, in the meantime, restrain its ships from attacking American shipping. France refused, and the talks were at a standstill.

At home, President Adams had resolved to continue his resistance to France. When he received the first of the dispatches outlining the reasons for the failed talks, he determined that no alternative remained between war and humiliation. Since Congress was unlikely to vote such a declaration, he removed the most belligerent passages from his message to Congress. Though his message of March 19 did not call for war, it did declare that a state of limited hostilities did exist between the two nations.

Reaction to the President's message was swift. Republicans claimed that it was absurd to take the side of Britain. On March 27, they called a caucus to plan their strategy. They adopted the Sprigg Resolutions, which declared that Adams acted inexpediently to declare war on France and that private ships should not be armed. They also insisted that Congress be given the complete test of the commissioner's dispatches. This was adopted by a vote of 65 to 27 by Congress on April 2. It was a decision they would soon regret as the dispatches showed the extent to which France had corrupted the American mission. Popular feeling turned against France, and the Democratic-Republicans, and Alexander Hamilton claimed that the opposition was totally destroyed. The political effect was soon forthcoming, as the elections for the Sixth Congress were determined to a large extent by the XYZ affair, and they gave the Federalists control of both houses for the first time since 1793.

*See also:* John Adams, Federalists, Elbridge Gerry, Charles Cotesworth Pinckney

*Daniel Dean Roland*

REFERENCES

Butterfield, Lyman H. 1961. *Diary of Autobiography of John Adams*. Cambridge: Harvard U. Pr.

Chambers, William Nisbett. 1963. *Political Parties in a New Nation*. New York: Oxford U. Pr.

Charles, Joseph. 1956. *The Origins of the American Party System*. Williamsburg: Inst. of Early American History and Culture.

Cunningham, Noble. 1957. *The Jeffersonian Republicans: The Formation of Party Organization, 1789–1801*. Chapel Hill: U. of North Carolina Pr.

De Conde, Alexander. 1966. *Quasi-War: The Politics and Diplomacy of the Undeclared War with France, 1797–1801*. New York: Scribner's.

Ford, Paul Leicester. 1892–1899. *Thomas Jefferson, Writings*. New York: Putnam's.

Hamilton, Stanislaus Murray. 1898–1903. *James Monroe, Writings*. New York: Putnam's.

Hunt, Gaillard. 1898–1910. *James Madison, Writings*. New York: Putnam's.

Miller, John C. 1960. *The Federalist Era*. New York: Harper.

Syrett, Harold. 1961–1987. *Papers of Alexander Hamilton*. New York: Columbia U. Pr.

## Daniel Yankelovich (1924– )

Prominent and unusual public opinion pollster. Daniel Yankelovich was born in Boston and received his B.A. and M.A. degrees in philosophy and psychology respectively from Harvard and did postgraduate work in philosophy at the Sorbonne. On returning to the United States in 1952, he began a career in marketing research. In 1958 he founded his own company, Daniel Yankelovich, Incorporated, eventually known as Yankelovich, Skelley, and White. Unlike most of the other well-known pollsters, Yankelovich has not made his mark doing surveys for and about politics and elections, though his predictions about presidential campaigns are frequently among the most accurate.

Instead, he has focused on the major changes of our age and how individuals cope with them. In *Ego and Instinct* (1969), Yankelovich argued that psychologists and philosophers had to work together and devise new models to help individuals cope with a changing world. In his most controversial book, *New Rules: Searching for Fulfillment in a World Turned Upside Down* (1981), he documented the decline of self-centered, indulgent, and even hedonistic values after the late 1960s.

Politically, Yankelovich has concentrated on understanding those important periods in American history when often fleeting and volatile public opinion turns into deeply held values about principle—something he calls public judgments, which, in turn, facilitate fundamental change in public policy. As an outgrowth of his polling work and his commitment to public service, Yankelovich and Cyrus Vance formed the Public Agenda Foundation in 1975 in an attempt to help people come to those kinds of informed decisions about vital issues through grass-roots education and dialogue.

In the 1980s, Yankelovich has been best known for his surveys about national security in both the United States and the Soviet Union. Along with a number of colleagues in both countries, Yankelovich has organized a joint project to investigate how attitudes about the arms race and questions of national security in general have changed since the early 1980s. In his book *Starting with the People* (1988), which he wrote with Sidney Harmon, Yankelovich details how Americans have reached judgments about the arms race and the Soviet Union that leave most people sharply at odds with government policy.

*Charles S. Hauss*

## Andrew J. Young, Jr. (1932– )

Leading civil rights activist and African-American political leader. Andrew Jackson Young, Jr. (called Andy) began his career in 1961 as a voter registration drive worker for the United Church of Christ (where he is an ordained minister). While engaged in this work, Young met Martin Luther King, Jr., and joined the Southern Christian Leadership Conference. In 1964 he became executive director of that organization and, after King's death executive vice president, second in command behind the Reverend Ralph Abernathy. While working for SCLC, Young helped draft the Civil Rights Act of 1964 and the Voting Rights Act of 1965.

Civil rights activism led Young into politics. A Democrat, Young became the first Black to represent Georgia in Congress since the end of Reconstruction when Atlanta's predominantly white Fifth Congressional District elected him to the United States House of Representatives in 1972. Reelected in 1974 and 1976, Young became an influential and effective leader largely owing to his willingness to negotiate and compromise. He served on the prestigious Rules Committee and the Banking and Currency Committee. His key areas of interest included federally funded rapid transit, housing for low income families, and the passage of the Equal Rights Amendment along with the maintenance and expansion of civil rights legislation.

While representing his district in the House, Young also developed a close relationship with Georgia's Jimmy Carter, advising him in his campaigns for governor of Georgia in 1970 and for President in 1976. Once elected President, Carter appointed Young United States ambassador to the United Nations, where he served until August 1979, when press revelations of his unauthorized meeting with representatives of the Palestine Liberation Organization forced his resignation. As ambassador, Young served as a strong spokesperson for the needs and interests of the Third World. Moreover, as the most influential African-American in Carter's administration, Young successfully pushed for better relations between the United States and Third World nations, especially those on the African continent.

In 1981 Young became the first Black mayor of Atlanta, Georgia, narrowly defeating white city council member Sidney Marcus in a bitter contest that split Atlanta along racial lines. Since winning office, however, Young expanded his base by gaining the support of Atlanta's white business community because of his successful policies. He is credited with creating an atmosphere conducive not only to economic growth but also to racial cooperation. In 1985, facing only token opposition, he won reelection with over 80 percent of the vote. Young also continues to have an influential voice in national Democratic politics where he is seen as a moderate realist.

*See also:* Jimmy Carter, Martin Luther King, Jr., Voting Rights Act of 1965 and Extensions

*Roberta Sue Alexander*

REFERENCES

Gardner, Carl. 1978. *Andrew Young; A Biography.* New York: Drake Publishers.

## Coleman A. Young (1918– )

First African-American mayor of Detroit. Coleman Alexander Young has also been one of the nation's longest-serving mayors. First elected in 1973, he won a record fifth term in 1989.

Detroit's politics is characterized by limited party organization and a strong union movement. The city's increasing Black population led to a near victory for an African-American mayoral candidate in 1969. In 1973 State Senator Coleman Young, a vocal and effective champion of labor, progressive, and minority causes, decided to seek the mayoralty. The union movement was caught between the white and Black communities, eventually providing little imme-diate support for Young. Young won because Black population and mobilization had increased substantially, but his base of white support was the lowest obtained by winning African-American mayoral candidates.

As mayor, Young undertook a major downtown revitalization, with the Renaissance Center as its focal point. He also ended the controversial STRESS program, a police effort seen as unfair to the Black community. Young's reelection base was extremely solid, combining the African-American community with the labor unions and media; he was reelected in 1977, 1981, 1985, and 1989. Remarkably, the racial division of the vote continued through 1977 in a pattern less prevalent in other cities with African-American mayors. During that period, he became a leading power in national Democratic Party, serving as vice chairman of the party (1977–1981) and chairman of the Democratic Convention Platform Committee in 1980.

*Raphael J. Sonenshein*

REFERENCES

O'Loughlin, John, and Dale A. Berg. 1977. "The Election of Black Mayors, 1969 and 1973." 67 *Annals of the Association of American Geographers* 223.

O'Loughlin, John. 1980. "The Election of Black Mayors, 1977." 70 *Annals of the Association of American Geographers.*

Rich, Wilbur C. 1987. "Coleman Young and Detroit Politics: 1973–1986." In Michael B. Preston, Lenneal J. Henderson, Jr., and Paul L. Puryear, eds. *The New Black Politics: The Search for Political Power.* New York: Longman.

## Young Americans for Freedom

A politically influential youth organization that promotes fundamental conservative ideals such as laissez faire capitalism and strong national defense, Young Americans for Freedom (YAF) was founded in 1960 and in the mid-1980s claimed a much disputed membership of 90,000. The organization was strongest in the 1960s, experiencing declining membership in the post-1970 period. YAF was active in supporting Senator Barry Goldwater's 1964 presidential campaign and favored Vice President Spiro Agnew for President in 1972 when President Richard M. Nixon's commitment to conservatism was doubted in the organization. Considered part of the "Old Right" with ties to such figures as William F. Buckley and M. Stanton Evans, YAF membership was a common experience for many of the new generation of conservative leaders who emerged in the 1980s.

YAF sponsors campus speakers, lobbying and legal activities, and publishes a quarterly magazine, *New Guard*. Its tax exempt affiliate, Young America's Foundation, distributes conservative information to high school and college students.

With regard to political action committees, the situation is a bit convoluted. Former YAF members founded the Fund for a Conservative Majority (FCM) in 1972, and it has been called by some "the political action committee of YAF." FCM has been among the PAC leaders in overall spending in the 1980s, especially in terms of millions of dollars on independent expenditures favoring President Ronald Reagan's election and reelection campaigns. The American Conservative Union (ACU), a major conservative group, absorbed the political action committee of Young Americans for Freedom in 1966. YAF currently maintains its own political action committee, YAF-PAC, but it is not politically prominent.

*See also:* Spiro Agnew, Barry Goldwater, Richard M. Nixon

*Clyde Brown*

REFERENCES

Crawford, Alan. 1980. *Thunder on the Right.* New York: Pantheon.

Roberts, James C. 1980. *The Conservative Decade.* Westport, CT: Arlington House.

## Young Democrats of America

In 1932, James A. Farley, the new chairman of the Democratic National Committee, helped to create the Young Democratic Clubs of America. Farley hoped the clubs would bring more young people into the party and into the presidential election effort of Franklin D. Roosevelt. The organization, which changed its name to the Young Democrats of America (YDA) in 1975, conducts such activities as voter registration, preparation and distribution of campaign literature, rally organization, campus mobilization, political workshops, fundraising, poll watching, membership recruitment, and publicity for Democratic candidates. Membership is open to Democrats age 18 to 35.

The YDA has been a consistent supporter of Democratic candidates nationally, though the group showed itself to be particularly enthusiastic about the candidacies of John F. Kennedy in 1960, Lyndon Johnson in 1964, and George McGovern in 1972. In 1968 many YDA members, opposed to the Vietnam policy of the Johnson administration, worked for Senator

Eugene McCarthy of Minnesota and Senator Robert F. Kennedy of New York. During the 1960s and 1970s, YDA members were active in the anti-Vietnam and civil rights movements, and some state chapters, to the dismay of many older Democrats, worked for gay rights, marijuana legalization, and legal abortion.

The YDA is entitled to two permanent seats on the Democratic National Committee, and about one-third of the members of Congress and over half of DNC members formerly belonged to the YDA. Quarterly, the organization publishes *The Young Democrat* as well as the monthly *Legislative Alerts*. The YDA reports a membership of 200,000 and is associated with the College Young Democrats of America.

*See also:* Democratic National Committee; Elections of 1960, 1964, 1968, and 1972; Lyndon B. Johnson; John F. Kennedy; Robert F. Kennedy; Eugene McCarthy; George McGovern; Franklin D. Roosevelt

*Tom A. Kazee*

REFERENCES

Koek, Karin E., Susan B. Martin, and Annette Novallo, eds. 1988. *Encyclopedia of Associations.* Detroit: Gale Research, Inc.

Schapsmeier, Edward L., and Frederick Schapsmeier. 1981. *The Greenwood Encyclopedia of American Institutions.* Westport, CT: Greenwood.

## Young Republican National Federation

Like its Democratic counterpart, the Young Democrats of America, the Young Republican National Federation (YRNF) was formed as a vehicle for the entry of young people into politics at the local, state, and national level. Founded in 1931 by Robert H. Lucas, executive director of the Republican National Committee (RNC), the YRNF was originally open to men and women between the ages of 21 and 36; later, Republicans 18 to 40 became eligible.

The YRNF affiliated officially with the RNC in 1934 and in 1936 adopted a constitution and by-laws written by New Hampshire governor Styles Bridges. Bridges was himself a former YRNF member, later elected to the U.S. Senate. Harold Stassen was the defeated candidate for chairman of the organization in its first election held under the new constitution; Stassen later was elected governor of Minnesota, served in the Dwight Eisenhower administration, and was a perennial candidate for President.

Many of the 500,000 YRers, as members are usually called, are drawn from college campuses. Among its activities, the YRNF maintains speakers' bureaus and a variety of issue-area committees, recruits campaign workers, and holds campaign seminars and regional conferences. The group places particular emphasis on training future candidates and holds an annual Young Republican Leadership Conference every spring in Washington, D.C. YRers also present every Republican member of Congress with a copy of the party's platform.

*See also:* Dwight D. Eisenhower, Republican National Committee

*Tom A. Kazee*

REFERENCES

Koek, Karin E., Susan B. Martin, and Annette Novallo, eds. 1988. *Encyclopedia of Associations.* Detroit: Gale Research, Inc.

Schapsmeier, Edward L., and Frederick Schapsmeier. 1981. *The Greenwood Encyclopedia of American Institutions.* Westport, CT: Greenwood.

# Appendices

# Table of Contents for Appendices

# Appendix 1

## Sessions of Congress

| Congress | Session | Date of Beginning | Date of Adjournment | Length in Days |
|---|---|---|---|---|
| 1st | 1 | Mar. 4, 1789 | Sept. 29, 1789 | 210 |
| | 2 | Jan. 4, 1790 | Aug. 12, 1790 | 221 |
| | 3 | Dec. 6, 1790 | Mar. 3, 1791 | 88 |
| 2nd | 1 | Oct. 24, 1791 | May 8, 1792 | 197 |
| | 2 | Nov. 5, 1792 | Mar. 2, 1793 | 119 |
| 3rd | 1 | Dec. 2, 1793 | June 9, 1794 | 190 |
| | 2 | Nov. 3, 1794 | Mar. 3, 1795 | 121 |
| 4th | 1 | Dec. 7, 1795 | June 1, 1796 | 177 |
| | 2 | Dec. 5, 1796 | Mar. 3, 1797 | 89 |
| 5th | 1 | May 15, 1797 | July 10, 1797 | 57 |
| | 2 | Nov. 13, 1797 | July 16, 1798 | 246 |
| | 3 | Dec. 3, 1798 | Mar. 3, 1799 | 91 |
| 6th | 1 | Dec. 2, 1799 | May 14, 1800 | 164 |
| | 2 | Nov. 17, 1800 | Mar. 3, 1801 | 107 |
| 7th | 1 | Dec. 7, 1801 | May 3, 1802 | 148 |
| | 2 | Dec. 6, 1802 | Mar. 3, 1803 | 88 |
| 8th | 1 | Oct. 17, 1803 | Mar. 27, 1804 | 163 |
| | 2 | Nov. 5, 1804 | Mar. 3, 1805 | 119 |
| 9th | 1 | Dec. 2, 1805 | Apr. 21, 1806 | 141 |
| | 2 | Dec. 1, 1806 | Mar. 3, 1807 | 93 |
| 10th | 1 | Oct. 26, 1807 | Apr. 25, 1808 | 182 |
| | 2 | Nov. 7, 1808 | Mar. 3, 1809 | 117 |
| 11th | 1 | May 22, 1809 | June 28, 1809 | 38 |
| | 2 | Nov. 27, 1809 | May 1, 1810 | 156 |
| | 3 | Dec. 3, 1810 | Mar. 3, 1811 | 91 |
| 12th | 1 | Nov. 4, 1811 | July 6, 1812 | 245 |
| | 2 | Nov. 2, 1812 | Mar. 3, 1813 | 122 |
| 13th | 1 | May 24, 1813 | Aug. 2, 1813 | 71 |
| | 2 | Dec. 6, 1813 | Apr. 18, 1814 | 134 |
| | 3 | Sept. 19, 1814 | Mar. 3, 1815 | 166 |
| 14th | 1 | Dec. 4, 1815 | Apr. 30. 1816 | 148 |
| | 2 | Dec. 2, 1816 | Mar. 3, 1817 | 92 |
| 15th | 1 | Dec. 1, 1817 | Apr. 20, 1818 | 141 |
| | 2 | Nov. 16, 1818 | Mar. 3, 1819 | 108 |
| 16th | 1 | Dec. 6, 1819 | May 15, 1820 | 162 |
| | 2 | Nov. 13, 1820 | Mar. 3, 1821 | 111 |
| 17th | 1 | Dec. 3, 1821 | May 8, 1822 | 157 |
| | 2 | Dec. 2, 1822 | Mar. 3, 1823 | 92 |
| 18th | 1 | Dec. 1, 1823 | May 27, 1824 | 178 |
| | 2 | Dec. 6, 1824 | Mar. 3, 1825 | 88 |
| 19th | 1 | Dec. 5, 1825 | May 22, 1826 | 169 |
| | 2 | Dec. 4, 1826 | Mar. 3, 1827 | 90 |
| 20th | 1 | Dec. 3, 1827 | May 26, 1828 | 175 |
| | 2 | Dec. 1, 1828 | Mar. 3, 1829 | 93 |
| 21st | 1 | Dec. 7, 1829 | May 31, 1830 | 176 |
| | 2 | Dec. 6, 1830 | Mar. 3, 1831 | 88 |
| 22nd | 1 | Dec. 5, 1831 | July 16, 1832 | 225 |
| | 2 | Dec. 3, 1832 | Mar. 2, 1833 | 91 |
| 23rd | 1 | Dec. 2, 1833 | June 30, 1834 | 211 |
| | 2 | Dec. 1, 1834 | Mar. 3, 1835 | 93 |
| 24th | 1 | Dec. 7, 1835 | July 4, 1836 | 211 |
| | 2 | Dec. 5, 1836 | Mar. 3, 1837 | 89 |
| 25th | 1 | Sept. 4, 1837 | Oct. 16, 1837 | 43 |
| | 2 | Dec. 4, 1837 | July 9, 1838 | 218 |
| | 3 | Dec. 3, 1838 | Mar. 3, 1839 | 91 |
| 26th | 1 | Dec. 2, 1839 | July 21, 1840 | 233 |
| | 2 | Dec. 7, 1840 | Mar. 3, 1941 | 87 |
| 27th | 1 | May 31, 1841 | Sept. 13, 1841 | 106 |
| | 2 | Dec. 6, 1841 | Aug. 31, 1842 | 269 |
| | 3 | Dec. 5, 1842 | Mar. 3, 1843 | 89 |
| 28th | 1 | Dec. 4, 1843 | June 17, 1844 | 196 |

| Congress | Session | Date of Beginning | Date of Adjournment | Length in Days |
|---|---|---|---|---|
| | 2 | Dec. 2, 1844 | Mar. 3, 1845 | 92 |
| 29th | 1 | Dec. 1, 1845 | Aug. 10, 1846 | 253 |
| | 2 | Dec. 7, 1846 | Mar. 3, 1847 | 87 |
| 30th | 1 | Dec. 6, 1847 | Aug. 14, 1848 | 254 |
| | 2 | Dec. 4, 1848 | Mar. 3, 1849 | 90 |
| 31st | 1 | Dec. 3, 1849 | Sept. 30, 1850 | 302 |
| | 2 | Dec. 2, 1850 | Mar. 3, 1851 | 92 |
| 32nd | 1 | Dec. 1, 1851 | Aug. 31, 1852 | 275 |
| | 2 | Dec. 6, 1852 | Mar. 3, 1853 | 88 |
| 33rd | 1 | Dec. 5, 1853 | Aug. 7, 1854 | 246 |
| | 2 | Dec. 4, 1854 | Mar. 3, 1855 | 90 |
| 34th | 1 | Dec. 3, 1855 | Aug. 18, 1856 | 260 |
| | 2 | Aug. 21, 1856 | Aug. 30, 1856 | 10 |
| | 3 | Dec. 1, 1856 | Mar. 3, 1857 | 93 |
| 35th | 1 | Dec. 7, 1857 | June 14, 1858 | 189 |
| | 2 | Dec. 6, 1858 | Mar. 3, 1859 | 88 |
| 36th | 1 | Dec. 5, 1859 | June 25, 1860 | 202 |
| | 2 | Dec. 3, 1860 | Mar. 3, 1861 | 93 |
| 37th | 1 | July 4, 1861 | Aug. 6, 1861 | 34 |
| | 2 | Dec. 2, 1861 | July 17, 1862 | 228 |
| | 3 | Dec. 1, 1862 | Mar. 3, 1863 | 93 |
| 38th | 1 | Dec. 7, 1863 | July 4, 1864 | 209 |
| | 2 | Dec. 5, 1864 | Mar. 3, 1865 | 89 |
| 39th | 1 | Dec. 4, 1865 | July 28, 1866 | 237 |
| | 2 | Dec. 3, 1866 | Mar. 3, 1867 | 91 |
| 40th | 1 | Mar. 4, 1867 | Dec. 2, 1867 | 274 |
| | 2 | Dec. 2, 1867 | Nov. 10, 1868 | 345 |
| | 3 | Dec. 7, 1868 | Mar. 3, 1869 | 87 |
| 41st | 1 | Mar. 4, 1869 | Apr. 10, 1869 | 38 |
| | 2 | Dec. 6, 1869 | July 15, 1870 | 222 |
| | 3 | Dec. 5, 1870 | Mar. 3, 1871 | 89 |
| 42nd | 1 | Mar. 4, 1871 | Apr. 20, 1871 | 48 |
| | 2 | Dec. 4, 1871 | June 10, 1872 | 190 |
| | 3 | Dec. 2, 1872 | Mar. 3, 1873 | 92 |
| 43rd | 1 | Dec. 1, 1873 | June 23, 1874 | 204 |
| | 2 | Dec. 7, 1874 | Mar. 3, 1875 | 87 |
| 44th | 1 | Dec. 6, 1875 | Aug. 15, 1876 | 254 |
| | 2 | Dec. 4, 1876 | Mar. 3, 1877 | 90 |
| 45th | 1 | Oct. 15, 1877 | Dec. 3, 1877 | 50 |
| | 2 | Dec. 3, 1877 | June 20, 1878 | 200 |
| | 3 | Dec. 2, 1878 | Mar. 3, 1879 | 92 |
| 46th | 1 | Mar. 18, 1879 | July 1, 1879 | 106 |
| | 2 | Dec. 1, 1879 | June 16, 1880 | 199 |
| | 3 | Dec. 6, 1880 | Mar. 3, 1881 | 88 |
| 47th | 1 | Dec. 5, 1881 | Aug. 8, 1882 | 247 |
| | 2 | Dec. 4, 1882 | Mar. 3, 1883 | 90 |
| 48th | 1 | Dec. 3, 1883 | July 7, 1884 | 218 |
| | 2 | Dec. 1, 1884 | Mar. 3, 1885 | 93 |
| 49th | 1 | Dec. 7, 1885 | Aug. 5, 1886 | 242 |
| | 2 | Dec. 6, 1886 | Mar. 3, 1877 | 88 |
| 50th | 1 | Dec. 5, 1887 | Oct. 20, 1888 | 321 |
| | 2 | Dec. 3, 1888 | Mar. 3, 1889 | 91 |
| 51st | 1 | Dec. 2, 1889 | Oct. 1, 1890 | 304 |
| | 2 | Dec. 1, 1890 | Mar. 3, 1891 | 93 |
| 52nd | 1 | Dec. 7, 1891 | Aug. 5, 1892 | 251 |
| | 2 | Dec. 5, 1892 | Mar. 3, 1893 | 89 |
| 53rd | 1 | Aug. 7, 1893 | Nov. 3, 1893 | 89 |
| | 2 | Dec. 4, 1893 | Aug. 28, 1894 | 268 |
| | 3 | Dec. 3, 1894 | Mar. 3, 1895 | 97 |
| 54th | 1 | Dec. 2, 1895 | June 11, 1896 | 193 |
| | 2 | Dec. 7, 1896 | Mars. 3, 1897 | 87 |
| 55th | 1 | Mar. 15, 1897 | July 24, 1897 | 131 |
| | 2 | Dec. 6, 1897 | July 8, 1898 | 215 |
| | 3 | Dec. 5, 1898 | Mar. 3, 1899 | 89 |
| 56th | 1 | Dec. 4, 1899 | June 7, 1900 | 186 |

| Congress | Session | Date of Beginning | Date of Adjournment | Length in Days |
|---|---|---|---|---|
| | 2 | Dec. 3, 1900 | Mar. 3, 1901 | 91 |
| 57th | 1 | Dec. 2, 1901 | July 1, 1902 | 212 |
| | 2 | Dec. 1, 1902 | Mar. 3, 1903 | 93 |
| 58th | 1 | Nov. 9, 1903 | Dec. 7, 1903 | 29 |
| | 2 | Dec. 7, 1903 | Apr. 28, 1904 | 144 |
| | 3 | Dec. 5, 1904 | Mar. 3, 1905 | 89 |
| 59th | 1 | Dec. 4, 1905 | June 30, 1906 | 209 |
| | 2 | Dec. 3, 1906 | Mar. 3, 1907 | 91 |
| 60th | 1 | Dec. 2, 1907 | May 30, 1908 | 181 |
| | 2 | Dec. 7, 1908 | Mar. 3, 1909 | 87 |
| 61st | 1 | Mar. 15, 1909 | Aug. 5, 1909 | 144 |
| | 2 | Dec. 6, 1909 | June 25, 1910 | 202 |
| | 3 | Dec. 5, 1910 | Mar. 3, 1911 | 89 |
| 62nd | 1 | Apr. 4, 1911 | Aug. 26, 1911 | 141 |
| | 2 | Dec. 4, 1911 | Aug. 26, 1912 | 267 |
| | 3 | Dec. 2, 1912 | Mar. 3, 1913 | 92 |
| 63rd | 1 | Apr. 7, 1913 | Dec. 1, 1913 | 239 |
| | 2 | Dec. 1, 1913 | Oct. 24, 1914 | 328 |
| | 3 | Dec. 7, 1914 | Mar. 3, 1915 | 87 |
| 64th | 1 | Dec. 6, 1915 | Sept. 8, 1916 | 278 |
| | 2 | Dec. 4, 1916 | Mar. 3, 1917 | 90 |
| 65th | 1 | Apr. 2, 1917 | Oct. 6, 1917 | 188 |
| | 2 | Dec. 3, 1917 | Nov. 21, 1918 | 354 |
| | 3 | Dec. 2, 1918 | Mar. 3, 1919 | 92 |
| 66th | 1 | May 19, 1919 | Nov. 19, 1919 | 185 |
| | 2 | Dec. 1, 1919 | June 5, 1920 | 188 |
| | 3 | Dec. 6, 1920 | Mar. 3, 1921 | 88 |
| 67th | 1 | Apr. 11, 1921 | Nov. 23, 1921 | 227 |
| | 2 | Dec. 5, 1921 | Sept. 22, 1922 | 292 |
| | 3 | Nov. 20, 1922 | Dec. 4, 1922 | 15 |
| | 4 | Dec. 4, 1922 | Mar. 3, 1923 | 90 |
| 68th | 1 | Dec. 3, 1923 | June 7, 1924 | 188 |
| | 2 | Dec. 1, 1924 | Mar. 3, 1925 | 93 |
| 69th | 1 | Dec. 7, 1925 | July 3, 1926 | 209 |
| | 2 | Dec. 6, 1926 | Mar. 3, 1927 | 88 |
| 70th | 1 | Dec. 5, 1927 | May 29, 1928 | 177 |
| | 2 | Dec. 3, 1928 | Mar. 3, 1929 | 91 |
| 71st | 1 | Apr. 15, 1929 | Nov. 22, 1929 | 222 |
| | 2 | Dec. 2, 1929 | July 3, 1930 | 214 |
| | 3 | Dec. 1, 1930 | Mar. 3, 1931 | 93 |
| 72nd | 1 | Dec. 7, 1931 | July 16, 1932 | 223 |
| | 2 | Dec. 5, 1932 | Mar. 3, 1933 | 89 |
| 73rd | 1 | Mar. 9, 1933 | June 15, 1933 | 99 |
| | 2 | Jan. 3, 1934 | June 18, 1934 | 167 |
| 74th | 1 | Jan. 3, 1935 | Aug. 26, 1935 | 236 |
| | 2 | Jan. 3, 1936 | Jun. 20, 1936 | 170 |
| 75th | 1 | Jan. 5, 1937 | Aug. 21, 1937 | 229 |
| | 2 | Nov. 15, 1937 | Dec. 21, 1937 | 37 |
| | 3 | Jan. 3, 1938 | June 16, 1938 | 165 |
| 76th | 1 | Jan. 3, 1939 | Aug. 5, 1939 | 215 |
| | 2 | Sept. 21, 1939 | Nov. 3, 1939 | 44 |
| | 3 | Jan. 3, 1940 | Jan. 3, 1941 | 366 |
| 77th | 1 | Jan. 3, 1941 | Jan. 2, 1942 | 365 |
| | 2 | Jan. 5, 1942 | Dec. 16, 1942 | 346 |
| 78th | 1 | Jan. 6, 1943 | Dec. 21, 1943 | 350 |
| | 2 | Jan. 10, 1944 | Dec. 19, 1944 | 345 |
| 79th | 1 | Jan. 3, 1945 | Dec. 21, 1945 | 353 |
| | 2 | Jan. 14, 1946 | Aug. 2, 1946 | 201 |
| 80th | 1 | Jan. 3, 1947 | Dec. 19, 1947 | 351 |
| | 2 | Jan. 6, 1948 | Dec. 31, 1948 | 361 |
| 81st | 1 | Jan. 3, 1949 | Oct. 19, 1949 | 290 |
| | 2 | Jan. 3, 1950 | Jan. 2, 1951 | 365 |
| 82nd | 1 | Jan. 3, 1951 | Oct. 20, 1951 | 291 |
| | 2 | Jan. 8, 1952 | July 7, 1952 | 182 |

| Congress | Session | Date of Beginning | Date of Adjournment | Length in Days |
|---|---|---|---|---|
| 83rd | 1 | Jan. 3, 1953 | Aug. 3, 1953 | 213 |
| | 2 | Jan. 6, 1954 | Dec. 2, 1954 | 331 |
| 84th | 1 | Jan. 5, 1955 | Aug. 2, 1955 | 210 |
| | 2 | Jan. 3, 1956 | July 27, 1956 | 207 |
| 85th | 1 | Jan. 3, 1957 | Aug. 30, 1957 | 239 |
| | 2 | Jan. 7, 1958 | Aug. 24, 1958 | 230 |
| 86th | 1 | Jan. 7, 1959 | Sept. 15, 1959 | 252 |
| | 2 | Jan. 6, 1960 | Sept. 1, 1960 | 240 |
| 87th | 1 | Jan. 3, 1961 | Sept. 27, 1961 | 268 |
| | 2 | Jan. 10, 1962 | Oct. 13, 1962 | 277 |
| 88th | 1 | Jan. 9, 1963 | Dec. 30, 1963 | 356 |
| | 2 | Jan. 7, 1964 | Oct. 3, 1964 | 270 |
| 89th | 1 | Jan. 4, 1965 | Oct. 23, 1965 | 293 |
| | 2 | Jan. 10, 1966 | Oct. 22, 1966 | 286 |
| 90th | 1 | Jan. 10, 1967 | Dec. 15, 1967 | 340 |
| | 2 | Jan. 15, 1968 | Oct. 14, 1968 | 274 |
| 91st | 1 | Jan. 3, 1969 | Dec. 23, 1969 | 355 |
| | 2 | Jan. 19, 1970 | Jan. 2, 1971 | 349 |
| 92nd | 1 | Jan. 21, 1971 | Dec. 17, 1971 | 331 |
| | 2 | Jan. 18, 1972 | Oct. 18, 1972 | 275 |
| 93rd | 1 | Jan. 3, 1973 | Dec. 22, 1973 | 354 |
| | 2 | Jan. 21, 1974 | Dec. 20, 1974 | 334 |
| 94th | 1 | Jan. 14, 1975 | Dec. 19, 1975 | 340 |
| | 2 | Jan. 19, 1976 | Oct. 1, 1976 | 257 |
| 95th | 1 | Jan. 4, 1977 | Dec. 15, 1977 | 346 |
| | 2 | Jan. 19, 1978 | Oct. 15, 1978 | 270 |
| 96th | 1 | Jan. 15, 1979 | Jan. 3, 1980 | 354 |
| | 2 | Jan. 3, 1980 | Dec. 16, 1980 | 349 |
| 97th | 1 | Jan. 5, 1981 | Dec. 16, 1981 | 347 |
| | 2 | Jan. 25, 1982 | Dec. 23, 1982 | 333 |
| 98th | 1 | Jan. 3, 1983 | Nov. 18, 1983 | 320 |
| | 2 | Jan. 23, 1984 | Oct. 12, 1984 | 264 |
| 99th | 1 | Jan. 3, 1985 | Dec. 20, 1985 | 352 |
| | 2 | Jan. 21, 1986 | Oct. 18, 1986 | 278 |
| 100th | 1 | Jan. 6, 1987 | Dec. 22, 1987 | 351 |
| | 2 | Jan. 25, 1988 | Oct. 22, 1988 | 272 |
| 101st | 1 | Jan. 3, 1989 | Nov. 22, 1989 | 323 |
| | 2 | Jan. 23, 1990 | Oct. 28, 1990 | 279 |

# Appendix 2

## *Speakers of the House*

Party designations: (Am) American; (D) Democratic; (DR) Democratic-Republican; (F) Federalist; (R) Republican; (W) Whig.

| Speaker | Congresses | Speaker | Congresses |
| --- | --- | --- | --- |
| Frederick A. C. Muhlenberg (F-PA) | 1st | Theodore M. Pomeroy (R-NY) | 40th |
| Jonathan Trumbull (F-CT) | 2nd | James G. Blaine (R-ME) | 41st–43rd |
| Frederick A. C. Muhlenberg (F-PA) | 3rd | Michael C. Kerr (D-IN) | 44th |
| Jonathan Dayton (F-NJ) | 4th–5th | Samuel J. Randall (D-PA) | 44th–46th |
| Theodore Sedgwick (F-MA) | 6th | J. Warren Keifer (R-OH) | 47th |
| Nathaniel Macon (DR-NC) | 7th–9th | John G. Carlisle (D-KY) | 48th–50th |
| Joseph B. Varnum (DR-MA) | 10th–11th | Thomas B. Reed (R-ME) | 51st |
| Henry Clay (DR-KY) | 12th–13th | Charles F. Crisp (D-GA) | 52nd–53rd |
| Langdon Cheeves (DR-SC) | 14th | Thomas B. Reed (R-ME) | 54th–55th |
| Henry Clay (DR-KY) | 14th–16th | David B. Henderson (R-IA) | 56th–57th |
| John W. Taylor (DR-NY) | 16th | Joseph G. Cannon (R-IL) | 58th–61st |
| Philip P. Barbour (DR-VA) | 17th | James Beauchamp (Champ) Clark (D-MO) | 62nd–65th |
| Henry Clay (DR-KY) | 18th | Frederick H. Gillett (R-MA) | 66th–68th |
| John W. Taylor (D-NY) | 19th | Nicholas Longworth (R-OH) | 69th–71st |
| Andrew Stevenson (D-VA) | 20th–23rd | John Nance Garner (D-TX) | 72nd |
| John Bell (D-TN) | 23rd | Henry T. Rainey (D-IL) | 73rd |
| James K. Polk (D-TN) | 24th–25th | Joseph W. Byrns (D-TN) | 74th |
| Robert M. T. Hunter (D-VA) | 26th | William B. Bankhead (D-AL) | 74th–76th |
| John White (W-KY) | 27th | Sam Rayburn (D-TX) | 76th–79th |
| John W. Jones (D-VA) | 28th | Joseph W. Martin, Jr. (R-MA) | 80th |
| John W. Davis (D-IN) | 29th | Sam Rayburn (D-TX) | 81st–82nd |
| Robert C. Winthrop (W-MA) | 30th | Joseph W. Martin, Jr. (R-MA) | 83rd |
| Howell Cobb (D-GA) | 31st | Sam Rayburn (D-TX) | 84th–87th |
| Linn Boyd (D-KY) | 32nd–33rd | John W. McCormack (D-MA) | 87th–91st |
| Nathaniel P. Banks (Am-MA) | 34th | Carl Albert (D-OK) | 92nd–94th |
| James L. Orr (D-SC) | 35th | Thomas P. (Tip) O'Neill, Jr. (D-MA) | 95th–99th |
| William Pennington (R-NJ) | 36th | James (Jim) Wright (D-TX) | 100th–101st |
| Galusha A. Grow (R-PA) | 37th | Thomas S. Foley (D-WA) | 101st– |
| Schuyler Colfax (R-IN) | 38th–40th | | |

# Appendix 3

## *Presidents* Pro Tempore *of the Senate*

| President *Pro Tempore* | Congresses | President *Pro Tempore* | Congresses |
|---|---|---|---|
| John Langdon (NH) | 1st | Thomas J. Rusk (TX) | 34th |
| Richard Henry Lee (VA) | 2nd | Benjamin Fitzpatrick (AL) | 35th–36th |
| John Langdon (NH) | 3rd | Jesse D. Bright (IN) | 36th |
| Ralph Izard (SC) | 3rd | Solomon Foot (VT) | 36th–38th |
| Henry Tazewell (VA) | 3rd–4th | Daniel Clark (NH) | 38th |
| Samuel Livermore (NH) | 4th | Lafayette S. Foster (CT) | 39th |
| William Bingham (PA) | 4th | Benjamin F. Wade (OH) | 39th–40th |
| William Bradford (RI) | 5th | Henry B. Anthony (RI) | 41st–42nd |
| Jacob Read (SC) | 5th | Matthew H. Carpenter (WI) | 43rd |
| Theodore Sedgwick (MA) | 5th | Henry B. Anthony (RI) | 43rd |
| John Laurence (NY) | 5th | Thomas W. Ferry (MI) | 44th–45th |
| James Ross (PA) | 5th | Allen G. Thurman (OH) | 46th |
| Samuel Livermore (NH) | 6th | Thomas F. Bayard (DE) | 47th |
| Uriah Tracy (CT) | 6th | David Davis (IL) | 47th |
| John E. Howard (MD) | 6th | George F. Edmunds (VT) | 47th–48th |
| James Hillhouse (CT) | 6th | John Sherman (OH) | 49th |
| Abraham Baldwin (GA) | 7th | John J. Ingalls (KS) | 49th–51st |
| Stephen R. Bradley (VT) | 7th | Charles F. Manderson (NE) | 51st |
| John Brown (KY) | 8th | Isham G. Harris (TN) | 52nd–53rd |
| Jesse Franklin (NC) | 8th | Matt W. Ransom (NC) | 53rd |
| Joseph Anderson (TN) | 8th | Isham G. Harris (TN) | 53rd |
| Samuel Smith (MD) | 9th–10th | William P. Frye (ME) | 54th–62nd |
| Stephen R. Bradley (VT) | 10th | Charles Curtis (KS) | 62nd |
| John Milledge (GA) | 10th | Augustus O. Bacon (GA) | 62nd |
| Andrew Gregg (PA) | 11th | Jacob H. Gallinger (NH) | 62nd |
| John Gaillard (SC) | 11th | Henry Cabot Lodge (MA) | 62nd |
| John Pope (KY) | 11th | Frank R. Brandegee (CT) | 62nd |
| William H. Crawford (GA) | 12th–13th | James P. Clarke (AR) | 63rd–64th |
| Joseph B. Varnum (MA) | 13th | Willard Saulsbury (DE) | 64th–65th |
| John Gaillard (SC) | 13th–15th | Albert B. Cummins (IA) | 66th–68th |
| James Barbour (VA) | 15th | George H. Moses (NH) | 69th–72nd |
| John Gaillard (SC) | 16th–18th | Key Pittman (NV) | 73rd–76th |
| Nathaniel Macon (NC) | 19th | William H. King (UT) | 76th |
| Samuel Smith (MD) | 20th–21st | Pat Harrison (MS) | 77th |
| Littleton Waller Tazewell (VA) | 21st–22nd | Carter Glass (VA) | 77th–78th |
| Hugh Lawson White (TN) | 22nd | Kenneth McKellar (TN) | 79th |
| George Poindexter (MS) | 23rd | Arthur H. Vandenberg (MI) | 80th |
| John Tyler (VA) | 23rd | Kenneth McKellar (TN) | 81st–82nd |
| William R. King (AL) | 24th–26th | Styles Bridges (NH) | 83rd |
| Samuel L. Southard (NJ) | 27th | Walter F. George (GA) | 84th |
| Willie P. Mangum (NC) | 27th–28th | Carl Hayden (AZ) | 85th–90th |
| David R. Atchison (MO) | 29th–30th | Richard B. Russell (GA) | 91st–92nd |
| William R. King (AL) | 31st–32nd | Allen J. Ellender (LA) | 92nd |
| David R. Atchison (MO) | 32nd–33rd | James O. Eastland (MS) | 92nd–95th |
| Jesse D. Bright (IN) | 33rd | Warren G. Magnuson (WA) | 96th |
| Lewis Cass (MI) | 33rd | Strom Thurmond (SC) | 97th–99th |
| Jesse D. Bright (IN) | 34th | John C. Stennis (MS) | 100th |
| James M. Mason (VA) | 34th | Robert C. Byrd (WV) | 101st– |

# Appendix 4

## *Leaders of the House of Representatives*

| Congress | Majority Leader | Minority Leader | Majority Whip | Minority Whip |
|---|---|---|---|---|
| 6th | Sereno E. Payne (R-NY) | James D. Richardson (D-TN) | James A. Tawney (R-MN) | Oscar W. Underwood (D-AL) |
| 7th | Payne | Richardson | Tawney | James T. Lloyd (D-MO) |
| 8th | Payne | John Sharp Williams (D-MS) | Tawney | Lloyd |
| 9th | Payne | Williams | James E. Watson (R-IN) | Lloyd |
| 0th | Payne | Williams/ Champ Clark (D-MO) | Watson | Lloyd |
| 1st | Payne | Clark | John W. Dwight (R-NY) | None |
| 2nd | Oscar W. Underwood (D-AL) | James R. Mann (R-IL) | None | John W. Dwight (R-NY) |
| 3rd | Underwood | Mann | Thomas M. Bell (D-GA) | Charles H. Burke (R-SD) |
| 4th | Claude Kitchin (D-NC) | Mann | None | Charles M. Hamilton (R-NY) |
| 5th | Kitchin | Mann | None | Hamilton |
| 6th | Franklin W. Mondell (R-WY) | Clark | Harold Knutson (R-MN) | None |
| 7th | Mondell | Claude Kitchin (D-NC) | Knutson | William A. Oldfield (D-AR) |
| 8th | Nicholas Longworth (R-OH) | Finis J. Garrett (D-TN) | Albert H. Vestal (R-IN) | Oldfield |
| 9th | John Q. Tilson (R-CT) | Garrett | Vestal | Oldfield |
| 0th | Tilson | Garrett | Vestal | Oldfield/ John McDuffie (D-AL) |
| 1st | Tilson | John N. Garner (D-TX) | Vestal | McDuffie |
| 2nd | Henry T. Rainey (D-IL) | Bertrand H. Snell (R-NY) | John McDuffie (D-AL) | Carl B. Bachmann (R-WV) |
| 3rd | Joseph W. Byrns (D-TN) | Snell | Arthur H. Greenwood (D-IN) | Harry L. Englebright (R-CA) |
| 4th | William B. Bankhead (D-AL) | Snell | Patrick J. Boland (D-PA) | Englebright |
| 5th | Sam Rayburn (D-TX) | Snell | Boland | Englebright |
| 6th | Rayburn/ John W. McCormack (D-MA) | Joseph W. Martin, Jr. (R-MA) | Boland | Englebright |
| 7th | McCormack | Martin | Boland/ Robert Ramspeck (D-GA) | Englebright |
| 8th | McCormack | Martin | Ramspeck | Leslie C. Arends (R-IL) |
| 9th | McCormack | Martin | Ramspeck/ John J. Sparkman (D-AL) | Arends |
| 0th | Charles A. Halleck (R-IN) | Sam Rayburn (D-TX) | Leslie C. Arends (R-IL) | John W. McCormack (D-MA) |
| 1st | McCormack | Martin | J. Percy Priest (D-TN) | Arends |
| 2nd | McCormack | Martin | Priest | Arends |
| 3rd | Halleck | Rayburn | Arends | McCormack |
| 4th | McCormack | Martin | Carl Albert (D-OK) | Arends |
| 5th | McCormack | Martin | Albert | Arends |
| 6th | McCormack | Charles A. Halleck (R-IN) | Albert | Arends |
| 7th | McCormack/Carl Albert (D-OK) | Halleck | Albert/Hale Boggs (D-LA) | Arends |
| 8th | Albert | Halleck | Boggs | Arends |
| 9th | Albert | Gerald R. Ford (R-MI) | Boggs | Arends |
| 0th | Albert | Ford | Boggs | Arends |
| 1st | Albert | Ford | Boggs | Arends |
| 2nd | Hale Boggs (D-LA) | Ford | Thomas P. O'Neill, Jr. (D-MA) | Arends |
| 3rd | Thomas P. O'Neill, Jr. (D-MA) | Ford/John J. Rhodes (R-AZ) | John J. McFall (D-CA) | Arends |
| 4th | O'Neill | Rhodes | McFall | Robert H. Michel (R-IL) |
| 5th | James C. Wright, Jr. (D-TX) | Rhodes | John Brademas (D-IN) | Michel |
| 6th | Wright | Rhodes | Brademas | Michel |
| 7th | Wright | Robert H. Michel (R-IL) | Thomas S. Foley (D-WA) | Trent Lott (R-MS) |
| 8th | Wright | Michel | Foley | Lott |
| 9th | Wright | Michel | Foley | Lott |
| 0th | Thomas S. Foley (D-WA) | Michel | Tony Coelho (D-CA) | Lott |
| 1st | Foley | Michel | Coelho | Newt Gingrich (D-GA) |
|  | Richard A. Gephardt (D-MO) | Michel | William H. Gray III (D-PA) | Gingrich |

# Appendix 5

## *Leaders of the Senate*

| Congress | Majority Leader | Minority Leader | Majority Whip | Minority Whip |
|---|---|---|---|---|
| 62nd | Shelby M. Cullom (R-IL) | Thomas S. Martin (D-VA) | None | None |
| 63rd | John W. Kern (D-IN) | Jacob H. Gallinger (R-NH) | J. Hamilton Lewis (D-IL) | None |
| 64th | Kern | Gallinger | Lewis | James W. Wadsworth, Jr. (R-NY)/ Charles Curtis (R-KS) |
| 65th | Thomas S. Martin (D-VA) | Gallinger/ Henry Cabot Lodge (R-MA) | Lewis | Curtis |
| 66th | Henry Cabot Lodge (R-MA) | Martin/ Oscar W. Underwood (D-AL) | Charles Curtis (R-KS) | Peter G. Gerry (D-RI) |
| 67th | Lodge | Underwood | Curtis | Gerry |
| 68th | Lodge/Charles Curtis (R-KS) | Joseph T. Robinson (D-AR) | Curtis/ Wesley L. Jones (R-WA) | Gerry |
| 69th | Curtis | Robinson | Jones | Gerry |
| 70th | Curtis | Robinson | Jones | Gerry |
| 71st | James E. Watson (R-IN) | Robinson | Simeon D. Fess (R-OH) | Morris Sheppard (D-TX) |
| 72nd | Watson | Robinson | Fess | Sheppard |
| 73rd | Joseph T. Robinson (D-AR) | Charles L. McNary (R-OR) | Lewis | Felix Hebert (R-RI) |
| 74th | Robinson | McNary | Lewis | None |
| 75th | Robinson/ Alben W. Barkley (D-KY) | McNary | Lewis | None |
| 76th | Barkley | McNary | Sherman Minton (D-IN) | None |
| 77th | Barkley | McNary | Lister Hill (D-AL) | None |
| 78th | Barkley | McNary | Hill | Kenneth Wherry (R-NE) |
| 79th | Barkley | Wallace H. White, Jr. (R-ME) | Hill | Wherry |
| 80th | Wallace H. White, Jr. (R-ME) | Alben W. Barkley (D-KY) | Kenneth Wherry (R-NE) | Scott Lucas (D-IL) |
| 81st | Scott W. Lucas (D-IL) | Kenneth S. Wherry (R-NE) | Francis Myers (D-PA) | Leverett Saltonstall (R-MA) |
| 82nd | Ernest W. McFarland (D-AZ) | Wherry/Styles Bridges (R-NH) | Lyndon B. Johnson (D-TX) | Saltonstall |
| 83rd | Robert A. Taft (R-OH) William F. Knowland (R-CA) | Lyndon B. Johnson (D-TX) | Leverett Saltonstall (R-MA) | Earle Clements (D-KY) |
| 84th | Lyndon B. Johnson (D-TX) | William F. Knowland (R-CA) | Earle Clements (D-KY) | Saltonstall |
| 85th | Johnson | Knowland | Mike Mansfield (D-MT) | Everett McKinley Dirksen (R-IL) |
| 86th | Johnson | Everett McKinley Dirksen (R-IL) | Mansfield | Thomas H. Kuchel (R-CA) |
| 87th | Mike Mansfield (D-MT) | Dirksen | Hubert H. Humphrey (D-MN) | Kuchel |
| 88th | Mansfield | Dirksen | Humphrey | Kuchel |
| 89th | Mansfield | Dirksen | Russell Long (D-LA) | Kuchel |
| 90th | Mansfield | Dirksen | Long | Kuchel |
| 91st | Mansfield | Dirksen/Hugh Scott (R-PA) | Edward M. Kennedy (D-MA) | Hugh Scott (R-PA)/ Robert P. Griffin (R-MI) |
| 92nd | Mansfield | Scott | Robert C. Byrd (D-WV) | Griffin |
| 93rd | Mansfield | Scott | Byrd | Griffin |
| 94th | Mansfield | Scott | Byrd | Griffin |
| 95th | Robert C. Byrd (D-WV) | Howard H. Baker, Jr. (R-TN) | Alan Cranston (D-CA) | Ted Stevens (R-AK) |
| 96th | Byrd | Baker | Cranston | Stevens |
| 97th | Howard H. Baker, Jr. (R-TN) | Robert C. Byrd (D-WV) | Ted Stevens (R-AK) | Alan Cranston (D-CA) |
| 98th | Baker | Byrd | Stevens | Cranston |
| 99th | Robert Dole (R-KS) | Byrd | Alan K. Simpson (R-WY) | Cranston |
| 100th | Byrd | Robert Dole (R-KS) | Cranston | Alan K. Simpson (R-WY) |
| 101st | George J. Mitchell (D-ME) | Dole | Cranston | Simpson |

# Appendix 6

## *Women in Congress*

### SENATE

| Name | Years of Service |
|---|---|
| Rebecca Latimer Felton (D-GA) | 1921–1922 |
| Hattie Wyatt Caraway (D-AR) | 1931–1944 |
| Rose McConnell Long (D-LA) | 1935–1936 |
| Dixie Bibb Graves (D-AL) | 1937–1938 |
| Gladys Pyle (R-SD) | 1937–1938 |
| Vera Cahalan Bushfield (R-SD) | 1947–1948 |
| Margaret Chase Smith (R-ME) | 1949–1972 |
| Hazel Hempel Abel (R-NE) | 1953–1954 |
| Eva Bowring (R-NE) | 1953–1954 |
| Maurine Brown Neuberger (D-OR) | 1961–1966 |
| Elaine S. Edwards (D-AL) | 1971–1972 |
| Maryon Pittman Allen (D-AL) | 1977–1978 |
| Muriel Buck Humphrey (D-MN) | 1977–1978 |
| Nancy Landon Kassebaum (R-KS) | 1978– |
| Paula Hawkins (R-FL) | 1981–1986 |
| Barbara Mikulski (D-MD) | 1986 |

### HOUSE

| Name | Years of Service |
|---|---|
| Jeannette Rankin (R-MT) | 1917-1918; 1941–1942 |
| Winnifred Sprague Mason Huck (R-IL) | 1921–1922 |
| Mae Ella Nolan (R-CA) | 1921–1924 |
| Alice Mary Robertson (R-OK) | 1921–1922 |
| Florence Prag Kahn (R-CA) | 1925–1936 |
| Mary Teresa Norton (D-NJ) | 1925–1950 |
| Edith Nourse Rogers (R-MA) | 1925–1960 |
| Katherine Gudger Langley (R-KY) | 1927–1930 |
| Pearl Peden Oldfield (D-AR) | 1927–1930 |
| Ruth Hanna McCormick (R-IL) | 1929–1930 |
| Ruth Bryan Owen (Rohde) (D-FL) | 1929–1932 |
| Ruth S. E. Prate (R-NY) | 1929–1932 |
| Effiegene Wingo (D-AR) | 1929–1932 |
| Willa McCord Blake Eslick (D-TN) | 1931–1932 |
| Marian Williams Clarke (R-NY) | 1933–1934 |
| Isabella Selmes Greenway (D-AZ) | 1933–1936 |
| Virginia Ellis Jenckes (D-IN) | 1933–1938 |
| Kathryn O'Loughlin McCarthy (D-KS) | 1933–1934 |
| Caroline Love Goodwin O'Day (D-NY) | 1935–1942 |
| Elizabeth H. Gasque (Van Exam) (D-SC) | 1937–1938 |
| Nan Wood Honeyman (D-OR) | 1937–1938 |
| Frances Payne Bolton (R-OH) | 1939–1968 |
| Florence Reville Gibbs (D-GA) | 1939–1940 |
| Clara Gooding McMillan (D-SC) | 1939–1940 |
| Margaret Chase Smith (R-ME) | 1939–1948 |
| Jessie Sumner (R-IL) | 1939–1946 |
| Veronica Grace Boland (D-PA) | 1941–1942 |
| Willa Lybrand Fulmer (D-SC) | 1943–1944 |
| Kathryne Edgar Bryon (D-MD) | 1941–1942 |
| Clare Booth Luce (R-CT) | 1943–1946 |
| Winifred Claire Stanley (R-NY) | 1943–1944 |
| Emily Taft Douglas (D-IL) | 1945–1950 |
| Helen Gahagan Douglas (D-CA) | 1945–1950 |
| Helen Douglas Mankin (D-GA) | 1945–1946 |
| Eliza Jane Pratt (D-NC) | 1945–1946 |

| Name | Years of Service |
|---|---|
| Chase Going Woodhouse (D-CT) | 1945–1946; 1949–1950 |
| Georgia Lee Lusk (D-NM) | 1947–1948 |
| Katherine Price Collier St. George (R-NY) | 1947–1964 |
| Reva Z. Beck Bosone (D-UT) | 1949–1952 |
| Cecil Murray Harden (R-IN) | 1949–1958 |
| Edna Flannery Kelly )D-NY) | 1949–1968 |
| Vera Daerr Buchanan (D-PA) | 1951–1956 |
| Marquerite Stitt Church (R-IL) | 1951–1962 |
| Maude Elizabeth Kee (D-WV) | 1951–1964 |
| Ruth Thompson (R-MI) | 1951–1956 |
| Mary Elizabeth Pruett Farrington (R-HI) | 1953–1956 |
| Gracie Bowers Pfost (D-ID) | 1953–1962 |
| Iris Faircloth Blitch (D-GA) | 1955–1962 |
| Kathryn Elizabeth Granahan (D-PA) | 1955–1962 |
| Edith Green (D-OR) | 1955–1974 |
| Martha Wright Griffiths (D-MI) | 1955–1974 |
| Coya Gjesdal Knutson (D-MN) | 1955–1958 |
| Florence Price Dwyer (R-NJ) | 1957–1972 |
| Julia Butler Hansen (D-WA) | 1959–1974 |
| Catherine D. May (Bedell) (R-WA) | 1959–1970 |
| Edna Oakes Simpson (R-IL) | 1959–1960 |
| Jessica McCullough Weis (R-NY) | 1959–1962 |
| Catherine D. Norell (D-AR) | 1961–1962 |
| Louise G. Reece (R-TN) | 1961–1962 |
| Corinne Boyd Riley (D-SC) | 1961–1962 |
| Irene B. Baker (R-TN) | 1963–1964 |
| Charlotte Thompson Reid (R-IL) | 1963–1972 |
| Patsy T. Mink (D-HI) | 1965–1976; 1990– |
| Lera M. Thomas (D-TX) | 1965–1966 |
| Margaret M. Heckler (R-MA) | 1967–1982 |
| Shirley Anita Chisholm (D-NY) | 1969–1982 |
| Bella Abzug (D-NY) | 1971–1976 |
| Elizabeth B. Andrews (D-AL) | 1971–1972 |
| Ella T. Grasso (D-CT) | 1971–1974 |
| Louise Day Hicks (D-MA) | 1971–1972 |
| Corrine Claiborne (Lindy) Boggs (D-LA) | 1973–1990 |
| Yvonne Braithwaite-Burke (D-CA) | 1973–1978 |
| Cardiss Collins (D-IL) | 1973– |
| Marjorie S. Holt (R-MD) | 1973–1986 |
| Elizabeth Holtzman (D-NY) | 1973–1980 |
| Barbara C. Jordan (D-TX) | 1973–1978 |
| Patricia Schroeder (D-CO) | 1973– |
| Leonor Kretzer Sullivan (D-MO) | 1973–1976 |
| Millicent Fenwick (R-NJ) | 1975–1982 |
| Martha E. Keys (D-KS) | 1975–1978 |
| Marilyn Lloyd (D-TN) | 1974– |
| Helen S. Meyner (D-NJ) | 1975–1978 |
| Shirley N. Pettis (R-CA) | 1975–1978 |
| Virginia Smith (R-NE) | 1975–1990 |
| Gladys Noon Spellman (D-MD) | 1975–1980 |
| Barbara Mikulski (D-MD) | 1977–1986 |
| Beverly B. Byron (D-MD) | 1979– |
| Mary Rose Oakar (D-OH) | 1977– |
| Geraldine Ferraro (D-NY) | 1979–1984 |
| Olympia J. Snowe (R-ME) | 1979– |

| Name | Years of Service | Name | Years of Service |
|------|------------------|------|------------------|
| Jean Ashbrook (R-OH) | 1981–1982 | Constance A. Morella (R-MD) | 1987– |
| Bobbi Fiedler (R-CA) | 1981–1986 | Liz J. Patterson (D-SC) | 1987– |
| Lynn Martin (R-IL) | 1981–1990 | Nancy Pelosi (D-CA) | 1987– |
| Marge Roukema (R-NJ) | 1981– | Patricia Saiki (R-HI) | 1987–1990 |
| Claudine Schneider (R-RI) | 1981–1990 | Louise Slaughter (D-NY) | 1987– |
| Barbara Boxer (D-CA) | 1983– | Jill Long (D-IN) | 1989– |
| Sala Burton (D-CA) | 1983–1988 | Nita M. Lowey (D-NY) | 1989– |
| Katie Hall (D-IN) | 1983–1984 | Jolene Unsoeld (D-WA) | 1989– |
| Nancy L. Johnson (R-CT) | 1983–1984 | Ileana Ros-Lehtinen (R-FL) | 1989– |
| Marcy Kaptur (D-OH) | 1983–1984 | Susan Molinari (R-NY) | 1990– |
| Barbara B. Kennelly (D-CT) | 1983– | Barbara-Rose Collins (D-MI) | 1991– |
| Barbara F. Vucanovich (R-NV) | 1983– | Rosa DeLauro (D-CT) | 1991– |
| Helen Delich Bentley (R-MD) | 1985– | Joan Kelly Horn (D-MO) | 1991– |
| Cathy Long (D-LA) | 1985–1986 | Eleanor Holmes Norton (D-DC) | 1991– |
| Jan Meyers (R-KS) | 1985– | Maxine Waters (D-CA) | 1991– |

Source: Information provided by the National Women's Political Caucus.

# Appendix 7

## African-Americans in the United States Congress

### SENATE

| Name | Years of Service |
|------|------------------|
| Hiram R. Revel (R-MS) | 1870–1871 |
| Blanche K. Bruce (R-MS) | 1875–1881 |
| Edward W. Brooke (R-MA) | 1967–1979 |

### HOUSE

| Name | Years of Service |
|------|------------------|
| Joseph H. Rainey (R-SC) | 1870–1879 |
| Jefferson F. Long (R-GA) | 1870–1871 |
| Robert B. Elliott (R-SC) | 1871–1874 |
| Robert C. DeLarge (R-SC) | 1871–1873 |
| Benjamin S. Turner (R-AL) | 1871–1873 |
| Josiah T. Walls (R-FL) | 1871–1873 |
| Richard H. Caine (R-SC) | 1873–1875; 1877–1879 |
| John R. Lynch (R-MS) | 1873–1877; 1882–1883 |
| James T. Rapier (R-AL) | 1873–1875 |
| Alonzo J. Ransier (R-SC) | 1873–1875 |
| Jeremiah Haralson (R-AL) | 1875–1877 |
| John A. Hyman (R-NC) | 1875–1877 |
| Charles E. Nash (R-LA) | 1875–1877 |
| Robert Smalls (R-SC) | 1875–1879 |
| James E. O'Hara (R-NC) | 1883–1887 |
| Henry P. Cheatham (R-NC) | 1889–1893 |
| John M. Langston (R-VA) | 1890–1891 |
| Thomas E. Miller (R-SC) | 1890–1891 |
| George W. Murray (R-SC) | 1893–1895; 1896–1897 |
| George W. White (R-NC) | 1897–1901 |
| Oscar DePriest (R-IL) | 1929–1935 |
| Arthur W. Mitchell (D-IL) | 1935–1943 |
| William L. Dawson (D-IL) | 1943–1970 |
| Adam Clayton Powell, Jr. (D-NY) | 1945–1967; 1969–1971 |
| Charles C. Diggs, Jr. (D-MI) | 1955–1980 |
| Robert N. C. Nix (D-PA) | 1958–1978 |
| Augustus F. Hawkins (D-CA) | 1963– |
| John Conyers, Jr. (D-MI) | 1965– |

| Name | Years of Service |
|------|------------------|
| William L. Clay (D-MO) | 1969– |
| Louis Stokes (D-OH) | 1969– |
| Shirley Chisholm (D-NY) | 1969–1982 |
| George W. Collins (D-IL) | 1970–1972 |
| Ronald V. Dellums (D-CA) | 1971– |
| Ralph H. Metcalfe (D-IL) | 1971–1978 |
| Parren J. Mitchell (D-MD) | 1971–1986 |
| Charles B. Rangel (D-NY) | 1971– |
| Walter E. Fauntroy (D-DC), Delegate | 1971–1991 |
| Yvonne B. Burke (D-CA) | 1973–1979 |
| Cardiss Collins (D-IL) | 1973– |
| Barbara C. Jordan (D-TX) | 1973–1978 |
| Andrew Young (D-GA) | 1973–1977 |
| Harold E. Ford (D-TN) | 1975– |
| Julian C. Dixon (D-CA) | 1979– |
| William H. Gray III (D-PA) | 1979– |
| Mickey Leland (D-TX) | 1979–1989 |
| Melvin Evans (R-VI), Delegate | 1979–1980 |
| Bennett McVey Steward (D-IL) | 1979–1980 |
| George W. Crockett (D-MI) | 1980–1990 |
| Mervyn M. Dymally (D-CA) | 1981– |
| Gus Savage (D-IL) | 1981– |
| Harold Washington (D-IL) | 1981–1983 |
| Katie Hall (D-IN) | 1982–1984 |
| Major Owens (D-NY) | 1983– |
| Edolphus Towns (D-NY) | 1983– |
| Alan Wheat (D-MO) | 1983– |
| Charles Hayes (D-IL) | 1983– |
| Alton R. Waldon, Jr. (D-NY) | 1986– |
| Mike Espy (D-MS) | 1987– |
| Floyd Flake (D-NY) | 1987– |
| John Lewis (D-GA) | 1987– |
| Kwesei Mfume (D-MD) | 1987– |
| Donald M. Payne (D-NJ) | 1989– |
| Craig Washington (D-TX) | 1989– |
| Barbara-Rose Collins (D-MI) | 1991– |
| Gary Franks (R-CT) | 1991– |
| William J. Jefferson (D-LA) | 1991– |
| Maxine Waters (D-CA) | 1991– |

Source: *101st Congress, 1988-1989*, pamphlet published by the Congressional Black Caucus.

# Appendix 8

## *Hispanic Members of the United States House of Representatives*

### Representatives

| Name | Years of Service |
|---|---|
| Romualdo Pacheco (R-CA) | 1879–1883 |
| Ladislas Lazaro (D-LA) | 1913–1927 |
| Benigno Cardenas Hernandez (R-NM) | 1915–1917; 1919–1921 |
| Nestor Montoyo (R-NM) | 1921–1923 |
| Joachim Octave Fernandez (D-LA) | 1931–1941 |
| Antonio Manuel Fernandez (D-LA) | 1943–1956 |
| Henry B. Gonzalez (D-TX) | 1961– |
| Edward R. Roybal (D-CA) | 1963– |
| E. Kika de la Garza (D-TX) | 1965– |
| Manuel Lujan, Jr. (R-NM) | 1969–1989 |
| Herman Badillo (D-NY) | 1971–1977 |
| Robert Garcia (D-NY) | 1978– |
| Tony Coehlo (D-CA) | 1979–1989 |
| Matthew G. Martinez (D-CA) | 1982– |
| Solomon P. Ortiz (D-TX) | 1983– |
| William B. Richardson (D-NM) | 1983– |
| Esteban E. Torres (D-CA) | 1983– |
| Albert G. Bustamente (D-TX) | 1985– |
| Ileana Ros-Lehtinen (R-FL) | 1989– |
| Jose E. Serrano (D-NY) | 1990– |

### Delegates

| Name | Years of Service |
|---|---|
| Joseph Marion Hernandex (W-FL) | 1822–1823 |
| Jose Manuel Gallegos (D-NM) | 1853–1855; 1871–1873 |
| Miguel Antonio Otero (D-NM) | 1856–1861 |
| Francisco Perea (R-NM) | 1863–1865 |
| Jose Francisco Chaves (R-NM) | 1865–1867 |
| Trinidad Romero (R-NM) | 1877–1879 |
| Mariano Sabino Otero (R-NM) | 1879–1881 |
| Tranquillino Luna (R-NM) | 1881–1884 |
| Francisco Manzanares (D-NM) | 1884–1885 |
| Pedro Perea (R-NM) | 1899–1901 |
| Julio Larringa (U-PR) | 1905–1911 |
| Luis Munoz Rivera (U-PR) | 1911–1916 |
| Felix Cordova Davila (U-PR) | 1917–1932 |
| Jose Lorenzo Pesquera (N.P.-PR) | 1932–1933 |
| Santiago Iglesias (C-PR) | 1933–1939 |
| Bolivar Pagan (C-PR) | 1939–1945 |
| Jesus T. Pinero (P.D.-PR) | 1945–1948 |
| Antonio Fernos-Isern (P.D.-PR) | 1949–1965 |
| Santiago Polanco-Abreu (P.D.-PR) | 1965–1969 |
| Jorge Luis Cordova (N.P.-PR) | 1969–1973 |
| Ron de Lugo (D-VI) | 1973–1979; 1981– |
| Jamie Benitez (P.D.-PR) | 1973–1979 |
| Baltasar Corrada (N.P.-PR) | 1977–1984 |
| Ben Blaz (R-Guam) | 1985– |
| Jamie B. Fuster (P.D.-PR) | 1985– |

Source: Congressional Hispanic Caucus.

# Appendix 9

## *Party Switchers in the United States Congress (1952–1990)*

| Name | State | House | Direction | Year |
|------|-------|-------|-----------|------|
| Wayne Morse | OR | Senate | R > I > D | 1952 |
| Strom Thurmond | SC | Senate | D > R | 1964 |
| Albert W. Watson | SC | House | D > R | 1965 |
| Harry F. Byrd, Jr. | VA | Senate | D > I | 1970 |
| Ogden R. Reid | NY | House | R > D | 1972 |
| Donald W. Reigle | MI | House | R > D | 1973 |
| John Jarman | OK | House | D > R | 1975 |
| Peter A. Peyser | NY | House | R > D | 1976 |
| Eugene V. Atkinson | PA | House | D > R | 1981 |
| Bob Stump | AZ | House | D > R | 1981 |
| Phil Gramm | TX | House | D > R | 1983 |
| Andy Ireland | FL | House | D > R | 1984 |
| Bill Grant | FL | House | D > R | 1989 |
| Tommy Robinson | OK | House | D > R | 1989 |

Source: *Congressional Quarterly Almanacs,* 1952–1989. Washington, DC: Congressional Quarterly.

# Appendix 10

## *Summary of Results of Presidential Elections*

Until 1804, electors cast two votes. The candidate with the highest total was elected President, second highest, Vice President. No popular votes were recorded.

### 1788-1789

| Electoral Votes | |
|---|---|
| 69 | George Washington |
| 34 | John Adams |
| 9 | John Jay |
| 6 | Robert Harrison |
| 6 | John Rutledge |
| 14 | (seven others) |

### 1792

| Electoral Votes | |
|---|---|
| 132 | George Washington |
| 77 | John Adams |
| 50 | George Clinton |
| 5 | (two others) |

### 1796

| Electoral Votes | |
|---|---|
| 71 | John Adams, *Federalist* |
| 68 | Thomas Jefferson, *Democratic-Republican* |
| 59 | Thomas Pinckney, *Federalist* |
| 30 | Aaron Burr, *Democratic-Republican* |
| 15 | Samuel Adams |
| 11 | Oliver Ellsworth |
| 22 | (seven others) |

### 1800

| Electoral Votes | |
|---|---|
| 73 | Thomas Jefferson, *Democratic-Republican* |
| 73 | Aaron Burr, *Democratic-Republican* |
| 65 | John Adams, *Federalist* |
| 64 | Charles C. Pinckney, *Federalist* |
| 1 | John Jay, *Federalist* (vote cast to keep Adams and Pinckney from tying) |

Since Jefferson and Burr tied, the House of Representatives decided the election; Jefferson won on the 36th ballot.

After the passage of the Twelfth Amendment to the Constitution, ratified in 1804, electors cast one ballot for President and Vice President, distinguishing which candidate was for which office.

### 1804

| Electoral Votes | |
|---|---|
| 162 | Thomas Jefferson and George Clinton, *Democratic-Republican* |
| 14 | Charles C. Pinckney and Rufus King, *Federalist* |

### 1808

| Electoral Votes | |
|---|---|
| 122 | James Madison and George Clinton, *Democratic-Republican* |
| 47 | Charles C. Pinckney and Rufus King, *Federalist* |
| 6 | George Clinton, *Democratic-Republican* |
| 1 | Not Voted |

### 1812

| Electoral Votes | |
|---|---|
| 128 | James Madison and Elbridge Gerry, *Democratic-Republican* |
| 89 | De Witt Clinton and Jared Ingersoll, *Federalist* |
| 1 | Not Voted |

### 1816

| Electoral Votes | |
|---|---|
| 183 | James Monroe and Daniel D. Tompkins, *Democratic-Republican* |
| 34 | Rufus King and John Howard, *Federalist* |
| 4 | Not Voted |

### 1820

| Electoral Votes | |
|---|---|
| 231 | James Monroe and Daniel D. Tompkins, *Democrati-Republican* (Tompkins actually received only 218 votes for Vice President) |
| 1 | John Quincy Adams, *Democratic-Republican* (4 others divided 14 votes for Vice-President) |

This election was essentially uncontested; the one vote for Adams was to assure that Monroe was not chosen unanimously.

### 1824

*For President*

| Electoral Votes | Popular Votes | |
|---|---|---|
| 84 | 108,740 | John Quincy Adams |
| 99 | 153,544 | Andrew Jackson |
| 37 | 47,136 | Henry Clay |
| 41 | 46,618 | William J. Crawford |

*For Vice President*

| Electoral Votes | |
|---|---|
| 182 | John C. Calhoun |
| 30 | Nathan Sanford |
| 24 | Nathaniel Macon |
| 13 | Andrew Jackson |
| 9 | Martin Van Buren |
| 2 | Henry Clay |

There were no national conventions—and essentially no partisan labels in this election. Various state legislatures nominated various candidates. Since no candidate received a majority of the electoral vote, the election was decided by the House of Representatives, under the terms of the Twelfth Amendment, with each state having one vote, to be determined by a majority of the members of its delegation. On February 9, 1825, thirteen states voted for Adams, who was elected; seven states cast their votes for Jackson; and four, for Crawford.

## 1828

| Electoral Votes | Popular Votes | |
|---|---|---|
| 178 | 647,286 | Andrew Jackson and John C. Calhoun, *Democratic-Republican* |
| 83 | 508,064 | John Quincy Adams and Richard Rush, *National Republican* |

## 1832

| Electoral Votes | Popular Votes | |
|---|---|---|
| 219 | 687,502 | Andrew Jackson and Martin Van Buren, *Democratic* |
| 49 | 530,189 | Henry Clay and John Sergeant, *National Republican* |
| 11 | | John Floyd and Henry Lee, *Nullifiers* (independent) |
| 7 | | William Wirt and Amos Ellmaker, *Antimasonic* |
| 2 | | Not Voted |

## 1836

| Electoral Votes | Popular Votes | |
|---|---|---|
| 219 | 765,483 | Martin Van Buren and Richard M Johnson, *Democratic* |
| 73 | 739,795 | William Henry Harrison |
| 26 | | Hugh L. White |
| 14 | | Daniel Webster and Frances Granger, John Tyler, *Whig* |
| 11 | | Willie P. Mangrim, *Anti-Jackson* |

The Whigs held no convention; various candidates ran under the Whig label in different states as a strategy to maximize anti-Jackson support, with the hopes of throwing the election into the House as had happened in 1824.

## 1840

| Electoral Votes | Popular Votes | |
|---|---|---|
| 234 | 1,274,624 | William H Harrison and John Tyler, *Whig* |
| 60 | 1,127,781 | Martin Van Buren and Richard M Johnson, Littleton W. Tazewill, James K. Polk, *Democratic* |

James G. Birney and Thomas Earle, *Liberty*

Various candidates were paired with Van Buren as vice presidential candidates in different states as the convention decided not to endorse any one of the many qualified candidates for Vice President.

## 1844

| Electoral Votes | Popular Votes | |
|---|---|---|
| 170 | 1,338,464 | James K. Polk and George M. Dallas, *Democratic* |
| 105 | 1,300,097 | Henry Clay and Theodore Frelinghuysen, *Whig* |
| 6 | 2,300 | James G. Birney and Thomas Morris, *Liberty* |
| | | John Tyler, *National Democratic* |

(eventually withdrew in favor of Polk)

## 1848

| Electoral Votes | Popular Votes | |
|---|---|---|
| 163 | 1,360,967 | Zachary Taylor and Millard Fillmore, *Whig* |
| 127 | 1,222,342 | Lewis Cass and William O. Butler, *Democratic* |
| | 291,263 | Martin Van Buren and Charles F. Adams, *Free Soil* |
| | 2,545 | Gerrit Smith and Charles C. Foote, *National Liberty* |
| | | John P. Hale and Leicester King, *Barnburners-Liberty* (later relinquished the nomination) |

## 1852

| Electoral Votes | Popular Votes | |
|---|---|---|
| 254 | 1,601,117 | Franklin Pierce and William R. de V. King, *Democratic* |
| 42 | 1,385,453 | Winfield Scott and William A. Graham, *Whig* |
| | 155,825 | John P. Hale and George W. Julian, *Free Soil* |

## 1856

| Electoral Votes | Popular Votes | |
|---|---|---|
| 174 | 1,832,955 | James Buchanan and John C. Breckinridge, *Democratic* |
| 114 | 1,339,932 | John C. Frémont and William L. Dayton, *Republican* |
| 8 | 871,731 | Millard Fillmore and Andrew J. Donelson, *American (Know-Nothing)* and *Whig (Silver Grays)* |
| | | Nathaniel P. Banks and William F. Johnson, *North American* (declined nomination, supported Republican candidates) |

## 1860

| Electoral Votes | Popular Votes | |
|---|---|---|
| 180 | 1,865,593 | Abraham Lincoln and Hannibal Hamlin, *Republican* |
| 12 | 1,382,713 | Steven A. Douglas and Herschel V. Johnson, *Democratic* |
| 72 | 848,356 | John C. Breckinridge and Joseph Lane, *Southern Democratic* |
| 39 | 592,906 | John Bell and Edward Everett, *Constitutional Union* |

## 1864

| Electoral Votes | Popular Votes | |
|---|---|---|
| 212 | 2,206,938 | Abraham Lincoln and Andrew Johnson, *Republican* |
| 21 | 1,803,787 | George B. McClellan and George Pendleton, *Democratic* John C. Frémont and John Cochrane, *Independent Republican* (declined nomination, supported Republican candidate) |
| 81 | Not Voted | |

## 1868

| Electoral Votes | Popular Votes | |
|---|---|---|
| 214 | 3,013,421 | Ulysses S. Grant and Schuyler Colfax, *Republican* |
| 80 | 2,706,829 | Horatio Seymour and Francis P. Blair, Jr., *Democratic* |
| 23 | Not Voted | |

## 1872

| Electoral Votes | Popular Votes | |
|---|---|---|
| 286 | 3,596,745 | Ulysses S. Grant and Henry Wilson, *Republican* and *National Working Men's Party* |
| * | 2,843,446 | Horace Greeley and Benjamin G. Brown, *Liberal Republican Democratic* and *Liberal Republican Party of Colored Men* William S. Groesbeck and Frederick Olmsted, *Independent Liberal Republican Party* |
| | 29,489 | Charles O'Conor and John Q. Adams, *Straight-Out Democratic* |
| | 3,371 | James Brack and John Russell, *Prohibition* Victoria Woodhull and Frederick Douglass, *People's Party (Equal Rights Party)* David Davis and Joel Parker, *Labor Reform* |
| 17 | Not Voted | |

*Greeley died shortly after the election. Electoral votes were cast for Thomas A. Hendricks (42), Benjamin G. Brown (18), Charles J. Jenkins (2), and David Davis (1).

## 1876

| Electoral Votes | Popular Votes | |
|---|---|---|
| 185 | 4,036,572 | Rutherford B. Hayes and William Wheeler, *Republican* |
| 184 | 4,284,020 | Samuel J. Tilden and Thomas A. Hendricks, *Democratic* |
| | 87,737 | Peter Cooper and Samuel F. Cary, *Greenback* |
| | 6,743 | Green C. Smith and Gideon T. Stewart, *Prohibition* |
| | 459 | James B. Walker and Donald Kirkpatrick, *American National* |

## 1880

| Electoral Votes | Popular Votes | |
|---|---|---|
| 214 | 4,453,295 | James A. Garfield and Chester A. Arthur, *Republican* |
| 155 | 4,414,082 | Winfield S. Hancock and William A. English, *Democratic* |
| | 308,578 | James B. Weaver and Benjamin J. Chambers, *Greenback Labor* |
| | 10,305 | Neal Dow and Henry A. Thompson, *Prohibition* |
| | 631 | John W. Phelps and Samuel C. Pomeroy, *American* |

## 1884

| Electoral Votes | Popular Votes | |
|---|---|---|
| 219 | 4,879,507 | Grover Cleveland and Thomas A. Hendricks, *Democratic* |
| 182 | 4,850,293 | James G. Blaine and John A. Logan, *Republican* |
| | 175,370 | Benjamin F. Butler and Absolom M. West, *Anti-Monopoly* and *Greenback-Labor* |
| | 150,369 | John P. St. John and William Daniel, *Prohibition* Samuel C. Pomeroy and John A. Conant, *American Prohibitio* Belva A. B. Lockwood and Marietta L. B. Stow, *Equal Rights* |

## 1888

| Electoral Votes | Popular Votes | |
|---|---|---|
| 223 | 5,447,129 | Benjamin Harrison and Levi P. Morton, *Republican* |
| 168 | 5,537,857 | Grover Cleveland and Allan G. Thurman, *Democratic* |
| | 249,506 | Clinton B. Fisk and John A. Brooks, *Prohibition* |
| | 146,935 | Alson J. Streeter and Charles E. Cunningham, *Union Labor* |
| | 1,020 | Robert H. Cowdrey and William Wakefield, *United Labor* |
| | 1,615 | James L. Curtis and Peter D. Wigginton, *American* Belva A. B. Lockwood and Alfred H. Love, *Equal Rights* Albert E. Redstone and John Colvin, *Industrial Reform* |

## 1892

| Electoral Votes | Popular Votes | |
|---|---|---|
| 277 | 5,555,426 | Grover Cleveland and Adlai E. Stevenson, *Democratic* |

| Electoral Votes | Popular Votes | |
|---|---|---|
| 145 | 5,182,690 | Benjamin Harrison and Whitelaw Reid, *Republican* |
| 22 | 1,029,846 | James B. Weaver and James G. Field, *People's Party of America* |
| | 264,133 | John Bidwell and James B. Cranfill, *Prohibition* |
| | 21,164 | Simon Wing and Charles H. Matchett, *Socialist Labor* |

## 1896

| Electoral Votes | Popular Votes | |
|---|---|---|
| 271 | 7,102,246 | William McKinley and Garret A. Hobart, *Republican* |
| 176 | 6,492,559 | William Jennings Bryan and Arthur Sewall, *Democratic* and *National Silver Party (Bi-Metallic League)* (Bryan also nominated by the *People's Party [Populist]* with Thomas E. Watson) |
| | 133,148 | John M. Palmer and Simon B. Buckner, *National Democratic* |
| | 132,007 | Joshua Levering and Hale Johnson, *Prohibition* |
| | 36,274 | Charles H. Matchett and Matthew Maguire, *Socialist Labor* |
| | 13,969 | Charles E. Bentley and James H. Southgate, *National* |

## 1900

| Electoral Votes | Popular Votes | |
|---|---|---|
| 292 | 7,218,491 | William McKinley and Theodore Roosevelt, *Republican* |
| 155 | 6,356,734 | William Jennings Bryan and Adlai E. Stevenson *Democratic* and *Silver Republican* |
| | 208,914 | John G. Wooley and Henry B. Metcalf, *Prohibition* |
| | 87,814 | Eugene V. Debs and Job Harriman, *Social Democratic* |
| | 50,373 | Wharton Barker and Ignatius Donnelly, *People's Party (Populist–Anti-Fusionist Faction)* |
| | 39,739 | Joseph F. Malloney and Valentine Remmel, *Socialist Labor* |
| | 5,693 | Seth H. Ellis and Samuel T. Nicholson, *Union Reform* |
| | 518 | Jonah F. R. Leonard and David H. Martin, *United Christian* |

## 1904

| Electoral Votes | Popular Votes | |
|---|---|---|
| 336 | 7,628,461 | Theodore Roosevelt and Charles Warren Fairbanks, *Republican* |
| 140 | 5,084,223 | Alton Brooks Parker and Henry G. Davis, *Democratic* |
| | 402,283 | Eugene V. Debs and Benjamin Hanford, *Socialist* |
| | 258,536 | Silas Comfort Swallow and George W. Carroll, *Prohibition* |
| | 117,183 | Thomas E. Watson and Thomas H. Tibbles, *People's Party (Populist)* |
| | 31,249 | Charles H. Corregan and William W. Cox, *Socialist Labor* |
| | 826 | Austin Holcomb and A. King, *Continental* |

## 1908

| Electoral Votes | Popular Votes | |
|---|---|---|
| 321 | 7,765,320 | William Howard Taft and James S. Sherman, *Republican* |
| 162 | 6,412,294 | William Jennings Bryan and John W. Kern, *Democratic* |
| | 420,793 | Eugene V. Debs and Benjamin Hanford, *Socialist* |
| | 253,840 | Eugene W. Chafin and Aaron S. Watkins, *Prohibition* |
| | 82,872 | Thomas L. Hisgen and John T. Graves, *Independence* |
| | 29,100 | Thomas E. Watson and Samuel Williams, *People's Party (Populist)* |
| | 14,021 | August Gillhaus and Donald L. Munro, *Socialist Labor* |
| | 461 | Daniel B. Turney and Lorenzo S. Coffin, *United Christian* |

## 1912

| Electoral Votes | Popular Votes | |
|---|---|---|
| 435 | 6,296,547 | Woodrow Wilson and Thomas R. Marshall, *Democratic* |
| 88 | 4,118,571 | Theodore Roosevelt and Hiram W. Johnson, *Progressive ("Bull Moose")* |
| 8 | 3,486,720 | William Howard Taft and James S. Sherman (Sherman died Oct. 30 and was replaced by Nicholas Murray Bulter), *Republican* |
| | 900,672 | Eugene V. Debs and Emil Seidel, *Socialist* |
| | 206,275 | Eugene W. Chafin and Aaron S. Watkins, *Prohibition* |
| | 28,750 | Arthur E. Reimer and August Gillhaus, *Socialist Labor* |

## 1916

| Electoral Votes | Popular Votes | |
|---|---|---|
| 277 | 9,127,695 | Woodrow Wilson and Thomas R. Marshall, *Democratic* |
| 254 | 8,533,507 | Charles Evans Hughes and Charles W. Fairbanks, *Republican* |
| | 585,113 | Allan L. Benson and George R. Kirkpatrick, *Socialist* |
| | 220,750 | James F. Hanly and Ira Landrith, *Prohibition* |
| | 28,750 | Arthur E. Reimer and Caleb Harrison, *Socialist Labor* |
| | 35,234 | Theodore Roosevelt and John M. Parker, *Progressive* (Roosevelt declined the nomination) |

## 1920

| Electoral Votes | Popular Votes | |
|---|---|---|
| 404 | 16,153,115 | Warren G. Harding and Calvin Coolidge, *Republican* |
| 127 | 9,133,092 | James M. Cox and Franklin D. Roosevelt, *Democratic* |
| | 915,490 | Eugene V. Debs and Seymour Stedman, *Socialist* |
| | 265,229 | Parley P. Christensen and Max S. Hayes, *Farmer-Labor* |
| | 189,339 | Aaron S. Watkins and D. Leigh Colvin, *Prohibition* |
| | 48,098 | James Ferguson and William J. Hough, *American* |
| | 30,594 | William W. Cox and August Gillhaus, *Socialist Labor* |
| | 5,833 | Robert C. Macauley and Richard C. Barnum, *Single Tax* |

## 1924

| Electoral Votes | Popular Votes | |
|---|---|---|
| 382 | 15,719,921 | Calvin Coolidge and Charles G. Dawes, *Republican* |
| 136 | 8,386,704 | John W. Davis and Charles W. Bryan, *Democratic* |
| 13 | 4,832,532 | Robert M. La Follette and Burton K. Wheeler, *Progressive* |
| | 56,292 | Herman P. Faris and Marie Caroline Brehm, *Prohibition* |
| | 34,174 | Frank T. Johns and Verne L. Reynolds, *Socialist Labor* |
| | 33,360 | William Z. Foster and Benjamin Gitlow, *Communist* |
| | 24,340 | Gilbert O. Nations and Leander L. Pickett, *American* |
| | 2,948 | William J. Wallace and John C. Lincoln, *Commonwealth Land* |

## 1928

| Electoral Votes | Popular Votes | |
|---|---|---|
| 444 | 21,437,277 | Herbert C. Hoover and Charles Curtis, *Republican* |
| 67 | 15,007,698 | Alfred E. Smith and Joseph T. Robinson, *Democratic* |
| | 265,583 | Norman Thomas and James H. Maurer, *Socialist* |
| | 46,896 | William Z. Foster and Benjamin Gitlow, *Communist* |
| | 21,586 | Verne L. Reynolds and John W. Aiken, *Socialist Labor* |
| | 20,101 | William F. Varney and James A. Edgerton, *Prohibition* |
| | 6,390 | Frank E. Webb and L. R. Tillman, *Farmer-Labor* |

## 1932

| Electoral Votes | Popular Votes | |
|---|---|---|
| 472 | 22,829,501 | Franklin D. Roosevelt and John N. Garner, *Democratic* |
| 59 | 15,760,684 | Herbert C. Hoover and Charles Curtis, *Republican* |

| | 884,649 | Norman Thomas and James H. Maurer, *Socialist* |
| | 103,253 | William Z. Foster and James W. Ford, *Communist* |
| | 81,872 | William D. Upshaw and Frank S. Regan, *Prohibition* |
| | 53,247 | William H. Harvey and Frank Hemenway, *Liberty* |
| | 34,043 | Verne L. Reynolds and Jeremiah D. Crowley, *Socialist Labor* |
| | 7,431 | Jacob S. Coxey and Julius J. Reiter, *Farmer-Labor* |
| | 1,645 | John Zahand and Florence Garvin, *National* |
| | 740 | James R. Cox and Victor C. Tisdal, *Jobless* |

## 1936

| Electoral Votes | Popular Votes | |
|---|---|---|
| 523 | 27,757,333 | Franklin D. Roosevelt and John N. Garner, *Democratic* |
| 8 | 16,684,231 | Alfred M. Landon and Frank Knox, *Republican* |
| | 892,267 | William Lemke and Thomas C. O'Brien, *Union* |
| | 187,833 | Norman Thomas and George A. Nelson, *Socialist* |
| | 80,171 | Earl Browder and James W. Ford, *Communist* |
| | 37,677 | D. Leigh Colvin and Claude A. Watson, *Prohibition* |
| | 12,829 | John W. Aiken and Emil F. Teichert, *Socialist Labor* |
| | 1,598 | William Dudley Pelley and Willard W. Kemp, *Christian* |

## 1940

| Electoral Votes | Popular Votes | |
|---|---|---|
| 449 | 27,313,041 | Franklin D. Roosevelt and Henry A. Wallace, *Democratic* |
| 82 | 22,348,480 | Wendell Willkie and Charles L. McNary, *Republican* |
| | 116,410 | Norman Thomas and Maynard C. Krueger, *Socialist* |
| | 58,708 | Roger Babson and Edgar V. Moorman, *Prohibition* |
| | 46,259 | Earl Browder and James W. Ford, *Communist* |
| | 14,892 | John W. Aiken and Aaron M. Orange, *Socialist Labor* |

## 1944

| Electoral Votes | Popular Votes | |
|---|---|---|
| 432 | 25,612,610 | Franklin D. Roosevelt and Harry S Truman, *Democratic* |
| 99 | 22,017,617 | Thomas E. Dewey and John W. Bricker, *Republican* |
| | 79,003 | Norman Thomas and Darlington Hoopes, *Socialist* |
| | 74,799 | Claude A. Watson and Andrew Johnson, *Prohibition* |
| | 5,191 | Edward A. Teichert and Arla A. Albaugh, *Socialist Labor* |

| | | |
|---|---|---|
| 1,780 | Gerald L. K. Smith and Harry Romer, *American First* | |

| | |
|---|---|
| 8 | Gerald L. K. Smith and Charles F. Robertson, *Christian Nationalist* |

## 1948

| Electoral Votes | Popular Votes | |
|---|---|---|
| 203 | 24,179,345 | Harry S Truman and Alben W. Barkley, *Democratic* |
| 189 | 21,991,291 | Thomas E. Dewey and Earl Warren, *Republican* |
| 39 | 1,176,125 | Strom Thurmond and Fielding L. Wright, *States' Rights* |
| | 1,157,326 | Henry A. Wallace and Glen H. Taylor, *Progressive* |
| | 139,572 | Norman Thomas and Tucker P. Smith, *Socialist* |
| | 103,900 | Claude A. Watson and Dale H. Learn, *Prohibition* |
| | 29,241 | Edward A. Teichert and Stephen Emery, *Socialist Labor* |
| | 13,614 | Farrell Dobbs and Grace Carlson, *Socialist Workers* |

## 1952

| Electoral Votes | Popular Votes | |
|---|---|---|
| 442 | 33,936,234 | Dwight D. Eisenhower and Richard M. Nixon, *Republican* |
| 89 | 27,314,992 | Adlai E. Stevenson and John J. Sparkman, *Democratic* |
| | 140,023 | Vincent Hallinan and Charlotta Bass, *Progressive* |
| | 72,949 | Stuart Hamblen and Enoch A. Holtwick, *Prohibition* |
| | 30,267 | Eric Hass and Stephen Emery, *Socialist Labor* |
| | 20,203 | Darlington Hoopes and Samuel H. Friedman, *Socialist* |
| | 10,321 | Farrell Dobbs and Myra Tanner Weiss, *Socialist Workers* |
| | 4,203 | Henry B. Krajewski and Frank Jenkins, *Poor Man's* |

## 1956

| Electoral Votes | Popular Votes | |
|---|---|---|
| 457 | 37,590,472 | Dwight D. Eisenhower and Richard M. Nixon, *Republican* |
| 73 | 26,022,752 | Adlai E. Stevenson and Estes Kefauver, *Democratic* |
| | 111,178 | T. Coleman Andrews and Thomas H. Werdel, *States' Rights* |
| | 44,450 | Eric Hass and Georgia Cozzini, *Socialist Labor* |
| | 41,937 | Enoch A. Holtwick and Edwin M. Cooper, *Prohibition* |
| | 7,797 | Farrell Dobbs and Myra Tanner Weiss, *Socialist Workers* |
| | 2,657 | Harry Flood Byrd and William E. Jenner, *States' Rights* |
| | 2,126 | Darlington Hoopes and Samuel H. Friedman, *Socialist* |
| | 1,829 | Henry B. Krajewski and Anne Marie Yezo, *American Third Party* |

## 1960

| Electoral Votes | Popular Votes | |
|---|---|---|
| 303 | 34,226,731 | John F. Kennedy and Lyndon B. Johnson, *Democratic* |
| 219 | 34,108,157 | Richard M. Nixon and Henry Cabot Lodge, *Republican* |
| | 47,522 | Eric Hass and Georgia Cozzini, *Socialist Labor* |
| | 46,203 | Rutherford L. Decker and E. Harold Munn, *Prohibition* |
| | 44,977 | Orval E. Faubus and John G. Crommelin, *National States' Rights* |
| | 40,165 | Farrell Dobbs and Myra Tanner Weiss, *Socialist Workers* |
| | 18,162 | Charles L. Sullivan and Merritt B. Curtis, *Constitution* |
| | 708 | J. Bracken Lee and Kent H. Courtney, *Conservative* |
| | 204 | C. Benton Coiner and Edward J. Silverman, *Conservative* |
| | 767 | Lar Daly and B. M. Miller, *Tax Cut* |
| | 485 | Clennon King and Reginald Carter, *Independent Afro-American* |
| | 401 | Merritt B. Curtis and B. M. Miller, *Constitution* |

## 1964

| Electoral Votes | Popular Votes | |
|---|---|---|
| 486 | 43,129,566 | Lyndon B. Johnson and Hubert H. Humphrey, *Democratic* |
| 52 | 27,178,188 | Barry M. Goldwater and William E. Miller, *Republican* |
| | 45,219 | Eric Hass and Henning A. Blomen, *Socialist Labor* |
| | 32,720 | Clifton DeBerry and Edward Shaw, *Socialist Workers* |
| | 23,267 | E. Harold Munn and Mark R. Shaw, *Prohibition* |
| | 6,953 | John Kasper and J. B. Stoner, *National States' Rights* |
| | 5,060 | Joseph B. Lightburn and T. C. Billings, *Constitution* |
| | 19 | James Hensley and John O. Hopkins, *Universal* |

## 1968

| Electoral Votes | Popular Votes | |
|---|---|---|
| 301 | 31,785,480 | Richard M. Nixon and Spiro T. Agnew, *Republican* |
| 191 | 31,275,166 | Hubert H. Humphrey and Edmund S. Muskie, *Democratic* |
| 46 | 9,906,473 | George C. Wallace and Curtis E. LeMay, *American Independent* |
| | 52,588 | Henning A. Blomen and George S. Taylor, *Socialist Labor* |

| | |
|---|---|
| 47,133 | Dick Gregory with various vice presidential candidates, *Peace and Freedom* |
| 41,388 | Fred Halstead and Paul Boutelle, *Socialist Workers* |
| 36,563 | Eldridge Cleaver with various vice presidential candidates, *Peace and Freedom* |
| 25,552 | Eugene J. McCarthy under various titles and written-in, but without indication of vice presidential candidates |
| 15,123 | E. Harold Munn and Rolland E. Fisher, *Prohibition* |
| 1,519 | Venture Chavez and Adelicio Moya, *People's Constitutional* |
| 1,075 | Charlene Mitchell and Michael Zagarell, *Communist* |
| 142 | James Hensley and Roscoe B. Mackenna, *Universal* |
| 34 | Richard K. Troxell and Merle Thayer, *Constitution* |
| 17 | Kent M. Soeters and James P. Powers, *Berkeley Defense Group* |

## 1972

| Electoral Votes | Popular Votes | |
|---|---|---|
| 520 | 47,169,911 | Richard M. Nixon and Spiro T. Agnew, *Republican* |
| 17 | 29,170,383 | George S. McGovern and R. Sargent Shriver, *Democratic* |
| | 1,099,482 | John G. Schmitz and Thomas J. Anderson, *American* |
| | 78,756 | Benjamin Spock and Julius Hobson, *People's* |
| | 66,677 | Linda Jenness and Andrew Pulley, *Socialist Workers* |
| | 53,814 | Louis Fisher and Genevieve Gunderson, *Socialist Labor* |
| | 25,595 | Gus Hall and Jarvis Tyner, *Communist* |
| | 13,505 | E. Harold Munn and Marshall E. Uncapher, *Prohibition* |
| | 3,673 | John Hospers and Theodora Nathan, *Libertarian* |
| | 1,743 | John V. Mahalchik and Irving Homer, *American First* |
| | 220 | Gabriel Green and Daniel Fry, *Universal* |

## 1976

| Electoral Votes | Popular Votes | |
|---|---|---|
| 297 | 40,830,763 | Jimmy Carter and Walter F. Mondale, *Democratic* |
| 240 | 39,147,793 | Gerald R. Ford and Robert Dole, *Republican* |
| | 756,691 | Eugene J. McCarthy with various vice-presidential candidates, *Independent* |
| | 173,001 | Roger L. MacBride and David D. Bergland, *Libertarian* |
| | 170,531 | Lester G. Maddox and William D. Dyke, *American Independent* |
| | 160,773 | Thomas J. Anderson and Rufus Shackelford, *American* |

| | |
|---|---|
| 91,341 | Peter Camejo and Willie Mae Reid, *Socialist Workers* |
| 58,992 | Gus Hall and Jarvis Tyner, *Communist* |
| 49,024 | Margaret Wright and Benjamin Spock, *People's* |
| 40,043 | Lyndon LaRouche and R. W. Evans, *United States Labor* |
| 15,934 | Benjamin C. Bubar and Earl F. Dodge, *Prohibition* |
| 9,616 | Julius Levin and Constance Blomen, *Socialist Labor* |
| 6,038 | Frank P. Zeidler and J. Q. Brisben, *Socialist* |
| 361 | Ernest L. Miller and Roy N. Eddy, *Restoration* |
| 36 | Frank Taylor and Henry Swan, *United American* |

## 1980

| Electoral Votes | Popular Votes | |
|---|---|---|
| 489 | 43,904,153 | Ronald Reagan and George Bush, *Republican* |
| 49 | 35,483,883 | Jimmy Carter and Walter F. Mondale, *Democratic* |
| | 5,720,060 | John B. Anderson and Patrick J. Lucey, *Independent* |
| | 921,299 | Edward E. Clark and David Koch, *Libertarian* |
| | 234,294 | Barry Commoner and LaDonna Harris, *Citizens* |
| | 45,023 | Gus Hall and Angela Davis, *Communist* |
| | 41,268 | John R. Rarick and Eileen M. Shearer, *American Independent* |
| | 38,737 | Clifton DeBerry and Matilde Zimmermann, *Socialist Workers* |
| | 32,327 | Ellen McCormack and Carroll Driscoll, *Right to Life* |
| | 18,116 | Maureen Smith and Elizabeth Barron, *Peace and Freedom* |
| | 13,300 | Deirdre Griswold and Larry Holmes, *Workers World* |
| | 7,212 | Benjamin C. Bubar and Earl F. Dodge, *Statesman* |
| | 6,898 | David McReynolds and Diane Dufenbrock, *Socialist* |
| | 6,647 | Percy L. Greaves and Frank L. Varnum, *American* |
| | 6,272 | Andrew Pulley and Matilde Zimmermann, *Socialist Workers* |
| | 4,029 | Richard Congress and Matilde Zimmermann, *Socialist Workers* |
| | 3,694 | Kurt Lynen and Harry Kieve, *Middle Class* |
| | 1,718 | Bill Gahres and J. F. Loughlin, *Down With Lawyers* |
| | 1,555 | Frank W. Shelton and George E. Jackson, *American* |
| | 923 | Martin E. Wendelken with no vice presidential candidate, *Independent* |
| | 296 | Harley McLain and Jewelie Goeller, *Natural Peoples* |

## 1984

| Electoral Votes | Popular Votes | |
|---|---|---|
| 525 | 54,455,075 | Ronald Reagan and George Bush, *Republican* |
| 13 | 37,577,185 | Walter F. Mondale and Geraldine A. Ferraro, *Democratic* |
| | 228,314 | David Bergland and James A. Lewis, *Libertarian* |
| | 78,807 | Lyndon H. LaRouche and Billy M. Davis, *Independent* |
| | 72,200 | Sonia Johnson and Richard Walton, *Citizens* |
| | 66,336 | Bob Richards and Maureen Salaman, *Populist* |
| | 46,868 | Dennis L. Serrette and Nancy Ross, *Alliance* |
| | 36,386 | Gus Hall and Angela Davis, *Communist* |
| | 24,706 | Mel Mason and Matilde Zimmermann, *Socialist Workers* |
| | 17,985 | Larry Holmes and Gloria LaRiva, *Workers World* |
| | 13,161 | Delmar Dennis and Traves Brownlee, *American* |
| | 10,801 | Ed Winn and Helen Halyard, *Workers League* |
| | 4,242 | Earl F. Dodge and Warren C. Martin, *Prohibition* |
| | 1,486 | John B. Anderson and Grace Pierce, *National Unity* |
| | 892 | Gerald Baker and Ferris Alger, *Big Deal* |
| | 825 | Arthur J. Lowery and Raymond L. Garland, *United States Citizens* |

## 1988

| Electoral Votes | Popular Votes | |
|---|---|---|
| 426 | 48,886,097 | George Bush and J. Danforth Quayle, *Republican* |
| 112 | 41,809,074 | Michael S. Dukakis and Lloyd Bentsen, *Democratic* |
| | 432,179 | Ron Paul and Andre V. Marrou, *Libertarian* |
| | 217,219 | Lenora B. Fulani and Joyce Dattner, *New Alliance* |
| | 47,074 | David E. Duke and Floyd C. Parker, *Populist* |
| | 30,905 | Eugene J. McCarthy and Florence Rice, *Consumer* |
| | 27,818 | James C. Griffin and Charles J. Morsa, *American Independent* |
| | 25,562 | Lyndon H. LaRouche and Debra H. Freeman, *National Economic Recovery* |
| | 20,504 | William A. Marra and Joan Andrews, *Right to Life* |
| | 18,693 | Ed Winn and Barry Porster, *Workers League* |
| | 15,604 | James Warren and Kathleen Mickells, *Socialist Workers* |
| | 10,370 | Herbert Lewin and Vikki Murdock, *Peace and Freedom* |
| | 8,002 | Earl F. Dodge and George Ormsby, *Prohibition* |
| | 7,846 | Larry Holmes and Gloria LaRiva, *Workers World* |
| | 3,882 | Willa Kenoyer and Ron Ehrenreich, *Socialist* |
| | 3,475 | Delmar Dennis and Earl Jeppson, *American* |
| | 1,949 | Jack Herer and Dana Beal, *Grassroots* |
| | 372 | Louie G. Youngkeit, with no vice presidential candidate, *Independent* |
| | 236 | John G. Martin and Cleveland Sparrow, *Third World Assembly* |

# Appendix 11

## *Political Parties Contesting Presidential Elections, 1789–1988*

Alliance Party, 1984
America First Party, 1944, 1972*
American Independent Party, 1968, 1976–1980, 1988
American Party, 1856, 1876, 1880, 1888, 1920, 1924,
    1968–1972, 1980–1988*
American Third Party, 1956
Anti-Federalist Party, 1796
Anti-Jackson Party, 1836
Antimasonic Party, 1832
Berkeley Defense Group, 1968
Big Deal Party, 1984
Christian Nationalist Party, 1956
Citizens Party, 1980–1984
Coalition Party, 1812
Commonwealth Candidates Party, 1924
Commonwealth Land Party, 1924
Communist Party, 1932–1940, 1972–1988
Conservative Party, 1960
Constitution Party, 1952, 1960–1968
Constitutional Party, 1960
Constitutional Union Party, 1860
Consumer Party, 1988
Democratic Party, 1828–present
Democratic-Republican Party, 1792–1812
Down With Lawyers Party, 1980
Farmer-Labor Party, 1920, 1932–1936
Federalist Party, 1789–1808, 1816
Free Soil Party, 1848–1852
Grassroots Party, 1988
Greenback Party, 1876
Greenback-Labor Party, 1880–1884
Independence Party, 1908
Independent Afro-American Party, 1960
Independent Alliance, 1984
Independent-Democratic Party, 1872
Independent-Federalist Party, 1796
Independent-Republican Party, 1808–1820
Jobless Party, 1932
Liberal Republican Party, 1872
Libertarian Party, 1972–1988
Liberty Party, 1844, 1932*
Middle Class Party, 1980
National Party, 1932

National Economic Recovery Party, 1988
National Unity Party, 1984
National Prohibition Party, 1896
National Republican Party, 1828, 1832
National States' Rights Party, 1960–1964
Nationalist Party, 1896
Native American Party, 1856
Natural People's Party, 1980
New Alliance Party, 1988
Nullifiers Party, 1832
Peace and Freedom Party, 1968, 1980–1988
People's Constitutional Party, 1968
People's Party, 1892, 1900–1908, 1972–1976*
Poor Man's Party, 1952
Populist Party, 1900–1908, 1984–1988*
Progressive Party, 1912, 1924, 1948–1952*
Prohibition Party, 1872–present
Republican Party, 1956–present
Restoration Party, 1976
Right to Life Party, 1980, 1988
Single Tax Party, 1920
Socialist Party, 1900–1952, 1976, 1980–1988
Socialist Labor Party, 1892–1976
Socialist Workers Party, 1948–present
Southern Rights Party, 1852
States' Rights Party, 1948, 1956
Statesman Party, 1980
Straight Democratic Party, 1872
Tax Cut Party, 1960
Third World Assembly, 1988
U.S. Labor Party, 1976
Union Party, 1936
Union Labor Party, 1888
Union Reform Party, 1900
United American Party, 1976
United Labor Party, 1888
United States Citizens Party, 1984
Universal Party, 1964
Whig Party, 1836–1852
Workers Party, 1924, 1928
Workers League, 1984–1988
Workers World Party, 1980–1988

*Parties of same name but not necessarily related

# Appendix 12

## *Major Party Convention Sites and Dates*

| Year | Democratic Party | Republican Party | Whig Party |
|------|------------------|------------------|------------|
| 1832 | The Athenaeum<br>Baltimore, MD<br>May 21–23 | | |
| 1836 | Fourth Presbyterian Church<br>Baltimore, MD<br>May 20–22, 1835 | | |
| 1840 | Hall of Musical Association<br>Baltimore, MD<br>May 5–6 | | Harrisburg, PA<br>December 4–6, 1839 |
| 1844 | Odd Fellows' Hall<br>Baltimore, MD<br>May 27–29 | | Universalist Church<br>Baltimore, MD<br>May 1 |
| 1848 | Universalist Church<br>Baltimore, MD<br>May 22–25 | | Museum Building<br>Philadelphia, PA<br>June 7–9 |
| 1852 | Maryland Institute Hall<br>Baltimore, MD<br>June 1–5 | | Maryland Institute Hall<br>Baltimore, MD<br>June 16–18 |
| 1856 | Smith and Nixon's Hall<br>Cincinnati, OH<br>June 2–6 | Music Fund Hall<br>Philadelphia, PA<br>June 17–19 | |
| 1860 | Hall of South Carolina Institute<br>Charleston, SC<br>April 23–28; May 1–3<br>Front St. Theater<br>Baltimore, MD<br>June 18–23 | The Wigwam<br>Chicago, IL<br>May 16–18 | |
| 1864 | The Amphitheater<br>Chicago, IL<br>August 29–31 | Front St. Theater<br>Baltimore, MD<br>June 7–8 | |
| 1868 | Tammany Hall<br>New York, NY<br>July 4–9 | Crosby's Opera House<br>Chicago, IL<br>May 20–21 | |
| 1872 | Ford's Opera House<br>Baltimore, MD<br>July 9–10, 1871 | Academy of Music<br>Philadelphia, PA<br>June 5–6 | |
| 1876 | Merchant's Exchange<br>St. Louis, MO<br>June 27–29 | Exposition Hall<br>Cincinnati, OH<br>June 14–16 | |
| 1880 | Music Hall<br>Cincinnati, OH<br>June 22–24 | Exposition Hall<br>Chicago, IL<br>June 2–5, 7–8 | |
| 1884 | Exposition Hall<br>Chicago, IL<br>July 8–11 | Exposition Hall<br>Chicago, IL<br>June 3–6 | |

| Year | Democratic Party | Republican Party |
|------|------------------|------------------|
| 1888 | Exposition Building<br>St. Louis, MO<br>June 5–7 | Civic Auditorium<br>Chicago, IL<br>June 19–25 |
| 1892 | Specially constructed building<br>Chicago, IL<br>June 21–23 | Industrial Exposition Hall<br>Minneapolis, MN<br>June 7–10 |
| 1896 | The Coliseum<br>Chicago, IL<br>July 7–11 | Specially built auditorium<br>St. Louis, MO<br>June 16–18 |
| 1900 | Convention Hall<br>Kansas City, MO<br>July 4–6 | Exposition Auditorium<br>Philadelphia, PA<br>June 19–21 |
| 1904 | The Coliseum<br>St. Louis, MO<br>July 6–9 | The Coliseum<br>Chicago, IL<br>June 21–23 |
| 1908 | Civic Auditorium<br>Denver, CO<br>July 7–10 | The Coliseum<br>Chicago, IL<br>June 16–19 |
| 1912 | Fifth Maryland Regiment Armory<br>Baltimore, MD<br>June 25–29; July 1–2 | The Coliseum<br>Chicago, IL<br>June 18–22 |
| 1916 | The Coliseum<br>St. Louis, MO<br>June 14–16 | The Coliseum<br>Chicago, IL<br>June 7–10 |
| 1920 | Civic Auditorium<br>San Francisco, CA<br>June 28–30; July 1–3, 5–6 | The Coliseum<br>Chicago, IL<br>June 8–12 |
| 1924 | Madison Square Garden<br>New York, NY<br>June 24–July 9 | Municipal Auditorium<br>Cleveland, OH<br>June 10–12 |
| 1928 | Sam Houston Hall<br>Houston, TX<br>June 26–29 | Civic Auditorium<br>Kansas City, MO<br>June 12–15 |
| 1932 | Chicago Stadium<br>Chicago, IL<br>June 27–30; July 1–2 | Chicago Stadium<br>Chicago, IL<br>June 14–16 |
| 1936 | Convention Hall<br>Philadelphia, PA<br>June 23-27 | Municipal Auditorium<br>Cleveland, OH<br>June 9–12 |
| 1940 | Chicago Stadium<br>Chicago, IL<br>July 15–18 | Convention Hall<br>Philadelphia, PA<br>June 24–28 |
| 1944 | Chicago Stadium<br>Chicago, IL<br>July 19–21 | Chicago Stadium<br>Chicago, IL<br>June 26–28 |
| 1948 | Convention Hall<br>Philadelphia, PA<br>July 12–14 | Convention Hall<br>Philadelphia, PA<br>June 21–25 |

| Year | Democratic Party | Republican Party |
|------|------------------|------------------|
| 1952 | International Amphitheater<br>Chicago, IL<br>July 21–26 | International Amphitheater<br>Chicago, IL<br>July 7–11 |
| 1956 | International Amphitheater<br>Chicago, IL<br>August 13–17 | Cow Palace<br>San Francisco, CA<br>August 20–23 |
| 1960 | Los Angeles Memorial Sports Arena<br>and Coliseum<br>Los Angeles, CA<br>July 11–15 | International Amphitheater<br>Chicago, IL<br>July 25–28 |
| 1964 | Atlantic City, NJ<br>August 24–27 | Cow Palace<br>San Francisco, CA<br>July 13-16 |
| 1968 | International Amphitheater<br>Chicago, IL<br>August 26–29 | Convention Hall<br>Miami Beach, FL<br>August 5–8 |
| 1972 | Convention Hall<br>Miami Beach, FL<br>July 10–13 | Convention Hall<br>Miami Beach, FL<br>August 21–23 |
| 1976 | Madison Square Garden<br>New York, NY<br>July 12-15 | Kemper Arena<br>Kansas City, MO<br>August 16–19 |
| 1980 | Madison Square Garden<br>New York, NY<br>August 11-14 | Joe Louis Arena<br>Detroit, MI<br>July 14–17 |
| 1984 | Moscone Center<br>San Francisco, CA<br>July 16–19 | Dallas Convention Center<br>Dallas, TX<br>August 20–23 |
| 1988 | The Omni<br>Atlanta, GA<br>July 18–21 | Louisiana Superdome<br>New Orleans, LA<br>August 15–18 |

Source: Elections 1800–1980

Presidential Also-Rans and Running Mates, 1788–1980
Leslie H. Southwick
Jefferson, NC: McFarland, 1984.

Election of 1984
*Congressional Quarterly Almanac, Vol. 40, 1984*
Washington, DC: Congressional Quarterly, 1985.

Election of 1988
*Congressional Quarterly Almanac, Vol. 44, 1988*
Washington, DC: Congressional Quarterly, 1989.

# Appendix 13

## *Chairs of the Democratic and Republican National Committees*

### *Democratic National Chairs*

| | Name | State | Term |
|---|---|---|---|
| 1 | Benjamin F. Hallett | MA | 1848–1852 |
| 2 | Robert M. McLane | MD | 1852–1856 |
| 3 | David A. Smalley | VT | 1856–1860 |
| 4 | August Belmont | NY | 1860–1872 |
| 5 | Augustus Schell | NY | 1872–1876 |
| 6 | Abram Stevens Hewitt | NY | 1876–1877 |
| 7 | William H. Barnum | CT | 1877–1889 |
| 8 | Calvin Stewart Brice | OH | 1889–1892 |
| 9 | William F. Harrity | PA | 1892–1896 |
| 10 | James K. Jones | AR | 1896–1904 |
| 11 | Thomas Taggart | IN | 1904–1908 |
| 12 | Norman E. Mack | NY | 1908–1912 |
| 13 | William F. McCombs | NY | 1912–1916 |
| 14 | Vance C. McCormick | PA | 1916–1919 |
| 15 | Homer S. Cummings | CT | 1919–1920 |
| 16 | George H. White | OH | 1920–1921 |
| 17 | Cordell Hull | TN | 1921–1924 |
| 18 | Clement L. Shaver | WV | 1924–1928 |
| 19 | John J. Raskob | MD | 1928–1932 |
| 20 | James A. Farley | NY | 1932–1940 |
| 21 | Edward J. Flynn | NY | 1940–1943 |
| 22 | Frank C. Walker | PA | 1943–1944 |
| 23 | Robert E. Hannegan | MO | 1944–1947 |
| 24 | J. Howard McGrath | RI | 1947–1949 |
| 25 | William M. Boyle, Jr. | MO | 1949–1951 |
| 26 | Frank E. McKinney | IN | 1951–1952 |
| 27 | Stephen A. Mitchell | IL | 1952–1955 |
| 28 | Paul M. Butler | IN | 1955–1960 |
| 29 | Henry M. Jackson | WA | 1960–1961 |
| 30 | John M. Bailey | CT | 1961–1968 |
| 31 | Lawrence O'Brien | MA | 1968–1969 |
| 32 | Fred R. Harris | OK | 1969–1970 |
| 33 | Lawrence O'Brien | MA | 1970–1972 |
| 34 | Jean Westwood | UT | 1972 |
| 35 | Robert Strauss | TX | 1972–1977 |
| 36 | Kenneth Curtis | ME | 1977 |
| 37 | John C. White | TX | 1977–1981 |
| 38 | Charles A. Manatt | IA | 1981–1985 |
| 39 | Paul G. Kirk, Jr. | MA | 1985–1989 |
| 40 | Ronald H. Brown | DC | 1989– |

### *Republican National Chairs*

| | Name | State | Term |
|---|---|---|---|
| 1 | Edwin D. Morgan | NY | 1856–1864 |
| 2 | Henry J. Raymond | NY | 1864–1866 |
| 3 | Marcus L. Ward | NJ | 1866–1868 |
| 4 | William Claflin | MA | 1868–1872 |
| 5 | Edwin D. Morgan | NY | 1872–1876 |
| 6 | Zachariah Chandler | MI | 1876–1879 |
| 7 | J. Donald Cameron | PA | 1879–1880 |
| 8 | Marshall Jewell | CT | 1880–1883 |
| 9 | D. M. Sabin | MN | 1883–1884 |
| 10 | Benjamin Franklin Jones | PA | 1884–1888 |
| 11 | Matthew S. Quay | PA | 1888–1891 |

| | Name | State | Term |
|---|---|---|---|
| 12 | James S. Clarkson | IA | 1891–1892 |
| 13 | Thomas H. Carter | MT | 1892–1896 |
| 14 | Marcus A. Hanna | OH | 1896–1904 |
| 15 | Henry C. Payne | WI | 1904 |
| 16 | George B. Cortelyou | NY | 1904–1907 |
| 17 | Harry S. New | IN | 1907–1908 |
| 18 | Frank H. Hitchcock | MA | 1908–1909 |
| 19 | John F. Hill | ME | 1911–1912 |
| 20 | Victor Rosewater | NE | 1912 |
| 21 | Charles D. Hilles | NY | 1912–1916 |
| 22 | William R. Wilcox | NY | 1916–1918 |
| 23 | Will Hays | IN | 1918–1921 |
| 24 | John T. Adams | IA | 1921–1924 |
| 25 | William M. Butler | MA | 1924–1928 |
| 26 | Herbert Work | CO | 1928–1929 |
| 27 | Claudius H. Huston | TN | 1929–1930 |
| 28 | Simeon D. Fess | OH | 1930–1932 |
| 29 | Everett Sanders | IN | 1932–1934 |
| 30 | Henry P. Fletcher | PA | 1934–1936 |
| 31 | John D. M. Hamilton | KS | 1936–1940 |
| 32 | Joseph W. Martin, Jr. | MA | 1940–1942 |
| 33 | Harrison E. Spangler | IA | 1942–1944 |
| 34 | Herbert Brownell | NY | 1944-1946 |
| 35 | Carroll Reece | TN | 1946–1948 |
| 36 | Hugh Scott | PA | 1948–1949 |
| 37 | Guy George Gabrielson | NJ | 1949–1952 |
| 38 | Arthur E. Summerfield | MI | 1952–1953 |
| 39 | Wesley Roberts | KS | 1953 |
| 40 | Leonard W. Hall | NY | 1953–1957 |
| 41 | Meade Alcorn | CT | 1957–1959 |
| 42 | Thruston B. Morton | KY | 1959–1961 |
| 43 | William E. Miller | NY | 1961–1964 |
| 44 | Dean Burch | AR | 1964–1965 |
| 45 | Ray C. Bliss | OH | 1965–1969 |
| 46 | Rogers C. B. Morton | MD | 1969–1971 |
| 47 | Bob Dole | KS | 1971–1973 |
| 48 | George Bush | TX | 1973–1974 |
| 49 | Mrs. Mary Louise Smith | IA | 1974–1977 |
| 50 | Bill Brock | TN | 1977–1981 |
| 51 | Richard Richards | UT | 1981–1983 |
| 52 | Frank J. Fahrenkopf, Jr. | NV | 1983–1989 |
| 53 | H. Lee Atwater | SC | 1989–1991 |
| 54 | Clayton Yeuter | NE | 1991– |

# Appendix 14A

## *Democratic State Committee Headquarters and Telephone Numbers*

ALABAMA
Alabama Democratic Party
4120 Third Avenue, South
Birmingham, AL  35222
205-595-9090

ALASKA
Alaska Democratic Party
P.O. Box 10-4199
Anchorage, AK  99510
907-258-3050

AMERICAN SAMOA
Democratic Party of American Samoa
P.O. Box 552
Pago Pago, American Samoa  96799
684-633-5121

ARIZONA
Arizona Democratic Party
P.O. Box 1944
Phoenix, AZ  85001
602-257-9136

ARKANSAS
Arkansas Democratic Party
1300 West Capitol
Little Rock, AR  72201
501-374-2361

CALIFORNIA
California Democratic Party
329 Bryant Street, Suite 3
San Francisco, CA  94107
415-896-5503

COLORADO
Colorado Democratic Party
1600 Downing Street, 6th Floor
Denver, CO  80218
303-830-8989

CONNECTICUT
Connecticut Democratic Party
634 Asylum Avenue
Hartford, CT  06105
203-278-6080

DELAWARE
Delaware Democratic Party
P.O. Box 2065
Wilmington, DE  19899
302-652-3051

DEMOCRATS ABROAD
Democrats Abroad
7400 Rebecca Drive
Alexandria, VA  22307
703-768-3174

DISTRICT OF COLUMBIA
D.C. Democratic Party
1012 14th Street NW, Suite 803
Washington, DC  20005
202-347-2489

FLORIDA
Florida Democratic Party
P.O. Box 1758
Tallahassee, FL  32302
904-222-3411

GEORGIA
Georgia Democratic Party
1100 Spring Street, Suite 350
Atlanta, GA  30367
404-872-1992

GUAM
Guam Democratic Party
P.O. Box CB-1
Agana, Guam  96910
671-472-3829

HAWAII
Hawaii Democratic Party
661 Auahi Street, #206
Honolulu, HI  96813
808-536-2258

IDAHO
Idaho Democratic Party
Box 445
Boise, ID  83701
208-336-1815

ILLINOIS
Illinois Democratic Party
218 North Jefferson Street
Chicago, IL  60606
312-930-5855

INDIANA
Indiana Democratic Party
P.O. Box 3366
Indianapolis, IN  46206
317-237-3366

IOWA
Iowa Democratic Party
2116 Grand Avenue
Des Moines, IA  50312
515-244-7292

KANSAS
Kansas Democratic Party
P.O. Box 1914
Topeka, KS  66601
913-234-0425

KENTUCKY
Kentucky Democratic Party
P.O. Box 694
Frankfort, KY 40602
502-695-4828

LOUISIANA
Louisiana Democratic Party
340 St. Joseph Street
Baton Rouge, LA 70802
504-336-4155

MAINE
Maine Democratic Party
P.O. Box 5258
Augusta, ME 04330
207-622-6233

MARYLAND
Maryland Democratic Party
224 Main Street
Annapolis, MD 21401
301-280-2300

MASSACHUSETTS
Massachusetts Democratic Party
45 Bromfield Street, 7th Floor
Boston, MA 02108
617-426-4760

MICHIGAN
Michigan Democratic Party
606 Townsend
Lansing, MI 48933
517-371-5410

MINNESOTA
Minnesota Democratic Farmer-Labor Party
525 Park Street, Suite 100
St. Paul, MN 55103
612-293-1200

MISSISSIPPI
Mississippi Democratic Party
P.O. Box 1583
Jackson, MS 39205
601-969-2913

MISSOURI
Missouri Democratic Party
P.O. Box 719
Jefferson City, MO 65102
314-636-5241

MONTANA
Montana Democratic Party
P.O. Box 802
Helena, MT 59624
406-442-9520

NEBRASKA
Nebraska Democratic Party
715 South 14th Street
Lincoln, NE 68508
402-475-4584

NEVADA
Nevada Democratic Party
1155 East Sahara Avenue, Suite 17
Las Vegas, NV 89104
702-732-3366

NEW HAMPSHIRE
New Hampshire Democratic Party
922 Elm Street, Suite 210
Manchester, NH 03101
603-622-9606

NEW JERSEY
New Jersey Democratic Party
48 West Lafayette Street
Trenton, NJ 08608
609-392-3367
201-731-7776

NEW MEXICO
New Mexico Democratic Party
315 8th Street, SW
Albuquerque, NM 87102
505-842-8208

NEW YORK
New York Democratic Party
60 East 42nd Street, Suite 1801
New York, NY 10165
212-986-2955

NORTH CAROLINA
North Carolina Democratic Party
P.O. Box 12196
Raleigh, NC 27605
919-821-2777

NORTH DAKOTA
North Dakota Democratic Party
1902 East Divide Avenue
Bismarck, ND 58501
701-255-0460

OHIO
Ohio Democratic Party
88 East Broad Street, Suite 1920
Columbus, OH 43215
614-221-6563

OKLAHOMA
Oklahoma Democratic Party
116 East Sheridan Street, Suite G 100
Oklahoma City, OK 73104
405-239-2700

OREGON
Oregon Democratic Party
P.O. Box 15057
Salem, OR 97309
503-370-8200

PENNSYLVANIA
Pennsylvania Democratic Party
510 North Third Street
Harrisburg, PA 17101
717-238-9381

PUERTO RICO
Puerto Rico Democratic Party
P.O. Box 306
Bayamon, PR   00621
809-785-6715
809-740-3620

RHODE ISLAND
Rhode Island Democratic Party
1991 Smith Street
North Providence, RI   02911
401-232-3800

SOUTH CAROLINA
South Carolina Democratic Party
P.O. Box 5965
Columbia, SC   29250
803-799-7798

SOUTH DAKOTA
South Dakota Democratic Party
P.O. Box 737
Sioux Falls, SD   57101
605-335-7337

TENNESSEE
Tennessee Democratic Party
42 Rutledge Street
Nashville, TN   37210
615-244-1336

TEXAS
Texas Democratic Party
815 Brazos Street, Suite 200
Austin, TX   78701
512-478-8746

UTAH
Utah Democratic Party
833 East 400 South, Suite 101
Salt Lake City, UT   84102
801-328-0239

VERMONT
Vermont Democratic Party
P.O. Box  336, 100 State Street
Montpelier, VT   05602
802-229-5986

VIRGIN ISLANDS
A. Winston Hodge, Chair
35 King Street
Christiansted, St. Croix, VI   00820
809-773-7725

VIRGINIA
Virginia Democratic Party
1001 East Broad Street, Suite LL25
Richmond, VA   23219
804-644-1966

WASHINGTON
Washington Democratic Party
P.O. Box 4027
Seattle, WA   98104
206-583-0664

WEST VIRGINIA
West Virginia Democratic Party
405 Capitol Street, Suite 804
Charleston, WV   25301
304-342-8121

WISCONSIN
Wisconsin Democratic Party
126 South Franklin Street
Madison, WI   53703-3494
608-255-5172

WYOMING
Wyoming Democratic Party
P.O. Box 1964
Casper, WY   82602
307-234-8862

# Appendix 14B

## *Republican State Committee Headquarters and Telephone Numbers*

ALABAMA
Alabama Republican Executive Committee
P.O. Box 320800
Birmingham, AL 35232-0800
205-324-1984
205-324-0682 FAX

ALASKA
Republican Party of Alaska
750 East Fireweed Lane, Suite 102
Anchorage, AK 99503
907-276-4467
907-258-4918 FAX

AMERICAN SAMOA
Republican Party of American Samoa
P.O. Box 3820
Pago Pago, American Samoa 96799
684-633-4116

ARIZONA
Arizona Republican State Committee
3501 North 24th Street
Phoenix, AZ 85016-6607
602-957-7770

ARKANSAS
Republican Party of Arkansas
One Riverfront Place, Suite 550
North Little Rock, AR 72114
501-372-7301

CALIFORNIA
California Republican Party
1903 West Magnolia
Burbank, CA 91506
818-841-5210
818-841-6668 FAX

COLORADO
Republican State Central Committee of Colorado
1275 Tremont Place
Denver, CO 80204
303-893-1776
303-893-1776 FAX (call first)

CONNECTICUT
Connecticut Republican State Central Committee
508 Tolland Street
East Hartford, CT 06108
203-289-6552
203-289-6505 FAX

DELAWARE
Delaware Republican State Committee
2 Mill Road
Wilmington, DE 19806
302-651-0260
302-651-0270 FAX

DISTRICT OF COLUMBIA
District of Columbia Republican Committee
440 First Street NW, 4th Floor
Washington, DC 20001
202-662-1382
202-628-6492 FAX

FLORIDA
Republican State Executive Committee of Florida
P.O. Box 311
Tallahassee, FL 32302
904-222-7920
904-681-0184 FAX

GEORGIA
Georgia Republican Party
3091 Maple Drive, NE, Suite 315
Atlanta, GA 30305
404-365-7700
404-365-7718 FAX

GUAM
Republican Party of Guam
P.O. Box 2846
Agana, Guam 96910
671-472-3450

HAWAII
Republican Party of Hawaii
100 North Beretania Street, Suite 203
Honolulu, HI 96817
808-526-1755

IDAHO
Idaho Republican State Central Committee
P.O. Box 2267
Boise, ID 83702
208-343-6405

ILLINOIS
Illinois Republican State Central Committee
223 South Third Street
Springfield, IL 62701
217-525-0011
217-753-4712 FAX

INDIANA
Indiana Republican State Central Committee
One North Capitol, Suite 1260
Indianapolis, IN 46204
317-635-7561
317-632-8510 FAX

IOWA
Republican State Central Committee of Iowa
521 East Locust Street
Des Moines, IA 50309
515-282-8105
515-282-9019 FAX

KANSAS
Kansas Republican State Committee
214 West 6th Street
Topeka, KS 66603
913-234-3416
913-234-3436 FAX

KENTUCKY
Republican Party of Kentucky
P.O. Box 1068, 105 West Third
Frankfort, KY 40602
502-875-5130
502-223-5625 FAX

LOUISIANA
Republican Party of Louisiana
650 North 6th Street
Baton Rouge, LA 70802
504-383-7234
504-383-8334 FAX

MAINE
Maine Republican Party
24 Stone Street
Augusta, ME 04330
207-622-6247

MARYLAND
Republican State Central Committee of Maryland
60 West Street, Suite 201
Annapolis, MD 21401
301-269-0113

MASSACHUSETTS
Massachusetts Republican State Committee
9 Galen Street, Suite 320
Watertown, MA 02172
617-924-8683
617-426-9469 FAX

MICHIGAN
Michigan Republican State Committee
2121 East Grand River
Lansing, MI 48912
517-487-5413
517-487-0090 FAX

MINNESOTA
Independent-Republicans of Minnesota
8030 Cedar Avenue, Suite 202
Bloomington, MN 55425
612-854-1446
612-854-8488 FAX

MISSISSIPPI
Mississippi Republican Party
P.O. Box 60
Jackson, MS 39205
601-948-5191

MISSOURI
Missouri Republican State Committee
P.O. Box 73
Jefferson City, MO 65102
314-636-3146
314-636-3273 FAX

MONTANA
Montana Republican State Central Committee
1425 Helena Avenue
Helena, MT 59601
406-442-6469
406-442-3293 FAX

NEBRASKA
Nebraska Republican State Central Committee
421 South 9th Street, Suite 102
Lincoln, NE 68508
402-475-2122
402-475-3541 FAX

NEVADA
Republican State Central Committee of Nevada
953 East Sahara Avenue, Suite 13B
Las Vegas, NV 89104
702-737-7031

NEW HAMPSHIRE
New Hampshire Republican State Committee
134 North Main Street
Concord, NH 03301
603-225-9341
603-225-7498 FAX

NEW JERSEY
New Jersey Republican State Committee
310 West State Street
Trenton, NJ 08618
609-989-7300
609-989-8685 FAX

NEW MEXICO
Republican Party of New Mexico
P.O. Box 36900
Albuquerque, NM 87176
505-883-7345
505-268-9958 FAX

NEW YORK
New York Republican State Committee
315 State Street
Albany, NY 12210
518-462-2601
518-449-7443 FAX

NORTH CAROLINA
North Carolina Republican Executive Committee
P.O. Box 12905, 1410 Hillsborough Street
Raleigh, NC 27605
919-828-6423
919-821-2724 FAX (call first)

NORTH DAKOTA
North Dakota Republican State Committee
P.O. Box 1917
Bismarck, ND 58502
701-255-0030
701-255-7513 FAX

OHIO
Republican State Central and Executive Committee of Ohio
172 East State Street, 4th Floor
Columbus, OH 43215
614-228-2481
614-228-1093 FAX

OKLAHOMA
Republican State Committee of Oklahoma
4031 North Lincoln Blvd.
Oklahoma City, OK 73105
405-528-3501

OREGON
Oregon Republican Party
10550 SW Allen Blvd., Room 224
Beaverton, OR 97005
503-627-0745
503-643-3332 FAX

PENNSYLVANIA
Republican State Committee of Pennsylvania
P.O. Box 1624
Harrisburg, PA 17105
717-234-4901
717-231-3842 FAX

PUERTO RICO
National Republican Party of Puerto Rico
Humacao Street, #A45
Villa Avila Guaxnavo, Puerto Rico 00657
809-731-3733
809-765-2251 FAX

REPUBLICANS ABROAD
Republicans Abroad
310 First Street SE
Washington, DC 20003
202-662-1390

RHODE ISLAND
Rhode Island Republican State Central Committee
400 Smith Street
Providence, RI 02908
401-421-2570

SOUTH CAROLINA
South Carolina Republican Party
P.O. Box 21765
Columbia, SC 29250
803-789-8999
803-799-4053 FAX

SOUTH DAKOTA
South Dakota Republican State Central Committee
P.O. Box 1099
Pierre, SD 57501
605-224-7347

TENNESSEE
Tennessee Republican State Executive Committee
2817 West End Avenue
Nashville, TN 37203
615-321-4521
615-327-1041 FAX

TEXAS
Republican Party of Texas
211 East 7th Street, Suite 620
Austin, TX 78701
512-477-9821
512-480-0709 FAX

UTAH
Utah Republican State Central Committee
643 East 400 South, Suite A
Salt Lake City, UT 84102
801-533-9777

VERMONT
Vermont Republican State Committee
P.O. Box 70
Montpelier, VT 05602
802-223-3411

VIRGIN ISLANDS
Republican Party of the Virgin Islands
P.O. Box 5396
St. Thomas, VI 00803
809-774-8410

VIRGINIA
Republican Party of Virginia
115 East Grace Street
Richmond, VA 23219
804-780-0111
804-343-1060 FAX

WASHINGTON
Republican State Committee of Washington
9 Lake Bellevue Drive, Suite 203
Bellevue, WA 98005
206-451-1988
206-451-9266 FAX

WEST VIRGINIA
Republican State Executive Committee of West Virginia
101 Dee Drive
Charleston, WV 25311
304-344-3446
304-344-3448 FAX (call first)

WISCONSIN
Republican Party of Wisconsin
P.O. Box 31
Madison, WI 53701
608-257-4765
608-257-4141 FAX

WYOMING
Wyoming Republican State Committee
P.O. Box 241
Casper, WY 82602
307-234-9166
307-234-9167 FAX (call first)

# Appendix 15

## *Federal Election Commission: Commissioners and Officers*

### Commissioners
Joan D. Aikens, 1975–
Thomas B. Curtis, 1975–1976
Thomas E. Harris, 1975–1985
Neil O. Staebler, 1975–1978
Vernon W. Thomson, 1975–1979; 1981
Robert O. Tiernan, 1975–1981
William L. Springer, 1975–1979
John Warren McGarry, 1978–
Max L. Friedersdorf, 1979–1980
Frank P. Reiche, 1979–1985
Lee Ann Elliot, 1981–
Danny L. McDonald, 1981–
Thomas J. Josefiak, 1985–
Scott E. Thomas, 1986–

### *Ex Officio* Commissioners

*Clerks of the House*
W. Pat Jennings, 1975
Edmund L. Henshaw, Jr., 1975–1983
Benjamin J. Guthrie, 1983–1986
Donald K. Anderson, 1987–

*Secretaries of the Senate*
Francis R. Valeo, 1975–1977
Joseph Stanley Kimmitt, 1977–1983
William F. Hildenbrand, 1981–1985
Jo-Anne L. Coe, 1985–1986
Walter J. Stewart, 1987–

### Statutory Officers

*Staff Directors*
Orlando B. Potter, 1975–1980
B. Allen Clutter III, 1980–1983
John C. Surina, 1983–

*General Counsels*
John G. Murphy, Jr., 1975–1976
William C. Oldaker, 1977–1979
Charles N. Steele, 1979–1987
Lawrence M. Noble, 1987–

Source: Federal Election Commission, *Federal Election Commission: The First Ten Years, 1975–1985*. Washington, DC: U.S. Government Printing Office, 1985. Updated by the F.E.C. through 1989.

# Appendix 16

## Governors of the States
*(by state, with terms of office and parties)*

### ALABAMA

Bibb, William Wyatt, 1819–1820 (D-R)
Bibb, Thomas, 1820–1821 (D-R)
Pickens, Israel, 1821–1825 (D-R)
Murphy, John, 1825–1829 (JD)
Moore, Gabriel, 1829–1831 (JD)
Moore, Samuel B., 1831 (D)
Gayle, John, 1831–1835 (D)
Clay, Clement Comer, 1835–1837 (D)
McVay, Hugh, 1837 (D)
Bagby, Arthur Pendleton, 1837–1841 (D)
Fitzpatrick, Benjamin, 1841–1845 (D)
Mattin, Joshua Lanier, 1845–1847 (I)
Chapman, Reuben, 1847–1849 (D)
Collier, Henry Watkins, 1849–1853 (D)
Winston, John Anthony, 1853–1857 (D)
Moore, Andrew Barry, 1857–1861 (D)
Shorter, John Gill, 1861–1863 (D)
Watts, Thomas Hill, 1863–1865 (W)
Parsons, Lewis E., 1865 (W–D-R)
Patten, Robert Miller, 1865–1868 (R)
Smith, William H., 1868–1870 (R)
Lindsay, Robert Burns, 1870–1872 (D)
Lewis, David Peter, 1872–1874 (R)
Houston, George Smith, 1874–1878 (D)
Cobb, James Edward, 1878–1882 (D)
O'Neal, Edward Ashbury, 1882–1886 (D)
Seay, Thomas, 1886–1890 (D)
Jones, Thomas Goode, 1890–1894 (D)
Oates, William Calvin, 1894–1896 (D)
Johnston, Joseph Forney, 1896–1900 (D)
Jelks, William Dorsey, 1900, 1901–1904, 1905–1907 (D)
Samford, William James, 1900–1901 (D)
Cunningham, Russell McWhortor, 1904–1905 (D)
Comer, Braxton Bragg, 1907–1911 (D)
O'Neal, Emmet, 1911–1915 (D)
Henderson, Charles, 1915–1919 (D)
Kilby, Thomas Erby, 1919–1923 (D)
Brandon, William Woodward, 1923–1927 (D)
Graves, David Bibb, 1927–1931, 1935–1939 (D)
Miller, Benjamin M., 1931–1935 (D)
Dixon, Frank Murray, 1939–1943 (D)
Sparks, Chauncey M., 1943–1947 (D)
Folsom, James Elisha, 1947–1951, 1955–1959 (D)
Persons, Seth Gordon, 1951–1955 (D)
Patterson, John Malcomb, 1959–1963 (D)
Wallace, George Corley, 1963–1967, 1971–1972, 1972–1979, 1983–1986 (D)
Wallace, Lurleen Burns, 1967–1968 (D)
Brewer, Albert Preston, 1968–1971 (D)
Beasley, Jere Locke, 1972 (D)
James, Forrest Hood, 1979–1983 (D)
Hunt, Harold Guy, 1987– (R)

### ALASKA

Egan, William Allen, 1958–1966, 1970–1974 (D)
Hickel, Walter Joseph, 1966–1969, 1990– (R)
Miller, Keith Harvey, 1969–1970 (R)
Hammond, Jay Sterner, 1974–1982 (R)
Sheffield, William Jennings, 1982–1986 (D)
Cowper, Steve, 1986–1990 (D)

### ARIZONA

Hunt, George Willey Paul, 1912–1917, 1917–1919, 1923–1929, 1931–1933 (D)
Campbell, Thomas Edward, 1917, 1919–1923 (R)
Phillips, John C., 1929–1931 (R)
Mouer, Benjamin Baker, 1933–1937 (D)
Stanford, Rawghile Clement, 1937–1939 (D)
Jones, Robert Taylor, 1939–1941 (D)
Osborn, Sidney Preston, 1941–1948 (D)
Garvey, Dan E., 1948–1951 (D)
Pyle, John Howard, 1951–1955 (R)
McFarland, Earnest William, 1955–1959 (D)
Fannin, Paul Jones, 1959–1965 (R)
Goddard, Samuel Pearson, 1965–1967 (D)
Williams, John Richard, 1967–1975 (R)
Castro, Raul Hector, 1975–1977 (D)
Bolin, Wesley H., 1977–1978 (D)
Babbitt, Bruce Edward, 1978–1986 (D)
Mecham, Evan, 1987–1988 (D)
Mofford, Rose, 1988–1991 (D)
Symington, Fife, 1991– (R)

### ARKANSAS

Conway, James Sevier, 1836–1840 (D)
Yell, Archibald, 1840–1844 (D)
Adams, Samuel, 1844 (D)
Drew, Thomas Stevenson, 1844–1849 (D)
Byrd, Richard C., 1849 (D)
Roane, John Selden, 1849–1852 (D)
Hampton, John R., 1851, 1857 (D)
Conway, Elias Nelson, 1852–1860 (D)
Recyor, Henry Massey, 1860–1862 (I–D)
Fletcher, Thomas, 1862 (D)
Flanagin, Harris, 1862–1864 (D)
Murphy, Issac 1864–1868 (D)
Clayton, Powell, 1868–1871 (R)
Hadley, Ozra A., 1871–1873 (R)
Baxter, Elisha 1873–1874 (R)
Garland, Augustus Hill, 1874–1877 (D)
Miller, William R., 1877–1881 (D)
Churchill, Thomas J., 1881–1883 (D)
Berry, James Henderson, 1883–1885 (D)
Hughes, Simeon P., 1885–1889 (D)
Eagle, James P., 1889–1893 (D)
Sloan, Clay, 1893 (D)
Fishback, William M., 1893–1895 (D)
Clarke, James P., 1895–1897 (D)
Jones, Daniel Webster, 1897–1901 (D)
Davis, Jefferson, 1901–1907 (D)
Little, John Sebastian, 1907 (D)
Moore, John I., 1907 (D)
Pindall, Xenophon O., 1907–1909 (D)
Donaghey, George W., 1909–1913 (D)
Robinson, Joseph, 1913 (D)
Oldham, William, 1913 (D)
Futrell, Junius Marion, 1913, 1933–1937 (D)
Hays, George, 1913–1917 (D)
Brough, Charles, 1917–1921 (D)
McRae, Thomas Chipman, 1921–1925 (D)
Terral, Thomas J., 1925–1927 (D)
Martineau, John Ellis, 1927–1928 (D)
Parnell, Harvey, 1928–1933 (D)
Bailey, Carl Edward, 1937–1941 (D)
Adkins, Homer Martin, 1941–1945 (D)
Laney, Benjamin T., 1945–1949 (D)
McMath, Sidney Sanders, 1949–1953 (D)
Cherry, Francis Adams, 1953–1955 (D)
Faubas, Orval Eugene, 1955–1967 (D)
Rockefeller, Winthrop, 1967–1971 (D)
Bumpers, Dale Leon, 1971–1975 (D)
Riley, Bob Cowley, 1975 (D)
Pryor, David, 1975–1979 (D)
Clinton, Bill, 1979–1981, 1983– (D)
White, Frank, 1981–1983 (R)

### CALIFORNIA

Burnett, Peter Hardeman, 1849–1851 (NP)
McDougal, John, 1851–1852 (I–D)
Bigler, John, 1852–1856 (D)
Johnson, James Neely, 1856–1858 (Am)
Weller, John B., 1858–1860 (D)
Lathem, Milton Slocum, 1860 (D)
Downey, John G., 1860–1862 (D)
Stanford, Amasa Leland, 1862–1863 (R)
Low, Frederick Ferdinand, 1863–1867 (U–R)
Haight, Henry Huntly, 1867–1871 (D)
Booth, Newton, 1871–1875 (R)
Pacheco, Romualdo, 1875 (R)
Irwin, William, 1875–1880 (D)
Perkins, George Clement, 1880–1883 (R)
Stoneman, George, 1883–1887 (D)

Bartlett, Washington, 1887 (D)
Waterman, Robert Whitney, 1887–1891 (R)
Markham, Henry Harrison, 1891–1895 (R)
Budd, James Herbert, 1895–1899 (D)
Gage, Henry Tifft, 1899–1903 (R)
Pardee, George Cooper, 1903–1907 (R)
Gillet, James Norris, 1907–1911 (D)
Johnson, Hiram, 1911–1917 (R)
Stephans, William Dennison, 1917–1923 (R)
Richardson, Friend William, 1923–1927 (R)
Young, Clement Calhoun, 1927–1931 (R)
Rolph, James, 1931–1934 (R)
Merriam, Frank Finley, 1934–1939 (R)
Olson, Culbert L., 1939–1943 (D)
Warren, Earl, 1943–1953 (R)
Knight, Goodwin Jess, 1953–1959 (R)
Brown, Edmund Gerald 1959–1967 (D)
Reagan, Ronald Wilson, 1967–1975 (R)
Brown, Edmund Gerald, Jr., 1975–1983 (D)
Deukmejian, George, 1983–1991 (R)
Wilson, Pete, 1991– (R)

## COLORADO

Routt, John L., 1876–1879, 1891–1893 (R)
Pitkin, Frederick Walter, 1879–1883 (R)
Grant, James Benton, 1883–1885 (D)
Eaton, Benjamin Harrison, 1885–1887 (R)
Adams, Alva, 1887–1889, 1897–1899, 1905 (D)
Cooper, Job Adams, 1889–1891 (R)
Waite, Davis Harrison, 1893–1895 (Pe)
McIntire, Albert Wills, 1895–1897 (R)
Thomas, Charles Spalding, 1899–1901 (D)
Orman, James Bradley, 1901–1903 (D)
Peabody, James Hamilton, 1903–1905 (R)
McDonald, Jesse Fuller, 1905–1907 (R)
Butchell, Henry Augustus, 1907–1909 (R)
Ammons, Elias Milton, 1913–1915 (D)
Carlson, George Alfred, 1915–1917 (R)
Gunter, Julias Caldeen, 1917–1919 (R)
Shoup, Oliver Henry Nelson, 1919–1923 (R)
Sweet, William Ellery, 1923–1925 (D)
Morley, Clarence J., 1925–1927 (R)
Adams, William Herbert, 1927–1933 (D)
Johnson, Edwin Carl, 1933–1937, 1955–1957 (D)
Talbot, Ray H., 1937 (D)
Ammons, Teller, 1937–1939 (D)
Carr, Ralph, 1939–1943 (R)
Vivian, John Charles, 1943–1947 (R)
Knous, William Lee, 1947–1950 (D)
Johnson, Walter Walfred, 1950–1951 (D)

Thornton, Daniel Isaac J., 1951–1955 (R)
McNichols, Stephan L. R., 1957–1963 (D)
Love, John A., 1963–1973 (R)
Vanderhoof, John David, 1973–1975 (R)
Lamm, Richard Davis, 1975–1987 (D)
Romer, Roy, 1987– (D)

## CONNECTICUT

Huntington, Samuel, 1786–1796 (NP)
Wolcott, Oliver, 1796–1797 (F)
Trumbull, Jonathan, 1797–1809 (F)
Treadwell, John, 1809–1811 (F)
Griswold, Roger, 1811–1812 (F)
Smith, John Cotton, 1812–1817 (F)
Wolcott, Oliver, II, 1817–1827 (R)
Tomlinson, Gideon, 1827–1831 (D-R)
Peters, John Samuel, 1831–1833 (NR)
Edwards, Henry Waggaman, 1833–1834, 1835–1838 (JD)
Foot, Samuel Augustus, 1834–1835 (R)
Ellsworth, William Wolcott, 1838–1842 (W)
Cleveland, Chauncey Fitch, 1842–1844 (D)
Baldwin, Roger Sherman, 1844–1846 (W)
Toucey, Isaac, 1846–1847 (D)
Bissell, Clark, 1847–1849 (W)
Trumbull, Joseph, 1849–1850 (W)
Seymour, Thomas Henry, 1850–1853 (D)
Pond, Charles Hobby, 1853–1854 (D)
Dutton, Henry, 1854–1855 (W)
Minor, William Thomas, 1855–1857 (A)
Holley, Alexander Hamilton, 1857–1858 (U)
Buckingham, William Alfred, 1858–1866 (R)
Hawley, Joseph Roswell, 1866–1867 (Pr)
English, James Edward, 1867–1869, 1870–1871 (D)
Jewell, Marshall, 1869–1870, 1871–1873 (R)
Ingersoll, Charles, Roberts 1873–1877 (D)
Hibbard, Richard Dudley, 1877–1879 (D)
Andrews, Charles Bartlett, 1879–1881 (R)
Bigelow, Hobart B., 1881–1883 (R)
Waller, Thomas MacDonald, 1883–1885 (D)
Harrison, Henry Baldwin, 1885–1887 (R)
Lounsbury, Phineas Chapman, 1887–1889 (R)
Bulkeley, Morgan Gardner, 1889–1893 (R)
Morris, Luzon Burritt, 1893–1895 (D)
Coffin, Owen Vincent, 1895–1897 (R)
Cooke, Lorrin Alamson, 1897–1899 (R)

Lounsbury, George Edward, 1899–1901 (R)
McLeon, George Payne, 1901–1903 (R)
Chamberlain, Abiram, 1903–1905 (R)
Roberts, Henry, 1905–1907 (R)
Woodruff, Rollin Simmons, 1907–1909 (R)
Lilley, George Leavens, 1909 (Pr)
Weeks, Frank Bentley, 1909–1911 (R)
Baldwin, Simeon Eben, 1911–1915 (D)
Holcomb, Marcus Hensey, 1915–1921 (R)
Lake, Everett John, 1921–1923 (R)
Templeton, Charles Augustus, 1923–1925 (R)
Bingham, Hiram, 1925 (R)
Trumbull, John H., 1925–1931 (R)
Cross, Wilbur Lucius, 1931–1939 (D)
Baldwin, Raymond Early, 1939–1941, 1943–1946 (R)
Hurley, Robert Augustine, 1941–1943 (D)
Snow, (Charles) Wilbert, 1946–1947 (D)
McConaughy, James Lukens, 1947–1948 (R)
Shannon, James C., 1848–1849 (R)
Bowles, Chester Bliss, 1949–1951 (D)
Lodge, John Davis, 1951–1955 (R)
Ribicoff, Abraham Alexander, 1955–1961 (D)
Dempsey, John Noel, 1961–1971 (D)
Meskill, Thomas J., 1971–1975 (R)
Grasso, Ella Tambussi, 1975–1980 (D)
O'Neil, Michael N., 1980–1991 (D)
Weicker, Lowell P., Jr., 1991– (I)

## DELAWARE

Clayton, Joshua, 1793–1796 (F)
Bedford, Gunning, 1796–1797 (F)
Rogers, Daniel, 1797–1799 (F)
Bassett, Richard, 1799–1801 (F)
Skyes, James, 1801–1802 (F)
Hall, Davia, 1802–1805 (D-R)
Mitchell, Nathaniel, 1805–1808 (F)
Truitt, George, 1808–1811 (F)
Haslet, Joseph, 1811–1814, 1823 (D-R)
Rodney, Daniel, 1814–1817 (F)
Clark, John, 1817–1820 (F)
Molleston, Henry [1820] (F)
Stout, Jacob, 1820–1821 (F)
Collins, John, 1821–1822 (D-R)
Rodney, Caleb, 1822–1823 (F)
Thomas, Charles, 1823–1824 (D-R)
Paynter, Samuel, 1824–1827 (F)
Polk, Charles, 1827–1830 (F)
Hazzard, David, 1830–1833 (A-R)
Bennett, Caleb Prew, 1833–1836 (D-R)
Comegys, Cornelius Parsons, 1837–1841 (W)
Cooper, William B., 1841–1845 (W)
Stockton, Thomas, 1845–1846 (W)
Maul, Joseph, 1846 (W)
Temple, William, 1846–1847 (W)
Tharp, William, 1847–1851 (D)
Ross, William Henry Harrison, 1851–1855 (D)

Causey, Peter Foster, 1855–1859 (W)
Burton, William, 1859–1863 (D)
Cannon, William, 1863–1865 (R)
Saulsbury, Gove, 1865–1871 (D)
Ponder, James, 1871–1875 (D)
Cochran, John P., 1875–1879 (D)
Hall, John Wood, 1879–1883 (D)
Stokley, Charles Clark, 1883–1887 (D)
Biggs, Benjamin Thomas, 1887–1891 (D)
Reynolds, Robert John, 1891–1895 (D)
Marvil, Joshua Hopkins, 1895 (R)
Watson, William T., 1895–1897 (D)
Tunnell, Ebe Walter, 1897–1901 (D)
Hinn, John, 1901–1905 (R)
Lea, Preston, 1905–1909 (R)
Pennwill, Simeon Selby, 1909–1913 (R)
Miller, Charles R., 1913–1917 (R)
Townsend, John G., 1917–1921 (R)
Denney, William du Hamel, 1921–1925 (R)
Robinson, Robert P., 1925–1929 (R)
Buck, Clayton Douglas, 1929–1937 (R)
McMullen, Richard Cann, 1937–1941 (D)
Bacon, Walter W., 1941–1949 (R)
Carvell, Elbert Nostrand, 1949–1953, 1961–1965 (D)
Boggs, James Caleb, 1953–1960 (R)
Buckson, David Penrose, 1960–1961 (R)
Tery, Charles Layman, 1965–1969 (D)
Peterson, Russel Wilbur, 1969–1973 (R)
Tribbitt, Sherman Willard, 1973–1977 (D)
DuPont, Pierre Samuel, IV, 1977–1985 (R)
Castle, Michael N., 1985– (R)

## FLORIDA

Moseley, William Dunn, 1845–1849 (D)
Brown, Thomas, 1849–1853 (W)
Broome, James E., 1853–1857 (D)
Perry, Madison Stark, 1857–1861 (D)
Milton, John, 1861–1865 (D)
Marvin, William, 1865
Walker, David Shelby, 1865–1868 (A)
Reed, Harrison, 1868–1873 (R)
Hart, Ossian Bingley, 1873–1874 (R)
Stearns, Marcellus Lovejoy, 1874–1877 (R)
Drew, George Franklin, 1877–1881 (D)
Bloxham, William Dunningham, 1881–1885, 1897–1901 (D)
Perry, Edward Alysworth, 1885–1889 (D)
Fleming, Francis Philip, 1889–1893 (D)
Mitchell, Henry Laurens, 1893–1897
Jennings, William Sherman, 1901–1905 (D)
Broward, Napoleon Bonaparte, 1905–1909 (D)
Gilchrist, Albert Waller, 1909–1913 (D)
Trammell, Park, 1913–1917 (D)
Catts, Sidney Johnson, 1917–1921 (D)
Hardee, Gary Augustus, 1921–1925 (D)
Martin, John Wellborn, 1925–1929 (D)

Carlton, Doyle Elam, 1929–1933 (D)
Sholtz, David, 1933–1937 (D)
Cone, Frederick, 1937–1941 (D)
Holland, Spessard Lindsey, 1941–1945 (D)
Caldwell, Millard Fillmore, 1945–1949 (D)
Warren, Fuller, 1949–1953 (D)
McCarty, Daniel Thomas, 1953 (D)
Johns, Charley Eugene, 1953–1955
Collins, [Thomas] Leroy, 1955–1961 (D)
Bryant, [Cecil] Farris, 1961–1965 (D)
Burns, Haydon William, 1965–1967 (D)
Kirk, Claude Roy, 1967–1971 (R)
Askew, Reubin O'Donovan, 1971–1979 (D)
Graham, Robert, 1979–1987 (D)
Martinez, Bob, 1987–1991 (R)
Chiles, Lawton, 1991– (D)

## GEORGIA

Walton, George, 1789 (JR)
Telfair, Edward, 1789–1793 (JR)
Mathews, George, 1793–1796 (JR)
Irwin, Jared, 1796–1798, 1806–1809 (D-R)
Jackson, James, 1798–1801 (D-R)
Emanuel, David, 1801 (D-R)
Tattanall, Josia, 1801–1802 (D-R)
Milledge, John, 1802–1806
Mitchell, David Brydie, 1809–1813, 1815–1817 (D-R)
Early, Peter, 1813–1815
Rabun, William, 1817–1819
Clark, John, 1819–1823
Troup, George M., 1823–1827 (D-R)
Forsyth, John, 1827–1829 (D)
Gilmer, George Rockingham, 1829–1931, 1837–1839 (D-R)
Lumpkin, Wilson, 1831–1835 (JD)
Schiley, William, 1835–1837 (D)
McDonald, Charles James, 1839–1843 (D)
Crawford, George Walker, 1843–1847 (W)
Towns, George Washington Bonaparte, 1847–1851 (U-D)
Cobb, Howell, 1851–1853 (D)
Johnson, Hershal Vespasian, 1853–1857 (D)
Brown, Joseph Emerson, 1857–1865 (D)
Johnson, James, 1865 (W)
Jenkins, Charles Jones, 1865–1868
Ruger, Thomas Howard, 1868
Bullock, Rufus Brown, 1868–1871 (R)
Conley, Benjamin F., 1871–1872 (R)
Smith, James Milton, 1872–1877 (D)
Colquitt, Alfred Holt, 1877–1882 (D)
Stephans, Alexander Hamilton, 1882–1883 (D)
Boynton, James S., 1883 (D)
McDaniel, Henry D., 1883–1886 (D)
Gordon, John B., 1886–1890 (D)
Northen, William J., 1890–1894 (D)
Atkinson, William Yates, 1894–1898 (D)

Candler, Allen D., 1898–1902 (D)
Terrell, Joseph M., 1902–1907 (D)
Smith, Hoke, 1907–1909, 1911 (D)
Brown, Joseph Mackey, 1909–1911, 1912–1913 (D)
Slaton, John Marshall, 1911–1912, 1913–1915 (D)
Harris, Nathaniel E., 1915–1917 (D)
Dorsey, Hugh Manson, 1917–1921 (D)
Hardwick, Thomas William, 1921–1923 (D)
Walker, Clifford Mitchell, 1923–1927 (D)
Hardman, Lamartine Griffon, 1927–1931 (D)
Russel, Richard B., 1931–1933 (D)
Talmadge, Eugene, 1933–1937, 1941–1943 (D)
Rivers, Eurith Dickenson, 1937–1941 (D)
Arnall, Ellis Gibbs, 1943–1947 (D)
Talmadge, Herman Eugene, 1947, 1948–1955 (D)
Thompson, Melvin Ernest, 1947–1948 (D)
Griffen, Samuel Marvin, 1955–1959 (D)
Vandiver, Samuel Earnest, 1959–1963 (D)
Sanders, Carl E., 1963–1967 (D)
Maddox, Lester Garfield, 1967–1971 (D)
Carter, James Earl, 1971–1975 (D)
Busbee, George Dekle, 1975–1983 (D)
Harris, Joe Frank, 1983–1991 (D)
Miller, Zell, 1991– (D)

## HAWAII

Quinn, William Francis, 1959–1962 (R)
Burns, John Anthony, 1962–1974 (D)
Ariyoshi, George Ryoichi, 1974–1986 (D)
Waihee, John D., III, 1986– (D)

## IDAHO

Shoup, George Laird, 1890 (R)
Wiley, Norman B., 1890–1893 (R)
McConnell, William John, 1893–1897 (R)
Steunenberg, Frank, 1897–1901 (D)
Hunt, Frank W., 1901–1903 (D)
Morrison, John T., 1903–1905 (R)
Gooding, Frank, 1905–1909 (R)
Brady, James H., 1909–1911 (R)
Hawley, James H., 1911–1913 (D)
Haines, John M., 1913–1915 (R)
Alexander, Moses, 1915–1919 (D)
Davis, David W., 1919–1923 (R)
Moore, Charles C., 1923–1927 (R)
Baldridge, H. Clarence, 1927–1931 (R)
Ross, C. Ben, 1931–1937 (D)
Clark, Barzilla Worth, 1937–1939 (D)
Bottolfsen, Clarence A., 1939–1941, 1943–1945 (R)
Clark, Chase A., 1941–1943 (D)
Gossett, Charles C., 1945 (D)
Williams, Arnold, 1945–1947 (D)
Robins, Clarence Armington, 1947–

1951 (R)
Jordon, Leonard Beck, 1951–1955 (R)
Smylie, Robert E., 1955–1967 (R)
Samuelson, Donald William, 1967–1971 (R)
Andrus, Cecil Dale, 1971–1977, 1987– (D)
Evans, John Victor, 1977–1987 (D)

## ILLINOIS

Bond, Shaderick, 1818–1822 (D-R)
Coles, Edward, 1822–1826 (D-R)
Edwards, Ninian, 1826–1830 (D)
Reynolds, John, 1830–1834 (D-R)
Ewing, William Lee Davidson, 1834 (JD)
Duncan, Joseph, 1834–1838 (JD)
Carlin, Thomas, 1838–1842 (D)
Ford, Thomas, 1842–1846 (D)
French, Augustus C., 1846–1853 (D)
Matteson, Joel Aldrich, 1853–1857 (D)
Bissell, William Henry, 1857–1860 ( R)
Wood, John, 1860–1861 (R)
Yates, Richard, 1861–1865 (R)
Oglesby, Richard James, 1865–1869, 1885–1889 (R)
Palmer, John McAuley, 1869–1873 (R)
Beveridge, John Lourie, 1873–1877 (R)
Cullom, Shelby Moore, 1877–1883 (R)
Hamilton, John Marshall, 1883–1885 (R)
Fifer, Joseph Wilson, 1889–1893 (R)
Altgeld, John Peter, 1893–1897 (D)
Tanner, John R., 1897–1901 (R)
Yates, Richard, Jr., 1901–1905 (R)
Deneen, Charles S., 1905–1913 (R)
Dunne, Edward F., 1913–1917 (D)
Lowden, Frank O., 1917–1921 (R)
Small, Lemington, 1921–1929 (R)
Emmerson, Louis L., 1929–1933 (R)
Horner, Henry, 1933–1940 (D)
Stelle, John H., 1940–1941 (D)
Green, Dwight H., 1941–1949 (R)
Stevenson, Adlai E., 1949–1953 (D)
Stratton, William G., 1953–1961 (R)
Kerner, Otto, 1961–1968 (D)
Shapiro, Samuel H., 1968–1969 (D)
Ogilvie, Richard Buell, 1969–1973 (R)
Walker, Daniel, 1973–1977 (D)
Thompson, James, 1977–1991 (R)
Edgar, Jim, 1991– (R)

## INDIANA

Jennings, Jonathan, 1816–1822 (JR)
Boon, Ratcliff, 1822 (JD)
Hendricks, William, 1822–1825 (D-R)
Ray, James Brown, 1825–1831 (D-R)
Noble, Noah, 1831–1837 (W)
Wallace, David, 1837–1840 (D-R)
Bigger, Samuel, 1840–1843 (W)
Whitcomb, James, 1843–1848 (D)
Dunning, Paris C., 1848–1849 (D)
Wright, Joseph A., 1849–1857 (D)
Willard, Ashbel P., 1857–1860 (D)
Hammond, Abram A., 1860–1861 (D)
Lane, Henry S., 1861 (R)

Morton, Oliver P., 1861–1867 (R)
Baker, Conrad, 1867–1873 (R)
Hendricks, Thomas, 1873–1877 (D)
Williams, James D., 1877–1880 (D)
Gray, Isaac P., 1880–1881, 1885–1889 (R)
Porter, Albert G., 1881–1885 (D)
Hovey, Alvin P., 1889–1891 (R)
Chase, Ira J., 1891–1893 (R)
Matthews, Claude, 1893–1897 (D)
Mount, James A., 1897–1901 (R)
Durbin, Winfield, 1901–1905 (R)
Hanly, James Franklin, 1905–1909 (R)
Marshall, Thomas R., 1909–1913 (D)
Ralston, Samuel, 1913–1917 (D)
Goodrich, James P., 1917–1921 (R)
McCray, Warren T., 1921–1924 (R)
Branch, Emmett F., 1924–1925 (R)
Jackson, Edward L., 1925–1929 (R)
Leslie, Henry G., 1929–1933 (R)
McNutt, Paul V., 1933–1937 (D)
Townsend, M. Clifford, 1937–1941 (D)
Shricker, Henry F., 1941–1945, 1949–1953 (D)
Gates, Ralph F., 1945–1949 (R)
Craig, George N., 1953–1957 (R)
Handley, Harold W., 1957–1961 (R)
Welsh, Matthew E., 1961–1965 (D)
Branigin, Roger D., 1965–1969 (D)
Whitcomb, Edgar D., 1969–1973 (R)
Bowen, Ottis R., 1973–1981 (R)
Orr, Robert D., 1981–1989 (R)
Bayh, Evan, 1989– (D)

## IOWA

Briggs, Ansel, 1846–1850 (D)
Hempstead, Stephan, 1850–1854 (D)
Grimes, James Wilson, 1854–1858 (W–Fus)
Lowe, Ralph P., 1858–1860 (R)
Kirkwood, Samuel Jordon, 1860–1864, 1876–1877 (R)
Stone, William M., 1864–1868 (R)
Merril, Samuel, 1868–1872 (R)
Carpenter, Cyrus C., 1872–1876 (R)
Newbold, Joshua G., 1877–1878 (R)
Gear, John H., 1878–1882 (R)
Sherman, Buren R., 1882–1886 (R)
Larrabee, William, 1886–1890 (R)
Boies, Horace, 1890–1894 (D)
Jackson, Frank Darr, 1894–1896 (R)
Drake, Francis, 1896–1898 (R)
Shaw, Leslie M., 1898–1902 (R)
Cumins, Albert Baird, 1902–1909 (R)
Carrol, Beryl F., 1909–1913 (R)
Clarke, George W., 1913–1917 (R)
Harding, William L., 1917–1921 (R)
Kendall, Nathan E., 1921–1925 (R)
Hammill, John, 1925–1931 (R)
Turner, Daniel W., 1931–1933 (R)
Herring, Clyde L., 1933–1937 (D)
Kraschel, Nelson G., 1937–1939 (D)
Wilson, George A., 1939–1943 (R)
Hickenlooper, Bourke Blakemore, 1943–1945 (R)
Blue, Robert D., 1945–1949 (R)
Beardsley, William S., 1949–1954 (R)

Elton, Les, 1954–1955
Hoegh, Leo A., 1955–1957 (R)
Loveless, Herschel C., 1957–1961 (D)
Erbie, Norman A., 1961–1963 (R)
Hughes, Harold E., 1963–1969 (D)
Fulton, Robert D., 1969 (D)
Ray, Robert D., 1969–1983 (R)
Bramsted, Terry E., 1983– (R)

## KANSAS

Robinson, Charles, 1861–1863 (R)
Carney, Thomas, 1863–1865 (R)
Crawford, Samuel Johnson, 1865–1868 (R)
Green, Nehemia, 1868–1869 (R)
Harvey, James Madison, 1869–1873 (R)
Osborn, Thomas Andrew, 1873–1877 (R)
Anthony, George Tobey, 1877–1879 (R)
St. John, John Pierce, 1879–1883 (R)
Glick, George Washington, 1883–1885 (D)
Martin, John Alexander, 1885–1889 (R)
Humphrey, Lyman Underwood, 1889–1893 (R)
Lewelling, Lorenzo Dow, 1893–1895 (Pe)
Morrill, Edmund Nedham, 1895–1897 (R)
Leedy, John Whitnah, 1897–1899 (D)
Stanley, William Eugene, 1899–1903 (R)
Bailey, Willis Joshua, 1903–1905 (R)
Hoch, Edward, 1905–1909 (R)
Stubbs, Walter Roscoe, 1909–1913 (R)
Hodges, George Hartshorn, 1913–1915 (D)
Capper, Arthur, 1915–1919 (R)
Allen, Henry Justin, 1919–1923 (R)
Davis, Jonathan McMillan, 1923–1925 (D)
Paulen, Benjamin Sanford, 1925–1929 (R)
Reed, Clyde Martin, 1929–1931 (R)
Woodring, Harry Hines, 1931–1933 (D)
Landon, Alfred Mossman, 1933–1937 (R)
Hoxman, Walter Augustus, 1937–1939 (D)
Fatner, Payne Harry, 1939–1943 (R)
Schoeppel, Andrew Frank, 1943–1947 (R)
Carlson, Frank, 1947–1950 (R)
Hagman, Frank Leslie, 1950–1951 (R)
Arn, Edward F., 1951–1955 (R)
Hall, Frederick Lee, 1955–1957 (R)
McCuish, John Berridge, 1957 (R)
Docking, George, 1957–1961 (D)
Anderson, John, 1961–1965 (R)
Avery, William Henry, 1965–1967 (R)
Docking, Robert Blackwell, 1967–1975 (D)
Bennett, Robert Frederick, 1975–1979 (R)
Carlin, John W., 1979–1987 (D)
Hayden, Mike, 1987–1991 (R)
Finney, Joan, 1991– (D)

# KENTUCKY

Shelby, Isaac, 1792–1796, 1812–1816 (JR)
Garred, James, 1796–1804 (JR)
Greenup, Christopher, 1804–1808 (JR)
Scott, Charles, 1808–1812 (D-R)
Madison, George, 1816
Slaughter, Gabriel, 1816–1820 (D-R)
Adair, John, 1820–1824 (D)
Desha, Joseph, 1824–1828 (D-R)
Metclaff, Thomas, 1828–1832 (D-R)
Breathitt, John, 1832–1834 (D)
Morehead, James Turner, 1834–1836 (R)
Clark, James, 1836–1839 (W)
Wickliffe, Charles Anderson, 1839–1840 (D)
Letcher, Robert Perkins, 1840–1844 (W)
Owsley, William, 1844–1848 (W)
Crittenden, John Jordon, 1848–1850 (W)
Helm, John Larue, 1850–1851, 1867 (W)
Powell, Lazarus Whitehead, 1851–1855 (D)
Morehead, Charles Slaughter, 1855–1859 (W–A)
Magoffin, Beriah, 1859–1862 (D)
Robinson, James Fisher, 1862–1863 (W)
Bramlette, Thomas E., 1863–1867 (U-D)
Stevenson, John White, 1867–1871 (D)
Leslie, Preston Hopkins, 1871–1875 (D)
McCreary, James Bennett, 1875–1879, 1911–1915 (D)
Blackburn, Luke Pryor, 1879–1883 (D)
Knott, James Proctor, 1883–1887 (D)
Buckner, Simon Bolivar, 1887–1891 (D)
Brown, John Young, 1891–1895 (D)
Bradley, William O'Connell, 1895–1899 (R)
Taylor, William Sylvester, 1899–1900 (R)
Goebel, William, 1900 (D)
Beckham, John Crepps Wickliffe, 1900–1907 (D)
Willson, Augustus Everett, 1907–1911 (R)
Stanley, Augustus Owsley, 1915–1919 (D)
Black, James Dixon, 1919 (D)
Morrow, Edwin Porch, 1919–1923 (R)
Fields, William Jason, 1923–1927 (D)
Sampson, Flem D., 1927–1931 (R)
Laffoon, Ruby, 1931–1935 (D)
Chandler, Albert Benjamin, 1935–1939, 1955–1959 (D)
Johnson, Keen, 1939–1943 (D)
Willis, Simeon, 1943–1947 (R)
Clements, Earle Chester, 1947–1950 (D)
Wetherby, Lawrence Winchester, 1950–1955 (D)
Combs, Bert Thomas, 1959–1963 (D)
Breathitt, Edward Thompson, 1963–1967 (D)
Nunn, Louie B., 1967–1971 (R)
Ford, Wendall Hampton, 1971–1974 (D)
Carroll, Julian Morton, 1974–1979 (D)
Brown, John Young, Jr., 1979–1983 (D)
Collins, Martha Layne, 1983–1987 (D)
Wilkinson, Wallace, 1987– (D)

# LOUISIANA

Claiborne, William Charles C., 1812–1816 (R)
Villere, Jacques Phillipe, 1816–1820 (D-R)
Robertson, Thomas Bolling, 1820–1824 (D-R)
Thibodeaux, Henry Schuyler, 1824 (D-R)
Johnson, Henry S., 1824–1828 (AR)
Derbigny, Pierre Auguste Charles Bourguignon, 1828–1829 (Am-R)
Beavais, Armand, 1829–1830 (NR)
Dupre, Jacques, 1830–1831 (NR)
Roman, Andres Bienvenu, 1831–1835, 1839–1843 (W)
White, Edward Douglas, 1835–1839 (R)
Mouton, Alexander, 1843–1846 (D)
Johnson, Isaac, 1846–1850 (D)
Walker, Joseph Marshall, 1850–1853 (D)
Herbert, Paul Octave, 1853–1856 (D)
Wickliffe, Robert Charles, 1856–1860 (D)
Moore, Thomas Overton, 1860–1864 (D)
Shepley, George Foster, 1862–1864
Allen, Henry Watkins, 1864–1865 (D)
Hahn, Michael, 1864–1865 (D)
Wells, James Madison, 1865–1867 (R)
Flanders, Benjamin Franklin, 1867–1868 (U)
Baker, Joshua, 1868 (D)
Warmouth, Henry Clay, 1868–1872 (R)
Pinchback, Pinckney Benton Stewart, 1872–1873 (R)
Kellogg, William Pitt, 1873–1877 (R)
Nicholas, Francis Redding Tillou, 1877–1880, 1888–1892 (D)
Wiltz, Louis Alfred, 1880–1881 (D)
McEnery, Samuel Douglas, 1881–1888 (D)
Foster, Murphy James, 1892–1900 (D)
Heard, William Wright, 1900–1904 (D)
Blanchard, Newton Crain, 1904–1908 (D)
Sanders, Jared Young, 1908–1912 (D)
Hall, Luther Egbert, 1912–1916 (D)
Pleasant, Ruffin Golson, 1916–1920 (D)
Parker, John, 1920–1924 (D)
Fiqua, Henry Luce, 1924–1926 (D)
Simpson, Oramel Hinckley, 1926–1928 (D)
Long, Huey Pierce, 1928–1932 (D)
King, Alvin Olin, 1932
Allen, Oscar Kelly, 1932–1936 (D)
Noe, James Albert, 1936 (D)
Leche, Richard Webster, 1936–1939 (D)
Long, Earl Kemp, 1939–1940, 1948–1952, 1956–1960 (D)
Jones, Sam Houston, 1940–1944 (D)
Davis, James Houston, 1944–1948, 1960–1964 (D)
Kennon, Robert Floyd, 1952–1956 (D)
McKeithan, John Julian, 1964–1972 (D)
Edwards, Edwin Washington, 1972–1980, 1984–1988 (D)
Treen, Dave C., 1980–1984 (R)
Roemer, Buddy, 1988– (D)

# MAINE

King, William, 1820–1821 (D-R)
Williamson, William Durkee, 1821 (D-R)
Aimes, Benjamin, 1821–1822
Rose, Daniel, 1822
Parris, Albion Keith, 1822–1827 (D-R)
Lincoln, Enoch, 1827–1829 (D-R)
Cutler, Nathan, 1829–1830 (D)
Hall, Joshua, 1830
Hunton, Jonathan G., 1830–1831 (NR)
Smith, Samuel Emerson, 1831–1834 (D-R)
Dunlap, Robert Pinckney, 1834–1838 (D)
Kent, Edward, 1838–1839, 1841–1842 (W)
Fairfield, John, 1839–1841, 1842–1843 (D)
Vose, Richard H., 1841
Kavanagh, Edward, 1843–1844 (D)
Dunn, David, 1844
Dana, John Winchester, 1844, 1847–1850 (D)
Anderson, Hugh Johnson, 1844–1847 (D)
Hubbard, John, 1850–1853 (D)
Crosby, William George, 1853–1855 (W)
Morrill, Anson Peaslee, 1855–1856 (D)
Wells, Samuel, 1856–1857 (D)
Hamlin, Hannibal, 1857 (JD)
Williams, Joseph Hartwell, 1857–1858 (R)
Morrill, Lot Myrick, 1858–1861 (R)
Washburn, Israel, 1861–1863 (R)
Coburn, Abner, 1863–1864 (R)
Cony, Samuel, 1864–1867 (R)
Chamberlain, Joshua Lawrence, 1867–1871 (R)
Perham, Sidney, 1871–1874 (R)
Dingley, Nelson, 1874–1876 (R)
Conner, Seldon, 1876–1879 (R)
Garcelon, Alonzo, 1879–1880 (D)
Davis, Daniel Franklin, 1880–1881 (R)
Plaisted, Harris Merrill, 1881–1883 (D)
Robie, Frederick, 1883–1887 (R)
Bodwell, Joseph Robinson, 1887 (R)
Marbie, Sebastian Streeter, 1887–1889 (R)
Burleigh, Edwin C., 1889–1893 (R)
Cleaves, Henry B., 1893–1897 (R)
Powers, Llewelyn, 1897–1901 (R)
Hill, John Fremont, 1901–1905 (R)
Cobb, William Titcomb, 1905–1909 (R)
Fernald, Bert Manfield, 1909–1911 (R)
Plaisted, Frederick William, 1911–1913 (D)
Haines, William Thomas, 1913–1915 (R)

Curtis, Oakley Chester, 1915–1917 (D)
Millikin, Carl E., 1917–1921 (R)
Parkhurst, Frederick Hale, 1921 (R)
Baxter, Percival P., 1921–1925 (R)
Brewster, Ralph Owen, 1925–1929 (R)
Gardiner, William Tudor, 1929–1933 (R)
Brann, Louis J., 1933–1937 (D)
Barrows, Lewis O., 1937–1941 (R)
Sewell, Sumner, 1941–1945 (R)
Hildreth, Horace A., 1945–1949 (R)
Payne, Frederick G., 1949–1953 (R)
Cross, Burton M., 1953–1955 (R)
Muskie, Edmund S., 1955–1959 (D)
Haskell, Robert N., 1959 (R)
Clauson, Clinton Amos, 1959 (D)
Reed, John H., 1959–1967 (R)
Curtis, Kennith M., 1967–1975 (D)
Longley, James Bernard, 1975–1979 (D)
Brennan, Joseph Edward, 1979–1987 (D)
McKernan, John R., Jr., 1987– (R)

## MARYLAND

Howard, John Eager, 1781–1791 (F)
Plater, George, 1791–1792 (F)
Lee, Thomas Sim, 1792–1794 (F)
Stone, John Hopkins, 1794–1797 (F)
Henry, John, 1797–1798 (F)
Ogle, Benjamin, 1798–1801 (F)
Mercer, John Francis, 1801–1803 (D-R)
Bowie, Robert, 1803–1806, 1811–1812 (R)
Wright, Robert, 1806–1809 (D-R)
Lloyd, Edward, 1809–1811 (D-R)
Winder, Levin, 1812–1816 (D-R)
Ridgely, Charles Carnan, 1816–1819 (F)
Goldsborough, Charles, 1819 (F)
Sprigg, Samuel, 1819–1822 (D-R)
Stevens, Samuel, 1822–1826 (D-R)
Kent, Joseph, 1826–1829 (D-R)
Martin, Daniel, 1829–1830, 1831 (R)
Carroll, Thomas King, 1830–1831 (D-R)
Howard, George, 1831–1833 (R)
Thomas, James, 1833–1836 (D)
Veazy, Thomas Ward, 1836–1839 (W)
Grason, William, 1839–1842 (F)
Thomas, Francis, 1842–1845 (D)
Pratt, Thomas George, 1845–1848 (W)
Thomas, Phillip Francis, 1848–1851 (D)
Lowe, Enoch Louis, 1851–1854 (D)
Ligon, Thomas Watkins, 1854–1858 (D)
Hicks, Thomas Holliday, 1858–1862 (W)
Bradford, Augustus Williamson, 1862–1866 (U-D)
Swan, Thomas, 1866–1869 (U–R)
Bowie, Oden, 1869–1872 (D)
Whyte, William Pickney, 1872–1874 (D)
Groome, James Black, 1874–1876 (D)
Carroll, John L., 1876–1880 (D)
Hamilton, William T., 1880–1884 (D)
McLane, Robert M., 1884–1885 (D)
Lloyd, Henry, 1885–1888 (D)
Jackson, Elihu Emory, 1888–1892 (D)
Brown, Frank, 1892–1896 (D)

Lowndes, Lloyd, 1896–1900 (R)
Smith, John W., 1900–1904 (D)
Warfield, Edwin, 1904–1908 (D)
Crothers, Austin Lane, 1908–1912 (D)
Goldsborough, Phillips Lee, 1912–1916 (R)
Harrington, Emerson Columbus, 1916–1920 (D)
Ritchie, Albert Cabell, 1920–1935 (D)
Nice, Harry Whinna, 1935–1939 (R)
O'Conor, Herbert Romulus, 1939–1947 (D)
Lane, William Preston, 1947–1951 (D)
McKeldin, Theodoore Roosevelt, 1951–1959 (R)
Tawes, John Millard, 1959–1967 (D)
Agnew, Spiro T., 1967–1969 (R)
Mandel, Marvin, 1969–1977, 1979 (D)
Lee, Blair, III, 1977–1979 (D)
Hughes, Harry Roe, 1979–1987 (D)
Schaefer, William Donald, 1987– (D)

## MASSACHUSETTS

Hancock, John, 1789–1793
Adams, Samuel, 1793–1797 (D-R)
Sumner, Increase, 1797–1799 (F)
OFFICE VACANT, 1799–1800
Strong, Caleb, 1800–1807, 1811–1816 (F)
Sullivan, James, 1807–1808 (D-R)
Lincoln, Levi, 1808–1809 (D-R)
Gore, Christopher, 1809–1810 (F)
Gerry, Elbridge, 1810–1811 (D-R)
Brooks, John, 1816–1823 (F)
Eustis, William, 1823–1825 (D-R)
Morton, Marcus, 1825, 1840–1841, 1843–1844 (D)
Lincoln, Levi, Jr., 1825–1834 (R)
Davis, John, 1834–1835, 1841–1843 (W)
Armstrong, Samuel Turell, 1835–1836 (W)
Everett, Edward, 1836–1840 (W)
Briggs, George Nixon, 1844–1851 (W)
Boutwell, George Sewell, 1851–1853 (D)
Clifford, John Henry, 1853–1854 (W)
Washburn, Emory, 1854–1855 (W)
Gardiner, Henry Joseph, 1855–1858 (A)
Banks, Nathaniel Prentice, 1858–1861 (D)
Andrew, John Albion, 1861–1866 (R)
Bullock, Alexander Hamilton, 1866–1869 (R)
Claflin, William, 1869–1872 (R)
Washburn, William Barrett, 1872–1874 (R)
Talbot, Thomas, 1874–1875, 1879–1880 (R)
Gaston, William, 1875–1876 (D)
Rice, Alexander Hamilton, 1876–1879 (R)
Long, John Davis, 1880–1883 (R)
Butler, Benjamin Franklin, 1883–1884 (D)
Robinson, George Dexter, 1884–1887 (R)

Ames, Oliver, 1887–1890 (R)
Brackett, John Quincy Adams, 1890–1891 (R)
Russell, William Eustis, 1891–1894 (D)
Greenhalge, Frederic Thomas, 1894–1896 (R)
Wolcott, Roger, 1896–1900 (R)
Crane, Winthrop Murray, 1900–1903 (R)
Bates, John Lewis, 1903–1905 (R)
Douglas, William Lewis, 1905–1906 (D)
Guild, Curtis, 1906–1909 (R)
Draper, Ebenezer Sumner, 1909–1911 (R)
Foss, Eugene Noble, 1911–1914 (D)
Walsh, David Ignatius, 1914–1916 (D)
McCall, Samuel Walker, 1916–1919 (R)
Claflin, William, 1919 (R)
Coolidge, Calvin, 1919–1921 (R)
Cox, Channing H., 1921–1925 (R)
Fuller, Alvin T., 1925–1929 (R)
Allen, Frank G., 1929–1931 (R)
Ely, Joseph Buell, 1931–1935 (D)
Curley, James M., 1935–1937 (D)
Hurley, Charles F., 1937–1939 (D)
Saltonstall, Leverett, 1939–1945 (R)
Tobin, Maurice J., 1945–1947 (D)
Bradford, Robert Fiske, 1947–1949 (R)
Dever, Paul Andrew, 1949–1953 (D)
Herter, Christian A., 1953–1957 (R)
Furcolo, Foster J., 1957–1961 (D)
Volpe, John A., 1961–1963, 1965–1969 (R)
Peabody, Endicott, 1963–1965 (D)
Sargent, Francis W., 1969–1975 (R)
Dukakis, Michael S., 1975–1979, 1983–1991 (D)
King, Edward Joseph, 1979–1983 (D)
Weld, William F., 1991– (R)

## MICHIGAN

Mason, Stevens Thomson, 1837–1840 (D)
Woodbridge, William, 1840–1841 (W)
Gordon, James Wright, 1841–1842 (W)
Barry, John Stewert, 1842–1846, 1850–1852 (D)
Felch, Alpheus, 1846–1847 (D)
Greenly, William L., 1847–1848 (D)
Ransom, Epaphroditus, 1848–1850 (D)
McClellend, Robert, 1852–1853 (D)
Parsons, Andrew, 1853–1855 (D)
Bingham, Kingsly Scott, 1855–1859 (R)
Wisner, Moses, 1859–1861 (R)
Blair, Austin, 1861–1865 (R)
Crapo, Henry Howland, 1865–1869 (R)
Baldwin, Henry Porter, 1869–1873 (R)
Bagley, John Judson, 1873–1877 (R)
Croswell, Charles Miller, 1877–1881 (R)
Jerome, David H., 1881–1883 (R)
Begole, Josiah, 1883–1885 (D)
Alger, Russell Alexander, 1885–1887 (R)
Luce, Cyrus, 1887–1891 (R)
Winans, Edwin, 1891–1893 (D)
Rich, John T., 1893–1897 (R)
Pingree, Hazen, 1897–1901 (R)
Bliss, Aaron T., 1901–1905 (R)

Warner, Fred Maltby, 1905–1911 (R)
Osborn, Chase Salmon, 1911–1913 (R)
Ferris, Woodbridge N., 1913–1917 (D)
Sleeper, Albert Edson, 1917–1921 (R)
Groesback, Alexander Joseph, 1921–1927 (R)
Green, Fred Warren, 1927–1931 (R)
Brucker, Wilbur, 1931–1933 (R)
Comstock, William A., 1933–1935 (D)
Fitzgerald, Frank D., 1935–1937, 1939 (R)
Murphy, Frank, 1937–1939 (D)
Dickenson, Luren Dudley, 1939–1941 (R)
Van Wagoner, Murray Delos, 1941–1943 (D)
Kelley, Harry Francis, 1943–1947 (R)
Sigler, Kim, 1947–1949 (R)
Williams, Gerhard Mennen, 1949–1961 (D)
Swainson, John Burley, 1961–1963 (D)
Romney, George, 1963–1969 (R)
Millikin, William, 1969–1983 (R)
Blanchard, James J., 1983–1991 (D)
Engler, John, 1991– (R)

## MINNESOTA

Sibley, Henry Hastings, 1858–1860 (D)
Ramsey, Alexander, 1860–1863 (W)
Swift, Henry Adoniram, 1863–1864 (R)
Marshall, William Rogerson, 1866–1870 (R)
Austin, Horace, 1870–1874 (R)
Davis, Cushman Kellogg, 1874–1876 (R)
Pillsbury, John Sargent, 1876–1882 (R)
Hubbard, Lucius Frederick, 1882–1887 (R)
McGill, Andrew Ryan, 1887–1889 (R)
Merriam, William Rush, 1889–1893 (R)
Nelson, Knute, 1893–1895 (R)
Clough, David Marston, 1895–1899 (R)
Lind, John, 1899–1901 (D)
Van Sant, Samuel Rinnah, 1901–1905 (R)
Johnson, John Albert, 1905–1909 (D)
Eberhart, Adolph Olson, 1909–1915 (R)
Hammond, Winfield Scott, 1915 (D)
Burnquist, Joseph Alfred Arner, 1915–1921 (R)
Preus, Jacob Aall Ottesen, 1921–1925 (R)
Christanson, Theodore, 1925–1931 (R)
Olson, Floyd Bjornstjerne, 1931–1936 (F–L)
Peterson, Hjalmar, 1936–1937 (F–L)
Benson, Elmer Austin, 1937–1939 (F–L)
Stassen, Harold Edward, 1939–1943 (R)
Thye, Edward John, 1943–1947 (R)
Youngdahl, Luther Wallace, 1947–1951 (R)
Anderson, C. Elmer, 1951–1955 (R)
Freeman, Orville Lothrop, 1955–1961 (D–F–L)
Anderson, Elmar Lee, 1961–1963 (R)
Rolvaag, Karl Fritjof, 1963–1967 (D)
LeVander, Harold, 1967–1971 (R)

Anderson, Wendall Richard, 1971–1976 (D)
Perpich, Rudy, 1976–1979, 1983–1991 (D)
Quie, Albert A., 1979–1983 (D)
Carlson, Arne, 1991– (R)

## MISSISSIPPI

Holmes, David, 1817–1820 (D-R)
Poindexter, George, 1820–1822 (D-R)
Leake, Walter, 1822–1825 (D-R)
Brandon, Gerard Chittocque, 1825–1826, 1826–1832 (D-R)
Scott, Charles, 1832–1833 (JD)
Lynch, Charles, 1833, 1836–1838 (W)
Runnels, Hiram G., 1833–1835 (JD)
Quitman, John Anthony, 1835–1836, 1850–1851 (D)
McNutt, Alexander, 1838–1842 (D)
Tucker, Tilgham Mayfield, 1842–1844 (D)
Brown, Albert Gallatin, 1844–1848 (D)
Matthews, Joseph W., 1848–1850 (D)
Guion, John Isaac, 1851 (D)
Whitfield, James, 1851–1852 (D)
Foote, Henry Stuart, 1852–1854 (D)
Pettus, John Jones, 1854, 1859–1863 (D)
McRae, John Jones, 1854–1857 (D)
McWillie, William, 1857–1859 (W)
Clark, Charles, 1863–1865 (D)
Sharkey, William Lewis, 1865
Humphreys, Benjamin Grubb, 1865–1868 (D)
Ames, Adelbert, 1868–1870, 1874–1876 (R)
Alcorn, James Lusk, 1870–1871 (R)
Powers, Ridgley Ceylon, 1871–1874 (R)
Stone, John Marshal, 1876–1882, 1890–1896 (D)
Lowry, Robert, 1882–1890 (D)
McLaurin, Anselm Joseph, 1896–1900 (D)
Longino, Andrew Houston, 1900–1904 (D)
Vardman, James Kimble, 1904–1908 (D)
Noel, Edmond Favor, 1908–1912 (D)
Brewer, Earl, 1912–1916 (D)
Bilbo, Theodore Gilmore, 1916–1920, 1928–1932 (D)
Russell, Lee Maurice, 1920–1924 (D)
Whitfield, Henry Lewis, 1924–1927 (D)
Murphree, Herron Dennis, 1927–1928, 1943–1944 (D)
Conner, Martin Sennett, 1932–1936 (D)
White, Hugh Lawson, 1936–1940, 1952–1956 (D)
Johnson, Paul Barney, 1940–1943 (D)
Bailey, Thomas L., 1944–1946 (D)
Wright, Fielding Lewis, 1946–1952 (D)
Coleman, James, 1956–1960 (D)
Barnett, Ross Robert, 1960–1964 (D)
Johnson, Paul Barney, Jr., 1964–1968 (D)
Williams, John Bell, 1968–1972 (D)
Waller, William Lowe, 1972–1976 (D)

Finch, Charles Clifton, 1976–1980 (D)
Winter, William Forrest, 1980–1984 (D)
Allain, William A., 1984–1988 (D)
Mabus, Ray, 1988– (D)

## MISSOURI

McNair, Alexander, 1820–1824 (D-R)
Bates, Frederick, 1824–1825 (NP)
Williams, Abraham, J. 1825–1826 (D-R)
Miller, John, 1826–1832 (JD)
Dunklin, Daniel, 1832–1836 (D)
Boggs, Lilburn W., 1836–1840 (D)
Reynolds, Thomas, 1840–1844 (D)
Marmaduke, Meredith M., 1844 (D)
Edwards, John Cummins, 1844–1848 (D)
King, Austin Augustus, 1848–1853 (D)
Price, Sterling, 1853–1857 (D)
Polk, Trusten, 1857 (D)
Jackson, Hancock Lee, 1857 (D)
Stewart, Robert Marcellus, 1857–1861 (D)
Jackson, Claiborne Fox, 1861 (D)
Gamble, Hamilton Rowan, 1861–1864 (U)
Hall, Willard Preble, 1864–1865 (U)
Fletcher, Thomas Clement, 1865–1869 (R)
McClung, Joseph W., 1869–1871 (R)
Brown, Benjamin Gratz, 1871–1873 (R)
Woodson, Silas, 1873–1875 (D)
Hardin, Charles Henry 1875–1877 (D)
Phelps, John Smith, 1877–1881 (D)
Crittenden, Thomas Theodore, 1881–1885 (D)
Marmaduke, John Sappington, 1885–1887 (D)
Morehouse, Albert P., 1887–1889 (D)
Francis, David Rowland, 1889–1893 (D)
Stone, William Joel, 1893–1897 (D)
Stephans, Lawrence Vest, 1897–1901 (D)
Dockery, Alexander Monroe, 1901–1905 (D)
Folk, Joseph Wingate, 1905–1909 (D)
Hadley, Herbert Spencer, 1909–1913 (R)
Major, Elliot Woolfolk, 1913–1917 (D)
Gardner, Frederick D., 1917–1921 (D)
Hyde, Arthur Mastick, 1921–1925 (R)
Baker, Samuel Aaron, 1925–1929 (R)
Caulfield, Henry Stewart, 1929–1933 (R)
Park, Guy B., 1933–1937 (D)
Stark, Lloyd Crow, 1937–1941 (D)
Donnell, Forrest C., 1941–1945 (R)
Donnelly, Phil M., 1945–1949, 1953–1957 (D)
Smith, Forrest, 1949–1953 (D)
Blair, James T., 1957–1961 (D)
Dalton, John M., 1961–1965 (D)
Hearnes, Warren E., 1965–1973 (D)
Bond, Christopher S., 1973–1977 (R)
Teasdale, Joseph Patrick, 1977–1985 (D)
Ashcroft, John, 1985– (R)

## MONTANA

Toole, Joseph Kemp, 1889–1893, 1901–1908 (D)
Rickards, John Ezra, 1893–1897 (R)
Smith, Robert Burns, 1897–1901 (PE)
Norris, Edwin L., 1908–1913 (D)
Stewart, Samuel Vernon, 1913–1921 (D)
Dixon, Joseph Moore, 1921–1925 (PR)
Erickson, John Edward, 1925–1933 (D)
Cooney, Frank H., 1933–1935 (D)
Holt, William Elmer, 1935–1937 (D)
Ayers, Roy Elmer, 1937–1941 (D)
Ford, Samuel Clarence, 1941–1949 (R)
Bonner, John Woodrow, 1949–1953 (D)
Aronson, J. Hugo, 1953–1961 (R)
Nutter, Donald Grant, 1961–1962 (R)
Babcock, Tim, 1962–1969 (R)
Anderson, Forrest Howard, 1969–1973 (D)
Judge, Thomas L., 1973–1981 (D)
Schwinden, Ted, 1981–1989 (D)
Stephens, Stan, 1989– (R)

## NEBRASKA

Butler, David C., 1867–1871 (R)
James, William Hartford, 1871–1873 (D)
Furnas, Robert Wilkinson, 1873–1875 (D)
Garber, Silas, 1875–1879 (R)
Nance, Albinus, 1879–1883 (R)
Dawes, James William, 1883–1887 (R)
Thayer, John Milton, 1887–1891, 1891–1892 (R)
Boyd, James E., 1891, 1892–1893 (D)
Crounse, Lorenzo, 1893–1895 (R)
Holcomb, Silas Alexander, 1895–1899 (Pop)
Poynter, William Amos, 1899–1901 (Pop)
Dietrich, Charles Henry, 1901 (R)
Savage, Ezra Perin, 1901–1903 (R)
Mickey, John Hopwood, 1903–1907 (R)
Sheldon, George Lawson, 1907–1909 (R)
Shallenberger, Ashton Cockayne, 1909–1911 (D)
Aldridge, Chester Hardy, 1911–1913 (R)
Morehead, John Henry, 1913–1917 (D)
Neville, M. Keith, 1917–1919 (D)
McKelvie, Samuel Roy, 1919–1923 (R)
Bryan, Charles Wayland, 1923–1925, 1931–1935 (D)
McMullen, Adam, 1925–1929 (R)
Weaver, Arthur J., 1929–1931 (R)
Cochran, Robert LeRoy, 1935–1941 (D)
Griswold, Dwight Palmer, 1941–1947 (R)
Peterson, Frederick Demar Erastus, 1947–1953 (R)
Crosby, Robert Berkey, 1953–1955 (R)
Anderson, Victor Emmanuel, 1955–1959 (R)
Brooks, Ralph Gilmour, 1959–1960 (D)

Burney, Dwight Willard, 1960–1961 (R)
Morrison, Frank Brener, 1961–1967 (D)
Tieman, Norbert Theodore, 1967–1971 (R)
Exon, John James, 1971–1979 (D)
Thone, Charles, 1979–1983 (R)
Kerrey, Robert, 1983–1987 (D)
Orr, Kay A., 1987–1991 (R)
Nelson, Ben, 1991– (D)

## NEVADA

Blasdel, Henry Goode, 1864–1871 (R)
Bradley, Lewis Rice, 1871–1879 (D)
Kinkead, John Henry, 1879–1883 (R)
Adams, Jewett William, 1883–1887 (D)
Stevenson, Charles Clark, 1887–1890 (R)
Bell, Francis Jardine, 1890–1891 (R)
Colcord, Roswell Keyes, 1891–1895 (R)
Jones, John Edward, 1895–1896 (Sil)
Sadler, Reinhold, 1896–1903 (Sil)
Sparks, John, 1903–1908 (Sil-D)
Dickerson, Denver Sylvester, 1908–1911 (D)
Oddie, Tasker Lowndes, 1911–1915 (R)
Boyle, Emmet Derby, 1915–1923 (D)
Scrugham, James Graves, 1923–1927 (D)
Balzar, Frederick Bennett, 1927–1934 (R)
Griswold, Morely, 1934–1935 (R)
Kirman, Richard, 1935–1939 (D)
Carville, Edward Peter, 1939–1945 (D)
Pittman, Vail Montgomery, 1945–1951 (D)
Russell, Charles H., 1951–1959 (R)
Sawyer, Grant, 1959–1967 (D)
Laxalt, Paul, 1967–1971 (R)
O'Callaghan, Donald Neil, 1971–1979 (D)
List, Robert Frank, 1979–1983 (R)
Bryan, Richard H., 1983–1988 (D)
Miller, Bob, 1988– (D)

## NEW HAMPSHIRE

Sullivan, John, 1789–1790
Bartlett, Josiah, 1790–1794
Gilman, John Taylor, 1794–1805, 1813–1816 (F)
Langdon, John, 1805–1809, 1810–1812 (D-R)
Smith, Jeremiah, 1809–1810 (JR)
Plumer, William, 1812–1813, 1816–1819 (F)
Bell, Samuel, 1819–1823 (D-R)
Woodbury, Levi, 1823–1824 (D-R)
Morril, David Lawrence, 1824–1827 (D-R)
Pierce, Benjamin, 1827–1828, 1829–1830 (D)
Bell, John, 1828–1829 (D)
Harvey, Matthew, 1830–1831 (D-R)
Harper, Joseph Morrill, 1831 (D)
Dinsmoor, Samuel, 1831–1834 (JD)
Badger, William, 1834–1836 (D)
Hill, Isaac, 1836–1839 (JD)

Page, John, 1839–1842 (D)
Hubbard, Henry, 1842–1844 (D)
Steele, John Hardy, 1844–1846 (D)
Colby, Anthony, 1846–1847 (D)
Williams, Jared Warner, 1847–1849 (D)
Dinsmoor, Samuel, Jr., 1849–1852 (D)
Martin, Noah, 1852–1854 (D)
Baker, Nathaniel Bradley, 1854–1855 (D)
Metcalf, Ralph, 1855–1857 (A)
Haile, William, 1857–1859 (R)
Goodwin, Ichabod, 1859–1861 (R)
Berry, Nathaniel Springer, 1861–1863 (R)
Gilmore, Joseph Albree, 1863–1865 (R)
Smyth, Frederick, 1865–1867 (R)
Harriman, Walter, 1867–1869 (D)
Stearns, Onslow, 1869–1871 (R)
Weston, James Adams, 1871–1872, 1874–1875 (D)
Straw, Ezekiel Albert, 1872–1874 (R)
Cheney, Person Colby, 1875–1877 (R)
Prescott, Benjamin Franklin, 1877–1879 (R)
Head, Natt, 1879–1881 (R)
Bell, Charles Henry, 1881–1883 (R)
Hale, Samuel Whitney, 1883–1885 (R)
Currier, Moody, 1885–1887 (R)
Sawyer, Charles Henry, 1887–1889 (R)
Goodell, David Harvey, 1889–1891 (R)
Tuttle, Hiram Americus, 1891–1893 (R)
Smith, John Butler, 1893–1895 (R)
Busiel, Charles Albert, 1895–1897 (R)
Ramsdell, George Allen, 1897–1899 (R)
Rollins, Frank West, 1899–1901 (R)
Jordan, Chester Bradley, 1901–1903 (R)
Bachelder, Nahum Josiah, 1903–1905 (R)
McLane, John, 1905–1907 (R)
Floyd, Charles Miller, 1907–1909 (R)
Quinby, Henry Brewer, 1909–1911 (R)
Bass, Robert Perkins, 1911–1913 (R)
Felker, Samuel Demeritt, 1913–1915 (D)
Spaulding, Roland Harty, 1915–1917 (R)
Keyes, Henry Wilder, 1917–1919 (R)
Bartlett, John Henry, 1919–1921 (R)
Brown, Albert Oscar, 1921–1923 (R)
Brown, Fred Herbert, 1923–1925 (D)
Winant, John Gilbert, 1925–1927, 1931–1935 (R)
Spaulding, Huntley Nowell, 1927–1929 (R)
Tobey, Charles William, 1929–1931 (R)
Bridges, Henry Styles, 1935–1937 (R)
Murphy, Francis Parnell, 1937–1941 (R)
Blood, Robert Oscar, 1941–1945 (R)
Dale, Charles Milby, 1945–1949 (R)
Adams, Llewelyn Sherman, 1949–1953 (R)
Gregg, Hugh, 1953–1955 (R)
Dwinell, Lane, 1955–1959 (R)
Powell, Wesley, 1959–1963 (R)
King, John William, 1963–1969 (D)
Peterson, Walter Rutherford, 1969–1973 (R)

Thomson, Meldrin, Jr., 1973–1979 (R)
Gallen, Hugh J., 1979–1982 (D)
Roy, Vesta M., 1982–1983 (R)
Sununu, John H., 1983–1989 (R)
Gregg, Judd, 1989– (R)

## NEW JERSEY

Livingston, William, 1776–1790
Paterson, William, 1790–1793 (D)
Henderson, Thomas, 1793
Howell, Richard, 1793–1801 (F)
Bloomfield, Joseph, 1801–1802, 1803–1812 (Jef-R)
Lambert, John, 1802–1803 (R)
Ogden, Aaron, 1812–1813 (F)
Pennington, William S., 1813–1815 (R)
Dickerson, Mahlon, 1815–1817 (R)
Williamson, Isaac H., 1817–1829 (R)
Vroom, Peter, 1829–1832, 1833–1836 (D)
Southard, Samuel Lewis, 1832–1833 (W)
Seeley, Elias P., 1833 (W)
Dickerson, Philemon, 1836–1837 (D)
Pennington, William, Jr., 1837–1843 (W)
Haines, Daniel, 1843–1845, 1848–1851 (D)
Stratton, Charles Creighton, 1845–1848 (W)
Fort, George Franklin, 1851–1854 (D)
Price, Rodman McCauley, 1854–1857 (D)
Newell, William Augustus, 1857–1860 (Fus-R)
Olden, Charles Smith, 1860–1863 (R)
Parker, Joel, 1863–1866, 1872–1875 (D)
Ward, Marcus Lawrence, 1866–1869 (R)
Randolph, Theodore Fitz, 1869–1872 (D)
Bedle, Joseph Dorsett, 1875–1878 (D)
McClellan, George, 1878–1881 (D)
Ludlow, George C., 1881–1884 (D)
Abbett, Leon, 1884–1887, 1890–1893 (D)
Green, Robert Stockton, 1887–1890 (D)
Werts, George Theodore, 1893–1896 (D)
Griggs, John William, 1896–1898 (R)
Voorhees, Foster MacGowan, 1898, 1899–1902 (R)
Watkins, David Ogden, 1898–1899 (R)
Murphy, Franklin, 1902–1905 (R)
Stokes, Edward Casper, 1905–1908 (R)
Fort, John Franklin, 1908–1911 (R)
Wilson, (Thomas) Woodrow, 1911–1913 (D)
Fielder, James Fairman, 1913, 1914–1917 (D)
Taylor, Leon R., 1913–1914 (D)
Edge, Walter Evans, 1917–1919, 1944–1947 (R)
Runyan, William Nelson, 1919–1920 (R)
Case, Clarence E., 1920 (R)
Edwards, Edward Irving, 1920–1923 (D)
Silzer, George Sebastian, 1923–1926 (D)

Moore, (Arthur) Harry, 1926–1929, 1932–1935, 1938–1941 (D)
Larson, Morgan Foster, 1929–1932 (R)
Prall, Horace Griggs, 1935 (R)
Hoffman, Harold Giles, 1935–1938 (R)
Edison, Charles, 1941–1944 (D)
Driscoll, Alfred Eastlack, 1947–1954 (R)
Meyner, Robert Baumle, 1954–1962 (D)
Hughes, Richard Joseph, 1962–1970 (D)
Cahill, William Thomas, 1970–1974 (R)
Byrne, Brendan Thomas, 1974–1982 (D)
Kean, Thomas. H., 1982–1990 (R)
Florio, James J., 1990– (D)

## NEW MEXICO

McDonald, William C., 1912–1917 (D)
DeBaca, Ezequiel Cabeza, 1917 (D)
Lindsey, Washington Elsworth, 1917–1919 (R)
Larrazolo, Octaviano Ambrosio, 1919–1921 (R)
Mechem, Merritt Cramer, 1921–1923 (R)
Hinkle, James Fielding, 1923–1925 (D)
Hannett, Arthur Thomas, 1925–1927 (D)
Dillon, Richard Charles, 1927–1931 (R)
Seligman, Arthur, 1931–1933 (D)
Hockenhull, Andrew W., 1933–1935 (D)
Tingley, Clyde, 1935–1939 (D)
Miles, John Esten, 1939–1943 (D)
Dempsey, John Joseph, 1943–1947 (D)
Mabry, Thomas Jewett, 1947–1951 (D)
Mechem, Edwin Leard, 1951–1955, 1957–1959, 1961–1962 (D)
Simms, John Field, 1955–1957 (D)
Burroughs, John, 1959–1961 (D)
Bolack, Thomas Felix, 1962–1963 (R)
Campbell, John M., 1963–1967 (D)
Cargo, David F., 1967–1971 (R)
King, Bruce, 1971–1975, 1979–1983 (D)
Apodaca, Jerry, 1975–1979 (D)
Anaya, Toney, 1983–1987 (D)
Carruthers, Garrey E., 1987–1991 (R)
King, Bruce, 1991– (D)

## NEW YORK

Clinton, George, 1789–1795, 1801–1804 (F)
Jay, John, 1795–1801 (F)
Lewis, Morgan, 1804–1807 (D-R)
Tompkins, Daniel D., 1807–1817 (Jef-R)
Taylor, John, 1817 (D-R)
Clinton, De Witt, 1817–1823, 1825–1828 (R)
Yates, Joseph C., 1823–1825 (Jef-R)
Pitcher, Nathaniel, 1828 (R)
Van Buren, Martin, 1829 (Jef-R)
Throop, Enos Thompson, 1829–1833 (Jef-R)
Marcy, William Learned, 1833–1839 (Jef-R)
Steward, William Henry, 1839–1843 (W)

Bouck, William C., 1843–1845 (D)
Wright, Silas, 1845–1847 (D)
Young, John, 1847–1849 (JD)
Fish, Hamilton, 1849–1851 (W)
Hunt, Washington, 1851–1853 (D)
Seymour, Horatio, 1853–1855, 1863–1865 (D)
Clark, Myron, 1855–1857 (W)
King, John Alsop, 1857–1859 (R)
Morgan, Edwin Denison, 1859–1863 (R)
Fenton, Reuben Eaton, 1865–1869 (R)
Hoffman, John Thompson, 1869–1873 (D)
Dix, John Adams, 1873–1875 (R)
Tilden, Samuel Jones, 1875–1877 (D)
Robinson, Lucius, 1877–1880 (D)
Cornell, Alonzo B., 1880–1883 (R)
Cleveland, Steven Grover, 1883–1885 (D)
Hill, David B., 1885–1892 (D)
Flower, Roswell Petibone, 1892–1895 (D)
Morton, Levi Parsons, 1895–1897 (R)
Black, Frank Swett, 1897–1899 (R)
Roosevelt, Theodore, 1899–1901 (R)
Odell, Benjamin Baker, 1901–1905 (R)
Higgins, Francis Wayland, 1905–1907 (R)
Hughes, Charles Evans, 1907–1910 (R)
White, Horace, 1910–1911
Dix, John Alden, 1911–1913 (D)
Sulzer, William, 1913 (D)
Glynn, Martin Henry, 1913–1915 (D)
Whitman, Charles Seymour, 1915–1919 (R)
Smith, Alfred E., 1919–1921, 1923–1929 (D)
Miller, Nathan L., 1921–1923 (R)
Roosevelt, Franklin Delano, 1929–1933 (D)
Lehman, Herbert Henry, 1933–1942 (D)
Poletti, Charles, 1942–1943 (D)
Dewey, Thomas Edmund, 1943–1955 (R)
Harriman, William Averell, 1955–1959 (D)
Rockefeller, Nelson Aldrich, 1959–1973 (R)
Wilson, Charles Malcolm, 1973–1975 (R)
Carey, Hugh L., 1975–1983 (D)
Cuomo, Mario M., 1983– (D)

## NORTH CAROLINA

Martin, Alexander, 1789–1792 (F)
Spaight, Richard Dobbs, 1792–1795 (F)
Ashe, Samuel, 1795–1798 (R)
Davie, William Richardson, 1798–1799 (F)
Williams, Benjamin, 1799–1802, 1807–1808 (R)
Turner, James, 1802–1805 (D-R)
Alexander, Nathaniel, 1805–1807 (D-R)
Stone, David, 1808–1810 (D-R)
Smith, Benjamin, 1810–1811 (R)
Hawkins, William, 1811–1814 (D-R)

Miller, William, 1814–1817
Branch, John, 1817–1820 (D)
Franklin, Jesse, 1820–1821 (D-R)
Holmes, Gabriel, 1821–1824 (D-R)
Burton, Hutchins Gordon, 1824–1827 (F)
Iredell, James, 1827–1828 (D)
Owen, John 1828–1830 (NR)
Stokes, Montford, 1830–1832 (J)
Swain, David Lowry, 1832–1835 (W)
Spaight, Richard Dobbs, Jr., 1835–1836 (R)
Dudley, Edward Bishop, 1836–1841 (W)
Morehead, John Motley, 1841–1845 (W)
Graham, William Alexander, 1845–1849 (W)
Manly, Charles, 1849–1850 (W)
Reid, David Settle, 1851–1854 (D)
Winslow, Warren, 1854–1855 (D)
Bragg, Thomas, 1855–1859 (D)
Ellis, John Willis, 1859–1861 (D)
Clark, Henry Toole, 1861–1862 (D)
Vance, Zebulon, 1862–1865, 1877–1879 (U-D)
Holden, William Woods, 1865, 1868–1870 (D)
Worth, Jonathan, 1865–1868 (U)
Caldwell, Ted Robinson, 1870–1874 (R)
Brogden, Curtis Hooks, 1874–1877 (R)
Jarvis, Thomas Jordon, 1879–1885 (D)
Robinson, James Lowry, 1885 (D)
Scales, Alfred Moore, 1885–1889 (D)
Fowle, Daniel Gould, 1889–1891 (D)
Holt, Thomas Michael, 1891–1893 (D)
Carr, Elias, 1893–1897 (FA)
Russell, Daniel Lindsey, 1897–1901 (R)
Aycoco, Charles Brantley, 1901–1905 (D)
Glenn, Robert Broadnax, 1905–1909 (D)
Kitchen, William Walton, 1909–1913 (D)
Craig, Locke, 1913–1917 (D)
Bickett, Thomas Walter, 1917–1921 (D)
Morrison, Cameron, 1921–1925 (D)
McLeon, Agnus Wilton, 1925–1929 (D)
Gardner, Oliver Max, 1929–1933 (D)
Ehringhaus, John Christoph Blucher, 1933–1937 (D)
Hoey, Clyde Roark, 1937–1941 (D)
Broughton, Joseph Melville, 1941–1945 (D)
Cherry, Robert Gregg, 1945–1949 (D)
Scott, William Kerr, 1949–1953 (D)
Umstead, William Bradley, 1953–1954 (D)
Hodges, Luther Hartwell, 1954–1961 (D)
Sanford, Terry, 1961–1965 (D)
Moore, Dan Killian, 1965–1969 (D)
Scott, Robert Walter, 1969–1973 (D)
Holshouser, James Eubert, 1973–1977 (R)
Hunt, James Baxter, 1977–1985 (D)
Martin, James G., 1985– (R)

## NORTH DAKOTA

Miller, John, 1889–1891 (R)
Burke, Andrew H., 1891–1893 (R)
Shortridge, Eli C. D., 1893–1895 (Pop)
Allin, Roger, 1895–1897 (R)
Briggs, Frank A., 1897–1898 (R)
Devine, Joseph M., 1898–1899 (R)
Fancher, Frederick Bartlett, 1899–1901 (R)
White, Frank, 1901–1905 (R)
Sharles, Elmore Yocum, 1905–1907 (R)
Burke, John, 1907–1913 (D)
Hanna, Lois Benjamin, 1913–1917 (R)
Frazier, Lynn Joseph, 1917–1921 (R)
Nestos, Ragnvald Anderson, 1921–1925 (R)
Sorlie, Arthur Gustav, 1925–1928 (R)
Maddock, Walter Jeremiah, 1928–1929 (NP)
Shafer, George F., 1929–1933 (R)
Langer, William, 1933–1934, 1937–1939 (R)
Olson, Ole H., 1934–1935 (R)
Moodie, Thomas Henry, 1935 (D)
Welford, Walter, 1935–1937 (NP)
Moses, John, 1939–1945 (D)
Aandahl, Fred George, 1945–1951 (R)
Brunsdale, Clarence Norman, 1951–1957 (R)
Davis, John Edward, 1957–1961 (R)
Guy, William Lewis, 1961–1973 (D)
Link, Arthur A., 1973–1981 (D)
Olson, Allen Ingvar, 1981–1985 (R)
Sinner, Richard F., 1985– (D)

## OHIO

Tiffin, Edward, 1803–1807 (D-R)
Kirker, Thomas, 1807–1808 (D-R)
Huntington, Samuel, 1808–1810 (D-R)
Meigs, Return J., 1810–1814 (D-R)
Looker, Othneil, 1814 (D-R)
Worthington, Thomas, 1814–1818 (D-R)
Brown, Ethan Allen, 1818–1822 (D-R)
Trimble, Allen, 1822, 1826–1830 (Con)
Morrow, Jeremiah, 1822–1826 (D-R)
McArthur, Duncan, 1830–1832 (R)
Lucas, Robert, 1832–1836 (D-R)
Vance, Joseph, 1836–1838 (W)
Shannon, Wilson, 1838–1840, 1842–1844 (D)
Corwin, Thomas, 1840–1842 (W)
Bartley, Thomas Welles, 1844 (D)
Bartley, Mordecai, 1844–1846 (W)
Bebb, Wiliam, 1846–1849 (W)
Ford, Seabury, 1849–1850 (W)
Wood, Reuban, 1850–1853 (D)
Medill, William, 1853–1856 (D)
Chase, Salmon Portland, 1856–1860 (R)
Dennison, William, 1860–1862 (R)
Tod, David, 1862–1864 (D)
Brough, John, 1864–1865 (U-R)
Anderson, Charles, 1865–1866 (R)
Cox, Jacob Dolson, 1866–1868 (R)
Hayes, Rutherford Birchard, 1868–1872, 1876–1877 (R)

Noyes, Edward F., 1872–1874 (R)
Allen, William, 1874–1876 (D)
Young, Thomas Lowry, 1877–1878 (D)
Bishop, Richard Moore, 1878–1880 (D)
Foster, Charles, 1880–1884 (R)
Hoadly, George, 1884–1886 (D)
Foraker, Joseph Benaon, 1886–1890 (R)
Campbell, James Edwin, 1890–1892 (D)
McKinley, William, 1892–1896 (R)
Bushnell, Asa S., 1896–1900 (R)
Nash, George Kilbon, 1900–1904 (R)
Herrick, Myron, 1904–1906 (R)
Pattison, John M., 1906 (D)
Harris, Andrew L., 1906–1909 (R)
Harmon, Judson, 1909–1913 (D)
Cox, James Middleton, 1913–1915, 1917–1921 (D)
Willis, Frank Bartlett, 1915–1917 (R)
Davis, Harry L., 1921–1923 (R)
Donahey, Alvin Victor, 1923–1929 (D)
Cooper, Myers Y., 1929–1931 (R)
White, George, 1931–1935 (D)
Davey, Martin Luther, 1935–1939 (D)
Bricker, John William, 1939–1945 (R)
Lausche, Frank John, 1945–1947, 1949–1957 (D)
Herbert, Thomas J., 1947–1949 (R)
Brown, John William, 1957 (R)
O'Neill, Crane William, 1957–1959 (R)
DiSalle, Michael Vincent, 1959–1963 (D)
Rhodes, James A., 1963–1971, 1975–1983 (R)
Gilligan, John Joyce, 1971–1974 (D)
Celeste, Richard F., 1983–1991 (D)
Voinovich, George V., 1991– (R)

## OKLAHOMA

Haskell, Charles Nathaniel, 1907–1911 (D)
Cruce, Lee, 1911–1915 (D)
Williams, Robert Lee, 1915–1919 (D)
Robertson, James Brooks Ayers, 1919–1923 (D)
Walton, John C., 1923 (D)
Trapp, Martin Edwin, 1923–1927 (D)
Johnston, Henry Simpson, 1927–1929 (D)
Holloway, William Judson, 1929–1931 (D)
Murray, William Henry, 1931–1935 (D)
Marland, Earnest Whitworth, 1935–1939 (D)
Phillips, Leon Chase, 1939–1943 (D)
Kerr, Robert Samuel, 1943–1947 (D)
Turner, Roy Joseph, 1947–1951 (D)
Murray, Johnston, 1951–1955 (D)
Gary, Raymond D., 1955–1959 (D)
Edmundson, James Howard, 1959–1963 (D)
Nigh, George Patterson, 1963, 1979–1987 (D)
Bellman, Henry Louis, 1963–1967, 1987–1991 (R)
Bartlett, Dewey Follet, 1967–1971 (R)
Hall, David, 1971–1975 (D)
Boren, David Lyle, 1975–1979 (D)
Walters, David, 1991– (D)

## OREGON

Whiteaker, John, 1859–1862 (D)
Gibbs, Addison C., 1862–1866 (D)
Woods, George Lemuel, 1866–1870 (R)
Grover, LaFayette, 1870–1877 (D)
Chadwick, Stephan Fowler, 1877–1878 (D)
Thayer, William Wallace, 1878–1882 (D)
Moody, Zenus Perry, 1882–1887 (R)
Pennoyer, Sylvester, 1887–1895 (D)
Lord, William Paine, 1895–1899 (R)
Geer, Theodore T., 1899–1903 (R)
Chamberlain, George Earle, 1903–1909 (D)
Benson, Frank W., 1909–1910 (R)
Bowerman, Jay, 1910–1911 (R)
West, Osaald, 1911–1915 (D)
Withycombe, James, 1915–1919 (R)
Olcott, Ben, 1919–1923 (R)
Pierce, Walter Marcus, 1923–1927 (D)
Patterson, Isaac Lee, 1927–1929 (R)
Norblad, Albin Walter, 1929–1931 (R)
Meier, Julius L., 1931–1935 (I)
Martin, Charles Henry, 1935–1939 (D)
Sprague, Charles Arthur, 1939–1943 (R)
Snell, Earl Wilcox, 1943–1947 (R)
Hall, John Hubert, 1947–1949 (R)
McKay, James Douglas, 1949–1952 (R)
Patterson, Paul Linton, 1952–1956 (R)
Smith, Elmo Everett, 1956–1957 (R)
Holmes, Robert Denison, 1957–1959 (D)
Hatfield, Mark, 1959–1967 (R)
McCall, Thomas Lawson, 1967–1975 (R)
Straub, Robert William, 1975–1979 (D)
Atiyeh, Victor G., 1979–1987 (R)
Goldschmidt, Neil, 1987–1991 (D)
Roberts, Barbara, 1991– (D)

## PENNSYLVANIA

Mifflin, Thomas, 1790–1799 (F)
McKean, Thomas, 1799–1808 (R)
Snyder, Simon, 1808–1817 (Jef)
Findlay, William, 1817–1820 (Jef)
Heister, Joseph, 1820–1823 (Jef)
Shulze, John Andrew, 1823–1829 (D)
Wolf, George, 1829–1835 (JD)
Ritner, Joseph, 1835–1839 (Jef)
Porter, David Rittenhouse, 1839–1845 (D)
Shunk, Francis Rawn, 1845–1848 (D)
Johnston, William Freame, 1848–1852 (W)
Rigler, William, 1852–1855 (D)
Pollack, James, 1855–1858 (W)
Packer, William Fisher, 1858–1861 (D)
Curtin, Andrew Gregg, 1861–1867 (Pe)
Geary, John White, 1867–1873 (R)
Hartranft, John Frederick, 1873–1879 (R)
Hoyt, Henry Martyn, 1879–1883 (R)
Pattison, Robert Emory, 1883–1887, 1891–1895 (D)
Beaver, James Adams, 1887–1891 (R)

Hastings, Daniel Hartman, 1895–1899 (R)
Stone, William Alexis, 1899–1903 (R)
Pennypacker, Samuel Whitaker, 1903–1907 (R)
Stuart, Edwin Sydney, 1907–1911 (R)
Tener, John Kinley, 1911–1915 (R)
Brumbagh, Martin Grove, 1915–1919 (R)
Sproul, William Cameron, 1919–1923 (R)
Pinchot, Gifford, 1923–1927, 1931–1935 (R)
Fisher, John Stuchell, 1927–1931 (R)
Earle, George Howard, 1935–1939 (D)
James, Arthur Horace, 1939–1943 (R)
Martin, Edward, 1943–1947 (R)
Bell, John Cromwell, 1947 (R)
Duff, James Henderson, 1947–1951 (R)
Fione, John Sydney, 1951–1955 (R)
Leader, George Michael, 1955–1959 (D)
Lawrence, David Lee, 1959–1963 (D)
Scranton, William Warren, 1963–1967 (R)
Shafer, Raymond Philip, 1967–1971 (R)
Shapp, Milton Jerrold, 1971–1979 (D)
Thornburgh, Richard Lewis, 1979–1987 (R)
Casey, Robert P., 1987– (D)

## RHODE ISLAND

Collins, John, 1786–1790 (A-F)
Fenner, Arthur, 1790–1805 (A-F)
Smith, Henry, 1805–1806 (D-R)
Wilbour, Isaac, 1806–1807
Fenner, James, 1807–1811, 1824–1831, 1843–1845 (D-R)
Jones, William, 1811–1817 (F)
Knight, Nehemiah Rice, 1817–1821 (W)
Gibbs, William Channing, 1821–1824 (D-R)
Arnold, Lemuel Hastings, 1831–1833 (D)
Francis, John Brown, 1833–1838 (D)
Sprague, William, 1838–1839 (W)
King, Samuel Ward, 1839–1843 (W)
Jackson, Charles, 1845–1846 (D-Lib)
Dimon, Byron, 1846–1847 (W)
Harris, Elisha, 1847–1849 (W)
Anthony, Henry Bowen, 1849–1851 (W)
Allen, Philip, 1851–1853 (D)
Dimond, Francis M., 1853–1854 (D)
Hoppin, William Warner, 1854–1857 (W)
Dyer, Elisha, 1857–1859 (W)
Turner, Thomas Goodwin, 1859–1860 (R)
Sprague, William, 1860–1863 (D)
Cozzens, William Cole, 1863 (D)
Smith, James Youngs, 1863–1866 (R)
Burnside, Ambrose Everett, 1866–1869 (R)
Padelford, Seth, 1869–1873 (R)
Howard, Henry, 1873–1875 (R)
Lippitt, Henry, 1875–1877 (R)

Van Zandyt, Charles Collins, 1877–1880 (R)
Littlefield, Alfred Henry, 1880–1883 (R)
Bourn, Augustus Osborn, 1883–1885 (R)
Wetmore, George Peabody, 1885–1887 (R)
Davis, John William, 1887–1888, 1890–1891 (D)
Taft, Royal Chapin, 1888–1889 (R)
Ladd, Herbert Warren, 1889–1890, 1891–1892 (R)
Brown, Daniel Russell, 1892–1895 (R)
Lippitt, Charles Warren, 1895–1897 (R)
Dyer, Elisha, Jr., 1897–1900 (R)
Gregory, William, 1900–1901 (R)
Kimball, Charles Dean, 1901–1903 (R)
Garvin, Lucius Fayette Clark, 1903–1905 (D)
Utter, George Herbert, 1905–1907 (R)
Higgins, James Henry, 1907–1909 (D)
Pothier, Aram, 1909–1915, 1925–1928 (R)
Beeckman, Robert Livingston, 1915–1921 (R)
San Souci, Emery J., 1921–1923 (R)
Flynn, William Smith, 1923–1925 (D)
Case, Norman Stanley, 1928–1933 (R)
Green, Theodore Francis, 1933–1937 (D)
Quinn, Robert Emmet, 1937–1939 (D)
Vanderbilt, William Henry, 1939–1941 (R)
McGrath, James Howard, 1941–1945 (D)
Pastore, John Orlando, 1945–1950 (D)
McKiernan, John Sammon, 1950–1951 (D)
Roberts, Dennis Joseph, 1951–1959 (D)
Del Sesto, Christopher, 1959–1961 (R)
Notte, John A., 1961–1963 (D)
Chaffe, John Hubbard, 1963–1969 (R)
Licht, Frank, 1969–1973 (D)
Noel, Philip William, 1973–1977 (D)
Garrahy, John Joseph, 1977–1985 (D)
DiPrete, Edward D., 1985–1991 (R)
Sundlun, Bruce, 1991– (D)

## SOUTH CAROLINA

Pinckney, Charles, 1789–1792, 1796–1798, 1806–1808 (D-R)
Moultrie, William, 1792–1794 (F)
Vanderhorst, Arnoldus, 1794–1796 (F)
Rutledge, Edward, 1798–1800 (F)
Drayton, John, 1800–1802, 1808–1810 (D-R)
Richardson, James Burchill, 1802–1804 (D-R)
Hamilton, Paul, 1804–1806 (D-R)
Middleton, Henry, 1810–1812 (D-R)
Alston, Joseph, 1812–1814 (D-R)
Williams, David Rogerson, 1814–1816 (D-R)
Pickens, Andrew, 1816–1818 (D-R)
Geddes, John, 1818–1820 (D-R)
Bennett, Thomas, 1820–1822 (D-R)

Wilson, John Lyde, 1822–1824 (D-R)
Manning, Richard Irvine, 1824–1826 (D-R)
Taylor, John, 1826–1828 (D-R)
Miller, Stephen Decatur, 1828–1830 (D)
Hamilton, James, 1830–1832 (D)
Hayne, Robert Young, 1832–1834 (D)
McDuffie, George, 1834–1836 (D)
Butler, Pierce Mason, 1836–1838 (D)
Noble, Patrick, 1838–1840 (D)
Henagan, Barnabus Kelet, 1840 (D)
Richardson, John Peter, 1840–1842 (D)
Hammond, James Henry, 1842–1844 (D)
Aiken, William, 1844–1846 (D)
Johnson, David, 1846–1848 (D)
Seabrook, Whitemarsh Benjamin, 1848–1850 (D)
Means, John Hugh, 1850–1852 (D)
Manning, John Laurence, 1852–1854 (D)
Adams, James Hopkins, 1854–1856 (D)
Allston, Robert Francis Withers, 1856–1858 (D)
Gist, William Henry, 1858–1860 (D)
Pickens, Francis Wilkinson, 1860–1862 (D)
Bonham, Milledge Luke, 1862–1864 (D)
Macgrath, Andrew Gordon, 1864–1865 (D)
Perry, Benjamin Franklin, 1865 (D)
Orr, James Lawrence, 1865–1868 (D)
Scott, Robert Kingston, 1868–1872 (R)
Moses, Franklin J., 1872–1874 (R)
Chamberlain, Daniel Henry, 1874–1876 (R)
Hampton, Wade, 1876–1879 (D)
Simpson, William Dunlap, 1879–1880 (D)
Jeter, Thomas Bothwell, 1880 (D)
Hagood, Johnson, 1880–1882 (D)
Thompson, Hugh Smith, 1882–1886 (D)
Sheppard, John Calhoun, 1886 (D)
Richardson, John Peter, Jr., 1886–1890 (D)
Tilman, Benjamin, 1890–1894 (D)
Evans, John Gary, 1894–1897 (D)
Ellerbe, William H., 1897–1899 (D)
McSweeney, Miles Benjamin, 1899–1903 (D)
Heyward, Duncan Clinch, 1903–1907 (D)
Ansel, Martin Frederick, 1907–1911 (D)
Blease, Coleman Livingston, 1911–1915 (D)
Smith, Charles A., 1915 (D)
Manning, Richard Irvine, III, 1915–1919 (D)
Cooper, Robert Archer, 1919–1922 (D)
Harvey, Wilson Godfrey, 1922–1923 (D)
McLeod, Thomas Gordon, 1923–1927 (D)
Richards, John Gardiner, 1927–1931 (D)

Blackwood, Irba Charles, 1931–1935 (D)
Johnston, Olin Dewitch Talmadge, 1935–1939, 1943–1945 (D)
Maybank, Burnet Rhett, 1939–1941 (D)
Harley, Joseph Emile, 1941–1942 (D)
Jeffries, Richard Manning, 1942–1943 (D)
Williams, Ransome Judson, 1945–1947 (D)
Thurmond, James Strom, 1947–1951 (D)
Byrnes, James Francis, 1951–1955 (D)
Timmerman, George Bell, 1955–1959 (D)
Hollings, Earnest Frederick, 1959–1963 (D)
Russell, Donald Stuart, 1963–1965 (D)
McNair, Robert Evander, 1965–1971 (D)
West, John Carl, 1971–1975 (D)
Edwards, James Burrows, 1975–1979 (R)
Riley, Richard Wilson, 1979–1987 (D)
Campbell, Carroll A., Jr., 1987– (R)

## SOUTH DAKOTA

Mellette, Arthur Calvin, 1889–1893 (R)
Sheldon, Charles Henry, 1893–1897 (R)
Lee, Andrew Ericson, 1897–1901 (Pe, Fus)
Herreid, Charles N., 1901–1905 (R)
Elrod, Samuel Harrison, 1905–1907 (R)
Crawford, Corie Isaac, 1907–1909 (R)
Vessey, Robert Scadden, 1909–1913 (R)
Byrne, Frank M., 1913–1917 (R)
Norbeck, Peter, 1917–1921 (R)
McMaster, William Henry, 1921–1925 (R)
Gunderson, Carl, 1925–1927 (R)
Bulow, William John, 1927–1931 (D)
Green, Warren Everett, 1931–1933 (R)
Berry, Thomas Matthew, 1933–1937 (D)
Jenson, Leslie, 1937–1939 (R)
Bushfield, Harlan John, 1939–1943 (R)
Sharpe, Merrell Quentin, 1943–1947 (R)
Mickelson, George Theodore, 1947–1951 (R)
Anderson, Sigurd, 1951–1955 (R)
Foss, Joseph Jacob, 1955–1959 (R)
Herseth, Ralph, 1959–1961 (D)
Gubbrud, Archie, 1961–1965 (R)
Boe, Nils Andrus, 1965–1969 (R)
Farrar, Frank Laroy, 1969–1971 (R)
Kneip, Richard Francis, 1971–1978 (D)
Wollman, Harvey, 1978–1979 (D)
Janklow, William John, 1979–1987 (R)
Mickelson, George S., 1987– (R)

## TENNESSEE

Sevier, John, 1796–1801, 1803–1809
Roane, Archibald, 1801–1803
Blount, William, 1809–1815 (JD)
McMinn, Joseph, 1815–1821
Carroll, William, 1821–1827, 1829–1835 (JD)

Houston, Sam, 1827–1829 (JD)
Hall, William, 1829 (D)
Cannon, Newton, 1835–1839 (W)
Polk, James Knox, 1839–1841 (D)
Jones, James Chamberlain, 1841–1845 (W)
Brown, Aaron Venable, 1845–1847 (D)
Brown, Neil Smith, 1847–1849 (W)
Trousdale, William, 1849–1851 (D)
Campbell, William Bowen, 1851–1853 (W)
Johnson, Andrew, 1853–1857, 1862–1865 (D)
Harris, Isham Green, 1857–1862 (D)
Brownlow, William Gannaway, 1865–1869 (W)
Senter, De Witt Clinton, 1869–1871 (U-R)
Brown, John Calvin, 1871–1875 (D)
Porter, James Davis, 1875–1879 (D)
Marks, Albert Smith, 1879–1881 (U-D)
Hawkins, Alvin, 1881–1883 (R)
Bate, William Brimage, 1883–1887 (D)
Taylor, Robert Love, 1887–1891, 1897–1899 (D)
Buchanan, John Price, 1891–1893 (D-All)
Turney, Peter, 1893–1897 (D)
McMillin, Benton, 1899–1903 (D)
Frazier, James Beriah, 1903–1905 (D)
Cox, John Isaac, 1905–1907 (D)
Patterson, Malcomb Rice, 1907–1911 (D)
Hooper, Ben Walter, 1911–1915 (R)
Rye, Thomas Clarke, 1915–1919 (D)
Roberts, Albert Houston, 1919–1921 (D)
Taylor, Alfred Alexander, 1921–1923 (R)
Peay, Austin, III, 1923–1927 (D)
Horton, Henry Hollis, 1927–1933 (D)
McAlister, Harry Hill, 1933–1937 (D)
Browning, Gordon, 1937–1939, 1949–1953 (D)
Cooper, William Prentice, 1939–1945 (D)
McCord, Jim Nance, 1945–1949 (D)
Clement, Frank Goad, 1953–1959, 1963–1967 (D)
Ellington, Earl Buford, 1959–1963, 1967–1971 (D)
Dunn, Bryant Winfield Culberson, 1971–1975 (R)
Blanton, Ray, 1975–1979 (D)
Alexander, Lamar, 1979–1987 (R)
McWherter, Ned Ray, 1987– (D)

## TEXAS

Henderson, James Pinckney, 1846–1847 (D)
Wood, George Thomas, 1847–1849 (D)
Bell, Peter Hansbourough, 1849–1853 (D)
Pease, Elisha Marshall, 1853–1857, 1867–1870 (D)
Runnels, Hardin Richard, 1857–1859 (D)

Houston, Sam, 1859–1861 (JD)
Clark, Edward, 1861 (I–D)
Lubbock, Francis Richard, 1861–1863 (D)
Murrah, Pendleton, 1863–1865 (D)
Stockdale, Fletcher S., 1865 (D)
Hamilton, Andrew Jackson, 1865–1866 (D)
Throckmorton, James Webb, 1866–1867 (Con)
Davis, Edmund Jackson, 1870–1874 (R)
Coke, Richard, 1874–1876 (D)
Hubbard, Richard Bennett, 1876–1879 (D)
Roberts, Oran Milo, 1879–1883 (D)
Ireland, John, 1883–1887 (D)
Ross, Lawrence Sullivan, 1887–1891 (D)
Hogg, James Stephan, 1891–1895 (D)
Culberson, Charles Allen, 1895–1899 (D)
Sayers, Joseph Draper, 1899–1903 (D)
Lanham, Samuel Tucker, 1903–1907 (D)
Campbell, Thomas Mitchell, 1907–1911 (D)
Colquitt, Oscar Branch, 1911–1915 (D)
Ferguson, James Edward, 1915–1917 (D)
Hobby, William Pettu, 1917–1921 (D)
Neff, Pat Morris, 1921–1925 (D)
Ferguson, Miriam A., 1925–1927, 1933–1935 (D)
Moody, Daniel J., 1927–1931 (D)
Sterling, Ross S., 1931–1933 (D)
Allred, James V., 1935–1939 (D)
O'Daniel, Wilbert Lee, 1939–1941 (D)
Stevenson, Coke R., 1941–1947 (D)
Jester, Beauford Halbert, 1947–1949 (D)
Shivers, Allen, 1949–1957 (D)
Daniel, Price, 1957–1963 (D)
Connally, John Bowdon, 1963–1969 (D)
Smith, Preston, 1969–1973 (D)
Briscoe, Dolph, 1973–1979 (D)
Clements, William P., Jr., 1979–1983, 1987–1991 (R)
White, Mark, 1983–1987 (D)
Richards, Ann W., 1991– (D)

## UTAH

Wells, Herber M., 1896–1905 (R)
Cutler, John Christopher, 1905–1909 (R)
Spry, William, 1909–1917 (R)
Bamberger, Simon, 1917–1921 (D)
Mabey, Charles Rendell, 1921–1925 (R)
Dern, George Henry, 1925–1933 (D)
Blood, Henry Hooper, 1933–1941 (D)
Maw, Herbert Brown, 1941–1949 (D)
Lee, Joseph Bracken, 1949–1957 (R)
Clyde, George Dewey, 1957–1965 (R)
Rampton, Calvin Lewellyn, 1965–1977 (D)
Matheson, Scott Milne, 1977–1985 (D)
Bangerter, Norman H., 1985– (R)

## VERMONT

Chittenden, Thomas, 1791–1797
Brigham, Paul, 1797 (F)
Ticheneor, Isaac, 1797–1807, 1808–1809 (F)
Smith, Israel, 1807–1808 (Jef-R)
Galusha, Jonus, 1809–1813, 1815–1820 (Jef-R)
Chittenden, Martin, 1813–1815 (F)
Skinner, Richard, 1820–1823 (D-R)
Van Ness, Cornelius P., 1923–1826 (D-R)
Butler, Ezra, 1826–1828 (D)
Crafts, Samuel C., 1828–1831 (W)
Palmer, William Adam, 1831–1835 (D)
Jenison, Silas H., 1835–1841 (W)
Paine, Charles, 1841–1843 (W)
Mattocks, John, 1843–1844 (W)
Slade, William, 1844–1846 (W)
Eaton, Horace, 1846–1848 (W)
Coolidge, Carlos, 1848–1850 (W)
Williams, Charles Kilborn, 1850–1852 (W)
Fairbanks, Erastus, 1852–1853, 1860–1861 (W)
Robinson, John Stanford, 1853–1854 (D)
Royce, Stephan, 1854–1856 (R)
Fletcher, Ryland, 1856–1858 (R)
Hall, Hiland, 1858–1860 (R)
Holbrook, Frederick, 1861–1863 (R)
Smith, John Gregory, 1863–1865 (R)
Dillingham, Paul, 1865–1867 (R)
Page, John B., 1867–1869 (R)
Washburn, Peter T., 1869–1870 (R)
Hendee, George Whitman, 1870 (R)
Stewart, John Wolcott, 1870–1872 (R)
Converse, Julius, 1872–1874 (R)
Peck, Asahe, 1874–1876 (R)
Fairbanks, Horace, 1876–1878 (R)
Proctor, Redfield, 1878–1880 (R)
Farnham, Roswell, 1880–1882 (R)
Barstow, John Lester, 1882–1884 (R)
Pingree, Samuel E., 1884–1886 (R)
Ormsbee, Ebenezer Jolls, 1886–1888 (R)
Dillingham, William Paul, 1888–1890 (R)
Page, Carroll Smalley, 1890–1892 (R)
Fuller, Levi Knight, 1892–1894 (R)
Woodbury, Urban Andrain, 1894–1896 (R)
Grout, Josiah, 1896–1898 (R)
Smith, Edward Curtis, 1898–1900 (R)
Stickney, William W., 1900–1902 (R)
McCullough, John Griffith, 1902–1904 (R)
Bell, Charles James, 1904–1906 (R)
Proctor, Fletcher Dutton, 1906–1908 (R)
Prouty, George, 1908–1910 (R)
Mead, John Abner, 1910–1912 (R)
Fletcher, Allen M., 1912–1915 (R)
Gates, Charles, 1915–1917 (R)
Graham, Horace French, 1917–1919 (R)
Clement, Percival W., 1919–1921 (R)
Hartness, James, 1921–1923 (R)
Proctor, Redfield, Jr., 1923–1925 (R)

Billings, Franklin Swift, 1925–1927 (R)
Weeks, John Eliakin, 1927–1931 (R)
Wilson, Stanley Calef, 1931–1935 (R)
Smith, Charles Manley, 1935–1937 (R)
Aiken, George D., 1937–1941 (R)
Wills, William H., 1941–1945 (R)
Proctor, Mortimer R., 1945–1947 (R)
Gibson, Ernest W., 1947–1950 (R)
Arthur, Harold John, 1950–1951 (R)
Emerson, Lee E., 1951–1955 (R)
Johnson, Joseph Blaine, 1955–1959 (R)
Stafford, Robert T., 1959–1961 (R)
Keyser, F. Ray, 1961–1963 (R)
Hoff, Philip Henderson, 1963–1969 (D)
Davis, Deane C., 1969–1973 (R)
Salmon, Thomas P., 1973–1977 (D)
Snelling, Richard Arkwright, 1977–1985, 1991– (R)
Kunin, Madeleine M., 1985–1991 (D)

## VIRGINIA

Randolph, Beverly, 1788–1791
Lee, Henry, 1791–1794 (F)
Brooke, Robert, 1794–1796
Wood, James, 1796–1799 (D-R)
Monroe, James, 1799–1802, 1811 (D-R)
Page, John, 1802–1805 (D-R)
Cabell, William Henry, 1805–1808 (D-R)
Tyler, John, 1808–1811 (D-R)
Smith, George William, 1811 (D-R)
Randolph, Peyton, 1811–1812 (D-R)
Barbour, James, 1812–1814 (D-R)
Nicholas, Wilson Cary, 1814–1816 (D-R)
Preston, James Patton, 1816–1819 (D-R)
Randolph, Thomas Mann, 1819–1822
Pleasants, James, 1822–1825 (D-R)
Tyler, John, Jr., 1825–1827 (D-R)
Giles, William Branch, 1827–1830 (D)
Floyd, John, 1830–1834 (D)
Tazewell, Littleton Waller, 1834–1836 (D)
Robertson, Wyndham, 1836–1837 (W)
Campbell, David, 1837–1840 (D)
Gilmer, Thomas Walker, 1840–1841 (W)
Patton, John Mercer, 1841 (W)
Rutherford, John, 1841–1842 (D)
Gregory, John Munford, 1842–1843 (W)
McDowell, James, 1843–1846 (W)
Smith, William, 1846–1849, 1864–1865 (D)
Floyd, John Buchanan, 1849–1852 (D)
Johnson, Joseph, 1852–1856 (D)
Wise, Henry Alexander, 1856–1860 (D)
Letcher, John, 1860–1864 (D)
Pierpoint, Francis Harrison, 1865–1868
Wells, Henry Horatio, 1868–1869 (R)
Walker, Gilbert Carlton, 1869–1874 (D)
Kemper, James Lawson, 1874–1878 (D)
Holliday, Frederick William Mackey, 1878–1882 (D)
Cameron, William Evelyn, 1882–1886 (Re)
Lee, Fitzhugh, 1886–1890 (D)

McKinney, Philip Watkins, 1890–1894 (D)

O'Ferral, Charles Triplett, 1894–1898 (D)

Tyler, James Hoge, 1898–1902 (D)

Montague, Andrew Jackson, 1902–1906 (D)

Swanson, Claude Augustus, 1906–1910 (D)

Mann, William Hodges, 1910–1914 (D)

Stuart, Henry Carter, 1914–1918 (D)

Davis, Westmoreland, 1918–1922 (D)

Trinkle, Elbert Lee, 1922–1926 (D)

Byrd, Harry Flood, 1926–1930 (D)

Pollard, John Garland, 1930–1934 (D)

Peery, George Campbell, 1934–1938 (D)

Price, James Hubert, 1938–1942 (D)

Darden, Colgate Whitehead, 1942–1946 (D)

Tuck, William Munford, 1946–1950 (D)

Battle, John Stewart, 1950–1954 (D)

Stanley, Thomas Bahnson, 1954–1958 (D)

Almond, James Lindsay, 1958–1962 (D)

Harrison, Albertis Sydney, 1962–1966 (D)

Godwin, Mills Edwin, 1966–1970, 1974–1978 (D)

Holton, Abner Linwood, 1970–1974 (R)

Dalton, John Nichols, 1978–1982 (R)

Robb, Charles S., 1982–1986 (D)

Baliles, Gerald L., 1986–1990 (D)

Wilder, L. Douglas, 1990– (D)

## WASHINGTON

Ferry, Elisha Peyre, 1889–1893 (R)

McGraw, John Harte, 1893–1897 (R)

Rogers, John Rankin, 1897–1901 (Pop-D)

McBride, Henry, 1901–1905 (R)

Mead, Albert E., 1905–1909 (R)

Cosgrove, Samuel G., 1909 (R)

Hay, Marion E., 1909–1913 (R)

Lister, Earnest, 1913–1919 (D)

Hart, Louis Folwell, 1919–1925 (R)

Hartley, Roland H., 1925–1933 (R)

Martin, Clarence Daniel, 1933–1941 (D)

Langlie, Arthur B., 1941–1945, 1949–1957 (R)

Wallgreen, Monrad Charles, 1945–1949 (D)

Rosellini, Albert Dean, 1957–1965 (D)

Evans, Daniel Jackson, 1965–1977 (R)

Ray, Dixy Lee, 1977–1981 (D)

Spellman, John Dennis, 1981–1985 (R)

Gardner, Booth, 1985– (D)

## WEST VIRGINIA

Boreman, Arthur Ingraham, 1863–1869 (U)

Farnsworth, Daniel Duane Yompkins, 1869 (R)

Stevenson, William Erskine, 1869–1871 (R)

Jacob, John Jeremiah, 1871–1877 (D)

Matthews, Henry Mason, 1877–1881 (D)

Jackson, Jacob Beeson, 1881–1885 (D)

Wilson, Emmanuel Willis, 1885–1890 (D)

Fleming, Aretas Brooks, 1890–1893 (D)

MacCorkle, William Alexander, 1893–1897 (D)

Atkinson, George Wesley, 1897–1901 (R)

White, Albert Blakeslee, 1901–1905 (R)

Dawson, William Mercer Owens, 1905–1909 (R)

Glasscook, William Ellsworth, 1909–1913 (R)

Hatfield, Henry Drury, 1913–1917 (R)

Cornwell, John Jacob, 1917–1921 (D)

Morgan, Ephriam Franklin, 1921–1925 (R)

Gore, Howard Mason, 1925–1929 (R)

Conley, William Gustavus, 1929–1933 (R)

Kump, Herman Guy, 1933–1937 (D)

Holt, Homer Adams, 1937–1941 (D)

Neely, Matthew Mansfield, 1941–1945 (D)

Meadows, Clarence Watson, 1945–1949 (D)

Patteson, Okey Leonidas, 1949–1953 (D)

Marland, William Casey, 1953–1957 (D)

Underwood, Cecil Harland, 1957–1961 (R)

Barron, William Wallace, 1961–1965 (D)

Smith, Hulett Carlson, 1965–1969 (D)

Moore, Arch Alfred, 1969–1977, 1985–1989 (R)

Rockefeller, John Davison, IV, 1977–1985 (D)

Caperton, Gaston, 1989– (D)

## WISCONSIN

Dewey, Nelson, 1848–1852 (D)

Farwell, Leonard James, 1852–1854 (W)

Barstow, William Augustus, 1854–1856 (D)

MacArthur, Arthur, 1856 (D)

Bashford, Coles, 1856–1858 (R)

Randell, Alexander Williams, 1858–1862 (D)

Harvey, Louis Powell, 1862 (R)

Soloman, Edward, 1862–1864 (D)

Lewis, James Taylor, 1864–1868 (D)

Fairchild, Lucius, 1866–1872 (R)

Washburn, Cadwallader Colden, 1872–1874 (R)

Taylor, William R., 1874–1876 (D)

Ludington, Harrison, 1876–1878 (R)

Smith, William E., 1878–1882 (R)

Rusk, Jeremiah M., 1882–1889 (R)

Hoard, William Dempster, 1889–1891 (R)

Peck, George W., 1891–1895 (D)

Upham, William H., 1895–1897 (R)

Scofield, Edward, 1897–1901 (R)

La Follette, Robert M., 1901–1906 (R)

Davidson, James O., 1906–1911 (R)

McGovern, Francis E., 1911–1915 (R)

Philipp, Emmanuel L., 1915–1921 (R)

Blaine, John L., 1921–1927 (R)

Zimmerman, Fred R., 1927–1929 (R)

Kohler, Walter J., 1929–1931 (R)

La Follette, Philip F., 1931–1933, 1935–1939 (R)

Schmedeman, Albert G., 1933–1935 (D)

Heil, Julius Peter, 1939–1943 (R)

Loomis, Orland S., [1943] (Pr)

Goodland, Walter S., 1943–1947 (R)

Rennebohm, Oscar, 1947–1951 (R)

Kohler, Walter, Jr., 1951–1957 (R)

Thomson, Vernon W., 1957–1959 (R)

Nelson, Gaylord Anton, 1959–1963 (D)

Reynolds, John W., 1963–1965 (D)

Knowles, Warren P., 1965–1971 (R)

Lucey, Patrick J., 1971–1977 (D)

Schreiber, Martin J., 1977–1979 (D)

Dreyfus, Lee Sherman, 1979–1983 (R)

Earl, Anthony S., 1983–1987 (D)

Thompson, Tommy G., 1987– (R)

## WYOMING

Warren, Francis Emroy, 1890 (R)

Barber, Amos Walker, 1890–1893 (R)

Osborne, John Eugene, 1893–1895 (D)

Richards, William Alford, 1895–1899 (R)

Richards, DeForest, 1899–1903 (R)

Chatterton, Fenimore, 1903–1905 (R)

Brooks, Bryant Butler, 1905–1911 (R)

Carey, Joseph Maull, 1911–1915 (D)

Kendrick, John Benjamin, 1915–1917 (D)

Houx, Frank L., 1917–1919 (D)

Carey, Robert Davis, 1919–1923 (R)

Ross, William Bradford, 1923–1924 (D)

Lucas, Franklin Earl, 1924–1925 (R)

Ross, Nellie Tayloe, 1925–1927 (D)

Emerson, Frank Collins, 1927–1931 (R)

Clark, Alonzo M., 1931–1933 (R)

Miller, Leslie A., 1933–1939 (R)

Smith, Nels H., 1939–1943 (R)

Hunt, Lester Calloway, 1943–1949 (D)

Crane, Arthur Griswold, 1949–1951 (R)

Barrett, Frank A., 1951–1953 (R)

Rogers, Clifford Joy, 1953–1955 (R)

Simpson, Milward L., 1955–1959 (R)

Hickey, John Joseph, 1959–1961 (D)

Gage, Jack Robert, 1961–1963 (D)

Hansen, Clifford P., 1963–1967 (R)

Hathaway, Stanley Knapp, 1967–1975 (R)

Herschler, Edgar J., 1975–1987 (D)

Sullivan, Michael, 1987– (D)

# Party designations:

(A-F) Anti-Federalist

(Am) American

(Am-R) American Republican

(Con) Conservative

(D) Democrat

(D-All) Democratic Alliance Party

(D-Lib) Democratic Liberationalist

(D-R) Democratic-Republican

(F) Federalist

(FA) Farmer's Alliance

(Fus-R) Fusion Party, Republican

(I) Independent

(I-D) Independent Democrat

(JD) Jacksonian Democrat

(JR) Jacksonian Republican

(Jef) Jeffersonian

(Jef-R) Jeffersonian Republican

(NP) Nonpartisan

(NR) National Republican

(Pe) People's Party

(Pop) Populist

(Pr) Progressive

(Re) Readjuster Party

(Sil) Free-Silver Party

(U) Unionist

(U-D) Union Democrat

(U-R) Union Republican

(W) Whig

# Appendix 17

## *Impeachments and Removals of Governors*

| Name and state | Year | Process of Impeachment and Outcome | | |
|---|---|---|---|---|
| Charles Robinson (KS) | 1862 | Impeached | Acquitted | |
| Harrison Reed (FL) | 1868 | Impeached | Acquitted | |
| William Holden (NC) | 1870 | Impeached | Convicted | Removed |
| Powell Clayton (AR) | 1871 | Impeached | Acquitted | |
| David Butler (NE) | 1871 | Impeached | Convicted | Removed |
| Henry Warmoth (LA) | 1872 | Impeached | | Term ended |
| Harrison Reed (FL) | 1873 | Impeached | Acquitted | |
| Adelbert Ames (MS) | 1876 | Impeached | | Resigned |
| Alexander Davis (MS) | 1876 | Impeached | Convicted | Removed |
| William P. Kellogg (LA) | 1876 | Impeached | Acquitted | |
| William Sulzer (NY) | 1913 | Impeached | Convicted | Removed |
| James 'Pa' Ferguson (TX) | 1917 | Impeached | Convicted | Resigned |
| John C. Walton (OK) | 1923 | Impeached | Convicted | Removed |
| Henry S. Johnston (OK) | 1928 | Impeached | Acquitted | |
| Henry S. Johnston (OK) | 1929 | Impeached | Convicted | Removed |
| Huey P. Long (LA) | 1929 | Impeached | Acquitted | |
| Henry Horton (TN) | 1931 | Impeached | Acquitted | |
| Richard Leche (LA) | 1939 | Threatened | | Resigned |
| Evan Mecham (AZ) | 1988 | Impeached | Convicted | Removed |

## *Other Removals of Incumbent Governors*

| Name and state | Year | Description |
|---|---|---|
| John A. Quitman (MS) | 1851 | Resigned after federal criminal indictment |
| Lynn J. Frazier (ND) | 1921 | Recalled by voters during third term |
| Warren T. McCray (IN) | 1924 | Resigned after federal criminal conviction |
| William Langer (ND) | 1934 | Removed by North Dakota Supreme Court |
| Thomas L. Moodie (ND) | 1935 | Removed by North Dakota Supreme Court |
| J. Howard Pyle (AZ) | 1955 | Recall petition certified, but term ended before date set for recall election[1] |
| Marvin Mandel (MD) | 1977 | Removed after federal criminal conviction |
| Ray Blanton (TN) | 1979 | Term shortened in bipartisan agreement[2] |

[1] From a discussion with Sean Griffin, reporter for the *Phoenix Gazette*, March 31, 1988.

[2] See Lamar Alexander, *Steps Along the Way: A Governor's Scrapbook* (Nashville, TN: Thomas Nelson, 1986), pp. 21–29, for a discussion of this unique transition between governors.

Source: *Book of the States*, 1988–1989, Vol. 27 (Lexington, KY: Council of State Governments, 1988).

# Appendix 18

| | Year | President | Vice President | Party |
|---|---|---|---|---|
| 1. | 1789 | George Washington | John Adams | Federalist |
| 2. | 1797 | John Adams | Federalist | |
| | | | Thomas Jefferson | Dem.–Rep. |
| 3. | 1801 | Thomas Jefferson | Aaron Burr | Dem.–Rep. |
| | 1805 | | George Clinton | Dem.–Rep. |
| 4. | 1809 | James Madison | George Clinton | Dem.–Rep. |
| | 1813 | | Elbridge Gerry | Dem.–Rep. |
| 5. | 1817 | James Monroe | D. D. Tompkins | Dem.–Rep. |
| 6. | 1825 | John Quincy Adams | John C. Calhoun | Dem.–Rep. |
| 7. | 1829 | Andrew Jackson | John C. Calhoun | Democrat |
| | 1833 | | Martin Van Buren | Democrat |
| 8. | 1837 | Martin Van Buren | Richard M. Johnson | Democrat |
| 9. | 1841 | William H. Harrison | John Tyler | Whig |
| 10. | 1841 | John Tyler | vacant | Whig & Democrat |
| 11. | 1845 | James K. Polk | George M. Dallas | Democrat |
| 12. | 1849 | Zachary Taylor | Millard Fillmore | Whig |
| 13. | 1850 | Millard Fillmore | vacant | Whig |
| 14. | 1853 | Franklin Pierce | William R. D. King | Democrat |
| 15. | 1857 | James Buchanan | John C. Breckinridge | Democrat |
| 16. | 1861 | Abraham Lincoln | Hannibal Hamlin | Republican |
| | 1865 | | Andrew Johnson | Unionist |
| 17. | 1865 | Andrew Johnson | vacant | Unionist |
| 18. | 1869 | Ulysses S. Grant | Schuyler Colfax | Republican |
| | 1873 | | Henry Wilson | Republican |
| 19. | 1877 | Rutherford B. Hayes | William A. Wheeler | Republican |
| 20. | 1881 | James A. Garfield | Chester A. Arthur | Republican |
| 21. | 1881 | Chester A. Arthur | vacant | Republican |
| 22. | 1885 | Grover Cleveland | T. A. Hendricks | Democrat |
| 23. | 1889 | Benjamin Harrison | Levi P. Morton | Republican |
| 24. | 1893 | Grover Cleveland | Adlai E. Stevenson | Democrat |
| 25. | 1897 | William McKinley | Garret A. Hobart | Republican |
| | 1901 | | Theodore Roosevelt | Republican |

| | Year | President | Vice President | Party |
|---|---|---|---|---|
| 26. | 1901 | Theodore Roosevelt | vacant | Republican |
| | 1905 | | Chas. W. Fairbanks | Republican |
| 27. | 1909 | William H. Taft | James S. Sherman | Republican |
| 28. | 1913 | Woodrow Wilson | Thomas R. Marshall | Democrat |
| 29. | 1921 | Warren G. Harding | Calvin Coolidge | Republican |
| 30. | 1923 | Calvin Coolidge | vacant | Republican |
| | 1925 | | Charles G. Dawes | Republican |
| 31. | 1929 | Herbert Hoover | Charles Curtis | Republican |
| 32. | 1933 | Franklin D. Roosevelt | John Nance Garner | Democrat |
| | 1941 | | Henry A. Wallace | Democrat |
| | 1945 | | Harry S Truman | Democrat |
| 33. | 1945 | Harry S Truman | vacant | Democrat |
| | 1949 | | Alben W. Barkley | Democrat |
| 34. | 1953 | Dwight D. Eisenhower | Richard M. Nixon | Republican |
| 35. | 1961 | John F. Kennedy | Lyndon B. Johnson | Democrat |
| 36. | 1963 | Lyndon B. Johnson | vacant | Democrat |
| | 1965 | | Hubert Humphrey | Democrat |
| 37. | 1969 | Richard M. Nixon | Spiro T. Agnew | Republican |
| | 1973 | | Gerald R. Ford | Republican |
| 38. | 1974 | Gerald R. Ford | Nelson Rockefeller | Republican |
| 39. | 1977 | Jimmy Carter | Walter Mondale | Democrat |
| 40. | 1981 | Ronald Reagan | George Bush | Republican |
| 41. | 1989 | George Bush | J. Danforth Quayle | Republican |

# Index